# Advanced Financial Accounting

# Advanced Financial Accounting

Eighth Edition

**Richard E. Baker**
*Northern Illinois University*

**Valdean C. Lembke**
*University of Iowa*

**Thomas E. King**
*Southern Illinois University Edwardsville*

**Cynthia G. Jeffrey**
*Iowa State University*

Boston   Burr Ridge, IL   Dubuque, IA   New York   San Francisco   St. Louis
Bangkok   Bogotá   Caracas   Kuala Lumpur   Lisbon   London   Madrid   Mexico City
Milan   Montreal   New Delhi   Santiago   Seoul   Singapore   Sydney   Taipei   Toronto

**McGraw-Hill Irwin**

ADVANCED FINANCIAL ACCOUNTING

Published by McGraw-Hill/Irwin, a business unit of The McGraw-Hill Companies, Inc., 1221 Avenue of the Americas, New York, NY, 10020. Copyright © 2009, 2008, 2005, 2002, 1999, 1996, 1993, 1989 by The McGraw-Hill Companies, Inc. All rights reserved. No part of this publication may be reproduced or distributed in any form or by any means, or stored in a database or retrieval system, without the prior written consent of The McGraw-Hill Companies, Inc., including, but not limited to, in any network or other electronic storage or transmission, or broadcast for distance learning.

Some ancillaries, including electronic and print components, may not be available to customers outside the United States.

Portions of **FASB Statement No. 52,** "Foreign Currency Translation," copyright by the Financial Accounting Standards Board, 401 Merritt 7, PO Box 5116, Norwalk, CT 06856-5116, U.S.A., are reproduced with permission. Complete copies of this document are available from the FASB.

Material from the Uniform CPA Examination and Unofficial Answers, Copyright 1969, 1970, 1972, 1973, 1974, 1975, 1976, 1977, 1978, 1979, 1980, 1981, 1982, 1983, 1984, 1985, 1986, 1987, 1988, 1989, 1990, 1991, 1992, 1993, 1994, 1995, 1996, 1997, 1998, by the American Institute of Certified Public Accountants, is reprinted (or adapted) with permission.

Material from the Certified Management Accountants Examination, Copyright 1974, 1975, 1976, 1977, 1979, 1980, 1981, 1982, 1983, 1984, 1985, 1986, 1987, 1988, 1989, by the Institute of Certified Management Accountants, is reprinted (or adapted) with permission.

This book is printed on acid-free paper.

1 2 3 4 5 6 7 8 9 0 QPD/QPD 0 9 8

ISBN 978-0-07-352691-1
MHID 0-07-352691-6

Publisher: *Tim Vertovec*
Editorial coordinator: *Christina Lane*
Associate marketing manager: *Dean Karampelas*
Senior project manager: *Harvey Yep*
Senior manager, EDP: *Heather D. Burbridge*
Designer: *Matt Diamond*
Media project manager: *Balaji Sundararaman, Hurix Systems Pvt. Ltd.*
Cover design: *Matt Diamond*
Cover image: © *Getty Images*
Typeface: *10.5/12 Times New Roman*
Compositor: *Laserwords Private Limited*
Printer: *Quebecor World Dubuque Inc.*

**Library of Congress Cataloging-in-Publication Data**

Advanced financial accounting/Richard E. Baker ... [et al.]—8th ed.
    p. cm.
   Includes index.
   ISBN-13: 978-0-07-352691-1 (alk. paper)
   ISBN-10: 0-07-352691-6 (alk. paper)
   1. Accounting.   I. Baker, Richard E.
HF5635.B165   2009
657'.046—dc22                2008032739

www.mhhe.com

# About the Authors

### Richard E. Baker

Richard E. Baker is a member of the faculty at Northern Illinois University. His academic recognitions include having been named the Ernst & Young Distinguished Professor of Accountancy at Northern Illinois University. In addition, he has been recognized as an inaugural University Presidential Teaching Professor, the highest teaching recognition of his university. He received his B.S. degree from the University of Wisconsin at River Falls and his MBA and Ph.D. from the University of Wisconsin at Madison. His activities in the American Accounting Association have been continuous over many years and include service on the AAA's Executive Committee as the Director of Education of the AAA; as a member of the AAA's Council; as the Chair of the Teaching and Curriculum Section; and as the President of the Midwest Region. His lengthy service to the Federation of Schools of Accountancy (FSA) includes the offices of the President, the Vice President, and the Secretary. Many of his extensive professional and academic organization committee service efforts have involved research in assessing teaching and learning outcomes, designing innovative curriculum models, developing meaningful measurement criteria for evaluating accounting programs, and continually integrating new electronic technology into the accounting classroom. Professor Baker has served as an Associate Editor for *Issues in Accounting Education* and previously served as a reviewer for this journal for several years. He has served as a reviewer and as an Associate Editor of *Advances in Accounting Education.* He has received numerous teaching awards at both the undergraduate and graduate levels and has been selected as the Illinois CPA Society's Outstanding Accounting Educator. His most recent published research studies have concentrated on ways to make the learning/teaching experience as effective as possible. Other published research includes studies in financial reporting and mergers and acquisitions. Professor Baker's major teaching areas include advanced financial accounting, financial theory, and international business management. He is a CPA and has taught advanced financial accounting topics in numerous CPA Examination review courses.

### Valdean C. Lembke

Valdean C. Lembke has been a faculty member in the Department of Accounting at the University of Iowa for many years. He received his B.S. degree from Iowa State University and his MBA and Ph.D. from the University of Michigan. He has internal audit and public accounting experience. He has been active in the American Accounting Association, including service as President of the Midwest Region and book review editor for *Issues in Accounting Education.* He was twice named recipient of the Gilbert P. Maynard Excellence in Accounting Instruction award. Professor Lembke has been actively involved in service to the Department of Accounting. He served two terms as department head and has been head of the Professional Program in Accounting. Professor Lembke has authored and coauthored articles in journals such as *The Accounting Review;* the *Journal of Accounting, Auditing and Finance;* the *Journal of Accountancy;* and the *Internal Auditor.* He also coauthored *Financial Accounting: A Decision Making Approach,* an introductory accounting text, and a chapter on business combinations and consolidated financial statements in the *Accountant's Encyclopedia.* His teaching has been primarily in undergraduate and graduate coursework in financial accounting and in governmental and not-for-profit accounting. He has taught advanced financial accounting on a continuing basis.

### Thomas E. King

Thomas E. King is a member of the faculty of the School of Business at Southern Illinois University Edwardsville. He received his B.S. degree from California State University, Northridge, and his MBA and Ph.D. from the University of California, Los Angeles. He is a CPA and received an Elijah Watt Sells Award and the Illinois gold medal for his scores on the Uniform CPA Examination. He has a number of years of business and consulting experience and has taught for more than 30 years. Professor King coauthored with Valdean Lembke the chapter on business combinations and consolidated financial statements in the *Accountant's Encyclopedia,* and he has authored and coauthored numerous articles in journals such as *The Accounting Review; Accounting Horizons;* the *Journal of Accountancy;* the *Journal of Accounting, Auditing and Finance;* the *Journal of Accounting Education;* and *Financial Executive.* He also coauthored *Financial Accounting: A Decision-Making Approach,* an introductory accounting text. Professor King has served on the editorial boards of *Advances in Accounting* and *Advances in Accounting Education* for a number of years. He served two terms on the Board of Governors of the St. Louis Chapter of the Institute of Internal Auditors, and he has been active in the Financial Executives Institute, the Institute of Management Accountants, and the Illinois CPA Society. Professor King has taught advanced financial accounting extensively, along with a wide variety of other financial and managerial accounting courses.

## Cynthia G. Jeffrey

Cynthia G. Jeffrey is an Associate Professor of Accounting in the College of Business at Iowa State University. She received her B.S. and M.S. at Iowa State University and her Ph.D. from the University of Minnesota. She is a CPA and is a member of the AICPA, American Accounting Association, and the Canadian Academic Accounting Association. Professor Jeffrey received the Graduate Teaching Award from Iowa State University in 2005 and was recognized as Teacher of the Year in 2000. She was Director of the Master of Accounting program from its inception in 1999 until 2004. Professor Jeffrey has authored and coauthored articles in journals such as *The Accounting Review; Journal of Accounting, Auditing and Finance; Business Ethics Quarterly; Behavioral Research in Accounting; The International Journal of Accounting;* the *Asia-Pacific Journal of Accounting;* and *Issues in Accounting Education.* Professor Jeffrey is the editor of *Research on Professional Responsibility and Ethics in Accounting.* Professor Jeffrey teaches both graduate and undergraduate courses. Her major teaching areas are financial accounting, financial accounting theory, and international accounting.

# Preface

The Eighth Edition of *Advanced Financial Accounting* is an up-to-date, comprehensive, and highly illustrated presentation of the accounting and reporting principles and procedures used in a variety of business entities. Every day, the business press carries stories about the merger and acquisition mania, the complexities of modern business entities, new organizational structures for conducting business, accounting scandals related to complex business transactions, the foreign activities of multinational firms, the operations of governmental and not-for-profit entities, bankruptcies of major firms, and other topics typically included in advanced accounting. Accountants must understand and know how to deal with the accounting and reporting ramifications of these issues.

## OVERVIEW

The Eighth Edition of *Advanced Financial Accounting* continues to provide strong coverage of advanced accounting topics, with clarity of presentation and integrated coverage based on continuous case examples. The text is highly illustrated with complete presentations of worksheets, schedules, and financial statements so that students can see the development of each topic. Inclusion of all recent FASB and GASB pronouncements and the continuing deliberations of the authoritative bodies provide a current and contemporary text for students preparing for the CPA Examination and current practice. This has become especially important given the recent rapid pace of the authoritative bodies in dealing with major issues having far-reaching implications. Of particular note is the recent issuance of **Financial Accounting Standards Board Statement No. 141 (revised 2007),** "Business Combinations" (FASB 141R) and **Financial Accounting Standards Board Statement No. 160,** "Noncontrolling Interests in Consolidated Financial Statements; an amendment of ARB No. 51" (FASB 160). Together, these pronouncements have made some of the most significant changes in accounting for business combinations and the presentation of consolidated financial statements in decades. The Eighth Edition provides extensive coverage of these and other recent pronouncements. Thus, many areas of the new edition of this text are significantly changed from previous editions.

The Eighth Edition continues the practice of previous editions in the consolidations chapters of demonstrating three alternative sets of consolidation procedures, depending on the method of accounting for the parent's investment in the subsidiary. The main body of each consolidation chapter focuses on consolidation following use of the basic equity method on the parent's books, with consolidation following use of the cost method and the fully adjusted equity method illustrated in appendices. This provides the opportunity for exploring the differences in the methods and seeing that the consolidated financial statements are the same regardless of the method the parent company uses to account for the investment.

The chapters dealing with global operations include a comprehensive discussion of accounting for foreign currency derivatives and other financial instruments and arrangements used in today's business arena. Also, the global chapters include increased discussion of International Financial Reporting Standards (IFRS). The governmental chapters include the many recent important developments with integration of recent GASB Statements and significant focus on the GASB's Exposure Draft entitled "Fund Balance Reporting and Governmental Fund Type Definitions." The not-for-profit chapter includes discussion of the FASB's Exposure Draft on mergers of not-for-profit entities.

## KEY FEATURES

The key strengths of this text are the clear and readable discussions of concepts and the detailed demonstrations of concepts through illustrations and explanations. The many favorable responses to prior editions from both students and instructors confirm our belief that clear presentation and comprehensive illustrations are essential to learning the sophisticated topics in an advanced accounting course. Key features of the Eighth Edition include:

- **A building-block approach based on a strong conceptual foundation.** For each major topic area, students are provided with a thorough conceptual understanding before advancing to the procedures. The discussion begins with the fundamental concepts and why they are important. The fundamentals are then illustrated, giving students a basic example before progressing. Once the conceptual foundation is established, the complexities are layered gradually in successive steps. The authors developed this methodology through years of teaching advanced accounting. Many adopters have commented favorably on the effectiveness of this approach.

- **The use of a continuous case for each major subject-matter area.** The comprehensive case of Peerless Products Corporation and its subsidiary, Special Foods Inc., is used throughout the for-profit chapters. For the governmental chapters, the Sol City case has been used to facilitate the development of governmental accounting and reporting concepts and procedures. Using a continuous case provides several benefits. First, students need only become familiar with one set of data and can then move more quickly through the subsequent discussion and illustrations without having to absorb a new set of data. Second, the case adds realism to the study of advanced accounting and permits students to see the effects of each successive step on the financial reports of an entity. Finally, comparing and contrasting alternative methods using a continuous case allows students to evaluate different methods and outcomes more readily.

- **Extensive illustrations of key concepts.** The book is heavily illustrated with complete, not partial, workpapers, financial statements, and other computations and comparisons useful for demonstrating each topic. The illustrations are cross-referenced to the relevant text discussion. In the consolidations portion of the text, the focus is on the basic equity method of accounting for an investment in a subsidiary, but two other methods—the cost method and the fully adjusted equity method—are fully discussed and illustrated in chapter appendices. Workpaper elimination entries presented in the consolidations chapters are separately identified with an (E) and are shaded to differentiate them clearly from book entries. The extensive use of illustrations makes the learning process more efficient by allowing students to see quickly and readily the applications of the concepts. In addition, the illustrations reinforce understanding of the concepts by demonstrating the effects on the financial statements. In this manner, students understand that the many workpaper procedures typically covered in advanced accounting represent the means to a desired end, not the end itself.

- **Comprehensive coverage with significant flexibility.** The subject matter of advanced accounting is expanding at an unprecedented rate. New topics are being added, and traditional topics require more extensive coverage. Flexibility is therefore essential in an advanced accounting text. Most one-term courses are unable to cover all the topics included in this text. In recognition of time constraints, this text is structured to provide the most efficient use of the time available. The self-contained units of subject matter allow for substantial flexibility in sequencing the course materials. In addition, individual chapters are organized to allow for going into greater depth on some topics through the use of the "Additional Considerations" sections. Several chapters include appendices containing discussions of alternative accounting procedures or illustrations of procedures or concepts that are of a supplemental nature.

- **Contemporary topical coverage.** The dynamic business environment requires accountants to continually learn about new types of transactions, new technologies available to the profession, and new requirements and standards for accounting and financial reporting. This textbook integrates the most recent professional standards and includes cases and examples from current practice. For example, the importance in recent years of topics such as the Sarbanes-Oxley Act, special-purpose entities (SPEs), variable interest entities (VIEs), derivatives, fair value reporting, and International Financial Reporting Standards (IFRS) has led to significant coverage of these topics in the current and recent editions of the text. The GASB's recent focus on enhanced financial statement disclosures for governmental entities is discussed and illustrated. Students are presented with an abundance of current information and learning opportunities to see that the topics in their advanced financial accounting courses are a significant part of today's profession of accountancy.

- **Extensive end-of-chapter materials.** A large number of questions, cases, exercises, and problems at the end of each chapter provide the opportunity to solidify understanding of the chapter material and assess mastery of the subject matter. The end-of-chapter materials progress from simple focused exercises to more complex integrated problems. Cases provide opportunities for extending thought, gaining exposure to different sources of accounting-related information, and applying the course material to real-world situations. These cases include Financial Accounting Research System (FARS) database searches, and Kaplan CPA Review simulations. The American Institute of CPAs has identified five skills to be examined as part of the CPA Exam: (*a*) analysis, (*b*) judgment, (*c*) communication, (*d*) research, and (*e*) understanding. The end-of-chapter materials provide abundant opportunities for students to enhance those skills with realistic and real-world applications of advanced financial accounting topics. Cases and exercises identified with a world globe icon provide special opportunities for students to access real-world data by using electronic databases, Internet search engines, or other inquiry processes to answer the questions presented on the topics in the chapters.

# ORGANIZATION: THE STORY OF PEERLESS PRODUCTS CORPORATION AND SPECIAL FOODS INC.

This textbook presents the complete story of a company, Peerless Products Corporation, from its beginning, through its growth to a multinational consolidated entity, and finally to its end. At each stage of the entity's development, including the acquisition of a subsidiary, Special Foods Inc., the text presents comprehensive examples and discussions of the accounting and financial reporting issues that accountants face. The discussions tied to the Peerless Products continuous case are easily identified by the company logos in the margin:

The following description explains how this text is organized and how continuing examples are used to demonstrate many of the topics.

## Business Combinations, Intercorporate Equity Investments, and Consolidation Concepts

Chapters 1, 2, and 3 of the textbook introduce the issue of complex organizational structures. These complex structures can be achieved in a number of ways, such as by creating them, investing in other entities, or through business combinations. These chapters discuss investments in entities such as special-purpose entities, variable interest entities, and partnerships. The chapters especially focus on investments in other corporations through acquisition of those corporations or through either subsidiary or nonsubsidiary investments in the common stock of those corporations.

## Business Combinations

Chapter 1 focuses primarily on business combinations, the acquisition of one business by another. The chapter discusses the ways in which one company can acquire another and how to account for acquisitions. The chapter provides in-depth coverage of acquisition accounting as required under **FASB 141R,** along with the important details of that pronouncement. In addition, many of the more detailed requirements of **FASB 141R** are presented in the "Additional Considerations" section of the chapter. Although the methods that were used to account for business combinations prior to 2009 are no longer acceptable, the effects of many business combinations accounted for using those methods are still found in current financial statements. Thus, students need some appreciation of the effects of those methods. Accordingly, brief consideration is given to those methods in the main part of the chapter, with more extensive coverage provided in an appendix.

## Interests in Other Entities

Chapters 2 and 3 deal with equity and other types of interests in entities that include partnerships, special-purpose entities, and variable interest entities. However, these chapters concentrate on investments in the common stock of other corporations. Chapter 2 focuses on investments in the common stock of other corporations that do not result in controlling financial interests. Chapter 3 deals with intercorporate investments that lead to the presentation of consolidated financial statements. This chapter provides a conceptual foundation for the study of consolidated financial statements and discusses and illustrates several different theories of consolidation. The chapter also discusses the significant impact **FASB 141R** and **FASB 160** have had on consolidated financial statements and the challenges yet facing the FASB in the development of a coherent consolidation policy. Based on the framework and overview presented in Chapter 3, Chapters 4 through 10 provide coverage of the more detailed concepts and procedures related to the preparation of consolidated financial statements.

## Consolidation of Wholly Owned Subsidiaries

The discussion of detailed consolidation procedures begins in Chapter 4 with the consolidation of wholly owned subsidiaries. Wholly owned subsidiaries provide a good starting point because most subsidiaries are wholly owned and basic consolidation procedures can be examined without the complexities of dealing with noncontrolling interests. This chapter initiates the story of Peerless Products Corporation, which purchases all of the stock of Special Foods Inc. and maintains Special Foods as a subsidiary. The consolidation workpaper is presented, with discussion of both a simple balance sheet workpaper as of the date of combination and a three-part workpaper for the preparation of a full set of consolidated financial statements subsequent to the acquisition date. Basic consolidation procedures for the date of combination and subsequent periods are presented. Illustrations for the consolidation of Peerless Products and its wholly owned subsidiary Special Foods are provided both for acquisition at book value and at amounts other than book value.

## Consolidation of Less-than-Wholly Owned Subsidiaries

Chapter 5 builds on the consolidation concepts introduced in Chapters 3 and 4 with an examination of the complexities added by a parent acquiring less than 100 percent ownership of a subsidiary. The consolidation of less-than-wholly owned subsidiaries is illustrated for two years of operations by assuming that Peerless Products acquires 80 percent of Special Foods' stock. The full impact of **FASB 141R** and **FASB 160** can be seen in the procedures presented in Chapter 5. Because **FASB 141R** and **FASB 160** may not be applied retrospectively, the consolidation of subsidiaries acquired prior to 2009 is also illustrated.

## Intercompany Transactions

As is common for affiliated companies, Peerless Products and Special Foods engage in a number of intercompany transactions. Chapters 6, 7, and 8 discuss intercorporate transfers of services, noncurrent assets, and inventory, as well as intercompany debt transactions.

## Complex Ownership Issues

Chapter 9 examines the special consolidation problems that arise from complex owner-ship structures. Included are the accounting issues that arise if: (1) Special Foods issues preferred stock, (2) Peerless's percentage ownership in Special Foods changes through its transactions in Special Foods' stock or through Special Foods' equity transactions, (3) Special Foods acquires a subsidiary of its own, (4) Special Foods acquires some of Peerless's stock, and (5) Special Foods issues stock dividends.

## Consolidation Reporting Issues

Chapter 10 completes the discussion of consolidated reporting by presenting several ad-ditional consolidation issues encountered by Peerless and Special Foods. First, the prep-aration of a consolidated cash flow statement is discussed and illustrated for Peerless Products and Special Foods. Second, the impact of interim acquisitions on consolidated financial statements is examined. Third, the chapter discusses tax considerations related to consolidated entities. Chapter 10 concludes with a discussion of the computation of consolidated earnings per share.

## Multinational Accounting

Chapters 11 and 12 present the accounting and reporting issues that arise when Peerless enters the multinational business environment. First, Peerless extends its sales to inter-national customers and begins dealing in foreign currency transactions. To manage its risk, Peerless uses forward exchange contracts and other financial derivatives for hedging purposes. Comprehensive appendices are presented that discuss using the time value of derivatives and accounting for other forms of derivatives. In Chapter 12, Peerless acquires a subsidiary located in Germany. The German company reports its operations in euros, and Peerless must translate the subsidiary's trial balance into U.S. dollars to consolidate the operations of its German subsidiary.

## Segment and Interim Reporting

Chapter 13 discusses segment reporting requirements, and examines the segment and related disclosures that Peerless must make in its consolidated financial statements. In-terim financial reporting also is discussed in this chapter and is illustrated with Peerless's interim reports.

## SEC Reporting

Chapter 14 presents a discussion of the issues that Peerless must understand if it wishes to "go public" and issue stock or debt in the capital markets. The Securities and Ex-change Commission has many specific rules, procedures, and reporting requirements that companies must follow if their securities are going to trade publicly. Coverage of the Sarbanes-Oxley Act is presented in this chapter so that students can gain some insights into this significant Act. The recent actions of the SEC to allow for IFRS in filings are presented and discussed.

## Partnership Accounting

Chapters 15 and 16 step back in chronology to review the origins of Peerless Prod-ucts. The process begins with C. Alt starting a software development business. Alt then forms a partnership with Blue, and, after operating for a year, the two partners bring Cha into the partnership because they need her business expertise. Accounting issues associated with partnership accounting are presented in these two chapters. Alternative approaches to partnership liquidation are illustrated. After operating the partnership for several years, the partners incorporate their business under the name of Peerless Products Corporation.

## Governmental and Nonprofit Accounting

Chapters 17 and 18 present the accounting and financial reporting for Sol City, the city in which Peerless Products is located. C. Alt serves on the city council, and the chapters present the accounting information needed by Alt to represent his constituents and by creditors and other financial statement users who wish to evaluate the government's service efforts and accomplishments. Chapter 19 presents the accounting and financial reporting requirements for Sol City University and for Sol City Community Hospital along with several other nonprofit agencies in Sol City.

## Corporations in Financial Difficulty

Chapter 20 closes the story of Peerless Products and Special Foods. Because of the poor health of C. Alt, the consolidated entity experiences a variety of financial problems. Attempts are made to restructure its debt and to reorganize with the help of a court-appointed receiver. However, the company has too many financial problems and is forced to enter into bankruptcy.

## Supplemental Chapters

The text's Web site (www.mhhe.com/baker8e) contains two supplemental chapters. The first is on Accounting for Branch Operations that presents illustrations and discussion on the issues of accounting and reporting for home office and branches. The second supplemental chapter is Estates and Trusts that presents the accounting for C. Alt's estate by Blue, the administrator of the estate and also the first partner brought into the Peerless Products partnership. These chapters include end-of-chapter material for which solutions may be obtained online by instructors. Material on creditor accounting for impaired loans and troubled debt restructuring has been moved to the book's Web site. This material is being covered in more intermediate financial accounting courses and the Web site information is available for those needing a quick review.

# CHANGES FOR THE EIGHTH EDITION

For the Eighth Edition, each of the chapters in the text has been revised to include comprehensive discussion and full illustration of relevant recently issued FASB and GASB standards and exposure drafts. In addition, end-of-chapter materials have been revised to best illustrate and explore both prior and new standards.

1. **Integration of new FASB standards on business combinations and consolidated financial statements.** The FASB recently issued two new standards that have a significant effect on accounting for business combinations and the presentation of consolidated financial statements. **FASB 141R** mandates the use of the acquisition method in accounting for business combinations and makes a number of significant changes that affect accounting for business combinations and the preparation of consolidated financial statements. **FASB 160** makes a number of significant changes relating to consolidated financial statements, such as how consolidated net income is calculated and the way in which the noncontrolling interest is reported. In addition, it clarifies how certain equity transactions are reported, how to account for interim acquisitions of subsidiaries, and how to account for deconsolidation. These new pronouncements are integrated where applicable throughout, but they receive special emphasis in Chapters 1, 3, 5, and 9. In addition, reduced coverage of prior standards is included because of the continued effect they have on financial statements. The end-of-chapter materials fully reflect the new standards and provide the opportunity to compare with previous standards.

2. **Inclusion of conceptual aspects of consolidation theories and issues.** Because both **FASB 141R** and **FASB 160** reflect a change in the basic approach to financial reporting subsequent to an acquisition, students need a strong foundation in the underlying concepts. The text, especially in Chapter 3, provides this conceptual foundation,

discussing the change in approach represented in the new standards and summarizing the related issues still being deliberated by the FASB.

3. **Expanded discussion of International Financial Reporting Standards (IFRS).** The SEC recently decided to allow foreign private issuers to submit financial statements prepared according to IFRS without requiring reconciliation to U.S. GAAP. In 2007, the SEC published a concept release exploring the potential for allowing U.S. issuers to prepare financial statements in accordance with IFRS. At an SEC Roundtable in December 2007, the majority of participants thought that the SEC should either require or allow U.S. issuers to report using IFRS within the near future. This new edition of the text discusses the issues related to convergence and the incentives driving convergence.

4. **Further integration of the Revised Uniform Partnership Act.** The model Revised Uniform Partnership Act (RUPA) continues to gain adoptions, now in about 40 states. Chapters 15 and 16 discuss and illustrate the essential provisions of RUPA, especially in a disassociation and for liquidation of a partnership.

5. **Increased focus on governmental and not-for-profit financial statements and disclosures.** Chapters 17 and 18 (on governmental entities) and Chapter 19 (not-for-profit entities) are updated for recent GASB and FASB standards and exposure drafts. For example, the GASB's recent action on fund balance reporting and governmental fund type definitions is discussed and illustrated. The discussion and end-of-chapter materials are enhanced to provide students with more opportunities to understand how the accounting and reporting standards affect the financial statements and other elements of the entities' annual reports.

6. **More "real-world" examples throughout the text.** Additional "real-world" examples have been added throughout the chapters to illustrate the topics and to show students that the topics covered are important for accountants to understand and be able to apply in the dynamic business environment. These examples make it "real" for students.

7. **End-of-chapter materials have been revised.**
   • *New cases:* Real-world cases included in the end-of-chapter materials have been updated and a number of new ones added throughout the text. These cases provide students with a sense of relevancy, an opportunity to engage in online research, and the chance to practice formal writing. Cases employing data from actual real-world companies or other forms of entities have been identified with a global icon.
   • *Recent major pronouncements:* The end-of-chapter materials include coverage of the most current pronouncements of the GASB and FASB.
   • *Supplemental problems:* Some of the longer complex problems in many of the chapters have been moved to the textbook's Web site (www.mhhe.com/baker8e) and are presented as Supplemental Problems. Advanced Financial Accounting classes that wish to intensively explore the accounting and reporting requirements of a chapter's topics can access the Web site and download the problem material. Moving some of the longer problems to the Web site allowed space to add real-world research cases to the text that are becoming so important for Advanced Financial Accounting courses.

## RETAINED FEATURES

The features that provided the strength of prior editions have been retained in the Eighth Edition:

1. The comprehensive continuous case approach has been retained because it provides students with the ability to see how each successive step affects the financial reporting model of an entity. The Peerless Products and Special Foods case is robust and serves as a foundation for the building-block approach used throughout the text. The Sol City case integrates coverage of governmental accounting and financial reporting.

2. Extensive efforts have been made to ensure retention of the clear writing style that faculty and students have valued very highly in previous editions as each chapter was revised to reflect recent FASB and GASB standards, as well as to refine and focus the discussion and presentations.

3. The full coverage of the FASB and GASB standards and exposure drafts that have direct applicability to the topics in Advanced Financial Accounting has been continued.

4. Cases at the end of each chapter requiring students to write essay-type responses reflecting alternative viewpoints or justifying a specific accounting choice have been retained and updated. Students are asked to explain their reasoning and often are asked to use library or Internet research tools and materials in support of their answers. These cases require students to go beyond the computational level in addressing the topics in Advanced Financial Accounting.

   Simulations relevant to Advanced Financial Accounting issues using the framework by Kaplan CPA Review have been retained. Students can work the simulations online to gain experience on the presentation and operation of simulations that appear on the computerized CPA exam.

5. The Study Guide for the text is written by the authors of the text to ensure full integration and compatible presentation of the topics. The Study Guide for the Eighth Edition has been revised to reflect all the updates and enhancements in the textbook coverage as a result of the new FASB and GASB standards, and every effort has been made to continue to provide a terrific learning tool for students.

6. Because Advanced Financial Accounting is often taken by students who plan to take the CPA Examination, numerous end-of-chapter materials are provided in the formats used for testing on the CPA Examination. A wide variety of multiple-choice questions and cases requiring database research and written presentations are provided.

# SUPPLEMENTS

This text is accompanied by a full ancillary program with items designed to enhance the learning process. Supplemental materials are available from McGraw-Hill/Irwin.

## For the Student

### Study Guide (0073360104)

Written by the authors of the text, the study guide contains summaries of the key concepts presented in each chapter and provides self-diagnostic and review materials in the form of objective-type and fill-in-the-blank questions, as well as both short and comprehensive exercises and problems. The solutions are provided so that achievement levels can be assessed readily and topics that need further review can be identified.

### Online Learning Center (URL: www.mhhe.com/baker8e), Student Edition

- *Learning Objectives:* The online material for each chapter begins with the Learning Objectives for that chapter. Students can gain an overview of the importance to accountants of the topics covered in each chapter.

- *Online Quizzes:* Prepared by ANSR Source India Private Limited, interactive quizzes give students a variety of multiple-choice and true/false questions related to the text for self-evaluation.

- *Excel Worksheets:* Prepared by Harlan Fuller, these worksheets for use with Excel are provided to facilitate completion of problems requiring numerous mechanical computations. Available only online.

- *Check Figures:* Prepared by the text authors, a list of answers is provided separately for many of the end-of-chapter materials in the text. Available only online.

- *Microsoft PowerPoint Slides®:* Authored by ANSR Source India Private Limited, copies of the Microsoft PowerPoint Slides® are available by chapter to facilitate note taking and review.
- *Supplemental Problems:* Additional problem materials for a number of the chapters are available online to enhance students' learning of the topics in the chapters. These supplemental problems tend to be longer problems that present a more comprehensive fact situation and can extend understanding of the topics in the chapters to a broader scope.
- *Supplemental Chapters:* Two chapters are available online for those persons wishing extended learning: (*a*) accounting for home office and branch operations; and (*b*) accounting and reporting for estates and trusts. Cases, exercises, and problems are also available for these two chapters.
- *PowerWeb:* This feature is a unique Web site that extends the learning experience beyond the core textbook and includes the following learning aids:

  ➢ Current readings
  ➢ Study tips and self-quizzes
  ➢ Links to related sites
  ➢ Web research guides
  ➢ Access to Northern Light Search Engine providing Internet access to additional articles

## For the Instructor

### *Instructor's Resource CD-ROM (0073360082)*

Only for instructors, this CD combines all instructor resource teaching supplements into one easy-to-use format:

- *Solutions Manual:* Created by the authors, solutions are provided for all questions, cases, exercises, and problems in the text. Solutions are carefully explained and logically presented. Answers for many of the multiple-choice questions include computations and explanations. Instructors can prepare transparencies directly from the Solutions Manual.
- *Instructors' Resource Manual:* Prepared by ANSR Source India Private Limited, the Instructor's Resource Manual includes chapter outlines, additional examples, teaching suggestions, and other materials to assist instructors in making the most effective use of the text.
- *Test Bank:* Authored by ANSR Source India Private Limited, this comprehensive collection of both conceptual and procedural test items has been revised. The material is organized by chapter and includes a large variety of multiple-choice questions, exercises, and problems that can be used to measure student achievement in the topics in each chapter. The test items are closely coordinated with the text to ensure consistency.

### *Online Learning Center (URL: www.mhhe.com/baker8e), Instructor Edition*

- Instructor supplements such as the *Solutions Manual, Instructor's Resource Manual,* and *Microsoft PowerPoint Slides®* are available in downloadable form and are password protected.
- *Supplemental Problems:* Downloadable additional exercises and problems are provided for a number of chapters on both the Student Edition and the Instructor Edition. Instructors can assign these additional exercises and problems to broaden their students' understanding of the topics in the chapters. The Instructor Edition includes downloadable solutions to those supplemental exercises and problems.
- *Supplemental Chapters:* Two chapters are available online: (*a*) accounting for home office and branch operations; and (*b*) accounting and reporting for estates and trusts. Cases, exercises, and problems are also available for these two chapters and the Instructor Edition includes solutions to those end-of-chapter items.

- *Instructor Updates:* Contains timely discussions and illustrations of major accounting or financial reporting issues under deliberation by standard-setting bodies. Instructors can choose to download these updates and share them with their students.
- *PowerWeb* delivers to instructors and students the latest news and developments pertinent to the course.

  ➢ Access to current articles related to advanced financial accounting
  ➢ Updates
  ➢ Links to related sites
  ➢ Web research guide
  ➢ Access to Northern Light Search Engine providing Internet access to additional articles

- *Online Course Support* provides course content cartridges available for course Web sites to support online class delivery when using products such as WebCT or Blackboard.
- *Page-Out* is McGraw-Hill's Course Management System that provides a "point and click" course Web site tool.

# Acknowledgments

This text includes the thoughts and contributions of many individuals, and we wish to express our sincere appreciation to them. First and foremost, we thank all the students in our advanced accounting classes, from whom we have learned so much. In many respects, this text is an outcome of the learning experiences we have shared with our students. Second, we wish to thank the many outstanding teachers we have had in our own educational programs, from whom we learned the joy of learning. We are indebted to our colleagues in advanced accounting for helping us reach our goal of writing the best possible advanced financial accounting text. We appreciate the many valuable comments and suggestions from the faculty who used recent editions of the text. Their comments and suggestions have contributed to making this text a more effective learning tool. We especially wish to thank: Jean C. Bedard, Bentley College; Mark Bettner, Bucknell University; John Bildersee, New York University; Bruce Bradford, Fairfield University; Bobby Carmichael, Texas A&M, Commerce; Charles Christianson, Luther College; David Doran, Pennsylvania State University, Erie; John Engstrom, Northern Illinois University; Sid Hasan, George Mason University; James Hopkins, Morningside College; Gordon Hosch, University of New Orleans; David Karmon, Central Michigan University; May H. Lo, Western New England College; Stephani Mason, Brooklyn College; Ralph McQuade, Jr., Bentley College; Scott Newman, Western State College of Colorado; Larry Prober, Rider University; Terence Reilly, Albright College; John Rhodes, Deloitte LLP; Andrew Rosman, University of Connecticut; Norlin Reuschhoff, University of Notre Dame; Victoria Rymer, University of Maryland at College Park; Pam Smith, Northern Illinois University; Nancy Starnes, Southern Illinois University Edwardsville; James Stice, Brigham Young University; Stuart Webster, University of Wyoming; and Scott Whisenant, University of Houston.

We thank Wendy A. Duffy for her development of FARS cases for several of the chapters. We also thank ANSR Source India Private Limited for their work in accuracy checking, as well as their revisions to the Instructor's Resource Manual, Test Bank, Microsoft PowerPoint Slides®, and Online Quizzes. Additionally, we thank Harlan Fuller for his revisions to the Excel Templates. We especially want to thank Lois Lembke for her many efforts on our Solutions Manual.

We are grateful for the assistance and direction of the McGraw-Hill/Irwin team: Stewart Mattson, Tim Vertovec, Christina Lane, Christa Selig, Michelle Gardner, Harvey Yep, Heather Burbridge, Matt Diamond, Dean Karampelas, and Balaji Sundararaman who all worked hard to champion our book through the production process

Permission has been received from the Institute of Certified Management Accountants of the Institute of Management Accountants to use questions and/or unofficial answers from past CMA examinations. We appreciate the cooperation of the American Institute of Certified Public Accountants for providing permission to adapt and use materials from past Uniform CPA Examinations. And we thank Kaplan CPA Review for providing their online framework for Advanced Financial Accounting students to gain important experience with the types of simulations that are included on the Uniform CPA Examination.

Above all, we extend our deepest appreciation to our families who continue to provide the encouragement and support necessary for this project.

*Richard E. Baker*
*Valdean C. Lembke*
*Thomas E. King*
*Cynthia G. Jeffrey*

# Brief Table of Contents

# Table of Contents

# Intercorporate Acquisitions and Investments in Other Entities

The business environment in the United States is perhaps the most dynamic and vibrant in the world. Each day, new companies and new products enter the marketplace, and others are forced to leave or to change substantially in order to survive. In this setting, existing companies often find it necessary to combine their operations with those of other companies or to establish new operating units in emerging areas of business activity.

In recent years, the business world has witnessed many corporate acquisitions and combinations, often involving some of the nation's largest and best-known companies. Some of these combinations have captured the attention of the public because of the personalities involved, the daring strategies employed, and the huge sums of money at stake.

Recent business practice has also experienced the creation of numerous less traditional types of enterprise structures and new, sometimes novel, entities for carrying out the enterprise's operating and financing activities. The creation of new structures and special entities is often a response to today's current operating environment, with its abundant operating risks, global considerations, and tax complexities. In some cases, however, as evidenced by numerous lawsuits, criminal investigations, congressional actions, and corporate bankruptcies, the legitimacy of the use of some of these structures and special entities has been questioned. The adequacy of some of the accounting methods also has been questioned.

Overall, today's business environment is one of the most exciting and challenging in history, characterized by rapid change and exceptional complexity. In this environment, regulators, such as the Securities and Exchange Commission (SEC), Financial Accounting Standards Board (FASB), and Public Company Accounting Oversight Board (PCAOB), are scrambling to respond to the rapid-paced changes in a manner that ensures the continued usefulness of accounting reports to reflect economic reality.

A number of accounting and reporting issues arise when two or more companies join under common ownership or a company creates a complex organizational structure involving any of a variety of forms of new financing or operating entities. The first 10 chapters of this text focus on a number of these issues. Chapter 1 lays the foundation by describing some of the factors that have led to corporate expansion and some of the types of complex organizational structures and relationships that have evolved. Then the chapter deals explicitly with the accounting and reporting issues related to formal business combinations. Chapter 2 focuses on investments in the common stock of other companies and on selected other types of investments in and relationships with other entities. The next eight chapters systematically develop the reporting procedures used by related companies when one controls the others and they present *consolidated financial statements* that portray the related companies as if they were actually a single company.

# THE DEVELOPMENT OF COMPLEX BUSINESS STRUCTURES

Today's business environment is complex. The complexity arises from doing business across different states and countries, each with its own laws and risks, the intricacies of tax provisions, the myriad of exceedingly complex business transactions and financial instruments, and various other factors. The simple business setting in which one company has two or three manufacturing plants and produces products for a local or regional market is much less common now than it was several decades ago. As companies grow in size, and as a response to the complex business environment, they often develop complex organizational and ownership structures.

## Enterprise Expansion

Most business enterprises seek to expand as a means of survival and profitability. Both the owners and managers of a business enterprise have an interest in seeing a company grow in size. This size often allows economies of scale to exist with regard to production and distribution. By expanding into new markets or acquiring other companies already in those markets, companies can develop new earning potential and those in cyclical industries can add greater stability to earnings through diversification. For example, Boeing, a company very strong in commercial aviation, acquired McDonnell Douglas, a company weak in commercial aviation but very strong in military aviation and other defense and space applications. When orders for commercial airliners plummeted following a precipitous decline in air travel, increased defense spending, partially related to the war in Iraq, helped level out Boeing's earnings.

Corporate management often is rewarded with higher salaries as company size increases. In addition, prestige frequently increases with the size of a company and with a reputation for the successful acquisition of other companies. As a result, corporate management often finds it personally advantageous to increase company size. For instance, Bernard Ebbers started his telecommunications career as the head of a small discount long-distance telephone service company and built it into one of the world's largest corporations, WorldCom. In the process, Ebbers became well known for his acquisition prowess and grew tremendously wealthy—until WorldCom was racked by accounting scandals and declared bankruptcy and Ebbers was sentenced to prison.

## Organizational Structure and Business Objectives

Complex organizational structures often evolve to help achieve a business's objectives, such as increasing profitability or reducing risk. For example, many companies establish subsidiaries to conduct certain business activities. A *subsidiary* is a corporation that is controlled by another corporation, referred to as a *parent company,* usually through majority ownership of its common stock. Because a subsidiary is a separate legal entity, the parent's risk associated with the subsidiary's activities is limited. Companies often transfer their receivables to subsidiaries or special-purpose entities that use the receivables as collateral for bonds issued to other entities (securitization). External parties may hold partial or complete ownership of those entities, allowing the transferring company to share its risk associated with the receivables. In some situations, tax benefits may be realized by conducting certain activities through a separate entity. Bank of America, for example, established a subsidiary to which it transferred bank-originated loans and was able to save $418 million in quarterly taxes.[1]

## Organizational Structure, Acquisitions, and Ethical Considerations

Acquisitions and complex organizational structures have sometimes been used to manipulate financial reporting with the aim of enhancing or enriching managers. Many major corporations, taking advantage of loopholes or laxness in financial reporting requirements, have used subsidiaries or other entities to borrow large amounts of money without

---

[1] "PNC Shakes Up Banking Sector; Investors Exit," *The Wall Street Journal,* January 30, 2002, p. C2.

reporting the debt on their balance sheets. Some companies have created special entities that have then been used to manipulate profits.

The term "special-purpose entity" has become well known in recent years because of the egregious abuse of these entities by companies such as Enron. A ***special-purpose entity*** (SPE) is, in general, a financing vehicle that is not a substantive operating entity, usually one created for a single specified purpose. An SPE may be in the form of a corporation, trust, or partnership. Enron Corp., one of the world's largest companies prior to its collapse in 2001, established many SPEs, at least some of which were intended to manipulate financial reporting. Some of Enron's SPEs apparently were created primarily to hide debt while others were used to create fictional transactions or to convert borrowings into reported revenues.

Accounting for mergers and acquisitions also is an area that can lend itself to manipulation. Arthur Levitt, former chairman of the SEC, referred to some of the accounting practices that have been used in accounting for mergers and acquisitions as "creative acquisition accounting" or "merger magic." For example, a previously widely used method of accounting for business combinations, pooling-of-interests, sometimes created earnings and, in the view of many, provided misleading financial reporting subsequent to a combination. WorldCom was a company built through acquisitions, many of which were accounted for using the pooling-of-interests method. Another approach used by many companies in accounting for their acquisitions was to assign a large portion of the purchase price of an acquired company to its in-process research and development, immediately charging off the full amount to expense and freeing financial reporting in future periods from the burden of those costs. These practices have since been eliminated by the FASB. However, the frequency and size of business combinations, the complexity of acquisition accounting, and the potential impact on financial statements of the accounting methods employed mean that the issues surrounding the accounting for business combinations are of critical importance.

The scandals and massive accounting failures at companies such as Enron, WorldCom, and Tyco, leading to heavy losses suffered by creditors, investors, employees, and others, focused considerable attention on weaknesses in accounting and the accounting profession. In the past several years, Congress, the SEC, and the FASB have taken actions to strengthen the financial reporting process and to clarify the accounting rules relating to special entities and to acquisitions.

# BUSINESS EXPANSION AND FORMS OF ORGANIZATIONAL STRUCTURE

Historically, businesses have expanded by internal growth through new product development and expansion of existing product lines into new markets. In recent decades, however, many companies have chosen to expand by combining with or acquiring other companies. Either approach may lead to a change in organizational structure.

## Expansion from Within

As companies expand from within, they often find it advantageous to conduct their expanded operations through new subsidiaries or other entities, such as partnerships, joint ventures, or special entities. In most of these situations, an identifiable segment of the company's existing assets is transferred to the new entity, and, in exchange, the transferring company receives equity ownership.

Companies may be motivated to establish new subsidiaries or other entities for a variety of reasons. Broadly diversified companies may place unrelated operations in separate subsidiaries to establish clear lines of control and facilitate the evaluation of operating results. In some cases, an entity that specializes in a particular type of activity or has its operations in a particular country may qualify for special tax incentives. Of particular importance in some industries is the fact that a separate legal entity may be permitted to operate in a regulatory environment without subjecting the entire entity to regulatory control. Also, by creating a separate legal entity, a parent company may be able to protect itself from exposing the entire company's assets to legal liability that may stem from a new product line or entry into a higher risk form of business activity.

Companies might also establish new subsidiaries or other entities, not as a means of expansion, but as a means of disposing of a portion of their existing operations through outright sale or a transfer of ownership to existing shareholders or others. In some cases, companies have used this approach in disposing of a segment of operations that no longer fits well with the overall mission of the company. In other cases, the approach has been used as a means of disposing of unprofitable operations or to gain regulatory or shareholder approval of a proposed merger with another company. A *spin-off* occurs when the ownership of a newly created or existing subsidiary is distributed to the parent's stockholders without the stockholders surrendering any of their stock in the parent company. A *split-off* occurs when the subsidiary's shares are exchanged for shares of the parent, thereby leading to a reduction in the outstanding shares of the parent company. Although a transfer of ownership to one or more unrelated parties normally results in a taxable transaction, properly designed transfers of ownership to existing shareholders generally qualify as nontaxable exchanges.

## Expansion through Business Combinations

Many times companies find that entry into new product areas or geographic regions is more easily accomplished by acquiring or combining with other companies than through internal expansion. For example, SBC Communications, a major telecommunications company and one of the "Baby Bells," significantly increased its service area by combining with Pacific Telesis and Ameritech, later acquiring AT&T (and adopting its name), and subsequently combining with BellSouth.

A *business combination* occurs when ". . . an acquirer obtains control of one or more businesses."[2] The concept of *control* relates to the ability to direct policies and management. Traditionally, control over a company has been gained by acquiring a majority of the company's common stock. However, the diversity of financial and operating arrangements employed in recent years also raises the possibility of gaining control with less than majority ownership or, in some cases, with no ownership at all.

The types of business combinations found in today's business environment and the terms of the combination agreements are as diverse as the firms involved. Companies enter into various types of formal and informal arrangements that may have at least some of the characteristics of a business combination. Most companies tend to avoid recording informal agreements on their books because of the potential difficulty of enforcing them. In fact, some types of informal arrangements, such as those aimed at fixing prices or apportioning potential customers, are illegal. Formal agreements generally are enforceable and are more likely to be recognized on the books of the participants.

### *Informal Arrangements*

Informal arrangements take many different forms. A simple gentlemen's agreement may be all that is needed to establish an amiable long-term relationship in a joint business venture. In other cases, companies with complementary products or services develop implicit working relationships. For example, a building contractor might always use a particular electrical or plumbing subcontractor. Some companies form *strategic alliances* for working together on a somewhat more formal basis. For example, Washington Mutual, the country's largest thrift organization, formed a strategic alliance with SAFECO Corporation to distribute SAFECO annuities through Washington Mutual's multistate branch network. Many airlines, such as American with Qantas and Delta with Air France-KLM, routinely enter into route-sharing or code-sharing agreements with one another, and many other well-known companies have entered into strategic agreements, such as Microsoft with Sun Microsystems, Microsoft with Nortel, eBay with VeriSign, Boeing

---

[2] *Financial Accounting Standards Board Statement No. 141 (revised 2007),* "Business Combinations," December 2007, para. 3e.

with IBM, and AOL with Google. Companies that partially depend on each other may use interlocking directorates, in which one or more members serve on the boards of directors of both companies, as a means of providing a degree of mutual direction without taking formal steps to join together.

The informality and freedom that make informal arrangements workable also are strong factors against combining financial statements and treating the companies as if they were a single entity. Another key factor in most informal arrangements is the continuing separation of ownership and the ease with which the informal arrangements can be terminated. Without some type of combined ownership, the essentials of a business combination generally are absent.

### *Formal Agreements*

Formal business combinations usually are accompanied by written agreements. These agreements specify the terms of the combination, including the form of the combined company, the consideration to be exchanged, the disposition of outstanding securities, and the rights and responsibilities of the participants. Consummation of such an agreement requires recognition on the books of one or more of the companies that are a party to the combination.

In some cases, a formal agreement may be equivalent in substance to a business combination, yet different in form. For example, a company entering into an agreement to lease all of another company's assets for a period of several decades is, in effect, acquiring the other company. Similarly, an operating agreement giving to one company full management authority over the operations of another company for an extended period of time may be viewed as a means of effecting a business combination.

## Frequency of Business Combinations

Very few major companies function as single legal entities in our modern business environment. Virtually all major companies have at least one subsidiary, with more than a few broadly diversified companies having several hundred subsidiaries. In some cases, subsidiaries are created to incorporate separately part of the ongoing operations previously conducted within the parent company. Other subsidiaries are acquired through business combinations.

Business combinations are a continuing and frequent part of the business environment. A merger boom occurred in the 1960s. This period was characterized by frantic and, in some cases, disorganized merger binges, resulting in creation of a large number of conglomerates, or companies operating in many different industries. Because many of the resulting companies lacked coherence in their operations, they often were less successful than anticipated, and many of the acquisitions of the 1960s have since been sold or abandoned. In the 1980s, the number of business combinations again increased. That period saw many leveraged buyouts, but the resulting debt has plagued many of those companies over the years.

The number of business combinations through the 1990s dwarfed previous merger booms, with all records for merger activity shattered. This pace continued into the new century, with a record-setting $3.3 trillion in deals closed in 2000.[3] However, with the downturn in the economy in the early 2000s, the number of mergers declined significantly. Many companies put their expansion plans on hold, and a number of the mergers that did occur were aimed at survival. Toward the middle of 2003, merger activity again increased and accelerated significantly through the middle of the decade. During one period of less than 100 hours in 2006, "around $110 billion in acquisition deals were sealed worldwide in sectors ranging from natural gas, to copper, to mouthwash to steel, linking investors and industrialists from India, to Canada, to Luxembourg to the U.S."[4]

[3] Dennis K. Berman and Jason Singer, "Big Mergers Are Making a Comeback as Companies, Investors Seek Growth," *The Wall Street Journal,* November 5, 2005, p. A1.
[4] Dennis K. Berman and Jason Singer, "Blizzard of Deals Heralds an Era of Megamergers," *The Wall Street Journal,* June 27, 2006, p. A1.

Through much of the middle of the decade, merger activity was fueled by a new phenomenon, the use of *private equity* money. Rather than the traditional merger activity that typically involves one publicly held company acquiring another, groups of investors, such as wealthy individuals, pension and endowment funds, and mutual funds, pooled their money to make acquisitions. Most such acquisitions did not result in lasting ownership relationships, with the private equity companies usually attempting to realize a return by selling their investments in a relatively short time. This activity was slowed dramatically by the credit crunch of 2007–2008. Nevertheless, business combinations will continue to be an important business activity into the foreseeable future.

Aside from private-equity acquisitions, business combinations have been common in telecommunications, defense, banking and financial services, information technology, energy and natural resources, entertainment, pharmaceuticals, and manufacturing. Some of the world's largest companies and best-known names have been involved in recent major acquisitions, such as Procter & Gamble, Gillette, Citicorp, Bank of America, AT&T, Whirlpool, Sprint, Verizon, Adobe Systems, Chrysler, Daimler-Benz, ConocoPhillips, British Petroleum, and Exxon.

## Complex Organizational Structures

While a parent-subsidiary structure has been standard for major corporations for a number of decades, more complex structures have started to become common in recent years. Many companies now conduct at least part of their operations through entities other than subsidiaries. As is discussed in Chapter 3, special-purpose and variable interest entities, including trusts, have gained widespread use as financing vehicles. Corporate joint ventures and partnerships are commonly found in energy development and distribution, construction, motion picture production, and various other industries. For example, Cingular Wireless, the largest provider of mobile wireless communications in the United States and now part of AT&T, was operated as a joint venture of AT&T and BellSouth prior to AT&T's acquisition of BellSouth. The adoption of less traditional, innovative organizational structures provides many challenges for financial reporting.

## Organizational Structure and Financial Reporting

When companies expand or change organizational structure by acquiring other companies or through internal division, the new structure must be examined to determine the appropriate financial reporting procedures. Several approaches are possible, depending on the circumstances:

1. **Merger**   A business combination in which the acquired company's assets and liabilities are combined with those of the acquiring company results in no additional organizational components. Thus, financial reporting is based on the original organizational structure.

2. **Controlling ownership**   A business combination in which the acquired company remains as a separate legal entity with a majority of its common stock owned by the purchasing company leads to a parent–subsidiary relationship. Accounting standards normally require that the financial statements of the parent and subsidiary be consolidated for general-purpose reporting so the companies appear as a single company. The treatment is the same if the subsidiary is created rather than purchased. The treatment is also the same when the other entity is unincorporated and the investor company has control and majority ownership.[5]

3. **Noncontrolling ownership**   The purchase of a less-than-majority interest in another corporation does not usually result in a business combination or controlling situation. A similar situation arises when a company creates another entity and holds less than a controlling position in it or purchases a less-than-controlling interest in an existing

---

[5] Majority ownership is generally a sufficient but not a necessary condition for the indicated treatment. Unlike the corporate case, percentage ownership does not fully describe the nature of a beneficial interest in a partnership. Investments in partnerships are discussed in later chapters.

partnership. In its financial statements, the investor company reports its interest in the investee as an investment with the specific method of accounting for the investment dictated by the circumstances.

4. **Other beneficial interest**   One company may have a beneficial interest in another entity even without a direct ownership interest. The beneficial interest may be defined by the agreement establishing the entity or by an operating or financing agreement. When the beneficial interest is based on factors other than percentage ownership, the reporting rules may be complex and depend on the circumstances. In general, a company that has the ability to make decisions significantly affecting the results of another entity's activities or is expected to receive a majority of the other entity's profits and losses is considered to be that entity's *primary beneficiary.* Normally, that entity's financial statements would be consolidated with those of the primary beneficiary.

These different situations, and the related accounting and reporting procedures, will be discussed throughout the first 10 chapters of the text. The primary focus will be on the first three situations, especially the purchase of all or part of another company's stock. The discussion of the fourth situation will be limited because of its complexity and the diversity of possible arrangements.

## CREATING BUSINESS ENTITIES

Companies that choose to conduct a portion of their operations through separate business entities usually do so through corporate subsidiaries, corporate joint ventures, or partnerships. The ongoing accounting and reporting for investments in corporate joint ventures and subsidiaries are discussed in Chapters 2 through 10. Ongoing accounting for investments in partnerships is discussed in Chapter 2, and accounting for partnerships themselves is discussed in Chapters 15 and 16. This section discusses the origination of these entities when the parent or investor creates them rather than purchases an interest in an existing corporation or partnership.

When a company transfers assets or operations to another entity that it has created, a vast number of variations in the types of entities and the types of agreements between the creating company and the created entity are possible. Accordingly, it is impossible to establish a single set of rules and procedures that will suffice in all situations. The discussion here focuses on the most straightforward and quite common cases in which the transferring company creates a subsidiary or partnership that it owns and controls, including cases in which the company intends to transfer ownership to its stockholders. The more complex situations will be reserved for later discussion.

In simple cases, the company transfers assets, and perhaps liabilities, to an entity that the company has created and controls and in which it holds majority ownership. The company transfers assets and liabilities to the created entity at book value, and the transferring company recognizes an ownership interest in the newly created entity equal to the book value of the net assets transferred. Recognition of fair values of the assets transferred in excess of their carrying values on the books of the transferring company normally is not appropriate in the absence of an arm's-length transaction. Thus, no gains or losses are recognized on the transfer by the transferring company. However, if the value of an asset transferred to a newly created entity has been impaired prior to the transfer and its fair value is less than the carrying value on the transferring company's books, the transferring company should recognize an impairment loss and transfer the asset to the new entity at the lower fair value.

The created entity begins accounting for the transferred assets and liabilities in the normal manner based on their book values at the time of transfer. Subsequent financial reporting involves consolidating the created entity's financial statements with those of the parent company. Overall, the consolidated financial statements appear the same as if the transfer had not taken place.

As an illustration of a created entity, assume that Allen Company creates a subsidiary, Blaine Company, and transfers the following assets to Blaine in exchange for all 100,000 shares of Blaine's $2 par common stock:

| Item | Cost | Book Value |
|------|------|------------|
| Cash | | $ 70,000 |
| Inventory | $ 50,000 | 50,000 |
| Land | 75,000 | 75,000 |
| Building | 100,000 | 80,000 |
| Equipment | 250,000 | 160,000 |
| | | $435,000 |

Allen records the transfer with the following entry:[6]

| (1) | Investment in Blaine Company Common Stock | 435,000 | |
|-----|-------------------------------------------|---------|---------|
| | Accumulated Depreciation | 110,000 | |
| | Cash | | 70,000 |
| | Inventory | | 50,000 |
| | Land | | 75,000 |
| | Building | | 100,000 |
| | Equipment | | 250,000 |

$110,000 = (\$100,000 - \$80,000) + (\$250,000 - \$160,000)$

Blaine Company records the transfer of assets and the issuance of stock at the book value of the assets transferred, as follows:

| (2) | Cash | 70,000 | |
|-----|------|--------|---------|
| | Inventory | 50,000 | |
| | Land | 75,000 | |
| | Building | 100,000 | |
| | Equipment | 250,000 | |
| | Accumulated Depreciation | | 110,000 |
| | Common Stock, $2 par | | 200,000 |
| | Additional Paid-In Capital | | 235,000 |

If Blaine Company had been created as a partnership rather than a corporation, the accounting would be similar. Assume that Allen invests the same assets as in the corporate case and an unrelated company, Chaney Corp., invests $65,000 cash for a 10 percent share of Blaine's profits and losses, with Allen operating and controlling the partnership. Allen Company records its investment as in entry (1), with a debit to Investment in Blaine Partnership replacing its investment in Blaine's common stock. Blaine records the receipt of assets from Allen and Chaney as follows:

| (3) | Cash | 135,000 | |
|-----|------|---------|---------|
| | Inventory | 50,000 | |
| | Land | 75,000 | |
| | Building | 100,000 | |
| | Equipment | 250,000 | |
| | Accumulated Depreciation | | 110,000 |
| | Capital, Allen Company | | 435,000 |
| | Capital, Chaney Corp. | | 65,000 |

[6] Journal entries used in the text to illustrate the various accounting procedures are numbered sequentially within individual chapters for easy reference. Each journal entry number appears only once in a chapter.

# BUSINESS COMBINATIONS

A business combination occurs when one party acquires control over one or more businesses. This usually involves two or more separate businesses being joined together under common control. The acquirer may obtain control by paying cash, transferring other assets, issuing debt, or issuing stock. In rare cases, the acquirer might obtain control by agreement or through other means without an exchange taking place. Business combinations can take one of several different forms and can be effected in different ways.

## Forms of Business Combinations

The three primary legal forms of business combinations are illustrated in Figure 1–1. A ***statutory merger*** is a type of business combination in which only one of the combining companies survives and the other loses its separate identity. The acquired company's assets and liabilities are transferred to the acquiring company, and the acquired company is dissolved, or ***liquidated.*** The operations of the previously separate companies are carried on in a single legal entity following the merger.

A ***statutory consolidation*** is a business combination in which both combining companies are dissolved and the assets and liabilities of both companies are transferred to

**FIGURE 1–1**
**Types of Business Combinations**

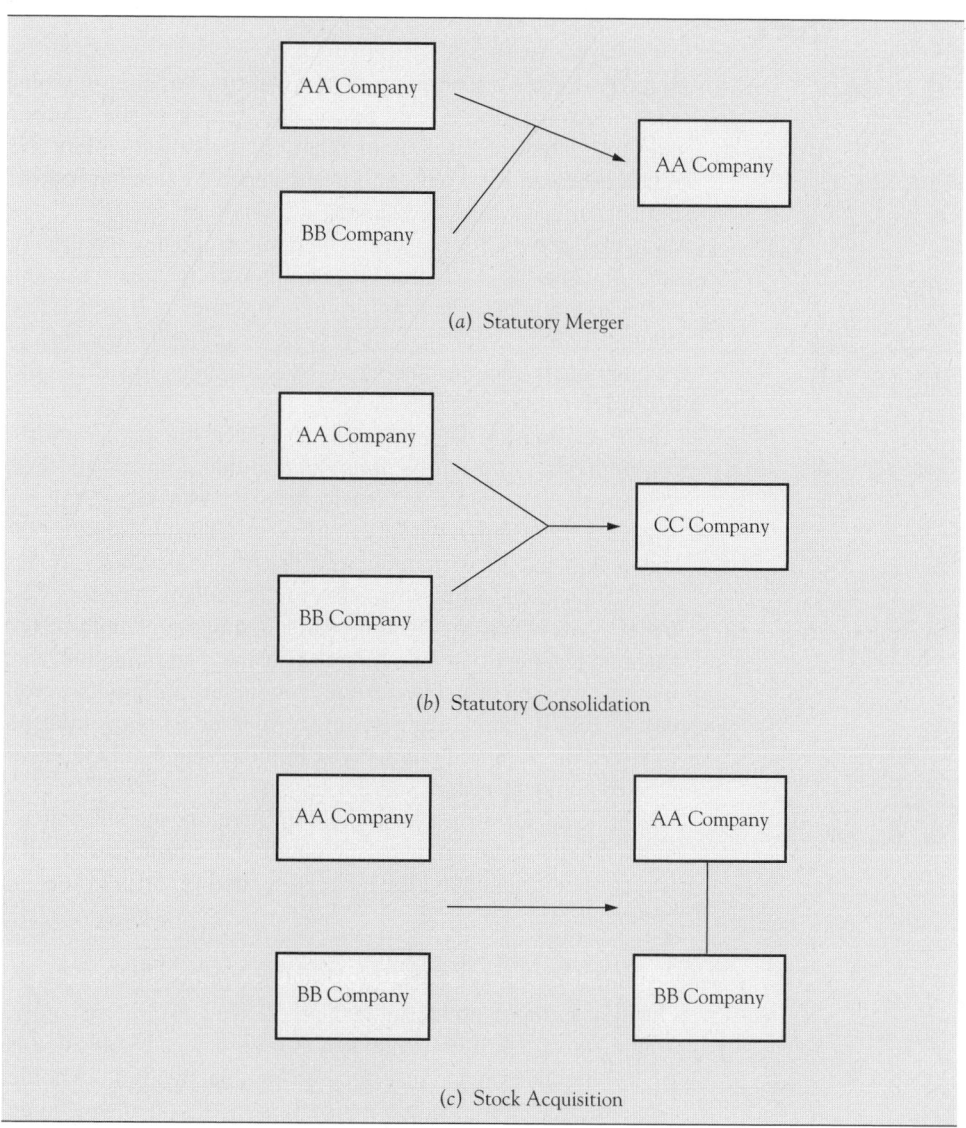

(a) Statutory Merger

(b) Statutory Consolidation

(c) Stock Acquisition

**FIGURE 1–2**
**Determining the
Type of Business
Combination**

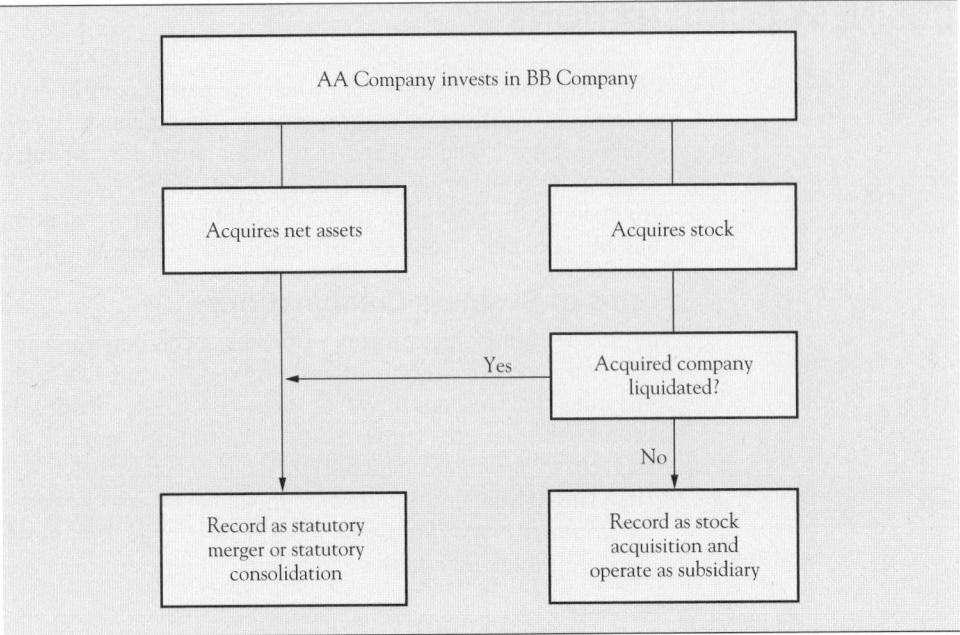

a newly created corporation. The operations of the previously separate companies are carried on in a single legal entity, and neither of the combining companies remains in existence after a statutory consolidation. In many situations, however, the resulting corporation is new in form only, and in substance it actually is one of the combining companies reincorporated with a new name.

A *stock acquisition* occurs when one company acquires the voting shares of another company and the two companies continue to operate as separate, but related, legal entities. Because neither of the combining companies is liquidated, the acquiring company accounts for its ownership interest in the other company as an investment. In a stock acquisition, the acquiring company need not acquire all the other company's stock to gain control.

The relationship that is created in a stock acquisition is referred to as a *parent–subsidiary relationship.* A *parent company* is one that controls another company, referred to as a *subsidiary,* usually through majority ownership of common stock. For general-purpose financial reporting, a parent company and its subsidiaries present consolidated financial statements that appear largely as if the companies had actually merged into one.

As illustrated in Figure 1–2, a stock acquisition occurs when one company acquires a majority of the voting stock of another company and both companies remain in existence as separate legal entities following the business combination. Statutory mergers and consolidations may be effected through acquisition of stock as well as through acquisition of net assets. To complete a statutory merger or consolidation following an acquisition of stock, the acquired company is liquidated and only the acquiring company or a newly created company remains in existence.

The legal form of a business combination, the substance of the combination agreement, and the circumstances surrounding the combination all affect how the combination is recorded initially and the accounting and reporting procedures used subsequent to the combination.

## Methods of Effecting Business Combinations

Business combinations can be characterized as either friendly or unfriendly. In a friendly combination, the managements of the companies involved come to agreement on the terms of the combination and recommend approval by the stockholders. Such combinations usually are effected in a single transaction involving an exchange of assets or voting shares.

In an unfriendly combination, or "hostile takeover," the managements of the companies involved are unable to agree on the terms of a combination, and the management of one of the companies makes a ***tender offer*** directly to the shareholders of the other company. A tender offer invites the shareholders of the other company to "tender," or exchange, their shares for securities or assets of the acquiring company. If sufficient shares are tendered, the acquiring company gains voting control of the other company and can install its own management by exercising its voting rights.

The specific procedures to be used in accounting for a business combination depend on whether the combination is effected through an acquisition of assets or an acquisition of stock.

### *Acquisition of Assets*

Sometimes one company acquires another company's assets through direct negotiations with its management. The agreement also may involve the acquiring company's assuming the other company's liabilities. Combinations of this sort take forms (*a*) or (*b*) in Figure 1–1. The selling company generally distributes to its stockholders the assets or securities received in the combination from the acquiring company and liquidates, leaving only the acquiring company as the surviving legal entity.

The acquiring company accounts for the combination by recording each asset acquired, each liability assumed, and the consideration given in exchange.

### *Acquisition of Stock*

A business combination effected through a stock acquisition does not necessarily have to involve the acquisition of all of a company's outstanding voting shares. For one company to gain control over another through stock ownership, a majority (i.e., more than 50 percent) of the outstanding voting shares usually is required unless other factors lead to the acquirer gaining control. The total of the shares of an acquired company not held by the controlling shareholder is called the ***noncontrolling interest,*** previously referred to as the ***minority interest.***

In those cases when control of another company is acquired and both companies remain in existence as separate legal entities following the business combination, the stock of the acquired company is recorded on the books of the acquiring company as an investment and subsequently is accounted for as an intercorporate investment. Alternatively, the acquired company may be liquidated and its assets and liabilities transferred to the acquiring company or a newly created company. To do so, all or substantially all of the acquired company's voting stock must be obtained. An acquisition of stock and subsequent liquidation of the acquired company is equivalent to an acquisition of assets.

### *Acquisition by Other Means*

Occasionally, a business combination may be effected without an exchange of assets or equities and without a change in ownership. In some cases, control might be acquired through agreement alone, or in rare cases, by some other means.

## Valuation of Business Entities

All parties involved in a business combination must believe they have an opportunity to benefit before they will agree to participate. Determining whether a particular combination proposal is advantageous can be difficult. Both the value of a company's assets and its future earning potential are important in assessing the value of the company. Also, the tax aspects must be considered. For example, one factor that may increase the value of a potential acquiree is the existence of accumulated net operating losses that can be used under U.S. tax law to shelter future income from taxes.

### *Value of Individual Assets and Liabilities*

The value of a company's individual assets and liabilities is usually determined by appraisal. For some items, the value may be determined with relative ease, such as investments that are traded actively in the securities markets, or short-term payables. For other items, the appraisal may be much more subjective, such as the value of land located in an area where few recent sales have occurred. In addition, certain intangibles typically are not reported on the balance sheet. For example, the costs of developing new ideas, new products, and new production methods normally are expensed as research and development costs in the period incurred.

Current liabilities often are viewed as having fair values equal to their book values because they will be paid at face amount within a short time. Long-term liabilities, however, must be valued based on current interest rates if different from the effective rates at the issue dates of the liabilities. For example, if $100,000 of 10-year, 6 percent bonds, paying interest annually, had been issued at par three years ago, and the current market rate of interest for the same type of security is 10 percent, the value of the liability currently is computed as follows:

| | |
|---|---:|
| Present value for 7 years at 10% of principal payment of $100,000 | |
| ($100,000 × .51316) | $51,316 |
| Present value at 10% of 7 interest payments of $6,000 | |
| ($6,000 × 4.86842) | 29,211 |
| Present value of bond | $80,527 |

Although accurate assessments of the value of assets and liabilities may be difficult, they form an important part of the overall determination of the value of an enterprise.

### Value of Potential Earnings

In many cases, assets operated together as a group have a value that exceeds the sum of their individual values. This "going-concern value" makes it desirable to operate the assets as an ongoing entity rather than sell them individually. A company's earning power as an ongoing enterprise is of obvious importance in valuing that company.

There are different approaches to measuring the value of a company's future earnings. Sometimes companies are valued based on a multiple of their current earnings. For example, if Bargain Company reports earnings of $35,000 for the current year, the company's value based on a multiple of 10 times current earnings is $350,000. The appropriate multiple to use is a matter of judgment and is based on factors such as the riskiness and variability of the earnings and the anticipated degree of growth.

Another method of valuing a company is to compute the present value of the anticipated future net cash flows generated by the company. This requires assessing the amount and timing of future cash flows and discounting them back to the present value at the discount rate determined to be appropriate for the type of enterprise. For example, if Bargain Company is expected to generate cash flows of $35,000 for each of the next 25 years, the present value of the firm at a discount rate of 10 percent is $317,696, computed as follows:

| | |
|---|---:|
| Annual cash flow generated | $ 35,000 |
| Present value factor for an annuity of 25 annual payments at 10% | × 9.07704 |
| Present value of future earnings | $ 317,696 |

Estimating the potential for future earnings requires numerous assumptions and estimates. Not surprisingly, the buyer and seller often have difficulty agreeing on the value of a company's expected earnings.

### Valuation of Consideration Exchanged

When one company acquires another, a value must be placed on the consideration given in the exchange. Little difficulty is encountered when cash is used in an acquisition, but valuation may be more difficult when securities are exchanged, particularly new untraded securities or securities with unusual features. For example, General Motors completed an acquisition a number of years ago using a new Series B common stock that paid dividends based on subsequent earnings of the acquired company rather than on the earnings of General Motors as a whole. Some companies have used non-interest-bearing bonds (zero coupon bonds), which have a fair value sufficiently below par value to compensate the holder for interest. Other companies have used various types of convertible securities. Unless these securities, or others that are considered equivalent, are being traded in the market, estimates of their value must be made. The approach generally followed is to use the value of some similar security with a determinable market value and adjust for the estimated value of the differences in the features of the two securities.

## ACCOUNTING FOR BUSINESS COMBINATIONS

For over half a century, accounting for business combinations remained largely unchanged. Two methods of accounting for business combinations, *purchase* and *pooling of interests,* were acceptable during that time. However, major changes in accounting for business combinations have occurred over the past decade. First, the FASB eliminated pooling of interests as an acceptable method of accounting for business combinations in 2001, leaving only a single method, purchase accounting. Then, in 2007, the FASB issued **FASB Statement No. 141,** "Business Combinations (revised 2007)" (FASB 141R), that replaced the purchase method with the *acquisition method,* now the only acceptable method of accounting for business combinations. The acquisition method must be used to account for all business combinations for which the acquisition date is in fiscal years beginning on or after December 15, 2008. **FASB 141R** may not be applied retroactively.

Although all business combinations must now be accounted for using the acquisition method, many companies' financial statements will continue to include the effects of previous business combinations recorded using the purchase and pooling-of-interests methods. Thus, a general understanding of those methods can be helpful. A numerical comparison of the three methods is presented in Appendix 1A.

The idea behind a pooling of interests was that no change in ownership had actually occurred in the business combination, often a questionable premise. Based on this idea, the book values of the combining companies were carried forward to the combined company and no revaluations to fair value were made. Managements often preferred pooling accounting because it did not result in asset write-ups or goodwill that might burden future earnings with additional depreciation or write-offs. Also, reporting practices often made acquisitions appear better than had purchase accounting been used.

Purchase accounting treated the purchase of a business much like the purchase of any asset: The acquired company was recorded based on the purchase price paid by the acquirer. Individual assets and liabilities of the acquired company were valued at their fair values, and the difference between the total purchase price and the fair value of the net identifiable assets acquired was recorded as goodwill. All direct costs of bringing about and consummating the combination were included in the total purchase price.

Acquisition accounting is consistent with the FASB's intention to move accounting in general more toward recognizing fair values. Under acquisition accounting, the acquirer in a business combination, in effect, values the acquired company based on the fair value of the consideration given in the combination and the fair value of any noncontrolling interest not acquired by the acquirer. Acquisition accounting is discussed in detail in the following section.

## ACQUISITION ACCOUNTING

As of the end of 2007, the FASB significantly changed the method of accounting for business combinations, requiring use of the acquisition method. Under the ***acquisition method,*** the acquirer recognizes all assets acquired and liabilities assumed in a business combination and measures them at their acquisition-date fair values. If less than 100 percent of the acquiree is acquired, the noncontrolling interest also is measured at its acquisition-date fair value. Note that a business combination does not affect the amounts at which the assets and liabilities of the acquirer are valued.

## Fair Value Measurements

Because accounting for business combinations is now based on fair values, the measurement of fair values takes on added importance. The acquirer must value at fair value the consideration it exchanges in a business combination, each of the individual assets and liabilities acquired, and any noncontrolling interest in the acquiree. Normally, a business combination involves an arm's-length exchange between two unrelated parties. The value of the consideration given in the exchange is usually the best measure of the value received and, therefore, reflects the value of the acquirer's interest in the acquiree. However, the FASB decided in **FASB 141R** to focus directly on the value of the consideration given rather than just using it to impute a fair value for the acquiree as a whole. In some cases, the value of the consideration given may be difficult to determine, or there may be no exchange, and valuation is better based on the value of the acquirer's interest in the acquiree or other valuation techniques. **FASB Statement No. 157,** "Fair Value Measurements" (FASB 157), provides a framework for applying fair value measurements in accounting.

## Applying the Acquisition Method

For all business combinations, an acquirer must be identified, and that party is the one gaining control over the other. In the past, some business combinations occurred under the dubious assertion that neither party acquired the other. In addition, an acquisition date must be determined. That date is usually the closing date when the exchange transaction actually occurs. However, in rare cases control may be acquired on a different date or without an exchange, so the circumstances must be examined to determine precisely when the acquirer gains control.

Under the acquisition method, the full acquisition-date fair values of the individual assets acquired, both tangible and intangible, and liabilities assumed in a business combination are recognized. This is true regardless of the percentage ownership acquired by the controlling entity. If the acquirer acquires all of the assets and liabilities of the acquiree in a merger, these assets and liabilities are recorded on the books of the acquiring company at their acquisition-date fair values. If the acquiring company acquires partial ownership of the acquiree in a stock acquisition, the assets acquired and liabilities assumed appear at their full acquisition-date fair values in a consolidated balance sheet prepared immediately after the combination.

Several other points related to assets and liabilities acquired in a business combination are as follows:

1. No separate asset valuation accounts related to assets acquired are recognized.
2. Long-lived assets classified at the acquisition date as held for sale are valued at fair value less cost to sell.
3. Deferred income taxes related to the business combination and assets and liabilities related to an acquiree's employee benefit plans are valued in accordance with the specific FASB standards relating to those topics.

Any excess of (1) the sum of the fair value of the consideration given by the acquirer in a business combination and the acquisition-date fair value of any noncontrolling interest over (2) the acquisition-date fair value of the net identifiable assets acquired in a business combination is considered goodwill. The amount of goodwill arising in a business combination is unaffected by the percentage of the acquiree acquired.

All costs of bringing about and consummating a business combination are charged to expense as incurred. The costs of issuing equity securities used to acquire the acquiree are treated in the same manner as stock issues costs are normally treated, as a reduction in the paid-in capital associated with the securities.

## Goodwill

Conceptually, *goodwill* as it relates to business combinations consists of all those intangible factors that allow a business to earn above-average profits. From an accounting perspective, the FASB has stated that **goodwill** "is an asset representing the future economic benefits arising from other assets acquired in a business combination that are not individually identified and separately recognized."[7] An asset is considered to be *identifiable,* and therefore must be separately recognized, if it is separable (can be separated from the business) or arises from a contractual or other right.

Under the acquisition method, an acquirer measures and recognizes goodwill from a business combination based on the relationship between the total fair value of the acquired company and the fair value of its net identifiable assets. However, the FASB decided, for several reasons, not to focus directly on the total fair value of the acquiree, but rather on the components that provide an indication of that fair value. The FASB identified three components that should be measured and summed for the total amount to be used in determining the amount of goodwill recognized in a business combination:

1. The fair value of the consideration given by the acquirer.
2. The fair value of any interest in the acquiree already held by the acquirer.
3. The fair value of the noncontrolling interest in the acquiree, if any.

The total of these three amounts, all measured at the acquisition date, is then compared with the acquisition-date fair value of the acquiree's net identifiable assets, and the difference is *goodwill.*

As an example of the computation of goodwill, assume that Albert Company acquires all of the assets of Zanfor Company for $400,000 when the fair value of Zanfor's net identifiable assets is $380,000. Goodwill is recognized for the $20,000 difference between the total consideration given and the fair value of the net identifiable assets acquired. If, instead of an acquisition of assets, Albert acquires 75 percent of the common stock of Zanfor for $300,000, and the fair value of the noncontrolling interest is $100,000, goodwill is computed as follows:

| | |
|---|---:|
| Fair value of consideration given by Albert | $300,000 |
| Fair value of noncontrolling interest | 100,000 |
| | $400,000 |
| Fair value of net identifiable assets acquired | (380,000) |
| Goodwill | $ 20,000 |

Note that the amount of goodwill is not affected by whether 100 percent of the acquiree is acquired or less than that. However, the fair value of the noncontrolling interest does have an effect on the amount of goodwill recognized. In the example given, the fair values of the controlling and noncontrolling interests are proportional (each is valued at an amount equal to its proportionate ownership share of the total) and imply a total fair value of the acquired company of $400,000. This is frequently the case and will always be assumed throughout the text unless indicated otherwise. However, that may not always be the case in practice. Situations might arise in a stock acquisition, for example, where the per-share value of the controlling interest is greater than that of the noncontrolling interest because of a premium associated with gaining control.

## Combination Effected through Acquisition of Net Assets

When one company acquires all the net assets of another in a business combination, the acquirer records on its books the individual assets acquired and liabilities assumed in the combination and the consideration given in exchange. Each identifiable asset and liability acquired (with minor exceptions) is recorded by the acquirer at its acquisition-date

---

[7] **FASB 141R,** para. 3j.

**FIGURE 1–3**
**Sharp Company**
**Balance Sheet**
**Information,**
**December 31, 20X0**

| Assets, Liabilities, and Equities | Book Value | Fair Value |
|---|---|---|
| Cash and Receivables | $ 45,000 | $ 45,000 |
| Inventory | 65,000 | 75,000 |
| Land | 40,000 | 70,000 |
| Buildings and Equipment | 400,000 | 350,000 |
| Accumulated Depreciation | (150,000) | |
| Patent | | 80,000 |
| Total Assets | $400,000 | $620,000 |
| Current Liabilities | $100,000 | 110,000 |
| Common Stock ($5 par) | 100,000 | |
| Additional Paid-In Capital | 50,000 | |
| Retained Earnings | 150,000 | |
| Total Liabilities and Equities | $400,000 | |
| Fair Value of Net Assets | | $510,000 |

fair value. Any excess of the fair value of the consideration exchanged over the fair value of the net identifiable assets is recorded by the acquiree as goodwill.

To illustrate the application of the acquisition method of accounting to a business combination effected through the acquisition of the acquiree's net assets, assume that Point Corporation acquires all of the assets and assumes all of the liabilities of Sharp Company in a statutory merger by issuing to Sharp 10,000 shares of $10 par common stock. The shares issued have a total market value of $610,000. Point incurs legal and appraisal fees of $40,000 in connection with the combination and stock issue costs of $25,000. Figure 1–3 shows the book values and fair values of Sharp's individual assets and liabilities on the date of combination.

The relationships among the fair value of the consideration exchanged, the fair value of Sharp's net assets, and the book value of Sharp's net assets are illustrated in the following diagram:

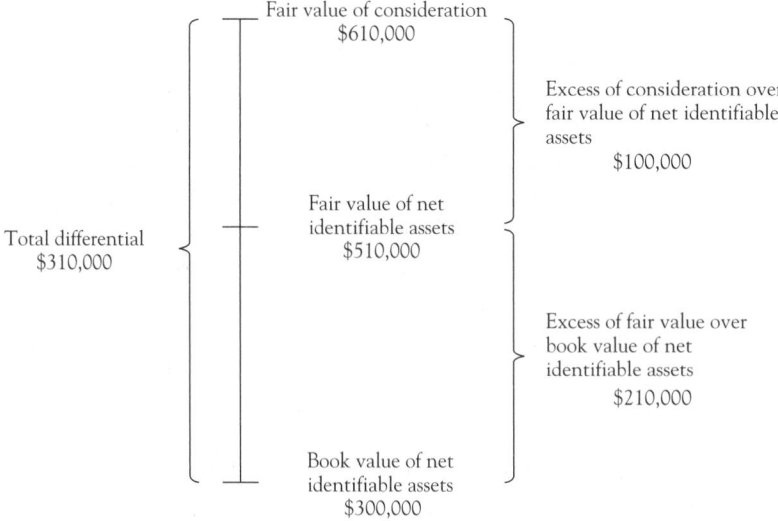

The total difference at the acquisition date between the fair value of the consideration exchanged and the book value of the net identifiable assets acquired is referred to as the differential. In more complex situations, the ***differential*** is equal to the difference between

(1) the acquisition-date fair value of the consideration transferred by the acquirer, plus the acquisition-date fair value of any equity interest in the acquiree previously held by the acquirer, plus the fair value of any noncontrolling interest in the acquiree and (2) the acquisition-date book values of the identifiable assets acquired and liabilities assumed.

In the Point/Sharp merger, the total differential of $310,000 reflects the difference between the total fair value of the shares issued by Point and the carrying amount of Sharp's net assets reflected on its books at the date of combination. A portion of that difference ($210,000) is attributable to the increased value of Sharp's net assets over book value. The remainder of the difference ($100,000) is considered to be goodwill.

The $40,000 of acquisition costs incurred by Point in bringing about the combination with Sharp are expensed as incurred:

| | | | |
|---|---|---|---|
| (4) | Merger Expense | 40,000 | |
| | Cash | | 40,000 |
| | Record costs related to acquisition of Sharp Company. | | |

Portions of the $25,000 of stock issue costs related to the shares issued to acquire Sharp may be incurred at various times. To facilitate accumulating these amounts before recording the combination, Point may record them in a separate temporary "suspense" account as incurred:

| | | | |
|---|---|---|---|
| (5) | Deferred Stock Issue Costs | 25,000 | |
| | Cash | | 25,000 |
| | Record costs related to issuance of common stock. | | |

On the date of combination, Point records the acquisition of Sharp with the following entry:

| | | | |
|---|---|---|---|
| (6) | Cash and Receivables | 45,000 | |
| | Inventory | 75,000 | |
| | Land | 70,000 | |
| | Buildings and Equipment | 350,000 | |
| | Patent | 80,000 | |
| | Goodwill | 100,000 | |
| | Current Liabilities | | 110,000 |
| | Common Stock | | 100,000 |
| | Additional Paid-In Capital | | 485,000 |
| | Deferred Stock Issue Costs | | 25,000 |
| | Record acquisition of Sharp Company. | | |

Entry (6) records all of Sharp's individual assets and liabilities, both tangible and intangible, on Point's books at their fair values on the date of combination. The fair value of Sharp's net assets recorded is $510,000 ($620,000 − $110,000). The $100,000 difference between the fair value of the shares given by Point ($610,000) and the fair value of Sharp's net assets is recorded as goodwill.

In recording the business combination, Sharp's book values are not relevant to Point; only the fair values are recorded. Because a change in ownership has occurred, the basis of accounting used by the acquired company is not relevant to the acquirer. Consistent with this view, accumulated depreciation recorded by Sharp on its buildings and equipment is not relevant to Point and is not recorded.

The stock issue costs incurred by Point in connection with Sharp's acquisition are initially recorded in a temporary account as incurred. They then are treated in the normal manner as a reduction in the proceeds received from the issuance of the stock. Thus, these costs are transferred from the temporary account to Additional Paid-In Capital as a reduction. Point records the $610,000 of stock issued at its value minus the stock issue costs, or $585,000. Of this amount, the $100,000 par value is recorded in the Common Stock account and the remainder in Additional Paid-In Capital.

### Entries Recorded by Acquired Company

On the date of the combination, Sharp records the following entry to recognize receipt of the Point shares and the transfer of all individual assets and liabilities to Point:

| | | | |
|---|---|---|---|
| (7) | Investment in Point Stock | 610,000 | |
| | Current Liabilities | 100,000 | |
| | Accumulated Depreciation | 150,000 | |
| | Cash and Receivables | | 45,000 |
| | Inventory | | 65,000 |
| | Land | | 40,000 |
| | Buildings and Equipment | | 400,000 |
| | Gain on Sale of Net Assets | | 310,000 |
| | Record transfer of assets to Point Corporation. | | |

Sharp recognizes the fair value of Point Corporation shares at the time of the exchange and records a gain of $310,000. The distribution of Point shares and the liquidation of Sharp are recorded on Sharp's books with the following entry:

| | | | |
|---|---|---|---|
| (8) | Common Stock | 100,000 | |
| | Additional Paid-In Capital | 50,000 | |
| | Retained Earnings | 150,000 | |
| | Gain on Sale of Net Assets | 310,000 | |
| | Investment in Point Stock | | 610,000 |
| | Record distribution of Point Corporation stock. | | |

### Subsequent Accounting for Goodwill by Acquirer

Goodwill arising in a merger is recorded by the acquirer for the difference between the fair value of the consideration exchanged and the fair value of the identifiable net assets acquired, as illustrated in entry (6). Once goodwill has been recorded by the acquirer, it must be accounted for in accordance with **FASB Statement No. 142,** "Goodwill and Other Intangible Assets" (FASB 142). Goodwill is carried forward at the originally recorded amount unless it becomes impaired. Goodwill must be reported as a separate line item in the balance sheet. A goodwill impairment loss that occurs subsequent to recording goodwill must be reported as a separate line item within income from continuing operations in the income statement unless the loss relates to discontinued operations, in which case the loss is reported within the discontinued operations section.

Goodwill must be tested for impairment at least annually, at the same time each year, and more frequently if events that are likely to impair the value of the goodwill occur. The process of testing goodwill for impairment is complex. It involves examining potential goodwill impairment by each of the company's reporting units, where a reporting unit is an operating segment[8] or a component of an operating segment that is a business for which management regularly reviews financial information from that component. When goodwill arises in a business combination, it must be assigned to individual reporting units. The goodwill is assigned to units that are expected to benefit from the combination, even if no other assets or liabilities of the acquired company are assigned to those units. To test for the impairment of goodwill, the fair value of the reporting unit is compared with its carrying amount. If the fair value of the reporting unit exceeds its carrying amount, the goodwill of that reporting unit is considered unimpaired. On the other hand,

[8] An operating segment is defined in *Financial Accounting Standards Board Statement No. 131,* "Disclosures about Segments of an Enterprise and Related Information," June 1997.

if the carrying amount of the reporting unit exceeds its fair value, an impairment of the reporting unit's goodwill is implied.

The amount of the reporting unit's goodwill impairment is measured as the excess of the carrying amount of the unit's goodwill over the implied value of its goodwill. The implied value of its goodwill is determined as the excess of the fair value of the reporting unit over the fair value of its net assets excluding goodwill. Goodwill impairment losses are recognized in income from continuing operations or income before extraordinary gains and losses.

As an example of goodwill impairment, assume that Reporting Unit A is assigned $100,000 of goodwill arising from a recent business combination. The following assets and liabilities are assigned to Reporting Unit A:

| Item | Carrying Amount | Fair Value |
|------|----------------:|-----------:|
| Cash and receivables | $ 50,000 | $ 50,000 |
| Inventory | 80,000 | 90,000 |
| Equipment | 120,000 | 150,000 |
| Goodwill | 100,000 | |
| Total assets | $350,000 | $290,000 |
| Current payables | (10,000) | (10,000) |
| Net assets | $340,000 | $280,000 |

By summing the carrying amounts of the assets and subtracting the carrying amount of the payables, the carrying amount of the reporting unit, including the goodwill, is determined to be $340,000. If the fair value of the reporting unit is estimated to be $360,000, no impairment of goodwill is indicated. On the other hand, if the fair value of the reporting unit is estimated to be $320,000, a second comparison must be made to determine the amount of any impairment loss. The implied value of Reporting Unit A's goodwill is determined by deducting the $280,000 fair value of the net assets, excluding goodwill, from the unit's $320,000 fair value. The $40,000 difference ($320,000 − $280,000) represents Reporting Unit A's implied goodwill. The impairment loss is measured as the excess of the carrying amount of the unit's goodwill ($100,000) over the implied value of the goodwill ($40,000), or $60,000. This goodwill impairment loss is combined with any impairment losses from other reporting units to determine the total impairment loss to be reported by the company as a whole. Goodwill is written down by the amount of the impairment loss. Once written down, goodwill may not be written up for recoveries.

### *Bargain Purchase*

Occasionally, the fair value of the consideration given in a business combination, along with the fair value of any equity interest in the acquiree already held and the fair value of any noncontrolling interest in the acquiree, may be less than the fair value of the acquiree's net identifiable assets, resulting in a ***bargain purchase.*** This might occur, for example, with a forced sale.

When a bargain purchase occurs (rarely), the acquirer must take steps to ensure that all acquisition-date valuations are appropriate. If they are, the acquirer recognizes a gain at the date of acquisition for the excess of the amount of the net identifiable assets acquired and liabilities assumed as valued under **FASB 141R** (usually at fair value) over the sum of the fair value of the consideration given in the exchange, the fair value of any equity interest in the acquiree held by the acquirer at the date of acquisition, and the fair value of any noncontrolling interest. The amount of the gain must be disclosed, along with where the gain is reported and the factors that led to the gain.

To illustrate accounting for a bargain purchase, assume that in the previous example of Point and Sharp, Point is able to acquire Sharp for $500,000 cash even though the fair value of Sharp's net identifiable assets is estimated to be $510,000. In this simple bargain-purchase case without an equity interest already held or a noncontrolling interest, the fair value of Sharp's net identifiable assets exceeds the consideration exchanged by Point, and, accordingly, a $10,000 gain attributable to Point is recognized.

In accounting for the bargain purchase (for cash) on Point's books, the following entry replaces previous entry (6):

| (9) | Cash and Receivables | 45,000 | |
|---|---|---|---|
| | Inventory | 75,000 | |
| | Land | 70,000 | |
| | Buildings and Equipment | 350,000 | |
| | Patent | 80,000 | |
| | Cash | | 500,000 |
| | Current Liabilities | | 110,000 |
| | Gain on Bargain Purchase of Sharp Company | | 10,000 |

This treatment is rather unusual because it recognizes a gain on an acquisition and, thus, represents an exception to the realization concept.

**FASB 141R** does not state a treatment for the situation opposite to that of a bargain purchase, that is, an overpayment. Acquirers do not knowingly overpay for an acquisition. Any overpayment presumably would be the result of misinformation, and the overpayment would not be discovered until a later time. The FASB avoided this issue by basing the computation of goodwill on the consideration given by the acquirer rather than the acquiree's total fair value. Thus, any overpayment would be included in goodwill and presumably eliminated in future periods by testing for goodwill impairment.

## Combination Effected through Acquisition of Stock

Many business combinations are effected by acquiring the voting stock of another company rather than by acquiring its net assets. In such a situation, the acquired company continues to exist, and the acquirer records an investment in the common stock of the acquiree rather than its individual assets and liabilities. The acquirer records its investment in the acquiree's common stock at the total fair value of the consideration given in exchange. For example, if Point Corporation (*a*) exchanges 10,000 shares of its stock with a total market value of $610,000 for all of Sharp Company's shares and (*b*) incurs merger costs of $40,000 and stock issue costs of $25,000, Point records the following entries upon receipt of the Sharp stock:

| (10) | Merger Expense | 40,000 | |
|---|---|---|---|
| | Deferred Stock Issue Costs | 25,000 | |
| | Cash | | 65,000 |
| | Record merger and stock issue costs related to acquisition of Sharp Company. | | |

| (11) | Investment in Sharp Stock | 610,000 | |
|---|---|---|---|
| | Common Stock | | 100,000 |
| | Additional Paid-In Capital | | 485,000 |
| | Deferred Stock Issue Costs | | 25,000 |
| | Record acquisition of Sharp Company stock. | | |

When a business combination is effected through a stock acquisition, the acquiree may continue to operate as a separate company, or it may lose its separate identity and be merged into the acquiring company. The accounting and reporting procedures for intercorporate investments in common stock when the acquiree continues in existence are discussed in the next nine chapters. If the acquired company is liquidated and its assets and liabilities are transferred to the acquirer, the dollar amounts recorded are identical to those in entry (6).

## Financial Reporting Subsequent to a Business Combination

Financial statements prepared subsequent to a business combination reflect the combined entity only from the date of combination. When a combination occurs during a fiscal period, income earned by the acquiree prior to the combination is not reported in the income of the combined enterprise. If the combined company presents comparative financial statements that include statements for periods before the combination, those statements include only the activities and financial position of the acquiring company, not those of the acquiree.

To illustrate financial reporting subsequent to a business combination, assume the following information for Point Corporation and Sharp Company:

|  | 20X0 | 20X1 |
|---|---|---|
| Point Corporation: |  |  |
| Separate income (excluding any income from Sharp) | $300,000 | $300,000 |
| Shares outstanding, December 31 | 30,000 | 40,000 |
| Sharp Company: |  |  |
| Net income | $ 60,000 | $ 60,000 |

Point Corporation acquires all of Sharp Company's stock at book value on January 1, 20X1, by issuing 10,000 shares of common stock. Subsequently, Point Corporation presents comparative financial statements for the years 20X0 and 20X1. The net income and earnings per share that Point presents in its comparative financial statements for the two years are as follows:

| 20X0: |  |
|---|---|
| Net Income | $300,000 |
| Earnings per Share ($300,000/30,000 shares) | $10.00 |
| 20X1: |  |
| Net Income ($300,000 + $60,000) | $360,000 |
| Earnings per Share ($360,000/40,000 shares) | $9.00 |

If Point Corporation had acquired Sharp Company in the middle of 20X1 instead of at the beginning, Point would include only Sharp's earnings subsequent to acquisition in its 20X1 income statement. If Sharp earned $25,000 in 20X1 before acquisition by Point and $35,000 after the combination, Point would report total net income for 20X1 of $335,000 ($300,000 + $35,000).

## Disclosure Requirements

**FASB 141R**[9] requires extensive disclosures relating to a company's business combinations so that financial statement users may assess the impact of the combinations. These disclosures include, among others items:

1. Identification and description of the acquired company, the acquisition date, and the percentage ownership acquired.
2. The main reasons for the acquisition and a description of the factors that led to the recognition of goodwill.
3. The acquisition-date fair value of the consideration transferred, the fair value of each component of the consideration, and a description of any contingent consideration.
4. The acquisition-date amounts recognized for each major class of assets acquired and liabilities assumed.

[9] **FASB 141R,** para. 68.

5. The business combination–related costs incurred, the amount expensed, and where they were reported, along with any issue costs not expensed and how they were recognized.
6. The acquiree's revenue and net income included in the consolidated income statement for the period since acquisition, and the results of operations for the combined company as if the business combination had occurred at the beginning of the reporting period.
7. The total amount of goodwill, the amount expected to be deductible for tax purposes, changes in goodwill during each subsequent period, and, if the company is required to report segment information, the amount of goodwill assigned to each segment.
8. For less-than-100-percent acquisitions, the acquisition-date fair value of the noncontrolling interest and the valuation method used.

# ADDITIONAL CONSIDERATIONS IN ACCOUNTING FOR BUSINESS COMBINATIONS

**FASB 141R** includes a number of requirements relating to specific items or aspects encountered in business combinations. Discussion of several of the more important situations follows.

## Uncertainty in Business Combinations

Uncertainty affects much of accounting measurement but is especially prevalent in business combinations. Although uncertainty relates to many aspects of business combination, three aspects of accounting for business combinations deserve particular attention: the measurement period, contingent consideration, and acquiree contingencies.

### *Measurement Period*

One type of uncertainty in business combinations arises from the requirement to value at acquisition-date fair value the assets and liabilities acquired in a business combination, the acquirer's interest in the acquiree, any noncontrolling interest, and the consideration given. Because the acquirer may not have sufficient information available immediately to properly ascertain fair values, **FASB 141R** allows for a period of time, called the **measurement period,** to acquire the necessary information. The measurement period ends once the acquirer obtains the necessary information about the facts as of the acquisition date, but may not exceed one year.

Assets that have been provisionally recorded as of the acquisition date are retrospectively adjusted in value during the measurement period for new information that clarifies the acquisition-date value. Usually, the offsetting entry is to goodwill. Retrospective adjustments may not be made for changes in value that occur subsequent to the acquisition date.

As an illustration, assume that Baine Company acquires land in a business combination and provisionally records the land at its estimated fair value of $100,000. During the measurement period, Baine receives a reliable appraisal that the land was worth $110,000 at the acquisition date. Subsequently, during the same accounting period, a change in the zoning of a neighboring parcel of land reduces the value of the land acquired by Baine to $75,000. Baine records the clarification of the acquisition-date fair value of the land and the subsequent impairment of value with the following entries:

| | | | |
|---|---|---:|---:|
| (12) | Land | 10,000 | |
| |     Goodwill | | 10,000 |
| | Adjust acquisition-date value of land acquired in business combination. | | |
| | | | |
| (13) | Impairment Loss | 35,000 | |
| |     Land | | 35,000 |
| | Recognize decline in value of land held. | | |

### *Contingent Consideration*

Sometimes the consideration exchanged by the acquirer in a business combination is not fixed in amount, but rather is contingent on future events. For example, the acquiree and acquirer may enter into a *contingent-share agreement* whereby, in addition to an initial issuance of shares, the acquirer may agree to issue a certain number of additional shares for each percentage point by which earnings exceeds a set amount over the next five years. Thus, total consideration exchanged in the business combination is not known within the measurement period because the number of shares to be issued is dependent on future events.

**FASB 141R** requires contingent consideration in a business combination to be valued at fair value as of the acquisition date and classified as either a liability or equity. The right to require the return of consideration given that is dependent on future events is classified as an asset. Contingent consideration classified as an asset or liability is remeasured each period to fair value and the change is recognized in income. Contingent consideration classified as equity is not remeasured.

### *Acquiree Contingencies*

Certain contingencies may relate to an acquiree in a business combination, such as pending lawsuits or loan guarantees made by the acquiree. Certainly, the acquirer considers such contingencies when entering into an acquisition agreement, and the accounting must also consider such contingencies. Under **FASB 141R,** the acquirer must recognize all contingencies that arise from contractual rights or obligations and other contingencies if it is more likely than not that they meet the definition of an asset or liability at the acquisition date. These contingencies are recorded by the acquirer at acquisition-date fair value.

For all acquired contingencies, the acquirer should provide a description of each, disclose the amount recognized at the acquisition date, and describe the estimated range of possible undiscounted outcomes. Subsequently, the acquirer should disclose changes in the amounts recognized and in the range of possible outcomes.

## In-Process Research and Development

In normal operations, research and development costs are required to be expensed as incurred, except under certain limited conditions. When a company acquires valuable ongoing research and development projects from an acquiree in a business combination, a question arises as to whether these should be recorded as assets. The FASB concluded that these projects are assets and should be recorded at their acquisition-date fair values, even if they have no alternative use. These projects should be classified as indefinite-lived and, therefore, should not be amortized until completed or abandoned. They should be tested for impairment in accordance with current standards. Subsequent expenditures for the previously acquired research and development projects would normally be expensed as incurred.

## Noncontrolling Equity Held Prior to Combination

In some cases an acquirer may hold an equity interest in an acquiree prior to obtaining control through a business combination. The total amount of the acquirer's investment in the acquiree subsequent to the combination is equal to the acquisition-date fair value of the equity interest previously held and the fair value of the consideration given in the business combination. For example, if Lemon Company held 10 percent of Aide Company's stock with a fair value of $500,000 and Lemon acquired the remaining shares of Aide for $4,500,000 cash, Lemon's total investment is considered to be $5,000,000.

An acquirer that held an equity position in an acquiree immediately prior to the acquisition date must revalue that equity position to its fair value at the acquisition date and recognize a gain or loss on the revaluation. Suppose that Lemon's 10 percent investment in Aide has a book value of $300,000 and fair value of $500,000 at the date Lemon acquires the remaining 90 percent of Aide's stock. Lemon revalues its original investment in Aide to its $500,000 fair value and recognizes a $200,000 gain on the revaluation at the date it acquires the remaining shares of Aide. Lemon records the following entries on its books in connection with the acquisition of Aide:

| | | | |
|---|---|---:|---:|
| (14) | Investment in Aide Company Stock | 200,000 | |
| |     Gain on revaluation of Aide Company Stock | | 200,000 |
| |     Revalue Aide Company stock to fair value at date | | |
| |     of business combination. | | |
| | | | |
| (15) | Investment in Aide Company Stock | 4,500,000 | |
| |     Cash | | 4,500,000 |
| |     Acquire controlling interest in Aide Company. | | |

## Acquisitions by Contract Alone

In rare instances, an acquirer may obtain control of an acquiree without transferring consideration or receiving an equity interest in the acquiree. Control is achieved by contract alone. In such cases, the amount of the acquiree's net assets at the date of acquisition is attributed to the noncontrolling interest and included in the noncontrolling interest reported in subsequent consolidated financial statements.

## Summary of Key Concepts

Business combinations and complex organizational structures are an important part of the global business scene. Many companies add organizational components by creating new corporations or partnerships through which to carry out a portion of their operations. In other cases, companies may enter into business combinations to acquire other companies through which to further their objectives.

When a company creates another corporation or a partnership through a transfer of assets, the book values of those assets are transferred to the new entity and no gain or loss is recognized. The creating company and the new entity will combine their financial statements for general-purpose financial reporting to appear as if they were a single company as long as the creating company continues to control the new entity.

Over the decades, business combinations have been occurring with increasing frequency. A business combination occurs when an acquirer obtains control of one or more other businesses. The three types of business combination that are commonly found are: (*a*) statutory mergers, where the acquiree loses its separate identity and the acquirer continues with the assets and liabilities of both companies; (*b*) statutory consolidations, where both combining companies join to form a new company; and (*c*) stock acquisitions, where both combining companies maintain their separate identities, with the acquirer owning the stock of the acquiree.

The FASB recently issued **FASB 141R,** which requires the acquisition method be used to account for business combinations. Under the acquisition method, all of the assets acquired and liabilities assumed by the acquirer in a business combination are valued at their fair values. The excess of the sum of the fair value of the acquirer's consideration transferred, the fair value of any equity interest in the acquiree already held, and the fair value of any noncontrolling interest in the acquiree over the fair value of the net identifiable assets acquired is goodwill. In subsequent financial statements, goodwill must be reported separately. Goodwill is not amortized, but it must be tested for impairment at least annually. If goodwill is impaired, it is written down to its new fair value and a loss recognized for the amount of the impairment. If the fair value of the consideration transferred by the acquirer in a business combination, along with the fair value of an equity interest already held and the noncontrolling interest, is less than the fair value of the acquiree's net identifiable assets, a situation referred to as a bargain purchase, the difference is recognized as a gain attributable to the acquirer.

All costs associated with a business combination are expensed as incurred. Any stock issue costs incurred in connection with a business combination are treated as a reduction in paid-in capital. A business combination is given effect as of the acquisition date for subsequent financial reporting.

## Key Terms

| | | |
|---|---|---|
| acquisition method *13* | liquidated, *9* | special-purpose entity, *3* |
| bargain purchase, *19* | measurement period *22* | spin-off, *4* |
| business combination, *4* | minority interest, *11* | split-off, *4* |
| consolidated financial statements, *1* | noncontrolling interest, *11* | statutory consolidation, *9* |
| | parent company, *2* | statutory merger, *9* |
| control, *4* | parent–subsidiary | stock acquisition, *10* |
| differential *16* | relationship, *10* | subsidiary, *2* |
| goodwill, *15* | primary beneficiary, *7* | tender offer, *11* |

# Appendix **1A** Methods of Accounting for Business Combinations

As discussed in the chapter, several different methods of accounting for business combinations have been acceptable over the years. While acquisition accounting is the only method acceptable for business combinations occurring after 2008, many companies' financial statements include the results of past business combinations recorded using either the purchase or pooling-of-interests method. Thus, accountants should understand the effects of these earlier methods even though they are no longer acceptable.

The example presented earlier in the chapter is used to illustrate the differences between the methods of accounting for business combinations. Point Corporation acquires all of the assets and assumes all of the liabilities of Sharp Company in a merger by issuing to Sharp 10,000 shares of $10 par common stock. The shares issued have a total market value of $610,000. Point incurs legal and appraisal fees of $40,000 in connection with the combination and stock issue costs of $25,000. See again Figure 1–3, which shows the book values and fair values of Sharp's individual assets and liabilities on the date of combination.

Figure 1–4 shows the journal entries on Point's books to record the business combination under the acquisition, purchase, and pooling-of-interests methods. Under the acquisition method, Point

**FIGURE 1–4**   **Different Methods of Accounting for Business Combinations**

| Acquisition Accounting | | | Purchase Accounting | | | Pooling Accounting | | |
|---|---|---|---|---|---|---|---|---|
| Merger Expenses | 40,000 | | Deferred Merger Costs | 40,000 | | Merger Expenses | 65,000 | |
| Deferred Stock Issue Costs | 25,000 | | Deferred Stock Issue Costs | 25,000 | | Cash | | 65,000 |
| Cash | | 65,000 | Cash | | 65,000 | | | |
| | | | | | | | | |
| Cash and Receivables | 45,000 | | Cash and Receivables | 45,000 | | Cash and Receivables | 45,000 | |
| Inventory | 75,000 | | Inventory | 75,000 | | Inventory | 65,000 | |
| Land | 70,000 | | Land | 70,000 | | Land | 40,000 | |
| Buildings and Equipment | 350,000 | | Buildings and Equipment | 350,000 | | Buildings and Equipment | 400,000 | |
| Patent | 80,000 | | Patent | 80,000 | | Accumulated Depreciation | | 150,000 |
| Goodwill | 100,000 | | Goodwill | 140,000 | | Current Liabilities | | 100,000 |
| Current Liabilities | | 110,000 | Current Liabilities | | 110,000 | Common Stock | | 100,000 |
| Common Stock | | 100,000 | Common Stock | | 100,000 | Additional Capital | | 50,000 |
| Additional Capital | | 485,000 | Additional Capital | | 485,000 | Retained Earnings | | 150,000 |
| Deferred Stock Issue Costs | | 25,000 | Deferred Merger Costs | | 40,000 | | | |
| | | | Deferred Stock Issue Costs | | 25,000 | | | |

records the identifiable assets and liabilities acquired in the business combination at their fair values and records goodwill for the $100,000 difference between the $610,000 fair value of the consideration transferred by Point and the $510,000 fair value of Sharp's net identifiable assets. Expenses related to the business combination are expensed, and the stock issue costs are treated as a reduction in the issue price of Point's stock.

The purchase method called for recording the acquired company at the amount of the total purchase price paid by the acquirer, including associated costs. Point records the identifiable assets and liabilities acquired at their fair values, as under the acquisition method. Point then records goodwill for the difference between the total purchase price paid for Sharp and the fair value of its net identifiable assets. The purchase method based the calculation of goodwill on the total purchase price while the acquisition method is based on the fair value of the consideration given. Also, the purchase method viewed the costs associated with bringing about the business combination as being part of the total purchase price, while the acquisition method expenses all such costs. The $140,000 of goodwill is calculated under the purchase method as the sum of the fair value of the consideration given by Point ($610,000) and the merger costs ($40,000), less the fair value of Sharp's net identifiable assets ($510,000).

The pooling-of-interests method assumed the view that the two companies were joining together and pooling their resources without either company acquiring the other and with a continuity of ownership. Thus, the book values of assets, liabilities, and equity were carried forward without adjustment to fair value. Consistent with the idea of the owners of both companies continuing as owners of the combined company, poolings could occur only when one company issued its common stock for the other combining company so that substantially all stockholders of both companies continued as owners. The issuing company recorded equity equal to that of the other combining company. The stock issued in the combination was recorded at the total amount of the other combining company's stock that it replaced, and the retained earnings of the other combining company was recorded on the books of the issuing company. All merger and stock issue costs were expensed. No goodwill was ever recorded in poolings, but unlike under purchase accounting, the retained earnings balances of both companies were carried forward. In this example, Point records on its books all of Sharp's recorded assets and liabilities at their book values from Sharp's books. Point records the stock it issues in the combination at the same total amount as Sharp's stock ($150,000, including both the par value and additional paid-in capital), and records Sharp's retained earnings ($150,000).

---

**Questions**

**Q1-1** What types of circumstances would encourage management to establish a complex organizational structure?

**Q1-2** How would the decision to dispose of a segment of operations using a split-off rather than a spin-off impact the financial statements of the company making the distribution?

**Q1-3** Why did companies such as Enron find the use of special-purpose entities to be advantageous?

**Q1-4** Describe each of the three legal forms that a business combination might take.

**Q1-5** What basis of accounting normally is used in recording the assets and liabilities transferred to a new wholly owned subsidiary?

**Q1-6** How might the concept of beneficial ownership impact the reporting of an interest in another company?

**Q1-7** When does a noncontrolling interest arise in a business combination?

**Q1-8** Why did corporate management often prefer pooling-of-interests accounting in recording business combinations?

**Q1-9** How is the amount reported as goodwill determined under the acquisition method?

**Q1-10** What impact does the level of ownership have on the amount of goodwill reported under the acquisition method?

**Q1-11** How is the amount of goodwill assigned to the noncontrolling interest determined when less than full ownership is acquired?

**Q1-12** What is a differential?

**Q1-13** When a business combination occurs after the beginning of the year, the income earned by the acquired company between the beginning of the year and the date of combination is excluded from the net income reported by the combined entity for the year. Why?

**Q1-14** What is the maximum balance in retained earnings that can be reported by the combined entity following a business combination?

**Q1-15** How is the amount of additional paid-in capital determined when recording a business combination?

**Q1-16** Which of the costs incurred in completing a business combination are capitalized under the acquisition method?

**Q1-17** Which of the costs incurred in completing a business combination should be treated as a reduction of additional paid-in capital?

**Q1-18** When is goodwill considered impaired following a business combination?

**Q1-19** When does a bargain purchase occur?

**Q1-20\*** Within the measurement period following a business combination, the acquisition-date fair value of buildings acquired is determined to be less than initially recorded. How is the reduction in value recognized?

**Q1-21\*** P Company reports its 10,000 shares of S Company at $40 per share. P Company then purchases an additional 60,000 shares of S Company for $65 each and gains control of S Company. What must be done with respect to the valuation of the shares previously owned?

**Q1-22A** P Company purchased 80 percent of the shares of S Company in 2006. How would the amount of goodwill reported differ from the amount to be reported under the acquisition method?

**Q1-23A** What major differences occur between using pooling of interests accounting for a business combination and using the acquisition method?

---

# Cases

### C1-1 Reporting Alternatives and International Harmonization

*Understanding*

Accounting procedures for business combinations historically have differed across countries. Pooling of interests, for many years a preferred method in the United States, was not acceptable in most countries. In some countries, accounting standards permit goodwill to be written off directly against stockholders' equity at the time of a business combination.

#### Required

*a.* Over the years, many U.S. companies complained they were at a disadvantage when competing against foreign companies in purchasing other business enterprises because, unlike U.S. companies, many foreign companies either did not have to capitalize goodwill or could write it off immediately against stockholders' equity. Historically, why were U.S. companies opposed to capitalizing goodwill? What happened during the past decade to improve the situation from the perspective of U.S. companies?

*b.* Should U.S. companies care about accounting standards other than those that are generally accepted in the United States? Explain.

### C1-2 Assignment of Acquisition Costs

*Research FARS*

Troy Company notified Kline Company's shareholders that it was interested in purchasing controlling ownership of Kline and offered to exchange one share of Troy's common stock for each share of Kline Company submitted by July 31, 2007. At the time of the offer, Troy's shares were trading for $35 per share and Kline's shares were trading at $28. Troy acquired all of the shares of Kline prior to December 31, 2007, and transferred the assets and liabilities of Kline to its books. In addition to issuing its shares, Troy paid a finder's fee of $200,000, stock registration and audit fees of $60,000, legal fees of $90,000 for transferring Kline's assets and liabilities to Troy, and $370,000 in legal fees to settle litigation brought by Kline's shareholders who alleged that the offering price was below the per share fair value of Kline's net assets.

Troy is currently negotiating to purchase Lad Company through an exchange of common stock and expects to incur additional costs comparable to those involved in the acquisition of Kline. The acquisition of Lad is expected to close sometime late in 2009.

\*Indicates that the item relates to "Additional Consideration."
"A" indicates that the item relates to "Appendix A."

### *Required*

Troy Company's vice president of finance has asked you to review the current accounting literature, including authoritative pronouncements, and prepare a memo reporting the required treatment of the additional costs at the time Kline Company was acquired and the current requirements for reporting the additional costs of acquiring Lad Company. Support your recommendations with citations and quotations from the authoritative financial reporting standards or other literature.

### C1-3   Evaluation of Merger

*Research*

One company may acquire another for a number of different reasons. The acquisition often has a significant impact on the financial statements. In 2005, 3M Corporation acquired CUNO Incorporated. Obtain a copy of the 3M 10-K filing for 2005. The 10-K reports the annual results for a company and is often available on the Investor Relations section of a company's Web site. It is also available on the SEC's Web site at www.SEC.gov.

### *Required*

Use the 10-K for 2005 to find the answers to the following questions about 3M's acquisition of CUNO Inc. (*Hint:* You can search on the term CUNO once you have accessed the 10-K online.)

*a.* Provide at least one reason why 3M acquired CUNO.

*b.* How was the acquisition funded?

*c.* What was the impact of the CUNO acquisition on net accounts receivable?

*d.* What was the impact of the CUNO acquisition on inventories?

### C1-4   Business Combinations

*Analysis*

A merger boom comparable to those of the 1960s and mid-1980s occurred in the 1990s and into the new century. The merger activity of the 1960s was associated with increasing stock prices and heavy use of pooling of interests accounting. The mid-1980s activity was associated with a number of leveraged buyouts and acquisitions involving junk bonds. Merger activity in the early 1990s, on the other hand, appeared to involve primarily purchases with cash and standard debt instruments. By the mid-1990s, however, many business combinations were being effected through exchanges of stock. In the first decade of the new century, the nature of many business acquisitions changed, and by late 2008, the merger boom had slowed dramatically.

*a.* Which factors do you believe were the most prominent in encouraging business combinations in the 1990s? Which of these was the most important? Explain why.

*b.* Why were so many of the business combinations in the middle and late 1990s effected through exchanges of stock?

*c.* What factors had a heavy influence on mergers during the mid-2000s. How did many of the business combinations of this period differ from earlier combinations? Why did the merger boom slow so dramatically late in 2008 and in 2009?

*d.* If a major review of the tax laws were undertaken, would it be wise or unwise public policy to establish greater tax incentives for corporate mergers? Propose three incentives that might be used.

*e.* If the FASB were interested in encouraging more mergers, what action should it take with regard to revising or eliminating existing accounting standards? Explain.

### C1-5   Determination of Goodwill Impairment

*Research*
*FARS*

Plush Corporation purchased 100 percent of Common Corporation's common stock on January 1, 20X3, and paid $450,000. The fair value of Common's identifiable net assets at that date was $430,000. By the end of 20X5, the fair value of Common, which Plush considers to be a reporting unit, had increased to $485,000; however, Plush's external auditor made a passing comment to the company's chief accountant that Plush may need to recognize impairment of goodwill on one or more of its investments.

### *Required*

Prepare a memo to Plush's chief accountant indicating the tests used in determining whether goodwill has been impaired. Include in your discussion one or more possible conditions under which Plush may be required to recognize impairment of goodwill on its investment in Common Corporation. In preparing your memo, review the current accounting literature, including authoritative pronouncements of the FASB and other appropriate bodies. Support your discussion with citations and quotations from the applicable literature.

### C1-6 Risks Associated with Acquisitions

*Analysis*

Not all business combinations are successful, and many entail substantial risk. Acquiring another company may involve a number of different types of risk. Obtain a copy of the 10-K report for Google, Inc., for the year ended December 31, 2006, available at the SEC's Web site (**www.sec.gov**). The report can also be accessed through Yahoo Finance or the company's Investor Relations page.

#### Required

On page 21 of the 10-K report, Google provides information to investors about its motivation for acquiring companies and the possible risks associated with such acquisitions. Briefly discuss the risks that Google sees inherent in potential acquisitions.

### C1-7 Numbers Game

*Communication*

Arthur Levitt's speech, "The Numbers Game," is available on the SEC's Web site at http://www.sec.gov/news/speech/speecharchive/1998/spch220.txt. Read the speech, and then answer the following questions.

#### Required

a. Briefly explain what motivations Levitt discusses for earnings management.
b. What specific techniques for earnings management does Levitt discuss?
c. According to Levitt, why is the issue of earnings management important?

### C1-8 MCI: A Succession of Mergers

*Research*

MCI WorldCom, Inc. (later MCI), was known as a high flying company, having had its roots in a small local company and rising to one of the world's largest communications giants. The company's spectacular growth was accomplished through a string of business combinations. However, not all went as planned, and MCI is no longer an independent company.

#### Required

Provide a brief history of, and indicate subsequent events related to, MCI WorldCom. Include in your discussion the following:

a. Trace the major acquisitions leading to MCI WorldCom and indicate the type of consideration used in the acquisitions.
b. Who is Bernard Ebbers, and where is he now?
c. What happened to MCI WorldCom, and where is it now?

### C1-9 Leveraged Buyouts

*Analysis*

A type of acquisition that was not discussed in the chapter is the *leveraged buyout*. Many experts argue that a leveraged buyout (LBO) is not a type of business combination but rather just a restructuring of ownership. Yet some would see an LBO as having many of the characteristics of a business combination. The number of LBOs in recent years has grown dramatically and, therefore, accounting for these transactions is of increased importance.

#### Required

a. What is a leveraged buyout? How does an LBO compare with a management buyout (MBO)?
b. What authoritative pronouncements, if any, deal with leveraged buyouts?
c. Is a leveraged buyout a type of business combination? Explain.
d. What is the major issue in determining the proper basis for an interest in a company purchased through a leveraged buyout?

### C1-10 Curtiss-Wright and Goodwill

Accounting standards continually evolve. One area where significant change has occurred over the past decade is in recording and accounting for goodwill. Prior to 2002, companies were required to amortize goodwill over its useful life, not to exceed 17 years. Beginning in 2002, goodwill was no

**Research**

longer required to be amortized. One company that has been affected by the changes in accounting for goodwill is Curtiss-Wright.

### Required

*a.* By what amounts did Curtiss-Wright's goodwill increase in 2001 and 2002, and what amounts did the company report at December 31, 2001 and 2002? What percentage of Curtis-Wright's total assets does goodwill represent at December 31, 2002? How does this compare to other companies?

*b.* What is the fair-value amount of assets Curtiss-Wright acquired in 2006 through business combinations? By what dollar amount did goodwill increase during 2006? What percentage increase does this represent? What percentage of Curtiss-Wright's total assets does goodwill represent at December 31, 2006?

*c.* What amount of goodwill impairment losses did Curtiss-Wright recognize for 2006 and 2005? What change did Curtiss-Wright make during 2006 in its goodwill impairment testing? Why was this change made? What effect did this change have on the financial statements for 2006 and prior years?

*d.* Do you think the management of Curtiss-Wright prefers the treatment that was required for goodwill before 2002 or the current treatment? Explain.

**C1-11** **Sears and Kmart: The Joining Together of Two of America's Oldest Retailers**

**Analysis**

Kmart started in 1899 as the S. S. Kresge Company, better known as the five-and-dime store. Sears has its roots in the 1880s and incorporated as Sears, Roebuck and Company in 1893. In 2005, the two companies joined together in a business combination.

### Required

*a.* What major event for Kmart occurred in 2002? How was that issued resolved?

*b.* What form of business combination brought Sears and Kmart together, and what was the resulting corporate structure?

*c.* In the business combination involving Sears and Kmart, which company acquired the other? On what basis was this determination made? What accounting implications did the choice of acquirer have?

---

**Exercises**

**E1-1** **Multiple-Choice Questions on Complex Organizations**

Select the correct answer for each of the following questions.

1. Growth in the complexity of the U.S. business environment:

    *a.* Has led to increased use of partnerships to avoid legal liability.

    *b.* Has led to increasingly complex organizational structures as management has attempted to achieve its business objectives.

    *c.* Has encouraged companies to reduce the number of operating divisions and product lines so they may better control those they retain.

    *d.* Has had no particular impact on the organizational structures or the way in which companies are managed.

2. Which of the following is *not* an appropriate reason for establishing a subsidiary?

    *a.* The parent wishes to protect existing operations by shifting new activities with greater risk to a newly created subsidiary.

    *b.* The parent wishes to avoid subjecting all of its operations to regulatory control by establishing a subsidiary that focuses its operations in regulated industries.

    *c.* The parent wishes to reduce its taxes by establishing a subsidiary that focuses its operations in areas where special tax benefits are available.

    *d.* The parent wishes to be able to increase its reported sales by transferring products to the subsidiary at the end of the fiscal year.

3. Which of the following actions is likely to result in recording goodwill on Randolph Company's books?

    a. Randolph acquires Penn Corporation in a business combination recorded as a merger.

    b. Randolph acquires a majority of Penn's common stock in a business combination and continues to operate it as a subsidiary.

    c. Randolph distributes ownership of a newly created subsidiary in a distribution considered to be a spin-off.

    d. Randolph distributes ownership of a newly created subsidiary in a distribution considered to be a split-off.

4. When an existing company creates a new subsidiary and transfers a portion of its assets and liabilities to the new entity:

    a. The new entity records both the assets and liabilities it received at fair values.

    b. The new entity records both the assets and liabilities it received at the carrying values of the original company.

    c. The original company records a gain or loss on the difference between its carrying values and the fair values of the assets transferred to the new entity.

    d. The original company records the difference between the carrying values and the fair values of the assets transferred to the new entity as goodwill.

5. When a company assigns goodwill to a reporting unit acquired in a business combination, it must:

    a. Record an impairment loss if the fair value of the net identifiable assets held by a reporting unit decreases.

    b. Record an impairment loss if the fair value of the reporting unit decreases.

    c. Record an impairment loss if the carrying value of the reporting unit is less than the fair value of the reporting unit.

    d. Record an impairment loss if the fair value of the reporting unit is less than its carrying value and the carrying value of goodwill is more than the implied value of its goodwill.

## E1-2 Multiple-Choice Questions on Recording Business Combinations [AICPA Adapted]

Select the correct answer for each of the following questions.

1. Goodwill represents the excess of the sum of the consideration given over the:

    a. Sum of the fair values assigned to identifiable assets acquired less liabilities assumed.

    b. Sum of the fair values assigned to tangible assets acquired less liabilities assumed.

    c. Sum of the fair values assigned to intangible assets acquired less liabilities assumed.

    d. Book value of an acquired company.

2. In a business combination, costs of registering equity securities to be issued by the acquiring company are a(n):

    a. Expense of the combined company for the period in which the costs were incurred.

    b. Direct addition to stockholders' equity of the combined company.

    c. Reduction of the otherwise determinable fair value of the securities.

    d. Addition to goodwill.

3. Which of the following is the appropriate basis for valuing fixed assets acquired in a business combination carried out by exchanging cash for common stock?

    a. Historical cost.

    b. Book value.

    c. Cost plus any excess of purchase price over book value of assets acquired.

    d. Fair value.

4. In a business combination, the fair value of the identifiable net assets acquired exceeds the fair value of the consideration given. The excess should be reported as a:

   a. Deferred credit.

   b. Reduction of the values assigned to current assets and a deferred credit for any unallocated portion.

   c. Pro rata reduction of the values assigned to current and noncurrent assets and a deferred credit for any unallocated portion.

   d. No answer listed is correct.

5. A and B Companies have been operating separately for five years. Each company has a minimal amount of liabilities and a simple capital structure consisting solely of voting common stock. A Company, in exchange for 40 percent of its voting stock, acquires 80 percent of the common stock of B Company. This is a "tax-free" stock-for-stock (type B) exchange for tax purposes. B Company assets have a total net fair market value of $800,000 and a total net book value of $580,000. The fair market value of the A stock used in the exchange is $700,000 and the fair value of the noncontrolling interest is $175,000. The goodwill reported following the acquisition would be:

   a. Zero.

   b. $60,000.

   c. $75,000.

   d. $295,000.

## E1-3    Multiple-Choice Questions on Reported Balances [AICPA Adapted]

Select the correct answer for each of the following questions.

1. On December 31, 20X3, Saxe Corporation was merged into Poe Corporation. In the business combination, Poe issued 200,000 shares of its $10 par common stock, with a market price of $18 a share, for all of Saxe's common stock. The stockholders' equity section of each company's balance sheet immediately before the combination was:

|  | Poe | Saxe |
|---|---|---|
| Common Stock | $3,000,000 | $1,500,000 |
| Additional Paid-In Capital | 1,300,000 | 150,000 |
| Retained Earnings | 2,500,000 | 850,000 |
|  | $6,800,000 | $2,500,000 |

In the December 31, 20X3, consolidated balance sheet, additional paid-in capital should be reported at:

   a. $950,000.

   b. $1,300,000.

   c. $1,450,000.

   d. $2,900,000.

2. On January 1, 20X1, Rolan Corporation issued 10,000 shares of common stock in exchange for all of Sandin Corporation's outstanding stock. Condensed balance sheets of Rolan and Sandin immediately before the combination follow:

|  | Rolan | Sandin |
|---|---|---|
| Total Assets | $1,000,000 | $500,000 |
| Liabilities | $ 300,000 | $150,000 |
| Common Stock ($10 par) | 200,000 | 100,000 |
| Retained Earnings | 500,000 | 250,000 |
| Total Liabilities and Equities | $1,000,000 | $500,000 |

Rolan's common stock had a market price of $60 per share on January 1, 20X1. The market price of Sandin's stock was not readily determinable. The fair value of Sandin's net identifiable assets was determined to be $570,000. Rolan's investment in Sandin's stock will be stated in Rolan's balance sheet immediately after the combination in the amount of:

  *a.* $350,000.

  *b.* $500,000.

  *c.* $570,000.

  *d.* $600,000.

3. On April 1, 20X2, Jack Company paid $800,000 for all of Ann Corporation's issued and outstanding common stock. Ann's recorded assets and liabilities on April 1, 20X2, were as follows:

| | |
|---|---|
| Cash | $ 80,000 |
| Inventory | 240,000 |
| Property and equipment (net of accumulated depreciation of $320,000) | 480,000 |
| Liabilities | (180,000) |

On April 1, 20X2, Ann's inventory was determined to have a fair value of $190,000 and the property and equipment had a fair value of $560,000. What is the amount of goodwill resulting from the business combination?

  *a.* $0.

  *b.* $50,000.

  *c.* $150,000.

  *d.* $180,000.

4. Action Corporation issued nonvoting preferred stock with a fair market value of $4,000,000 in exchange for all the outstanding common stock of Master Corporation. On the date of the exchange, Master had tangible net assets with a book value of $2,000,000 and a fair value of $2,500,000. In addition, Action issued preferred stock valued at $400,000 to an individual as a finder's fee in arranging the transaction. As a result of this transaction, Action should record an increase in net assets of:

  *a.* $2,000,000.

  *b.* $2,500,000.

  *c.* $4,000,000.

  *d.* $4,400,000.

### E1-4 Multiple-Choice Questions Involving Account Balances

Select the correct answer for each of the following questions.

1. Topper Company established a subsidiary and transferred equipment with a fair value of $72,000 to the subsidiary. Topper had purchased the equipment with an expected life of 10 years 4 years earlier for $100,000 and has used straight-line depreciation with no expected residual value. At the time of the transfer, the subsidiary should record:

  *a.* Equipment at $72,000 and no accumulated depreciation.

  *b.* Equipment at $60,000 and no accumulated depreciation.

  *c.* Equipment at $100,000 and accumulated depreciation of $40,000.

  *d.* Equipment at $120,000 and accumulated depreciation of $48,000.

2. Lead Corporation established a new subsidiary and transferred to it assets with a cost of $90,000 and a book value of $75,000. The assets had a fair value of $100,000 at the time of transfer. The transfer will result in:

  *a.* A reduction of net assets reported by Lead Corporation of $90,000.

  *b.* A reduction of net assets reported by Lead Corporation of $75,000.

  *c.* No change in the reported net assets of Lead Corporation.

  *d.* An increase in the net assets reported by Lead Corporation of $25,000.

3. Tear Company, a newly established subsidiary of Stern Corporation, received assets with an original cost of $260,000, a fair value of $200,000, and a book value of $140,000 from the parent in exchange for 7,000 shares of Tear's $8 par value common stock. Tear should record:

 a. Additional paid-in capital of $0.
 b. Additional paid-in capital of $84,000.
 c. Additional paid-in capital of $144,000.
 d. Additional paid-in capital of $204,000.

4. Grout Company reports assets with a carrying value of $420,000 (including goodwill with a carrying value of $35,000) assigned to an identifiable reporting unit purchased at the end of the prior year. The fair value of the net assets held by the reporting unit is currently $350,000, and the fair value of the reporting unit is $395,000. At the end of the current period, Grout should report goodwill of:

 a. $45,000.
 b. $35,000.
 c. $25,000.
 d. $10,000.

5. Twill Company has a reporting unit with the fair value of its net identifiable assets of $500,000. The carrying value of the reporting unit's net assets on Twill's books is $575,000, which includes $90,000 of goodwill. The fair value of the reporting unit is $560,000. Twill should report impairment of goodwill of:

 a. $60,000.
 b. $30,000.
 c. $15,000.
 d. $0.

### E1-5 Asset Transfer to Subsidiary

Pale Company was established on January 1, 20X1. Along with other assets, it immediately purchased land for $80,000, a building for $240,000, and equipment for $90,000. On January 1, 20X5, Pale transferred these assets, cash of $21,000, and inventory costing $37,000 to a newly created subsidiary, Bright Company, in exchange for 10,000 shares of Bright's $6 par value stock. Pale uses straight-line depreciation and useful lives of 40 years and 10 years for the building and equipment, respectively, with no estimated residual values.

#### Required

 a. Give the journal entry that Pale recorded when it transferred the assets to Bright.
 b. Give the journal entry that Bright recorded for the receipt of assets and issuance of common stock to Pale.

### E1-6 Creation of New Subsidiary

Lester Company transferred the following assets to a newly created subsidiary, Mumby Corporation, in exchange for 40,000 shares of its $3 par value stock:

| | Cost | Book Value |
| --- | --- | --- |
| Cash | $ 40,000 | $ 40,000 |
| Accounts Receivable | 75,000 | 68,000 |
| Inventory | 50,000 | 50,000 |
| Land | 35,000 | 35,000 |
| Buildings | 160,000 | 125,000 |
| Equipment | 240,000 | 180,000 |

#### Required

 a. Give the journal entry in which Lester recorded the transfer of assets to Mumby Corporation.

*b.* Give the journal entry in which Mumby recorded the receipt of assets and issuance of common stock to Lester.

## E1-7   Balance Sheet Totals of Parent Company

Foster Corporation established Kline Company as a wholly owned subsidiary. Foster reported the following balance sheet amounts immediately before and after it transferred assets and accounts payable to Kline Company in exchange for 4,000 shares of $12 par value common stock:

| | Amount Reported | | | |
|---|---|---|---|---|
| | Before Transfer | | After Transfer | |
| Cash | | $ 40,000 | | $ 25,000 |
| Accounts Receivable | | 65,000 | | 41,000 |
| Inventory | | 30,000 | | 21,000 |
| Investment in Kline Company | | | | 66,000 |
| Land | | 15,000 | | 12,000 |
| Depreciable Assets | $180,000 | | $115,000 | |
| Accumulated Depreciation | 75,000 | 105,000 | 47,000 | 68,000 |
| Total Assets | | $255,000 | | $233,000 |
| Accounts Payable | | $ 40,000 | | $ 18,000 |
| Bonds Payable | | 80,000 | | 80,000 |
| Common Stock | | 60,000 | | 60,000 |
| Retained Earnings | | 75,000 | | 75,000 |
| Total Liabilities and Equities | | $255,000 | | $233,000 |

### Required

*a.* Give the journal entry that Foster recorded when it transferred its assets and accounts payable to Kline.

*b.* Give the journal entry that Kline recorded upon receipt of the assets and accounts payable from Foster.

## E1-8   Creation of Partnership

Glover Corporation entered into an agreement with Renfro Company to establish G&R Partnership. Glover agreed to transfer the following assets to G&R for 90 percent ownership, and Renfro agreed to transfer $50,000 cash to the partnership for 10 percent ownership.

| | Cost | Book Value |
|---|---|---|
| Cash | $ 10,000 | $ 10,000 |
| Accounts Receivable | 19,000 | 19,000 |
| Inventory | 35,000 | 35,000 |
| Land | 16,000 | 16,000 |
| Buildings | 260,000 | 200,000 |
| Equipment | 210,000 | 170,000 |

### Required

*a.* Give the journal entry that Glover recorded at the time of its transfer of assets to G&R.

*b.* Give the journal entry that Renfro recorded at the time of its transfer of cash to G&R.

*c.* Give the journal entry that G&R recorded upon the receipt of assets from Glover and Renfro.

## E1-9   Acquisition of Net Assets

Sun Corporation concluded the fair value of Tender Company was $60,000 and paid that amount to acquire its net assets. Tender reported assets with a book value of $55,000 and fair value of

$71,000 and liabilities with a book value and fair value of $20,000 on the date of combination. Sun also paid $4,000 to a search firm for finder's fees related to the acquisition.

### Required

Give the journal entries to be made by Sun to record its investment in Tender and its payment of the finder's fees.

**E1-10** **Reporting Goodwill**

Samper Company reported the book value of its net assets at $160,000 when Public Corporation acquired 100 percent ownership for $310,000. The fair value of Samper's net assets was determined to be $190,000 on that date.

### Required

Determine the amount of goodwill to be reported in consolidated financial statements presented immediately following the combination and the amount at which Public will record its investment in Samper if the amount paid by Public is:

*a.* $310,000.

*b.* $196,000.

*c.* $150,000.

**E1-11** **Stock Acquisition**

McDermott Corporation has been in the midst of a major expansion program. Much of its growth had been internal, but in 20X1 McDermott decided to continue its expansion through the acquisition of other companies. The first company acquired was Tippy Inc., a small manufacturer of inertial guidance systems for aircraft and missiles. On June 10, 20X1, McDermott issued 17,000 shares of its $25 par common stock for all 40,000 of Tippy's $10 par common shares. At the date of combination, Tippy reported additional paid-in capital of $100,000 and retained earnings of $350,000. McDermott's stock was selling for $58 per share immediately prior to the combination. Subsequent to the combination, Tippy operated as a subsidiary of McDermott.

### Required

Present the journal entry or entries that McDermott would make to record the business combination with Tippy.

**E1-12** **Balances Reported Following Combination**

Elm Corporation and Maple Company have announced terms of an exchange agreement under which Elm will issue 8,000 shares of its $10 par value common stock to acquire all of Maple Company's assets. Elm shares currently are trading at $50, and Maple $5 par value shares are trading at $18 each. Historical cost and fair value balance sheet data on January 1, 20X2, are as follows:

| Balance Sheet Item | Elm Corporation Book Value | Elm Corporation Fair Value | Maple Company Book Value | Maple Company Fair Value |
|---|---|---|---|---|
| Cash and Receivables | $150,000 | $150,000 | $ 40,000 | $ 40,000 |
| Land | 100,000 | 170,000 | 50,000 | 85,000 |
| Buildings and Equipment (net) | 300,000 | 400,000 | 160,000 | 230,000 |
| Total Assets | $550,000 | $720,000 | $250,000 | $355,000 |
| Common Stock | $200,000 | | $100,000 | |
| Additional Paid-In Capital | 20,000 | | 10,000 | |
| Retained Earnings | 330,000 | | 140,000 | |
| Total Equities | $550,000 | | $250,000 | |

### Required

What amount will be reported immediately following the business combination for each of the following items in the combined company's balance sheet?

a. Common Stock.

b. Cash and Receivables.

c. Land.

d. Buildings and Equipment (net).

e. Goodwill.

f. Additional Paid-In Capital.

g. Retained Earnings.

### E1-13 Goodwill Recognition

Spur Corporation reported the following balance sheet amounts on December 31, 20X1:

| Balance Sheet Item | Historical Cost | Fair Value |
|---|---|---|
| Cash and Receivables | $ 50,000 | $ 40,000 |
| Inventory | 100,000 | 150,000 |
| Land | 40,000 | 30,000 |
| Plant and Equipment | 400,000 | 350,000 |
| Less: Accumulated Depreciation | (150,000) | |
| Patent | | 130,000 |
| Total Assets | $440,000 | $700,000 |
| Accounts Payable | $ 80,000 | $ 85,000 |
| Common Stock | 200,000 | |
| Additional Paid-In Capital | 20,000 | |
| Retained Earnings | 140,000 | |
| Total Liabilities and Equities | $440,000 | |

#### Required

Blanket acquired Spur Corporation's assets and liabilities for $670,000 cash on December 31, 20X1. Give the entry that Blanket made to record the purchase.

### E1-14 Acquisition Using Debentures

Fortune Corporation used debentures with a par value of $625,000 to acquire 100 percent of Sorden Company's net assets on January 1, 20X2. On that date, the fair value of the bonds issued by Fortune was $608,000. The following balance sheet data were reported by Sorden:

| Balance Sheet Item | Historical Cost | Fair Value |
|---|---|---|
| Cash and Receivables | $ 55,000 | $ 50,000 |
| Inventory | 105,000 | 200,000 |
| Land | 60,000 | 100,000 |
| Plant and Equipment | 400,000 | 300,000 |
| Less: Accumulated Depreciation | (150,000) | |
| Goodwill | 10,000 | |
| Total Assets | $480,000 | $650,000 |
| Accounts Payable | $ 50,000 | $ 50,000 |
| Common Stock | 100,000 | |
| Additional Paid-In Capital | 60,000 | |
| Retained Earnings | 270,000 | |
| Total Liabilities and Equities | $480,000 | |

#### Required

Give the journal entry that Fortune recorded at the time of exchange.

### E1-15 Bargain Purchase

Using the data presented in E1-14 determine the amount Fortune Corporation would record as a gain on bargain purchase and prepare the journal entry Fortune would record at the time of the exchange if Fortune issued bonds with a par value of $580,000 and a fair value of $564,000 in completing the acquisition of Sorden.

### E1-16 Impairment of Goodwill

Mesa Corporation purchased Kwick Company's net assets and assigned goodwill of $80,000 to Reporting Division K. The following assets and liabilities are assigned to Reporting Division K:

|  | Carrying Amount | Fair Value |
|---|---|---|
| Cash | $ 14,000 | $ 14,000 |
| Inventory | 56,000 | 71,000 |
| Equipment | 170,000 | 190,000 |
| Goodwill | 80,000 |  |
| Accounts Payable | 30,000 | 30,000 |

#### Required

Determine the amount of goodwill to be reported for Division K and the amount of goodwill impairment to be recognized, if any, if Division K's fair value is determined to be:

a. $340,000.

b. $280,000.

c. $260,000.

### E1-17 Assignment of Goodwill

Double Corporation acquired all of the common stock of Simple Company for $450,000 on January 1, 20X4. On that date, Simple's identifiable net assets had a fair value of $390,000. The assets acquired in the purchase of Simple are considered to be a separate reporting unit of Double. The carrying value of Double's investment at December 31, 20X4, is $500,000.

#### Required

Determine the amount of goodwill impairment, if any, that should be recognized at December 31, 20X4, if the fair value of the net assets (excluding goodwill) at that date is $440,000 and the fair value of the reporting unit is determined to be:

a. $530,000.

b. $485,000.

c. $450,000.

### E1-18 Goodwill Assigned to Reporting Units

Groft Company purchased Strobe Company's net assets and assigned them to four separate reporting units. Total goodwill of $186,000 is assigned to the reporting units as indicated:

|  | Reporting Unit | | | |
|---|---|---|---|---|
|  | A | B | C | D |
| Carrying value of investment | $700,000 | $330,000 | $380,000 | $520,000 |
| Goodwill included in carrying value | 60,000 | 48,000 | 28,000 | 50,000 |
| Fair value of net identifiable assets at year-end | 600,000 | 300,000 | 400,000 | 500,000 |
| Fair value of reporting unit at year-end | 690,000 | 335,000 | 370,000 | 585,000 |

### Required

Determine the amount of goodwill that Groft should report at year-end. Show how you computed it.

## E1-19 Goodwill Measurement

Washer Company has a reporting unit resulting from an earlier business combination. The reporting unit's current assets and liabilities are:

|  | Carrying Amount | Fair Value |
|---|---|---|
| Cash | $ 30,000 | $ 30,000 |
| Inventory | 70,000 | 100,000 |
| Land | 30,000 | 60,000 |
| Buildings | 210,000 | 230,000 |
| Equipment | 160,000 | 170,000 |
| Goodwill | 150,000 | |
| Notes Payable | 100,000 | 100,000 |

### Required

Determine the amount of goodwill to be reported and the amount of goodwill impairment, if any, if the fair value of the reporting unit is determined to be:

a. $580.000.

b. $540,000.

c. $500,000.

d. $460,000.

## E1-20 Computation of Fair Value

Grant Company acquired all of Bedford Corporation's assets and liabilities on January 1, 20X2, in a business combination. At that date, Bedford reported assets with a book value of $624,000 and liabilities of $356,000. Grant noted that Bedford had $40,000 of research and development costs on its books at the acquisition date that did not appear to be of value. Grant also determined that patents developed by Bedford had a fair value of $120,000 but had not been recorded by Bedford. Except for buildings and equipment, Grant determined the fair value of all other assets and liabilities reported by Bedford approximated the recorded amounts. In recording the transfer of assets and liabilities to its books, Grant recorded goodwill of $93,000. Grant paid $517,000 to acquire Bedford's assets and liabilities. If the book value of Bedford's buildings and equipment was $341,000 at the date of acquisition, what was their fair value?

## E1-21 Computation of Shares Issued and Goodwill

Dunyain Company acquired Allsap Corporation on January 1, 20X1, through an exchange of common shares. All of Allsap's assets and liabilities were immediately transferred to Dunyain, which reported total par value of shares outstanding of $218,400 and $327,600 and additional paid-in capital of $370,000 and $650,800 immediately before and after the business combination, respectively.

### Required

a. Assuming that Dunyain's common stock had a market value of $25 per share at the time of exchange, what number of shares was issued?

b. What is the par value per share of Dunyain's common stock?

c. Assuming that Allsap's identifiable assets had a fair value of $476,000 and its liabilities had a fair value of $120,000, what amount of goodwill did Dunyain record at the time of the business combination?

## E1-22 Combined Balance Sheet

The following balance sheets were prepared for Adam Corporation and Best Company on January 1, 20X2, just before they entered into a business combination:

| Item | Adam Corporation | | Best Company | |
|---|---|---|---|---|
| | Book Value | Fair Value | Book Value | Fair Value |
| Cash and Receivables | $150,000 | $150,000 | $ 90,000 | $ 90,000 |
| Inventory | 300,000 | 380,000 | 70,000 | 160,000 |
| Buildings and Equipment | 600,000 | 430,000 | 250,000 | 240,000 |
| Less: Accumulated Depreciation | (250,000) | | (80,000) | |
| Total Assets | $800,000 | $960,000 | $330,000 | $490,000 |
| Accounts Payable | $ 75,000 | $ 75,000 | $ 50,000 | $ 50,000 |
| Notes Payable | 200,000 | 215,000 | 30,000 | 35,000 |
| Common Stock: | | | | |
| $8 par value | 180,000 | | | |
| $6 par value | | | 90,000 | |
| Additional Paid-In Capital | 140,000 | | 55,000 | |
| Retained Earnings | 205,000 | | 105,000 | |
| Total Liabilities and Equities | $800,000 | | $330,000 | |

Adam acquired all of Best Company's assets and liabilities on January 1, 20X2, in exchange for its common shares. Adam issued 8,000 shares of stock to complete the business combination.

### Required

Prepare a balance sheet of the combined company immediately following the acquisition, assuming Adam's shares were trading at $60 each.

**E1-23  Recording a Business Combination**

The following financial statement information was prepared for Blue Corporation and Sparse Company at December 31, 20X2:

**Balance Sheets**
**December 31, 20X2**

| | Blue Corporation | | Sparse Company | |
|---|---|---|---|---|
| Cash | | $  140,000 | | $  70,000 |
| Accounts Receivable | | 170,000 | | 110,000 |
| Inventory | | 250,000 | | 180,000 |
| Land | | 80,000 | | 100,000 |
| Buildings and Equipment | $ 680,000 | | $ 450,000 | |
| Less: Accumulated Depreciation | (320,000) | 360,000 | (230,000) | 220,000 |
| Goodwill | | 70,000 | | 20,000 |
| Total Assets | | $1,070,000 | | $700,000 |
| Accounts Payable | | $   70,000 | | $195,000 |
| Bonds Payable | | 320,000 | | 100,000 |
| Bond Premium | | | | 10,000 |
| Common Stock | | 120,000 | | 150,000 |
| Additional Paid-In Capital | | 170,000 | | 60,000 |
| Retained Earnings | | 390,000 | | 185,000 |
| Total Liabilities and Equities | | $1,070,000 | | $700,000 |

Blue and Sparse agreed to combine as of January 1, 20X3. To effect the merger, Blue paid finder's fees of $30,000 and legal fees of $24,000. Blue also paid $15,000 of audit fees related to the issuance of stock, stock registration fees of $8,000, and stock listing application fees of $6,000.

At January 1, 20X3, book values of Sparse Company's assets and liabilities approximated market value except for inventory with a market value of $200,000, buildings and equipment with a market value of $350,000, and bonds payable with a market value of $105,000. All assets and liabilities were immediately recorded on Blue's books.

### Required
Give all journal entries that Blue recorded assuming Blue issued 40,000 shares of $8 par value common stock to acquire all of Sparse's assets and liabilities in a business combination. Blue common stock was trading at $14 per share on January 1, 20X3.

**E1-24**  **Reporting Income**

On July 1, 20X2, Alan Enterprises merged with Cherry Corporation through an exchange of stock and the subsequent liquidation of Cherry. Alan issued 200,000 shares of its stock to effect the combination. The book values of Cherry's assets and liabilities were equal to their fair values at the date of combination, and the value of the shares exchanged was equal to Cherry's book value. Information relating to income for the companies is as follows:

|  | 20X1 | Jan. 1–June 30, 20X2 | July 1–Dec. 31, 20X2 |
|---|---|---|---|
| Net Income: |  |  |  |
| Alan Enterprises | $4,460,000 | $2,500,000 | $3,528,000 |
| Cherry Corporation | 1,300,000 | 692,000 | — |

Alan Enterprises had 1,000,000 shares of stock outstanding prior to the combination.

### Required
Compute the net income and earnings-per-share amounts that would be reported in Alan's 20X2 comparative income statements for both 20X2 and 20X1.

## Problems

**P1-25**  **Assets and Accounts Payable Transferred to Subsidiary**

Tab Corporation decided to establish Collon Company as a wholly owned subsidiary by transferring some of its existing assets and liabilities to the new entity. In exchange, Collon issued Tab 30,000 shares of $6 par value common stock. The following information is provided on the assets and accounts payable transferred:

|  | Cost | Book Value | Fair Value |
|---|---|---|---|
| Cash | $ 25,000 | $ 25,000 | $ 25,000 |
| Inventory | 70,000 | 70,000 | 70,000 |
| Land | 60,000 | 60,000 | 90,000 |
| Buildings | 170,000 | 130,000 | 240,000 |
| Equipment | 90,000 | 80,000 | 105,000 |
| Accounts Payable | 45,000 | 45,000 | 45,000 |

### Required

a.  Give the journal entry that Tab recorded for the transfer of assets and accounts payable to Collon.

b.  Give the journal entry that Collon recorded for the receipt of assets and accounts payable from Tab.

**P1-26**  **Creation of New Subsidiary**

Eagle Corporation established a subsidiary to enter into a new line of business considered to be substantially more risky than Eagle's current business. Eagle transferred the following assets and accounts payable to Sand Corporation in exchange for 5,000 shares of $10 par value stock of Sand:

|  | Cost | Book Value |
|---|---|---|
| Cash | $ 30,000 | $ 30,000 |
| Accounts Receivable | 45,000 | 40,000 |
| Inventory | 60,000 | 60,000 |
| Land | 20,000 | 20,000 |
| Buildings and Equipment | 300,000 | 260,000 |
| Accounts Payable | 10,000 | 10,000 |

### Required

a. Give the journal entry that Eagle recorded for the transfer of assets and accounts payable to Sand.

b. Give the journal entry that Sand recorded for receipt of the assets and accounts payable from Eagle.

**P1-27 Incomplete Data on Creation of Subsidiary**

Thumb Company created New Company as a wholly owned subsidiary by transferring assets and accounts payable to New in exchange for its common stock. New recorded the following entry when it received the assets and accounts payable:

| | | |
|---|---|---|
| Cash | 3,000 | |
| Accounts Receivable | 16,000 | |
| Inventory | 27,000 | |
| Land | 9,000 | |
| Buildings | 70,000 | |
| Equipment | 60,000 | |
| Accounts Payable | | 14,000 |
| Accumulated Depreciation—Buildings | | 21,000 |
| Accumulated Depreciation—Equipment | | 12,000 |
| Common Stock | | 40,000 |
| Additional Paid-In Capital | | 98,000 |

### Required

a. What was Thumb's book value of the total assets transferred to New Company?

b. What amount did Thumb report as its investment in New after the transfer?

c. What number of shares of $5 par value stock did New issue to Thumb?

d. What impact did the transfer of assets and accounts payable have on the amount reported by Thumb as total assets?

e. What impact did the transfer of assets and accounts payable have on the amount that Thumb and the consolidated entity reported as shares outstanding?

**P1-28 Establishing a Partnership**

Krantz Company and Dull Corporation decided to form a partnership. Krantz agreed to transfer the following assets and accounts payable to K&D Partnership in exchange for 60 percent ownership:

|  | Cost | Book Value |
|---|---|---|
| Cash | $ 10,000 | $ 10,000 |
| Inventory | 30,000 | 30,000 |
| Land | 70,000 | 70,000 |
| Buildings | 200,000 | 150,000 |
| Equipment | 120,000 | 90,000 |
| Accounts Payable | 50,000 | 50,000 |

Dull agreed to contribute cash of $200,000 to K&D Partnership.

### Required

a. Give the journal entries that K&D recorded for its receipt of assets and accounts payable from Krantz and Dull.

b. Give the journal entries that Krantz and Dull recorded for their transfer of assets and accounts payable to K&D Partnership.

**P1-29   Balance Sheet Data for Companies Establishing a Partnership**

Good Corporation and Nevall Company formed G&W Partnership in which Good received 75 percent ownership and Nevall received 25 percent ownership. The following assets were transferred by Good and Nevall:

| | Good Corporation | | Nevall Company | |
|---|---|---|---|---|
| | Cost | Book Value | Cost | Book Value |
| Cash | $ 21,000 | $21,000 | $ 3,000 | $ 3,000 |
| Inventory | 4,000 | 4,000 | 25,000 | 25,000 |
| Land | 15,000 | 15,000 | | |
| Buildings | 100,000 | 70,000 | | |
| Equipment | 60,000 | 40,000 | 36,000 | 22,000 |

### Required

a. Give the journal entry that Good recorded for its transfer of assets to G&W Partnership.

b. Give the journal entry that Nevall recorded for its transfer of assets to G&W Partnership.

c. Give the journal entry that G&W recorded for its receipt of assets from Good and Nevall.

**P1-30   Acquisition in Multiple Steps**

Deal Corporation issued 4,000 shares of its $10 par value stock with a market value of $85,000 to acquire 85 percent ownership of Mead Company on August 31, 20X3. The fair value of Mead was determined to be $100,000 on that date. Deal had earlier purchased 15 percent of Mead's shares for $9,000 and used the cost method in accounting for its investment in Mead. Deal later paid appraisal fees of $3,500 and stock issue costs of $2,000 incurred in completing the acquisition of the additional shares.

### Required

Give the journal entries to be recorded by Deal in completing the acquisition of the additional shares of Mead.

**P1-31   Journal Entries to Record a Business Combination**

On January 1, 20X2, Frost Company acquired all of TKK Corporation's assets and liabilities by issuing 24,000 shares of its $4 par value common stock. At that date, Frost shares were selling at $22 per share. Historical cost and fair value balance sheet data for TKK at the time of acquisition were as follows:

| Balance Sheet Item | Historical Cost | Fair Value |
|---|---|---|
| Cash and Receivables | $ 28,000 | $ 28,000 |
| Inventory | 94,000 | 122,000 |
| Buildings and Equipment | 600,000 | 470,000 |
| Less: Accumulated Depreciation | (240,000) | |
| Total Assets | $482,000 | $620,000 |
| Accounts Payable | $ 41,000 | $ 41,000 |
| Notes Payable | 65,000 | 63,000 |
| Common Stock ($10 par value) | 160,000 | |
| Retained Earnings | 216,000 | |
| Total Liabilities and Equities | $482,000 | |

Frost paid legal fees for the transfer of assets and liabilities of $14,000. Frost also paid audit fees of $21,000 and listing application fees of $7,000, both related to the issuance of new shares.

### Required

Prepare the journal entries made by Frost to record the business combination.

P1-32    **Recording Business Combinations**

Flint Corporation exchanged shares of its $2 par common stock for all of Mark Company's assets and liabilities in a planned merger. Immediately prior to the combination, Mark's assets and liabilities were as follows:

| Assets | |
| --- | ---: |
| Cash and Equivalents | $    41,000 |
| Accounts Receivable | 73,000 |
| Inventory | 144,000 |
| Land | 200,000 |
| Buildings | 1,520,000 |
| Equipment | 638,000 |
| Accumulated Depreciation | (431,000) |
| Total Assets | $2,185,000 |

| Liabilities and Equities | |
| --- | ---: |
| Accounts Payable | $    35,000 |
| Short-Term Notes Payable | 50,000 |
| Bonds Payable | 500,000 |
| Common Stock ($10 par) | 1,000,000 |
| Additional Paid-In Capital | 325,000 |
| Retained Earnings | 275,000 |
| Total Liabilities and Equities | $2,185,000 |

Immediately prior to the combination, Flint reported $250,000 additional paid-in capital and $1,350,000 retained earnings. The fair values of Mark's assets and liabilities were equal to their book values on the date of combination except that Mark's buildings were worth $1,500,000 and its equipment was worth $300,000. Costs associated with planning and completing the business combination totaled $38,000, and stock issue costs totaled $22,000. The market value of Flint's stock at the date of combination was $4 per share.

### Required

Prepare the journal entries that would appear on Flint's books to record the combination if Flint issued 450,000 shares.

P1-33    **Business Combination with Goodwill**

Anchor Corporation paid cash of $178,000 to acquire Zink Company's net assets on February 1, 20X3. The balance sheet data for the two companies and fair value information for Zink immediately before the business combination were:

| Balance Sheet Item | Anchor Corporation Book Value | Zink Company Book Value | Zink Company Fair Value |
|---|---|---|---|
| Cash | $240,000 | $ 20,000 | $ 20,000 |
| Accounts Receivable | 140,000 | 35,000 | 35,000 |
| Inventory | 170,000 | 30,000 | 50,000 |
| Patents | 80,000 | 40,000 | 60,000 |
| Buildings and Equipment | 380,000 | 310,000 | 150,000 |
| Less: Accumulated Depreciation | (190,000) | (200,000) | |
| Total Assets | $820,000 | $235,000 | $315,000 |
| Accounts Payable | $ 85,000 | $ 55,000 | $ 55,000 |
| Notes Payable | 150,000 | 120,000 | 120,000 |
| Common Stock: | | | |
| $10 par value | 200,000 | | |
| $6 par value | | 18,000 | |
| Additional Paid-In Capital | 160,000 | 10,000 | |
| Retained Earnings | 225,000 | 32,000 | |
| Total Liabilities and Equities | $820,000 | $235,000 | |

### Required

*a.* Give the journal entry recorded by Anchor Corporation when it acquired Zink's net assets.

*b.* Prepare a balance sheet for Anchor immediately following the acquisition.

*c.* Give the journal entry to be recorded by Anchor if it acquires all of Zink's common stock for $178,000.

**P1-34   Bargain Purchase**

Bower Company purchased Lark Corporation's net assets on January 3, 20X2, for $625,000 cash. In addition, $5,000 of direct costs were incurred in consummating the combination. At the time of acquisition, Lark reported the following historical cost and current market data:

| Balance Sheet Item | Book Value | Fair Value |
|---|---|---|
| Cash and Receivables | $ 50,000 | $ 50,000 |
| Inventory | 100,000 | 150,000 |
| Buildings and Equipment (net) | 200,000 | 300,000 |
| Patent | — | 200,000 |
| Total Assets | $350,000 | $700,000 |
| Accounts Payable | $ 30,000 | $ 30,000 |
| Common Stock | 100,000 | |
| Additional Paid-In Capital | 80,000 | |
| Retained Earnings | 140,000 | |
| Total Liabilities and Equities | $350,000 | |

### Required

Give the journal entry or entries with which Bower recorded its acquisition of Lark's net assets.

**P1-35   Computation of Account Balances**

Aspro Division is considered to be an individual reporting unit of Tabor Company. Tabor acquired the division by issuing 100,000 shares of its common stock with a market price of $7.60 each. Tabor management was able to identify assets with fair values of $810,000 and liabilities of $190,000 at the date of acquisition. At the end of the first year, the reporting unit had assets with a fair value of $950,000, and the fair value of the reporting entity was $930,000. Tabor's accountants concluded it must recognize impairment of goodwill in the amount of $30,000 at the end of the first year.

### Required

a. Determine the fair value of the reporting unit's liabilities at the end of the first year. Show your computation.

b. If the reporting unit's liabilities at the end of the period had been $70,000, what would the fair value of the reporting unit had to have been to avoid recognizing an impairment of goodwill? Show your computation.

**P1-36** **Goodwill Assigned to Multiple Reporting Units**

The fair values of assets and liabilities held by three reporting units and other information related to the reporting units owned by Rover Company are as follows:

|  | Reporting Unit | | |
|  | A | B | C |
|---|---|---|---|
| Cash and Receivables | $ 30,000 | $ 80,000 | $ 20,000 |
| Inventory | 60,000 | 100,000 | 40,000 |
| Land | 20,000 | 30,000 | 10,000 |
| Buildings | 100,000 | 150,000 | 80,000 |
| Equipment | 140,000 | 90,000 | 50,000 |
| Accounts Payable | 40,000 | 60,000 | 10,000 |
| Fair Value of Reporting Unit | 400,000 | 440,000 | 265,000 |
| Carrying Value of Investment | 420,000 | 500,000 | 290,000 |
| Goodwill Included in Carrying Value | 70,000 | 80,000 | 40,000 |

### Required

a. Determine the amount of goodwill that Rover should report in its current financial statements.

b. Determine the amount, if any, that Rover should report as impairment of goodwill for the current period.

**P1-37** **Journal Entries**

On January 1, 20X3, PURE Products Corporation issued 12,000 shares of its $10 par value stock to acquire the net assets of Light Steel Company. Underlying book value and fair value information for the balance sheet items of Light Steel at the time of acquisition follow:

| Balance Sheet Item | Book Value | Fair Value |
|---|---|---|
| Cash | $ 60,000 | $ 60,000 |
| Accounts Receivable | 100,000 | 100,000 |
| Inventory (LIFO basis) | 60,000 | 115,000 |
| Land | 50,000 | 70,000 |
| Buildings and Equipment | 400,000 | 350,000 |
| Less: Accumulated Depreciation | (150,000) | — |
| Total Assets | $520,000 | $695,000 |
| | | |
| Accounts Payable | $ 10,000 | $ 10,000 |
| Bonds Payable | 200,000 | 180,000 |
| Common Stock ($5 par value) | 150,000 | |
| Additional Paid-In Capital | 70,000 | |
| Retained Earnings | 90,000 | |
| Total Liabilities and Equities | $520,000 | |

Light Steel shares were selling at $18 and PURE Products shares were selling at $50 just before the merger announcement. Additional cash payments made by PURE Products in completing the acquisition were:

| | |
|---|---:|
| Finder's fee paid to firm that located Light Steel | $10,000 |
| Audit fee for stock issued by PURE Products | 3,000 |
| Stock registration fee for new shares of PURE Products | 5,000 |
| Legal fees paid to assist in transfer of net assets | 9,000 |
| Cost of SEC registration of PURE Products shares | 1,000 |

### Required

Prepare all journal entries to record the business combination on PURE Products' books.

**P1-38**   **Purchase at More than Book Value**

Ramrod Manufacturing acquired all the assets and liabilities of Stafford Industries on January 1, 20X2, in exchange for 4,000 shares of Ramrod's $20 par value common stock. Balance sheet data for both companies just before the merger are given as follows:

| | Ramrod Manufacturing | | Stafford Industries | |
|---|---|---|---|---|
| **Balance Sheet Items** | **Book Value** | **Fair Value** | **Book Value** | **Fair Value** |
| Cash | $ 70,000 | $ 70,000 | $ 30,000 | $ 30,000 |
| Accounts Receivable | 100,000 | 100,000 | 60,000 | 60,000 |
| Inventory | 200,000 | 375,000 | 100,000 | 160,000 |
| Land | 50,000 | 80,000 | 40,000 | 30,000 |
| Buildings and Equipment | 600,000 } | | 400,000 } | |
| Less: Accumulated Depreciation | (250,000) } | 540,000 | (150,000) } | 350,000 |
| Total Assets | $770,000 | $1,165,000 | $480,000 | $630,000 |
| Accounts Payable | $ 50,000 | $ 50,000 | $ 10,000 | $ 10,000 |
| Bonds Payable | 300,000 | 310,000 | 150,000 | 145,000 |
| Common Stock: | | | | |
| $20 par value | 200,000 | | | |
| $5 par value | | | 100,000 | |
| Additional Paid-In Capital | 40,000 | | 20,000 | |
| Retained Earnings | 180,000 | | 200,000 | |
| Total Liabilities and Equities | $770,000 | | $480,000 | |

Ramrod shares were selling for $150 on the date of acquisition.

### Required

Prepare the following:

*a.* Journal entries to record the acquisition on Ramrod's books.

*b.* A balance sheet for the combined enterprise immediately following the business combination.

**P1-39**   **Business Combination**

Following are the balance sheets of Boogie Musical Corporation and Toot-Toot Tuba Company as of December 31, 20X5.

**BOOGIE MUSICAL CORPORATION**
**Balance Sheet**
**December 31, 20X5**

| *Assets* | | *Liabilities and Equities* | |
|---|---:|---|---:|
| Cash | $ 23,000 | Accounts Payable | $ 48,000 |
| Accounts Receivable | 85,000 | Notes Payable | 65,000 |
| Allowance for Uncollectible Accounts | (1,200) | Mortgage Payable | 200,000 |
| Inventory | 192,000 | Bonds Payable | 200,000 |
| Plant and Equipment | 980,000 | Capital Stock ($10 par) | 500,000 |
| Accumulated Depreciation | (160,000) | Premium on Capital Stock | 1,000 |
| Other Assets | 14,000 | Retained Earnings | 118,800 |
| Total Assets | $1,132,800 | Total Liabilities and Equities | $1,132,800 |

**TOOT-TOOT TUBA COMPANY**
**Balance Sheet**
**December 31, 20X5**

| Assets | | Liabilities and Equities | |
|---|---:|---|---:|
| Cash | $ 300 | Accounts Payable | $ 8,200 |
| Accounts Receivable | 17,000 | Notes Payable | 10,000 |
| Allowance for Uncollectible Accounts | (600) | Mortgage Payable | 50,000 |
| Inventory | 78,500 | Bonds Payable | 100,000 |
| Plant and Equipment | 451,000 | Capital Stock ($50 par) | 100,000 |
| Accumulated Depreciation | (225,000) | Premium on Capital Stock | 150,000 |
| Other Assets | 25,800 | Retained Earnings | (71,200) |
| Total Assets | $347,000 | Total Liabilities and Equities | $347,000 |

In preparation for a possible business combination, a team of experts from Boogie Musical made a thorough examination and audit of Toot-Toot Tuba. They found that Toot-Toot's assets and liabilities were correctly stated except that they estimated uncollectible accounts at $1,400. The experts also estimated the market value of the inventory at $35,000 and the market value of the plant and equipment at $500,000. The business combination took place on January 1, 20X6, and on that date Boogie Musical acquired all the assets and liabilities of Toot-Toot Tuba. On that date, Boogie's common stock was selling for $55 per share.

### Required
Record the combination on Boogie's books assuming that Boogie issued 9,000 of its $10 par common shares in exchange for Toot-Toot's assets and liabilities.

**P1-40 Combined Balance Sheet**
Bilge Pumpworks and Seaworthy Rope Company agreed to merge on January 1, 20X3. On the date of the merger agreement, the companies reported the following data:

| Balance Sheet Items | Bilge Pumpworks | | Seaworthy Rope Company | |
|---|---|---|---|---|
| | Book Value | Fair Value | Book Value | Fair Value |
| Cash and Receivables | $ 90,000 | $ 90,000 | $ 20,000 | $ 20,000 |
| Inventory | 100,000 | 150,000 | 30,000 | 42,000 |
| Land | 100,000 | 140,000 | 10,000 | 15,000 |
| Plant and Equipment | 400,000 | | 200,000 | |
| Less: Accumulated Depreciation | (150,000) | 300,000 | (80,000) | 140,000 |
| Total Assets | $540,000 | $680,000 | $180,000 | $217,000 |
| Current Liabilities | $ 80,000 | $ 80,000 | $ 20,000 | $ 20,000 |
| Capital Stock | 200,000 | | 20,000 | |
| Capital in Excess of Par Value | 20,000 | | 5,000 | |
| Retained Earnings | 240,000 | | 135,000 | |
| Total Liabilities and Equities | $540,000 | | $180,000 | |

Bilge Pumpworks has 10,000 shares of its $20 par value shares outstanding on January 1, 20X3, and Seaworthy has 4,000 shares of $5 par value stock outstanding. The market values of the shares are $300 and $50, respectively.

### Required

*a.* Bilge issues 700 shares of stock in exchange for all of Seaworthy's net assets. Prepare a balance sheet for the combined entity immediately following the merger.

*b.* Prepare the stockholders' equity section of the combined company's balance sheet, assuming Bilge acquires all of Seaworthy's net assets by issuing:

1. 1,100 shares of common.
2. 1,800 shares of common.
3. 3,000 shares of common.

**P1-41**  **Incomplete Data Problem**

On January 1, 20X2, End Corporation acquired all of Cork Corporation's assets and liabilities by issuing shares of its common stock. Partial balance sheet data for the companies prior to the business combination and immediately following the combination are as follows:

| | End Corp. Book Value | Cork Corp. Book Value | Combined Entity |
|---|---|---|---|
| Cash | $ 40,000 | $ 10,000 | $ 50,000 |
| Accounts Receivable | 60,000 | 30,000 | 88,000 |
| Inventory | 50,000 | 35,000 | 96,000 |
| Buildings and Equipment (net) | 300,000 | 110,000 | 430,000 |
| Goodwill | | | ? |
| Total Assets | $450,000 | $185,000 | $    ? |
| Accounts Payable | $ 32,000 | $ 14,000 | $ 46,000 |
| Bonds Payable | 150,000 | 70,000 | 220,000 |
| Bond Premium | 6,000 | | 6,000 |
| Common Stock, $5 par | 100,000 | 40,000 | 126,000 |
| Additional Paid-In Capital | 65,000 | 28,000 | 247,000 |
| Retained Earnings | 97,000 | 33,000 | ? |
| Total Liabilities and Equities | $450,000 | $185,000 | $    ? |

### Required

*a.* What number of shares did End issue to acquire Cork's assets and liabilities?

*b.* What was the market value of the shares issued by End?

*c.* What was the fair value of the inventory held by Cork at the date of combination?

*d.* What was the fair value of the net assets held by Cork at the date of combination?

*e.* What amount of goodwill, if any, will be reported by the combined entity immediately following the combination?

*f.* What balance in retained earnings will the combined entity report immediately following the combination?

*g.* If the depreciable assets held by Cork had an average remaining life of 10 years at the date of acquisition, what amount of depreciation expense will be reported on those assets in 20X2?

**P1-42**  **Incomplete Data Following Purchase**

On January 1, 20X1, Alpha Corporation acquired all of Bravo Company's assets and liabilities by issuing shares of its $3 par value stock to the owners of Bravo Company in a business combination. Alpha also made a cash payment to Banker Corporation for stock issue costs. Partial balance sheet data for Alpha and Bravo, before the cash payment and issuance of shares, and a combined balance sheet following the business combination are as follows:

| | Alpha Corporation | Bravo Company | | Combined Entity |
|---|---|---|---|---|
| | Book Value | Book Value | Fair Value | |
| Cash | $ 65,000 | $ 15,000 | $ 15,000 | $ 56,000 |
| Accounts Receivable | 105,000 | 30,000 | 30,000 | 135,000 |
| Inventory | 210,000 | 90,000 | ? | 320,000 |
| Buildings and Equipment (net) | 400,000 | 210,000 | 293,000 | 693,000 |
| Goodwill | | | | ? |
| Total Assets | $780,000 | $345,000 | $448,000 | $    ? |
| | | | | |
| Accounts Payable | $ 56,000 | $ 22,000 | $ 22,000 | $ 78,000 |
| Bonds Payable | 200,000 | 120,000 | 120,000 | 320,000 |
| Common Stock | 96,000 | 70,000 | | 117,000 |
| Additional Paid-In Capital | 234,000 | 42,000 | | 553,000 |
| Retained Earnings | 194,000 | 91,000 | | ? |
| Total Liabilities and Equities | $780,000 | $345,000 | $142,000 | $    ? |

### Required

a. What number of its $5 par value shares did Bravo have outstanding at January 1, 20X1?

b. Assuming that all of Bravo's shares were issued when the company was started, what was the price per share received at the time of issue?

c. How many shares of Alpha were issued at the date of combination?

d. What amount of cash did Alpha pay as stock issue costs?

e. What was the market value of Alpha's shares issued at the date of combination?

f. What was the fair value of Bravo's inventory at the date of combination?

g. What was the fair value of Bravo's net assets at the date of combination?

h. What amount of goodwill, if any, will be reported in the combined balance sheet following the combination?

**P1-43**   ### Comprehensive Business Combination Problem

Bigtime Industries Inc. entered into a business combination agreement with Hydrolized Chemical Corporation (HCC) to ensure an uninterrupted supply of key raw materials and to realize certain economies from combining the operating processes and the marketing efforts of the two companies. Under the terms of the agreement, Bigtime issued 180,000 shares of its $1 par common stock in exchange for all of HCC's assets and liabilities. The Bigtime shares then were distributed to HCC's shareholders, and HCC was liquidated.

Immediately prior to the combination, HCC's balance sheet appeared as follows, with fair values also indicated:

|  | Book Values | Fair Values |
|---|---|---|
| **Assets** | | |
| Cash | $    28,000 | $    28,000 |
| Accounts Receivable | 258,000 | 251,500 |
| Less: Allowance for Bad Debts | (6,500) | |
| Inventory | 381,000 | 395,000 |
| Long-Term Investments | 150,000 | 175,000 |
| Land | 55,000 | 100,000 |
| Rolling Stock | 130,000 | 63,000 |
| Plant and Equipment | 2,425,000 | 2,500,000 |
| Less: Accumulated Depreciation | (614,000) | |
| Patents | 125,000 | 500,000 |
| Special Licenses | 95,800 | 100,000 |
| Total Assets | $3,027,300 | $4,112,500 |
| **Liabilities** | | |
| Current Payables | $  137,200 | $  137,200 |
| Mortgages Payable | 500,000 | 520,000 |
| Equipment Trust Notes | 100,000 | 95,000 |
| Debentures Payable | 1,000,000 | 950,000 |
| Less: Discount on Debentures | (40,000) | |
| Total Liabilities | $1,697,200 | $1,702,200 |
| **Stockholders' Equity** | | |
| Common Stock ($5 par) | 600,000 | |
| Additional Paid-In Capital from Common Stock | 500,000 | |
| Additional Paid-In Capital from | | |
| Reirement of Preferred Stock | 22,000 | |
| Retained Earnings | 220,100 | |
| Less: Treasury Stock (1,500 shares) | (12,000) | |
| Total Liabilities and Equity | $3,027,300 | |

Immediately prior to the combination, Bigtime's common stock was selling for $14 per share. Bigtime incurred direct costs of $135,000 in arranging the business combination and $42,000 of costs associated with registering and issuing the common stock used in the combination.

### Required

*a.* Prepare all journal entries that Bigtime should have entered on its books to record the business combination.

*b.* Present all journal entries that should have been entered on HCC's books to record the combination and the distribution of the stock received.

# Chapter **Two**

# Reporting Intercorporate Interests

Companies often acquire ownership or other interests in other companies through a variety of arrangements and for a variety of reasons. Some companies invest in other companies simply to earn a favorable return by taking advantage of potentially profitable situations. However, companies can have many other reasons for acquiring interests in other entities, including to (1) gain control over other companies, (2) enter new market or product areas through companies established in those areas, (3) ensure a supply of raw materials or other production inputs, (4) ensure a customer for production output, (5) gain economies associated with greater size, (6) diversify, (7) gain new technology, (8) lessen competition, and (9) limit risk. Examples of intercorporate investments include IBM's acquisition of a sizable portion of Intel's stock to ensure a supply of computer components, AT&T's purchase of the stock of McCaw Cellular Communications to gain a foothold in the cellular phone market, and Texaco's acquisition of Getty Oil's stock to acquire oil and gas reserves.

Accounting for intercorporate ownership investments and various types of interests in other companies can differ in a number of respects from accounting for other types of investments. This chapter presents the accounting and reporting procedures for investments in common stock and for selected other types of interests in different entities.

## ACCOUNTING FOR INVESTMENTS IN COMMON STOCK

The method used to account for investments in common stock depends, in part, on the level of influence or control that the investor is able to exercise over the investee. It also depends on choices made by the investor because of options available. For financial reporting, consolidated financial statements that include both the investor and the investee must be presented if the investor can exercise control over the investee. If the investor is unable to exercise control over the investee, the investment must be reported on the investor's balance sheet using either the cost method (adjusted to market value, if appropriate) or equity method, or the fair value option. Figure 2–1 summarizes the relationship between methods used to report intercorporate investments in common stock and levels of ownership and influence. Note that, while use of the cost or equity method is dictated by the level of influence, the investor can elect the fair value option in place of either method.

*Consolidation* involves combining for financial reporting the individual assets, liabilities, revenues, and expenses of two or more related companies as if they were part of a single company. This process includes the elimination of all intercompany ownership and activities. Consolidation normally is appropriate when one company, referred to as the *parent,* controls another company, referred to as a *subsidiary.* The specific requirements for consolidation are discussed in Chapter 3. A subsidiary that is not consolidated with the parent is referred to as an *unconsolidated subsidiary* and is shown as an investment on the parent's balance sheet. Under current accounting standards, most subsidiaries are consolidated.

**FIGURE 2–1**  **Financial Reporting Basis by Level of Common Stock Ownership**

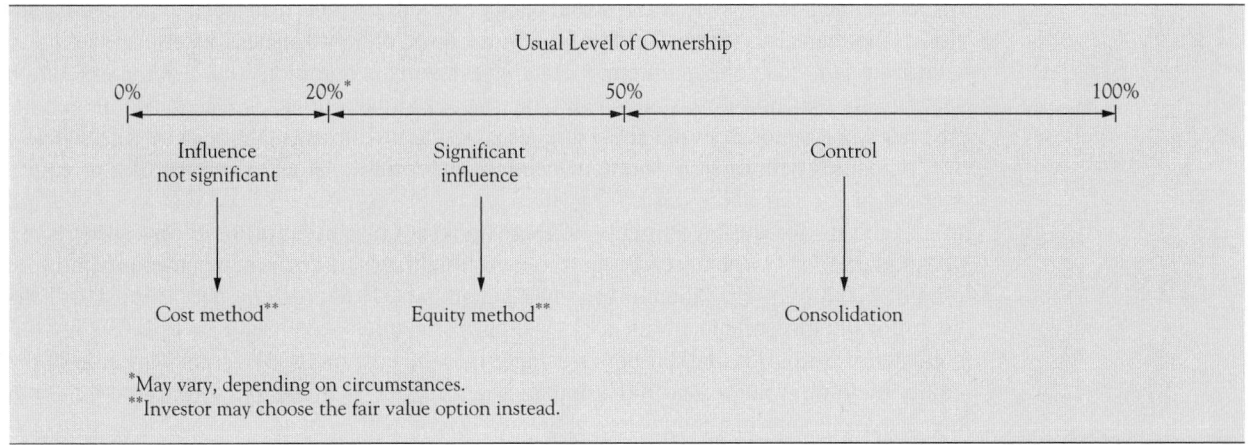

*May vary, depending on circumstances.
**Investor may choose the fair value option instead.

The ***equity method*** is used for external reporting when the investor exercises ***significant influence*** over the operating and financial policies of the investee and consolidation is not appropriate. The equity method may not be used in place of consolidation when consolidation is appropriate, and therefore its primary use is in reporting nonsubsidiary investments. This method is used most often when one company holds between 20 and 50 percent of another company's common stock. Under the equity method, the investor recognizes income from the investment as the investee earns the income. Instead of combining the individual assets, liabilities, revenues, and expenses of the investee with those of the investor, as in consolidation, the investment is reported as one line in the investor's balance sheet, and income recognized from the investee is reported as one line in the investor's income statement. The investment represents the investor's share of the investee's net assets, and the income recognized is the investor's share of the investee's net income.

The ***cost method*** is used for reporting investments in equity securities when both consolidation and equity-method reporting are inappropriate. If cost-method equity securities have readily determinable fair values, they must be adjusted to market value at year-end under **FASB Statement 115**.[1] Under the cost method, the investor recognizes income from the investment when the income is distributed by the investee as dividends.

Coca-Cola's balance sheet provides a good example of the financial reporting of cost and equity investments:

| | December 31 | |
| --- | --- | --- |
| | **2007** | **2006** |
| **Investments** | | |
| Equity-method investments: | | |
| Coca-Cola Enterprises Inc. | **$1,637** | $1,312 |
| Coca-Cola Hellenic Bottling Company S.A. | **1,549** | 1,251 |
| Coca-Cola FEMSA, S.A.B de C.V. | **996** | 835 |
| Coca-Cola Amatil Limited | **806** | 817 |
| Other, principally bottling companies | **2,301** | 2,095 |
| Cost-method investments, principally bottling companies | **488** | 473 |
| **Total Investments** | **$7,777** | $6,783 |

[1] *Financial Accounting Standards Board Statement No. 115,* "Accounting for Certain Investments in Debt and Equity Securities," May 1993. Because the provisions of **FASB 115** are normally discussed in Intermediate Accounting, detailed coverage is not provided here. Note, however, that equity investments accounted for using the cost method are accounted for as discussed in this chapter, with the provisions of **FASB 115** applied as end-of-period adjustments. **FASB 115** is not applicable to equity-method investments.

Under the FASB's recently effective fair value option,[2] companies have the choice of using traditional methods, such as the cost and equity methods, to report financial assets and liabilities, or they can elect to report at fair value some or all of their financial assets and liabilities. Under the fair value option, intercorporate investments in common stock are remeasured to fair value at the end of each period and the unrealized gain or loss is recognized in income. The fair value option does not apply to intercorporate investments that must be consolidated.

Companies with intercorporate investments in common stock using the cost or equity method or the fair value option for financial reporting normally use that same method in accounting for the investments on their books. When intercorporate investments are consolidated for financial reporting, the investment and related income accounts must be eliminated in preparing the consolidated statements. However, the parent must still account for the investments on its books. Parent companies account for investments in consolidated subsidiaries on their books using either the cost method or some variation of the equity method. A survey of 900 companies conducted by the authors indicated that both the cost and equity methods were being used by companies in accounting for their investments in consolidated subsidiaries. The preparation of consolidated financial statements is discussed in Chapters 3 through 10.

# THE COST METHOD

Intercorporate investments accounted for by the cost method are carried by the investor at historical cost. Income is recorded by the investor as dividends are declared by the investee. The cost method is used when the investor lacks the ability either to control or to exercise significant influence over the investee. The inability of an investor to exercise either control or significant influence over an investee may result from the size of the investment, usually at common stock ownership levels of less than 20 percent. In some situations, other factors, such as the bankruptcy of the investee, prevent the investor from exercising control or significant influence regardless of the size of the investment.

## Accounting Procedures under the Cost Method

The cost method is consistent with the treatment normally accorded noncurrent assets. At the time of purchase, the investor records its investment in common stock at the total cost incurred in making the purchase. Subsequently, the carrying amount of the investment remains unchanged under the cost method; the investment continues to be carried at its original cost until the time of sale. Income from the investment is recognized by the investor as dividends are declared by the investee. Once the investee declares a dividend, the investor has a legal claim against the investee for a proportionate share of the dividend, and realization of the income is considered certain enough to be recognized. Recognition of investment income before a dividend declaration is considered inappropriate because the investee's income is not available to the owners until a dividend is declared.

To illustrate the cost method, assume that ABC Company purchases 20 percent of XYZ Company's common stock for $100,000 at the beginning of the year but does not gain significant influence over XYZ. During the year, XYZ has net income of $60,000 and pays dividends of $20,000. ABC Company records the following entries relating to its investment in XYZ:

| | | | |
|---|---|---|---|
| (1) | Investment in XYZ Company Stock | 100,000 | |
| | Cash | | 100,000 |
| | Record purchase of XYZ Company stock. | | |

[2] *Financial Accounting Standards Board Statement No. 159,* "The Fair Value Option for Financial Assets and Liabilities," February 2007.

| (2) | Cash | 4,000 | |
|---|---|---|---|
| | Dividend Income | | 4,000 |
| | Record dividend income from XYZ Company: | | |
| | $20,000 \times .20$ | | |

Note that ABC records only its share of the distributed earnings of XYZ and makes no entry regarding the undistributed portion. The carrying amount of the investment remains at its original cost of $100,000.

## Declaration of Dividends in Excess of Earnings since Acquisition

A special treatment is required under the cost method in situations in which an investor holds common stock in a company that declares dividends in excess of the income it has earned since the investor acquired its stock. The dividends received are viewed first as representing earnings of the investee from the purchase date of the investment to the declaration date of the dividend. All dividends declared by the investee in excess of its earnings since acquisition by the investor are viewed by the investor as *liquidating dividends.* The investor's share of these liquidating dividends is treated as a return of capital, and the investment account balance is reduced by that amount. Blocks of an investee's stock acquired at different times should be treated separately for purposes of computing liquidating dividends.

### *Liquidating Dividends Illustrated*

To illustrate the computation of liquidating dividends received by the investor, assume that Investor Company purchases 10 percent of the common stock of Investee Company on January 2, 20X1. The annual income and dividends of Investee, the amount of dividend income recognized by Investor each year under the cost method, and the reduction of the carrying amount of Investor's investment in Investee when appropriate are as follows:

| | Investee Company | | | Investor Company | | |
|---|---|---|---|---|---|---|
| Year | Net Income | Dividends | Cumulative Undistributed Income | Cash Received | Dividend Income | Reduction of Investment |
| 20X1 | $100,000 | $ 70,000 | $30,000 | $ 7,000 | $ 7,000 | |
| 20X2 | 100,000 | 120,000 | 10,000 | 12,000 | 12,000 | |
| 20X3 | 100,000 | 120,000 | –0– | 12,000 | 11,000 | $1,000 |
| 20X4 | 100,000 | 120,000 | –0– | 12,000 | 10,000 | 2,000 |
| 20X5 | 100,000 | 70,000 | 30,000 | 7,000 | 7,000 | |

Investor Company records its 10 percent share of Investee's dividend as income in 20X1 because the income of Investee exceeds its dividend. In 20X2, Investee's dividend exceeds earnings for the year, but the cumulative dividends declared since January 2, 20X1, the date Investor acquired Investee's stock, do not exceed Investee's earnings since that date. Hence, Investor again records its 10 percent share of the dividend as income. By the end of 20X3, dividends declared by Investee since January 2, 20X1, total $310,000, while Investee's income since that date totals only $300,000. Thus, from Investor's point of view, $10,000 of the 20X3 dividend represents a return of capital while the remaining $110,000 represents a distribution of earnings. Investor's share of each amount is 10 percent. The entry to record the 20X3 dividend on Investor's books is:

| (3) | Cash | 12,000 | |
| | Investment in Investee Company Stock | | 1,000 |
| | Dividend Income | | 11,000 |

Record receipt of 20X3 dividend from Investee Company:

$12,000 = $120,000 × .10

$1,000 = ($310,000 − $300,000) × .10

$11,000 = ($120,000 − $10,000) × .10

Once the investor has recorded a liquidating dividend, the comparison in future periods between cumulative earnings and dividends of the investee should be based on the date of the last liquidating dividend rather than the date the investor acquired the investee's stock. In the example, Investor Company records liquidating dividends in 20X3 and 20X4. In years after 20X4, Investor compares earnings and dividends of Investee from the date of the most recent liquidating dividend in 20X4 rather than comparing from January 2, 20X1. All the dividend paid in 20X5 is considered by Investor to be a distribution of earnings.

### Liquidating Dividends following Switch from Equity Method

If the investor previously carried the investment using the equity method and, because of the sale of a portion of the investment, switches to the cost method, the date of the switch in methods replaces the date of acquisition as the reference date for distinguishing liquidating dividends. From that point forward, the investor should compare earnings and dividends of the investee starting at the date of the switch to the cost method.

### Investee's View of Liquidating Dividends

Dividends received by an investor in excess of earnings since acquisition, while viewed as liquidating dividends by the investor, usually are not liquidating dividends from the investee's point of view. This type of dividend might occur, for example, when an investee's stock is acquired shortly before a dividend is declared. The investee does not consider a dividend to be a liquidating dividend unless the investee's retained earnings is insufficient or the investee specifically declares a liquidating dividend for all common shareholders.

## Acquisition at Interim Date

The acquisition of an investment at other than the beginning or end of a fiscal period generally does not create any major problems when the cost method is used in accounting for the investment. The only potential difficulty involves determining whether some part of the payment received by the investor is a liquidating dividend when the investee declares a dividend soon after the investor purchases stock in the investee. In this situation, the investor must estimate the amount of the investee's earnings for the portion of the period during which the investor held the investee's stock and may record dividend income only on that portion.

## Changes in the Number of Shares Held

Changes in the number of investment shares resulting from stock dividends, stock splits, or reverse splits receive no formal recognition in the accounts of the investor. The carrying value of the investment before the stock dividend or split becomes the carrying amount of the new, greater or lesser number of shares. Purchases and sales of shares, of course, do require journal entries but do not result in any unusual difficulties under the cost method.

### Purchases of Additional Shares

A purchase of additional shares of a stock already held is recorded at cost in the same way as an initial purchase of shares. The investor's new percentage ownership of the investee then is calculated, and other evidence, if available, is evaluated to determine whether the total investment still should be carried at cost or if the investor should switch to the equity method. When the additional shares give the investor the ability to exercise significant influence over the investee, the equity method should be applied retroactively from the date of the original investment, as illustrated later in this chapter.

### Sales of Shares

If all or part of an intercorporate investment in stock is sold, the transaction is accounted for in the same manner as the sale of any other noncurrent asset. A gain or loss on the sale is recognized for the difference between the proceeds received and the carrying amount of the investment sold.

If shares of the stock have been purchased at more than one price, a determination must be made at the time of sale as to which of the shares have been sold. The specific shares sold may be identified through segregation, numbered stock certificates, or other means. When specific identification is impractical, either a FIFO or weighted-average cost flow assumption may be used; however, the weighted-average method seldom is used in practice because it is not acceptable for tax purposes.

# THE EQUITY METHOD

The equity method of accounting for intercorporate investments in common stock is intended to reflect the investor's changing equity or interest in the investee. This method is a rather curious one in that the balance in the investment account generally does not reflect either cost or market value, and it does not necessarily represent a pro rata share of the investee's book value. Instead, the investment is recorded at the initial purchase price and adjusted each period for the investor's share of the investee's profits or losses and the dividends declared by the investee.

## Use of the Equity Method

**APB Opinion No. 18** (as amended), "The Equity Method of Accounting for Investments in Common Stock" (APB 18), requires that the equity method be used for reporting investments in common stock of the following:[3]

1. Corporate joint ventures. A ***corporate joint venture*** is a corporation owned and operated by a small group of businesses, none of which owns a majority of the joint venture's common stock.
2. Companies in which the investor's voting stock interest gives the investor the "ability to exercise significant influence over operating and financial policies" of that company.

The second condition is the broader of the two and establishes the "significant influence" criterion. Because assessing the degree of influence may be difficult in some cases, **APB 18** establishes a 20 percent rule.[4] In the absence of evidence to the contrary, an investor holding 20 percent or more of an investee's voting stock is presumed to have the ability to exercise significant influence over the investee. On the other hand, an investor holding less than 20 percent of an investee's voting stock is presumed not to have the ability to exercise significant influence in the absence of evidence to the contrary.

In most cases, an investment of 20 to 50 percent in another company's voting stock is reported under the equity method. Notice, however, that the 20 percent rule does not apply if other evidence is available that provides a better indication of the ability or inability of the investor to significantly influence the investee.

Regardless of the level of ownership, the equity method is not appropriate if the investor's influence is limited by circumstances other than stock ownership, such as bankruptcy of the investee or severe restrictions placed on the availability of a foreign investee's earnings or assets by a foreign government.

---

[3] *Accounting Principles Board Opinion No. 18,* "The Equity Method of Accounting for Investments in Common Stock," March 1971, para. 16.
[4] Ibid., para. 17.

## Investor's Equity in the Investee

Under the equity method, the investor records its investment at the original cost. This amount is adjusted periodically for changes in the investee's stockholders' equity occasioned by the investee's profits, losses, and dividend declarations. The effect of the investee's income, losses, and dividends on the investor's investment account and other accounts can be characterized in the following way:

| Reported by Investee | Effect on Investor's Accounts |
|---|---|
| Net income | Record income from investment<br>Increase investment account |
| Net loss | Record loss from investment<br>Decrease investment account |
| Dividend declaration | Record asset (cash or receivable)<br>Decrease investment account |

## Recognition of Income

Under the equity method, the investor's income statement includes the investor's proportionate share of the investee's income or loss each period. The carrying amount of the investment is adjusted by the same amount to reflect the change in the net assets of the investee resulting from the investee's income.

To illustrate, assume ABC Company acquires significant influence over XYZ Company by purchasing 20 percent of the common stock of the XYZ Company at the beginning of the year. XYZ reports income of $60,000 for the year. ABC records its $12,000 share of XYZ's income with the following entry:

| | | | |
|---|---|---|---|
| (4) | Investment in XYZ Company Stock | 12,000 | |
| | Income from Investee | | 12,000 |
| | Record income from investment in XYZ Company: | | |
| | $60,000 × .20 | | |

This entry may be referred to as the *equity accrual* and normally is made as an adjusting entry at the end of the period. If the investee reports a loss for the period, the investor recognizes its share of the loss and reduces the carrying amount of the investment by that amount.

Because of the ability to exercise significant influence over the policies of the investee, realization of income from the investment is considered to be sufficiently ensured to warrant recognition by the investor as the income is earned by the investee. This differs from the case in which the investor does not have the ability to significantly influence the investee and the investment must be reported using the cost method; in that case, income from the investment is recognized only upon declaration of a dividend by the investee.

## Recognition of Dividends

Dividends from an investment are not recognized as income under the equity method because the investor's share of the investee's income is recognized as it is earned by the investee. Instead, such dividends are viewed as distributions of previously recognized income that already has been capitalized in the carrying amount of the investment. The investor must consider investee dividends declared as a reduction in its equity in the investee and, accordingly, reduce the carrying amount of its investment. In effect, all dividends from the investee are treated as liquidating dividends under the equity method. Thus, if ABC Company owns 20 percent of XYZ Company's common stock and XYZ declares and pays a $20,000 dividend, the following entry is recorded on the books of ABC to record its share of the dividend:

| (5) | Cash | 4,000 | |
| | Investment in XYZ Company Stock | | 4,000 |

Record receipt of dividend from XYZ: $20,000 × .20

## Carrying Amount of the Investment

Because the investment account on the investor's books under the equity method is adjusted for the investor's share of the investee's income or losses and dividends, the carrying amount of the investment usually is not the same as the original cost to the investor. Only if the investee pays dividends in the exact amount of its earnings will the carrying amount of the investment subsequent to acquisition be equal to its original cost. If the earnings of the investee subsequent to investment by the investor exceed the investee's dividends during that time, the carrying amount of the investment will be greater than its original cost. On the other hand, if the investee's dividends exceed its income, the carrying amount of the investment will be less than its original cost.

To illustrate the change in the carrying amount of the investment under the equity method, assume that after ABC acquires 20 percent of XYZ's common stock for $100,000, XYZ earns income of $60,000 and pays dividends of $20,000. The carrying amount of the investment starts with the original cost of $100,000 and is increased by ABC's share of XYZ's income, which is $12,000. The carrying amount is reduced by ABC's share of XYZ's dividends, which is $4,000. Thus, the carrying amount of the investment at the end of the period is $108,000 ($100,000 + $12,000 − $4,000). The investment account on ABC's books appears as follows:

| Investment in XYZ Common Stock | | | |
|---|---|---|---|
| Original cost | 100,000 | | |
| Equity accrual | | Dividends | |
| ($60,000 × .20) | 12,000 | ($20,000 × .20) | 4,000 |
| Ending balance | 108,000 | | |

The $8,000 increase in the investment account represents ABC's 20 percent share of XYZ's undistributed earnings ($60,000 − $20,000) for the period.

## Acquisition at Interim Date

When an investment is purchased, the investor begins accruing income from the investee under the equity method at the date of acquisition. No income earned by the investee before the date of acquisition of the investment may be accrued by the investor. When the purchase occurs between balance sheet dates, the amount of income earned by the investee from the date of acquisition to the end of the fiscal period may need to be estimated by the investor in recording the equity accrual.

To illustrate, assume that ABC acquires 20 percent of XYZ's common stock on October 1 for $109,000. XYZ earns income of $60,000 uniformly throughout the year and pays dividends of $20,000 on December 20. The carrying amount of the investment is increased by $3,000, which represents ABC's share of XYZ's net income earned between October 1 and December 31, and is decreased by $4,000 as a result of dividends received at year end:

| Investment in XYZ Common Stock | | | |
|---|---|---|---|
| Original cost | 109,000 | | |
| Equity accrual | | Dividends | |
| ($60,000 × ¼ × .20) | 3,000 | ($20,000 × .20) | 4,000 |
| Ending balance | 108,000 | | |

## Difference between Cost of Investment and Underlying Book Value

When an investor purchases the common stock of another company, the purchase price normally is based on the market value of the shares acquired rather than the book value of the investee's assets and liabilities. Not surprisingly, a difference is usually found between the cost of the investment to the investor and the book value of the investor's proportionate share of the investee's net assets. This difference is referred to as a **differential.** Note that in the case of an equity-method investment, the differential on the parent's books relates only to the parent's share of any difference between an total investee's fair value and book value. The differential in the case of an equity-method investment is implicit in the investment account on the parent's books and is not recorded separately.

The cost of an investment might exceed the book value of the underlying net assets, giving rise to a positive differential, for any of several reasons. One reason is that the investee's assets may be worth more than their book values. Another reason could be the existence of unrecorded goodwill associated with the excess earning power of the investee. In either case, the portion of the differential pertaining to each asset of the investee, including goodwill, must be ascertained. When the equity method is applied, that portion of the differential pertaining to limited-life assets of the investee, including identifiable intangibles, must be amortized over the remaining economic lives of those assets. Any portion of the differential that represents goodwill (referred to as *equity-method goodwill*) is not amortized or written off because of impairment. However, an impairment loss on the investment itself should be recognized if it suffers a material decline in value that is other than temporary.

### Amortization or Write-Off of the Differential

When the equity method is used, each portion of the differential must be treated in the same manner as the investee treats the assets or liabilities to which the differential relates. Thus, any portion of the differential related to depreciable or amortizable assets of the investee should be amortized over the remaining time that the cost of the asset is being allocated by the investee. Amortization of the differential associated with depreciable or amortizable assets of the investee is necessary on the investor's books to reflect the decline in the future benefits the investor expects from that portion of the investment cost associated with those assets. The investee recognizes the reduction in service potential of assets with limited lives as depreciation or amortization expense based on the amount it has invested in those assets. This reduction, in turn, is recognized by the investor through its share of the investee's net income. When the cost of the investor's interest in the investee's assets is greater than the investee's cost (as reflected in a positive differential), the additional cost must be amortized as well.

The approach to amortizing the differential that is most consistent with the idea of reflecting all aspects of the investment in just one line on the balance sheet and one line on the income statement is to reduce the income recognized by the investor from the investee and the balance of the investment account:

| | | |
|---|---|---|
| Income from Investee | XXX | |
| Investment in Common Stock of Investee | | XXX |

The differential represents the amount paid by the investor in excess of the book value of the investment and is included in the investment amount. Hence, the amortization or reduction of the differential involves the reduction of the investment account. At the same time, the investor's net income must be reduced by an equal amount to recognize that a portion of the amount paid for the investment has expired.

### Treatment of the Differential Illustrated

To illustrate the equity method when the cost of the investment exceeds the book value of the underlying net assets, assume that Ajax Corporation purchases 40 percent of the common stock of Barclay Company on January 1, 20X1, for $200,000. Barclay has net assets on that date with a book value of $400,000 and fair value of $465,000. Ajax's share of the book value of Barclay's net assets at acquisition is $160,000 ($400,000 × .40). A $40,000 differential is computed as follows:

| | |
|---|---|
| Cost of investment to Ajax | $ 200,000 |
| Book value of Ajax's share of Barclay's net assets | (160,000) |
| Differential | $ 40,000 |

The $65,000 excess of the fair value over the book value of Barclay's net assets consists of a $15,000 increase in the value of Barclay's land and a $50,000 increase in the value of Barclay's equipment. Ajax's 40 percent share of the increase in the value of Barclay's assets is as follows:

| | Total Increase | Ajax's 40% Share |
|---|---|---|
| Land | $15,000 | $ 6,000 |
| Equipment | 50,000 | 20,000 |
| | $65,000 | $26,000 |

Thus, $26,000 of the differential is assigned to land and equipment, with the remaining $14,000 attributed to goodwill. The allocation of the differential can be illustrated as follows:

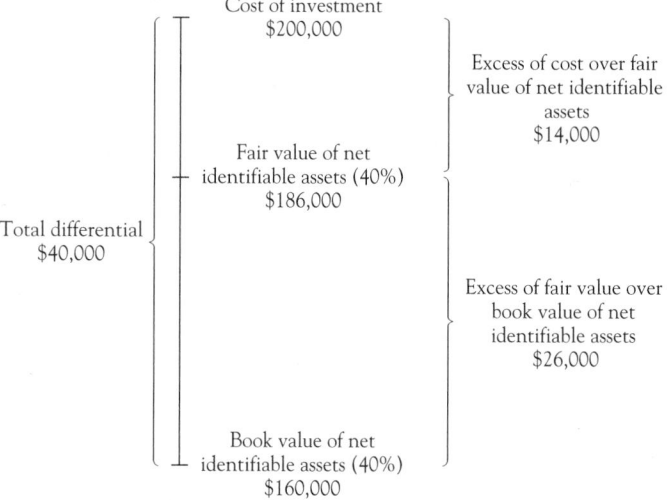

Although the differential relates to assets of Barclay, the additional cost incurred by Ajax to acquire a claim on the assets of Barclay is reflected in Ajax's investment in Barclay. No separate differential account is established, and no separate accounts are recorded on Ajax's books to reflect the apportionment of the differential to specific assets. Similarly, no separate expense account is established on Ajax's books. Amortization or write-off of the differential is accomplished by reducing Ajax's investment account and the income Ajax recognizes from its investment in Barclay.

Because land has an unlimited economic life, the portion of the differential related to land is not amortized. The $20,000 portion of the differential related to Barclay's equipment is amortized over the equipment's remaining life. If the equipment's remaining life is five years, Ajax's annual amortization of the differential is $4,000 ($20,000 ÷ 5).

Beginning in 1970, financial reporting standards required that goodwill be amortized over its useful life, not to exceed 40 years. In 2001, however, the FASB issued **Statement No. 142,** "Goodwill and Other Intangible Assets," under which equity-method goodwill is neither amortized nor written off. That portion of the differential remains imbedded in the investment account. Thus, in this example, the only amortization of the differential is the $4,000 related to Barclay's equipment.

Barclay declares dividends of $20,000 during 20X1 and at year-end reports net income of $80,000 for the year. Using the equity method, Ajax records the following entries on its books during 20X1:

| (6) | Investment in Barclay Stock | 200,000 | |
| | Cash | | 200,000 |
| | Record purchase of Barclay stock. | | |

| (7) | Cash | 8,000 | |
| | Investment in Barclay Stock | | 8,000 |
| | Record dividend from Barclay: $20,000 × .40 | | |

| (8) | Investment in Barclay Stock | 32,000 | |
| | Income from Investee | | 32,000 |
| | Record equity-method income: $80,000 × .40 | | |

| (9) | Income from Investee | 4,000 | |
| | Investment in Barclay Stock | | 4,000 |
| | Amortize differential related to equipment. | | |

With these entries, Ajax recognizes $28,000 of income from Barclay and adjusts its investment in Barclay to an ending balance of $220,000.

The amortization on Ajax's books of the portion of the differential related to Barclay's equipment is the same ($4,000) for each of the first five years (20X1 through 20X5). This amortization stops after 20X5 because this portion of the differential is fully amortized after five years.

Notice that no special accounts are established on the books of the investor with regard to the differential or the amortization of the differential. The only two accounts involved are "Income from Investee" and "Investment in Barclay Stock." As the Investment in Barclay Stock account is amortized, the differential between the carrying amount of the investment and the book value of the underlying net assets decreases.

### *Disposal of Differential-Related Assets*

Although the differential is included on the books of the investor as part of the investment account, it relates to specific assets of the investee. Thus, if the investee disposes of any asset to which the differential relates, that portion of the differential must be removed from the investment account on the investor's books. When this is done, the investor's share of the investee's gain or loss on disposal of the asset must be adjusted to reflect the fact that the investor paid more for its proportionate share of that asset than did the investee. For example, if in the previous illustration Barclay Company sells the land to which $6,000 of Ajax's differential relates, Ajax does not recognize a full 40 percent of the gain or loss on the sale. Assume that Barclay originally had purchased the land in 20X0 for $75,000 and sells the land in 20X2 for $125,000. Barclay recognizes a gain on the sale of $50,000, and Ajax's share of that gain is 40 percent, or $20,000. The portion of the gain actually recognized by Ajax, however, must be adjusted as follows because of the amount in excess of book value paid by Ajax for its investment in Barclay:

| | |
| --- | --- |
| Ajax's share of Barclay's reported gain | $20,000 |
| Portion of Ajax's differential related to the land | (6,000) |
| Gain to be recognized by Ajax | $14,000 |

Thus, if Barclay reports net income (including gain on sale of land) of $150,000 for 20X2, Ajax records the following entries (disregarding dividends and amortization of the differential relating to equipment):

| (10) | Investment in Barclay Stock | 60,000 | |
|------|------------------------------|--------|--------|
| | Income from Investee | | 60,000 |
| | Record equity-method income: $150,000 × .40 | | |

| (11) | Income from Investee | 6,000 | |
|------|------------------------------|--------|--------|
| | Investment in Barclay Stock | | 6,000 |
| | Remove differential related to Barclay's land sold. | | |

The same approach applies when dealing with a limited-life asset. The unamortized portion of the original differential relating to the asset sold is removed from the investment account, and the investor's share of the investee's income is adjusted by that amount.

Note that the investor does not separately report its share of ordinary gains or losses included in the investee's net income, such as the gain on the sale of the fixed asset or the write-off of the unamortized differential. Consistent with the idea of using only a single line in the income statement to report the impact of the investee's activities on the investor, all such items are included in the Income from Investee account. Current standards do require the investor to report its share of an investee's extraordinary gains and losses, prior-period adjustments, and elements of other comprehensive income, if material to the investor, as separate items in the same manner as the investor reports its own.

### *Impairment of Investment Value*

As with many assets, accounting standards require that equity-method investments be written down if their value is impaired. If the market value of the investment declines materially below its equity-method carrying amount, and the decline in value is considered other than temporary, the carrying amount of the investment should be written down to the market value and a loss recognized. The new lower value serves as a starting point for continued application of the equity method. Subsequent recoveries in the value of the investment may not be recognized.

## Changes in the Number of Shares Held

Some changes in the number of common shares held by an investor are handled easily under the equity method, but others require a bit more attention. A change resulting from a stock dividend, split, or reverse split is treated in the same way as under the cost method. No formal accounting recognition is required on the books of the investor. On the other hand, purchases and sales of shares do require formal recognition.

### *Purchases of Additional Shares*

A purchase of additional shares of a common stock already held by an investor and accounted for using the equity method simply involves adding the cost of the new shares to the investment account and applying the equity method in the normal manner from the date of acquisition forward. The new and old investments in the same stock are combined for financial reporting purposes. Income accruing to the new shares can be recognized by the investor only from the date of acquisition forward.

To illustrate, assume that ABC Company purchases 20 percent of XYZ Company's common stock on January 2, 20X1, and another 10 percent on July 1, 20X1, and that the stock purchases are at book value. If XYZ earns income of $25,000 from January 2 to June 30 and earns $35,000 from July 1 to December 31, the total income recognized in 20X1 by ABC from its investment in XYZ is $15,500, computed as follows:

| Income, January 2 to June 30: $25,000 × .20 | $ 5,000 |
|---|---|
| Income, July 1 to December 31: $35,000 × .30 | 10,500 |
| Income from investment, 20X1 | $15,500 |

If XYZ declares and pays a $10,000 dividend on January 15 and again on July 15, ABC reduces its investment account by $2,000 ($10,000 × .20) on January 15 and by $3,000 ($10,000 × .30) on July 15.

When an investment in common stock is carried using the cost method and purchases of additional shares give the investor the ability to significantly influence the investee, a retroactive switch from the cost method to the equity method is required. This change to the equity method must be applied retroactively to the date of the first acquisition of the investee's stock.

To illustrate a change to the equity method, assume that Aron Corporation purchases 15 percent of Zenon Company's common stock on January 2, 20X1, and another 10 percent on January 2, 20X4. Furthermore, assume that Aron switches to the equity method on January 2, 20X4, because it gains the ability to significantly influence Zenon. Given the following income and dividend data for Zenon, and assuming the purchases of stock are at book value, the investment income figures reported by Aron originally and as restated are as follows:

| | Zenon | | Investment Income Reported by Aron | |
|---|---|---|---|---|
| Year | Net Income | Dividends | Originally under Cost[a] | Restated under Equity[b] |
| 20X1 | $15,000 | $10,000 | $1,500 | $2,250 |
| 20X2 | 18,000 | 10,000 | 1,500 | 2,700 |
| 20X3 | 22,000 | 10,000 | 1,500 | 3,300 |
| | $55,000 | $30,000 | $4,500 | $8,250 |

[a] 15 percent of Zenon's dividends for the year.
[b] 15 percent of Zenon's net income for the year.

Thus, in Aron's 20X4 financial report, the comparative statements for 20X1, 20X2, and 20X3 are restated to include Aron's 15 percent share of Zenon's profit and to exclude from income Aron's share of dividends recognized under the cost method. In addition, the investment account and retained earnings of Aron are restated as if the equity method had been applied from the date of the original acquisition. This restatement is accomplished on Aron's books with the following journal entry on January 2, 20X4:

| (12) | Investment in Zenon Company Stock | 3,750 | |
|---|---|---|---|
| | Retained Earnings | | 3,750 |
| | Restate investment account from cost to equity method: | | |
| | $8,250 − $4,500 | | |

In 20X4, if Zenon reports net income of $30,000, Aron's investment income is $7,500 (25 percent of Zenon's net income).

### Sales of Shares

The sale of all or part of an investment in common stock carried using the equity method is treated the same as the sale of any noncurrent asset. First, the investment account is adjusted to the date of sale for the investor's share of the investee's current earnings. Then, a gain or loss is recognized for the difference between the proceeds received and the carrying amount of the shares sold.

If only part of the investment is sold, the investor must decide whether to continue using the equity method to account for the remaining shares or to change to the cost method. The choice is based on evidence available after the sale as to whether the investor still is able to exercise significant influence over the investee. If the equity method no longer is appropriate after the date of sale, the carrying value of the remaining investment is treated as the cost of that investment, and the cost method is applied in the normal manner from the date of sale forward. No retroactive restatement of the investment to actual cost is made.

# THE COST AND EQUITY METHODS COMPARED

Some of the key features of the cost and equity methods are summarized and compared in Figure 2–2.

The cost method of accounting for intercorporate investments is consistent with the historical cost basis for most other assets. This method is subject to the usual criticisms leveled against historical cost. In particular, questions arise as to the relevance of reporting the purchase price of an investment acquired some years earlier. The cost method does conform more closely to the traditional accounting and legal views of the realization of income in that the investee's earnings are not available to the investor until transferred as dividends. Income based on dividend distributions sometimes can be manipulated, however. The significant influence criterion, which must be met to use the equity method, takes into consideration that the declaration of dividends by the investee can be influenced by the investor. Recognizing equity-method income from the investee without regard to investee dividends provides protection against manipulating the investor's net income by influencing investee dividend declarations.

On the other hand, the equity method is criticized because the asset valuation departs from historical cost but stops short of a market value approach. Instead, the carrying amount of the investment is composed of a number of components and is not similar to the valuation of any other assets.

Over the years there has been considerable criticism of the use of the equity method as a substitute for the consolidation of certain types of subsidiaries. Although the equity

**FIGURE 2–2**
**Summary Comparison of the Cost and Equity Methods**

| Item | Cost Method | Equity Method |
|---|---|---|
| Recorded amount of investment at date of acquisition | Original cost | Original cost |
| Usual carrying amount of investment subsequent to acquisition | Original cost | Original cost increased (decreased) by investor's share of investee's income (loss) and decreased by investor's share of investee's dividends and by amortization or write-off of the differential |
| Differential | Not amortized or written off | Amortized or written down if related to limited-life assets of investee or assets disposed of |
| Income recognition by investor | Investor's share of investee's dividends declared from earnings since acquisition | Investor's share of investee's earnings since acquisition, whether distributed or not, reduced by any amortization or write-off of the differential |
| Investee dividends from earnings since acquisition by investor | Income | Reduction of investment |
| Investee dividends in excess of earnings since acquisition by investor | Reduction of investment | Reduction of investment |

method has been viewed as a "one-line consolidation," the amount of detail reported is considerably different under the equity method than with consolidation. For example, an investor would report the same equity-method income from the following two investees even though their income statements are quite different in composition:

|  | Investee 1 | Investee 2 |
|---|---|---|
| Sales | $50,000 | $ 500,000 |
| Operating Expenses | (30,000) | (620,000) |
| Operating Income (Loss) | $20,000 | $(120,000) |
| Gain on Sale of Land |  | 140,000 |
| Net Income | $20,000 | $ 20,000 |

Similarly, an investment in the stock of another company is reported under the equity method as a single amount in the balance sheet of the investor regardless of the asset and capital structure of the investee. In the past, some companies borrowed heavily through unconsolidated subsidiaries and reported their investments in the subsidiaries using the equity method. Because the debt was not reported in these situations, concerns were raised over the use of the equity method to facilitate "off-balance sheet" financing.

As a result of these concerns, the Financial Accounting Standards Board eliminated the use of the equity method for reporting investments in subsidiaries by requiring the consolidation of virtually all majority-owned subsidiaries. The FASB is expected in the future to study the use of the equity method for investments in corporate joint ventures and other types of investees.

## THE FAIR VALUE OPTION

**FASB 159** permits but does not require companies to measure many financial assets and liabilities at fair value. Companies holding investments in the common stock of other companies have this option for investments that are not required to be consolidated. Thus, rather than using the cost or equity method to report nonsubsidiary investments in common stock, investors may report those investments at fair value.

Under the fair value option, the investor remeasures the investment to its fair value at the end of each period. The change in value is then recognized in income for the period. Although the FASB does not specify how to account for dividends received from the investment, normally the investor recognizes dividend income in the same manner as under the cost method.

To illustrate use of the fair value method, assume that Ajax Corporation purchases 40 percent of Barclay Company's common stock on January 1, 20X1, for $200,000. Barclay has net assets on that date with a book value of $400,000 and fair value of $465,000. Ajax issues financial statements at the end of each calendar quarter. On March 1, 20X1, Ajax receives a cash dividend of $1,500 from Barclay. On March 31, 20X1, Ajax determines the fair value of its investment in Barclay to be $207,000. During the first quarter of 20X1, Ajax records the following entries on its books in relation to its investment in Barclay:

January 1, 20X1

| (13) | Investment in Barclay Stock | 200,000 | |
|---|---|---|---|
| | Cash | | 200,000 |
| | Record purchase of Barclay Company stock. | | |

March 1, 20X1

| (14) | Cash | 1,500 | |
| | Dividend Income | | 1,500 |
| | Record dividend income from Barclay Company. | | |

March 31, 20X1

| (15) | Investment in Barclay Stock | 7,000 | |
| | Unrealized Gain on Increase in Value of Barclay Stock | | 7,000 |
| | Record increase in value of Barclay stock. | | |

Notice that under the fair value option, no special treatment is accorded the differential.

# INTERESTS OTHER THAN INVESTMENTS IN COMMON STOCK

Increasingly in recent years, companies have acquired interests in other entities that are not represented by investments in common stock. Such interests may involve equity investments in partnerships, or the interests might reflect no ownership at all. Because of the diversity and complexity of these types of arrangements, the accounting rules, if they exist at all, are often complex or, in some cases, not well specified.

## Investments in Partnerships

FASB pronouncements generally relate to corporations rather than partnerships. Thus, companies holding equity investments in partnerships generally have more flexibility but less guidance in reporting their investments.

Equity investments in partnerships do not provide the clear-cut measures found with common stock investments. An investment in the common stock of a corporation almost always provides for a proportionate share of profits, a proportionate share of distributions, a proportionate claim on net assets, and proportionate voting rights. The same is not true of equity investments in partnerships. A partner contributing a specified share of the partnership's capital may have a different share of profits (but not necessarily the same share of losses), a different proportion of distributions (drawing rights), and a greater or lesser degree of control than indicated by the capital share. For partnerships, all of these ownership rights are determined by the partnership agreement (or state law) rather than by percentage ownership. Thus, the convenient measures available to determine the financial reporting methods for investments in common stock are not available for investments in partnerships.

Companies with ownership investments in partnerships have traditionally chosen one of several methods of reporting those investments:

1. Cost method
2. Equity method
3. Pro rata consolidation
4. Consolidation

### *Reporting Methods Illustrated*

As an illustration of the methods of accounting for ownership investments in partnerships, assume that on January 1, 20X5, Albers Company invests $200,000 for a 40 percent share of initial capital of AB Partnership and a 40 percent share of the profits and losses. For the year 20X5, Albers reports the following, excluding its investment in AB Partnership:

| | |
|---|---|
| Revenues, 20X5 | $ 700,000 |
| Expenses, 20X5 | 400,000 |
| Assets, 12/31/20X5 (excluding investment in AB) | 1,000,000 |
| Liabilities, 12/31/20X5 | 300,000 |

Also assume that the AB Partnership reports $80,000 of revenues and $50,000 of expenses; no amounts are distributed to or withdrawn by the partners. The financial statements for AB Partnership and Albers Company's financial statements under several possible reporting alternatives are presented in Figure 2–3.

**FIGURE 2–3**  **Reporting Alternatives for Equity Interests in Partnerships**

**Balance Sheet**

| | AB Partnership | Cost Method | Equity Method | Pro Rata Consolidation | Full Consolidation |
|---|---|---|---|---|---|
| | | **Albers Company Consolidated Balance Sheet** | | | |
| Assets | $630,000 | $1,000,000 | $1,000,000 | $ 1,252,000[a] | $ 1,630,000[b] |
| Investment in AB Partnership | | 200,000 | 212,000[c] | | |
| | $630,000 | $1,200,000 | $1,212,000 | $ 1,252,000 | $ 1,630,000 |
| Liabilities | $100,000 | $ 300,000 | $ 300,000 | $ 340,000[d] | $ 400,000[e] |
| Interest of Outside Partner | | | | | 318,000[f] |
| Owners' Equity | 530,000[g] | 900,000 | 912,000[h] | 912,000[h] | 912,000[h] |
| | $630,000 | $1,200,000 | $1,212,000 | $ 1,252,000 | $ 1,630,000 |

[a]$1,252,000 = $1,000,000 + ($630,000 × .40)
[b]$1,630,000 = $1,000,000 + $630,000
[c]$212,000 = $200,000 + ($30,000 × .40)
[d]$340,000 = $300,000 + ($100,000 × .40)
[e]$400,000 = $300,000 + $100,000
[f]$318,000 = $530,000 × .60
[g]Capital, Albers Company      $212,000
  Capital, Outside Partner      $318,000
[h]$912,000 = $900,000 + ($30,000 × .40)

**Income Statement**

| | AB Partnership | Cost Method | Equity Method | Pro Rata Consolidation | Full Consolidation |
|---|---|---|---|---|---|
| | | **Consolidated Income Statement** | | | |
| Revenues | $80,000 | $700,000 | $700,000 | $732,000[a] | $780,000[b] |
| Expenses | (50,000) | (400,000) | (400,000) | (420,000)[c] | (450,000)[d] |
| Income from Partnership | | | 12,000[e] | | |
| Income to Outside Partner | | | | | (18,000)[f] |
| Net Income | $30,000[g] | $300,000 | $312,000 | $312,000 | $312,000 |

[a]$732,000 = $700,000 + ($80,000 × .40)
[b]$780,000 = $700,000 + $80,000
[c]$420,000 = $400,000 + ($50,000 × .40)
[d]$450,000 = $400,000 + $50,000
[e]$12,000 = $30,000 × .40
[f]$18,000 = $30,000 × .60
[g]Allocation of income:
  Albers (40%)           $12,000
  Outside Partner (60%)  $18,000

The cost and equity methods of accounting for investments in partnerships are applied largely in the same manner as for investments in common stock. In the AB Partnership example, no income is distributed by the partnership (withdrawn by the partners), and, accordingly, the investor recognizes no income from the partnership under the cost method. The equity method is more generally used in accounting for partnership interests, and the investor recognizes its share of partnership income even though the income is not withdrawn from the partnership.

Authoritative bodies generally view pro rata consolidation as an unacceptable reporting method for investments in other corporations (e.g., corporate joint ventures). Nevertheless, pro rata consolidation has been used in practice to at least a small degree to account for certain investments in common stock and to a greater degree to account for investments in partnerships and unincorporated joint ventures (e.g., two or three partners with nearly equal investments or profit shares). This method involves combining the investor's proportionate share of the partnership's assets, liabilities, revenues, and expenses with those of the investor. This approach provides the same overall results as the equity method (e.g., same net income and net assets), but the details within the financial statements differ.

Full consolidation of a partnership with one of the partners has not been widespread in practice. This method involves combining the full amount of the partnership's assets, liabilities, revenues, and expenses with the like items of one of the partners. Because the consolidating partner has only a partial claim on the income and net assets of the partnership, the claim of the outside partner(s) must be recognized in the consolidated income statement and balance sheet, as indicated in Figure 2–3. Also as shown in Figure 2–3, full consolidation leads to the same overall results as the equity method and pro rata consolidation. However, while net income (after deducting income to outside partners) and net assets (after deducting the claim of outside partners) are the same under each of the three methods, the details of the financial statements differ.

### *Standards for Reporting Partnership Interests*

The method of reporting partnership interests can have a significant effect on the financial statements, especially for companies that conduct a large portion of their activities through partnerships (such as some construction companies). The cost method provides little information relating to the partnership investment and, thus, is generally not an appropriate method to use. The equity method can hide partnership debt and disguise the type of income earned by the partnership because, in effect, the partnership assets and liabilities are netted against one another and the partner's share is reported as a single line in the balance sheet; similarly, all of the partnership's income and expense items are combined and the partner's share of income is reported as a single line in the income statement.

Both pro rata consolidation, especially for unincorporated joint ventures, and full consolidation have received significant support for reporting partnership interests. Unfortunately, partnership arrangements relating to control, veto power, share of profits and losses, distribution of different types of assets, responsibility for partnership debt, and other factors are often so complex and varied that establishing standards for reporting partnership interests has been extremely difficult. The FASB is continuing to grapple with issues surrounding the reporting of interests in partnerships and joint ventures. One step the FASB has taken is to issue **Interpretation No. 46,** "Consolidation of Variable Interest Entities, an interpretation of **ARB No. 51.**" While this pronouncement does not address accounting for partnership interests directly, its provisions do apply in some instances. Specifically, the interpretation establishes standards for when certain types of entities should be consolidated by a particular investor. This topic is discussed in Chapter 3.

One other approach that might be taken in accounting for partnership interests is to measure them at fair value. As mentioned earlier in the chapter, **FASB 159** allows companies the option of measuring financial assets, including investments in partnerships, at fair value.

### Nonequity Interests in Other Entities

In some situations, a company may have a nonownership interest in another entity, which might be a corporation, partnership, or trust. For example, a company might share in the profits of another entity through an operating agreement without having an ownership interest. In another common situation, a company might sell assets to another entity and provide some type of guarantee with respect to those assets, the debt of the other entity, or the return to be received by the owners of the entity. Because of the diversity of the types of arrangements found in practice, no standards exist to cover all potential situations. Some existing standards may have an indirect bearing on various aspects of nonownership interests, such as the FASB's requirement to report guarantees at fair value. The FASB's pronouncements on variable interest entities and certain types of special-purpose entities are applicable in some cases to nonownership interests. Variable interest entities and special-purpose entities are discussed in Chapter 3.

## ADDITIONAL CONSIDERATIONS RELATING TO THE EQUITY METHOD

### Determination of Significant Influence

The general rule established in **APB 18** is that the equity method is appropriate when the investor, by virtue of its common stock interest in an investee, is able to exercise significant influence over the operating and financial policies of the investee. In the absence of other evidence, common stock ownership of 20 percent or more is viewed as indicating that the investor is able to exercise significant influence over the investee. However, the APB also stated a number of factors that could constitute other evidence of the ability to exercise significant influence:[5]

1. Representation on board of directors.
2. Participation in policy making.
3. Material intercompany transactions.
4. Interchange of managerial personnel.
5. Technological dependency.
6. Size of investment in relation to concentration of other shareholdings.

Conversely, the FASB provides in **FASB Interpretation No. 35** some examples of evidence that an investor is unable to exercise significant influence over an investee.[6] These situations include legal or regulatory challenges to the investor's influence by the investee, agreement by the investor to give up important shareholder rights, concentration of majority ownership among a small group of owners who disregard the views of the investor, and unsuccessful attempts by the investor to obtain information from the investee or representation on the investee's board of directors.

### Unrealized Intercompany Profits

The equity method as applied under **APB 18** often is referred to as a *one-line consolidation* because (*a*) the investor's income and stockholders' equity are the same as if the investee were consolidated and (*b*) all equity method adjustments are made through the investment and related income accounts, which are reported in only a single line in the balance sheet and a single line in the income statement.[7] The view currently taken in consolidation is that intercompany sales do not result in the realization of income until the intercompany profit is confirmed in some way, usually through a transaction with an unrelated third party. For

---

[5] **APB 18,** para. 17.
[6] *Financial Accounting Standards Board Interpretation No. 35,* "Criteria for Applying the Equity Method of Accounting for Investments in Common Stock," May 1981, para. 4.
[7] Although **APB 18** established the requirement for an equity-method investor's income and stockholders' equity to be the same as if the investee were consolidated, the FASB's recent decision to not permit the write-off of equity-method goodwill may lead to differences in situations in which such goodwill has been impaired.

example, if a parent company sells inventory to a subsidiary at a profit, that profit cannot be recognized in the consolidated financial statements until it is confirmed by resale of the inventory to an external party. Because profits from sales to related companies are viewed from a consolidated perspective as being unrealized until there is a resale to unrelated parties, such profits must be eliminated when preparing consolidated financial statements.

The consolidated financial statements are not the only ones affected, however, because **APB 18** requires that the income of an investor that reports an investment using the equity method must be the same as if the investee were consolidated. Therefore, the investor's equity-method income from the investee must be adjusted for unconfirmed profits on intercompany sales as well. The term for the application of the equity method that includes the adjustment for unrealized profit on sales to affiliates is ***fully adjusted equity method.***

### Adjusting for Unrealized Intercompany Profits

An intercompany sale normally is recorded on the books of the selling affiliate in the same manner as any other sale, including the recognition of profit. In applying the equity method, any intercompany profit remaining unrealized at the end of the period must be deducted from the amount of income that otherwise would be reported.

Under the one-line consolidation approach, the income recognized from the investment and the carrying amount of the investment are reduced to remove the effects of the unrealized intercompany profits. In future periods when the intercompany profit actually is realized, the entry is reversed.

### Unrealized Profit Adjustments Illustrated

To illustrate the adjustment for unrealized intercompany profits under the equity method, assume that Palit Corporation owns 40 percent of the common stock of Label Manufacturing. During 20X1, Palit sells inventory to Label for $10,000; the inventory originally cost Palit $7,000. Label resells one-third of the inventory to outsiders during 20X1 and retains the other two-thirds in its ending inventory. The amount of unrealized profit is computed as follows:

| | |
|---|---|
| Total intercompany profit | $10,000 − $7,000 = $3,000 |
| Unrealized portion | $3,000 × ⅔ = $2,000 |

Assuming that Label reports net income of $60,000 for 20X1 and declares no dividends, the following entries are recorded on Palit's books at the end of 20X1:

December 31, 20X1

| | | | |
|---|---|---|---|
| (16) | Investment in Label Manufacturing Stock | 24,000 | |
| |     Income from Label Manufacturing | | 24,000 |
| |     Record equity-method income: | | |
| |     $60,000 ×.40 | | |
| | | | |
| (17) | Income from Label Manufacturing | 2,000 | |
| |     Investment in Label Manufacturing Stock | | 2,000 |
| |     Remove unrealized intercompany profit. | | |

If all the remaining inventory is sold in 20X2, the following entry is made on Palit's books at the end of 20X2 to record the realization of the previously unrealized intercompany profit:

December 31, 20X2

| | | | |
|---|---|---|---|
| (18) | Investment in Label Manufacturing Stock | 2,000 | |
| |     Income from Label Manufacturing | | 2,000 |
| |     Recognize realized intercompany profit. | | |

## Additional Requirements of APB 18

**APB 18,** the governing pronouncement dealing with equity-method reporting, includes several additional requirements:

1. The investor's share of the investee's extraordinary items and prior-period adjustments should be reported as such by the investor, if material.

2. If an investor's share of investee losses exceeds the carrying amount of the investment, the equity method should be discontinued once the investment has been reduced to zero. No further losses are to be recognized by the investor unless the investor is committed to provide further financial support for the investee or unless the investee's imminent return to profitability appears assured. If, after the equity method has been suspended, the investee reports net income, the investor again should apply the equity method, but only after the investor's share of net income equals its share of losses not previously recognized.

3. Preferred dividends of the investee should be deducted from the investee's net income if declared or, whether declared or not, if the preferred stock is cumulative, before the investor computes its share of investee earnings.

**APB 18** also includes a number of required financial statement disclosures. When using the equity method, the investor must disclose:[8]

1. The name and percentage ownership of each investee.

2. The investor's accounting policies with respect to its investments in common stock, including the reasons for any departures from the 20 percent criterion established by **APB 18.**

3. The amount and accounting treatment of any differential.

4. The aggregate market value of each identified nonsubsidiary investment where a quoted market price is available.

5. Either separate statements for or summarized information as to assets, liabilities, and results of operations of corporate joint ventures of the investor, if material in the aggregate.

## Investor's Share of Other Comprehensive Income

When an investor uses the equity method to account for its investment in another company, the investor's comprehensive income should include its proportionate share of each of the amounts reported as "Other Comprehensive Income" by the investee. For example, assume that Ajax Corporation purchases 40 percent of the common stock of Barclay Company on January 1, 20X1. For the year 20X1, Barclay reports net income of $80,000 and comprehensive income of $115,000, which includes other comprehensive income (in addition to net income) of $35,000. This other comprehensive income (OCI) reflects an unrealized $35,000 gain (net of tax) resulting from an increase in the fair value of an investment in stock classified as available-for-sale under the criteria established by **FASB 115.** In addition to recording the normal equity-method entries, Ajax recognizes its proportionate share of the unrealized gain on available-for-sale securities reported by Barclay during 20X1 with the following entry:

| | | | |
|---|---|---|---|
| (19) | Investment in Barclay Stock | 14,000 | |
| | Unrealized Gain on Investments of Investee (OCI) | | 14,000 |
| | Recognize share of investee's unrealized gain on available-for-sale securities. | | |

[8] **FASB 159** requires most of the same disclosures for investments in common stock reported under the fair value option that otherwise would have been reported using the equity method.

Entry (19) has no effect on Ajax's net income for 20X1, but it does increase Ajax's other comprehensive income, and thus its total comprehensive income, by $14,000. Ajax will make a similar entry at the end of each period for its proportionate share of any increase or decrease in Barclay's accumulated unrealized holding gain.

## Tax Allocation Procedures

Intercompany income accruals and dividend transfers must be taken into consideration in computing income tax expense for the period. The impact depends on the level of ownership and the filing status of the companies. Because corporations generally are permitted to deduct 80 percent of the dividends received (100 percent if at least 80 percent of all voting stock is owned), they are taxed at relatively low effective tax rates (20 percent times the marginal tax rate) on those dividends.

When an investor and an investee file a consolidated tax return, intercompany dividends and income accruals are eliminated in determining taxable income. Deferred tax accruals, therefore, are not needed even though temporary differences occur between the recognition of investment income by the investor and realization through dividend transfers from the investee. Consolidated tax returns may be filed when an investor owns at least 80 percent of a subsidiary's stock and elects to file a consolidated return. Otherwise, an investor and investee must file separate returns.

If an investor and an investee file separate tax returns, the investor is taxed on the dividends received from the investee rather than on the amount of investment income reported. The amount of tax expense reported in the income statement of the investor each period should be based on income from the investor's own operations as well as on income recognized from its intercompany investments. **FASB Statement No. 109,** "Accounting for Income Taxes" (FASB 109), specifies those situations in which additional deferred tax accruals are required as a result of temporary differences in the recognition of income for financial reporting purposes and that used in determining taxable income.

### *Tax Expense under the Cost Method*

If the investor reports its investment using the cost method, income tax expense recorded by the investor on the investment income and the amount of taxes actually paid are both based on dividends received from the investee. No interperiod income tax allocation is required under the cost method because the income is recognized in the same period for both financial reporting and tax purposes; there are no temporary differences.

### *Tax Expense under the Equity Method*

If the investment is reported using the equity method and separate tax returns are filed, the investor reports its share of the investee's income in the income statement but reports only its share of the investee's dividends in the tax return. When the amount of the investee's dividends is different from its earnings, a temporary difference arises and interperiod tax allocation is required for the investor. In this situation, deferred income taxes must be recognized on the difference between the equity-method income reported by the investor in its income statement and the dividend income reported in its tax return. Current accounting standards generally require that the investor's reported income tax expense be computed as if all the investment income recognized by the investor under the equity method actually had been received. Thus, the investor's tax expense is recorded in excess of the taxes actually paid when the investee's earnings are greater than its dividends and normally is recorded at less than taxes actually paid when dividends are greater than earnings.

The requirements for computing the investor's income tax expense on income from intercorporate investments in common stock are summarized in Figure 2–4.

**FIGURE 2–4**
**Investor Income Tax Expense Computation**

| Type of Investee | Computation of Investor's Income Tax Expense Related to Income from Investee |
|---|---|
| Equity-method investees | Ordinary tax rate × (investor's share of investee net income − dividend deduction)[a] |
| Cost-method investees | Ordinary tax rate × (dividends received − dividend deduction) |

[a]Need not accrue taxes if the earnings will be distributed in a tax-free transfer or if there is evidence that the earnings of a foreign subsidiary or foreign corporate joint venture are to be reinvested permanently.

## Accounting for Investments in Subsidiaries

Companies are free to adopt whatever procedures they wish in accounting for investments in controlled subsidiaries on their books. Because investments in consolidated subsidiaries are eliminated when consolidated statements are prepared, the consolidated statements are not affected by the procedures used to account for the investments on the parent's books.

In practice, companies follow three different approaches in accounting for their consolidated subsidiaries:

1. Fully adjusted equity method.
2. Modified version of the equity method.
3. Cost method.

Several modified versions of the equity method are found in practice, and all usually are referred to as the ***modified equity method.*** Some companies apply the equity method without making adjustments for unrealized intercompany profits and the amortization of the differential. Others adjust for the amortization of the differential but omit the adjustments for unrealized intercompany profits. This latter approach is referred to in this text as the ***basic equity method*** and is used through many of the later chapters on consolidations. While modified versions of the equity method are not acceptable for financial reporting purposes, they may provide some clerical savings for the parent if used on the books when consolidation of the subsidiary is required.

## Summary of Key Concepts

Companies owning investments in the common stock of other companies generally report those investments by consolidating them or reporting them using the cost method (adjusted to market, if appropriate) or equity method, depending on the circumstances. Consolidation generally is appropriate if one entity controls the investee, usually through majority ownership of the investee's voting stock. The equity method is required when an investor has sufficient stock ownership in an investee to significantly influence the operating and financial policies of the investee but owns less than a majority of the investee's stock. In the absence of other evidence, ownership of 20 percent or more of an investee's voting stock is viewed as giving the investor the ability to exercise significant influence over the investee. The cost method is used when consolidation and the equity method are not appropriate, usually when the investor is unable to exercise significant influence over the investee. If the cost method is used in reporting an investment in common stock and the common stock is marketable, an adjustment to market is required for financial reporting purposes.

The cost method is similar to the approach used in accounting for other noncurrent assets. The investment is carried at its original cost to the investor. Consistent with the realization concept, income from the investment is recognized when distributed by the investee in the form of dividends.

The equity method is unique in that the carrying value of the investment is adjusted periodically to reflect the investor's changing equity in the underlying investee. Income from the investment is recognized by the investor under the equity method as the investee reports the income rather than when it is distributed.

Companies also have the choice of reporting nonconsolidated investments using the fair value option instead of the cost or equity method. Under the fair value option, the investment is remeasured to fair value at the end of each reporting period and the change in value recognized as an unrealized gain or loss in income.

| Key Terms | | | |
|---|---|---|---|
| | basic equity method, *74* | equity method, *53* | one-line consolidation, *70* |
| | consolidation, *52* | fully adjusted equity | parent, *52* |
| | corporate joint venture, *57* | method, *71* | significant influence, *53* |
| | cost method, *53* | liquidating dividends, *55* | subsidiary, *52* |
| | differential, *60* | modified equity | unconsolidated |
| | equity accrual, *58* | method, *74* | subsidiary, *52* |

**Questions**

**Q2-1** What types of investments in common stock normally are accounted for using (*a*) the equity method and (*b*) the cost method?

**Q2-2** How is the ability to significantly influence the operating and financial policies of a company normally demonstrated?

**Q2-3** When is equity-method reporting considered inappropriate even though sufficient common shares are owned to allow the exercise of significant influence?

**Q2-4** When will the balance in the intercorporate investment account be the same under the cost method and the equity method?

**Q2-5** Describe an investor's treatment of an investee's prior-period dividends and earnings when the investor acquires significant influence through a purchase of additional stock.

**Q2-6** From the point of view of an investor in common stock, what is a liquidating dividend? Is a liquidating dividend viewed in the same way by the investee?

**Q2-7** What effect does a liquidating dividend have on the balance in the investment account under the cost method and the equity method?

**Q2-8** When is the carrying value of the investment account reduced under equity-method reporting?

**Q2-9** What is a corporate joint venture? How should an investment in the common stock of a corporate joint venture normally be reported?

**Q2-10** What is a differential? How is a differential treated by an investor in computing income from an investee under (*a*) cost-method and (*b*) equity-method reporting?

**Q2-11** How is the receipt of a dividend recorded under the equity method? Under the cost method?

**Q2-12** Turner Manufacturing Corporation owns 40 percent of the common shares of Straight Lace Company. If Straight Lace reports net income of $100,000 for 20X5, what factors may cause Turner to report less than $40,000 of income from the investee?

**Q2-13** How does the fair value method differ from the cost method and equity method in reporting income from nonsubsidiary investments?

**Q2-14** How is the total amount of income from a nonsubsidiary investment computed using the fair value method?

**Q2-15** What types of complexities arise in applying the equity method to accounting for an investment in a partnership?

**Q2-16** In what types of situations could it be appropriate to use equity-method reporting even though the investor does not hold voting common stock of the investee?

**Q2-17*** When must tax allocation procedures be used in recording income tax expense under the equity method?

**Q2-18*** Will the expected amount of deferred income taxes be larger under the cost method or the equity method? Explain.

**Q2-19*** How does the fully adjusted equity method differ from the basic equity method?

**Q2-20*** Explain the concept of a one-line consolidation.

**Q2-21*** What is the basic equity method? When might a company choose to use the basic equity method rather than the fully adjusted equity method?

**Q2-22*** How are extraordinary items of the investee disclosed by the investor under equity-method reporting?

*Indicates that the item relates to "Additional Considerations."

## Cases

### C2-1 Choice of Accounting Method

*Understanding*

Slanted Building Supplies purchased 32 percent of the voting shares of Flat Flooring Company in March 20X3. On December 31, 20X3, the officers of Slanted Building Supplies indicated they needed advice on whether to use the equity method or cost method in reporting their ownership in Flat Flooring.

#### Required

a. What factors should be considered in determining whether equity-method reporting is appropriate?

b. Which of the two methods is likely to show the larger reported contribution to Slanted's earnings in 20X4? Explain.

c. Why might the use of the equity method become more appropriate as the percentage of ownership increases?

### C2-2 Intercorporate Ownership

*Research FARS*

Most Company purchased 90 percent of the voting common stock of Port Company on January 1, 20X4, and 15 percent of the voting common stock of Adams Company on July 1, 20X4. In preparing the financial statements for Most Company at December 31, 20X4, you discover that Port Company purchased 10 percent of the common stock of Adams Company in 20X2 and continues to hold those shares. Adams Company reported net income of $200,000 for 20X4 and paid a dividend of $70,000 on December 20, 20X4.

#### Required

Most Company's chief accountant instructs you to review the current accounting literature, including pronouncements of the FASB and other appropriate bodies, and prepare a memo discussing whether the cost or equity method should be used in reporting the investment in Adams Company in Most's consolidated statements prepared at December 31, 20X4. Support your recommendations with citations and quotations from the authoritative financial reporting standards or other literature.

### C2-3 Application of the Equity Method

*Research FARS*

Forth Company owned 85,000 of Brown Company's 100,000 shares of common stock until January 1, 20X2, at which time it sold 70,000 of the shares to a group of seven investors, each of whom purchased 10,000 shares. On December 3, 20X2, Forth received a dividend of $9,000 from Brown. Forth continues to purchase a substantial portion of Brown's output under a contract that runs until the end of 20X9. Because of this arrangement, Forth is permitted to place two of its employees on the board of directors of Brown.

#### Required

Forth Company's controller is not sure whether the company should use the cost or equity method in accounting for its investment in Brown Company. The controller asked you to review the relevant accounting literature and prepare a memo containing your recommendations. Support your recommendations with citations and quotations from the appropriate authoritative financial reporting standards or other literature.

### C2-4 Complex Organizational Structures

*Analysis*

Major companies often have very complex organizational structures, sometimes consisting of different types of entities. Some organizational structures include combinations of corporations, partnerships, and perhaps other types of entities. Complex organizational structures often present challenges for financial reporting.

#### Required

a. What type of entity is Atlas America, Inc. (i.e., corporation, partnership, trust)? What is the company's business?

b. Atlas America lists a number of subsidiaries in its Form 10-K filed with the SEC (in a separate exhibit). What types of entities are included among the subsidiaries? How does the company report its subsidiaries and interests in energy partnerships?

c. Atlas America lists subsidiaries with the names Atlas Pipeline Partners and Atlas Pipeline Holdings. What is the relationship between these companies?

d. What type of entity is Atlas Pipeline Partners, L.P.? What types of entities are its subsidiaries? What arrangement is there for the management of Atlas Pipeline Partners?

*e.* Does Atlas Pipeline Partners present separate or consolidated financial statements? What type of entity is NOARK Pipeline System, and what is Atlas Pipeline's relationship to NOARK? How is NOARK reflected in Atlas Pipeline's financial statements?

*f.* Was Atlas America previously owned by another company? Is Atlas America currently owned by another company? Explain.

### C2-5   Evaluating Investments

*Understanding*

Major companies often have investments in a number of other entities. The types of entities, ownership shares, and circumstances may differ considerably for these various investments, thus leading to different reporting methods for the different investments. The Dow Chemical Company is a company with numerous investments in other corporations, joint ventures, and partnerships.

#### Required

*a.* Approximately how many subsidiaries (10, 50, or more than 100) does Dow Chemical have? What is Dow's consolidation policy?

*b.* For what types of entities does Dow use the equity method of reporting? What is the highest percentage ownership for affiliates actually owned by Dow and reported using the equity method? Exclusive of Dow Corning, MEGlobal, Equipolymers, and EQUATE Petrochemical, what was the total differential associated with Dow's equity-method investments at December 31, 2005? What was the nature of the differential relating to MEGlobal, Equipolymers, and EQUATE Petrochemical?

*c.* In conjunction with what activity does Dow evaluate goodwill for impairment?

*d.* An investment that suffers a significant decline in value that is judged as being other than temporary must be written down to its fair value and a loss recognized. Did Dow Chemical experience such a loss in the past with respect to any of its partnership or joint venture investments? Explain.

### C2-6   Reporting Significant Investments in Common Stock

*Analysis*

The reporting treatment for investments in common stock depends on the level of ownership and the ability to influence policies of the investee. The reporting treatment may even change over time as ownership levels or other factors change. When investees are not consolidated, the investments typically are reported in the Investments section of the investor's balance sheet. However, the investor's income from those investments is not always easy to find in the investor's income statement.

#### Required

*a.* Harley-Davidson, Inc., holds an investment in the common stock of Buell Motorcycle Company. How did Harley-Davidson report this investment before 1998? How does it report the investment now? Why did Harley change its method of reporting its investment in Buell?

*b.* How does Chevron Corporation account for its investments in affiliated companies? How does the company account for issuances of additional stock by affiliates that change the company's proportionate dollar share of the affiliates' equity? How does Chevron treat a differential associated with an equity-method investment? How does Chevron account for the impairment of an equity investment? How does Chevron account for its investment in Dynegy common stock? Why is the carrying amount of Chevron's investment in Dynegy common stock different from its proportionate interest in Dynegy's net assets?

*c.* Prior to 1999, where did PepsiCo report its share of the net income or loss of its unconsolidated affiliates over which it exercised significant influence but not control? What rationale might be given for this treatment? How does PepsiCo now report this type of income?

*d.* Does Sears have any investments in companies that it accounts for using the equity method? Where are these investments reported in the balance sheet, and where is the income from these investments reported in the income statement?

## Exercises

### E2-1   Multiple-Choice Questions on Use of Cost and Equity Methods [AICPA Adapted]

Select the correct answer for each of the following questions.

1. Peel Company received a cash dividend from a common stock investment. Should Peel report an increase in the investment account if it uses the cost method or equity method of accounting?

| | Cost | Equity |
|---|---|---|
| *a.* | No | No |
| *b.* | Yes | Yes |
| *c.* | Yes | No |
| *d.* | No | Yes |

2. In 20X0, Neil Company held the following investments in common stock:

   - 25,000 shares of B&K Inc.'s 100,000 outstanding shares. Neil's level of ownership gives it the ability to exercise significant influence over the financial and operating policies of B&K.
   - 6,000 shares of Amal Corporation's 309,000 outstanding shares.

   During 20X0, Neil received the following distributions from its common stock investments:

   | | |
   |---|---|
   | November 6 | $30,000 cash dividend from B&K |
   | November 11 | $1,500 cash dividend from Amal |
   | December 26 | 3 percent common stock dividend from Amal |
   | | The closing price of this stock was $115 per share. |

   What amount of dividend revenue should Neil report for 20X0?

   *a.* $1,500.

   *b.* $4,200.

   *c.* $31,500.

   *d.* $34,200.

3. What is the most appropriate basis for recording the acquisition of 40 percent of the stock in another company if the acquisition was a noncash transaction?

   *a.* At the book value of the consideration given.

   *b.* At the par value of the stock acquired.

   *c.* At the book value of the stock acquired.

   *d.* At the fair value of the consideration given.

4. An investor uses the equity method to account for investments in common stock. The purchase price implies a fair value of the investee's depreciable assets in excess of the investee's net asset carrying values. The investor's amortization of the excess:

   *a.* Decreases the investment account.

   *b.* Decreases the goodwill account.

   *c.* Increases the investment revenue account.

   *d.* Does not affect the investment account.

5. A corporation exercises significant influence over an affiliate in which it holds a 40 percent common stock interest. If its affiliate completed a fiscal year profitably but paid no dividends, how would this affect the investor corporation?

   *a.* Result in an increased current ratio.

   *b.* Result in increased earnings per share.

   *c.* Increase several turnover ratios.

   *d.* Decrease book value per share.

6. An investor in common stock received dividends in excess of the investor's share of investee's earnings subsequent to the date of the investment. How will the investor's investment account be affected by those dividends under each of the following methods?

   | | Cost Method | Equity Method |
   |---|---|---|
   | *a.* | No effect | No effect |
   | *b.* | Decrease | No effect |
   | *c.* | No effect | Decrease |
   | *d.* | Decrease | Decrease |

7. An investor uses the cost method to account for an investment in common stock. A portion of the dividends received this year was in excess of the investor's share of investee's earnings subsequent to the date of investment. The amount of dividend revenue that should be reported in the investor's income statement for this year would be:

   a. Zero.

   b. The total amount of dividends received this year.

   c. The portion of the dividends received this year that was in excess of the investor's share of investee's earnings subsequent to the date of investment.

   d. The portion of the dividends received this year that was not in excess of the investor's share of investee's earnings subsequent to the date of investment.

### E2-2   Multiple-Choice Questions on Intercorporate Investments

Select the correct answer for each of the following questions.

1. Companies often acquire ownership in other companies using a variety of ownership arrangements. Equity-method reporting should be used by the investor whenever:

   a. The investor purchases voting common stock of the investee.

   b. The investor has significant influence over the operating and financing decisions of the investee.

   c. The investor purchases goods and services from the investee.

   d. The carrying value of the investment is less than the market value of the investee's shares held by the investor.

2. The carrying amount of an investment should be written down by the investor if:

   a. The carrying amount of the investment is more than the market value of the shares held, and the decline is considered to be temporary.

   b. The carrying amount of the investment is less than the market value of the shares held, and the increase is considered to be temporary.

   c. The carrying amount of the investment is more than the market value of the shares held, and the decline is considered to be other than temporary.

   d. The carrying amount of the investment is less than the market value of the shares held, and the increase is considered to be other than temporary.

3. An investment in a partnership potentially may be reported using:

   a. Cost method.

   b. Equity method.

   c. Full consolidation.

   d. All of the above.

4. Prescott Company holds a 40 percent interest in G&K Partnership, which has operated profitably since its formation and has made no distributions of earnings to its owners. Prescott's total assets at the end of the fourth year of ownership will be highest if it uses:

   a. Full consolidation.

   b. Pro rata consolidation.

   c. Equity-method reporting.

   d. Cost-method reporting.

5. Using equity-method reporting for investments in partnerships as opposed to investments in corporations:

   a. May be more difficult because factors other than the percent of assets contributed to the partnership may determine whether the equity method is appropriate.

   b. Is more difficult to apply because partnerships generally do not follow generally accepted accounting principles in recording everyday transactions.

   c. Is easier because the dollar amounts typically are much smaller.

   d. Is easier because corporations must pay income taxes and partnerships do not.

**E2-3    Multiple-Choice Questions on Applying Equity Method [AICPA Adapted]**

Select the correct answer for each of the following questions.

1. Green Corporation owns 30 percent of the outstanding common stock and 100 percent of the outstanding noncumulative nonvoting preferred stock of Axel Corporation. In 20X1, Axel declared dividends of $100,000 on its common stock and $60,000 on its preferred stock. Green exercises significant influence over Axel's operations. What amount of dividend revenue should Green report in its income statement for the year ended December 31, 20X1?

   a. $0.
   b. $30,000.
   c. $60,000.
   d. $90,000.

2. On January 2, 20X3, Kean Company purchased a 30 percent interest in Pod Company for $250,000. On this date, Pod's stockholders' equity was $500,000. The carrying amounts of Pod's identifiable net assets approximated their fair values, except for equipment whose fair value exceeded its carrying amount by $200,000 and had an expected remaining useful life of 15 years at January 2, 20X3. Pod reported net income of $100,000 for 20X3 and paid no dividends. Kean accounts for this investment using the equity method. In its December 31, 20X3, balance sheet, what amount should Kean report as its investment in Pod?

   a. $210,000.
   b. $220,000.
   c. $270,000.
   d. $276,000.

3. On January 1, 20X8, Mega Corporation acquired 10 percent of the outstanding voting stock of Penny Inc. On January 2, 20X9, Mega gained the ability to exercise significant influence over Penny's financial and operating decisions by acquiring an additional 20 percent of Penny's outstanding stock. The two purchases were made at prices proportionate to the value assigned to Penny's net assets, which equaled their carrying amounts. For the years ended December 31, 20X8 and 20X9, Penny reported the following:

|  | 20X8 | 20X9 |
|---|---|---|
| Dividends Paid | $200,000 | $300,000 |
| Net Income | 600,000 | 650,000 |

In 20X9, what amounts should Mega report as current year investment income and as an adjustment, before income taxes, to 20X8 investment income?

|  | 20X9 Investment Income | Adjustment to 20X8 Investment Income |
|---|---|---|
| a. | $195,000 | $160,000 |
| b. | $195,000 | $100,000 |
| c. | $195,000 | $ 40,000 |
| d. | $105,000 | $ 40,000 |

4. Investor Inc. owns 40 percent of Alimand Corporation. During the calendar year 20X5, Alimand had net earnings of $100,000 and paid dividends of $10,000. Investor mistakenly recorded these transactions using the cost method rather than the equity method of accounting. What effect would this have on the investment account, net earnings, and retained earnings, respectively?

   a. Understate, overstate, overstate.
   b. Overstate, understate, understate.
   c. Overstate, overstate, overstate.
   d. Understate, understate, understate.

5. A corporation using the equity method of accounting for its investment in a 40 percent-owned investee, which earned $20,000 and paid $5,000 in dividends, made the following entries:

| | | |
|---|---|---|
| Investment in Investee | 8,000 | |
|     Equity in Earnings of Investee | | 8,000 |
| Cash | 2,000 | |
|     Dividend Revenue | | 2,000 |

What effect will these entries have on the investor's statement of financial position?

a. Financial position will be fairly stated.

b. Investment in the investee will be overstated, retained earnings understated.

c. Investment in the investee will be understated, retained earnings understated.

d. Investment in the investee will be overstated, retained earnings overstated.

### E2-4   Cost versus Equity Reporting

Roller Corporation purchased 20 percent ownership of Steam Company on January 1, 20X5, for $70,000. On that date, the book value of Steam's reported net assets was $200,000. The excess over book value paid is attributable to depreciable assets with a remaining useful life of 10 years. Net income and dividend payments of Steam in the following periods were:

| Year | Net Income | Dividends |
|---|---|---|
| 20X5 | $20,000 | $ 5,000 |
| 20X6 | 40,000 | 15,000 |
| 20X7 | 20,000 | 35,000 |

#### Required

Prepare journal entries on Roller Corporation's books relating to its investment in Steam Company for each of the three years, assuming it accounts for the investment using (*a*) the cost method and (*b*) the equity method.

### E2-5   Cost versus Equity Reporting

Winston Corporation purchased 40 percent of the stock of Fullbright Company on January 1, 20X2, at underlying book value. The companies reported the following operating results and dividend payments during the first three years of intercorporate ownership:

| | Winston Corporation | | Fullbright Company | |
|---|---|---|---|---|
| Year | Operating Income | Dividends | Net Income | Dividends |
| 20X2 | $100,000 | $ 40,000 | $70,000 | $30,000 |
| 20X3 | 60,000 | 80,000 | 40,000 | 60,000 |
| 20X4 | 250,000 | 120,000 | 25,000 | 50,000 |

#### Required

Compute the net income reported by Winston for each of the three years, assuming it accounts for its investment in Fullbright using (*a*) the cost method and (*b*) the equity method.

### E2-6   Acquisition Price

Phillips Company bought 40 percent ownership in Jones Bag Company on January 1, 20X1, at underlying book value. In 20X1, 20X2, and 20X3, Jones Bag reported net income of $8,000, $12,000, $20,000, and dividends of $15,000, $10,000, and $10,000, respectively. The balance in Phillips Company's investment account on December 31, 20X3, was $54,000.

#### Required

In each of the following independent cases, determine the amount that Phillips paid for its investment in Jones Bag stock assuming that Phillips accounted for its investment using the (*a*) cost method and (*b*) equity method.

### E2-7 Investment Income

Ravine Corporation purchased 30 percent ownership of Valley Industries for $90,000 on January 1, 20X6, when Valley had capital stock of $240,000 and retained earnings of $60,000. The following data were reported by the companies for the years 20X6 through 20X9:

| Year | Operating Income, Ravine Corporation | Net Income, Valley Industries | Dividends Declared Ravine | Dividends Declared Valley |
|------|------|------|------|------|
| 20X6 | $140,000 | $30,000 | $ 70,000 | $20,000 |
| 20X7 | 80,000 | 50,000 | 70,000 | 40,000 |
| 20X8 | 220,000 | 10,000 | 90,000 | 40,000 |
| 20X9 | 160,000 | 40,000 | 100,000 | 20,000 |

#### Required

*a.* What net income would Ravine Corporation have reported for each of the years, assuming Ravine accounts for the intercorporate investment using (1) the cost method and (2) the equity method?

*b.* Give all appropriate journal entries for 20X8 that Ravine made under both the cost and the equity methods.

### E2-8 Impairment of Investment Value

Port Company purchased 30,000 of the 100,000 outstanding shares of Sund Company common stock on January 1, 20X2, for $180,000. The purchase price was equal to the book value of the shares purchased. Sund reported net income of $40,000, $30,000, and $5,000 for 20X2, 20X3, and 20X4, respectively. It paid a dividend of $25,000 in 20X2, but paid no dividends in 20X3 and 20X4. Due to the expiration of patent rights, Sund's net income for 20X4 declined substantially and it expected relatively large operating losses in 20X5 and beyond. In December 20X4 Sund's shares suffered a decline in value that is apparently other than temporary. The shares were trading at $4.50 each on December 31, 20X4.

#### Required

Compute the amounts Port Company should report as the carrying values of its investment in Sund Company at December 31, 20X2, 20X3, and 20X4.

### E2-9 Alternative Reporting for Investment in Partnership

Moss Company invested $90,000 in TF Partnership on January 1, 20X1, for a 45 percent share of its profits and losses. At December 31, 20X2, Moss reported total assets of $510,000 (excluding its investment in TF) and liabilities of $40,000, and TF reported total assets of $250,000 and liabilities of $30,000.

#### Required

Present the balance sheets for Moss Company at December 31, 20X2, assuming they are prepared using the following reporting alternatives for its investment in TF Partnership:

*a.* Cost method.

*b.* Equity method.

*c.* Pro rata consolidation.

*d.* Consolidation.

### E2-10 Differential Assigned to Patents

Power Corporation purchased 35 percent of the common stock of Snow Corporation on January 1, 20X2, by issuing 15,000 shares of its $6 par value common stock. The market price of Power's shares at the date of issue was $24. Snow reported net assets with a book value of $980,000 on that date. The amount paid in excess of the book value of Snow's net assets was attributed to the increased value of patents held by Snow with a remaining useful life of eight years. Snow reported net income of $56,000 and paid dividends of $20,000 in 20X2 and reported a net loss of $44,000 and paid dividends of $10,000 in 20X3.

*Required*

Assuming that Power Corporation uses the equity method in accounting for its investment in Snow Corporation, prepare all journal entries for Power for 20X2 and 20X3.

### E2-11 Differential Assigned to Copyrights

Best Corporation acquired 25 percent of the voting common stock of Flair Company on January 1, 20X7, by issuing bonds with a par value and fair value of $170,000 and making a cash payment of $26,000. At the date of acquisition, Flair reported assets of $740,000 and liabilities of $140,000. The book values and fair values of Flair's net assets were equal except for land and copyrights. Flair's land had a fair value $16,000 greater than its book value. All of the remaining purchase price was attributable to the increased value of Flair's copyrights with a remaining useful life of eight years. Flair Company reported a loss of $88,000 in 20X7 and net income of $120,000 in 20X8. Flair paid dividends of $24,000 each year.

*Required*

Assuming that Best Corporation uses the equity method in accounting for its investment in Flair Company, prepare all journal entries for Best for 20X7 and 20X8.

### E2-12 Differential Attributable to Depreciable Assets

Capital Corporation purchased 40 percent of Cook Company's stock on January 1, 20X4, for $136,000. On that date, Cook reported net assets of $300,000 valued at historical cost and $340,000 stated at fair value. The difference was due to the increased value of buildings with a remaining life of 10 years. During 20X4 and 20X5 Cook reported net income of $10,000 and $20,000 and paid dividends of $6,000 and $9,000, respectively.

*Required*

Assuming that Capital Corporation uses (*a*) the equity method and (*b*) the cost method in accounting for its ownership of Cook Company, give the journal entries that Capital recorded in 20X4 and 20X5.

### E2-13 Investment Income

Brindle Company purchased 25 percent of Monroe Company's voting common stock for $162,000 on January 1, 20X4. At that date, Monroe reported assets of $690,000 and liabilities of $230,000. The book values and fair values of Monroe's assets were equal except for land, which had a fair value $30,000 greater than book value, and equipment, which had a fair value $80,000 greater than book value. The remaining economic life of all depreciable assets at January 1, 20X4, was five years. The amount of the differential assigned to goodwill is not impaired. Monroe reported net income of $68,000 and paid dividends of $34,000 in 20X4.

*Required*

Compute the amount of investment income to be reported by Brindle for 20X4.

### E2-14 Determination of Purchase Price

Branch Corporation purchased 30 percent of Hardy Company's common stock on January 1, 20X5, and paid $28,000 above book value. The full amount of the additional payment was attributed to amortizable assets with a life of eight years remaining at January 1, 20X5. During 20X5 and 20X6, Hardy reported net income of $110,000 and $20,000 and paid dividends of $50,000 and $40,000, respectively. Branch uses the equity method in accounting for its investment in Hardy and reported a balance in its investment account of $161,000 on December 31, 20X6.

*Required*

Compute the amount paid by Branch to purchase Hardy shares.

### E2-15 Correction of Error

During review of the adjusting entries to be recorded on December 31, 20X8, Grand Corporation discovered that it had inappropriately been using the cost method in accounting for its investment in Case Products Corporation. Grand purchased 40 percent ownership of Case Products on January 1, 20X6, for $56,000, at which time Case Products reported retained earnings of $60,000 and capital stock outstanding of $40,000. The differential was attributable to patents with a life of eight years. Income and dividends of Case Products were:

| Year | Net Income | Dividends |
|------|-----------|-----------|
| 20X6 | $40,000 | $15,000 |
| 20X7 | 60,000 | 20,000 |
| 20X8 | 80,000 | 20,000 |

### Required

Give the correcting entry required on December 31, 20X8, to properly report the investment under the equity method, assuming the books have not been closed. Case Products' dividends were declared in early November and paid in early December each year.

### E2-16 Differential Assigned to Land and Equipment

Rod Corporation purchased 30 percent ownership of Stafford Corporation on January 1, 20X4, for $65,000, which was $10,000 above the underlying book value. Half the additional amount was attributable to an increase in the value of land held by Stafford, and half was due to an increase in the value of equipment. The equipment had a remaining economic life of five years on January 1, 20X4. During 20X4, Stafford reported net income of $40,000 and paid dividends of $15,000.

### Required

Give the journal entries that Rod Corporation recorded during 20X4 related to its investment in Stafford Corporation, assuming Rod uses the equity method in accounting for its investment.

### E2-17 Equity Entries with Goodwill

Turner Corporation reported the following balances at January 1, 20X9:

| Item | Book Value | Fair Value |
|------|-----------|-----------|
| Cash | $ 45,000 | $ 45,000 |
| Accounts Receivable | 60,000 | 60,000 |
| Inventory | 120,000 | 130,000 |
| Buildings and Equipment | 300,000 | 240,000 |
| Less: Accumulated Depreciation | (150,000) | |
| Total Assets | $375,000 | $475,000 |
| Accounts Payable | $ 75,000 | $ 75,000 |
| Common Stock ($10 par value) | 100,000 | |
| Additional Paid-In Capital | 30,000 | |
| Retained Earnings | 170,000 | |
| Total Liabilities and Equities | $375,000 | |

On January 1, 20X9, Gross Corporation purchased 40 percent of Turner's stock. All tangible assets had a remaining economic life of 10 years at January 1, 20X9. Both companies use the FIFO inventory method. Turner reported net income of $40,000 in 20X9 and paid dividends of $8,000. Gross uses the equity method in accounting for its investment in Turner.

### Required

Give all journal entries that Gross recorded during 20X9 with respect to its investment assuming Gross paid $175,000 for the ownership of Turner on January 1, 20X9. The amount of the differential assigned to goodwill is not impaired.

### E2-18 Income Reporting

Grandview Company purchased 40 percent of the stock of Spinet Corporation on January 1, 20X8, at underlying book value. Spinet recorded the following income for 20X9:

| | |
|---|---|
| Income before Extraordinary Gain | $60,000 |
| Extraordinary Gain | 30,000 |
| Net Income | $90,000 |

*Required*

Prepare all journal entries on Grandview's books for 20X9 to account for its investment in Spinet.

**E2-19    Fair Value Method**

Small Company reported 20X7 net income of $40,000 and paid dividends of $15,000 during the year. Mock Corporation acquired 20 percent of Small's shares on January 1, 20X7, for $105,000. At December 31, 20X7, Mock determined the fair value of the shares of Small to be $121,000. Mock reported operating income of $90,000 for 20X7.

*Required*

Compute Mock's net income for 20X7 assuming it uses:

*a.* The cost method in accounting for its investment in Small.

*b.* The equity method in accounting for its investment in Small.

*c.* The fair value method in accounting for its investment in Small.

**E2-20    Fair Value Recognition**

Kent Company purchased 35 percent ownership of Lomm Company on January 1, 20X8, for $140,000. Lomm reported 20X8 net income of $80,000 and paid dividends of $20,000. At December 31, 20X8, Kent determined the fair value of its investment in Lomm to be $174,000.

*Required*

Give all journal entries recorded by Kent with respect to its investment in Lomm in 20X8 assuming it uses:

*a.* The equity method.

*b.* The fair value method.

**E2-21\*    Investee with Preferred Stock Outstanding**

Reden Corporation purchased 45 percent of Montgomery Company's common stock on January 1, 20X9, at underlying book value of $288,000. Montgomery's balance sheet contained the following stockholders' equity balances:

| | |
|---|---:|
| Preferred Stock ($5 par value, 50,000 shares issued and outstanding) | $250,000 |
| Common Stock ($1 par value, 150,000 shares issued and outstanding) | 150,000 |
| Additional Paid-In Capital | 180,000 |
| Retained Earnings | 310,000 |
| Total Stockholders' Equity | $890,000 |

Montgomery's preferred stock is cumulative and pays a 10 percent annual dividend. Montgomery reported net income of $95,000 for 20X9 and paid total dividends of $40,000.

*Required*

Give the journal entries recorded by Reden Corporation for 20X9 related to its investment in Montgomery Company common stock.

**E2-22\*    Other Comprehensive Income Reported by Investee**

Callas Corporation paid $380,000 to acquire 40 percent ownership of Thinbill Company on January 1, 20X9. The amount paid was equal to underlying book value. During 20X9, Thinbill reported operating income of $45,000, an increase of $10,000 in the market value of trading securities held for the year, and an increase of $20,000 in the market value of available-for-sale securities held for the year. Thinbill paid dividends of $9,000 on December 10, 20X9.

*Required*

Give all journal entries that Callas Corporation recorded in 20X9, including closing entries at December 31, 20X9, associated with its investment in Thinbill Company.

**E2-23\*    Other Comprehensive Income Reported by Investee**

Baldwin Corporation purchased 25 percent of Gwin Company's common stock on January 1, 20X8, at underlying book value. In 20X8 Gwin reported a net loss of $20,000 and paid dividends of $10,000, and in 20X9 the company reported net income of $68,000 and paid dividends of

$16,000. Gwin also purchased marketable securities classified as available-for-sale on February 8, 20X9, and reported an increase of $12,000 in their fair value at December 31, 20X9. Baldwin reported a balance of $67,000 in its investment in Gwin at December 31, 20X9.

**Required**

Compute the amount paid by Baldwin Corporation to purchase the shares of Gwin Company.

**E2-24\*** **Deferred Income Taxes**

Special Corporation reported net income of $250,000 for 20X5 and paid dividends of $50,000. Power Company owns 40 percent of Special's shares and uses the equity method in accounting for its investment. Power Company reports taxable income of $300,000 on its separate operations and has an effective tax rate of 35 percent. Eighty percent of dividends received from Special are exempt from income tax.

**Required**

Compute the following:

*a.* Income tax expense for 20X5.

*b.* Income taxes payable for 20X5.

---

**Problems** **P2-25** **Multiple-Choice Questions on Applying the Equity Method [AICPA Adapted]**

Select the correct answer for each of the following questions.

1. On July 1, 20X3, Barker Company purchased 20 percent of Acme Company's outstanding common stock for $400,000 when the fair value of Acme's net assets was $2,000,000. Barker does not have the ability to exercise significant influence over Acme's operating and financial policies. The following data concerning Acme are available for 20X3:

| | Twelve Months Ended December 31, 20X3 | Six Months Ended December 31, 20X3 |
|---|---|---|
| Net income | $300,000 | $160,000 |
| Dividends declared and paid | 190,000 | 100,000 |

In its income statement for the year ended December 31, 20X3, how much income should Barker report from this investment?

*a.* $20,000.

*b.* $32,000.

*c.* $38,000.

*d.* $60,000.

2. On January 1, 20X3, Miller Company purchased 25 percent of Wall Corporation's common stock; no goodwill resulted from the purchase. Miller appropriately carries this investment at equity, and the balance in Miller's investment account was $190,000 on December 31, 20X3. Wall reported net income of $120,000 for the year ended December 31, 20X3, and paid dividends on its common stock totaling $48,000 during 20X3. How much did Miller pay for its 25 percent interest in Wall?

*a.* $172,000.

*b.* $202,000.

*c.* $208,000.

*d.* $232,000.

3. On January 1, 20X7, Robohn Company purchased for cash 40 percent of Lowell Company's 300,000 shares of voting common stock for $1,800,000 when 40 percent of the underlying equity in Lowell's net assets was $1,740,000. The payment in excess of underlying equity was assigned to amortizable assets with a remaining life of six years. The amortization is not

deductible for income tax reporting. As a result of this transaction, Robohn has the ability to exercise significant influence over Lowell's operating and financial policies. Lowell's net income for the year ended December 31, 20X7, was $600,000. During 20X7, Lowell paid $325,000 in dividends to its shareholders. The income reported by Robohn for its investment in Lowell should be:

*a.* $120,000.

*b.* $130,000.

*c.* $230,000.

*d.* $240,000.

4. In January 20X0, Farley Corporation acquired 20 percent of Davis Company's outstanding common stock for $800,000. This investment gave Farley the ability to exercise significant influence over Davis. The book value of the acquired shares was $600,000. The excess of cost over book value was attributed to an identifiable intangible asset, which was undervalued on Davis's balance sheet and which had a remaining economic life of 10 years. For the year ended December 31, 20X0, Davis reported net income of $180,000 and paid cash dividends of $40,000 on its common stock. What is the proper carrying value of Farley's investment in Davis on December 31, 20X0?

*a.* $772,000.

*b.* $780,000.

*c.* $800,000.

*d.* $808,000.

**P2-26  Amortization of Differential**

Ball Corporation purchased 30 percent of Krown Company's common stock on January 1, 20X5, by issuing preferred stock with a par value of $50,000 and a market price of $120,000. The following amounts relate to Krown's balance sheet items at that date:

|  | Book Value | Fair Value |
|---|---|---|
| Cash and Receivables | $200,000 | $200,000 |
| Buildings and Equipment | 400,000 | 360,000 |
| Less: Accumulated Depreciation | (100,000) |  |
| Total Assets | $500,000 |  |
| Accounts Payable | $ 50,000 | 50,000 |
| Bonds Payable | 200,000 | 200,000 |
| Common Stock | 100,000 |  |
| Retained Earnings | 150,000 |  |
| Total Liabilities and Equities | $500,000 |  |

Krown purchased buildings and equipment on January 1, 20X0, with an expected economic life of 20 years. No change in overall expected economic life occurred as a result of the acquisition of Ball's stock. The amount paid in excess of the fair value of Krown's reported net assets is attributed to unrecorded copyrights with a remaining useful life of eight years. During 20X5, Krown reported net income of $40,000 and paid dividends of $10,000.

**Required**

Give all journal entries to be recorded on Ball Corporation's books during 20X5, assuming it uses the equity method in accounting for its ownership of Krown Company.

**P2-27  Computation of Account Balances**

Easy Chair Company purchased 40 percent ownership of Stuffy Sofa Corporation on January 1, 20X1, for $150,000. Stuffy Sofa's balance sheet at the time of acquisition was as follows:

**STUFFY SOFA CORPORATION**
**Balance Sheet**
**January 1, 20X1**

| | | | | | |
|---|---|---|---|---|---|
| Cash | | $ 30,000 | Current Liabilities | | $ 40,000 |
| Accounts Receivable | | 120,000 | Bonds Payable | | 200,000 |
| Inventory | | 80,000 | Common Stock | | 200,000 |
| Land | | 150,000 | Additional | | |
| Buildings and Equipment | $300,000 | | Paid-In Capital | | 40,000 |
| Less: Accumulated | | | Retained Earnings | | 80,000 |
| Depreciation | (120,000) | 180,000 | | | |
| Total Assets | | $560,000 | Total Liabilities and Equities | | $560,000 |

During 20X1 Stuffy Sofa Corporation reported net income of $30,000 and paid dividends of $9,000. The fair values of Stuffy Sofa's assets and liabilities were equal to their book values at the date of acquisition, with the exception of buildings and equipment, which had a fair value $35,000 above book value. All buildings and equipment had remaining lives of five years at the time of the business combination. The amount attributed to goodwill as a result of its purchase of Stuffy Sofa shares is not impaired.

### Required

a. What amount of investment income will Easy Chair Company record during 20X1 under equity-method accounting?

b. What amount of income will be reported under the cost method?

c. What will be the balance in the investment account on December 31, 20X1, under (1) cost-method and (2) equity-method accounting?

**P2-28    Retroactive Recognition**

Idle Corporation has been acquiring shares of Fast Track Enterprises at book value for the last several years. Data provided by Fast Track included the following:

| | 20X2 | 20X3 | 20X4 | 20X5 |
|---|---|---|---|---|
| Net Income | $40,000 | $60,000 | $40,000 | $50,000 |
| Dividends | 20,000 | 20,000 | 10,000 | 20,000 |

Fast Track declares and pays its annual dividend on November 15 each year. Its net book value on January 1, 20X2, was $250,000. Idle purchased shares of Fast Track on three occasions:

| | **Percent of Ownership** | |
|---|---|---|
| **Date** | **Purchased** | **Amount Paid** |
| January 1, 20X2 | 10% | $25,000 |
| July 1, 20X3 | 5 | 15,000 |
| January 1, 20X5 | 10 | 34,000 |

### Required

Give the journal entries to be recorded on Idle's books in 20X5 related to its investment in Fast Track.

**P2-29    Multistep Acquisition**

Jackson Corporation purchased shares of Phillips Corporation in the following sequence:

| Date | Number of Shares Purchased | Amount Paid |
|------|----------------------------|-------------|
| January 1, 20X6 | 1,000 shares | $25,000 |
| January 1, 20X8 | 500 shares | 15,000 |
| January 1, 20X9 | 2,000 shares | 70,000 |

The book value of Phillips's net assets at January 1, 20X6, was $200,000. Each year since Jackson first purchased shares, Phillips has reported net income of $70,000 and paid dividends of $20,000. The amount paid in excess of the book value of Phillips's net assets was attributed to the increase in the value of identifiable intangible assets with a remaining life of five years at the date the shares of Phillips were purchased. Phillips has had 10,000 shares of voting common stock outstanding throughout the four-year period.

### Required
Give the journal entries recorded on Jackson Corporation's books in 20X9 related to its investment in Phillips Corporation.

### P2-30  Investment in Joint Venture
Tye Corporation invested in an unincorporated joint venture and elected to use pro rata consolidation in preparing its financial statements. For the year ended December 31, 20X3, Tye reported income of $52,000 from its separate operations and net income of $60,000. The joint venture reported assets of $293,000 and liabilities of $45,000 on January 1, 20X3, and assets of $330,000 and liabilities of $50,000 on December 31, 20X3. It made no distributions to owners during the year.

### Required
a. Determine the percentage ownership of the joint venture held by Tye.

b. If Tye reports total assets (excluding its investment in the unincorporated joint venture) of $700,000 at December 31, 20X3, what amount of total assets will Tye report in its balance sheet on that date?

### P2-31  Investment in Partnership
Down Corporation paid $96,000 to acquire 30 percent of the ownership of DF Partnership on January 1, 20X4, and shares in its profits and losses at 30 percent. DF Partnership did not make any distribution to its owners during 20X4. At December 31, 20X4, Down and DF reported the following amounts when Down used the equity method in accounting for its investment in DF:

|  | Down Corporation | DF Partnership |
|--|------------------|----------------|
| Assets (other than investments) | $800,000 | $380,000 |
| Investment in DF Partnership | 105,000 | |
| Liabilities | 175,000 | 30,000 |
| Owners' Equity | 730,000 | 350,000 |
| Sales Revenue for 20X4 | 500,000 | 400,000 |
| Expenses for 20X4 | 345,000 | 370,000 |

### Required
Present the balance sheets at December 31, 20X4, and income statements for 20X4 for Down Corporation, assuming they are prepared using the following reporting alternatives for Down's investment in DF Partnership:

a. Cost method.

b. Equity method.

c. Pro rata consolidation.

d. Consolidation.

**P2-32** **Complex Differential**

Essex Company issued common shares with a par value of $50,000 and a market value of $165,000 in exchange for 30 percent ownership of Tolliver Corporation on January 1, 20X2. Tolliver reported the following balances on that date:

**TOLLIVER CORPORATION**
**Balance Sheet**
**January 1, 20X2**

|  | Book Value | Fair Value |
|---|---|---|
| **Assets** | | |
| Cash | $ 40,000 | $ 40,000 |
| Accounts Receivable | 80,000 | 80,000 |
| Inventory (FIFO basis) | 120,000 | 150,000 |
| Land | 50,000 | 65,000 |
| Buildings and Equipment | 500,000 | |
| Less: Accumulated Depreciation | (240,000) | 320,000 |
| Patent | | 25,000 |
| Total Assets | $550,000 | $680,000 |
| | | |
| **Liabilities and Equities** | | |
| Accounts Payable | $ 30,000 | $ 30,000 |
| Bonds Payable | 100,000 | 100,000 |
| Common Stock | 150,000 | |
| Additional Paid-In Capital | 20,000 | |
| Retained Earnings | 250,000 | |
| Total Liabilities and Equities | $550,000 | |

The estimated economic life of the patents held by Tolliver is 10 years. The buildings and equipment are expected to last 12 more years on average. Tolliver paid dividends of $9,000 during 20X2 and reported net income of $80,000 for the year.

**Required**

Compute the amount of investment income (loss) reported by Essex from its investment in Tolliver for 20X2 and the balance in the investment account on December 31, 20X2, assuming the equity method is used in accounting for the investment.

**P2-33** **Equity Entries with Differential**

On January 1, 20X0, Hunter Corporation issued 6,000 of its $10 par value shares to acquire 45 percent of the shares of Arrow Manufacturing. Arrow Manufacturing's balance sheet immediately before the acquisition contained the following items:

**ARROW MANUFACTURING**
**Balance Sheet**
**January 1, 20X0**

|  | Book Value | Fair Value |
|---|---|---|
| **Assets** | | |
| Cash and Receivables | $ 30,000 | $ 30,000 |
| Land | 70,000 | 80,000 |
| Buildings and Equipment (net) | 120,000 | 150,000 |
| Patent | 80,000 | 80,000 |
| Total Assets | $300,000 | |
| **Liabilities and Equities** | | |
| Accounts Payable | $ 90,000 | 90,000 |
| Common Stock | 150,000 | |
| Retained Earnings | 60,000 | |
| Total Liabilities and Equities | $300,000 | |

On the date of the stock acquisition, Hunter's shares were selling at $35, and Arrow Manufacturing's buildings and equipment had a remaining economic life of 10 years. The amount of the differential assigned to goodwill is not impaired.

In the two years following the stock acquisition, Arrow Manufacturing reported net income of $80,000 and $50,000 and paid dividends of $20,000 and $40,000, respectively. Hunter used the equity method in accounting for its ownership of Arrow Manufacturing.

### Required

*a.* Give the entry recorded by Hunter Corporation at the time of acquisition.

*b.* Give the journal entries recorded by Hunter during 20X0 and 20X1 related to its investment in Arrow Manufacturing.

*c.* What balance will be reported in Hunter's investment account on December 31, 20X1?

### P2-34   Equity Entries with Differential

Ennis Corporation acquired 35 percent of Jackson Corporation's stock on January 1, 20X8, by issuing 25,000 shares of its $2 par value common stock. Jackson Corporation's balance sheet immediately before the acquisition contained the following items:

**JACKSON CORPORATION**
Balance Sheet
January 1, 20X8

| | Book Value | Fair Value |
|---|---|---|
| **Assets** | | |
| Cash and Receivables | $ 40,000 | $ 40,000 |
| Inventory (FIFO basis) | 80,000 | 100,000 |
| Land | 50,000 | 70,000 |
| Buildings and Equipment (net) | 240,000 | 320,000 |
| Total Assets | $410,000 | $530,000 |
| | | |
| **Liabilities and Equities** | | |
| Accounts Payable | $ 70,000 | $ 70,000 |
| Common Stock | 130,000 | |
| Retained Earnings | 210,000 | |
| Total Liabilities and Equities | $410,000 | |

Shares of Ennis were selling at $8 at the time of the acquisition. On the date of acquisition, the remaining economic life of buildings and equipment held by Jackson was 20 years. The amount of the differential assigned to goodwill is not impaired. For the year 20X8, Jackson reported net income of $70,000 and paid dividends of $10,000.

### Required

*a.* Give the journal entries recorded by Ennis Corporation during 20X8 related to its investment in Jackson Corporation.

*b.* What balance will Ennis report as its investment in Jackson at December 31, 20X8?

### P2-35   Additional Ownership Level

Balance sheet and income and dividend data for Amber Corporation, Blair Corporation, and Carmen Corporation at January 1, 20X3, were as follows:

| Account Balances | Amber Corporation | Blair Corporation | Carmen Corporation |
|---|---|---|---|
| Cash | $ 70,000 | $ 60,000 | $ 20,000 |
| Accounts Receivable | 120,000 | 80,000 | 40,000 |
| Inventory | 100,000 | 90,000 | 65,000 |
| Fixed Assets (net) | 450,000 | 350,000 | 240,000 |
| Total Assets | $740,000 | $580,000 | $365,000 |

(continued)

*(continued)*

| Account Balances | Amber Corporation | Blair Corporation | Carmen Corporation |
|---|---|---|---|
| Accounts Payable | $105,000 | $110,000 | $ 45,000 |
| Bonds Payable | 300,000 | 200,000 | 120,000 |
| Common Stock | 150,000 | 75,000 | 90,000 |
| Retained Earnings | 185,000 | 195,000 | 110,000 |
| Total Liabilities and Equity | $740,000 | $580,000 | $365,000 |
| Income from Operations in 20X3 | $220,000 | $100,000 | |
| Net Income for 20X3 | | | $ 50,000 |
| Dividends Declared and Paid | 60,000 | 30,000 | 25,000 |

On January 1, 20X3, Amber Corporation purchased 40 percent of the voting common stock of Blair Corporation by issuing common stock with a par value of $40,000 and fair value of $130,000. Immediately after this transaction, Blair purchased 25 percent of the voting common stock of Carmen Corporation by issuing bonds payable with a par value and market value of $51,500.

On January 1, 20X3, the book values of Blair's net assets were equal to their fair values except for equipment that had a fair value $30,000 greater than book value and patents that had a fair value $25,000 greater than book value. At that date the equipment had a remaining economic life of eight years and the patents had a remaining economic life of five years. The book values of Carmen's assets were equal to their fair values except for inventory that had a fair value $6,000 in excess of book value and was accounted for on a FIFO basis.

### Required

a. Compute the net income reported by Amber Corporation for 20X3, assuming the equity method is used by Amber and Blair in accounting for their intercorporate investments.

b. Give all journal entries recorded by Amber relating to its investment in Blair during 20X3.

**P2-36**   **Fair Value Method**

Gant Company purchased 20 percent of the outstanding shares of Temp Company for $70,000 on January 1, 20X6. The following results are reported for Temp Company:

| | 20X6 | 20X7 | 20X8 |
|---|---|---|---|
| Net income | $40,000 | $35,000 | $60,000 |
| Dividends paid | 15,000 | 30,000 | 20,000 |
| Fair value of shares held by Gant: | | | |
| January 1 | 70,000 | 89,000 | 86,000 |
| December 31 | 89,000 | 86,000 | 97,000 |

### Required

Determine the amounts reported by Gant as income from its investment in Temp for each year and the balance in Gant's investment in Temp at the end of each year assuming Gant uses the following methods in accounting for its investment in Temp:

a. Cost method.

b. Equity method.

c. Fair value method.

**P2-37**   **Fair Value Journal Entries**

Marlow Company acquired 40 percent of the voting shares of Brown Company on January 1, 20X8, for $85,000. The following results are reported for Brown Company:

|  | 20X8 | 20X9 |
|---|---|---|
| Net income | $20,000 | $30,000 |
| Dividends paid | 10,000 | 15,000 |
| Fair value of shares held by Marlow: |  |  |
| January 1 | 85,000 | 97,000 |
| December 31 | 97,000 | 92,000 |

### Required

Give all journal entries recorded by Marlow for 20X8 and 20X9 assuming it uses the fair value method in accounting for its investment in Brown.

**P2-38  Correction of Error**

Hill Company paid $164,000 to acquire 40 percent ownership of Dale Company on January 1, 20X2. Net book value of Dale's assets on that date was $300,000. Book values and fair values of net assets held by Dale were the same except for equipment and patents. Equipment held by Dale had a book value of $70,000 and fair value of $120,000. All of the remaining purchase price was attributable to the increased value of patents with a remaining useful life of eight years. The remaining economic life of all depreciable assets held by Dale was five years.

Dale Company's net income and dividends for the three years immediately following the purchase of shares were:

| Year | Net Income | Dividends |
|---|---|---|
| 20X2 | $40,000 | $15,000 |
| 20X3 | 60,000 | 20,000 |
| 20X4 | 70,000 | 25,000 |

The computation of Hill's investment income for 20X4 and entries in its investment account since the date of purchase were as follows:

|  |  | 20X4 Investment Income |
|---|---|---|
| Pro rata income accrual ($70,000 × .40) |  | $28,000 |
| Amortize patents ($44,000 ÷ 8 years) | $5,500 |  |
| Dividends received ($25,000 × .40) |  | 10,000 |
| 20X4 investment income |  | $32,500 |

| Investment in Dale Company | | |
|---|---|---|
| 1/1/X2 purchase price | $164,000 |  |
| 20X2 income accrual | 16,000 |  |
| Amortize patents |  | $5,500 |
| 20X3 income accrual | 24,000 |  |
| Amortize patents |  | 5,500 |
| 20X4 income accrual | 28,000 |  |
| Amortize patents |  | 5,500 |
| 12/31/X4 balance | $215,500 |  |

Before making closing entries at the end of 20X4, Hill's new controller reviewed the reports and was convinced that both the balance in the investment account and the investment income that Hill reported for 20X4 were in error.

### Required

Prepare a correcting entry, along with supporting computations, to properly state the balance in the investment account and all related account balances at the end of 20X4.

**P2-39\* Other Comprehensive Income Reported by Investee**

Dewey Corporation owns 30 percent of the common stock of Jimm Company, which it purchased at underlying book value on January 1, 20X5. Dewey reported a balance of $245,000 for its investment in Jimm Company on January 1, 20X5, and $276,800 at December 31, 20X5. During 20X5, Dewey and Jimm Company reported operating income of $340,000 and $70,000, respectively. Jimm received dividends from investments in marketable equity securities in the amount of $7,000 during 20X5. It also reported an increase of $18,000 in the market value of its portfolio of trading securities and an increase in the value of its portfolio of securities classified as available-for-sale. Jimm paid dividends of $20,000 in 20X5. Ignore income taxes in determining your solution.

### Required

a. Assuming that Dewey uses the equity method in accounting for its investment in Jimm, compute the amount of income from Jimm recorded by Dewey in 20X5.

b. Compute the amount added to the investment account during 20X5.

c. Compute the amount reported by Jimm as other comprehensive income in 20X5.

d. If all of Jimm's other comprehensive income arose solely from its investment in available-for-sale securities purchased on March 10, 20X5, for $130,000, what was the market value of those securities at December 31, 20X5?

**P2-40\* Equity-Method Income Statement**

Wealthy Manufacturing Company purchased 40 percent of the voting shares of Diversified Products Corporation on March 23, 20X4. On December 31, 20X8, Wealthy Manufacturing's controller attempted to prepare income statements and retained earnings statements for the two companies using the following summarized 20X8 data:

|  | Wealthy Manufacturing | Diversified Products |
|---|---|---|
| Net Sales | $850,000 | $400,000 |
| Cost of Goods Sold | 670,000 | 320,000 |
| Other Expenses | 90,000 | 25,000 |
| Dividends Paid | 30,000 | 10,000 |
| Retained Earnings, 1/1/X8 | 420,000 | 260,000 |

Wealthy Manufacturing uses the equity method in accounting for its investment in Diversified Products. The controller was also aware of the following specific transactions for Diversified Products in 20X8, which were not included in the preceding data:

1. On June 30, 20X8, Diversified incurred a $5,000 extraordinary loss from a volcanic eruption near its Greenland facility.

2. Diversified sold its entire Health Technologies division on September 30, 20X8, for $375,000. The book value of Health Technologies division's net assets on that date was $331,000. The division incurred an operating loss of $15,000 in the first nine months of 20X8.

3. On January 1, 20X8, Diversified switched from FIFO inventory costing to the weighted-average method. Had Diversified always used the weighted-average method, prior years' income would have been lower by $20,000.

4. During 20X8, Diversified sold one of its delivery trucks after it was involved in an accident and recorded a gain of $10,000.

### Required

*a.* Prepare an income statement and retained earnings statement for Diversified Products for 20X8.

*b.* Prepare an income statement and retained earnings statement for Wealthy Manufacturing for 20X8.

**P2-41\***   **Net Income after Tax**

Baltic Corporation owns 30 percent of the voting shares of Cumberland Company. Cumberland reported net income of $70,000 and paid dividends of $30,000 in 20X8. Baltic accounts for its ownership of Cumberland using the equity method. Baltic reported operating income of $95,000 in 20X8.

### Required

What would Baltic report as net income for the year assuming an 80 percent exemption of intercompany dividends and an effective tax rate of 40 percent?

**P2-42\***   **Income Tax Expense and Net Income**

Long Company owns 25 percent of Computech Company's common stock, purchased December 28, 20X3, at book value. During the two years following the acquisition of its stock by Long, Computech reported net income and dividends and Long reported operating income as follows :

|  | 20X4 | 20X5 |
|---|---|---|
| Computech's net income | $20,000 | $ 8,000 |
| Computech's dividends | 4,000 | 10,000 |
| Long Company's operating income | 50,000 | 64,000 |

### Required

Compute the amount of income tax expense and net income Long Company should report for each year assuming an 80 percent exemption of intercompany dividends and assuming that Long has an effective tax rate of 40 percent and reports its investment in Computech using:

*a.* The cost method

*b.* The equity method.

# The Reporting Entity and Consolidated Financial Statements

Today, nearly all major corporations prepare consolidated financial statements. While people often think of the world's corporate giants as being single companies, closer examination reveals that each actually is composed of a number of separate companies. For example, General Motors Corporation and Ford Motor Company both own dozens of other companies. The Walt Disney Company is famous for spectacular theme parks and immortal cartoon characters, but it also owns many subsidiaries that include the following businesses: Miramax Films, Touchstone Pictures, Buena Vista Home Entertainment, Hollywood Records, the ABC Television Network, ESPN, many local television stations, and Disney Cruise Line. Similarly, Time Warner Inc. owns more than 1,500 subsidiaries, including AOL, Netscape, MapQuest, Moviefone, Time Warner Cable (which owns many subsidiaries), Turner Broadcasting (which owns many subsidiaries), Warner Bros. Entertainment, Warner Bros. Television, New Line Cinema, Warner Home Entertainment, DC Comics, Home Box Office, the Atlanta Braves (professional baseball), Time, and CNN (Cable News Network). General Motors, Ford, The Walt Disney Company, and Time Warner each present consolidated financial statements, as do nearly all corporations that are publicly held.

*Consolidated financial statements* present the financial position and results of operations for a *parent* (controlling entity) and one or more *subsidiaries* (controlled entities) as if all the individual entities actually were a single company or entity. Consolidation is required when a corporation owns a majority of another corporation's outstanding common stock. As discussed later in the chapter, consolidation also may be appropriate in certain other situations, and not all units subject to consolidation need necessarily be corporations or even business (for profit) enterprises.

Two companies are considered to be *related companies* or *affiliates* when one controls the other or both are under the common control of another entity. Consolidated financial statements are generally considered to be more useful than the separate financial statements of the individual companies when the companies are related. The accounting principles applied in the preparation of consolidated financial statements are the same accounting principles applied in preparing separate-company financial statements. The process of preparing consolidated financial statements involves bringing together the separate financial statements of related companies as if the related companies were actually a single company.

Any business combination results in one of two situations: either (1) the net assets of one or both of the combining companies are transferred to a single company (a merger or statutory consolidation) or (2) the combining companies each remain as *separate legal entities* (a stock acquisition). In the first case, no consolidation questions arise because only a single corporation emerges from the business combination. The financial statements of the resulting reporting entity are those of a single corporation. The matter of consolidated financial statements arises in the second instance because of the existence of two or more legally separate but related companies. A similar situation also arises if a company creates rather than purchases a subsidiary. Whether the subsidiary is acquired or created, each individual company maintains its own accounting records, but consolidated statements are needed to present the companies together as a single economic entity for general-purpose financial reporting.

## USEFULNESS OF CONSOLIDATED FINANCIAL STATEMENTS

Consolidated financial statements are presented primarily for those parties having a long-run interest in the parent company, including the parent's shareholders, creditors, and other resource providers. Consolidated statements often provide the only means of obtaining a clear picture of the total resources of the combined entity that are under the parent's control and the results of employing those resources. Especially when the number of related companies is substantial, consolidated statements may provide the only means of conveniently summarizing the vast amount of information relating to the individual companies and how the positions and operations of the individual companies affect the overall consolidated entity.

Current and prospective stockholders of the parent company are usually more interested in the consolidated financial statements than those of the individual companies because the well-being of the parent company is affected by the operations of its subsidiaries. When subsidiaries are profitable, profits accrue to the parent, and, similarly, the parent cannot escape the ill effects of unprofitable subsidiaries. By examining the consolidated statements, owners and potential owners are better able to assess the effectiveness with which management employs all the resources under its control.

The parent's long-term creditors also find the consolidated statements useful because the effects of subsidiary operations on the overall health and future of the parent are relevant to their decisions. In addition, although the parent and its subsidiaries are separate companies, the parent's creditors have an indirect claim on the subsidiaries' assets. The parent's short-term creditors, however, even though they also have an indirect claim on the subsidiaries' assets, are usually more interested in the parent's immediate solvency rather than its long-term profitability. Accordingly, they tend to rely more on the parent's separate financial statements, especially the balance sheet.

The parent company's management has a continuing need for current information both about the combined operations of the consolidated entity and about the individual companies forming the consolidated entity. For example, individual subsidiaries might have substantial volatility in their operations, and not until operating results and balance sheets are combined can the manager understand the overall impact of the activities for the period. On the other hand, information about individual companies within the consolidated entity may also be useful. For example, it may allow a manager to offset a cash shortfall in one subsidiary with excess cash from another without resorting to costly outside borrowing. The parent company's management may be particularly concerned with the consolidated financial statements because top management generally is evaluated, and sometimes compensated, based on the overall performance of the entity as reflected in the consolidated statements.

The creditors and any outside stockholders of subsidiaries generally are most interested in the separate financial statements of those subsidiaries. Subsidiary resource providers have no claim on the parent company unless the parent has provided guarantees or entered into other arrangements for the benefit of the subsidiaries.

## LIMITATIONS OF CONSOLIDATED FINANCIAL STATEMENTS

While consolidated financial statements are useful, their limitations also must be kept in mind. Some information is lost any time data sets are aggregated; this is particularly true when the information involves an aggregation across companies that have substantially different operating characteristics.

Some of the more important limitations of consolidated financial statements are as follows:

1. Because the operating results and financial position of individual companies included in the consolidation are not disclosed, the poor performance or position of one or more companies may be hidden by the good performance and position of others.

2. Not all the consolidated retained earnings balance is necessarily available for dividends of the parent because a portion may represent the parent's share of undistributed subsidiary earnings. Similarly, because the consolidated statements include the subsidiary's assets, not all assets shown are available for dividend distributions of the parent company.

3. Because financial ratios based on the consolidated statements are calculated on aggregated information, they are not necessarily representative of any single company in the consolidation, including the parent.

4. Similar accounts of different companies that are combined in the consolidation may not be entirely comparable. For example, the length of operating cycles of different companies may vary, causing receivables of similar length to be classified differently.

5. Additional information about individual companies or groups of companies included in the consolidation often is necessary for a fair presentation; such additional disclosures may require voluminous footnotes.

## SUBSIDIARY FINANCIAL STATEMENTS

Some financial statement users may be interested in the separate financial statements of individual subsidiaries, either instead of or in addition to consolidated financial statements. While the parent company's management is concerned with the entire consolidated entity as well as individual subsidiaries, the creditors, preferred stockholders, and noncontrolling common stockholders of subsidiary companies are most interested in the separate financial statements of the subsidiaries in which they have an interest. Because subsidiaries are legally separate from their parents, a subsidiary's creditors and stockholders generally have no claim on the parent and the subsidiary's stockholders do not share in the parent's profits. Therefore, consolidated financial statements usually are of little use to those interested in obtaining information about the assets, capital, or income of individual subsidiaries.

## CONSOLIDATED FINANCIAL STATEMENTS: CONCEPTS AND STANDARDS

Consolidated financial statements are intended to provide a meaningful representation of the overall position and activities of a single economic entity comprising a number of related companies. Current consolidation standards have been established by **Accounting Research Bulletin No. 51,** "Consolidated Financial Statements" (ARB 51),[1] issued in 1959, **FASB Statement No. 94,** "Consolidation of All Majority-Owned Subsidiaries" (FASB 94),[2] issued in 1987, and **FASB Statement No. 160,** "Noncontrolling Interests in Consolidated Financial Statements, an amendment of ARB No. 51" (FASB 160),[3] issued in 2007.[4] Under current standards, subsidiaries must be consolidated unless the parent is

---

[1] *Accounting Research Bulletin No. 51,* "Consolidated Financial Statements," Committee on Accounting Procedure, American Institute of Certified Public Accountants, August 1959.

[2] *Financial Accounting Standards Board Statement No. 94,* "Consolidation of All Majority-Owned Subsidiaries," October 1987.

[3] *Financial Accounting Standards Board Statement No. 160,* "Noncontrolling Interests in Consolidated Financial Statements, an amendment of ARB No. 51," December 2007.

[4] **FASB 141R,** "Business Combinations," does not deal directly with consolidation standards, but many of its requirements have a significant impact on consolidated financial statements.

precluded from exercising control. When consolidation of a subsidiary is not appropriate, the subsidiary is reported as an intercorporate investment.

## Traditional View of Control

Over the years, the single most important criterion for determining when an individual subsidiary should be consolidated has been that of control. **ARB 51** indicates that consolidated financial statements normally are appropriate for a group of companies when one company "has a controlling financial interest in the other companies." It also states that "the usual condition for a controlling financial interest is ownership of a majority voting interest. . . ." In practice, control has been determined by the proportion of voting shares of a company's stock owned directly or indirectly by another company. This criterion was formalized by **FASB 94,** which requires consolidation of all majority-owned subsidiaries unless the parent is unable to exercise control.

Although majority ownership is the most common means of acquiring control, a company may be able to direct the operating and financing policies of another with less than majority ownership, such as when the remainder of the stock is widely held. **FASB 94** does not preclude consolidation with less than majority ownership, but such consolidations have seldom been found in practice. More directly, **FASB 141R** indicates that control can be obtained without majority ownership of a company's common stock.

## Indirect Control

The traditional view of control includes both direct and indirect control. ***Direct control*** typically occurs when one company owns a majority of another company's common stock. ***Indirect control*** or *pyramiding* occurs when a company's common stock is owned by one or more other companies that are all under common control. Examples of indirect control of Z Company by P Company include the following ownership situations:

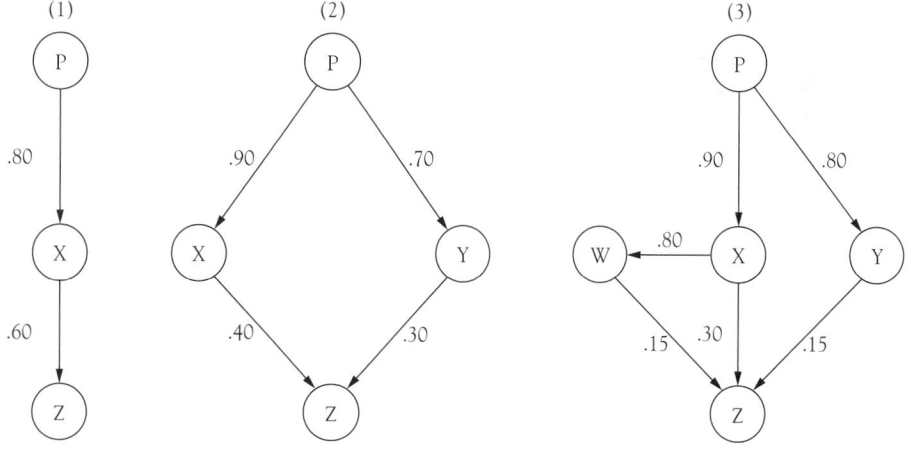

In (1), P owns 80 percent of X, which owns 60 percent of Z.

In (2), P owns 90 percent of X and 70 percent of Y; X owns 40 percent of Z; Y owns 30 percent of Z.

In (3), P owns 90 percent of X and 80 percent of Y; X owns 80 percent of W and 30 percent of Z; Y owns 15 percent of Z; W owns 15 percent of Z.

In each case, P's control over Z is indirect because it is gained by controlling other companies that control Z.

## Ability to Exercise Control

Under certain circumstances, a subsidiary's majority stockholders may not be able to exercise control even though they hold more than 50 percent of its outstanding voting stock. This might occur, for instance, if the subsidiary was in legal reorganization or in bankruptcy; while the parent might hold majority ownership, control would rest with the courts or a court-appointed trustee. Similarly, if the subsidiary was located in a foreign country and that country had placed restrictions on the subsidiary that prevented the re-mittance of profits or assets back to the parent company, consolidation of that subsidiary would not be appropriate because of the parent's inability to control important aspects of the subsidiary's operations.

## Differences in Fiscal Periods

A difference in the fiscal periods of a parent and subsidiary should not preclude con-solidation of that subsidiary. Often the subsidiary's fiscal period, if different from the parent's, is changed to coincide with that of the parent. Another alternative is to adjust the financial statement data of the subsidiary each period to place the data on a basis con-sistent with the fiscal period of the parent. Both the Securities and Exchange Commis-sion and current accounting standards permit the consolidation of a subsidiary's financial statements without adjusting the fiscal period of the subsidiary if that period does not dif-fer from the parent's by more than three months and if recognition is given to intervening events that have a material effect on financial position or results of operations.

## Changing Concept of the Reporting Entity

For nearly three decades, **ARB 51** served without significant revision as the primary source of consolidation policy. Over those years, many changes occurred in the busi-ness environment, including widespread diversification of companies and the increased emphasis on financial services by manufacturing and merchandising companies such as General Electric and Harley-Davidson.

In addition, the criteria used in determining whether to consolidate specific subsidiar-ies were subject to varying interpretations. Companies exercised great latitude in select-ing which subsidiaries to consolidate and which to report as intercorporate investments. The lack of consistency in consolidation policy became of increasing concern as many manufacturing and merchandising companies engaged in "off-balance sheet financing" by borrowing heavily through finance subsidiaries and then excluding those subsidiaries from consolidation.

In 1982, the FASB began a project aimed at developing a comprehensive consolidation policy. In 1987, **FASB 94,** requiring consolidation of all majority-owned subsidiaries, was issued to eliminate the inconsistencies found in practice until a more comprehensive standard could be issued. Unfortunately, the issues have been more difficult to resolve than anticipated. After grappling with these issues for more than two decades, the FASB has still been unable to provide a comprehensive consolidation policy.

Completion of the FASB's consolidation project has been hampered by, among other things, the inability to resolve issues related to two important concepts: (1) control and (2) the reporting entity. Regarding the first issue, the FASB has been attempting to move beyond the traditional notion of control based on majority ownership of common stock to requiring consolidation of entities under ***effective control.*** This idea reflects the ability to direct the policies of another entity even though majority ownership is lacking. Adopting the concept of effective control can lead to the consolidation of companies in which little, or even no, ownership is held and to the consolidation of entities other than corporations, such as partnerships and trusts. Although the FASB has indicated in its new standard on business combinations, **FASB 141R,** that control can be achieved without majority own-ership, a comprehensive consolidation policy has yet to be achieved.

With respect to the second issue, defining the accounting entity would go a long way toward resolving the issue of when to prepare consolidated financial statements and what entities should be included. Unfortunately, the FASB has found both the entity and con-trol issues so complex that they are not easily resolved and require further study. Ac-cordingly, the FASB issued **FASB 160,** which deals only with selected issues related to consolidated financial statements, leaving a comprehensive consolidation policy until a later time.

# OVERVIEW OF THE CONSOLIDATION PROCESS

The consolidation process adds together the financial statements of two or more legally separate companies, creating a single set of financial statements. The following chapters discuss the specific procedures used to produce consolidated financial statements in considerable detail. An understanding of the procedures is important because they facilitate the accurate and efficient preparation of consolidated statements. However, the focus should continue to be on the end product, the financial statements. The procedures are intended to produce financial statements that appear as if the consolidated companies are actually a single company.

The separate financial statements of the companies involved serve as the starting point each time consolidated statements are prepared. These separate statements are added together, after some adjustments and eliminations, to generate consolidated statements. The adjustments and eliminations relate to intercompany transactions and holdings. While the individual companies within a consolidated entity may legitimately report sales and receivables or payables to one another, the consolidated entity as a whole must report only transactions with parties outside the consolidated entity and receivables from or payables to external parties. Thus, the adjustments and eliminations required as part of the consolidation process aim at ensuring that the consolidated financial statements are presented as if they were the statements of a single enterprise.

After all the consolidation procedures have been applied, the preparer should review the resulting statements and ask: "Do these statements appear as if the consolidated companies were actually a single company?" To answer this question, two other questions must be answered:

1. Are items included in the statements that would not appear, or that would be stated at different amounts, in the statements of a single company?
2. Do any items not appear in these statements that would appear if the consolidated entity were actually a single company?

These questions are answered based not on a knowledge of consolidation procedures, but on a thorough knowledge of generally accepted accounting principles. If the statements are not equivalent to those of a single company, additional procedures must be completed to provide statements as they would be presented by a single reporting entity.

# THE CONSOLIDATION PROCESS ILLUSTRATED

The basic concepts that apply to the preparation of consolidated financial statements are illustrated in the following example. The focus of the example is on the balance sheet, but the concepts apply equally to the other financial statements as well. Assume that on January 1, 20X1, Popper Company purchases at book value all of Sun Corporation's common stock. At the acquisition date, the fair values of Sun's assets and liabilities are equal to their book values. At the end of 20X1, the balance sheets of the two companies appear as follows:

|  | Balance Sheets December 31, 20X1 | |
| --- | --- | --- |
|  | **Popper** | **Sun** |
| **Assets** | | |
| Cash | $ 5,000 | $ 3,000 |
| Receivables (net) | 84,000 | 30,000 |
| Inventory | 95,000 | 60,000 |
| Fixed Assets (net) | 375,000 | 250,000 |
| Other Assets | 25,000 | 15,000 |
| Investment in Sun Stock | 300,000 | |
| Total Assets | $884,000 | $358,000 |

*(continued)*

*(continued)*

|  | Popper | Sun |
|---|---|---|
| **Liabilities and Equities** | | |
| Short-Term Payables | $ 60,000 | $ 8,000 |
| Long-Term Payables | 200,000 | 50,000 |
| Common Stock | 500,000 | 200,000 |
| Retained Earnings | 124,000 | 100,000 |
| Total Liabilities and Equities | $884,000 | $358,000 |

Additional information regarding Popper and Sun is as follows:

1. Popper uses the basic equity method to account for its investment in Sun. The investment account is carried at the book value of Sun's net assets and is adjusted for Popper's share of Sun's earnings and dividends.
2. Sun owes Popper $1,000 on account at the end of the year.
3. Sun purchases $6,000 of inventory from Popper during 20X1. The inventory originally cost Popper $4,000. Sun still holds all the inventory at the end of the year.

## The Consolidated Entity

The following diagram can be helpful in understanding the consolidated entity:

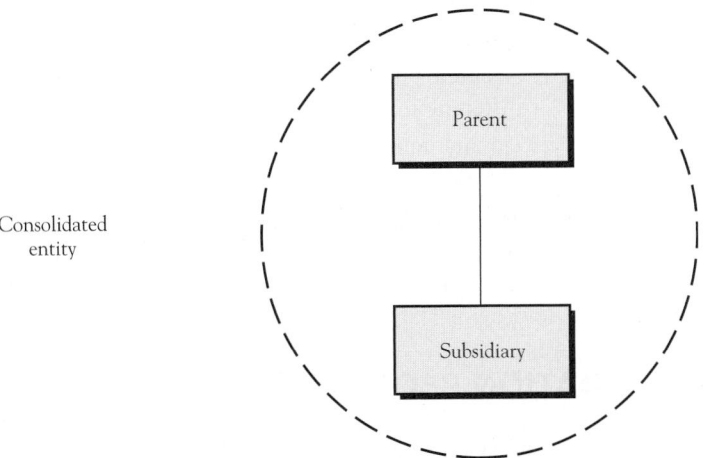

Consolidated
entity

The boxes representing the parent and the subsidiary indicate legal entities. Transactions are recorded in the accounts of these legal entities. The dashed circular line can be viewed as defining the consolidated entity, which encompasses both the parent and the subsidiary. This consolidated entity has no legal existence but is considered to have economic reality.

Transactions or ownership relations that cross over the dashed line can be viewed as involving outsiders and are properly reflected in the consolidated financial statements. Those transactions or relations that are entirely within the consolidated entity are not reflected in the consolidated financial statements because they do not involve outsiders. Instead, they are viewed as occurring within a single accounting entity and, therefore, do not qualify for inclusion in the consolidated statements.

The consolidated balance sheet for Popper and Sun appears in Figure 3–1, along with the computations used in deriving the balances reported. The like accounts from the parent and subsidiary financial statements are added together and then adjusted, when appropriate, to remove the effects of intercompany ownership and transactions. For example, the totals reported for cash, fixed assets, other assets, and long-term payables in this example are derived by simply adding together the amounts reported by the two companies. An adjustment is required to reduce receivables (net) and short-term payables for intercompany debt. Similarly, inventory and retained earnings are adjusted to remove the

**FIGURE 3–1**
**Consolidated Balance Sheet**

### POPPER COMPANY
#### Consolidated Balance Sheet
#### December 31, 20X1

| Assets | | Liabilities and Equities | |
|---|---|---|---|
| Cash | $ 8,000ᵃ | Short-Term Payables | $ 67,000ᶠ |
| Receivables (net) | 113,000ᵇ | Long-Term Payables | 250,000ᵍ |
| Inventory | 153,000ᶜ | | |
| Fixed Assets (net) | 625,000ᵈ | Common Stock | 500,000ʰ |
| Other Assets | 40,000ᵉ | Retained Earnings | 122,000ⁱ |
| Total Assets | $939,000 | Total Liabilities and Equities | $939,000 |

The consolidated balances were obtained as follows:
ᵃ Cash: $5,000 + $3,000 = $8,000
ᵇ Receivables (net): $84,000 + $30,000 − $1,000 = $113,000
ᶜ Inventory: $95,000 + $60,000 − $2,000 = $153,000
ᵈ Fixed Assets (net): $375,000 + $250,000 = $625,000
ᵉ Other Assets: $25,000 + $15,000 = $40,000
ᶠ Short-Term Payables: $60,000 + $8,000 − $1,000 = $67,000
ᵍ Long-Term Payables: $200,000 + $50,000 = $250,000
ʰ Common Stock: $500,000 + $200,000 − $200,000 = $500,000
ⁱ Retained Earnings: $124,000 + $100,000 − $100,000 − $2,000 = $122,000

write-up in carrying value that occurred when Sun purchased the inventory from Popper. For corporate ownership, only the stockholders' equity balances of Popper, as the parent company, are included in the consolidated balance sheet. A discussion of the rationale for each of the adjustments is presented in the sections that follow.

In the Popper and Sun example, several items need to be given special attention to ensure that the consolidated financial statements appear as if they are the statements of a single company:

1. Intercorporate stockholdings.
2. Intercompany receivables and payables.
3. Intercompany sales.

### Intercorporate Stockholdings

In the example given, Popper Company's common stock is held by those outside the consolidated entity and is properly viewed as the common stock of the entire entity. Sun's common stock, on the other hand, is held entirely within the consolidated entity and is not stock outstanding from a consolidated viewpoint. These relationships are illustrated as follows:

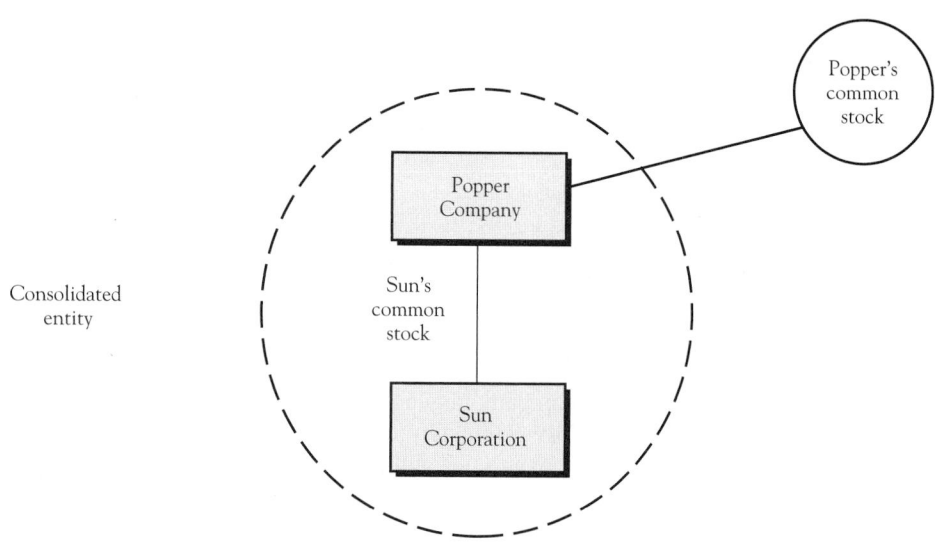

Because a company cannot report in its financial statements an investment in itself, Sun's common stock and Popper's investment in that stock both must be eliminated. Popper's common stock remains as the common stock of the consolidated entity, and Popper's retained earnings (less the unrealized intercompany profit) remains as the only retained earnings figure in the consolidated balance sheet.

### Intercompany Receivables and Payables

The intercompany receivable/payable can be viewed as follows:

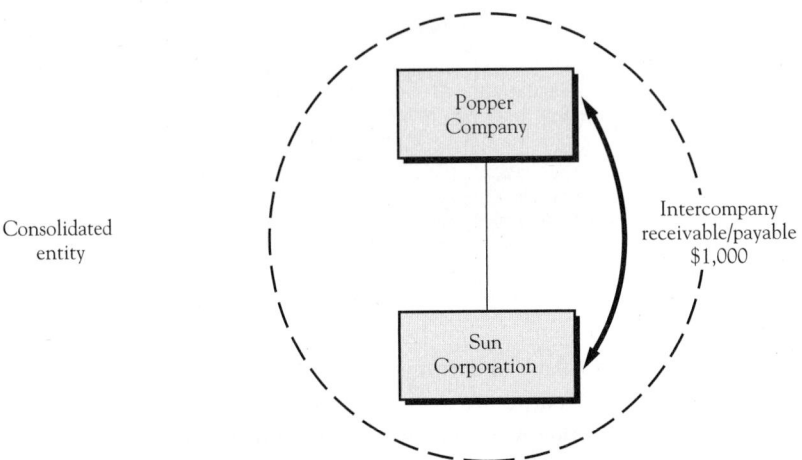

A single company cannot owe itself money. While as separate companies Popper properly reports a $1,000 trade receivable from Sun and Sun properly reports a $1,000 trade payable to Popper, such a receivable/payable does not exist from a consolidated viewpoint. Therefore, the $1,000 is eliminated from both receivables and payables in preparing the consolidated balance sheet.

### Intercompany Sales

The sale of inventory by Popper to Sun also must be viewed in the context of a single entity, as illustrated in the following diagram:

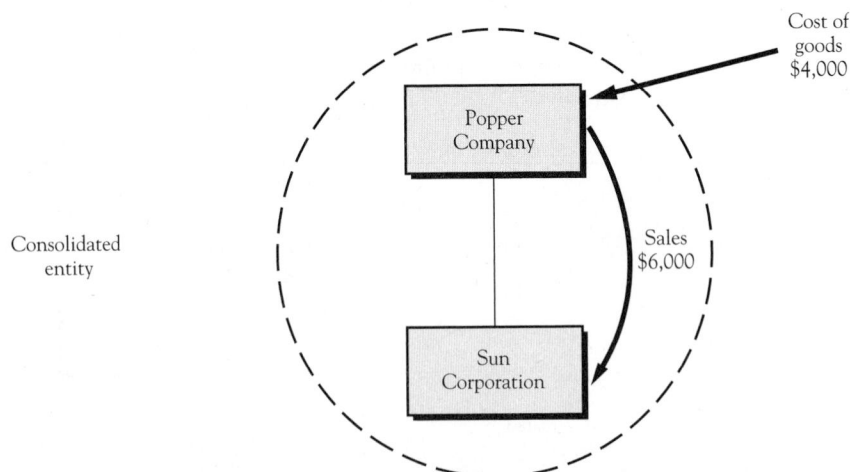

A single company may not recognize a profit and write up its inventory simply because the inventory is transferred from one department or division to another. This also applies to intercompany sales within a consolidated entity. In this example, the intercompany inventory remaining at the end of the period ($6,000) must be restated to its original cost to the consolidated entity, the $4,000 paid by Popper. Similarly, the $2,000 profit recognized on the intercompany sale and included in Popper's retained earnings may not be included in the consolidated amounts. Therefore, both the inventory and the consolidated retained earnings must be reduced by the $2,000 unrealized intercompany profit when preparing the consolidated balance sheet. In preparing a consolidated income statement, the $6,000 intercompany sale would have to be removed from the combined revenues of Popper and Sun because it does not represent a sale to an external party.

### Difference between Fair Value and Book Value

In the current example, an assumption is made that the fair value of the consideration given by Popper to acquire Sun is equal to the fair value of Sun's net assets, and the fair values of Sun's assets and liabilities are equal to their book values. In reality, the fair value of the consideration given usually reflects the fair value of the acquired company and differs from its book value. This difference or differential is treated in the same way when preparing consolidated financial statements as for a merger, discussed in Chapter 1. An acquiree's assets and liabilities must be valued based on their acquisition-date fair values, and any excess of the consideration given over the fair values of the net assets is considered goodwill.

### Single-Entity Viewpoint

The various adjustments discussed in this simplified example illustrate the type of thinking involved in the preparation of consolidated financial statements. To understand each of the adjustments needed in preparing consolidated statements, the reader should focus on (1) identifying the treatment accorded a particular item by each of the separate companies and (2) identifying the amount that would appear in the financial statements with respect to that item if the consolidated entity were actually a single company.

## Mechanics of the Consolidation Process

A worksheet is used to facilitate the process of combining and adjusting the account balances involved in a consolidation. The parent company and each subsidiary maintains its own set of books. No set of books exists for the consolidated entity. Instead, the balances of the accounts are taken at the end of each period from the books of the parent and each subsidiary and entered in the consolidation workpaper.

A consolidation workpaper for the preparation of Popper Company's consolidated balance sheet appears in Figure 3–2. The account balances for Popper and Sun, taken from their separate books, are listed in the first two columns beside one another so the amounts for each asset, liability, and equity item may be added across to obtain the consolidated balances.

When simply adding the amounts from the two companies leads to a consolidated figure different from the amount that would appear if the two companies were actually one, the combined amount must be adjusted to the desired figure. This is done through the preparation of *eliminating entries.* Separate debit and credit columns are provided for the eliminating entries in the workpaper in Figure 3–2. The final column in the workpaper presents the amounts to appear in the consolidated balance sheet. These amounts are obtained by summing across each line and including the effects of each debit or credit elimination or adjustment. The consolidated amounts then appear in the consolidated balance sheet as in Figure 3–1.

The following chapters discuss consolidation workpapers and eliminating entries in more detail. The consolidation procedures and workpapers are important because they facilitate the preparation of the consolidated statements, help ensure clerical accuracy, and provide a trail for the verification of the account balances in the consolidated statements. At this point, however, the reader should focus on understanding what numbers appear in the financial statements when adopting a single-entity viewpoint rather than concentrating on specific procedures or workpaper techniques.

**FIGURE 3–2**
Consolidated Balance
Sheet Workpaper

| | | | Eliminations | | |
| Item | Popper Company | Sun Corporation | Debit | Credit | Consolidated |
|---|---|---|---|---|---|
| **POPPER COMPANY AND SUBSIDIARY** | | | | | |
| **Consolidated Balance Sheet Workpaper** | | | | | |
| **December 31, 20X1** | | | | | |
| Cash | 5,000 | 3,000 | | | 8,000 |
| Receivables (net) | 84,000 | 30,000 | | (a) 1,000 | 113,000 |
| Inventory | 95,000 | 60,000 | | (b) 2,000 | 153,000 |
| Fixed Assets (net) | 375,000 | 250,000 | | | 625,000 |
| Other Assets | 25,000 | 15,000 | | | 40,000 |
| Investment in Sun Stock | 300,000 | | | (c) 300,000 | |
| | 884,000 | 358,000 | | | 939,000 |
| Short-Term Payables | 60,000 | 8,000 | (a) 1,000 | | 67,000 |
| Long-Term Payables | 200,000 | 50,000 | | | 250,000 |
| Common Stock | 500,000 | 200,000 | (c) 200,000 | | 500,000 |
| Retained Earnings | 124,000 | 100,000 | (c) 100,000 | | |
| | | | (b) 2,000 | | 122,000 |
| | 884,000 | 358,000 | 303,000 | 303,000 | 939,000 |

Elimination entries:
(a) Eliminate intercompany receivable/payable.
(b) Eliminate unrealized intercompany profit included in ending inventory against consolidated retained earnings.
(c) Eliminate intercorporate investment against subsidiary's stockholders' equity.

# NONCONTROLLING INTEREST

A parent company does not always own 100 percent of a subsidiary's outstanding common stock. The parent may have acquired less than 100 percent of a company's stock in a business combination, or it may originally have held 100 percent but sold or awarded some shares to others. For the parent to consolidate the subsidiary, only a controlling interest is needed. Those shareholders of the subsidiary other than the parent are referred to as "noncontrolling" or "minority" shareholders. The claim of these shareholders on the income and net assets of the subsidiary is referred to as the ***noncontrolling interest*** or the ***minority interest.***

The noncontrolling shareholders clearly have a claim on the subsidiary's assets and earnings through their stock ownership. Because 100 percent of a subsidiary's assets, liabilities, and earnings is included in the consolidated financial statements, regardless of the parent's percentage ownership, the noncontrolling shareholders' claim on these items must be reported.

## Computation of Noncontrolling Interest

In uncomplicated situations, the noncontrolling interest's share of consolidated net income is a simple proportionate share of the subsidiary's net income. For example, if a subsidiary has net income of $150,000 and the noncontrolling shareholders own 10 percent of the subsidiary's common stock, their share of income is $15,000 ($150,000 × .10).

The noncontrolling shareholders' claim on the net assets of the subsidiary is based on the acquisition-date fair value of the noncontrolling interest, adjusted over time for a proportionate share of the subsidiary's income and dividends. The noncontrolling interest is discussed in detail in Chapter 5.

## Presentation of Noncontrolling Interest

Historically, the portion of the subsidiary's net income assigned to the noncontrolling interest normally has been deducted from the combined earnings of the entire entity (including both the parent and subsidiary) to arrive at consolidated net income in the consolidated income statement. The label "consolidated net income" has been applied to the parent's share of the consolidated entity's income. Even though income assigned to the noncontrolling interest does not meet the definition of an expense, it normally has been accorded this expense-type treatment. For example, Century Telephone generally has referred to the minority interest's share of income as an expense in the notes to its consolidated financial statements.

The FASB's new standard on reporting noncontrolling interests, **FASB 160,** requires that the term "consolidated net income" be applied to the income available to all stockholders, with the allocation of that income between the controlling and noncontrolling stockholders shown. For example, assume that Parent Company owns 90 percent of Sub Company's stock, acquired without a differential, and that the two companies report revenues and expenses as follows:

|  | Parent | Sub |
|---|---|---|
| Revenues | $300,000 | $100,000 |
| Expenses | 225,000 | 65,000 |

An abbreviated consolidated income statement for Parent and its subsidiary would appear as follows:

| | |
|---|---|
| Revenues | $400,000 |
| Expenses | (290,000) |
| Consolidated net income | $110,000 |
| Less consolidated net income attributable to noncontrolling interest in subsidiary | (3,500) |
| Consolidated net income attributable to controlling interest | $106,500 |

The noncontrolling interest's claim on the net assets of the subsidiary was previously reported in the balance sheet most frequently (e.g., by Ford Motor Company) in the "mezzanine" between liabilities and stockholders' equity. Some companies reported the minority interest as a liability, although it clearly did not meet the definition of a liability. **FASB 160** makes clear that the noncontrolling interest's claim on net assets is an element of equity, not a liability. It requires reporting the noncontrolling interest in equity, in the following manner:

| | |
|---|---|
| Controlling interest: | |
| Common stock | $700,000 |
| Additional paid-in capital | 50,000 |
| Retained earnings | 80,000 |
| Total controlling interest | $830,000 |
| Noncontrolling interest in subsidiary | 75,000 |
| Total stockholders' equity | $905,000 |

Several different consolidation theories that affect the computation and treatment of the noncontrolling interest have been proposed. These theories are discussed briefly later in the chapter.

# COMBINED FINANCIAL STATEMENTS

Financial statements sometimes are prepared for a group of companies when no one company in the group owns a majority of the common stock of any other company in the group. Financial statements that include a group of related companies without including the parent company or other owner are referred to as ***combined financial statements.***

Combined financial statements are commonly prepared when an individual, rather than a corporation, owns or controls a number of companies and wishes to include them all in a single set of financial statements. In some cases, a parent company may prepare financial statements that include only its subsidiaries, not the parent. In other cases, a parent may prepare financial statements for its subsidiaries by operating group, with all the subsidiaries engaged in a particular type of operation, or those located in a particular geographical region, reported together.

The procedures used to prepare combined financial statements are essentially the same as those used in preparing consolidated financial statements. All intercompany receivables and payables, intercompany transactions, and unrealized intercompany profits and losses must be eliminated in the same manner as in the preparation of consolidated statements. Although no parent company is included in the reporting entity, any intercompany ownership, and the associated portion of stockholders' equity, must be eliminated in the same way as the parent's investment in a subsidiary is eliminated in preparing consolidated financial statements. The remaining stockholders' equity of the companies in the reporting entity is divided into the portions accruing to the controlling and noncontrolling interests.

# SPECIAL-PURPOSE AND VARIABLE INTEREST ENTITIES

While consolidation standards pertaining to related corporations have at times lacked clarity and needed updating, consolidation standards relating to partnerships or other types of entities such as trusts have been virtually nonexistent. Even corporate consolidation standards have not been adequate in situations in which other relationships such as guarantees and operating agreements overshadow the lack of a significant ownership element. As a result, companies such as Enron have taken advantage of the lack of standards to avoid reporting debt or losses by hiding them in special entities that were not consolidated. Although many companies have used special entities for legitimate purposes, financial reporting has not always captured the economic substance of the relationships. Only in the past few years have consolidation standards for these special entities started to provide some uniformity in the financial reporting for corporations having relationships with such entities.

**ARB 51** established consolidation standards in terms of one company controlling another and set majority voting interest as the usual condition leading to consolidation. Similarly, **FASB 94** requires consolidation for majority-owned subsidiaries. In recent years, however, new types of relationships have been established between corporations and other entities that often are difficult to characterize in terms of voting, controlling, or ownership interests. Such entities often are structured to provide financing and/or control through forms other than those used by traditional operating companies. Some entities have no governing boards, or they may have boards or managers with only a limited ability to direct the entity's activities. Such entities may be governed instead by their incorporation or partnership documents, or by other agreements or documents. Some entities may have little equity investment, and the equity investors may have little or no control over the entity. For these special types of entities, **ARB 51** does not provide a clear basis for consolidation.

These special types of entities have generally been referred to as ***special-purpose entities (SPEs).*** In general, SPEs are corporations, trusts, or partnerships created for a single specified purpose. They usually have no substantive operations and are used only for financing purposes. SPEs have been used for several decades for asset securitization, risk sharing, and taking advantage of tax statutes. Prior to 2003, no comprehensive reporting framework had been established for SPEs. Several different pronouncements from various bodies dealt with selected issues or types of SPEs, but the guidance provided by these issuances was incomplete, vague, and not always correctly interpreted in practice.

## Off-Balance Sheet Financing

Imagine that Genergy, Inc., needs $1 billion to finance building a gas pipeline in central Asia. Potential investors may want their risk/reward exposure limited to the pipeline without other aspects of Genergy's business. They might also want the pipeline to be a self-supporting independent entity with cash flows that are separate from Genergy's other business activities, and they may want to eliminate the possibility that Genergy will sell the pipeline. These objectives might be achieved by forming an SPE or what the FASB refers to as a *variable interest entity (VIE),* with a charter that specifies these limited operating activities.

Once the VIE is established, the pipeline assets and the debt used to finance the pipeline may, under certain circumstances, be excluded from Genergy's balance sheet. In this manner, Genergy has achieved *off-balance sheet financing* of the pipeline. As long as the VIE is not consolidated, Genergy's financial statements will not reflect the assets, liabilities, cash flows, revenues, and expenses associated with owning and operating the pipeline. Further, any transactions between Genergy and the pipeline entity are not eliminated in preparing Genergy's financial statements.

Some estimates have indicated that well over half of American companies use some type of off-balance sheet financing, involving perhaps trillions of dollars. These transactions are often facilitated by the use of some type of special entity, such as a VIE. There is concern that VIEs can be motivated either by a genuine business purpose, such as risk sharing among investors and isolation of project risk from company risk, or by a desire to meet specific financial reporting goals that may or may not be supported by the underlying economic substance of the transactions.

Companies might prefer to keep debt and the related assets financed by that debt off the balance sheet for a number of reasons, but the main one often has to do with making the company appear better to investors. One effect is to reduce the company's leverage and debt/equity ratios. Net income also may be increased as neither the interest on the debt nor the depreciation on the related assets is included in expenses. Further, the smaller asset base, because the assets are not shown on the balance sheet, combined with the higher net income produces a higher calculated return on assets.

Several means of keeping debt and related assets off a company's balance sheet have become common in practice. A company may lease assets from a third party such as a VIE, which borrows the money to buy the assets. Careful engineering of the lease terms so that it qualifies for treatment as an operating rather than a capital lease avoids recognition of the asset and lease obligation. Another possibility is for a company to sell assets such as accounts receivable outright rather than borrowing against them. A third option found with increasing frequency is for a company to create a new VIE and transfer both assets and liabilities to it. Not only does this allow the sponsoring corporation to remove the asset and related debt from its balance sheet, but the company may also be able to recognize a gain on the disposal of the asset.

Complex organizational structures increase the need for accounting standards aimed at ensuring that financial statements reflect the economic substance of those structures and the related transactions. However, the very complexity of these organizational structures makes the development of these standards a challenging endeavor.

## Qualifying Special-Purpose Entities

Certain types of SPEs that are widely used for servicing financial assets and meet very restrictive conditions established by **FASB Statement No. 140** are referred to as *qualifying SPEs.* Although the conditions are complex, in general they require that the SPE be "demonstrably distinct from the transferor," its activities be significantly limited, and it hold only certain types of financial assets.[5] For example, a finance-type company making many car loans, such as GMAC, might sell all of the car loans to an SPE especially established for the purpose. The SPE would then issue bonds (collateralized asset obligations) to the public using the car loans as collateral. The SPE would collect the payments on the car loans and make the payments on the bonds. While the SPE would have a significant amount of long-term debt, it might have little or no equity ownership. If the conditions of **FASB 140** are met, this type of SPE is not consolidated by the transferor of assets to the SPE.

## Variable Interest Entities

In January 2003, the FASB issued **FASB Interpretation No. 46,** *Consolidation of Variable Interest Entities,* an interpretation of **ARB No. 51,** with a revised version issued in December 2003 (FIN 46R).[6] For clarification, the interpretation uses the term *variable interest entities* to encompass SPEs and any other entities falling within its conditions. This pronouncement does not apply to entities that are considered qualifying SPEs under **FASB No. 140.**

A ***variable interest entity (VIE)*** is a legal structure used for business purposes, usually a corporation, trust, or partnership, that either (1) does not have equity investors that have voting rights and share in all of the entity's profits and losses or (2) has equity investors that do not provide sufficient financial resources to support the entity's activities. In a variable interest entity, specific agreements may limit the extent to which the equity investors, if any, share in the entity's profits or losses, and the agreements may limit the control that equity investors have over the entity's activities. For the equity investment to be considered sufficient financial support for the entity's activities (condition 2), it must be able to absorb the entity's expected future losses. A total equity investment that is less than 10 percent of the entity's total assets is, in general, considered to be insufficient by itself to allow the entity to finance its activities, and an investment of more than 10 percent might be needed, depending on the circumstances.

A typical variable interest entity might be created (or sponsored) by a corporation for a particular purpose, such as purchasing the sponsoring company's receivables or leasing facilities to the sponsoring company. The sponsoring company may acquire little or no stock (or other equity interest) in the VIE. Instead, the sponsoring company may enlist another party to purchase most or all of the common stock. The majority of the VIE's capital, however, normally comes from borrowing. Because lenders may be reluctant to lend (at least at reasonable interest rates) to an entity with only a small amount of equity, the sponsoring company often guarantees the VIE's loans. Thus, the sponsoring company may have little or no equity investment in the VIE, but the loan guarantees represent a type of interest in the VIE.

A corporation having an interest in a VIE cannot simply rely on its percentage stock ownership, if any, to determine whether to consolidate the entity. Instead each party having a variable interest in the VIE must determine the extent to which it shares in the VIE's expected profits and losses. **FIN 46R** (para. 2c) defines a *variable interest* in a VIE as a contractual, ownership (with or without voting rights), or other money-related interest in an entity that changes with changes in the fair value of the entity's net assets exclusive of variable interests. In other words, variable interests increase with the VIE's profits and decrease with its losses. The VIE's variable interests will absorb portions of the losses, if they occur, or receive portions of the residual returns.

Variable interests may be of a number of different types. The designation of several common types of interests in a VIE are as follows:

---

[5] *Financial Accounting Standards Board Statement No. 140,* "Accounting for Transfers and Servicing of Financial Assets and Extinguishments of Liabilities," September 2000, para. 35.

[6] *Financial Accounting Standards Board Interpretation No. 46 (revised December 2003),* "Consolidation of Variable Interest Entities, an interpretation of **ARB No. 51,**" December 2003.

| Type of Interest | Variable Interest? |
|---|---|
| Common stock, with no special features or provisions | Yes |
| Common stock, with loss protection or other provisions | Maybe |
| Senior debt | Usually not |
| Subordinated debt | Yes |
| Loan or asset guarantees | Yes |

Common stock that places the owners' investment at risk is a variable interest. In some cases, certain common stock may have, by agreement, special provisions that protect the investor against losses or provide a fixed return. These special types of shares may not involve significant risk on the part of the investor and might, depending on the provisions, result in an interest that is not a variable interest. Senior debt usually carries a fixed return and is protected against loss by subordinated interests. Subordinated debt represents a variable interest because, if the entity's cash flows are insufficient to pay off the subordinated debt, the holders of that debt will sustain losses. They do not have the same protection against loss that holders of the senior debt have. Parties that guarantee the value of assets or liabilities can sustain losses if they are called on to make good on their guarantees, and, therefore, the guarantees represent variable interests.

The nature of each party's variable interest determines whether consolidation by that party is appropriate. An enterprise that will absorb a majority of the VIE's expected losses, receive a majority of the VIE's expected residual returns, or both, is called the ***primary beneficiary*** of the variable interest entity. The primary beneficiary must consolidate the VIE. If the entity's profits and losses are divided differently, the enterprise absorbing a majority of the losses will consolidate the VIE.

As an example of the financial reporting determinations that must be made by parties having an interest in a VIE, suppose that Young Company and Zebra Corporation, both financially stable companies, create YZ Corporation to lease equipment to Young and other companies. Zebra purchases all of YZ's common stock. Young guarantees Zebra a 7 percent dividend on its stock, agrees to absorb all of YZ's losses, and, in addition, guarantees fixed-rate bank loans that are made to YZ. All profits in excess of the 7 percent payout to Zebra are split evenly between Young and Zebra.

In this case, the bank loans are not variable interests because they carry a fixed interest rate and are guaranteed by Young, a company capable of honoring the guarantee. Common stock of a VIE is a variable interest if the investment is at risk. In this case, Zebra's investment is not at risk, but it does share in the profits of YZ, and the amount of profits is not fixed. Therefore, the common stock is a variable interest. However, Zebra will not consolidate YZ because Zebra does not share in the losses, all of which Young will bear. Young would consolidate YZ because Young's guarantees represent a variable interest and it will absorb a majority (all) of the losses.

If consolidation of a VIE is appropriate, the amounts to be consolidated with those of the primary beneficiary are based on fair values at the date the enterprise first becomes the primary beneficiary. However, assets and liabilities transferred to a VIE by its primary beneficiary are valued at their book values, with no gain or loss recognized on the transfer. Subsequent to the initial determination of consolidation values, a VIE is accounted for in consolidated financial statements in accordance with **ARB 51** in the same manner as if it were consolidated based on voting interests. Intercompany balances and transactions are eliminated so the resulting consolidated financial statements appear as if there were just a single entity. These procedures are consistent with those used when consolidating parent and subsidiary corporations. Appendix 3A at the end of the chapter presents a simple illustration of the consolidation of a VIE.

## ADDITIONAL CONSIDERATIONS— DIFFERENT APPROACHES TO CONSOLIDATION

The previous sections gave a brief overview of the concepts, issues, and procedures to be discussed in Chapters 4 through 10. Before these matters are covered in detail in subsequent chapters, this section addresses the various theories underlying the consolidation process.

Several different accounting theories have been suggested that might serve as a basis for preparing consolidated financial statements. The choice of theory can have a significant impact on the consolidated financial statements in cases when the parent company owns less than 100 percent of the subsidiary's common stock. This discussion focuses on three alternative theories of consolidation: (1) proprietary, (2) parent company, and (3) entity. The proprietary and entity theories may be viewed as falling near opposite ends of a spectrum, with the parent company theory falling somewhere in between:

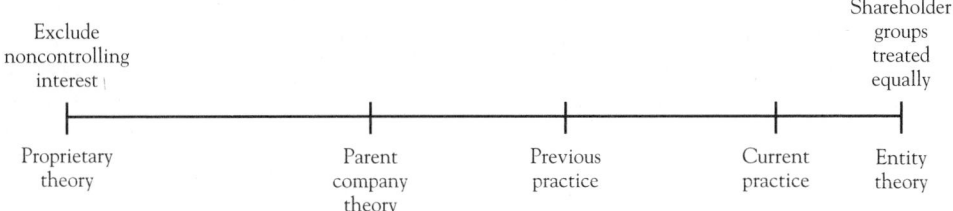

Until recently, the accounting profession had not adopted any of the three theories in its entirety, although practice was most closely aligned with the parent company approach. With the issuance of **FASB 141R** in 2007, however, the FASB's approach to consolidation has moved very much toward the entity theory.

### Theories of Consolidation

The ***proprietary theory*** of accounting views the firm as an extension of the owners. The firm's assets, liabilities, revenues, and expenses are viewed as those of the owners themselves. When applied to consolidated financial statements, the proprietary concept results in a ***pro rata consolidation*** in which the parent company consolidates only its proportionate share of a less-than-wholly owned subsidiary's assets, liabilities, revenues, and expenses.

The ***parent company theory*** is perhaps better suited to the modern corporation and the preparation of consolidated financial statements than is the proprietary approach. The parent company theory recognizes that the parent has the ability to effectively control all of the assets and liabilities of a majority-owned subsidiary, not just a proportionate share, even though the parent does not actually own the subsidiary's assets or have any obligation for its liabilities. The consolidated financial statements include all of the subsidiary's assets, liabilities, revenues, and expenses. Separate recognition is given in the consolidated balance sheet to the noncontrolling interest's claim on the subsidiary's net assets and in the consolidated income statement to the earnings assigned to the noncontrolling shareholders.

As a general ownership theory, the ***entity theory*** focuses on the firm as a separate economic entity rather than on the ownership rights of the shareholders. Emphasis under the entity approach is on the consolidated entity itself, with the controlling and noncontrolling shareholders viewed as two separate groups, each having an equity in the consolidated entity. Neither of the two groups is emphasized over the other or over the consolidated entity. Accordingly, all of the assets, liabilities, revenues, and expenses of a less-than-wholly owned subsidiary are included in the consolidated financial statements, with no special treatment accorded either the controlling or noncontrolling interest.

**FIGURE 3–3**
**Recognition of**
**Subsidiary Net Assets**

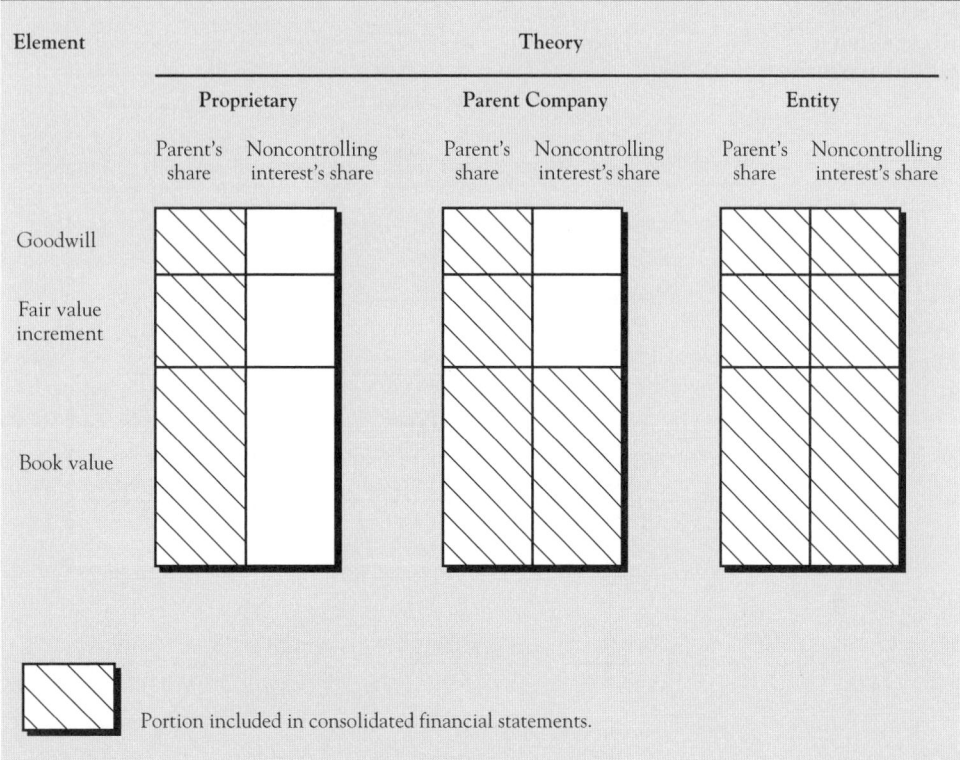

## Comparison of Alternative Theories

Figure 3–3 provides a comparison of the amounts included in a consolidated balance sheet (lined areas) for a parent and less-than-wholly owned subsidiary under the different approaches to consolidation. With the proprietary theory, only the parent's share of a subsidiary's assets and liabilities is included in the consolidated balance sheet, with the amount based on the fair values of those assets and liabilities on the date majority ownership in the subsidiary is acquired. Goodwill is included for the excess of the purchase price over the fair value of the parent's share of the subsidiary's net identifiable assets. The portion of the subsidiary's identifiable assets and liabilities claimed by the noncontrolling interest is excluded from the consolidated balance sheet, as is any implied goodwill assignable to the noncontrolling interest.

The parent company approach includes all of the subsidiary's assets and liabilities in the consolidated balance sheet, as can be seen from the lined areas in Figure 3–3. However, only the parent's share of any fair value increment and goodwill is included. As a result, subsidiary assets are included at their full fair values only when the parent purchases full ownership of the subsidiary. The noncontrolling shareholder's claim is reported in the consolidated balance sheet based on a proportionate share of the book value of the subsidiary's net assets.

All subsidiary assets and liabilities are also included in the consolidated balance sheet under the entity approach. However, the amounts included are based on the full fair values at the date of combination, and the full amount of any goodwill is included regardless of the percentage ownership held by the parent. The amount of noncontrolling interest reported in the consolidated balance sheet is based on a proportionate share of the total amount of subsidiary net assets, including goodwill.

Figure 3–4 provides a comparison of amounts included in the consolidated income statement under the different approaches when a less-than-wholly owned subsidiary is consolidated. In general, the income statement treatment is consistent with the balance sheet treatment shown in Figure 3–3 under each theory. As can be seen from the lined areas, the proprietary theory results in consolidation of just the parent's share of the revenues,

**FIGURE 3–4**
**Recognition of Subsidiary Income**

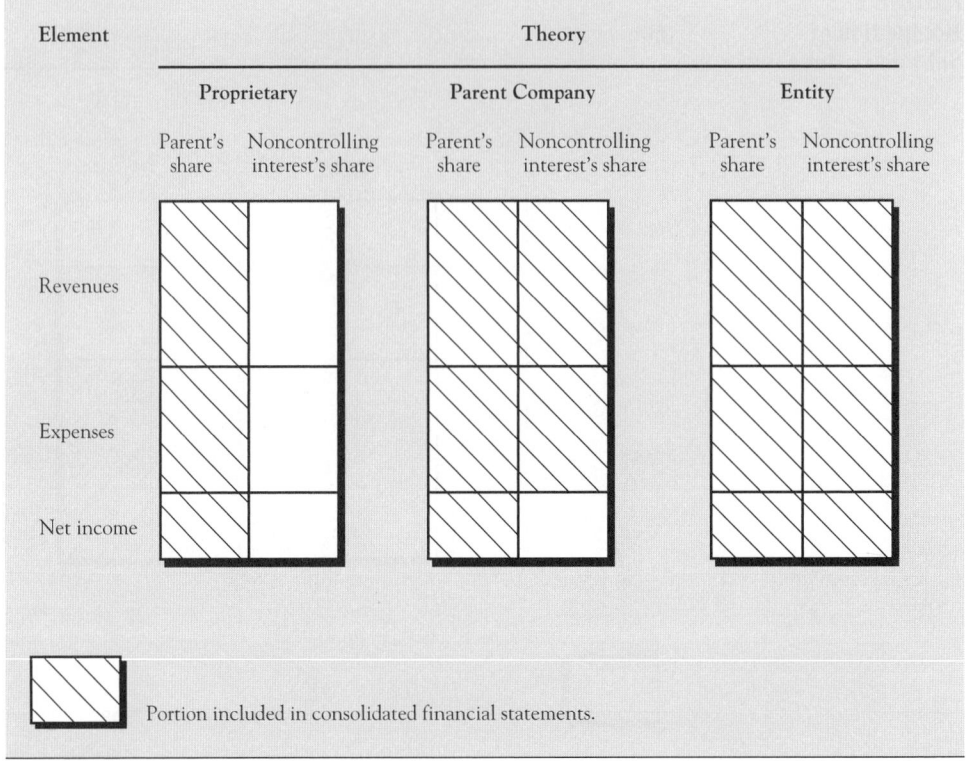

Portion included in consolidated financial statements.

expenses, and net income of the subsidiary. On the other hand, both the parent company and entity theories result in consolidation of all of the subsidiary's revenues and expenses, regardless of degree of majority ownership. Under the parent company theory, however, the noncontrolling interest's share of income is deducted to arrive at consolidated net income.

Figure 3–5 provides a numerical comparison of the different consolidation approaches. The example assumes that P Company acquires 80 percent of the stock of S Company on

**FIGURE 3–5**
**Illustration of the Effects of Different Approaches to the Preparation of Consolidated Financial Statements**

| | Theory | | |
|---|---|---|---|
| **Item** | **Proprietary** | **Parent Company** | **Entity** |
| Value of subsidiary net assets recognized at acquisition: | | | |
| Book value: | | | |
| $100,000 × .80 | $ 80,000 | | |
| $100,000 × 1.00 | | $100,000 | $100,000 |
| Fair value increment: | | | |
| $20,000 × .80 | 16,000 | 16,000 | |
| $20,000 × 1.00 | | | 20,000 |
| Total net assets | $ 96,000 | $116,000 | $120,000 |
| Amount of noncontrolling interest recognized at acquisition | | $ 20,000 | $ 24,000 |
| Amount of fair value increment amortized* | $  1,600 | $  1,600 | $  2,000 |
| Consolidated net income | $222,400[a] | $222,400[a] | $228,000[b] |
| Income assigned to noncontrolling interest | | $  6,000[c] | $  5,600[d] |

[a]$222,400 = $200,000 + ($30,000 × .80) − $1,600*
[b]$228,000 = $200,000 + $30,000 − $2,000*
[c]$6,000 = $30,000 × .20
[d]$5,600 = ($30,000 − $2,000) × .20
*Amortization of fair value increment using straight-line basis over 10 years.

January 1, 20X1, for $96,000. On that date, S Company has a total fair value of $120,000 and the 20 percent noncontrolling interest has a fair value of $24,000. S Company holds assets with a book value of $100,000 and fair value of $120,000. The $20,000 fair value increment relates entirely to S Company's buildings and equipment, with a remaining life of 10 years. Straight-line depreciation is used. For the year 20X1, P Company reports income from its own operations of $200,000, and S Company reports net income of $30,000. The example assumes the income includes no unrealized profits from intercompany sales. If unrealized intercompany profits were included in income, additional differences between the approaches could be seen.

## Current Practice

**FASB 141R** has significantly changed the preparation of consolidated financial statements subsequent to the acquisition of less-than-wholly owned subsidiaries. In the past, only the parent's share of a subsidiary's fair value increment and goodwill at the date of combination was recognized, consistent with a parent company approach. Now, under **FASB 141R,** consolidation follows largely an entity-theory approach. Accordingly, the full entity fair value increment and the full amount of goodwill are recognized.

Current practice follows the entity approach in most important aspects, but it does deviate in certain respects. In the income statement, consolidated net income refers to the income of the consolidated entity as a whole, rather than just the parent's share as in the past. Still, more emphasis continues to be placed on the parent's share of consolidated net income than on the noncontrolling interest's share. For example, only the parent's portion of consolidated net income is included in the computation of consolidated earnings per share. In addition, the only retained earnings figure reported in the consolidated balance sheet is that related to the controlling interest, with all amounts relating to the noncontrolling interest's share of equity reported in a single figure. If a strict entity approach were followed, the emphasis would be on the entire entity without emphasizing either the controlling or noncontrolling interest over the other. Nevertheless, the current approach clearly follows the entity theory with minor modifications aimed at the practical reality that consolidated financial statements are used primarily by those having a long-run interest in the parent company.

## Summary of Key Concepts

Consolidated financial statements present the financial position and results of operations of a parent and one or more subsidiaries as if they were actually a single company. As a result, a group of legally separate companies is portrayed as a single economic entity by the consolidated financial statements. All indications of intercorporate ownership and the effects of all intercompany transactions are excluded from the consolidated statements. The basic approach to the preparation of consolidated financial statements is to combine the separate financial statements of the individual consolidating companies and then to eliminate or adjust those items that would not appear, or that would appear differently, if the companies actually were one.

Current consolidation standards require that the consolidated financial statements include all companies under common control unless control is questionable. Consolidated financial statements are prepared primarily for those with a long-run interest in the parent company, especially the parent's stockholders and long-term creditors. While consolidated financial statements allow interested parties to view a group of related companies as a single economic entity, such statements have some limitations. In particular, information about the characteristics and operations of the individual companies within the consolidated entity is lost in the process of combining financial statements.

New types of business arrangements have proved troublesome for financial reporting. In particular, special types of entities, called *special-purpose entities* and *variable interest entities,* have been used to hide or transform various types of transactions, in addition to being used for many legitimate purposes such as risk sharing. Often these entities were disclosed only through vague notes to the financial statements. Reporting standards now require that the party that is the primary beneficiary of a variable interest entity consolidate that entity.

Several different theories or approaches underlie the preparation of consolidated financial statements, and the approach used can significantly affect the consolidated statements when the subsidiaries are not wholly owned. The proprietary and entity theories can be viewed as lying at opposite ends of a spectrum, with the parent company theory in the middle. Until recently, practice largely followed the parent company approach. Now, following issuance of **FASB 141R** and **FASB 160,** practice conforms most closely with the entity approach, but with somewhat more emphasis on the controlling interest than on the noncontrolling interest.

## Key Terms

affiliates, *96*
combined financial
    statements, *108*
consolidated financial
    statements, *96*
direct control, *99*
effective control, *100*
eliminating entries, *105*

entity theory, *112*
indirect control, *99*
minority interest, *106*
noncontrolling interest, *106*
parent, *96*
parent company theory, *112*
primary beneficiary, *111*
proprietary theory, *112*

pro rata consolidation, *112*
related companies, *96*
separate legal entities, *96*
special-purpose entities
    (SPEs), *108*
subsidiaries, *96*
variable interest entity
    (VIE), *110*

## Appendix **3A**    Consolidation of Variable Interest Entities

The standards for determining whether a party with an interest in a variable interest entity (VIE) should consolidate the VIE were discussed earlier in the chapter. Once a party has determined that it must consolidate a VIE, the consolidation procedures are similar to those used when consolidating a subsidiary. As an illustration, assume that Ignition Petroleum Company joins with Mammoth Financial Corporation to create a special corporation, Exploration Equipment Company, that would lease equipment to Ignition and other companies. Ignition purchases 10 percent of Exploration's stock for $1,000,000, and Mammoth purchases the other 90 percent for $9,000,000. Profits are to be split equally between the two owners, but Ignition agrees to absorb the first $500,000 of annual losses. Immediately after incorporation, Exploration borrows $120,000,000 from a syndicate of banks, and Ignition guarantees the loan. Exploration then purchases plant, equipment, and supplies for its own use and equipment for lease to others. The balance sheets of Ignition and Exploration appear as follows just prior to the start of Exploration's operations:

| Item | Ignition | Exploration |
|---|---|---|
| Cash and Receivables | $100,000,000 | $ 23,500,000 |
| Inventory and Supplies | 50,000,000 | 200,000 |
| Equipment Held for Lease | | 105,000,000 |
| Investment in Exploration Equipment Co. | 1,000,000 | |
| Plant and Equipment (net) | 180,000,000 | 1,350,000 |
| Total Assets | $331,000,000 | $130,050,000 |
| | | |
| Accounts Payable | $    900,000 | $    50,000 |
| Bank Loans Payable | 30,000,000 | 120,000,000 |
| Common Stock Issued and Outstanding | 200,000,000 | 10,000,000 |
| Retained Earnings | 100,100,000 | |
| Total Liabilities and Equity | $331,000,000 | $130,050,000 |

Both Ignition and Mammoth hold variable interests in Exploration. Ignition's variable interests include both its common stock and its guarantees. Ignition is the primary beneficiary of Exploration because it shares equally in the profits with Mammoth but must absorb a larger share of the expected losses than Mammoth, both through its profit and loss sharing agreement with Mammoth and its loan guarantee. Accordingly, Ignition must consolidate Exploration.

Ignition's consolidated balance sheet that includes Exploration appears as in Figure 3–6. The balances in Exploration's asset and liability accounts are added to the balances of Ignition's like accounts. Ignition's investment in Exploration is eliminated against the common stock of Exploration,

**FIGURE 3–6**
Balance Sheet
Consolidating a
Variable Interest
Entity

| IGNITION PETROLEUM COMPANY | | |
|---|---|---|
| **Consolidated Balance Sheet** | | |
| **Assets** | | |
| Cash and Receivables | | $123,500,000 |
| Inventory and Supplies | | 50,200,000 |
| Equipment Held for Lease | | 105,000,000 |
| Plant and Equipment (net) | | 181,350,000 |
| Total Assets | | $460,050,000 |
| **Liabilities** | | |
| Accounts Payable | $ 950,000 | |
| Bank Loans Payable | 150,000,000 | |
| Total Liabilities | | $150,950,000 |
| **Stockholders' Equity** | | |
| Common Stock | $200,000,000 | |
| Retained Earnings | 100,100,000 | |
| Noncontrolling Interest | 9,000,000 | |
| Total Stockholders' Equity | | 309,100,000 |
| Total Liabilities and Stockholders' Equity | | $460,050,000 |

and Exploration's remaining common stock is labeled as noncontrolling interest and reported within the equity section of the consolidated balance sheet.

## Questions

**Q3-1** What is the basic idea underlying the preparation of consolidated financial statements?

**Q3-2** How might consolidated statements help an investor assess the desirability of purchasing shares of the parent company?

**Q3-3** Are consolidated financial statements likely to be more useful to the owners of the parent company or to the noncontrolling owners of the subsidiaries? Why?

**Q3-4** What is meant by "parent company"? When is a company considered to be a parent?

**Q3-5** Are consolidated financial statements likely to be more useful to the creditors of the parent company or the creditors of the subsidiaries? Why?

**Q3-6** Why is ownership of a majority of the common stock of another company considered important in consolidation?

**Q3-7** What major criteria must be met before a company is consolidated?

**Q3-8** When is consolidation considered inappropriate even though the parent holds a majority of the voting common shares of another company?

**Q3-9** How has reliance on legal control as a consolidation criterion led to off-balance sheet financing?

**Q3-10** What types of entities are referred to as *special-purpose entities,* and how have they generally been used?

**Q3-11** How does a variable interest entity typically differ from a traditional corporate business entity?

**Q3-12** What characteristics are normally examined in determining whether a company is a primary beneficiary of a variable interest entity?

**Q3-13** What is meant by "indirect control"? Give an illustration.

**Q3-14** What means other than majority ownership might be used to gain control over a company? Can consolidation occur if control is gained by other means?

**Q3-15** Why must intercompany receivables and payables be eliminated when consolidated financial statements are prepared?

**Q3-16** Why are subsidiary shares not reported as stock outstanding in the consolidated balance sheet?

**Q3-17** What must be done if the fiscal periods of the parent and its subsidiary are not the same?

**Q3-18** What is the noncontrolling interest in a subsidiary?

**Q3-19** What is the difference between consolidated and combined financial statements?

**Q3-20\*** How does the proprietary theory of consolidation differ from current accounting practice?

**Q3-21\*** How does the entity theory of consolidation differ from current accounting practice?

**Q3-22\*** Which theory of consolidation is closest to current accounting practice?

## Cases

**C3-1**

*Understanding*

### Computation of Total Asset Values

A reader of Gigantic Company's consolidated financial statements received from another source copies of the financial statements of the individual companies included in the consolidation. He is confused by the fact that the total assets in the consolidated balance sheet differ rather substantially from the sum of the asset totals reported by the individual companies.

#### Required

Will this relationship always be true? What factors may cause this difference to occur?

**C3-2**

*Understanding*

### Accounting Entity [AICPA Adapted]

The concept of the accounting entity often is considered to be the most fundamental of accounting concepts, one that pervades all of accounting.

#### Required

*a.* (1) What is an accounting entity? Explain.

   (2) Explain why the accounting entity concept is so fundamental that it pervades all of accounting.

*b.* For each of the following, indicate whether the entity concept is applicable; discuss and give illustrations.

   (1) A unit created by or under law.

   (2) The product-line segment of an enterprise.

   (3) A combination of legal units.

   (4) All the activities of an owner or a group of owners.

   (5) The economy of the United States.

**C3-3**

*Research*
*FARS*

### Recognition of Fair Value and Goodwill

March Corporation acquired 65 percent of Ember Corporation's ownership on January 2, 2008, for $708,500. At that time, Ember's net assets had a book value of $810,000 and a fair value of $960,000. The difference between the book value and fair value of Ember's net assets all related to depreciable assets. The total fair value of Ember's shares not acquired by March Corporation was $381,500.

FASB Statement No. 141R, which was not in effect at the time of Ember's acquisition, requires recognition of 100 percent of the fair value of the assets and liabilities of an acquired company and 100 percent of the implied goodwill, even in less-than-100-percent acquisitions. Because March's top managers are considering additional acquisitions, they are concerned with how to account for those acquisitions under the FASB's current standards.

#### Required

Analyze how March's consolidated financial statements would have been different if March had acquired Ember after FASB Statement No. 141R became effective. Prepare a memo to Mr. R. U. Cleer, CFO of March Corporation, explaining how the amounts appearing in the consolidated financial statements relating to Ember would differ between the prior reporting standards and those established by FASB No. 141R. Include in your memo citations to and quotations from the appropriate accounting literature.

**C3-4**

*Research*
*FARS*

### Joint Venture Investment

Dell Computer Corp. and CIT Group, Inc., established Dell Financial Services L.P. (DFS) as a joint venture to provide financing services for Dell customers. Dell owns 70 percent of the equity of DFS and CIT owns 30 percent. In the initial agreement, losses were allocated entirely to CIT, although CIT would recoup any losses before any future income was allocated. At the time the joint venture was formed, both Dell and CIT indicated that they had no plans to consolidate DFS. The joint venture agreement was extended and modified in 2004.

\*Indicates that the item relates to "Additional Considerations."

**Required**

a. How could both Dell and CIT avoid consolidating DFS?

b. What treatment did Dell accord DFS in the latest financial statements available in which the joint venture is reported? What might be the reasoning behind this treatment?

c. Does Dell currently employ off-balance sheet financing? Explain.

### C3-5 Need for Consolidation [AICPA Adapted]

*Analysis*

Sharp Company will acquire 90 percent of Moore Company in a business combination. The total consideration has been agreed on, but the nature of Sharp's payment has not. It is expected that on the date the business combination is to be consummated, the fair value will exceed the book value of Moore's assets minus liabilities. Sharp desires to prepare consolidated financial statements that will include Moore's financial statements.

**Required**

a. Explain how the amount of goodwill is determined.

b. From a theoretical standpoint, why should consolidated financial statements be prepared?

c. From a theoretical standpoint, what is usually the first necessary condition to be met before consolidated financial statements can be prepared?

### C3-6 What Company Is That?

*Analysis*

Many well-known products and names come from companies that may be less well known or may be known for other reasons. In some cases, an obscure parent company may have well-known subsidiaries, and often familiar but diverse products may be produced under common ownership.

**Required**

a. Viacom is not necessarily a common name easily identified because it operates through numerous subsidiaries, but its brand names are seen every day. What are some of the well-known brand names from Viacom's subsidiaries? What changes occurred in its organizational structure in 2006? Who is Sumner Redstone?

b. ConAgra Foods, Inc., is one of the world's largest food processors and distributors. Although it produces many products with familiar names, the company's name generally is not well known. What are some of ConAgra's brand names?

c. What type of company is Yum! Brands, Inc.? What are some of its well-known brands? What is the origin of the company, and what was its previous name?

### C3-7 Subsidiaries and Core Businesses

*Analysis*

During previous merger booms, a number of companies acquired many subsidiaries that often were in businesses unrelated to the acquiring company's central operations. In many cases, the acquiring company's management was unable to manage effectively the many diverse types of operations found in the numerous subsidiaries. More recently, many of these subsidiaries have been sold or, in a few cases, liquidated so the parent companies could concentrate on their core businesses.

**Required**

a. In 1986, General Electric acquired nearly all of the common stock of the large brokerage firm Kidder, Peabody Inc. Unfortunately, the newly acquired subsidiary's performance was very poor. What ultimately happened to this subsidiary of General Electric?

b. What major business has Sears, Roebuck been in for many decades? What other businesses was it in during the 1980s and early 1990s? What were some of its best-known subsidiaries during that time? Does Sears still own those subsidiaries? What additional acquisitions have occurred?

c. PepsiCo is best known as a soft-drink company. What well-known subsidiaries did PepsiCo own during the mid-1990s? Does PepsiCo still own them?

d. When a parent company and its subsidiaries are in businesses that are considerably different in nature, such as retailing and financial services, how meaningful are their consolidated financial statements in your opinion? Explain. How might financial reporting be improved in such situations?

### C3-8 International Consolidation Issues

The International Accounting Standards Board (IASB) is charged with developing a set of high-quality standards and encouraging their adoption globally. Standards promulgated by the IASB are called International Financial Reporting Standards (IFRS). The European Union (EU) requires statements prepared using IFRS for all companies that list on the EU stock exchanges. While the United States does not yet accept IFRS, the SEC has indicated that it is working toward allowing international companies that list on U.S. exchanges to use IFRS for financial reporting in the United States.

*Research*        The differences between U.S. GAAP and IFRS are described in many different publications. For example, PricewaterhouseCoopers has a publication available for download on its Web site (http://www.pwc.com/extweb/pwcpublications.nsf/docid/74d6c09e0a4ee610802569a1003354c8) entitled "Similarities and Differences—A Comparison of IFRS and U.S. GAAP" that provides a topic-based comparison. Based on the information in this publication or others, answer the following questions about the preparation of consolidated financial statements.

#### Required

a. Under U.S. GAAP, consolidated financial statements must be prepared for the parent and all majority-owned subsidiaries, with an exception only if the parent is unable to exercise control over a subsidiary. What is required by IFRS?

b. Under U.S. GAAP, negative goodwill (a bargain purchase) arising in a business combination results in the recognition of a gain in the income statement in the period of the combination (as discussed in Chapter 1). What is the treatment of negative goodwill required by the IASB?

c. U.S. GAAP requires a two-step process to evaluate goodwill for potential impairment (as discussed in Chapter 1). What is required by IFRS with respect to goodwill impairment?

### C3-9 Off-Balance Sheet Financing and VIEs

*Understanding*  A variable interest entity (VIE) is a structure frequently used for off-balance sheet financing. VIEs have become quite numerous in recent years and have been the subject of some controversy.

#### Required

a. Briefly explain what is meant by off-balance sheet financing.

b. What are three techniques used to keep debt off the balance sheet?

c. What are some legitimate uses of VIEs?

d. How can VIEs be used to manage earnings to meet financial reporting goals? How does this relate to the importance of following the intent of the guidelines for consolidations?

### C3-10 Alternative Accounting Methods

*Analysis*  The use of proportionate or pro rata consolidation generally has not been acceptable in the United States. Normally, a significant investment in the common stock of another company must either be fully consolidated or reported using the equity method.

#### Required

a. What method does Amerada Hess use to account for its investments in affiliates and joint ventures?

b. What method does EnCana Corporation use to account for its investments in jointly controlled ventures? In what country is EnCana based? Does this make a difference?

c. Should the method used to account for investments in affiliates be different depending on whether the affiliate is a corporation or an unincorporated partnership? Explain.

### C3-11 Consolidation Differences among Major Companies

*Research*  A variety of organizational structures are used by major companies, and different approaches to consolidation are sometimes found. Two large and familiar U.S. corporations are Union Pacific and Exxon Mobil.

#### Required

a. Many large companies have tens or even hundreds of subsidiaries. List the significant subsidiaries of Union Pacific Corporation.

*b.* Exxon Mobil Corporation is a major energy company. Does Exxon Mobil consolidate all of its majority-owned subsidiaries? Explain. Does Exxon Mobil consolidate any entities in which it does not hold majority ownership? Explain. What methods does Exxon Mobil use to account for investments in the common stock of companies in which it holds less than majority ownership?

---

**Exercises**     **E3-1**   **Multiple-Choice Questions on Consolidation Overview [AICPA Adapted]**
Select the correct answer for each of the following questions.

1. When a parent–subsidiary relationship exists, consolidated financial statements are prepared in recognition of the accounting concept of:

   *a.* Reliability.
   *b.* Materiality.
   *c.* Legal entity.
   *d.* Economic entity.

2. Consolidated financial statements are typically prepared when one company has a controlling interest in another unless:

   *a.* The subsidiary is a finance company.
   *b.* The fiscal year-ends of the two companies are more than three months apart.
   *c.* Circumstances prevent the exercise of control.
   *d.* The two companies are in unrelated industries, such as real estate and manufacturing.

3. Penn Inc., a manufacturing company, owns 75 percent of the common stock of Sell Inc., an investment company. Sell owns 60 percent of the common stock of Vane Inc., an insurance company. In Penn's consolidated statements, should consolidation accounting or equity-method accounting be used for Sell and Vane?

   *a.* Consolidation used for Sell and equity method used for Vane.
   *b.* Consolidation used for both Sell and Vane.
   *c.* Equity method used for Sell and consolidation used for Vane.
   *d.* Equity method used for both Sell and Vane.

4. Shep Company has a receivable from its parent, Pep Company. Should this receivable be separately reported on Shep's balance sheet and in Pep's consolidated balance sheet?

|  | Shep's Balance Sheet | Pep's Consolidated Balance Sheet |
|---|---|---|
| *a.* | Yes | No |
| *b.* | Yes | Yes |
| *c.* | No | No |
| *d.* | No | Yes |

5. Which of the following is the best theoretical justification for consolidated financial statements?

   *a.* In form the companies are one entity; in substance they are separate.
   *b.* In form the companies are separate; in substance they are one entity.
   *c.* In form and substance the companies are one entity.
   *d.* In form and substance the companies are separate.

**E3-2**   **Multiple-Choice Questions on Variable Interest Entities**
Select the correct answer for each of the following questions.

1. Special-purpose entities generally:

   *a.* Have a much larger portion of assets financed by equity shareholders than do companies such as General Motors.
   *b.* Have relatively large amounts of preferred stock and convertible securities outstanding.

    *c.* Have a much smaller portion of their assets financed by equity shareholders than do companies such as General Motors.

    *d.* Pay out a relatively high percentage of their earnings as dividends to facilitate the sale of additional shares.

2. Variable interest entities may be established as:

    *a.* Corporations.

    *b.* Trusts.

    *c.* Partnerships.

    *d.* All of the above.

3. An enterprise that will absorb a majority of a variable interest entity's expected losses is called the:

    *a.* Primary beneficiary.

    *b.* Qualified owner.

    *c.* Major facilitator.

    *d.* Critical management director.

4. In determining whether or not a variable interest entity is to be consolidated, the FASB focused on:

    *a.* Legal control.

    *b.* Share of profits and obligation to absorb losses.

    *c.* Frequency of intercompany transfers.

    *d.* Proportionate size of the two entities.

5. A qualified special-purpose entity:

    *a.* Must always be consolidated.

    *b.* Meets the criteria to be exempted from consolidation.

    *c.* Permits consolidation of only those activities of the special-purpose entity that are related to the activities of the transferor.

    *d.* Permits proportionate consolidation based on the proportion of ownership held by the transferor.

**E3-3** **Multiple-Choice Questions on Consolidated Balances [AICPA Adapted]**

Select the correct answer for each of the following questions.

1. Par Corporation owns 60 percent of Sub Corporation's outstanding capital stock. On May 1, 20X8, Par advanced Sub $70,000 in cash, which was still outstanding at December 31, 20X8. What portion of this advance should be eliminated in the preparation of the December 31, 20X8, consolidated balance sheet?

    *a.* $70,000.

    *b.* $42,000.

    *c.* $28,000.

    *d.* $0.

Items 2 and 3 are based on the following:

On January 2, 20X8, Pare Company acquired 75 percent of Kidd Company's outstanding common stock. Selected balance sheet data at December 31, 20X8, are as follows:

| | Pare Company | Kidd Company |
|---|---|---|
| Total Assets | $420,000 | $180,000 |
| Liabilities | $120,000 | $ 60,000 |
| Common Stock | 100,000 | 50,000 |
| Retained Earnings | 200,000 | 70,000 |
| | $420,000 | $180,000 |

2. In Pare's December 31, 20X8, consolidated balance sheet, what amount should be reported as minority interest in net assets?

   *a.* $0.
   *b.* $30,000.
   *c.* $45,000.
   *d.* $105,000.

3. In its consolidated balance sheet at December 31, 20X8, what amount should Pare report as common stock outstanding?

   *a.* $50,000.
   *b.* $100,000.
   *c.* $137,500.
   *d.* $150,000.

4. At the time Hyman Corporation became a subsidiary of Duane Corporation, Hyman switched depreciation of its plant assets from the straight-line method to the sum-of-the-years'-digits method used by Duane. As to Hyman, this change was a:

   *a.* Change in an accounting estimate.
   *b.* Correction of an error.
   *c.* Change of accounting principle.
   *d.* Change in the reporting entity.

5. Consolidated statements are proper for Neely Inc., Randle Inc., and Walker Inc., if:

   *a.* Neely owns 80 percent of the outstanding common stock of Randle and 40 percent of Walker; Randle owns 30 percent of Walker.
   *b.* Neely owns 100 percent of the outstanding common stock of Randle and 90 percent of Walker; Neely bought the Walker stock one month before the foreign country in which Walker is based imposed restrictions preventing Walker from remitting profits to Neely.
   *c.* Neely owns 100 percent of the outstanding common stock of Randle and Walker; Walker is in legal reorganization.
   *d.* Neely owns 80 percent of the outstanding common stock of Randle and 40 percent of Walker; Reeves Inc. owns 55 percent of Walker.

**E3-4**  **Multiple-Choice Questions on Consolidation Overview [AICPA Adapted]**

Select the correct answer for each of the following questions.

1. Consolidated financial statements are typically prepared when one company has:

   *a.* Accounted for its investment in another company by the equity method.
   *b.* Accounted for its investment in another company by the cost method.
   *c.* Significant influence over the operating and financial policies of another company.
   *d.* The controlling financial interest in another company.

2. Aaron Inc. owns 80 percent of the outstanding stock of Belle Inc. Compare the consolidated net earnings of Aaron and Belle (X) and Aaron's net earnings if it does not consolidate Belle (Y).

   *a.* X is greater than Y.
   *b.* X is equal to Y.
   *c.* X is less than Y.
   *d.* Cannot be determined.

3. On October 1, X Company acquired for cash all of Y Company's outstanding common stock. Both companies have a December 31 year-end and have been in business for many years. Consolidated net income for the year ended December 31 should include net income of:

   *a.* X Company for three months and Y Company for three months.
   *b.* X Company for 12 months and Y Company for 3 months.
   *c.* X Company for 12 months and Y Company for 12 months.
   *d.* X Company for 12 months, but no income from Y Company until Y Company distributes a dividend.

4. Ownership of 51 percent of the outstanding voting stock of a company would usually result in:

   a. The use of the cost method.
   b. The use of the lower-of-cost-or-market method.
   c. The use of the equity method.
   d. A consolidation.

### E3-5   Balance Sheet Consolidation

On January 1, 20X3, Guild Corporation reported total assets of $470,000, liabilities of $270,000, and stockholders' equity of $200,000. At that date, Bristol Corporation reported total assets of $190,000, liabilities of $135,000, and stockholders' equity of $55,000. Following lengthy negotiations, Guild paid Bristol's existing shareholders $55,000 in cash for 100 percent of the voting common shares of Bristol.

#### Required

Immediately after Guild purchased the Bristol shares:

a. What amount of total assets did Guild report in its balance sheet?
b. What amount of total assets was reported in the consolidated balance sheet?
c. What amount of total liabilities was reported in the consolidated balance sheet?
d. What amount of stockholders' equity was reported in the consolidated balance sheet?

### E3-6   Balance Sheet Consolidation with Intercompany Transfer

Potter Company acquired 100 percent of the voting common shares of Stately Corporation by issuing bonds with a par value and fair value of $135,000 to Stately's existing shareholders. Immediately prior to the acquisition, Potter reported total assets of $510,000, liabilities of $320,000, and stockholders' equity of $190,000. At that date, Stately reported total assets of $350,000, liabilities of $215,000, and stockholders' equity of $135,000. Included in Stately's liabilities was an account payable to Potter in the amount of $15,000, which Potter included in its accounts receivable.

#### Required

Immediately after Potter acquired Stately's shares:

a. What amount of total assets did Potter report in its balance sheet?
b. What amount of total assets was reported in the consolidated balance sheet?
c. What amount of total liabilities was reported in the consolidated balance sheet?
d. What amount of stockholders' equity was reported in the consolidated balance sheet?

### E3-7   Intercompany Transfers

Route Manufacturing acquired 80 percent of the stock of Hampton Mines Inc. in 20X3. In preparing the consolidated financial statements at the end of 20X5, Route's controller discovered that Route had purchased $75,000 of raw materials from Hampton Mines during the year and that the parent company had not paid for the last purchase of $12,000. All the inventory purchased was still on hand at year-end. Hampton Mines had spent $50,000 in producing the items sold to Route.

#### Required

a. What effect, if any, will failure to eliminate or adjust for these items have on total current assets reported in the consolidated balance sheet on December 31, 20X5?
b. What effect, if any, will failure to eliminate or adjust for these items have on the consolidated entity's net working capital?
c. What effect, if any, will failure to eliminate or adjust for these items have on the computation of income when the inventory is sold in the following period?

### E3-8   Subsidiary Acquired for Cash

Fineline Pencil Company acquired 100 percent of Smudge Eraser Corporation's stock on January 2, 20X3, for $150,000 cash. Summarized balance sheet data for the companies on December 31, 20X2, are as follows:

| | Fineline Pencil Company | | Smudge Eraser Corporation | |
|---|---|---|---|---|
| | **Book Value** | **Fair Value** | **Book Value** | **Fair Value** |
| Cash | $200,000 | $200,000 | $ 50,000 | $ 50,000 |
| Other Assets | 400,000 | 650,000 | 120,000 | 180,000 |
| Total Debits | $600,000 | | $170,000 | |
| Current Liabilities | $100,000 | 100,000 | $ 80,000 | 80,000 |
| Common Stock | 300,000 | | 50,000 | |
| Retained Earnings | 200,000 | | 40,000 | |
| Total Credits | $600,000 | | $170,000 | |

*Required*

Prepare a consolidated balance sheet immediately following the acquisition.

### E3-9  Subsidiary Acquired with Bonds

Byte Computer Corporation acquired 100 percent of Nofail Software Company's stock on January 2, 20X3, by issuing bonds with a par value of $140,000 and a fair value of $150,000 in exchange for the shares. Summarized balance sheet data presented for the companies just before the acquisition are as follows:

| | Byte Computer Corporation | | Nofail Software Company | |
|---|---|---|---|---|
| | **Book Value** | **Fair Value** | **Book Value** | **Fair Value** |
| Cash | $200,000 | $200,000 | $ 50,000 | $ 50,000 |
| Other Assets | 400,000 | 650,000 | 120,000 | 180,000 |
| Total Debits | $600,000 | | $170,000 | |
| Current Liabilities | $100,000 | 100,000 | $ 80,000 | 80,000 |
| Common Stock | 300,000 | | 50,000 | |
| Retained Earnings | 200,000 | | 40,000 | |
| Total Credits | $600,000 | | $170,000 | |

*Required*

Prepare a consolidated balance sheet immediately following the acquisition.

### E3-10  Subsidiary Acquired by Issuing Preferred Stock

Byte Computer Corporation acquired 100 percent of Nofail Software Company's common stock on January 2, 20X3, by issuing preferred stock with a par value of $6 per share and a market value of $10 per share. A total of 15,000 shares of preferred stock was issued. Balance sheet data for the two companies immediately before the business combination are presented in E3-9.

*Required*

Prepare a consolidated balance sheet for the companies immediately after Byte obtains ownership of Nofail by issuing the preferred stock.

### E3-11  Reporting for a Variable Interest Entity

Gamble Company convinced Conservative Corporation that the two companies should establish Simpletown Corporation to build a new gambling casino in Simpletown Corner. Although chances for the casino's success were relatively low, a local bank loaned $140,000,000 to the new corporation, which built the casino at a cost of $130,000,000. Conservative purchased 100 percent of the initial capital stock offering for $5,600,000, and Gamble agreed to supply 100 percent of the management and guarantee the bank loan. Gamble also guaranteed a 20 percent return to Conservative on its investment for the first 10 years. Gamble will receive all profits in excess of the 20 percent return to Conservative. Immediately after the casino's construction, Gamble reported the following amounts:

| | |
|---|---:|
| Cash | $ 3,000,000 |
| Buildings and Equipment | 240,600,000 |
| Accumulated Depreciation | 10,100,000 |
| Accounts Payable | 5,000,000 |
| Bonds Payable | 20,300,000 |
| Common Stock | 103,000,000 |
| Retained Earnings | 105,200,000 |

The only disclosure that Gamble currently provides in its financial reports about its relationships to Conservative and Simpletown is a brief footnote indicating that a contingent liability exists on its guarantee of Simpletown Corporation's debt.

### Required

Prepare a balance sheet in good form for Gamble immediately following the casino's construction.

### E3-12   Consolidation of a Variable Interest Entity

Teal Corporation is the primary beneficiary of a variable interest entity with total assets of $500,000, liabilities of $470,000, and owners' equity of $30,000. Because Teal owns 25 percent of the VIE's voting stock, it reported a $7,500 investment in the VIE in its balance sheet. Teal reported total assets of $190,000 (including its investment in the VIE), liabilities of $80,000, common stock of $15,000, and retained earnings of $95,000 in its balance sheet.

### Required

Prepare a condensed balance sheet in good form for Teal, taking into consideration that it is the primary beneficiary of the variable interest entity.

### E3-13   Computation of Subsidiary Net Income

Frazer Corporation owns 70 percent of Messer Company's stock. In the 20X9 consolidated income statement, the noncontrolling interest was assigned $18,000 of income.

### Required

What amount of net income did Messer Company report for 20X9?

### E3-14   Incomplete Consolidation

Belchfire Motors' accountant was called away after completing only half of the consolidated statements at the end of 20X4. The data left behind included the following:

| Item | Belchfire Motors | Premium Body Shop | Consolidated |
|---|---:|---:|---:|
| Cash | $ 40,000 | $ 20,000 | $   60,000 |
| Accounts Receivable | 180,000 | 30,000 | 200,000 |
| Inventory | 220,000 | 50,000 | 270,000 |
| Buildings and Equipment (net) | 300,000 | 290,000 | 590,000 |
| Investment in Premium Body Shop | 150,000 | | |
| Total Debits | $890,000 | $390,000 | $1,120,000 |
| | | | |
| Accounts Payable | $ 30,000 | $ 40,000 | |
| Bonds Payable | 400,000 | 200,000 | |
| Common Stock | 200,000 | 100,000 | |
| Retained Earnings | 260,000 | 50,000 | |
| Total Credits | $890,000 | $390,000 | |

### Required

a. Belchfire Motors acquired shares of Premium Body Shop at underlying book value on January 1, 20X1. What portion of the ownership of Premium Body Shop does Belchfire apparently hold?

b. Compute the consolidated totals for each of the remaining balance sheet items.

**E3-15**    **Noncontrolling Interest**

Sanderson Corporation acquired 70 percent of Kline Corporation's common stock on January 1, 20X7, for $294,000 in cash. At the acquisition date, the book values and fair values of Kline's assets and liabilities were equal, and the fair value of the noncontrolling interest was equal to 30 percent of the total book value of Kline. The stockholders' equity accounts of the two companies at the date of purchase are:

|  | Sanderson Corporation | Kline Corporation |
|---|---|---|
| Common Stock ($10 par value) | $ 400,000 | $ 180,000 |
| Additional Paid-In Capital | 222,000 | 65,000 |
| Retained Earnings | 358,000 | 175,000 |
| Total Stockholders' Equity | $ 980,000 | $ 420,000 |

### Required

a. What amount will be assigned to the noncontrolling interest on January 1, 20X7, in the consolidated balance sheet?

b. Prepare the stockholders' equity section of Sanderson and Kline's consolidated balance sheet as of January 1, 20X7.

c. Sanderson acquired ownership of Kline to ensure a constant supply of electronic switches, which it purchases regularly from Kline. Why might Sanderson not feel compelled to purchase all of Kline's shares?

**E3-16**    **Computation of Consolidated Net Income**

Ambrose Corporation owns 75 percent of Kroop Company's common stock, acquired at underlying book value on January 1, 20X4. At the acquisition date, the book values and fair values of Kroop's assets and liabilities were equal, and the fair value of the noncontrolling interest was equal to 25 percent of the total book value of Kroop. The income statements for Ambrose and Kroop for 20X4 include the following amounts:

|  | Ambrose Corporation | Kroop Company |
|---|---|---|
| Sales | $528,000 | $150,000 |
| Dividend Income | 9,000 | |
| Total Income | $537,000 | $150,000 |
| Less: Cost of Goods Sold | $380,000 | $ 87,000 |
| Depreciation Expense | 32,000 | 20,000 |
| Other Expenses | 66,000 | 23,000 |
| Total Expenses | $478,000 | $130,000 |
| Net Income | $ 59,000 | $ 20,000 |

Ambrose uses the cost method in accounting for its ownership of Kroop. Kroop paid dividends of $12,000 in 20X4.

### Required

a. What amount should Ambrose report in its income statement as income from its investment in Kroop using equity-method accounting?

b. What amount of income should be assigned to noncontrolling interest in the consolidated income statement for 20X4?

c. What amount should Ambrose report as consolidated net income for 20X4?

d. Why should Ambrose not report consolidated net income of $79,000 ($59,000 + $20,000) for 20X4?

### E3-17 Computation of Subsidiary Balances

Tall Corporation acquired 75 percent of Light Corporation's voting common stock on January 1, 20X2, at underlying book value. At the acquisition date, the book values and fair values of Light's assets and liabilities were equal, and the fair value of the noncontrolling interest was equal to 25 percent of the total book value of Light. Noncontrolling interest was assigned income of $8,000 in Tall's consolidated income statement for 20X2 and a balance of $65,500 in Tall's consolidated balance sheet at December 31, 20X2. Light reported retained earnings of $70,000 and additional paid-in capital of $40,000 on January 1, 20X2. Light did not pay dividends or issue stock in 20X2.

### Required

a. Compute the amount of net income reported by Light for 20X2.

b. Prepare the stockholders' equity section of Light's balance sheet at December 31, 20X2.

### E3-18 Subsidiary Acquired at Net Book Value

Banner Corporation acquired all of Dwyer Company's common stock at underlying book value. At the acquisition date, the book values and fair values of all of Dwyer's assets and liabilities were equal. Banner uses the equity method in accounting for its investment. Balance sheet information provided by the companies at December 31, 20X8, is as follows:

|  | Banner Corporation | Dwyer Company |
| --- | --- | --- |
| Cash | $ 40,000 | $ 20,000 |
| Accounts Receivable | 120,000 | 70,000 |
| Inventory | 180,000 | 90,000 |
| Fixed Assets (net) | 350,000 | 240,000 |
| Investment in Dwyer Company Stock | 170,000 | |
| Total Debits | $860,000 | $420,000 |
| Accounts Payable | $ 65,000 | $ 30,000 |
| Notes Payable | 350,000 | 220,000 |
| Common Stock | 150,000 | 90,000 |
| Retained Earnings | 295,000 | 80,000 |
| Total Credits | $860,000 | $420,000 |

### Required

Prepare a consolidated balance sheet for Banner at December 31, 20X8.

### E3-19* Applying Alternative Accounting Theories

Noway Manufacturing owns 75 percent of Positive Piston Corporation's stock. During 20X9, Noway and Positive Piston reported sales of $400,000 and $200,000 and expenses of $280,000 and $160,000, respectively.

### Required

Compute the amount of total revenue, total expenses, and net income to be reported in the 20X9 consolidated income statement under the following alternative approaches:

a. Proprietary theory.

b. Parent company theory.

c. Entity theory.

d. Current accounting practice.

### E3-20* Measurement of Goodwill

Rank Corporation acquired 60 percent of Fresh Company's stock on December 31, 20X4. In preparing the consolidated financial statements at December 31, 20X4, goodwill of $240,000 was reported. The goodwill is attributable to Rank's purchase of Fresh shares, and the parent company approach was used in determining the amount of goodwill reported.

#### Required

Determine the amount of goodwill to be reported under each of the following consolidation alternatives:

a. Proprietary theory.

b. Entity theory.

c. Current accounting practice.

### E3-21* Valuation of Assets under Alternative Accounting Theories

Garwood Corporation acquired 75 percent of Zorn Company's voting common stock on January 1, 20X4. At the time of acquisition, Zorn reported buildings and equipment at book value of $240,000; however, an appraisal indicated a fair value of $290,000.

#### Required

If consolidated statements are prepared, determine the amount at which buildings and equipment will be reported using the following consolidation alternatives:

a. Entity theory.

b. Parent company theory.

c. Proprietary theory.

d. Current accounting practice.

### E3-22* Reported Income under Alternative Accounting Theories

Placer Corporation acquired 80 percent of Billings Company's voting common stock on January 1, 20X4. Placer and Billings reported total revenue of $410,000 and $200,000 and total expenses of $320,000 and $150,000, respectively, for the year ended December 31, 20X4.

#### Required

Determine the amount of total revenue, total expense, and net income to be reported in the consolidated income statement for 20X4 under the following consolidation alternatives:

a. Entity theory.

b. Parent company theory.

c. Proprietary theory.

d. Current accounting practice.

### E3-23* Acquisition of Majority Ownership

Lang Company reports net assets with a book value of $120,000 and fair value of $170,000. The overall fair value of Lang is determined to be $200,000 when Pace Corporation acquires 75 percent ownership for $150,000. Pace reports net assets with a book value of $520,000 and a fair value of $640,000 at that time, excluding its investment in Lang.

#### Required

For each of the following, compute the amounts that would be reported immediately after the combination under current accounting practice:

a. Net identifiable assets.

b. Goodwill.

c. Noncontrolling interest.

## Problems

**P3-24   Multiple-Choice Questions on Consolidated and Combined Financial Statements [AICPA Adapted]**

Select the correct answer for each of the following questions.

1. What is the theoretically preferred method of presenting a noncontrolling interest in a consolidated balance sheet?

   a. As a separate item within the liability section.

   b. As a deduction from (contra to) goodwill from consolidation, if any.

   c. By means of notes or footnotes to the balance sheet.

   d. As a separate item within the stockholders' equity section.

2. Presenting consolidated financial statements this year when statements of individual companies were presented last year is:

   a. The correction of an error.

   b. An accounting change that should be reported prospectively.

   c. An accounting change that should be reported by restating the financial statements of all prior periods presented.

   d. Not an accounting change.

3. A subsidiary, acquired for cash in a business combination, owned equipment with a market value in excess of book value as of the date of combination. A consolidated balance sheet prepared immediately after the acquisition would treat this excess as:

   a. Goodwill.

   b. Plant and equipment.

   c. Retained earnings.

   d. Deferred credit.

4. Mr. Cord owns four corporations. Combined financial statements are being prepared for these corporations, which have intercompany loans of $200,000 and intercompany profits of $500,000. What amount of these intercompany loans and profits should be included in the combined financial statements?

|  | Intercompany | |
|---|---|---|
|  | **Loans** | **Profits** |
| a. | $200,000 | $0 |
| b. | $200,000 | $500,000 |
| c. | $0 | $0 |
| d. | $0 | $500,000 |

**P3-25   Intercompany Sales**

Knight Corporation owns 100 percent of Spahn Company's voting shares. During 20X6, Spahn purchased inventory items for $20,000 and sold them to Knight for $50,000. Knight continues to hold the items in inventory on December 31, 20X6. Sales for the two companies during 20X6 totaled $300,000, and total cost of goods sold was $200,000.

### Required

a. If no adjustment is made to eliminate the intercorporate sale when a consolidated income statement is prepared for 20X6, by what amount will consolidated net income be overstated or understated?

b. Prepare a consolidated income statement for 20X6 without any adjustment for the intercorporate sale.

c. Prepare a consolidated income statement for 20X6 adjusted for the intercorporate sale.

d. What items in the consolidated income statements are different in requirements *b* and *c?*

**P3-26    Intercompany Inventory Transfer**

River Products Corporation purchases all its inventory from its wholly owned subsidiary, Clayborn Corporation. In 20X2, Clayborn produced inventory at a cost of $10,000 and sold it to River Products for $25,000. The parent held all the items in inventory on January 1, 20X3. During 20X3, River Products sold all the units for $55,000.

*Required*

Assuming the companies had no other transactions during either year, indicate the appropriate amounts to be reported in the consolidated financial statements for the following items:

*a.* Inventory on January 1, 20X3.

*b.* Cost of goods sold for 20X2.

*c.* Cost of goods sold for 20X3.

*d.* Sales for 20X2.

*e.* Sales for 20X3.

**P3-27    Determining Net Income of Parent Company**

Tally Corporation and its subsidiary reported consolidated net income of $164,300 for 20X2. Tally owns 60 percent of the common shares of its subsidiary, acquired at book value. Noncontrolling interest was assigned income of $15,200 in the consolidated income statement for 20X2.

*Required*

Determine the amount of separate operating income reported by Tally for 20X2.

**P3-28    Reported Balances**

Roof Corporation acquired 80 percent of the stock of Gable Company by issuing shares of its common stock with a fair value of $192,000. At that time, the fair value of the noncontrolling interest was estimated to be $48,000 and the fair values of its identifiable assets and liabilities were $310,000 and $95,000, respectively. Gable's assets and liabilities had book values of $220,000 and $95,000, respectively.

*Required*

Compute the following amounts to be reported immediately after the combination:

*a.* Investment in Gable reported by Roof.

*b.* Increase in identifiable assets of the combined entity.

*c.* Increase in total liabilities of the combined entity.

*d.* Goodwill for the combined entity.

*e.* Noncontrolling interest reported in the consolidated balance sheet.

**P3-29    Acquisition Price**

Darwin Company holds assets with a fair value of $120,000 and a book value of $90,000 and liabilities with a book value and fair value of $25,000.

*Required*

Compute the following amounts if Brad Corporation acquires 60 percent ownership of Darwin:

*a.* What amount did Brad pay for the shares if no goodwill and no gain on a bargain purchase are reported?

*b.* What amount did Brad pay for the shares if the fair value of the noncontrolling interest at acquisition is $54,000 and goodwill of $40,000 is reported?

*c.* What balance will be assigned to the noncontrolling interest in the consolidated balance sheet if Brad pays $73,200 to acquire its ownership and goodwill of $27,000 is reported?

**P3-30    Consolidation of a Variable Interest Entity**

On December 28, 20X3, Stern Corporation and Ram Company established S&R Partnership, with cash contributions of $10,000 and $40,000, respectively. The partnership's purpose is to purchase from Stern accounts receivable that have an average collection period of 80 days and hold them to collection. The partnership borrows cash from Midtown Bank and purchases the receivables without recourse but at an amount equal to the expected percent to be collected, less a financing fee of 3 percent of the gross receivables. Stern and Ram hold 20 percent and 80 percent of the ownership of the partnership, respectively, and Stern guarantees both the bank loan made to the partnership and a 15 percent annual return on the investment made by Ram. Stern receives any income in excess of the 15 percent return guaranteed to Ram. The partnership agreement provides Stern total control over the partnership's activities. On December 31, 20X3, Stern sold $8,000,000 of accounts receivable to the partnership. The partnership immediately borrowed $7,500,000 from the bank and paid Stern $7,360,000. Prior to the sale, Stern had established a $400,000 allowance for uncollectibles on the receivables sold to the partnership. The balance sheets of Stern and S&R immediately after the sale of receivables to the partnership contained the following:

|  | Stern Corporation | S&R Partnership |
|---|---|---|
| Cash | $7,960,000 | $ 190,000 |
| Accounts Receivable | 4,200,000 | 8,000,000 |
| Allowance for Uncollectible Accounts | (210,000) | (400,000) |
| Other Assets | 5,400,000 | |
| Prepaid Finance Charges | 240,000 | |
| Investment in S&R Partnership | 10,000 | |
| Accounts Payable | 950,000 | |
| Deferred Revenue | | 240,000 |
| Bank Notes Payable | | 7,500,000 |
| Bonds Payable | 9,800,000 | |
| Common Stock | 700,000 | |
| Retained Earnings | 6,150,000 | |
| Capital, Stern Corporation | | 10,000 |
| Capital, Ram Company | | 40,000 |

### Required

Assuming that Stern is S&R's primary beneficiary, prepare a consolidated balance sheet in good form for Stern at January 1, 20X4.

**P3-31** ### Reporting for Variable Interest Entities

Purified Oil Company and Midwest Pipeline Corporation established Venture Company to conduct oil exploration activities in North America to reduce their dependence on imported crude oil. Midwest Pipeline purchased all 20,000 shares of the newly created company for $10 each. Purified Oil agreed to purchase all of Venture's output at market price, guarantee up to $5,000,000 of debt for Venture, and absorb all losses if the company proved unsuccessful. Purified and Midwest agreed to share equally the profits up to $80,000 per year and to allocate 70 percent of those in excess of $80,000 to Purified and 30 percent to Midwest.

Venture immediately borrowed $3,000,000 from Second National Bank and purchased land, drilling equipment, and supplies to start its operations. Following these asset purchases, Venture and Purified Oil reported the following balances:

|  | Venture Company | Purified Oil Company |
|---|---|---|
| Cash | $ 230,000 | $ 410,000 |
| Drilling Supplies | 420,000 | |
| Accounts Receivable | | 640,000 |
| Equipment (net) | 1,800,000 | 6,700,000 |
| Land | 900,000 | 4,200,000 |
| Accounts Payable | 150,000 | 440,000 |
| Bank Loans Payable | 3,000,000 | 8,800,000 |
| Common Stock | 200,000 | 560,000 |
| Retained Earnings | | 2,150,000 |

The only disclosure that Purified Oil currently provides in its financial statements with respect to its relationship with Midwest Pipeline and Venture is a brief note indicating that a contingent liability exists on the guarantee of Venture Company debt.

### Required

Assuming that Venture is considered to be a variable interest entity and Purified Oil is the primary beneficiary, prepare a balance sheet in good form for Purified Oil.

**P3-32** ## Consolidated Income Statement Data

Master Products acquired 100 percent ownership of LoCal Bakeries on January 1, 20X3, when the fair value of LoCal's depreciable assets was $50,000 greater than book value. The depreciable assets had an eight-year economic life at the date of the acquisition.

| | Master Products | | LoCal Bakeries | |
|---|---|---|---|---|
| Sales | | $300,000 | | $200,000 |
| Cost of Goods Sold | $200,000 | | $130,000 | |
| Depreciation Expense | 40,000 | (240,000) | 30,000 | (160,000) |
| Income before Income from Subsidiary | | $ 60,000 | | |
| Net Income | | | | $ 40,000 |

During 20X3, Master Products purchased a special imported yeast for $35,000 and resold it to LoCal for $50,000. LoCal did not resell any of the yeast before year-end.

### Required

Determine the amounts to be reported for each of the following items in the consolidated income statement for 20X3:

*a.* Sales.

*b.* Investment income from LoCal Bakeries.

*c.* Cost of goods sold.

*d.* Depreciation expense.

**P3-33** ## Incomplete Company and Consolidated Data

Beryl Corporation acquired 100 percent of Stargel Enterprises' common stock on December 31, 20X4. At that date, the book values and fair values of Stargel's identifiable assets and liabilities were identical. Balance sheet data for the individual companies and the consolidated entity on January 1, 20X5, are as follows:

| | Beryl Corporation | Stargel Enterprises | Consolidated Entity |
|---|---|---|---|
| Cash | $ 60,000 | $ 35,000 | $ 95,000 |
| Accounts Receivable | 90,000 | 50,000 | 130,000 |
| Inventory | 120,000 | 90,000 | ? |
| Land | 70,000 | 50,000 | 105,000 |
| Buildings and Equipment | 340,000 | 220,000 | 560,000 |
| Less: Accumulated Depreciation | (180,000) | (90,000) | (270,000) |
| Investment in Stargel Enterprises Stock | 110,000 | | |
| Goodwill | | | 30,000 |
| Total Assets | $610,000 | $355,000 | $ ? |
| Accounts Payable | $ 75,000 | $ 55,000 | $ ? |
| Wages Payable | 30,000 | 20,000 | 50,000 |
| Notes Payable | 250,000 | 200,000 | 450,000 |
| Common Stock | ? | 30,000 | 100,000 |
| Retained Earnings | 155,000 | 50,000 | 140,000 |
| Total Liabilities and Stockholders' Equity | $610,000 | $355,000 | $ ? |

### Required

a. Assuming there were no inventory transactions between the companies, what balance for inventory should be reported in the consolidated balance sheet?

b. What amount did Beryl pay to acquire Stargel? Was this amount equal to, greater than, or less than underlying book value? How do you know?

c. Beryl sold land it had purchased 12 years earlier for $10,000 to Stargel immediately after it acquired Stargel. At what price did Beryl sell the land to Stargel? How do you know?

d. What balance will be reported as accounts payable in the consolidated balance sheet?

e. What is the par value of Beryl's common stock outstanding at January 1, 20X5?

**P3-34**  ## Consolidation Following Intercompany Sale of Equipment

Potash Company acquired 100 percent of Bortz Corporation's common stock at underlying book value on December 31, 20X4, which was equal to the fair value of Bortz as a whole. Potash uses the equity method in accounting for its investment in Bortz. On December 31, 20X6, Potash sold equipment with a book value of $85,000 to Bortz for $110,000. Bortz made immediate payment of $93,000 and will pay the remainder on March 15, 20X7. Balance sheet data on January 1, 20X7, are as follows:

|  | Potash Company | Bortz Corporation |
|---|---|---|
| Cash | $ 50,000 | $ 35,000 |
| Accounts Receivable | 110,000 | 60,000 |
| Merchandise Inventory | 95,000 | 75,000 |
| Equipment (net) | 230,000 | 105,000 |
| Investment in Bortz Corporation Stock | 140,000 | |
| Total Assets | $625,000 | $275,000 |
| Accounts Payable | $ 82,000 | $ 28,000 |
| Notes Payable | 200,000 | 107,000 |
| Common Stock | 180,000 | 50,000 |
| Additional Paid-In Capital | | 25,000 |
| Retained Earnings | 163,000 | 65,000 |
| Total Liabilities and Stockholders' Equity | $625,000 | $275,000 |

### Required

Prepare a consolidated balance sheet for Potash as of January 1, 20X7.

**P3-35**  ## Parent Company and Consolidated Amounts

Quoton Corporation acquired 80 percent of Tempro Company's common stock on December 31, 20X5, at underlying book value. The book values and fair values of Tempro's assets and liabilities were equal, and the fair value of the noncontrolling interest was equal to 20 percent of the total book value of Tempro. Tempro provided the following trial balance data at December 31, 20X5:

|  | Debit | Credit |
|---|---|---|
| Cash | $ 28,000 | |
| Accounts Receivable | 65,000 | |
| Inventory | 90,000 | |
| Buildings and Equipment (net) | 210,000 | |
| Cost of Goods Sold | 105,000 | |
| Depreciation Expense | 24,000 | |
| Other Operating Expenses | 31,000 | |
| Dividends Declared | 15,000 | |
| Accounts Payable | | $ 33,000 |
| Notes Payable | | 120,000 |
| Common Stock | | 90,000 |
| Retained Earnings | | 130,000 |
| Sales | | 195,000 |
| Total | $568,000 | $568,000 |

### Required

a. How much did Quoton pay to purchase its shares of Tempro?

b. If consolidated financial statements are prepared at December 31, 20X5, what amount will be assigned to the noncontrolling interest in the consolidated balance sheet?

c. If Quoton reported income of $143,000 from its separate operations for 20X5, what amount of consolidated net income will be reported for 20X5?

d. If Quoton had purchased its ownership of Tempro on January 1, 20X5, at underlying book value and Quoton reported income of $143,000 from its separate operations for 20X5, what amount of consolidated net income would be reported for 20X5?

**P3-36** **Parent Company and Consolidated Balances**

Exacto Company reported net assets of $260,000 on January 1, 20X5, and reported the following net income and dividends for the years indicated:

| Year | Net Income | Dividends |
|------|-----------|-----------|
| 20X5 | $35,000 | $12,000 |
| 20X6 | 45,000 | 20,000 |
| 20X7 | 30,000 | 14,000 |

True Corporation acquired 75 percent of Exacto's common stock on January 1, 20X5. At that date, the fair value of Exacto's net assets was equal to the fair value of Exacto as a whole. The excess of the fair value of Exacto's net assets over book value was due to an increase in the value of equipment with a remaining economic life of 10 years at January 1, 20X5. True uses the equity method in accounting for its ownership in Exacto and reported a balance of $259,800 in its investment account on December 31, 20X7.

### Required

a. What amount in excess of book value did True pay when it purchased Exacto's shares?

b. What amount will be added to buildings and equipment when the consolidated balance sheet is prepared at December 31, 20X7?

c. What amount will be added to accumulated depreciation when the consolidated balance sheet is prepared at December 31, 20X7?

d. What amount will be assigned to the noncontrolling shareholders in the consolidated balance sheet prepared at December 31, 20X7?

**P3-37** **Indirect Ownership**

Purple Corporation recently attempted to expand by acquiring ownership in Green Company. The following ownership structure was reported on December 31, 20X9:

| Investor | Investee | Percentage of Ownership Held |
|----------|----------|------------------------------|
| Purple Corporation | Green Company | 70 |
| Green Company | Orange Corporation | 10 |
| Orange Corporation | Blue Company | 60 |
| Green Company | Yellow Company | 40 |

The following income from operations (excluding investment income) and dividend payments were reported by the companies during 20X9:

| Company | Operating Income | Dividends Paid |
|---------|------------------|----------------|
| Purple Corporation | $ 90,000 | $60,000 |
| Green Company | 20,000 | 10,000 |
| Orange Corporation | 40,000 | 30,000 |
| Blue Company | 100,000 | 80,000 |
| Yellow Company | 60,000 | 40,000 |

**Required**

Compute the amount reported as consolidated net income for 20X9.

## P3-38 Comprehensive Problem: Consolidated Financial Statements

Bishop Enterprises acquired 100 percent of Mangle Manufacturing Company's common shares on January 1, 20X7, for $1,250,000, a price that was $55,000 in excess of the book value of the shares acquired. The excess of the $1,220,000 fair value of the net assets held by Mangle over book value was related to equipment with a five-year remaining life at the date of acquisition.

Balance sheets for the two companies as of December 31, 20X7, were as follows:

|  | Bishop Enterprises | Mangle Manufacturing |
|---|---|---|
| Cash | $ 71,000 | $ 33,000 |
| Receivables (net) | 431,000 | 122,000 |
| Inventory | 909,000 | 370,000 |
| Investment in Mangle Stock (at cost) | 1,250,000 | — |
| Land | 510,000 | 100,000 |
| Buildings (net) | 1,303,000 | 250,000 |
| Equipment (net) | 1,528,000 | 475,000 |
| Total Assets | $6,002,000 | $1,350,000 |
| Current Payables | $ 227,000 | $ 95,000 |
| Bonds Payable | 500,000 | — |
| Common Stock | 1,000,000 | 500,000 |
| Additional Paid-In Capital | 3,550,000 | 400,000 |
| Retained Earnings | 725,000 | 355,000 |
| Total Liabilities and Equity | $6,002,000 | $1,350,000 |

For the year 20X7, the separate income statements of Bishop and Mangle included, among other items, the following:

|  | Bishop Enterprises | Mangle Manufacturing |
|---|---|---|
| Sales Revenue | $8,325,000 | $2,980,000 |
| Cost of Goods Sold | 5,150,000 | 2,010,000 |
| Depreciation Expense | 302,000 | 85,000 |

The only intercompany transaction during 20X7 was the sale of inventory at year-end from Bishop to Mangle. Bishop originally purchased the goods for $34,000 and sold them to Mangle for $45,000 on account. Mangle still had all of the goods in its inventory at year-end but had not yet paid for them.

**Required**

Indicate the amount at which Bishop and its subsidiary would report each of the following items in the 20X7 consolidated financial statements:

a. Cash.

b. Receivables (net).

c. Inventory.

d. Investment in Mangle Stock.

e. Equipment (net).

f. Goodwill.

  g. Current Payables.

  h. Common Stock (par).

  i. Sales Revenue.

  j. Cost of Goods Sold.

  k. Depreciation Expense.

**P3-39\***  **Balance Sheet Amounts under Alternative Accounting Theories**

Parsons Corporation purchased 75 percent ownership of Tumble Company on December 31, 20X7, for $210,000. Summarized balance sheet amounts for the companies on December 31, 20X7, prior to the purchase, were as follows:

| | Parsons Corporation | Tumble Company Book Value | Tumble Company Fair Value |
|---|---|---|---|
| Cash and Inventory | $300,000 | $ 80,000 | $ 80,000 |
| Buildings and Equipment (net) | 400,000 | 120,000 | 180,000 |
| Total Assets | $700,000 | $200,000 | $260,000 |
| Common Stock | $380,000 | $ 90,000 | |
| Retained Earnings | 320,000 | 110,000 | |
| Total Liabilities and Stockholders' Equity | $700,000 | $200,000 | |

## *Required*

If consolidated financial statements are prepared, determine the amounts that would be reported as cash and inventory, buildings and equipment (net), and goodwill using the following consolidation alternatives:

  a. Proprietary theory.

  b. Parent company theory.

  c. Entity theory.

  d. Current accounting practice.

# Consolidation of Wholly Owned Subsidiaries

Consolidated and unconsolidated financial statements are prepared using the same generally accepted accounting principles. The unique aspect of consolidated statements is that they bring together the operating results and financial positions of two or more separate legal entities into a single set of statements for the economic entity as a whole. To accomplish this, the consolidation process includes procedures that eliminate all effects of intercorporate ownership and intercompany transactions.

This chapter and the next provide a thorough introduction to the process of preparing consolidated financial statements. Then, using these chapters as a foundation and following a building-block approach, Chapters 6 through 10 deal with intercorporate transfers and other consolidation issues.

## CONSOLIDATION PROCEDURES

Consolidation procedures, including the use of a consolidation workpaper, are established to bring together the accounts of a parent and its subsidiaries so they appear as a single entity. The starting point for preparing consolidated financial statements is the books of the separate consolidating companies. Because the consolidated entity has no books, all amounts in the consolidated financial statements originate on the books of the parent or a subsidiary or in the consolidation workpaper.

The term *subsidiary* has been defined as "an entity . . . in which another entity, known as its *parent,* holds a controlling financial interest."[1] A parent company may hold all or less than all of a corporate subsidiary's common stock, but at least majority ownership is normally required for the presentation of consolidated financial statements. Most, but not all, corporate subsidiaries are wholly owned by their parents.

Because most subsidiaries are wholly owned, this chapter begins the in-depth examination of consolidation procedures by focusing on the procedures for wholly owned subsidiaries. The chapter begins with basic consolidation procedures applied to the preparation of a consolidated balance sheet immediately following the establishment of a parent–subsidiary relationship, either through creation or acquisition of the subsidiary. Then, it introduces the use of a simple consolidation workpaper for the balance sheet only. The chapter then moves to the preparation of a full set of consolidated financial statements in subsequent periods and the use of a three-part workpaper designed to facilitate the preparation of a consolidated income statement, retained earnings statement, and balance sheet. Chapter 5 extends the discussion by dealing with the preparation of consolidated financial statements for less-than-wholly owned subsidiaries.

---

[1] *Financial Accounting Standards Board Statement No. 160,* "Noncontrolling Interests in Consolidated Financial Statements, an amendment of ARB No. 51," December 2007, para. B1.

**FIGURE 4–1**
**Format for
Consolidation
Workpaper**

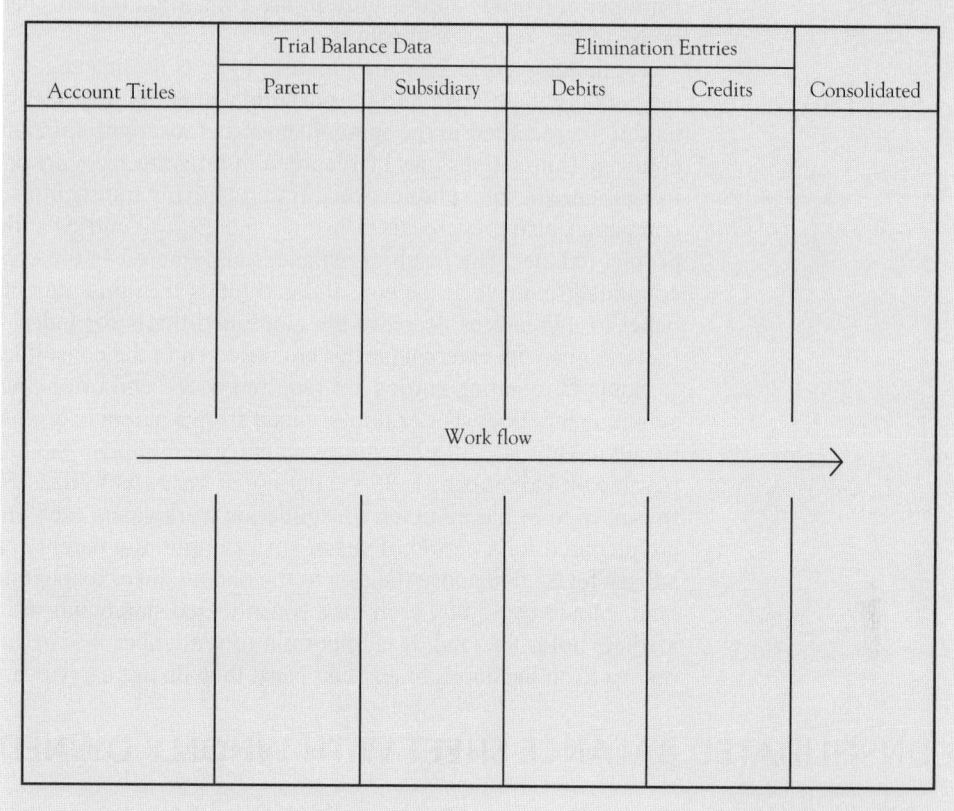

| Account Titles | Trial Balance Data | | Elimination Entries | | Consolidated |
|---|---|---|---|---|---|
| | Parent | Subsidiary | Debits | Credits | |
| | | | | | |

Work flow →

# CONSOLIDATION WORKPAPERS

The **consolidation workpaper** provides a mechanism for efficiently combining the accounts of the separate companies involved in the consolidation and for adjusting the combined balances to the amounts that would be reported if all consolidating companies were actually a single company. Keep in mind that no set of books exists for the consolidated entity. The parent and its subsidiaries, as separate legal and accounting entities, maintain their own books. When consolidated financial statements are prepared, the account balances are taken from the separate books of the parent and each subsidiary and placed in the consolidation workpaper. The consolidated statements are prepared, after adjustments and eliminations, from the amounts in the consolidation workpaper.

## Workpaper Format

The basic form of a consolidation workpaper is shown in Figure 4–1. The titles of the accounts of the consolidating companies are listed in the first column of the workpaper. The account balances from the books or trial balances of the individual companies are listed in the next set of columns, with a separate column for each company included in the consolidation. Entries are made in the columns labeled Elimination Entries to adjust or eliminate balances so that the resulting amounts are those that would appear in the financial statements if all the consolidating companies actually formed a single company. The balances in the last column are obtained by summing all amounts algebraically across the workpaper by account. These are the balances that appear in the consolidated financial statements.

## Nature of Eliminating Entries

**Eliminating entries** are used in the consolidation workpaper to adjust the totals of the individual account balances of the separate consolidating companies to reflect the amounts that would appear if all the legally separate companies were actually a single company.

Eliminating entries appear only in the consolidating workpapers and do not affect the books of the separate companies.

For the most part, companies that are to be consolidated record their transactions during the period without regard to the consolidated entity. Transactions with related companies tend to be recorded in the same manner as those with unrelated parties, although intercompany transactions may be recorded in separate accounts or other records may be kept to facilitate the later elimination of intercompany transactions. Each of the consolidating companies also prepares its adjusting and closing entries at the end of the period in the normal manner. The resulting balances are entered in the consolidation workpaper and combined to arrive at the consolidated totals. Eliminating entries are used in the workpaper to increase or decrease the combined totals for individual accounts so that only transactions with external parties are reflected in the consolidated amounts.

Some eliminating entries are required at the end of one period but not at the end of subsequent periods. For example, a loan from a parent to a subsidiary in December 20X1, repaid in February 20X2, requires an entry to eliminate the intercompany receivable and payable on December 31, 20X1, but not at the end of 20X2. Some other eliminating entries need to be placed in the consolidation workpapers each time consolidated statements are prepared for a period of years. For example, if a parent company sells land to a subsidiary for $5,000 above the cost to the parent, a workpaper entry is needed to reduce the land amount by $5,000 each time consolidated statements are prepared for as long as an affiliate holds the land. It is important to remember that because eliminating entries are not made on the books of any company, they do not carry over from period to period.

## CONSOLIDATED BALANCE SHEET WITH WHOLLY OWNED SUBSIDIARY

The simplest consolidation setting occurs when the financial statements of related companies are consolidated immediately after a parent–subsidiary relationship is established through a business combination or creation of a new subsidiary. A series of examples follows to illustrate the preparation of a consolidated balance sheet. Consolidation procedures are the same whether a subsidiary is created or acquired. The case of an acquired subsidiary is used to illustrate the consolidation procedures in the examples that follow. In each example, Peerless Products Corporation purchases all or part of the common stock of Special Foods Inc. on January 1, 20X1, and immediately prepares a consolidated balance sheet. The separate balance sheets of the two companies immediately before the combination appear in Figure 4–2.

**FIGURE 4–2**
**Balance Sheets of Peerless Products and Special Foods, January 1, 20X1, Immediately before Combination**

|  | Peerless Products | Special Foods |
|---|---|---|
| Assets |  |  |
| Cash | $ 350,000 | $ 50,000 |
| Accounts Receivable | 75,000 | 50,000 |
| Inventory | 100,000 | 60,000 |
| Land | 175,000 | 40,000 |
| Buildings and Equipment | 800,000 | 600,000 |
| Accumulated Depreciation | (400,000) | (300,000) |
| Total Assets | $1,100,000 | $500,000 |
|  |  |  |
| Liabilities and Stockholders' Equity |  |  |
| Accounts Payable | $ 100,000 | $100,000 |
| Bonds Payable | 200,000 | 100,000 |
| Common Stock | 500,000 | 200,000 |
| Retained Earnings | 300,000 | 100,000 |
| Total Liabilities and Equity | $1,100,000 | $500,000 |

In the discussion that follows, all journal entries and workpaper eliminating entries are numbered sequentially throughout the chapter. Eliminating entries appearing in the workpapers are also discussed in the text of the chapter. To avoid confusing the eliminating entries with journal entries that appear on the separate books of the parent or subsidiary, all workpaper eliminating entries appearing in the text are shaded and designated by an entry number preceded by an E.

## 100 Percent Ownership Acquired at Book Value

In the first example, Peerless acquires all of Special Foods' outstanding common stock for $300,000, an amount equal to the fair value of Special Foods as a whole. On the date of combination, the fair values of Special Foods' individual assets and liabilities are equal to their book values shown in Figure 4–2. Because Peerless acquires all of Special Foods' common stock and because Special Foods has only the one class of stock outstanding, the total book value of the shares acquired equals the total stockholders' equity of Special Foods ($200,000 + $100,000). The $300,000 of consideration exchanged is equal to the book value of the shares acquired. This ownership situation can be characterized as follows:

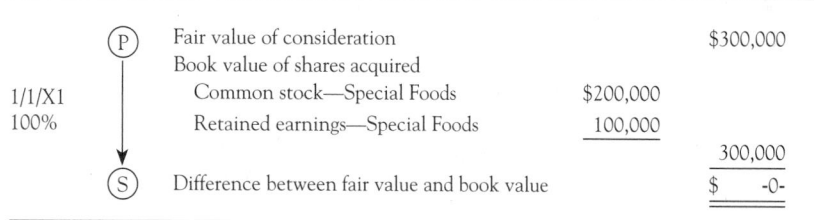

Peerless records the stock acquisition on its books with the following entry on the date of combination:

| | January 1, 20X1 | | |
|---|---|---|---|
| (1) | Investment in Special Foods Stock | 300,000 | |
| | Cash | | 300,000 |
| | Record purchase of Special Foods stock. | | |

The separate financial statements of Peerless and Special Foods immediately after the combination appear in Figure 4–3. Special Foods' balance sheet in Figure 4–3 is the same as in Figure 4–2, but Peerless's balance sheet has changed to reflect the $300,000 reduction in cash and the recording of the investment in Special Foods stock for the same amount. Note that the $300,000 of cash was paid to the former stockholders of Special Foods and not to the company itself. Accordingly, that cash is no longer in the consolidated entity.

### Consolidation Workpaper

The workpaper for the preparation of a consolidated balance sheet immediately following the acquisition is presented in Figure 4–4. The first two columns of the workpaper in Figure 4–4 are the account balances taken from the books of Peerless and Special Foods, as shown in Figure 4–3. The balances of like accounts are placed side by side so that they may be added together. If more than two companies were to be consolidated, a separate column would be included in the workpaper for each additional subsidiary.

The accounts are placed in the workpaper so that those having debit balances are in the upper half of the workpaper and those having credit balances are in the lower half. Total debit items must equal total credit items for each of the companies and for the consolidated totals.

**FIGURE 4–3**
**Balance Sheets of Peerless Products and Special Foods, January 1, 20X1, Immediately after Combination**

| | Peerless Products | Special Foods |
|---|---|---|
| **Assets** | | |
| Cash | $ 50,000 | $ 50,000 |
| Accounts Receivable | 75,000 | 50,000 |
| Inventory | 100,000 | 60,000 |
| Land | 175,000 | 40,000 |
| Buildings and Equipment | 800,000 | 600,000 |
| Accumulated Depreciation | (400,000) | (300,000) |
| Investment in Special Foods Stock | 300,000 | |
| Total Assets | $1,100,000 | $500,000 |
| **Liabilities and Stockholders' Equity** | | |
| Accounts Payable | $ 100,000 | $100,000 |
| Bonds Payable | 200,000 | 100,000 |
| Common Stock | 500,000 | 200,000 |
| Retained Earnings | 300,000 | 100,000 |
| Total Liabilities and Equity | $1,100,000 | $500,000 |

**FIGURE 4–4**   **Workpaper for Consolidated Balance Sheet, January 1, 20X1, Date of Combination; 100 Percent Acquisition at Book Value**

| Item | Peerless Products | Special Foods | Eliminations Debit | Eliminations Credit | Consolidated |
|---|---|---|---|---|---|
| Cash | 50,000 | 50,000 | | | 100,000 |
| Accounts Receivable | 75,000 | 50,000 | | | 125,000 |
| Inventory | 100,000 | 60,000 | | | 160,000 |
| Land | 175,000 | 40,000 | | | 215,000 |
| Buildings and Equipment | 800,000 | 600,000 | | | 1,400,000 |
| Investment in Special Foods Stock | 300,000 | | | (2) 300,000 | |
| Total Debits | 1,500,000 | 800,000 | | | 2,000,000 |
| Accumulated Depreciation | 400,000 | 300,000 | | | 700,000 |
| Accounts Payable | 100,000 | 100,000 | | | 200,000 |
| Bonds Payable | 200,000 | 100,000 | | | 300,000 |
| Common Stock | 500,000 | 200,000 | (2) 200,000 | | 500,000 |
| Retained Earnings | 300,000 | 100,000 | (2) 100,000 | | 300,000 |
| Total Credits | 1,500,000 | 800,000 | 300,000 | 300,000 | 2,000,000 |

Elimination entry:
   (2)  Eliminate investment balance and stockholders' equity of Special Foods.
   (*Note:* Elimination entries are keyed to those in the text; all entries are numbered sequentially throughout the chapter.)

The two columns labeled Eliminations in Figure 4–4 are used to adjust the amounts reported by the individual companies to the amounts appropriate for the consolidated statement. All eliminations made in the workpapers are made in double-entry form; the debit amounts of each entry must equal the credit amounts. All parts of the same eliminating entry are keyed with the same number or other symbol so that whole entries can be identified. When the workpaper is completed, total debits entered in the Debit Eliminations column must equal total credits entered in the Credit Eliminations column. After the appropriate eliminating entries have been entered in the Eliminations columns, summing algebraically across the individual accounts provides the consolidated totals.

### Investment Elimination Entry

The only eliminating entry in the workpaper in Figure 4–4 is one needed to eliminate the Investment in Special Foods Stock account and the subsidiary's stockholders' equity accounts. This is accomplished through entry E(2) in the workpaper:

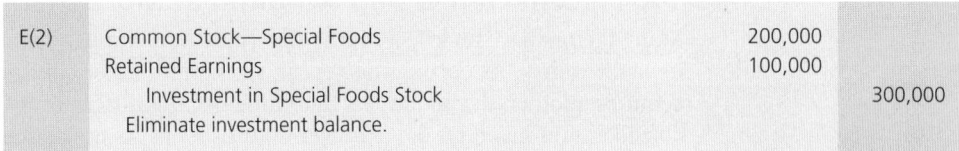

| E(2) | Common Stock—Special Foods | 200,000 | |
| | Retained Earnings | 100,000 | |
| | Investment in Special Foods Stock | | 300,000 |
| | Eliminate investment balance. | | |

Remember that this entry is made in the consolidation workpaper, not on the books of either the parent or the subsidiary, and is presented here in general journal form only for instructional purposes.

The investment account must be eliminated because, from a single entity viewpoint, a company cannot hold an investment in itself. The subsidiary's stock and the related stockholders' equity accounts must be eliminated because the subsidiary's stock is held entirely within the consolidated entity and none represents claims by outsiders.

From a somewhat different viewpoint, the investment account on the parent's books can be thought of as a single account representing the parent's investment in the net assets of the subsidiary, a so-called *one-line consolidation.* In a full consolidation, the subsidiary's individual assets and liabilities are combined with those of the parent. Including both the net assets of the subsidiary, as represented by the balance in the investment account, and the subsidiary's individual assets and liabilities would double count the same set of assets. Therefore, the investment account is eliminated and not carried to the consolidated balance sheet.

In this example, Peerless's purchase price for the stock acquired is equal to the fair value of Special Foods as a whole. This reflects the normal situation where the acquisition price paid by the parent is equal to the fair value of its proportionate share of the subsidiary. In addition, this example assumes that the subsidiary's fair value is equal to its book value, a generally unrealistic assumption. Given the assumption, however, the balance of Peerless's investment account is equal to Special Foods' stockholders' equity, and entry E(2) fully eliminates the investment account against Special Foods' stockholders' equity accounts, with no difference between the accounts.

### The Consolidated Balance Sheet

The consolidated balance sheet presented in Figure 4–5 is prepared directly from the last column of the consolidation workpaper in Figure 4–4. The total debit and credit balances shown on the balance sheet differ from the debit and credit totals given in the workpaper because contra asset accounts are included with the credits in the workpaper but are

**FIGURE 4–5** Consolidated Balance Sheet, January 1, 20X1, Date of Combination; 100 Percent Acquisition at Book Value

**PEERLESS PRODUCTS CORPORATION AND SUBSIDIARY**
**Consolidated Balance Sheet**
**January 1, 20X1**

| Assets | | | Liabilities | |
|---|---|---|---|---|
| Cash | | $ 100,000 | Accounts Payable | $ 200,000 |
| Accounts Receivable | | 125,000 | Bonds Payable | 300,000 |
| Inventory | | 160,000 | | |
| Land | | 215,000 | Stockholders' Equity | |
| Buildings and Equipment | $1,400,000 | | Common Stock | 500,000 |
| Accumulated Depreciation | (700,000) | 700,000 | Retained Earnings | 300,000 |
| Total Assets | | $1,300,000 | Total Liabilities and Equity | $1,300,000 |

offset against the related assets in the consolidated balance sheet. Because no operations occurred between the date of combination and the preparation of the consolidated balance sheet, the stockholders' equity section of the consolidated balance sheet is identical to that of Peerless in Figure 4–2.

## 100 Percent Ownership Acquired at More than Book Value

Many factors have an effect on the fair value of a company and its stock price, including its asset values, its earning power, and general market conditions. When one company acquires another, the acquiree's fair value usually differs from its book value, and so the consideration given by the acquirer does as well. As discussed in Chapter 1, this difference between the fair value of the consideration given and the book value of the acquiree's net identifiable assets is referred to as a *differential.*

The process of preparing a consolidated balance sheet immediately after a business combination is complicated only slightly when 100 percent of a company's stock is acquired at a price that differs from the acquiree's book value. To illustrate the acquisition of a subsidiary when the consideration given is greater than the book value of the acquiree, assume that Peerless Products acquires all of Special Foods' outstanding stock on January 1, 20X1, by paying $340,000 cash, an amount equal to Special Foods' fair value as a whole. The consideration given by Peerless is $40,000 in excess of Special Foods' book value of $300,000. The resulting ownership situation can be viewed as follows:

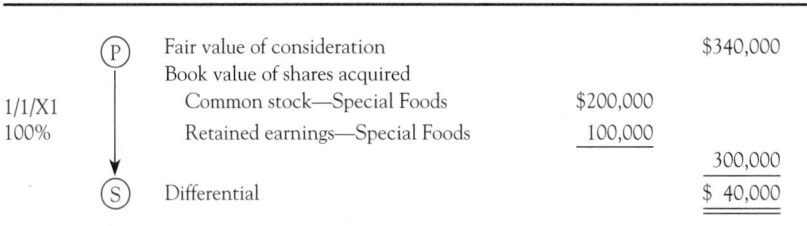

| | | |
|---|---|---|
| Fair value of consideration | | $340,000 |
| Book value of shares acquired | | |
| Common stock—Special Foods | $200,000 | |
| Retained earnings—Special Foods | 100,000 | |
| | | 300,000 |
| Differential | | $ 40,000 |

1/1/X1
100%

Peerless records the stock acquisition with the following entry:

January 1, 20X1

| (3) | Investment in Special Foods Stock | 340,000 | |
|---|---|---|---|
| | Cash | | 340,000 |
| | Record purchase of Special Foods stock. | | |

In a business combination, and therefore in consolidation following a business combination, the full amount of the consideration given by the acquirer must be assigned to the individual assets and liabilities acquired and to goodwill. The consolidation workpaper procedures used in adjusting to the proper consolidated amounts follow a consistent pattern. The first workpaper entry eliminates the parent's investment account and each of the subsidiary's stockholders' equity accounts. When the acquisition-date fair value of the consideration is more than the acquiree's book value at that date, the first eliminating entry includes a debit to a workpaper clearing account to balance the entry. This clearing account can be titled *Excess of Acquisition Consideration over Acquiree Book Value,* or just *Differential.* The differential represents (in simple situations involving a 100 percent acquisition in a single step) the total difference between the acquisition-date fair value of the consideration given by the acquirer and the acquiree's book value. The amount recorded by the parent as its investment in the subsidiary is equal to the acquisition-date fair value of the consideration given. Thus, the differential can be seen in eliminating entry E(4) to be equal to the difference between the book value of Special Foods' stockholders' equity and the cost of Peerless's investment in Special Foods. Note that the Differential account is simply a workpaper clearing account and is not found on the books of the parent or subsidiary and does not appear in the consolidated financial statements.

The workpaper entry to eliminate Peerless's investment account and the stockholders' equity accounts of Special Foods is as follows:

| E(4) | Common Stock—Special Foods | 200,000 | |
| | Retained Earnings | 100,000 | |
| | Differential | 40,000 | |
| | Investment in Special Foods Stock | | 340,000 |
| | Eliminate investment balance. | | |

The balance assigned to Differential in this initial eliminating entry is subsequently cleared from that account through one or more additional workpaper entries. These additional workpaper entries adjust the various account balances to reflect the fair values of the subsidiary's assets and liabilities at the time the parent acquired the subsidiary and to establish goodwill, if appropriate.

## Treatment of a Positive Differential

The fair value, and hence acquisition price, of a subsidiary might exceed the book value for several reasons, such as the following:

1. Errors or omissions on the books of the subsidiary.
2. Excess of fair value over the book value of the subsidiary's net identifiable assets.
3. Existence of goodwill.

### Errors or Omissions on the Books of the Subsidiary

An examination of an acquired company's books may reveal material errors. In some cases, the acquired company may have expensed rather than capitalized assets or, for other reasons, omitted them from the books. An acquired company that previously had been closely held may not have followed generally accepted accounting principles in maintaining its accounting records. In some cases, the recordkeeping may have simply been inadequate.

Where such errors or omissions exist, corrections should be made directly on the subsidiary's books as of the date of acquisition. These corrections are treated as prior-period adjustments in accordance with **FASB Statement No. 16,** "Prior Period Adjustments" (FASB 16). Once the subsidiary's books are stated in accordance with generally accepted accounting principles, that portion of the differential attributable to the errors or omissions will no longer exist.

### Excess of Fair Value over Book Value of Subsidiary's Net Identifiable Assets

The fair value of a company's assets is an important factor in the overall determination of the company's fair value. In many cases, the fair value of an acquired company's net assets exceeds the book value. Consequently, the consideration given by an acquirer may exceed the acquiree's book value. The procedures used in preparing the consolidated balance sheet should lead to reporting all of the acquired company's assets and liabilities based on their fair values on the date of combination. This valuation may be accomplished in one of two ways: (1) the assets and liabilities of the subsidiary may be revalued directly on the books of the subsidiary or (2) the accounting basis of the subsidiary may be maintained and the revaluations made each period in the consolidation workpaper.

Revaluing the assets and liabilities on the subsidiary's books generally is the simplest approach if all of the subsidiary's common stock is acquired. On the other hand, it generally is not appropriate to revalue the assets and liabilities on the subsidiary's books if there is a significant noncontrolling interest in that subsidiary. From a noncontrolling shareholder's point of view, the subsidiary is a continuing company, and the basis of accounting should not change. More difficult to resolve is the situation in which the parent acquires all of the subsidiary's common stock but continues to issue separate financial statements of the subsidiary to holders of the subsidiary's bonds or preferred stock.

Revaluing the assets and liabilities of the subsidiary directly on the subsidiary's books is referred to as ***push-down accounting*** and is discussed later in this chapter.

When the assets and liabilities are revalued directly on the subsidiary's books, that portion of the differential then no longer exists. However, if the assets and liabilities are not revalued on the subsidiary's books, an entry to revalue those assets and allocate the differential is needed in the consolidation workpaper each time consolidated financial statements are prepared, for as long as the related assets are held.

In the example introduced earlier, Peerless Products acquired all of Special Foods' stock for $340,000. This gives rise to a $40,000 debit differential. In preparing a consolidated balance sheet immediately after acquisition, the investment elimination entry appearing in the consolidation workpaper is (as given earlier):

| | | | |
|---|---|---|---|
| E(4) | Common Stock—Special Foods | 200,000 | |
| | Retained Earnings | 100,000 | |
| | Differential | 40,000 | |
| | Investment in Special Foods Stock | | 340,000 |
| | Eliminate investment balance. | | |

If the fair value of Special Foods' land is determined to be $40,000 more than its book value, and all other assets and liabilities have fair values equal to their book values, the entire amount of the differential is allocated to the subsidiary's land. This allocation of the differential is made in the consolidation workpaper with the following entry:

| | | | |
|---|---|---|---|
| E(5) | Land | 40,000 | |
| | Differential | | 40,000 |
| | Assign differential to land. | | |

The consolidation workpaper reflecting the allocation of the differential to the subsidiary's land is illustrated in Figure 4–6. The workpaper is based on the data in Figure 4–2 and an acquisition price of $340,000.

**FIGURE 4–6** **Workpaper for Consolidated Balance Sheet, January 1, 20X1, Date of Combination; 100 Percent Acquisition at More than Book Value**

| | Peerless Products | Special Foods | Eliminations | | Consolidated |
|---|---|---|---|---|---|
| **Item** | | | **Debit** | **Credit** | |
| Cash | 10,000 | 50,000 | | | 60,000 |
| Accounts Receivable | 75,000 | 50,000 | | | 125,000 |
| Inventory | 100,000 | 60,000 | | | 160,000 |
| Land | 175,000 | 40,000 | (5) 40,000 | | 255,000 |
| Buildings and Equipment | 800,000 | 600,000 | | | 1,400,000 |
| Investment in Special Foods Stock | 340,000 | | | (4) 340,000 | |
| Differential | | | (4) 40,000 | (5) 40,000 | |
| Total Debits | 1,500,000 | 800,000 | | | 2,000,000 |
| Accumulated Depreciation | 400,000 | 300,000 | | | 700,000 |
| Accounts Payable | 100,000 | 100,000 | | | 200,000 |
| Bonds Payable | 200,000 | 100,000 | | | 300,000 |
| Common Stock | 500,000 | 200,000 | (4) 200,000 | | 500,000 |
| Retained Earnings | 300,000 | 100,000 | (4) 100,000 | | 300,000 |
| Total Credits | 1,500,000 | 800,000 | 380,000 | 380,000 | 2,000,000 |

Elimination entries:
(4) Eliminate investment balance and stockholders' equity of Special Foods.
(5) Assign differential to land.

The amounts reported in the consolidated balance sheet are those in the Consolidated column of the workpaper in Figure 4–6. Land is included in the consolidated balance sheet at $255,000, the amount carried on Peerless's books ($175,000) plus the amount carried on Special Foods' books ($40,000) plus the differential reflecting the increased value of Special Foods' land ($40,000).

This example is sufficiently simple that the assignment of the differential to land could be made directly in eliminating entry E(4) rather than through the use of the differential clearing account. In practice, however, the differential often relates to more than a single asset, and the allocation of the differential may be considerably more complex than in this example. The possibilities for clerical errors are reduced in complex situations by making two separate entries rather than one complicated entry.

### Existence of Goodwill

If the acquisition-date fair value of the consideration exchanged for an acquired subsidiary is greater than the total fair value of the subsidiary's net identifiable assets, the difference is considered to be related to the future economic benefits associated with other assets of the subsidiary that are not separately identified and recognized and is referred to as ***goodwill.*** Thus, once a subsidiary's identifiable assets and liabilities are revalued to their fair values, any remaining debit differential is normally allocated to goodwill. For example, assuming that in the Peerless Products and Special Foods illustration the acquisition-date fair values of Special Foods' assets and liabilities are equal to their book values, then the $40,000 difference between the $340,000 consideration exchanged and the $300,000 fair value of the subsidiary's net identifiable assets should be attributed to goodwill. The following entry to assign the differential is needed in the consolidation workpaper prepared immediately after the combination:

| | | | |
|---|---|---|---|
| E(6) | Goodwill | 40,000 | |
| | Differential | | 40,000 |
| | Assign differential to goodwill. | | |

The consolidation workpaper would appear as in Figure 4–6 except that elimination entry E(6) would replace elimination entry E(5). Goodwill, which does not appear on the books of either Peerless or Special Foods, would appear at $40,000 in the consolidated balance sheet prepared immediately after acquisition.

In the past, some companies have included in goodwill the fair-value increment related to certain identifiable assets of the subsidiary rather than separately recognizing those assets. Such treatment is not acceptable, and any fair-value increment related to an intangible asset that arises from a contractual or legal right or that is separable from the entity must be allocated to that asset.

## Illustration of Treatment of Debit Differential

In many situations, the differential relates to a number of different assets and liabilities. As a means of illustrating the allocation of the differential to various assets and liabilities, assume that the acquisition-date book values and fair values of Special Foods' assets and liabilities are as shown in Figure 4–7. The inventory and land have fair values in excess of their book values, while the buildings and equipment are worth less than their book values.

Bond prices fluctuate as interest rates change. In this example, the value of Special Foods' bonds payable is higher than the book value. This indicates that the nominal interest rate on the bonds is higher than the current market rate of interest, and, therefore, investors are willing to pay a price higher than par for the bonds. In determining the value of Special Foods, Peerless must recognize that it is assuming a liability that pays an interest rate higher than the current market rate. Accordingly, Special Foods' value will be less than if the liability carried a lower interest rate. The resulting consolidated financial statements must recognize the acquisition-date fair values of Special Foods' liabilities as well as its assets.

Assume that Peerless Products acquires all of Special Foods' capital stock for $400,000 on January 1, 20X1, by issuing $100,000 of 9 percent bonds, with a fair value of $100,000,

**FIGURE 4–7**
**Balance Sheet for Special Foods Inc., January 1, 20X1, Date of Combination**

| | Book Value | Fair Value | Difference between Fair Value and Book Value |
|---|---|---|---|
| Cash | $ 50,000 | $ 50,000 | |
| Accounts Receivable | 50,000 | 50,000 | |
| Inventory | 60,000 | 75,000 | $15,000 |
| Land | 40,000 | 100,000 | 60,000 |
| Buildings and Equipment $ 600,000 | | | |
| Accumulated Depreciation (300,000) | 300,000 | 290,000 | (10,000) |
| | $500,000 | $565,000 | |
| Accounts Payable | $100,000 | $100,000 | |
| Bonds Payable | 100,000 | 135,000 | (35,000) |
| Common Stock | 200,000 | | |
| Retained Earnings | 100,000 | | |
| | $500,000 | $235,000 | $30,000 |

and paying cash of $300,000. The resulting ownership situation can be pictured as follows:

| | | | |
|---|---|---|---|
| (P) | Fair value of consideration | | $400,000 |
| | Book value of shares acquired | | |
| 1/1/X1 | Common stock—Special Foods | $200,000 | |
| 100% | Retained earnings—Special Foods | 100,000 | |
| | | | 300,000 |
| (S) | Differential | | $100,000 |

Peerless records the investment on its books with the following entry:

January 1, 20X1

| (7) | Investment in Special Foods Stock | 400,000 | |
|---|---|---|---|
| | Bonds Payable | | 100,000 |
| | Cash | | 300,000 |
| | Record purchase of Special Foods stock. | | |

The relationship between the fair value of the consideration given for Special Foods, the fair value of Special Foods' net assets, and the book value of Special Foods' net assets is as follows:

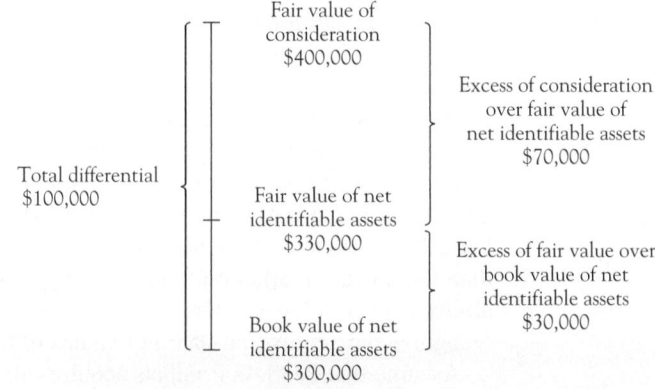

The total $400,000 consideration exceeds by $100,000 the book value of Special Foods' net assets (assets of $500,000 less liabilities of $200,000). Thus, the total differential is $100,000. The total fair value of the net identifiable assets acquired in the combination is $330,000 ($565,000 − $235,000), based on the data in Figure 4–7. The amount by which the total consideration of $400,000 exceeds the $330,000 fair value of the net identifiable assets is $70,000, and that amount is assigned to goodwill in the consolidated balance sheet.

The eliminations entered in the consolidation workpaper in preparing the consolidated balance sheet immediately after the combination are:

| E(8) | Common Stock—Special Foods | 200,000 | |
| | Retained Earnings | 100,000 | |
| | Differential | 100,000 | |
| |     Investment in Special Foods Stock | | 400,000 |
| |     Eliminate investment balance. | | |
| | | | |
| E(9) | Inventory | 15,000 | |
| | Land | 60,000 | |
| | Goodwill | 70,000 | |
| |     Buildings and Equipment | | 10,000 |
| |     Premium on Bonds Payable | | 35,000 |
| |     Differential | | 100,000 |
| |     Assign differential. | | |

These entries are reflected in the workpaper in Figure 4–8. While entry E(9) is somewhat more complex than in the previous example, the differential allocation is conceptually the same in both cases. In each case, the end result is a consolidated balance sheet with the subsidiary's assets and liabilities valued at their fair values at the date of combination.

**FIGURE 4–8**  **Workpaper for Consolidated Balance Sheet, January 1, 20X1, Date of Combination; 100 Percent Acquisition at More than Book Value**

| Item | Peerless Products | Special Foods | Eliminations Debit | Eliminations Credit | Consolidated |
|---|---|---|---|---|---|
| Cash | 50,000 | 50,000 | | | 100,000 |
| Accounts Receivable | 75,000 | 50,000 | | | 125,000 |
| Inventory | 100,000 | 60,000 | (9)  15,000 | | 175,000 |
| Land | 175,000 | 40,000 | (9)  60,000 | | 275,000 |
| Buildings and Equipment | 800,000 | 600,000 | | (9)  10,000 | 1,390,000 |
| Goodwill | | | (9)  70,000 | | 70,000 |
| Investment in Special Foods Stock | 400,000 | | | (8) 400,000 | |
| Differential | | | (8) 100,000 | (9) 100,000 | |
| Total Debits | 1,600,000 | 800,000 | | | 2,135,000 |
| | | | | | |
| Accumulated Depreciation | 400,000 | 300,000 | | | 700,000 |
| Accounts Payable | 100,000 | 100,000 | | | 200,000 |
| Bonds Payable | 300,000 | 100,000 | | | 400,000 |
| Premium on Bonds Payable | | | | (9)  35,000 | 35,000 |
| Common Stock | 500,000 | 200,000 | (8) 200,000 | | 500,000 |
| Retained Earnings | 300,000 | 100,000 | (8) 100,000 | | 300,000 |
| Total Credits | 1,600,000 | 800,000 | 545,000 | 545,000 | 2,135,000 |

Elimination entries:
(8) Eliminate investment balance and stockholders' equity of Special Foods.
(9) Assign differential.

## 100 Percent Ownership Acquired at Less than Fair Value of Net Assets

Numerous instances have been seen of companies with common stock trading in the market at prices less than the fair value of their net assets. These companies are often singled out as prime acquisition targets. The acquisition price of an acquired company may be less than the fair value of its net assets because some of the acquiree's assets or liabilities may have been incorrectly specified or because the transaction reflects a forced sale, where the seller was required to sell quickly and was unable to fully market the sale.

Obviously, if assets or liabilities acquired in a business combination have been incorrectly specified, the errors must be corrected and the assets and liabilities valued at their fair values. Once this is done, if the fair value of the consideration given is still less than the fair value of the net assets acquired, a gain attributable to the acquirer is recognized for the difference. In general, as discussed in Chapter 1, a business combination where (1) the sum of the acquisition-date fair values of the consideration given, any equity interest already held by the acquirer, and any noncontrolling interest is less than (2) the amounts at which the identifiable net assets must be valued at the acquisition date as specified by **FASB 141R** (usually fair values) is considered a *bargain purchase,* and a gain attributable to the acquirer is recognized for the difference.

## Illustration of Treatment of Bargain-Purchase Differential

Using the example of Peerless Products and Special Foods, assume that the acquisition-date book values and fair values of Special Foods' assets and liabilities are equal except that the fair value of Special Foods' land is $40,000 greater than its book value. On January 1, 20X1, Peerless acquires all of Special Foods' common stock for $310,000, resulting in a bargain purchase. The resulting ownership situation is as follows:

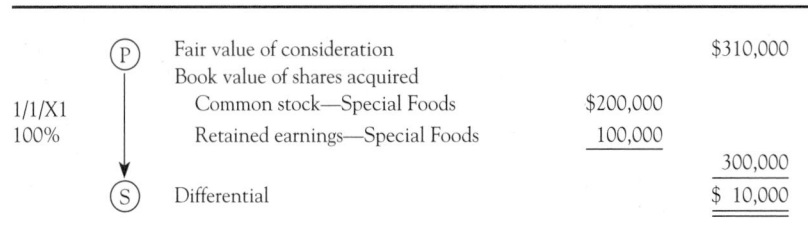

|  |  |  |  |  |
|---|---|---|---|---|
| | ⓅP | Fair value of consideration | | $310,000 |
| | | Book value of shares acquired | | |
| 1/1/X1 | | Common stock—Special Foods | $200,000 | |
| 100% | | Retained earnings—Special Foods | 100,000 | |
| | | | | 300,000 |
| | ⓈS | Differential | | $ 10,000 |

Peerless records its investment in Special Foods with the following entry on its books:

January 1, 20X1

| (10) | Investment in Special Foods Stock | 310,000 | |
|---|---|---|---|
| | Cash | | 310,000 |
| | Record purchase of Special Foods stock. | | |

In this example, the acquisition-date fair value of Special Foods' net assets is greater than their book value by $40,000. However, the purchase price exceeds Special Foods' book value by only $10,000 and, thus, is less than the fair value of the net identifiable assets acquired. This business combination, therefore, represents a bargain purchase. All of the acquiree's assets and liabilities must be valued at fair value, which in this case requires only Special Foods' land to be revalued. Assuming push-down accounting is not employed, this revaluation is accomplished in the consolidation workpaper.

If a consolidated balance sheet is prepared immediately after the combination, the following eliminating entries are included in the consolidation workpaper:

| E(11) | Common Stock—Special Foods | 200,000 | |
|---|---|---|---|
| | Retained Earnings | 100,000 | |
| | Differential | 10,000 | |
| | Investment in Special Foods Stock | | 310,000 |
| | Eliminate investment balance. | | |

| E(12) | Land | 40,000 | |
| | Differential | | 10,000 |
| | Retained Earnings (Gain on Bargain Purchase) | | 30,000 |
| | Assign differential in bargain purchase. | | |

Once all of Special Foods' assets and liabilities are valued at their fair values in the consolidation workpaper, a gain is recognized for the $30,000 excess of the $340,000 fair value of Special Foods' net assets over the $310,000 fair value of the consideration given by Peerless in the exchange. In entry E(12), the gain is carried directly to Retained Earnings because no income statement is being prepared, only a balance sheet.

If the consideration given in the exchange had been less than the book value of Special Foods, the same procedures would be followed except the differential would have a credit balance. For example, assume that Peerless paid $295,000 for all of the common stock of Special Foods. The eliminating entries included in a workpaper to prepare a consolidated balance sheet immediately following the combination would be as follows:

| E(13) | Common Stock—Special Foods | 200,000 | |
| | Retained Earnings | 100,000 | |
| | Differential | | 5,000 |
| | Investment in Special Foods Stock | | 295,000 |
| | Eliminate investment balance. | | |
| | | | |
| E(14) | Land | 40,000 | |
| | Differential | 5,000 | |
| | Retained Earnings (Gain on Bargain Purchase) | | 45,000 |
| | Assign differential in bargain purchase. | | |

# CONSOLIDATION SUBSEQUENT TO ACQUISITION

The preceding portion of the chapter introduced the procedures used to prepare a consolidated balance sheet as of the date of acquisition. More than a consolidated balance sheet, however, is needed to provide a comprehensive picture of the consolidated entity's activities following acquisition. As with a single company, the set of basic financial statements for a consolidated entity consists of a balance sheet, an income statement, a statement of changes in retained earnings, and a statement of cash flows.

This portion of the chapter presents the procedures used to prepare a consolidated balance sheet, income statement, and retained earnings statement subsequent to the date of combination. The preparation of a consolidated statement of cash flows is discussed in Chapter 10.

The discussion that follows first deals with the important concepts of consolidated net income and consolidated retained earnings, followed by a description of the workpaper format used to facilitate the preparation of a full set of consolidated financial statements. The specific procedures used to prepare consolidated financial statements subsequent to the date of combination are then discussed.

This and subsequent chapters focus on procedures for consolidation when the parent company accounts for its investment in subsidiary stock using the equity method. If the parent accounts for its investment using the cost method, the general approach to the preparation of consolidated financial statements is the same, but the specific procedures differ somewhat. Consolidation procedures using the cost method are discussed in Appendix 5A. Regardless of the method the parent uses to account for its subsidiary investment, however, the consolidated statements will be the same because the investment and related accounts are eliminated in the consolidation process.

The approach followed to prepare a complete set of consolidated financial statements subsequent to a business combination is quite similar to that used to prepare a consolidated balance sheet as of the date of combination. However, in addition to the assets and liabilities, the revenues and expenses of the consolidating companies must be combined. As the accounts are combined, eliminations must be made in the consolidation workpaper so that the consolidated financial statements appear as if they are the financial statements of a single company.

When a full set of consolidated financial statements is prepared subsequent to the date of combination, two of the important concepts affecting the statements are those of consolidated net income and consolidated retained earnings. Although accounting practice in the United States and Canada has largely reflected the parent company approach to consolidation, as discussed in Chapter 3, that has recently changed to more of an entity focus, but with special consideration for the parent.

## Consolidated Net Income

All revenues and expenses of the individual consolidating companies arising from transactions with unaffiliated companies are included in the consolidated financial statements. The consolidated income statement includes 100 percent of the revenues and expenses regardless of the parent's percentage ownership. As with single-company financial statements, the difference between revenues and expenses is net income, in this case, consolidated net income. In the absence of transactions among the consolidating companies, ***consolidated net income*** is equal to the parent's income from its own operations, excluding any investment income from consolidated subsidiaries, plus the net income from each of the consolidated subsidiaries, adjusted for any differential write-off. Intercorporate investment income from consolidated subsidiaries included in the parent's net income under either the cost or equity method must be eliminated in computing consolidated net income to avoid double counting.

If all subsidiaries are wholly owned, all of the consolidated net income accrues to the parent company, or the controlling interest. If one or more of the consolidated subsidiaries is less than wholly owned, a portion of the consolidated net income accrues to the noncontrolling shareholders. In that case, the income attributable to the noncontrolling interest is deducted from consolidated net income on the face of the income statement to arrive at consolidated net income attributable to the controlling interest.

Consolidated net income and consolidated net income attributable to the controlling interest are the same when all consolidated subsidiaries are wholly owned. For example, assume that Push Corporation purchases all of the stock of Shove Company at an amount equal to its book value. During 20X1, Shove reports net income of $25,000, while Push reports net income of $125,000, including equity-method income from Shove of $25,000. Consolidated net income for 20X1 is computed as follows:

| | |
|---|---:|
| Push's net income | $125,000 |
| Less: Equity-method income from Shove | (25,000) |
| Shove's net income | 25,000 |
| Consolidated net income | $125,000 |

Note that when all subsidiaries are wholly owned, and absent any intercompany transactions and goodwill impairment, consolidated net income is equal to the parent's equity-method net income.

## Consolidated Retained Earnings

Although the computation of consolidated net income has changed to an entity-theory basis, the treatment of retained earnings is still more consistent with the traditional parent company approach. The only retained earnings figure reported in the consolidated balance sheet is that attributable to the controlling interest. For subsidiaries that are not wholly owned, the noncontrolling stockholders' share of subsidiary retained earnings is included in the noncontrolling interest amount reported in the equity section of the consolidated balance sheet.

***Consolidated retained earnings,*** as it appears in the consolidated balance sheet, is that portion of the consolidated enterprise's undistributed earnings accruing to the parent company shareholders. Consolidated retained earnings at the end of the period is equal to the beginning consolidated retained earnings balance plus consolidated net income attributable to the controlling interest, less dividends declared by the parent company.

### Computing Consolidated Retained Earnings

Consolidated retained earnings is computed by adding together the parent's retained earnings from its own operations (excluding any income from consolidated subsidiaries recognized by the parent) and the parent's proportionate share of the net income of each subsidiary since the date of acquisition, adjusted for differential write-off and goodwill impairment. This is the same approach used to compute the parent's retained earnings when the parent accounts for subsidiaries using the equity method on its books. In the absence of unrealized profits from intercompany transactions and goodwill impairment, consolidated retained earnings and the parent's equity-method retained earnings are normally equal.

If the parent accounts for subsidiaries using the equity method on its books, the retained earnings of each subsidiary is completely eliminated when the subsidiary is consolidated. This is necessary because (1) retained earnings cannot be purchased, and so subsidiary retained earnings at the date of a business combination cannot be included in the combined company's retained earnings; (2) the parent's share of the subsidiary's income since acquisition is already included in the parent's equity-method retained earnings; and (3) the noncontrolling interest's share (if any) of the subsidiary's retained earnings is not included in consolidated retained earnings.

### Computation of Consolidated Retained Earnings Illustrated

In the simple example given earlier, assume that on the date of combination, January 1, 20X1, Push's retained earnings balance is $400,000 and Shove's is $250,000. During 20X1, Shove reports $25,000 of net income and declares $10,000 of dividends. Push reports $100,000 of separate operating earnings plus $25,000 of equity-method income from its 100 percent interest in Shove; Push declares dividends of $30,000. Based on this information, the retained earnings balances for Push and Shove on December 31, 20X1, are computed as follows:

|  | Push | Shove |
| --- | --- | --- |
| Balance, January 1, 20X1 | $400,000 | $250,000 |
| Net income, 20X1 | 125,000 | 25,000 |
| Dividends declared in 20X1 | (30,000) | (10,000) |
| Balance, December 31, 20X1 | $495,000 | $265,000 |

Consolidated retained earnings is computed by first determining the parent's retained earnings from its own operations. This computation involves removing from the parent's retained earnings the $25,000 of subsidiary income since acquisition recognized by the parent, leaving $470,000 ($495,000 − $25,000) of retained earnings resulting from the parent's own operations. The parent's 100 percent share of the subsidiary's net income since the date of acquisition is then added to this number, resulting in consolidated retained earnings of $495,000. This number is the same as the parent's equity-method retained earnings.

## Workpaper Format

Several different workpaper formats for preparing consolidated financial statements are used in practice. One of the most widely used formats is the three-part workpaper, consisting of one part for each of three financial statements: the income statement, the statement of retained earnings, and the balance sheet. In recent years, the retained earnings statement has been dropped by many companies in favor of the statement of changes in stockholders' equity. Nevertheless, the information normally found in a retained earnings

**FIGURE 4–9**   **Format for Comprehensive Three-Part Consolidation Workpaper**

| Item | Trial Balance Data | | Elimination Entries | | Consolidated |
|---|---|---|---|---|---|
| | Parent | Subsidiary | Debits | Credits | |
| Credit Accounts:<br>  Revenues<br>  Gains<br><br>Debit Accounts:<br>  Contra Revenues<br>  Expenses<br>  Losses<br><br>Net Income | | | INCOME STATEMENT SECTION | | |
| Beginning Retained<br>  Earnings<br><br>Add: Net Income<br>Deduct: Dividends<br><br>Ending Retained<br>  Earnings | | | RETAINED EARNINGS STATEMENT SECTION | | |
| Debit Accounts:<br>  Assets<br>  Contra Liabilities<br><br>Credit Accounts:<br>  Contra Assets<br>  Liabilities<br>  Stockholders' Equity:<br>    Capital Stock<br>    Paid-In Capital<br>    Retained Earnings | | | BALANCE SHEET SECTION | | |

statement is included in the statement of stockholders' equity, along with additional information, and so the three-part workpaper described continues to provide a useful format.

Figure 4–9 presents the format for the comprehensive three-part consolidation workpaper. The columns are the same as those for the balance sheet workpaper discussed earlier in this chapter. The final column in the workpaper contains the totals of each line summed algebraically across and is the basis for preparing the consolidated financial statements.

The top portion of the workpaper is used in preparing the consolidated income statement. All income statement accounts with credit balances are listed first, with those having debit balances listed next. When the income statement portion of the workpaper is completed, a total for each column is entered at the bottom of the income statement portion of the workpaper. The bottom line in this part of the workpaper shows the parent's net income, the subsidiary's net income, the totals of the debit and credit eliminations for this section of the workpaper, and consolidated net income. The entire bottom line is carried down to the retained earnings statement portion of the workpaper immediately below.

The retained earnings statement section of the workpaper is in the same format as a retained earnings statement, or the retained earnings section of a statement of stockholders' equity. Net income and the other totals from the bottom line of the income statement portion of the workpaper are brought down from above. Similarly, the final line in the retained earnings statement section of the workpaper is carried down in its entirety to the balance sheet section.

The bottom portion of the workpaper reflects the balance sheet amounts at the end of the period. Debits and credits are separated in the same manner as in the consolidated balance sheet workpaper presented earlier. The retained earnings amounts appearing in the balance sheet section of the workpaper are the totals carried forward from the bottom line of the retained earnings statement section.

The examples in the following sections of this chapter demonstrate the use of the comprehensive three-part consolidation workpaper.

# CONSOLIDATED FINANCIAL STATEMENTS—100 PERCENT OWNERSHIP ACQUIRED AT BOOK VALUE

Each of the consolidated financial statements is prepared as if it is taken from a single set of books that is being used to account for the overall consolidated entity. There is, of course, no set of books for the consolidated entity, and as in the preparation of the consolidated balance sheet, the consolidation process starts with the data recorded on the books of the individual consolidating companies. The account balances from the books of the individual companies are placed in the three-part workpaper, and entries are made to eliminate the effects of intercorporate ownership and transactions. The consolidation approach and procedures are the same whether the subsidiary being consolidated was acquired or created.

To understand the process of consolidation subsequent to the start of a parent–subsidiary relationship, assume that on January 1, 20X1, Peerless Products Corporation acquires all of the common stock of Special Foods Inc. for $300,000, an amount equal to the book value of Special Foods on that date. At that time, Special Foods has $200,000 of common stock outstanding and retained earnings of $100,000. The resulting ownership situation is as follows:

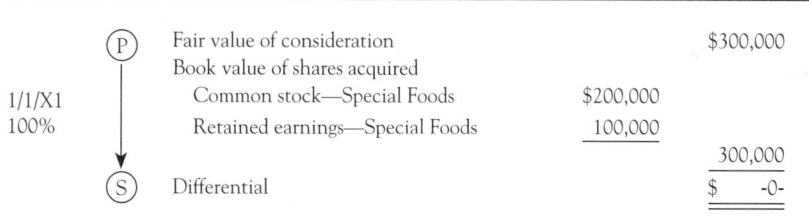

| | | |
|---|---|---|
| (P) Fair value of consideration | | $300,000 |
| Book value of shares acquired | | |
| 1/1/X1    Common stock—Special Foods | $200,000 | |
| 100%    Retained earnings—Special Foods | 100,000 | |
| | | 300,000 |
| (S) Differential | | $ -0- |

Peerless accounts for its investment in Special Foods stock using the equity method. Information about Peerless and Special Foods as of the date of combination and for the years 20X1 and 20X2 appears in Figure 4–10.

**FIGURE 4–10**
**Selected Information about Peerless Products and Special Foods on January 1, 20X1, and for the Years 20X1 and 20X2**

| | Peerless Products | Special Foods |
|---|---|---|
| Common Stock, January 1, 20X1 | $500,000 | $200,000 |
| Retained Earnings, January 1, 20X1 | 300,000 | 100,000 |
| 20X1: | | |
|    Separate Operating Income, Peerless | 140,000 | |
|    Net Income, Special Foods | | 50,000 |
|    Dividends | 60,000 | 30,000 |
| 20X2: | | |
|    Separate Operating Income, Peerless | 160,000 | |
|    Net Income, Special Foods | | 75,000 |
|    Dividends | 60,000 | 40,000 |

## Initial Year of Ownership

On January 1, 20X1, Peerless records its purchase of Special Foods common stock with the following entry:

January 1, 20X1

| (15) | Investment in Special Foods Stock | 300,000 | |
| | Cash | | 300,000 |
| | Record purchase of Special Foods stock. | | |

During 20X1, Peerless records operating earnings of $140,000, excluding its income from investing in Special Foods, and declares dividends of $60,000. Special Foods reports 20X1 net income of $50,000 and declares dividends of $30,000.

### *Parent Company Entries*

Peerless records its 20X1 income and dividends from Special Foods under the equity method with the following entries:

| (16) | Cash | 30,000 | |
| | Investment in Special Foods Stock | | 30,000 |
| | Record dividends from Special Foods: | | |
| | $30,000 \times 1.00$ | | |

| (17) | Investment in Special Foods Stock | 50,000 | |
| | Income from Subsidiary | | 50,000 |
| | Record equity-method income: | | |
| | $50,000 \times 1.00$ | | |

### *Consolidation Workpaper—Initial Year of Ownership*

After all appropriate entries, including year-end adjustments, have been made on the books of Peerless and Special Foods, a consolidation workpaper is prepared as in Figure 4–11. The adjusted account balances from the books of Peerless and Special Foods are placed in the first two columns of the workpaper. Then all amounts that reflect intercorporate transactions or ownership are eliminated in the consolidation process.

The distinction between journal entries recorded on the books of the individual companies and the eliminating entries recorded only on the consolidation workpaper is an important one. Book entries affect balances on the books and the amounts that are carried to the consolidation workpaper; workpaper eliminating entries affect only those balances carried to the consolidated financial statements in the period. As mentioned previously, the eliminating entries presented in this text are identified with an "E" prefix to the left of the journal entry number whenever they are shown outside the workpaper.

In this example, the accounts that must be eliminated because of intercorporate ownership are the stockholders' equity accounts of Special Foods, including dividends declared, Peerless's investment in Special Foods stock, and Peerless's income from Special Foods. While these accounts can be eliminated in a single entry, two entries often are used to avoid the complexity of a single, large entry.

The first eliminating entry, E(18), removes both the investment income reflected in the parent's income statement and the parent's portion of any dividends declared by the subsidiary during the period:

| E(18) | Income from Subsidiary | 50,000 | |
| | Dividends Declared | | 30,000 |
| | Investment in Special Foods Stock | | 20,000 |
| | Eliminate income from subsidiary. | | |

**FIGURE 4–11**   **December 31, 20X1, Equity-Method Workpaper for Consolidated Financial Statements, Initial Year of Ownership; 100 Percent Acquisition at Book Value**

| Item | Peerless Products | Special Foods | Eliminations Debit | Eliminations Credit | Consolidated |
|---|---|---|---|---|---|
| Sales | 400,000 | 200,000 | | | 600,000 |
| Income from Subsidiary | 50,000 | | (18)  50,000 | | |
| Credits | 450,000 | 200,000 | | | 600,000 |
| Cost of Goods Sold | 170,000 | 115,000 | | | 285,000 |
| Depreciation and Amortization | 50,000 | 20,000 | | | 70,000 |
| Other Expenses | 40,000 | 15,000 | | | 55,000 |
| Debits | (260,000) | (150,000) | | | (410,000) |
| Net Income, carry forward | 190,000 | 50,000 | 50,000 | | 190,000 |
| Retained Earnings, January 1 | 300,000 | 100,000 | (19) 100,000 | | 300,000 |
| Net Income, from above | 190,000 | 50,000 | 50,000 | | 190,000 |
| | 490,000 | 150,000 | | | 490,000 |
| Dividends Declared | (60,000) | (30,000) | | (18)  30,000 | (60,000) |
| Retained Earnings, December 31, carry forward | 430,000 | 120,000 | 150,000 | 30,000 | 430,000 |
| Cash | 210,000 | 75,000 | | | 285,000 |
| Accounts Receivable | 75,000 | 50,000 | | | 125,000 |
| Inventory | 100,000 | 75,000 | | | 175,000 |
| Land | 175,000 | 40,000 | | | 215,000 |
| Buildings and Equipment | 800,000 | 600,000 | | | 1,400,000 |
| Investment in Special Foods Stock | 320,000 | | | (18)  20,000 (19) 300,000 | |
| Debits | 1,680,000 | 840,000 | | | 2,200,000 |
| Accumulated Depreciation | 450,000 | 320,000 | | | 770,000 |
| Accounts Payable | 100,000 | 100,000 | | | 200,000 |
| Bonds Payable | 200,000 | 100,000 | | | 300,000 |
| Common Stock | 500,000 | 200,000 | (19) 200,000 | | 500,000 |
| Retained Earnings, from above | 430,000 | 120,000 | 150,000 | 30,000 | 430,000 |
| Credits | 1,680,000 | 840,000 | 350,000 | 350,000 | 2,200,000 |

Elimination entries:
(18) Eliminate income from subsidiary.
(19) Eliminate beginning investment balance.

Under the equity method, the parent recognized on its separate books its share (100 percent) of the subsidiary's income. In the consolidated income statement, however, the individual revenue and expense accounts of the subsidiary are combined with those of the parent. Income recognized by the parent from all consolidated subsidiaries, therefore, must be eliminated to avoid double counting. The subsidiary's dividends paid to the parent company must be eliminated when consolidated statements are prepared so that only dividend declarations related to the parent's shareholders are treated as dividends of the consolidated entity.

The investment account is credited for the difference between investment income and the parent's portion of subsidiary dividends. This difference represents the net change in the investment account for the period. The investment account balance increased by $20,000 during 20X1. Entering a $20,000 credit to the investment account in the workpaper takes the account balance back to the $300,000 balance at the beginning of the period.

The second eliminating entry removes the intercorporate ownership claim and stockholders' equity accounts of the subsidiary as of the beginning of the period:

| E(19) | Common Stock—Special Foods | 200,000 | |
|---|---|---|---|
| | Retained Earnings, January 1 | 100,000 | |
| | Investment in Special Foods Stock | | 300,000 |
| | Eliminate beginning investment balance. | | |

This entry credits the investment account for its balance at the beginning of the period and, together with entry E(18), fully eliminates the balance of the investment account at the end of the period. Note that the parent's investment in the stock of a consolidated subsidiary never appears in the consolidated balance sheet.

Common stock and retained earnings are debited in entry E(19) for the balances in the accounts at the beginning of the period. Ending retained earnings never is adjusted directly when a three-part workpaper is prepared. Instead, the three components of ending retained earnings are eliminated individually: the beginning retained earnings balance is eliminated by entry E(19) in the retained earnings statement portion of the workpaper, and income (from the subsidiary) and dividends are eliminated by entry E(18).

### Workpaper Relationships

Both of the eliminating entries are entered in Figure 4–11 and the amounts totaled across and down to complete the workpaper. Some specific points to recognize with respect to the full workpaper are as follows:

1. Each of the first two sections of the workpaper "telescopes" into the section below in a logical progression. As part of the normal accounting cycle, net income is closed to retained earnings, and retained earnings is reflected in the balance sheet. Similarly, in the consolidation workpaper, the net income is carried into the retained earnings statement section of the workpaper, and the ending retained earnings line is carried into the balance sheet section of the workpaper. Note that in both cases the entire line, including total eliminations, is carried forward.

2. Double-entry bookkeeping requires total debits to equal total credits for any single eliminating entry and for the workpaper as a whole. Because some eliminating entries extend to more than one section of the workpaper, however, the totals of the debit and credit eliminations are not likely to be equal in either of the first two sections of the workpaper. The totals of all debits and credits at the bottom of the balance sheet section are equal because the cumulative balances from the two upper sections are carried forward to the balance sheet section.

3. In the balance sheet portion of the workpaper, total debit balances must equal total credit balances for each company and the consolidated entity.

4. When (1) the parent uses the equity method of accounting for the investment, (2) there are no unrealized profits from intercorporate transactions, and (3) goodwill is not impaired, consolidated net income should equal the parent's net income and consolidated retained earnings should equal the parent's retained earnings. This means the existing balance in subsidiary retained earnings must be eliminated to avoid double counting.

5. Certain other clerical safeguards are incorporated into the workpaper. The amounts reflected in the bottom line of the income statement section, when summed (algebraically) across, must equal the number reported as consolidated net income. Similarly,

the amounts in the last line of the retained earnings statement section must equal consolidated retained earnings when summed across.

## Second and Subsequent Years of Ownership

The consolidation procedures employed at the end of the second and subsequent years are basically the same as those used at the end of the first year. Adjusted trial balance data of the individual companies are used as the starting point each time consolidated statements are prepared because no separate books are kept for the consolidated entity. An additional check is needed in each period following acquisition to ensure that the beginning balance of consolidated retained earnings shown in the completed workpaper equals the balance reported at the end of the prior period. In all other respects the eliminating entries and workpaper are comparable with those shown for the first year.

### Parent Company Entries

Consolidation after two years of ownership is illustrated by continuing the example of Peerless Products and Special Foods, based on the data in Figure 4–10. Peerless's separate income from its own operations for 20X2 is $160,000, and its dividends total $60,000. Special Foods reports net income of $75,000 in 20X2 and pays dividends of $40,000. Equity-method entries recorded by Peerless in 20X2 are as follows:

| | | | |
|---|---|---:|---:|
| (20) | Cash | 40,000 | |
| |     Investment in Special Foods Stock | | 40,000 |
| |     Record dividends from Special Foods: | | |
| |     $40,000 \times 1.00$ | | |
| | | | |
| (21) | Investment in Special Foods Stock | 75,000 | |
| |     Income from Subsidiary | | 75,000 |
| |     Record equity-method income: | | |
| |     $75,000 \times 1.00$ | | |

With these entries, the balance in the investment account reported by Peerless increases from $320,000 on January 1, 20X2, to $355,000 on December 31, 20X2, and reported net income of Peerless totals $235,000 ($160,000 + $75,000).

### Consolidation Workpaper—Second Year of Ownership

The workpaper to prepare consolidated statements for 20X2 is illustrated in Figure 4–12. Entry E(22) eliminates Peerless's 20X2 income from Special Foods and the dividend payment made to Peerless by Special Foods. The credit to the investment account in entry E(22) removes the change in the investment account recorded by Peerless during the period:

| | | | |
|---|---|---:|---:|
| E(22) | Income from Subsidiary | 75,000 | |
| |     Dividends Declared | | 40,000 |
| |     Investment in Special Foods Stock | | 35,000 |
| |     Eliminate income from subsidiary. | | |

The second workpaper entry eliminates the beginning balance in the investment account and the stockholders' equity accounts of the subsidiary at the beginning of 20X2:

| | | | |
|---|---|---:|---:|
| E(23) | Common Stock—Special Foods | 200,000 | |
| | Retained Earnings, January 1 | 120,000 | |
| |     Investment in Special Foods Stock | | 320,000 |
| |     Eliminate beginning investment balance. | | |

**FIGURE 4–12** December 31, 20X2, Equity-Method Workpaper for Consolidated Financial Statements, Second Year of Ownership; 100 Percent Acquisition at Book Value

| Item | Peerless Products | Special Foods | Eliminations Debit | Eliminations Credit | Consolidated |
|---|---|---|---|---|---|
| Sales | 450,000 | 300,000 | | | 750,000 |
| Income from Subsidiary | 75,000 | | (22)  75,000 | | |
| Credits | 525,000 | 300,000 | | | 750,000 |
| Cost of Goods Sold | 180,000 | 160,000 | | | 340,000 |
| Depreciation and Amortization | 50,000 | 20,000 | | | 70,000 |
| Other Expenses | 60,000 | 45,000 | | | 105,000 |
| Debits | (290,000) | (225,000) | | | (515,000) |
| Net Income, carry forward | 235,000 | 75,000 | 75,000 | | 235,000 |
| Retained Earnings, January 1 | 430,000 | 120,000 | (23) 120,000 | | 430,000 |
| Net Income, from above | 235,000 | 75,000 | 75,000 | | 235,000 |
| | 665,000 | 195,000 | | | 665,000 |
| Dividends Declared | (60,000) | (40,000) | | (22)  40,000 | (60,000) |
| Retained Earnings, December 31, carry forward | 605,000 | 155,000 | 195,000 | 40,000 | 605,000 |
| Cash | 245,000 | 85,000 | | | 330,000 |
| Accounts Receivable | 150,000 | 80,000 | | | 230,000 |
| Inventory | 180,000 | 90,000 | | | 270,000 |
| Land | 175,000 | 40,000 | | | 215,000 |
| Buildings and Equipment | 800,000 | 600,000 | | | 1,400,000 |
| Investment in Special Foods Stock | 355,000 | | | (22)  35,000 (23) 320,000 | |
| Debits | 1,905,000 | 895,000 | | | 2,445,000 |
| Accumulated Depreciation | 500,000 | 340,000 | | | 840,000 |
| Accounts Payable | 100,000 | 100,000 | | | 200,000 |
| Bonds Payable | 200,000 | 100,000 | | | 300,000 |
| Common Stock | 500,000 | 200,000 | (23) 200,000 | | 500,000 |
| Retained Earnings, from above | 605,000 | 155,000 | 195,000 | 40,000 | 605,000 |
| Credits | 1,905,000 | 895,000 | 395,000 | 395,000 | 2,445,000 |

Elimination entries:
  (22) Eliminate income from subsidiary.
  (23) Eliminate beginning investment balance.

Because the parent purchased all of the subsidiary's common stock at book value and is accounting for the investment using the equity method, the balance in its investment account is equal to the stockholders' equity of the subsidiary. The full balance of the subsidiary's retained earnings must be eliminated each period. Special Foods' retained earnings of $100,000 on the date of combination cannot be purchased by Peerless and therefore must be excluded from consolidated retained earnings. Further, the $20,000 increase in Special Foods' retained earnings during 20X1 already is reflected in Peerless's retained earnings as a result of using the equity method.

After placement of entries E(22) and E(23) in the consolidation workpaper, the workpaper is completed in the normal manner as shown in Figure 4–12. All workpaper relationships discussed in conjunction with Figure 4–11 continue in the second year as well. The beginning consolidated retained earnings balance for 20X2, as shown in Figure 4–12, should be compared with the ending consolidated retained earnings balance for 20X1, as shown in Figure 4–11, to ensure that they are the same.

## Consolidated Net Income and Retained Earnings

In the consolidation workpapers illustrated in Figures 4–11 and 4–12, consolidated net income for 20X1 and 20X2 appears as the last number in the income statement section of the workpapers in the Consolidated column on the far right. The numbers can be computed as follows:

|  | 20X1 | 20X2 |
| --- | --- | --- |
| Peerless's net income | $190,000 | $235,000 |
| Peerless's equity income from Special Foods | (50,000) | (75,000) |
| Special Foods' net income | 50,000 | 75,000 |
| Consolidated net income | $190,000 | $235,000 |

In this simple illustration, with no noncontrolling interest, consolidated net income is the same as the parent's equity-method net income. Had the parent used the cost method to account for its investment in Special Foods, the consolidated net income would not be the same as the parent's net income.

In Figures 4–11 and 4–12, consolidated retained earnings is the last figure in the retained earnings statement section of the workpapers, in the Consolidated column. Consolidated retained earnings is equal to the beginning balance of consolidated retained earnings plus consolidated net income, less dividends declared on the parent's common stock. It also can be computed as follows:

|  | 20X1 | 20X2 |
| --- | --- | --- |
| Peerless's beginning retained earnings from its own operations | $300,000 | $380,000 |
| Peerless's income from its own operations | 140,000 | 160,000 |
| Peerless's income from Special Foods since acquisition (cumulative) | 50,000 | 125,000 |
| Peerless's dividends declared | (60,000) | (60,000) |
| Consolidated retained earnings | $430,000 | $605,000 |

As with income, consolidated retained earnings is the same as the parent's equity-method retained earnings in simple cases.

# CONSOLIDATED FINANCIAL STATEMENTS—100 PERCENT OWNERSHIP ACQUIRED AT MORE THAN BOOK VALUE

Most frequently, an investment in a subsidiary is acquired at a price that is in excess of the acquiree's book value. In consolidation, the excess or differential must be allocated to specific assets and liabilities, with the identifiable assets and liabilities revalued based on their acquisition-date fair values and any excess recognized as goodwill. If this revaluation is not accomplished on the separate books of the subsidiary through the use of push-down accounting, as illustrated in Appendix 4A, it must be made in the consolidation workpaper each time consolidated statements are prepared. In addition, if the revaluations relate to assets or liabilities that must be depreciated, amortized, or otherwise written off, appropriate entries must be made in the consolidation workpaper to reduce consolidated net income accordingly.

When an investor company accounts for an investment using the equity method, as illustrated in Chapter 2, it records the amount of differential viewed as expiring during the period as a reduction of the income recognized from the investee. In consolidation, the differential is assigned to the appropriate asset and liability balances, and consolidated income is adjusted for the amounts expiring during the period by assigning them to the related expense items (e.g., depreciation expense).

## Initial Year of Ownership

As an illustration of the acquisition of 100 percent ownership acquired at an amount greater than book value, assume that Peerless Products acquires all of Special Foods' common stock on January 1, 20X1, for $387,500, an amount $87,500 in excess of the book value. The acquisition price includes cash of $300,000 and a 60-day note for $87,500 (paid at maturity during 20X1). At the date of combination, Special Foods is holding the assets and liabilities shown in Figure 4–2. The resulting ownership situation is as follows:

| | | | |
|---|---|---|---|
| | (P) Fair value of consideration | | $387,500 |
| | Book value of shares acquired | | |
| 1/1/X1 | Common stock—Special Foods | $200,000 | |
| 100% | Retained earnings—Special Foods | 100,000 | |
| | | | 300,000 |
| | (S) Differential | | $ 87,500 |

On the date of combination, all of Special Foods' assets and liabilities have fair values equal to their book values, except as follows:

| | Book Value | Fair Value | Fair Value Increment |
|---|---|---|---|
| Inventory | $ 60,000 | $ 65,000 | $ 5,000 |
| Land | 40,000 | 50,000 | 10,000 |
| Buildings and Equipment | 300,000 | 360,000 | 60,000 |
| | $400,000 | $475,000 | $75,000 |

Of the $87,500 total differential, $75,000 relates to identifiable assets of Special Foods. The remaining $12,500 is attributable to goodwill. The apportionment of the differential appears as follows:

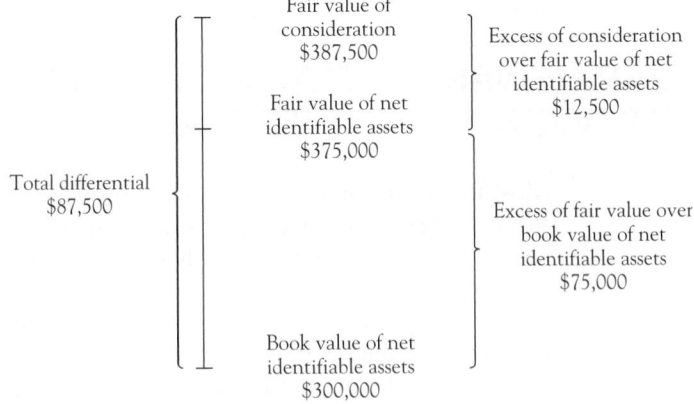

All the inventory to which the differential relates is sold during 20X1; none is left in ending inventory. The buildings and equipment have a remaining economic life of 10 years from the date of combination, and straight-line depreciation is used. At the end of 20X1, Peerless's management determines that the goodwill acquired in the combination with Special Foods has been impaired. Management determines that a $3,000 goodwill impairment loss should be recognized in the consolidated income statement.

For the first year immediately after the date of combination, 20X1, Peerless Products earns income from its own separate operations of $140,000 and pays dividends of $60,000. Special Foods reports net income of $50,000 and pays dividends of $30,000.

### Parent Company Entries

During 20X1, Peerless makes the normal equity-method entries on its books to record its purchase of Special Foods stock and its income and dividends from Special Foods:

| | | | |
|---|---|---:|---:|
| (24) | Investment in Special Foods Stock | 387,500 | |
| | Cash | | 300,000 |
| | Notes Payable | | 87,500 |
| | Record purchase of Special Foods stock. | | |

| | | | |
|---|---|---:|---:|
| (25) | Cash | 30,000 | |
| | Investment in Special Foods Stock | | 30,000 |
| | Record dividends from Special Foods. | | |

| | | | |
|---|---|---:|---:|
| (26) | Investment in Special Foods Stock | 50,000 | |
| | Income from Subsidiary | | 50,000 |
| | Record equity-method income. | | |

Entries (25) and (26) are the same as if Peerless had acquired its investment at underlying book value. In this case, however, Peerless paid an amount for its investment that was $87,500 in excess of the book value of the shares acquired. As discussed in Chapter 2, this difference is a differential that is implicit in the recorded amount of the investment account on Peerless's books. Because Peerless acquired 100 percent of Special Foods' stock, Peerless's differential included in its investment account is equal to the total differential arising from the business combination. However, while the differential arising from the business combination must be allocated to specific assets and liabilities in consolidation, the differential on Peerless's books does not appear separate from the Investment in Special Foods account. Nevertheless, this differential must be written off on Peerless's books to recognize any cost expiration related to the service expiration of Special Foods' assets to which it relates. Because on Peerless's books the differential is included in the investment account, the investment account is reduced to reflect the write-off of the differential:

| | | | |
|---|---|---:|---:|
| (27) | Income from Subsidiary | 5,000 | |
| | Investment in Special Foods Stock | | 5,000 |
| | Adjust income for differential related to inventory sold. | | |

| | | | |
|---|---|---:|---:|
| (28) | Income from Subsidiary | 6,000 | |
| | Investment in Special Foods Stock | | 6,000 |
| | Amortize differential related to buildings and equipment. | | |

A portion of the differential ($5,000) in the investment account on Peerless's books relates to inventory of Special Foods that is sold during 20X1. Because the asset to which that portion of the differential relates is no longer held by Special Foods at the end of the year, that portion of the differential must be written off by reducing the investment account and Peerless's income from Special Foods. This is done through entry (27).

An additional $60,000 of the differential is attributable to the excess of the acquisition-date fair value over book value of Special Foods' buildings and equipment. As the service potential of the underlying assets expires, Peerless must amortize the additional cost it incurred because of the higher fair value of those assets. This is accomplished through annual amortization of $6,000 ($60,000 ÷ 10) over the remaining 10-year life, reflected in entry (28) for 20X1.

The $12,500 portion of the differential representing equity-method goodwill is not adjusted on Peerless's books. Although the goodwill will be written down and a goodwill impairment loss recognized when preparing consolidated financial statements, the FASB has indicated that no equity-method adjustment should be made to reflect this impairment of goodwill.

### Consolidation Workpaper—Year of Combination

After the subsidiary income accruals are entered on Peerless's books, the adjusted trial balance data of the consolidating companies are entered in the three-part consolidation workpaper as shown in Figure 4–13.

**FIGURE 4–13** December 31, 20X1, Equity-Method Workpaper for Consolidated Financial Statements, Initial Year of Ownership; 100 Percent Acquisition at More than Book Value

| Item | Peerless Products | Special Foods | Eliminations Debit | Eliminations Credit | Consolidated |
|---|---|---|---|---|---|
| Sales | 400,000 | 200,000 | | | 600,000 |
| Income from Subsidiary | 39,000 | | (29)  39,000 | | |
| Credits | 439,000 | 200,000 | | | 600,000 |
| Cost of Goods Sold | 170,000 | 115,000 | (31)  5,000 | | 290,000 |
| Depreciation and Amortization | 50,000 | 20,000 | (32)  6,000 | | 76,000 |
| Goodwill Impairment Loss | | | (33)  3,000 | | 3,000 |
| Other Expenses | 40,000 | 15,000 | | | 55,000 |
| Debits | (260,000) | (150,000) | | | (424,000) |
| Net Income, carry forward | 179,000 | 50,000 | 53,000 | | 176,000 |
| Retained Earnings, January 1 | 300,000 | 100,000 | (30) 100,000 | | 300,000 |
| Net Income, from above | 179,000 | 50,000 | 53,000 | | 176,000 |
| | 479,000 | 150,000 | | | 476,000 |
| Dividends Declared | (60,000) | (30,000) | | (29)  30,000 | (60,000) |
| Retained Earnings, December 31, carry forward | 419,000 | 120,000 | 153,000 | 30,000 | 416,000 |
| Cash | 122,500 | 75,000 | | | 197,500 |
| Accounts Receivable | 75,000 | 50,000 | | | 125,000 |
| Inventory | 100,000 | 75,000 | | | 175,000 |
| Land | 175,000 | 40,000 | (31)  10,000 | | 225,000 |
| Buildings and Equipment | 800,000 | 600,000 | (31)  60,000 | | 1,460,000 |
| Investment in Special Foods Stock | 396,500 | | | (29)  9,000 | |
| | | | | (30) 387,500 | |
| Goodwill | | | (31)  12,500 | (33)  3,000 | 9,500 |
| Differential | | | (30)  87,500 | (31)  87,500 | |
| Debits | 1,669,000 | 840,000 | | | 2,192,000 |
| Accumulated Depreciation | 450,000 | 320,000 | | (32)  6,000 | 776,000 |
| Accounts Payable | 100,000 | 100,000 | | | 200,000 |
| Bonds Payable | 200,000 | 100,000 | | | 300,000 |
| Common Stock | 500,000 | 200,000 | (30) 200,000 | | 500,000 |
| Retained Earnings, from above | 419,000 | 120,000 | 153,000 | 30,000 | 416,000 |
| Credits | 1,669,000 | 840,000 | 523,000 | 523,000 | 2,192,000 |

Elimination entries:
  (29)  Eliminate income from subsidiary.
  (30)  Eliminate beginning investment balance.
  (31)  Assign beginning differential.
  (32)  Amortize differential related to buildings and equipment.
  (33)  Write down goodwill for impairment.

The first two workpaper entries eliminate the subsidiary income and dividends recorded by Peerless and eliminate the investment account and the stockholders' equity accounts of Special Foods:

| E(29) | Income from Subsidiary | 39,000 | |
|---|---|---|---|
| | Dividends Declared | | 30,000 |
| | Investment in Special Foods Stock | | 9,000 |
| | Eliminate income from subsidiary. | | |
| | | | |
| E(30) | Common Stock—Special Foods | 200,000 | |
| | Retained Earnings, January 1 | 100,000 | |
| | Differential | 87,500 | |
| | Investment in Special Foods Stock | | 387,500 |
| | Eliminate beginning investment balance. | | |

Entry E(29) removes the net effect of the income accrual recorded by the parent during 20X1 in entries (26), (27), and (28) and removes the dividends declared by the subsidiary during the period. The second elimination entry, E(30), removes the stockholders' equity balances of the subsidiary and the investment account of the parent as of the beginning of the period. Because the acquisition-date fair value of the consideration exchanged in the combination exceeded the book value of Special Foods, a differential appears as the balancing figure in this entry. The differential established in this entry represents the unamortized amount as of the beginning of the period. Because the combination occurred on the first day of 20X1, the amount equals the differential on the date of combination, $87,500. As before, the differential account serves as a clearing account in the workpaper and is entered in the balance sheet portion of the workpaper at the bottom of the asset section.

Three additional eliminating entries are needed in the workpaper in Figure 4–13 to allocate and write down the differential:

| E(31) | Cost of Goods Sold | 5,000 | |
|---|---|---|---|
| | Land | 10,000 | |
| | Buildings and Equipment | 60,000 | |
| | Goodwill | 12,500 | |
| | Differential | | 87,500 |
| | Assign beginning differential. | | |
| | | | |
| E(32) | Depreciation Expense | 6,000 | |
| | Accumulated Depreciation | | 6,000 |
| | Amortize differential related to buildings and equipment: | | |
| | $60,000 \div 10$ years | | |
| | | | |
| E(33) | Goodwill Impairment Loss | 3,000 | |
| | Goodwill | | 3,000 |
| | Write down goodwill for impairment. | | |

Entry E(31) assigns the original amount of the differential to the appropriate asset and expense accounts based on the fair value differences computed previously.

Because all inventory on hand on the date of combination has been sold during the year, the $5,000 of differential applicable to inventory is allocated directly to cost of goods sold. The cost of goods sold recorded on the books of Special Foods is correct for that company's separate financial statements. However, the cost of the inventory to the consolidated entity is viewed as being $5,000 higher, and this additional cost must be included in consolidated cost of goods sold.

No workpaper entry is needed in future periods with respect to the inventory because the inventory has been expensed and no longer is on the subsidiary's books. The portion of the differential related to the inventory no longer exists on Peerless's books after 20X1 because it is removed from the investment account by entry (27).

The differential assigned to depreciable assets in entry E(31) must be charged to depreciation expense over the remaining lives of those assets. From a consolidated viewpoint, the acquisition-date fair value increment associated with the depreciable assets acquired becomes part of the assets' depreciation base. Depreciation already is recorded on the subsidiary's books based on the original cost of the assets to the subsidiary, and these amounts are carried to the consolidation workpaper as depreciation expense. Depreciation on the acquisition-date fair value increment of those assets is entered in the workpaper through entry E(32).

The difference between the $387,500 fair value of the consideration exchanged and the $375,000 fair value of Special Foods' net identifiable assets is assumed to be related to the excess earning power of Special Foods. This difference is entered in the workpaper in Figure 4–13 with entry E(31) as goodwill of $12,500. The $3,000 impairment of this goodwill is recognized with eliminating entry E(33). Although goodwill is not amortized, it must be written down when its value is impaired. This entry reduces the amount of goodwill to be reported in the consolidated balance sheet and establishes a loss to be reported in the consolidated income statement.

A distinction must be made between journal entries recorded on the parent's books under equity-method reporting and the eliminating entries needed in the workpaper to prepare the consolidated financial statements. The eliminating entry to record depreciation expense in the workpaper is needed even though Peerless amortizes the differential on its books at the end of 20X1 with entry (28). The entry on Peerless's books alters the balance in its investment account and the amount of income recognized from Special Foods. However, both account balances are eliminated in the consolidation process, thereby removing any effect of entry (28) on the consolidated totals. Consequently, consolidated income does not reflect the amortization of the differential unless eliminating entry (32) is made.

Once the appropriate eliminating entries are placed in the consolidation workpaper in Figure 4–13, the workpaper is completed by summing each row across, taking into consideration the debit or credit effect of the eliminations.

### *Consolidated Net Income and Retained Earnings*

As can be seen from the workpaper, consolidated net income for 20X1 is $176,000 and consolidated retained earnings on December 31, 20X1, is $416,000. These amounts can be computed as shown in Figure 4–14. Note that both consolidated net income and retained earnings are reduced by the write-off of the purchase differential and the impairment of goodwill.

## Second Year of Ownership

The consolidation procedures employed at the end of the second year, and in periods thereafter, are basically the same as those used at the end of the first year. Consolidation two years after acquisition is illustrated by continuing the example used for 20X1. During 20X2, Peerless Products earns income from its own separate operations of $160,000 and pays dividends of $60,000; Special Foods reports net income of $75,000 and pays dividends of $40,000. No further impairment of the goodwill from the business combination occurs during 20X2.

### *Parent Company Entries*

Peerless Products records the following entries on its separate books during 20X2:

| | | | |
|---|---|---|---|
| (34) | Cash | 40,000 | |
| | Investment in Special Foods Stock | | 40,000 |
| | Record dividends from Special Foods. | | |

**FIGURE 4–14**
**Consolidated Net Income and Retained Earnings, 20X1; 100 Percent Acquisition at More than Book Value**

| Consolidated net income, 20X1: | |
| --- | --- |
| Peerless's separate operating income | $140,000 |
| Special Foods' net income | 50,000 |
| Write-off of differential related to inventory sold during 20X1 | (5,000) |
| Amortization of differential related to buildings and equipment in 20X1 | (6,000) |
| Goodwill impairment loss | (3,000) |
| Consolidated net income, 20X1 | $176,000 |
| Consolidated retained earnings, December 31, 20X1: | |
| Peerless's retained earnings on date of combination, January 1, 20X1 | $300,000 |
| Peerless's separate operating income, 20X1 | 140,000 |
| Special Foods' 20X1 net income | 50,000 |
| Write-off of differential related to inventory sold during 20X1 | (5,000) |
| Amortization of differential related to buildings and equipment in 20X1 | (6,000) |
| Goodwill impairment loss | (3,000) |
| Dividends declared by Peerless, 20X1 | (60,000) |
| Consolidated retained earnings, December 31, 20X1 | $416,000 |

| (35) | Investment in Special Foods Stock | 75,000 | |
| --- | --- | --- | --- |
| | Income from Subsidiary | | 75,000 |
| | Record equity-method income. | | |

| (36) | Income from Subsidiary | 6,000 | |
| --- | --- | --- | --- |
| | Investment in Special Foods Stock | | 6,000 |
| | Amortize differential related to buildings and equipment. | | |

Entry (36) to record the 20X2 amortization of the differential related to buildings and equipment is identical to entry (28) recorded by Peerless in 2001 because the straight-line method is used.

The changes in the parent's investment account for 20X1 and 20X2 can be summarized as follows:

| | 20X1 | | 20X2 | |
| --- | --- | --- | --- | --- |
| Balance at start of year | | $387,500 | | $396,500 |
| Income from subsidiary: | | | | |
| Parent's accrual of subsidiary's income | $50,000 | | $75,000 | |
| Differential write-off for inventory sold | (5,000) | | | |
| Amortization of differential | (6,000) | | (6,000) | |
| | | 39,000 | | 69,000 |
| Less: Dividends received from subsidiary | | (30,000) | | (40,000) |
| Balance at end of year | | $396,500 | | $425,500 |

### Consolidation Workpaper—Second Year Following Combination

The workpaper to prepare a complete set of consolidated financial statements for the year 20X2 is illustrated in Figure 4–15. Eliminating entries at the end of 20X2 are similar to those at the end of 20X1.

The first workpaper entry, E(37), eliminates Peerless's income from Special Foods and Special Foods' dividends for 20X2:

| E(37) | Income from Subsidiary | 69,000 | |
| --- | --- | --- | --- |
| | Dividends Declared | | 40,000 |
| | Investment in Special Foods Stock | | 29,000 |
| | Eliminate income from subsidiary. | | |

**FIGURE 4–15**  December 31, 20X2, Equity-Method Workpaper for Consolidated Financial Statements, Second Year of Ownership; 100 Percent Acquisition at More than Book Value

| Item | Peerless Products | Special Foods | Eliminations Debit | Eliminations Credits | Consolidated |
|---|---|---|---|---|---|
| Sales | 450,000 | 300,000 | | | 750,000 |
| Income from Subsidiary | 69,000 | | (37)  69,000 | | |
| Credits | 519,000 | 300,000 | | | 750,000 |
| Cost of Goods Sold | 180,000 | 160,000 | | | 340,000 |
| Depreciation and Amortization | 50,000 | 20,000 | (40)  6,000 | | 76,000 |
| Other Expenses | 60,000 | 45,000 | | | 105,000 |
| Debits | (290,000) | (225,000) | | | 521,000 |
| Net Income, carry forward | 229,000 | 75,000 | 75,000 | | 229,000 |
| Retained Earnings, January 1 | 419,000 | 120,000 | (38) 120,000 | | |
| | | | (41)  3,000 | | 416,000 |
| Net Income, from above | 229,000 | 75,000 | 75,000 | | 229,000 |
| | 648,000 | 195,000 | | | 645,000 |
| Dividends Declared | (60,000) | (40,000) | | (37)  40,000 | (60,000) |
| Retained Earnings, December 31, carry forward | 588,000 | 155,000 | 198,000 | 40,000 | 585,000 |
| Cash | 157,500 | 85,000 | | | 242,500 |
| Accounts Receivable | 150,000 | 80,000 | | | 230,000 |
| Inventory | 180,000 | 90,000 | | | 270,000 |
| Land | 175,000 | 40,000 | (39)  10,000 | | 225,000 |
| Buildings and Equipment | 800,000 | 600,000 | (39)  60,000 | | 1,460,000 |
| Investment in Special Foods Stock | 425,500 | | | (37)  29,000 | |
| | | | | (38) 396,500 | |
| Goodwill | | | (39)  12,500 | (41)  3,000 | 9,500 |
| Differential | | | (38)  76,500 | (39)  76,500 | |
| Debits | 1,888,000 | 895,000 | | | 2,437,000 |
| Accumulated Depreciation | 500,000 | 340,000 | | (39)  6,000 | |
| | | | | (40)  6,000 | 852,000 |
| Accounts Payable | 100,000 | 100,000 | | | 200,000 |
| Bonds Payable | 200,000 | 100,000 | | | 300,000 |
| Common Stock | 500,000 | 200,000 | (38) 200,000 | | 500,000 |
| Retained Earnings, from above | 588,000 | 155,000 | 198,000 | 40,000 | 585,000 |
| Credits | 1,888,000 | 895,000 | 557,000 | 557,000 | 2,437,000 |

Elimination entries:
  (37)  Eliminate income from subsidiary.
  (38)  Eliminate beginning investment balance.
  (39)  Assign beginning differential.
  (40)  Amortize differential related to buildings and equipment.
  (41)  Adjust for 20X1 impairment of goodwill.

The net credit to the investment account of $29,000 represents the increase in the account balance during the period and takes the account balance back to the amount on January 1, 20X2, the beginning of the second year.

Entry E(38) eliminates the balances in Peerless's investment account and Special Foods' stockholders' equity accounts as of the beginning of the period:

| E(38) | Common Stock—Special Foods | 200,000 | |
|---|---|---|---|
| | Retained Earnings, January 1 | 120,000 | |
| | Differential | 76,500 | |
| | Investment in Special Foods Stock | | 396,500 |
| | Eliminate beginning investment balance. | | |

Together, entries E(37) and E(38) fully eliminate the ending balance in the parent's investment account.

Entry E(38) also establishes the differential as of the beginning of 20X2. The differential at the beginning of 20X1, the date of combination, was $87,500 and was reduced by the amounts written off during 20X1. During 20X1, Peerless wrote off the $5,000 of the differential related to the inventory sold in 20X1 and amortized $6,000 of the differential related to buildings and equipment. Thus, the unamortized balance of the differential at the beginning of 20X2 is $76,500 ($87,500 − $5,000 − $6,000).

In the consolidation workpaper, allocation of the differential in 20X2 is different from the allocation in the first year in several respects:

1. No allocation is made to inventory or cost of goods sold.
2. The balance in the Goodwill account in 20X2 should be only $9,500 because of the $3,000 write-off of goodwill in 20X1 to reflect an impairment loss. However, because the differential was not written down on Peerless's books to reflect the goodwill impairment and goodwill is not amortized (in accordance with the FASB's requirements), the original $12,500 amount of goodwill is established in the workpaper. The prior-period impairment is then recognized in a separate eliminating entry.
3. Accumulated depreciation must be entered in the workpaper to reflect the additional depreciation on the buildings and equipment taken in the 20X1 consolidation workpaper. This should be part of the 20X2 consolidated total, but it does not automatically carry forward from the previous year's workpaper.

Entry E(39) assigns the January 1, 20X2, differential:

| E(39) | Land | 10,000 | |
|---|---|---|---|
| | Buildings and Equipment | 60,000 | |
| | Goodwill | 12,500 | |
| | Differential | | 76,500 |
| | Accumulated Depreciation | | 6,000 |
| | Assign beginning differential. | | |

Because each year's workpaper is prepared from the trial balance data reported by the separate companies, not from the previous year's workpaper, the $6,000 of additional accumulated depreciation entered in the consolidation workpaper at the end of 20X1 does not automatically carry over to the 20X2 workpaper. Thus, the workpaper entry to allocate the differential each time also must establish the additional accumulated depreciation for all prior years on any differential amounts assigned to depreciable assets.

The 20X2 depreciation of the portion of the differential assigned to buildings and equipment is given in entry E(40):

| E(40) | Depreciation Expense | 6,000 | |
|---|---|---|---|
| | Accumulated Depreciation | | 6,000 |
| | Amortize differential related to buildings and equipment: | | |
| | $60,000 ÷ 10 years | | |

| Consolidated net income, 20X2: | |
|---|---:|
| Peerless's separate operating income | $160,000 |
| Special Foods' net income | 75,000 |
| Amortization of differential related to buildings and equipment in 20X2 | (6,000) |
| Consolidated net income, 20X2 | $229,000 |
| | |
| Consolidated retained earnings, December 31, 20X2: | |
| Consolidated retained earnings, December 31, 20X1 | $416,000 |
| Peerless's separate operating income, 20X2 | 160,000 |
| Special Foods' 20X2 net income | 75,000 |
| Amortization of differential related to buildings and equipment in 20X2 | (6,000) |
| Dividends declared by Peerless, 20X2 | (60,000) |
| Consolidated retained earnings, December 31, 20X2 | $585,000 |

The amount of additional depreciation expense each period remains the same from year to year unless (1) a depreciation method other than straight-line is used, (2) some of the underlying assets are sold, or (3) some of the assets become fully depreciated.

Entry E(41) corrects the beginning consolidated retained earnings and the goodwill balance for the impairment loss recognized in the 20X1 consolidated income statement:

| E(41) | Retained Earnings, January 1 | 3,000 | |
|---|---|---:|---:|
| | Goodwill | | 3,000 |
| | Adjust for 20X1 impairment of goodwill. | | |

Because the differential on Peerless's books is not written down under the equity method to reflect the 20X1 impairment of goodwill, the differential established in the 20X2 workpaper through entry E(39) includes the full $12,500 differential originally representing goodwill. Also, because the impairment loss did not affect Peerless's equity-method net income, and Peerless's retained earnings becomes consolidated retained earnings, beginning consolidated retained earnings will be overstated unless it is reduced by the amount of the prior period's impairment loss. Thus, both beginning consolidated retained earnings and goodwill must be reduced each period in the consolidation workpaper for the 20X1 impairment.

### Consolidated Net Income and Retained Earnings

The computation of 20X2 consolidated net income and consolidated retained earnings at the end of 20X2 is shown in Figure 4–16.

## INTERCOMPANY RECEIVABLES AND PAYABLES

All forms of intercompany receivables and payables need to be eliminated when consolidated financial statements are prepared. From a single-company viewpoint, a company cannot owe itself money. If a company owes an affiliate $1,000 on account, one company carries a $1,000 receivable on its separate books, and the other has a payable for the same amount. When consolidated financial statements are prepared, the following elimination entry is needed in the consolidation workpaper:

| E(42) | Accounts Payable | 1,000 | |
|---|---|---:|---:|
| | Accounts Receivable | | 1,000 |
| | Eliminate intercompany receivable/payable. | | |

If no eliminating entry is made, both the consolidated assets and liabilities are overstated by an equal amount.

If the intercompany receivable/payable bears interest, all accounts related to the intercompany claim must be eliminated in the preparation of consolidated statements, including the receivable/payable, interest income, interest expense, and any accrued interest on the intercompany claim. Other forms of intercorporate claims, such as bonds, are discussed in subsequent chapters. In all cases, failure to eliminate these claims can distort consolidated balances. As a result, the magnitude of debt of the combined entity may appear to be greater than it is, working capital ratios may be incorrect, and other types of comparisons may be distorted.

# PUSH-DOWN ACCOUNTING

The term *push-down accounting* refers to the practice of revaluing an acquired subsidiary's assets and liabilities to their fair values directly on that subsidiary's books at the date of acquisition. If this practice is followed, the revaluations are recorded once on the subsidiary's books at the date of acquisition and, therefore, are not made in the consolidation workpapers each time consolidated statements are prepared.

Those who favor push-down accounting argue that the change in the subsidiary's ownership in an acquisition is reason for adopting a new basis of accounting for the subsidiary's assets and liabilities, and this new basis of accounting should be reflected directly on the subsidiary's books. This argument is most persuasive when the subsidiary is wholly owned and is consolidated or has its separate financial statements included with the statements of the parent.

On the other hand, when a subsidiary has a significant noncontrolling interest or the subsidiary has bonds or preferred stock held by the public, push-down accounting may be inappropriate. The use of push-down accounting in the financial statements issued to the noncontrolling shareholders or to those holding bonds or preferred stock results in a new basis of accounting even though, from the perspective of those statement users, the entity has not changed. From their viewpoint, push-down accounting results in the revaluation of the assets and liabilities of a continuing enterprise, a practice that normally is not acceptable.

**SEC Staff Accounting Bulletin No. 54** requires push-down accounting whenever a business combination results in the acquired subsidiary becoming substantially wholly owned. The staff accounting bulletin encourages but does not require the use of push-down accounting in situations in which the subsidiary is less than wholly owned or the subsidiary has outstanding debt or preferred stock held by the public.

The revaluation of assets and liabilities on a subsidiary's books involves making an entry to debit or credit each asset and liability account to be revalued, with the balancing entry to a revaluation capital account. The revaluation capital account is part of the subsidiary's stockholders' equity. Once the revaluations are made on the books of the subsidiary, the new book values of the subsidiary's assets, including goodwill, are equal to the acquisition cost of the subsidiary. Thus, no differential arises in the consolidation process. The investment elimination entry in a consolidation workpaper prepared immediately after acquisition of a subsidiary and revaluation of its assets on its books might appear as follows:

| E(43) | Capital Stock—Subsidiary | XXX | |
| | Retained Earnings | XXX | |
| | Revaluation Capital | XXX | |
| |     Investment in Subsidiary Stock | | XXX |
| |     Eliminate investment balance. | | |

Note that the Revaluation Capital account, as part of the subsidiary's stockholders' equity, is eliminated in preparing consolidated statements. A more detailed example of push-down accounting is given in Appendix 4A.

## Summary of Key Concepts

Consolidated financial statements present the financial position and results of operations of two or more separate legal entities as if they were a single company. A consolidated balance sheet prepared on the date a parent acquires a subsidiary appears the same as if the acquired company had been merged into the parent.

A consolidation workpaper provides a means of efficiently developing the data needed to prepare consolidated financial statements. The workpaper includes a separate column for the trial balance data of each of the consolidating companies, a debit and a credit column for the elimination entries, and a column for the consolidated totals that appear in the consolidated financial statements. A three-part consolidation workpaper facilitates preparation of a consolidated income statement, retained earnings statement, and balance sheet, and it includes a section for each statement. Eliminating entries are needed in the workpaper to remove the effects of intercompany ownership and intercompany transactions so the consolidated financial statements appear as if the separate companies are actually one. Workpaper eliminating entries are needed to (1) eliminate the parent's subsidiary investment and the subsidiary's stockholders' equity accounts, (2) eliminate the subsidiary's income recognized by the parent during the period and the subsidiary's dividends declared, (3) assign any differential to specific assets and liabilities, (4) amortize or write off a portion of the differential, if appropriate, and (5) eliminate intercompany receivables and payables.

Consolidated net income is computed in simple cases for a parent and a wholly owned subsidiary as the total of the parent's income from its own operations and the subsidiary's net income, adjusted for the write-off of differential, if appropriate. In this situation, consolidated retained earnings is computed as the total of the parent's retained earnings, excluding any income from the subsidiary, plus the subsidiary's cumulative net income since acquisition.

When a subsidiary is acquired for an amount greater than its book value, some parents may prefer to assign the differential to individual assets and liabilities directly on the books of the subsidiary at the time of acquisition, thereby eliminating the need for revaluation entries in the consolidation workpaper each period. This procedure is called push-down accounting.

## Key Terms

bargain purchase, *150*
consolidated net income, *152*
consolidated retained earnings, *153*
consolidation workpaper, *139*
differential, *144*
eliminating entries, *139*
goodwill, *147*
parent, *138*
push-down accounting, *146*
subsidiary, *138*

# Appendix 4A    Push-Down Accounting Illustrated

When a subsidiary is acquired in a business combination, its assets and liabilities must be revalued to their fair values as of the date of combination for consolidated reporting. If *push-down accounting* is employed, the revaluations are made as of the date of combination directly on the books of the subsidiary and no eliminating entries related to the differential are needed in the workpapers.

The following example illustrates the consolidation process when assets and liabilities are revalued directly on a subsidiary's books rather than using consolidation workpaper entries to accomplish the revaluation. Assume that Peerless Products purchases all of Special Foods' common stock on January 1, 20X1, for $370,000 cash. The purchase price is $70,000 in excess of Special Foods' book value. Of the $70,000 total differential, $10,000 is related to land held by Special Foods and $60,000 is related to buildings and equipment having a 10-year remaining life. Peerless accounts for its investment in Special Foods stock using the equity method.

Peerless records the acquisition of stock on its books with the following entry:

January 1, 20X1

| | | | |
|---|---|---|---|
| (44) | Investment in Special Foods Stock | 370,000 | |
| | Cash | | 370,000 |
| | Record purchase of Special Foods stock. | | |

In contrast to a workpaper revaluation, the use of push-down accounting involves the revaluation of the assets on the separate books of Special Foods and alleviates the need for revaluation entries in the consolidation workpaper each period. If push-down accounting is used to revalue Special Foods' assets, the following entry is made directly on Special Foods' books:

January 1, 20X1

| | | | |
|---|---|---|---|
| (45) | Land | 10,000 | |
| | Buildings and Equipment | 60,000 | |
| | Revaluation Capital | | 70,000 |
| | Revalue assets to reflect fair values at date of combination. | | |

This entry increases the amount at which the land and the buildings and equipment are shown in Special Foods' separate financial statements and gives rise to a revaluation capital account that is shown in the stockholders' equity section of Special Foods' balance sheet. Special Foods records $6,000 additional depreciation on its books to reflect the amortization over 10 years of the $60,000 write-up of buildings and equipment. This additional depreciation decreases Special Foods' reported net income for 20X1 from $50,000 to $44,000.

On its books, Peerless records its income and dividends from Special Foods:

| | | | |
|---|---|---|---|
| (46) | Cash | 30,000 | |
| | Investment in Special Foods Stock | | 30,000 |
| | Record dividends from Special Foods. | | |

| | | | |
|---|---|---|---|
| (47) | Investment in Special Foods Stock | 44,000 | |
| | Income from Subsidiary | | 44,000 |
| | Record equity-method income. | | |

The equity-method income recorded by Peerless in entry (47) is less than had push-down accounting not been employed because Special Foods' income is reduced by the additional depreciation on the write-up of the buildings and equipment recorded on Special Foods' books. Because the revaluation is recorded on the subsidiary's books, Special Foods' book value is then equal to the fair value of the consideration given in the combination. Therefore, no differential exists, and Peerless need not record any amortization associated with the investment. The net amount of income from Special Foods recorded by Peerless is the same regardless of whether or not push-down accounting is employed.

Figure 4–17 shows the consolidation workpaper prepared at the end of 20X1 and includes the effects of revaluing Special Foods' assets. Note that Special Foods' Land and its Buildings and Equipment have been increased by $10,000 and $60,000, respectively. Also note the Revaluation Capital account in Special Foods' stockholders' equity.

Because the revaluation was accomplished directly on the books of Special Foods, only the two investment elimination entries are needed in the workpaper illustrated in Figure 4–17:

| | | | |
|---|---|---|---|
| E(48) | Income from Subsidiary | 44,000 | |
| | Dividends Declared | | 30,000 |
| | Investment in Special Foods Stock | | 14,000 |
| | Eliminate income from subsidiary. | | |

| | | | |
|---|---|---|---|
| E(49) | Common Stock—Special Foods | 200,000 | |
| | Retained Earnings, January 1 | 100,000 | |
| | Revaluation Capital | 70,000 | |
| | Investment in Special Foods Stock | | 370,000 |
| | Eliminate beginning investment balance. | | |

**FIGURE 4-17**   December 31, 20X1, Equity-Method Workpaper for Consolidated Financial Statements, Initial Year of Ownership; 100 Percent Acquisition at More than Book Value; Push-Down Accounting

| Item | Peerless Products | Special Foods | Eliminations Debit | Eliminations Credit | Consolidated |
|---|---|---|---|---|---|
| Sales | 400,000 | 200,000 | | | 600,000 |
| Income from Subsidiary | 44,000 | | (48)   44,000 | | |
| Credits | 444,000 | 200,000 | | | 600,000 |
| Cost of Goods Sold | 170,000 | 115,000 | | | 285,000 |
| Depreciation and Amortization | 50,000 | 26,000 | | | 76,000 |
| Other Expenses | 40,000 | 15,000 | | | 55,000 |
| Debits | (260,000) | (156,000) | | | (416,000) |
| Net Income, carry forward | 184,000 | 44,000 | 44,000 | | 184,000 |
| Retained Earnings, January 1 | 300,000 | 100,000 | (49) 100,000 | | 300,000 |
| Net Income, from above | 184,000 | 44,000 | 44,000 | | 184,000 |
| | 484,000 | 144,000 | | | 484,000 |
| Dividends Declared | (60,000) | (30,000) | | (48)   30,000 | (60,000) |
| Retained Earnings, December 31, carry forward | 424,000 | 114,000 | 144,000 | 30,000 | 424,000 |
| Cash | 140,000 | 75,000 | | | 215,000 |
| Accounts Receivable | 75,000 | 50,000 | | | 125,000 |
| Inventory | 100,000 | 75,000 | | | 175,000 |
| Land | 175,000 | 50,000 | | | 225,000 |
| Buildings and Equipment | 800,000 | 660,000 | | | 1,460,000 |
| Investment in Special Foods Stock | 384,000 | | | (48)   14,000 | |
| | | | | (49) 370,000 | |
| Debits | 1,674,000 | 910,000 | | | 2,200,000 |
| Accumulated Depreciation | 450,000 | 326,000 | | | 776,000 |
| Accounts Payable | 100,000 | 100,000 | | | 200,000 |
| Bonds Payable | 200,000 | 100,000 | | | 300,000 |
| Common Stock | 500,000 | 200,000 | (49) 200,000 | | 500,000 |
| Retained Earnings, from above | 424,000 | 114,000 | 144,000 | 30,000 | 424,000 |
| Revaluation Capital | | 70,000 | (49)   70,000 | | |
| Credits | 1,674,000 | 910,000 | 414,000 | 414,000 | 2,200,000 |

Elimination entries:
(48) Eliminate income from subsidiary.
(49) Eliminate beginning investment balance.

**Questions**

**Q4-1**   How does an eliminating entry differ from an adjusting entry?

**Q4-2**   What is the term *differential* used to indicate?

**Q4-3**   What conditions must exist for a negative differential to occur?

**Q4-4**   What portion of the balances of subsidiary stockholders' equity accounts are included in the consolidated balance sheet?

**Q4-5**   What portion of the book value of the net assets held by a subsidiary at acquisition is included in the consolidated balance sheet?

**Q4-6**   What portion of the fair value of a subsidiary's net assets normally is included in the consolidated balance sheet following a business combination?

**Q4-7**   What is the justification for using a differential clearing account in preparing consolidated statements?

Q4-8   What happens to the differential in the consolidation workpaper prepared as of the date of combination? How is it reestablished so that the proper balances can be reported the following year?

Q4-9   Explain why consolidated financial statements become increasingly important when the differential is very large.

Q4-10   How does the elimination process change when consolidated statements are prepared after—rather than at—the date of acquisition?

Q4-11   What are the three parts of the consolidation workpaper, and what sequence is used in completing the workpaper parts?

Q4-12   How are a subsidiary's dividend declarations reported in the consolidated retained earnings statement?

Q4-13   Give a definition of *consolidated net income*.

Q4-14   How is consolidated net income computed in a consolidation workpaper?

Q4-15   Give a definition of *consolidated retained earnings*.

Q4-16   How is the amount reported as consolidated retained earnings determined?

Q4-17   Why is the beginning retained earnings balance for each company entered in the three-part consolidation workpaper rather than just the ending balance?

Q4-18   When Ajax was preparing its consolidation workpaper, the differential was properly assigned to buildings and equipment. What additional entry generally must be made in the workpaper?

Q4-19   What determines whether the balance assigned to the differential remains constant or decreases each period?

Q4-20   What does the term *push-down accounting* mean?

Q4-21   Under what conditions is push-down accounting considered appropriate?

Q4-22   What happens to the differential when push-down accounting is used following a business combination?

---

# Cases

**C4-1**   **Need for Consolidation Process**

At a recent staff meeting, the vice president of marketing appeared confused. The controller had assured him that the parent company and each of the subsidiary companies had properly accounted for all transactions during the year. After several other questions, he finally asked, "If it has been done properly, then why must you spend so much time and make so many changes to the amounts reported by the individual companies when you prepare the consolidated financial statements each month? You should be able to just add the reported balances together."

*Communication*

### Required
Prepare an appropriate response to help the controller answer the marketing vice president's question.

**C4-2**   **Account Presentation**

Prime Company has been expanding rapidly and is now an extremely diversified company for its size. It currently owns three companies with manufacturing facilities, two companies primarily in retail sales, a consumer finance company, and two natural gas pipeline companies. This has led to some conflict between the company's chief accountant and its treasurer. The treasurer advocates presenting no more than five assets and three liabilities on its balance sheet. The chief accountant has resisted combining balances from substantially different subsidiaries and has asked for your assistance.

*Research
FARS*

### Required
Review the appropriate authoritative pronouncements or other relevant accounting literature to see what guidance is provided and prepare a memo to the chief accountant with your findings. Include citations to and quotations from the most relevant references. Include in your memo at least two examples of situations in which it may be inappropriate to combine similar appearing accounts of two subsidiaries.

**C4-3**   **Consolidating an Unprofitable Subsidiary**

Amazing Chemical Corporation's president had always wanted his own yacht and crew and concluded that Amazing Chemical should diversify its investments by purchasing an existing boatyard

*Research
FARS*

and repair facility on the lake shore near his summer home. He could then purchase a yacht and have a convenient place to store it and have it repaired. Although the board of directors was never formally asked to approve this new venture, the president moved forward with optimism and a rather substantial amount of corporate money to purchase full ownership of the boatyard, which had lost rather significant amounts of money each of the five prior years and had never reported a profit for the original owners.

Not surprisingly, the boatyard continued to lose money after Amazing Chemical purchased it, and the losses grew larger each month. Amazing Chemical, a very profitable chemical company, reported net income of $780,000 in 20X2 and $850,000 in 20X3 even though the boatyard reported net losses of $160,000 in 20X2 and $210,000 in 20X3 and was fully consolidated.

### Required

Amazing Chemical's chief accountant has become concerned that members of the board of directors or company shareholders will accuse him of improperly preparing the consolidated statements. The president does not plan to tell anyone about the losses, which do not show up in the consolidated income statement that the chief accountant prepared. You have been asked to prepare a memo to the chief accountant indicating the way to include subsidiaries in the consolidated income statement and to provide citations to or quotations from the authoritative accounting literature that would assist the chief accountant in dealing with this matter. You have also been asked to search the accounting literature to see whether any reporting requirements require disclosure of the boatyard in notes to the financial statements or in management's discussion and analysis.

**C4-4**

*Analysis*

### Assigning an Acquisition Differential

Ball Corporation's owners recently offered to sell 60 percent of their ownership to Timber Corporation for $450,000. Timber's business manager was told that Ball's book value was $300,000, and she estimates the fair value of its net assets at approximately $600,000. Ball has relatively old equipment and manufacturing facilities and uses a LIFO basis for inventory valuation of some items and a FIFO basis for others.

### Required

If Timber accepts the offer and acquires a controlling interest in Ball, what difficulties are likely to be encountered in assigning the differential?

**C4-5**

*Understanding*

### Negative Retained Earnings

Although Sloan Company had good earnings reports in 20X5 and 20X6, it had a negative retained earnings balance on December 31, 20X6. Jacobs Corporation purchased 80 percent of Sloan's common stock on January 1, 20X7.

### Required

a. Explain how Sloan's negative retained earnings balance is reflected in the consolidated balance sheet immediately following the acquisition.

b. Explain how the existence of negative retained earnings changes the consolidation workpaper entries.

c. Can goodwill be recorded if Jacobs pays more than book value for Sloan's shares? Explain.

**C4-6**

*Judgment*

### Balance Sheet Reporting Issues

Crumple Car Rentals is planning to expand into the western part of the United States and needs to acquire approximately 400 additional automobiles for rental purposes. Because Crumple's cash reserves were substantially depleted in replacing the bumpers on existing automobiles with new "fashion plate" bumpers, the expansion funds must be acquired through other means. Crumple's management has identified three options:

1. Issue additional debt.

2. Create a wholly owned leasing subsidiary that would borrow the money with a guarantee for payment from Crumple. The subsidiary would then lease the cars to the parent.

3. Create a trust that would borrow the money with a guarantee for repayment from Crumple and lease the cars to it. In the event of liquidation, the residual value of the trust would go to the Historical Preservation Society of Pleasantville.

The acquisition price of the cars is approximately the same under all three alternatives.

### Required

*a.* You have been asked to compare and contrast the three alternatives from the perspective of:

(1) The impact on Crumple's consolidated balance sheet.

(2) Their legal ramifications.

(3) The ability to control the maintenance, repair, and replacement of automobiles.

*b.* You are to consider any alternatives that might be used in acquiring the required automobiles.

*c.* You are to select the preferred alternative and show why it is the best choice.

**C4-7   Subsidiary Ownership: AMR Corporation and International Lease**

*Research*

Most subsidiaries are wholly owned, although only majority ownership is usually all that is required for consolidation. The parent's ownership may be direct or indirect. Frequently, a parent's direct subsidiaries have subsidiaries of their own, thus providing the parent with indirect ownership of the subsidiary's subsidiaries.

### Required

*a.* AMR Corporation is one of the largest corporations in the United States, with significant visibility.

(1) What is AMR Corporation's principal business?

(2) What is the name of AMR's principal directly owned subsidiary?

(3) In what city is AMR headquartered?

(4) In what state is AMR incorporated?

(5) Where are most of AMR's subsidiaries incorporated?

(6) Where is AMR's common stock traded?

(7) How many subsidiaries, if any, does AMR's principal subsidiary have?

(8) Approximately what percentage of AMR's subsidiaries are wholly owned?

*b.* International Lease Finance Corporation is a very large leasing company. It leases equipment that everyone is familiar with and many have used.

(1) Specifically, what is the principal business of International Lease Finance Corporation?

(2) Who are the direct owners of International Lease?

(3) In what city is International Lease headquartered?

(4) In what state is International Lease incorporated?

(5) Where is International Lease's common stock traded?

(6) What company is the parent in the consolidated financial statements in which International Lease is included, and what is that company's principal business?

---

**Exercises**

**E4-1   Multiple-Choice Questions on Consolidation Process**

Select the most appropriate answer for each of the following questions.

1. Goodwill is:

*a.* Seldom reported because it is too difficult to measure.

*b.* Reported when more than book value is paid in purchasing another company.

*c.* Reported when the fair value of the acquire is greater than the fair value of the net identifiable assets acquired.

*d.* Generally smaller for small companies and increases in amount as the companies acquired increase in size.

2. [AICPA Adapted] Wright Corporation includes several subsidiaries in its consolidated financial statements. In its December 31, 20X2, trial balance, Wright had the following intercompany balances before eliminations:

| | Debit | Credit |
|---|---|---|
| Current receivable due from Main Company | $ 32,000 | |
| Noncurrent receivable from Main Company | 114,000 | |
| Cash advance to Corn Corporation | 6,000 | |
| Cash advance from King Company | | $ 15,000 |
| Intercompany payable to King Company | | 101,000 |

In its December 31, 20X2, consolidated balance sheet, what amount should Wright report as intercompany receivables?

a. $152,000.

b. $146,000.

c. $36,000.

d. $0.

3. Beni Corporation acquired 100 percent of Carr Corporation's outstanding capital stock for $430,000 cash. Immediately before the purchase, the balance sheets of both corporations reported the following:

| | Beni | Carr |
|---|---|---|
| Assets | $2,000,000 | $750,000 |
| | | |
| Liabilities | $ 750,000 | $400,000 |
| Common Stock | 1,000,000 | 310,000 |
| Retained Earnings | 250,000 | 40,000 |
| Liabilities and Stockholders' Equity | $2,000,000 | $750,000 |

At the date of purchase, the fair value of Carr's assets was $50,000 more than the aggregate carrying amounts. In the consolidated balance sheet prepared immediately after the purchase, the consolidated stockholders' equity should amount to:

a. $1,680,000.

b. $1,650,000.

c. $1,600,000.

d. $1,250,000.

*Note:* Questions 4 and 5 are based on the following information:
Nugget Company's balance sheet on December 31, 20X6, was as follows:

| Assets | | Liabilities and Stockholders' Equity | |
|---|---|---|---|
| Cash | $ 100,000 | Current Liabilities | $ 300,000 |
| Accounts Receivable | 200,000 | Long-Term Debt | 500,000 |
| Inventories | 500,000 | Common Stock (par $1 per share) | 100,000 |
| Property, Plant, and Equipment (net) | 900,000 | Additional Paid-In Capital | 200,000 |
| | | Retained Earnings | 600,000 |
| | | Total Liabilities and | |
| Total Assets | $1,700,000 | Stockholders' Equity | $1,700,000 |

On December 31, 20X6, Gold Company acquired all of Nugget's outstanding common stock for $1,500,000 cash. On that date, the fair (market) value of Nugget's inventories was $450,000, and the fair value of Nugget's property, plant, and equipment was $1,000,000. The fair values of all other assets and liabilities of Nugget were equal to their book values.

4. As a result of Gold's acquisition of Nugget, the consolidated balance sheet of Gold and Nugget should reflect goodwill in the amount of:

a. $500,000.

b. $550,000.

c. $600,000.

d. $650,000.

5. Assuming that the balance sheet of Gold (unconsolidated) on December 31, 20X6, reflected retained earnings of $2,000,000, what amount of retained earnings should be shown in the December 31, 20X6, consolidated balance sheet of Gold and its new subsidiary, Nugget?

  *a.* $2,000,000.

  *b.* $2,600,000.

  *c.* $2,800,000.

  *d.* $3,150,000.

**E4-2**  **Multiple-Choice Questions on Consolidation [AICPA Adapted]**

Select the correct answer for each of the following questions.

1. On January 1, 20X1, Prim Inc. acquired all of Scrap Inc.'s outstanding common shares for cash equal to the stock's book value. The carrying amounts of Scrap's assets and liabilities approximated their fair values, except that the carrying amount of its building was more than fair value. In preparing Prim's 20X1 consolidated income statement, which of the following adjustments would be made?

   *a.* Decrease depreciation expense and recognize goodwill amortization.

   *b.* Increase depreciation expense and recognize goodwill amortization.

   *c.* Decrease depreciation expense and recognize no goodwill amortization.

   *d.* Increase depreciation expense and recognize no goodwill amortization.

2. The first examination of Rudd Corporation's financial statements was made for the year ended December 31, 20X8. The auditor found that Rudd had acquired another company on January 1, 20X8, and had recorded goodwill of $100,000 in connection with this acquisition. Although a friend of the auditor believes the goodwill will last no more than five years, Rudd's management has found no impairment of goodwill during 20X8. In its 20X8 financial statements, Rudd should report:

|  | Amortization Expense | Goodwill |
|---|---|---|
| *a.* | $     0 | $100,000 |
| *b.* | $100,000 | $     0 |
| *c.* | $ 20,000 | $ 80,000 |
| *d.* | $     0 | $     0 |

3. Consolidated financial statements are being prepared for a parent and its four subsidiaries that have intercompany loans of $100,000 and intercompany profits of $300,000. How much of these intercompany loans and profits should be eliminated?

|  | Intercompany | |
|---|---|---|
|  | Loans | Profits |
| *a.* | $     0 | $     0 |
| *b.* | $     0 | $300,000 |
| *c.* | $100,000 | $     0 |
| *d.* | $100,000 | $300,000 |

4. On April 1, 20X8, Plum Inc. paid $1,700,000 for all of Long Corp.'s issued and outstanding common stock. On that date, the costs and fair values of Long's recorded assets and liabilities were as follows:

|  | Cost | Fair Value |
|---|---|---|
| Cash | $ 160,000 | $ 160,000 |
| Inventory | 480,000 | 460,000 |
| Property, plant and equipment (net) | 980,000 | 1,040,000 |
| Liabilities | (360,000) | (360,000) |
| Net assets | $1,260,000 | $1,300,000 |

In Plum's March 31, 20X9, consolidated balance sheet, what amount of goodwill should be reported as a result of this business combination?

   *a.* $360,000.

   *b.* $396,000.

   *c.* $400,000.

   *d.* $440,000.

### E4-3 Basic Elimination Entry

On December 31, 20X3, Broadway Corporation reported common stock outstanding of $200,000, additional paid-in capital of $300,000, and retained earnings of $100,000. On January 1, 20X4, Johe Company acquired control of Broadway in a business combination.

#### Required

Give the eliminating entry that would be needed in preparing a consolidated balance sheet immediately following the combination if Johe acquired all of Broadway's outstanding common stock for $600,000.

### E4-4 Eliminating Entries with Differential

On June 10, 20X8, Tower Corporation acquired 100 percent of Brown Company's common stock. Summarized balance sheet data for the two companies immediately after the stock acquisition are as follows:

| Item | Tower Corp. | Brown Company Book Value | Fair Value |
|---|---|---|---|
| Cash | $ 15,000 | $ 5,000 | $ 5,000 |
| Accounts Receivable | 30,000 | 10,000 | 10,000 |
| Inventory | 80,000 | 20,000 | 25,000 |
| Buildings and Equipment (net) | 120,000 | 50,000 | 70,000 |
| Investment in Brown Stock | 100,000 | | |
| Total | $345,000 | $85,000 | $110,000 |
| Accounts Payable | $ 25,000 | $ 3,000 | $ 3,000 |
| Bonds Payable | 150,000 | 25,000 | 25,000 |
| Common Stock | 55,000 | 20,000 | |
| Retained Earnings | 115,000 | 37,000 | |
| Total | $345,000 | $85,000 | $ 28,000 |

#### Required

*a.* Give the eliminating entries required to prepare a consolidated balance sheet immediately after the acquisition of Brown Company shares.

*b.* Explain how eliminating entries differ from other types of journal entries recorded in the normal course of business.

### E4-5 Balance Sheet Consolidation

Reed Corporation acquired 100 percent of Thorne Corporation's voting common stock on December 31, 20X4, for $395,000. At the date of combination, Thorne reported the following:

| | | | |
|---|---|---|---|
| Cash | $120,000 | Current Liabilities | $ 80,000 |
| Inventory | 100,000 | Long-Term Liabilities | 200,000 |
| Buildings (net) | 420,000 | Common Stock | 120,000 |
| | | Retained Earnings | 240,000 |
| Total | $640,000 | Total | $640,000 |

At December 31, 20X4, the book values of Thorne's net assets and liabilities approximated their fair values, except for buildings, which had a fair value of $20,000 less than book value, and inventories, which had a fair value $36,000 more than book value.

### Required

Reed Corporation wishes to prepare a consolidated balance sheet immediately following the business combination. Give the eliminating entry or entries needed to prepare a consolidated balance sheet at December 31, 20X4.

### E4-6 Acquisition with Differential

Road Corporation acquired all of Conger Corporation's voting shares on January 1, 20X2, for $470,000. At that time Conger reported common stock outstanding of $80,000 and retained earnings of $130,000. The book values of Conger's assets and liabilities approximated fair values, except for land, which had a book value of $80,000 and a fair value of $100,000, and buildings, which had a book value of $220,000 and a fair value of $400,000. Land and buildings are the only noncurrent assets that Conger holds.

### Required

a. Compute the amount of goodwill at the date of acquisition.

b. Give the eliminating entry or entries required immediately following the acquisition to prepare a consolidated balance sheet.

### E4-7 Balance Sheet Workpaper

Blank Corporation acquired 100 percent of Faith Corporation's common stock on December 31, 20X2, for $150,000. Data from the balance sheets of the two companies included the following amounts as of the date of acquisition:

| Item | Blank Corporation | Faith Corporation |
|---|---|---|
| Cash | $ 65,000 | $ 18,000 |
| Accounts Receivable | 87,000 | 37,000 |
| Inventory | 110,000 | 60,000 |
| Buildings and Equipment (net) | 220,000 | 150,000 |
| Investment in Faith Corporation Stock | 150,000 | |
| Total Assets | $632,000 | $265,000 |
| Accounts Payable | $ 92,000 | $ 35,000 |
| Notes Payable | 150,000 | 80,000 |
| Common Stock | 100,000 | 60,000 |
| Retained Earnings | 290,000 | 90,000 |
| Total Liabilities and Stockholders' Equity | $632,000 | $265,000 |

At the date of the business combination, the book values of Faith's net assets and liabilities approximated fair value.

### Required

a. Give the eliminating entry or entries needed to prepare a consolidated balance sheet immediately following the business combination.

b. Prepare a consolidated balance sheet workpaper.

### E4-8 Balance Sheet Workpaper with Differential

Blank Corporation acquired 100 percent of Faith Corporation's common stock on December 31, 20X2, for $189,000. Data from the balance sheets of the two companies included the following amounts as of the date of acquisition:

| Item | Blank Corporation | Faith Corporation |
|---|---|---|
| Cash | $ 26,000 | $ 18,000 |
| Accounts Receivable | 87,000 | 37,000 |
| Inventory | 110,000 | 60,000 |
| Buildings and Equipment (net) | 220,000 | 150,000 |
| Investment in Faith Corporation Stock | 189,000 | |
| Total Assets | $632,000 | $265,000 |
| Accounts Payable | $ 92,000 | $ 35,000 |
| Notes Payable | 150,000 | 80,000 |
| Common Stock | 100,000 | 60,000 |
| Retained Earnings | 290,000 | 90,000 |
| Total Liabilities and Stockholders' Equity | $632,000 | $265,000 |

At the date of the business combination, Faith's net assets and liabilities approximated fair value except for inventory, which had a fair value of $84,000 and buildings and equipment (net), which had a fair value of $165,000.

### Required

a. Give the eliminating entry or entries needed to prepare a consolidated balance sheet immediately following the business combination.

b. Prepare a consolidation balance sheet workpaper.

**E4-9   Workpaper for Wholly Owned Subsidiary**

Gold Enterprises acquired 100 percent of Premium Builders' stock on December 31, 20X4. Balance sheet data for Gold and Premium on January 1, 20X5, are as follows:

| | Gold Enterprises | Premium Builders |
|---|---|---|
| Cash and Receivables | $ 80,000 | $ 30,000 |
| Inventory | 150,000 | 350,000 |
| Buildings and Equipment (net) | 430,000 | 80,000 |
| Investment in Premium Stock | 167,000 | |
| Total Assets | $827,000 | $460,000 |
| Current Liabilities | $100,000 | $110,000 |
| Long-Term Debt | 400,000 | 200,000 |
| Common Stock | 200,000 | 140,000 |
| Retained Earnings | 127,000 | 10,000 |
| Total Liabilities and Stockholders' Equity | $827,000 | $460,000 |

At the date of the business combination, Premium's cash and receivables had a fair value of $28,000, inventory had a fair value of $357,000, and buildings and equipment had a fair value of $92,000.

### Required

a. Give all eliminating entries needed to prepare a consolidated balance sheet on January 1, 20X5.

b. Complete a consolidated balance sheet workpaper.

c. Prepare a consolidated balance sheet in good form.

**E4-10   Computation of Consolidated Balances**

Astor Corporation's balance sheet at January 1, 20X7, reflected the following balances:

| | | | |
|---|---|---|---|
| Cash and Receivables | $ 80,000 | Accounts Payable | $ 40,000 |
| Inventory | 120,000 | Income Taxes Payable | 60,000 |
| Land | 70,000 | Bonds Payable | 200,000 |
| Buildings and Equipment (net) | 480,000 | Common Stock | 250,000 |
| | | Retained Earnings | 200,000 |
| Total Assets | $750,000 | Total Liabilities and Stockholders' Equity | $750,000 |

Phel Corporation, which had just entered into an active acquisition program, acquired 100 percent of Astor's common stock on January 2, 20X7, for $576,000. A careful review of the fair value of Astor's assets and liabilities indicated the following:

| | Book Value | Fair Value |
|---|---|---|
| Inventory | $120,000 | $140,000 |
| Land | 70,000 | 60,000 |
| Buildings and Equipment (net) | 480,000 | 550,000 |

### Required

Compute the appropriate amount to be included in the consolidated balance sheet immediately following the acquisition for each of the following items:

*a.* Inventory.

*b.* Land.

*c.* Buildings and Equipment (net).

*d.* Goodwill.

*e.* Investment in Astor Corporation.

### E4-11    Multiple-Choice Questions on Balance Sheet Consolidation

Top Corporation acquired 100 percent of Sun Corporation's common stock on December 31, 20X2. Balance sheet data for the two companies immediately following the acquisition follow:

| Item | Top Corporation | Sun Corporation |
|---|---|---|
| Cash | $ 49,000 | $ 30,000 |
| Accounts Receivable | 110,000 | 45,000 |
| Inventory | 130,000 | 70,000 |
| Land | 80,000 | 25,000 |
| Buildings and Equipment | 500,000 | 400,000 |
| Less: Accumulated Depreciation | (223,000) | (165,000) |
| Investment in Sun Corporation Stock | 198,000 | |
| Total Assets | $844,000 | $405,000 |
| Accounts Payable | $ 61,500 | $ 28,000 |
| Taxes Payable | 95,000 | 37,000 |
| Bonds Payable | 280,000 | 200,000 |
| Common Stock | 150,000 | 50,000 |
| Retained Earnings | 257,500 | 90,000 |
| Total Liabilities and Stockholders' Equity | $844,000 | $405,000 |

At the date of the business combination, the book values of Sun's net assets and liabilities approximated fair value except for inventory, which had a fair value of $85,000, and land, which had a fair value of $45,000.

### Required

For each question on the next page, indicate the appropriate total that should appear in the consolidated balance sheet prepared immediately after the business combination.

1. What amount of inventory will be reported?

    a. $70,000.

    b. $130,000.

    c. $200,000.

    d. $215,000.

2. What amount of goodwill will be reported?

    a. $0.

    b. $23,000.

    c. $43,000.

    d. $58,000.

3. What amount of total assets will be reported?

    a. $84,400.

    b. $1,051,000.

    c. $1,109,000.

    d. $1,249,000.

4. What amount of total liabilities will be reported?

    a. $265,000.

    b. $436,500.

    c. $701,500.

    d. $1,249,000.

5. What amount of consolidated retained earnings will be reported?

    a. $547,500.

    b. $397,500.

    c. $347,500.

    d. $257,500.

6. What amount of total stockholders' equity will be reported?

    a. $407,500.

    b. $547,500.

    c. $844,000.

    d. $1,249,000.

## E4-12 Consolidation Entries for Wholly Owned Subsidiary

Trim Corporation acquired 100 percent of Round Corporation's voting common stock on January 1, 20X2, for $400,000. At that date, the book values and fair values of Round's assets and liabilities were equal. Round reported the following summarized balance sheet data:

| Assets | $700,000 | Accounts Payable | $100,000 |
|--------|----------|------------------|----------|
|        |          | Bonds Payable    | 200,000 |
|        |          | Common Stock     | 120,000 |
|        |          | Retained Earnings | 280,000 |
| Total  | $700,000 | Total            | $700,000 |

Round reported net income of $80,000 for 20X2 and paid dividends of $25,000.

### Required

a. Give the journal entries recorded by Trim Corporation during 20X2 on its books if Trim accounts for its investment in Round using the equity method.

b. Give the eliminating entries needed at December 31, 20X2, to prepare consolidated financial statements.

**E4-13  Basic Consolidation Entries for Fully Owned Subsidiary**

Amber Corporation reported the following summarized balance sheet data on December 31, 20X6:

| | | | |
|---|---|---|---|
| Assets | $600,000 | Liabilities | $100,000 |
| | | Common Stock | 300,000 |
| | | Retained Earnings | 200,000 |
| Total | $600,000 | Total | $600,000 |

On January 1, 20X7, Purple Company acquired 100 percent of Amber's stock for $500,000. At the acquisition date, the book values and fair values of Amber's assets and liabilities were equal. Amber reported net income of $50,000 for 20X7 and paid dividends of $20,000.

### Required

a. Give the journal entries recorded by Purple on its books during 20X7 if it accounts for its investment in Amber using the equity method.

b. Give the eliminating entries needed on December 31, 20X7, to prepare consolidated financial statements.

**E4-14  Wholly Owned Subsidiary with Differential**

Canton Corporation is a wholly owned subsidiary of Winston Corporation. Winston acquired ownership of Canton on January 1, 20X3, for $28,000 above Canton's reported net assets. At that date, Canton reported common stock outstanding of $60,000 and retained earnings of $90,000. The differential is assigned to equipment with an economic life of seven years at the date of the business combination. Canton reported net income of $30,000 and paid dividends of $12,000 in 20X3.

### Required

a. Give the journal entries recorded by Winston Corporation during 20X3 on its books if Winston accounts for its investment in Canton using the equity method.

b. Give the eliminating entries needed at December 31, 20X3, to prepare consolidated financial statements.

**E4-15  Basic Consolidation Workpaper**

Blake Corporation acquired 100 percent of Shaw Corporation's voting shares on January 1, 20X3, at underlying book value. At that date, the book values and fair values of Shaw's assets and liabilities were equal. Blake uses the equity method in accounting for its investment in Shaw. Adjusted trial balances for Blake and Shaw on December 31, 20X3, are as follows:

| | Blake Corporation | | Shaw Corporation | |
|---|---|---|---|---|
| Item | Debit | Credit | Debit | Credit |
| Current Assets | $145,000 | | $105,000 | |
| Depreciable Assets (net) | 325,000 | | 225,000 | |
| Investment in Shaw Corporation Stock | 170,000 | | | |
| Depreciation Expense | 25,000 | | 15,000 | |
| Other Expenses | 105,000 | | 75,000 | |
| Dividends Declared | 40,000 | | 10,000 | |
| Current Liabilities | | $ 50,000 | | $ 40,000 |
| Long-Term Debt | | 100,000 | | 120,000 |
| Common Stock | | 200,000 | | 100,000 |
| Retained Earnings | | 230,000 | | 50,000 |
| Sales | | 200,000 | | 120,000 |
| Income from Subsidiary | | 30,000 | | |
| | $810,000 | $810,000 | $430,000 | $430,000 |

### Required

a. Give all eliminating entries required on December 31, 20X3, to prepare consolidated financial statements.

b. Prepare a three-part consolidation workpaper as of December 31, 20X3.

### E4-16 Basic Consolidation Workpaper for Second Year

Blake Corporation acquired 100 percent of Shaw Corporation's voting shares on January 1, 20X3, at underlying book value. At that date, the book values and fair values of Shaw's assets and liabilities were equal. Blake uses the equity method in accounting for its investment in Shaw. Adjusted trial balances for Blake and Shaw on December 31, 20X4, are as follows:

| Item | Blake Corporation | | Shaw Corporation | |
| --- | --- | --- | --- | --- |
| | Debit | Credit | Debit | Credit |
| Current Assets | $210,000 | | $150,000 | |
| Depreciable Assets (net) | 300,000 | | 210,000 | |
| Investment in Shaw Corporation Stock | 190,000 | | | |
| Depreciation Expense | 25,000 | | 15,000 | |
| Other Expenses | 150,000 | | 90,000 | |
| Dividends Declared | 50,000 | | 15,000 | |
| Current Liabilities | | $ 70,000 | | $ 50,000 |
| Long-Term Debt | | 100,000 | | 120,000 |
| Common Stock | | 200,000 | | 100,000 |
| Retained Earnings | | 290,000 | | 70,000 |
| Sales | | 230,000 | | 140,000 |
| Income from Subsidiary | | 35,000 | | |
| | $925,000 | $925,000 | $480,000 | $480,000 |

### Required

a. Give all eliminating entries required on December 31, 20X4, to prepare consolidated financial statements.

b. Prepare a three-part consolidation workpaper as of December 31, 20X4.

### E4-17 Consolidation Workpaper with Differential

Kennelly Corporation acquired all of Short Company's common shares on January 1, 20X5, for $180,000. On that date, the book value of the net assets reported by Short was $150,000. The entire differential was assigned to depreciable assets with a six-year remaining economic life from January 1, 20X5.

The adjusted trial balances for the two companies on December 31, 20X5, are as follows:

| Item | Kennelly Corporation | | Short Company | |
| --- | --- | --- | --- | --- |
| | Debit | Credit | Debit | Credit |
| Cash | $ 15,000 | | $ 5,000 | |
| Accounts Receivable | 30,000 | | 40,000 | |
| Inventory | 70,000 | | 60,000 | |
| Depreciable Assets (net) | 325,000 | | 225,000 | |
| Investment in Short Company Stock | 195,000 | | | |
| Depreciation Expense | 25,000 | | 15,000 | |
| Other Expenses | 105,000 | | 75,000 | |
| Dividends Declared | 40,000 | | 10,000 | |
| Accounts Payable | | $ 50,000 | | $ 40,000 |
| Notes Payable | | 100,000 | | 120,000 |
| Common Stock | | 200,000 | | 100,000 |
| Retained Earnings | | 230,000 | | 50,000 |
| Sales | | 200,000 | | 120,000 |
| Income from Subsidiary | | 25,000 | | |
| | $805,000 | $805,000 | $430,000 | $430,000 |

Kennelly uses the equity method in accounting for its investment in Short. Short declared and paid dividends on December 31, 20X5.

### Required

a. Prepare the eliminating entries needed as of December 31, 20X5, to complete a consolidation workpaper.

b. Prepare a three-part consolidation workpaper as of December 31, 20X5.

### E4-18  Consolidation Workpaper for Subsidiary

Land Corporation acquired 100 percent of Growth Company's voting stock on January 1, 20X4, at underlying book value. Land uses the equity method in accounting for its ownership of Growth. On December 31, 20X4, the trial balances of the two companies are as follows:

| Item | Land Corporation Debit | Land Corporation Credit | Growth Company Debit | Growth Company Credit |
|------|------:|------:|------:|------:|
| Current Assets | $ 238,000 | | $150,000 | |
| Depreciable Assets (net) | 500,000 | | 300,000 | |
| Investment in Growth Company Stock | 190,000 | | | |
| Depreciation Expense | 25,000 | | 15,000 | |
| Other Expenses | 150,000 | | 90,000 | |
| Dividends Declared | 50,000 | | 15,000 | |
| Accumulated Depreciation | | $ 200,000 | | $ 90,000 |
| Current Liabilities | | 70,000 | | 50,000 |
| Long-Term Debt | | 100,000 | | 120,000 |
| Common Stock | | 200,000 | | 100,000 |
| Retained Earnings | | 318,000 | | 70,000 |
| Sales | | 230,000 | | 140,000 |
| Income from Subsidiary | | 35,000 | | |
| | $1,153,000 | $1,153,000 | $570,000 | $570,000 |

### Required

a. Give all eliminating entries required on December 31, 20X4, to prepare consolidated financial statements.

b. Prepare a three-part consolidation workpaper as of December 31, 20X4.

### E4-19  Push-Down Accounting

Jefferson Company acquired all of Louis Corporation's common shares on January 2, 20X3, for $789,000. At the date of combination, Louis's balance sheet appeared as follows:

| Assets | | Liabilities | |
|--------|------:|-------------|------:|
| Cash and Receivables | $ 34,000 | Current Payables | $ 25,000 |
| Inventory | 165,000 | Notes Payable | 100,000 |
| Land | 60,000 | Stockholders' Equity | |
| Buildings (net) | 250,000 | Common Stock | 200,000 |
| Equipment (net) | 320,000 | Additional Capital | 425,000 |
| | | Retained Earnings | 79,000 |
| Total | $829,000 | Total | $829,000 |

The fair values of all of Louis's assets and liabilities were equal to their book values except for its fixed assets. Louis's land had a fair value of $75,000; the buildings, a fair value of $300,000; and the equipment, a fair value of $340,000.

Jefferson Company decided to employ push-down accounting for the acquisition of Louis Corporation. Subsequent to the combination, Louis continued to operate as a separate company.

### Required

a. Record the acquisition of Louis's stock on Jefferson's books.

b. Present any entries that would be made on Louis's books related to the business combination, assuming push-down accounting is used.

c. Present, in general journal form, all elimination entries that would appear in a consolidation workpaper for Jefferson and its subsidiary prepared immediately following the combination.

## Problems

### P4-20 Assignment of Differential in Workpaper

Teresa Corporation acquired all the voting shares of Sally Enterprises on January 1, 20X4. Balance sheet amounts for the companies on the date of acquisition were as follows:

| | Teresa Corporation | Sally Enterprises |
|---|---|---|
| Cash and Receivables | $ 40,000 | $ 20,000 |
| Inventory | 95,000 | 40,000 |
| Land | 80,000 | 90,000 |
| Buildings and Equipment | 400,000 | 230,000 |
| Investment in Sally Enterprises | 290,000 | |
| Total Debits | $905,000 | $380,000 |
| Accumulated Depreciation | $175,000 | $ 65,000 |
| Accounts Payable | 60,000 | 15,000 |
| Notes Payable | 100,000 | 50,000 |
| Common Stock | 300,000 | 100,000 |
| Retained Earnings | 270,000 | 150,000 |
| Total Credits | $905,000 | $380,000 |

Sally Enterprises' buildings and equipment were estimated to have a market value of $175,000 on January 1, 20X4. All other items appeared to have market values approximating current book values.

### Required

a. Complete a consolidated balance sheet workpaper for January 1, 20X4.

b. Prepare a consolidated balance sheet in good form.

### P4-21 Computation of Consolidated Balances

Retail Records Inc. acquired all of Decibel Studios' voting shares on January 1, 20X2, for $280,000. Retail's balance sheet immediately after the combination contained the following balances:

**RETAIL RECORDS INC.**
**Balance Sheet**
**January 1, 20X2**

| | | | |
|---|---|---|---|
| Cash and Receivables | $120,000 | Accounts Payable | $ 75,000 |
| Inventory | 110,000 | Taxes Payable | 50,000 |
| Land | 70,000 | Notes Payable | 300,000 |
| Buildings and Equipment (net) | 350,000 | Common Stock | 400,000 |
| Investment in Decibel Stock | 280,000 | Retained Earnings | 105,000 |
| Total Assets | $930,000 | Total Liabilities and Stockholders' Equity | $930,000 |

Decibel's balance sheet at acquisition contained the following balances:

---

**DECIBEL STUDIOS**
**Balance Sheet**
**January 1, 20X2**

| | | | |
|---|---|---|---|
| Cash and Receivables | $ 40,000 | Accounts Payable | $ 90,000 |
| Inventory | 180,000 | Notes Payable | 250,000 |
| Buildings and Equipment (net) | 350,000 | Common Stock | 100,000 |
| Goodwill | 30,000 | Additional Paid-In Capital | 200,000 |
| | | Retained Earnings | (40,000) |
| Total Assets | $600,000 | Total Liabilities and Stockholders' Equity | $600,000 |

---

On the date of combination, the inventory held by Decibel had a fair value of $170,000, and its buildings and recording equipment had a value of $375,000. Goodwill reported by Decibel resulted from a purchase of Sound Stage Enterprises in 20X1. Sound Stage was liquidated and its assets and liabilities were brought onto Decibel's books.

### Required

Compute the balances to be reported in the consolidated balance sheet immediately after the acquisition for:

*a.* Inventory.

*b.* Buildings and Equipment (net).

*c.* Investment in Decibel Stock.

*d.* Goodwill.

*e.* Common Stock.

*f.* Retained Earnings.

**P4-22   Balance Sheet Consolidation [AICPA Adapted]**

Case Inc. acquired all Frey Inc.'s outstanding $25 par common stock on December 31, 20X3, in exchange for 40,000 shares of its $25 par common stock. Case's common stock closed at $56.50 per share on a national stock exchange on December 31, 20X3. Both corporations continued to operate as separate businesses maintaining separate accounting records with years ending December 31.

On December 31, 20X4, after year-end adjustments and the closing of nominal accounts, the companies had condensed balance sheet accounts as follows:

| | Case | Frey |
|---|---|---|
| **Assets** | | |
| Cash | $   825,000 | $  330,000 |
| Accounts and Other Receivables | 2,140,000 | 835,000 |
| Inventories | 2,310,000 | 1,045,000 |
| Land | 650,000 | 300,000 |
| Depreciable Assets (net) | 4,575,000 | 1,980,000 |
| Investment in Frey Inc. | 2,680,000 | |
| Long-Term Investments and Other Assets | 865,000 | 385,000 |
| Total Assets | $14,045,000 | $4,875,000 |
| **Liabilities and Stockholders' Equity** | | |
| Accounts Payable and Other Current Liabilities | $ 2,465,000 | $1,145,000 |
| Long-Term Debt | 1,900,000 | 1,300,000 |
| Common Stock, $25 Par Value | 3,200,000 | 1,000,000 |
| Additional Paid-In Capital | 2,100,000 | 190,000 |
| Retained Earnings | 4,380,000 | 1,240,000 |
| Total Liabilities and Stockholders' Equity | $14,045,000 | $4,875,000 |

### Additional Information

1. Case uses the equity method of accounting for its investment in Frey.

2. On December 31, 20X3, Frey's assets and liabilities had fair values equal to the book balances with the exception of land, which had a fair value of $550,000. Frey had no land transactions in 20X4.

3. On June 15, 20X4, Frey paid a cash dividend of $4 per share on its common stock.

4. On December 10, 20X4, Case paid a cash dividend totaling $256,000 on its common stock.

5. On December 31, 20X3, immediately before the combination, the stockholders' equities were:

|  | Case | Frey |
|---|---|---|
| Common Stock | $2,200,000 | $1,000,000 |
| Additional Paid-In Capital | 1,660,000 | 190,000 |
| Retained Earnings | 3,166,000 | 820,000 |
|  | $7,026,000 | $2,010,000 |

6. The 20X4 net income amounts according to the separate books of Case and Frey were $890,000 (exclusive of equity in Frey's earnings) and $580,000, respectively.

### Required

Prepare a consolidated balance sheet workpaper for Case and its subsidiary, Frey, for December 31, 20X4. A formal consolidated balance sheet is not required.

**P4-23** **Consolidated Balance Sheet**

Thompson Company spent $240,000 to acquire all of Lake Corporation's stock on January 1, 20X2. The balance sheets of the two companies on December 31, 20X3, showed the following amounts:

|  | Thompson Company | Lake Corporation |
|---|---|---|
| Cash | $ 30,000 | $ 20,000 |
| Accounts Receivable | 100,000 | 40,000 |
| Land | 60,000 | 50,000 |
| Buildings and Equipment | 500,000 | 350,000 |
| Less: Accumulated Depreciation | (230,000) | (75,000) |
| Investment in Lake Corporation | 252,000 |  |
|  | $712,000 | $385,000 |
|  |  |  |
| Accounts Payable | $ 80,000 | $ 10,000 |
| Taxes Payable | 40,000 | 70,000 |
| Notes Payable | 100,000 | 85,000 |
| Common Stock | 200,000 | 100,000 |
| Retained Earnings | 292,000 | 120,000 |
|  | $712,000 | $385,000 |

Lake reported retained earnings of $100,000 at the date of acquisition. The difference between the acquisition price and underlying book value is assigned to buildings and equipment with a remaining economic life of 10 years from the date of acquisition.

### Required

*a.* Give the appropriate eliminating entry or entries needed to prepare a consolidated balance sheet as of December 31, 20X3.

*b.* Prepare a consolidated balance sheet workpaper as of December 31, 20X3.

**P4-24** **Comprehensive Problem: Consolidation in Subsequent Period**

Thompson Company spent $240,000 to acquire all of Lake Corporation's stock on January 1, 20X2. On December 31, 20X4, the trial balances of the two companies were as follows:

| Item | Thompson Company Debit | Thompson Company Credit | Lake Corporation Debit | Lake Corporation Credit |
|---|---|---|---|---|
| Cash | $ 74,000 | | $ 42,000 | |
| Accounts Receivable | 130,000 | | 53,000 | |
| Land | 60,000 | | 50,000 | |
| Buildings and Equipment | 500,000 | | 350,000 | |
| Investment in Lake Corporation Stock | 268,000 | | | |
| Cost of Services Provided | 470,000 | | 130,000 | |
| Depreciation Expense | 35,000 | | 18,000 | |
| Other Expenses | 57,000 | | 60,000 | |
| Dividends Declared | 30,000 | | 12,000 | |
| Accumulated Depreciation | | $ 265,000 | | $ 93,000 |
| Accounts Payable | | 71,000 | | 17,000 |
| Taxes Payable | | 58,000 | | 60,000 |
| Notes Payable | | 100,000 | | 85,000 |
| Common Stock | | 200,000 | | 100,000 |
| Retained Earnings | | 292,000 | | 120,000 |
| Service Revenue | | 610,000 | | 240,000 |
| Income from Subsidiary | | 28,000 | | |
| | $1,624,000 | $1,624,000 | $715,000 | $715,000 |

Lake Corporation reported retained earnings of $100,000 at the date of acquisition. The difference between the acquisition price and underlying book value is assigned to buildings and equipment with a remaining economic life of 10 years from the date of acquisition. At December 31, 20X4, Lake owed Thompson $2,500 for services provided.

***Required***

*a.* Give all journal entries recorded by Thompson with regard to its investment in Lake during 20X4.

*b.* Give all eliminating entries required on December 31, 20X4, to prepare consolidated financial statements.

*c.* Prepare a three-part consolidation workpaper as of December 31, 20X4.

**P4-25** **Acquisition at Other than Fair Value of Net Assets**

Mason Corporation acquired 100 percent ownership of Best Company on February 12, 20X9. At the date of acquisition, Best Company reported assets and liabilities with book values of $420,000 and $165,000, respectively, common stock outstanding of $80,000, and retained earnings of $175,000. The book values and fair values of Best's assets and liabilities were identical except for land which had increased in value by $20,000 and inventories which had decreased by $7,000. The estimated fair value of Best as a whole at the date of acquisition was $295,000.

***Required***

Give the eliminating entries required to prepare a consolidated balance sheet immediately after the business combination assuming Mason acquired its ownership of Best for:

*a.* $280,000.

*b.* $251,000.

**P4-26** **Intercorporate Receivables and Payables**

Kim Corporation acquired 100 percent of Normal Company's outstanding shares on January 1, 20X7. Balance sheet data for the two companies immediately after the purchase follow:

| | Kim Corporation | Normal Company |
|---|---|---|
| Cash | $ 70,000 | $ 35,000 |
| Accounts Receivable | 90,000 | 65,000 |
| Inventory | 84,000 | 80,000 |
| Buildings and Equipment | 400,000 | 300,000 |
| Less: Accumulated Depreciation | (160,000) | (75,000) |
| Investment in Normal Company Stock | 305,000 | |
| Investment in Normal Company Bonds | 50,000 | |
| Total Assets | $839,000 | $405,000 |
| Accounts Payable | $ 50,000 | $ 20,000 |
| Bonds Payable | 200,000 | 100,000 |
| Common Stock | 300,000 | 150,000 |
| Capital in Excess of Par | | 140,000 |
| Retained Earnings | 289,000 | (5,000) |
| Total Liabilities and Equities | $839,000 | $405,000 |

As indicated in the parent company balance sheet, Kim purchased $50,000 of Normal's bonds from the subsidiary immediately after it acquired the stock. An analysis of intercompany receivables and payables also indicates that the subsidiary owes the parent $10,000. On the date of combination, the book values and fair values of Normal's assets and liabilities were the same.

### Required

a. Give all eliminating entries needed to prepare a consolidated balance sheet for January 1, 20X7.

b. Complete a consolidated balance sheet workpaper.

c. Prepare a consolidated balance sheet in good form.

**P4-27** **Balance Sheet Consolidation**

On January 2, 20X8, Primary Corporation acquired 100 percent of Street Company's outstanding common stock. In exchange for Street's stock, Primary issued bonds payable with a par and fair value of $650,000 directly to the selling stockholders of Street. The two companies continued to operate as separate entities subsequent to combination.

Immediately prior to the combination, the book values and fair values of the companies' assets and liabilities were as follows:

| | Primary | | Street | |
|---|---|---|---|---|
| | Book Value | Fair Value | Book Value | Fair Value |
| Cash | $ 12,000 | $ 12,000 | $ 9,000 | $ 9,000 |
| Receivables | 41,000 | 39,000 | 31,000 | 30,000 |
| Allowance for Bad Debts | (2,000) | | (1,000) | |
| Inventory | 86,000 | 89,000 | 68,000 | 72,000 |
| Land | 55,000 | 200,000 | 50,000 | 70,000 |
| Buildings and Equipment | 960,000 | 650,000 | 670,000 | 500,000 |
| Accumulated Depreciation | (411,000) | | (220,000) | |
| Patent | | | | 40,000 |
| Total Assets | $741,000 | $990,000 | $607,000 | $721,000 |
| Current Payables | $ 38,000 | $ 38,000 | $ 29,000 | $ 29,000 |
| Bonds Payable | 200,000 | 210,000 | 100,000 | 90,000 |
| Common Stock | 300,000 | | 200,000 | |
| Additional Paid-In Capital | 100,000 | | 130,000 | |
| Retained Earnings | 103,000 | | 148,000 | |
| Total Liabilities and Equity | $741,000 | | $607,000 | |

At the date of combination, Street owed Primary $6,000 plus accrued interest of $500 on a short-term note. Both companies have properly recorded these amounts.

### Required

*a.* Record the business combination on the books of Primary Corporation.

*b.* Present in general journal form all elimination entries needed in a workpaper to prepare a consolidated balance sheet immediately following the business combination on January 2, 20X8.

*c.* Prepare and complete a consolidated balance sheet workpaper as of January 2, 20X8, immediately following the business combination.

*d.* Present a consolidated balance sheet for Primary and its subsidiary as of January 2, 20X8.

**P4-28**  **Consolidation Workpaper at End of First Year of Ownership**

Mill Corporation acquired 100 percent ownership of Roller Company on January 1, 20X8, for $128,000. At that date, the fair value of Roller's buildings and equipment was $20,000 more than book value. Buildings and equipment are depreciated on a 10-year basis. Although goodwill is not amortized, the management of Mill concluded at December 31, 20X8, that goodwill involved in its acquisition of Roller shares had been impaired and the correct carrying value was $2,500.

Trial balance data for Mill and Roller on December 31, 20X8, are as follows:

| | Mill Corporation | | Roller Company | |
|---|---|---|---|---|
| Item | Debit | Credit | Debit | Credit |
| Cash | $ 19,500 | | $ 21,000 | |
| Accounts Receivable | 70,000 | | 12,000 | |
| Inventory | 90,000 | | 25,000 | |
| Land | 30,000 | | 15,000 | |
| Buildings and Equipment | 350,000 | | 150,000 | |
| Investment in Roller Co. Stock | 134,000 | | | |
| Cost of Goods Sold | 125,000 | | 110,000 | |
| Wage Expense | 42,000 | | 27,000 | |
| Depreciation Expense | 25,000 | | 10,000 | |
| Interest Expense | 12,000 | | 4,000 | |
| Other Expenses | 13,500 | | 5,000 | |
| Dividends Declared | 30,000 | | 16,000 | |
| Accumulated Depreciation | | $145,000 | | $ 40,000 |
| Accounts Payable | | 45,000 | | 16,000 |
| Wages Payable | | 17,000 | | 9,000 |
| Notes Payable | | 150,000 | | 50,000 |
| Common Stock | | 200,000 | | 60,000 |
| Retained Earnings | | 102,000 | | 40,000 |
| Sales | | 260,000 | | 180,000 |
| Income from Subsidiary | | 22,000 | | |
| | $941,000 | $941,000 | $395,000 | $395,000 |

### Required

*a.* Give all eliminating entries needed to prepare a three-part consolidation workpaper as of December 31, 20X8.

*b.* Prepare a three-part consolidation workpaper for 20X8 in good form.

**P4-29**  **Consolidation Workpaper at End of Second Year of Ownership**

Mill Corporation acquired 100 percent ownership of Roller Company on January 1, 20X8, for $128,000. At that date, the fair value of Roller's buildings and equipment was $20,000 more than book value. Buildings and equipment are depreciated on a 10-year basis. Although goodwill is not amortized, the management of Mill concluded at December 31, 20X8, that goodwill involved in its acquisition of Roller shares had been impaired and the correct carrying value was $2,500. No additional impairment occurred in 20X9.

Trial balance data for Mill and Roller on December 31, 20X9, are as follows:

| | Mill Corporation | | Roller Company | |
|---|---|---|---|---|
| **Item** | **Debit** | **Credit** | **Debit** | **Credit** |
| Cash | $   45,500 | | $  32,000 | |
| Accounts Receivable | 85,000 | | 14,000 | |
| Inventory | 97,000 | | 24,000 | |
| Land | 50,000 | | 25,000 | |
| Buildings and Equipment | 350,000 | | 150,000 | |
| Investment in Roller Co. Stock | 148,000 | | | |
| Cost of Goods Sold | 145,000 | | 114,000 | |
| Wage Expense | 35,000 | | 20,000 | |
| Depreciation Expense | 25,000 | | 10,000 | |
| Interest Expense | 12,000 | | 4,000 | |
| Other Expenses | 23,000 | | 16,000 | |
| Dividends Declared | 30,000 | | 20,000 | |
| Accumulated Depreciation | | $  170,000 | | $  50,000 |
| Accounts Payable | | 51,000 | | 15,000 |
| Wages Payable | | 14,000 | | 6,000 |
| Notes Payable | | 150,000 | | 50,000 |
| Common Stock | | 200,000 | | 60,000 |
| Retained Earnings | | 136,500 | | 48,000 |
| Sales | | 290,000 | | 200,000 |
| Income from Subsidiary | | 34,000 | | |
| | $1,045,500 | $1,045,500 | $429,000 | $429,000 |

### Required

a. Give all eliminating entries needed to prepare a three-part consolidation workpaper as of December 31, 20X9.

b. Prepare a three-part consolidation workpaper for 20X9 in good form.

c. Prepare a consolidated balance sheet, income statement, and retained earnings statement for 20X9.

**P4-30    Comprehensive Problem: Wholly Owned Subsidiary**

Power Corporation acquired 100 percent ownership of Upland Products Company on January 1, 20X1, for $200,000. On that date Upland reported retained earnings of $50,000 and had $100,000 of common stock outstanding. Power has used the equity method in accounting for its investment in Upland.

Trial balance data for the two companies on December 31, 20X5, are as follows:

| | Power Corporation | | Upland Products Company | |
|---|---|---|---|---|
| **Item** | **Debit** | **Credit** | **Debit** | **Credit** |
| Cash and Receivables | $   43,000 | | $  65,000 | |
| Inventory | 260,000 | | 90,000 | |
| Land | 80,000 | | 80,000 | |
| Buildings and Equipment | 500,000 | | 150,000 | |
| Investment in Upland Products Stock | 235,000 | | | |
| Cost of Goods Sold | 120,000 | | 50,000 | |
| Depreciation Expense | 25,000 | | 15,000 | |
| Inventory Losses | 15,000 | | 5,000 | |
| Dividends Declared | 30,000 | | 10,000 | |
| Accumulated Depreciation | | $  205,000 | | $105,000 |
| Accounts Payable | | 60,000 | | 20,000 |

*(continued)*

| | | |
|---|---|---|
| Notes Payable | 200,000 | 50,000 |
| Common Stock | 300,000 | 100,000 |
| Retained Earnings | 318,000 | 90,000 |
| Sales | 200,000 | 100,000 |
| Income from Subsidiary | 25,000 | |
| | $1,308,000  $1,308,000 | $465,000  $465,000 |

### Additional Information

1. On the date of combination, the fair value of Upland's depreciable assets was $50,000 more than book value. The differential assigned to depreciable assets should be written off over the following 10-year period.

2. There was $10,000 of intercorporate receivables and payables at the end of 20X5.

### Required

a. Give all journal entries that Power recorded during 20X5 related to its investment in Upland.

b. Give all eliminating entries needed to prepare consolidated statements for 20X5.

c. Prepare a three-part workpaper as of December 31, 20X5.

**P4-31**  **Comprehensive Problem: Differential Apportionment**

Jersey Corporation acquired 100 percent of Lime Company on January 1, 20X7, for $203,000. The trial balances for the two companies on December 31, 20X7, included the following amounts:

| Item | Jersey Corporation | | Lime Company | |
|---|---|---|---|---|
| | Debit | Credit | Debit | Credit |
| Cash | $   82,000 | | $  25,000 | |
| Accounts Receivable | 50,000 | | 55,000 | |
| Inventory | 170,000 | | 100,000 | |
| Land | 80,000 | | 20,000 | |
| Buildings and Equipment | 500,000 | | 150,000 | |
| Investment in Lime Company Stock | 240,000 | | | |
| Cost of Goods Sold | 500,000 | | 250,000 | |
| Depreciation Expense | 25,000 | | 15,000 | |
| Other Expenses | 75,000 | | 75,000 | |
| Dividends Declared | 50,000 | | 20,000 | |
| Accumulated Depreciation | | $  155,000 | | $  75,000 |
| Accounts Payable | | 70,000 | | 35,000 |
| Mortgages Payable | | 200,000 | | 50,000 |
| Common Stock | | 300,000 | | 50,000 |
| Retained Earnings | | 290,000 | | 100,000 |
| Sales | | 700,000 | | 400,000 |
| Income from Subsidiary | | 57,000 | | |
| | $1,772,000 | $1,772,000 | $710,000 | $710,000 |

### Additional Information

1. On January 1, 20X7, Lime reported net assets with a book value of $150,000. A total of $20,000 of the acquisition price is applied to goodwill, which was not impaired in 20X7.

2. Lime's depreciable assets had an estimated economic life of 11 years on the date of combination. The difference between fair value and book value of tangible assets is related entirely to buildings and equipment.

3. Jersey used the equity method in accounting for its investment in Lime.

4. Detailed analysis of receivables and payables showed that Lime owed Jersey $16,000 on December 31, 20X7.

### Required

*a.* Give all journal entries recorded by Jersey with regard to its investment in Lime during 20X7.

*b.* Give all eliminating entries needed to prepare a full set of consolidated financial statements for 20X7.

*c.* Prepare a three-part consolidation workpaper as of December 31, 20X7.

**P4-32A    Push-Down Accounting**

On December 31, 20X6, Greenly Corporation and Lindy Company entered into a business combination in which Greenly acquired all of Lindy's common stock for $935,000. At the date of combination, Lindy had common stock outstanding with a par value of $100,000, additional paid-in capital of $400,000, and retained earnings of $175,000. The fair values and book values of all Lindy's assets and liabilities were equal at the date of combination, except for the following:

|  | Book Value | Fair Value |
|---|---|---|
| Inventory | $  50,000 | $  55,000 |
| Land | 75,000 | 160,000 |
| Buildings | 400,000 | 500,000 |
| Equipment | 500,000 | 570,000 |

The buildings had a remaining life of 20 years, and the equipment was expected to last another 10 years. In accounting for the business combination, Greenly decided to use push-down accounting on Lindy's books.

During 20X7, Lindy earned net income of $88,000 and paid a dividend of $50,000. All of the inventory on hand at the end of 20X6 was sold during 20X7. During 20X8, Lindy earned net income of $90,000 and paid a dividend of $50,000.

### Required

*a.* Record the acquisition of Lindy's stock on Greenly's books on December 31, 20X6.

*b.* Record any entries that would be made on December 31, 20X6, on Lindy's books related to the business combination if push-down accounting is employed.

*c.* Present all eliminating entries that would appear in the workpaper to prepare a consolidated balance sheet immediately after the combination.

*d.* Present all entries that Greenly would record during 20X7 related to its investment in Lindy if Greenly uses the equity method of accounting for its investment.

*e.* Present all eliminating entries that would appear in the workpaper to prepare a full set of consolidated financial statements for the year 20X7.

*f.* Present all eliminating entries that would appear in the workpaper to prepare a full set of consolidated financial statements for the year 20X8.

---

**Kaplan CPA Review**

**SCHWESER**

**Kaplan CPA Review Simulation on Comprehensive Consolidation Procedures**

Access to the online CPA Simulation can be attained by visiting the text's Web site: www.mhhe.com/baker8e

### Situation

On January 1, Year One, Big Corporation acquires for $700,000 in cash all of the outstanding voting stock of Little Corporation. It was the first such acquisition for either company. On the day prior to the transaction, Big and Little reported assets of $2 million and $800,000, liabilities of $900,000 and $330,000, contributed capital of $300,000 and $100,000, and retained earnings of $800,000 and $370,000, respectively. Unless otherwise stated, assume Little Corporation holds a building with a book value of $200,000 but a fair value of $300,000. The building has a 10-year remaining life. All of Little's other assets and liabilities are fairly valued in its financial records.

### Topics Covered in the Simulation

*a.* Computation of consolidated assets.

*b.* Goodwill measurement.

*c.* Computation of consolidated expenses.

*d.* Allocation of purchase differentials.

*e.* Equity-method reporting.

*f.* Valuation of other intangibles.

*g.* Determining when control exists.

*h.* Testing for goodwill impairment.

# Consolidation of Less-than-Wholly Owned Subsidiaries

A controlling financial interest in a subsidiary is normally required for a parent to consolidate that subsidiary. In practice, this means that only majority ownership is required for consolidation, not total ownership. Consolidated financial statements often include one or more subsidiaries that are less than wholly owned by the parent. The stockholders who own the shares of the subsidiary not held by the parent are referred to collectively as the *noncontrolling interest* or *minority interest.*

All of a subsidiary's assets, liabilities, revenues, and expenses are included in consolidated financial statements whether or not that subsidiary is wholly owned. The parent's percentage ownership of a subsidiary does not affect the portion of the subsidiary's financial statement amounts included in the consolidated statements—100 percent must be included. Because of this, whenever a parent company holds less than total ownership of a subsidiary, the claim of the noncontrolling shareholders must be reflected in the consolidated financial statements. The noncontrolling interest's share of subsidiary income is deducted from consolidated net income at the bottom of the consolidated income statement to arrive at the income attributable to the controlling interest. The noncontrolling interest's claim on the net assets of the subsidiary is shown at the bottom of the stockholders' equity section of the consolidated balance sheet.

## EFFECT OF A NONCONTROLLING INTEREST

When a subsidiary is less than wholly owned, the general approach to consolidation is the same as discussed in Chapter 4, but the consolidation procedures must be modified slightly to recognize the noncontrolling interest. Before examining the specific procedures used in consolidating a less-than-wholly owned subsidiary, the computation of consolidated net income, consolidated retained earnings, the differential, and the noncontrolling interest's claim on income and net assets is examined, and modifications to the consolidation workpaper are discussed.

### Consolidated Net Income

Consolidated net income, as it appears in the consolidated income statement, is the difference between consolidated revenues and expenses. In the absence of transactions between companies included in the consolidation, *consolidated net income* is equal to the parent's income from its own operations, excluding any investment income from consolidated subsidiaries, plus the net income from each of the consolidated subsidiaries, adjusted for any differential write-off.

When all subsidiaries are wholly owned, all of the consolidated net income accrues to the parent company, or the controlling interest. If one or more of the consolidated subsidiaries is less than wholly owned, a portion of the consolidated net income accrues to the noncontrolling shareholders. In that case, the income attributable to the subsidiary noncontrolling interest is deducted from consolidated net income on the face of the income statement to arrive at consolidated net income attributable to the controlling interest.

Income attributable to a noncontrolling interest in a subsidiary is based on a proportionate share of that subsidiary's net income. The subsidiary's net income available to common shareholders is divided between the parent and noncontrolling stockholders based on their relative common stock ownership of the subsidiary. Note that the noncontrolling shareholders in a particular subsidiary have a proportionate claim only on the income of that subsidiary and not on the income of the parent or any other subsidiary. If a differential is present and a portion of the differential is written off during the period, the noncontrolling interest's share of the write-off must be deducted from its share of income.

As an example of the computation and allocation of consolidated net income, assume that Push Corporation purchases 80 percent of the stock of Shove Company for an amount equal to 80 percent of Shove's total book value. During 20X1, Shove reports net income of $25,000, while Push reports net income of $120,000, including equity-method income from Shove of $20,000 ($25,000 × .80). Consolidated net income for 20X1 is computed and allocated as follows:

| | |
|---|---:|
| Push's net income | $120,000 |
| Less: Equity-method income from Shove | (20,000) |
| Shove's net income | 25,000 |
| Consolidated net income | $125,000 |
| Income attributable to noncontrolling interest | (5,000) |
| Income attributable to controlling interest | $120,000 |

Consolidated net income is equal to the separate income of Push from its own operations ($100,000) plus Shove's net income ($25,000). The $20,000 of equity-method income from Shove that had been recognized by Push must be excluded from the computation to avoid double counting the same income. Consolidated net income is allocated to the noncontrolling stockholders based on their 20 percent share of Shove's net income. The amount of income allocated to the controlling interest is equal to the parent's income from its own operations ($100,000) and the parent's 80 percent share of Shove's income ($20,000). If Push had acquired Shove for a price that exceeded Shove's book value and part of the differential was written off during the period, consolidated net income and income attributable to the noncontrolling and controlling interests would all be lower.

## Consolidated Retained Earnings

The only retained earnings figure reported in the consolidated balance sheet is not entirely consistent with the computation of consolidated net income. Retained earnings in the consolidated balance sheet is that portion of the consolidated entity's undistributed earnings accruing to the parent's stockholders. It is calculated by adding the parent's share of subsidiary cumulative net income since acquisition to the parent's retained earnings from its own operations (excluding any income from the subsidiary included in the parent's retained earnings) and subtracting the parent's share of any differential write-off. Any retained earnings related to subsidiary noncontrolling shareholders is included in the Noncontrolling Interest amount reported in the equity section of the consolidated balance sheet. Thus, the consolidated retained earnings figure is more consistent with the parent company theory rather than the entity approach assumed in the computation of consolidated net income.

As an illustration of the computation of consolidated retained earnings when a noncontrolling interest exists, assume that Push purchases 80 percent of the stock of Shove on January 1, 20X1, and accounts for its investment in Shove using the equity method.

Net income and dividends are as follows for Push and Shove during the two years following acquisition:

|  | Push | Shove |
|---|---|---|
| Retained earnings, January 1, 20X1 | $400,000 | $250,000 |
| Net income, 20X1 | 120,000 | 25,000 |
| Dividends, 20X1 | (30,000) | (10,000) |
| Retained earnings December 31, 20X1 | $490,000 | $265,000 |
| Net income, 20X2 | 148,000 | 35,000 |
| Dividends, 20X2 | (30,000) | (10,000) |
| Retained earnings, December 31, 20X2 | $608,000 | $290,000 |

Consolidated retained earnings at December 31, 20X2, two years after the date of combination, is computed as follows, assuming no differential:

| | |
|---|---|
| Push's retained earnings, December 31, 20X2 | $608,000 |
| Equity accrual from Shove since acquisition ($25,000 + $35,000) × .80 | (48,000) |
| Push's retained earnings from its own operations, December 31, 20X2 | $560,000 |
| Push's share of Shove's net income since acquisition $60,000 × .8 | 48,000 |
| Consolidated retained earnings, December 31, 20X2 | $608,000 |

Several important points can be noted from the example. First, the subsidiary's retained earnings is not combined with that of the parent. Only the parent's share of the subsidiary's cumulative net income since the date of combination is included. Second, consolidated retained earnings is equal to the parent's retained earnings in this example because the parent uses the equity method to account for its investment in the subsidiary. If the parent accounted for the investment using the cost method, the parent's retained earnings and consolidated retained earnings would differ. Finally, the cumulative income from the subsidiary recognized by the parent on its books must be removed from the parent's retained earnings to arrive at retained earnings from the parent's own operations so that all or part (depending on whether the equity or cost method is used) of the same income will not be included twice.

## Differential

As discussed in earlier chapters, when the total consideration given for an acquiree in a business combination is greater than the book value of the acquiree's net identifiable assets, a *differential* arises for the difference. If the acquiring company acquires less than 100 percent of the other company's stock in a stock-acquisition type of business combination, the differential, in effect, is shared by both the controlling and noncontrolling interests. Although the differential is usually attributable to the controlling and noncontrolling interests proportionately, situations may arise where that is not the case, as when a premium is associated with gaining control.

## Noncontrolling Interest

The noncontrolling shareholders of a less-than-wholly owned subsidiary have a claim on the income and net assets of the subsidiary even though the subsidiary is consolidated with its parent and, perhaps, other subsidiaries. In the absence of a differential and intercompany transactions, the noncontrolling interest's share of subsidiary income is simply a proportionate share of the subsidiary's income available for common stockholders. As seen earlier in the Push and Shove example, the noncontrolling interest's claim on Shove's $25,000 income is $5,000, equal to the noncontrolling interest's 20 percent share. In the consolidated income statement, this amount is shown as an allocation of consolidated net income to the noncontrolling interest.

The noncontrolling interest's claim on the subsidiary's net assets is valued initially at its fair value at the date of combination. This amount is usually a proportionate share of the total fair value of the subsidiary at that date, but it may differ in some cases. Once the noncontrolling interest has been valued at the date of combination, it increases each period by a proportionate share of the subsidiary's undistributed earnings for the period, less the appropriate share of any differential write-off. The amount of the noncontrolling interest's claim on subsidiary assets is reported in the consolidated balance sheet at the bottom of the stockholders' equity section.

### Workpaper Format

The same three-part workpaper described in Chapter 4 can be used when consolidating less-than-wholly owned subsidiaries, with only minor modifications. The workpaper must allow for including the noncontrolling interest's claim on the income and assets of the subsidiaries. The noncontrolling interest's claim on the income of a subsidiary is deducted from consolidated net income at the bottom of the workpaper's income statement section in the Consolidated column to arrive at consolidated net income attributable to the controlling interest. The noncontrolling interest's claim on the subsidiary's net assets is placed at the bottom of the workpaper's credit portion of the balance sheet section. The noncontrolling interest's claims on both income and net assets are entered in the workpaper through eliminating entries and then carried over to the Consolidated column. As discussed in Chapter 4, the amounts in the Consolidated column are used to prepare the consolidated financial statements.

# CONSOLIDATED BALANCE SHEET WITH MAJORITY-OWNED SUBSIDIARY

The consolidation process for a less-than-wholly owned subsidiary is the same as for a wholly owned subsidiary except that the claims of the noncontrolling interest must be included. The example of Peerless Products Corporation and Special Foods Inc. from Chapter 4 will serve as a basis for illustrating consolidation procedures when less than full ownership of a subsidiary is held. Assume that on January 1, 20X1, Peerless acquires 80 percent of the common stock of Special Foods for $310,000. At that date, the fair value of the noncontrolling interest is estimated to be $77,500. The ownership situation can be viewed as follows, where the total fair value indicated is equal to the sum of the fair value of the consideration given and the fair value of the noncontrolling interest:

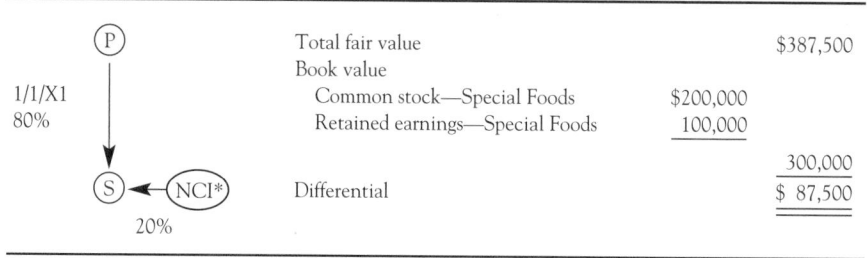

| | | |
|---|---|---|
| Total fair value | | $387,500 |
| Book value | | |
| Common stock—Special Foods | $200,000 | |
| Retained earnings—Special Foods | 100,000 | |
| | | 300,000 |
| Differential | | $ 87,500 |

1/1/X1
80%

S ← NCI*
20%

* Noncontrolling interest

Peerless records the acquisition on its books with the following entry:

| (1) | Investment in Special Foods Stock | 310,000 | |
|---|---|---|---|
| | Cash | | 310,000 |
| | Record purchase of Special Foods stock. | | |

**FIGURE 5–1**
**Balance Sheets of Peerless Products and Special Foods, January 1, 20X1, Immediately after Combination**

| | Peerless Products | Special Foods |
|---|---|---|
| Assets | | |
| Cash | $ 40,000 | $ 50,000 |
| Accounts Receivable | 75,000 | 50,000 |
| Inventory | 100,000 | 60,000 |
| Land | 175,000 | 40,000 |
| Buildings and Equipment | 800,000 | 600,000 |
| Accumulated Depreciation | (400,000) | (300,000) |
| Investment in Special Foods Stock | 310,000 | |
| Total Assets | $1,100,000 | $500,000 |
| | | |
| Liabilities and Stockholders' Equity | | |
| Accounts Payable | $ 100,000 | $100,000 |
| Bonds Payable | 200,000 | 100,000 |
| Common Stock | 500,000 | 200,000 |
| Retained Earnings | 300,000 | 100,000 |
| Total Liabilities and Equity | $1,100,000 | $500,000 |

**FIGURE 5–2**
**Values of Select Assets of Special Foods**

| | Book Value | Fair Value | Fair Value Increment |
|---|---|---|---|
| Inventory | $ 60,000 | $ 65,000 | $ 5,000 |
| Land | 40,000 | 50,000 | 10,000 |
| Buildings and Equipment | 300,000 | 360,000 | 60,000 |
| | $400,000 | $475,000 | $75,000 |

The balance sheets of Peerless and Special Foods appear immediately after acquisition as in Figure 5–1. The fair values of all of Special Foods' assets and liabilities are equal to their book values except as shown in Figure 5–2.

The excess of the $387,500 total fair value of the consideration given and the noncontrolling interest on the date of combination over the $300,000 book value of Special Foods is $87,500. Of this total $87,500 differential, $75,000 relates to the excess of the acquisition-date fair value over the book value of Special Foods' net identifiable assets, as can be seen from Figure 5–2. The remaining $12,500 of the differential, the excess of the consideration given and the noncontrolling interest over the fair value of Special Foods' net identifiable assets, is assigned to goodwill. The total differential can be viewed as follows, where the total fair value refers to the combined fair values of the consideration given and the noncontrolling interest:

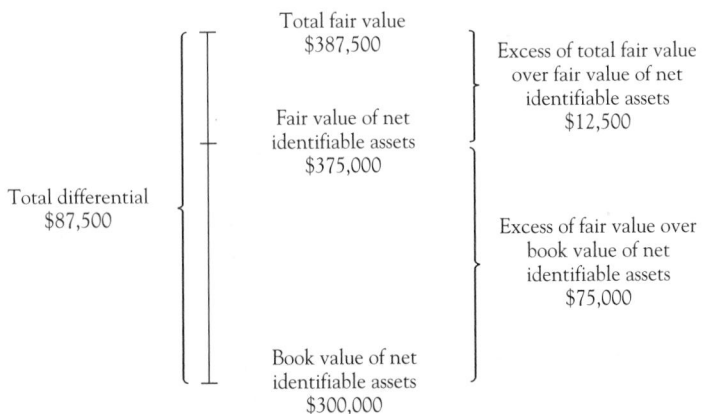

**FIGURE 5–3**  **Workpaper for Consolidated Balance Sheet, January 1, 20X1, Date of Combination; 80 Percent Acquisition at More than Book Value**

| Item | Peerless Products | Special Foods | Eliminations Debit | Eliminations Credit | Consolidated |
|------|------------------:|-------------:|------------------:|-------------------:|------------:|
| Cash | 40,000 | 50,000 | | | 90,000 |
| Accounts Receivable | 75,000 | 50,000 | | | 125,000 |
| Inventory | 100,000 | 60,000 | (3)   5,000 | | 165,000 |
| Land | 175,000 | 40,000 | (3)  10,000 | | 225,000 |
| Buildings and Equipment | 800,000 | 600,000 | (3)  60,000 | | 1,460,000 |
| Goodwill | | | (3)  12,500 | | 12,500 |
| Investment in Special Foods Stock | 310,000 | | | (2) 310,000 | |
| Differential | | | (2)  87,500 | (3)  87,500 | |
| Total Debits | 1,500,000 | 800,000 | | | 2,077,500 |
| Accumulated Depreciation | 400,000 | 300,000 | | | 700,000 |
| Accounts Payable | 100,000 | 100,000 | | | 200,000 |
| Bonds Payable | 200,000 | 100,000 | | | 300,000 |
| Common Stock | 500,000 | 200,000 | (2) 200,000 | | 500,000 |
| Retained Earnings | 300,000 | 100,000 | (2) 100,000 | | 300,000 |
| Noncontrolling Interest | | | | (2)  77,500 | 77,500 |
| Total Credits | 1,500,000 | 800,000 | 475,000 | 475,000 | 2,077,500 |

Elimination entries:
(2)  Eliminate investment balance and stockholders' equity of Special Foods; establish noncontrolling interest.
(3)  Assign differential.

If a consolidated balance sheet is prepared immediately after the combination of Peerless and Special Foods, the consolidation workpaper appears as in Figure 5–3. The following eliminating entries are included in the workpaper:

| E(2) | Common Stock—Special Foods | 200,000 | |
|------|---------------------------|--------:|--------:|
| | Retained Earnings | 100,000 | |
| | Differential | 87,500 | |
| | Investment in Special Foods Stock | | 310,000 |
| | Noncontrolling Interest | | 77,500 |
| | Eliminate investment balance and establish noncontrolling interest. | | |

| E(3) | Inventory | 5,000 | |
|------|-----------|------:|------:|
| | Land | 10,000 | |
| | Buildings and Equipment | 60,000 | |
| | Goodwill | 12,500 | |
| | Differential | | 87,500 |
| | Assign differential. | | |

The first workpaper entry eliminates Peerless's investment account and the stockholders' equity accounts of Special Foods. This entry also establishes the noncontrolling shareholders' claim on the subsidiary's assets in the workpaper. This $77,500 amount is the fair value of the noncontrolling interest at the date of combination. Note that the amount of the noncontrolling interest is equal to its fair value and is not based on the book value of the subsidiary. Thus, the amount of the noncontrolling interest is affected by the increased fair value of Special Foods' net identifiable assets and by the goodwill.

The $77,500 noncontrolling interest amount is not taken from the books of either the parent or the subsidiary; it enters the workpaper only through eliminating entry E(2). This entry is an example of an eliminating entry that does more than just eliminate balances carried over from the books of the separate companies; it establishes a new item in the workpaper. The noncontrolling interest is placed in the workpaper at the bottom of the credit portion of the workpaper shown in Figure 5–3 and is carried across to the Consolidated column.

Entry E(2) also establishes in the workpaper the $87,500 differential at the date of combination for the difference between (1) the sum of the fair values of the consideration given and the noncontrolling interest and (2) the book value of Special Foods. In eliminating entry E(2), the two elements in item (1) are represented by the parent's investment account and the noncontrolling interest on the credit side of the entry. Item (2) is represented by the subsidiary's stockholders' equity accounts on the other side of the entry. The Differential also is an account that does not appear on the books of either the parent or the subsidiary but is entered in the consolidation workpaper through an eliminating entry. Entry E(3) allocates the differential to Special Foods' identifiable assets based on the amounts in Figure 5–2 to bring them to their acquisition-date fair values. It also assigns the remaining $12,500 of the differential to goodwill.

Once the eliminating entries are placed in the workpaper, each row is summed across to get the consolidated totals. Note that the asset amounts included in the Consolidated column, and thus in the consolidated balance sheet, consist of book values for Peerless's assets and liabilities, plus acquisition-date fair values for Special Foods' assets and liabilities, plus goodwill.

# CONSOLIDATED FINANCIAL STATEMENTS WITH MAJORITY-OWNED SUBSIDIARY

Consolidation subsequent to acquisition involves the preparation of a complete set of consolidated financial statements, as discussed in Chapter 4. To continue the illustration from the previous section beyond the date of acquisition, assume Peerless Products and Special Foods report the income and dividends shown in Figure 5–4. With respect to the assets to which the $87,500 differential relates, assume that all of the inventory is sold during 20X1, the buildings and equipment have a remaining economic life of 10 years from the date of combination, and straight-line depreciation is used. Further, assume that management determines at the end of 20X1 that the goodwill is impaired and should be written down by $3,125. Management has determined that the goodwill arising in the acquisition of Special Foods relates proportionately to the controlling and noncontrolling interests, as does the impairment. Finally, assume that Peerless accounts for its investment in Special Foods using the equity method.

## Initial Year of Ownership

The business combination of Peerless Products and Special Foods occurs at the beginning of 20X1. Accordingly, Peerless recognizes income and dividends from Special Foods on its books for the entire year, and the consolidated statements portray the two companies

**FIGURE 5–4**
**Income and Dividend Information about Peerless Products and Special Foods for the Years 20X1 and 20X2**

| | Peerless Products | Special Foods |
|---|---|---|
| 20X1: | | |
| Separate operating income, Peerless | $140,000 | |
| Net income, Special Foods | | $50,000 |
| Dividends | 60,000 | 30,000 |
| 20X2: | | |
| Separate operating income, Peerless | 160,000 | |
| Net income, Special Foods | | 75,000 |
| Dividends | 60,000 | 40,000 |

as if they were one entity for the entire year. The procedures are basically the same as those in Chapter 4 except the parent claims only its share of the subsidiary's income and dividends, and the consolidation procedures must allow for the claims of the noncontrolling shareholders.

### Parent Company Entries

During 20X1, Peerless Products makes the normal entry on its books to record its purchase of Special Foods stock. Peerless also makes the usual equity-method entries to record income and dividends from its subsidiary, but, unlike in Chapter 4, Peerless must share Special Foods' income and dividends with the subsidiary's other stockholders. Accordingly, Peerless recognizes only its proportionate share of Special Foods' net income and dividends. Peerless records the following entries during 20X1:

| | | | |
|---|---|---|---|
| (4) | Investment in Special Foods Stock | 310,000 | |
| |     Cash | | 310,000 |
| |     Record purchase of Special Foods stock. | | |
| | | | |
| (5) | Cash | 24,000 | |
| |     Investment in Special Foods Stock | | 24,000 |
| |     Record dividends from Special Foods: | | |
| |     $30,000 × .80 | | |
| | | | |
| (6) | Investment in Special Foods Stock | 40,000 | |
| |     Income from Subsidiary | | 40,000 |
| |     Record equity-method income: | | |
| |     $50,000 × .80 | | |

In addition, Peerless must write off a portion of the differential with the following entries:

| | | | |
|---|---|---|---|
| (7) | Income from Subsidiary | 4,000 | |
| |     Investment in Special Foods Stock | | 4,000 |
| |     Adjust income for differential related to inventory sold: | | |
| |     $5,000 × .80 | | |
| | | | |
| (8) | Income from Subsidiary | 4,800 | |
| |     Investment in Special Foods Stock | | 4,800 |
| |     Amortize differential related to buildings and equipment: | | |
| |     ($60,000 × .80) ÷ 10 years | | |

Special Foods' inventory to which $5,000 of the total differential relates was sold during the year. Therefore, Peerless's $4,000 portion of the differential must be written off by taking it out of the investment account, and the parent's income from the subsidiary must be reduced. Also, Peerless's $48,000 portion of the increased value of Special Foods' buildings and equipment must be amortized at $4,800 per year ($48,000 ÷ 10) over the remaining 10-year life with entry (8).

Peerless's $10,000 portion of the differential related to goodwill is not adjusted on the parent's books. Even though the goodwill of the consolidated entity is impaired, current standards dictate against writing down the investment account unless the value of the investment declines significantly and the decline is judged as being other than temporary.

### Consolidation Workpaper—Initial Year of Ownership

After the subsidiary income accruals are entered on Peerless's books, the adjusted trial balance data of the consolidating companies are entered in the three-part consolidation workpaper as shown in Figure 5–5. The last column in the workpaper will serve as a basis for preparing consolidated financial statements at the end of 20X1.

**FIGURE 5–5** December 31, 20X1, Equity-Method Workpaper for Consolidated Financial Statements, Initial Year of Ownership; 80 Percent Acquisition at More than Book Value

| Item | Peerless Products | Special Foods | Eliminations | | Consolidated |
|---|---|---|---|---|---|
| | | | Debit | Credit | |
| Sales | 400,000 | 200,000 | | | 600,000 |
| Income from Subsidiary | 31,200 | | (9) 31,200 | | |
| Credits | 431,200 | 200,000 | | | 600,000 |
| Cost of Goods Sold | 170,000 | 115,000 | (12) 5,000 | | 290,000 |
| Depreciation and Amortization | 50,000 | 20,000 | (13) 6,000 | | 76,000 |
| Goodwill Impairment Loss | | | (14) 3,125 | | 3,125 |
| Other Expenses | 40,000 | 15,000 | | | 55,000 |
| Debits | (260,000) | (150,000) | | | (424,125) |
| Consolidated Net Income | | | | | 175,875 |
| Income to Noncontrolling Interest | | | (10) 7,175 | | (7,175) |
| Income, carry forward | 171,200 | 50,000 | 52,500 | | 168,700 |
| Retained Earnings, January 1 | 300,000 | 100,000 | (11) 100,000 | | 300,000 |
| Income, from above | 171,200 | 50,000 | 52,500 | | 168,700 |
| | 471,200 | 150,000 | | | 468,700 |
| Dividends Declared | (60,000) | (30,000) | | (9) 24,000 | |
| | | | | (10) 6,000 | (60,000) |
| Retained Earnings, December 31, carry forward | 411,200 | 120,000 | 152,500 | 30,000 | 408,700 |
| Cash | 194,000 | 75,000 | | | 269,000 |
| Accounts Receivable | 75,000 | 50,000 | | | 125,000 |
| Inventory | 100,000 | 75,000 | | | 175,000 |
| Land | 175,000 | 40,000 | (12) 10,000 | | 225,000 |
| Buildings and Equipment | 800,000 | 600,000 | (12) 60,000 | | 1,460,000 |
| Investment in Special Foods Stock | 317,200 | | | (9) 7,200 | |
| | | | | (11) 310,000 | |
| Goodwill | | | (12) 12,500 | (14) 3,125 | 9,375 |
| Differential | | | (11) 87,500 | (12) 87,500 | |
| Debits | 1,661,200 | 840,000 | | | 2,263,375 |
| Accumulated Depreciation | 450,000 | 320,000 | | (13) 6,000 | 776,000 |
| Accounts Payable | 100,000 | 100,000 | | | 200,000 |
| Bonds Payable | 200,000 | 100,000 | | | 300,000 |
| Common Stock | 500,000 | 200,000 | (11) 200,000 | | 500,000 |
| Retained Earnings, from above | 411,200 | 120,000 | 152,500 | 30,000 | 408,700 |
| Noncontrolling Interest | | | | (10) 1,175 | |
| | | | | (11) 77,500 | 78,675 |
| Credits | 1,661,200 | 840,000 | 522,500 | 522,500 | 2,263,375 |

Elimination entries:

(9) Eliminate income from subsidiary.

(10) Assign income to noncontrolling interest.

(11) Eliminate beginning investment balance.

(12) Assign beginning differential.

(13) Amortize differential related to buildings and equipment.

(14) Write down goodwill for impairment.

The first three workpaper entries eliminate the subsidiary income and dividends recorded by Peerless, eliminate the investment account and the stockholders' equity accounts of Special Foods, and establish the noncontrolling interest:

| E(9) | Income from Subsidiary | 31,200 | |
| |     Dividends Declared | | 24,000 |
| |     Investment in Special Foods Stock | | 7,200 |
| |     Eliminate income from subsidiary. | | |
| | | | |
| E(10) | Income to Noncontrolling Interest | 7,175 | |
| |     Dividends Declared | | 6,000 |
| |     Noncontrolling Interest | | 1,175 |
| |     Assign income to noncontrolling interest. | | |
| | | | |
| E(11) | Common Stock—Special Foods | 200,000 | |
| | Retained Earnings, January 1 | 100,000 | |
| | Differential | 87,500 | |
| |     Investment in Special Foods Stock | | 310,000 |
| |     Noncontrolling Interest | | 77,500 |
| |     Eliminate beginning investment balance. | | |

Entry E(9) removes the net effect of the income accrual recorded by the parent during 20X1 in entries (6), (7), and (8) and removes the parent's portion of dividends declared by the subsidiary during the period, as recorded in entry (5). Elimination entry E(10) places the noncontrolling interest's share of subsidiary income in the workpaper and eliminates the noncontrolling interest's share of subsidiary dividends ($30,000 × .20). The income assigned to the noncontrolling interest is based on its proportionate share of the subsidiary's income. However, because the noncontrolling interest's claim on subsidiary assets is based on its acquisition-date fair value and includes its share of the differential, as seen in eliminating entry E(2) at the date of combination, the noncontrolling interest must also bear its share of the differential write-offs. Accordingly, the income assigned to the noncontrolling interest in the 20X1 consolidated income statement is computed as shown in Figure 5–6.

Entry E(10) also recognizes the $1,175 increase in the noncontrolling interest during the period because the noncontrolling interest's share of subsidiary income ($7,175) exceeds its share of dividends ($6,000). This increase in the noncontrolling interest is included in the balance assigned to the noncontrolling interest at the bottom of the balance sheet section of the workpaper.

The third elimination entry, E(11), removes Peerless's beginning investment balance and Special Foods' beginning stockholders' equity balances, and it establishes the beginning-of-the-period balance of the noncontrolling interest in the workpaper. Because this entry deals with balances as of the beginning of the period, it is the same as elimination entry E(2) that appeared in the workpaper to prepare a consolidated balance sheet at the date of combination. A reconciliation between the book value of Special Foods and the fair value of the noncontrolling interest at the date of combination is shown in Figure 5–6. Subsequently, the amount assigned to the noncontrolling interest at a particular date is usually equal to a proportionate share of the sum of Special Foods' book value at that date and any remaining differential. The amount of the noncontrolling interest to be reported in the consolidated balance sheet at December 31, 20X1, can be seen as the last figure in the Consolidated column in the Figure 5–5 workpaper and can be computed as in Figure 5–6.

Entry E(11) also establishes the beginning balance of the differential in the workpaper. In this case, Peerless acquired Special Foods at the beginning of the period, so the beginning balance of the differential is the $87,500 balance at the date of combination.

| | |
|---|---:|
| Income to noncontrolling interest, 20X1: | |
| Special Foods' net income | $ 50,000 |
| Write-off of differential related to inventory sold in 20X1 | (5,000) |
| Amortization of differential related to buildings and equipment in 20X1 | (6,000) |
| Goodwill impairment loss | (3,125) |
| Special Foods' adjusted income | $ 35,875 |
| Noncontrolling stockholders' proportionate share | × .20 |
| Income assigned to noncontrolling interest | $ 7,175 |
| | |
| Noncontrolling interest, January 1, 20X1: | |
| Special Foods' common stock | $200,000 |
| Special Foods' retained earnings | 100,000 |
| Special Foods' book value | $300,000 |
| Differential related to inventory | 5,000 |
| Differential related to land | 10,000 |
| Differential related to buildings and equipment | 60,000 |
| Differential related to goodwill | 12,500 |
| Special Foods' book value plus differential | $387,500 |
| Noncontrolling stockholders' proportionate share | × .20 |
| Noncontrolling interest, January 1, 20X1 | $ 77,500 |
| | |
| Noncontrolling interest, December 31, 20X1: | |
| Special Foods' common stock | $200,000 |
| Special Foods' retained earnings | 120,000 |
| Special Foods' book value | $320,000 |
| Differential related to land | 10,000 |
| Unamortized differential related to buildings and equipment ($60,000 − $6,000) | 54,000 |
| Unimpaired goodwill ($12,500 − $3,125) | 9,375 |
| Special Foods' book value plus differential | $393,375 |
| Noncontrolling stockholders' proportionate share | × .20 |
| Noncontrolling interest, December 31, 20X1 | $ 78,675 |

Three additional eliminating entries are needed in the workpaper in Figure 5–5, all having to do with the differential that was established in the workpaper with entry E(11):

| | | | |
|---|---|---:|---:|
| E(12) | Cost of Goods Sold | 5,000 | |
| | Land | 10,000 | |
| | Buildings and Equipment | 60,000 | |
| | Goodwill | 12,500 | |
| | Differential | | 87,500 |
| | Assign beginning differential. | | |
| | | | |
| E(13) | Depreciation Expense | 6,000 | |
| | Accumulated Depreciation | | 6,000 |
| | Amortize differential related to buildings and equipment: $60,000 ÷ 10 | | |
| | | | |
| E(14) | Goodwill Impairment Loss | 3,125 | |
| | Goodwill | | 3,125 |
| | Write down goodwill for impairment. | | |

Eliminating entry E(12) allocates the differential to bring Special Foods' assets to their acquisition-date fair values and to enter goodwill in the workpaper. Because all inventory on hand on the date of combination was sold during the year, the $5,000 of differential applicable to the inventory is allocated directly to cost of goods sold. The consolidated entity's cost of the inventory sold is viewed as being its acquisition-date fair value.

Entry E(13) recognizes the depreciation of that portion of the differential related to Special Foods' buildings and equipment. The acquisition-date fair value of the buildings and equipment is viewed as the appropriate amount for the consolidated entity to allocate to expense over the remaining useful lives. The subsidiary has already recorded depreciation on the buildings and equipment based on their original cost to the subsidiary, and that amount has been carried into the consolidation workpaper. Depreciation on the fair value increment must be added to that amount, and this is accomplished through entry E(13).

The $12,500 excess of the $387,500 sum of the acquisition-date fair values of the consideration given for Special Foods and its noncontrolling interest over the $375,000 fair value of its net identifiable assets is considered goodwill and is entered in the workpaper through entry E(12). During the year, however, management determines that the acquisition-date goodwill has become impaired and must be written down by $3,125. Entry E(14) recognizes in the workpaper the goodwill impairment loss incurred during 20X1 and reduces goodwill by that amount.

Note that the distinction between journal entries recorded on the parent's books under the equity method and the eliminating entries in the consolidation workpaper is important. Even though Peerless amortizes the differential related to Special Foods' buildings and equipment on its books with entry (8), eliminating entry E(13) is still needed in the workpaper to record depreciation expense. All effects of Peerless's subsidiary income accrual, including the effects of entry (8), are eliminated in the workpaper by entry E(9). Consequently, eliminating entry E(13) is required for consolidated net income to reflect the amortization of the additional cost of Special Foods' buildings and equipment to the consolidated entity.

Once the appropriate eliminating entries are placed in the consolidation workpaper in Figure 5–5, the workpaper is completed by summing each row across, taking into consideration the debit or credit effect of the eliminations.

### Consolidated Net Income and Retained Earnings

As can be seen from the workpaper in Figure 5–5, consolidated net income for 20X1 is $175,875 and the amount of that income accruing to the controlling interest, shown as the last number in the income statement section of the workpaper in the Consolidated column, is $168,700. The amount of retained earnings reported in the consolidated balance sheet at December 31, 20X1, shown as the last number in the retained earnings section of the workpaper in the Consolidated column, is $408,700. The computation of these amounts is shown in Figure 5–7.

**FIGURE 5–7**
**Consolidated Net Income and Retained Earnings, 20X1; 80 Percent Acquisition at More than Book Value**

| | |
|---|---:|
| Consolidated net income, 20X1: | |
|   Peerless's separate operating income | $140,000 |
|   Special Foods' net income | 50,000 |
|   Write-off of differential related to inventory sold in 20X1 | (5,000) |
|   Amortization of differential related to buildings | |
|     and equipment in 20X1 | (6,000) |
|   Goodwill impairment loss | (3,125) |
|   Consolidated net income | $175,875 |
| | |
| Income to controlling interest, 20X1: | |
|   Consolidated net income | $175,875 |
|   Income to noncontrolling interest | (7,175) |
|   Income to controlling interest | $168,700 |
| | |
| Consolidated retained earnings, December 31, 20X1: | |
|   Peerless's retained earnings on date of combination, | |
|     January 1, 20X1 | $300,000 |
|   Income to controlling interest, 20X1 | 168,700 |
|   Dividends declared by Peerless, 20X1 | (60,000) |
|   Consolidated retained earnings | $408,700 |

## Second Year of Ownership

The equity-method and consolidation procedures employed during the second and subsequent years of ownership are the same as in the first year and are illustrated by continuing the Peerless Products and Special Foods example through 20X2. No further impairment of the goodwill arising from the business combination occurs in 20X2.

### *Parent Company Entries*

Given the income and dividends as shown in Figure 5–4, Peerless Products records the following entries on its separate books during 20X2:

| (15) | Cash | 32,000 | |
| | Investment in Special Foods Stock | | 32,000 |
| | Record dividends from Special Foods: | | |
| | $40,000 × .80 | | |

| (16) | Investment in Special Foods Stock | 60,000 | |
| | Income from Subsidiary | | 60,000 |
| | Record equity-method income: | | |
| | $75,000 × .80 | | |

| (17) | Income from Subsidiary | 4,800 | |
| | Investment in Special Foods Stock | | 4,800 |
| | Amortize differential related to buildings and equipment. | | |

The changes in the parent's investment account for 20X1 and 20X2 can be summarized as follows:

| | 20X1 | | 20X2 | |
|---|---|---|---|---|
| Balance at start of year | | $310,000 | | $317,200 |
| Income from subsidiary: | | | | |
|   Parent's share of subsidiary's income | $40,000 | | $60,000 | |
|   Differential write-off for inventory sold | (4,000) | | | |
|   Amortization of differential | (4,800) | | (4,800) | |
| | | 31,200 | | 55,200 |
| Less: Dividends received from subsidiary | | (24,000) | | (32,000) |
| Balance at end of year | | $317,200 | | $340,400 |

### *Consolidation Workpaper—Second Year Following Combination*

The workpaper to prepare a complete set of consolidated financial statements for the year 20X2 is illustrated in Figure 5–8. Eliminating entries at the end of 20X2 are similar to those at the end of 20X1.

The first workpaper entry eliminates Peerless's income from Special Foods and Peerless's share of Special Foods' dividends for 20X2:

| E(18) | Income from Subsidiary | 55,200 | |
| | Dividends Declared | | 32,000 |
| | Investment in Special Foods Stock | | 23,200 |
| | Eliminate income from subsidiary. | | |

**FIGURE 5–8**   December 31, 20X2, Equity-Method Workpaper for Consolidated Financial Statements, Second Year of Ownership; 80 Percent Acquisition at More than Book Value

| Item | Peerless Products | Special Foods | Eliminations Debit | Eliminations Credit | Consolidated |
|---|---|---|---|---|---|
| Sales | 450,000 | 300,000 | | | 750,000 |
| Income from Subsidiary | 55,200 | | (18)   55,200 | | |
| Credits | 505,200 | 300,000 | | | 750,000 |
| Cost of Goods Sold | 180,000 | 160,000 | | | 340,000 |
| Depreciation and Amortization | 50,000 | 20,000 | (22)   6,000 | | 76,000 |
| Other Expenses | 60,000 | 45,000 | | | 105,000 |
| Debits | (290,000) | (225,000) | | | (521,000) |
| Consolidated Net Income | | | | | 229,000 |
| Income to Noncontrolling Interest | | | (19)   13,800 | | (13,800) |
| Income, carry forward | 215,200 | 75,000 | 75,000 | | 215,200 |
| Retained Earnings, January 1 | 411,200 | 120,000 | (20) 122,500 | | 408,700 |
| Income, from above | 215,200 | 75,000 | 75,000 | | 215,200 |
| | 626,400 | 195,000 | | | 623,900 |
| Dividends Declared | (60,000) | (40,000) | | (18)   32,000 | |
| | | | | (19)     8,000 | (60,000) |
| Retained Earnings, December 31, carry forward | 566,400 | 155,000 | 197,500 | 40,000 | 563,900 |
| Cash | 221,000 | 85,000 | | | 306,000 |
| Accounts Receivable | 150,000 | 80,000 | | | 230,000 |
| Inventory | 180,000 | 90,000 | | | 270,000 |
| Land | 175,000 | 40,000 | (21)   10,000 | | 225,000 |
| Buildings and Equipment | 800,000 | 600,000 | (21)   60,000 | | 1,460,000 |
| Investment in Special Foods Stock | 340,400 | | | (18)   23,200 | |
| | | | | (20) 317,200 | |
| Goodwill | | | (21)     9,375 | | 9,375 |
| Differential | | | (20)   73,375 | (21)   73,375 | |
| Debits | 1,866,400 | 895,000 | | | 2,500,375 |
| Accumulated Depreciation | 500,000 | 340,000 | | (21)     6,000 | |
| | | | | (22)     6,000 | 852,000 |
| Accounts Payable | 100,000 | 100,000 | | | 200,000 |
| Bonds Payable | 200,000 | 100,000 | | | 300,000 |
| Common Stock | 500,000 | 200,000 | (20) 200,000 | | 500,000 |
| Retained Earnings, from above | 566,400 | 155,000 | 197,500 | 40,000 | 563,900 |
| Noncontrolling Interest | | | | (19)     5,800 | |
| | | | | (20)   78,675 | 84,475 |
| Credits | 1,866,400 | 895,000 | 550,250 | 550,250 | 2,500,375 |

Elimination entries:
  (18) Eliminate income from subsidiary.
  (19) Assign income to noncontrolling interest.
  (20) Eliminate beginning investment balance.
  (21) Assign beginning differential.
  (22) Amortize differential related to buildings and equipment.

The net credit to the investment account of $23,200 represents the increase in the account balance during the period and takes the account balance back to the amount on January 1, 20X2, the beginning of the second year.

**FIGURE 5–9**
**Noncontrolling Interest, 20X2; 80 Percent Acquisition at More than Book Value**

| | |
|---|---|
| Income to noncontrolling interest, 20X2: | |
| Special Foods' net income | $ 75,000 |
| Amortization of differential related to buildings and equipment in 20X2 | (6,000) |
| Special Foods' adjusted income | $ 69,000 |
| Noncontrolling stockholders' proportionate share | × .20 |
| Income assigned to noncontrolling interest | $ 13,800 |
| | |
| Noncontrolling interest, December 31, 20X2: | |
| Special Foods' common stock | $200,000 |
| Special Foods' retained earnings | 155,000 |
| Special Foods' book value | $355,000 |
| Differential related to land | 10,000 |
| Unamortized differential related to buildings and equipment ($60,000 − $12,000) | 48,000 |
| Unimpaired goodwill ($12,500 − $3,125) | 9,375 |
| Special Foods' book value plus differential | $422,375 |
| Noncontrolling stockholders' proportionate share | × .20 |
| Noncontrolling interest, December 31, 20X2 | $ 84,475 |

Entry E(19) enters in the workpaper the amount of subsidiary income assigned to the noncontrolling interest:

| E(19) | Income to Noncontrolling Interest | 13,800 | |
|---|---|---|---|
| | Dividends Declared | | 8,000 |
| | Noncontrolling Interest | | 5,800 |
| | Assign income to noncontrolling interest. | | |

The computation of the income assigned to the noncontrolling interest for 20X1 is shown in Figure 5–9. The $13,800 of income assigned to the noncontrolling interest is subtracted from consolidated net income in the Consolidated column of the income statement portion of the workpaper in Figure 5–8 to arrive at the amount of income assigned to the controlling interest. Entry E(19) also includes a credit to Dividends Declared to eliminate the noncontrolling interest's portion of Special Foods' dividends. Entries E(18) and E(19) together totally eliminate the dividends of Special Foods. The $5,800 difference between the noncontrolling stockholders' share of subsidiary income and dividends represents the increase in the noncontrolling interest for 20X2 and is placed in the balance sheet portion of the workpaper.

Entry E(20) eliminates the balances in Peerless's investment account and Special Foods' stockholders' equity accounts as of the beginning of the period:

| E(20) | Common Stock—Special Foods | 200,000 | |
|---|---|---|---|
| | Retained Earnings, January 1 | 122,500 | |
| | Differential | 73,375 | |
| | Investment in Special Foods Stock | | 317,200 |
| | Noncontrolling Interest | | 78,675 |
| | Eliminate beginning investment balance: | | |
| | $122,500 = $120,000 + $2,500 | | |

Together entries E(18) and E(20) fully eliminate the ending balance in the parent's investment account. The noncontrolling interest is credited for its balance at the beginning of the period, equal to its ending balance for 20X1, as shown in Figure 5–6. This amount is added to the 20X2 increase in the noncontrolling interest established in entry E(19) to arrive at the total noncontrolling interest that appears as the last figure in the Consolidated column in the Figure 5–8 workpaper. This amount is carried to the consolidated balance sheet. The noncontrolling interest at December 31, 20X2, can also be computed as in Figure 5–9.

Entry E(20) also establishes the beginning differential in the workpaper. This amount is calculated as follows:

| | |
|---|---:|
| Land | $10,000 |
| Buildings and equipment ($60,000 − $6,000) | 54,000 |
| Unimpaired goodwill ($12,500 − $3,125) | 9,375 |
| Differential, December 31, 20X1 | $73,375 |

The differential was reduced in 20X1 by the $5,000 of inventory sold, the $6,000 of amortization related to buildings and equipment, and the $3,125 impairment of the goodwill.

One other point about entry E(20) needs to be noted. Normally, if the parent has used the equity method to account for its subsidiary investment, the debit to Retained Earnings, January 1, is for the amount of the subsidiary's retained earnings on that date, $120,000 in this case. In entry E(20), however, the debit is for $122,500. The additional $2,500 relates to the parent's share of the goodwill impairment loss recognized in the 20X1 consolidated income statement. Because, in accordance with current accounting standards, the parent did not recognize its share of the impairment loss in 20X1 under the equity method, its retained earnings has not been reduced by the loss. Once the amount of Special Foods' beginning retained earnings is eliminated, Peerless's beginning retained earnings becomes consolidated retained earnings at that date. Thus, beginning retained earnings will be overstated unless it is reduced by the parent's share ($3,125 × .80) of the 20X1 impairment loss. Accordingly, the total elimination of beginning retained earnings in the workpaper is for the amount of Special Foods' beginning retained earnings ($120,000) plus Peerless's share of the 20X1 goodwill impairment loss ($2,500).

Entry E(21) assigns the January 1, 20X2, differential:

| E(21) | Land | 10,000 | |
|---|---|---:|---:|
| | Buildings and Equipment | 60,000 | |
| | Goodwill | 9,375 | |
| |     Differential | | 73,375 |
| |       Accumulated Depreciation | | 6,000 |
| |     Assign beginning differential. | | |

Keep in mind that each year's workpaper is prepared from the trial balance data reported by the separate companies, not from the previous year's workpaper. The $6,000 of accumulated depreciation entered in the consolidation workpaper at the end of 20X1 does not automatically carry over to the 20X2 workpaper. Therefore, the workpaper entry to allocate the differential each time also must establish the additional accumulated depreciation for all prior years on any differential amounts assigned to depreciable assets.

The 20X2 depreciation of the portion of the differential assigned to buildings and equipment is given in entry E(22):

| E(22) | Depreciation Expense | 6,000 | |
|---|---|---:|---:|
| |     Accumulated Depreciation | | 6,000 |
| |     Amortize differential related to buildings and equipment: | | |
| |       $60,000 ÷ 10 years | | |

**FIGURE 5–10**
Consolidated Net
Income and Retained
Earnings, 20X2; 80
Percent Acquisition at
More than Book Value

| | |
|---|---:|
| Consolidated net income, 20X2: | |
| Peerless's separate operating income | $160,000 |
| Special Foods' net income | 75,000 |
| Amortization of differential related to buildings and equipment in 20X2 | (6,000) |
| Consolidated net income | $229,000 |
| | |
| Income to controlling interest, 20X2: | |
| Consolidated net income | $229,000 |
| Income to noncontrolling interest | (13,800) |
| Income to controlling interest | $215,200 |
| | |
| Consolidated retained earnings, December 31, 20X2: | |
| Peerless's retained earnings on date of combination, January 1, 20X1 | $300,000 |
| Income to controlling interest, 20X1 | 168,700 |
| Dividends declared by Peerless, 20X1 | (60,000) |
| Consolidated retained earnings, December 31, 20X1 | $408,700 |
| Income to controlling interest, 20X2 | 215,200 |
| Dividends declared by Peerless, 20X2 | (60,000) |
| Consolidated retained earnings, December 31, 20X2 | $563,900 |

### Consolidated Net Income and Retained Earnings

The computation of 20X2 consolidated net income and consolidated retained earnings at the end of 20X2 is shown in Figure 5–10.

### Consolidated Financial Statements

A consolidated income statement and retained earnings statement for the year 20X2 and a consolidated balance sheet as of December 31, 20X2, are presented in Figure 5–11.

## DISCONTINUANCE OF CONSOLIDATION

A parent that has been including a subsidiary in its consolidated financial statements should exclude that company from future consolidation if the parent can no longer exercise control over it. Control might be lost for a number of reasons, such as the parent sells some or all of its interest in the subsidiary, the subsidiary issues additional common stock, the parent enters into an agreement to relinquish control, or the subsidiary comes under the control of the government or other regulator.

If a parent loses control of a subsidiary and no longer holds an equity interest in the former subsidiary, it recognizes a gain or loss for the difference between any proceeds received from the event leading to loss of control (e.g., sale of interest, expropriation of subsidiary) and the carrying amount of the parent's equity interest. If the parent loses control but maintains a noncontrolling equity interest in the former subsidiary, it must recognize in income a gain or loss for the difference, at the date control is lost, between (1) the sum of any proceeds received by the parent and the fair value of its remaining equity interest in the former subsidiary, and (2) the carrying amount of the parent's total interest in the subsidiary.

As an example, assume that Peerless Products sells three-quarters of its 80 percent interest in Special Foods on January 1, 20X2, for $246,000, leaving it holding 20 percent of Special Foods' outstanding stock. On that date, assume that the fair value of Special Foods as a whole is $410,000 and the carrying amount of Peerless's 80 percent share of Special Foods is $317,200 (as shown earlier in the chapter). Assume the fair value of Peerless's remaining 20 percent interest in Special Foods is $82,000. Peerless's gain on the sale of Special Foods stock is computed as follows:

**FIGURE 5–11** **Consolidated Financial Statements for Peerless Products Corporation and Special Foods Inc., 20X2**

**PEERLESS PRODUCTS CORPORATION AND SUBSIDIARY**
**Consolidated Income Statement**
**For the Year Ended December 31, 20X2**

| | | |
|---|---:|---:|
| Sales | | $ 750,000 |
| Cost of Goods Sold | | (340,000) |
| Gross Margin | | $ 410,000 |
| Expenses: | | |
| Depreciation and Amortization | $ 76,000 | |
| Other Expenses | 105,000 | |
| Total Expenses | | (181,000) |
| Consolidated Net Income | | $ 229,000 |
| Income to Noncontrolling Interest | | (13,800) |
| Income to Controlling Interest | | $ 215,200 |

**PEERLESS PRODUCTS CORPORATION AND SUBSIDIARY**
**Consolidated Retained Earnings Statement**
**For the Year Ended December 31, 20X2**

| | |
|---|---:|
| Retained Earnings, January 1, 20X2 | $408,700 |
| Income to Controlling Interest, 20X2 | 215,200 |
| Dividends Declared, 20X2 | (60,000) |
| Retained Earnings, December 31, 20X2 | $563,900 |

**PEERLESS PRODUCTS CORPORATION AND SUBSIDIARY**
**Consolidated Balance Sheet**
**December 31, 20X2**

| Assets | | | Liabilities | | |
|---|---:|---:|---|---:|---:|
| Cash | | $ 306,000 | Accounts Payable | $200,000 | |
| Accounts Receivable | | 230,000 | Bonds Payable | 300,000 | |
| Inventory | | 270,000 | | | $ 500,000 |
| Land | | 225,000 | Stockholders' Equity | | |
| Buildings and Equipment | $1,460,000 | | Controlling Interest | | |
| Accumulated Depreciation | (852,000) | | Common Stock | $500,000 | |
| | | 608,000 | Retained Earnings | 563,900 | |
| Goodwill | | 9,375 | Total Controlling Interest | | 1,063,900 |
| | | | Noncontrolling Interest | | 84,475 |
| Total Assets | | $1,648,375 | Total Liabilities and Equity | | $1,648,375 |

| | |
|---|---:|
| Cash proceeds received | $246,000 |
| Fair value of Peerless's remaining equity interest in Special Foods | 82,000 |
| | $328,000 |
| Peerless's total interest in Special Foods at date of sale | 317,200 |
| Gain on sale of 60 percent interest in Special Foods | $ 10,800 |

Peerless reports the $10,800 gain in 20X2 income.

# TREATMENT OF OTHER COMPREHENSIVE INCOME

**FASB Statement No. 130,** "Reporting Comprehensive Income" (FASB 130), requires that companies separately report *other comprehensive income,* which includes all revenues, expenses, gains, and losses that under generally accepted accounting principles are excluded from net income.[1] Comprehensive income is the sum of net income and other comprehensive income. **FASB 130** permits several different options for reporting comprehensive income, but the consolidation process is the same regardless of the reporting format.

Other comprehensive income accounts are temporary accounts that are closed at the end of each period. Instead of being closed to Retained Earnings as revenue and expense accounts are, other comprehensive income accounts are closed to a special stockholders' equity account, Accumulated Other Comprehensive Income.

## Modification of the Consolidation Workpaper

When a parent or subsidiary has recorded other comprehensive income, the consolidation workpaper normally includes an additional section for other comprehensive income. This section of the workpaper facilitates computation of the amount of other comprehensive income to be reported, the portion, if any, of other comprehensive income to be assigned to the noncontrolling interest, and the amount of accumulated other comprehensive income to be reported in the consolidated balance sheet. Although this extra section of the workpaper for comprehensive income could be placed after the income statement section of the standard workpaper, the format used here is to place it at the bottom of the workpaper. If neither the parent nor any subsidiary reports other comprehensive income, the section can be omitted from the workpaper. When other comprehensive income is reported, the workpaper is prepared in the normal manner, with the additional section added to the bottom. The only modification within the standard workpaper is an additional stockholders' equity account included in the balance sheet portion of the workpaper for the cumulative effects of the other comprehensive income.

To illustrate the consolidation process when a subsidiary reports other comprehensive income, assume that during 20X2 Special Foods purchases $20,000 of investments classified as available-for-sale. By December 31, 20X2, the fair value of the securities increases to $30,000. Other than the effects of accounting for Special Foods' investment in securities, the financial statement information reported by Peerless Products and Special Foods at December 31, 20X2, is identical to that presented in Figure 5–8.

## Adjusting Entry Recorded by Subsidiary

At December 31, 20X2, Special Foods recognizes the increase in the fair value of its available-for-sale securities by recording the following adjusting entry:

| (23) | Investment in Available-for-Sale Securities | 10,000 | |
| | Unrealized Gain on Investments (OCI) | | 10,000 |
| | Record increase in fair value of available-for-sale securities. | | |

The unrealized gain is not included in the subsidiary's net income but is reported by the subsidiary as an element of other comprehensive income (OCI).

## Adjusting Entry Recorded by Parent Company

In 20X2, Peerless records all its normal entries [(15) through (17)] relating to its investment in Special Foods as if the subsidiary had not reported other comprehensive income. In addition, at December 31, 20X2, Peerless Products separately recognizes its proportionate share of the subsidiary's unrealized gain from the increase in the value of the available-for-sale securities:

| (17a) | Investment in Special Foods Stock | 8,000 | |
| | Other Comprehensive Income from Subsidiary—Unrealized | | |
| | Gain on Investments (OCI) | | 8,000 |
| | Record Peerless's proportionate share of the increase in value | | |
| | of available-for-sale securities held by subsidiary. | | |

---

[1] Other comprehensive income elements include foreign currency translation adjustments, unrealized gains and losses on certain derivatives and investments in certain types of securities, and certain minimum pension liability adjustments.

## Consolidation Workpaper—Second Year following Combination

The workpaper to prepare a complete set of consolidated financial statements for the year 20X2 is illustrated in Figure 5–12. In the workpaper, Peerless's balance in the Investment in Special Foods Stock account is greater than the balance in Figure 5–8 because of entry (17a), and Peerless's $8,000 proportionate share of Special Foods' unrealized gain is included in the separate section of the workpaper for comprehensive income (Other Comprehensive Income from Subsidiary—Unrealized Gain on Investments). Special Foods' trial balance has been changed to reflect (1) the reduction in the cash balance resulting from the investment acquisition, (2) the investment in available-for-sale securities, and (3) an unrealized gain of $10,000 on the investment.

## Consolidation Procedures

Eliminating entries E(18) through E(22) were used in preparing the consolidation workpaper for 20X2 presented in Figure 5–8. When other comprehensive income is introduced, the parent's income from its subsidiary is eliminated in the normal manner with entry E(18), and a proportionate share of the subsidiary's income is allocated to the noncontrolling interest with entry E(19); both of these entries are as shown in Figure 5–8. Entry E(20) in Figure 5–8 eliminates the beginning balances of the investment account and the beginning stockholders' equity balances of the subsidiary. Although this entry remains unchanged in this example, it would have included the elimination of the beginning balance of the subsidiary's accumulated Other Comprehensive Income if the subsidiary had had a balance as of the beginning of the period because that account is properly included in the subsidiary's stockholders' equity; further, a portion of the balance of that account would have been allocated to the beginning noncontrolling interest, as with the other stockholders' equity accounts of the subsidiary.

Eliminating entries E(21) and E(22) dealing with the differential also are unchanged from Figure 5–8. However, two additional entries are needed for the treatment of the subsidiary's other comprehensive income. First, the proportionate share of the subsidiary's other comprehensive income recorded by the parent with entry (17a) must be eliminated to avoid double counting the subsidiary's other comprehensive income. Thus, entry (17a) is reversed in the workpaper:

| E(24) | Other Comprehensive Income from Subsidiary—Unrealized Gain on Investments (OCI) | 8,000 | |
| | Investment in Special Foods Stock | | 8,000 |
| | Eliminate other comprehensive income from subsidiary. | | |

Second, a proportionate share of the subsidiary's other comprehensive income must be allocated to the noncontrolling interest:

| E(25) | Other Comprehensive Income to Noncontrolling Interest | 2,000 | |
| | Noncontrolling Interest | | 2,000 |
| | Assign other comprehensive income to noncontrolling interest. | | |

The amount of consolidated other comprehensive income reported in the consolidated financial statements is equal to the subsidiary's $10,000 amount. The noncontrolling interest's $2,000 proportionate share of the subsidiary's other comprehensive income is deducted to arrive at the $8,000 other comprehensive income allocated to the controlling interest.

While consolidated net income is the same in Figure 5–12 as in Figure 5–8, the other comprehensive income section of the workpaper in Figure 5–12 gives explicit recognition to the unrealized gain on available-for-sale securities held by Special Foods. This permits recognition in the consolidated financial statements under any of the alternative formats permitted by the FASB.

**FIGURE 5–12**  December 31, 20X2, Comprehensive Income Illustration, Second Year of Ownership; 80 Percent Acquisition at More than Book Value

| Item | Peerless Products | Special Foods | Eliminations Debit | Eliminations Credit | Consolidated |
|---|---|---|---|---|---|
| Sales | 450,000 | 300,000 | | | 750,000 |
| Income from Subsidiary | 55,200 | | (18) 55,200 | | |
| Credits | 505,200 | 300,000 | | | 750,000 |
| Cost of Goods Sold | 180,000 | 160,000 | | | 340,000 |
| Depreciation and Amortization | 50,000 | 20,000 | (22) 6,000 | | 76,000 |
| Other Expenses | 60,000 | 45,000 | | | 105,000 |
| Debits | (290,000) | (225,000) | | | (521,000) |
| Consolidated Net Income | | | | | 229,000 |
| Income to Noncontrolling Interest | | | (19) 13,800 | | (13,800) |
| Income, carry forward | 215,200 | 75,000 | 75,000 | | 215,200 |
| Retained Earnings, January 1 | 411,200 | 120,000 | (20) 122,500 | | 408,700 |
| Income, from above | 215,200 | 75,000 | 75,000 | | 215,200 |
| | 626,400 | 195,000 | | | 623,900 |
| Dividends Declared | (60,000) | (40,000) | | (18) 32,000 | |
| | | | | (19) 8,000 | (60,000) |
| Retained Earnings, December 31, carry forward | 566,400 | 155,000 | 197,500 | 40,000 | 563,900 |
| Cash | 221,000 | 65,000 | | | 286,000 |
| Accounts Receivable | 150,000 | 80,000 | | | 230,000 |
| Inventory | 180,000 | 90,000 | | | 270,000 |
| Land | 175,000 | 40,000 | (21) 10,000 | | 225,000 |
| Buildings and Equipment | 800,000 | 600,000 | (21) 60,000 | | 1,460,000 |
| Investment in AFS Securities | | 30,000 | | | 30,000 |
| Investment in Special Foods Stock | 348,400 | | | (18) 23,200 | |
| | | | | (20) 317,200 | |
| | | | | (24) 8,000 | |
| Goodwill | | | (21) 9,375 | | 9,375 |
| Differential | | | (20) 73,375 | (21) 73,375 | |
| Debits | 1,874,400 | 905,000 | | | 2,510,375 |
| Accumulated Depreciation | 500,000 | 340,000 | | (21) 6,000 | |
| | | | | (22) 6,000 | 852,000 |
| Accounts Payable | 100,000 | 100,000 | | | 200,000 |
| Bonds Payable | 200,000 | 100,000 | | | 300,000 |
| Common Stock | 500,000 | 200,000 | (20) 200,000 | | 500,000 |
| Retained Earnings, from above | 566,400 | 155,000 | 197,500 | 40,000 | 563,900 |
| Accumulated Other Comprehensive Income, from below | 8,000 | 10,000 | 10,000 | | 8,000 |
| Noncontrolling Interest | | | | (19) 5,800 | |
| | | | | (20) 78,675 | |
| | | | | (26) 2,000 | 86,475 |
| Credits | 1,874,400 | 905,000 | 560,250 | 560,250 | 2,510,375 |
| Other Comprehensive Income: | | | | | |
| OCI from Subsidiary—Unrealized Gain on Investments | 8,000 | | (24) 8,000 | | |
| Unrealized Gain on Investments | | 10,000 | | | 10,000 |
| Other Comprehensive Income to Noncontrolling Interest | | | (25) 2,000 | | (2,000) |
| Accumulated Other Comprehensive Income, January 1 | | | | | |
| Accumulated Other Comprehensive Income, December 31, carry up | 8,000 | 10,000 | 10,000 | | 8,000 |

Elimination entries:

(18) Eliminate income from subsidiary.

(19) Assign income to noncontrolling interest.

(20) Eliminate beginning investment balance.

(21) Assign beginning differential.

(22) Amortize differential related to buildings and equipment.

(24) Eliminate other comprehensive income from subsidiary.

(25) Assign other comprehensive income to noncontrolling interest.

Consolidated financial statements for the other comprehensive income example are presented in Figure 5–13. Note that consolidated other comprehensive income includes the full $10,000 unrealized gain. The noncontrolling interest's share is then deducted, along with

**FIGURE 5–13**
**Consolidated Financial Statements for Peerless Products Corporation and Special Foods Inc., 20X2, Including Other Comprehensive Income**

**PEERLESS PRODUCTS CORPORATION AND SUBSIDIARY**
**Consolidated Income Statement**
**For the Year Ended December 31, 20X2**

| | | |
|---|---|---|
| Sales | | $750,000 |
| Cost of Goods Sold | | (340,000) |
| Gross Margin | | $410,000 |
| Expenses: | | |
| Depreciation and Amortization | $ 76,000 | |
| Other Expenses | 105,000 | |
| Total Expenses | | (181,000) |
| Consolidated Net Income | | $229,000 |
| Income to Noncontrolling Interest | | (13,800) |
| Income to Controlling Interest | | $215,200 |

**PEERLESS PRODUCTS CORPORATION AND SUBSIDIARY**
**Consolidated Statement of Comprehensive Income**
**For the Year Ended December 31, 20X2**

| | |
|---|---|
| Consolidated Net Income | $229,000 |
| Other Comprehensive Income: | |
| Unrealized Gain on Investments | 10,000 |
| Total Consolidated Comprehensive Income | $239,000 |
| Less: Comprehensive Income Attributable to Noncontrolling Interest | 15,800 |
| Comprehensive Income Attributable to Controlling Interest | $223,200 |

**PEERLESS PRODUCTS CORPORATION AND SUBSIDIARY**
**Consolidated Statement of Financial Position**
**December 31, 20X2**

| | | |
|---|---|---|
| Assets | | |
| Cash | | $ 286,000 |
| Accounts Receivable | | 230,000 |
| Inventory | | 270,000 |
| Investment in Available-for-Sale Securities | | 30,000 |
| Land | | 225,000 |
| Buildings and Equipment | $1,460,000 | |
| Accumulated Depreciation | (852,000) | |
| | | 608,000 |
| Goodwill | | 9,375 |
| Total Assets | | $1,658,375 |
| Liabilities | | |
| Accounts Payable | $ 200,000 | |
| Bonds Payable | 300,000 | |
| Total Liabilities | | $ 500,000 |
| Stockholders' Equity | | |
| Controlling Interest: | | |
| Common Stock | $ 500,000 | |
| Retained Earnings | 563,900 | |
| Accumulated Other Comprehensive Income | 8,000 | |
| Total Controlling Interest | $1,071,900 | |
| Noncontrolling Interest | 86,475 | |
| Total Stockholders' Equity | | 1,158,375 |
| Total Liabilities and Stockholders' Equity | | $1,658,375 |

its share of consolidated net income, to arrive at the consolidated comprehensive income allocated to the controlling interest. The amount of other comprehensive income allocated to the controlling interest is carried to the Accumulated Other Comprehensive Income that is reported in the consolidated balance sheet, while the noncontrolling interest's share is included in the Noncontrolling Interest amount in the consolidated balance sheet. The FASB requires that the amount of each other comprehensive income element allocated to the controlling and noncontrolling interests be disclosed in the consolidated statements or notes.

## Consolidation Workpaper—Comprehensive Income in Subsequent Years

Each year following 20X2, Special Foods will adjust the unrealized gain on investments on its books for the change in fair value of the available-for-sale securities. For example, if Special Foods' investment increased in value by an additional $5,000 during 20X3, Special Foods would increase by $5,000 the carrying amount of its investment in securities and recognize as an element of 20X3's other comprehensive income an unrealized gain of $5,000. Under equity-method recording, Peerless would increase its Investment in Special Foods Stock account and record its $4,000 share of the subsidiary's other comprehensive income.

The eliminating entries required to prepare the consolidation workpaper at December 31, 20X3, would include the normal eliminating entries corresponding to E(18), E(19), E(21), and E(22). In addition, the normal investment elimination entry corresponding to E(20) would be expanded to eliminate the subsidiary's $10,000 beginning Accumulated Other Comprehensive Income balance and to increase the noncontrolling interest by its proportionate share of the subsidiary's beginning Accumulated Other Comprehensive Income amount ($10,000 $\times$ .20). Two additional eliminating entries corresponding to E(24) and E(25) also would be needed:

| E(24a) | Other Comprehensive Income from Subsidiary—Unrealized | | |
| | Gain on Investments (OCI) | 4,000 | |
| | Investment in Special Foods Stock | | 4,000 |
| | Eliminate other comprehensive income from subsidiary. | | |
| | | | |
| E(25a) | Other Comprehensive Income to Noncontrolling Interest | 1,000 | |
| | Noncontrolling Interest | | 1,000 |
| | Assign other comprehensive income to noncontrolling interest. | | |

# CONSOLIDATION OF SUBSIDIARIES ACQUIRED PRIOR TO 2009

The FASB's current standard on business combinations, **FASB 141R,** governs accounting for business combinations that are completed in fiscal years that begin on or after December 15, 2008. However, most acquired subsidiaries currently held by parent companies and included in their consolidated financial statements were acquired prior to the effective date of **FASB 141R.** Because companies are prohibited from applying **FASB 141R** retroactively, they are faced with consolidating numerous subsidiaries under the previous accounting standards. Thus, accountants must be familiar not only with current standards relating to the consolidation of acquired subsidiaries, but also with the standards that were in effect prior to **FASB 141R.**

## Differences in Consolidation Procedures

Fortunately, the general approach to consolidation is the same under both current and prior standards. The major differences are that the current standards place greater emphasis on fair value than previous standards, and the computation of the differential relates to the entire subsidiary rather than just the parent's share of less-than-wholly owned subsidiaries.

Currently, an acquired subsidiary is valued at the fair value of the consideration given to acquire it plus the fair value of any noncontrolling interest. Previously, an acquired subsidiary was valued at its cost to the acquiring company, plus the book value of any noncontrolling interest. Acquisition costs, such as legal, accounting, and appraisal fees, were previously included in the total recorded purchase price for an acquired company in addition to the consideration given the sellers, but under current standards those costs are expensed as incurred. Expensing these costs may somewhat lower the amount of goodwill recognized in a business combination.

Under current standards, the differential is equal to the difference between (1) the sum of the fair values of the consideration exchanged and the noncontrolling interest and (2) the book value of the net identifiable assets acquired. The differential relates to the claims of both the controlling and noncontrolling interests. Previously, when a company acquired less than 100 percent of a subsidiary's common stock, the differential was computed as the difference between the cost of the investment and the parent's proportionate share of the subsidiary's book value. In other words, only the parent's share of the total differential was recognized. Thus, the practical effect of the current standards' approach to the differential for less-than-wholly owned subsidiaries is often to increase the amount of goodwill recognized in a business combination, along with increasing the amount recognized for the subsidiary's assets and liabilities that are now valued at their total fair values rather than only the parent's portion.

## Illustration of Consolidation under Previous Accounting Standards

To illustrate the consolidation of a partially owned subsidiary under previous standards, the Peerless Products and Special Foods example used earlier in the chapter will again be used. As before, the relevant information is given in Figures 5–1, 5–2, and 5–4. Peerless acquires its 80 percent interest in Special Foods on January 1, 20X1, for a total cost of $310,000, and records the investment with entry (4) given earlier. Assume that Peerless acquires Special Foods prior to the effective date of **FASB 141R.**

### *Consolidation in Initial Year of Ownership*

Peerless accounts for its investment in Special Foods in the normal manner using the equity method. At the end of 20X1, Peerless records entries (5), (6), (7), and (8) given earlier in the chapter to recognize its share of Special Foods' dividends and to accrue and adjust its income from Special Foods. In the current example, the entries on Peerless's books are the same under both current and prior standards. If, however, Peerless had incurred additional acquisition costs such as legal fees, they would have been included under prior standards in the recorded amount of the investment at the date of combination, resulting in a higher carrying amount and a larger differential. In the current example, the differential is $70,000, the difference between Peerless's $310,000 purchase price for its stock in Special Foods and the $240,000 book value of the shares it acquired ($300,000 × .80). Assume that, during 20X1, management determines that the goodwill is impaired and must be written down by $2,500.

The workpaper to prepare consolidated financial statements for 20X1 using the prior accounting standards is shown in Figure 5–14. The workpaper includes the following elimination entries:

| | | | |
|---|---|---:|---:|
| E(9) | Income from Subsidiary | 31,200 | |
| | Dividends Declared | | 24,000 |
| | Investment in Special Foods Stock | | 7,200 |
| | Eliminate income from subsidiary. | | |
| E(10a) | Income to Noncontrolling Interest | 10,000 | |
| | Dividends Declared | | 6,000 |
| | Noncontrolling Interest | | 4,000 |
| | Assign income to noncontrolling interest: | | |
| | $10,000 = $50,000 × .20 | | |

**FIGURE 5–14** **December 31, 20X1, Equity-Method Workpaper for Consolidated Financial Statements, Initial Year of Ownership; 80 Percent Purchase at More than Book Value; Prior Standards**

| Item | Peerless Products | Special Foods | Eliminations Debit | | Eliminations Credit | | Consolidated |
|---|---|---|---|---|---|---|---|
| Sales | 400,000 | 200,000 | | | | | 600,000 |
| Income from Subsidiary | 31,200 | | (9) | 31,200 | | | |
| Credits | 431,200 | 200,000 | | | | | 600,000 |
| Cost of Goods Sold | 170,000 | 115,000 | (12a) | 4,000 | | | 289,000 |
| Depreciation and Amortization | 50,000 | 20,000 | (13a) | 4,800 | | | 74,800 |
| Goodwill Impairment Loss | | | (14a) | 2,500 | | | 2,500 |
| Other Expenses | 40,000 | 15,000 | | | | | 55,000 |
| Debits | (260,000) | (150,000) | | | | | (421,300) |
| | | | | | | | 178,700 |
| Income to Noncontrolling Interest | | | (10a) | 10,000 | | | (10,000) |
| Net Income, carry forward | 171,200 | 50,000 | | 52,500 | | | 168,700 |
| Retained Earnings, January 1 | 300,000 | 100,000 | (11a) | 100,000 | | | 300,000 |
| Net Income, from above | 171,200 | 50,000 | | 52,500 | | | 168,700 |
| | 471,200 | 150,000 | | | | | 468,700 |
| Dividends Declared | (60,000) | (30,000) | | | (9) | 24,000 | |
| | | | | | (10a) | 6,000 | (60,000) |
| Retained Earnings, December 31, carry forward | 411,200 | 120,000 | | 152,500 | | 30,000 | 408,700 |
| Cash | 194,000 | 75,000 | | | | | 269,000 |
| Accounts Receivable | 75,000 | 50,000 | | | | | 125,000 |
| Inventory | 100,000 | 75,000 | | | | | 175,000 |
| Land | 175,000 | 40,000 | (12a) | 8,000 | | | 223,000 |
| Buildings and Equipment | 800,000 | 600,000 | (12a) | 48,000 | | | 1,448,000 |
| Investment in Special Foods Stock | 317,200 | | | | (9) | 7,200 | |
| | | | | | (11a) | 310,000 | |
| Goodwill | | | (12a) | 10,000 | (14a) | 2,500 | 7,500 |
| Differential | | | (11a) | 70,000 | (12a) | 70,000 | |
| Debits | 1,661,200 | 840,000 | | | | | 2,247,500 |
| Accumulated Depreciation | 450,000 | 320,000 | | | (13a) | 4,800 | 774,800 |
| Accounts Payable | 100,000 | 100,000 | | | | | 200,000 |
| Bonds Payable | 200,000 | 100,000 | | | | | 300,000 |
| Common Stock | 500,000 | 200,000 | (11a) | 200,000 | | | 500,000 |
| Retained Earnings, from above | 411,200 | 120,000 | | 152,500 | | 30,000 | 408,700 |
| Noncontrolling Interest | | | | | (10a) | 4,000 | |
| | | | | | (11a) | 60,000 | 64,000 |
| Credits | 1,661,200 | 840,000 | | 488,500 | | 488,500 | 2,247,500 |

Elimination entries:

(9) Eliminate income from subsidiary.

(10a) Assign income to noncontrolling interest.

(11a) Eliminate beginning investment balance.

(12a) Assign beginning differential.

(13a) Amortize differential related to buildings and equipment.

(14a) Write down goodwill for impairment.

| E(11a) | Common Stock—Special Foods | 200,000 | |
| | Retained Earnings, January 1 | 100,000 | |
| | Differential | 70,000 | |
| |     Investment in Special Foods Stock | | 310,000 |
| |     Noncontrolling Interest | | 60,000 |
| |     Eliminate beginning investment balance. | | |
| | | | |
| E(12a) | Cost of Goods Sold | 4,000 | |
| | Land | 8,000 | |
| | Buildings and Equipment | 48,000 | |
| | Goodwill | 10,000 | |
| |     Differential | | 70,000 |
| |     Assign beginning differential. | | |
| | | | |
| E(13a) | Depreciation Expense | 4,800 | |
| |     Accumulated Depreciation | | 4,800 |
| |     Amortize differential related to buildings and equipment: | | |
| |         $48,000 ÷ 10 | | |
| | | | |
| E(14a) | Goodwill Impairment Loss | 2,500 | |
| |     Goodwill | | 2,500 |
| |     Write down goodwill for impairment. | | |

All of the eliminating entries except E(9) are different in the example of prior standards as compared with the example of current standards discussed earlier because of the difference in the differential. Entry E(9) in this example is the same as in the earlier example because it simply removes the effects of entries (6), (7), and (8) that were recorded by Peerless, and the entries on Peerless's books are the same in both examples.

Elimination entry E(10a) differs from E(10) in the earlier example because under prior standards the noncontrolling interest did not share in the differential and therefore its income was not burdened by any write-off of the differential. Under current standards, however, the amount of the noncontrolling interest is affected by the fair values of the subsidiary's net identifiable assets and goodwill. Thus, the noncontrolling interest is reduced by its share of the differential write-off, as can be seen in Figure 5–6 from the earlier example. In the current example under prior standards, the noncontrolling interest's share of income is a proportionate share of the subsidiary's net income ($50,000 × .20).

All of the remaining elimination entries, E(11a) through E(14a), differ from their counterparts in the earlier example. E(11a) through E(14a) differ because the earlier entries were based on a differential of $87,500, the excess of the $387,500 sum of the consideration given and the fair value of the noncontrolling interest over the $300,000 book value of Special Foods. In the current example under prior standards, the differential is the difference between Peerless's cost of $310,000 and Peerless's share of Special Foods' book value ($300,000 × .80). Accordingly, the differential in this example under prior standards is equal to only 80 percent of the differential in the example under current standards ($87,500 × .80), as can be seen by comparing entries E(11) and E(11a). Because the differential in Entry E(11a) represents only the parent's 80 percent share, the amounts in all of the rest of the elimination entries relating to the differential also are equal to just the parent's share and are 80 percent of the amounts in the respective entries in the earlier example under current standards.

Note several additional points from the consolidation workpaper in Figure 5–14. First, the workpaper and the general consolidation procedures are the same as under current standards. Only the eliminating entries, and the resulting consolidated amounts, are different, and those differ only by the amounts related to the differential. Second, Special Foods' assets and liabilities, including goodwill, are not valued based on their full acquisition-date fair values but only on their acquisition-date book values plus the parent's share of the fair value increment. Thus, the consolidated asset amounts in this illustration of the prior standards are lower than under current standards because they include only the parent's share of the fair value increment. Third, because the noncontrolling interest was not affected by the differential under prior standards, it is reported in the balance sheet at its 20 percent share of Special Foods' book value, as can be seen from the stockholders' equity section of the workpaper. Thus, the noncontrolling interest appears in the balance sheet section of the workpaper at a lower amount than under current standards (assuming a positive differential). Fourth, the income to the noncontrolling interest has not been reduced by any write-off of the differential in the example illustrating prior standards. The differential write-off, which is based on a less-than-full-entity differential, reduces the controlling interest's share of income only and does not affect the noncontrolling interest. Thus, the noncontrolling interest's share of income in the illustration of prior standards is a proportionate share of the subsidiary's net income ($50,000 × .10), as can be seen in the Figure 5–14 workpaper.

Two additional points should also be noted. First, the definition of consolidated net income has changed under the new standards. Under the previous standards, consolidated net income generally referred to the parent's share of the income of the consolidated entity, the amount remaining after deducting the income allocated to the noncontrolling interest. Thus, in Figure 5–14, consolidated net income is $168,700, the last figure in the Consolidated column in the income statement section of the workpaper. Under current standards, consolidated net income refers to the income of the entire consolidated entity before any allocation to the controlling or noncontrolling interests. Thus, in Figure 5–5, consolidated net income is $175,875, the figure in the Consolidated column that appears in the income statement section of the workpaper immediately before deducting income to the noncontrolling interest. The final figure in the income statement section of the Figure 5–5 workpaper, $168,700, is the portion of consolidated net income attributed to the controlling interest.

The second point is that the noncontrolling interest's claim on the net assets of the subsidiary is reported in the stockholders' equity section of the consolidated balance sheet under current standards. Previously, the presentation of the noncontrolling interest was not specified. Most companies reported the noncontrolling interest in the consolidated balance sheet as a "mezzanine" item between liabilities and stockholders' equity. However, some companies reported the noncontrolling interest as a liability or in stockholders' equity.

### Consolidation in Second Year of Ownership

During 20X2, Peerless records the normal equity-method entries on its books to record dividends and income from Special Foods. These entries are the same as entries (15), (16), and (17) in the earlier example under current standards.

The workpaper to prepare consolidated financial statements for 20X2 using the prior accounting standards is basically the same as under current standards. The only difference from the workpaper previously illustrated in Figure 5–8 is that the amounts of most elimination entries are different because of the difference in the differential, and accordingly the consolidated amounts are different. The workpaper would include the following elimination entries:

| E(18) | Income from Subsidiary | 55,200 | |
| | Dividends Declared | | 32,000 |
| | Investment in Special Foods Stock | | 23,200 |
| | Eliminate income from subsidiary. | | |
| E(19a) | Income to Noncontrolling Interest | 15,000 | |
| | Dividends Declared | | 8,000 |
| | Noncontrolling Interest | | 7,000 |
| | Assign income to noncontrolling interest: | | |
| | $15,000 = $75,000 × .20 | | |

| E(20a) | Common Stock—Special Foods | 200,000 | |
| | Retained Earnings, January 1 | 122,500 | |
| | Differential | 58,700 | |
| |     Investment in Special Foods Stock | | 317,200 |
| |     Noncontrolling Interest | | 64,000 |
| | Eliminate beginning investment balance: | | |
| | $122,500 = $120,000 + $2,500 | | |
| | $58,700 = $70,000 − $4,000 − $4,800 − $2,500 | | |
| | | | |
| E(21a) | Land | 8,000 | |
| | Buildings and Equipment | 48,000 | |
| | Goodwill | 7,500 | |
| |     Differential | | 58,700 |
| |     Accumulated Depreciation | | 4,800 |
| | Assign beginning differential: | | |
| | $7,500 = $10,000 − $2,500 | | |
| | | | |
| E(22a) | Depreciation Expense | 4,800 | |
| |     Accumulated Depreciation | | 4,800 |
| | Amortize differential related to buildings and equipment: | | |
| | $48,000 ÷ 10 | | |

Eliminating entry E(18) is the same under both current and prior accounting standards because it just eliminates Peerless's equity-method entries, and those entries are the same under both sets of standards. The amounts in the other four eliminating entries differ from current standards because of the differential. Entry E(19a) places the income to the noncontrolling interest in the workpaper, calculated as the noncontrolling interest's 20 percent share of Special Foods' net income. It differs from entry E(19) by the noncontrolling stockholders' $1,200 share of the differential amortization that the noncontrolling interest must bear under current standards but did not under prior standards. This $1,200 difference can also be seen in comparing entries E(22a) and E(22). Each of the entries E(20a) through E(22a) differs from their counterparts under current standards only in that these entries deal just with the parent's share of the differential and entries under current standards deal with the entire differential. These differences in elimination entries result in consolidated amounts that differ between current standards and prior standards by the differential-related amounts.

# ADDITIONAL CONSIDERATIONS

Chapters 3, 4, and 5 have provided a conceptual foundation for consolidated financial statements and a description of the basic procedures used in preparing consolidated statements. Before moving on to the issue of intercompany transactions in Chapters 6 through 8, several additional items should be considered to provide completeness and clarity.

## Subsidiary Valuation Accounts at Acquisition

**FASB 141R** indicates that all assets and liabilities acquired in a business combination should be valued at their acquisition-date fair values and no valuation accounts are to be carried over. While the application of this rule is clear-cut in merger-type business combinations, its application in consolidation following a stock acquisition is less clear. A subsidiary maintains an ongoing set of books and, unless push-down accounting is employed, it will carry forward its accounts. For some valuation accounts, such as accumulated depreciation, theory has dictated that the acquisition-date amount of the valuation account should be offset against the related asset account each time consolidated statements are prepared. Nevertheless, as an expediency, and because of a lack of materiality, companies generally have not made this offset, with no effect on the net amount of the asset. That is not expected to change under **FASB 141R.** For some other valuation accounts, depending on their nature and materiality, and how the amounts work out over time, they may have to be offset each time consolidated statements are prepared, at least for some number of periods.

## Negative Retained Earnings of Subsidiary at Acquisition

A parent company may acquire a subsidiary with a negative or debit balance in its retained earnings account. An accumulated deficit of a subsidiary at acquisition causes no special problems in the consolidation process. The normal investment elimination entry is made in the consolidation workpaper except that the debit balance in the subsidiary's Retained Earnings account is eliminated with a credit entry. Thus, the investment elimination entry appears as follows:

| E(26) | Capital Stock—Subsidiary | XXX | |
|---|---|---|---|
| | Differential | XXX | |
| |     Retained Earnings | | XXX |
| |     Investment in Subsidiary | | XXX |
| |   Eliminate investment balance. | | |

## Other Stockholders' Equity Accounts

The discussion of consolidated statements up to this point has dealt with companies having stockholders' equity consisting only of retained earnings and a single class of capital stock issued at par. Typically, companies have more complex stockholders' equity structures, often including preferred stock and various types of additional contributed capital. In general, all stockholders' equity accounts accruing to the common shareholders receive the same treatment as common stock and are eliminated at the time common stock is eliminated. The treatment of preferred stock in the consolidation process is discussed in Chapter 9.

## Subsidiary's Disposal of Differential-Related Assets

The disposal of an asset usually has income statement implications. If the asset is held by a subsidiary and is one to which a differential is assigned in the consolidation workpaper, both the parent's equity-method income and consolidated net income are affected. On the parent's books, the portion of the differential included in the subsidiary investment account that relates to the asset sold must be written off by the parent under the equity method as a reduction in both the income from the subsidiary and the investment account. In consolidation, the portion of the differential related to the asset sold is treated as an adjustment to consolidated income.

### Inventory

Any inventory-related differential is assigned to inventory for as long as the subsidiary holds the inventory units. In the period in which the inventory units are sold, the inventory-related differential is assigned to Cost of Goods Sold, as illustrated previously in Figure 5–5.

The inventory costing method used by the subsidiary determines the period in which the differential cost of goods sold is recognized. When the subsidiary uses FIFO inventory costing, the inventory units on hand on the date of combination are viewed as being the first units sold after the combination. Therefore, the differential normally is assigned to cost of goods sold in the period immediately after the combination. When the subsidiary uses LIFO inventory costing, the inventory units on the date of combination are viewed as remaining in the subsidiary's inventory. Only if the inventory level drops below its level at the date of combination is a portion of the differential assigned to cost of goods sold.

### Fixed Assets

A differential related to land held by a subsidiary is added to the Land balance in the consolidation workpaper each time a consolidated balance sheet is prepared. If the subsidiary sells the land to which the differential relates, the differential is treated in the consolidation workpaper as an adjustment to the gain or loss on the sale of the land in the period of the sale.

To illustrate, assume that on January 1, 20X1, Bright purchases all the common stock of Star at $10,000 more than book value. All the differential relates to land that Star had purchased earlier for $25,000. So long as Star continues to hold the land, the $10,000 differential is assigned to Land in the consolidation workpaper. If Star sells the land to an unrelated company for $40,000, the following entry is recorded on Star's books:

| (27) | Cash | 40,000 | |
|------|------|--------|--------|
| | Land | | 25,000 |
| | Gain on Sale of Land | | 15,000 |
| | Record sale of land. | | |

While a gain of $15,000 is appropriate for Star to report, the accounting basis of the land to the consolidated entity is $35,000 ($25,000 + $10,000). Therefore, the consolidated enterprise must report a gain of only $5,000. To reduce the $15,000 gain reported by Star to the $5,000 gain that should be reported by the consolidated entity, the following elimination is included in the consolidation workpaper for the year of the sale:

| E(28) | Gain on Sale of Land | 10,000 | |
|-------|----------------------|--------|--------|
| | Differential | | 10,000 |
| | Assign beginning differential. | | |

If, instead, Star sells the land for $32,000, the $7,000 ($32,000 − $25,000) gain recorded by Star is eliminated, and a loss of $3,000 ($32,000 − $35,000) is recognized in the consolidated income statement. The eliminating entry in this case is:

| E(29) | Gain on Sale of Land | 7,000 | |
|-------|----------------------|--------|--------|
| | Loss on Sale of Land | 3,000 | |
| | Differential | | 10,000 |
| | Assign beginning differential. | | |

When the equity method is used on the parent's books, the parent must adjust the carrying amount of the investment and its equity-method income in the period of the sale to write off the differential, as discussed in Chapter 2. Thereafter, the $10,000 differential no longer exists.

The sale of differential-related equipment is treated in the same manner as land except that the amortization for the current and previous periods must be considered.

## Summary of Key Concepts

The procedures and workpaper for consolidating less-than-wholly owned subsidiaries are the same as discussed in Chapter 4 for wholly owned subsidiaries, with several modifications. The workpaper elimination entries are modified to include the noncontrolling shareholders' claim on the income and assets of the subsidiary. The noncontrolling interest has a claim on subsidiary assets based on its acquisition-date fair value. If the acquisition-date fair value of the consideration given in a business combination, plus the fair value of any noncontrolling interest, exceeds the book value of the subsidiary, the difference is referred to as a differential and increases both the controlling and noncontrolling interests. The subsidiary's assets and liabilities are valued in consolidation based on their full acquisition-date fair values, with goodwill recognized at acquisition for the difference between (1) the sum of the fair value of the consideration given in the combination and the fair value of the noncontrolling interest and (2) the fair value of the subsidiary's net identifiable assets. Any subsequent write-off of the differential reduces both the controlling and noncontrolling interests.

Consolidated net income is equal to the parent's income from its own operations plus the subsidiary's net income adjusted for any amortization or write-off of the differential. The amount of consolidated net income attributable to the noncontrolling interest is equal to the noncontrolling interest's proportionate share of the subsidiary's net income less a proportionate share of any differential write-off. The income attributable to the controlling interest is equal to consolidated net income less the income attributable to the noncontrolling interest.

A subsidiary's other comprehensive income for the period must be recognized in consolidated other comprehensive income and allocated between the controlling and noncontrolling interests. The consolidation workpaper is modified to accommodate the other comprehensive income items by adding a special section at the bottom.

| **Key Terms** | consolidated net income, *198* | minority interest, *198* | other comprehensive |
|---|---|---|---|
| | differential, *200* | noncontrolling interest, *198* | income, *215* |

## Appendix **5A**   Consolidation and the Cost Method

Not all parent companies use the equity method to account for their subsidiary investments that are to be consolidated. The choice of the cost or equity method has no effect on the consolidated financial statements. This is so because the balance in the parent's investment account, the parent's income from the subsidiary, and related items are eliminated in preparing the consolidated statements. Thus, the parent is free to use on its separate books either the cost method or some version of the equity method in accounting for investments in subsidiaries that are to be consolidated.

Because the cost method uses different parent-company entries than the equity method, it also requires different eliminating entries in preparing the consolidation workpaper. Keep in mind that the consolidated financial statements appear the same regardless of whether the parent uses the cost or the equity method on its separate books.

### CONSOLIDATION—YEAR OF COMBINATION

To illustrate the preparation of consolidated financial statements when the parent company carries its subsidiary investment using the cost method, the Peerless Products and Special Foods example is used once again. Assume that Peerless purchases 80 percent of the common stock of Special Foods on January 1, 20X1, for $310,000. At that date, the book value of Special Foods as a whole is $300,000, and the fair value of the 20 percent noncontrolling interest is $77,500. The total differential is $87,500 [($310,000 + $77,500) − $300,000]. Of the total differential, $5,000 relates to inventory that is sold in 20X1, $10,000 relates to land, $60,000 relates to buildings and equipment having a remaining life of 10 years from the date of combination, and $12,500 relates to goodwill that is reduced by a $3,125 impairment loss during 20X1 and remains constant thereafter. All other data are the same as presented in Figures 5–1 and 5–4.

### Parent Company Cost-Method Entries

When the cost method is used, only two journal entries are recorded by Peerless during 20X1 related to its investment in Special Foods. Entry (30) records Peerless's purchase of Special Foods stock; entry (31) recognizes dividend income based on the $24,000 ($30,000 × .80) of dividends received during the period:

| | | | |
|---|---|---|---|
| (30) | Investment in Special Foods Stock | 310,000 | |
| | Cash | | 310,000 |
| | Record purchase of Special Foods stock. | | |
| | | | |
| (31) | Cash | 24,000 | |
| | Dividend Income | | 24,000 |
| | Record dividends from Special Foods: | | |
| | $30,000 × .80 | | |

No entries are made on the parent's books to amortize or write off the portion of the differential that expires during 20X1, as would be done under the equity method.

## Consolidation Workpaper—Year of Combination

The workpaper to prepare consolidated financial statements for December 31, 20X1, is shown in Figure 5–15. The trial balance data for Peerless and Special Foods included in the workpaper in Figure 5–15 differ from those presented in Figure 5–5 only by the effects of using the cost

**FIGURE 5–15**   **December 31, 20X1, Cost-Method Workpaper for Consolidated Financial Statements, Year of Combination; 80 Percent Acquisition at More than Book Value**

| Item | Peerless Products | Special Foods | Eliminations Debit | | Eliminations Credit | | Consolidated |
|---|---|---|---|---|---|---|---|
| Sales | 400,000 | 200,000 | | | | | 600,000 |
| Dividend Income | 24,000 | | (32) | 24,000 | | | |
| Credits | 424,000 | 200,000 | | | | | 600,000 |
| Cost of Goods Sold | 170,000 | 115,000 | (35) | 5,000 | | | 290,000 |
| Depreciation and Amortization | 50,000 | 20,000 | (36) | 6,000 | | | 76,000 |
| Goodwill Impairment Loss | | | (36) | 3,125 | | | 3,125 |
| Other Expenses | 40,000 | 15,000 | | | | | 55,000 |
| Debits | (260,000) | (150,000) | | | | | (424,125) |
| Consolidated Net Income | | | | | | | 175,875 |
| Income to Noncontrolling Interest | | | (33) | 7,175 | | | (7,175) |
| Income, carry forward | 164,000 | 50,000 | | 45,300 | | | 168,700 |
| Retained Earnings, January 1 | 300,000 | 100,000 | (34) | 100,000 | | | 300,000 |
| Income, from above | 164,000 | 50,000 | | 45,300 | | | 168,700 |
| | 464,000 | 150,000 | | | | | 468,700 |
| Dividends Declared | (60,000) | (30,000) | | | (32) | 24,000 | |
| | | | | | (33) | 6,000 | (60,000) |
| Retained Earnings, December 31, carry forward | 404,000 | 120,000 | | 145,300 | | 30,000 | 408,700 |
| Cash | 194,000 | 75,000 | | | | | 269,000 |
| Accounts Receivable | 75,000 | 50,000 | | | | | 125,000 |
| Inventory | 100,000 | 75,000 | | | | | 175,000 |
| Land | 175,000 | 40,000 | (35) | 10,000 | | | 225,000 |
| Buildings and Equipment | 800,000 | 600,000 | (35) | 60,000 | | | 1,460,000 |
| Investment in Special Foods Stock | 310,000 | | | | (34) | 310,000 | |
| Goodwill | | | (35) | 12,500 | (36) | 3,125 | 9,375 |
| Differential | | | (34) | 87,500 | (35) | 87,500 | |
| Debits | 1,654,000 | 840,000 | | | | | 2,263,375 |
| Accumulated Depreciation | 450,000 | 320,000 | | | (36) | 6,000 | 776,000 |
| Accounts Payable | 100,000 | 100,000 | | | | | 200,000 |
| Bonds Payable | 200,000 | 100,000 | | | | | 300,000 |
| Common Stock | 500,000 | 200,000 | (34) | 200,000 | | | 500,000 |
| Retained Earnings, from above | 404,000 | 120,000 | | 145,300 | | 30,000 | 408,700 |
| Noncontrolling Interest | | | | | (33) | 1,175 | |
| | | | | | (34) | 77,500 | 78,675 |
| Credits | 1,654,000 | 840,000 | | 515,300 | | 515,300 | 2,263,375 |

Elimination entries:
(32) Eliminate dividend income from subsidiary.
(33) Assign income to noncontrolling interest.
(34) Eliminate investment balance at date of acquisition.
(35) Assign differential at date of acquisition.
(36) Amortize differential and reduce goodwill for impairment.

method rather than the equity method on Peerless's books. Note that all of the amounts in the Consolidated column are the same as in Figure 5–5 because the method used by the parent to account for its subsidiary investment on its books has no effect on the consolidated financial statements.

Five eliminating entries are used to prepare the consolidation workpaper:

| | | | |
|---|---|--:|--:|
| E(32) | Dividend Income | 24,000 | |
| | Dividends Declared | | 24,000 |
| | Eliminate dividend income from subsidiary. | | |
| | | | |
| E(33) | Income to Noncontrolling Interest | 7,175 | |
| | Dividends Declared | | 6,000 |
| | Noncontrolling Interest | | 1,175 |
| | Assign income to noncontrolling interest. | | |
| | | | |
| E(34) | Common Stock—Special Foods | 200,000 | |
| | Retained Earnings, January 1 | 100,000 | |
| | Differential | 87,500 | |
| | Investment in Special Foods Stock | | 310,000 |
| | Noncontrolling Interest | | 77,500 |
| | Eliminate investment balance at date of acquisition. | | |
| | | | |
| E(35) | Cost of Goods Sold | 5,000 | |
| | Land | 10,000 | |
| | Buildings and Equipment | 60,000 | |
| | Goodwill | 12,500 | |
| | Differential | | 87,500 |
| | Assign differential at date of acquisition. | | |
| | | | |
| E(36) | Depreciation Expense | 6,000 | |
| | Goodwill Impairment Loss | 3,125 | |
| | Accumulated Depreciation | | 6,000 |
| | Goodwill | | 3,125 |
| | Amortize differential related to buildings and equipment and reduce goodwill for impairment. | | |

Entry E(32) eliminates the dividend income recorded by Peerless during the period along with Special Foods' dividend declaration related to the stockholdings of Peerless. Entry E(33) assigns income to the noncontrolling shareholders, as computed previously in Figure 5–6, and eliminates their portion of the subsidiary dividends ($30,000 × .20). This entry is the same as under the equity method and is not affected by the method used on the parent's books.

Entry E(34) eliminates the balances in the stockholders' equity accounts of Special Foods and the balance in Peerless's investment account as of the date of combination. A differential clearing account is established, representing the $87,500 differential at that date. Entry E(34) also establishes the noncontrolling interest in the workpaper at its acquisition-date fair value of $77,500. Entry E(35) assigns the differential to the appropriate expense and asset categories. Entry E(36) recognizes the additional depreciation related to the portion of the differential assigned to buildings and equipment. This entry also establishes in the workpaper the loss from the impairment of the goodwill included in the differential and reduces the goodwill by the amount of the impairment.

The investment elimination entry, E(34), is the same as the corresponding entry made when using the equity method. This occurs only in the year of acquisition because the balances eliminated are those at the beginning of the year, the date of combination. The balances on the date of combination are the same regardless of the method used to account for the investment subsequent to the combination. In all subsequent years, the investment elimination entries differ.

As mentioned previously, the amounts in the Consolidated column of the workpaper in Figure 5–15 are the same as those in Figure 5–5 because the method used on the parent's books to account for the subsidiary investment does not affect the consolidated financial statements.

# CONSOLIDATION—SECOND YEAR OF OWNERSHIP

Consolidation differences between cost-method accounting and equity-method accounting tend to be more evident in the second year of ownership. To see this, assume that Peerless earns income from its own separate operations of $160,000 during 20X2 and pays dividends of $60,000; Special Foods reports net income of $75,000 for 20X2 and pays dividends of $40,000.

## Parent Company Cost-Method Entry

Only a single entry is recorded by the parent in 20X2 in relation to its subsidiary investment:

| (37) | Cash | 32,000 | |
| |    Dividend Income | | 32,000 |
| |   Record dividends from Special Foods: | | |
| |   $40,000 × .80 | | |

## Consolidation Workpaper—Second Year Following Combination

The trial balance data for Peerless and Special Foods are entered in the consolidation workpaper at December 31, 20X2, as shown in Figure 5–16.

The first two elimination entries are similar to those used in the first year. Entry E(38) eliminates the dividend income from Special Foods recorded by Peerless and the dividend declaration of Special Foods related to Peerless's investment:

| E(38) | Dividend Income | 32,000 | |
| |    Dividends Declared | | 32,000 |
| |   Eliminate dividend income from subsidiary. | | |

Entry E(39) assigns to the noncontrolling shareholders their share of the subsidiary's income, as computed previously in Figure 5–9, and eliminates the noncontrolling interest's portion of subsidiary dividends ($40,000 × .20):

| E(39) | Income to Noncontrolling Interest | 13,800 | |
| |    Dividends Declared | | 8,000 |
| |    Noncontrolling Interest | | 5,800 |
| |   Assign income to noncontrolling interest. | | |

Under the cost method, the parent company has not recognized its portion of the undistributed earnings of the subsidiary on the parent company's books. Therefore, the parent company's retained earnings at the beginning of the second period is less than consolidated retained earnings, and the investment account balance reported by the parent is less than its proportionate share of the subsidiary's net assets at that date. The approach used in completing the consolidation workpaper in Figure 5–16 is to eliminate the balances reported by the parent company under the cost method and to carry the parent's portion of the increase in the subsidiary's retained earnings across to the Consolidated column.

Because the balance in the parent's investment account usually remains constant under the cost method, the investment elimination entry also remains constant. Entry E(40) eliminates the balance in Peerless's investment account and the balances in the stockholders' equity accounts of Special Foods as they existed at the date of combination:

| E(40) | Common Stock—Special Foods | 200,000 | |
| | Retained Earnings, January 1 | 100,000 | |
| | Differential | 87,500 | |
| |    Investment in Special Foods Stock | | 310,000 |
| |    Noncontrolling Interest | | 77,500 |
| |   Eliminate investment balance at date of acquisition. | | |

**FIGURE 5–16** December 31, 20X2, Cost-Method Workpaper for Consolidated Financial Statements, Second Year of Ownership; 80 Percent Acquisition at More than Book Value

| Item | Peerless Products | Special Foods | Eliminations Debit | Eliminations Credit | Consolidated |
|---|---|---|---|---|---|
| Sales | 450,000 | 300,000 | | | 750,000 |
| Dividend Income | 32,000 | | (38) 32,000 | | |
| Credits | 482,000 | 300,000 | | | 750,000 |
| Cost of Goods Sold | 180,000 | 160,000 | | | 340,000 |
| Depreciation and Amortization | 50,000 | 20,000 | (43) 6,000 | | 76,000 |
| Other Expenses | 60,000 | 45,000 | | | 105,000 |
| Debits | (290,000) | (225,000) | | | (521,000) |
| Consolidated Net Income | | | | | 229,000 |
| Income to Noncontrolling Interest | | | (39) 13,800 | | (13,800) |
| Income, carry forward | 192,000 | 75,000 | 51,800 | | 215,200 |
| Retained Earnings, January 1 | 404,000 | 120,000 | (40) 100,000 | | |
| | | | (41) 4,000 | | |
| | | | (42) 11,300 | | 408,700 |
| Income, from above | 192,000 | 75,000 | 51,800 | | 215,200 |
| | 596,000 | 195,000 | | | 623,900 |
| Dividends Declared | (60,000) | (40,000) | | (38) 32,000 | |
| | | | | (39) 8,000 | (60,000) |
| Retained Earnings, December 31, carry forward | 536,000 | 155,000 | 167,100 | 40,000 | 563,900 |
| Cash | 221,000 | 85,000 | | | 306,000 |
| Accounts Receivable | 150,000 | 80,000 | | | 230,000 |
| Inventory | 180,000 | 90,000 | | | 270,000 |
| Land | 175,000 | 40,000 | (42) 10,000 | | 225,000 |
| Buildings and Equipment | 800,000 | 600,000 | (42) 60,000 | | 1,460,000 |
| Investment in Special Foods Stock | 310,000 | | | (40) 310,000 | |
| Goodwill | | | (42) 9,375 | | 9,375 |
| Differential | | | (40) 87,500 | (42) 87,500 | |
| Debits | 1,836,000 | 895,000 | | | 2,500,375 |
| Accumulated Depreciation | 500,000 | 340,000 | | (42) 6,000 | |
| | | | | (43) 6,000 | 852,000 |
| Accounts Payable | 100,000 | 100,000 | | | 200,000 |
| Bonds Payable | 200,000 | 100,000 | | | 300,000 |
| Common Stock | 500,000 | 200,000 | (40) 200,000 | | 500,000 |
| Retained Earnings, from above | 536,000 | 155,000 | 167,100 | 40,000 | 563,900 |
| Noncontrolling Interest | | | (42) 2,825 | (39) 5,800 | |
| | | | | (40) 77,500 | |
| | | | | (41) 4,000 | 84,475 |
| Credits | 1,836,000 | 895,000 | 536,800 | 536,800 | 2,500,375 |

Elimination entries:
(38) Eliminate dividend income from subsidiary.
(39) Assign income to noncontrolling interest.
(40) Eliminate investment balance at date of acquisition.
(41) Assign undistributed prior earnings of subsidiary to noncontrolling interest.
(42) Assign differential remaining at beginning of year.
(43) Amortize differential related to buildings and equipment.

This entry is exactly the same as investment elimination entry E(34) made in the first year. The investment elimination entry continues to be the same in each subsequent year unless there is a change in ownership level or a change in the number of subsidiary shares outstanding or unless the subsidiary declares dividends in excess of earnings since acquisition by the parent.

Another workpaper entry is needed to establish the proper balance for noncontrolling shareholders in the consolidated balance sheet. Entry E(39) assigns to the noncontrolling shareholders their share of the increase in the stockholders' equity of the subsidiary during 20X2. Entry E(40) places the acquisition-date fair value of the noncontrolling interest in the workpaper. An additional entry is needed to assign to the noncontrolling shareholders their share of the increase in the subsidiary's stockholders' equity that occurred between the date of combination and the beginning of the current period. This increase is computed as follows:

| | |
|---|---:|
| Balance in retained earnings of Special Foods on January 1, 20X2 | $120,000 |
| Balance in retained earnings of Special Foods at acquisition | (100,000) |
| Undistributed earnings | $ 20,000 |
| Noncontrolling interest's share | × .20 |
| Increase assignable to noncontrolling interest | $ 4,000 |

Entry E(41) assigns to the noncontrolling interest its share of the increase in the stockholders' equity of Special Foods that occurred between the date of combination and the beginning of the current period:

| | | | |
|---|---|---:|---:|
| E(41) | Retained Earnings, January 1 | 4,000 | |
| | Noncontrolling Interest | | 4,000 |
| | Assign undistributed prior earnings of subsidiary to noncontrolling interest. | | |

A comparable computation and eliminating entry are necessary each time consolidated statements are prepared.

The final two entries in the consolidation workpaper are related to the differential:

| | | | |
|---|---|---:|---:|
| E(42) | Land | 10,000 | |
| | Buildings and Equipment | 60,000 | |
| | Goodwill | 9,375 | |
| | Retained Earnings, January 1 | 11,300 | |
| | Noncontrolling Interest | 2,825 | |
| | Differential | | 87,500 |
| | Accumulated Depreciation | | 6,000 |
| | Assign differential remaining at beginning of year: | | |
| | $9,375 = $12,500 − $3,125 | | |
| | $11,300 = ($5,000 + $6,000 + $3,125) × .8 | | |
| | $2,825 = ($5,000 + $6,000 + $3,125) × .2 | | |
| | | | |
| E(43) | Depreciation Expense | 6,000 | |
| | Accumulated Depreciation | | 6,000 |
| | Amortize differential related to buildings and equipment. | | |

Entry E(42) assigns the original amount of the differential so that the subsidiary's asset and contra asset accounts are brought to their appropriate consolidated balances as of the beginning of 20X2. Entry E(43) amortizes for 20X2 the portion of the differential related to buildings and equipment.

The assignment of the differential in entry E(42) is based on the acquisition-date fair values of Special Foods' assets. The inventory to which $5,000 of differential applied at the date of combination was sold in 20X1 and so does not appear. The goodwill balance reflects the $3,125 impairment reduction from 20X1. The $6,000 of additional depreciation recognized in the 20X1 workpaper is added to accumulated depreciation in this period's workpaper because workpaper entries do not carry over from year to year.

Entry E(42) also reduces the two ownership interests, the controlling and noncontrolling interests, for their proportionate shares of the 20X1 differential write-offs. Because under the cost method the parent does not reduce its investment income from the subsidiary on its separate books for differential write-offs, the beginning retained earnings balance is overstated from a consolidated viewpoint. Similarly, the 20X2 beginning balance of the noncontrolling interest was established in the workpaper with entry E(40) at its unreduced amount. Accordingly, the beginning balances of both the controlling and noncontrolling interests are overstated in the workpaper and must be reduced through entry E(42). The total differential write-offs in 20X1 were as follows:

| | |
|---|---:|
| Inventory sold in 20X1 | $ 5,000 |
| Additional depreciation | 6,000 |
| Goodwill impairment | 3,125 |
| Total write-off | $14,125 |

The beginning balance of the controlling interest is reduced by 80 percent of the prior year's write-off with a debit to Retained Earnings, January 1, and the noncontrolling interest is reduced by its 20 percent share.

Once all elimination entries are placed in the workpaper, the workpaper is completed in the normal manner. Note that the amounts in the Consolidated column in Figure 5–16 are the same as when the equity method is used on the parent's books (Figure 5–8) because all entries on the parent's books relating to the investment in its subsidiary are eliminated in the workpaper, resulting in the same amounts in the consolidated financial statements regardless of the method used on the parent's books to account for the subsidiary.

## Consolidated Retained Earnings

Consolidated Retained Earnings on January 1, 20X2, is derived in the consolidation workpaper by combining the parent's Retained Earnings and the subsidiary's Retained Earnings with the debits and credits from the various eliminating entries. The January 1, 20X2, $408,700 balance computed in this manner is equal to the December 31, 20X1, balance shown in Figure 5–15.

The beginning balance of the subsidiary's Retained Earnings is not fully eliminated under the cost method because the parent's Retained Earnings does not include undistributed earnings of the subsidiary since acquisition. As a result, some portion of subsidiary Retained Earnings must be carried across and included in consolidated Retained Earnings. Keep in mind that the only retained earnings figure reported in the consolidated balance sheet is the amount related to just the controlling interest, unlike consolidated net income. Thus, the amount reported in the consolidated balance sheet for retained earnings is equal to the parent's retained earnings (under the cost method), plus the parent's share of the subsidiary's undistributed earnings since acquisition, less the parent's share of the differential write-off since acquisition.

---

**Questions**

**Q5-1** Where is the balance assigned to the noncontrolling interest reported in the consolidated balance sheet?

**Q5-2** Why must a noncontrolling interest be reported in the consolidated balance sheet?

**Q5-3** How does the introduction of noncontrolling shareholders change the consolidation workpaper?

**Q5-4** How is the amount assigned to the noncontrolling interest normally determined when a consolidated balance sheet is prepared immediately after a business combination?

**Q5-5** What portion of consolidated retained earnings is assigned to the noncontrolling interest in the consolidated balance sheet?

**Q5-6** When majority ownership is acquired, what portion of the fair value of assets held by the subsidiary at acquisition is reported in the consolidated balance sheet?

**Q5-7** When majority ownership is acquired, what portion of the goodwill reported in the consolidated balance sheet is assigned to the noncontrolling interest?

**Q5-8** How is the income assigned to the noncontrolling interest normally computed?

**Q5-9** How is income assigned to the noncontrolling interest shown in the consolidation workpaper?

**Q5-10** How are dividends paid by a subsidiary to noncontrolling shareholders treated in the consolidation workpaper?

**Q5-11** Does a noncontrolling shareholder have access to any information other than the consolidated financial statements to determine how well the subsidiary is doing? Explain.

**Q5-12** How do other comprehensive income elements reported by a subsidiary affect the consolidated financial statements?

**Q5-13** What portion of other comprehensive income reported by a subsidiary is included in the consolidated statement of comprehensive income as accruing to parent company shareholders?

**Q5-14** Prior to the adoption of **FASB 141R,** how was the amount of the differential determined?

**Q5-15** Prior to the adoption of **FASB 141R,** how was the amount reported as goodwill determined when majority ownership was acquired at an amount greater than book value?

**Q5-16** Prior to the adoption of **FASB 141R,** how was the amount of consolidated net income of a less-than-wholly owned subsidiary determined?

**Q5-17\*** What effect does a negative retained earnings balance on the subsidiary's books have on consolidation procedures?

**Q5-18\*** What type of adjustment must be made in the consolidation workpaper if a differential is assigned to land and the subsidiary disposes of the land in the current period?

**Q5-19A** Why are eliminating entries in the consolidation workpaper different when the parent accounts for its investment in a subsidiary using the cost method rather than the equity method? What is the major difference in eliminating entries?

---

**Cases**

**C5-1** **Consolidation Workpaper Preparation**

The newest clerk in the accounting office recently entered trial balance data for the parent company and its subsidiaries in the company's consolidation program. After a few minutes of additional work needed to eliminate the intercompany investment account balances, he expressed his satisfaction at having completed the consolidation workpaper for 20X5. In reviewing the printout of the consolidation workpaper, other employees raised several questions, and you are asked to respond.

*Required*

*Analysis*

Indicate whether each of the following items can be answered by looking at the data in the consolidation workpaper (indicate why or why not):

a. Is it possible to tell if the parent is using the equity method in recording its ownership of each subsidiary?

b. Is it possible to tell if the correct amount of consolidated net income has been reported?

c. One of the employees thought the parent company had paid well above the fair value of net assets for a subsidiary purchased on January 1, 20X5. Is it possible to tell by reviewing the consolidation workpaper?

d. Is it possible to determine from the workpaper the percentage ownership of a subsidiary held by the parent?

**C5-2** **Consolidated Income Presentation**

*Research*
*FARS*

Standard Company has a relatively high profit margin on its sales, and Jewel Company has a substantially lower profit margin. Standard holds 55 percent of Jewel's common stock and includes Jewel in its consolidated statements. Standard and Jewel reported sales of $100,000 and $60,000, respectively, in 20X4. Sales increased to $120,000 and $280,000 for the two companies in 20X5. The average profit margins of the two companies remained constant over the two years at 60 percent and 10 percent, respectively.

Standard's treasurer was aware that the subsidiary was awarded a major new contract in 20X5 and anticipated a substantial increase in net income for the year. She was disappointed to learn that consolidated net income allocated to the controlling interest had increased by only 38 percent

*\*Indicates that the item relates to "Additional Considerations."*

*"A" indicates that the item relates to "Appendix A."*

even though sales were 2.5 times higher than in 20X4. She is not trained in accounting and does not understand the fundamental processes used in preparing Standard's consolidated income statement. She does know, however, that the earnings per share figures reported in the consolidated income statement are based on income allocated to the controlling interest and she wonders why that number isn't higher.

### Required

As a member of the accounting department, you have been asked to prepare a memo to the treasurer explaining how consolidated net income is computed and the procedures used to allocate income to the parent company and to the subsidiary's noncontrolling shareholders. Include in your memo citations to or quotations from the authoritative literature. To assist the treasurer in gaining a better understanding, prepare an analysis showing the income statement amounts actually reported for 20X4 and 20X5.

**C5-3** **Pro Rata Consolidation**

*Research*
*FARS*

Rose Corporation and Krome Company established a joint venture to manufacture components for both companies' use on January 1, 20X1, and have operated it quite successfully for the past four years. Rose and Krome both contributed 50 percent of the equity when the joint venture was created. Rose purchases roughly 70 percent of the output of the joint venture and Krome purchases 30 percent. Rose and Krome have equal numbers of representatives on the joint venture's board of directors and participate equally in its management. Joint venture profits are distributed at year-end on the basis of total purchases by each company.

### Required

Rose has been using the equity method to report its investment in the joint venture; however, Rose's financial vice president believes that each company should use pro rata consolidation. As a senior accountant at Rose, you have been asked to prepare a memo discussing those situations in which pro rata consolidation may be appropriate and to offer your recommendation as to whether Rose should continue to use the equity method or switch to pro rata consolidation. Include in your memo citations of and quotations from the authoritative literature to support your arguments.

**C5-4** **Elimination Procedures**

*Communication*

A new employee has been given responsibility for preparing the consolidated financial statements of Sample Company. After attempting to work alone for some time, the employee seeks assistance in gaining a better overall understanding of the way in which the consolidation process works.

### Required

You have been asked to provide assistance in explaining the consolidation process.

*a.* Why must the eliminating entries be entered in the consolidation workpaper each time consolidated statements are prepared?

*b.* How is the beginning-of-period noncontrolling interest balance determined?

*c.* How is the end-of-period noncontrolling interest balance determined?

*d.* Which of the subsidiary's account balances must always be eliminated?

*e.* Which of the parent company's account balances must always be eliminated?

**C5-5** **Changing Accounting Standards: Monsanto Company**

*Research*

Monsanto Company, a St. Louis-based company, is a leading provider of agricultural products for farmers. It sells seeds, biotechnology trait products, and herbicides worldwide.

### Required

*a.* How did Monsanto Company report its income to noncontrolling (minority) shareholders of consolidated subsidiaries in its 2007 consolidated income statement?

*b.* How did Monsanto Company report its subsidiary noncontrolling (minority) interest in its 2007 consolidated balance sheet?

*c.* Comment on Monsanto's treatment of its subsidiary noncontrolling interest.

*d.* In 2007, Monsanto had several affiliates that were special purpose or variable interest entities. What level of ownership did Monsanto have in these entities? Were any of these consolidated? Why?

**Exercises**

**E5-1  Multiple-Choice Questions on Consolidation Process**

Select the most appropriate answer for each of the following questions.

1. If A Company acquires 80 percent of the stock of B Company on January 1, 20X2, immediately after the acquisition:

   a. Consolidated retained earnings will be equal to the combined retained earnings of the two companies.
   b. Goodwill will be reported in the consolidated balance sheet.
   c. A Company's additional paid-in capital may be reduced to permit the carryforward of B Company retained earnings.
   d. Consolidated retained earnings and A Company retained earnings will be the same.

2. Which of the following is correct?

   a. The noncontrolling shareholders' claim on the subsidiary's net assets is based on the book value of the subsidiary's net assets.
   b. Only the parent's portion of the difference between book value and fair value of the subsidiary's assets is assigned to those assets.
   c. Goodwill represents the difference between the book value of the subsidiary's net assets and the amount paid by the parent to buy ownership.
   d. Total assets reported by the parent generally will be less than total assets reported on the consolidated balance sheet.

3. Which of the following statements is correct?

   a. Foreign subsidiaries do not need to be consolidated if they are reported as a separate operating group under segment reporting.
   b. Consolidated retained earnings does not include the noncontrolling interest's claim on the subsidiary's retained earnings.
   c. The noncontrolling shareholders' claim should be adjusted for changes in the fair value of the subsidiary assets but should not include goodwill.
   d. Consolidation is expected any time the investor holds significant influence over the investee.

4. [AICPA Adapted] At December 31, 20X9, Grey Inc. owned 90 percent of Winn Corporation, a consolidated subsidiary, and 20 percent of Carr Corporation, an investee in which Grey cannot exercise significant influence. On the same date, Grey had receivables of $300,000 from Winn and $200,000 from Carr. In its December 31, 20X9, consolidated balance sheet, Grey should report accounts receivable from its affiliates of:

   a. $500,000.
   b. $340,000.
   c. $230,000.
   d. $200,000.

**E5-2  Multiple-Choice Questions on Consolidation [AICPA Adapted]**

Select the correct answer for each of the following questions.

1. A 70 percent owned subsidiary company declares and pays a cash dividend. What effect does the dividend have on the retained earnings and minority interest balances in the parent company's consolidated balance sheet?

   a. No effect on either retained earnings or minority interest.
   b. No effect on retained earnings and a decrease in minority interest.
   c. Decreases in both retained earnings and minority interest.
   d. A decrease in retained earnings and no effect on minority interest.

2. How is the portion of consolidated earnings to be assigned to the noncontrolling interest in consolidated financial statements determined?

   a. The parent's net income is subtracted from the subsidiary's net income to determine the noncontrolling interest.
   b. The subsidiary's net income is extended to the noncontrolling interest.

c. The amount of the subsidiary's earnings recognized for consolidation purposes is multiplied by the noncontrolling interest's percentage of ownership.

d. The amount of consolidated earnings on the consolidated workpapers is multiplied by the noncontrolling interest percentage on the balance sheet date.

3. On January 1, 20X5, Post Company acquired an 80 percent investment in Stake Company. The acquisition cost was equal to Post's equity in Stake's net assets at that date. On January 1, 20X5, Post and Stake had retained earnings of $500,000 and $100,000, respectively. During 20X5, Post had net income of $200,000, which included its equity in Stake's earnings, and declared dividends of $50,000; Stake had net income of $40,000 and declared dividends of $20,000. There were no other intercompany transactions between the parent and subsidiary. On December 31, 20X5, what should the consolidated retained earnings be?

a. $650,000.

b. $666,000.

c. $766,000.

d. $770,000.

*Note:* Items 4 and 5 are based on the following information:

On January 1, 20X8, Ritt Corporation acquired 80 percent of Shaw Corporation's $10 par common stock for $956,000. On this date, the fair value of the noncontrolling interest was $239,000, and the carrying amount of Shaw's net assets was $1,000,000. The fair values of Shaw's identifiable assets and liabilities were the same as their carrying amounts except for plant assets (net) with a remaining life of 20 years, which were $100,000 in excess of the carrying amount. For the year ended December 31, 20X8, Shaw had net income of $190,000 and paid cash dividends totaling $125,000.

4. In the January 1, 20X8, consolidated balance sheet, the amount of goodwill reported should be:

a. $0.

b. $76,000.

c. $95,000.

d. $156,000.

5. In the December 31, 20X8, consolidated balance sheet, the amount of noncontrolling interest reported should be:

a. $200,000.

b. $239,000.

c. $251,000.

d. $252,000.

### E5-3 Eliminating Entries with Differential

On June 10, 20X8, Game Corporation acquired 60 percent of Amber Company's common stock. The fair value of the noncontrolling interest was $32,800 on that date. Summarized balance sheet data for the two companies immediately after the stock purchase are as follows:

| Item | Game Corp. Book Value | Amber Company Book Value | Amber Company Fair Value |
|---|---|---|---|
| Cash | $ 25,800 | $ 5,000 | $ 5,000 |
| Accounts Receivable | 30,000 | 10,000 | 10,000 |
| Inventory | 80,000 | 20,000 | 25,000 |
| Buildings and Equipment (net) | 120,000 | 50,000 | 70,000 |
| Investment in Amber Stock | 49,200 | | |
| Total | $305,000 | $85,000 | $110,000 |
| Accounts Payable | $ 25,000 | $ 3,000 | $ 3,000 |
| Bonds Payable | 150,000 | 25,000 | 25,000 |
| Common Stock | 55,000 | 20,000 | |
| Retained Earnings | 75,000 | 37,000 | |
| Total | $305,000 | $85,000 | $ 28,000 |

**Required**

a. Give the eliminating entries required to prepare a consolidated balance sheet immediately after the purchase of Amber Company shares.

b. Explain how eliminating entries differ from other types of journal entries recorded in the normal course of business.

### E5-4   Computation of Consolidated Balances

Slim Corporation's balance sheet at January 1, 20X7, reflected the following balances:

| | | | |
|---|---|---|---|
| Cash and Receivables | $ 80,000 | Accounts Payable | $ 40,000 |
| Inventory | 120,000 | Income Taxes Payable | 60,000 |
| Land | 70,000 | Bonds Payable | 200,000 |
| Buildings and Equipment (net) | 480,000 | Common Stock | 250,000 |
| | | Retained Earnings | 200,000 |
| Total Assets | $750,000 | Total Liabilities and Stockholders' Equity | $750,000 |

Ford Corporation entered into an active acquisition program and acquired 80 percent of Slim's common stock on January 2, 20X7, for $470,000. The fair value of the noncontrolling interest at that date was determined to be $117,500. A careful review of the fair value of Slim's assets and liabilities indicated the following:

| | Book Value | Fair Value |
|---|---|---|
| Inventory | $120,000 | $140,000 |
| Land | 70,000 | 60,000 |
| Buildings and Equipment (net) | 480,000 | 550,000 |

Goodwill is assigned proportionately to Ford and the noncontrolling shareholders.

**Required**

Compute the appropriate amount to be included in the consolidated balance sheet immediately following the acquisition for each of the following items:

a. Inventory.

b. Land.

c. Buildings and Equipment (net).

d. Goodwill.

e. Investment in Slim Corporation.

f. Noncontrolling Interest.

### E5-5   Balance Sheet Workpaper

Power Company owns 90 percent of Pleasantdale Dairy's stock. The balance sheets of the two companies immediately after the Pleasantdale acquisition showed the following amounts:

| | Power Company | Pleasantdale Dairy |
|---|---|---|
| Cash and Receivables | $ 130,000 | $ 70,000 |
| Inventory | 210,000 | 90,000 |
| Land | 70,000 | 40,000 |
| Buildings and Equipment (net) | 390,000 | 220,000 |
| Investment in Pleasantdale Stock | 270,000 | |
| Total Assets | $1,070,000 | $420,000 |
| Current Payables | $ 80,000 | $ 40,000 |
| Long-Term Liabilities | 200,000 | 100,000 |
| Common Stock | 400,000 | 60,000 |
| Retained Earnings | 390,000 | 220,000 |
| Total Liabilities and Stockholders' Equity | $1,070,000 | $420,000 |

The fair value of the noncontrolling interest at the date of acquisition was determined to be $30,000. The full amount of the increase over book value is assigned to land held by Pleasantdale. At the date of acquisition, Pleasantdale owed Power $8,000 plus $900 accrued interest. Pleasantdale had recorded the accrued interest, but Power had not.

### Required
Prepare and complete a consolidated balance sheet workpaper.

**E5-6  Majority-Owned Subsidiary Acquired at Greater than Book Value**

Zenith Corporation acquired 70 percent of Down Corporation's common stock on December 31, 20X4, for $102,200. The fair value of the noncontrolling interest at that date was determined to be $43,800. Data from the balance sheets of the two companies included the following amounts as of the date of acquisition:

| Item | Zenith Corporation | Down Corporation |
|---|---|---|
| Cash | $ 50,300 | $ 21,000 |
| Accounts Receivable | 90,000 | 44,000 |
| Inventory | 130,000 | 75,000 |
| Land | 60,000 | 30,000 |
| Buildings and Equipment | 410,000 | 250,000 |
| Less: Accumulated Depreciation | (150,000) | (80,000) |
| Investment in Down Corporation Stock | 102,200 | |
| Total Assets | $692,500 | $340,000 |
| Accounts Payable | $152,500 | $ 35,000 |
| Mortgage Payable | 250,000 | 180,000 |
| Common Stock | 80,000 | 40,000 |
| Retained Earnings | 210,000 | 85,000 |
| Total Liabilities and Stockholders' Equity | $692,500 | $340,000 |

At the date of the business combination, the book values of Down's assets and liabilities approximated fair value except for inventory, which had a fair value of $81,000, and buildings and equipment, which had a fair value of $185,000. At December 31, 20X4, Zenith reported accounts payable of $12,500 to Down, which reported an equal amount in its accounts receivable.

### Required
a. Give the eliminating entry or entries needed to prepare a consolidated balance sheet immediately following the business combination.
b. Prepare a consolidated balance sheet workpaper.
c. Prepare a consolidated balance sheet in good form.

**E5-7  Consolidation with Minority Interest**

Temple Corporation acquired 75 percent of Dynamic Corporation's voting common stock on December 31, 20X4, for $390,000. At the date of combination, Dynamic reported the following:

| | | | | |
|---|---|---|---|---|
| Current Assets | $220,000 | Current Liabilities | $ 80,000 |
| Long-Term Assets (net) | 420,000 | Long-Term Liabilities | 200,000 |
| | | Common Stock | 120,000 |
| | | Retained Earnings | 240,000 |
| Total | $640,000 | Total | $640,000 |

At December 31, 20X4, the book values of Dynamic's net assets and liabilities approximated their fair values, except for buildings, which had a fair value of $80,000 more than book value, and inventories, which had a fair value of $36,000 more than book value. The fair value of the noncontrolling interest was determined to be $130,000 at that date.

*Required*

Temple Corporation wishes to prepare a consolidated balance sheet immediately following the business combination. Give the eliminating entry or entries needed to prepare a consolidated balance sheet at December 31, 20X4.

### E5-8 Workpaper for Majority-Owned Subsidiary

Glitter Enterprises acquired 60 percent of Lowtide Builders' stock on December 31, 20X4. Glitter acquired its shares for $90,000, the book value of the shares acquired. At that date, the fair value of the noncontrolling interest was equal to 40 percent of the book value of Lowtide. Balance sheet data for Glitter and Lowtide on January 1, 20X5, are as follows:

| | Glitter Enterprises | Lowtide Builders |
|---|---|---|
| Cash and Receivables | $ 80,000 | $ 30,000 |
| Inventory | 150,000 | 350,000 |
| Buildings and Equipment (net) | 430,000 | 80,000 |
| Investment in Lowtide Stock | 90,000 | |
| Total Assets | $750,000 | $460,000 |
| Current Liabilities | $100,000 | $110,000 |
| Long-Term Debt | 400,000 | 200,000 |
| Common Stock | 200,000 | 140,000 |
| Retained Earnings | 50,000 | 10,000 |
| Total Liabilities and Stockholders' Equity | $750,000 | $460,000 |

*Required*

a. Give all eliminating entries needed to prepare a consolidated balance sheet on January 1, 20X5.

b. Complete a consolidated balance sheet workpaper.

c. Prepare a consolidated balance sheet in good form.

### E5-9 Multiple-Choice Questions on Balance Sheet Consolidation

Power Corporation acquired 70 percent of Silk Corporation's common stock on December 31, 20X2. Balance sheet data for the two companies immediately following the acquisition follow:

| Item | Power Corporation | Silk Corporation |
|---|---|---|
| Cash | $ 44,000 | $ 30,000 |
| Accounts Receivable | 110,000 | 45,000 |
| Inventory | 130,000 | 70,000 |
| Land | 80,000 | 25,000 |
| Buildings and Equipment | 500,000 | 400,000 |
| Less: Accumulated Depreciation | (223,000) | (165,000) |
| Investment in Silk Corporation Stock | 150,500 | |
| Total Assets | $791,500 | $405,000 |
| Accounts Payable | $ 61,500 | $ 28,000 |
| Taxes Payable | 95,000 | 37,000 |
| Bonds Payable | 280,000 | 200,000 |
| Common Stock | 150,000 | 50,000 |
| Retained Earnings | 205,000 | 90,000 |
| Total Liabilities and Stockholders' Equity | $791,500 | $405,000 |

At the date of the business combination, the book values of Silk's net assets and liabilities approximated fair value except for inventory, which had a fair value of $85,000, and land, which had a fair value of $45,000. The fair value of the noncontrolling interest was $64,500 on December 31, 20X2.

### Required

For each question below, indicate the appropriate total that should appear in the consolidated balance sheet prepared immediately after the business combination.

1. What amount of inventory will be reported?

   a. $179,000.

   b. $200,000.

   c. $210,500.

   d. $215,000.

2. What amount of goodwill will be reported?

   a. $0.

   b. $28,000.

   c. $40,000.

   d. $52,000.

3. What amount of total assets will be reported?

   a. $1,081,000.

   b. $1,121,000.

   c. $1,196,500.

   d. $1,231,500.

4. What amount of total liabilities will be reported?

   a. $265,000.

   b. $436,500.

   c. $622,000.

   d. $701,500.

5. What amount will be reported as noncontrolling interest?

   a. $42,000.

   b. $52,500.

   c. $60,900.

   d. $64,500.

6. What amount of consolidated retained earnings will be reported?

   a. $295,000.

   b. $268,000.

   c. $232,000.

   d. $205,000.

7. What amount of total stockholders' equity will be reported?

   a. $355,000.

   b. $397,000.

   c. $419,500.

   d. $495,000.

### E5-10 Basic Consolidation Entries for Majority-Owned Subsidiary

Farmstead Company reported the following summarized balance sheet data on December 31, 20X8:

| Assets | $350,000 | Accounts Payable | $ 50,000 |
|--------|----------|------------------|----------|
|        |          | Common Stock     | 100,000 |
|        |          | Retained Earnings | 200,000 |
| Total  | $350,000 | Total            | $350,000 |

On January 1, 20X9, Horrigan Corporation acquired 70 percent of Farmstead's stock for $210,000, the book value of the shares acquired. At that date the fair value of the noncontrolling interest was equal to 30 percent of the book value of Farmstead. Farmstead reported net income of $20,000 for 20X9 and paid dividends of $5,000.

### Required

a. Give the equity-method journal entries recorded by Horrigan on its books during 20X9 related to its ownership of Farmstead.

b. Give the eliminating entries needed on December 31, 20X9, to prepare consolidated financial statements.

**E5-11   Majority-Owned Subsidiary with Differential**

Canton Corporation is a majority-owned subsidiary of West Corporation. West acquired 75 percent ownership on January 1, 20X3, for $133,500. At that date, Canton reported common stock outstanding of $60,000 and retained earnings of $90,000, and the fair value of the noncontrolling interest was $44,500. The differential is assigned to equipment, which had a fair value $28,000 greater than book value and a remaining economic life of seven years at the date of the business combination. Canton reported net income of $30,000 and paid dividends of $12,000 in 20X3.

### Required

a. Give the journal entries recorded by West during 20X3 on its books if it accounts for its investment in Canton using the equity method.

b. Give the eliminating entries needed at December 31, 20X3, to prepare consolidated financial statements.

**E5-12   Differential Assigned to Amortizable Asset**

Major Corporation acquired 90 percent of Lancaster Company's voting common stock on January 1, 20X1, for $486,000. At the time of the combination, Lancaster reported common stock outstanding of $120,000 and retained earnings of $380,000, and the fair value of the noncontrolling interest was $54,000. The book value of Lancaster's net assets approximated market value except for patents that had a market value of $40,000 more than their book value. The patents had a remaining economic life of five years at the date of the business combination. Lancaster reported net income of $60,000 and paid dividends of $20,000 during 20X1.

### Required

a. What balance did Major report as its investment in Lancaster at December 31, 20X1, assuming Major uses the equity method in accounting for its investment?

b. Give the eliminating entry or entries needed to prepare consolidated financial statements at December 31, 20X1.

**E5-13   Consolidation after One Year of Ownership**

Pioneer Corporation purchased 80 percent of Lowe Corporation's stock on January 1, 20X2. At that date Lowe reported retained earnings of $80,000 and had $120,000 of stock outstanding. The fair value of its buildings was $32,000 more than the book value.

Pioneer paid $190,000 to acquire the Lowe shares. At that date, the noncontrolling interest had a fair value of $47,500. The remaining economic life for all Lowe's depreciable assets was eight years on the date of combination. The amount of the differential assigned to goodwill is not impaired. Lowe reported net income of $40,000 in 20X2 and declared no dividends.

### Required

a. Give the eliminating entries needed to prepare a consolidated balance sheet immediately after Pioneer purchased Lowe stock.

b. Give all eliminating entries needed to prepare a full set of consolidated financial statements for 20X2.

**E5-14   Consolidation Following Three Years of Ownership**

Knox Corporation purchased 60 percent of Conway Company ownership on January 1, 20X7, for $277,500. Conway reported the following net income and dividend payments:

| Year | Net Income | Dividends Paid |
|------|-----------|----------------|
| 20X7 | $45,000 | $25,000 |
| 20X8 | 55,000 | 35,000 |
| 20X9 | 30,000 | 10,000 |

On January 1, 20X7, Conway had $250,000 of $5 par value common stock outstanding and retained earnings of $150,000, and the fair value of the noncontrolling interest was $185,000. Conway held land with a book value of $22,500 and a market value of $30,000 and equipment with a book value of $320,000 and a market value of $360,000 at the date of combination. The remainder of the differential at acquisition was attributable to an increase in the value of patents, which had a remaining useful life of 10 years. All depreciable assets held by Conway at the date of acquisition had a remaining economic life of eight years.

### Required

a. Compute the increase in the fair value of patents held by Conway.

b. Prepare the eliminating entries needed at January 1, 20X7, to prepare a consolidated balance sheet.

c. Compute the balance reported by Knox as its investment in Conway at January 1, 20X9.

d. Prepare the journal entries recorded by Knox with regard to its investment in Conway during 20X9.

e. Prepare the eliminating entries needed at December 31, 20X9, to prepare a three-part consolidation workpaper.

**E5-15** **Consolidation Workpaper for Majority-Owned Subsidiary**

Proud Corporation acquired 80 percent of Stergis Company's voting stock on January 1, 20X3, at underlying book value. The fair value of the noncontrolling interest was equal to 20 percent of the book value of Stergis at that date. Proud uses the equity method in accounting for its ownership of Stergis during 20X3. On December 31, 20X3, the trial balances of the two companies are as follows:

| Item | Proud Corporation | | Stergis Company | |
|------|-------|--------|-------|--------|
| | Debit | Credit | Debit | Credit |
| Current Assets | $173,000 | | $105,000 | |
| Depreciable Assets | 500,000 | | 300,000 | |
| Investment in Stergis Company Stock | 136,000 | | | |
| Depreciation Expense | 25,000 | | 15,000 | |
| Other Expenses | 105,000 | | 75,000 | |
| Dividends Declared | 40,000 | | 10,000 | |
| Accumulated Depreciation | | $175,000 | | $ 75,000 |
| Current Liabilities | | 50,000 | | 40,000 |
| Long-Term Debt | | 100,000 | | 120,000 |
| Common Stock | | 200,000 | | 100,000 |
| Retained Earnings | | 230,000 | | 50,000 |
| Sales | | 200,000 | | 120,000 |
| Income from Subsidiary | | 24,000 | | |
| | $979,000 | $979,000 | $505,000 | $505,000 |

### Required

a. Give all eliminating entries required as of December 31, 20X3, to prepare consolidated financial statements.

b. Prepare a three-part consolidation workpaper.

c. Prepare a consolidated balance sheet, income statement, and retained earnings statement for 20X3.

**E5-16  Consolidation Workpaper for Majority-Owned Subsidiary for Second Year**

Proud Corporation acquired 80 percent of Stergis Company's voting stock on January 1, 20X3, at underlying book value. The fair value of the noncontrolling interest was equal to 20 percent of the book value of Stergis at that date. Proud uses the equity method in accounting for its ownership of Stergis. On December 31, 20X4, the trial balances of the two companies are as follows:

| Item | Proud Corporation Debit | Proud Corporation Credit | Stergis Company Debit | Stergis Company Credit |
|---|---|---|---|---|
| Current Assets | $ 235,000 | | $150,000 | |
| Depreciable Assets (net) | 500,000 | | 300,000 | |
| Investment in Stergis Company Stock | 152,000 | | | |
| Depreciation Expense | 25,000 | | 15,000 | |
| Other Expenses | 150,000 | | 90,000 | |
| Dividends Declared | 50,000 | | 15,000 | |
| Accumulated Depreciation | | $ 200,000 | | $ 90,000 |
| Current Liabilities | | 70,000 | | 50,000 |
| Long-Term Debt | | 100,000 | | 120,000 |
| Common Stock | | 200,000 | | 100,000 |
| Retained Earnings | | 284,000 | | 70,000 |
| Sales | | 230,000 | | 140,000 |
| Income from Subsidiary | | 28,000 | | |
| | $1,112,000 | $1,112,000 | $570,000 | $570,000 |

**Required**

a. Give all eliminating entries required on December 31, 20X4, to prepare consolidated financial statements.

b. Prepare a three-part consolidation workpaper as of December 31, 20X4.

**E5-17  Preparation of Stockholders' Equity Section with Other Comprehensive Income**

Broadmore Corporation acquired 75 percent of Stem Corporation's common stock on January 1, 20X8, for $435,000. At that date, Stem reported common stock outstanding of $300,000 and retained earnings of $200,000, and the fair value of the noncontrolling interest was $145,000. The book values and fair values of Stem's assets and liabilities were equal, except for other intangible assets which had a fair value $80,000 greater than book value and a 10-year remaining life. Broadmore and Stem reported the following data for 20X8 and 20X9:

| | Stem Corporation | | | Broadmore Corporation | |
|---|---|---|---|---|---|
| Year | Net Income | Comprehensive Income | Dividends Paid | Operating Income | Dividends Paid |
| 20X8 | $40,000 | $50,000 | $15,000 | $120,000 | $70,000 |
| 20X9 | 60,000 | 65,000 | 30,000 | 140,000 | 70,000 |

**Required**

a. Compute consolidated comprehensive income for 20X8 and 20X9.

b. Compute comprehensive income attributable to the controlling interest for 20X8 and 20X9.

c. Assuming that Broadmore reported capital stock outstanding of $320,000 and retained earnings of $430,000 at January 1, 20X8, prepare the stockholders' equity section of the consolidated balance sheet at December 31, 20X8 and 20X9.

**E5-18  Eliminating Entries for Subsidiary with Other Comprehensive Income**

Palmer Corporation acquired 70 percent of Krown Corporation's ownership on January 1, 20X8, for $140,000. At that date, Krown reported capital stock outstanding of $120,000 and retained earnings of $80,000, and the fair value of the noncontrolling interest was equal to 30 percent of the book value of Krown. During 20X8, Krown reported net income of $30,000 and comprehensive income of $36,000 and paid dividends of $25,000.

### Required

a. Present all equity-method entries that Palmer would have recorded in accounting for its investment in Krown during 20X8.

b. Present all eliminating entries needed at December 31, 20X8, to prepare a complete set of consolidated financial statements for Palmer Corporation and its subsidiary.

### E5-19 Majority-Owned Subsidiary with Differential—Prior Procedures

Using the data presented in E5-11, prepare a solution assuming the business combination occurred prior to the effective date of **FASB 141R.**

### E5-20 Consolidation after One Year of Ownership—Prior Procedures

Using the data presented in E5-13, prepare a solution assuming the business combination occurred prior to the effective date of **FASB 141R.**

### E5-21 Balance Sheet Workpaper—Prior Procedures

Using the data presented in E5-5, prepare a solution assuming the business combination occurred prior to the effective date of **FASB 141R.**

### E5-22* Consolidation of Subsidiary with Negative Retained Earnings

General Corporation acquired 80 percent of Strap Company's voting common stock on January 1, 20X4, for $138,000. At that date, the fair value of the noncontrolling interest was $34,500. Strap's balance sheet at the date of acquisition contained the following balances:

|  |  |  |  |
|---|---:|---|---:|
| **STRAP COMPANY** | | | |
| **Balance Sheet** | | | |
| **January 1, 20X4** | | | |
| Cash | $ 20,000 | Accounts Payable | $ 35,000 |
| Accounts Receivable | 35,000 | Notes Payable | 180,000 |
| Land | 90,000 | Common Stock | 100,000 |
| Building and Equipment | 300,000 | Additional Paid-In Capital | 75,000 |
| Less: Accumulated Depreciation | (85,000) | Retained Earnings | (30,000) |
| Total Assets | $360,000 | Total Liabilities and Stockholders' Equity | $360,000 |

At the date of acquisition, the reported book values of Strap's assets and liabilities approximated fair value.

### Required

Give the eliminating entry or entries needed to prepare a consolidated balance sheet immediately following the business combination.

### E5-23* Complex Assignment of Differential

On December 31, 20X4, Worth Corporation acquired 90 percent of Brinker Inc.'s common stock for $864,000. At that date, the fair value of the noncontrolling interest was $96,000. Of the $240,000 differential, $5,000 related to the increased value of Brinker's inventory, $75,000 related to the increased value of its land, $60,000 related to the increased value of its equipment, and $50,000 was associated with a change in the value of its notes payable due to increasing interest rates. Brinker's equipment had a remaining life of 15 years from the date of combination. Brinker sold all inventory it held at the end of 20X4 during 20X5; the land to which the differential related also was sold during the year for a large gain. The amortization of the differential relating to Brinker's notes payable was $7,500 for 20X5.

At the date of combination, Brinker reported retained earnings of $120,000, common stock outstanding of $500,000, and premium on common stock of $100,000. For the year 20X5, it reported net income of $150,000, but paid no dividends. Worth accounts for its investment in Brinker using the equity method.

### Required

a. Present all entries that Worth would have recorded during 20X5 with respect to its investment in Brinker.

b. Present all elimination entries that would have been included in the workpaper to prepare a full set of consolidated financial statements for the year 20X5.

**E5-24A** **Basic Cost-Method Workpaper**

Blake Corporation purchased 100 percent of Shaw Corporation's voting shares on January 1, 20X3, at underlying book value. Blake uses the cost method in accounting for its investment in Shaw. Shaw's retained earnings, as shown in the 20X3 trial balance, was $50,000 on January 1, 20X3. On December 31, 20X3, the trial balance data for the two companies are as follows:

| Item | Blake Corporation Debit | Blake Corporation Credit | Shaw Corporation Debit | Shaw Corporation Credit |
|---|---|---|---|---|
| Current Assets | $145,000 | | $105,000 | |
| Depreciable Assets (net) | 325,000 | | 225,000 | |
| Investment in Shaw Corporation Stock | 150,000 | | | |
| Depreciation Expense | 25,000 | | 15,000 | |
| Other Expenses | 105,000 | | 75,000 | |
| Dividends Declared | 40,000 | | 10,000 | |
| Current Liabilities | | $ 50,000 | | $ 40,000 |
| Long-Term Debt | | 100,000 | | 120,000 |
| Common Stock | | 200,000 | | 100,000 |
| Retained Earnings | | 230,000 | | 50,000 |
| Sales | | 200,000 | | 120,000 |
| Dividend Income | | 10,000 | | |
| | $790,000 | $790,000 | $430,000 | $430,000 |

### Required

a. Give all eliminating entries needed to prepare a three-part consolidation workpaper as of December 31, 20X3.

b. Prepare the workpaper in good form.

**E5-25A** **Cost-Method Workpaper in Subsequent Period**

The trial balances for Blake Corporation and Shaw Corporation as of December 31, 20X4, follow:

| Item | Blake Corporation Debit | Blake Corporation Credit | Shaw Corporation Debit | Shaw Corporation Credit |
|---|---|---|---|---|
| Current Assets | $170,000 | | $110,000 | |
| Depreciable Assets (net) | 300,000 | | 210,000 | |
| Investment in Shaw Corporation Stock | 150,000 | | | |
| Depreciation Expense | 25,000 | | 15,000 | |
| Other Expenses | 250,000 | | 160,000 | |
| Dividends Declared | 20,000 | | 15,000 | |
| Current Liabilities | | $ 30,000 | | $ 20,000 |
| Long-Term Debt | | 100,000 | | 120,000 |
| Common Stock | | 200,000 | | 100,000 |
| Retained Earnings | | 270,000 | | 70,000 |
| Sales | | 300,000 | | 200,000 |
| Dividend Income | | 15,000 | | |
| | $915,000 | $915,000 | $510,000 | $510,000 |

Blake acquired 100 percent ownership of Shaw on January 1, 20X3, at a cost of $150,000, which was equal to the book value of Shaw's net assets at that date. Shaw reported $50,000 of retained earnings at acquisition. Blake uses the cost method in accounting for its investment in Shaw.

### Required

a. Give all eliminating entries required to prepare a full set of consolidated statements for 20X4.

b. Prepare a three-part consolidation workpaper in good form as of December 31, 20X4.

### E5-26A Cost-Method Consolidation for Majority-Owned Subsidiary

Lintner Corporation purchased 80 percent of Knight Company's voting stock on January 1, 20X6, at underlying book value. At that date, the fair value of the noncontrolling interest was equal to 20 percent of the book value of Knight. Lintner uses the cost method in accounting for its investment in Knight. Knight reported $50,000 of retained earnings at the time of acquisition. Trial balance data for the two companies on December 31, 20X7, are as follows:

| Item | Lintner Corporation Debit | Lintner Corporation Credit | Knight Company Debit | Knight Company Credit |
|---|---|---|---|---|
| Current Assets | $ 183,000 | | $ 80,000 | |
| Depreciable Assets | 500,000 | | 300,000 | |
| Investment in Knight Company Stock | 120,000 | | | |
| Depreciation Expense | 25,000 | | 15,000 | |
| Other Expenses | 251,000 | | 155,000 | |
| Dividends Declared | 25,000 | | 20,000 | |
| Accumulated Depreciation | | $ 200,000 | | $ 90,000 |
| Accounts Payable | | 120,000 | | 110,000 |
| Common Stock | | 200,000 | | 100,000 |
| Retained Earnings | | 268,000 | | 70,000 |
| Sales | | 300,000 | | 200,000 |
| Dividend Income | | 16,000 | | |
| | $1,104,000 | $1,104,000 | $570,000 | $570,000 |

### Required

a. Prepare eliminating entries as of December 31, 20X7, for a full set of consolidated statements.

b. Prepare a three-part consolidation workpaper as of December 31, 20X7.

c. Prepare a consolidated income statement, balance sheet, and retained earnings statement for 20X7.

## Problems

### P5-27 Majority-Owned Subsidiary Acquired at Book Value

Cameron Corporation acquired 70 percent of Darla Corporation's common stock on December 31, 20X4, for $87,500. Data from the balance sheets of the two companies included the following amounts as of the date of acquisition:

| Item | Cameron Corporation | Darla Corporation |
|---|---|---|
| Cash | $ 65,000 | $ 21,000 |
| Accounts Receivable | 90,000 | 44,000 |
| Inventory | 130,000 | 75,000 |
| Land | 60,000 | 30,000 |
| Buildings and Equipment | 410,000 | 250,000 |
| Less: Accumulated Depreciation | (150,000) | (80,000) |
| Investment in Darla Corporation Stock | 87,500 | |
| Total Assets | $692,500 | $340,000 |

(continued)

| | | |
|---|---:|---:|
| Accounts Payable | $152,500 | $ 35,000 |
| Mortgage Payable | 250,000 | 180,000 |
| Common Stock | 80,000 | 40,000 |
| Retained Earnings | 210,000 | 85,000 |
| Total Liabilities and Stockholders' Equity | $692,500 | $340,000 |

At the date of the business combination, the book values of Darla Corporation's assets and liabilities approximated fair value, and the fair value of the noncontrolling interest was equal to 30 percent of the book value of Darla Corporation. At December 31, 20X4, Cameron reported accounts payable of $12,500 to Darla, which reported an equal amount in its accounts receivable.

### Required

a. Give the eliminating entry or entries needed to prepare a consolidated balance sheet immediately following the business combination.

b. Prepare a consolidated balance sheet workpaper.

c. Prepare a consolidated balance sheet in good form.

**P5-28**  **Majority-Owned Subsidiary Acquired at Greater than Book Value**

Porter corporation acquired 70 percent of Darla Corporation's common stock on December 31, 20X4, for $102,200. At that date, the fair value of the noncontrolling interest was $43,800. Data from the balance sheets of the two companies included the following amounts as of the date of acquisition:

| Item | Porter Corporation | Darla Corporation |
|---|---:|---:|
| Cash | $ 50,300 | $ 21,000 |
| Accounts Receivable | 90,000 | 44,000 |
| Inventory | 130,000 | 75,000 |
| Land | 60,000 | 30,000 |
| Buildings and Equipment | 410,000 | 250,000 |
| Less: Accumulated Depreciation | (150,000) | (80,000) |
| Investment in Darla Corporation Stock | 102,200 | |
| Total Assets | $692,500 | $340,000 |
| Accounts Payable | $152,500 | $ 35,000 |
| Mortgage Payable | 250,000 | 180,000 |
| Common Stock | 80,000 | 40,000 |
| Retained Earnings | 210,000 | 85,000 |
| Total Liabilities and Stockholders' Equity | $692,500 | $340,000 |

At the date of the business combination, the book values of Darla's assets and liabilities approximated fair value except for inventory, which had a fair value of $81,000, and buildings and equipment, which had a fair value of $185,000. At December 31, 20X4, Porter reported accounts payable of $12,500 to Darla, which reported an equal amount in its accounts receivable.

### Required

a. Give the eliminating entry or entries needed to prepare a consolidated balance sheet immediately following the business combination.

b. Prepare a consolidated balance sheet workpaper.

c. Prepare a consolidated balance sheet in good form.

**P5-29**  **Balance Sheet Consolidation of Majority-Owned Subsidiary**

On January 2, 20X8, Total Corporation acquired 75 percent of Ticken Tie Company's outstanding common stock. In exchange for Ticken Tie's stock, Total issued bonds payable with a par value of $500,000 and fair value of $510,000 directly to the selling stockholders of Ticken Tie. At that date, the fair value of the noncontrolling interest was $170,000. The two companies continued to operate as separate entities subsequent to the combination.

Immediately prior to the combination, the book values and fair values of the companies' assets and liabilities were as follows:

| | Total | | Ticken Tie | |
|---|---|---|---|---|
| | **Book Value** | **Fair Value** | **Book Value** | **Fair Value** |
| Cash | $ 12,000 | $ 12,000 | $ 9,000 | $ 9,000 |
| Receivables | 41,000 | 39,000 | 31,000 | 30,000 |
| Allowance for Bad Debts | (2,000) | | (1,000) | |
| Inventory | 86,000 | 89,000 | 68,000 | 72,000 |
| Land | 55,000 | 200,000 | 50,000 | 70,000 |
| Buildings and Equipment | 960,000 | 650,000 | 670,000 | 500,000 |
| Accumulated Depreciation | (411,000) | | (220,000) | |
| Patent | | | | 40,000 |
| Total Assets | $741,000 | $990,000 | $607,000 | $721,000 |
| Current Payables | $ 38,000 | $ 38,000 | $ 29,000 | $ 29,000 |
| Bonds Payable | 200,000 | 210,000 | 100,000 | 100,000 |
| Common Stock | 300,000 | | 200,000 | |
| Additional Paid-In Capital | 100,000 | | 130,000 | |
| Retained Earnings | 103,000 | | 148,000 | |
| Total Liabilities and Equity | $741,000 | | $607,000 | |

At the date of combination, Ticken Tie owed Total $6,000 plus accrued interest of $500 on a short-term note. Both companies have properly recorded these amounts.

### Required

a. Record the business combination on the books of Total Corporation.

b. Present in general journal form all elimination entries needed in a workpaper to prepare a consolidated balance sheet immediately following the business combination on January 2, 20X8.

c. Prepare and complete a consolidated balance sheet workpaper as of January 2, 20X8, immediately following the business combination.

d. Present a consolidated balance sheet for Total and its subsidiary as of January 2, 20X8.

**P5-30** **Incomplete Data**

Blue Corporation acquired controlling ownership of Skyler Corporation on December 31, 20X3, and a consolidated balance sheet was prepared immediately. Partial balance sheet data for the two companies and the consolidated entity at that date follow:

**BLUE CORPORATION AND SKYLER CORPORATION**
**Balance Sheet Data**
**December 31, 20X3**

| Item | Blue Corporation | Skyler Corporation | Consolidated Entity |
|---|---|---|---|
| Cash | $ 63,650 | $ 35,000 | $ 98,650 |
| Accounts Receivable | 98,000 | ? | 148,000 |
| Inventory | 105,000 | 80,000 | 195,000 |
| Buildings and Equipment | 400,000 | 340,000 | 780,000 |
| Less: Accumulated Depreciation | (215,000) | (140,000) | (355,000) |
| Investment in Skyler Corporation Stock | ? | | |
| Goodwill | | | 9,000 |
| Total Assets | $620,000 | $380,000 | $875,650 |

*(continued)*

| | | | |
|---|---|---|---|
| Accounts Payable | $115,000 | $ 46,000 | $146,000 |
| Wages Payable | ? | ? | 94,000 |
| Notes Payable | 200,000 | 110,000 | 310,000 |
| Common Stock | 120,000 | 75,000 | ? |
| Retained Earnings | 115,000 | 125,000 | ? |
| Noncontrolling Interest | | | 90,650 |
| Total Liabilities and Equities | $    ? | $380,000 | $875,650 |

During 20X3, Blue provided engineering services to Skyler and has not yet been paid for them. There were no other receivables or payables between Blue and Skyler at December 31, 20X3.

### Required

a.  What is the amount of unpaid engineering services at December 31, 20X3, on work done by Blue for Skyler?

b.  What balance in accounts receivable did Skyler report at December 31, 20X3?

c.  What amounts of wages payable did Blue and Skyler report at December 31, 20X3?

d.  What was the fair value of Skyler as a whole at the date of acquisition?

e.  What percentage of Skyler's shares were purchased by Blue?

f.  What amounts of capital stock and retained earnings must be reported in the consolidated balance sheet?

**P5-31**  **Income and Retained Earnings**

Quill Corporation acquired 70 percent of North Company's stock on January 1, 20X9, for $105,000. At that date, the fair value of the noncontrolling interest was equal to 30 percent of the book value of North Company. The companies reported the following stockholders' equity balances immediately after the acquisition:

| | Quill Corporation | North Company |
|---|---|---|
| Common Stock | $120,000 | $ 30,000 |
| Additional Paid-In Capital | 230,000 | 80,000 |
| Retained Earnings | 290,000 | 40,000 |
| Total | $640,000 | $150,000 |

Quill and North reported 20X9 operating incomes of $90,000 and $35,000 and dividend payments of $30,000 and $10,000, respectively.

### Required

a.  Compute the amount reported as net income by each company for 20X9, assuming Quill uses equity-method accounting for its investment in North.

b.  Compute consolidated net income for 20X9.

c.  Compute the reported balance in retained earnings at December 31, 20X9, for both companies.

d.  Compute consolidated retained earnings at December 31, 20X9.

e.  How would the computation of consolidated retained earnings at December 31, 20X9, change if Quill uses the cost method in accounting for its investment in North?

**P5-32**  **Consolidation Workpaper at End of First Year of Ownership**

Power Corporation acquired 75 percent of Best Company's ownership on January 1, 20X8, for $96,000. At that date, the fair value of the noncontrolling interest was $32,000. The book value of Best's net assets at acquisition was $100,000. The book values and fair values of Best's assets and liabilities were equal, except for Best's buildings and equipment, which were worth $20,000 more than book value. Buildings and equipment are depreciated on a 10-year basis.

Although goodwill is not amortized, the management of Power concluded at December 31, 20X8, that goodwill from its purchase of Best shares had been impaired and the correct carrying amount was $2,500. Goodwill and goodwill impairment were assigned proportionately to the controlling and noncontrolling shareholders. (Note that Power Company does not adjust its Income from Subsidiary for goodwill impairment under the basic equity method.)

Trial balance data for Power and Best on December 31, 20X8, are as follows:

| Item | Power Corporation Debit | Power Corporation Credit | Best Company Debit | Best Company Credit |
|---|---|---|---|---|
| Cash | $ 47,500 | | $ 21,000 | |
| Accounts Receivable | 70,000 | | 12,000 | |
| Inventory | 90,000 | | 25,000 | |
| Land | 30,000 | | 15,000 | |
| Buildings and Equipment | 350,000 | | 150,000 | |
| Investment in Best Co. Stock | 100,500 | | | |
| Cost of Goods Sold | 125,000 | | 110,000 | |
| Wage Expense | 42,000 | | 27,000 | |
| Depreciation Expense | 25,000 | | 10,000 | |
| Interest Expense | 12,000 | | 4,000 | |
| Other Expenses | 13,500 | | 5,000 | |
| Dividends Declared | 30,000 | | 16,000 | |
| Accumulated Depreciation | | $145,000 | | $ 40,000 |
| Accounts Payable | | 45,000 | | 16,000 |
| Wages Payable | | 17,000 | | 9,000 |
| Notes Payable | | 150,000 | | 50,000 |
| Common Stock | | 200,000 | | 60,000 |
| Retained Earnings | | 102,000 | | 40,000 |
| Sales | | 260,000 | | 180,000 |
| Income from Subsidiary | | 16,500 | | |
| | $935,500 | $935,500 | $395,000 | $395,000 |

### Required

a. Give all eliminating entries needed to prepare a three-part consolidation workpaper as of December 31, 20X8.

b. Prepare a three-part consolidation workpaper for 20X8 in good form.

**P5-33** **Consolidation Workpaper at End of Second Year of Ownership**

Power Corporation acquired 75 percent of Best Company's ownership on January 1, 20X8, for $96,000. At that date, the fair value of the noncontrolling interest was $32,000. The book value of Best's net assets at acquisition was $100,000. The book values and fair values of Best's assets and liabilities were equal, except for Best's buildings and equipment, which were worth $20,000 more than book value. Buildings and equipment are depreciated on a 10-year basis.

Although goodwill is not amortized, the management of Power concluded at December 31, 20X8, that goodwill from its purchase of Best shares had been impaired and the correct carrying amount was $2,500. Goodwill and goodwill impairment were assigned proportionately to the controlling and noncontrolling shareholders. (Note that Power Company does not adjust its Income from Subsidiary for goodwill impairment under the basic equity method.) No additional impairment occurred in 20X9.

Trial balance data for Power and Best on December 31, 20X9, are as follows:

| Item | Power Corporation Debit | Power Corporation Credit | Best Company Debit | Best Company Credit |
|---|---|---|---|---|
| Cash | $ 68,500 | | $ 32,000 | |
| Accounts Receivable | 85,000 | | 14,000 | |
| Inventory | 97,000 | | 24,000 | |
| Land | 50,000 | | 25,000 | |
| Buildings and Equipment | 350,000 | | 150,000 | |
| Investment in Best Co. Stock | 111,000 | | | |

*(continued)*

| | | | | |
|---|---|---|---|---|
| Cost of Goods Sold | 145,000 | | 114,000 | |
| Wage Expense | 35,000 | | 20,000 | |
| Depreciation Expense | 25,000 | | 10,000 | |
| Interest Expense | 12,000 | | 4,000 | |
| Other Expenses | 23,000 | | 16,000 | |
| Dividends Declared | 30,000 | | 20,000 | |
| Accumulated Depreciation | | $ 170,000 | | $ 50,000 |
| Accounts Payable | | 51,000 | | 15,000 |
| Wages Payable | | 14,000 | | 6,000 |
| Notes Payable | | 150,000 | | 50,000 |
| Common Stock | | 200,000 | | 60,000 |
| Retained Earnings | | 131,000 | | 48,000 |
| Sales | | 290,000 | | 200,000 |
| Income from Subsidiary | | 25,500 | | |
| | $1,031,500 | $1,031,500 | $429,000 | $429,000 |

### Required

*a.* Give all eliminating entries needed to prepare a three-part consolidation workpaper as of December 31, 20X9.

*b.* Prepare a three-part consolidation workpaper for 20X9 in good form.

*c.* Prepare a consolidated balance sheet, income statement, and retained earnings statement for 20X9.

**P5-34  Comprehensive Problem: Majority-Owned Subsidiary**

Master Corporation acquired 80 percent ownership of Stanley Wood Products Company on January 1, 20X1, for $160,000. On that date, the fair value of the noncontrolling interest was $40,000, and Stanley reported retained earnings of $50,000 and had $100,000 of common stock outstanding. Master has used the equity method in accounting for its investment in Stanley.

Trial balance data for the two companies on December 31, 20X5, are as follows:

| Item | Master Corporation Debit | Credit | Stanley Wood Products Company Debit | Credit |
|---|---|---|---|---|
| Cash and Receivables | $ 81,000 | | $ 65,000 | |
| Inventory | 260,000 | | 90,000 | |
| Land | 80,000 | | 80,000 | |
| Buildings and Equipment | 500,000 | | 150,000 | |
| Investment in Stanley Wood Products Stock | 188,000 | | | |
| Cost of Goods Sold | 120,000 | | 50,000 | |
| Depreciation Expense | 25,000 | | 15,000 | |
| Inventory Losses | 15,000 | | 5,000 | |
| Dividends Declared | 30,000 | | 10,000 | |
| Accumulated Depreciation | | $ 205,000 | | $105,000 |
| Accounts Payable | | 60,000 | | 20,000 |
| Notes Payable | | 200,000 | | 50,000 |
| Common Stock | | 300,000 | | 100,000 |
| Retained Earnings | | 314,000 | | 90,000 |
| Sales | | 200,000 | | 100,000 |
| Income from Subsidiary | | 20,000 | | |
| | $1,299,000 | $1,299,000 | $465,000 | $465,000 |

### Additional Information

1. On the date of combination, the fair value of Stanley's depreciable assets was $50,000 more than book value. The differential assigned to depreciable assets should be written off over the following 10-year period.
2. There was $10,000 of intercorporate receivables and payables at the end of 20X5.

### Required

*a.* Give all journal entries that Master recorded during 20X5 related to its investment in Stanley.

*b.* Give all eliminating entries needed to prepare consolidated statements for 20X5.

*c.* Prepare a three-part workpaper as of December 31, 20X5.

**P5-35** **Comprehensive Problem: Differential Apportionment**

Mortar Corporation acquired 80 percent ownership of Granite Company on January 1, 20X7, for $173,000. At that date, the fair value of the noncontrolling interest was $43,250. The trial balances for the two companies on December 31, 20X7, included the following amounts:

| Item | Mortar Corporation Debit | Mortar Corporation Credit | Granite Company Debit | Granite Company Credit |
|---|---|---|---|---|
| Cash | $ 38,000 | | $ 25,000 | |
| Accounts Receivable | 50,000 | | 55,000 | |
| Inventory | 240,000 | | 100,000 | |
| Land | 80,000 | | 20,000 | |
| Buildings and Equipment | 500,000 | | 150,000 | |
| Investment in Granite Company Stock | 202,000 | | | |
| Cost of Goods Sold | 500,000 | | 250,000 | |
| Depreciation Expense | 25,000 | | 15,000 | |
| Other Expenses | 75,000 | | 75,000 | |
| Dividends Declared | 50,000 | | 20,000 | |
| Accumulated Depreciation | | $ 155,000 | | $ 75,000 |
| Accounts Payable | | 70,000 | | 35,000 |
| Mortgages Payable | | 200,000 | | 50,000 |
| Common Stock | | 300,000 | | 50,000 |
| Retained Earnings | | 290,000 | | 100,000 |
| Sales | | 700,000 | | 400,000 |
| Income from Subsidiary | | 45,000 | | |
| | $1,760,000 | $1,760,000 | $710,000 | $710,000 |

### Additional Information

1. On January 1, 20X7, Granite reported net assets with a book value of $150,000 and a fair value of $191,250.

2. Granite's depreciable assets had an estimated economic life of 11 years on the date of combination. The difference between fair value and book value of Granite's net assets is related entirely to buildings and equipment.

3. Mortar used the equity method in accounting for its investment in Granite.

4. Detailed analysis of receivables and payables showed that Granite owed Mortar $16,000 on December 31, 20X7.

### Required

*a.* Give all journal entries recorded by Mortar with regard to its investment in Granite during 20X7.

*b.* Give all eliminating entries needed to prepare a full set of consolidated financial statements for 20X7.

*c.* Prepare a three-part consolidation workpaper as of December 31, 20X7.

**P5-36**  **Comprehensive Problem: Differential Apportionment in Subsequent Period**

Mortar Corporation acquired 80 percent ownership of Granite Company on January 1, 20X7, for $173,000. At that date, the fair value of the noncontrolling interest was $43,250. The trial balances for the two companies on December 31, 20X8, included the following amounts:

| Item | Mortar Corporation | | Granite Company | |
|------|-------|--------|-------|--------|
|      | Debit | Credit | Debit | Credit |
| Cash | $   59,000 | | $  31,000 | |
| Accounts Receivable | 83,000 | | 71,000 | |
| Inventory | 275,000 | | 118,000 | |
| Land | 80,000 | | 30,000 | |
| Buildings and Equipment | 500,000 | | 150,000 | |
| Investment in Granite Company Stock | 215,000 | | | |
| Cost of Goods Sold | 490,000 | | 310,000 | |
| Depreciation Expense | 25,000 | | 15,000 | |
| Other Expenses | 62,000 | | 100,000 | |
| Dividends Declared | 45,000 | | 25,000 | |
| Accumulated Depreciation | | $  180,000 | | $  90,000 |
| Accounts Payable | | 86,000 | | 30,000 |
| Mortgages Payable | | 200,000 | | 70,000 |
| Common Stock | | 300,000 | | 50,000 |
| Retained Earnings | | 385,000 | | 140,000 |
| Sales | | 650,000 | | 470,000 |
| Income from Subsidiary | | 33,000 | | |
| | $1,834,000 | $1,834,000 | $850,000 | $850,000 |

### Additional Information

1. On January 1, 20X7, Granite reported net assets with a book value of $150,000 and a fair value of $191,250. The difference between fair value and book value of Granite's net assets is related entirely to Buildings and Equipment. Granite's depreciable assests had an estimated economic life of 11 years on the date of combination.

2. At December 31, 20X8, Mortar's management reviewed the amount attributed to goodwill and concluded goodwill was impaired and should be reduced to $14,000. Goodwill and goodwill impairment were assigned proportionately to the controlling and noncontrolling shareholders.

3. Mortar used the equity method in accounting for its investment in Granite.

4. Detailed analysis of receivables and payables showed that Mortar owed Granite $9,000 on December 31, 20X8.

### Required

*a.* Give all journal entries recorded by Mortar with regard to its investment in Granite during 20X8.

*b.* Give all eliminating entries needed to prepare a full set of consolidated financial statements for 20X8.

*c.* Prepare a three-part consolidation workpaper as of December 31, 20X8.

**P5-37**  **Subsidiary with Other Comprehensive Income in Year of Acquisition**

Amber Corporation acquired 60 percent ownership of Sparta Company on January 1, 20X8, at underlying book value. At that date, the fair value of the noncontrolling interest was equal to

40 percent of the book value of Sparta Company. Trial balance data at December 31, 20X8, for Amber and Sparta are as follows:

| Item | Amber Corporation Debit | Amber Corporation Credit | Sparta Company Debit | Sparta Company Credit |
|---|---|---|---|---|
| Cash | $ 27,000 | | $ 8,000 | |
| Accounts Receivable | 65,000 | | 22,000 | |
| Inventory | 40,000 | | 30,000 | |
| Buildings and Equipment | 500,000 | | 235,000 | |
| Investment in Row Company Securities | | | 40,000 | |
| Investment in Sparta Company | 108,000 | | | |
| Cost of Goods Sold | 150,000 | | 110,000 | |
| Depreciation Expense | 30,000 | | 10,000 | |
| Interest Expense | 8,000 | | 3,000 | |
| Dividends Declared | 24,000 | | 15,000 | |
| Accumulated Depreciation | | $140,000 | | $ 85,000 |
| Accounts Payable | | 63,000 | | 20,000 |
| Bonds Payable | | 100,000 | | 50,000 |
| Common Stock | | 200,000 | | 100,000 |
| Retained Earnings | | 208,000 | | 60,000 |
| Other Comprehensive Income from Subsidiary (OCI)—Unrealized Gain on Investments | | 6,000 | | |
| Unrealized Gain on Investments (OCI) | | | | 10,000 |
| Sales | | 220,000 | | 148,000 |
| Income from Subsidiary | | 15,000 | | |
| | $952,000 | $952,000 | $473,000 | $473,000 |

### Additional Information

Sparta purchased stock of Row Company on January 1, 20X8, for $30,000 and classified the investment as available-for-sale securities. The value of Row's securities increased to $40,000 at December 31, 20X8.

### Required

a. Give all eliminating entries needed to prepare a three-part consolidation workpaper as of December 31, 20X8.

b. Prepare a three-part consolidation workpaper for 20X8 in good form.

c. Prepare a consolidated balance sheet, income statement, and statement of comprehensive income for 20X8.

**P5-38** **Subsidiary with Other Comprehensive Income in Year Following Acquisition**

Amber Corporation acquired 60 percent ownership of Sparta Company on January 1, 20X8, at underlying book value. At that date, the fair value of the noncontrolling interest was equal to 40 percent of the book value of Sparta Company. Trial balance data at December 31, 20X9, for Amber and Sparta are as follows:

| Item | Amber Corporation Debit | Amber Corporation Credit | Sparta Company Debit | Sparta Company Credit |
|---|---|---|---|---|
| Cash | $ 18,000 | | $ 11,000 | |
| Accounts Receivable | 45,000 | | 21,000 | |
| Inventory | 40,000 | | 30,000 | |
| Buildings and Equipment | 585,000 | | 257,000 | |
| Investment in Row Company Securities | | | 44,000 | |
| Investment in Sparta Company | 116,400 | | | |
| Cost of Goods Sold | 170,000 | | 97,000 | |
| Depreciation Expense | 30,000 | | 10,000 | |
| Interest Expense | 8,000 | | 3,000 | |
| Dividends Declared | 40,000 | | 20,000 | |

*(continued)*

| | | | |
|---|---:|---:|---:|
| Accumulated Depreciation | | $ 170,000 | $ 95,000 |
| Accounts Payable | | 75,000 | 24,000 |
| Bonds Payable | | 100,000 | 50,000 |
| Common Stock | | 200,000 | 100,000 |
| Retained Earnings | | 231,000 | 70,000 |
| Accumulated Other Comprehensive Income | | 6,000 | 10,000 |
| Other Comprehensive Income from Subsidiary (OCI)—Unrealized Gain on Investments | | 2,400 | |
| Unrealized Gain on Investments (OCI) | | | 4,000 |
| Sales | | 250,000 | 140,000 |
| Income from Subsidiary | | 18,000 | |
| | | $1,052,400  $1,052,400 | $493,000  $493,000 |

### Additional Information

Sparta purchased stock of Row Company on January 1, 20X8, for $30,000 and classified the investment as available-for-sale securities. The value of Row's securities increased to $40,000 and $44,000, respectively, at December 31, 20X8, and 20X9.

### Required

*a.* Give all eliminating entries needed to prepare a three-part consolidation workpaper as of December 31, 20X9.

*b.* Prepare a three-part consolidation workpaper for 20X9 in good form.

**P5-39  Income and Retained Earnings—Prior Procedures**

Using the data presented in P5-31, prepare a solution using the accounting procedures in effect prior to the effective date of **FASB 141R.**

**P5-40  Majority-Owned Subsidiary Acquired at Greater than Book Value—Prior Procedures**

Using the data presented in P5-28, prepare a solution using the accounting procedures in effect prior to the effective date of **FASB 141R.**

**P5-41  Consolidation Workpaper at End of First Year of Ownership—Prior Procedures**

Using the data presented in P5-32, prepare a solution as if the business combination occurred prior to the effective date of **FASB 141R.**

*Note:* Goodwill at acquisition will be reported as the excess of the amount paid by the parent in acquiring ownership over its share of the fair value of the net assets of the subsidiary. Ignore the instruction in the problem that indicates goodwill impairment is assigned proportionately to the controlling and noncontrolling shareholders.

**P5-42  Consolidation Workpaper at End of Second Year of Ownership—Prior Procedures**

Using the data presented in P5-33, prepare a solution as if the business combination occurred prior to the effective date of **FASB 141R.**

*Note:* Goodwill at acquisition will be reported as the excess of the amount paid by the parent in acquiring ownership over its share of the fair value of the net assets of the subsidiary. Ignore the instruction in the problem that indicates goodwill impairment is assigned proportionately to the controlling and noncontrolling shareholders.

**P5-43A  Cost-Method Workpaper with Differential**

Trial balance data for Light Corporation and Star Company on December 31, 20X5, are as follows:

| | Light Corporation | | Star Company | |
|---|---:|---:|---:|---:|
| Item | Debit | Credit | Debit | Credit |
| Cash | $ 37,000 | | $ 20,000 | |
| Accounts Receivable | 50,000 | | 30,000 | |
| Inventory | 70,000 | | 60,000 | |
| Buildings and Equipment | 300,000 | | 240,000 | |
| Investment in Star Company Stock (at cost) | 220,000 | | | |
| Cost of Goods Sold | 210,000 | | 85,000 | |

*(continued)*

*(continued)*

| Item | Light Corporation Debit | Light Corporation Credit | Star Company Debit | Star Company Credit |
|---|---|---|---|---|
| Depreciation Expense | 25,000 | | 20,000 | |
| Other Expenses | 23,000 | | 25,000 | |
| Dividends Declared | 20,000 | | 10,000 | |
| Accumulated Depreciation | | $105,000 | | $ 65,000 |
| Accounts Payable | | 40,000 | | 20,000 |
| Taxes Payable | | 70,000 | | 55,000 |
| Common Stock | | 200,000 | | 150,000 |
| Retained Earnings, January 1 | | 230,000 | | 50,000 |
| Sales | | 300,000 | | 150,000 |
| Dividend Income | | 10,000 | | |
| | $955,000 | $955,000 | $490,000 | $490,000 |

Light acquired all of Star's shares on January 1, 20X5, for $220,000. The full differential is assigned to goodwill. At December 31, 20X5, the management of Light reviewed the amount attributed to goodwill and concluded goodwill had been impaired and should be reported at $8,000. Light uses the cost method in accounting for its investment in Star.

### Required
Present all eliminating entries needed to prepare consolidated financial statements for the year 20X5, and prepare a three-part consolidation workpaper in good form as of December 31, 20X5.

**P5-44A** **Cost-Method Consolidation in Subsequent Period**

Trial balance data for Light Corporation and Star Company on December 31, 20X6, are as follows:

| Item | Light Corporation Debit | Light Corporation Credit | Star Company Debit | Star Company Credit |
|---|---|---|---|---|
| Cash | $ 46,000 | | $ 30,000 | |
| Accounts Receivable | 55,000 | | 40,000 | |
| Inventory | 75,000 | | 65,000 | |
| Buildings and Equipment | 300,000 | | 240,000 | |
| Investment in Star Company (at cost) | 220,000 | | | |
| Cost of Goods Sold | 270,000 | | 135,000 | |
| Depreciation Expense | 25,000 | | 20,000 | |
| Other Expenses | 21,000 | | 10,000 | |
| Dividends Declared | 20,000 | | 20,000 | |
| Accumulated Depreciation | | $ 130,000 | | $ 85,000 |
| Accounts Payable | | 20,000 | | 30,000 |
| Taxes Payable | | 50,000 | | 35,000 |
| Common Stock | | 200,000 | | 150,000 |
| Retained Earnings, January 1 | | 262,000 | | 60,000 |
| Sales | | 350,000 | | 200,000 |
| Dividend Income | | 20,000 | | |
| | $1,032,000 | $1,032,000 | $560,000 | $560,000 |

Light acquired all of Star's shares on January 1, 20X5, for $220,000, which was equal to the fair value of Star as a whole. Star's retained earnings balance at the date of acquisition was $50,000.

The full purchase differential is assigned to goodwill. At December 31, 20X5, the management of Light reviewed the amount attributed to goodwill and concluded goodwill had been impaired and should be reported at $8,000. No further impairment occurred during 20X6. Light uses the cost method in accounting for its investment in Star.

### Required

Present all eliminating entries needed to prepare consolidated financial statements for the year 20X6, and prepare a three-part consolidation workpaper in good form as of December 31, 20X6.

**P5-45A**  ## Cost-Method Consolidation of Majority-Owned Subsidiary

Rapid Delivery Corporation was created on January 1, 20X2, and quickly became successful. On January 1, 20X6, the owner sold 80 percent of the stock to Samuelson Company at underlying book value. At the date of acquisition, the fair value of the noncontrolling interest was equal to 20 percent of the book value of Rapid Delivery. Samuelson has continued to operate the subsidiary as a separate legal entity and uses the cost method in recording investment income.

Trial balance data for the two companies on December 31, 20X6, consist of the following:

| Item | Samuelson Company Debit | Samuelson Company Credit | Rapid Delivery Corporation Debit | Rapid Delivery Corporation Credit |
|---|---|---|---|---|
| Cash and Receivables | $ 141,000 | | $ 80,000 | |
| Inventory | 240,000 | | 100,000 | |
| Land | 80,000 | | 20,000 | |
| Buildings and Equipment | 500,000 | | 150,000 | |
| Investment in Rapid Delivery Stock | 120,000 | | | |
| Cost of Goods Sold | 500,000 | | 250,000 | |
| Depreciation Expense | 25,000 | | 15,000 | |
| Wage Expense | 45,000 | | 35,000 | |
| Other Expenses | 30,000 | | 40,000 | |
| Dividends Declared | 50,000 | | 20,000 | |
| Accumulated Depreciation | | $ 155,000 | | $ 75,000 |
| Accounts Payable | | 70,000 | | 35,000 |
| Notes Payable | | 200,000 | | 50,000 |
| Common Stock | | 300,000 | | 50,000 |
| Retained Earnings | | 290,000 | | 100,000 |
| Sales | | 700,000 | | 400,000 |
| Dividend Income | | 16,000 | | |
| | $1,731,000 | $1,731,000 | $710,000 | $710,000 |

Rapid Delivery's retained earnings on the date of acquisition was $100,000.

### Required

Samuelson's controller has asked you to prepare a three-part consolidation workpaper in good form and to prepare a consolidated income statement, balance sheet, and statement of changes in retained earnings for the year 20X6.

**P5-46A**  ## Comprehensive Cost-Method Consolidation Problem

Master Corporation acquired 80 percent ownership of Stanley Wood Products Company on January 1, 20X1, for $160,000. On that date, the fair value of the noncontrolling interest was $40,000, and Stanley reported retained earnings of $50,000 and had $100,000 of common stock outstanding. Master has used the cost method in recording its investment in Stanley.

Trial balance data for the two companies on December 31, 20X5, are as follows:

| Item | Master Corporation | | Stanley Wood Products Company | |
|---|---|---|---|---|
| | Debit | Credit | Debit | Credit |
| Cash and Receivables | $ 81,000 | | $ 65,000 | |
| Inventory | 260,000 | | 90,000 | |
| Land | 80,000 | | 80,000 | |
| Buildings and Equipment | 500,000 | | 150,000 | |
| Investment in Stanley Wood Products Stock | 160,000 | | | |
| Cost of Goods Sold | 120,000 | | 50,000 | |
| Depreciation Expense | 25,000 | | 15,000 | |
| Inventory Losses | 15,000 | | 5,000 | |
| Dividends Declared | 30,000 | | 10,000 | |
| Accumulated Depreciation | | $ 205,000 | | $105,000 |
| Accounts Payable | | 60,000 | | 20,000 |
| Notes Payable | | 200,000 | | 50,000 |
| Common Stock | | 300,000 | | 100,000 |
| Retained Earnings | | 298,000 | | 90,000 |
| Sales | | 200,000 | | 100,000 |
| Dividend Income | | 8,000 | | |
| | $1,271,000 | $1,271,000 | $465,000 | $465,000 |

## Additional Information

1. On the date of combination, the fair value of Stanley's depreciable assets was $50,000 more than book value. The differential assigned to depreciable assets should be written off over the following 10-year period.
2. There was $10,000 of intercorporate receivables and payables at the end of 20X5.

## Required

a. Give all journal entries that Master recorded during 20X5 related to its investment in Stanley.

b. Give all eliminating entries needed to prepare consolidated statements for 20X5.

c. Prepare a three-part consolidation workpaper as of December 31, 20X5.

# Chapter **Six**

# Intercompany Transfers of Services and Noncurrent Assets

A parent company and its subsidiaries often engage in a variety of transactions among themselves. For example, manufacturing companies often have subsidiaries that develop raw materials or produce components to be included in the products of affiliated companies. Some companies sell consulting or other services to affiliated companies. A number of major retailers, such as J. C. Penney Company, transfer receivables to their credit subsidiaries in return for operating cash. United States Steel Corporation and its subsidiaries engage in numerous transactions with one another, including sales of raw materials, fabricated products, and transportation services. Such transactions often are critical to the operations of the overall consolidated entity. These transactions between related companies are referred to as *intercompany* or *intercorporate transfers*.

The central idea of consolidated financial statements is that they report on the activities of the consolidating affiliates as if the separate affiliates actually constitute a single company. Because single companies are not permitted to reflect internal transactions in their financial statements, consolidated entities also must exclude from their financial statements the effects of transactions that are totally within the consolidated entity.

Building on the basic consolidation procedures presented in earlier chapters, this chapter and the next two deal with the effects of intercompany transfers. This chapter deals with intercompany services and sales of fixed assets, and Chapters 7 and 8 discuss intercompany sales of inventory and intercompany debt transfers.

## OVERVIEW OF THE CONSOLIDATED ENTITY

The consolidated entity is an aggregation of a number of different companies. The financial statements prepared by the individual affiliates are consolidated into a single set of financial statements representing the financial position and operating results of the entire economic entity as if it were a single company.

Figure 6–1 illustrates a consolidated entity with each of the affiliated companies engaging in both intercompany transfers and transactions with external parties. From a consolidated viewpoint, only transactions with parties outside the economic entity are included in the income statement. Thus, the arrows crossing the perimeter of the consolidated entity in Figure 6–1 represent transactions that are included in the operating results of the consolidated entity for the period. Transfers between the affiliated companies, shown in Figure 6–1 as those arrows not crossing the boundary of the consolidated entity, are equivalent to transfers between operating divisions of a single company and are not reported in the consolidated statements.

**FIGURE 6–1**
**Transactions of Affiliated Companies**

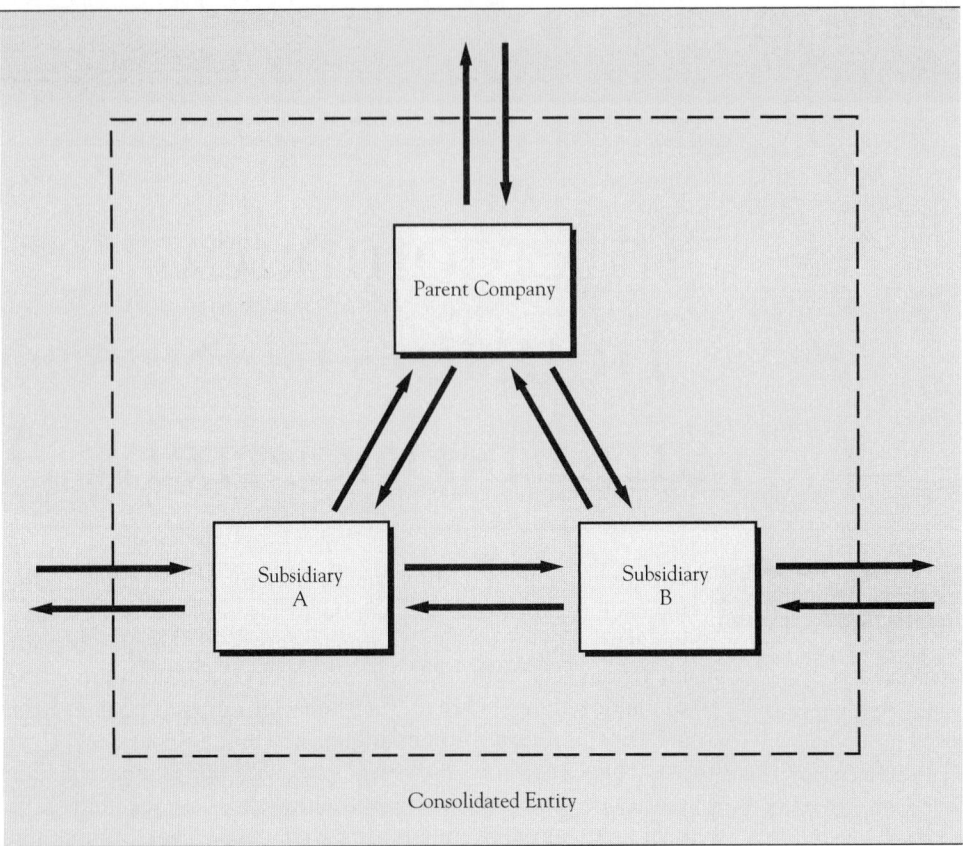

Consolidated Entity

## Elimination of Intercompany Transfers

All aspects of intercompany transfers must be eliminated in preparing consolidated financial statements so that the statements appear as if they were those of a single company. **Accounting Research Bulletin No. 51,** "Consolidated Financial Statements" (ARB 51), mentions open account balances, security holdings, sales and purchases, and interest and dividends as examples of the intercompany balances and transactions that must be eliminated.[1]

No distinction is made between wholly owned and less-than-wholly owned subsidiaries with regard to the elimination of intercompany transfers. The focus in consolidation is on the single-entity concept rather than on the percentage of ownership. Once the conditions for consolidation are met, a company becomes part of a single economic entity, and all transactions with related companies become internal transfers that must be eliminated fully, regardless of the level of ownership held.

## Elimination of Unrealized Profits and Losses

Companies usually record transactions with affiliates on the same basis as transactions with nonaffiliates, including recognition of profits and losses. Profit or loss from selling an item to a related party normally is considered realized at the time of the sale from the selling company's perspective, but the profit is not considered realized for consolidation purposes until confirmed, usually through resale to an unrelated party. This unconfirmed profit from an intercompany transfer is referred to as *unrealized intercompany profit*.

The following illustrations provide an overview of the intercompany sale process using land as an example. Figure 6–2 shows a series of transactions involving a parent company and its subsidiary. Land first is purchased by Parent Company from an unrelated party, then sold to a subsidiary of Parent Company, and finally sold by the subsidiary to an unrelated party. The three transactions, and the amounts, are as follows:

[1]*Accounting Research Bulletin No. 51,* "Consolidated Financial Statements," August 1959, para. 6.

**FIGURE 6–2**
**Intercompany Sales**

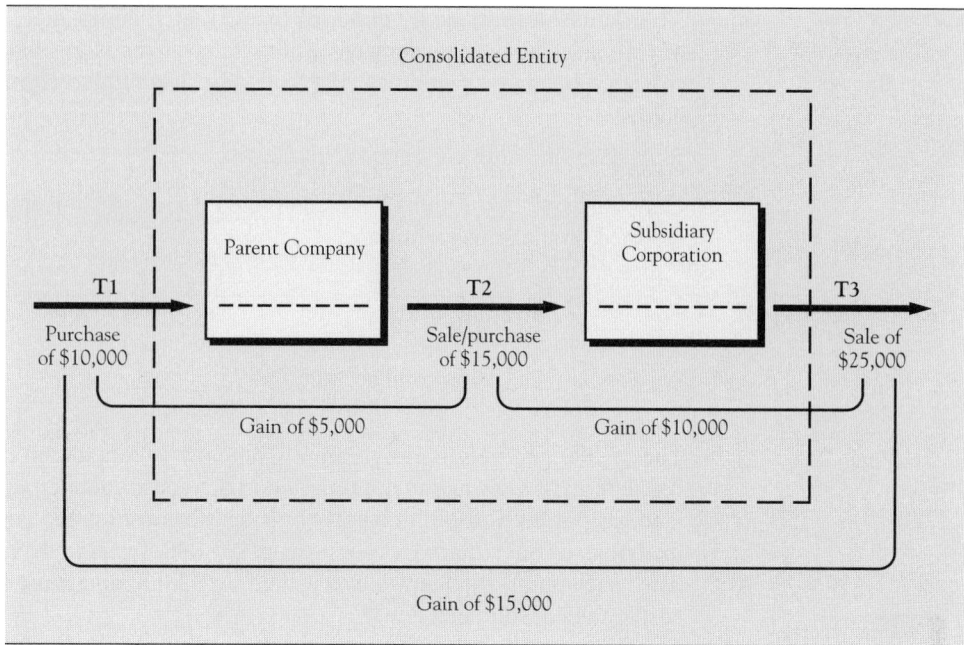

T1—Purchase by Parent Company from outsider for $10,000.

T2—Sale from Parent Company to Subsidiary Corporation for $15,000.

T3—Sale from Subsidiary Corporation to outsider for $25,000.

As shown in the following cases, the amount of gain reported by each of the individual companies and by the consolidated entity in a period depends on which of the transactions occur during that period.

### Case A

All three transactions are completed in the same accounting period. The gain amounts reported on the transactions are:

| | |
|---|---|
| Parent Company | $ 5,000 ($15,000 − $10,000) |
| Subsidiary Corporation | 10,000 ($25,000 − $15,000) |
| Consolidated Entity | 15,000 ($25,000 − $10,000) |

The gain reported by each of the entities is considered to be realized because the land is resold to an unrelated party during the period. The total gain reported by the consolidated entity is the difference between the $10,000 price paid by the consolidated entity and the $25,000 price at which the consolidated entity sold the land to an outsider. This $15,000 gain is reported in the consolidated income statement. From a consolidated viewpoint, the sale from Parent Company to Subsidiary Corporation, transaction T2, is an internal transaction and is not reported in the consolidated financial statements.

### Case B

Only transaction T1 is completed during the current period. The gain amounts reported on the transactions are:

| | |
|---|---|
| Parent Company | $-0- |
| Subsidiary Corporation | -0- |
| Consolidated Entity | -0- |

No sale has been made by either of the affiliated companies, and no gains are reported or realized. The land is reported both in Parent Company's balance sheet and in the consolidated balance sheet at its cost to Parent, which also is the cost to the consolidated entity.

### Case C

Only transactions T1 and T2 are completed during the current period. The gain amounts reported on the transactions are:

| | |
|---|---|
| Parent Company | $5,000 ($15,000 − $10,000) |
| Subsidiary Corporation | -0- |
| Consolidated Entity | -0- |

The $5,000 gain reported by Parent Company is considered unrealized from a consolidated point of view and is not reported in the consolidated income statement because the land has not been resold to a party outside the consolidated entity. The land is carried on the books of Subsidiary Corporation at $15,000, the cost to Subsidiary. From a consolidated viewpoint, the land is overvalued by $5,000 and must be reported at its $10,000 cost to the consolidated entity.

### Case D

Only transaction T3 is completed during the current period, T1 and T2 having occurred in a prior period. The gain amounts reported on the transactions in the current period are:

| | |
|---|---|
| Parent Company | $    -0- |
| Subsidiary Corporation | 10,000 ($25,000 − $15,000) |
| Consolidated Entity | 15,000 ($25,000 − $10,000) |

Subsidiary recognizes a gain equal to the difference between its selling price of $25,000 and cost of $15,000 while the consolidated entity reports a gain equal to the difference between its selling price of $25,000 and cost of $10,000.

From a consolidated viewpoint, the sale of an asset wholly within the consolidated entity involves only a change in the location of the asset and does not represent the culmination of the earning process. To culminate the earning process with respect to the consolidated entity, a sale must be made to a party external to the consolidated entity. The key to deciding when to report a transaction in the consolidated financial statements is to visualize the consolidated entity and determine whether a particular transaction occurs totally within the consolidated entity, in which case its effects must be excluded from the consolidated statements, or involves outsiders and thus constitutes a transaction of the consolidated entity.

## INTERCOMPANY TRANSFERS OF SERVICES

Related companies frequently purchase services from one another. These services may be of many different types; intercompany purchases of consulting, engineering, marketing, and maintenance services are common.

When one company purchases services from a related company, the purchaser typically records an expense and the seller records a revenue. When consolidated financial statements are prepared, both the expense and revenue must be eliminated. For example, if the parent sells consulting services to the subsidiary for $50,000, the parent would recognize $50,000 of consulting revenue on its books and the subsidiary would recognize $50,000 of consulting expense. In the consolidation workpaper, an eliminating entry would be needed to reduce both consulting revenue (debit) and consulting expense (credit) by $50,000. Because the revenue and expense are equal and both are eliminated, income is unaffected by the elimination. Even though income is not affected, the elimination is still important, however, because otherwise both revenues and expenses are overstated.

Generally, a simplistic approach is taken in eliminating intercompany transfers of services by assuming that the services benefit the current period and, therefore, any intercompany profit on the services becomes realized within the period of transfer. Accordingly, no eliminating entries relating to the current period's transfer of services are needed in future periods because the intercompany profit is considered realized in the transfer period.

Usually the assumption that the profit on intercompany sales of services is realized in the period of sale is a realistic assumption. In some cases, however, realization of intercompany profit on the services does not occur in the period the services are provided and the amounts are significant. For example, if the parent company charges a subsidiary for architectural services to design a new manufacturing facility for the subsidiary, the subsidiary would include that cost in the capitalized cost of the new facility. From a consolidated point of view, however, any profit the parent recognized on the intercompany sale of services (revenue over the cost of providing the service) would have to be eliminated from the reported cost of the new facility until the intercompany profit became realized. Realization would be viewed as occurring over the life of the facility. Thus, eliminating entries would be needed each year similar to those illustrated later in the chapter for intercompany transfers of fixed assets.

# INTERCOMPANY TRANSFERS OF LAND

When intercorporate transfers of noncurrent assets occur, adjustments often are needed in the preparation of consolidated financial statements for as long as the assets are held by the acquiring company. The simplest example of an intercorporate asset transfer is the intercorporate sale of land.

## Overview of the Profit Elimination Process

When land is transferred between related companies at book value, no special adjustments or eliminations are needed in preparing the consolidated statements. If, for example, a company purchases land for $10,000 and sells it to its subsidiary for $10,000, the asset continues to be valued at the $10,000 original cost to the consolidated entity:

| Parent | | | Subsidiary | | |
|---|---|---|---|---|---|
| Cash | 10,000 | | Land | 10,000 | |
| Land | | 10,000 | Cash | | 10,000 |

Because the seller records no gain or loss, both income and assets are stated correctly from a consolidated viewpoint.

Land transfers at more or less than book value do require special treatment in the consolidation process. The selling entity's gain or loss must be eliminated because the land is still held by the consolidated entity, and no gain or loss may be reported in the consolidated financial statements until the land is sold to a party outside the consolidated entity. Likewise, the land must be reported at its original cost in the consolidated financial statements as long as it is held within the consolidated entity, regardless of which affiliate holds the land.

As an illustration, assume that Peerless Products Corporation acquires land for $20,000 on January 1, 20X1, and sells the land to its subsidiary, Special Foods Incorporated, on July 1, 20X1, for $35,000, as follows:

Consolidated Entity

Peerless records the purchase of the land and its sale to Special Foods with the following entries:

January 1, 20X1

| | | | |
|---|---|---|---|
| (1) | Land | 20,000 | |
| | Cash | | 20,000 |
| | Record purchase of land. | | |

July 1, 20X1

| | | | |
|---|---|---|---|
| (2) | Cash | 35,000 | |
| | Land | | 20,000 |
| | Gain on Sale of Land. | | 15,000 |
| | Record sale of land to Special Foods. | | |

Special Foods records the purchase of the land from Peerless as follows:

July 1, 20X1

| | | | |
|---|---|---|---|
| (3) | Land | 35,000 | |
| | Cash | | 35,000 |
| | Record purchase of land from Peerless. | | |

The intercorporate transfer causes the seller to recognize a $15,000 gain and the carrying value of the land to increase by the same amount. Neither of these amounts may be reported in the consolidated financial statements because the $15,000 intercompany gain is unrealized from a consolidated viewpoint. The land has not been sold to a party outside the consolidated entity but only transferred within; consequently, the land must continue to be reported in consolidated financial statements at its original cost to the consolidated entity. The gain must be eliminated in the preparation of consolidated statements and the land restated from the $35,000 recorded on Special Foods' books to its original cost of $20,000. This is accomplished with the following eliminating entry in the consolidation workpaper prepared at the end of 20X1:

| | | | |
|---|---|---|---|
| E(4) | Gain on Sale of Land | 15,000 | |
| | Land | | 15,000 |
| | Eliminate unrealized gain on sale of land. | | |

## Assignment of Unrealized Profit Elimination

Unrealized intercompany gains and losses must be eliminated fully when preparing consolidated financial statements. Regardless of the parent's percentage ownership of a subsidiary, the full amount of any unrealized gains and losses must be eliminated and must be excluded from consolidated net income. Although the full amount of an unrealized gain or loss is excluded from consolidated net income, a question arises when the parent owns less than 100 percent of a subsidiary as to whether the unrealized profit elimination should reduce the controlling or noncontrolling interest, or both.

A gain or loss on an intercompany transfer is recognized by the selling affiliate and ultimately accrues to the stockholders of that affiliate. When a sale is from a parent to a subsidiary, referred to as a ***downstream sale,*** any gain or loss on the transfer accrues to the parent company's stockholders. When the sale is from a subsidiary to its parent, an ***upstream sale,*** any gain or loss accrues to the subsidiary's stockholders. If the subsidiary is wholly owned, all gain or loss ultimately accrues to the parent company as the sole stockholder. If, however, the selling subsidiary is not wholly owned, the gain or loss on the upstream sale is apportioned between the parent company and the noncontrolling shareholders.

Generally, gains and losses are not considered realized by the consolidated entity until a sale is made to an external party. Unrealized gains and losses are eliminated in preparing consolidated financial statements against the interests of those shareholders who recognized the gains and losses in the first place: the shareholders of the selling affiliate. Therefore, the direction of the sale determines which shareholder group absorbs the elimination of unrealized intercompany gains and losses. Specifically, unrealized intercompany gains and losses are eliminated in consolidation in the following ways:

| Sale | Elimination |
|---|---|
| Downstream (parent to subsidiary) | Against controlling interest |
| Upstream (subsidiary to parent): | |
|     Wholly owned subsidiary | Against controlling interest |
|     Majority-owned subsidiary | Proportionately against controlling and noncontrolling interests |

As an illustration, assume that Purity Company owns 75 percent of the common stock of Southern Corporation. Purity reports operating income from its own activities, excluding any investment income from Southern, of $100,000; Southern reports net income of $60,000. Included in the income of the selling affiliate is an unrealized gain of $10,000 on the intercompany transfer of an asset. If the sale is a downstream transfer, all unrealized profit is eliminated from the controlling interest's share of income when consolidated statements are prepared. Thus, consolidated net income is computed and allocated as follows:

| | |
|---|---|
| Purity's separate income | $100,000 |
| Less: Unrealized intercompany gain on downstream asset sale | (10,000) |
| Purity's separate realized income | $ 90,000 |
| Southern's net income | 60,000 |
| Consolidated net income | $150,000 |
| Income to noncontrolling interest ($60,000 × .25) | (15,000) |
| Income to controlling interest | $135,000 |

If, instead, the intercompany transfer is from subsidiary to parent, the unrealized profit on the upstream sale is eliminated proportionately from the interests of the controlling and noncontrolling shareholders. In this situation, consolidated net income is computed and allocated as follows:

| | | |
|---|---:|---:|
| Purity's separate income | | $100,000 |
| Southern's net income | $60,000 | |
| Less: Unrealized intercompany gain on upstream asset sale | (10,000) | |
| Southern's realized net income | | 50,000 |
| Consolidated net income | | $150,000 |
| Income to noncontrolling interest ($50,000 × .25) | | (12,500) |
| Income to controlling interest | | $137,500 |

Consolidated net income is the same whether the intercompany sale is upstream or downstream, but the allocation of the income reduction differs. Because Purity recognized all of the gain in the downstream case, the controlling interest's share of income is reduced by the full unrealized gain elimination. In the upstream case, the intercompany gain was recognized by Southern and shared proportionately by Southern's controlling and noncontrolling interests. Therefore, the elimination is made proportionately against the controlling and noncontrolling interest's share of income.

Note that unrealized intercompany gains and losses are always fully eliminated in preparing consolidated financial statements. The existence of a noncontrolling interest in a selling subsidiary affects only the allocation of the eliminated unrealized gain or loss and not the amount eliminated.

### *Income to Noncontrolling Interest*

The income assigned to the noncontrolling interest is the noncontrolling interest's proportionate share of the subsidiary's income realized in transactions with parties external to the consolidated entity. Income assigned to the noncontrolling interest in the downstream example is computed as follows:

| | |
|---|---:|
| Southern's net income | $60,000 |
| Proportionate share to noncontrolling interest | × .25 |
| Income assigned to noncontrolling interest | $15,000 |

Income assigned to the noncontrolling interest in the upstream example is computed as follows:

| | |
|---|---:|
| Southern's net income | $60,000 |
| Less: Unrealized gain on upstream asset sale | (10,000) |
| Southern's realized net income | $50,000 |
| Proportionate share to noncontrolling interest | × .25 |
| Income assigned to noncontrolling interest | $12,500 |

In the downstream example, the $10,000 of unrealized intercompany profit is recognized on the parent company's books; therefore, the noncontrolling interest is not affected by the unrealized gain on the downstream intercompany transaction. The entire $60,000 of the subsidiary's income is realized in transactions with parties external to the consolidated entity. In the upstream example, the subsidiary's income includes $10,000 of unrealized intercompany profit. The amount of the subsidiary's income realized in transactions with external parties is only $50,000 ($60,000 less $10,000 of unrealized intercompany profit).

## Downstream Sale

To illustrate more fully the treatment of unrealized intercompany profits, assume the following with respect to the Peerless and Special Foods example used previously:

1. Peerless Products Corporation purchases 80 percent of Special Foods Inc.'s stock on December 31, 20X0, at the stock's book value of $240,000. The fair value of Special Foods' noncontrolling interest on that date is $60,000, the book value of those shares.

2. On July 1, 20X1, Peerless sells land to Special Foods for $35,000. Peerless had originally purchased the land on January 1, 20X1, for $20,000. Special Foods continues to hold the land through 20X1 and subsequent years.

3. During 20X1, Peerless reports separate income of $155,000, consisting of income from regular operations of $140,000 and a $15,000 gain on the sale of land; Peerless declares dividends of $60,000. Special Foods reports net income of $50,000 and declares dividends of $30,000.

4. Peerless accounts for its investment in Special Foods using the basic equity method, under which it records its share of Special Foods' net income and dividends but does not adjust for unrealized intercompany profits.

Peerless records the sale of the land and the resulting gain of $15,000 ($35,000 − $20,000) with entry (2), given previously. Special Foods records the purchase of the land for $35,000 with entry (3).

### Basic Equity-Method Entries—20X1

During 20X1, Peerless records its share of income and dividends from Special Foods with the usual entries under the basic equity method:

| | | | |
|---|---|---|---|
| (5) | Cash | 24,000 | |
| |     Investment in Special Foods Stock | | 24,000 |
| |     Record dividends from Special Foods: | | |
| |     $30,000 × .80 | | |
| | | | |
| (6) | Investment in Special Foods Stock | 40,000 | |
| |     Income from Subsidiary | | 40,000 |
| |     Record equity-method income: | | |
| |     $50,000 × .80 | | |

On December 31, 20X1, the investment account on Peerless's books appears as follows:

| | **Investment in Special Foods Stock** | | | | | |
|---|---|---|---|---|---|---|
| | Original cost | 240,000 | | | | |
| (6) | Equity accrual | | (5) | Dividends | | |
| | ($50,000 × .80) | 40,000 | | ($30,000 × .80) | 24,000 | |
| | Balance, 12/31/X1 | 256,000 | | | | |

### Consolidation Workpaper—20X1

The consolidation workpaper used in preparing consolidated financial statements for 20X1 is shown in Figure 6–3. The normal workpaper entries are included:

| | | | |
|---|---|---|---|
| E(7) | Income from Subsidiary | 40,000 | |
| |     Dividends Declared | | 24,000 |
| |     Investment in Special Foods Stock | | 16,000 |
| |     Eliminate income from subsidiary. | | |

**FIGURE 6–3**  December 31, 20X1, Consolidation Workpaper, Period of Intercompany Sale; Downstream Sale of Land

| Item | Peerless Products | Special Foods | Eliminations Debit | Eliminations Credit | Consolidated |
|---|---|---|---|---|---|
| Sales | 400,000 | 200,000 | | | 600,000 |
| Gain on Sale of Land | 15,000 | | (10) 15,000 | | |
| Income from Subsidiary | 40,000 | | (7) 40,000 | | |
| Credits | 455,000 | 200,000 | | | 600,000 |
| Cost of Goods Sold | 170,000 | 115,000 | | | 285,000 |
| Depreciation and Amortization | 50,000 | 20,000 | | | 70,000 |
| Other Expenses | 40,000 | 15,000 | | | 55,000 |
| Debits | (260,000) | (150,000) | | | (410,000) |
| Consolidated Net Income | | | | | 190,000 |
| Income to Noncontrolling Interest | | | (8) 10,000 | | (10,000) |
| Income, carry forward | 195,000 | 50,000 | 65,000 | | 180,000 |
| Retained Earnings, January 1 | 300,000 | 100,000 | (9) 100,000 | | 300,000 |
| Income, from above | 195,000 | 50,000 | 65,000 | | 180,000 |
| | 495,000 | 150,000 | | | 480,000 |
| Dividends Declared | (60,000) | (30,000) | | (7) 24,000 | |
| | | | | (8) 6,000 | (60,000) |
| Retained Earnings, December 31, carry forward | 435,000 | 120,000 | 165,000 | 30,000 | 420,000 |
| Cash | 299,000 | 40,000 | | | 339,000 |
| Accounts Receivable | 75,000 | 50,000 | | | 125,000 |
| Inventory | 100,000 | 75,000 | | | 175,000 |
| Land | 155,000 | 75,000 | | (10) 15,000 | 215,000 |
| Buildings and Equipment | 800,000 | 600,000 | | | 1,400,000 |
| Investment in Special Foods Stock | 256,000 | | | (7) 16,000 | |
| | | | | (9) 240,000 | |
| Debits | 1,685,000 | 840,000 | | | 2,254,000 |
| Accumulated Depreciation | 450,000 | 320,000 | | | 770,000 |
| Accounts Payable | 100,000 | 100,000 | | | 200,000 |
| Bonds Payable | 200,000 | 100,000 | | | 300,000 |
| Common Stock | 500,000 | 200,000 | (9) 200,000 | | 500,000 |
| Retained Earnings, from above | 435,000 | 120,000 | 165,000 | 30,000 | 420,000 |
| Noncontrolling Interest | | | | (8) 4,000 | |
| | | | | (9) 60,000 | 64,000 |
| Credits | 1,685,000 | 840,000 | 365,000 | 365,000 | 2,254,000 |

Elimination entries:

(7) Eliminate income from subsidiary.
(8) Assign income to noncontrolling interest.
(9) Eliminate beginning investment balance.
(10) Eliminate unrealized gain on downstream sale of land.

| | | | |
|---|---|---|---|
| E(8) | Income to Noncontrolling Interest | 10,000 | |
| | Dividends Declared | | 6,000 |
| | Noncontrolling Interest | | 4,000 |
| | Assign income to noncontrolling interest. | | |
| | $10,000 = \$50,000 \times .20$ | | |
| | $6,000 = \$30,000 \times .20$ | | |

| E(9) | Common Stock—Special Foods | 200,000 | |
| | Retained Earnings, January 1 | 100,000 | |
| |     Investment in Special Foods Stock | | 240,000 |
| |     Noncontrolling Interest | | 60,000 |
| | Eliminate beginning investment balance. | | |

Entry E(7) eliminates the changes in Peerless's investment account for the year, the income from Special Foods recognized by Peerless in entry (6), and Peerless's share of Special Foods' dividends recognized in entry (5). Entry E(8) assigns a share of Special Foods' income to the noncontrolling stockholders ($50,000 × .20) and eliminates their share of Special Foods' dividends. Income assigned to the noncontrolling interest is not affected by the unrealized intercompany gain because the transfer was a downstream sale. Entry E(9) eliminates Peerless's beginning investment balance and the beginning stockholders' equity amounts of Special Foods. This entry also establishes the noncontrolling interest in the workpaper as of the beginning of the year at its acquisition-date fair value because the combination occurred at the beginning of the year.

One additional entry is needed to eliminate the unrealized gain on the intercompany sale of the land:

| E(10) | Gain on sale of Land | 15,000 | |
| |     Land | | 15,000 |
| | Eliminate unrealized gain on downstream sale of land. | | |

Because the land still is held within the consolidated entity, the $15,000 gain recognized on Peerless's books must be eliminated in the consolidation workpaper so that it does not appear in the consolidated income statement. Similarly, the land must appear in the consolidated balance sheet at its $20,000 original cost to the consolidated entity and, therefore, must be reduced from the $35,000 amount carried on Special Foods' books.

### Consolidated Net Income

The 20X1 consolidated net income is computed and allocated as follows:

| | |
| --- | --- |
| Peerless's separate income | $155,000 |
| Less: Unrealized intercompany gain on downstream land sale | (15,000) |
| Peerless's separate realized income | $140,000 |
| Special Foods' net income | 50,000 |
| Consolidated net income, 20X1 | $190,000 |
| Income to noncontrolling interest ($50,000 × .20) | (10,000) |
| Income to controlling interest | $180,000 |

### Noncontrolling Interest

The noncontrolling stockholders' share of consolidated net income is limited to their proportionate share of the subsidiary's income. Special Foods' net income for 20X1 is $50,000, and the noncontrolling stockholders' ownership interest is 20 percent. Therefore, income of $10,000 ($50,000 × .20) is allocated to the noncontrolling interest.

As shown in Figure 6–3, the total noncontrolling interest at the end of 20X1 is $64,000. Normally the noncontrolling interest's claim on the subsidiary's net assets at a particular date is equal to a proportionate share of the subsidiary's book value and remaining differential at that date. In this example, the subsidiary's acquisition-date fair value and book value are equal, and, thus, no differential is associated with the combination. Accordingly, the noncontrolling interest on December 31, 20X1, is equal to a proportionate share of Special Foods' book value:

| | |
|---|---:|
| Book value of Special Foods, December 31, 20X1: | |
| Common stock | $200,000 |
| Retained earnings | 120,000 |
| Total book value | $320,000 |
| Noncontrolling stockholders' proportionate share | × .20 |
| Noncontrolling interest, December 31, 20X1 | $ 64,000 |

The noncontrolling interest is unaffected by the unrealized gain on the downstream sale.

## Upstream Sale

An upstream sale results in the recording of intercompany profits on the subsidiary's books. If the profits are unrealized from a consolidated viewpoint, they must not be included in the consolidated financial statements. The unrealized intercompany profits are eliminated from the consolidation workpaper in the same manner as in the downstream case. However, the profit elimination reduces both the controlling and the noncontrolling interests in proportion to their ownership.

The treatment of an upstream sale may be illustrated with the same example used to illustrate a downstream sale. In this case, Special Foods recognizes a $15,000 gain from selling the land to Peerless in addition to the $50,000 of income earned from its regular operations; thus, Special Foods' net income for 20X1 is $65,000. Peerless's separate income is $140,000 and comes entirely from its normal operations.

The upstream sale from Special Foods to Peerless is as follows:

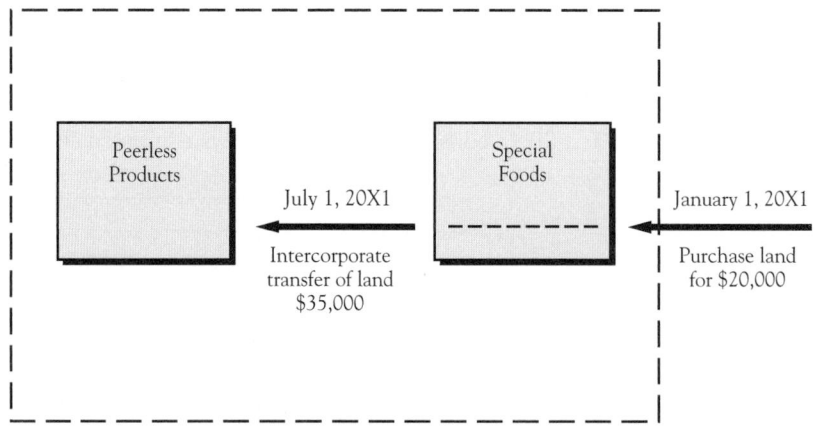

Consolidated Entity

### *Basic Equity-Method Entries—20X1*

During 20X1, Peerless records the normal entries under the basic equity method, reflecting its share of Special Foods' income and dividends:

| | | | |
|---|---|---:|---:|
| (11) | Cash | 24,000 | |
| | Investment in Special Foods Stock | | 24,000 |
| | Record dividends from Special Foods: | | |
| | $30,000 × .80 | | |

| (12) | Investment in Special Foods Stock | 52,000 | |
| | Income from Subsidiary | | 52,000 |
| | Record equity-method income: | | |
| | $65,000 × .80 | | |

Note that Peerless's equity accrual in entry (12) includes its share of both Special Foods' operating income and Special Foods' gain on the transfer of the land.

The investment account on Peerless's books appears as follows at the end of 20X1:

| Investment in Special Foods Stock | | | |
|---|---|---|---|
| Original cost | 240,000 | | |
| (12) Equity accrual | | (11) Dividends | |
| ($65,000 × .80) | 52,000 | ($30,000 × .80) | 24,000 |
| Balance, 12/31/X1 | 268,000 | | |

### Consolidation Workpaper—20X1

The consolidation workpaper prepared at the end of 20X1 appears in Figure 6–4. The four eliminating entries needed to prepare consolidated statements in the upstream case are nearly identical with those in the downstream case:

| E(13) | Income from Subsidiary | 52,000 | |
| | Dividends Declared | | 24,000 |
| | Investment in Special Foods Stock | | 28,000 |
| | Eliminate income from subsidiary. | | |
| | | | |
| E(14) | Income to Noncontrolling Interest | 10,000 | |
| | Dividends Declared | | 6,000 |
| | Noncontrolling Interest | | 4,000 |
| | Assign income to noncontrolling interest: | | |
| | $10,000 = ($65,000 − $15,000) × .20 | | |
| | $6,000 = $30,000 × .20 | | |
| | | | |
| E(15) | Common Stock—Special Foods | 200,000 | |
| | Retained Earnings, January 1 | 100,000 | |
| | Investment in Special Foods Stock | | 240,000 |
| | Noncontrolling Interest | | 60,000 |
| | Eliminate beginning investment balance. | | |
| | | | |
| E(16) | Gain on Sale of Land | 15,000 | |
| | Land | | 15,000 |
| | Eliminate unrealized gain on upstream sale of land. | | |

The only difference between these elimination entries and those in the downstream example is in entry E(13). This difference results from the subsidiary's reporting $65,000 as its income in the upstream example rather than the $50,000 reported in the downstream example, with the additional $15,000 being the gain on the sale of the land.

Entry E(14), which assigns income to the noncontrolling interest, is the same as in the downstream example. The assignment of income to the controlling and noncontrolling interests is based on the subsidiary's realized income, which is the same in both cases, $50,000.

The only procedural difference in the upstream and downstream elimination process is that unrealized intercompany profits of the subsidiary from upstream sales are eliminated

**FIGURE 6–4** **December 31, 20X1, Consolidation Workpaper, Period of Intercompany Sale; Upstream Sale of Land**

| Item | Peerless Products | Special Foods | Eliminations Debit | Eliminations Credit | Consolidated |
|---|---|---|---|---|---|
| Sales | 400,000 | 200,000 | | | 600,000 |
| Gain on Sale of Land | | 15,000 | (16) 15,000 | | |
| Income from Subsidiary | 52,000 | | (13) 52,000 | | |
| Credits | 452,000 | 215,000 | | | 600,000 |
| Cost of Goods Sold | 170,000 | 115,000 | | | 285,000 |
| Depreciation and Amortization | 50,000 | 20,000 | | | 70,000 |
| Other Expenses | 40,000 | 15,000 | | | 55,000 |
| Debits | (260,000) | (150,000) | | | (410,000) |
| Consolidated Net Income | | | | | 190,000 |
| Income to Noncontrolling Interest | | | (14) 10,000 | | (10,000) |
| Income, carry forward | 192,000 | 65,000 | 77,000 | | 180,000 |
| Retained Earnings, January 1 | 300,000 | 100,000 | (15) 100,000 | | 300,000 |
| Income, from above | 192,000 | 65,000 | 77,000 | | 180,000 |
| | 492,000 | 165,000 | | | 480,000 |
| Dividends Declared | (60,000) | (30,000) | | (13) 24,000 | |
| | | | | (14) 6,000 | (60,000) |
| Retained Earnings, December 31, carry forward | 432,000 | 135,000 | 177,000 | 30,000 | 420,000 |
| Cash | 229,000 | 110,000 | | | 339,000 |
| Accounts Receivable | 75,000 | 50,000 | | | 125,000 |
| Inventory | 100,000 | 75,000 | | | 175,000 |
| Land | 210,000 | 20,000 | | (16) 15,000 | 215,000 |
| Buildings and Equipment | 800,000 | 600,000 | | | 1,400,000 |
| Investment in Special Foods Stock | 268,000 | | | (13) 28,000 | |
| | | | | (15) 240,000 | |
| Debits | 1,682,000 | 855,000 | | | 2,254,000 |
| Accumulated Depreciation | 450,000 | 320,000 | | | 770,000 |
| Accounts Payable | 100,000 | 100,000 | | | 200,000 |
| Bonds Payable | 200,000 | 100,000 | | | 300,000 |
| Common Stock | 500,000 | 200,000 | (15) 200,000 | | 500,000 |
| Retained Earnings, from above | 432,000 | 135,000 | 177,000 | 30,000 | 420,000 |
| Noncontrolling Interest | | | | (14) 4,000 | |
| | | | | (15) 60,000 | 64,000 |
| Credits | 1,682,000 | 855,000 | 377,000 | 377,000 | 2,254,000 |

Elimination entries:
(13) Eliminate income from subsidiary.
(14) Assign income to noncontrolling interest.
(15) Eliminate beginning investment balance.
(16) Eliminate unrealized gain on upstream sale of land.

proportionately against the controlling and noncontrolling interests while unrealized intercompany profits of the parent from downstream sales are eliminated totally against the controlling interest. Thus, in the downstream example, the entire $15,000 unrealized intercompany gain was eliminated against the controlling interest's share of income to derive consolidated net income. In the upstream case, $3,000 of the unrealized intercompany gain is subtracted from the noncontrolling stockholders' share of income. The noncontrolling stockholders' share of the subsidiary's total net income is $13,000 ($65,000 × .20) but is reduced by their $3,000 ($15,000 × .20) share of the unrealized gain on the intercompany sale.

Particularly note that the elimination of the unrealized intercompany profit is the same for the upstream case in entry E(16) as for the downstream case in entry E(10). The full amount of the unrealized intercompany profit, $15,000 in this example, is always eliminated. The only difference between the upstream and downstream cases involves how the income reduction for unrealized profit is allocated between the controlling and noncontrolling interests.

### Consolidated Net Income

When intercompany profits that are unrealized from a consolidated point of view are included in the income of a subsidiary, consolidated net income and the noncontrolling stockholders' share of income both must be adjusted for the unrealized profits. Consolidated net income for 20X1 is computed and allocated as follows:

| | | |
|---|---:|---:|
| Peerless's separate income | | $140,000 |
| Special Foods' net income | $65,000 | |
| Less: Unrealized intercompany gain on upstream land sale | (15,000) | |
| Special Foods' realized net income | | 50,000 |
| Consolidated net income, 20X1 | | $190,000 |
| Income to noncontrolling interest ($50,000 × .20) | | (10,000) |
| Income to controlling interest | | $180,000 |

Consolidated net income in this year is the same whether or not there is an intercompany sale because the gain is unrealized. The unrealized gain must be eliminated fully, with consolidated net income based only on the realized income of the two affiliates.

### Noncontrolling Interest

The income assigned to the noncontrolling shareholders is computed as their proportionate share of the realized income of Special Foods, as follows:

| | |
|---|---:|
| Special Foods' net income | $65,000 |
| Less: Unrealized intercompany profit on upstream land sale | (15,000) |
| Special Foods' realized income | $50,000 |
| Proportionate share to noncontrolling interest | ×   .20 |
| Income to noncontrolling interest | $10,000 |

Total noncontrolling interest is computed, in the absence of a differential, as the noncontrolling stockholders' proportionate share of the stockholders' equity of Special Foods, excluding unrealized gains and losses. On December 31, 20X1, noncontrolling interest totals $64,000, computed as follows:

| | |
|---|---:|
| Book value of Special Foods, December 31, 20X1: | |
| Common stock | $200,000 |
| Retained earnings | 135,000 |
| Total book value | $335,000 |
| Unrealized intercompany gain on upstream land sale | (15,000) |
| Realized book value of Special Foods | $320,000 |
| Noncontrolling stockholders' proportionate share | ×   .20 |
| Noncontrolling interest, December 31, 20X1 | $ 64,000 |

## Eliminating Unrealized Profits after the First Year

In the period in which unrealized profits arise from an intercorporate sale, workpaper eliminating entries are used in the consolidation process to remove the gain or loss recorded by the seller and to adjust the reported amount of the asset back to the price originally paid by the selling affiliate. Each period thereafter while the asset is held by the purchasing affiliate, the reported asset balance and the shareholder claims of the selling affiliate are adjusted to remove the effects of the unrealized gain or loss. Income in those subsequent periods is not affected.

In the case of a downstream sale, the parent recognizes the entire profit on the intercompany transfer and includes it in its retained earnings in subsequent years. Therefore, the following eliminating entry is needed in the consolidation workpaper each year after the year of the downstream sale of the land, for as long as the subsidiary holds the land:

| E(17) | Retained Earnings, January 1 | 15,000 | |
| | Land | | 15,000 |
| | Eliminate unrealized gain on prior-period downstream sale of land. | | |

This entry reduces beginning consolidated retained earnings and the reported balance of the land to exclude the unrealized intercompany gain.

In the upstream case, the subsidiary recognizes the intercompany profit. The parent recognizes its proportionate share of the gain, and that amount is included in the parent's beginning retained earnings in subsequent years. In the consolidation workpaper prepared in years subsequent to the intercompany transfer while the land is held by the parent, the unrealized intercompany gain is eliminated from the reported balance of the land and proportionately from the subsidiary ownership interests with the following entry:

| E(18) | Retained Earnings, January 1 | 12,000 | |
| | Noncontrolling Interest | 3,000 | |
| | Land | | 15,000 |
| | Eliminate unrealized gain on prior-period upstream sale of land. | | |

Thus, in periods subsequent to an upstream intercompany transfer, consolidated retained earnings is reduced by the parent's share of the unrealized intercompany gain, and the noncontrolling interest is reduced by the remainder. All other elimination entries are made as if there is no unrealized intercompany gain.

## Subsequent Disposition of Asset

Unrealized profits on intercompany sales of assets are viewed as being realized at the time the assets are resold to external parties. When a transferred asset is subsequently sold to an external party, the gain or loss recognized by the affiliate selling to the external party must be adjusted for consolidated reporting by the amount of the previously unrealized intercompany gain or loss. While the seller's reported profit on the external sale is based on that affiliate's cost, the gain or loss reported by the consolidated entity is based on the cost of the asset to the consolidated entity, which is the cost incurred by the affiliate that purchased the asset originally from an outside party.

When previously unrealized intercompany profits are realized, the effects of the profit elimination process must be reversed. At the time of realization, the full amount of the deferred intercompany profit is added back into the consolidated income computation and assigned to the shareholder interests from which it originally was eliminated.

To illustrate the treatment of unrealized intercompany profits once the transferred asset is resold, assume that Peerless purchases land from an outside party for $20,000 on January 1, 20X1, and sells the land to Special Foods on July 1, 20X1, for $35,000.

Special Foods subsequently sells the land to an outside party on March 1, 20X5, for $45,000, as follows:

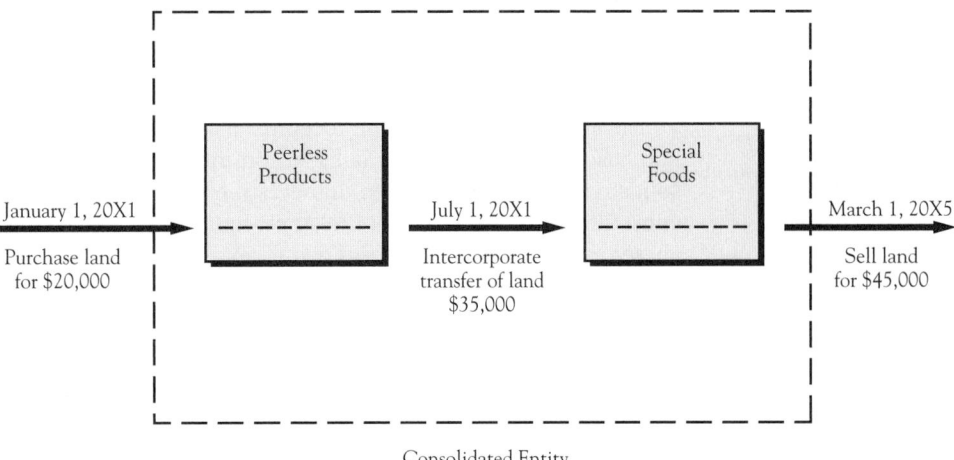

Consolidated Entity

Special Foods recognizes a gain on the sale to the outside party of $10,000 ($45,000 − $35,000). From a consolidated viewpoint, however, the gain is $25,000, the difference between the price at which the land left the consolidated entity ($45,000) and the price at which the land entered the consolidated entity ($20,000) when purchased originally by Peerless.

In the consolidation workpaper, the land no longer needs to be reduced by the unrealized intercompany gain because the gain now is realized and the consolidated entity no longer holds the land. Instead, the $10,000 gain recognized by Special Foods on the sale of the land to an outsider must be adjusted to reflect a total gain for the consolidated entity of $25,000. Thus, the following eliminating entry is made in the consolidation workpaper prepared at the end of 20X5:

| E(19) | Retained Earnings, January 1 | 15,000 | |
| | Gain on Sale of Land | | 15,000 |
| | Adjust for previously unrealized intercompany gain on sale of land. | | |

In addition to adjusting the gain, this entry reduces beginning consolidated retained earnings by the amount of the unrealized intercompany gain previously recognized by Peerless. All other elimination entries are the same as if there were no unrealized intercompany profits at the beginning of the period.

No additional consideration need be given the intercompany transfer in periods subsequent to the external sale. From a consolidated viewpoint, all aspects of the transaction are complete, and the profit is realized once the sale to an external party occurs.

In the example, if the sale to the external party had been made by Peerless following an upstream intercompany transfer from Special Foods, the workpaper treatment would be the same as in the case of the downstream transfer except that the debit in elimination entry E(19) would be prorated between beginning Retained Earnings ($12,000) and Noncontrolling Interest ($3,000) based on the relative ownership interests. In addition, the income assigned to the noncontrolling interest in the workpaper would be based on the subsidiary's realized net income. Because the $15,000 intercompany gain becomes realized during the year through an exchange with an external party, the subsidiary's realized net income includes the subsidiary's reported net income plus the intercompany gain.

# INTERCOMPANY TRANSFERS OF DEPRECIABLE ASSETS

Unrealized intercompany profits on a depreciable or amortizable asset are viewed as being realized gradually over the remaining economic life of the asset as it is used by the purchasing affiliate in generating revenue from unaffiliated parties. In effect, a portion of the unrealized gain or loss is realized each period as benefits are derived from the asset and its service potential expires.

The amount of depreciation recognized on a company's books each period on an asset purchased from an affiliate is based on the intercorporate transfer price. From a consolidated viewpoint, however, depreciation must be based on the cost of the asset to the consolidated entity, which is the asset's cost to the related company that originally purchased it from an outsider. Eliminating entries are needed in the consolidation workpaper to restate the asset, associated accumulated depreciation, and depreciation expense to the amounts that would appear in the financial statements if there had been no intercompany transfer. Because the intercompany sale takes place totally within the consolidated entity, the consolidated financial statements must appear as if the intercompany transfer had never occurred.

## Downstream Sale

The example of Peerless Products and Special Foods is modified to illustrate the downstream sale of a depreciable asset. Assume that Peerless sells equipment to Special Foods on December 31, 20X1, for $7,000, as follows:

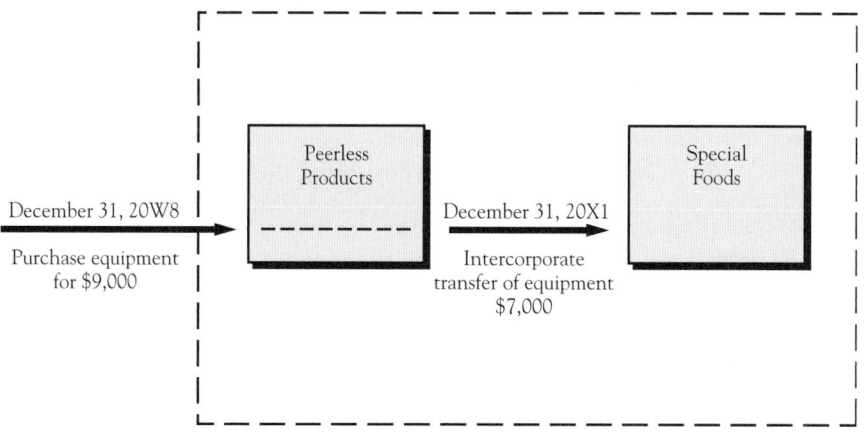

Consolidated Entity

The equipment originally cost Peerless $9,000 when purchased on December 31, 20W8, three years before December 31, 20X1, and is being depreciated over a total life of 10 years using straight-line depreciation with no residual value. The book value of the equipment immediately before the sale by Peerless is computed as follows:

| | | |
|---|---:|---:|
| Original cost to Peerless | | $9,000 |
| Accumulated depreciation on December 31, 20X1: | | |
|     Annual depreciation ($9,000 ÷ 10 years) | $900 | |
|     Number of years | × 3 | |
| | | (2,700) |
| Book value on December 31, 20X1 | | $6,300 |

The gain recognized by Peerless on the intercompany sale of the equipment is:

| | |
|---|---:|
| Sale price of the equipment | $7,000 |
| Book value of the equipment | (6,300) |
| Gain on sale of the equipment | $ 700 |

### Separate-Company Entries—20X1

Special Foods records the purchase of the equipment at its cost:

December 31, 20X1

| (20) | Equipment | 7,000 | |
|---|---|---|---|
| | Cash | | 7,000 |
| | Record purchase of equipment. | | |

Special Foods does not depreciate the equipment during 20X1 because the equipment is purchased at the very end of 20X1.

Peerless must record depreciation on the equipment for 20X1 because it held the asset until the end of the year:

December 31, 20X1

| (21) | Depreciation Expense | 900 | |
|---|---|---|---|
| | Accumulated Depreciation | | 900 |
| | Record 20X1 depreciation expense on equipment sold. | | |

Peerless also records the sale of the equipment at the end of 20X1 and recognizes the $700 ($7,000 − $6,300) gain on the sale:

December 31, 20X1

| (22) | Cash | 7,000 | |
|---|---|---|---|
| | Accumulated Depreciation | 2,700 | |
| | Equipment | | 9,000 |
| | Gain on Sale of Equipment | | 700 |
| | Record sale of equipment. | | |

In addition, Peerless records the normal basic equity-method entries to recognize its share of Special Foods' income and dividends for 20X1:

| (23) | Cash | 24,000 | |
|---|---|---|---|
| | Investment in Special Foods Stock | | 24,000 |
| | Record dividends from Special Foods: | | |
| | $30,000 × .80 | | |

| (24) | Investment in Special Foods Stock | 40,000 | |
|---|---|---|---|
| | Income from Subsidiary | | 40,000 |
| | Record equity-method income: | | |
| | $50,000 × .80 | | |

### Consolidation Workpaper—20X1

The workpaper to prepare consolidated financial statements at the end of 20X1 appears in Figure 6–5. The first three elimination entries in the workpaper are the normal entries to (1) eliminate the income and dividends from Special Foods recognized by Peerless and the change in the investment account for the year, (2) assign income to the noncontrolling

**FIGURE 6–5** December 31, 20X1, Consolidation Workpaper, Period of Intercompany Sale; Downstream Sale of Equipment

| Item | Peerless Products | Special Foods | Eliminations Debit | Eliminations Credit | Consolidated |
|---|---|---|---|---|---|
| Sales | 400,000 | 200,000 | | | 600,000 |
| Gain on Sale of Equipment | 700 | | (28) 700 | | |
| Income from Subsidiary | 40,000 | | (25) 40,000 | | |
| Credits | 440,700 | 200,000 | | | 600,000 |
| Cost of Goods Sold | 170,000 | 115,000 | | | 285,000 |
| Depreciation and Amortization | 50,000 | 20,000 | | | 70,000 |
| Other Expenses | 40,000 | 15,000 | | | 55,000 |
| Debits | (260,000) | (150,000) | | | (410,000) |
| Consolidated Net Income | | | | | 190,000 |
| Income to Noncontrolling Interest | | | (26) 10,000 | | (10,000) |
| Income, carry forward | 180,700 | 50,000 | 50,700 | | 180,000 |
| Retained Earnings, January 1 | 300,000 | 100,000 | (27) 100,000 | | 300,000 |
| Income, from above | 180,700 | 50,000 | 50,700 | | 180,000 |
| | 480,700 | 150,000 | | | 480,000 |
| Dividends Declared | (60,000) | (30,000) | | (25) 24,000 | |
| | | | | (26) 6,000 | (60,000) |
| Retained Earnings, December 31, carry forward | 420,700 | 120,000 | 150,700 | 30,000 | 420,000 |
| Cash | 271,000 | 68,000 | | | 339,000 |
| Accounts Receivable | 75,000 | 50,000 | | | 125,000 |
| Inventory | 100,000 | 75,000 | | | 175,000 |
| Land | 175,000 | 40,000 | | | 215,000 |
| Buildings and Equipment | 791,000 | 607,000 | (28) 2,000 | | 1,400,000 |
| Investment in Special Foods Stock | 256,000 | | | (25) 16,000 | |
| | | | | (27) 240,000 | |
| Debits | 1,668,000 | 840,000 | | | 2,254,000 |
| Accumulated Depreciation | 447,300 | 320,000 | | (28) 2,700 | 770,000 |
| Accounts Payable | 100,000 | 100,000 | | | 200,000 |
| Bonds Payable | 200,000 | 100,000 | | | 300,000 |
| Common Stock | 500,000 | 200,000 | (27) 200,000 | | 500,000 |
| Retained Earnings, from above | 420,700 | 120,000 | 150,700 | 30,000 | 420,000 |
| Noncontrolling Interest | | | | (26) 4,000 | |
| | | | | (27) 60,000 | 64,000 |
| Credits | 1,668,000 | 840,000 | 352,700 | 352,700 | 2,254,000 |

Elimination entries:
(25) Eliminate income from subsidiary.
(26) Assign income to noncontrolling interest.
(27) Eliminate beginning investment balance.
(28) Eliminate unrealized gain on downstream sale of equipment.

interest, and (3) eliminate the stockholders' equity accounts of Special Foods and the investment account as of the beginning of the year, assuming no differential:

| E(25) | Income from Subsidiary | 40,000 | |
|---|---|---|---|
| | Dividends Declared | | 24,000 |
| | Investment in Special Foods Stock | | 16,000 |
| | Eliminate income from subsidiary. | | |

| E(26) | Income to Noncontrolling Interest | 10,000 | |
|---|---|---|---|
| | Dividends Declared | | 6,000 |
| | Noncontrolling Interest | | 4,000 |
| | Assign income to noncontrolling interest: | | |
| | $10,000 = $50,000 × .20 | | |
| | | | |
| E(27) | Common Stock—Special Foods | 200,000 | |
| | Retained Earnings, January 1 | 100,000 | |
| | Investment in Special Foods Stock | | 240,000 |
| | Noncontrolling Interest | | 60,000 |
| | Eliminate beginning investment balance. | | |

An additional workpaper entry is needed to eliminate the unrealized intercompany gain on the sale of the equipment from consolidated net income and to restate the equipment to the amounts that would appear in the consolidated statements if there had been no intercompany sale. The amounts in the trial balances of the parent and subsidiary include the effects of the intercompany transfer and need to be adjusted in the consolidation workpaper to the balances immediately before the transfer:

| | Amounts from Trial Balances | Elimination | Consolidated Amounts |
|---|---|---|---|
| Buildings and equipment | $7,000 | $2,000 | $9,000 |
| Accumulated depreciation | -0- | (2,700) | (2,700) |
| Gain on sale of equipment | (700) | 700 | -0- |

Thus, the following entry is needed in the workpaper:

| E(28) | Buildings and Equipment | 2,000 | |
|---|---|---|---|
| | Gain on Sale of Equipment | 700 | |
| | Accumulated Depreciation | | 2,700 |
| | Eliminate unrealized gain on downstream sale of equipment. | | |

As a result of this entry, the equipment, stated at $7,000 on Special Foods' books, is reported in the consolidated balance sheet at $9,000 ($7,000 + $2,000), its original cost to Peerless. While Special Foods has not depreciated the equipment, elimination entry E(28) provides for $2,700 of accumulated depreciation ($900 × 3), the amount that would have been shown on Peerless's books had the equipment not been sold. Entry E(28) also eliminates the $700 intercompany gain that is unrealized and cannot appear when Peerless and Special Foods are viewed together as a single entity. The overall effect of entry E(28) is to report exactly the same numbers in the consolidated financial statements as if the parent company had continued to own the equipment and there had been no intercompany transfer.

### Separate-Company Entries—20X2

During 20X2, Special Foods begins depreciating the $7,000 cost of the equipment acquired from Peerless Products over its remaining life of seven years using straight-line depreciation. The resulting depreciation is $1,000 per year ($7,000 ÷ 7 years):

| (29) | Depreciation Expense | 1,000 | |
|---|---|---|---|
| | Accumulated Depreciation | | 1,000 |
| | Record depreciation expense for 20X2. | | |

This amount is $100 more per year than the depreciation that would have been recorded each year if Peerless had continued to hold the equipment.

Peerless records its normal equity-method entries for 20X2 to reflect its share of Special Foods' $74,000 income and dividends of $40,000:

| (30) | Cash | 32,000 | |
| |     Investment in Special Foods Stock | | 32,000 |
| |     Record dividends from Special Foods: | | |
| |     $40,000 × .80 | | |

| (31) | Investment in Special Foods Stock | 59,200 | |
| |     Income from Subsidiary | | 59,200 |
| |     Record equity-method income: | | |
| |     $74,000 × .80 | | |

Special Foods' net income is only $74,000 in 20X2 because it has been reduced by the $1,000 of depreciation on the transferred asset. Accordingly, Peerless's share of that income is $59,200 ($74,000 × .80).

The investment account on Peerless's books appears as follows:

| **Investment in Special Foods Stock** | | | | |
|---|---|---|---|---|
| Original cost | 240,000 | | | |
| (24) 20X1 equity accrual ($50,000 × .80) | 40,000 | (23) 20X1 dividends ($30,000 × .80) | 24,000 | |
| Balance, 12/31/X1 | 256,000 | | | |
| (31) 20X2 equity accrual ($74,000 × .80) | 59,200 | (30) 20X2 dividends ($40,000 × .80) | 32,000 | |
| Balance, 12/31/X2 | 283,200 | | | |

### Consolidation Workpaper—20X2

The consolidation workpaper for 20X2 is presented in Figure 6–6. The trial balance amounts from the basic example have been adjusted to reflect the intercompany asset sale. The first three elimination entries are the normal entries to eliminate income and dividends from the subsidiary, the investment account, and the stockholders' equity accounts of the subsidiary, and to establish the noncontrolling interest in the workpaper:

| E(32) | Income from Subsidiary | 59,200 | |
| |     Dividends Declared | | 32,000 |
| |     Investment in Special Foods Stock | | 27,200 |
| |     Eliminate income from subsidiary. | | |

| E(33) | Income to Noncontrolling Interest | 14,800 | |
| |     Dividends Declared | | 8,000 |
| |     Noncontrolling Interest | | 6,800 |
| |     Assign income to noncontrolling interest: | | |
| |     $14,800 = $74,000 × .20 | | |

| E(34) | Common Stock—Special Foods | 200,000 | |
| | Retained Earnings, January 1 | 120,000 | |
| |     Investment in Special Foods Stock | | 256,000 |
| |     Noncontrolling Interest | | 64,000 |
| |     Eliminate beginning investment balance. | | |

**FIGURE 6–6** December 31, 20X2, Consolidation Workpaper, Next Period following Intercompany Sale; Downstream Sale of Equipment

| Item | Peerless Products | Special Foods | Eliminations Debit | | Eliminations Credit | | Consolidated |
|---|---|---|---|---|---|---|---|
| Sales | 450,000 | 300,000 | | | | | 750,000 |
| Income from Subsidiary | 59,200 | | (32) | 59,200 | | | |
| Credits | 509,200 | 300,000 | | | | | 750,000 |
| Cost of Goods Sold | 180,000 | 160,000 | | | | | 340,000 |
| Depreciation and Amortization | 49,100 | 21,000 | | | (36) | 100 | 70,000 |
| Other Expenses | 60,000 | 45,000 | | | | | 105,000 |
| Debits | (289,100) | (226,000) | | | | | (515,000) |
| Consolidated Net Income | | | | | | | 235,000 |
| Income to Noncontrolling Interest | | | (33) | 14,800 | | | (14,800) |
| Income, carry forward | 220,100 | 74,000 | | 74,000 | | 100 | 220,200 |
| Retained Earnings, January 1 | 420,700 | 120,000 | (34) | 120,000 | | | |
| | | | (35) | 700 | | | 420,000 |
| Income, from above | 220,100 | 74,000 | | 74,000 | | 100 | 220,200 |
| | 640,800 | 194,000 | | | | | 640,200 |
| Dividends Declared | (60,000) | (40,000) | | | (32) | 32,000 | |
| | | | | | (33) | 8,000 | (60,000) |
| Retained Earnings, December 31, carry forward | 580,800 | 154,000 | | 194,700 | | 40,100 | 580,200 |
| Cash | 298,000 | 78,000 | | | | | 376,000 |
| Accounts Receivable | 150,000 | 80,000 | | | | | 230,000 |
| Inventory | 180,000 | 90,000 | | | | | 270,000 |
| Land | 175,000 | 40,000 | | | | | 215,000 |
| Buildings and Equipment | 791,000 | 607,000 | (35) | 2,000 | | | 1,400,000 |
| Investment in Special Foods Stock | 283,200 | | | | (32) | 27,200 | |
| | | | | | (34) | 256,000 | |
| Debits | 1,877,200 | 895,000 | | | | | 2,491,000 |
| Accumulated Depreciation | 496,400 | 341,000 | (36) | 100 | (35) | 2,700 | 840,000 |
| Accounts Payable | 100,000 | 100,000 | | | | | 200,000 |
| Bonds Payable | 200,000 | 100,000 | | | | | 300,000 |
| Common Stock | 500,000 | 200,000 | (34) | 200,000 | | | 500,000 |
| Retained Earnings, from above | 580,800 | 154,000 | | 194,700 | | 40,100 | 580,200 |
| Noncontrolling Interest | | | | | (33) | 6,800 | |
| | | | | | (34) | 64,000 | 70,800 |
| Credits | 1,877,200 | 895,000 | | 396,800 | | 396,800 | 2,491,000 |

Elimination entries:
  (32) Eliminate income from subsidiary.
  (33) Assign income to noncontrolling interest.
  (34) Eliminate beginning investment balance.
  (35) Eliminate unrealized gain on equipment.
  (36) Eliminate excess depreciation.

Entry E(33) assigns the noncontrolling interest its full 20 percent of the $74,000 reported income of Special Foods, given that the unrealized profits are on the books of the parent.

In addition to the normal elimination entries, entry E(35) is needed to eliminate the effects of the 20X1 intercompany transaction as of the beginning of 20X2:

| E(35) | Buildings and Equipment | 2,000 | |
|---|---|---|---|
| | Retained Earnings, January 1 | 700 | |
| | Accumulated Depreciation | | 2,700 |
| | Eliminate unrealized gain on equipment. | | |

Entry E(35) restates the balance of the equipment to $9,000 ($7,000 + $2,000), the original cost to the consolidated entity when purchased by Peerless. Accumulated depreciation on the equipment is credited for $2,700. This is the amount at which accumulated depreciation would have been stated as of January 1, 20X2, if the asset had not been transferred to Special Foods:

| | |
|---|---|
| Depreciation per year ($9,000 ÷ 10 years) | $ 900 |
| Number of years to December 31, 20X1 | × 3 |
| Accumulated depreciation, December 31, 20X1 | $2,700 |

Entry E(35) also reduces beginning retained earnings by the amount of intercompany profit unrealized at the beginning of the year. The full amount of the unrealized gain is included in Peerless's beginning retained earnings. If this amount were reported in consolidated retained earnings, the balance would be overstated because the gain has not been realized from a consolidated viewpoint.

One additional eliminating entry is needed in the December 31, 20X2, consolidation workpaper. Special Foods started depreciating the transferred asset at the beginning of 20X2 and recorded depreciation of $1,000 ($7,000 ÷ 7 years) on its separate books. From a consolidated point of view, however, the depreciation expense for 20X2 should be based on the $6,300 ($9,000 − $2,700) remaining book value of the equipment on Peerless's books immediately before the transfer. This $6,300 is allocated over the remaining seven-year life of the equipment, resulting in depreciation of $900 per year ($6,300 ÷ 7 years) from a consolidated perspective. Therefore, consolidated depreciation expense and the associated accumulated depreciation must be reduced by $100 from the amount recorded by Special Foods:

| E(36) | Accumulated Depreciation | 100 | |
|---|---|---|---|
| | Depreciation Expense | | 100 |
| | Eliminate excess depreciation. | | |

Note that this entry increases consolidated net income by $100. The $700 unrealized gain on the intercorporate sale is viewed as being realized at $100 per year over the seven years following the transfer. After seven years, the intercompany gain will be fully realized, and no further eliminations of depreciation or retained earnings will be needed.

Separating entries (35) and (36) is purely a matter of preference. Some prefer to combine the two entries and establish the consolidated balances at the end of the year in a single entry:

| E(36a) | Buildings and Equipment | 2,000 | |
|---|---|---|---|
| | Retained Earnings, January 1 | 700 | |
| | Depreciation Expense | | 100 |
| | Accumulated Depreciation | | 2,600 |

The $2,600 credit to Accumulated Depreciation represents the difference between the $3,600 ($900 × 4 years) amount at which consolidated accumulated depreciation should be stated on December 31, 20X2, and the $1,000 amount at which accumulated depreciation is stated on Special Foods' books.

Once all the eliminating entries have been made in the workpaper, the adjusted balances exclude the effects of the intercorporate transfer:

|  | Subsidiary Trial Balance | Elimination | Consolidated Amounts |
|---|---|---|---|
| Buildings and Equipment | $7,000 | $2,000 | $9,000 |
| Accumulated Depreciation | (1,000) | (2,600) | (3,600) |
| Depreciation Expense | 1,000 | (100) | 900 |

### Consolidated Net Income and Retained Earnings

Computation of consolidated net income for 20X2 must include an adjustment for the realization of profit on the 20X1 sale of equipment to Special Foods:

| | |
|---|---|
| Peerless's separate income | $160,900 |
| Partial realization of intercompany gain on downstream sale of equipment | 100 |
| Peerless's separate realized income | $161,000 |
| Special Foods' net income | 74,000 |
| Consolidated net income, 20X2 | $235,000 |
| Income to noncontrolling interest ($74,000 × .20) | (14,800) |
| Income to controlling interest | $220,200 |

Because Peerless does not adjust its investment income from Special Foods for unrealized gains and losses, Peerless's retained earnings includes the unrealized intercompany gain and therefore exceeds the amount that should be reported as consolidated retained earnings. Accordingly, consolidated retained earnings at December 31, 20X2, can be computed by subtracting the remaining unrealized intercompany gain from Peerless's retained earnings:

| | | |
|---|---|---|
| Peerless's retained earnings, December 31, 20X2 | | $580,800 |
| Less: Unrealized 20X1 intercompany gain | $700 | |
| 20X2 partial realization of gain | (100) | (600) |
| Consolidated retained earnings, December 31, 20X2 | | $580,200 |

### Noncontrolling Interest

Income allocated to the noncontrolling stockholders in 20X2 is equal to their proportionate share of the subsidiary's realized and reported income. Special Foods' net income for 20X2 is $74,000, and the noncontrolling interest's 20 percent share is $14,800 ($74,000 × .20).

The total noncontrolling interest at the end of 20X2 is $70,800, equal to the noncontrolling stockholders' proportionate share of the total book value of the subsidiary:

| | |
|---|---|
| Book value of Special Foods, December 31, 20X2: | |
| Common stock | $200,000 |
| Retained earnings | 154,000 |
| Total book value | $354,000 |
| Noncontrolling stockholders' proportionate share | × .20 |
| Noncontrolling interest, December 31, 20X2 | $ 70,800 |

Normally the noncontrolling interest at a particular date is equal to a proportionate share of the subsidiary's book value plus the noncontrolling interest's share of the remaining differential at that date. In this example, however, no differential was recognized at the date of combination.

### Consolidation in Subsequent Years

The consolidation procedures in subsequent years are quite similar to those in 20X2. As long as Special Foods continues to hold and depreciate the equipment, consolidation procedures must include:

1. Restating the asset and accumulated depreciation balances.
2. Adjusting depreciation expense for the year.
3. Reducing beginning retained earnings by the amount of the intercompany gain unrealized at the beginning of the year.

For example, selected entries from the December 31, 20X3, consolidation workpaper for Peerless Products and Special Foods are as follows:

| | | | |
|---|---|---|---|
| E(37) | Buildings and Equipment | 2,000 | |
| | Retained Earnings, January 1 | 600 | |
| | Accumulated Depreciation | | 2,600 |
| | Eliminate unrealized gain on equipment. | | |
| | | | |
| E(38) | Accumulated Depreciation | 100 | |
| | Depreciation Expense | | 100 |
| | Eliminate excess depreciation. | | |

These entries are the same as entries E(35) and E(36) for 20X2, except that an additional $100 of the intercompany gain is considered realized by the end of 20X2. Therefore, the reduction of beginning retained earnings in entry E(37) is for $600, the $700 original amount of the intercompany gain less the $100 portion of the gain considered realized in 20X2.

The credit to Accumulated Depreciation in entry E(37) is $100 less than in entry E(35) for 20X2 because Special Foods credited $100 more to Accumulated Depreciation on its books in 20X2 than was appropriate for consolidated reporting. Because this amount is brought into the workpaper, the restatement of the beginning accumulated depreciation in entry E(37) is $100 less than in the previous year:

| | |
|---|---|
| Accumulated depreciation that would have been recorded by Peerless as of December 31, 20X2, if asset had not been transferred [($9,000 ÷ 10) × 4] | $3,600 |
| Accumulated depreciation recorded by Special Foods as of December 31, 20X2 [($7,000 ÷ 7) × 1] | (1,000) |
| Workpaper adjustment to accumulated depreciation | $2,600 |

Both the debit to beginning Retained Earnings and the credit to Accumulated Depreciation will decrease by $100 each year until the asset is fully depreciated and the intercompany gain is fully recognized.

## Change in Estimated Life of Asset upon Transfer

When a depreciable asset is transferred between companies, a change in the remaining estimated economic life may be appropriate. For example, the acquiring company may use the asset in a different type of production process, or the frequency of use may change. When a change in the estimated life of a depreciable asset occurs at the time of an intercorporate transfer, the treatment is no different than if the change occurred while the asset remained on the books of the transferring affiliate. The new remaining useful life is used as a basis for depreciation both by the purchasing affiliate and for purposes of preparing consolidated financial statements.

## Upstream Sale

The treatment of unrealized profits arising from upstream intercompany sales is identical to that of downstream sales except that the unrealized profit, and subsequent realization, must be allocated between the controlling and noncontrolling interests. The case of an upstream sale can be illustrated using the same example as for the downstream sale. Assume that Special Foods sells equipment to Peerless Products for $7,000 on December 31, 20X1, and reports total income for 20X1 of $50,700 ($50,000 + $700), including the $700 gain on the sale of the equipment. Special Foods originally purchased the equipment for $9,000 three years before the intercompany sale.[2] The book value of the equipment at the date of sale is as follows:

| | | |
|---|---:|---:|
| Original cost to Special Foods | | $9,000 |
| Accumulated depreciation on December 31, 20X1: | | |
|    Annual depreciation ($9,000 ÷ 10 years) | $900 | |
|    Number of years | × 3 | |
| | | (2,700) |
| Book value on December 31, 20X1 | | $6,300 |

### *Separate-Company Entries—20X1*

Special Foods records depreciation on the equipment for the year and the sale of the equipment to Peerless on December 31, 20X1, with the following entries:

December 31, 20X1

| | | | |
|---|---|---:|---:|
| (39) | Depreciation Expense | 900 | |
| |    Accumulated Depreciation | | 900 |
| | Record 20X1 depreciation expense on equipment sold. | | |

| | | | |
|---|---|---:|---:|
| (40) | Cash | 7,000 | |
| | Accumulated Depreciation | 2,700 | |
| |    Equipment | | 9,000 |
| |    Gain on Sale of Equipment | | 700 |
| | Record sale of equipment. | | |

Peerless records the purchase of the equipment from Special Foods with the following entry:

December 31, 20X1

| | | | |
|---|---|---:|---:|
| (41) | Equipment | 7,000 | |
| |    Cash | | 7,000 |
| | Record purchase of equipment. | | |

In addition, Peerless records the following basic equity-method entries to recognize its share of Special Foods' reported income and dividends:

| | | | |
|---|---|---:|---:|
| (42) | Cash | 24,000 | |
| |    Investment in Special Foods Stock | | 24,000 |
| | Record dividends from Special Foods: | | |
| | $30,000 × .80 | | |

| | | | |
|---|---|---:|---:|
| (43) | Investment in Special Foods Stock | 40,560 | |
| |    Income from Subsidiary | | 40,560 |
| | Record equity-method income: | | |
| | ($50,000 + $700) × .80 | | |

[2] To avoid additional complexity, the equipment's fair value is assumed to be equal to its book value on the date of combination. There is, therefore, no differential related to the equipment.

**FIGURE 6–7** December 31, 20X1, Consolidation Workpaper, Period of Intercompany Sale; Upstream Sale of Equipment

| Item | Peerless Products | Special Foods | Eliminations Debit | Eliminations Credit | Consolidated |
|---|---|---|---|---|---|
| Sales | 400,000 | 200,000 | | | 600,000 |
| Gain on Sale of Equipment | | 700 | (47) 700 | | |
| Income from Subsidiary | 40,560 | | (44) 40,560 | | |
| Credits | 440,560 | 200,700 | | | 600,000 |
| Cost of Goods Sold | 170,000 | 115,000 | | | 285,000 |
| Depreciation and Amortization | 50,000 | 20,000 | | | 70,000 |
| Other Expenses | 40,000 | 15,000 | | | 55,000 |
| Debits | (260,000) | (150,000) | | | (410,000) |
| Consolidated Net Income | | | | | 190,000 |
| Income to Noncontrolling Interest | | | (45) 10,000 | | (10,000) |
| Income, carry forward | 180,560 | 50,700 | 51,260 | | 180,000 |
| Retained Earnings, January 1 | 300,000 | 100,000 | (46) 100,000 | | 300,000 |
| Income, from above | 180,560 | 50,700 | 51,260 | | 180,000 |
| | 480,560 | 150,700 | | | 480,000 |
| Dividends Declared | (60,000) | (30,000) | | (44) 24,000 | |
| | | | | (45) 6,000 | (60,000) |
| Retained Earnings, December 31, carry forward | 420,560 | 120,700 | 151,260 | 30,000 | 420,000 |
| Cash | 257,000 | 82,000 | | | 339,000 |
| Accounts Receivable | 75,000 | 50,000 | | | 125,000 |
| Inventory | 100,000 | 75,000 | | | 175,000 |
| Land | 175,000 | 40,000 | | | 215,000 |
| Buildings and Equipment | 807,000 | 591,000 | (47) 2,000 | | 1,400,000 |
| Investment in Special Foods Stock | 256,560 | | | (44) 16,560 | |
| | | | | (46) 240,000 | |
| Debits | 1,670,560 | 838,000 | | | 2,254,000 |
| Accumulated Depreciation | 450,000 | 317,300 | | (47) 2,700 | 770,000 |
| Accounts Payable | 100,000 | 100,000 | | | 200,000 |
| Bonds Payable | 200,000 | 100,000 | | | 300,000 |
| Common Stock | 500,000 | 200,000 | (46) 200,000 | | 500,000 |
| Retained Earnings, from above | 420,560 | 120,700 | 151,260 | 30,000 | 420,000 |
| Noncontrolling Interest | | | | (45) 4,000 | |
| | | | | (46) 60,000 | 64,000 |
| Credits | 1,670,560 | 838,000 | 353,260 | 353,260 | 2,254,000 |

Elimination entries:
(44) Eliminate income from subsidiary.
(45) Assign income to noncontrolling interest.
(46) Eliminate beginning investment balance.
(47) Eliminate unrealized gain on upstream sale of equipment.

### Consolidation Workpaper—20X1

The consolidation workpaper for 20X1 is presented in Figure 6–7. It is the same as that presented in Figure 6–5 except where modified to reflect the upstream sale of the equipment.

Four eliminating entries appear in the consolidation workpaper for 20X1:

| E(44) | Income from Subsidiary | 40,560 | |
| | Dividends Declared | | 24,000 |
| | Investment in Special Foods Stock | | 16,560 |
| | Eliminate income from subsidiary. | | |
| | | | |
| E(45) | Income to Noncontrolling Interest | 10,000 | |
| | Dividends Declared | | 6,000 |
| | Noncontrolling Interest | | 4,000 |
| | Assign income to noncontrolling interest: | | |
| | $10,000 = ($50,700 − $700) × .20 | | |
| | | | |
| E(46) | Common Stock—Special Foods | 200,000 | |
| | Retained Earnings, January 1 | 100,000 | |
| | Investment in Special Foods Stock | | 240,000 |
| | Noncontrolling Interest | | 60,000 |
| | Eliminate beginning investment balance. | | |
| | | | |
| E(47) | Buildings and Equipment | 2,000 | |
| | Gain on Sale of Equipment | 700 | |
| | Accumulated Depreciation | | 2,700 |
| | Eliminate unrealized gain on upstream sale of equipment. | | |

Entry E(44) is the normal workpaper entry to eliminate the income and dividends from Special Foods recorded by Peerless and is based on the amounts recorded by Peerless on its books during 20X1. Entry E(45) assigns income to the noncontrolling shareholders based on their share of Special Foods' realized income, computed as follows:

| | |
|---|---|
| Net income of Special Foods for 20X1 | $50,700 |
| Unrealized gain on intercompany sale | (700) |
| Realized net income of Special Foods for 20X1 | $50,000 |
| Noncontrolling stockholders' proportionate share | ×   .20 |
| Income to noncontrolling interest, 20X1 | $10,000 |

In the upstream case, as in the downstream case, consolidated net income is reduced by the amount of the current period's unrealized gain on the intercompany transfer. However, in the upstream case the unrealized gain reduces both the controlling and noncontrolling interests proportionately because both are owners of Special Foods and shared in the gain. The allocation of Special Foods' income to the controlling and noncontrolling interests is based on Special Foods' realized net income after having deducted the unrealized gain. The computation and allocation of 20X1 consolidated net income is as follows:

| | | |
|---|---|---|
| Peerless's separate income | | $140,000 |
| Special Foods' net income | $50,700 | |
| Less: Unrealized intercompany gain on upstream sale of equipment | (700) | |
| Special Foods' realized net income | | 50,000 |
| Consolidated net income, 20X1 | | $190,000 |
| Income to noncontrolling interest ($50,000 × .20) | | (10,000) |
| Income to controlling interest | | $180,000 |

Eliminating entries E(46) and E(47) are identical to those used in the downstream case. Entry E(46) is not affected by the transfer. Entry E(47) is not affected by the direction of the sale in the period in which the sale occurs.

### Separate-Company Books—20X2

In the year following the intercorporate transfer, Special Foods reports net income of $75,900 (with the $900 of depreciation expense on the transferred asset now excluded). Peerless records the normal basic equity-method entries on its books to recognize its share of Special Foods' 20X2 income and dividends. At the end of 20X2, the investment account on Peerless's books appears as follows:

| Investment in Special Foods Stock | | | | |
|---|---|---|---|---|
| | Original cost | 240,000 | | |
| (43) | 20X1 equity accrual | | (42) 20X1 dividends | |
| | ($50,700 × .80) | 40,560 | ($30,000 × .80) | 24,000 |
| | Balance, 12/31/X1 | 256,560 | | |
| | 20X2 equity accrual | | 20X2 dividends | |
| | ($75,900 × .80) | 60,720 | ($40,000 × .80) | 32,000 |
| | Balance, 12/31/X2 | 285,280 | | |

### Consolidation Elimination Entries—20X2

The consolidation workpaper for 20X2 is presented in Figure 6–8. The elimination entries used in the preparation of consolidated financial statements for 20X2 are as follows:

| | | | |
|---|---|---|---|
| E(48) | Income from Subsidiary | 60,720 | |
| | Dividends Declared | | 32,000 |
| | Investment in Special Foods Stock | | 28,720 |
| | Eliminate income from subsidiary: | | |
| | $60,720 = $75,900 × .80 | | |
| E(49) | Income to Noncontrolling Interest | 15,200 | |
| | Dividends Declared | | 8,000 |
| | Noncontrolling Interest | | 7,200 |
| | Assign income to noncontrolling interest: | | |
| | $15,200 = ($75,900 + $100) × .20 | | |
| E(50) | Common Stock—Special Foods | 200,000 | |
| | Retained Earnings, January 1 | 120,700 | |
| | Investment in Special Foods Stock | | 256,560 |
| | Noncontrolling Interest | | 64,140 |
| | Eliminate beginning investment balance: | | |
| | $256,560 = ($200,000 + $120,700) × .80 | | |
| | $64,140 = ($200,000 + $120,700) × .20 | | |
| E(51) | Buildings and Equipment | 2,000 | |
| | Retained Earnings, January 1 | 560 | |
| | Noncontrolling Interest | 140 | |
| | Accumulated Depreciation | | 2,700 |
| | Eliminate unrealized gain on upstream sale of equipment. | | |
| E(52) | Accumulated Depreciation | 100 | |
| | Depreciation Expense | | 100 |
| | Eliminate excess depreciation. | | |

**FIGURE 6–8**   December 31, 20X2, Consolidation Workpaper, Next Period following Intercompany Sale; Upstream Sale of Equipment

| Item | Peerless Products | Special Foods | Eliminations Debit | Eliminations Credit | Consolidated |
|---|---|---|---|---|---|
| Sales | 450,000 | 300,000 | | | 750,000 |
| Income from Subsidiary | 60,720 | | (48)   60,720 | | |
| Credits | 510,720 | 300,000 | | | 750,000 |
| Cost of Goods Sold | 180,000 | 160,000 | | | 340,000 |
| Depreciation and Amortization | 51,000 | 19,100 | | (52)   100 | 70,000 |
| Other Expenses | 60,000 | 45,000 | | | 105,000 |
| Debits | (291,000) | (224,100) | | | (515,000) |
| Consolidated Net Income | | | | | 235,000 |
| Income to Noncontrolling Interest | | | (49)   15,200 | | (15,200) |
| Income, carry forward | 219,720 | 75,900 | 75,920 | 100 | 219,800 |
| Retained Earnings, January 1 | 420,560 | 120,700 | (50) 120,700 | | |
| | | | (51)      560 | | 420,000 |
| Income, from above | 219,720 | 75,900 | 75,920 | 100 | 219,800 |
| | 640,280 | 196,600 | | | 639,800 |
| Dividends Declared | (60,000) | (40,000) | | (48)   32,000 | |
| | | | | (49)    8,000 | (60,000) |
| Retained Earnings, December 31, carry forward | 580,280 | 156,600 | 197,180 | 40,100 | 579,800 |
| Cash | 284,000 | 92,000 | | | 376,000 |
| Accounts Receivable | 150,000 | 80,000 | | | 230,000 |
| Inventory | 180,000 | 90,000 | | | 270,000 |
| Land | 175,000 | 40,000 | | | 215,000 |
| Buildings and Equipment | 807,000 | 591,000 | (51)    2,000 | | 1,400,000 |
| Investment in Special Foods Stock | 285,280 | | | (48)   28,720 | |
| | | | | (50) 256,560 | |
| Debits | 1,881,280 | 893,000 | | | 2,491,000 |
| Accumulated Depreciation | 501,000 | 336,400 | (52)      100 | (51)    2,700 | 840,000 |
| Accounts Payable | 100,000 | 100,000 | | | 200,000 |
| Bonds Payable | 200,000 | 100,000 | | | 300,000 |
| Common Stock | 500,000 | 200,000 | (50) 200,000 | | 500,000 |
| Retained Earnings, from above | 580,280 | 156,600 | 197,180 | 40,100 | 579,800 |
| Noncontrolling Interest | | | (51)      140 | (49)    7,200 | |
| | | | | (50)   64,140 | 71,200 |
| Credits | 1,881,280 | 893,000 | 399,420 | 399,420 | 2,491,000 |

Elimination entries:
(48) Eliminate income from subsidiary.
(49) Assign income to noncontrolling interest.
(50) Eliminate beginning investment balance.
(51) Eliminate unrealized gain on upstream sale of equipment.
(52) Eliminate excess depreciation.

The second-year elimination entries differ little between the upstream and downstream cases except that the amount of unrealized intercompany gain at the beginning of the period is allocated proportionally between the controlling interest (retained earnings) and the noncontrolling interest in entry E(51); it was allocated entirely to the controlling interest in entry E(35) for the downstream case. The $700 unrealized gain on the upstream sale was eliminated proportionally against both the controlling and the noncontrolling interests at the end of 20X1. Therefore, elimination of the unrealized gain at the beginning of 20X2 must be treated as a reduction of both consolidated retained earnings and the noncontrolling interest.

The difference in the annual depreciation recorded by the purchasing affiliate, Peerless in this case, and the amount that would have been recorded by the selling affiliate, Special Foods, is $100:

| | |
|---|---:|
| Depreciation recorded by Peerless ($7,000 ÷ 7 years) | $1,000 |
| Depreciation that would have been recorded by Special Foods if asset had not been transferred ($9,000 ÷ 10 years) | (900) |
| | $ 100 |

Entry E(52) adjusts depreciation expense and accumulated depreciation for this difference and has the effect of increasing total income by $100.

The $100 increase in income is viewed as resulting from the realization of a portion of the gain on the intercompany transfer. The $700 unrealized gain is considered realized at $100 per year over the seven-year period following the intercorporate transfer. As $100 of the gain is realized each year, the controlling interest is increased by $80, its 80 percent share, and the noncontrolling interest is increased by $20, its 20 percent share. Entry E(49) allocates a proportionate share of Special Foods' income to the noncontrolling interest and is based on Special Foods' reported income ($75,900) plus the portion of the intercompany gain considered realized during 20X2 ($100). The remaining $80 of realized gain accrues to the controlling interest.

Entry E(50) is the normal entry to eliminate the investment account and subsidiary stockholders' equity balances as of the beginning of the year. The entry also assigns to the noncontrolling interest a pro rata portion of the subsidiary stockholders' equity balances ($320,700 × .20) as of the beginning of the year. This amount ($64,140), however, is greater than the actual amount assigned to the noncontrolling interest at the end of last period (see Figure 6–7). This increase is attributed to the $140 noncontrolling stockholders' share of the unrealized intercompany profit at the beginning of the period ($700 × .20). Entry E(51) reduces the noncontrolling interest by a proportionate share of the unrealized intercompany profit at the beginning of the year, and the two entries together establish the correct beginning balance of the noncontrolling interest.

### Consolidated Net Income

Peerless Products' separate income for 20X2 is $159,000 after deducting an additional $1,000 for the depreciation on the transferred asset. Consolidated net income for 20X2 is computed and allocated as follows:

| | | |
|---|---:|---:|
| Peerless's separate income | | $159,000 |
| Special Foods' net income | $75,900 | |
| Partial realization of intercompany gain on upstream sale of equipment | 100 | |
| Special Foods' realized net income | | 76,000 |
| Consolidated net income, 20X2 | | $235,000 |
| Income to noncontrolling interest ($76,000 × .20) | | (15,200) |
| Income to controlling interest | | $219,800 |

Note that the consolidated net income allocated to the controlling interest can also be calculated as follows:

| | | |
|---|---:|---:|
| Peerless's separate income | | $159,000 |
| Special Foods' net income | $75,900 | |
| Partial realization of intercompany gain on upstream sale of equipment | 100 | |
| Special Foods' realized net income | $76,000 | |
| Peerless's proportionate share | × .80 | |
| Peerless's share of Special Foods' realized net income | | 60,800 |
| Income to controlling interest | | $219,800 |

### Noncontrolling Interest

The noncontrolling interest's share of income is $15,200 for 20X2, computed as the noncontrolling stockholders' proportionate share of the realized income of Special Foods ($76,000 × .20). Total noncontrolling interest in the absence of a differential is computed as the noncontrolling stockholders' proportionate share of the stockholders' equity of Special Foods, excluding unrealized gains and losses. On December 31, 20X2, the noncontrolling interest totals $71,200, computed as follows:

| | | |
|---|---:|---:|
| Book value of Special Foods, December 31, 20X2: | | |
| Common Stock | $200,000 | |
| Retained earnings ($120,700 + $75,900 − $40,000) | 156,600 | |
| Total book value | $356,600 | |
| Unrealized 20X1 intercompany gain on upstream sale | (700) | |
| Intercompany gain realized in 20X2 | 100 | |
| Realized book value of Special Foods | $356,000 | |
| Noncontrolling stockholders' share | × .20 | |
| Noncontrolling interest, December 31, 20X2 | $ 71,200 | |

## Asset Transfers before Year-End

In cases in which an intercorporate asset transfer occurs during a period rather than at the end, a portion of the intercompany gain or loss is considered realized in the period of the transfer. When this occurs, the workpaper eliminating entries at the end of the year must include an adjustment of depreciation expense and accumulated depreciation. The amount of this adjustment is equal to the difference between the depreciation recorded by the purchaser and that which would have been recorded by the seller during the portion of the year elapsing after the intercorporate sale.

If, for example, the upstream sale of equipment from Special Foods to Peerless occurred on January 1, 20X1, rather than on December 31, 20X1, an additional eliminating entry identical to E(52) would be needed in the consolidation workpaper prepared for December 31, 20X1.

# INTERCOMPANY TRANSFERS OF AMORTIZABLE ASSETS

Production rights, patents, and other types of intangible assets may be sold to affiliated enterprises. Accounting for intangible assets usually differs from accounting for tangible assets in that amortizable intangibles normally are reported at the remaining unamortized balance without the use of a contra account. Other than netting the accumulated amortization on an intangible asset against the asset cost, the intercompany sale of intangibles is treated the same in consolidation as the intercompany sale of tangible assets.

## Summary of Key Concepts

Transactions between affiliated companies within a consolidated entity must be viewed as if they occurred within a single company. Under generally accepted accounting principles, the effects of transactions that are internal to an enterprise may not be included in external accounting reports. Therefore, the effects of all transactions between companies within the consolidated entity must be eliminated in preparing consolidated financial statements.

The elimination of intercompany transactions must include the removal of unrealized intercompany profits. When one company sells an asset to an affiliate within the consolidated entity, any intercompany profit is not considered realized until confirmed by subsequent events. If the asset has an unlimited life, as with land, the unrealized intercompany gain or loss is realized at the time the asset is resold to a party outside the consolidated entity. If the asset has a limited life, the unrealized intercompany gain or loss is considered to be realized over the remaining life of the asset as the asset is used and depreciated or amortized.

Consolidation procedures relating to unrealized gains and losses on intercompany transfers of assets involve workpaper adjustments to restate the assets and associated accounts, such as accumulated depreciation, to the balances that would be reported if there had been no intercompany transfer. In the period of transfer, the income assigned to the shareholders of the selling affiliate must be reduced by their share of the unrealized intercompany profit. If the sale is a downstream sale, the unrealized intercompany gain or loss is eliminated against the controlling interest. When an upstream sale occurs, the unrealized intercompany gain or loss is eliminated proportionately against the controlling and noncontrolling interests.

## Key Terms

downstream sale, *267*  
intercompany transfers, *261*  
intercorporate transfers, *261*

unrealized intercompany profit, *262*

upstream sale, *267*

---

## Appendix 6A Intercompany Transfers of Noncurrent Assets— Fully Adjusted Equity Method and Cost Method

A parent company may account for a subsidiary using any of several methods. So long as the subsidiary is to be consolidated, the method of accounting for the subsidiary on the parent's books will have no impact on the consolidated financial statements. While the primary focus of Chapter 6 is on consolidation following use of the basic equity method on the parent's books, two other methods are used in practice with some frequency as well. These methods are the fully adjusted equity method and the cost method.

### FULLY ADJUSTED EQUITY METHOD

A company that chooses to account for an investment using the fully adjusted equity method records its proportionate share of subsidiary income and dividends in the same manner as under the basic equity method. In addition, the investor's share of any unrealized profits from intercompany transactions is removed from the parent's income in the period of intercompany sale by reducing both the investment account and the income recognized from the investee. When the intercompany profits subsequently are realized, the investor increases both the investment account and the income recognized from the investee. With these adjustments, parent company net income normally equals the amount of consolidated net income allocated to the controlling interest.

As an illustration, assume the same facts as in the upstream sale of equipment discussed previously and reflected in Figure 6–7. Special Foods sells equipment to Peerless Products for $7,000 on December 31, 20X1, and reports total income for 20X1 of $50,700, including the $700 gain on the sale of the equipment. Special Foods originally purchased the equipment for $9,000 three years before the intercompany sale. Both companies use straight-line depreciation.

As illustrated previously, Special Foods records 20X1 depreciation on the equipment and the gain on the December 31, 20X1, sale of the equipment to Peerless with the following entries:

December 31, 20X1

| (53) | Depreciation Expense | 900 | |
| | Accumulated Depreciation | | 900 |
| | Record 20X1 depreciation expense on equipment sold. | | |

| (54) | Cash | 7,000 | |
| | Accumulated Depreciation | 2,700 | |
| | Equipment | | 9,000 |
| | Gain on Sale of Equipment | | 700 |
| | Record sale of equipment. | | |

Peerless records the purchase of the equipment from Special Foods with the following entry:

December 31, 20X1

| (55) | Equipment | 7,000 | |
| | Cash | | 7,000 |
| | Record purchase of equipment. | | |

## Fully Adjusted Equity-Method Entries—20X1

In applying the fully adjusted equity method, Peerless recognizes its 80 percent share of Special Foods' income and dividends for 20X1 in the same way as under the basic equity method:

| (56) | Cash | 24,000 | |
| | Investment in Special Foods Stock | | 24,000 |
| | Record dividends from Special Foods: | | |
| | $30,000 × .80 | | |

| (57) | Investment in Special Foods Stock | 40,560 | |
| | Income from Subsidiary | | 40,560 |
| | Record equity-method income: | | |
| | $50,700 × .80 | | |

An additional entry is needed under the fully adjusted equity method to reduce income by Peerless's proportionate share of the $700 unrealized intercompany gain:

| (58) | Income from Subsidiary | 560 | |
| | Investment in Special Foods Stock | | 560 |
| | Remove unrealized gain on sale of equipment: $700 × .80 | | |

Entries (57) and (58) together record total income from Special Foods of $40,000. This amount is equal to Peerless's share of the realized net income of Special Foods, computed as follows:

| | |
|---|---:|
| Reported net income of Special Foods for 20X1 | $50,700 |
| Unrealized gain on intercompany sale | (700) |
| Realized net income of Special Foods for 20X1 | $50,000 |
| Peerless's proportionate share | × .80 |
| Peerless's income from Special Foods, 20X1 | $40,000 |

Because the intercompany sale is an upstream sale, only the parent's share of the unrealized gain is deducted in deriving equity-method net income. If the sale were downstream, the full $700 amount of the unrealized gain would be deducted in entry (58).

After the equity-method adjustments for December 31, 20X1, the investment account has a balance of $256,000:

| | |
|---|---:|
| Original purchase price of Special Foods stock | $240,000 |
| Peerless's proportionate share of Special Foods' income ($50,700 × .80) | 40,560 |
| Peerless's share of Special Foods' dividends ($30,000 × .80) | (24,000) |
| Peerless's share of unrealized gain ($700 × .80) | (560) |
| Balance of investment account, December 31, 20X1 | $256,000 |

Note that at the end of 20X1, Peerless's income and the investment account both are lower than had the basic equity method been used to account for the investment in Special Foods. The $560 difference is equal to Peerless's share of the unrealized intercompany gain ($700 × .80).

## Consolidation Workpaper—20X1

The consolidation workpaper prepared as of December 31, 20X1, is presented in Figure 6–9. It is the same as that presented in Figure 6–7, except where modified to reflect use of the fully adjusted equity method.

Four eliminating entries appear in the consolidation workpaper prepared as of December 31, 20X1:

| | | | |
|---|---|---:|---:|
| E(59) | Income from Subsidiary | 40,000 | |
| | Dividends Declared | | 24,000 |
| | Investment in Special Foods Stock | | 16,000 |
| | Eliminate income from subsidiary. | | |
| | | | |
| E(60) | Income to Noncontrolling Interest | 10,000 | |
| | Dividends Declared | | 6,000 |
| | Noncontrolling Interest | | 4,000 |
| | Assign income to noncontrolling interest: | | |
| | $10,000 = ($50,700 – $700) × .20 | | |
| | | | |
| E(61) | Common Stock—Special Foods | 200,000 | |
| | Retained Earnings, January 1 | 100,000 | |
| | Investment in Special Foods Stock | | 240,000 |
| | Noncontrolling Interest | | 60,000 |
| | Eliminate beginning investment balance. | | |
| | | | |
| E(62) | Buildings and Equipment | 2,000 | |
| | Gain on Sale of Equipment | 700 | |
| | Accumulated Depreciation | | 2,700 |
| | Eliminate unrealized gain on upstream sale of equipment. | | |

All these entries are the same as those in Figure 6–7 prepared following use of the basic equity method, except for entry E(59). This entry eliminates the income recorded by Peerless under the equity method and differs from entry E(44) in Figure 6–7 by the amount of the unrealized profit adjustment recorded by Peerless with entry (58). The remainder of the workpaper is completed the same way as when the basic equity method is used.

Although entry (58) removed a pro rata share of the unrealized gain from the income reported on Peerless's books, it did not eliminate the gain from consolidated net income. Entry (58) changes only the amount of income from the subsidiary recognized by Peerless and the balance in the investment account. These balances, in turn, are eliminated by entries E(59) and E(61). The gain account entered on Special Foods' books at the time the equipment is sold is unaffected by the entries recorded by Peerless and, therefore, carries over to the consolidation workpaper. Entry E(62) is needed to prevent the gain from appearing in the consolidated income statement.

**FIGURE 6–9**  December 31, 20X1, Fully Adjusted Equity-Method Consolidation Workpaper, Period of Intercompany Sale; Upstream Sale of Equipment

| Item | Peerless Products | Special Foods | Eliminations Debit | Eliminations Credit | Consolidated |
|---|---|---|---|---|---|
| Sales | 400,000 | 200,000 | | | 600,000 |
| Gain on Sale of Equipment | | 700 | (62) 700 | | |
| Income from Subsidiary | 40,000 | | (59) 40,000 | | |
| Credits | 440,000 | 200,700 | | | 600,000 |
| Cost of Goods Sold | 170,000 | 115,000 | | | 285,000 |
| Depreciation and Amortization | 50,000 | 20,000 | | | 70,000 |
| Other Expenses | 40,000 | 15,000 | | | 55,000 |
| Debits | (260,000) | (150,000) | | | (410,000) |
| Consolidated Net Income | | | | | 190,000 |
| Income to Noncontrolling Interest | | | (60) 10,000 | | (10,000) |
| Income, carry forward | 180,000 | 50,700 | 50,700 | | 180,000 |
| Retained Earnings, January 1 | 300,000 | 100,000 | (61) 100,000 | | 300,000 |
| Income, from above | 180,000 | 50,700 | 50,700 | | 180,000 |
| | 480,000 | 150,700 | | | 480,000 |
| Dividends Declared | (60,000) | (30,000) | | (59) 24,000 | |
| | | | | (60) 6,000 | (60,000) |
| Retained Earnings, December 31, carry forward | 420,000 | 120,700 | 150,700 | 30,000 | 420,000 |
| Cash | 257,000 | 82,000 | | | 339,000 |
| Accounts Receivable | 75,000 | 50,000 | | | 125,000 |
| Inventory | 100,000 | 75,000 | | | 175,000 |
| Land | 175,000 | 40,000 | | | 215,000 |
| Buildings and Equipment | 807,000 | 591,000 | (62) 2,000 | | 1,400,000 |
| Investment in Special Foods Stock | 256,000 | | | (59) 16,000 | |
| | | | | (61) 240,000 | |
| Debits | 1,670,000 | 838,000 | | | 2,254,000 |
| Accumulated Depreciation | 450,000 | 317,300 | | (62) 2,700 | 770,000 |
| Accounts Payable | 100,000 | 100,000 | | | 200,000 |
| Bonds Payable | 200,000 | 100,000 | | | 300,000 |
| Common Stock | 500,000 | 200,000 | (61) 200,000 | | 500,000 |
| Retained Earnings, from above | 420,000 | 120,700 | 150,700 | 30,000 | 420,000 |
| Noncontrolling Interest | | | | (60) 4,000 | |
| | | | | (61) 60,000 | 64,000 |
| Credits | 1,670,000 | 838,000 | 352,700 | 352,700 | 2,254,000 |

Elimination entries:
(59) Eliminate income from subsidiary.
(60) Assign income to noncontrolling interest.
(61) Eliminate beginning investment balance.
(62) Eliminate unrealized gain on upstream sale of equipment.

## Fully Adjusted Equity-Method Entries—20X2

In 20X2, Peerless records its share of Special Foods' $75,900 income and $40,000 of dividends with the following entries:

| (63) | Cash | 32,000 | |
| | Investment in Special Foods Stock | | 32,000 |
| | Record dividends from Special Foods: | | |
| | $40,000 × .80 | | |

| (64) | Investment in Special Foods Stock | 60,720 | |
| | Income from Subsidiary | | 60,720 |
| | Record equity-method income: | | |
| | $75,900 × .80 | | |

Peerless records an additional entry under the fully adjusted equity method to increase income for the partial realization of the unrealized intercompany gain:

| (65) | Investment in Special Foods Stock | 80 | |
| | Income from Subsidiary | | 80 |
| | Recognize portion of gain on sale of equipment: | | |
| | ($700 ÷ 7 years) × .80 | | |

The gain on the 20X1 intercompany transfer is viewed as being realized over a seven-year period. The $100 of intercompany gain realized each year is equal to the difference between the amount of depreciation recorded by Peerless ($1,000) and the amount that would have been recorded by Special Foods had there been no intercompany transfer ($900). Because depreciation expense will be adjusted in the preparation of consolidated financial statements to the amount that would have been reported if there had been no intercompany transfer, consolidated net income will be increased by $100. This increase will be allocated between the controlling and noncontrolling interests in the upstream case.

Entry (65) adds to Peerless's equity-method income a proportionate share of the part of the gain considered realized during 20X2. Recall that Peerless's 20X1 income was reduced by a proportionate share of the unrealized gain. Therefore, Peerless's portion of the realized part of the gain ($100 × .80) is put back into its income and the investment account in 20X2.

## Consolidation Workpaper—20X2

The consolidation workpaper for 20X2 is shown in Figure 6–10. The following elimination entries are included in the workpaper:

| E(66) | Income from Subsidiary | 60,800 | |
| | Dividends Declared | | 32,000 |
| | Investment in Special Foods Stock | | 28,800 |
| | Eliminate income from subsidiary: | | |
| | $60,800 = ($75,900 + $100) × .80 | | |

| E(67) | Income to Noncontrolling Interest | 15,200 | |
| | Dividends Declared | | 8,000 |
| | Noncontrolling Interest | | 7,200 |
| | Assign income to noncontrolling interest: | | |
| | $15,200 = ($75,900 + $100) × .20 | | |

| E(68) | Common Stock—Special Foods | 200,000 | |
| | Retained Earnings, January 1 | 120,700 | |
| | Investment in Special Foods Stock | | 256,560 |
| | Noncontrolling Interest | | 64,140 |
| | Eliminate beginning investment balance: | | |
| | $256,560 = ($200,000 + $120,700) × .80 | | |
| | $64,140 = ($200,000 + $120,700) × .20 | | |

| E(69) | Buildings and Equipment | 2,000 | |
| | Investment in Special Foods Stock | 560 | |
| | Noncontrolling Interest | 140 | |
| | Accumulated Depreciation | | 2,700 |
| | Eliminate unrealized gain on upstream sale of equipment. | | |

| E(70) | Accumulated Depreciation | 100 | |
| | Depreciation Expense | | 100 |
| | Eliminate excess depreciation. | | |

**FIGURE 6–10** December 31, 20X2, Fully Adjusted Equity-Method Consolidation Workpaper, Next Period following Intercompany Sale; Upstream Sale of Equipment

| Item | Peerless Products | Special Foods | Eliminations Debit | Eliminations Credit | Consolidated |
|---|---|---|---|---|---|
| Sales | 450,000 | 300,000 | | | 750,000 |
| Income from Subsidiary | 60,800 | | (66) 60,800 | | |
| Credits | 510,800 | 300,000 | | | 750,000 |
| Cost of Goods Sold | 180,000 | 160,000 | | | 340,000 |
| Depreciation and Amortization | 51,000 | 19,100 | | (70) 100 | 70,000 |
| Other Expenses | 60,000 | 45,000 | | | 105,000 |
| Debits | (291,000) | (224,100) | | | (515,000) |
| Consolidated Net Income | | | | | 235,000 |
| Income to Noncontrolling Interest | | | (67) 15,200 | | (15,200) |
| Income, carry forward | 219,800 | 75,900 | 76,000 | 100 | 219,800 |
| Retained Earnings, January 1 | 420,000 | 120,700 | (68) 120,700 | | 420,000 |
| Income, from above | 219,800 | 75,900 | 76,000 | 100 | 219,800 |
| | 639,800 | 196,600 | | | 639,800 |
| Dividends Declared | (60,000) | (40,000) | | (66) 32,000 | |
| | | | | (67) 8,000 | (60,000) |
| Retained Earnings, December 31, carry forward | 579,800 | 156,600 | 196,700 | 40,100 | 579,800 |
| Cash | 284,000 | 92,000 | | | 376,000 |
| Accounts Receivable | 150,000 | 80,000 | | | 230,000 |
| Inventory | 180,000 | 90,000 | | | 270,000 |
| Land | 175,000 | 40,000 | | | 215,000 |
| Buildings and Equipment | 807,000 | 591,000 | (69) 2,000 | | 1,400,000 |
| Investment in Special Foods Stock | 284,800 | | (69) 560 | (66) 28,800 | |
| | | | | (68) 256,560 | |
| Debits | 1,880,800 | 893,000 | | | 2,491,000 |
| Accumulated Depreciation | 501,000 | 336,400 | (70) 100 | (69) 2,700 | 840,000 |
| Accounts Payable | 100,000 | 100,000 | | | 200,000 |
| Bonds Payable | 200,000 | 100,000 | | | 300,000 |
| Common Stock | 500,000 | 200,000 | (68) 200,000 | | 500,000 |
| Retained Earnings, from above | 579,800 | 156,600 | 196,700 | 40,100 | 579,800 |
| Noncontrolling Interest | | | (69) 140 | (67) 7,200 | |
| | | | | (68) 64,140 | 71,200 |
| Credits | 1,880,800 | 893,000 | 399,500 | 399,500 | 2,491,000 |

Elimination entries:
(66) Eliminate income from subsidiary.
(67) Assign income to noncontrolling interest.
(68) Eliminate beginning investment balance.
(69) Eliminate unrealized gain on upstream sale of equipment.
(70) Eliminate excess depreciation.

These entries are the same as the eliminating entries used following application of the basic equity method, with two differences. First, entry E(66) eliminates Special Foods' income and dividends recognized by Peerless. Because the 20X2 income recognized by Peerless under the fully adjusted equity method includes Peerless's share of the realized 20X1 intercompany gain, which is not included when using the basic equity method, the income elimination is $80 ($100 × .80) higher following use of the fully adjusted equity method.

The second difference is in entry E(69). When the basic equity method is used, the parent's share of the intercompany gain unrealized at the beginning of 20X2 is included in its retained earnings and must be eliminated when consolidating. This was accomplished in the basic equity illustration through entry E(51). When the fully adjusted equity method is used, however, the parent's share of the unrealized gain is deducted from income on the parent's books in the year of the intercompany transfer and subsequently is not included in retained earnings. Therefore, no additional elimination of retained earnings is needed.

Replacing the debit to Retained Earnings in entry E(51) is a debit to the investment account in entry E(69). Because the investment account is reduced at the same time that the unrealized income is deducted from the parent's income, eliminating entry E(68), which credits the investment account for an amount equal to the parent's proportionate share of the beginning subsidiary stockholders' equity balances, eliminates an amount greater than the actual beginning investment account balance. The additional amount is equal to the parent's share of the intercompany gain unrealized at the beginning of the year. Entry E(69) debits the investment account for that amount, and the two entries together, E(68) and E(69), fully eliminate the beginning balance of the investment.

All other eliminations are the same under both the basic and the fully adjusted equity methods.

# COST METHOD

When using the cost method of accounting for an investment in a subsidiary, the parent records dividends received from the subsidiary during the period as income. No entries are made under the cost method to record the parent's share of undistributed subsidiary earnings, amortize differential, or remove unrealized intercompany profits.

To illustrate consolidation following an intercompany sale of equipment when the parent accounts for its subsidiary investment using the cost method, assume the same facts as in the previous illustrations of an upstream sale.

## Consolidation Workpaper—20X1

The workpaper illustrated in Figure 6–11 is used in preparing consolidated financial statements for 20X1 following the upstream sale of equipment to Peerless by Special Foods. The following elimination entries appear in the workpaper, assuming Peerless uses the cost method to account for its investment:

| | | | |
|---|---|---:|---:|
| E(71) | Dividend Income | 24,000 | |
| |     Dividends Declared | | 24,000 |
| | Eliminate dividend income from subsidiary: | | |
| |     $30,000 \times .80$ | | |
| E(72) | Income to Noncontrolling Interest | 10,000 | |
| |     Dividends Declared | | 6,000 |
| |     Noncontrolling Interest | | 4,000 |
| | Assign income to noncontrolling interest: | | |
| |     $10,000 = (\$50,700 - \$700) \times .20$ | | |
| E(73) | Common Stock—Special Foods | 200,000 | |
| | Retained Earnings, January 1 | 100,000 | |
| |     Investment in Special Foods Stock | | 240,000 |
| |     Noncontrolling Interest | | 60,000 |
| | Eliminate investment balance at date of acquisition. | | |
| E(74) | Buildings and Equipment | 2,000 | |
| | Gain on Sale of Equipment | 700 | |
| |     Accumulated Depreciation | | 2,700 |
| | Eliminate unrealized gain on upstream sale of equipment. | | |

Entry E(71) eliminates Peerless's share of Special Foods' 20X1 dividends. All other eliminating entries are the same as under the basic equity method in the year of acquisition.

## Consolidation Workpaper—20X2

The consolidation workpaper prepared for December 31, 20X2, is presented in Figure 6–12. The following eliminating entries are needed in the workpaper:

**FIGURE 6–11**  December 31, 20X1, Cost-Method Consolidation Workpaper, Period of Intercompany Sale; Upstream Sale of Equipment

| Item | Peerless Products | Special Foods | Eliminations Debit | Eliminations Credit | Consolidated |
|------|------:|------:|------|------|------:|
| Sales | 400,000 | 200,000 | | | 600,000 |
| Gain on Sale of Equipment | | 700 | (74) 700 | | |
| Dividend Income | 24,000 | | (71) 24,000 | | |
| Credits | 424,000 | 200,700 | | | 600,000 |
| Cost of Goods Sold | 170,000 | 115,000 | | | 285,000 |
| Depreciation and Amortization | 50,000 | 20,000 | | | 70,000 |
| Other Expenses | 40,000 | 15,000 | | | 55,000 |
| Debits | (260,000) | (150,000) | | | (410,000) |
| Consolidated Net Income | | | | | 190,000 |
| Income to Noncontrolling Interest | | | (72) 10,000 | | (10,000) |
| Income, carry forward | 164,000 | 50,700 | 34,700 | | 180,000 |
| Retained Earnings, January 1 | 300,000 | 100,000 | (73) 100,000 | | 300,000 |
| Income, from above | 164,000 | 50,700 | 34,700 | | 180,000 |
| | 464,000 | 150,700 | | | 480,000 |
| Dividends Declared | (60,000) | (30,000) | | (71) 24,000 | |
| | | | | (72) 6,000 | (60,000) |
| Retained Earnings, December 31, carry forward | 404,000 | 120,700 | 134,700 | 30,000 | 420,000 |
| Cash | 257,000 | 82,000 | | | 339,000 |
| Accounts Receivable | 75,000 | 50,000 | | | 125,000 |
| Inventory | 100,000 | 75,000 | | | 175,000 |
| Land | 175,000 | 40,000 | | | 215,000 |
| Buildings and Equipment | 807,000 | 591,000 | (74) 2,000 | | 1,400,000 |
| Investment in Special Foods Stock | 240,000 | | | (73) 240,000 | |
| Debits | 1,654,000 | 838,000 | | | 2,254,000 |
| Accumulated Depreciation | 450,000 | 317,300 | | (74) 2,700 | 770,000 |
| Accounts Payable | 100,000 | 100,000 | | | 200,000 |
| Bonds Payable | 200,000 | 100,000 | | | 300,000 |
| Common Stock | 500,000 | 200,000 | (73) 200,000 | | 500,000 |
| Retained Earnings, from above | 404,000 | 120,700 | 134,700 | 30,000 | 420,000 |
| Noncontrolling Interest | | | | (72) 4,000 | |
| | | | | (73) 60,000 | 64,000 |
| Credits | 1,654,000 | 838,000 | 336,700 | 336,700 | 2,254,000 |

Elimination entries:
(71) Eliminate dividend income from subsidiary.
(72) Assign income to noncontrolling interest.
(73) Eliminate investment balance at date of acquisition.
(74) Eliminate unrealized gain on upstream sale of equipment.

| | | | | |
|------|------|------|------:|------:|
| E(75) | Dividend Income | | 32,000 | |
| | Dividends Declared | | | 32,000 |
| | Eliminate dividend income from subsidiary: | | | |
| | $40,000 \times .80$ | | | |
| E(76) | Income to Noncontrolling Interest | | 15,200 | |
| | Dividends Declared | | | 8,000 |
| | Noncontrolling Interest | | | 7,200 |
| | Assign income to noncontrolling interest: | | | |
| | $15,200 = ($75,900 + $100) \times .20$ | | | |

**FIGURE 6–12** December 31, 20X2, Cost-Method Consolidation Workpaper, Next Period following Intercompany Sale; Upstream Sale of Equipment

| Item | Peerless Products | Special Foods | Eliminations Debit | | Eliminations Credit | | Consolidated |
|---|---|---|---|---|---|---|---|
| Sales | 450,000 | 300,000 | | | | | 750,000 |
| Dividend Income | 32,000 | | (75) | 32,000 | | | |
| Credits | 482,000 | 300,000 | | | | | 750,000 |
| Cost of Goods Sold | 180,000 | 160,000 | | | | | 340,000 |
| Depreciation and Amortization | 51,000 | 19,100 | | | (80) | 100 | 70,000 |
| Other Expenses | 60,000 | 45,000 | | | | | 105,000 |
| Debits | (291,000) | (224,100) | | | | | (515,000) |
| Consolidated Net Income | | | | | | | 235,000 |
| Income to Noncontrolling Interest | | | (76) | 15,200 | | | (15,200) |
| Income, carry forward | 191,000 | 75,900 | | 47,200 | | 100 | 219,800 |
| Retained Earnings, January 1 | 404,000 | 120,700 | (77) | 100,000 | | | |
| | | | (78) | 4,140 | | | |
| | | | (79) | 560 | | | 420,000 |
| Income, from above | 191,000 | 75,900 | | 47,200 | | 100 | 219,800 |
| | 595,000 | 196,600 | | | | | 639,800 |
| Dividends Declared | (60,000) | (40,000) | | | (75) | 32,000 | |
| | | | | | (76) | 8,000 | (60,000) |
| Retained Earnings, December 31, carry forward | 535,000 | 156,600 | | 151,900 | | 40,100 | 579,800 |
| Cash | 284,000 | 92,000 | | | | | 376,000 |
| Accounts Receivable | 150,000 | 80,000 | | | | | 230,000 |
| Inventory | 180,000 | 90,000 | | | | | 270,000 |
| Land | 175,000 | 40,000 | | | | | 215,000 |
| Buildings and Equipment | 807,000 | 591,000 | (79) | 2,000 | | | 1,400,000 |
| Investment in Special Foods Stock | 240,000 | | | | (77) | 240,000 | |
| Debits | 1,836,000 | 893,000 | | | | | 2,491,000 |
| Accumulated Depreciation | 501,000 | 336,400 | (80) | 100 | (79) | 2,700 | 840,000 |
| Accounts Payable | 100,000 | 100,000 | | | | | 200,000 |
| Bonds Payable | 200,000 | 100,000 | | | | | 300,000 |
| Common Stock | 500,000 | 200,000 | (77) | 200,000 | | | 500,000 |
| Retained Earnings, from above | 535,000 | 156,600 | | 151,900 | | 40,100 | 579,800 |
| Noncontrolling Interest | | | (79) | 140 | (76) | 7,200 | |
| | | | | | (77) | 60,000 | |
| | | | | | (78) | 4,140 | 71,200 |
| Credits | 1,836,000 | 893,000 | | 354,140 | | 354,140 | 2,491,000 |

Elimination entries:
(75) Eliminate dividend income from subsidiary.
(76) Assign income to noncontrolling interest.
(77) Eliminate investment balance at date of acquisition.
(78) Assign undistributed prior earnings of subsidiary to noncontrolling interest.
(79) Eliminate unrealized gain on upstream sale of equipment.
(80) Eliminate excess depreciation.

| E(77) | Common Stock—Special Foods | 200,000 | |
|---|---|---|---|
| | Retained Earnings, January 1 | 100,000 | |
| | Investment in Special Foods Stock | | 240,000 |
| | Noncontrolling Interest | | 60,000 |
| | Eliminate investment balance at date of acquisition. | | |

| | | | |
|---|---|---|---|
| E(78) | Retained Earnings, January 1 | 4,140 | |
| | Noncontrolling Interest | | 4,140 |
| | Assign undistributed prior earnings of subsidiary to | | |
| | noncontrolling interest: ($120,700 − $100,000) × .20 | | |
| | | | |
| E(79) | Buildings and Equipment | 2,000 | |
| | Retained Earnings, January 1 | 560 | |
| | Noncontrolling Interest | 140 | |
| | Accumulated Depreciation | | 2,700 |
| | Eliminate unrealized gain on upstream sale of equipment. | | |
| | | | |
| E(80) | Accumulated Depreciation | 100 | |
| | Depreciation Expense | | 100 |
| | Eliminate excess depreciation. | | |

Entry E(75) eliminates Peerless's share of Special Foods' dividends. Entry E(76) assigns income to the noncontrolling interest in the normal manner, taking into consideration a proportionate share of the $100 of intercompany gain considered realized during 20X2. The investment elimination entry normally does not change under the cost method because the carrying amount of the investment does not change. Therefore, entry E(77) is the same as the investment elimination entry in 20X1. However, an additional entry, E(78), is needed to assign a proportionate share of Special Foods' undistributed prior years' income since the date of combination to the noncontrolling interest [($50,700 − $30,000) × .20]. The portion of beginning retained earnings that is neither eliminated nor assigned to the noncontrolling interest carries over in the workpaper to the Consolidated column as the beginning balance of consolidated retained earnings.

Entries E(79) and E(80) eliminate the effects of the intercompany transfer and are the same as when consolidation follows use of the basic equity method.

---

**Questions**

**Q6-1** When are profits on intercorporate sales considered to be realized? Explain.

**Q6-2** What is an upstream sale? Which company may have unrealized profits on its books in an upstream sale?

**Q6-3** What dollar amounts in the consolidated financial statements will be incorrect if intercompany services are not eliminated?

**Q6-4** How are unrealized profits on current-period intercorporate sales treated in preparing the income statement for (*a*) the selling company and (*b*) the consolidated entity?

**Q6-5** How are unrealized profits treated in the consolidated income statement if the intercorporate sale occurred in a prior period and the transferred item is sold to a nonaffiliate in the current period?

**Q6-6** How are unrealized intercorporate profits treated in the consolidated statements if the intercorporate sale occurred in a prior period and the profits have not been realized by the end of the current period?

**Q6-7** What is a downstream sale? Which company may have unrealized profits on its books in a downstream sale?

**Q6-8** What portion of the unrealized intercorporate profit is eliminated in a downstream sale? In an upstream sale?

**Q6-9** How is the effect of unrealized intercorporate profits on consolidated net income different between an upstream and a downstream sale?

**Q6-10** Unrealized profits from a prior-year upstream sale were realized in the current period. What effect will this event have on income assigned to the noncontrolling interest in the consolidated income statement for the current period?

**Q6-11** A subsidiary sold a depreciable asset to the parent company at a profit in the current period. Will the income assigned to the noncontrolling interest in the consolidated income statement for the current period be more than, less than, or equal to a proportionate share of the reported net income of the subsidiary? Why?

**Q6-12** A subsidiary sold a depreciable asset to the parent company at a profit of $1,000 in the current period. Will the income assigned to the noncontrolling interest in the consolidated income statement for the current period be more if the intercorporate sale occurs on January 1 or on December 31? Why?

**Q6-13** If a company sells a depreciable asset to its subsidiary at a profit on December 31, 20X3, what account balances must be eliminated or adjusted in preparing the consolidated income statement for 20X3?

**Q6-14** If the sale in the preceding question occurs on January 1, 20X3, what additional account will require adjustment in preparing the consolidated income statement?

**Q6-15** In the period in which an intercorporate sale occurs, how do the consolidation eliminating entries differ when unrealized profits pertain to an intangible asset rather than a tangible asset?

**Q6-16** When is unrealized profit on an intercompany sale of land considered realized? When is profit on an intercompany sale of equipment considered realized? Why do the treatments differ?

**Q6-17** In the elimination of a prior-period unrealized intercorporate gain on depreciable assets, why does the debit to Retained Earnings decrease over time?

**Q6-18A** A parent company may use on its books one of several different methods of accounting for its ownership of a subsidiary: (*a*) cost method, (*b*) basic equity method, or (*c*) fully adjusted equity method. How will the choice of method affect the reported balance in the investment account when there are unrealized intercorporate profits on the parent's books at the end of the period?

---

## Cases

### C6-1 Correction of Elimination Procedures

Plug Corporation purchased 60 percent of Coy Company's common stock approximately 10 years ago. On January 1, 20X2, Coy sold equipment to Plug for $850,000 and recorded a $150,000 loss on the sale. Coy had purchased the equipment for $1,200,000 on January 1, 20X0, and was depreciating it on a straight-line basis over 12 years with no assumed residual value.

*Research*
*FARS*

In preparing Plug's consolidated financial statements for 20X2, its chief accountant increased the reported amount of the equipment by $150,000 and eliminated the loss on the sale of equipment recorded by Coy. No other eliminations or adjustments related to the equipment were made.

#### Required

As a member of the audit firm Gotcha and Gotcha, you have been asked, after reviewing Plug's consolidated income statement, to prepare a memo to Plug's controller detailing the elimination procedures that should be followed in transferring equipment between subsidiary and parent. Include citations to or quotations from the authoritative literature to support your recommendations. Your memo should include the correct eliminating entry and explain why each debit and credit is needed.

### C6-2 Elimination of Intercorporate Services

Dream Corporation owns 90 percent of Classic Company's common stock and 70 percent of Plain Company's stock. Dream provides legal services to each subsidiary and bills it for 150 percent of the cost of the services provided. During 20X3, Classic recorded legal expenses of $80,000 when it paid Dream for legal assistance in an unsuccessful patent infringement suit against another company, and Plain recorded legal expenses of $150,000 when it paid Dream for legal work associated with the purchase of additional property in Montana to expand an existing strip mine owned by Plain. In preparing the consolidated statements at December 31, 20X3, no eliminations were made for intercompany services. When asked why no entries had been made to eliminate the intercompany services, Dream's chief accountant replied that intercompany services are not mentioned in the company accounting manual and can be ignored.

*Research*
*FARS*

#### Required

Prepare a memo detailing the appropriate treatment of legal services provided by Dream to Plain and Classic during 20X3. Include citations to or quotations from authoritative accounting standards to support your recommendations. In addition, provide the eliminating entries at December 31, 20X3, and 20X4, needed as a result of the services provided in 20X3, and explain why each debit or credit is necessary.

### C6-3 Noncontrolling Interest

Current reporting standards require the consolidated entity to include all the revenues, expenses, assets, and liabilities of the parent and its subsidiaries in the consolidated financial statements.

"A" indicates that the item relates to "Appendix A."

*Understanding*  When the parent does not own all of a subsidiary's shares, various rules and procedures exist with regard to the assignment of income and net assets to noncontrolling shareholders and the way in which the noncontrolling interest is to be reported.

### Required

*a.* How is the amount of income assigned to noncontrolling shareholders in the consolidated income statement computed if there are no unrealized intercorporate profits on the subsidiary's books?

*b.* How is the amount reported for the noncontrolling interest in the consolidated balance sheet computed if there are no unrealized intercorporate profits on the subsidiary's books?

*c.* What effect do unrealized intercorporate profits have on the computation of income assigned to the noncontrolling interest if the profits arose from a transfer of (1) land or (2) equipment?

*d.* Are the noncontrolling shareholders of a subsidiary likely to find the amounts assigned to them in the consolidated financial statements useful? Explain.

### C6-4  Intercompany Sale of Services

Diamond Manufacturing Company regularly purchases janitorial and maintenance services from its wholly owned subsidiary, Schwartz Maintenance Services Inc. Schwartz bills Diamond monthly
*Analysis*  at its regular rates for the services provided, with the services consisting primarily of cleaning, groundskeeping, and small repairs. The cost of providing the services that Schwartz sells consists mostly of salaries and associated labor costs that total about 60 percent of the amount billed. Diamond issues consolidated financial statements annually.

### Required

*a.* When Diamond prepares consolidated financial statements, what account balances of Diamond and Schwartz related to the intercompany sale of services must be adjusted or eliminated in the consolidation workpaper? What impact do these adjustments or eliminations have on consolidated net income?

*b.* In the case of intercompany sales of services at a profit, at what point in time are the intercompany profits considered to be realized? Explain.

### C6-5  Intercompany Profits

Companies have many different practices for pricing transfers of goods and services from one affiliate to another. Regardless of the approaches used for internal decision making and performance
*Analysis*  evaluation or for tax purposes, all intercompany profits, unless immaterial, are supposed to be eliminated when preparing consolidated financial statements until confirmed through transactions with external parties.

### Required

*a.* Century Telephone Enterprises Inc. provides certain services to its subsidiaries, and some of its service subsidiaries provide services and materials to Century's telephone subsidiaries. How are these transactions billed among the affiliates? Are intercompany profits eliminated when consolidated financial statements are prepared? Explain.

*b.* Verizon Communications also is in the telephone business, although it is larger and more diversified than Century Telephone. How does it treat intercompany profits for consolidation?

*c.* Harley-Davidson operates in two business areas: (1) motorcycles and related products and (2) financial services. Does Harley eliminate all effects of intercompany transactions when preparing consolidated financial statements? Explain. What effect does its treatment have on consolidated net income?

---

**Exercises**  **E6-1**  ### Multiple-Choice Questions on Intercompany Transfers [AICPA Adapted]

For each question, select the single best answer.

1. Water Company owns 80 percent of Fire Company's outstanding common stock. On December 31, 20X9, Fire sold equipment to Water at a price in excess of Fire's carrying amount, but less than its original cost. On a consolidated balance sheet at December 31, 20X9, the carrying amount of the equipment should be reported at:

   *a.* Water's original cost.

   *b.* Fire's original cost.

    *c.* Water's original cost less Fire's recorded gain.

    *d.* Water's original cost less 80 percent of Fire's recorded gain.

2. Company J acquired all of Company K's outstanding common stock in exchange for cash. The acquisition price exceeds the fair value of net assets acquired. How should Company J determine the amounts to be reported for the plant and equipment and long-term debt acquired from Company K?

| Plant and Equipment | Long-Term Debt |
|---|---|
| *a.* K's carrying amount | K's carrying amount |
| *b.* K's carrying amount | Fair value |
| *c.* Fair value | K's carrying amount |
| *d.* Fair value | Fair value |

3. Port Inc. owns 100 percent of Salem Inc. On January 1, 20X2, Port sold delivery equipment to Salem at a gain. Port had owned the equipment for two years and used a five-year straight-line depreciation rate with no residual value. Salem is using a three-year straight-line depreciation rate with no residual value for the equipment. In the consolidated income statement, Salem's recorded depreciation expense on the equipment for 20X2 will be decreased by:

    *a.* 20 percent of the gain on the sale.

    *b.* 33⅓ percent of the gain on the sale.

    *c.* 50 percent of the gain on the sale.

    *d.* 100 percent of the gain on the sale.

4. On January 1, 20X0, Poe Corporation sold a machine for $900,000 to Saxe Corporation, its wholly owned subsidiary. Poe paid $1,100,000 for this machine, which had accumulated depreciation of $250,000. Poe estimated a $100,000 salvage value and depreciated the machine using the straight-line method over 20 years, a policy that Saxe continued. In Poe's December 31, 20X0, consolidated balance sheet, this machine should be included in fixed-asset cost and accumulated depreciation as:

| | Cost | Accumulated Depreciation |
|---|---|---|
| *a.* | $1,100,000 | $300,000 |
| *b.* | $1,100,000 | $290,000 |
| *c.* | $ 900,000 | $ 40,000 |
| *d.* | $ 850,000 | $ 42,500 |

5. Scroll Inc., a wholly owned subsidiary of Pirn Inc., began operations on January 1, 20X1. The following information is from the condensed 20X1 income statements of Pirn and Scroll:

| | Pirn | Scroll |
|---|---|---|
| Sales | $500,000 | $300,000 |
| Cost of Goods Sold | (350,000) | (270,000) |
| Gross Profit | $150,000 | $ 30,000 |
| Depreciation | (40,000) | (10,000) |
| Other Expenses | (60,000) | (15,000) |
| Income from Operations | $ 50,000 | $ 5,000 |
| Gain on Sale of Equipment to Scroll | 12,000 | |
| Income before Taxes | $ 62,000 | $ 5,000 |

Equipment purchased by Scroll from Pirn for $36,000 on January 1, 20X1, is depreciated using the straight-line method over four years. What amount should be reported as depreciation expense in Pirn's 20X1 consolidated income statement?

    *a.* $50,000.

    *b.* $47,000.

    *c.* $44,000.

    *d.* $41,000.

## E6-2   Multiple-Choice Questions on Intercompany Transactions

Select the correct answer for each of the following questions.

1. Upper Company holds 60 percent of Lower Company's voting shares. During the preparation of consolidated financial statements for 20X5, the following eliminating entry was made:

| | | |
|---|---|---|
| Retained Earnings, January 1 | 10,000 | |
|     Land | | 10,000 |

    Which of the following statements is correct?

    *a.* Upper Company purchased land from Lower Company during 20X5.

    *b.* Upper Company purchased land from Lower Company before January 1, 20X5.

    *c.* Lower Company purchased land from Upper Company during 20X5.

    *d.* Lower Company purchased land from Upper Company before January 1, 20X5.

2. Middle Company holds 60 percent of Bottom Corporation's voting shares. Bottom has developed a new type of production equipment that appears to be quite marketable. It spent $40,000 in developing the equipment; however, Middle agreed to purchase the production rights for the machine for $100,000. If the intercompany sale occurred on January 1, 20X2, and the production rights are expected to have value for five years, at what amount should the rights be reported in the consolidated balance sheet for December 31, 20X2?

    *a.* $0.

    *b.* $32,000.

    *c.* $80,000.

    *d.* $100,000.

*Note:* Questions 3 through 6 are based on the following information:

On January 1, 20X4, Gold Company purchased a computer with an expected economic life of five years. On January 1, 20X6, Gold sold the computer to TLK Corporation and recorded the following entry:

| | | |
|---|---|---|
| Cash | 39,000 | |
| Accumulated Depreciation | 16,000 | |
|     Computer Equipment | | 40,000 |
|     Gain on Sale of Equipment | | 15,000 |

TLK Corporation holds 60 percent of Gold's voting shares. Gold reported net income of $45,000, and TLK reported income from its own operations of $85,000 for 20X6. There is no change in the estimated economic life of the equipment as a result of the intercorporate transfer.

3. In the preparation of the 20X6 consolidated income statement, depreciation expense will be:

    *a.* Debited for $5,000 in the eliminating entries.

    *b.* Credited for $5,000 in the eliminating entries.

    *c.* Debited for $13,000 in the eliminating entries.

    *d.* Credited for $13,000 in the eliminating entries.

4. In the preparation of the 20X6 consolidated balance sheet, computer equipment will be:

    *a.* Debited for $1,000.

    *b.* Debited for $15,000.

    *c.* Credited for $24,000.

    *d.* Debited for $40,000.

5. Income assigned to the noncontrolling interest in the 20X6 consolidated income statement will be:

    *a.* $12,000.

    *b.* $14,000.

    *c.* $18,000.

    *d.* $52,000.

6. Consolidated net income for 20X6 will be:

    *a.* $106,000.

    *b.* $112,000.

    *c.* $120,000.

    *d.* $130,000.

### E6-3 Elimination Entries for Land Transfer

Huckster Corporation purchased land on January 1, 20X1, for $20,000. On June 10, 20X4, it sold the land to its subsidiary, Lowly Corporation, for $30,000. Huckster owns 60 percent of Lowly's voting shares.

#### Required

*a.* Give the workpaper eliminating entries needed to remove the effects of the intercompany sale of land in preparing the consolidated financial statements for 20X4 and 20X5.

*b.* Give the workpaper eliminating entries needed on December 31, 20X4 and 20X5, if Lowly had initially purchased the land for $20,000 and then sold it to Huckster on June 10, 20X4, for $30,000.

### E6-4 Intercompany Services

Power Corporation owns 75 percent of Swift Company's stock. Swift provides health care services to its employees and those of Power. During 20X2, Power recorded $45,000 as health care expense for medical care given to its employees by Swift. Swift's costs incurred in providing the services to Power were $32,000.

#### Required

*a.* By what amount will consolidated net income change when the intercompany services are eliminated in preparing Power's consolidated statements for 20X2?

*b.* What would be the impact of eliminating the intercompany services on consolidated net income if Power owned 100 percent of Swift's stock rather than 75 percent? Explain.

*c.* If in its consolidated income statement for 20X2 Power had reported total health care costs of $70,000, what was the cost to Swift of providing health care services to its own employees?

### E6-5 Elimination Entries for Intercompany Services

On January 1, 20X5, Block Corporation started using a wholly owned subsidiary to deliver all its sales overnight to its customers. During 20X5, Block recorded delivery service expense of $76,000 and made payments of $58,000 to the subsidiary.

#### Required

Give the workpaper eliminating entries related to the intercompany services needed on December 31, 20X5, to prepare consolidated financial statements.

### E6-6 Elimination Entries for Depreciable Asset Transfer: Year-End Sale

Pam Corporation holds 70 percent ownership of Northern Enterprises. On December 31, 20X6, Northern paid Pam $40,000 for a truck that Pam had purchased for $45,000 on January 1, 20X2. The truck was considered to have a 15-year life from January 1, 20X2, and no residual value. Both companies depreciate equipment using the straight-line method.

#### Required

*a.* Give the workpaper eliminating entry or entries needed on December 31, 20X6, to remove the effects of the intercompany sale.

*b.* Give the workpaper eliminating entry or entries needed on December 31, 20X7, to remove the effects of the intercompany sale.

### E6-7 Transfer of Land

Bowen Corporation owns 70 percent of Roan Corporation's voting common stock. On March 12, 20X2, Roan sold land it had purchased for $140,000 to Bowen for $185,000. Bowen plans to build a new warehouse on the property in 20X3.

*Required*

a. Give the workpaper eliminating entries to remove the effects of the intercompany sale of land in preparing the consolidated financial statements at December 31, 20X2 and 20X3.

b. Give the workpaper eliminating entries needed at December 31, 20X3 and 20X4, if Bowen had initially purchased the land for $150,000 and sold it to Roan on March 12, 20X2, for $180,000.

### E6-8 Transfer of Depreciable Asset at Year-End

Frazer Corporation purchased 60 percent of Minnow Corporation's voting common stock on January 1, 20X1. On December 31, 20X5, Frazer received $210,000 from Minnow for a truck Frazer had purchased on January 1, 20X2, for $300,000. The truck is expected to have a 10-year useful life and no salvage value. Both companies depreciate trucks on a straight-line basis.

*Required*

a. Give the workpaper eliminating entry or entries needed at December 31, 20X5, to remove the effects of the intercompany sale.

b. Give the workpaper eliminating entry or entries needed at December 31, 20X6, to remove the effects of the intercompany sale.

### E6-9 Transfer of Depreciable Asset at Beginning of Year

Frazer Corporation purchased 60 percent of Minnow Corporation's voting common stock on January 1, 20X1. On January 1, 20X5, Frazer received $245,000 from Minnow for a truck Frazer had purchased on January 1, 20X2, for $300,000. The truck is expected to have a 10-year useful life and no salvage value. Both companies depreciate trucks on a straight-line basis.

*Required*

a. Give the workpaper eliminating entry or entries needed at December 31, 20X5, to remove the effects of the intercompany sale.

b. Give the workpaper eliminating entry or entries needed at December 31, 20X6, to remove the effects of the intercompany sale.

### E6-10 Sale of Equipment to Subsidiary in Current Period

On January 1, 20X7, Wainwrite Corporation sold to Lance Corporation equipment it had purchased for $150,000 and used for eight years. Wainwrite recorded a gain of $14,000 on the sale. The equipment has a total useful life of 15 years and is depreciated on a straight-line basis. Wainwrite holds 70 percent of Lance's voting common shares.

*Required*

a. Give the journal entry made by Wainwrite on January 1, 20X7, to record the sale of equipment.

b. Give the journal entries recorded by Lance during 20X7 to record the purchase of equipment and year-end depreciation expense.

c. Give the eliminating entry or entries related to the intercompany sale of equipment needed at December 31, 20X7, to prepare a full set of consolidated financial statements.

d. Give the eliminating entry or entries related to the equipment required at January 1, 20X8, to prepare a consolidated balance sheet only.

### E6-11 Upstream Sale of Equipment in Prior Period

Baywatch Industries has owned 80 percent of Tubberware Corporation for many years. On January 1, 20X6, Baywatch paid Tubberware $270,000 to acquire equipment that Tubberware had purchased on January 1, 20X3, for $300,000. The equipment is expected to have no scrap value and is depreciated over a 15-year useful life.

Baywatch reported operating earnings of $100,000 for 20X8 and paid dividends of $40,000. Tubberware reported net income of $40,000 and paid dividends of $20,000 in 20X8.

*Required*

a. Compute the amount reported as consolidated net income for 20X8.

b. By what amount would consolidated net income change if the equipment sale had been a downstream sale rather than an upstream sale?

c. Give the eliminating entry or entries required to eliminate the effects of the intercompany sale of equipment in preparing a full set of consolidated financial statements at December 31, 20X8.

### E6-12 Elimination Entries for Midyear Depreciable Asset Transfer

Kline Corporation holds 90 percent ownership of Andrews Company. On July 1, 20X3, Kline sold equipment that it had purchased for $30,000 on January 1, 20X1, to Andrews for $28,000. The equipment's original six-year estimated total economic life remains unchanged. Both companies use straight-line depreciation. The equipment's residual value is considered negligible.

#### Required

a. Give the eliminating entry or entries in the consolidation workpaper prepared as of December 31, 20X3, to remove the effects of the intercompany sale.

b. Give the eliminating entry or entries in the consolidation workpaper prepared as of December 31, 20X4, to remove the effects of the intercompany sale.

### E6-13 Consolidated Net Income Computation

Verry Corporation owns 75 percent of Spawn Corporation's voting common stock. Verry reported income from its separate operations of $90,000 and $110,000 in 20X4 and 20X5, respectively. Spawn reported net income of $60,000 and $40,000 in 20X4 and 20X5, respectively.

#### Required

a. Compute consolidated net income and the income assigned to the controlling interest for 20X4 and 20X5 if Verry sold land with a book value of $95,000 to Spawn for $120,000 on June 30, 20X4.

b. Compute consolidated net income and the amount of income assigned to the controlling interest in the consolidated statements for 20X4 and 20X5 if Spawn sold land with a book value of $95,000 to Verry for $120,000 on June 30, 20X4.

### E6-14 Elimination Entries for Intercompany Transfers

Grand Delivery Service acquired at book value 80 percent of the voting shares of Acme Real Estate Company. On that date, the fair value of the noncontrolling interest was equal to 20 percent of Acme's book value. Acme Real Estate reported common stock of $300,000 and retained earnings of $100,000. During 20X3 Grand Delivery provided courier services for Acme Real Estate in the amount of $15,000. Also during 20X3, Acme Real Estate purchased land for $1,000. It sold the land to Grand Delivery Service for $26,000 so that Grand Delivery could build a new transportation center. Grand Delivery reported $65,000 of operating income from its delivery operations in 20X3. Acme Real Estate reported net income of $40,000 and paid dividends of $10,000 in 20X3.

#### Required

a. Compute consolidated net income for 20X3.

b. Give all journal entries recorded by Grand Delivery Service related to its investment in Acme Real Estate assuming Grand uses the basic equity method in accounting for the investment.

c. Give all eliminating entries required in preparing a consolidation workpaper as of December 31, 20X3.

### E6-15 Sale of Building to Parent in Prior Period

Turner Company purchased 70 percent of Split Company's stock approximately 20 years ago. On December 31, 20X8, Turner purchased a building from Split for $300,000. Split had purchased the building on January 1, 20X1, at a cost of $400,000 and used straight-line depreciation on an expected life of 20 years. The asset's total estimated economic life is unchanged as a result of the intercompany sale.

#### Required

a. What amount of depreciation expense on the building will Turner report for 20X9?

b. What amount of depreciation expense would Split have reported for 20X9 if it had continued to own the building?

c. Give the eliminating entry or entries needed to eliminate the effects of the intercompany building transfer in preparing a full set of consolidated financial statements at December 31, 20X9.

 *d.* What amount of income will be assigned to the noncontrolling interest in the consolidated income statement for 20X9 if Split reports net income of $40,000 for 20X9?

 *e.* Split reports assets with a book value of $350,000 and liabilities of $150,000 at January 1, 20X9, and reports net income of $40,000 and dividends of $15,000 for 20X9. What amount will be assigned to the noncontrolling interest in the consolidated balance sheet at December 31, 20X9, assuming the fair value of the noncontrolling interest at the date of acquisition was equal to 30 percent of the book value of Split Company.

## E6-16   Intercompany Sale at a Loss

Parent Company holds 90 percent of Sunway Company's voting common shares. On December 31, 20X8, Parent recorded a loss of $16,000 on the sale of equipment to Sunway. At the time of the sale, the equipment's estimated remaining economic life was eight years.

### Required

 *a.* Will consolidated net income be increased or decreased when eliminating entries associated with the sale of equipment are made at December 31, 20X8? By what amount?

 *b.* Will consolidated net income be increased or decreased when eliminating entries associated with the sale of equipment are made at December 31, 20X9? By what amount?

## E6-17   Eliminating Entries following Intercompany Sale at a Loss

Brown Corporation holds 70 percent of Transom Company's voting common stock. On January 1, 20X2, Transom paid $300,000 to acquire a building with a 15-year expected economic life. Transom uses straight-line depreciation for all depreciable assets. On December 31, 20X7, Brown purchased the building from Transom for $144,000. Brown reported income, excluding investment income from Transom, of $125,000 and $150,000 for 20X7 and 20X8, respectively. Transom reported net income of $15,000 and $40,000 for 20X7 and 20X8, respectively.

### Required

 *a.* Give the appropriate eliminating entry or entries needed to eliminate the effects of the intercompany sale of the building in preparing consolidated financial statements for 20X7.

 *b.* Compute the amount to be reported as consolidated net income for 20X7 and the income to be allocated to the controlling interest.

 *c.* Give the appropriate eliminating entry or entries needed to eliminate the effects of the intercompany sale of the building in preparing consolidated financial statements for 20X8.

 *d.* Compute consolidated net income and the amount of income assigned to the controlling shareholders in the consolidated income statement for 20X8.

## E6-18   Multiple Transfers of Asset

Swanson Corporation purchased land from Clayton Corporation for $240,000 on December 20, 20X3. This purchase followed a series of transactions between Swanson-controlled subsidiaries. On February 7, 20X3, Sullivan Corporation purchased the land from a nonaffiliate for $145,000. It sold the land to Kolder Company for $130,000 on October 10, 20X3, and Kolder sold the land to Clayton for $180,000 on November 27, 20X3. Swanson has control of the following companies:

| Subsidiary | Level of Ownership | 20X3 Net Income |
|---|---|---|
| Sullivan Corporation | 80 percent | $120,000 |
| Kolder Company | 70 percent | 60,000 |
| Clayton Corporation | 90 percent | 80,000 |

Swanson reported income from its separate operations of $150,000 for 20X3.

### Required

 *a.* At what amount should the land be reported in the consolidated balance sheet as of December 31, 20X3?

 *b.* What amount of gain or loss on sale of land should be reported in the consolidated income statement for 20X3?

 *c.* What amount of income should be assigned to the controlling shareholders in the consolidated income statement for 20X3?

  *d.* Give any elimination entry related to the land that should appear in the workpaper used to prepare consolidated financial statements for 20X3.

**E6-19**   **Elimination Entry in Period of Transfer**

Blank Corporation owns 60 percent of Grand Corporation's voting common stock. On December 31, 20X4, Blank paid Grand $276,000 for dump trucks Grand had purchased on January 1, 20X2. Both companies use straight-line depreciation. The eliminating entry included in preparing consolidated financial statements at December 31, 20X4, was:

| | | |
|---|---:|---:|
| Trucks | 24,000 | |
| Gain on Sale of Trucks | 36,000 | |
|     Accumulated Depreciation | | 60,000 |

### Required

  *a.* What amount was paid by Grand to purchase the trucks on January 1, 20X2?

  *b.* What was the economic life of the trucks on January 1, 20X2?

  *c.* Give the workpaper eliminating entry needed in preparing the consolidated financial statements at December 31, 20X5.

**E6-20**   **Elimination Entry Computation**

Stern Manufacturing purchased an ultrasound drilling machine with a remaining 10-year economic life from a 70 percent owned subsidiary for $360,000 on January 1, 20X6. Both companies use straight-line depreciation. The subsidiary recorded the following entry when it sold the machine to Stern:

| | | |
|---|---:|---:|
| Cash | 360,000 | |
| Accumulated Depreciation | 150,000 | |
|     Equipment | | 450,000 |
|     Gain on Sale of Equipment | | 60,000 |

### Required

Give the workpaper elimination entry or entries needed to remove the effects of the intercorporate sale of equipment when consolidated financial statements are prepared as of (*a*) December 31, 20X6, and (*b*) December 31, 20X7.

**E6-21**   **Using the Eliminating Entry to Determine Account Balances**

Pastel Corporation acquired controlling interest of Somber Corporation in 20X5 at underlying book value. At the date of acquisition, the fair value of the noncontrolling interest was equal to its proportionate share of the book value of Somber Corporation. In preparing a consolidated balance sheet workpaper at January 1, 20X9, Pastel's controller included the following eliminating entry:

| | | |
|---|---:|---:|
| Equipment | 53,500 | |
| Retained Earnings | 9,450 | |
| Noncontrolling Interest | 1,050 | |
|     Accumulated Depreciation | | 64,000 |

A note at the bottom of the consolidation workpaper at January 1, 20X9, indicates the equipment was purchased from a nonaffiliate on January 1, 20X1, for $120,000 and was sold to an affiliate on December 31, 20X8. The equipment is being depreciated on a 15-year straight-line basis. Somber reported stock outstanding of $300,000 and retained earnings of $200,000 at January 1, 20X9. Somber reported net income of $25,000 and paid dividends of $6,000 for 20X9.

### Required

  *a.* What percentage ownership of Somber Corporation does Pastel hold?

  *b.* Was the parent or subsidiary the owner prior to the intercorporate sale of equipment? Explain.

  *c.* What was the intercompany transfer price of the equipment on December 31, 20X8?

  *d.* What amount of income will be assigned to the noncontrolling interest in the consolidated income statement for 20X9?

e. Assuming Pastel and Somber report depreciation expense of $15,000 and $9,000, respectively, for 20X9, what depreciation amount will be reported in the consolidated income statement for 20X9?

f. Give all eliminating entries needed at December 31, 20X9, to prepare a complete set of consolidated financial statements.

### E6-22 Intercompany Sale of Services

Norgaard Corporation is provided management consulting services by its 75 percent owned subsidiary, Bline Inc. During 20X3, Norgaard paid Bline $123,200 for its services. For the year 20X4, Bline billed Norgaard $138,700 for such services and collected all but $6,600 by year-end. Bline's labor cost and other associated costs for the employees providing services to Norgaard totaled $91,000 in 20X3 and $112,000 in 20X4. Norgaard reported $2,342,000 of income from its own separate operations for 20X4, and Bline reported net income of $631,000.

#### Required

a. Present all elimination entries related to the intercompany sale of services that would be needed in the consolidation workpaper used to prepare a complete set of consolidated financial statements for 20X4.

b. Compute consolidated net income for 20X4 and the amount of income assigned to the controlling interest.

### E6-23A Fully Adjusted Equity Method and Cost Method

Newtime Products purchased 65 percent of TV Sales Company's stock at underlying book value on January 1, 20X3. At that date, the fair value of the noncontrolling interest was equal to 35 percent of the book value of TV Sales. TV Sales reported shares outstanding of $300,000 and retained earnings of $100,000. During 20X3, TV Sales reported net income of $50,000 and paid dividends of $5,000. In 20X4, TV Sales reported net income of $70,000 and paid dividends of $20,000.

The following transactions occurred between Newtime Products and TV Sales in 20X3 and 20X4:

1. TV Sales sold camera equipment to Newtime for a $40,000 profit on December 31, 20X3. The equipment had a five-year estimated economic life remaining at the time of intercompany transfer and is depreciated on a straight-line basis.
2. Newtime sold land costing $30,000 to TV Sales on June 30, 20X4, for $41,000.

#### Required

a. Assuming that Newtime uses the fully adjusted equity method to account for its investment in TV Sales:
   (1) Give the journal entries recorded on Newtime's books in 20X4 related to its investment in TV Sales.
   (2) Give all eliminating entries needed to prepare a consolidation workpaper for 20X4.

b. Assuming that Newtime uses the cost method to account for its investment in TV Sales:
   (1) Give the journal entries recorded on Newtime's books in 20X4 related to its investment in TV Sales.
   (2) Give all eliminating entries needed to prepare a consolidation workpaper for 20X4.

## Problems

### P6-24 Computation of Consolidated Net Income

Petime Corporation acquired 90 percent ownership of United Grain Company on January 1, 20X4, for $108,000 when the fair value of United's net assets was $10,000 greater than its $110,000 book value. The increase in value was attributed to amortizable assets with a remaining life of 10 years. At that date, the fair value of the noncontrolling interest was equal to $12,000.

During 20X4, United sold land to Petime at a $7,000 profit. United Grain reported net income of $19,000 and paid dividends of $4,000 in 20X4. Petime reported income, exclusive of its income from United Grain, of $34,000 and paid dividends of $15,000 in 20X4.

#### Required

a. Compute the amount of income assigned to the controlling interest in the consolidated income statement for 20X4.

b. By what amount will the 20X4 income assigned to the controlling interest increase or decrease if the sale of land had been from Petime to United Grain and the gain on the sale of land had been included in Petime's $34,000 income?

**P6-25** **Subsidiary Net Income**

Bold Corporation acquired 75 percent of Toll Corporation's voting common stock on January 1, 20X4, for $348,000, when the fair value of its net identifiable assets was $464,000 and the fair value of the noncontrolling interest was $116,000. Toll reported common stock outstanding of $150,000 and retained earnings of $270,000. The excess of fair value over book value of Toll's net assets was attributed to amortizable assets with a remaining life of 10 years. On December 31, 20X4, Toll sold a building to Bold and recorded a gain of $20,000. Income assigned to the noncontrolling shareholders in the 20X4 consolidated income statement was $17,500.

### Required

a. Compute the amount of net income Toll reported for 20X4.

b. Compute the amount reported as consolidated net income if Bold reported operating income of $234,000 for 20X4.

c. Compute the amount of income assigned to the controlling interest in the 20X4 consolidated income statement.

**P6-26** **Transfer of Asset from One Subsidiary to Another**

Pelts Company holds a total of 70 percent of Bugle Corporation and 80 percent of Cook Products Corporation stock. Bugle purchased a warehouse with an expected life of 20 years on January 1, 20X1, for $40,000. On January 1, 20X6, it sold the warehouse to Cook Products for $45,000.

### Required

Complete the following table showing selected information that would appear in the separate 20X6 income statements and balance sheets of Bugle Corporation and Cook Products Corporation and in the 20X6 consolidated financial statements.

| | Bugle Corporation | Cook Products Corporation | Consolidated Entity |
|---|---|---|---|
| Depreciation expense | | | |
| Fixed assets—warehouse | | | |
| Accumulated depreciation | | | |
| Gain on sale of warehouse | | | |

**P6-27** **Consolidated Eliminating Entry**

In preparing its consolidated financial statements at December 31, 20X7, the following eliminating entry was included in the consolidation workpaper of Master Corporation:

| | | |
|---|---|---|
| Buildings | 140,000 | |
| Gain on Sale of Building | 28,000 | |
| Depreciation Expense | | 2,000 |
| Accumulated Depreciation | | 166,000 |

Master owns 60 percent of Rakel Corporation's voting common stock. On January 1, 20X7, Rakel sold Master a building it had purchased for $600,000 on January 1, 20X1, and depreciated on a 20-year straight-line basis. Master recorded depreciation for 20X7 using straight-line depreciation and the same useful life and residual value as Rakel.

### Required

a. What amount did Master pay Rakel for the building?

b. What amount of accumulated depreciation did Rakel report at January 1, 20X7, prior to the sale?

c. What annual depreciation expense did Rakel record prior to the sale?

d. What expected residual value did Rakel use in computing its annual depreciation expense?

e. What amount of depreciation expense did Master record in 20X7?

f. If Rakel reported net income of $80,000 for 20X7, what amount of income will be assigned to the noncontrolling interest in the consolidated income statement for 20X7?

g. If Rakel reported net income of $65,000 for 20X8, what amount of income will be assigned to the noncontrolling interest in the consolidated income statement for 20X8?

**P6-28** **Multiple-Choice Questions**

Select the correct answer for each of the following questions.

1. In the preparation of a consolidated income statement:

   a. Income assigned to noncontrolling shareholders always is computed as a pro rata portion of the reported net income of the consolidated entity.

   b. Income assigned to noncontrolling shareholders always is computed as a pro rata portion of the reported net income of the subsidiary.

   c. Income assigned to noncontrolling shareholders in the current period is likely to be less than a pro rata portion of the reported net income of the subsidiary in the current period if the subsidiary had an unrealized gain on an intercorporate sale of depreciable assets in the preceding period.

   d. Income assigned to noncontrolling shareholders in the current period is likely to be more than a pro rata portion of the reported net income of the subsidiary in the current period if the subsidiary had an unrealized gain on an intercorporate sale of depreciable assets in the preceding period.

2. When a 90 percent owned subsidiary records a gain on the sale of land to an affiliate during the current period and the land is not resold before the end of the period:

   a. Ninety percent of the gain will be excluded from consolidated net income.

   b. Consolidated net income will be increased by the full amount of the gain.

   c. A proportionate share of the unrealized gain will be excluded from income assigned to non-controlling interest.

   d. The full amount of the unrealized gain will be excluded from income assigned to noncon-trolling interest.

3. During 20X5, Subsidiary Corporation sells land to Parent Corporation and records a gain of $15,000 on the sale. Subsidiary reports 20X5 net income of $55,000. Parent holds 60 percent of the voting shares of Subsidiary. Parent plans to build a new general headquarters on the land in 20X7. If no adjustment is made for unrealized profits in preparing the consolidated financial statements as of December 31, 20X5:

   a. Consolidated net income will be overstated by $15,000.

   b. Consolidated retained earnings will be overstated by $15,000.

   c. Income assigned to the noncontrolling interest in the consolidated income statement will be overstated by $9,000.

   d. Consolidated net income will be overstated by $9,000.

   e. Both answers *a* and *b* are correct.

4. Minor Company sold land to Major Company on November 15, 20X4, and recorded a gain of $30,000 on the sale. Major owns 80 percent of Minor's common shares. Which of the following statements is correct?

   a. A proportionate share of the $30,000 must be treated as a reduction of income assigned to the noncontrolling interest in the consolidated income statement unless the land is resold to a nonaffiliate in 20X4.

   b. The $30,000 will not be treated as an adjustment in computing income assigned to the non-controlling interest in the consolidated income statement in 20X4 unless the land is resold to a nonaffiliate in 20X4.

   c. In computing consolidated net income it does not matter whether the land is or is not resold to a nonaffiliate before the end of the period; the $30,000 will not affect the computation of consolidated net income in 20X4 because the profits are on the subsidiary's books.

   d. Minor's trial balance as of December 31, 20X4, should be adjusted to remove the $30,000 gain since the gain is not yet realized.

5. Lewis Company owns 80 percent of Tomassini Corporation's stock. You are told that Tomassini has sold equipment to Lewis and that the following eliminating entry is needed to prepare consolidated statements for 20X9:

| | | |
|---|---|---|
| Equipment | 20,000 | |
| Gain on Sale of Equipment | 40,000 | |
| Depreciation Expense | | 5,000 |
| Accumulated Depreciation | | 55,000 |

Which of the following is incorrect?

a. The parent paid $40,000 in excess of the subsidiary's carrying amount to acquire the asset.

b. From a consolidated viewpoint, depreciation expense as Lewis recorded it is overstated.

c. The asset transfer occurred in 20X9 before the end of the year.

d. Consolidated net income will be reduced by $40,000 when this entry is used as an eliminating entry.

### P6-29 Intercompany Services Provided to Subsidiary

During 20X4, Plate Company paid its employees $80,000 for work done in helping its wholly owned subsidiary build a new office building that was completed on December 31, 20X4. Plate recorded the $110,000 payment from the subsidiary for the work done as service revenue. The subsidiary included the payment in the cost of the building and is depreciating the building over 25 years with no assumed residual value.

#### Required

Present the eliminating entries needed at December 31, 20X4 and 20X5, to prepare Plate's consolidated financial statements.

### P6-30 Consolidated Net Income with Intercorporate Transfers

In its 20X7 consolidated income statement, Bower Development Company reported consolidated net income of $961,000 and $39,000 of income assigned to the 30 percent noncontrolling interest in its only subsidiary, Subsidence Mining, Inc. During the year, Subsidence had sold a previously mined parcel of land to Bower for a new housing development; the sales price to Bower was $500,000, and the land had a carrying amount at the time of sale of $560,000. At the beginning of the previous year, Bower had sold excavation and grading equipment to Subsidence for $240,000; the equipment had a remaining life of six years as of the date of sale and a book value of $210,000. The equipment originally had cost $350,000 when Bower purchased it on January 2, 20X2. The equipment never was expected to have any salvage value.

Bower had acquired 70 percent of the voting shares of Subsidence 12 years earlier when the fair value of its net assets was $200,000 greater than book value and the fair value of the noncontrolling interest was $60,000 more than a proportionate share of the book value of Subsidence's net assets. All the excess over the book value was attributable to intangible assets with a remaining life of 10 years from the date of combination. Both parent and subsidiary use straight-line amortization and depreciation.

#### Required

a. Present the journal entry made by Bower to record the sale of equipment in 20X6 to Subsidence.

b. Present all elimination entries related to the intercompany transfers of land and equipment that should appear in the consolidation workpaper used to prepare a complete set of consolidated financial statements for 20X7.

c. Compute Subsidence's 20X7 net income.

d. Compute Bower's 20X7 income from its own separate operations, excluding any investment income from its investment in Subsidence Mining.

### P6-31 Computation of Retained Earnings following Multiple Transfers

Great Company acquired 80 percent of Meager Corporation's common stock on January 1, 20X4, for $280,000. The fair value of the noncontrolling interest was $70,000 at the date of acquisition. Great's corporate controller has lost the consolidation files for the past three years and has asked you to compute the proper retained earnings balances for the consolidated entity at January 1, 20X8, and December 31, 20X8. The controller has been able to determine the following:

1. The book value of Meager's net assets at January 1, 20X4, was $290,000 and the fair value of its net assets was $325,000. This difference was due to an increase in the value of equipment. All depreciable assets had a remaining life of 10 years at the date of combination. At December 31, 20X8, Great's management reviewed the amount attributed to goodwill as a result of its purchase of Meager common stock and concluded an impairment loss of $17,500 should be recognized in 20X8 and shared proportionately between the controlling and noncontrolling shareholders.

2. Great uses the basic equity method in accounting for its investment in Meager.

3. Meager has reported net income of $30,000 and paid dividends of $20,000 each year since Great purchased its ownership.

4. Great reported retained earnings of $450,000 in its December 31, 20X7, balance sheet. For 20X8, Great reported operating income of $65,000 and paid dividends of $45,000.

5. Meager sold land costing $40,000 to Great for $56,000 on December 31, 20X7.

6. On January 1, 20X6, Great sold depreciable assets with a remaining useful life of 10 years to Meager and recorded a $22,000 gain on the sale.

### Required

Compute the appropriate amounts to be reported as consolidated retained earnings at January 1, 20X8, and December 31, 20X8.

**P6-32  Preparation of Consolidated Balance Sheet**

Lofton Company owns 60 percent of Temple Corporation's voting shares, purchased on May 17, 20X1, at book value. At that date, the fair value of the noncontrolling interest was equal to 40 percent of the book value of Temple Corporation. The companies' permanent accounts on December 31, 20X6, contained the following balances:

| | Lofton Company | Temple Corporation |
|---|---|---|
| Cash and Receivables | $101,000 | $ 20,000 |
| Inventory | 80,000 | 40,000 |
| Land | 150,000 | 90,000 |
| Buildings and Equipment | 400,000 | 300,000 |
| Investment in Temple Corporation Stock | 150,000 | |
| | $881,000 | $450,000 |
| | | |
| Accumulated Depreciation | $135,000 | $ 85,000 |
| Accounts Payable | 90,000 | 25,000 |
| Notes Payable | 200,000 | 90,000 |
| Common Stock | 100,000 | 200,000 |
| Retained Earnings | 356,000 | 50,000 |
| | $881,000 | $450,000 |

On January 1, 20X2, Lofton paid $100,000 for equipment with a 10-year expected total economic life. The equipment was depreciated on a straight-line basis with no residual value. Temple purchased the equipment from Lofton on December 31, 20X4, for $91,000.

Temple sold land it had purchased for $30,000 on February 23, 20X4, to Lofton for $20,000 on October 14, 20X5.

### Required

a. Prepare a consolidated balance sheet workpaper in good form as of December 31, 20X6.

b. Prepare a consolidated balance sheet as of December 31, 20X6.

**P6-33  Consolidation Workpaper with Intercompany Transfers**

Mist Company acquired 65 percent of Blank Corporation's voting common stock on June 20, 20X2, at underlying book value. At that date, the fair value of the noncontrolling interest was equal to 35 percent of the book value of Blank Corporation. The balance sheets and income statements for the companies at December 31, 20X4, are as follows:

## MIST COMPANY AND BLANK CORPORATION
### Balance Sheets
### December 31, 20X4

| Item | Mist Company | Blank Corp. |
|---|---|---|
| Cash | $ 32,500 | $ 22,000 |
| Accounts Receivable | 62,000 | 37,000 |
| Inventory | 95,000 | 71,000 |
| Land | 40,000 | 15,000 |
| Buildings and Equipment (net) | 200,000 | 125,000 |
| Investment in Blank Corp. Stock | 110,500 | |
| Total Assets | $540,000 | $270,000 |
| Accounts Payable | $ 35,000 | $ 20,000 |
| Bonds Payable | 180,000 | 80,000 |
| Common Stock, $5 par value | 100,000 | 60,000 |
| Retained Earnings | 225,000 | 110,000 |
| Total Liabilities and Stockholders' Equity | $540,000 | $270,000 |

## MIST COMPANY AND BLANK CORPORATION
### Combined Income and Retained Earnings Statements
### Year Ended December 31, 20X4

| Item | Mist Company | | Blank Corp. | |
|---|---|---|---|---|
| Sales and Service Revenue | | $286,500 | | $128,500 |
| Gain on Sale of Land | | 4,000 | | |
| Gain on Sale of Building | | | | 13,200 |
| Income from Subsidiary | | 19,500 | | |
| | | $310,000 | | $141,700 |
| Cost of Goods and Services Sold | $160,000 | | $75,000 | |
| Depreciation Expense | 22,000 | | 19,000 | |
| Other Expenses | 76,000 | (258,000) | 17,700 | (111,700) |
| Net Income | | $ 52,000 | | $ 30,000 |
| Dividends Paid | | (25,000) | | (5,000) |
| Change in Retained Earnings | | $ 27,000 | | $ 25,000 |

### Additional Information

1. Mist uses the basic equity method in accounting for its investment in Blank.
2. During 20X4, Mist charged Blank $24,000 for consulting services to Blank during the year. The services cost Mist $17,000.
3. On January 1, 20X4, Blank sold Mist a building for $13,200 above its carrying value on Blank's books. The building had a 12-year remaining economic life at the time of transfer.
4. On June 14, 20X4, Mist sold land it had purchased for $3,000 to Blank for $7,000. Blank continued to hold the land at December 31, 20X4.

### Required

a. Give all eliminating entries needed to prepare a full set of consolidated financial statements for 20X4.
b. Prepare a consolidation workpaper for 20X4.
c. Prepare the 20X4 consolidated balance sheet, income statement, and retained earnings statement.

**P6-34   Consolidation Workpaper in Year of Intercompany Transfer**

Prime Company holds 80 percent of Lane Company's stock, acquired on January 1, 20X2, for $160,000. On the acquisition date, the fair value of the noncontrolling interest was $40,000. Lane reported retained earnings of $50,000 and had $100,000 of common stock outstanding. Prime uses the basic equity method in accounting for its investment in Lane.

Trial balance data for the two companies on December 31, 20X6, are as follows:

| Item | Prime Company | | Lane Company | |
|---|---|---|---|---|
| | Debit | Credit | Debit | Credit |
| Cash and Accounts Receivable | $ 113,000 | | $ 35,000 | |
| Inventory | 260,000 | | 90,000 | |
| Land | 80,000 | | 80,000 | |
| Buildings and Equipment | 500,000 | | 150,000 | |
| Investment in Lane Company Stock | 232,000 | | | |
| Cost of Goods Sold | 140,000 | | 60,000 | |
| Depreciation and Amortization | 25,000 | | 15,000 | |
| Other Expenses | 15,000 | | 5,000 | |
| Dividends Declared | 30,000 | | 5,000 | |
| Accumulated Depreciation | | $ 205,000 | | $ 45,000 |
| Accounts Payable | | 60,000 | | 20,000 |
| Bonds Payable | | 200,000 | | 50,000 |
| Common Stock | | 300,000 | | 100,000 |
| Retained Earnings | | 338,000 | | 105,000 |
| Sales | | 240,000 | | 120,000 |
| Gain on Sale of Equipment | | 20,000 | | |
| Income from Subsidiary | | 32,000 | | |
| Total | $1,395,000 | $1,395,000 | $440,000 | $440,000 |

### Additional Information

1. At the date of combination, the book values and fair values of all separably identifiable assets and liabilities of Lane were the same. At December 31, 20X6, the management of Prime reviewed the amount attributed to goodwill as a result of its purchase of Lane stock and concluded an impairment loss of $18,000 should be recognized in 20X6 and shared proportionately between the controlling and noncontrolling shareholders.
2. On January 1, 20X5, Lane sold land that had cost $8,000 to Prime for $18,000.
3. On January 1, 20X6, Prime sold to Lane equipment that it had purchased for $75,000 on January 1, 20X1. The equipment has a total economic life of 15 years and was sold to Lane for $70,000. Both companies use straight-line depreciation.
4. There was $7,000 of intercompany receivables and payables on December 31, 20X6.

### Required

*a.* Give all eliminating entries needed to prepare a consolidation workpaper for 20X6.
*b.* Prepare a three-part workpaper for 20X6 in good form.
*c.* Prepare a consolidated balance sheet, income statement, and retained earnings statement for 20X6.

**P6-35   Intercorporate Sales in Prior Years**

On January 1, 20X5, Pond Corporation acquired 80 percent of Skate Company's stock by issuing common stock with a fair value of $180,000. At that date, Skate reported net assets of $150,000. The fair value of the noncontrolling interest was $45,000. The balance sheets for Pond and Skate at January 1, 20X8, and December 31, 20X8, and income statements for 20X8 were reported as follows:

### 20X8 Balance Sheet Data

| | Pond Corporation | | Skate Company | |
|---|---|---|---|---|
| | January 1 | December 31 | January 1 | December 31 |
| Cash | $ 40,400 | $ 68,400 | $ 10,000 | $ 47,000 |
| Accounts Receivable | 120,000 | 130,000 | 60,000 | 65,000 |
| Interest and Other Receivables | 40,000 | 45,000 | 8,000 | 10,000 |
| Inventory | 100,000 | 140,000 | 50,000 | 50,000 |
| Land | 50,000 | 50,000 | 22,000 | 22,000 |
| Buildings and Equipment | 400,000 | 400,000 | 240,000 | 240,000 |
| Accumulated Depreciation | (150,000) | (185,000) | (70,000) | (94,000) |
| Investment in Skate Company Stock | 211,000 | 224,000 | | |
| Investment in Tin Co. Bonds | 135,000 | 134,000 | | |
| Total Assets | $946,400 | $1,006,400 | $320,000 | $340,000 |
| Accounts Payable | $ 60,000 | $ 65,000 | $ 16,500 | $ 11,000 |
| Interest and Other Payables | 40,000 | 45,000 | 7,000 | 12,000 |
| Bonds Payable | 300,000 | 300,000 | 100,000 | 100,000 |
| Bond Discount | | | (3,500) | (3,000) |
| Common Stock | 150,000 | 150,000 | 30,000 | 30,000 |
| Additional Paid-In Capital | 155,000 | 155,000 | 20,000 | 20,000 |
| Retained Earnings | 241,400 | 291,400 | 150,000 | 170,000 |
| Total Liabilities and Equities | $946,400 | $1,006,400 | $320,000 | $340,000 |

### 20X8 Income Statement Data

| | Pond Corporation | | Skate Company | |
|---|---|---|---|---|
| Sales | | $450,000 | | $ 250,000 |
| Income from Subsidiary | | 21,000 | | |
| Interest Income | | 14,900 | | |
| Total Revenue | | $485,900 | | $ 250,000 |
| Cost of Goods Sold | $285,000 | | $136,000 | |
| Other Operating Expenses | 50,000 | | 40,000 | |
| Depreciation Expense | 35,000 | | 24,000 | |
| Interest Expense | 24,000 | | 10,500 | |
| Miscellaneous Expenses | 11,900 | (405,900) | 9,500 | (220,000) |
| Net Income | | $ 80,000 | | $ 30,000 |

### Additional Information

1. In 20X2 Skate developed a patent for a high-speed drill bit that Pond planned to market more extensively. In accordance with generally accepted accounting standards, Skate charges all research and development costs to expense in the year the expenses are incurred. At January 1, 20X5, the market value of the patent rights was estimated to be $50,000. Pond believes the patent will be of value for the next 20 years. The remainder of the differential is assigned to buildings and equipment, which also had a 20-year estimated economic life at January 1, 20X5. All of Skate's other assets and liabilities identified by Pond at the date of acquisition had book values and fair values that were relatively equal.

2. On December 31, 20X7, Pond sold a building to Skate for $65,000 that it had purchased for $125,000 and depreciated on a straight-line basis over 25 years. At the time of sale, Pond reported accumulated depreciation of $75,000 and a remaining life of 10 years.

3. On July 1, 20X6, Skate sold land that it had purchased for $22,000 to Pond for $35,000. Pond is planning to build a new warehouse on the property prior to the end of 20X9.

4. Both Pond and Skate paid dividends in 20X8.

### Required

*a.* Give all eliminating entries required to prepare a three-part consolidation working paper at December 31, 20X8.

*b.* Prepare a three-part workpaper for 20X8 in good form.

**P6-36** ## Intercorporate Sale of Land and Depreciable Asset

Topp Corporation acquired 70 percent of Morris Company's voting common stock on January 31, 20X3, for $158,900. Morris reported common stock outstanding of $100,000 and retained earnings of $85,000. The fair value of the noncontrolling interest was $68,100 at the date of acquisition. Buildings and equipment held by Morris had a fair value $25,000 greater than book value. The remainder of the differential was assigned to a copyright held by Morris. Buildings and equipment had a 10-year remaining life and the copyright had a five-year life at the date of acquisition.

Trial balances for Topp and Morris on December 31, 20X5, are as follows:

|  | Topp Corporation | | Morris Company | |
| --- | --- | --- | --- | --- |
|  | Debit | Credit | Debit | Credit |
| Cash | $ 15,850 | | $ 58,000 | |
| Accounts Receivable | 65,000 | | 70,000 | |
| Interest and Other Receivables | 30,000 | | 10,000 | |
| Inventory | 150,000 | | 180,000 | |
| Land | 80,000 | | 60,000 | |
| Buildings and Equipment | 315,000 | | 240,000 | |
| Bond Discount | | | 15,000 | |
| Investment in Morris Company Stock | 174,510 | | | |
| Cost of Goods Sold | 375,000 | | 110,000 | |
| Depreciation Expense | 25,000 | | 10,000 | |
| Interest Expense | 24,000 | | 33,000 | |
| Other Expense | 28,000 | | 17,000 | |
| Dividends Declared | 30,000 | | 5,000 | |
| Accumulated Depreciation— | | | | |
| Buildings and Equipment | | $ 120,000 | | $ 60,000 |
| Accounts Payable | | 61,000 | | 28,000 |
| Other Payables | | 30,000 | | 20,000 |
| Bonds Payable | | 250,000 | | 300,000 |
| Common Stock | | 150,000 | | 100,000 |
| Additional Paid-In Capital | | 30,000 | | |
| Retained Earnings | | 176,240 | | 100,000 |
| Sales | | 450,000 | | 190,400 |
| Other Income | | 28,250 | | |
| Gain on Sale of Equipment | | | | 9,600 |
| Income from Subsidiary | | 16,870 | | |
| Total | $1,312,360 | $1,312,360 | $808,000 | $808,000 |

Topp sold land it had purchased for $21,000 to Morris on September 20, 20X4, for $32,000. Morris plans to use the land for future plant expansion. On January 1, 20X5, Morris sold equipment to Topp for $91,600. Morris purchased the equipment on January 1, 20X3, for $100,000 and depreciated it on a 10-year basis, including an estimated residual value of $10,000. The residual value and estimated economic life of the equipment remained unchanged as a result of the transfer and both companies use straight-line depreciation.

### Required

*a.* Compute the amount of income assigned to the nonconcontrolling interest in the consolidated income statement for 20X5.

*b.* Prepare a reconciliation between the balance in the Investment in Morris Company Stock account reported by Topp at December 31, 20X5, and the underlying book value of net assets reported by Morris at that date.

*c.* Give all eliminating entries needed to prepare a full set of consolidated financial statements at December 31, 20X5, for Topp and Morris.

*d.* Prepare a three-part workpaper for 20X5 in good form.

**P6-37**  **Consolidation Workpaper in Year following Intercompany Transfer**

Prime Company holds 80 percent of Lane Company's stock, acquired on January 1, 20X2, for $160,000. On the date of acquisition, Lane reported retained earnings of $50,000 and $100,000 of common stock outstanding, and the fair value of the noncontrolling interest was $40,000. Prime uses the basic equity method in accounting for its investment in Lane.

Trial balance data for the two companies on December 31, 20X7, are as follows:

| Item | Prime Company Debit | Prime Company Credit | Lane Company Debit | Lane Company Credit |
|---|---|---|---|---|
| Cash and Accounts Receivable | $ 151,000 | | $ 55,000 | |
| Inventory | 240,000 | | 100,000 | |
| Land | 100,000 | | 80,000 | |
| Buildings and Equipment | 500,000 | | 150,000 | |
| Investment in Lane Company Stock | 240,000 | | | |
| Cost of Goods Sold | 160,000 | | 80,000 | |
| Depreciation and Amortization | 25,000 | | 15,000 | |
| Other Expenses | 20,000 | | 10,000 | |
| Dividends Declared | 60,000 | | 35,000 | |
| Accumulated Depreciation | | $ 230,000 | | $ 60,000 |
| Accounts Payable | | 60,000 | | 25,000 |
| Bonds Payable | | 200,000 | | 50,000 |
| Common Stock | | 300,000 | | 100,000 |
| Retained Earnings | | 420,000 | | 140,000 |
| Sales | | 250,000 | | 150,000 |
| Income from Subsidiary | | 36,000 | | |
| Total | $1,496,000 | $1,496,000 | $525,000 | $525,000 |

### Additional Information

1. At the date of combination, the book values and fair values of Lane's separably identifiable assets and liabilities were equal. The full amount of the increased value of the entity was attributed to goodwill. At December 31, 20X6, the management of Prime reviewed the amount attributed to goodwill as a result of its purchase of Lane stock and recognized an impairment loss of $25,000. No further impairment occurred in 20X7.

2. On January 1, 20X5, Lane sold land that had cost $8,000 to Prime for $18,000.

3. On January 1, 20X6, Prime sold to Lane equipment that it had purchased for $75,000 on January 1, 20X1. The equipment has a total 15-year economic life and was sold to Lane for $70,000. Both companies use straight-line depreciation.

4. Intercorporate receivables and payables total $4,000 on December 31, 20X7.

### Required

*a.* Prepare a reconciliation between the balance in Prime's Investment in Lane Company Stock account reported on December 31, 20X7, and the book value of Lane.

*b.* Prepare all workpaper eliminating entries needed as of December 31, 20X7, and complete a three-part consolidation workpaper for 20X7.

## P6-38 Incomplete Data

Partial trial balance data for Mound Corporation, Shadow Company, and the consolidated entity at December 31, 20X7, are as follows:

| Item | Mound Corporation | Shadow Company | Consolidated Entity |
|---|---|---|---|
| Cash | $ 65,300 | $ 25,000 | $ 90,300 |
| Accounts Receivable | (d) | 35,000 | 126,000 |
| Inventory | 160,000 | 75,000 | 235,000 |
| Buildings and Equipment | 345,000 | 150,000 | (i) |
| Land | 70,000 | 90,000 | 153,000 |
| Investment in Shadow Company Stock | (f) | | |
| Cost of Goods Sold | 230,000 | 195,000 | 425,000 |
| Depreciation Expense | 45,000 | 10,000 | 52,000 |
| Amortization Expense | | | (e) |
| Miscellaneous Expense | 18,000 | 15,000 | 33,000 |
| Dividends Declared | 25,000 | 20,000 | 25,000 |
| Income to Noncontrolling Interest | | | (l) |
| Copyrights | | | 9,000 |
| Total Debits | $1,189,700 | $615,000 | $1,674,200 |
| Accumulated Depreciation | $ 180,000 | $ 80,000 | $ (j) |
| Accounts Payable | 25,000 | 85,000 | 101,000 |
| Common Stock | 100,000 | 50,000 | (a) |
| Additional Paid-In Capital | (b) | 70,000 | 140,000 |
| Retained Earnings | 379,400 | 80,000 | (k) |
| Income from Subsidiary | 15,300 | | |
| Sales | 343,000 | (c) | 593,000 |
| Gain on Sale of Land | (g) | | (h) |
| Noncontrolling Interest | | | 86,400 |
| Total Credits | $1,189,700 | $615,000 | $1,674,200 |

### Additional Information

1. Mound Corporation acquired 60 percent ownership of Shadow Company on January 1, 20X4, for $106,200. Shadow reported net assets of $150,000 at that date, and the fair value of the noncontrolling interest was estimated to be $70,800. The full amount of the differential at acquisition is assigned to copyrights that are being amortized over a six-year life.

2. On August 13, 20X7, Mound sold land to Shadow for $28,000. Mound also has accounts receivable from Shadow on services performed prior to the end of 20X7.

3. Shadow sold equipment it had purchased for $60,000 on January 1, 20X4, to Mound on January 1, 20X6, for $45,000. The equipment is depreciated on a straight-line basis and had a total expected useful life of five years when Shadow purchased it. No change in life expectancy resulted from the intercompany transfer.

### Required

Compute the dollar amount for each of the balances identified by a letter.

## P6-39 Intercompany Sale of Equipment at a Loss in Prior Period

Block Corporation was created on January 1, 20X0, to develop computer software. On January 1, 20X5, Foster Company acquired 90 percent of Block's common stock at underlying book value.

At that date, the fair value of the noncontrolling interest was equal to 10 percent of the book value of Block Corporation. Trial balances for Foster and Block on December 31, 20X9, follow:

| | Foster Company | | Block Corporation | |
| --- | --- | --- | --- | --- |
| | **Debit** | **Credit** | **Debit** | **Credit** |
| Cash | $ 82,000 | | $ 32,400 | |
| Accounts Receivable | 80,000 | | 90,000 | |
| Other Receivables | 40,000 | | 10,000 | |
| Inventory | 200,000 | | 130,000 | |
| Land | 80,000 | | 60,000 | |
| Buildings and Equipment | 500,000 | | 250,000 | |
| Investment in Block Corporation Stock | 216,000 | | | |
| Cost of Goods Sold | 500,000 | | 250,000 | |
| Depreciation Expense | 45,000 | | 15,000 | |
| Other Expense | 95,000 | | 75,000 | |
| Dividends Declared | 40,000 | | 20,000 | |
| Accumulated Depreciation | | $ 155,000 | | $ 75,000 |
| Accounts Payable | | 63,000 | | 35,000 |
| Other Payables | | 95,000 | | 20,000 |
| Bonds Payable | | 250,000 | | 200,000 |
| Bond Premium | | | | 2,400 |
| Common Stock | | 210,000 | | 50,000 |
| Additional Paid-In Capital | | 110,000 | | |
| Retained Earnings | | 235,000 | | 150,000 |
| Sales | | 680,000 | | 385,000 |
| Other Income | | 26,000 | | 15,000 |
| Income from Subsidiary | | 54,000 | | |
| Total | $1,878,000 | $1,878,000 | $932,400 | $932,400 |

On January 1, 20X7, Block sold equipment to Foster for $48,000. Block had purchased the equipment for $90,000 on January 1, 20X5, and was depreciating it on a straight-line basis with a 10-year expected life and no anticipated scrap value. The equipment's total expected life is unchanged as a result of the intercompany sale.

### Required

*a.* Give all eliminating entries required to prepare a three-part consolidated working paper at December 31, 20X9.

*b.* Prepare a three-part workpaper for 20X9 in good form.

**P6-40** **Comprehensive Problem: Intercorporate Transfers**

Rossman Corporation holds 75 percent of the common stock of Schmid Distributors Inc., purchased on December 31, 20X1, for $2,340,000. At the date of acquisition, Schmid reported common stock with a par value of $1,000,000, additional paid-in capital of $1,350,000, and retained earnings of $620,000. The fair value of the noncontrolling interest at acquisition was $780,000. The differential at acquisition was attributable to the following items:

| | |
| --- | --- |
| Inventory (sold in 20X2) | $ 30,000 |
| Land | 56,000 |
| Goodwill | 64,000 |
| Total Differential | $150,000 |

During 20X2, Rossman sold to Schmid at a gain of $23,000 a piece of land that it had purchased several years before; Schmid continues to hold the land. In 20X6, Rossman and Schmid entered into a five-year contract under which Rossman provides management consulting services to Schmid on a continuing basis; Schmid pays Rossman a fixed fee of $80,000 per year for these services. At December 31, 20X8, Schmid owed Rossman $20,000 as the final 20X8 quarterly payment under the contract.

On January 2, 20X8, Rossman purchased from Schmid for $250,000 equipment that Schmid was then carrying at $290,000. Schmid had purchased that equipment on December 27, 20X2, for $435,000. The equipment is expected to have a total 15-year life and no salvage value. The amount of the differential assigned to goodwill has not been impaired.

At December 31, 20X8, trial balances for Rossman and Schmid appeared as follows:

| | Rossman Corporation | | Schmid Distributors Inc. | |
|---|---|---|---|---|
| Item | Debit | Credit | Debit | Credit |
| Cash | $    50,700 | | $    38,000 | |
| Current Receivables | 101,800 | | 89,400 | |
| Inventory | 286,000 | | 218,900 | |
| Investment in Schmid Stock | 2,970,000 | | | |
| Land | 400,000 | | 1,200,000 | |
| Buildings and Equipment | 2,400,000 | | 2,990,000 | |
| Cost of Goods Sold | 2,193,000 | | 525,000 | |
| Depreciation and Amortization | 202,000 | | 88,000 | |
| Other Expenses | 1,381,000 | | 227,000 | |
| Dividends Declared | 50,000 | | 20,000 | |
| Accumulated Depreciation | | $ 1,105,000 | | $   420,000 |
| Current Payables | | 86,200 | | 76,300 |
| Bonds Payable | | 1,000,000 | | 200,000 |
| Common Stock | | 100,000 | | 1,000,000 |
| Additional Paid-In Capital | | 1,272,000 | | 1,350,000 |
| Retained Earnings, January 1 | | 1,497,800 | | 1,400,000 |
| Sales | | 4,801,000 | | 985,000 |
| Other Income or Loss | | 90,000 | 35,000 | |
| Income from Subsidiary | | 82,500 | | |
| Total | $10,034,500 | $10,034,500 | $5,431,300 | $5,431,300 |

As of December 31, 20X8, Schmid had declared but not yet paid its fourth-quarter dividend of $5,000. Both companies use straight-line depreciation and amortization. Rossman uses the basic equity method to account for its investment in Schmid.

### Required

*a.* Compute the amount of the differential as of January 1, 20X8.

*b.* Verify the balance in Rossman's Investment in Schmid Stock account as of December 31, 20X8.

*c.* Present all elimination entries that would appear in a three-part consolidation workpaper as of December 31, 20X8.

*d.* Prepare and complete a three-part workpaper for the preparation of consolidated financial statements for 20X8.

**P6-41A** ### Fully Adjusted Equity Method

On December 31, 20X7, Prime Company recorded the following entry on its books to adjust its investment in Lane Company from the basic equity method to the fully adjusted equity method:

| | | |
|---|---|---|
| Retained Earnings | 26,000 | |
|     Income from Subsidiary | | 2,000 |
|     Investment in Lane Company Stock | | 24,000 |

### Required

a. Adjust the data reported by Prime in the trial balance in Problem P6-37 for the effects of the adjusting entry presented on page 325.

b. Prepare the journal entries that would have been recorded on Prime's books during 20X7 if it had always used the fully adjusted equity method.

c. Prepare all eliminating entries needed to complete a consolidation workpaper as of December 31, 20X7, assuming Prime has used the fully adjusted equity method.

d. Complete a three-part consolidation workpaper as of December 31, 20X7.

**P6-42A**  **Cost Method**

The trial balance data presented in Problem P6-37 can be converted to reflect use of the cost method by inserting the following amounts in place of those presented for Prime Company:

| | |
|---|---:|
| Investment in Lane Company Stock | $160,000 |
| Retained Earnings | 348,000 |
| Income from Subsidiary | -0- |
| Dividend Income | 28,000 |

### Required

a. Prepare the journal entries that would have been recorded on Prime's books during 20X7 under the cost method.

b. Prepare all eliminating entries needed to complete a consolidation workpaper as of December 31, 20X7, assuming Prime has used the cost method.

c. Complete a three-part consolidation workpaper as of December 31, 20X7.

# Intercompany Inventory Transactions

Inventory transactions are the most common form of intercompany exchange. Conceptually, the elimination of inventory transfers between related companies is no different than for other types of intercompany transactions. All revenue and expense items recorded by the participants must be eliminated fully in preparing the consolidated income statement, and all profits and losses recorded on the transfers are deferred until the items are sold to a nonaffiliate.

The recordkeeping process for intercompany transfers of inventory may be more complex than for other forms of transfers. Companies often have many different types of inventory items, and some may be transferred from affiliate to affiliate. Also, the problems of keeping tabs on which items have been resold and which items are still on hand are greater in the case of inventory transactions because part of a shipment may be sold immediately by the purchasing company and other units may remain on hand for several accounting periods. Nevertheless, the consolidation procedures relating to inventory transfers are quite similar to those discussed in Chapter 6 relating to fixed assets.

## GENERAL OVERVIEW

The workpaper eliminating entries used in preparing consolidated financial statements must eliminate fully the effects of all transactions between related companies. When there have been intercompany inventory transactions, eliminating entries are needed to remove the revenue and expenses related to the intercompany transfers recorded by the individual companies. The eliminations ensure that only the cost of the inventory to the consolidated entity is included in the consolidated balance sheet when the inventory is still on hand and is charged to cost of goods sold in the period the inventory is resold to nonaffiliates.

### Transfers at Cost

Merchandise sometimes is sold to related companies at the seller's cost or carrying value. When an intercorporate sale includes no profit or loss, the balance sheet inventory amounts at the end of the period require no adjustment for consolidation because the purchasing affiliate's inventory carrying amount is the same as the cost to the transferring affiliate and the consolidated entity. At the time the inventory is resold to a nonaffiliate, the amount recognized as cost of goods sold by the affiliate making the outside sale is the cost to the consolidated entity.

Even when the intercorporate sale includes no profit or loss, however, an eliminating entry is needed to remove both the revenue from the intercorporate sale and the related cost of goods sold recorded by the seller. This avoids overstating these two accounts. Consolidated net income is not affected by the eliminating entry when the transfer is made at cost because both revenue and cost of goods sold are reduced by the same amount.

### Transfers at a Profit or Loss

Companies use many different approaches in setting intercorporate transfer prices. In some companies, the sale price to an affiliate is the same as the price to any other customer. Some companies routinely mark up inventory transferred to affiliates by a certain percentage of cost. Other companies have elaborate transfer pricing policies designed to encourage internal sales. Regardless of the method used in setting intercorporate transfer prices, the elimination process must remove the effects of such sales from the consolidated statements.

When intercompany sales include unrealized profits or losses, the workpaper eliminations needed for consolidation in the period of transfer must adjust accounts in both the consolidated income statement and balance sheet:

> **Income statement: Sales and cost of goods sold.** The sales revenue from the intercompany sale and the related cost of goods sold recorded by the transferring affiliate must be removed.
>
> **Balance sheet: Inventory.** The profit or loss on the intercompany sale must be removed so the inventory is reported at the cost to the consolidated entity.

The resulting financial statements appear as if the intercompany transfer had not occurred.

### Effect of Type of Inventory System

Most companies use either a perpetual or a periodic inventory control system to keep track of inventory and cost of goods sold. Under a perpetual inventory system, a purchase of merchandise is debited directly to the Inventory account; a sale requires a debit to Cost of Goods Sold and a credit to Inventory for the cost of the item. When a periodic system is used, a purchase of merchandise is debited to a Purchases account rather than to Inventory, and no entry is made to recognize cost of goods sold until the end of the accounting period.

The choice between periodic and perpetual inventory systems results in different entries on the books of the individual companies and, therefore, slightly different workpaper eliminating entries in preparing consolidated financial statements. Because most companies use perpetual inventory systems, the discussion in the chapter focuses on the consolidation procedures used in connection with perpetual inventories.

## DOWNSTREAM SALE OF INVENTORY

For consolidation purposes, profits recorded on an intercorporate inventory sale are recognized in the period in which the inventory is resold to an unrelated party. Until the point of resale, all intercorporate profits must be deferred. Consolidated net income must be based on the realized income of the transferring affiliate. Because intercompany profits from downstream sales are on the parent's books, consolidated net income and the overall claim of parent company shareholders must be reduced by the full amount of the unrealized profits.

When a company sells an inventory item to an affiliate, one of three situations results: (1) the item is resold to a nonaffiliate during the same period, (2) the item is resold to a nonaffiliate during the next period, or (3) the item is held for two or more periods by the purchasing affiliate. The continuing example of Peerless Products Corporation and Special Foods Inc. is used to illustrate the consolidation process under each of the alternatives. As in Chapter 6, assume that Peerless Products purchases 80 percent of the common stock of Special Foods on December 31, 20X0, for its book value of $240,000, and that the fair value of Special Foods' noncontrolling interest on that date is equal to its book value of $60,000.

As an illustration of the effects of a downstream sale, assume that on March 1, 20X1, Peerless buys inventory for $7,000 and resells it to Special Foods for $10,000 on April 1. Peerless records the following entries on its books:

March 1, 20X1

| (1) | Inventory | 7,000 | |
| |     Cash | | 7,000 |
| | Purchase of inventory. | | |

April 1, 20X1

| (2) | Cash | 10,000 | |
| |     Sales | | 10,000 |
| | Sale of inventory to Special Foods. | | |

| (3) | Cost of Goods Sold | 7,000 | |
| |     Inventory | | 7,000 |
| | Cost of inventory sold to Special Foods. | | |

Special Foods records the purchase of the inventory from Peerless with the following entry:

April 1, 20X1

| (4) | Inventory | 10,000 | |
| |     Cash | | 10,000 |
| | Purchase of inventory from Peerless. | | |

## Resale in Period of Intercorporate Transfer

To illustrate consolidation when inventory is sold to an affiliate and then resold to a nonaffiliate during the same period, assume that on November 5, 20X1, Special Foods sells the inventory purchased from Peerless to Nonaffiliated Corporation for $15,000, as follows:

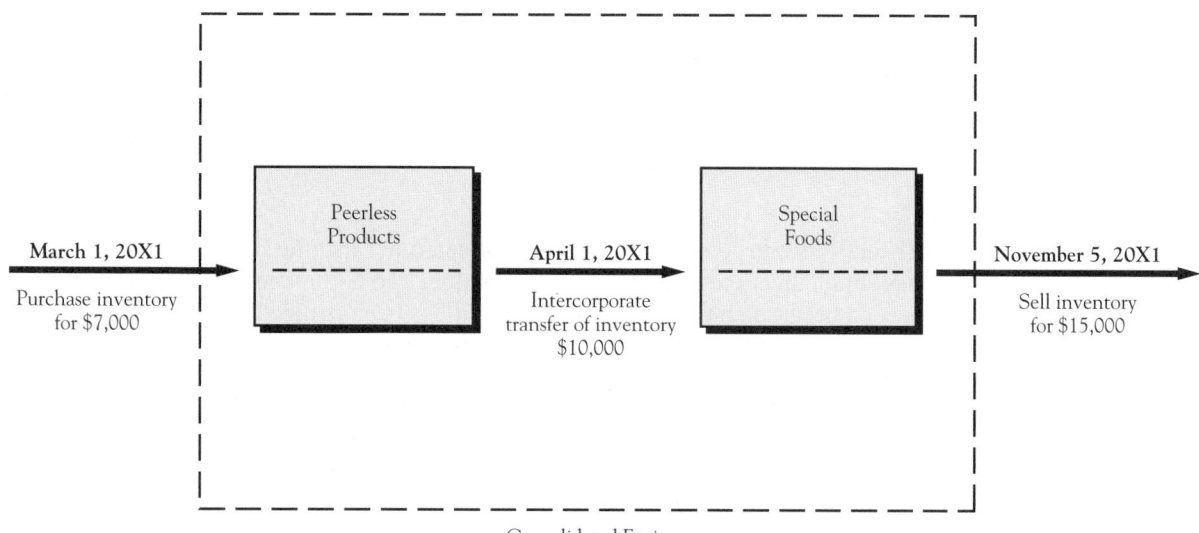

Consolidated Entity

Special Foods records the sale to Nonaffiliated with the following entries:

| | | | |
|---|---|---|---|
| November 5, 20X1 | | | |
| (5) | Cash | 15,000 | |
| | Sales | | 15,000 |
| | Sale of inventory to Nonaffiliated. | | |
| | | | |
| (6) | Cost of Goods Sold | 10,000 | |
| | Inventory | | 10,000 |
| | Cost of inventory sold to Nonaffiliated. | | |

A review of all entries recorded by the individual companies indicates that incorrect balances will be reported in the consolidated income statement if the effects of the intercorporate sale are not removed:

| Item | Peerless Products | Special Foods | Unadjusted Totals | Consolidated Amounts |
|---|---|---|---|---|
| Sales | $10,000 | $15,000 | $25,000 | $15,000 |
| Cost of Goods Sold | (7,000) | (10,000) | (17,000) | (7,000) |
| Gross Profit | $ 3,000 | $ 5,000 | $ 8,000 | $ 8,000 |

Although consolidated gross profit is correct even if no adjustments are made, the totals for sales and cost of goods sold derived by simply adding the amounts on the books of Peerless and Special Foods are overstated for the consolidated entity. The selling price of the inventory to Nonaffiliated Corporation is $15,000, and the original cost to Peerless Products is $7,000. Thus, gross profit of $8,000 is correct from a consolidated viewpoint, but consolidated sales and cost of goods sold should be $15,000 and $7,000, respectively, rather than $25,000 and $17,000. In the consolidation workpaper, the amount of the intercompany sale must be eliminated from both sales and cost of goods sold to correctly state the consolidated totals:

| | | | |
|---|---|---|---|
| E(7) | Sales | 10,000 | |
| | Cost of Goods Sold | | 10,000 |
| | Eliminate intercompany inventory sale. | | |

Note that this entry does not affect consolidated net income because sales and cost of goods sold both are reduced by the same amount. No elimination of intercompany profit is needed because all the intercompany profit has been realized through resale of the inventory to the external party during the current period.

## Resale in Period following Intercorporate Transfer

When inventory is sold to an affiliate at a profit but is not resold during the same period, appropriate adjustments are needed to prepare consolidated financial statements in the period of the intercompany sale and in each subsequent period until the inventory is sold to a nonaffiliate. By way of illustration, assume that Peerless Products purchases inventory in 20X1 for $7,000 and sells the inventory during the year to Special Foods for $10,000. Special Foods sells the inventory to Nonaffiliated Corporation for $15,000 on January 2, 20X2, as follows:

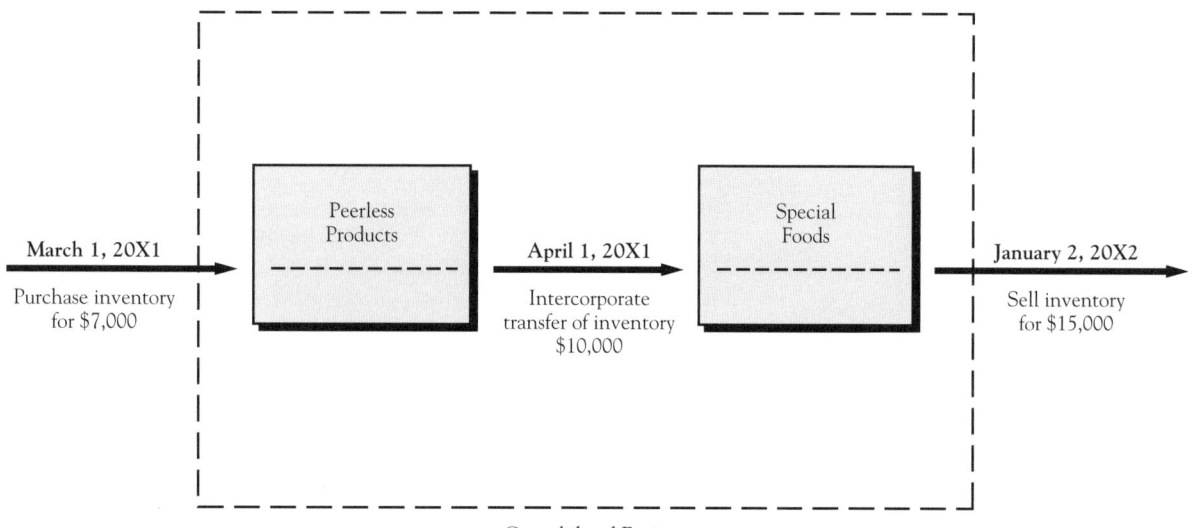

Consolidated Entity

During 20X1, Peerless records the purchase of the inventory and the sale to Special Foods with journal entries (1) through (3), given previously; Special Foods records the purchase of the inventory from Peerless with entry (4). In 20X2, Special Foods records the sale of the inventory to Nonaffiliated with entries (5) and (6), given earlier.

### Basic Equity-Method Entries—20X1

Using the basic equity method, Peerless records its share of Special Foods' income and dividends for 20X1 in the normal manner:

| | | | |
|---|---|---|---|
| (8) | Cash | 24,000 | |
| |     Investment in Special Foods Stock | | 24,000 |
| |     Record dividends from Special Foods: | | |
| |     $30,000 \times .80$ | | |
| | | | |
| (9) | Investment in Special Foods Stock | 40,000 | |
| |     Income from Subsidiary | | 40,000 |
| |     Record equity-method income: | | |
| |     $50,000 \times .80$ | | |

As a result of these entries, the ending balance of the investment account is $256,000 ($240,000 + $40,000 − $24,000).

### Consolidation Workpaper—20X1

The consolidation workpaper prepared at the end of 20X1 appears in Figure 7–1. Four elimination entries are included in the workpaper:

| | | | |
|---|---|---|---|
| E(10) | Income from Subsidiary | 40,000 | |
| |     Dividends Declared | | 24,000 |
| |     Investment in Special Foods Stock | | 16,000 |
| |     Eliminate income from subsidiary. | | |
| | | | |
| E(11) | Income to Noncontrolling Interest | 10,000 | |
| |     Dividends Declared | | 6,000 |
| |     Noncontrolling Interest | | 4,000 |
| |     Assign income to noncontrolling interest. | | |
| |     $10,000 = $50,000 \times .20$ | | |

**FIGURE 7–1** December 31, 20X1, Consolidation Workpaper, Period of Intercompany Sale; Downstream Inventory Sale

| Item | Peerless Products | Special Foods | Eliminations Debit | Eliminations Credit | Consolidated |
|---|---|---|---|---|---|
| Sales | 400,000 | 200,000 | (13) 10,000 | | 590,000 |
| Income from Subsidiary | 40,000 | | (10) 40,000 | | |
| Credits | 440,000 | 200,000 | | | 590,000 |
| Cost of Goods Sold | 170,000 | 115,000 | | (13) 7,000 | 278,000 |
| Depreciation and Amortization | 50,000 | 20,000 | | | 70,000 |
| Other Expenses | 40,000 | 15,000 | | | 55,000 |
| Debits | (260,000) | (150,000) | | | (403,000) |
| Consolidated Net Income | | | | | 187,000 |
| Income to Noncontrolling Interest | | | (11) 10,000 | | (10,000) |
| Income, carry forward | 180,000 | 50,000 | 60,000 | 7,000 | 177,000 |
| Retained Earnings, January 1 | 300,000 | 100,000 | (12) 100,000 | | 300,000 |
| Income, from above | 180,000 | 50,000 | 60,000 | 7,000 | 177,000 |
| | 480,000 | 150,000 | | | 477,000 |
| Dividends Declared | (60,000) | (30,000) | | (10) 24,000 | |
| | | | | (11) 6,000 | (60,000) |
| Retained Earnings, December 31, carry forward | 420,000 | 120,000 | 160,000 | 37,000 | 417,000 |
| Cash | 264,000 | 75,000 | | | 339,000 |
| Accounts Receivable | 75,000 | 50,000 | | | 125,000 |
| Inventory | 100,000 | 75,000 | | (13) 3,000 | 172,000 |
| Land | 175,000 | 40,000 | | | 215,000 |
| Buildings and Equipment | 800,000 | 600,000 | | | 1,400,000 |
| Investment in Special Foods Stock | 256,000 | | | (10) 16,000 | |
| | | | | (12) 240,000 | |
| Debits | 1,670,000 | 840,000 | | | 2,251,000 |
| Accumulated Depreciation | 250,000 | 220,000 | | | 470,000 |
| Accounts Payable | 100,000 | 100,000 | | | 200,000 |
| Bonds Payable | 400,000 | 200,000 | | | 600,000 |
| Common Stock | 500,000 | 200,000 | (12) 200,000 | | 500,000 |
| Retained Earnings, from above | 420,000 | 120,000 | 160,000 | 37,000 | 417,000 |
| Noncontrolling Interest | | | | (11) 4,000 | |
| | | | | (12) 60,000 | 64,000 |
| Credits | 1,670,000 | 840,000 | 360,000 | 360,000 | 2,251,000 |

Elimination entries:
(10) Eliminate income from subsidiary.
(11) Assign income to noncontrolling interest.
(12) Eliminate beginning investment balance.
(13) Eliminate intercompany downstream sale of inventory.

| | | | |
|---|---|---|---|
| E(12) | Common Stock—Special Foods | 200,000 | |
| | Retained Earnings, January 1 | 100,000 | |
| | Investment in Special Foods Stock | | 240,000 |
| | Noncontrolling Interest | | 60,000 |
| | Eliminate beginning investment balance. | | |
| E(13) | Sales | 10,000 | |
| | Cost of Goods Sold | | 7,000 |
| | Inventory | | 3,000 |
| | Eliminate intercompany downstream sale of inventory. | | |

Only entry E(13) relates to the elimination of unrealized inventory profits; the other entries are the type normally found in the workpaper.

Entry E(10) is based on entries (8) and (9) on Peerless's books and eliminates both Peerless's share of Special Foods' income and dividends and the change in the investment account for the period. The noncontrolling interest is not affected by the downstream inventory transfer and is assigned a pro rata portion ($50,000 × .20) of the net income of Special Foods in workpaper entry E(11). This entry also eliminates the noncontrolling stockholders' share of Special Foods' dividends ($30,000 × .20) and establishes the $4,000 increase in the noncontrolling interest for the period due to the excess of Special Foods' net income over its dividends [($50,000 − $30,000) × .20]. Entry E(12) eliminates the beginning balances of Special Foods' stockholders' equity accounts and Peerless's investment account. Entry E(12) also establishes in the workpaper the beginning balance of the noncontrolling interest. Because the combination occurred at the beginning of the period, the amount of the noncontrolling interest at the beginning of the period is equal to its fair value at that date, which in this example is equal to its book value. The intercompany inventory sale has no effect on this entry because the entry eliminates balances as of the beginning of the year while the intercompany transaction occurred during the year.

Entry E(13) is needed to eliminate the effects of the intercompany sale of inventory. The journal entries recorded by Peerless Products and Special Foods in 20X1 on their separate books will result in an overstatement of consolidated gross profit for 20X1 and the consolidated inventory balance at year-end unless the amounts are adjusted in the consolidation workpaper. The amounts resulting from the intercompany inventory transactions from the separate books of Peerless Products and Special Foods, and the appropriate consolidated amounts, are as follows:

| Item | Peerless Products | Special Foods | Unadjusted Totals | Consolidated Amounts |
|---|---|---|---|---|
| Sales | $10,000 | $    -0- | $10,000 | $    -0- |
| Cost of Goods Sold | (7,000) | -0- | (7,000) | -0- |
| Gross Profit | $ 3,000 | $    -0- | $ 3,000 | $    -0- |
| Inventory | $    -0- | $10,000 | $10,000 | $7,000 |

Eliminating entry E(13) corrects the unadjusted totals to the appropriate consolidated amounts. Both Sales and Cost of Goods Sold taken from the trial balance of Peerless Products are reduced in preparing the consolidated income statement. In doing so, income is reduced by the difference of $3,000 ($10,000 − $7,000). In addition, ending inventory reported on Special Foods' books is stated at the intercompany exchange price rather than the historical cost to the consolidated entity. Until resold to an external party by Special Foods, the inventory must be reduced by the amount of unrealized intercompany profit each time consolidated statements are prepared.

### Consolidated Net Income—20X1

Consolidated net income for 20X1 is shown as $187,000 in the Figure 7–1 workpaper. This amount is computed and allocated as follows:

| | |
|---|---|
| Peerless's separate income | $140,000 |
| Less: Unrealized intercompany profit on downstream inventory sale | (3,000) |
| Peerless's separate realized income | $137,000 |
| Special Foods' net income | 50,000 |
| Consolidated net income, 20X1 | $187,000 |
| Income to noncontrolling interest ($50,000 × .20) | (10,000) |
| Income to controlling interest | $177,000 |

### Basic Equity-Method Entries—20X2

During 20X2, Special Foods receives $15,000 when it sells to Nonaffiliated Corporation the inventory that it had purchased for $10,000 from Peerless in 20X1. Also, Peerless records its pro rata portion of Special Foods' net income and dividends for 20X2 with the normal basic equity-method entries:

| | | | |
|---|---|---:|---:|
| (14) | Cash | 32,000 | |
| |     Investment in Special Foods Stock | | 32,000 |
| |     Record dividends from Special Foods: | | |
| |     $40,000 × .80 | | |
| | | | |
| (15) | Investment in Special Foods Stock | 60,000 | |
| |     Income from Subsidiary | | 60,000 |
| |     Record equity-method income: | | |
| |     $75,000 × .80 | | |

### Investment Account Balance

The investment account on Peerless's books appears as follows:

| Investment in Special Foods Stock | | | | |
|---|---:|---|---|---:|
| Original cost | 240,000 | | | |
| (9) 20X1 Equity accrual | | | (8) 20X1 Dividends | |
|     ($50,000 × .80) | 40,000 | |     ($30,000 × .80) | 24,000 |
| Balance, 12/31/X1 | 256,000 | | | |
| (15) 20X2 Equity accrual | | | (14) 20X2 Dividends | |
|     ($75,000 × .80) | 60,000 | |     ($40,000 × .80) | 32,000 |
| Balance, 12/31/X2 | 284,000 | | | |

### Consolidation Workpaper—20X2

The consolidation workpaper prepared at the end of 20X2 is shown in Figure 7–2. Four elimination entries are needed:

| | | | |
|---|---|---:|---:|
| E(16) | Income from Subsidiary | 60,000 | |
| |     Dividends Declared | | 32,000 |
| |     Investment in Special Foods Stock | | 28,000 |
| |     Eliminate income from subsidiary. | | |
| | | | |
| E(17) | Income to Noncontrolling Interest | 15,000 | |
| |     Dividends Declared | | 8,000 |
| |     Noncontrolling Interest | | 7,000 |
| |     Assign income to noncontrolling interest. | | |
| |     $15,000 = $75,000 × .20 | | |
| | | | |
| E(18) | Common Stock—Special Foods | 200,000 | |
| | Retained Earnings, January 1 | 120,000 | |
| |     Investment in Special Foods Stock | | 256,000 |
| |     Noncontrolling Interest | | 64,000 |
| |     Eliminate beginning investment balance. | | |
| | | | |
| E(19) | Retained Earnings, January 1 | 3,000 | |
| |     Cost of Goods Sold | | 3,000 |
| |     Eliminate beginning inventory profit. | | |

**FIGURE 7–2**   December 31, 20X2, Consolidation Workpaper, Next Period following Intercompany Sale; Downstream Inventory Sale

| Item | Peerless Products | Special Foods | Eliminations Debit | Eliminations Credit | Consolidated |
|---|---|---|---|---|---|
| Sales | 450,000 | 300,000 | | | 750,000 |
| Income from Subsidiary | 60,000 | | (16)   60,000 | | |
| Credits | 510,000 | 300,000 | | | 750,000 |
| Cost of Goods Sold | 180,000 | 160,000 | | (19)    3,000 | 337,000 |
| Depreciation and Amortization | 50,000 | 20,000 | | | 70,000 |
| Other Expenses | 60,000 | 45,000 | | | 105,000 |
| Debits | (290,000) | (225,000) | | | (512,000) |
| Consolidated Net Income | | | | | 238,000 |
| Income to Noncontrolling Interest | | | (17)   15,000 | | (15,000) |
| Income, carry forward | 220,000 | 75,000 | 75,000 | 3,000 | 223,000 |
| Retained Earnings, January 1 | 420,000 | 120,000 | (18) 120,000 | | |
| | | | (19)    3,000 | | 417,000 |
| Income, from above | 220,000 | 75,000 | 75,000 | 3,000 | 223,000 |
| | 640,000 | 195,000 | | | 640,000 |
| Dividends Declared | (60,000) | (40,000) | | (16)   32,000 | |
| | | | | (17)    8,000 | (60,000) |
| Retained Earnings, December 31, carry forward | 580,000 | 155,000 | 198,000 | 43,000 | 580,000 |
| Cash | 291,000 | 85,000 | | | 376,000 |
| Accounts Receivable | 150,000 | 80,000 | | | 230,000 |
| Inventory | 180,000 | 90,000 | | | 270,000 |
| Land | 175,000 | 40,000 | | | 215,000 |
| Buildings and Equipment | 800,000 | 600,000 | | | 1,400,000 |
| Investment in Special Foods Stock | 284,000 | | | (16)   28,000 | |
| | | | | (18) 256,000 | |
| Debits | 1,880,000 | 895,000 | | | 2,491,000 |
| Accumulated Depreciation | 300,000 | 240,000 | | | 540,000 |
| Accounts Payable | 100,000 | 100,000 | | | 200,000 |
| Bonds Payable | 400,000 | 200,000 | | | 600,000 |
| Common Stock | 500,000 | 200,000 | (18) 200,000 | | 500,000 |
| Retained Earnings, from above | 580,000 | 155,000 | 198,000 | 43,000 | 580,000 |
| Noncontrolling Interest | | | | (17)    7,000 | |
| | | | | (18)   64,000 | 71,000 |
| Credits | 1,880,000 | 895,000 | 398,000 | 398,000 | 2,491,000 |

Elimination entries:
   (16) Eliminate income from subsidiary.
   (17) Assign income to noncontrolling interest.
   (18) Eliminate beginning investment balance.
   (19) Eliminate beginning inventory profit.

Entry E(16) eliminates the effects of basic equity-method entries (14) and (15) recorded by Peerless Products during 20X2. Entry E(17) assigns the noncontrolling shareholders their share of income ($75,000 × .20) and establishes in the workpaper the 20X2 increase in the claim of the noncontrolling shareholders on Special Foods' net assets. Because the sale is downstream, the amount of income assigned to noncontrolling shareholders and the balance of the noncontrolling interest are not affected by the intercompany profit. Entry E(18) eliminates Special Foods' beginning stockholders' equity balances and Peerless's beginning investment balance, and it establishes the beginning noncontrolling interest with a balance, in the absence of a differential, equal to 20 percent of Special Foods' book value.

Entry E(19) is needed to adjust cost of goods sold to the proper consolidated balance and to reduce beginning retained earnings. The unrealized intercompany profit included in Special Foods' beginning inventory was charged to Cost of Goods Sold when Special Foods sold the inventory during the period. Thus, consolidated cost of goods sold will be overstated for 20X2 if it is reported in the consolidated income statement at the unadjusted total from the books of Peerless and Special Foods:

| Item | Peerless Products | Special Foods | Unadjusted Totals | Consolidated Amounts |
|---|---|---|---|---|
| Sales | $  -0- | $15,000 | $15,000 | $15,000 |
| Cost of Goods Sold | -0- | (10,000) | (10,000) | (7,000) |
| Gross Profit | $  -0- | $ 5,000 | $ 5,000 | $ 8,000 |

Unlike the period in which the intercompany transfer occurs, no adjustment to sales is required in a subsequent period when the inventory is sold to a nonaffiliate. The amount reported by Special Foods reflects the sale outside the economic entity and is the appropriate amount to be reported for consolidation. By removing the $3,000 of intercorporate profit from Cost of Goods Sold in entry E(19), the original acquisition price paid by Peerless Products is reported, and $8,000 of gross profit is correctly reported in the consolidated income statement.

Elimination entry E(19) also reduces the beginning balance of retained earnings by the amount of the intercompany profit unrealized at the beginning of 20X2. Because Peerless had recognized all the intercompany profit on the downstream sale in 20X1 and it is included in Peerless's beginning retained earnings balance, beginning consolidated retained earnings will be overstated if the full balance reported by Peerless is carried to the consolidated financial statements. Entry E(19) results in the reporting of beginning consolidated retained earnings and cost of goods sold for the year as if there had been no unrealized intercompany profit at the beginning of the year.

Once the sale is made to an external party, the transaction is complete and no adjustments or eliminations related to the intercompany transaction are needed in future periods.

### Consolidated Net Income—20X2

Consolidated net income for 20X2 is shown as $238,000 in the Figure 7–2 workpaper. This amount is verified and allocated as follows:

| | |
|---|---|
| Peerless's separate income | $160,000 |
| Realization of deferred intercompany profit on downstream inventory sale | 3,000 |
| Peerless's separate realized income | $163,000 |
| Special Foods' net income | 75,000 |
| Consolidated net income, 20X2 | $238,000 |
| Income to noncontrolling interest ($75,000 × .20) | (15,000) |
| Income to controlling interest | $223,000 |

## Inventory Held Two or More Periods

Companies may carry the cost of inventory purchased from an affiliate for more than one accounting period. For example, the cost of an item may be in a LIFO inventory layer and would be included as part of the inventory balance until the layer is liquidated. Prior to liquidation, an eliminating entry is needed in the consolidation workpaper each time consolidated statements are prepared to restate the inventory to its cost to the consolidated entity. For example, if Special Foods continues to hold the inventory purchased from Peerless Products, the following eliminating entry is needed in the consolidation workpaper each time a consolidated balance sheet is prepared for years following the year of intercompany sale, for as long as the inventory is held:

| E(20) | Retained Earnings, January 1 | 3,000 | |
|---|---|---|---|
| | Inventory | | 3,000 |
| | Eliminate beginning inventory profit. | | |

No income statement adjustments are needed in the periods following the intercorporate sale until the inventory is resold to parties external to the consolidated entity.

## UPSTREAM SALE OF INVENTORY

When an upstream sale of inventory occurs and the inventory is resold by the parent to a nonaffiliate during the same period, all the parent's equity-method entries and the eliminating entries in the consolidation workpaper are identical to those in the downstream case.

When the inventory is not resold to a nonaffiliate before the end of the period, workpaper eliminating entries are different from the downstream case only by the apportionment of the unrealized intercompany profit to both the controlling and noncontrolling interests. The intercompany profit in an upstream sale is recognized by the subsidiary and shared between the controlling and noncontrolling stockholders of the subsidiary. Therefore, the elimination of the unrealized intercompany profit must reduce the interests of both ownership groups each period until the profit is confirmed by resale of the inventory to a nonaffiliated party.

An upstream sale can be illustrated using the same example as used for the downstream sale. Assume an intercompany sale of inventory from Special Foods to Peerless Products, as follows:

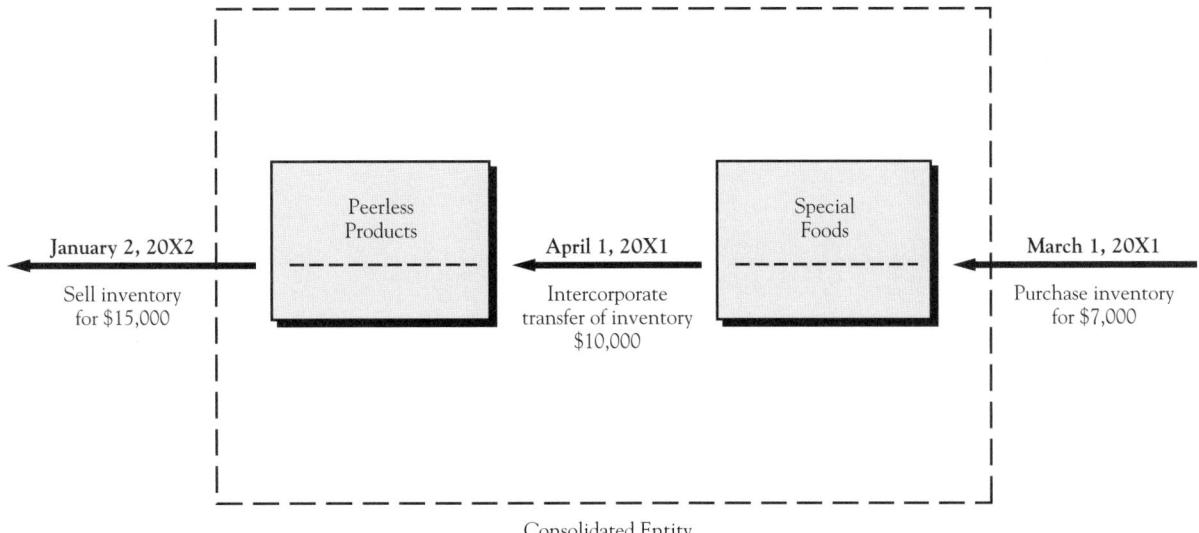

Consolidated Entity

Special Foods purchases the inventory on March 1, 20X1, for $7,000 and sells it to Peerless for $10,000 during the same year. Peerless holds the inventory until January 2 of the following year, at which time Peerless sells it to Nonaffiliated Corporation for $15,000.

## Basic Equity-Method Entries—20X1

Peerless Products records the following basic equity-method entries in 20X1:

| | | | |
|---|---|---|---|
| (21) | Cash | 24,000 | |
| | Investment in Special Foods Stock | | 24,000 |
| | Record dividends from Special Foods: | | |
| | $30,000 × .80 | | |
| | | | |
| (22) | Investment in Special Foods Stock | 40,000 | |
| | Income from Subsidiary | | 40,000 |
| | Record equity-method income: | | |
| | $50,000 × .80 | | |

These entries are the same as in the illustration of the downstream sale.

## Consolidation Workpaper—20X1

The workpaper for the preparation of the 20X1 consolidated financial statements is shown in Figure 7–3. Four eliminating entries are included in the workpaper:

| | | | |
|---|---|---|---|
| E(23) | Income from Subsidiary | 40,000 | |
| | Dividends Declared | | 24,000 |
| | Investment in Special Foods Stock | | 16,000 |
| | Eliminate income from subsidiary. | | |
| | | | |
| E(24) | Income to Noncontrolling Interest | 9,400 | |
| | Dividends Declared | | 6,000 |
| | Noncontrolling Interest | | 3,400 |
| | Assign income to noncontrolling interest: | | |
| | $9,400 = ($50,000 − $3,000) × .20 | | |
| | | | |
| E(25) | Common Stock—Special Foods | 200,000 | |
| | Retained Earnings, January 1 | 100,000 | |
| | Investment in Special Foods Stock | | 240,000 |
| | Noncontrolling Interest | | 60,000 |
| | Eliminate beginning investment balance. | | |
| | | | |
| E(26) | Sales | 10,000 | |
| | Cost of Goods Sold | | 7,000 |
| | Inventory | | 3,000 |
| | Eliminate intercompany upstream sale of inventory. | | |

All workpaper eliminating entries in the year of the intercorporate transfer are the same in the upstream case as in the downstream case except for entry E(24). Because the intercompany profit recognized by Special Foods on the upstream sale was shared by both the controlling and noncontrolling interests, both must be reduced by the unrealized profit elimination. Income assigned to the noncontrolling interest in entry E(24) is based on the realized income of Special Foods ($50,000 − $3,000) and, therefore, is reduced by the noncontrolling stockholders' share of the unrealized intercompany profit.

Because the unrealized profit elimination is allocated proportionately between the controlling and noncontrolling interests in the upstream case, the income assigned to the noncontrolling shareholders is $600 ($3,000 × .20) less in Figure 7–3 for the upstream case than in Figure 7–1 for the downstream case. Accordingly, the amount of income assigned

**FIGURE 7–3**  December 31, 20X1, Consolidation Workpaper, Period of Intercompany Sale; Upstream Inventory Sale

| Item | Peerless Products | Special Foods | Eliminations Debit | Eliminations Credit | Consolidated |
|---|---|---|---|---|---|
| Sales | 400,000 | 200,000 | (26) 10,000 | | 590,000 |
| Income from Subsidiary | 40,000 | | (23) 40,000 | | |
| Credits | 440,000 | 200,000 | | | 590,000 |
| Cost of Goods Sold | 170,000 | 115,000 | | (26) 7,000 | 278,000 |
| Depreciation and Amortization | 50,000 | 20,000 | | | 70,000 |
| Other Expenses | 40,000 | 15,000 | | | 55,000 |
| Debits | (260,000) | (150,000) | | | (403,000) |
| Consolidated Net Income | | | | | 187,000 |
| Income to Noncontrolling Interest | | | (24) 9,400 | | (9,400) |
| Income, carry forward | 180,000 | 50,000 | 59,400 | 7,000 | 177,600 |
| Retained Earnings, January 1 | 300,000 | 100,000 | (25) 100,000 | | 300,000 |
| Income, from above | 180,000 | 50,000 | 59,400 | 7,000 | 177,600 |
| | 480,000 | 150,000 | | | 477,600 |
| Dividends Declared | (60,000) | (30,000) | | (23) 24,000 | |
| | | | | (24) 6,000 | (60,000) |
| Retained Earnings, December 31, carry forward | 420,000 | 120,000 | 159,400 | 37,000 | 417,600 |
| Cash | 264,000 | 75,000 | | | 339,000 |
| Accounts Receivable | 75,000 | 50,000 | | | 125,000 |
| Inventory | 100,000 | 75,000 | | (26) 3,000 | 172,000 |
| Land | 175,000 | 40,000 | | | 215,000 |
| Buildings and Equipment | 800,000 | 600,000 | | | 1,400,000 |
| Investment in Special Foods Stock | 256,000 | | | (23) 16,000 | |
| | | | | (25) 240,000 | |
| Debits | 1,670,000 | 840,000 | | | 2,251,000 |
| Accumulated Depreciation | 250,000 | 220,000 | | | 470,000 |
| Accounts Payable | 100,000 | 100,000 | | | 200,000 |
| Bonds Payable | 400,000 | 200,000 | | | 600,000 |
| Common Stock | 500,000 | 200,000 | (25) 200,000 | | 500,000 |
| Retained Earnings, from above | 420,000 | 120,000 | 159,400 | 37,000 | 417,600 |
| Noncontrolling Interest | | | | (24) 3,400 | |
| | | | | (25) 60,000 | 63,400 |
| Credits | 1,670,000 | 840,000 | 359,400 | 359,400 | 2,251,000 |

Elimination entries:
(23) Eliminate income from subsidiary.
(24) Assign income to noncontrolling interest.
(25) Eliminate beginning investment balance.
(26) Eliminate intercompany upstream sale of inventory.

to the controlling interest is $600 higher. Note that consolidated net income and all other income statement amounts are the same whether the sale is upstream or downstream.

## Consolidated Net Income—20X1

Consolidated net income for 20X1 is shown in the workpaper as $187,000. Consolidated net income is computed and allocated to the controlling and noncontrolling stockholders as follows:

| | | |
|---|---:|---:|
| Peerless's separate income | | $140,000 |
| Special Foods' net income | $50,000 | |
| Less: Unrealized intercompany profit on upstream inventory sale | (3,000) | |
| Special Foods' realized net income | | 47,000 |
| Consolidated net income, 20X1 | | $187,000 |
| Income to noncontrolling interest ($47,000 × .20) | | (9,400) |
| Income to controlling interest | | $177,600 |

## Basic Equity-Method Entries—20X2

Peerless recognizes its share of Special Foods' income and dividends for 20X2 with the normal basic equity-method entries:

| (27) | Cash | 32,000 | |
|---|---|---:|---:|
| | Investment in Special Foods Stock | | 32,000 |
| | Record dividends from Special Foods: | | |
| | $40,000 × .80 | | |

| (28) | Investment in Special Foods Stock | 60,000 | |
|---|---|---:|---:|
| | Income from Subsidiary | | 60,000 |
| | Record equity-method income: | | |
| | $75,000 × .80 | | |

As in the downstream illustration, the investment account balance at the end of 20X2 is $284,000.

## Consolidation Workpaper—20X2

The consolidation workpaper used to prepare consolidated financial statements at the end of 20X2 appears in Figure 7–4. The workpaper includes the following elimination entries:

| E(29) | Income from Subsidiary | 60,000 | |
|---|---|---:|---:|
| | Dividends Declared | | 32,000 |
| | Investment in Special Foods Stock | | 28,000 |
| | Eliminate income from subsidiary. | | |

| E(30) | Income to Noncontrolling Interest | 15,600 | |
|---|---|---:|---:|
| | Dividends Declared | | 8,000 |
| | Noncontrolling Interest | | 7,600 |
| | Assign income to noncontrolling interest: | | |
| | $15,600 = ($75,000 + $3,000) × .20 | | |

| E(31) | Common Stock—Special Foods | 200,000 | |
|---|---|---:|---:|
| | Retained Earnings, January 1 | 120,000 | |
| | Investment in Special Foods Stock | | 256,000 |
| | Noncontrolling Interest | | 64,000 |
| | Eliminate beginning investment balance. | | |

| E(32) | Retained Earnings, January 1 | 2,400 | |
|---|---|---:|---:|
| | Noncontrolling Interest | 600 | |
| | Cost of Goods Sold | | 3,000 |
| | Eliminate beginning inventory profit: | | |
| | $2,400 = $3,000 × .80 | | |
| | $600 = $3,000 × .20 | | |

**FIGURE 7–4**   **December 31, 20X2, Consolidation Workpaper, Next Period following Intercompany Sale; Upstream Inventory Sale**

| Item | Peerless Products | Special Foods | Eliminations Debit | Eliminations Credit | Consolidated |
|---|---|---|---|---|---|
| Sales | 450,000 | 300,000 | | | 750,000 |
| Income from Subsidiary | 60,000 | | (29)   60,000 | | |
| Credits | 510,000 | 300,000 | | | 750,000 |
| Cost of Goods Sold | 180,000 | 160,000 | | (32)   3,000 | 337,000 |
| Depreciation and Amortization | 50,000 | 20,000 | | | 70,000 |
| Other Expenses | 60,000 | 45,000 | | | 105,000 |
| Debits | (290,000) | (225,000) | | | (512,000) |
| Consolidated Net Income | | | | | 238,000 |
| Income to Noncontrolling Interest | | | (30)   15,600 | | (15,600) |
| Income, carry forward | 220,000 | 75,000 | 75,600 | 3,000 | 222,400 |
| Retained Earnings, January 1 | 420,000 | 120,000 | (31)   120,000 | | |
| | | | (32)   2,400 | | 417,600 |
| Income, from above | 220,000 | 75,000 | 75,600 | 3,000 | 222,400 |
| | 640,000 | 195,000 | | | 640,000 |
| Dividends Declared | (60,000) | (40,000) | | (29)   32,000 | |
| | | | | (30)   8,000 | (60,000) |
| Retained Earnings, December 31, carry forward | 580,000 | 155,000 | 198,000 | 43,000 | 580,000 |
| Cash | 291,000 | 85,000 | | | 376,000 |
| Accounts Receivable | 150,000 | 80,000 | | | 230,000 |
| Inventory | 180,000 | 90,000 | | | 270,000 |
| Land | 175,000 | 40,000 | | | 215,000 |
| Buildings and Equipment | 800,000 | 600,000 | | | 1,400,000 |
| Investment in Special Foods Stock | 284,000 | | | (29)   28,000 | |
| | | | | (31)   256,000 | |
| Debits | 1,880,000 | 895,000 | | | 2,491,000 |
| Accumulated Depreciation | 300,000 | 240,000 | | | 540,000 |
| Accounts Payable | 100,000 | 100,000 | | | 200,000 |
| Bonds Payable | 400,000 | 200,000 | | | 600,000 |
| Common Stock | 500,000 | 200,000 | (31)   200,000 | | 500,000 |
| Retained Earnings, from above | 580,000 | 155,000 | 198,000 | 43,000 | 580,000 |
| Noncontrolling Interest | | | (32)   600 | (30)   7,600 | |
| | | | | (31)   64,000 | 71,000 |
| Credits | 1,880,000 | 895,000 | 398,600 | 398,600 | 2,491,000 |

Elimination entries:
(29) Eliminate income from subsidiary.
(30) Assign income to noncontrolling interest.
(31) Eliminate beginning investment balance.
(32) Eliminate beginning inventory profit.

Entry E(30) assigns income of $15,600 [($75,000 + $3,000) × .20] to the noncontrolling stockholders based on the realized net income of the subsidiary. The income assigned to the noncontrolling interest consists of a proportionate share of both the $75,000 reported net income of Special Foods and the $3,000 of intercompany inventory profit realized in 20X2.

Workpaper entry E(32) deals explicitly with the elimination of the inventory profit on the upstream sale. In the preparation of the 20X1 consolidated financial statements, the unrealized profit was deducted proportionately from the income assigned to the controlling and noncontrolling interests. The unrealized profit at the beginning of 20X2 is apportioned against both controlling and noncontrolling shareholders in entry E(32). As in the downstream case, Cost of Goods Sold must be credited in the consolidation workpaper to reflect the original cost to the consolidated entity ($7,000) of the inventory sold.

### Consolidated Net Income—20X2

Consolidated net income for 20X2 is shown as $238,000 in the Figure 7–4 workpaper. This amount is computed and allocated as follows:

| | | |
|---|---:|---:|
| Peerless's separate income | | $160,000 |
| Special Foods' net income | $75,000 | |
| Realization of deferred intercompany profit on upstream inventory sale | 3,000 | |
| Special Foods' realized net income | | 78,000 |
| Consolidated net income, 20X2 | | $238,000 |
| Income to noncontrolling interest ($78,000 × .20) | | (15,600) |
| Income to controlling interest | | $222,400 |

# ADDITIONAL CONSIDERATIONS

The frequency of intercompany inventory transfers and the varied circumstances under which they may occur raise a number of additional implementation issues. Several of these are discussed briefly in this section.

### Sale from One Subsidiary to Another

Transfers of inventory often occur between companies that are under common control or ownership. When one subsidiary sells merchandise to another subsidiary, the eliminating entries are identical to those presented earlier for sales from a subsidiary to its parent. The full amount of any unrealized intercompany profit is eliminated, with the profit elimination allocated proportionately against the ownership interests of the selling subsidiary.

As an illustration, assume that Peerless Products owns 90 percent of the outstanding stock of Super Industries in addition to its 80 percent interest in Special Foods. If Special Foods sells inventory at a $3,000 profit to Super Industries for $10,000 and Super Industries holds all of the inventory at the end of the period, the following elimination entry is among those needed in the consolidation workpaper prepared at the end of the period:

| E(33) | Sales | 10,000 | |
|---|---|---:|---:|
| | Cost of Goods Sold | | 7,000 |
| | Inventory | | 3,000 |
| | Eliminate intercompany sale of inventory. | | |

The $3,000 elimination of unrealized intercompany profit is allocated proportionately between the two shareholder groups of the selling affiliate. Consolidated net income is reduced by the full $3,000 unrealized intercompany profit. The income allocated to the controlling interest is reduced by Peerless's 80 percent share of the intercompany profit, or $2,400, and Special Foods' noncontrolling interest is reduced by its 20 percent share, or $600.

## Costs Associated with Transfers

When one affiliate transfers inventory to another, some additional cost, such as freight, is often incurred in the transfer. This cost should be treated in the same way as if the affiliates were operating divisions of a single company. If the additional cost would be inventoried in transferring the units from one location to another within the same company, that treatment also would be appropriate for consolidation.

## Lower of Cost or Market

A company might write down inventory purchased from an affiliate under the lower-of-cost-or-market rule if the market value at the end of the period is less than the intercompany transfer price. Such a situation can be illustrated by assuming that a parent company purchases inventory for $20,000 and sells it to its subsidiary for $35,000. The subsidiary still holds the inventory at year-end and determines that its market value (replacement cost) is $25,000 at that time.

The subsidiary writes the inventory down from $35,000 to its lower market value of $25,000 at the end of the year and records the following entry:

| | | | |
|---|---|---|---|
| (34) | Loss on Decline in Value of Inventory | 10,000 | |
| | Inventory | | 10,000 |
| | Write down inventory to market value. | | |

While this entry revalues the inventory to $25,000 on the subsidiary's books, the appropriate valuation from a consolidated viewpoint is the $20,000 original cost of the inventory to the parent. Therefore, the following eliminating entry is needed in the consolidation workpaper:

| | | | |
|---|---|---|---|
| E(35) | Sales | 35,000 | |
| | Cost of Goods Sold | | 20,000 |
| | Inventory | | 5,000 |
| | Loss on Decline in Value of Inventory | | 10,000 |
| | Eliminate intercompany sale of inventory. | | |

The inventory loss recorded by the subsidiary must be eliminated because the $20,000 inventory valuation for consolidation purposes is below the $25,000 market value of the inventory.

## Sales and Purchases before Affiliation

Sometimes companies that have sold inventory to one another later join together in a business combination. The consolidation treatment of profits on inventory transfers that occurred before the business combination depends on whether the companies were at that time independent and the sale transaction was the result of arm's-length bargaining. As a general rule, the effects of transactions that are not the result of arm's-length bargaining must be eliminated. However, the combining of two companies does not necessarily mean that their prior transactions with one another were not conducted at arm's length. The circumstances surrounding the prior transactions, such as the price and quantity of units transferred, would have to be examined.

In the absence of evidence to the contrary, companies that have joined together in a business combination are viewed as having been separate and independent prior to the combination. Thus, if the prior sales were the result of arm's-length bargaining, they are viewed as transactions between unrelated parties. Accordingly, no elimination or adjustment is needed in preparing consolidated statements subsequent to the combination, even if an affiliate still holds the inventory.

## Summary of Key Concepts

Consolidated financial statements are prepared for the consolidated entity as if it were a single company. Therefore, the effects of all transactions between companies within the entity must be eliminated in preparing consolidated financial statements.

The treatment of intercompany inventory transactions is similar to the treatment of intercompany transfers of noncurrent assets discussed in Chapter 6. Each time consolidated statements are prepared, all effects of intercompany transactions occurring during that period, and the effects of unrealized profits from transactions in prior periods, must be eliminated. For intercompany inventory transactions, the intercompany sale and cost of goods sold must be eliminated. In addition, the intercompany profit may not be recognized in consolidation until it is confirmed by resale of the inventory to an external party. Unrealized intercompany profits must be eliminated fully and are allocated proportionately against the stockholder groups of the selling affiliate. If inventory containing unrealized intercompany profits is sold during the period, consolidated cost of goods sold must be adjusted to reflect the actual cost to the consolidated entity of the inventory sold; if the inventory is still held at the end of the period, it must be adjusted to its actual cost to the consolidated entity.

## Appendix 7A Intercompany Inventory Transactions—Fully Adjusted Equity Method and Cost Method

Consolidation procedures following use of first the fully adjusted equity method and then the cost method are illustrated with the example of the upstream sale of inventory presented earlier. Assume that Special Foods purchases inventory for $7,000 in 20X1 and, in the same year, sells the inventory to Peerless Products for $10,000. Peerless Products sells the inventory to external parties in 20X2. Both companies use perpetual inventory control systems.

### FULLY ADJUSTED EQUITY METHOD

The journal entries on Peerless's books and the elimination entries in the consolidation workpaper are the same under the fully adjusted equity method as under the basic equity method except for differences related to unrealized intercompany profits. When using the fully adjusted equity method, the parent reduces its income and the balance of the investment account for its share of unrealized intercompany profits that arise during the period. Subsequently, the parent increases its income and the carrying amount of the investment account when the intercompany profits are realized through transactions with external parties.

#### Fully Adjusted Equity-Method Entries—20X1

In 20X1, Peerless Products records the normal equity-method entries reflecting its share of Special Foods' income and dividends, and an additional entry to reduce income and the investment account by the parent's share of the unrealized intercompany profit arising during the year:

| | | | |
|---|---|---|---|
| (36) | Cash | 24,000 | |
| | Investment in Special Foods Stock | | 24,000 |
| | Record dividends from Special Foods: $30,000 × .80 | | |
| (37) | Investment in Special Foods Stock | 40,000 | |
| | Income from Subsidiary | | 40,000 |
| | Record equity-method income: | | |
| | $50,000 × .80 | | |
| (38) | Income from Subsidiary | 2,400 | |
| | Investment in Special Foods Stock | | 2,400 |
| | Remove unrealized profit on upstream sale of inventory: $3,000 × .80 | | |

Entry (38) is used under the fully adjusted equity method to reduce the parent's income and the investment account by the parent's share of unrealized profits and, consequently, to bring the parent's net income into agreement with consolidated net income allocated to the controlling interest.

## Consolidation Elimination Entries—20X1

Four eliminating entries are needed in the workpaper to prepare consolidated financial statements for 20X1:

| | | | |
|---|---|---|---|
| E(39) | Income from Subsidiary | 37,600 | |
| | Dividends Declared | | 24,000 |
| | Investment in Special Foods Stock | | 13,600 |
| | Eliminate income from subsidiary. | | |
| | | | |
| E(40) | Income to Noncontrolling Interest | 9,400 | |
| | Dividends Declared | | 6,000 |
| | Noncontrolling Interest | | 3,400 |
| | Assign income to noncontrolling interest: | | |
| | $9,400 = ($50,000 − $3,000) × .20 | | |
| | | | |
| E(41) | Common Stock—Special Foods | 200,000 | |
| | Retained Earnings, January 1 | 100,000 | |
| | Investment in Special Foods Stock | | 240,000 |
| | Noncontrolling Interest | | 60,000 |
| | Eliminate beginning investment balance. | | |
| | | | |
| E(42) | Sales | 10,000 | |
| | Cost of Goods Sold | | 7,000 |
| | Inventory | | 3,000 |
| | Eliminate intercompany upstream sale of inventory. | | |

All these workpaper entries are the same as those following use of the basic equity method except for entry E(39). Because the parent's recorded income from Special Foods is $2,400 less under the fully adjusted equity method than under the basic equity method, the elimination of that income in entry E(39) is for the lesser amount. Similarly, the increase in the investment account on the parent's books during 20X1 under the fully adjusted equity method is reduced by the parent's share of the unrealized intercompany profit, and that difference is reflected in elimination entry E(39).

## Fully Adjusted Equity-Method Entries—20X2

With resale of the inventory to an external party in 20X2, the parent company recognizes its portion of the $3,000 of deferred inventory profit in addition to its pro rata portion of the reported net income of the subsidiary:

| | | | |
|---|---|---|---|
| (43) | Cash | 32,000 | |
| | Investment in Special Foods Stock | | 32,000 |
| | Record dividends from Special Foods: | | |
| | $40,000 × .80 | | |
| | | | |
| (44) | Investment in Special Foods Stock | 60,000 | |
| | Income from Subsidiary | | 60,000 |
| | Record equity-method income: | | |
| | $75,000 × .80 | | |
| | | | |
| (45) | Investment in Special Foods Stock | 2,400 | |
| | Income from Subsidiary | | 2,400 |
| | Recognize deferred profit on upstream sale of inventory: | | |
| | $3,000 × .80 | | |

Once the inventory is sold to a nonaffiliate, the intercompany profit is considered realized by the consolidated entity and is included in consolidated net income. Peerless records entry (45) to bring its equity-method net income into agreement with consolidated net income allocated to the controlling interest.

## Consolidation Elimination Entries—20X2

Workpaper eliminating entries needed for the preparation of consolidated financial statements at the end of 20X2 are as follows:

| | | | |
|---|---|---:|---:|
| E(46) | Income from Subsidiary | 62,400 | |
| | Dividends Declared | | 32,000 |
| | Investment in Special Foods Stock | | 30,400 |
| | Eliminate income from subsidiary. | | |
| | | | |
| E(47) | Income to Noncontrolling Interest | 15,600 | |
| | Dividends Declared | | 8,000 |
| | Noncontrolling Interest | | 7,600 |
| | Assign income to noncontrolling interest: | | |
| | $15,600 = ($75,000 + $3,000) \times .20$ | | |
| | | | |
| E(48) | Common Stock—Special Foods | 200,000 | |
| | Retained Earnings, January 1 | 120,000 | |
| | Investment in Special Foods Stock | | 256,000 |
| | Noncontrolling Interest | | 64,000 |
| | Eliminate beginning investment balance. | | |
| | | | |
| E(49) | Investment in Special Foods Stock | 2,400 | |
| | Noncontrolling Interest | 600 | |
| | Cost of Goods Sold | | 3,000 |
| | Eliminate beginning inventory profit. | | |

Peerless's equity-method income and share of Special Foods' dividends are eliminated in entry E(46). Just as the equity-method entries on the parent's books include the parent's share of the realized inventory profit, income assigned to noncontrolling shareholders for 20X2 in entry E(47) must include 20 percent of both the $75,000 reported net income of Special Foods and the $3,000 deferred intercompany inventory profit realized in 20X2. Thus, income assigned to the noncontrolling interest in the 20X2 income statement is $15,600 [($75,000 + $3,000) × .20].

Entry E(48) is the normal workpaper entry to eliminate the beginning balances of the subsidiary's stockholders' equity accounts and the investment account, assuming no differential. The credit to the investment account is for Peerless's share of the book value of Special Foods. Because Peerless reduced the balance of the investment account in 20X1 with entry (38) to remove unrealized intercompany profits, entry E(48) credits the investment account for $2,400 more than its beginning balance.

Workpaper entry E(49) deals explicitly with the elimination of the inventory profit on the upstream sale. Cost of Goods Sold is credited in the consolidation workpaper to reflect the original cost to the consolidated entity ($7,000) of the inventory sold. The unrealized profit at the beginning of the period is allocated against both controlling and noncontrolling shareholders. The parent's share of the unrealized intercompany profit already has been removed from its beginning retained earnings by entry (38) in 20X1. This entry reduced Peerless's income and ending retained earnings for 20X1 and brought Peerless's retained earnings into agreement with consolidated retained earnings on December 31, 20X1. Thus, Peerless's 20X2 beginning retained earnings is equal to consolidated retained earnings at the beginning of 20X2 and may be included in the 20X2 consolidation workpaper without additional adjustment.

The debit to the investment account for $2,400 in entry E(49) is needed because entry E(48) over-eliminates the investment account owing to the reduction by entry (38). Together, entries E(46), E(48), and E(49) fully eliminate the balance in the investment account.

## COST METHOD

When using the cost method, the parent records dividends received from the subsidiary as income but makes no adjustments with respect to undistributed income of the subsidiary or unrealized intercompany profits. As an example of consolidation following an upstream intercompany sale of inventory when the parent accounts for its investment in the subsidiary using the cost method, assume the same facts as in previous illustrations dealing with an upstream sale.

## Consolidation Elimination Entries—20X1

The following eliminating entries are needed in the workpaper used to prepare consolidated financial statements for 20X1:

| | | | |
|---|---|---:|---:|
| E(50) | Dividend Income | 24,000 | |
| | Dividends Declared | | 24,000 |
| | Eliminate dividend income from subsidiary: | | |
| | $30,000 × .80 | | |
| E(51) | Income to Noncontrolling Interest | 9,400 | |
| | Dividends Declared | | 6,000 |
| | Noncontrolling Interest | | 3,400 |
| | Assign income to noncontrolling interest: | | |
| | $9,400 = ($50,000 − $3,000) × .20 | | |
| E(52) | Common Stock—Special Foods | 200,000 | |
| | Retained Earnings, January 1 | 100,000 | |
| | Investment in Special Foods Stock | | 240,000 |
| | Noncontrolling Interest | | 60,000 |
| | Eliminate investment balance at date of acquisition. | | |
| E(53) | Sales | 10,000 | |
| | Cost of Goods Sold | | 7,000 |
| | Inventory | | 3,000 |
| | Eliminate intercompany upstream sale of inventory. | | |

These eliminating entries are the same as those following use of the basic equity method, except for entry E(50). This entry eliminates the parent's dividend income from Special Foods rather than its share of Special Foods' net income.

## Consolidation Elimination Entries—20X2

Elimination entries needed in the consolidation workpaper prepared at the end of 20X2 are as follows:

| | | | |
|---|---|---:|---:|
| E(54) | Dividend Income | 32,000 | |
| | Dividends Declared | | 32,000 |
| | Eliminate dividend income from subsidiary: | | |
| | $40,000 × .80 | | |
| E(55) | Income to Noncontrolling Interest | 15,600 | |
| | Dividends Declared | | 8,000 |
| | Noncontrolling Interest | | 7,600 |
| | Assign income to noncontrolling interest: | | |
| | $15,600 = ($75,000 + $3,000) × .20 | | |
| E(56) | Common Stock—Special Foods | 200,000 | |
| | Retained Earnings, January 1 | 100,000 | |
| | Investment in Special Foods Stock | | 240,000 |
| | Noncontrolling Interest | | 60,000 |
| | Eliminate investment balance at date of acquisition. | | |
| E(57) | Retained Earnings, January 1 | 4,000 | |
| | Noncontrolling Interest | | 4,000 |
| | Assign undistributed prior earnings of subsidiary | | |
| | to noncontrolling interest: $20,000 × .20 | | |
| E(58) | Retained Earnings, January 1 | 2,400 | |
| | Noncontrolling Interest | 600 | |
| | Cost of Goods Sold | | 3,000 |
| | Eliminate beginning inventory profit. | | |

Entries E(55) and E(58) are the same as those following the use of the basic equity method. Entry E(54) eliminates the dividend income recorded by Peerless in 20X2. Entry E(56) eliminates the balances at the date of combination of Special Foods' stockholders' equity accounts and the investment account. This entry is the same each year. Because this entry does not change, it assigns to the noncontrolling stockholders only their share of Special Foods' book value at the date of combination. Therefore, entry E(57) is needed to assign to the noncontrolling interest a proportionate share of the undistributed earnings of Special Foods from the date of combination to the beginning of the current year.

---

## Questions

**Q7-1**   Why must inventory transfers to related companies be eliminated in preparing consolidated financial statements?

**Q7-2**   Why is there need for an eliminating entry when an intercompany inventory transfer is made at cost?

**Q7-3**   Distinguish between an upstream sale of inventory and a downstream sale. Why is it important to know whether a sale is upstream or downstream?

**Q7-4**   How do unrealized intercompany profits on a downstream sale of inventory made during the current period affect the computation of consolidated net income and income to the controlling interest?

**Q7-5**   How do unrealized intercompany profits on an upstream sale of inventory made during the current period affect the computation of consolidated net income and income to the controlling interest?

**Q7-6**   Will the elimination of unrealized intercompany profits on an upstream sale or on a downstream sale in the current period have a greater effect on income assigned to the noncontrolling interest? Why?

**Q7-7**   What is the basic eliminating entry needed when inventory is sold to an affiliate at a profit and is resold to an unaffiliated party before the end of the period? (Assume both affiliates use perpetual inventory systems.)

**Q7-8**   What is the basic eliminating entry needed when inventory is sold to an affiliate at a profit and is not resold before the end of the period? (Assume both affiliates use perpetual inventory systems.)

**Q7-9**   How is the amount to be reported as cost of goods sold by the consolidated entity determined when there have been intercorporate sales during the period?

**Q7-10**   How is the amount to be reported as consolidated retained earnings determined when there have been intercorporate sales during the period?

**Q7-11**   How is the amount of consolidated retained earnings assigned to the noncontrolling interest affected by unrealized inventory profits at the end of the year?

**Q7-12**   How do unrealized intercompany inventory profits from a prior period affect the computation of consolidated net income when the inventory is resold in the current period? Is it important to know if the sale was upstream or downstream? Why, or why not?

**Q7-13**   How will the elimination of unrealized intercompany inventory profits recorded on the parent's books affect consolidated retained earnings?

**Q7-14**   How will the elimination of unrealized intercompany inventory profits recorded on the subsidiary's books affect consolidated retained earnings?

**Q7-15\***   Is an inventory sale from one subsidiary to another treated in the same manner as an upstream sale or a downstream sale? Why?

**Q7-16\***   Par Company regularly purchases inventory from Eagle Company. Recently, Par Company purchased a majority of the voting shares of Eagle Company. How should it treat inventory profits recorded by Eagle Company before the day of acquisition? Following the day of acquisition?

*\*Indicates that the item relates to "Additional Considerations."*

---

## Cases

**C7-1**   **Measuring Cost of Goods Sold**

*Judgment*   Shortcut Charlie usually manages to develop some simple rule to handle even the most complex situations. In providing for the elimination of the effects of inventory transfers between the parent company and a subsidiary or between subsidiaries, Shortcut started with the following rules:

1. When the buyer continues to hold the inventory at the end of the period, credit cost of goods sold for the amount recorded as cost of goods sold by the company that made the intercompany sale.

2. When the buyer resells the inventory before the end of the period, credit cost of goods sold for the amount recorded as cost of goods sold by the company that made the intercompany sale plus the profit recorded by that company.

3. Debit sales for the total amount credited in rule 1 or 2 above.

One of the new employees is seeking some assistance in understanding how the rules work and why.

### Required

*a.* Explain why rule 1 is needed when consolidated statements are prepared.

*b.* Explain what is missing from rule 1, and prepare an alternative or additional statement for the elimination of unrealized profit when the purchasing affiliate does not resell to an unaffiliated company in the period in which it purchases inventory from an affiliate.

*c.* Does rule 2 lead to the correct result? Explain your answer.

*d.* The rules do not provide assistance in determining how much profit was recorded by either of the two companies. Where should the employee look to determine the amount of profit referred to in rule 2?

### C7-2 Inventory Values and Intercompany Transfers

*Research FARS*

Water Products Corporation has been supplying high-quality bathroom fixtures to its customers for several decades and uses a LIFO inventory system. Rapid increases in the cost of fixtures have resulted in inventory values substantially below current replacement cost. To bring its inventory carrying costs up to more reasonable levels, Water Products sold its entire inventory to Plumbers Products Corporation and purchased an entirely new supply of inventory items from Growinkle Manufacturing. Water Products owns common stock of both Growinkle and Plumbers Products.

Water Products' external auditor immediately pointed out that under some ownership levels of these two companies, Water Products could accomplish its goal and under other levels it could not.

### Required

Prepare a memo to Water Products' president describing the effects of intercompany transfers on the valuation of inventories and discuss the effects that different ownership levels of Growinkle and Plumbers Products would have on the success of Water Products' plan. Include citations to or quotations from the authoritative accounting literature to support your position.

### C7-3 Intercompany Inventory Transfers

*Research FARS*

On December 20, 20X2, Evert Corporation paid Frankle Company $180,000 for inventory that Frankle had purchased for $240,000. Frankle had not previously recognized a loss and reduced the inventory's carrying value because the drop in prices was considered temporary. A resurgence in demand for the product occurred in early 20X3, and Evert sold the entire inventory for $310,000.

Evert owns 90 percent of Frankle's stock. Evert prepared consolidated financial statements at December 31, 20X2 and 20X3, but failed to make adjustments to the reported data provided by Evert and Frankle for the intercorporate sale.

### Required

Prepare a memo to Evert's treasurer describing the required treatment of intercorporate sales of inventory. Include citations to or quotations from the authoritative accounting literature to support your position. You should include in your memo an analysis of the effects that eliminating the intercompany transfer would have had on Evert's reported revenues and expenses for 20X2 and 20X3 and on its balance sheet accounts at December 31, 20X2 and 20X3.

### C7-4 Unrealized Inventory Profits

*Understanding*

Morrison Company owns 80 percent of Bloom Corporation's stock, acquired when Bloom's fair value as a whole was equal to its book value. The companies frequently engage in intercompany inventory transactions.

### Required

Name the conditions that would make it possible for each of the following statements to be true. Treat each statement independently.

a. Income assigned to the noncontrolling interest in the consolidated income statement for 20X3 is greater than a pro rata share of the reported net income of Bloom.

b. Income assigned to the noncontrolling interest in the consolidated income statement for 20X3 is greater than a pro rata share of Bloom's reported net income, but consolidated net income is reduced as a result of the elimination of intercompany inventory transfers.

c. Cost of goods sold reported in the income statement of Morrison is greater than consolidated cost of goods sold for 20X3.

d. Consolidated inventory is greater than the amounts reported by the separate companies.

### C7-5 Eliminating Inventory Transfers

*Analysis*

Ready Building Products has six subsidiaries that sell building materials and supplies to the public and to the parent and other subsidiaries. Because of the invoicing system Ready uses, it is not possible to keep track of which items have been purchased from related companies and which have been bought from outside sources. Due to the nature of the products purchased, there are substantially different profit margins on different product groupings.

#### Required

a. If no effort is made to eliminate intercompany sales for the period or unrealized profits at year-end, what elements of the financial statements are likely to be misstated?

b. What type of control system would you recommend to Ready's controller to provide the information needed to make the required eliminating entries?

c. Would it matter if the buyer and seller used different inventory costing methods (FIFO, LIFO, or weighted average)? Explain.

d. Assume you believe that the adjustments for unrealized profit would be material. How would you go about determining what amounts must be eliminated at the end of the current period?

### C7-6 Intercompany Profits and Transfers of Inventory

*Analysis*

Many companies transfer inventories from one affiliate to another. Often the companies have integrated operations in which one affiliate provides the raw materials, another manufactures finished products, another distributes the products, and perhaps another sells the products at retail. In other cases, various affiliates may be established for selling the company's products in different geographic locations, especially in different countries. Often tax considerations also have an effect on intercompany transfers.

#### Required

a. Are Xerox Corporation's intercompany transfers significant? How does Xerox treat intercompany transfers for consolidation purposes?

b. How does ExxonMobil Corporation price its products for intercompany transfers? Are these transfers significant? How does ExxonMobil treat intercompany profits for consolidation purposes?

c. What types of intercompany and intersegment sales does Ford Motor Company have? Are they significant? How are they treated for consolidation?

---

## Exercises

### E7-1 Multiple-Choice Questions on Intercompany Inventory Transfers [AICPA Adapted]

Select the correct answer for each of the following questions.

1. Perez Inc. owns 80 percent of Senior Inc. During 20X2, Perez sold goods with a 40 percent gross profit to Senior. Senior sold all of these goods in 20X2. For 20X2 consolidated financial statements, how should the summation of Perez and Senior income statement items be adjusted?

   a. Sales and cost of goods sold should be reduced by the intercompany sales.

   b. Sales and cost of goods sold should be reduced by 80 percent of the intercompany sales.

   c. Net income should be reduced by 80 percent of the gross profit on intercompany sales.

   d. No adjustment is necessary.

2. Parker Corporation owns 80 percent of Smith Inc.'s common stock. During 20X1, Parker sold inventory to Smith for $250,000 on the same terms as sales made to third parties. Smith sold all of the inventory purchased from Parker in 20X1. The following information pertains to Smith and Parker's sales for 20X1:

|  | Parker | Smith |
|---|---|---|
| Sales | $1,000,000 | $700,000 |
| Cost of Sales | (400,000) | (350,000) |
| Gross Profit | $ 600,000 | $350,000 |

What amount should Parker report as cost of sales in its 20X1 consolidated income statement?

a. $750,000.

b. $680,000.

c. $500,000.

d. $430,000.

*Note:* Items 3 and 4 are based on the following information:

Nolan owns 100 percent of the capital stock of both Twill Corporation and Webb Corporation. Twill purchases merchandise inventory from Webb at 140 percent of Webb's cost. During 20X0, Webb sold merchandise that had cost it $40,000 to Twill. Twill sold all of this merchandise to unrelated customers for $81,200 during 20X0. In preparing combined financial statements for 20X0, Nolan's bookkeeper disregarded the common ownership of Twill and Webb.

3. What amount should be eliminated from cost of goods sold in the combined income statement for 20X0?

a. $56,000.

b. $40,000.

c. $24,000.

d. $16,000.

4. By what amount was unadjusted revenue overstated in the combined income statement for 20X0?

a. $16,000.

b. $40,000.

c. $56,000.

d. $81,200.

5. Clark Company had the following transactions with affiliated parties during 20X2:

- Sales of $60,000 to Dean Inc., with $20,000 gross profit. Dean had $15,000 of this inventory on hand at year-end. Clark owns a 15 percent interest in Dean and does not exert significant influence.

- Purchases of raw materials totaling $240,000 from Kent Corporation, a wholly owned subsidiary. Kent's gross profit on the sales was $48,000. Clark had $60,000 of this inventory remaining on December 31, 20X2.

Before eliminating entries, Clark had consolidated current assets of $320,000. What amount should Clark report in its December 31, 20X2, consolidated balance sheet for current assets?

a. $320,000.

b. $317,000.

c. $308,000.

d. $303,000.

6. Selected data for two subsidiaries of Dunn Corporation taken from the December 31, 20X8, preclosing trial balances are as follows:

|  | Banks Co. (Debits) | Lamm Co. (Credits) |
|---|---|---|
| Shipments to Banks | $ — | $150,000 |
| Shipments from Lamm | 200,000 | — |
| Intercompany Inventory Profit on Total Shipments |  | 50,000 |

Additional data relating to the December 31, 20X8, inventory are as follows:

| | |
|---|---:|
| Inventory acquired by Banks from outside parties | $175,000 |
| Inventory acquired by Lamm from outside parties | 250,000 |
| Inventory acquired by Banks from Lamm | 60,000 |

At December 31, 20X8, the inventory reported on the combined balance sheet of the two subsidiaries should be:

a. $425,000.

b. $435,000.

c. $470,000.

d. $485,000.

### E7-2 Multiple-Choice Questions on the Effects of Inventory Transfers [AICPA Adapted]

Select the correct answer for each of the following questions.

1. During 20X3, Park Corporation recorded sales of inventory costing $500,000 to Small Company, its wholly owned subsidiary, on the same terms as sales made to third parties. At December 31, 20X3, Small held one-fifth of these goods in its inventory. The following information pertains to Park and Small's sales for 20X3:

| | Park | Small |
|---|---:|---:|
| Sales | $2,000,000 | $1,400,000 |
| Cost of Sales | (800,000) | (700,000) |
| Gross Profit | $1,200,000 | $ 700,000 |

In its 20X3 consolidated income statement, what amount should Park report as cost of sales?

a. $1,000,000.

b. $1,060,000.

c. $1,260,000.

d. $1,500,000.

*Note:* Items 2 through 6 are based on the following information:

Selected information from the separate and consolidated balance sheets and income statements of Power Inc. and its subsidiary, Spin Company, as of December 31, 20X8, and for the year then ended is as follows:

| | Power | Spin | Consolidated |
|---|---:|---:|---:|
| **Balance Sheet Accounts** | | | |
| Accounts Receivable | $ 26,000 | $ 19,000 | $ 39,000 |
| Inventory | 30,000 | 25,000 | 52,000 |
| Investment in Spin | 56,000 | — | — |
| Patents | — | — | 20,000 |
| Noncontrolling Interest | — | — | 14,000 |
| Stockholders' Equity | 154,000 | 50,000 | 154,000 |
| **Income Statement Accounts** | | | |
| Revenues | $200,000 | $140,000 | $308,000 |
| Cost of Goods Sold | 150,000 | 110,000 | 231,000 |
| Gross Profit | $ 50,000 | $ 30,000 | $ 77,000 |
| Equity in Earnings of Spin | 10,400 | — | — |
| Amortization of Patents | — | — | 2,000 |
| Net Income | 36,000 | 15,000 | 40,000 |

### Additional Information

During 20X8, Power sold goods to Spin at the same markup that Power uses for all sales. At December 31, 20X8, Spin had not paid for all of these goods and still held 37.5 percent of them in inventory.

Power acquired its interest in Spin on January 2, 20X5, when the book values and fair values of the assets and liabilities of Spin were equal, except for patents, which had a fair value of $28,000. The fair value of the noncontrolling interest was equal to a proportionate share of fair value of Spin's net assets.

2. What was the amount of intercompany sales from Power to Spin during 20X8?

    *a.* $3,000.

    *b.* $6,000.

    *c.* $29,000.

    *d.* $32,000.

3. At December 31, 20X8, what was the amount of Spin's payable to Power for intercompany sales?

    *a.* $3,000.

    *b.* $6,000.

    *c.* $29,000.

    *d.* $32,000.

4. In Power's consolidated balance sheet, what was the carrying amount of the inventory that Spin purchased from Power?

    *a.* $3,000.

    *b.* $6,000.

    *c.* $9,000.

    *d.* $12,000.

5. What is the percent of noncontrolling interest ownership of Spin?

    *a.* 10 percent.

    *b.* 20 percent.

    *c.* 25 percent.

    *d.* 45 percent.

6. Over how many years has Power chosen to amortize patents?

    *a.* 10 years.

    *b.* 14 years.

    *c.* 23 years.

    *d.* 40 years.

**E7-3**  **Multiple-Choice Questions—Consolidated Income Statement**

Select the correct answer for each of the following questions.

Blue Company purchased 60 percent ownership of Kelly Corporation in 20X1. On May 10, 20X2, Kelly purchased inventory from Blue for $60,000. Kelly sold all of the inventory to an unaffiliated company for $86,000 on November 10, 20X2. Blue produced the inventory sold to Kelly for $47,000. The companies had no other transactions during 20X2.

1. What amount of sales will be reported in the 20X2 consolidated income statement?

    *a.* $51,600.

    *b.* $60,000.

    *c.* $86,000.

    *d.* $146,000.

2. What amount of cost of goods sold will be reported in the 20X2 consolidated income statement?

    *a.* $36,000.

    *b.* $47,000.

    *c.* $60,000.

    *d.* $107,000.

3. What amount of consolidated net income will be assigned to the controlling shareholders for 20X2?

    *a.* $13,000.

    *b.* $26,000.

    *c.* $28,600.

    *d.* $39,000.

**E7-4**    **Multiple-Choice Questions—Consolidated Balances**

Select the correct answer for each of the following questions.

Lorn Corporation purchased inventory from Dresser Corporation for $120,000 on September 20, 20X1, and resold 80 percent of the inventory to unaffiliated companies prior to December 31, 20X1, for $140,000. Dresser produced the inventory sold to Lorn for $75,000. Lorn owns 70 percent of Dresser's voting common stock. The companies had no other transactions during 20X1.

1. What amount of sales will be reported in the 20X1 consolidated income statement?

    *a.* $98,000.

    *b.* $120,000.

    *c.* $140,000.

    *d.* $260,000.

2. What amount of cost of goods sold will be reported in the 20X1 consolidated income statement?

    *a.* $60,000.

    *b.* $75,000.

    *c.* $96,000.

    *d.* $120,000.

    *e.* $171,000.

3. What amount of consolidated net income will be assigned to the controlling interest for 20X1?

    *a.* $20,000.

    *b.* $30,800.

    *c.* $44,000.

    *d.* $45,000.

    *e.* $69,200.

    *f.* $80,000.

4. What inventory balance will be reported by the consolidated entity on December 31, 20X1?

    *a.* $15,000.

    *b.* $16,800.

    *c.* $24,000.

    *d.* $39,000.

**E7-5**    **Multiple-Choice Questions—Consolidated Income Statement**

Select the correct answer for each of the following questions.

Amber Corporation holds 80 percent of the stock of Movie Productions Inc. During 20X4, Amber purchased an inventory of snack bar items for $40,000 and resold $30,000 to Movie Productions for $48,000. Movie Productions Inc. reported sales of $67,000 in 20X4 and had inventory of $16,000 on December 31, 20X4. The companies held no beginning inventory and had no other transactions in 20X4.

1. What amount of cost of goods sold will be reported in the 20X4 consolidated income statement?

    *a.* $20,000.

    *b.* $30,000.

    *c.* $32,000.

    *d.* $52,000.

    *e.* $62,000.

2. What amount of net income will be reported in the 20X4 consolidated income statement?

    *a.* $12,000.

    *b.* $18,000.

    *c.* $40,000.

    *d.* $47,000.

    *e.* $53,000.

3. What amount of income will be assigned to the noncontrolling interest in the 20X4 consolidated income statement?

    *a.* $7,000.

    *b.* $8,000.

    *c.* $9,400.

    *d.* $10,200.

    *e.* $13,400.

**E7-6  Realized Profit on Intercompany Sale**

Nordway Corporation acquired 90 percent of Olman Company's voting shares of stock in 20X1. During 20X4, Nordway purchased 40,000 Playday doghouses for $24 each and sold 25,000 of the doghouses to Olman for $30 each. Olman sold all of the doghouses to retail establishments prior to December 31, 20X4, for $45 each. Both companies use perpetual inventory systems.

### Required

*a.* Give the journal entries Nordway recorded for the purchase of inventory and resale to Olman Company in 20X4.

*b.* Give the journal entries Olman recorded for the purchase of inventory and resale to retail establishments in 20X4.

*c.* Give the workpaper eliminating entry(ies) needed in preparing consolidated financial statements for 20X4 to remove all effects of the intercompany sale.

**E7-7  Sale of Inventory to Subsidiary**

Nordway Corporation acquired 90 percent of Olman Company's voting shares of stock in 20X1. During 20X4, Nordway purchased 40,000 Playday doghouses for $24 each and sold 25,000 of the doghouses to Olman for $30 each. Olman sold 18,000 of the doghouses to retail establishments prior to December 31, 20X4, for $45 each. Both companies use perpetual inventory systems.

### Required

*a.* Give all journal entries Nordway recorded for the purchase of inventory and resale to Olman Company in 20X4.

*b.* Give the journal entries Olman recorded for the purchase of inventory and resale to retail establishments in 20X4.

*c.* Give the workpaper eliminating entry(ies) needed in preparing consolidated financial statements for 20X4 to remove the effects of the intercompany sale.

**E7-8  Inventory Transfer between Parent and Subsidiary**

Karlow Corporation owns 60 percent of Draw Company's voting shares. During 20X3, Karlow produced 25,000 computer desks at a cost of $82 each and sold 10,000 desks to Draw for $94 each. Draw sold 7,000 of the desks to unaffiliated companies for $130 each prior to December 31, 20X3, and sold the remainder in early 20X4 for $140 each. Both companies use perpetual inventory systems.

### Required

*a.* What amounts of cost of goods sold did Karlow and Draw record in 20X3?

*b.* What amount of cost of goods sold must be reported in the consolidated income statement for 20X3?

*c.* Give the workpaper eliminating entry or entries needed in preparing consolidated financial statements at December 31, 20X3, relating to the intercorporate sale of inventory.

*d.* Give the workpaper eliminating entry or entries needed in preparing consolidated financial statements at December 31, 20X4, relating to the intercorporate sale of inventory.

e. Give the workpaper eliminating entry or entries needed in preparing consolidated financial statements at December 31, 20X4, relating to the intercorporate sale of inventory if Draw had produced the computer desks at a cost of $82 each and sold 10,000 desks to Karlow for $94 each in 20X3, with Karlow selling 7,000 desks to unaffiliated companies in 20X3 and the remaining 3,000 in 20X4.

**E7-9** **Income Statement Effects of Unrealized Profit**

Holiday Bakery owns 60 percent of Farmco Products Company's stock. During 20X8, Farmco produced 100,000 bags of flour, which it sold to Holiday Bakery for $900,000. On December 31, 20X8, Holiday had 20,000 bags of flour purchased from Farmco Products on hand. Farmco prices its sales at cost plus 50 percent of cost for profit. Holiday, which purchased all its flour from Farmco in 20X8, had no inventory on hand on January 1, 20X8.

Holiday Bakery reported income from its baking operations of $400,000, and Farmco Products reported net income of $150,000 for 20X8.

### Required

a. Compute the amount reported as cost of goods sold in the 20X8 consolidated income statement.
b. Give the workpaper eliminating entry or entries required to remove the effects of the intercompany sale in preparing consolidated statements at the end of 20X8.
c. Compute the amounts reported as consolidated net income and income assigned to the controlling interest in the 20X8 consolidated income statement.

**E7-10** **Prior-Period Unrealized Inventory Profit**

Holiday Bakery owns 60 percent of Farmco Products Company's stock. On January 1, 20X9, inventory reported by Holiday included 20,000 bags of flour purchased from Farmco at $9 per bag. By December 31, 20X9, all the beginning inventory purchased from Farmco Products had been baked into products and sold to customers by Holiday. There were no transactions between Holiday and Farmco during 20X9.

Both Holiday Bakery and Farmco Products price their sales at cost plus 50 percent markup for profit. Holiday reported income from its baking operations of $300,000, and Farmco reported net income of $250,000 for 20X9.

### Required

a. Compute the amount reported as cost of goods sold in the 20X9 consolidated income statement for the flour purchased from Farmco in 20X8.
b. Give the eliminating entry or entries required to remove the effects of the unrealized profit in beginning inventory in preparing the consolidation workpaper as of December 31, 20X9.
c. Compute the amounts reported as consolidated net income and income assigned to the controlling interest in the 20X9 consolidated income statement.

**E7-11** **Computation of Consolidated Income Statement Data**

Prem Company acquired 60 percent ownership of Cooper Company's voting shares on January 1, 20X2. During 20X5, Prem purchased inventory for $20,000 and sold the full amount to Cooper Company for $30,000. On December 31, 20X5, Cooper's ending inventory included $6,000 of items purchased from Prem. Also in 20X5, Cooper purchased inventory for $50,000 and sold the units to Prem for $80,000. Prem included $20,000 of its purchase from Cooper in ending inventory on December 31, 20X5.

Summary income statement data for the two companies revealed the following:

|  | Prem Company | Cooper Company |
|---|---|---|
| Sales | $ 400,000 | $ 200,000 |
| Income from Subsidiary | 27,000 | |
|  | $ 427,000 | $ 200,000 |
| Cost of Goods Sold | $ 250,000 | $ 120,000 |
| Other Expenses | 70,000 | 35,000 |
| Total Expenses | $(320,000) | $(155,000) |
| Net Income | $ 107,000 | $ 45,000 |

### Required

a. Compute the amount to be reported as sales in the 20X5 consolidated income statement.

b. Compute the amount to be reported as cost of goods sold in the 20X5 consolidated income statement.

c. What amount of income will be assigned to the noncontrolling shareholders in the 20X5 consolidated income statement?

d. What amount of income will be assigned to the controlling interest in the 20X5 consolidated income statement?

**E7-12**  **Sale of Inventory at a Loss**

The price of high-quality burnwhistles fluctuates substantially from month to month. As a result, it is not uncommon for a company that deals in burnwhistles to report a substantial gain in one period, followed by a substantial loss in the following period. The price of burnwhistles was relatively high during the first three months of 20X8, declined substantially for the next four months, and then recovered nicely by year-end. On February 6, 20X8, Trent Company purchased burnwhistles for $400,000 and sold them to Gord Corporation on July 10, 20X8, for $300,000. Gord held its purchase for several months before selling 60 percent to nonaffiliates for $360,000 in late November. The remaining units were held at year-end and are expected to be sold in early 20X9 for approximately $240,000. Gord owns 75 percent of the stock of Trent Company.

### Required

a. Give the journal entries Trent and Gord recorded during 20X8 related to the initial purchase, intercorporate sale, and resale of inventory.

b. What amount should be reported as cost of goods sold in the 20X8 consolidated income statement?

c. If Gord reported operating income of $230,000 and Trent reported net income of $80,000, what amount of income should be assigned to the controlling interest in the 20X8 consolidated income statement?

d. Give the workpaper eliminating entry or entries needed in preparing consolidated financial statements for 20X8 to remove all effects of the intercompany transfer.

**E7-13**  **Intercompany Sales**

Hollow Corporation acquired 70 percent of Surg Corporation's voting stock on May 18, 20X1. The companies reported the following data with respect to intercompany sales in 20X4 and 20X5:

| Year | Purchased by | Purchase Price | Sold to | Sale Price | Unsold at End of Year | Year Sold to Unaffilliated Co. |
|------|--------------|----------------|---------|------------|-----------------------|--------------------------------|
| 20X4 | Surg Corp. | $120,000 | Hollow Corp. | $180,000 | $ 45,000 | 20X5 |
| 20X5 | Surg Corp. | 90,000 | Hollow Corp. | 135,000 | 30,000 | 20X6 |
| 20X5 | Hollow Corp. | 140,000 | Surg Corp. | 280,000 | 110,000 | 20X6 |

Hollow reported operating income (excluding income from its investment in Surg) of $160,000 and $220,000 in 20X4 and 20X5, respectively. Surg reported net income of $90,000 and $85,000 in 20X4 and 20X5, respectively.

### Required

a. Compute consolidated net income for 20X4.

b. Compute the inventory balance reported in the consolidated balance sheet at December 31, 20X5, for the transactions shown.

c. Compute the amount included in consolidated cost of goods sold for 20X5 relating to the transactions shown.

d. Compute the amount of income assigned to the controlling interest in the 20X5 consolidated income statement.

**E7-14**  **Consolidated Balance Sheet Workpaper**

The December 31, 20X8, balance sheets for Doorst Corporation and its 70 percent owned subsidiary Hingle Company contained the following summarized amounts:

**DOORST CORPORATION AND HINGLE COMPANY**
**Balance Sheets**
**December 31, 20X8**

|  | Doorst Corporation | Hingle Company |
|---|---|---|
| Cash and Receivables | $ 98,000 | $ 40,000 |
| Inventory | 150,000 | 100,000 |
| Buildings and Equipment (net) | 310,000 | 280,000 |
| Investment in Hingle Company Stock | 280,000 | |
| Total Assets | $838,000 | $420,000 |
| Accounts Payable | $ 70,000 | $ 20,000 |
| Common Stock | 200,000 | 150,000 |
| Retained Earnings | 568,000 | 250,000 |
| Total Liabilities and Equity | $838,000 | $420,000 |

Doorst acquired the shares of Hingle Company on January 1, 20X7. On December 31, 20X8, Doorst's balance sheet contains inventory items purchased from Hingle for $95,000. The items cost Hingle $55,000 to produce. In addition, Hingle's inventory contains goods it purchased from Doorst for $25,000 that Doorst had produced for $15,000.

### Required

*a.* Prepare all eliminating entries needed to complete a consolidated balance sheet workpaper as of December 31, 20X8.

*b.* Prepare a consolidated balance sheet workpaper as of December 31, 20X8.

**E7-15\*** ### Multiple Transfers between Affiliates

Klon Corporation owns 70 percent of Brant Company's stock and 60 percent of Torkel Company's stock. During 20X8, Klon sold inventory purchased in 20X7 for $100,000 to Brant for $150,000. Brant then sold the inventory at its cost of $150,000 to Torkel. Prior to December 31, 20X8, Torkel sold $90,000 of inventory to a nonaffiliate for $120,000 and held $60,000 in inventory at December 31, 20X8.

### Required

*a.* Give the journal entries recorded by Klon, Brant, and Torkel during 20X8 relating to the intercorporate sale and resale of inventory.

*b.* What amount should be reported in the 20X8 consolidated income statement as cost of goods sold?

*c.* What amount should be reported in the December 31, 20X8, consolidated balance sheet as inventory?

*d.* Give the eliminating entry needed at December 31, 20X8, to remove the effects of the inventory transfers.

**E7-16** ### Inventory Sales

Herb Corporation holds 60 percent ownership of Spice Company. Each year, Spice purchases large quantities of a gnarl root used in producing health drinks. Spice purchased $150,000 of roots in 20X7 and sold $40,000 of these purchases to Herb for $60,000. By the end of 20X7, Herb had resold all but $15,000 of its purchase from Spice. Herb generated $90,000 on the sale of roots to various health stores during the year.

### Required

*a.* Give the journal entries recorded by Herb and Spice during 20X7 relating to the initial purchase, intercorporate sale, and resale of gnarl roots.

*b.* Give the workpaper eliminating entries needed as of December 31, 20X7, to remove all effects of the intercompany transfer in preparing the 20X7 consolidated financial statements.

### E7-17   Prior-Period Inventory Profits

Home Products Corporation sells a broad line of home detergent products. Home Products owns 75 percent of the stock of Level Brothers Soap Company. During 20X8, Level Brothers sold soap products to Home Products for $180,000, which it had produced for $120,000. Home Products sold $150,000 of its purchase from Level Brothers in 20X8 and the remainder in 20X9. In addition, Home Products purchased $240,000 of inventory from Level Brothers in 20X9 and resold $90,000 of the items before year-end. Level Brothers' cost to produce the items sold to Home Products in 20X9 was $160,000.

#### Required

a. Give all workpaper eliminating entries needed for December 31, 20X9, to remove the effects of the intercompany inventory transfers in 20X8 and 20X9.

b. Compute the amount of income assigned to noncontrolling shareholders in the 20X8 and 20X9 consolidated income statements if Level Brothers reported net income of $350,000 for 20X8 and $420,000 for 20X9.

## Problems

### P7-18   Consolidated Income Statement Data

Sweeny Corporation owns 60 percent of Bitner Company's shares. Partial 20X2 financial data for the companies and consolidated entity were as follows:

|  | Sweeny Corporation | Bitner Company | Consolidated Totals |
|---|---|---|---|
| Sales | $550,000 | $450,000 | $820,000 |
| Cost of Goods Sold | 310,000 | 300,000 | 420,000 |
| Inventory, Dec. 31 | 180,000 | 210,000 | 375,000 |

On January 1, 20X2, Sweeny's inventory contained items purchased from Bitner for $75,000. The cost of the units to Bitner was $50,000. All intercorporate sales during 20X2 were made by Bitner to Sweeny.

#### Required

a. What amount of intercorporate sales occurred in 20X2?

b. How much unrealized intercompany profit existed on January 1, 20X2? On December 31, 20X2?

c. Give the workpaper eliminating entries relating to inventory and cost of goods sold needed to prepare consolidated financial statements for 20X2.

d. If Bitner reports net income of $90,000 for 20X2, what amount of income is assigned to the noncontrolling interest in the 20X2 consolidated income statement?

### P7-19   Unrealized Profit on Upstream Sales

Carroll Company sells all its output at 25 percent above cost. Pacific Corporation purchases all its inventory from Carroll. Selected information on the operations of the companies over the past three years is as follows:

|  | Carroll Company | | Pacific Corporation | |
|---|---|---|---|---|
| Year | Sales to Pacific Corp. | Net Income | Inventory, Dec. 31 | Operating Income |
| 20X2 | $200,000 | $100,000 | $ 70,000 | $150,000 |
| 20X3 | 175,000 | 90,000 | 105,000 | 240,000 |
| 20X4 | 225,000 | 160,000 | 120,000 | 300,000 |

Pacific acquired 60 percent of the ownership of Carroll on January 1, 20X1, at underlying book value.

### Required

Compute consolidated net income and income assigned to the controlling interest for 20X2, 20X3, and 20X4.

**P7-20** **Net Income of Consolidated Entity**

Master Corporation acquired 70 percent of Crown Corporation's voting stock on January 1, 20X2, for $416,500. The fair value of the noncontrolling interest was $178,500 at the date of acquisition. Crown reported common stock outstanding of $200,000 and retained earnings of $350,000. The differential is assigned to buildings with an expected life of 15 years at the date of acquisition.

On December 31, 20X4, Master had $25,000 of unrealized profits on its books from inventory sales to Crown, and Crown had $40,000 of unrealized profit on its books from inventory sales to Master. All inventory held at December 31, 20X4, was sold during 20X5.

On December 31, 20X5, Master had $14,000 of unrealized profit on its books from inventory sales to Crown, and Crown had unrealized profit on its books of $55,000 from inventory sales to Master.

Master reported income from its separate operations (excluding income on its investment in Crown and amortization of purchase differential) of $118,000 in 20X5, and Crown reported net income of $65,000.

### Required

Compute consolidated net income and income assigned to the controlling interest in the 20X5 consolidated income statement.

**P7-21** **Correction of Eliminating Entries**

In preparing the consolidation workpaper for Bolger Corporation and its 60 percent owned subsidiary, Feldman Company, the following eliminating entries were proposed by Bolger's bookkeeper:

| | | | |
|---|---|---|---|
| E(1) | Cash | 80,000 | |
| | Accounts Payable | | 80,000 |
| | To eliminate the unpaid balance for intercorporate inventory sales in 20X5. | | |
| E(2) | Cost of Goods Sold | 12,000 | |
| | Income from Subsidiary | | 12,000 |
| | To eliminate unrealized inventory profits at December 31, 20X5. | | |
| E(3) | Income from Subsidiary | 140,000 | |
| | Sales | | 140,000 |
| | To eliminate intercompany sales for 20X5. | | |

Bolger's bookkeeper recently graduated from Oddball University, and while the dollar amounts recorded are correct, he had some confusion in determining which accounts needed adjustment. All intercorporate sales in 20X5 were from Feldman to Bolger, and Feldman sells inventory at cost plus 40 percent of cost. Bolger uses the basic equity method in accounting for its ownership in Feldman.

### Required

*a.* What percentage of the intercompany inventory transfer was resold prior to the end of 20X5?

*b.* Give the appropriate eliminating entries needed at December 31, 20X5, to prepare consolidated financial statements.

**P7-22** **Incomplete Data**

Lever Corporation acquired 75 percent of the ownership of Tropic Company on January 1, 20X1. The fair value of the noncontrolling interest at acquisition was equal to its proportionate share of the fair value of the net assets of Tropic. The full amount of the differential at acquisition was attributable to buildings and equipment which had a remaining useful life of eight years. Financial statement data for the two companies and the consolidated entity at December 31, 20X6, are as follows:

---

**LEVER CORPORATION AND TROPIC COMPANY**
**Balance Sheet Data**
**December 31, 20X6**

| Item | Lever Corporation | Tropic Company | Consolidated Entity |
|---|---|---|---|
| Cash | $ 67,000 | $ 45,000 | $ 112,000 |
| Accounts Receivable | ? | 55,000 | 145,000 |
| Inventory | 125,000 | 90,000 | 211,000 |
| Buildings and Equipment | 400,000 | 240,000 | 680,000 |
| Less: Accumulated Depreciation | (180,000) | (110,000) | ( ? ) |
| Investment in Tropic Company | ? | | |
| Total Assets | $ ? | $320,000 | $ ? |
| Accounts Payable | $ 86,000 | $ 20,000 | $ 89,000 |
| Other Payables | ? | 8,000 | ? |
| Notes Payable | 250,000 | 120,000 | 370,000 |
| Common Stock | 120,000 | 60,000 | 120,000 |
| Retained Earnings | 175,500 | 112,000 | 172,500 |
| Noncontrolling Interest | | | 44,500 |
| Total Liabilities and Equity | $ ? | $320,000 | $ ? |

---

**LEVER CORPORATION AND TROPIC COMPANY**
**Income Statement Data**
**For the Year Ended December 31, 20X6**

| Item | Lever Corporation | Tropic Company | Consolidated Entity |
|---|---|---|---|
| Sales | $420,000 | $260,000 | $650,000 |
| Income from Subsidiary | 26,250 | | |
| Total Income | $446,250 | $260,000 | $650,000 |
| Cost of Goods Sold | $310,000 | $170,000 | $445,000 |
| Depreciation Expense | 20,000 | 25,000 | 50,000 |
| Interest Expense | 25,000 | 9,500 | 34,500 |
| Other Expenses | 22,000 | 15,500 | 37,500 |
| Total Expenses | ($377,000) | ($220,000) | ($567,000) |
| Consolidated Net Income | | | $ 83,000 |
| Income to Noncontrolling Interest | | | (7,750) |
| Net Income and Income to Controlling Interest | $ 69,250 | $ 40,000 | $ 75,250 |

---

All unrealized profit on intercompany inventory sales on January 1, 20X6, were on Lever's books. All unrealized inventory profits at December 31, 20X6, were on Tropic's books.

### Required

*a.* For the buildings and equipment held by Tropic when it was acquired by Lever and still on hand on December 31, 20X6, by what amount had they increased in value from their aquisition to the date of combination with Lever?

b. What amount should be reported as accumulated depreciation for the consolidated entity at December 31, 20X6?

c. If Tropic reported capital stock outstanding of $60,000 and retained earnings of $30,000 on January 1, 20X1, what amount did Lever pay to acquire its ownership of Tropic?

d. What balance does Lever report as its investment in Tropic at December 31, 20X6?

e. What amount of intercorporate sales of inventory occurred in 20X6?

f. What amount of unrealized inventory profit exists at December 31, 20X6?

g. Give the eliminating entry used in eliminating intercompany inventory sales during 20X6.

h. What was the amount of unrealized inventory profit at January 1, 20X6?

i. What balance in accounts receivable did Lever report at December 31, 20X6?

**P7-23** **Eliminations for Upstream Sales**

Clean Air Products owns 80 percent of the stock of Superior Filter Company, which it acquired at underlying book value on August 30, 20X6. At that date, the fair value of the noncontrolling interest was equal to 20 percent of the book value of Superior Filter. Summarized trial balance data for the two companies as of December 31, 20X8, are as follows:

| | Clean Air Products | | Superior Filter Company | |
|---|---|---|---|---|
| | Debit | Credit | Debit | Credit |
| Cash and Accounts Receivable | $ 145,000 | | $ 90,000 | |
| Inventory | 220,000 | | 110,000 | |
| Buildings and Equipment (net) | 270,000 | | 180,000 | |
| Investment in Superior Filter Stock | 280,000 | | | |
| Cost of Goods Sold | 175,000 | | 140,000 | |
| Depreciation Expense | 30,000 | | 20,000 | |
| Current Liabilities | | $ 150,000 | | $ 30,000 |
| Common Stock | | 200,000 | | 90,000 |
| Retained Earnings | | 488,000 | | 220,000 |
| Sales | | 250,000 | | 200,000 |
| Income from Subsidiary | | 32,000 | | |
| Total | $1,120,000 | $1,120,000 | $540,000 | $540,000 |

On January 1, 20X8, Clean Air's inventory contained filters purchased for $60,000 from Superior Filter, which had produced the filters for $40,000. In 20X8, Superior Filter spent $100,000 to produce additional filters, which it sold to Clean Air for $150,000. By December 31, 20X8, Clean Air had sold all filters that had been on hand January 1, 20X8, but continued to hold in inventory $45,000 of the 20X8 purchase from Superior Filter.

### Required

a. Prepare all eliminating entries needed to complete a consolidation workpaper for 20X8.

b. Compute consolidated net income and income assigned to the controlling interest in the 20X8 consolidated income statement.

c. Compute the balance assigned to the noncontrolling interest in the consolidated balance sheet as of December 31, 20X8.

**P7-24** **Multiple Inventory Transfers**

Ajax Corporation purchased at book value 70 percent of Beta Corporation's ownership and 90 percent of Cole Corporation's ownership in 20X5. At the dates the ownership was acquired, the fair value of the noncontrolling interest was equal to a proportionate share of book value. There are frequent intercompany transfers among the companies. Activity relevant to 20X8 follows:

| Year | Producer | Production Cost | Buyer | Transfer Price | Unsold at End of Year | Year Sold |
|------|----------|----------------|-------|---------------|----------------------|-----------|
| 20X7 | Beta Corporation | $24,000 | Ajax Corporation | $30,000 | $10,000 | 20X8 |
| 20X7 | Cole Corporation | 60,000 | Beta Corporation | 72,000 | 18,000 | 20X8 |
| 20X8 | Ajax Corporation | 15,000 | Beta Corporation | 35,000 | 7,000 | 20X9 |
| 20X8 | Beta Corporation | 63,000 | Cole Corporation | 72,000 | 12,000 | 20X9 |
| 20X8 | Cole Corporation | 27,000 | Ajax Corporation | 45,000 | 15,000 | 20X9 |

For the year ended December 31, 20X8, Ajax reported $80,000 of income from its separate operations (excluding income from intercorporate investments), Beta reported net income of $37,500, and Cole reported net income of $20,000.

### Required

*a.* Compute the amount to be reported as consolidated net income for 20X8.

*b.* Compute the amount to be reported as inventory in the December 31, 20X8, consolidated balance sheet for the preceding items.

*c.* Compute the amount to be reported as income assigned to noncontrolling shareholders in the 20X8 consolidated income statement.

**P7-25**  **Consolidation with Inventory Transfers and Other Comprehensive Income**

On January 1, 20X1, Priority Corporation purchased 90 percent of Tall Corporation's common stock at underlying book value. At that date, the fair value of the noncontrolling interest was equal to 10 percent of the book value of Tall Corporation. Priority uses the equity method in accounting for its investment in Tall. The stockholders' equity section of Tall at January 1, 20X5, contained the following balances:

| | |
|---|---|
| Common Stock ($5 par) | $ 400,000 |
| Additional Paid-In Capital | 200,000 |
| Retained Earnings | 790,000 |
| Accumulated Other Comprehensive Income | 10,000 |
| Total | $1,400,000 |

During 20X4, Tall sold goods costing $30,000 to Priority for $45,000, and Priority resold 60 percent prior to year-end. It sold the remainder in 20X5. Also in 20X4, Priority sold inventory items costing $90,000 to Tall for $108,000. Tall resold $60,000 of its purchases in 20X4 and the remaining $48,000 in 20X5.

In 20X5, Priority sold additional inventory costing $30,000 to Tall for $36,000, and Tall resold $24,000 of it prior to year-end. Tall sold inventory costing $60,000 to Priority in 20X5 for $90,000, and Priority resold $48,000 of its purchase by December 31, 20X5.

Priority reported 20X5 income of $240,000 from its separate operations and paid dividends of $150,000. Tall reported 20X5 net income of $90,000 and comprehensive income of $110,000. Tall reported other comprehensive income of $10,000 in 20X4. In both years, other comprehensive income arose from an increase in the market value of securities classified as available-for-sale. Tall paid dividends of $60,000 in 20X5.

### Required

*a.* Compute the balance in the investment account reported by Priority at December 31, 20X5.

*b.* Compute the amount of investment income reported by Priority on its investment in Tall for 20X5.

*c.* Compute the amount of income assigned to noncontrolling shareholders in the 20X5 consolidated income statement.

*d.* Compute the balance assigned to noncontrolling shareholders in the consolidated balance sheet prepared at December 31, 20X5.

e. Priority and Tall report inventory balances of $120,000 and $100,000, respectively, at December 31, 20X5. What amount should be reported as inventory in the consolidated balance sheet at December 31, 20X5?

f. Compute the amount reported as consolidated net income for 20X5.

g. Prepare the eliminating entries needed to complete a consolidation workpaper as of December 31, 20X5.

### P7-26  Multiple Inventory Transfers between Parent and Subsidiary

Proud Company and Slinky Company both produce and purchase equipment for resale each period and frequently sell to each other. Since Proud Company holds 60 percent ownership of Slinky Company, Proud's controller compiled the following information with regard to intercompany transactions between the two companies in 20X5 and 20X6:

| Year | Produced by | Sold to | Percent Resold to Nonaffiliate in 20X5 | Percent Resold to Nonaffiliate in 20X6 | Cost to Produce | Sale Price to Affiliate |
|------|-------------|---------|------|------|---------|---------|
| 20X5 | Proud Company | Slinky Company | 60% | 40% | $100,000 | $150,000 |
| 20X5 | Slinky Company | Proud Company | 30 | 50 | 70,000 | 100,000 |
| 20X6 | Proud Company | Slinky Company | | 90 | 40,000 | 60,000 |
| 20X6 | Slinky Company | Proud Company | | 25 | 200,000 | 240,000 |

### Required

a. Give the eliminating entries required at December 31, 20X6, to eliminate the effects of the inventory transfers in preparing a full set of consolidated financial statements.

b. Compute the amount of cost of goods sold to be reported in the consolidated income statement for 20X6.

### P7-27  Consolidation following Inventory Transactions

Bell Company purchased 60 percent ownership of Troll Corporation on January 1, 20X1, for $82,800. On that date, the noncontrolling interest had a fair value of $55,200 and Troll reported common stock outstanding of $100,000 and retained earnings of $20,000. The full amount of the differential is assigned to land to be used as a future building site. Bell uses the basic equity method in accounting for its ownership of Troll. On December 31, 20X2, the trial balances of the two companies are as follows:

| Item | Bell Company Debit | Bell Company Credit | Troll Corporation Debit | Troll Corporation Credit |
|------|-------|--------|-------|--------|
| Cash and Accounts Receivable | $ 69,400 | | $ 51,200 | |
| Inventory | 60,000 | | 55,000 | |
| Land | 40,000 | | 30,000 | |
| Buildings and Equipment | 520,000 | | 350,000 | |
| Investment in Troll Corporation Stock | 112,800 | | | |
| Cost of Goods Sold | 99,800 | | 61,000 | |
| Depreciation Expense | 25,000 | | 15,000 | |
| Interest Expense | 6,000 | | 14,000 | |
| Dividends Declared | 40,000 | | 10,000 | |
| Accumulated Depreciation | | $175,000 | | $ 75,000 |
| Accounts Payable | | 68,800 | | 41,200 |
| Bonds Payable | | 80,000 | | 200,000 |
| Bond Premium | | 1,200 | | |
| Common Stock | | 200,000 | | 100,000 |
| Retained Earnings | | 230,000 | | 50,000 |
| Sales | | 200,000 | | 120,000 |
| Income from Subsidiary | | 18,000 | | |
| | $973,000 | $973,000 | $586,200 | $586,200 |

Troll sold inventory costing $25,500 to Bell for $42,500 in 20X1. Bell resold 80 percent of the purchase in 20X1 and the remainder in 20X2. Troll sold inventory costing $21,000 to Bell in 20X2 for $35,000, and Bell resold 70 percent prior to December 31, 20X2. In addition, Bell sold inventory costing $14,000 to Troll for $28,000 in 20X2, and Troll resold all but $13,000 of its purchase prior to December 31, 20X2.

### Required

a. Record the journal entry or entries for 20X2 on Bell's books related to its investment in Troll Corporation, using the basic equity method.

b. Prepare the elimination entries needed to complete a consolidated workpaper for 20X2.

c. Prepare a three-part consolidation workpaper for 20X2.

**P7-28   Consolidation Workpaper**

Crow Corporation purchased 70 percent of West Company's voting common stock on January 1, 20X5, for $291,200. On that date, the noncontrolling interest had a fair value of $124,800 and the book value of West's net assets was $380,000. The book values and fair values of West's assets and liabilities were equal, except for land that had a fair value $14,000 greater than book value. The amount attributed to goodwill as a result of the acquisition is not amortized and has not been impaired.

### CROW CORPORATION AND WEST COMPANY
#### Trial Balance Data
#### December 31, 20X9

| Item | Crow Corporation Debit | Crow Corporation Credit | West Company Debit | West Company Credit |
|---|---|---|---|---|
| Cash and Receivables | $   81,300 | | $  85,000 | |
| Inventory | 200,000 | | 110,000 | |
| Land, Buildings, and Equipment (net) | 270,000 | | 250,000 | |
| Investment in West Company Stock | 315,700 | | | |
| Cost of Goods and Services | 200,000 | | 150,000 | |
| Depreciation Expense | 40,000 | | 30,000 | |
| Dividends Declared | 35,000 | | 5,000 | |
| Sales and Service Revenue | | $  300,000 | | $200,000 |
| Income from Subsidiary | | 14,000 | | |
| Accounts Payable | | 60,000 | | 30,000 |
| Common Stock | | 200,000 | | 150,000 |
| Retained Earnings | | 568,000 | | 250,000 |
| Total | $1,142,000 | $1,142,000 | $630,000 | $630,000 |

On January 1, 20X9, Crow's inventory contained unrealized intercompany profits recorded by West in the amount of $30,000. West's inventory on that date contained $15,000 of unrealized intercompany profits recorded on Crow's books. Both companies sold their ending 20X8 inventories to unrelated companies in 20X9.

During 20X9, West sold inventory costing $37,000 to Crow for $62,000. Crow held all inventory purchased from West during 20X9 on December 31, 20X9. Also during 20X9, Crow sold goods costing $54,000 to West for $90,000. West continues to hold $20,000 of its purchase from Crow on December 31, 20X9.

On January 1, 20X6, Crow paid $95,000 to West for equipment purchased by West on January 1, 20X1, for $120,000. The total estimated economic life of 15 years for the equipment remains unchanged.

### Required

a. Prepare all eliminating entries needed to complete a consolidation workpaper as of December 31, 20X9.

b. Prepare a consolidation workpaper as of December 31, 20X9.

c. Prepare a reconciliation between the balance in retained earnings reported by Crow on December 31, 20X9, and consolidated retained earnings.

**P7-29   Computation of Consolidated Totals**

Bunker Corporation owns 80 percent of Harrison Company's stock. At the end of 20X8, Bunker and Harrison reported the following partial operating results and inventory balances:

| | Bunker Corporation | Harrison Company |
|---|---|---|
| Total sales | $660,000 | $510,000 |
| Sales to Harrison Company | 140,000 | |
| Sales to Bunker Corporation | | 240,000 |
| Net income | | 20,000 |
| Operating income (excluding investment income from Harrison) | 70,000 | |
| Inventory on hand, December 31, 20X8, purchased from: | | |
| Harrison Company | 48,000 | |
| Bunker Corporation | | 42,000 |

Bunker regularly prices its products at cost plus a 40 percent markup for profit. Harrison prices its sales at cost plus a 20 percent markup. The total sales reported by Bunker and Harrison include both intercompany sales and sales to nonaffiliates.

***Required***

*a.* What amount of sales will be reported in the consolidated income statement for 20X8?

*b.* What amount of cost of goods sold will be reported in the 20X8 consolidated income statement?

*c.* What amount of consolidated net income and income to controlling interest will be reported in the 20X8 consolidated income statement?

*d.* What balance will be reported for inventory in the consolidated balance sheet for December 31, 20X8?

**P7-30   Intercompany Transfer of Inventory and Land**

Pine Corporation acquired 70 percent of Bock Company's voting common shares on January 1, 20X2, for $108,500. At that date, the noncontrolling interest had a fair value of $46,500 and Bock reported $70,000 of common stock outstanding and retained earnings of $30,000. The differential is assigned to buildings and equipment, which had a fair value $20,000 greater than book value and a remaining 10-year life, and to patents, which had a fair value $35,000 greater than book value and a remaining life of five years at the date of the business combination. Trial balances for the companies as of December 31, 20X3, are as follows:

| | Pine Corporation | | Bock Company | |
|---|---|---|---|---|
| Item | Debit | Credit | Debit | Credit |
| Cash and Accounts Receivable | $ 15,400 | | $ 21,600 | |
| Inventory | 165,000 | | 35,000 | |
| Land | 80,000 | | 40,000 | |
| Buildings and Equipment | 340,000 | | 260,000 | |
| Investment in Bock Company Stock | 123,900 | | | |
| Cost of Goods Sold | 186,000 | | 79,800 | |
| Depreciation Expense | 20,000 | | 15,000 | |
| Interest Expense | 16,000 | | 5,200 | |
| Dividends Declared | 30,000 | | 15,000 | |
| Accumulated Depreciation | | $140,000 | | $ 80,000 |
| Accounts Payable | | 92,400 | | 35,000 |
| Bonds Payable | | 200,000 | | 100,000 |
| Bond Premium | | | | 1,600 |
| Common Stock | | 120,000 | | 70,000 |
| Retained Earnings | | 139,100 | | 60,000 |
| Sales | | 260,000 | | 125,000 |
| Other Income | | 13,600 | | |
| Income from Subsidiary | | 11,200 | | |
| | $976,300 | $976,300 | $471,600 | $471,600 |

On December 31, 20X2, Bock purchased inventory for $32,000 and sold it to Pine for $48,000. Pine resold $27,000 of the inventory during 20X3 and had the remaining balance in inventory at December 31, 20X3.

During 20X3, Bock sold inventory purchased for $60,000 to Pine for $90,000, and Pine resold all but $24,000 of its purchase. On March 10, 20X3, Pine sold inventory purchased for $15,000 to Bock for $30,000. Bock sold all but $7,600 of the inventory prior to December 31, 20X3.

During 20X2, Bock sold land it had purchased for $22,000 to Pine for $37,000. Pine plans to build a warehouse on the property in the near future.

### Required

*a.* Give all eliminating entries needed to prepare a full set of consolidated financial statements at December 31, 20X3, for Pine and Bock.

*b.* Prepare a three-part consolidation workpaper for 20X3.

**P7-31  Consolidation Using Financial Statement Data**

Bower Corporation acquired 60 percent of Concerto Company's stock on January 1, 20X3, for $24,000 in excess of book value. On that date, the book values and fair values of Concerto's assets and liabilities were equal and the fair value of the noncontrolling interest was $16,000 in excess of book value. The full amount of the differential at acquisition was assigned to goodwill. At December 31, 20X6, the management of Bower reviewed the amount assigned to goodwill and concluded it had been impaired. They concluded the correct carrying value at that date should be $30,000 and the impairment loss should be assigned proportionately between the controlling and noncontrolling interests.

Balance sheet data for January 1, 20X6, and December 31, 20X6, and income statement data for 20X6 for the two companies are as follows:

---

**BOWER CORPORATION AND CONCERTO COMPANY**
**Balance Sheet Data**
**January 1, 20X6**

| Item | Bower Corporation | | Concerto Company | |
|---|---|---|---|---|
| Cash | $ 9,800 | | $ 10,000 | |
| Accounts Receivable | 60,000 | | 50,000 | |
| Inventory | 100,000 | | 80,000 | |
| Total Current Assets | | $169,800 | | $140,000 |
| Land | | 70,000 | | 20,000 |
| Buildings and Equipment | $300,000 | | $200,000 | |
| Less: Accumulated Depreciation | (140,000) | 160,000 | (70,000) | 130,000 |
| Investment in Concerto Company Stock | | 144,000 | | |
| Total Assets | | $543,800 | | $290,000 |
| Accounts Payable | | $ 30,000 | | $ 20,000 |
| Bonds Payable | | 120,000 | | 70,000 |
| Common Stock | $100,000 | | $ 50,000 | |
| Retained Earnings | 293,800 | 393,800 | 150,000 | 200,000 |
| Total Liabilities and Stockholders' Equity | | $543,800 | | $290,000 |

---

**BOWER CORPORATION AND CONCERTO COMPANY**
**Balance Sheet Data**
**December 31, 20X6**

| Item | Bower Corporation | | Concerto Company | |
|---|---|---|---|---|
| Cash | $ 26,800 | | $ 35,000 | |
| Accounts Receivable | 80,000 | | 40,000 | |
| Inventory | 120,000 | | 90,000 | |
| Total Current Assets | | $226,800 | | $165,000 |
| Land | | 70,000 | | 20,000 |

*(continued)*

(continued)

| Item | Bower Corporation | | Concerto Company | |
|---|---|---|---|---|
| Buildings and Equipment | $340,000 | | $200,000 | |
| Less: Accumulated Depreciation | (165,000) | 175,000 | (85,000) | 115,000 |
| Investment in Concerto Company Stock | | 153,000 | | |
| Total Assets | | $624,800 | | $300,000 |
| Accounts Payable | | $ 80,000 | | $ 15,000 |
| Bonds Payable | | 120,000 | | 70,000 |
| Common Stock | $100,000 | | $ 50,000 | |
| Retained Earnings | 324,800 | 424,800 | 165,000 | 215,000 |
| Total Liabilities and Stockholders' Equity | | $624,800 | | $300,000 |

**BOWER CORPORATION AND CONCERTO COMPANY**
**Income Statement Data**
**Year Ended December 31, 20X6**

| Item | Bower Corporation | | Concerto Company | |
|---|---|---|---|---|
| Sales | $400,000 | | $200,000 | |
| Income from Subsidiary | 21,000 | | | |
| | $421,000 | | $200,000 | |
| Cost of Goods Sold | $280,000 | | $120,000 | |
| Depreciation and Amortization Expense | 25,000 | | 15,000 | |
| Other Expenses | 35,000 | (340,000) | 30,000 | (165,000) |
| Net Income | | $ 81,000 | | $ 35,000 |

In 20X4, Concerto purchased a piece of land for $35,000 and later in the year sold it to Bower for $45,000. Bower is still using the land in its operations.

On January 1, 20X6, Bower held inventory purchased from Concerto for $48,000. During 20X6, Bower purchased an additional $90,000 of goods from Concerto and held $54,000 of its purchases on December 31, 20X6. Concerto sells inventory to the parent at 20 percent above cost.

Concerto also purchases inventory from Bower Corporation. On January 1, 20X6, Concerto held inventory purchased from Bower for $14,000, and on December 31, 20X6, it held inventory purchased from Bower for $7,000. Concerto's total purchases from Bower Corporation were $22,000 in 20X6. Bower Corporation sells items to Concerto Company at 40 percent above cost.

During 20X6, Bower paid dividends of $50,000, and Concerto paid dividends of $20,000.

### Required

a. Prepare all eliminating entries needed to complete a consolidation workpaper as of December 31, 20X6.

b. Prepare a three-part consolidation workpaper as of December 31, 20X6.

**P7-32 Intercorporate Transfers of Inventory and Equipment**

Block Corporation was created on January 1, 20X0, to develop computer software. On January 1, 20X5, Foster Company purchased 90 percent of Block's common stock at underlying book value. At that date, the fair value of the noncontrolling interest was equal to 10 percent of the book value of Block Corporation. Trial balances for Foster and Block on December 31, 20X9, are as follows:

| | 20X9 Trial Balance Data | | | |
| | Foster Company | | Block Corporation | |
| Item | Debit | Credit | Debit | Credit |
|---|---|---|---|---|
| Cash | $ 187,000 | | $ 57,400 | |
| Accounts Receivable | 80,000 | | 90,000 | |
| Other Receivables | 40,000 | | 10,000 | |
| Inventory | 137,000 | | 130,000 | |
| Land | 80,000 | | 60,000 | |
| Buildings and Equipment | 500,000 | | 250,000 | |
| Investment in Block Corporation Stock | 238,500 | | | |
| Cost of Goods Sold | 593,000 | | 270,000 | |
| Depreciation Expense | 45,000 | | 15,000 | |
| Other Expenses | 95,000 | | 75,000 | |
| Dividends Declared | 40,000 | | 20,000 | |
| Accumulated Depreciation | | $ 155,000 | | $ 75,000 |
| Accounts Payable | | 63,000 | | 35,000 |
| Other Payables | | 95,000 | | 20,000 |
| Bonds Payable | | 250,000 | | 200,000 |
| Bond Premium | | | | 2,400 |
| Common Stock | | 210,000 | | 50,000 |
| Additional Paid-In Capital | | 110,000 | | |
| Retained Earnings | | 248,500 | | 165,000 |
| Sales | | 815,000 | | 415,000 |
| Other Income | | 26,000 | | 15,000 |
| Income from Subsidiary | | 63,000 | | |
| Total | $2,035,500 | $2,035,500 | $977,400 | $977,400 |

On January 1, 20X7, Block sold equipment to Foster for $48,000. Block had purchased the equipment for $90,000 on January 1, 20X5; it was depreciated on a straight-line basis with an expected life of 10 years and no anticipated scrap value. The equipment's total expected life is unchanged as a result of the intercompany transfer.

During 20X9, Block produced inventory for $20,000 and sold it to Foster for $30,000. Foster resold 60 percent of the inventory in 20X9. Also in 20X9, Foster sold inventory purchased from Block in 20X8. It had cost Block $60,000 to produce the inventory, and Foster purchased it for $75,000.

### Required

*a.* What amount of cost of goods sold will be reported in the 20X9 consolidated income statement?

*b.* What inventory balance will be reported in the December 31, 20X9, consolidated balance sheet?

*c.* What amount of income will be assigned to noncontrolling shareholders in the 20X9 consolidated income statement?

*d.* What amount will be assigned to noncontrolling interest in the consolidated balance sheet prepared at December 31, 20X9?

*e.* What amount of retained earnings will be reported in the consolidated balance sheet at December 31, 20X9?

*f.* Give all eliminating entries required to prepare a three-part consolidation workpaper at December 31, 20X9.

*g.* Prepare a three-part consolidation workpaper at December 31, 20X9.

**P7-33 Consolidated Balance Sheet Workpaper [AICPA Adapted]**

The December 31, 20X6, condensed balance sheets of Pine Corporation and its 90 percent–owned subsidiary, Slim Corporation, are presented in the accompanying worksheet.

### Additional Information

- Pine's investment in Slim was acquired for $1,170,000 cash on January 1, 20X6, and is accounted for by the basic equity method. The fair value of the noncontrolling interest at that date was $130,000.
- At January 1, 20X6, Slim's retained earnings amounted to $600,000, and its common stock amounted to $200,000.
- Slim declared a $1,000 cash dividend in December 20X6, payable in January 20X7.
- As of December 31, 20X6, Pine had not recorded any portion of Slim's 20X6 net income or dividend declaration.
- Slim borrowed $100,000 from Pine on June 30, 20X6, with the note maturing on June 30, 20X7, at 10 percent interest. Correct accruals have been recorded by both companies.
- During 20X6, Pine sold merchandise to Slim at an aggregate invoice price of $300,000, which included a profit of $60,000. At December 31, 20X6, Slim had not paid Pine for $90,000 of these purchases, and 5 percent of the total merchandise purchased from Pine still remained in Slim's inventory.
- Pine's excess cost over book value of its investment in Slim has appropriately been identified as goodwill. At December 31, 20X6, Pine's management reviewed the amount attributed to goodwill and found no evidence of impairment.

### Required

Complete the accompanying workpaper for Pine and its subsidiary, Slim, at December 31, 20X6.

---

### PINE CORPORATION AND SUBSIDIARY
### Consolidated Balance Sheet Workpaper
### December 31, 20X6

| | Pine Corporation | Slim Corporation | Adjustments and Eliminations Debit | Adjustments and Eliminations Credit | Consolidated |
|---|---|---|---|---|---|
| **Assets** | | | | | |
| Cash | 105,000 | 15,000 | | | |
| Accounts and Other Current Receivables | 410,000 | 120,000 | | | |
| Merchandise Inventory | 920,000 | 670,000 | | | |
| Plant and Equipment, Net | 1,000,000 | 400,000 | | | |
| Investment in Slim | 1,170,000 | | | | |
| Totals | 3,605,000 | 1,205,000 | | | |
| | | | | | |
| **Liabilities and Stockholders' Equity:** | | | | | |
| Accounts Payable and Other Current Liabilities | 140,000 | 305,000 | | | |
| Common Stock ($10 par) | 500,000 | 200,000 | | | |
| Retained Earnings | 2,965,000 | 700,000 | | | |
| Totals | 3,605,000 | 1,205,000 | | | |

---

**P7-34 Comprehensive Worksheet Problem**

Randall Corporation acquired 80 percent of Sharp Company's voting shares on January 1, 20X4, for $280,000 in cash and marketable securities. At that date, the noncontrolling interest had a fair value of $70,000 and Sharp reported net assets of $300,000. Trial balances for the two companies on December 31, 20X7, are as follows:

| Item | Randall Corporation | | Sharp Company | |
|---|---|---|---|---|
| | **Debit** | **Credit** | **Debit** | **Credit** |
| Cash | $ 130,300 | | $ 10,000 | |
| Accounts Receivable | 80,000 | | 70,000 | |
| Inventory | 170,000 | | 110,000 | |
| Buildings and Equipment | 600,000 | | 400,000 | |
| Investment in Sharp Company Stock | 304,000 | | | |
| Cost of Goods Sold | 416,000 | | 202,000 | |
| Depreciation and Amortization | 30,000 | | 20,000 | |
| Other Expenses | 24,000 | | 18,000 | |
| Dividends Declared | 50,000 | | 25,000 | |
| Accumulated Depreciation | | $ 310,000 | | $120,000 |
| Accounts Payable | | 100,000 | | 15,200 |
| Bonds Payable | | 300,000 | | 100,000 |
| Bond Premium | | | | 4,800 |
| Common Stock | | 200,000 | | 100,000 |
| Additional Paid-In Capital | | | | 20,000 |
| Retained Earnings | | 345,900 | | 215,000 |
| Sales | | 500,000 | | 250,000 |
| Other Income | | 20,400 | | 30,000 |
| Income from Subsidiary | | 28,000 | | |
| | $1,804,300 | $1,804,300 | $855,000 | $855,000 |

### Additional Information

a. The full amount of the differential at acquisition was assigned to buildings and equipment with a remaining 10-year economic life.

b. Randall and Sharp regularly purchase inventory from each other. During 20X6, Sharp sold inventory costing $40,000 to Randall Corporation for $60,000, and Randall resold 60 percent of the inventory in 20X6 and 40 percent in 20X7. Also in 20X6, Randall sold inventory costing $20,000 to Sharp for $26,000. Sharp resold two-thirds of the inventory in 20X6 and one-third in 20X7.

c. During 20X7, Sharp sold inventory costing $30,000 to Randall for $45,000, and Randall sold items purchased for $9,000 to Sharp for $12,000. Before the end of the year, Randall resold one-third of the inventory it purchased from Sharp in 20X7. Sharp continues to hold all the units purchased from Randall during 20X7.

d. Randall sold equipment originally purchased for $75,000 to Sharp for $50,000 on December 31, 20X5. Accumulated depreciation over the 12 years of use before the intercorporate sale was $45,000. The estimated remaining life at the time of transfer was eight years. Straight-line depreciation is used by both companies.

e. Sharp owes Randall $10,000 on account on December 31, 20X7.

### Required

a. Prepare the 20X7 journal entries recorded on Randall's books related to its investment in Sharp if Randall uses the basic equity method.

b. Prepare all eliminating entries needed to complete a consolidation workpaper as of December 31, 20X7.

c. Prepare a three-part consolidation workpaper as of December 31, 20X7.

d. Prepare, in good form, a consolidated income statement, balance sheet, and retained earnings statement for 20X7.

**P7-35   Comprehensive Consolidation Workpaper; Equity Method [AICPA Adapted]**

Fran Corporation acquired all outstanding $10 par value voting common stock of Brey Inc. on January 1, 20X9, in exchange for 25,000 shares of its $20 par value voting common stock.

On December 31, 20X8, Fran's common stock had a closing market price of $30 per share on a national stock exchange. The acquisition was appropriately accounted for under the acquisition method. Both companies continued to operate as separate business entities maintaining separate accounting records with years ending December 31. Fran accounts for its investment in Brey stock using the equity method without adjusting for unrealized intercompany profits.

On December 31, 20X9, the companies had condensed financial statements as follows:

| | Fran Corporation | | Brey Inc. | |
|---|---|---|---|---|
| | **Dr** | **(Cr)** | **Dr** | **(Cr)** |
| **Income Statement** | | | | |
| Net Sales | | $(3,800,000) | | $(1,500,000) |
| Equity in Brey's Income | | (181,000) | | |
| Gain on Sale of Warehouse | | (30,000) | | |
| Cost of Goods Sold | 2,360,000 | | 870,000 | |
| Operating Expenses (including depreciation) | 1,100,000 | | 440,000 | |
| Net Income | | $ (551,000) | | $ (190,000) |
| **Retained Earnings Statement** | | | | |
| Balance, 1/1/X9 | | $ (440,000) | | $ (156,000) |
| Net Income | | (551,000) | | (190,000) |
| Dividends Paid | | | 40,000 | |
| Balance, 12/31/X9 | | $ (991,000) | | $ (306,000) |
| **Balance Sheet** | | | | |
| Assets: | | | | |
| Cash | $ 570,000 | | $ 150,000 | |
| Accounts Receivable (net) | 860,000 | | 350,000 | |
| Inventories | 1,060,000 | | 410,000 | |
| Land, Plant, and Equipment | 1,320,000 | | 680,000 | |
| Accumulated Depreciation | | (370,000) | | (210,000) |
| Investment in Brey | 891,000 | | | |
| Total Assets | $ 4,331,000 | | $ 1,380,000 | |
| Liabilities and Stockholders' Equity: | | | | |
| Accounts Payable and Accrued Expenses | | $(1,340,000) | | $ (594,000) |
| Common Stock | | (1,700,000) | | (400,000) |
| Additional Paid-In Capital | | (300,000) | | (80,000) |
| Retained Earnings | | (991,000) | | (306,000) |
| Total Liabilities and Equity | | $(4,331,000) | | $(1,380,000) |

### Additional Information

There were no changes in the Common Stock and Additional Paid-In Capital accounts during 20X9 except the one necessitated by Fran's acquisition of Brey.

At the acquisition date, the fair value of Brey's machinery exceeded its book value by $54,000. The excess cost will be amortized over the estimated average remaining life of six years. The fair values of all of Brey's other assets and liabilities were equal to their book values. At December 31, 20X9, Fran's management reviewed the amount attributed to goodwill as a result of its purchase of Brey's common stock and concluded an impairment loss of $35,000 should be recognized in 20X9.

On July 1, 20X9, Fran sold a warehouse facility to Brey for $129,000 cash. At the date of sale, Fran's book values were $33,000 for the land and $66,000 for the undepreciated cost of the building. Based on a real estate appraisal, Brey allocated $43,000 of the purchase price to the land and $86,000 to the building. Brey is depreciating the building over its estimated five-year remaining useful life by the straight-line method with no salvage value.

During 20X9, Fran purchased merchandise from Brey at an aggregate invoice price of $180,000, which included a 100 percent markup on Brey's cost. At December 31, 20X9, Fran owed Brey $86,000 on these purchases, and $36,000 of this merchandise remained in Fran's inventory.

### Required

Develop and complete a consolidation workpaper that would be used to prepare a consolidated income statement and a consolidated retained earnings statement for the year ended December 31, 20X9, and a consolidated balance sheet as of December 31, 20X9. List the accounts in the workpaper in the same order as they are listed in the financial statements provided. Formal consolidated statements are not required. Ignore income tax considerations. Supporting computations should be in good form.

**P7-36A**  ### Fully Adjusted Equity Method

On December 31, 20X7, Randall Corporation recorded the following entry on its books to adjust from the basic equity method to the fully adjusted equity method for its investment in Sharp Company stock:

| | | |
|---|---|---|
| Retained Earnings | 25,900 | |
| Income from Subsidiary | 100 | |
| Investment in Sharp Company Stock | | 26,000 |

### Required

a. Adjust the data reported by Randall in the trial balance contained in Problem P7-34 for the effects of the preceding adjusting entry.

b. Prepare the journal entries that would have been recorded on Randall's books during 20X7 under the fully adjusted equity method.

c. Prepare all eliminating entries needed to complete a consolidation workpaper at December 31, 20X7, assuming Randall has used the fully adjusted equity method.

d. Complete a three-part consolidation workpaper as of December 31, 20X7.

**P7-37A**  ### Cost Method

The trial balance data presented in Problem P7-34 can be converted to reflect use of the cost method by inserting the following amounts in place of those presented for Randall Corporation:

| | |
|---|---|
| Investment in Sharp Company Stock | $280,000 |
| Retained Earnings | 329,900 |
| Income from Subsidiary | -0- |
| Dividend Income | 20,000 |

### Required

a. Prepare the journal entries that would have been recorded on Randall's books during 20X7 under the cost method.

b. Prepare all eliminating entries needed to complete a consolidation workpaper as of December 31, 20X7, assuming Randall uses the cost method.

c. Complete a three-part consolidation workpaper as of December 31, 20X7.

"A" indicates that the item relates to "Appendix A."

# Intercompany Indebtedness

One advantage of having control over other companies is that management has the ability to transfer resources from one legal entity to another as needed by the individual companies. Companies often find it beneficial to lend excess funds to affiliates and to borrow from affiliates when cash shortages arise. The borrower often benefits from lower borrowing rates, less restrictive credit terms, and the informality and lower debt issue costs of intercompany borrowing relative to public debt offerings. The lending affiliate may benefit by being able to invest excess funds in a company about which it has considerable knowledge, perhaps allowing it to earn a given return on the funds invested while incurring less risk than if it invested in unrelated companies. Also, the combined entity may find it advantageous for the parent company or another affiliate to borrow funds for the entire enterprise rather than having each affiliate going directly to the capital markets.

## CONSOLIDATION OVERVIEW

Figure 8–1 illustrates two types of intercompany debt transfers. A **direct intercompany debt transfer** involves a loan from one affiliate to another without the participation of an unrelated party, as in Figure 8–1(*a*). Examples include a trade receivable/payable arising from an intercompany sale of inventory on credit and the issuance of a note payable by one affiliate to another in exchange for operating funds.

An **indirect intercompany debt transfer** involves the issuance of debt to an unrelated party and the subsequent purchase of the debt instrument by an affiliate of the issuer. For example, in Figure 8–1(*b*), Special Foods borrows funds by issuing a debt instrument, such as a note or a bond, to Nonaffiliated Corporation. The debt instrument subsequently is purchased from Nonaffiliated Corporation by Special Foods' parent, Peerless Products. Thus, Peerless Products acquires the debt of Special Foods indirectly through Nonaffiliated Corporation.

All account balances arising from intercorporate financing arrangements must be eliminated when consolidated statements are prepared. The consolidated financial statements portray the consolidated entity as a single company. Therefore, in Figure 8–1, transactions that do not cross the boundary of the consolidated entity are not reported in the consolidated financial statements. Although in illustration (*a*) Special Foods borrows funds from Peerless, the consolidated entity as a whole does not borrow, and the intercompany loan is not reflected in the consolidated financial statements.

In illustration (*b*), Special Foods borrows funds from Nonaffiliated Corporation. Because this transaction is with an unrelated party and crosses the boundary of the consolidated entity, it is reflected in the consolidated financial statements. In effect, the consolidated entity is borrowing from an outside party, and the liability is included in the consolidated balance sheet. When Peerless purchases Special Foods' debt instrument from Nonaffiliated, this transaction also crosses the boundary of the consolidated entity.

**FIGURE 8–1**  **Intercompany Debt Transactions**

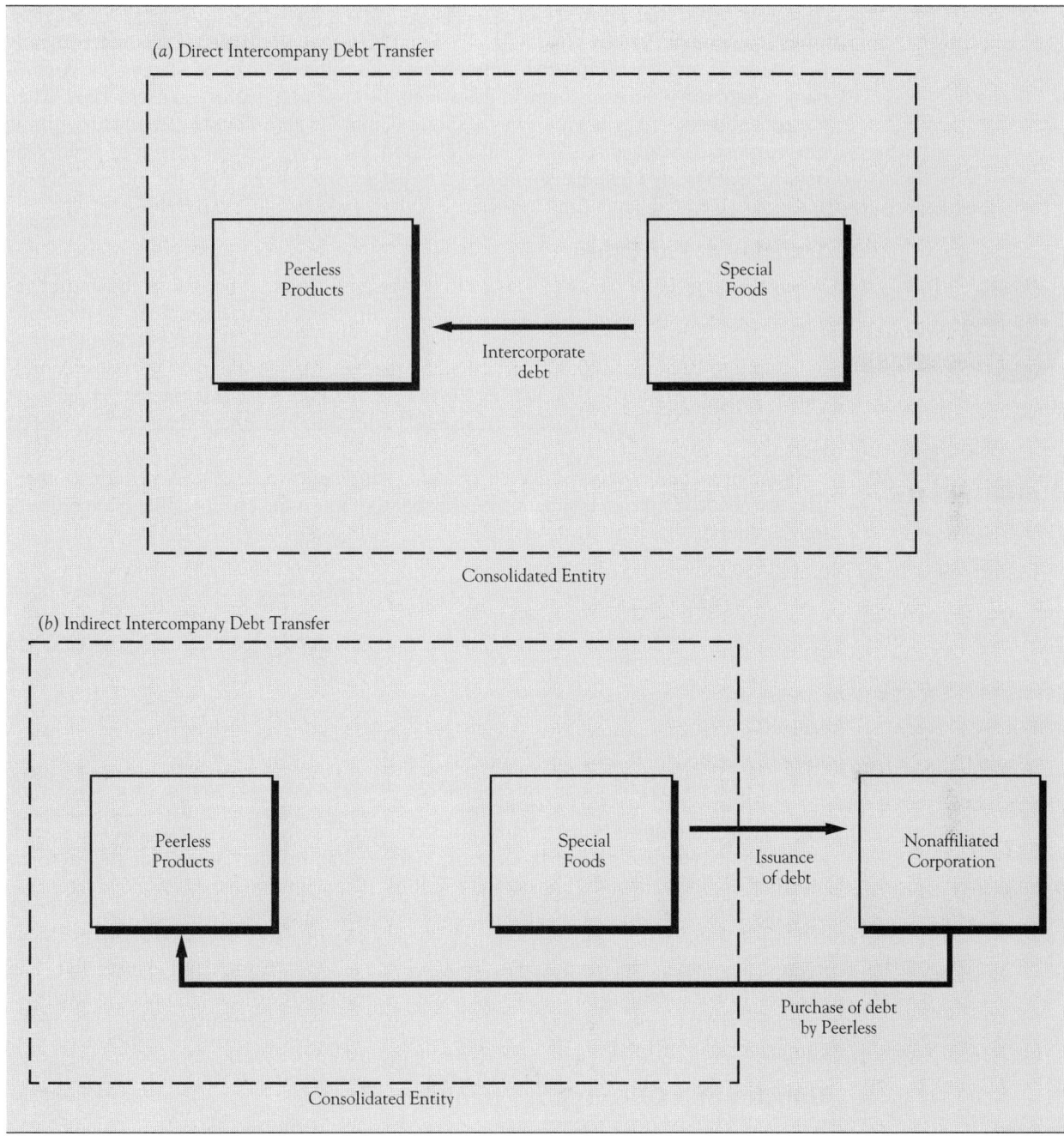

In effect, the consolidated entity repurchases its debt and needs to report the purchase as a debt retirement. As with most retirements of debt before maturity, a purchase of an affiliate's bonds usually gives rise to a gain or loss on the retirement; the gain or loss is reported in the consolidated income statement even though it does not appear in the separate income statement of either affiliate.

This chapter discusses the procedures used to prepare consolidated financial statements when intercorporate indebtedness arises from either direct or indirect debt transfers. Although the discussion focuses on bonds, the same concepts and procedures also apply to notes and other types of intercorporate indebtedness.

# BOND SALE DIRECTLY TO AN AFFILIATE

When one company sells bonds directly to an affiliate, all effects of the intercompany indebtedness must be eliminated in preparing consolidated financial statements. A company cannot report an investment in its own bonds or a bond liability to itself. Thus, when the consolidated entity is viewed as a single company, all amounts associated with the intercorporate indebtedness must be eliminated, including the investment in bonds, the bonds payable, any unamortized discount or premium on the bonds, the interest income and expense on the bonds, and any accrued interest receivable and payable.

## Transfer at Par Value

When a note or bond payable is sold directly to an affiliate at par value, the entries recorded by the investor and the issuer should be mirror images of each other. To illustrate, assume that on January 1, 20X1, Special Foods borrows $100,000 from Peerless Products by issuing to Peerless $100,000 par value, 12 percent, 10-year bonds. This transaction is represented by Figure 8–1(*a*). During 20X1, Special Foods records interest expense on the bonds of $12,000 ($100,000 × .12), and Peerless records an equal amount of interest income.

In the preparation of consolidated financial statements for 20X1, two elimination entries are needed in the consolidation workpaper to remove the effects of the intercompany indebtedness:

| | | | |
|---|---|---:|---:|
| E(1) | Bonds Payable | 100,000 | |
| |     Investment in Special Foods Bonds | | 100,000 |
| |     Eliminate intercorporate bond holdings. | | |
| | | | |
| E(2) | Interest Income | 12,000 | |
| |     Interest Expense | | 12,000 |
| |     Eliminate intercompany interest. | | |

These entries eliminate from the consolidated statements the bond investment and associated income recorded on Peerless's books and the liability and related interest expense recorded on Special Foods' books. The resulting statements appear as if the indebtedness does not exist, which from a consolidated viewpoint it does not.

Note that these entries have no effect on consolidated net income because they reduce interest income and interest expense by the same amount. Eliminating entries E(1) and E(2) are required at the end of each period for as long as the intercorporate indebtedness continues. If any interest had accrued on the bonds at year-end, that too would have to be eliminated.

## Transfer at a Discount or Premium

When the coupon or nominal interest rate on a bond is different from the yield demanded by those who lend funds, a bond sells at a discount or premium. In such cases, the amount of bond interest income or expense recorded no longer equals the cash interest payments. Instead, interest income and expense amounts are adjusted for the amortization of the discount or premium.

As an illustration of the treatment of intercompany bond transfers at other than par, assume that on January 1, 20X1, Peerless Products purchases $100,000 par value, 12 percent, 10-year bonds from Special Foods for $90,000. Interest on the bonds is payable on January 1 and July 1. The interest expense recognized by Special Foods and the interest income recognized by Peerless each year include straight-line amortization of the discount, as follows:

| | |
|---|---:|
| Cash interest ($100,000 × .12) | $12,000 |
| Amortization of discount ($10,000 ÷ 20 semiannual interest periods) × 2 periods | 1,000 |
| Interest expense or income | $13,000 |

Half of these amounts are recognized in each of the two interest payment periods during a year. Although the interest method of amortization usually is required for amortizing discounts and premiums, the straight-line method is acceptable when it does not depart materially from the interest method and when transactions are between parent and subsidiary companies or between subsidiaries of a common parent.

### *Entries by the Debtor*

Special Foods records the issuance of the bonds on January 1 at a discount of $10,000. It recognizes interest expense on July 1, when the first semiannual interest payment is made, and on December 31, when interest is accrued for the second half of the year. The amortization of the bond discount causes interest expense to be greater than the cash interest payment and causes the balance of the discount to decrease. Special Foods records the following entries related to the bonds during 20X1:

| | | | |
|---|---|---:|---:|
| January 1, 20X1 | | | |
| (3) | Cash | 90,000 | |
| | Discount on Bonds Payable | 10,000 | |
| | Bonds Payable | | 100,000 |
| | Issue bonds to Peerless Products. | | |
| | | | |
| July 1, 20X1 | | | |
| (4) | Interest Expense | 6,500 | |
| | Discount on Bonds Payable | | 500 |
| | Cash | | 6,000 |
| | Semiannual payment of interest. | | |
| | | | |
| December 31, 20X1 | | | |
| (5) | Interest Expense | 6,500 | |
| | Discount on Bonds Payable | | 500 |
| | Interest Payable | | 6,000 |
| | Accrue interest expense at year-end. | | |

### *Entries by the Bond Investor*

Peerless Products records the purchase of the bonds and the interest income derived from the bonds during 20X1 with the following entries:

| | | | |
|---|---|---:|---:|
| January 1, 20X1 | | | |
| (6) | Investment in Special Foods Bonds | 90,000 | |
| | Cash | | 90,000 |
| | Purchase of bonds from Special Foods. | | |
| | | | |
| July 1, 20X1 | | | |
| (7) | Cash | 6,000 | |
| | Investment in Special Foods Bonds | 500 | |
| | Interest Income | | 6,500 |
| | Receive interest on bond investment. | | |

December 31, 20X1

| | | | | |
|---|---|---|---|---|
| (8) | Interest Receivable | | 6,000 | |
| | Investment in Special Foods Bonds | | 500 | |
| | Interest Income | | | 6,500 |
| | Accrue interest income at year-end. | | | |

The amortization of the discount by Peerless increases interest income to an amount greater than the cash interest payment and causes the balance of the bond investment account to increase.

### Elimination Entries at Year-End

The December 31, 20X1, bond-related amounts taken from the books of Peerless Products and Special Foods and the appropriate consolidated amounts are as follows:

| Item | Peerless Products | Special Foods | Unadjusted Totals | Consolidated Amounts |
|---|---|---|---|---|
| Bonds Payable | -0- | $(100,000) | $(100,000) | -0- |
| Discount on Bonds Payable | -0- | 9,000 | 9,000 | -0- |
| Interest Payable | -0- | (6,000) | (6,000) | -0- |
| Investment in Bonds | $ 91,000 | -0- | 91,000 | -0- |
| Interest Receivable | 6,000 | -0- | 6,000 | -0- |
| Interest Expense | -0- | $ 13,000 | $ 13,000 | -0- |
| Interest Income | $(13,000) | -0- | (13,000) | -0- |

All account balances relating to the intercorporate bond holdings must be eliminated in the preparation of consolidated financial statements. Toward that end, the consolidation workpaper prepared on December 31, 20X1, includes the following eliminating entries related to the intercompany bond holdings:

| | | | |
|---|---|---|---|
| E(9) | Bonds Payable | 100,000 | |
| | Investment in Special Foods Bonds | | 91,000 |
| | Discount on Bonds Payable | | 9,000 |
| | Eliminate intercorporate bond holdings. | | |
| E(10) | Interest Income | 13,000 | |
| | Interest Expense | | 13,000 |
| | Eliminate intercompany interest. | | |
| E(11) | Interest Payable | 6,000 | |
| | Interest Receivable | | 6,000 |
| | Eliminate intercompany interest receivable/payable. | | |

Entry E(9) eliminates the bonds payable and associated discount against the investment in bonds. The book value of the bond liability on Special Foods' books and the investment in bonds on Peerless's books will be the same so long as both companies amortize the discount in the same way.

Entry E(10) eliminates the bond interest income recognized by Peerless during 20X1 against the bond interest expense recognized by Special Foods. Because the interest for the second half of 20X1 was accrued but not paid, an intercompany receivable/payable exists at the end of the year. Entry E(11) eliminates the interest receivable against the interest payable.

Consolidation at the end of 20X2 requires elimination entries similar to those at the end of 20X1. Because $1,000 of the discount is amortized each year, the bond investment balance on Peerless's books increases to $92,000 ($90,000 + $1,000 + $1,000). Similarly, the bond discount on Special Foods' books decreases to $8,000, resulting in an effective bond liability of $92,000. The consolidation elimination entries related to the bonds at the end of 20X2 are as follows:

| E(12) | Bonds Payable | 100,000 | |
| |     Investment in Special Foods Bonds | | 92,000 |
| |     Discount on Bonds Payable | | 8,000 |
| |     Eliminate intercorporate bond holdings. | | |
| | | | |
| E(13) | Interest Income | 13,000 | |
| |     Interest Expense | | 13,000 |
| |     Eliminate intercompany interest. | | |
| | | | |
| E(14) | Interest Payable | 6,000 | |
| |     Interest Receivable | | 6,000 |
| |     Eliminate intercompany interest receivable/payable. | | |

# BONDS OF AFFILIATE PURCHASED FROM A NONAFFILIATE

A more complex situation occurs when bonds that were issued to an unrelated party are acquired later by an affiliate of the issuer. From the viewpoint of the consolidated entity, an acquisition of an affiliate's bonds retires the bonds at the time they are purchased. The bonds no longer are held outside the consolidated entity once they are purchased by another company within the consolidated entity, and they must be treated as if repurchased by the debtor. Acquisition of the bonds of an affiliate by another company within the consolidated entity is referred to as *constructive retirement*. Although the bonds actually are not retired, they are treated as if they were retired in preparing consolidated financial statements.

When a constructive retirement occurs, the consolidated income statement for the period reports a gain or loss on debt retirement based on the difference between the carrying value of the bonds on the books of the debtor and the purchase price paid by the affiliate in acquiring the bonds. Neither the bonds payable nor the purchaser's investment in the bonds is reported in the consolidated balance sheet because the bonds are no longer considered outstanding.

## Purchase at Book Value

In the event that a company purchases an affiliate's debt from an unrelated party at a price equal to the liability reported by the debtor, the elimination entries required in preparing the consolidated financial statements are identical to those used in eliminating a direct intercorporate debt transfer. In this case, the total of the bond liability and the related premium or discount reported by the debtor equal the balance in the investment account shown by the bondholder, and the interest income reported by the bondholder each period equals the interest expense reported by the debtor. All of these amounts need to be eliminated to avoid misstating the accounts in the consolidated financial statements.

## Purchase at an Amount Less than Book Value

Continuing movement in the level of interest rates and the volatility of other factors influencing the securities markets make it unlikely that a company's bonds will sell after issuance at a price identical to their book value. When the price paid to acquire the bonds of an affiliate differs from the liability reported by the debtor, a gain or loss is reported in the consolidated income statement in the period of constructive retirement. In addition, the bond interest income and interest expense reported by the two affiliates subsequent

to the purchase must be eliminated in preparing consolidated statements. Interest income reported by the investing affiliate and interest expense reported by the debtor are not equal in this case because of the different bond carrying amounts on the books of the two companies. The difference in the bond carrying amounts is reflected in the amortization of the discount or premium and, in turn, causes interest income and expense to differ.

As an example of consolidation following the purchase of an affiliate's bonds at less than book value, assume that Peerless Products Corporation purchases 80 percent of the common stock of Special Foods Inc. on December 31, 20X0, for its underlying book value of $240,000. At that date, the fair value of the noncontrolling interest is equal to its book value of $60,000. In addition, the following conditions occur:

1. On January 1, 20X1, Special Foods issues 10-year, 12 percent bonds payable with a par value of $100,000; the bonds are issued at 102. Nonaffiliated Corporation purchases the bonds from Special Foods.
2. The bonds pay interest on June 30 and December 31.
3. Both Peerless Products and Special Foods amortize bond discount and premium using the straight-line method.
4. On December 31, 20X1, Peerless Products purchases the bonds from Nonaffiliated for $91,000.
5. Special Foods reports net income of $50,000 for 20X1 and $75,000 for 20X2. Special Foods declares dividends of $30,000 in 20X1 and $40,000 in 20X2.
6. Peerless earns $140,000 in 20X1 and $160,000 in 20X2 from its own separate operations. Peerless declares dividends of $60,000 in both 20X1 and 20X2.

The bond transactions of Special Foods and Peerless appear as follows:

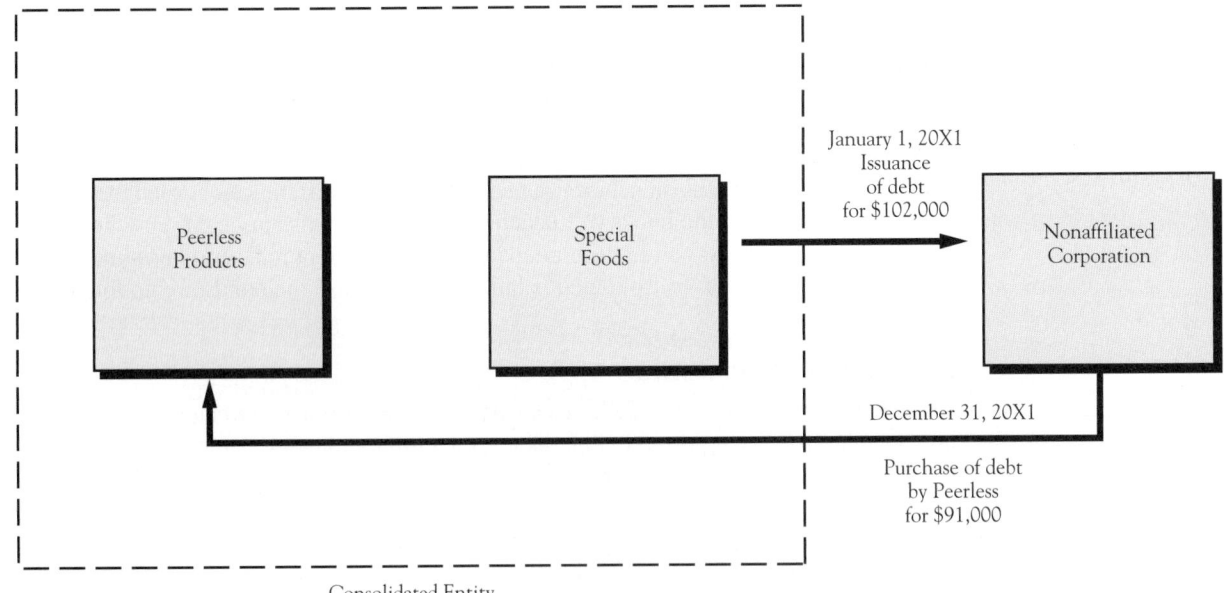

### Bond Liability Entries—20X1

Special Foods records the following entries related to its bonds during 20X1:

| January 1, 20X1 | | |
|---|---|---|
| (15) Cash | 102,000 | |
| Bonds Payable | | 100,000 |
| Premium on Bonds Payable | | 2,000 |
| Sale of bonds to Nonaffiliated. | | |

June 30, 20X1

| (16) | Interest Expense | 5,900 | |
| | Premium on Bonds Payable | 100 | |
| |    Cash | | 6,000 |

Semiannual payment of interest:

$5,900 = $6,000 − $100

$100 = $2,000 ÷ 20 interest periods

$6,000 = $100,000 × .12 × 6/12

December 31, 20X1

| (17) | Interest Expense | 5,900 | |
| | Premium on Bonds Payable | 100 | |
| |    Cash | | 6,000 |

Semiannual payment of interest.

Entry (15) records the issuance of the bonds to Nonaffiliated Corporation for $102,000. Entries (16) and (17) record the payment of interest and the amortization of the bond premium at each of the two interest payment dates during 20X1. Total interest expense for 20X1 is $11,800 ($5,900 × 2), and the book value of the bonds on December 31, 20X1, is as follows:

| | |
|---|---|
| Book value of bonds at issuance | $102,000 |
| Amortization of premium, 20X1 | (200) |
| Book value of bonds, December 31, 20X1 | $101,800 |

### Bond Investment Entries—20X1

Peerless Products records the purchase of Special Foods' bonds from Nonaffiliated with the following entry:

December 31, 20X1

| (18) | Investment in Special Foods Bonds | 91,000 | |
| |    Cash | | 91,000 |

Purchase of Special Foods bonds from Nonaffiliated Corporation.

This entry is the same as if the bonds purchased were those of an unrelated company. Peerless purchases the bonds at the very end of the year after payment of the interest to Nonaffiliated; therefore, Peerless earns no interest on the bonds during 20X1, nor is there any interest accrued on the bonds at the date of purchase.

### Computation of Gain on Constructive Retirement of Bonds

From a consolidated viewpoint, the purchase of Special Foods' bonds by Peerless is considered a retirement of the bonds by the consolidated entity. Therefore, in the preparation of consolidated financial statements, a gain or loss must be recognized for the difference between the book value of the bonds on the date of repurchase and the amount paid by the consolidated entity in reacquiring the bonds:

| | |
|---|---|
| Book value of Special Foods' bonds, December 31, 20X1 | $101,800 |
| Price paid by Peerless to purchase bonds | (91,000) |
| Gain on constructive retirement of bonds | $ 10,800 |

This gain is included in the consolidated income statement as a gain on the retirement of bonds.

### Assignment of Gain on Constructive Retirement

Four approaches have been used in practice for assigning the gain or loss on the constructive retirement of the bonds of an affiliate to the shareholders of the participating companies. Depending upon the method selected, the gain or loss may be assigned to any of the following:

1. The affiliate issuing the bonds.
2. The affiliate purchasing the bonds.
3. The parent company.
4. The issuing and purchasing companies, based on the difference between the carrying amounts of the bonds on their books at the date of purchase and the par value of the bonds.

No compelling reasons seem to exist for choosing one of these methods over the others, and in practice the choice often is based on expediency and lack of materiality. The FASB's approach is to assign the gain or loss to the issuing company. In previous chapters, gains and losses on intercompany transactions were viewed as accruing to the shareholders of the selling affiliate. When this approach is applied in the case of intercorporate debt transactions, gains and losses arising from the intercompany debt transactions are viewed as accruing to the shareholders of the selling or issuing affiliate. In effect, the purchasing affiliate is viewed as acting on behalf of the issuing affiliate by acquiring the bonds.

An important difference exists between the intercompany gains and losses discussed in previous chapters and the gains and losses arising from intercorporate debt transactions. Gains and losses from intercorporate transfers of assets are recognized by the individual affiliates and are eliminated in consolidation. Gains and losses from intercorporate debt transactions are not recognized by the individual affiliates but must be included in consolidation.

When the subsidiary is the issuing affiliate, the gain or loss on constructive retirement of the bonds is viewed as accruing to the subsidiary's shareholders. Thus, the gain or loss is apportioned between the controlling and noncontrolling interests based on the relative ownership interests in the common stock. If the parent is the issuing affiliate, the entire gain or loss on the constructive retirement accrues to the controlling interest and none is apportioned to the noncontrolling interest.

As a result of the interest income and expense entries recorded annually by the companies involved, the constructive gain or loss is recognized over the remaining term of the bond issue; accordingly, the total amount of the unrecognized gain or loss decreases each period and is fully amortized at the time the bond matures. Thus, no permanent gain or loss is assigned to the debtor company's shareholders.

### Basic Equity-Method Entries—20X1

In addition to recording the bond investment with entry (18), Peerless records the following basic equity-method entries during 20X1 to account for its investment in Special Foods stock:

| | | | |
|---|---|---|---|
| (19) | Cash | 24,000 | |
| |     Investment in Special Foods Stock | | 24,000 |
| |     Record dividends from Special Foods: | | |
| |     $30,000 × .80 | | |
| (20) | Investment in Special Foods Stock | 40,000 | |
| |     Income from Subsidiary | | 40,000 |
| |     Record equity-method income: | | |
| |     $50,000 × .80 | | |

These entries result in a $256,000 balance in the investment account at the end of 20X1.

### Consolidation Workpaper—20X1

The December 31, 20X1, workpaper to prepare consolidated financial statements for Peerless Products and Special Foods is presented in Figure 8–2. The following eliminating entries are included in the workpaper:

| | | | |
|---|---|---:|---:|
| E(21) | Income from Subsidiary | 40,000 | |
| | Dividends Declared | | 24,000 |
| | Investment in Special Foods Stock | | 16,000 |
| | Eliminate income from subsidiary. | | |
| | | | |
| E(22) | Income to Noncontrolling Interest | 12,160 | |
| | Dividends Declared | | 6,000 |
| | Noncontrolling Interest | | 6,160 |
| | Assign income to noncontrolling interest: | | |
| | $12,160 = ($50,000 + $10,800) × .20 | | |
| | | | |
| E(23) | Common Stock—Special Foods | 200,000 | |
| | Retained Earnings, January 1 | 100,000 | |
| | Investment in Special Foods Stock | | 240,000 |
| | Noncontrolling Interest | | 60,000 |
| | Eliminate beginning investment balance. | | |
| | | | |
| E(24) | Bonds Payable | 100,000 | |
| | Premium on Bonds Payable | 1,800 | |
| | Investment in Special Foods Bonds | | 91,000 |
| | Gain on Bond Retirement | | 10,800 |
| | Eliminate intercorporate bond holdings. | | |

Workpaper entry E(21) eliminates the changes in the investment account during 20X1, the parent's share of the subsidiary's net income, and the dividends recognized by Peerless during the year. Income of $12,160 is assigned to the noncontrolling interest in entry E(22), computed as follows:

| | |
|---|---:|
| Net income of Special Foods | $50,000 |
| Gain on constructive retirement of bonds | 10,800 |
| Realized net income of Special Foods | $60,800 |
| Noncontrolling stockholders' share | × .20 |
| Noncontrolling interest's share of income | $12,160 |

The full gain on constructive retirement is included in consolidated net income. That gain is attributed to the shareholders of the issuing company, Special Foods. Therefore, a proportionate share of the gain ($10,800 × .20) is assigned to the noncontrolling interest along with a proportionate share of Special Foods' reported net income. If Peerless had been the issuing affiliate, all of the gain would have been included in its share of consolidated net income and none would have been allocated to the noncontrolling interest.

Entry E(22) also eliminates the noncontrolling interest's share of Special Foods' dividends declared during 20X1 and recognizes the increase in the noncontrolling interest's claim on the subsidiary's net assets. Entry E(23) eliminates Peerless's investment account and the stockholders' equity balances of Special Foods at the beginning of the year, and it establishes in the workpaper the amount of the noncontrolling interest at the beginning of the year, an amount equal to its acquisition-date fair value.

The final entry in the workpaper, E(24), eliminates the intercompany bond holdings and recognizes the gain on constructive retirement of the bonds. The appropriate

**FIGURE 8–2    December 31, 20X1, Consolidation Workpaper; Repurchase of Bonds at Less than Book Value**

| Item | Peerless Products | Special Foods | Eliminations Debit | Eliminations Credit | Consolidated |
|---|---|---|---|---|---|
| Sales | 400,000 | 200,000 | | | 600,000 |
| Income from Subsidiary | 40,000 | | (21)  40,000 | | |
| Gain on Bond Retirement | | | | (24)  10,800 | 10,800 |
| Credits | 440,000 | 200,000 | | | 610,800 |
| Cost of Goods Sold | 170,000 | 115,000 | | | 285,000 |
| Depreciation and Amortization | 50,000 | 20,000 | | | 70,000 |
| Other Expenses | 20,000 | 3,200 | | | 23,200 |
| Interest Expense | 20,000 | 11,800 | | | 31,800 |
| Debits | (260,000) | (150,000) | | | (410,000) |
| Consolidated Net Income | | | | | 200,800 |
| Income to Noncontrolling Interest | | | (22)  12,160 | | (12,160) |
| Income, carry forward | 180,000 | 50,000 | 52,160 | 10,800 | 188,640 |
| Retained Earnings, January 1 | 300,000 | 100,000 | (23)  100,000 | | 300,000 |
| Income, from above | 180,000 | 50,000 | 52,160 | 10,800 | 188,640 |
| | 480,000 | 150,000 | | | 488,640 |
| Dividends Declared | (60,000) | (30,000) | | (21)  24,000 | |
| | | | | (22)  6,000 | (60,000) |
| Retained Earnings, December 31, carry forward | 420,000 | 120,000 | 152,160 | 40,800 | 428,640 |
| Cash | 173,000 | 76,800 | | | 249,800 |
| Accounts Receivable | 75,000 | 50,000 | | | 125,000 |
| Inventory | 100,000 | 75,000 | | | 175,000 |
| Land | 175,000 | 40,000 | | | 215,000 |
| Buildings and Equipment | 800,000 | 600,000 | | | 1,400,000 |
| Investment in Special Foods Bonds | 91,000 | | | (24)  91,000 | |
| Investment in Special Foods Stock | 256,000 | | | (21)  16,000 | |
| | | | | (23)  240,000 | |
| Debits | 1,670,000 | 841,800 | | | 2,164,800 |
| Accumulated Depreciation | 450,000 | 320,000 | | | 770,000 |
| Accounts Payable | 100,000 | 100,000 | | | 200,000 |
| Bonds Payable | 200,000 | 100,000 | (24)  100,000 | | 200,000 |
| Premium on Bonds Payable | | 1,800 | (24)  1,800 | | |
| Common Stock | 500,000 | 200,000 | (23)  200,000 | | 500,000 |
| Retained Earnings, from above | 420,000 | 120,000 | 152,160 | 40,800 | 428,640 |
| Noncontrolling Interest | | | | (22)  6,160 | |
| | | | | (23)  60,000 | 66,160 |
| Credits | 1,670,000 | 841,800 | 453,960 | 453,960 | 2,164,800 |

Elimination entries:

(21) Eliminate income from subsidiary.

(22) Assign income to noncontrolling interest.

(23) Eliminate beginning investment balance.

(24) Eliminate intercompany bond holdings.

consolidated balances and the amounts recorded on the books of Peerless and Special Foods are as follows:

| Item | Peerless Products | Special Foods | Unadjusted Totals | Consolidated Amounts |
|------|------|------|------|------|
| Bonds Payable | -0- | $(100,000) | $(100,000) | -0- |
| Premium on Bonds Payable | -0- | (1,800) | (1,800) | -0- |
| Investment in Bonds | $91,000 | -0- | 91,000 | -0- |
| Interest Expense | -0- | $  11,800 | $  11,800 | $11,800 |
| Interest Income | -0- | -0- | -0- | -0- |
| Gain on Bond Retirement | -0- | -0- | -0- | (10,800) |

Special Foods' bonds payable and Peerless's investment in Special Foods' bonds cannot appear in the consolidated balance sheet because the bond holdings involve parties totally within the single economic entity. Note that the gain recognized on the constructive retirement of the bonds does not appear on the books of either Peerless or Special Foods because the bonds still are outstanding from the perspective of the separate companies. From the viewpoint of the consolidated entity, the bonds are retired at the end of 20X1, and a gain must be entered in the consolidation workpaper so that it appears in the consolidated income statement.

No eliminations are needed with respect to interest income or interest expense in preparing the consolidated statements for December 31, 20X1. Because Peerless purchased the bonds at the end of the year, no interest income is recorded by Peerless until 20X2. The interest expense of $11,800 ($12,000 − $200) recorded by Special Foods is viewed appropriately as interest expense of the consolidated entity because the bonds were held by an unrelated party during all of 20X1.

### *Consolidated Net Income—20X1*

Consolidated net income of $200,800 is shown in the workpaper in Figure 8–2. This amount is computed and allocated as follows:

| | | |
|---|---:|---:|
| Peerless's separate income | | $140,000 |
| Special Foods' net income | $50,000 | |
| Gain on constructive retirement of bonds | 10,800 | |
| Special Foods' realized net income | | 60,800 |
| Consolidated net income, 20X1 | | $200,800 |
| Income to noncontrolling interest ($60,800 × .20) | | (12,160) |
| Income to controlling interest | | $188,640 |

Consolidated net income is $10,800 higher than it would have been had Peerless not purchased the bonds.

### *Noncontrolling Interest—December 31, 20X1*

Total noncontrolling interest on December 31, 20X1, in the absence of a differential, includes a proportionate share of both the reported book value of Special Foods and the gain on constructive bond retirement. The balance of the noncontrolling interest on December 31, 20X1, is computed as follows:

| | | |
|---|---|---:|
| Book value of Special Foods, December 31, 20X1: | | |
| Common stock | $200,000 | |
| Retained earnings | 120,000 | |
| Total reported book value | $320,000 | |
| Gain on constructive retirement of bonds | 10,800 | |
| Realized book value of Special Foods | $330,800 | |
| Noncontrolling stockholders' share | × .20 | |
| Noncontrolling interest, December 31, 20X1 | $ 66,160 | |

### Bond Liability Entries—20X2

Special Foods records interest on its bonds during 20X2 with the following entries:

June 30, 20X2

| | | | |
|---|---|---:|---:|
| (25) | Interest Expense | 5,900 | |
| | Premium on Bonds Payable | 100 | |
| | Cash | | 6,000 |
| | Semiannual payment of interest. | | |

December 31, 20X2

| | | | |
|---|---|---:|---:|
| (26) | Interest Expense | 5,900 | |
| | Premium on Bonds Payable | 100 | |
| | Cash | | 6,000 |
| | Semiannual payment of interest. | | |

### Bond Investment Entries—20X2

Peerless Products accounts for its investment in Special Foods' bonds in the same way as if the bonds were those of a nonaffiliate. The $91,000 purchase price paid by Peerless reflects a $9,000 ($100,000 − $91,000) discount from the par value of the bonds. This discount is amortized over the nine-year remaining term of the bonds at $1,000 per year ($9,000 ÷ 9 years), or $500 per six-month interest payment period. Peerless's entries to record interest income for 20X2 are as follows:

June 30, 20X2

| | | | |
|---|---|---:|---:|
| (27) | Cash | 6,000 | |
| | Investment in Special Foods Bonds | 500 | |
| | Interest Income | | 6,500 |
| | Record receipt of bond interest. | | |

December 31, 20X2

| | | | |
|---|---|---:|---:|
| (28) | Cash | 6,000 | |
| | Investment in Special Foods Bonds | 500 | |
| | Interest Income | | 6,500 |
| | Record receipt of bond interest. | | |

This $13,000 of interest income is earned by Peerless in addition to its $160,000 of separate operating income for 20X2.

### Subsequent Recognition of Gain on Constructive Retirement

In the year of the constructive bond retirement, 20X1, the entire $10,800 gain on the retirement was recognized in the consolidated income statement but not on the books of either Peerless or Special Foods. The total gain on the constructive bond retirement in 20X1 was equal to the sum of the discount on Peerless's bond investment and the premium on Special Foods' bond liability at the time of the constructive retirement:

| Peerless's discount on bond investment | $ 9,000 |
|---|---|
| Special Foods' premium on bond liability | 1,800 |
| Total gain on constructive retirement of bonds | $10,800 |

This can be visualized as in the following figure:

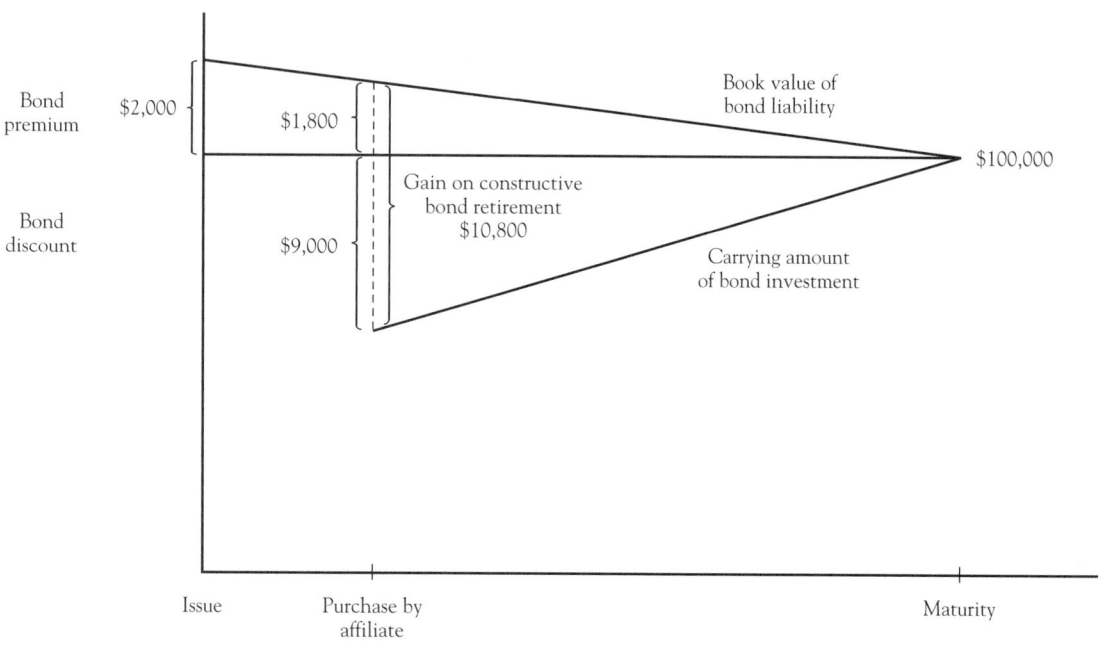

In each year subsequent to 20X1, both Peerless and Special Foods recognize a portion of the constructive gain as they amortize the discount on the bond investment and the premium on the bond liability:

| Peerless's amortization of discount on bond investment ($9,000 ÷ 9 years) | $1,000 |
|---|---|
| Special Foods' amortization of premium on bonds payable ($1,800 ÷ 9 years) | 200 |
| Annual increase in combined incomes of separate companies | $1,200 |

Thus, the $10,800 gain on constructive bond retirement, previously recognized in the consolidated income statement, is recognized on the books of Peerless and Special Foods at the rate of $1,200 each year. Over the remaining nine-year term of the bonds, Peerless and Special Foods will recognize the full $10,800 gain ($1,200 × 9).

### Basic Equity-Method Entries—20X2

In addition to the entries related to its investment in Special Foods' bonds, Peerless records the following entries during 20X2 under the basic equity method:

| (29) | Cash | 32,000 | |
|---|---|---|---|
| | Investment in Special Foods Stock | | 32,000 |
| | Record dividends from Special Foods: | | |
| | $40,000 × .80 | | |

| (30) | Investment in Special Foods Stock | 60,000 | |
|---|---|---|---|
| | Income from Subsidiary | | 60,000 |
| | Record equity-method income: | | |
| | $75,000 × .80 | | |

### Investment Account—20X2

At the end of 20X2, Peerless's account for its investment in the common stock of Special Foods appears as follows:

| Investment in Special Foods Stock | | | | |
|---|---|---|---|---|
| | Original cost | 240,000 | | |
| (20) | 20X1 equity accrual ($50,000 × .80) | 40,000 | (19) 20X1 dividends ($30,000 × .80) | 24,000 |
| | Balance, 12/31/X1 | 256,000 | | |
| (30) | 20X2 equity accrual ($75,000 × .80) | 60,000 | (29) 20X2 dividends ($40,000 × .80) | 32,000 |
| | Balance, 12/31/X2 | 284,000 | | |

### Consolidation Workpaper—20X2

The consolidation workpaper prepared for December 31, 20X2, is presented in Figure 8–3. The following elimination entries are needed in the workpaper:

| | | | |
|---|---|---|---|
| E(31) | Income from Subsidiary | 60,000 | |
| | Dividends Declared | | 32,000 |
| | Investment in Special Foods Stock | | 28,000 |
| | Eliminate income from subsidiary. | | |
| E(32) | Income to Noncontrolling Interest | 14,760 | |
| | Dividends Declared | | 8,000 |
| | Noncontrolling Interest | | 6,760 |
| | Assign income to noncontrolling interest: | | |
| | $14,760 = ($75,000 − $1,200) × .20 | | |
| E(33) | Common Stock—Special Foods | 200,000 | |
| | Retained Earnings, January 1 | 120,000 | |
| | Investment in Special Foods Stock | | 256,000 |
| | Noncontrolling Interest | | 64,000 |
| | Eliminate beginning investment balance. | | |
| E(34) | Bonds Payable | 100,000 | |
| | Premium on Bonds Payable | 1,600 | |
| | Interest Income | 13,000 | |
| | Investment in Special Foods Bonds | | 92,000 |
| | Interest Expense | | 11,800 |
| | Retained Earnings, January 1 | | 8,640 |
| | Noncontrolling Interest | | 2,160 |
| | Eliminate intercorporate bond holdings: | | |
| | $1,600 = $2,000 − $200 − $200 | | |
| | $13,000 = ($100,000 × .12) + $1,000 | | |
| | $92,000 = $91,000 + $1,000 | | |
| | $11,800 = ($100,000 × .12) − $200 | | |
| | $8,640 = $10,800 × .80 | | |
| | $2,160 = $10,800 × .20 | | |

**FIGURE 8–3**   December 31, 20X2, Consolidation Workpaper; Next Year following Repurchase of Bonds at Less than Book Value

| Item | Peerless Products | Special Foods | Eliminations Debit | Eliminations Credit | Consolidated |
|---|---|---|---|---|---|
| Sales | 450,000 | 300,000 | | | 750,000 |
| Interest Income | 13,000 | | (34)   13,000 | | |
| Income from Subsidiary | 60,000 | | (31)   60,000 | | |
| Credits | 523,000 | 300,000 | | | 750,000 |
| Cost of Goods Sold | 180,000 | 160,000 | | | 340,000 |
| Depreciation and Amortization | 50,000 | 20,000 | | | 70,000 |
| Other Expenses | 40,000 | 33,200 | | | 73,200 |
| Interest Expense | 20,000 | 11,800 | | (34)   11,800 | 20,000 |
| Debits | (290,000) | (225,000) | | | (503,200) |
| Consolidated Net Income | | | | | 246,800 |
| Income to Noncontrolling Interest | | | (32)   14,760 | | (14,760) |
| Income, carry forward | 233,000 | 75,000 | 87,760 | 11,800 | 232,040 |
| Retained Earnings, January 1 | 420,000 | 120,000 | (33) 120,000 | (34)     8,640 | 428,640 |
| Income, from above | 233,000 | 75,000 | 87,760 | 11,800 | 232,040 |
| | 653,000 | 195,000 | | | 660,680 |
| Dividends Declared | (60,000) | (40,000) | | (31)   32,000 | |
| | | | | (32)     8,000 | (60,000) |
| Retained Earnings, December 31, carry forward | 593,000 | 155,000 | 207,760 | 60,440 | 600,680 |
| Cash | 212,000 | 86,600 | | | 298,600 |
| Accounts Receivable | 150,000 | 80,000 | | | 230,000 |
| Inventory | 180,000 | 90,000 | | | 270,000 |
| Land | 175,000 | 40,000 | | | 215,000 |
| Buildings and Equipment | 800,000 | 600,000 | | | 1,400,000 |
| Investment in Special Foods Bonds | 92,000 | | | (34)   92,000 | |
| Investment in Special Foods Stock | 284,000 | | | (31)   28,000 | |
| | | | | (33) 256,000 | |
| Debits | 1,893,000 | 896,600 | | | 2,413,600 |
| Accumulated Depreciation | 500,000 | 340,000 | | | 840,000 |
| Accounts Payable | 100,000 | 100,000 | | | 200,000 |
| Bonds Payable | 200,000 | 100,000 | (34) 100,000 | | 200,000 |
| Premium on Bonds Payable | | 1,600 | (34)     1,600 | | |
| Common Stock | 500,000 | 200,000 | (33) 200,000 | | 500,000 |
| Retained Earnings, from above | 593,000 | 155,000 | 207,760 | 60,440 | 600,680 |
| Noncontrolling Interest | | | | (32)     6,760 | |
| | | | | (33)   64,000 | |
| | | | | (34)     2,160 | 72,920 |
| Credits | 1,893,000 | 896,600 | 509,360 | 509,360 | 2,413,600 |

Elimination entries:
(31)  Eliminate income from subsidiary.
(32)  Assign income to noncontrolling interest.
(33)  Eliminate beginning investment balance.
(34)  Eliminate intercompany bond holdings.

Entry E(31) eliminates the net effect of the 20X2 equity-method entries recorded on Peerless's books. Entry E(32) assigns income to the noncontrolling interest, as follows:

| | |
|---|---:|
| Net income of Special Foods, 20X2 | $75,000 |
| Less: 20X1 gain on constructive retirement | |
| of debt recognized in 20X2 by affiliates: | |
| Amortization of Peerless's bond discount | (1,000) |
| Amortization of Special Foods' bond premium | (200) |
| Special Foods' realized net income | $73,800 |
| Noncontrolling interest's proportionate share | × .20 |
| Noncontrolling interest's share of income | $14,760 |

In 20X1, the gain on the constructive retirement of the bonds was included in consolidated net income and in the computation of income assigned to noncontrolling shareholders. As the gain is recognized on the books of the two affiliates through their amortization of the bond discount and premium, its effect must be eliminated from consolidated net income and from the amount of income assigned to the noncontrolling interest in entry E(32).

Entry E(33) is the normal entry to eliminate the 20X2 beginning balances of Special Foods' stockholders' equity accounts and the beginning balance of Peerless's Investment in Special Foods Stock account and to establish the amount of the noncontrolling interest at the beginning of 20X2. Entry E(33) establishes the beginning amount of the noncontrolling interest as if there were no constructive gain. The entries to the investment account and to noncontrolling interest are based, in the absence of a differential, on each shareholder group's proportionate share of the book value of Special Foods at the beginning of the period:

| | |
|---|---:|
| Book value of Special Foods, January 1, 20X2: | |
| Common stock | $200,000 |
| Retained earnings | 120,000 |
| Total book value | $320,000 |
| | |
| Controlling interest's share of book value ($320,000 × .80) | $256,000 |
| Noncontrolling interest's share of book value ($320,000 × .20) | 64,000 |
| Total assigned | $320,000 |

The impact of the constructive gain on the beginning noncontrolling interest balance and on the beginning consolidated retained earnings balance is reflected in entry E(34) in the workpaper. Entry E(34) increases the beginning balance of consolidated retained earnings by Peerless's $8,640 share ($10,800 × .80) of the gain on constructive retirement of the bonds that has not been recorded on the books of the affiliates as of the beginning of the period. Similarly, the noncontrolling interest is increased by its $2,160 proportionate share ($10,800 × .20) of the unrecorded gain. Because the gain on constructive retirement of the bonds was recognized in the 20X1 consolidated income statement but not on the separate books of Peerless and Special Foods, the beginning balances of consolidated retained earnings and the noncontrolling interest will be understated unless the gain amount is added into the workpaper in 20X2 and apportioned to each.

Entry E(34) also eliminates all aspects of the intercorporate bond holdings, including (1) Peerless's investment in bonds, (2) Special Foods' bonds payable and the associated premium, (3) Peerless's bond interest income, and (4) Special Foods' bond interest expense. The amounts related to the bonds from the books of Peerless and Special Foods and the appropriate consolidated amounts are as follows:

| Item | Peerless Products | Special Foods | Unadjusted Totals | Consolidated Amounts |
|------|------------------:|--------------:|------------------:|---------------------:|
| Bonds Payable | -0- | $(100,000) | $(100,000) | -0- |
| Premium on Bonds Payable | -0- | (1,600) | (1,600) | -0- |
| Investment in Bonds | $ 92,000 | -0- | 92,000 | -0- |
| Interest Expense | -0- | $ 11,800 | $ 11,800 | -0- |
| Interest Income | $(13,000) | -0- | (13,000) | -0- |

All balances related to the intercompany bond holdings are eliminated in entry E(34) so that none of the unadjusted totals appear in the consolidated financial statements.

### Consolidated Net Income—20X2

Consolidated net income of $246,800 is shown in the workpaper in Figure 8–3. This amount is computed and allocated as follows:

| | | |
|---|---:|---:|
| Peerless's separate income | | $173,000 |
| Special Foods' net income | $75,000 | |
| Peerless's amortization of bond discount | (1,000) | |
| Special Foods' amortization of bond premium | (200) | |
| Special Foods' realized net income | | 73,800 |
| Consolidated net income, 20X1 | | $246,800 |
| Income to noncontrolling interest ($73,800 × .20) | | (14,760) |
| Income to controlling interest | | $232,040 |

### Noncontrolling Interest—December 31, 20X2

Total noncontrolling interest on December 31, 20X2, includes a proportionate share of both the reported book value of Special Foods and the portion of the gain on constructive bond retirement not yet recognized by the affiliates:

| | | |
|---|---:|---:|
| Book value of Special Foods, December 31, 20X2: | | |
| Common stock | | $200,000 |
| Retained earnings | | 155,000 |
| Total book value | | $355,000 |
| Gain on constructive retirement of bonds | $10,800 | |
| Less: Portion recognized by affiliates during 20X2 | (1,200) | |
| Constructive gain not yet recognized by affiliates | | 9,600 |
| Realized book value of Special Foods | | $364,600 |
| Noncontrolling stockholders' share | | × .20 |
| Noncontrolling interest, December 31, 20X2 | | $ 72,920 |

### Bond Elimination Entry in Subsequent Years

In years after 20X2, the workpaper entry to eliminate the intercompany bonds and to adjust for the gain on constructive retirement of the bonds is similar to entry E(34). The unamortized bond discount and premium decrease each year by $1,000 and $200, respectively. As of the beginning of 20X3, $9,600 of the gain on the constructive retirement of the bonds remains unrecognized by the affiliates, computed as follows:

| | | |
|---|---:|---:|
| Gain on constructive retirement of bonds | | $10,800 |
| Less: Portion recognized by affiliates during 20X2: | | |
| Peerless's amortization of bond discount | $1,000 | |
| Special Foods' amortization of bond premium | 200 | |
| Total gain recognized by affiliates | | (1,200) |
| Unrecognized gain on constructive retirement of bonds, January 1, 20X3 | | $ 9,600 |

In the bond elimination entry in the consolidation workpaper prepared at the end of 20X3, this amount is allocated between beginning retained earnings and the noncontrolling interest:

| | | | |
|---|---|---:|---:|
| E(35) | Bonds Payable | 100,000 | |
| | Premium on Bonds Payable | 1,400 | |
| | Interest Income | 13,000 | |
| |     Investment in Special Foods Bonds | | 93,000 |
| |     Interest Expense | | 11,800 |
| |     Retained Earnings, January 1 | | 7,680 |
| |     Noncontrolling Interest | | 1,920 |
| | Eliminate intercorporate bond holdings: | | |
| | $1,400 = $2,000 − $200 − $200 − $200 | | |
| | $13,000 = ($100,000 × .12) + $1,000 | | |
| | $93,000 = $91,000 + $1,000 + $1,000 | | |
| | $11,800 = ($100,000 × .12) − $200 | | |
| | $7,680 = ($10,800 − $1,200) × .80 | | |
| | $1,920 = ($10,800 − $1,200) × .20 | | |

## Purchase at an Amount Greater than Book Value

When an affiliate's bonds are purchased from a nonaffiliate at an amount greater than their book value, the consolidation procedures are virtually the same as previously illustrated except that a loss is recognized on the constructive retirement of the debt. For example, assume that Special Foods issues 10-year 12 percent bonds on January 1, 20X1, at par of $100,000. The bonds are purchased from Special Foods by Nonaffiliated Corporation, which sells the bonds to Peerless Products on December 31, 20X1, for $104,500. Special Foods recognizes $12,000 ($100,000 × .12) of interest expense each year. Peerless recognizes interest income of $11,500 in each year after 20X1, computed as follows:

| | |
|---|---:|
| Annual cash interest payment ($100,000 × .12) | $12,000 |
| Less: Amortization of premium on bond investment ($4,500 ÷ 9 years) | (500) |
| Interest income | $11,500 |

Because the bonds were issued at par, the carrying amount on Special Foods' books remains at $100,000. Thus, once Peerless purchases the bonds from Nonaffiliated Corporation for $104,500, a loss on the constructive retirement must be recognized in the consolidated income statement for $4,500 ($104,500 − $100,000). The bond elimination entry in the consolidation workpaper prepared at the end of 20X1 removes the bonds payable and the bond investment and recognizes the loss on the constructive retirement:

| | | | |
|---|---|---:|---:|
| E(36) | Bonds Payable | 100,000 | |
| | Loss on Bond Retirement | 4,500 | |
| |     Investment in Special Foods Bonds | | 104,500 |
| | Eliminate intercorporate bond holdings. | | |

In subsequent years, Peerless amortizes the premium on the bond investment, reducing interest income and the bond investment balance by $500 each year. This, in effect, recognizes a portion of the loss on the constructive retirement. When consolidated statements are prepared, the amount of the loss on constructive retirement that has not been recognized by the separate affiliates at the beginning of the period is allocated proportionately against the ownership interests of the issuing affiliate. The bond elimination entry needed in the consolidation workpaper prepared at the end of 20X2 is as follows:

| E(37) | Bonds Payable | 100,000 | |
| | Interest Income | 11,500 | |
| | Retained Earnings, January 1 | 3,600 | |
| | Noncontrolling Interest | 900 | |
| | Investment in Special Foods Bonds | | 104,000 |
| | Interest Expense | | 12,000 |
| | Eliminate intercorporate bond holdings: | | |
| | $11,500 = ($100,000 × .12) − $500 | | |
| | $3,600 = $4,500 × .80 | | |
| | $900 = $4,500 × .20 | | |
| | $104,000 = $104,500 − $500 | | |
| | $12,000 = $100,000 × .12 | | |

Similarly, the following entry is needed in the consolidation workpaper at the end of 20X3:

| E(38) | Bonds Payable | 100,000 | |
| | Interest Income | 11,500 | |
| | Retained Earnings, January 1 | 3,200 | |
| | Noncontrolling Interest | 800 | |
| | Investment in Special Foods Bonds | | 103,500 |
| | Interest Expense | | 12,000 |
| | Eliminate intercorporate bond holdings: | | |
| | $3,200 = ($4,500 − $500) × .80 | | |
| | $800 = ($4,500 − $500) × .20 | | |
| | $103,500 = $104,500 − $500 − $500 | | |

## Summary of Key Concepts

The effects of intercompany debt transactions must be eliminated completely in preparing consolidated financial statements, just as with other types of intercompany transactions. Only debt transactions between the consolidated entity and unaffiliated parties are reported in the consolidated statements.

When one affiliate issues bonds that are purchased directly by another affiliate, the bonds are viewed from a consolidated point of view as never having been issued. Thus, all aspects of the intercompany bond holding are eliminated in consolidation. Items requiring elimination include (1) the bond investment from the purchasing affiliate's books, (2) the bond liability and any associated discount or premium from the issuer's books, (3) the interest income recognized by the investing affiliate and the interest expense recognized by the issuer, and (4) any intercompany interest receivable/payable as of the date of the consolidated statements.

When a company purchases the bonds of an affiliate from a nonaffiliate, the bonds are treated in consolidation as if they had been issued and subsequently repurchased by the consolidated entity. If the price paid by the purchasing affiliate is different from the issuer's book value of the bonds, a gain or loss from retirement of the bonds is recognized in the consolidated income statement. In addition, all aspects of the intercompany bond holding are eliminated because the bonds are treated as if the consolidated entity had retired them.

| **Key Terms** | constructive retirement, *379* | direct intercompany debt transfer, *374* | indirect intercompany debt transfer, *374* |
| --- | --- | --- | --- |

## Appendix **8A**  Intercompany Indebtedness—Fully Adjusted Equity Method and Cost Method

Consolidation procedures following use of (1) the fully adjusted equity method and (2) the cost method are illustrated with the example of the intercompany bond transaction presented earlier. Assume that Special Foods issues bonds with a par value of $100,000 and a term of 10 years to Nonaffiliated Corporation for $102,000 on January 1, 20X1. Peerless Products purchases the bonds from Nonaffiliated Corporation on December 31, 20X1, for $91,000.

## FULLY ADJUSTED EQUITY METHOD

The accounting procedures under the fully adjusted equity method are the same as under the basic equity method except that the parent (1) adjusts its income and the investment account by its proportionate share of the gain or loss on the constructive retirement of the bonds in the year of repurchase and (2) adjusts for the implicit recognition of the gain or loss by it and its subsidiary as they amortize the discount and premium in subsequent years.

The 20X1 gain on the constructive retirement in this illustration is $10,800, computed as follows:

| | |
| --- | --- |
| Book value of Special Foods' bonds, December 31, 20X1 ($102,000 − $200) | $101,800 |
| Price paid by Peerless to purchase bonds | (91,000) |
| Gain on constructive retirement of bonds | $ 10,800 |

### Fully Adjusted Equity-Method Entries—20X1

Peerless records the following entries under the fully adjusted equity method during 20X1 to account for its investment in Special Foods stock:

| | | | |
| --- | --- | --- | --- |
| (39) | Cash | 24,000 | |
| |     Investment in Special Foods Stock | | 24,000 |
| |     Record dividends from Special Foods: | | |
| |     $30,000 × .80 | | |
| | | | |
| (40) | Investment in Special Foods Stock | 40,000 | |
| |     Income from Subsidiary | | 40,000 |
| |     Record equity-method income: | | |
| |     $50,000 × .80 | | |
| | | | |
| (41) | Investment in Special Foods Stock | 8,640 | |
| |     Income from Subsidiary | | 8,640 |
| |     Recognize income from bond retirement: | | |
| |     ($101,800 − $91,000) × .80 | | |

Entry (41) adjusts equity-method net income by a proportionate share of the gain on the constructive retirement of Special Foods' bonds. Although the gain itself is not recognized by Peerless, its net income under the fully adjusted equity method must equal its allocated share of consolidated net income. In keeping with the concept of a one-line consolidation, Peerless's share of the gain on constructive retirement of Special Foods' bonds is included in its share of income from Special Foods.

Entries (39), (40), and (41) record income from Special Foods of $48,640 and increase the carrying amount of the investment on Peerless's books to $264,640 as of December 31, 20X1.

## Consolidation Elimination Entries—20X1

The December 31, 20X1, workpaper to prepare consolidated financial statements for Peerless Products and Special Foods contains the following eliminating entries:

| | | | |
|---|---|---:|---:|
| E(42) | Income from Subsidiary | 48,640 | |
| |     Dividends Declared | | 24,000 |
| |     Investment in Special Foods Stock | | 24,640 |
| |     Eliminate income from subsidiary. | | |
| | | | |
| E(43) | Income to Noncontrolling Interest | 12,160 | |
| |     Dividends Declared | | 6,000 |
| |     Noncontrolling Interest | | 6,160 |
| |     Assign income to noncontrolling interest: | | |
| |     $12,160 = ($50,000 + $10,800) \times .20$ | | |
| | | | |
| E(44) | Common Stock—Special Foods | 200,000 | |
| | Retained Earnings, January 1 | 100,000 | |
| |     Investment in Special Foods Stock | | 240,000 |
| |     Noncontrolling Interest | | 60,000 |
| |     Eliminate beginning investment balance. | | |
| | | | |
| E(45) | Bonds Payable | 100,000 | |
| | Premium on Bonds Payable | 1,800 | |
| |     Investment in Special Foods Bonds | | 91,000 |
| |     Gain on Bond Retirement | | 10,800 |
| |     Eliminate intercorporate bond holdings. | | |

## Fully Adjusted Equity-Method Entries—20X2

In addition to the entries related to its investment in Special Foods' bonds, Peerless records the following entries during 20X2 under the fully adjusted equity method:

| | | | |
|---|---|---:|---:|
| (46) | Cash | 32,000 | |
| |     Investment in Special Foods Stock | | 32,000 |
| |     Record dividends from Special Foods: | | |
| |     $40,000 \times .80$ | | |
| | | | |
| (47) | Investment in Special Foods Stock | 60,000 | |
| |     Income from Subsidiary | | 60,000 |
| |     Record equity-method income: | | |
| |     $75,000 \times .80$ | | |
| | | | |
| (48) | Income from Subsidiary | 960 | |
| |     Investment in Special Foods Stock | | 960 |
| |     Adjust for portion of gain on constructive | | |
| |     bond retirement recognized: | | |
| |     ($10,800 \div 9) \times .80$ | | |

Entry (48) adjusts for Peerless's portion of the gain on the constructive bond retirement recognized on the separate books of Peerless and Special Foods during 20X2 as a result of the excess of Peerless's $13,000 interest income accrual over Special Foods' $11,800 charge to interest expense.

Whereas neither Peerless nor Special Foods recognized any of the gain from the constructive bond retirement on its separate books in 20X1, Peerless adjusted its equity-method income from Special Foods for its 80 percent share of the $10,800 gain, $8,640. Therefore, as Peerless and Special Foods recognize the gain over the remaining term of the bonds, Peerless must reverse its 20X1 entry for its share of the gain. This adjustment is needed to avoid double counting Peerless's share of the gain. Thus, the original adjustment of $8,640 is reversed by $960 ($8,640 ÷ 9 years) each year. This is accomplished in 20X2 through entry (48).

The amount of entry (48) also equals Peerless's 80 percent share of the difference in interest expense and interest income to be eliminated in consolidation:

| | |
|---|---:|
| Elimination of Peerless's interest income | $13,000 |
| Elimination of Special Foods' interest expense | (11,800) |
| Net reduction in consolidated net income | $ 1,200 |
| Peerless's proportionate share | × .80 |
| Reduction in Peerless's share of consolidated net income | $   960 |

When the bond interest expense and bond interest income are eliminated in the preparation of consolidated financial statements, Peerless's share of consolidated net income is reduced by $960. Entry (48) adjusts Peerless's equity-method income to equal its share of consolidated net income.

Peerless's account relating to its investment in Special Foods' common stock appears as follows at the end of 20X2:

| **Investment in Special Foods Stock** | | | | |
|---|---:|---|---|---:|
| Original cost | 240,000 | | | |
| (40) 20X1 equity accrual ($50,000 × .80) | 40,000 | (39) | 20X1 dividends ($30,000 × .80) | 24,000 |
| (41) Gain on constructive bond retirement ($10,800 × .80) | 8,640 | | | |
| Balance, 12/31/X1 | 264,640 | | | |
| (47) 20X2 equity accrual ($75,000 × .80) | 60,000 | (46) | 20X2 dividends ($40,000 × .80) | 32,000 |
| | | (48) | Recognized portion of constructive gain ($8,640 ÷ 9 years) | 960 |
| Balance, 12/31/X2 | 291,680 | | | |

## Consolidation Elimination Entries—20X2

The following elimination entries are needed in the workpaper to prepare consolidated financial statements for 20X2:

| E(49) | Income from Subsidiary | 59,040 | |
|---|---|---:|---:|
| | Dividends Declared | | 32,000 |
| | Investment in Special Foods Stock | | 27,040 |
| | Eliminate income from subsidiary. | | |
| | | | |
| E(50) | Income to Noncontrolling Interest | 14,760 | |
| | Dividends Declared | | 8,000 |
| | Noncontrolling Interest | | 6,760 |
| | Assign income to noncontrolling interest: | | |
| | $14,760 = ($75,000 − $1,200) × .20 | | |

| E(51) | Common Stock—Special Foods | 200,000 | |
|---|---|---|---|
| | Retained Earnings, January 1 | 120,000 | |
| |     Investment in Special Foods Stock | | 256,000 |
| |     Noncontrolling Interest | | 64,000 |
| |   Eliminate beginning investment balance. | | |

| E(52) | Bonds Payable | 100,000 | |
|---|---|---|---|
| | Premium on Bonds Payable | 1,600 | |
| | Interest Income | 13,000 | |
| |     Investment in Special Foods Bonds | | 92,000 |
| |     Interest Expense | | 11,800 |
| |     Investment in Special Foods Stock | | 8,640 |
| |     Noncontrolling Interest | | 2,160 |

Eliminate intercorporate bond holdings:

$1,600 = $2,000 − $200 − $200

$13,000 = ($100,000 × .12) + $1,000

$92,000 = $91,000 + $1,000

$11,800 = ($100,000 × .12) − $200

$8,640 = $10,800 × .80

$2,160 = $10,800 × .20

# COST METHOD

Preparation of consolidated financial statements when the cost method has been used is illustrated with the same example employed for the fully adjusted equity method. Peerless recognizes dividend income of $24,000 ($30,000 × .80) in 20X1 and $32,000 ($40,000 × .80) in 20X2 under the cost method. Peerless makes no adjustments with respect to Special Foods' undistributed earnings or the gain on the constructive bond retirement.

## Consolidation Elimination Entries—20X1

The following eliminating entries are needed in the consolidation workpaper prepared at the end of 20X1, following use of the cost method:

| E(53) | Dividend Income | 24,000 | |
|---|---|---|---|
| |     Dividends Declared | | 24,000 |
| |   Eliminate dividend income from subsidiary: $30,000 × .80 | | |

| E(54) | Income to Noncontrolling Interest | 12,160 | |
|---|---|---|---|
| |     Dividends Declared | | 6,000 |
| |     Noncontrolling Interest | | 6,160 |
| |   Assign income to noncontrolling interest: | | |

$12,160 = ($50,000 + $10,800) × .20

| E(55) | Common Stock—Special Foods | 200,000 | |
|---|---|---|---|
| | Retained Earnings, January 1 | 100,000 | |
| |     Investment in Special Foods Stock | | 240,000 |
| |     Noncontrolling Interest | | 60,000 |
| |   Eliminate investment balance at date of acquisition. | | |

| E(56) | Bonds Payable | 100,000 | |
|---|---|---|---|
| | Premium on Bonds Payable | 1,800 | |
| |     Investment in Special Foods Bonds | | 91,000 |
| |     Gain on Bond Retirement | | 10,800 |
| |   Eliminate intercorporate bond holdings. | | |

## Consolidation Elimination Entries—20X2

Elimination entries needed in the consolidation workpaper at the end of 20X2 are as follows:

| | | | |
|---|---|---|---|
| E(57) | Dividend Income | 32,000 | |
| | Dividends Declared | | 32,000 |
| | Eliminate dividend income from subsidiary: $40,000 × .80 | | |
| | | | |
| E(58) | Income to Noncontrolling Interest | 14,760 | |
| | Dividends Declared | | 8,000 |
| | Noncontrolling Interest | | 6,760 |
| | Assign income to noncontrolling interest: | | |
| | $14,760 = ($75,000 − $1,200) × .20 | | |
| | | | |
| E(59) | Common Stock—Special Foods | 200,000 | |
| | Retained Earnings, January 1 | 100,000 | |
| | Investment in Special Foods Stock | | 240,000 |
| | Noncontrolling Interest | | 60,000 |
| | Eliminate investment balance at date of acquisition. | | |
| | | | |
| E(60) | Retained Earnings, January 1 | 4,000 | |
| | Noncontrolling Interest | | 4,000 |
| | Assign undistributed prior earnings of subsidiary to noncontrolling interest: $20,000 × .20 | | |
| | | | |
| E(61) | Bonds Payable | 100,000 | |
| | Premium on Bonds Payable | 1,600 | |
| | Interest Income | 13,000 | |
| | Investment in Special Foods Bonds | | 92,000 |
| | Interest Expense | | 11,800 |
| | Retained Earnings, January 1 | | 8,640 |
| | Noncontrolling Interest | | 2,160 |
| | Eliminate intercorporate bond holdings: | | |
| | $1,600 = $2,000 − $200 − $200 | | |
| | $13,000 = ($100,000 × .12) + $1,000 | | |
| | $92,000 = $91,000 + $1,000 | | |
| | $11,800 = ($100,000 × .12) − $200 | | |
| | $8,640 = $10,800 × .80 | | |
| | $2,160 = $10,800 × .20 | | |

---

**Questions**

**Q8-1**  When is a gain or loss on bond retirement included in the consolidated income statement?

**Q8-2**  What is meant by a constructive bond retirement in a multi-corporate setting? How does a constructive bond retirement differ from an actual bond retirement?

**Q8-3**  When a bond issue has been placed directly with an affiliate, what account balances will be stated incorrectly in the consolidated statements if the intercompany bond ownership is not eliminated in preparing the consolidation workpaper?

**Q8-4**  When an affiliate's bonds are purchased from a nonaffiliate during the period, what balances will be stated incorrectly in the consolidated financial statements if the intercompany bond ownership is not eliminated in preparing the consolidation workpaper?

**Q8-5**  For a multi-corporate entity, how is the recognition of gains or losses on bond retirement changed when emphasis is placed on the economic entity rather than the legal entity?

**Q8-6**  When a parent company sells land to a subsidiary at more than book value, the consolidation eliminating entries at the end of the period include a debit to the gain on the sale of land. When a parent purchases the bonds of a subsidiary from a nonaffiliate at less than book value, the eliminating entries at the end of the period contain a credit to a gain on bond retirement. Why are these two situations not handled in the same manner in the consolidation workpaper?

**Q8-7**   What is the effect of eliminating intercompany interest income and interest expense on consolidated net income when there has been a direct sale of bonds to an affiliate? Why?

**Q8-8**   What is the effect of eliminating intercompany interest income and interest expense on consolidated net income when a loss on bond retirement has been reported in a prior year's consolidated financial statements as a result of a constructive retirement of an affiliate's bonds? Why?

**Q8-9**   If an affiliate's bonds are purchased from a nonaffiliate at the beginning of the current year, how can the amount of the gain or loss on constructive retirement be computed by looking at the two companies' year-end trial balances?

**Q8-10**   When the parent company purchases a subsidiary's bonds from a nonaffiliate for more than book value, what income statement accounts will be affected in preparing consolidated financial statements? What will be the effect on income assigned to the controlling interest in the consolidated income statement?

**Q8-11**   When a subsidiary purchases the bonds of its parent from a nonaffiliate for less than book value, what will be the effect on consolidated net income and income to the controlling interest?

**Q8-12**   How is the amount of income assigned to the noncontrolling interest affected by the direct placement of a subsidiary's bonds with the parent company?

**Q8-13**   How is the amount of income assigned to the noncontrolling interest affected when the parent purchases the bonds of its subsidiary from an unaffiliated company for less than book value?

**Q8-14**   How would the relationship between interest income recorded by a subsidiary and interest expense recorded by the parent be expected to change when a direct placement of the parent's bonds with the subsidiary is compared with a constructive retirement in which the subsidiary purchases the bonds of the parent from a nonaffiliate?

**Q8-15**   A subsidiary purchased bonds of its parent company from a nonaffiliate in the preceding period, and a gain on bond retirement was reported in the consolidated income statement as a result of the purchase. What effect will that event have on the amount of consolidated net income and income to the noncontrolling interest reported in the current period?

**Q8-16**   A parent company purchased its subsidiary's bonds from a nonaffiliate in the preceding year, and a loss on bond retirement was reported in the consolidated income statement. How will income assigned to the noncontrolling interest be affected in the year following the constructive retirement?

**Q8-17**   A parent purchases a subsidiary's bonds directly from the subsidiary. The parent later sells the bonds to a nonaffiliate. From a consolidated viewpoint, what occurs when the parent sells the bonds? Is a gain or loss reported in the consolidated income statement when the parent sells the bonds? Why?

**Q8-18**   Shortly after a parent company purchased its subsidiary's bonds from a nonaffiliate, the subsidiary retired the entire issue. How is the gain or loss on bond retirement reported by the subsidiary treated for consolidation purposes?

---

# Cases

### C8-1   Recognition of Retirement Gains and Losses

Bradley Corporation sold bonds to Flood Company in 20X2 at 90. At the end of 20X4, Century Corporation purchased the bonds from Flood at 105. Bradley then retired the full bond issue on December 31, 20X7, at 101. Century holds 80 percent of Bradley's voting stock. Neither Century nor Bradley owns stock of Flood Company.

*Analysis*

### Required

*a.* Indicate how each of the three bond transactions should be recorded by the companies involved.

*b.* Indicate when, if at all, the consolidated entity headed by Century should recognize a gain or loss on bond retirement, and indicate whether a gain or a loss should be recognized.

*c.* Will income assigned to Bradley's noncontrolling shareholders be affected by the bond transactions? If so, in which years?

### C8-2    Borrowing by Variable Interest Entities

*Research FARS*

Hydro Corporation needed to build a new production facility. Because it already had a relatively high debt ratio, the company decided to establish a joint venture with Rich Corner Bank. This arrangement permitted the joint venture to borrow $30,000,000 for 20 years on a fixed interest rate basis at an interest rate nearly 2 percent less than Hydro would have paid if it had borrowed the money. Rich Corner Bank purchased 100 percent of the joint venture's equity for $200,000, and Hydro provided a guarantee of the debt to the bond holders and a guarantee to Rich Corner Bank that it would earn a 20 percent annual return on its investment.

On completion of the production facility, Hydro entered into a 10-year lease with the joint venture for use of the new facility. Due to the lease agreement terms, Hydro has reported the lease as an operating lease. Hydro does not report an investment in the joint venture because it holds no equity interest.

#### Required

As a senior member of Hydro's accounting staff, you have been asked to investigate the financial reporting standards associated with accounting for variable interest entities and determine whether Hydro's reporting is appropriate. Prepare a memo to Hydro's president stating your findings and conclusions and analyzing the impact on Hydro's financial statements if the current reporting procedures are inappropriate. Include citations to or quotations from the authoritative accounting literature in support of your findings and conclusions.

### C8-3    Subsidiary Bond Holdings

*Research FARS*

Farflung Corporation has in excess of 60 subsidiaries worldwide. It owns 65 percent of the voting common stock of Micro Company and 80 percent of the shares of Eagle Corporation. Micro sold $400,000 par value first mortgage bonds at par value on January 2, 20X0, to Independent Company. No intercorporate ownership exists between Farflung and its subsidiaries and Independent.

On December 31, 20X4, Independent determined the need for cash for other purposes and sold the Micro bonds to Eagle for $424,000. Farflung's accounting department was not aware of the bond purchase by Eagle and included the Micro Company bonds among its long-term liabilities in the consolidated balance sheet prepared at December 31, 20X4.

#### Required

In reviewing the financial statements of Farflung and its subsidiaries at December 31, 20X5, you discovered Eagle Corporation's investment in Micro's bonds and immediately brought it to the attention of Farflung's financial vice president. You have been asked to prepare a memo to the financial vice president detailing the appropriate reporting treatment when intercorporate bond ownership occurs in this way and to provide recommendations as to the actions, if any, Farflung should take in preparing its consolidated statements at December 31, 20X5. Include in your memo citations to or quotations from applicable authoritative accounting standards in support of your position.

### C8-4    Interest Income and Expense

*Understanding*

Snerd Corporation's controller is having difficulty explaining the impact of several of the company's intercorporate bond transactions.

#### Required

a.  Snerd receives interest payments in excess of the amount of interest income it records on its investment in Snort bonds. Did Snerd purchase the bonds at par value, at a premium, or at a discount? How can you tell?

b.  The 20X3 consolidated income statement reported a gain on the retirement of a subsidiary's bonds. If Snerd purchased the bonds from a nonaffiliate at par value:

  (1)  Were the subsidiary's bonds originally sold at a premium or a discount? How can you tell?

  (2)  Will the annual interest payments received by Snerd be more or less than the interest expense recorded by the subsidiary? Explain.

  (3)  How is the difference between the interest income recorded by Snerd and the interest expense recorded by the subsidiary treated in preparing consolidated financial statements at the end of each period?

### C8-5    Intercompany Debt

Intercompany debt, both long term and short term, arises frequently. In some cases, intercorporate borrowings may arise because one affiliate can borrow at a cheaper rate than others, and lending to

*Analysis*  other affiliates may reduce the overall cost of borrowing. In other cases, intercompany receivables/payables arise because of intercompany sales of goods or services or other types of intercompany transactions.

### Required

a.  What major problem might arise with intercompany debt between a domestic parent and a foreign subsidiary or between subsidiaries in different countries? How has Hershey Foods dealt with this problem?

b.  Did Hershey Foods' intercompany loans arise because of direct loans or because of intercompany sales of goods and services on credit?

---

**Exercises**

### E8-1  Bond Sale from Parent to Subsidiary

Lamar Corporation owns 60 percent of Humbolt Corporation's voting shares. On January 1, 20X2, Lamar Corporation sold $150,000 par value 6 percent first mortgage bonds to Humbolt for $156,000. The bonds mature in 10 years and pay interest semiannually on January 1 and July 1.

### Required

a.  Prepare the journal entries for 20X2 for Humbolt related to its ownership of Lamar's bonds.

b.  Prepare the journal entries for 20X2 for Lamar related to the bonds.

c.  Prepare the workpaper eliminating entries needed on December 31, 20X2, to remove the effects of the intercorporate ownership of bonds.

### E8-2  Computation of Transfer Price

Nettle Corporation sold $100,000 par value 10-year first mortgage bonds to Timberline Corporation on January 1, 20X5. The bonds, which bear a nominal interest rate of 12 percent, pay interest semiannually on January 1 and July 1. The entry to record interest income by Timberline Corporation on December 31, 20X7, was as follows:

| | | |
|---|---:|---:|
| Interest Receivable | 6,000 | |
| Interest Income | | 5,750 |
| Investment in Nettle Corporation Bonds | | 250 |

Timberline Corporation owns 65 percent of the voting stock of Nettle Corporation, and consolidated statements are prepared on December 31, 20X7.

### Required

a.  What was the original purchase price of the bonds to Timberline Corporation?

b.  What is the balance in Timberline's bond investment account on December 31, 20X7?

c.  Give the workpaper eliminating entry or entries needed to remove the effects of the intercompany ownership of bonds in preparing consolidated financial statements for 20X7.

### E8-3  Bond Sale at Discount

Wood Corporation owns 70 percent of Carter Company's voting shares. On January 1, 20X3, Carter sold bonds with a par value of $600,000 at 98. Wood purchased $400,000 par value of the bonds; the remainder was sold to nonaffiliates. The bonds mature in five years and pay an annual interest rate of 8 percent. Interest is paid semiannually on January 1 and July 1.

### Required

a.  What amount of interest expense should be reported in the 20X4 consolidated income statement?

b.  Give the journal entries recorded by Wood during 20X4 with regard to its investment in Carter bonds.

c.  Give all workpaper eliminating entries needed to remove the effects of the intercorporate bond ownership in preparing consolidated financial statements for 20X4.

### E8-4  Evaluation of Intercorporate Bond Holdings

Stellar Corporation purchased bonds of its subsidiary from a nonaffiliate during 20X6. Although Stellar purchased the bonds at par value, a loss on bond retirement is reported in the 20X6 consolidated income statement as a result of the purchase.

### Required

a. Were the bonds originally sold by the subsidiary at a premium or a discount? Explain.

b. Will the annual interest payments received by Stellar be more or less than the interest expense recorded by the subsidiary each period? Explain.

c. As a result of the entry recorded at December 31, 20X7, to eliminate the effects of the intercompany bond holding, will consolidated net income be increased or decreased? Explain.

### E8-5 Multiple-Choice Questions

Select the correct answer for each of the following questions.

1. **[AICPA Adapted]** Wagner, a holder of a $1,000,000 Palmer Inc. bond, collected the interest due on March 31, 20X8, and then sold the bond to Seal Inc. for $975,000. On that date, Palmer, a 75 percent owner of Seal, had a $1,075,000 carrying amount for this bond. What was the effect of Seal's purchase of Palmer's bond on the retained earnings and noncontrolling interest amounts reported in Palmer's March 31, 20X8, consolidated balance sheet?

   | | Retained Earnings | Noncontrolling Interest |
   |---|---|---|
   | a. | $100,000 increase | No effect |
   | b. | $75,000 increase | $25,000 increase |
   | c. | No effect | $25,000 increase |
   | d. | No effect | $100,000 increase |

2. **[AICPA Adapted]** P Company purchased term bonds at a premium on the open market. These bonds represented 20 percent of the outstanding class of bonds issued at a discount by S Company, P's wholly owned subsidiary. P intends to hold the bonds to maturity. In a consolidated balance sheet, the difference between the bond carrying amounts of the two companies would be:

   a. Included as a decrease to retained earnings.

   b. Included as an increase in retained earnings.

   c. Reported as a deferred debit to be amortized over the remaining life of the bonds.

   d. Reported as a deferred credit to be amortized over the remaining life of the bonds.

*Note.* The following information relates to questions 3–6:

Kruse Corporation holds 60 percent of the voting common shares of Gary's Ice Cream Parlors. On January 1, 20X6, Gary's purchased $50,000 par value 10 percent first mortgage bonds of Kruse from Cane for $58,000. Kruse originally issued the bonds to Cane on January 1, 20X4, for $53,000. The bonds have a 10-year maturity from the date of issue.

Gary's reported net income of $20,000 for 20X6, and Kruse reported income (excluding income from ownership of Gary's stock) of $40,000.

3. What amount of interest expense does Kruse record annually?

   a. $4,000.

   b. $4,700.

   c. $5,000.

   d. $10,000.

4. What amount of interest income does Gary's Ice Cream Parlors record for 20X6?

   a. $4,000.

   b. $5,000.

   c. $9,000.

   d. $10,000.

5. What gain or loss on the retirement of bonds should be reported in the 20X6 consolidated income statement?

   a. $2,400 gain.

   b. $5,600 gain.

   c. $5,600 loss.

   d. $8,000 loss.

6. What amount of consolidated net income should be reported for 20X6?

   *a.* $47,100.

   *b.* $54,400.

   *c.* $55,100.

   *d.* $60,000.

### E8-6   Multiple-Choice Questions

On January 1, 20X4, Passive Heating Corporation paid $104,000 for $100,000 par value 9 percent bonds of Solar Energy Corporation. Solar had issued $300,000 of the 10-year bonds on January 1, 20X2, for $360,000. Passive previously had purchased 80 percent of the common stock of Solar on January 1, 20X1, at underlying book value.

Passive reported operating income (excluding income from subsidiary) of $50,000, and Solar reported net income of $30,000 for 20X4.

#### *Required*

Select the correct answer for each of the following questions.

1. What amount of interest expense should be included in the 20X4 consolidated income statement?

   *a.* $14,000.

   *b.* $18,000.

   *c.* $21,000.

   *d.* $27,000.

2. What amount of gain or loss on bond retirement should be included in the 20X4 consolidated income statement?

   *a.* $4,000 gain.

   *b.* $4,000 loss.

   *c.* $12,000 gain.

   *d.* $16,000 loss.

3. Income assigned to the noncontrolling interest in the 20X4 consolidated income statement should be:

   *a.* $6,000.

   *b.* $8,100.

   *c.* $8,400.

   *d.* $16,000.

### E8-7   Constructive Retirement at End of Year

Able Company issued $600,000 of 9 percent first mortgage bonds on January 1, 20X1, at 103. The bonds mature in 20 years and pay interest semiannually on January 1 and July 1. Prime Corporation purchased $400,000 of Able's bonds from the original purchaser on December 31, 20X5, for $397,000. Prime owns 60 percent of Able's voting common stock.

#### *Required*

*a.* Prepare the workpaper elimination entry or entries needed to remove the effects of the intercorporate bond ownership in preparing consolidated financial statements for 20X5.

*b.* Prepare the workpaper elimination entry or entries needed to remove the effects of the intercorporate bond ownership in preparing consolidated financial statements for 20X6.

### E8-8   Constructive Retirement at Beginning of Year

Able Company issued $600,000 of 9 percent first mortgage bonds on January 1, 20X1, at 103. The bonds mature in 20 years and pay interest semiannually on January 1 and July 1. Prime Corporation purchased $400,000 of Able's bonds from the original purchaser on January 1, 20X5, for $396,800. Prime owns 60 percent of Able's voting common stock.

#### *Required*

*a.* Prepare the workpaper elimination entry or entries needed to remove the effects of the intercorporate bond ownership in preparing consolidated financial statements for 20X5.

*b.* Prepare the workpaper elimination entry or entries needed to remove the effects of the intercorporate bond ownership in preparing consolidated financial statements for 20X6.

### E8-9 Retirement of Bonds Sold at a Discount

Farley Corporation owns 70 percent of Snowball Enterprises's stock. On January 1, 20X1, Farley sold $1,000,000 par value 7 percent, 20-year, first mortgage bonds to Kling Corporation at 97. On January 1, 20X8, Snowball purchased $300,000 par value of the Farley bonds directly from Kling for $296,880.

#### Required

Prepare the eliminating entry needed at December 31, 20X8, to remove the effects of the intercorporate bond ownership in preparing consolidated financial statements.

### E8-10 Loss on Constructive Retirement

Apple Corporation holds 60 percent of Shortway Publishing Company's voting shares. Apple issued $500,000 of 10 percent bonds with a 10-year maturity on January 1, 20X2, at 90. On January 1, 20X8, Shortway purchased $100,000 of the Apple bonds for $108,000. Partial trial balances for the two companies on December 31, 20X8, are as follows:

|  | Apple Corporation | Shortway Publishing Company |
|---|---|---|
| Investment in Shortway Publishing Company Stock | $141,000 | |
| Investment in Apple Corporation Bonds | | $106,000 |
| Bonds Payable | 500,000 | |
| Discount on Bonds Payable | 15,000 | |
| Interest Expense | 55,000 | |
| Interest Income | | 8,000 |
| Interest Payable | 25,000 | |
| Interest Receivable | | 5,000 |

#### Required

Prepare the workpaper eliminating entry or entries needed on December 31, 20X8, to remove the effects of the intercorporate bond ownership in preparing consolidated financial statements.

### E8-11 Determining the Amount of Retirement Gain or Loss

Online Enterprises owns 95 percent of Downlink Corporation. On January 1, 20X1, Downlink issued $200,000 of five-year bonds at 115. Annual interest of 12 percent is paid semiannually on January 1 and July 1. Online purchased $100,000 of the bonds on August 31, 20X3, at par value. The following balances are taken from the separate 20X3 financial statements of the two companies:

|  | Online Enterprises | Downlink Corporation |
|---|---|---|
| Investment in Downlink Corporation Bonds | $100,000 | |
| Interest Income | 4,000 | |
| Interest Receivable | 6,000 | |
| Bonds Payable | | $200,000 |
| Bond Premium | | 12,000 |
| Interest Expense | | 18,000 |
| Interest Payable | | 12,000 |

#### Required

a. Compute the amount of interest expense that should be reported in the consolidated income statement for 20X3.

b. Compute the gain or loss on constructive bond retirement that should be reported in the 20X3 consolidated income statement.

c. Prepare the consolidation workpaper eliminating entry or entries as of December 31, 20X3, to remove the effects of the intercorporate bond ownership.

### E8-12 Evaluation of Bond Retirement

Bundle Company issued $500,000 par value 10-year bonds at 104 on January 1, 20X3, which Mega Corporation purchased. The coupon rate on the bonds is 11 percent. Interest payments are made semiannually on July 1 and January 1. On July 1, 20X6, Parent Company purchased $200,000 par value of the bonds from Mega for $192,200. Parent owns 70 percent of Bundle's voting shares.

#### Required

*a.* What amount of gain or loss will be reported in Bundle's 20X6 income statement on the retirement of bonds?

*b.* Will a gain or loss be reported in the 20X6 consolidated financial statements for Parent for the constructive retirement of bonds? What amount will be reported?

*c.* How much will Parent's purchase of the bonds change consolidated net income for 20X6?

*d.* Prepare the workpaper eliminating entry or entries needed to remove the effects of the intercorporate bond ownership in preparing consolidated financial statements at December 31, 20X6.

*e.* Prepare the workpaper eliminating entry or entries needed to remove the effects of the intercorporate bond ownership in preparing consolidated financial statements at December 31, 20X7.

*f.* If Bundle reports net income of $50,000 for 20X7, what amount of income will be assigned to the noncontrolling interest in the consolidated income statement?

### E8-13 Elimination of Intercorporate Bond Holdings

Stang Corporation issued to Bradley Company $400,000 par value 10-year bonds with a coupon rate of 12 percent on January 1, 20X5, at 105. The bonds pay interest semiannually on July 1 and January 1. On January 1, 20X8, Purple Corporation purchased $100,000 of the bonds from Bradley for $104,900.

Purple owns 65 percent of the voting common shares of Stang and prepares consolidated financial statements.

#### Required

*a.* Prepare the workpaper eliminating entry or entries needed to remove the effects of the intercorporate bond ownership in preparing consolidated financial statements for 20X8.

*b.* Assuming that Stang reports net income of $20,000 for 20X8, compute the amount of income assigned to noncontrolling shareholders in the 20X8 consolidated income statement.

*c.* Prepare the workpaper eliminating entry or entries needed to remove the effects of the intercorporate bond ownership in preparing consolidated financial statements for 20X9.

## Problems

### P8-14 Consolidation Workpaper with Sale of Bonds to Subsidiary

Porter Company purchased 60 percent ownership of Temple Corporation on January 1, 20X1, at underlying book value. At that date, the fair value of the noncontrolling interest was equal to 40 percent of the book value of Temple. On January 1, 20X1, Porter sold $80,000 par value 8 percent five-year bonds directly to Temple for $82,000. The bonds pay interest annually on December 31. Porter uses the basic equity method in accounting for its ownership of Temple. On December 31, 20X2, the trial balances of the two companies are as follows:

| Item | Porter Company Debit | Porter Company Credit | Temple Corporation Debit | Temple Corporation Credit |
|---|---|---|---|---|
| Cash and Accounts Receivable | $ 80,200 | | $ 40,000 | |
| Inventory | 120,000 | | 65,000 | |
| Buildings and Equipment | 500,000 | | 300,000 | |
| Investment in Temple Corporation Stock | 102,000 | | | |
| Investment in Porter Company Bonds | | | 81,200 | |
| Cost of Goods Sold | 99,800 | | 61,000 | |
| Depreciation Expense | 25,000 | | 15,000 | |
| Interest Expense | 6,000 | | 14,000 | |
| Dividends Declared | 40,000 | | 10,000 | |

*(continued)*

(*continued*)

| Item | Porter Company Debit | Porter Company Credit | Temple Corporation Debit | Temple Corporation Credit |
|---|---|---|---|---|
| Accumulated Depreciation | | $175,000 | | $ 75,000 |
| Accounts Payable | | 68,800 | | 41,200 |
| Bonds Payable | | 80,000 | | 200,000 |
| Bond Premium | | 1,200 | | |
| Common Stock | | 200,000 | | 100,000 |
| Retained Earnings | | 230,000 | | 50,000 |
| Sales | | 200,000 | | 114,000 |
| Interest Income | | | | 6,000 |
| Income from Subsidiary | | 18,000 | | |
| | $973,000 | $973,000 | $586,200 | $586,200 |

## Required

*a.* Record the journal entry or entries for 20X2 on Porter's books related to its investment in Temple.

*b.* Record the journal entry or entries for 20X2 on Porter's books related to its bonds payable.

*c.* Record the journal entry or entries for 20X2 on Temple's books related to its investment in Porter's bonds.

*d.* Prepare the elimination entries needed to complete a consolidated workpaper for 20X2.

*e.* Prepare a three-part consolidated workpaper for 20X2.

**P8-15    Consolidation Workpaper with Sale of Bonds to Parent**

Mega Corporation purchased 90 percent of Tarp Company's voting common shares on January 1, 20X2, at underlying book value. At that date, the fair value of the noncontrolling interest was equal to 10 percent of the book value of Tarp Company. Mega also purchased $100,000 of 6 percent five-year bonds directly from Tarp on January 1, 20X2, for $104,000. The bonds pay interest annually on December 31. The trial balances of the companies as of December 31, 20X4, are as follows:

| Item | Mega Corporation Debit | Mega Corporation Credit | Tarp Company Debit | Tarp Company Credit |
|---|---|---|---|---|
| Cash and Receivables | $ 22,000 | | $ 36,600 | |
| Inventory | 165,000 | | 75,000 | |
| Buildings and Equipment | 400,000 | | 240,000 | |
| Investment in Tarp Company Stock | 121,500 | | | |
| Investment in Tarp Company Bonds | 101,600 | | | |
| Cost of Goods Sold | 86,000 | | 79,800 | |
| Depreciation Expense | 20,000 | | 15,000 | |
| Interest Expense | 16,000 | | 5,200 | |
| Dividends Declared | 30,000 | | 20,000 | |
| Accumulated Depreciation | | $140,000 | | $ 80,000 |
| Current Payables | | 92,400 | | 35,000 |
| Bonds Payable | | 200,000 | | 100,000 |
| Bond Premium | | | | 1,600 |
| Common Stock | | 120,000 | | 80,000 |
| Retained Earnings | | 242,000 | | 50,000 |
| Sales | | 140,000 | | 125,000 |
| Interest Income | | 5,200 | | |
| Income from Subsidiary | | 22,500 | | |
| | $962,100 | $962,100 | $471,600 | $471,600 |

### Required

a. Record the journal entry or entries for 20X4 on Mega's books related to its investment in Tarp Common stock.

b. Record the journal entry or entries for 20X4 on Mega's books related to its investment in Tarp Company bonds.

c. Record the journal entry or entries for 20X4 on Tarp's books related to its bonds payable.

d. Prepare the elimination entries needed to complete a consolidated workpaper for 20X4.

e. Prepare a three-part consolidated workpaper for 20X4.

**P8-16  Direct Sale of Bonds to Parent**

On January 1, 20X1, Fern Corporation paid Morton Advertising $116,200 to acquire 70 percent of Vincent Company's stock. Fern also paid $45,000 to acquire $50,000 par value 8 percent 10-year bonds directly from Vincent on that date. Interest payments are made on January 1 and July 1. The fair value of the noncontrolling interest at January 1, 20X1, was $49,800, and book value of Vincent's net assets was $110,000. The book values and fair values of Vincent's assets and liabilities were equal except for buildings and equipment, which had a fair value $56,000 greater than book value and a remaining economic life of 14 years at January 1, 20X1.

The trial balances for the two companies as of December 31, 20X3, are as follows:

| Item | Fern Corporation Debit | Fern Corporation Credit | Vincent Company Debit | Vincent Company Credit |
|---|---|---|---|---|
| Cash and Current Receivables | $ 30,300 | | $ 46,000 | |
| Inventory | 170,000 | | 70,000 | |
| Land, Buildings, and Equipment (net) | 320,000 | | 180,000 | |
| Investment in Vincent Bonds | 46,500 | | | |
| Investment in Vincent Stock | 149,800 | | | |
| Discount on Bonds Payable | | | 7,000 | |
| Operating Expenses | 198,500 | | 161,000 | |
| Interest Expense | 27,000 | | 9,000 | |
| Dividends Declared | 60,000 | | 10,000 | |
| Current Liabilities | | $ 35,000 | | $ 33,000 |
| Bonds Payable | | 300,000 | | 100,000 |
| Common Stock | | 100,000 | | 50,000 |
| Retained Earnings | | 244,400 | | 100,000 |
| Sales | | 300,000 | | 200,000 |
| Interest Income | | 4,500 | | |
| Income from Subsidiary | | 18,200 | | |
| Total | $1,002,100 | $1,002,100 | $483,000 | $483,000 |

On July 1, 20X2, Vincent sold land that it had purchased for $17,000 to Fern for $25,000. Fern continues to hold the land at December 31, 20X3.

### Required

a. Record the journal entries for 20X3 on Fern's books related to its investment in Vincent's stock and bonds.

b. Record the entries for 20X3 on Vincent's books related to its bond issue.

c. Prepare elimination entries needed to complete a consolidation workpaper for 20X3.

d. Prepare a three-part consolidation workpaper for 20X3.

**P8-17  Information Provided in Eliminating Entry**

Gross Corporation issued $500,000 par value 10-year bonds at 104 on January 1, 20X1, which Independent Corporation purchased. On July 1, 20X5, Rupp Corporation purchased $200,000 of Gross bonds from Independent. The bonds pay 9 percent interest annually on December 31. The preparation of consolidated financial statements for Gross and Rupp at December 31, 20X7, required the following eliminating entry:

| | | |
|---|---:|---:|
| Bonds Payable | 200,000 | |
| Premium on Bonds Payable | 2,400 | |
| Interest Income | 18,600 | |
| Investment in Gross Corporation Bonds | | 198,200 |
| Interest Expense | | 17,200 |
| Retained Earnings, January 1 | | 4,200 |
| Noncontrolling Interest | | 1,400 |

### Required

With the information given, answer each of the following questions. Show how you derived your answer.

a. Is Gross or Rupp the parent company? How do you know?

b. What percentage of the subsidiary's ownership does the parent hold?

c. What amount did Rupp pay when it purchased the bonds on July 1, 20X5?

d. Was a gain or a loss on bond retirement included in the 20X5 consolidated income statement? What amount was reported?

e. If 20X7 consolidated net income of $70,000 would have been reported without the preceding eliminating entry, what amount will actually be reported?

f. Will income to the noncontrolling interest reported in 20X7 increase or decrease as a result of the preceding eliminating entry? By what amount?

g. Prepare the eliminating entry needed to remove the effects of the intercorporate bond ownership in completing a three-part consolidation workpaper at December 31, 20X8.

**P8-18** ### Prior Retirement of Bonds

Amazing Corporation purchased $100,000 par value bonds of its subsidiary, Broadway Company, on December 31, 20X5, from Lemon Corporation. The 10-year bonds bear a 9 percent coupon rate and were originally sold by Broadway on January 1, 20X3, to Lemon. Interest is paid annually on December 31. Amazing owns 85 percent of the stock of Broadway.

In preparing the consolidation workpaper at December 31, 20X6, Amazing's controller made the following entry to eliminate the effects of the intercorporate bond ownership:

| | | |
|---|---:|---:|
| Bonds Payable | 100,000 | |
| Interest Income | 8,600 | |
| Retained Earnings, January 1 | 5,355 | |
| Noncontrolling Interest | 945 | |
| Investment in Broadway Company Bonds | | 102,400 |
| Discount on Bonds Payable | | 3,000 |
| Interest Expense | | 9,500 |

### Required

With the information given, answer the following questions:

a. What amount did Amazing pay when it purchased Broadway's bonds?

b. Prepare the journal entry made by Broadway in 20X6 to record its interest expense for the year.

c. Prepare the journal entry made by Amazing in 20X6 to record its interest income on the Broadway bonds that it holds.

d. Prepare the eliminating entry to remove the effects of the intercorporate bond ownership in completing a three-part consolidation workpaper at December 31, 20X5.

e. Broadway reported net income of $60,000 and $80,000 for 20X5 and 20X6, respectively. Amazing reported income from its separate operations of $120,000 and $150,000 for 20X5 and 20X6, respectively. What amount of consolidated net income and income to the controlling interest will be reported in the consolidated income statements for 20X5 and 20X6?

**P8-19** ### Incomplete Data

Ballard Corporation purchased 70 percent of Condor Company's voting shares on January 1, 20X4, at underlying book value. On that date it also purchased $100,000 par value 12 percent Condor bonds, which had been issued on January 1, 20X1, with a 10-year maturity.

During preparation of the consolidated financial statements for December 31, 20X4, the following eliminating entry was made in the workpaper:

| | | |
|---|---:|---:|
| Bonds Payable | 100,000 | |
| Bond Premium | 6,000 | |
| Loss on Bond Retirement | 3,500 | |
| Interest Income | ? | |
|      Investment in Condor Company Bonds | | 109,000 |
|      Interest Expense | | ? |

### Required

a. What price did Ballard pay to purchase the Condor bonds?

b. What was the carrying amount of the bonds on Condor's books on the date of purchase?

c. If Condor reports net income of $30,000 in 20X5, what amount of income should be assigned to the noncontrolling interest in the 20X5 consolidated income statement?

**P8-20**   **Balance Sheet Eliminations**

Bath Corporation acquired 80 percent of Stang Brewing Company's stock on January 1, 20X1, at underlying book value. At that date, the fair value of the noncontrolling interest was equal to 20 percent of the book value of Stang Brewing. On January 1, 20X1, Stang Brewing issued $300,000 par value 8 percent 10-year bonds to Sidney Malt Company. Bath subsequently purchased $100,000 of the bonds from Sidney Malt for $102,000 on January 1, 20X3. Interest is paid semiannually on January 1 and July 1.

Summarized balance sheets for Bath and Stang as of December 31, 20X4, follow:

**BATH CORPORATION**
**Balance Sheet**
**December 31, 20X4**

| | | | |
|---|---:|---|---:|
| Cash and Receivables | $122,500 | Accounts Payable | $ 40,000 |
| Inventory | 200,000 | Bonds Payable | 400,000 |
| Buildings and Equipment (net) | 320,000 | Common Stock | 200,000 |
| Investment in Stang Brewing: | | Retained Earnings | 320,000 |
|   Bonds | 101,500 | | |
|   Stock | 216,000 | | |
| Total Assets | $960,000 | Total Liabilities and Owners' Equity | $960,000 |

**STANG BREWING COMPANY**
**Balance Sheet**
**December 31, 20X4**

| | | | |
|---|---:|---|---:|
| Cash and Receivables | $124,000 | Accounts Payable | $ 28,000 |
| Inventory | 150,000 | Bonds Payable | 300,000 |
| Buildings and Equipment (net) | 360,000 | Bond Premium | 36,000 |
| | | Common Stock | 100,000 |
| | | Retained Earnings | 170,000 |
| Total Assets | $634,000 | Total Liabilities and Owners' Equity | $634,000 |

At December 31, 20X4, Stang holds $42,000 of inventory purchased from Bath, and Bath holds $26,000 of inventory purchased from Stang. Stang and Bath sell at cost plus markups of 30 percent and 40 percent, respectively.

### Required

a. Prepare all elimination entries needed on December 31, 20X4, to complete a consolidated balance sheet workpaper.

    *b.* Prepare a consolidated balance sheet workpaper.

    *c.* Prepare a consolidated balance sheet in good form.

**P8-21** **Computations Relating to Bond Purchase from Nonaffiliate**

Bliss Perfume Company issued $300,000 of 10 percent bonds on January 1, 20X2, at 110. The bonds mature 10 years from issue and have semiannual interest payments on January 1 and July 1. Parsons Corporation owns 80 percent of Bliss Perfume stock. On April 1, 20X4, Parsons purchased $100,000 par value of Bliss Perfume bonds in the securities markets.

    Partial trial balances for the two companies on December 31, 20X4, are as follows:

|  | Parsons Corporation | Bliss Perfume Company |
|---|---|---|
| Investment in Bliss Perfume Company Bonds | $105,600 | |
| Interest Income | 6,900 | |
| Interest Receivable | 5,000 | |
| Bonds Payable | | $300,000 |
| Bond Premium | | 21,000 |
| Interest Expense | | 27,000 |
| Interest Payable | | 15,000 |

### Required

*a.* What was the purchase price of the Bliss Perfume bonds to Parsons?

*b.* What amount of gain or loss on bond retirement should be reported in the consolidated income statement for 20X4?

*c.* Prepare the necessary workpaper eliminating entries as of December 31, 20X4, to remove the effects of the intercorporate bond ownership.

**P8-22** **Computations following Parent's Acquisition of Subsidiary Bonds**

Mainstream Corporation holds 80 percent of Offenberg Company's voting shares, acquired on January 1, 20X1, at underlying book value. On January 1, 20X4, Mainstream purchased Offenberg bonds with a par value of $40,000. The bonds pay 10 percent interest annually on December 31 and mature on December 31, 20X8. Mainstream uses the basic equity method in accounting for its ownership in Offenberg. Partial balance sheet data for the two companies on December 31, 20X5, are as follows:

|  | Mainstream Corporation | Offenberg Company |
|---|---|---|
| Investment in Offenberg Company Stock | $120,000 | |
| Investment in Offenberg Company Bonds | 42,400 | |
| Interest Income | 3,200 | |
| Bonds Payable | | $100,000 |
| Bond Premium | | 11,250 |
| Interest Expense | | 6,250 |
| Common Stock | 300,000 | 100,000 |
| Retained Earnings, December 31, 20X5 | 500,000 | 50,000 |

### Required

*a.* Compute the gain or loss on bond retirement reported in the 20X4 consolidated income statement.

*b.* Prepare the eliminating entry needed to remove the effects of the intercorporate bond ownership in completing the consolidation workpaper for 20X5.

*c.* What balance should be reported as consolidated retained earnings on December. 31, 20X5?

**P8-23** **Consolidation Workpaper—Year of Retirement**

Tyler Manufacturing purchased 60 percent of the ownership of Brown Corporation stock on January 1, 20X1, at underlying book value. At that date, the fair value of the noncontrolling interest was equal to 40 percent of the book value of Brown Corporation. Tyler also purchased $50,000 of Brown bonds at par value on December 31, 20X3. Brown sold the bonds on January 1, 20X1, at 120; they have a stated interest rate of 12 percent. Interest is paid semiannually on June 30 and December 31.

On December 31, 20X1, Brown sold to Tyler for $30,000 a building with a remaining life of 15 years. Brown had purchased the building 10 years earlier for $40,000. It is being depreciated based on a 25-year expected life.

Trial balances for the two companies on December 31 20X3, are as follows:

| Item | Tyler Manufacturing | | Brown Corporation | |
|---|---|---|---|---|
| | Debit | Credit | Debit | Credit |
| Cash | $ 68,000 | | $ 55,000 | |
| Accounts Receivable | 100,000 | | 75,000 | |
| Inventory | 120,000 | | 110,000 | |
| Investment in Brown Bonds | 50,000 | | | |
| Investment in Brown Stock | 102,000 | | | |
| Depreciable Assets (net) | 360,000 | | 210,000 | |
| Interest Expense | 20,000 | | 20,000 | |
| Operating Expenses | 302,200 | | 150,000 | |
| Dividends Declared | 40,000 | | 10,000 | |
| Accounts Payable | | $ 94,200 | | $ 52,000 |
| Bonds Payable | | 200,000 | | 200,000 |
| Bond Premium | | | | 28,000 |
| Common Stock | | 300,000 | | 100,000 |
| Retained Earnings | | 150,000 | | 50,000 |
| Sales | | 400,000 | | 200,000 |
| Income from Subsidiary | | 18,000 | | |
| Total | $1,162,200 | $1,162,200 | $630,000 | $630,000 |

### Required

*a.* Prepare a consolidation workpaper for 20X3, in good form.

*b.* Prepare a consolidated balance sheet, income statement, and statement of changes in retained earnings for 20X3.

**P8-24 Consolidation Workpaper—Year after Retirement**

Bennett Corporation owns 60 percent of the stock of Stone Container Company, which it acquired at book value in 20X1. At that date, the fair value of the noncontrolling interest was equal to 40 percent of the book value of Stone. On December 31, 20X3, Bennett purchased $100,000 par value bonds of Stone. Stone originally issued the bonds at par value. The bonds' coupon rate is 9 percent. Interest is paid semiannually on June 30 and December 31. Trial balances for the two companies on December 31, 20X4, are as follows:

| Item | Bennett Corporation | | Stone Container Company | |
|---|---|---|---|---|
| | Debit | Credit | Debit | Credit |
| Cash | $ 61,600 | | $ 20,000 | |
| Accounts Receivable | 100,000 | | 80,000 | |
| Inventory | 120,000 | | 110,000 | |
| Other Assets | 340,000 | | 250,000 | |
| Investment in Stone Container Bonds | 106,000 | | | |
| Investment in Stone Container Stock | 126,000 | | | |
| Interest Expense | 20,000 | | 18,000 | |
| Other Expenses | 368,600 | | 182,000 | |
| Dividends Declared | 40,000 | | 10,000 | |

(*continued*)

(*continued*)

| Item | Bennett Corporation Debit | Bennett Corporation Credit | Stone Container Company Debit | Stone Container Company Credit |
|---|---|---|---|---|
| Accounts Payable | | $   80,000 | | $  50,000 |
| Bonds Payable | | 200,000 | | 200,000 |
| Common Stock | | 300,000 | | 100,000 |
| Retained Earnings | | 214,200 | | 70,000 |
| Sales | | 450,000 | | 250,000 |
| Interest Income | | 8,000 | | |
| Income from Subsidiary | | 30,000 | | |
| Total | $1,282,200 | $1,282,200 | $670,000 | $670,000 |

All interest income recognized by Bennett is related to its investment in Stone bonds.

### Required

*a.*  Prepare a consolidation workpaper for 20X4 in good form.

*b.*  Prepare a consolidated balance sheet, income statement, and retained earnings statement for 20X4.

**P8-25**    ### Intercorporate Inventory and Debt Transfers

Lance Corporation purchased 75 percent of Avery Company's common stock at underlying book value on January 1, 20X3. At that date, the fair value of the noncontrolling interest was equal to 25 percent of the book value of Avery. Trial balances for Lance and Avery on December 31, 20X7, are as follows:

| | 20X7 Trial Balance Data | | | |
|---|---|---|---|---|
| Item | Lance Corporation Debit | Lance Corporation Credit | Avery Company Debit | Avery Company Credit |
| Cash | $   37,900 | | $  48,800 | |
| Accounts Receivable | 110,000 | | 105,000 | |
| Other Receivables | 30,000 | | 15,000 | |
| Inventory | 167,000 | | 120,000 | |
| Land | 90,000 | | 40,000 | |
| Buildings and Equipment | 500,000 | | 250,000 | |
| Investment in Avery Company: | | | | |
| Bonds | 78,800 | | | |
| Stock | 183,000 | | | |
| Cost of Goods Sold | 620,000 | | 240,000 | |
| Depreciation Expense | 45,000 | | 15,000 | |
| Interest and Other Expenses | 35,000 | | 22,000 | |
| Dividends Declared | 50,000 | | 24,000 | |
| Accumulated Depreciation | | $  155,000 | | $  75,000 |
| Accounts Payable | | 118,000 | | 35,000 |
| Other Payables | | 40,000 | | 20,000 |
| Bonds Payable | | 250,000 | | 200,000 |
| Bond Premium | | | | 4,800 |
| Common Stock | | 250,000 | | 50,000 |
| Additional Paid-In Capital | | 40,000 | | |
| Retained Earnings | | 291,700 | | 170,000 |
| Sales | | 750,000 | | 320,000 |
| Interest and Other Income | | 16,000 | | 5,000 |
| Income from Subsidiary | | 36,000 | | |
| Total | $1,946,700 | $1,946,700 | $879,800 | $879,800 |

During 20X7, Lance resold inventory purchased from Avery in 20X6. It had cost Avery $44,000 to produce the inventory, and Lance purchased it for $59,000. In 20X7, Lance purchased inventory for $40,000 and sold it to Avery for $60,000. At December 31, 20X7, Avery continued to hold $27,000 of the inventory.

Avery issued $200,000 of 8 percent, 10-year bonds on January 1, 20X4, at 104. Lance purchased $80,000 of the bonds from one of the original owners for $78,400 on December 31, 20X5. Both companies use straight-line write-off of premiums and discounts. Interest is paid annually on December 31.

### Required

a. What amount of cost of goods sold will be reported in the 20X7 consolidated income statement?

b. What inventory balance will be reported in the December 31, 20X7, consolidated balance sheet?

c. Prepare the journal entry to record interest expense for Avery for 20X7.

d. Prepare the journal entry to record interest income for Lance for 20X7.

e. What amount will be assigned to the noncontrolling interest in the consolidated balance sheet prepared at December 31, 20X7?

f. Prepare all eliminating entries needed at December 31, 20X7, to complete a three-part consolidation workpaper.

g. Prepare a consolidation workpaper for 20X7 in good form.

**P8-26** ### Intercorporate Bond Holdings and Other Transfers

On January 1, 20X5, Pond Corporation purchased 75 percent of Skate Company's stock at underlying book value. At that date, the fair value of the noncontrolling interest was equal to 25 percent of the book value of Skate. The balance sheets for Pond and Skate at January 1, 20X8, and December 31, 20X8, and income statements for 20X8 were reported as follows:

| | 20X8 Balance Sheets | | | |
|---|---|---|---|---|
| | **Pond Corporation** | | **Skate Company** | |
| | January 1 | December 31 | January 1 | December 31 |
| Cash | $ 57,600 | $ 53,100 | $ 10,000 | $ 47,000 |
| Accounts Receivable | 130,000 | 176,000 | 60,000 | 65,000 |
| Interest and Other Receivables | 40,000 | 45,000 | 8,000 | 10,000 |
| Inventory | 100,000 | 140,000 | 50,000 | 50,000 |
| Land | 50,000 | 50,000 | 22,000 | 22,000 |
| Buildings and Equipment | 400,000 | 400,000 | 240,000 | 240,000 |
| Accumulated Depreciation | (150,000) | (185,000) | (70,000) | (94,000) |
| Investment in Skate Company: | | | | |
|   Stock | 150,000 | 165,000 | | |
|   Bonds | 42,800 | 42,400 | | |
| Investment in Tin Co. Bonds | 135,000 | 134,000 | | |
| Total Assets | $955,400 | $1,020,500 | $320,000 | $340,000 |
| Accounts Payable | $ 60,000 | $ 65,000 | $ 16,500 | $ 11,000 |
| Interest and Other Payables | 40,000 | 45,000 | 7,000 | 12,000 |
| Bonds Payable | 300,000 | 300,000 | 100,000 | 100,000 |
| Bond Discount | | | (3,500) | (3,000) |
| Common Stock | 150,000 | 150,000 | 30,000 | 30,000 |
| Additional Paid-In Capital | 155,000 | 155,000 | 20,000 | 20,000 |
| Retained Earnings | 250,400 | 305,500 | 150,000 | 170,000 |
| Total Liabilities and Equities | $955,400 | $1,020,500 | $320,000 | $340,000 |

| | 20X8 Income Statements | |
|---|---|---|
| | **Pond Corporation** | **Skate Company** |
| Sales | $450,000 | $250,000 |
| Income from Subsidiary | 22,500 | |
| Interest Income | 18,500 | |
| Total Revenue | $491,000 | $250,000 |
| Cost of Goods Sold | $285,000 | $136,000 |
| Other Operating Expenses | 50,000 | 40,000 |
| Depreciation Expense | 35,000 | 24,000 |
| Interest Expense | 24,000 | 10,500 |
| Miscellaneous Expenses | 11,900    405,900 | 9,500    220,000 |
| Net Income | $ 85,100 | $ 30,000 |

### Additional Information

1. Pond sold a building to Skate for $65,000 on December 31, 20X7. Pond had purchased the building for $125,000 and was depreciating it on a straight-line basis over 25 years. At the time of sale, Pond reported accumulated depreciation of $75,000 and a remaining life of 10 years.

2. On July 1, 20X6, Skate sold land that it had purchased for $22,000 to Pond for $35,000. Pond is planning to build a new warehouse on the property prior to the end of 20X9.

3. Skate issued $100,000 par value 10-year bonds with a coupon rate of 10 percent on January 1, 20X5, at $95,000. On December 31, 20X7, Pond purchased $40,000 par value of Skate's bonds for $42,800. Both companies amortize bond premiums and discounts on a straight-line basis. Interest payments are made on July 1 and January 1.

4. Pond and Skate paid dividends of $30,000 and $10,000, respectively, in 20X8.

### Required

a. Prepare all eliminating entries needed at December 31, 20X8, to complete a three-part consolidation workpaper.

b. Prepare a three-part workpaper for 20X8 in good form.

### P8-27 Comprehensive Multiple-Choice Questions

Panther Enterprises owns 80 percent of Grange Corporation's voting stock. Panther acquired the shares on January 1, 20X4, for $234,500. On that date, the fair value of the noncontrolling interest was $58,625, and Grange reported common stock outstanding of $200,000 and retained earnings of $50,000. The book values and fair values of Grange's assets and liabilities were equal, except for buildings with a fair value $30,000 more than book value at the time of combination. The buildings had an expected 10-year remaining economic life from the date of combination. On December 31, 20X6, Panther's management reviewed the amount attributed to goodwill as a result of the acquisition of Grange and concluded an impairment loss of $7,500 should be recorded in 20X6, with the loss shared proportionately between the controlling and noncontrolling interests.

The following trial balances were prepared by the companies on December 31, 20X6:

| | Panther Enterprises | | Grange Corporation | |
|---|---|---|---|---|
| **Item** | **Debit** | **Credit** | **Debit** | **Credit** |
| Cash | $ 194,220 | | $183,000 | |
| Inventory | 200,000 | | 180,000 | |
| Buildings and Equipment | 500,000 | | 400,000 | |
| Investment in Grange Corporation Bonds | 106,400 | | | |
| Investment in Grange Corporation Stock | 287,300 | | | |
| Cost of Goods Sold | 220,000 | | 140,000 | |
| Depreciation and Amortization | 50,000 | | 30,000 | |
| Interest Expense | 24,000 | | 16,000 | |

*(continued)*

| | | | | |
|---|---|---|---|---|
| Other Expenses | 16,000 | | 14,000 | |
| Dividends Declared | 20,000 | | 15,000 | |
| Accumulated Depreciation | | $ 250,000 | | $180,000 |
| Current Liabilities | | 100,000 | | 50,000 |
| Bonds Payable | | 400,000 | | 200,000 |
| Bond Premium | | | | 8,000 |
| Common Stock | | 300,000 | | 200,000 |
| Retained Earnings | | 202,400 | | 100,000 |
| Sales | | 300,000 | | 240,000 |
| Other Income | | 35,920 | | |
| Income from Subsidiary | | 29,600 | | |
| Total | $1,617,920 | $1,617,920 | $978,000 | $978,000 |

Panther purchases much of its inventory from Grange. The inventory Panther held on January 1, 20X6, contained $2,000 of unrealized intercompany profit. During 20X6, Grange sold goods costing $50,000 to Panther for $70,000. Panther resold the inventory held at the beginning of the year and 70 percent of the inventory it purchased in 20X6 prior to the end of the year. The inventory remaining at the end of 20X6 was sold in 20X7.

On January 1, 20X6, Panther purchased from Kirkwood Corporation $100,000 par value bonds of Grange Corporation. Kirkwood had purchased the 10-year bonds on January 1, 20X1. The coupon rate is 9 percent, and interest is paid annually on December 31.

### Required

Select the correct answer for each of the following questions.

1. What should be the total amount of inventory reported in the consolidated balance sheet as of December 31, 20X6?

    a. $360,000.

    b. $374,000.

    c. $375,200.

    d. $380,000.

2. What amount of cost of goods sold should be reported in the 20X6 consolidated income statement?

    a. $288,000.

    b. $294,000.

    c. $296,000.

    d. $360,000.

3. What amount of interest income did Panther Enterprises record from its investment in Grange Corporation bonds during 20X6?

    a. $7,400.

    b. $7,720.

    c. $9,000.

    d. $10,600.

4. What amount of interest expense should be reported in the 20X6 consolidated income statement?

    a. $24,000.

    b. $32,000.

    c. $33,000.

    d. $40,000.

5. What amount of goodwill would be reported by the consolidated entity at January 1, 20X4?

    a. $10,500.

    b. $13,125.

    c. $34,500.

    d. $43,125.

6. What amount of depreciation and amortization expense should be reported in the 20X6 consolidated income statement?

 a. $77,000.

 b. $80,000.

 c. $82,400.

 d. $83,000.

7. What amount of gain or loss on bond retirement should be included in the 20X6 consolidated income statement?

 a. $2,400.

 b. $3,000.

 c. $4,000.

 d. $6,400.

8. What amount of income should be assigned to the noncontrolling interest in the 20X6 consolidated income statement?

 a. $4,620.

 b. $6,120.

 c. $6,720.

 d. $8,000.

9. What amount should be assigned to the noncontrolling interest in the consolidated balance sheet as of December 31, 20X6?

 a. $60,000.

 b. $63,320.

 c. $65,000.

 d. $68,645.

10. What amount of goodwill, if any, should be reported in the consolidated balance sheet as of December 31, 20X6?

 a. $0.

 b. $5,625.

 c. $10,500.

 d. $13,125.

**P8-28 Comprehensive Problem: Intercorporate Transfers**

Topp Manufacturing Company acquired 90 percent of Bussman Corporation's outstanding common stock on December 31, 20X5, for $1,152,000. At that date, the fair value of the noncontrolling interest was $128,000, and Bussman reported common stock outstanding of $500,000, premium on common stock of $280,000, and retained earnings of $420,000. The book values and fair values of Bussman's assets and liabilities were equal, except for land, which was worth $30,000 more than its book value.

On April 1, 20X6, Topp issued at par $200,000 of 10 percent bonds directly to Bussman; interest on the bonds is payable March 31 and September 30. On January 2, 20X7, Topp purchased all of Bussman's outstanding 10-year 12 percent bonds from an unrelated institutional investor at 98. The bonds originally had been issued on January 2, 20X1, for 101. Interest on the bonds is payable December 31 and June 30.

Since the date it was acquired by Topp Manufacturing, Bussman has sold inventory to Topp on a regular basis. The amount of such intercompany sales totaled $64,000 in 20X6 and $78,000 in 20X7, including a 30 percent gross profit. All inventory transferred in 20X6 had been resold by December 31, 20X6, except inventory for which Topp had paid $15,000 and did not resell until January 20X7. All inventory transferred in 20X7 had been resold at December 31, 20X7, except merchandise for which Topp had paid $18,000.

At December 31, 20X7, trial balances for Topp and Bussman appeared as follows:

| Item | Topp Manufacturing Debit | Topp Manufacturing Credit | Bussman Corporation Debit | Bussman Corporation Credit |
|---|---|---|---|---|
| Cash | $ 39,500 | | $ 29,000 | |
| Current Receivables | 112,500 | | 85,100 | |
| Inventory | 301,000 | | 348,900 | |
| Investment in Bussman Stock | 1,251,000 | | | |
| Investment in Bussman Bonds | 985,000 | | | |
| Investment in Topp Bonds | | | 200,000 | |
| Land | 1,231,000 | | 513,000 | |
| Buildings and Equipment | 2,750,000 | | 1,835,000 | |
| Cost of Goods Sold | 2,009,000 | | 430,000 | |
| Depreciation and Amortization | 195,000 | | 85,000 | |
| Other Expenses | 643,000 | | 206,000 | |
| Dividends Declared | 50,000 | | 40,000 | |
| Accumulated Depreciation | | $1,210,000 | | $ 619,000 |
| Current Payables | | 98,000 | | 79,000 |
| Bonds Payable | | 200,000 | | 1,000,000 |
| Premium on Bonds Payable | | | | 3,000 |
| Common Stock | | 1,000,000 | | 500,000 |
| Premium on Common Stock | | 700,000 | | 280,000 |
| Retained Earnings, January 1 | | 3,033,000 | | 470,000 |
| Sales | | 3,101,000 | | 790,000 |
| Other Income | | 135,000 | | 31,000 |
| Income from Subsidiary | | 90,000 | | |
| Total | $9,567,000 | $9,567,000 | $3,772,000 | $3,772,000 |

As of December 31, 20X7, Bussman had declared but not yet paid its fourth-quarter dividend of $10,000. Both Topp and Bussman use straight-line depreciation and amortization, including the amortization of bond discount and premium. On December 31, 20X7, Topp's management reviewed the amount attributed to goodwill as a result of its purchase of Bussman common stock and concluded that an impairment loss in the amount of $25,000 had occurred during 20X7 and should be shared proportionately between the controlling and noncontrolling interests. Topp uses the basic equity method to account for its investment in Bussman.

### Required

a. Compute the amount of the goodwill as of January 1, 20X7.

b. Compute the balance of Topp's Investment in Bussman Stock account as of January 1, 20X7.

c. Compute the gain or loss on the constructive retirement of Bussman's bonds that should appear in the 20X7 consolidated income statement.

d. Compute the income that should be assigned to the noncontrolling interest in the 20X7 consolidated income statement.

e. Compute the total noncontrolling interest as of December 31, 20X6.

f. Present all elimination entries that would appear in a three-part consolidation workpaper as of December 31, 20X7.

g. Prepare and complete a three-part workpaper for the preparation of consolidated financial statements for 20X7.

**P8-29A   Fully Adjusted Equity Method**

On December 31, 20X4, Bennett Corporation recorded the following entry on its books to adjust its investment in Stone Container Company stock from the basic equity method to the fully adjusted equity method:

"A" indicates that the item relates to "Appendix A."

| | | |
|---|---|---|
| Retained Earnings | 4,200 | |
| Income from Subsidiary | | 600 |
| Investment in Stone Container Company Stock | | 3,600 |

### Required

*a.* Adjust the data reported by Bennett in the trial balance contained in Problem P8-24 for the effects of the preceding adjusting entry.

*b.* Prepare the journal entries that would have been recorded on Bennett's books during 20X4 under the fully adjusted equity method.

*c.* Prepare all eliminating entries needed to complete a consolidation workpaper as of December 31, 20X4, assuming Bennett has used the fully adjusted equity method.

*d.* Complete a three-part consolidation workpaper as of December 31, 20X4.

**P8-30A**   **Cost Method**

The trial balance data presented in Problem P8-24 can be converted to reflect use of the cost method by inserting the following amounts in place of those presented for Bennett Corporation:

| | |
|---|---|
| Investment in Stone Container Stock | $ 75,000 |
| Retained Earnings | 187,200 |
| Income from Subsidiary | -0- |
| Dividend Income | 6,000 |

Stone reported retained earnings of $25,000 on the date Bennett purchased 60 percent of the stock.

### Required

*a.* Prepare the journal entries that would have been recorded on Bennett's books during 20X4 under the cost method.

*b.* Prepare all eliminating entries needed to complete a consolidation workpaper as of December 31, 20X4, assuming Bennett uses the cost method.

*c.* Complete a three-part consolidation workpaper as of December 31, 20X4.

---

**Kaplan CPA Review**

**Kaplan CPA Review Simulation on Basic Consolidation Procedures**

Access to the online CPA Simulation can be attained by visiting the text's Web site: www.mhhe.com/baker8e.

SCHWESER

### Situation

Giant Company acquired all of the outstanding common stock of Tiny Corporation 4 years ago for $240,000 more than book value. This excess was assigned equally to a building (10-year life), inventory (sold within 1 year), and goodwill. On its separate financial statements for the current year, Giant reported sales of $900,000, cost of goods sold of $500,000, and operating expenses of $200,000. No investment income was included in these figures. On its separate financial statements for the current year, Tiny reported sales of $500,000, cost of goods sold of $200,000, and operating expenses of $100,000. Both companies paid dividends of $20,000 this year and reported positive current ratios of above 1-to-1.

### Topics Covered in the Simulation

*a.* Intercompany inventory transfers.

*b.* Intercompany equipment transfers.

*c.* Intercompany land transfers.

*d.* Intercompany loans.

*e.* Equity-method reporting.

*f.* Push-down accounting.

*g.* Reporting noncontrolling interest (minority interest).

*h.* Bargain purchase.

# Consolidation Ownership Issues

Only simple ownership situations have been presented in the preceding illustrations of consolidations. In practice, however, relatively complex ownership structures are often found. For example, a subsidiary may have preferred stock outstanding in addition to its common stock, and in some cases a parent may acquire shares of both a subsidiary's common and preferred stock. Other times, one or more subsidiaries may acquire stock of the parent or of other related companies. Sometimes the parent's ownership claim on a subsidiary may change through its purchase or sale of subsidiary shares or through stock transactions of the subsidiary.

The discussion in this chapter is intended to provide a basic understanding of some of the consolidation problems arising from complex ownership situations commonly encountered in practice. The following topics are discussed:

1. Subsidiary preferred stock outstanding.
2. Changes in the parent's ownership interest in the subsidiary.
3. Multiple ownership levels.
4. Reciprocal or mutual ownership.
5. Subsidiary stock dividends.

## SUBSIDIARY PREFERRED STOCK OUTSTANDING

Many companies have more than one type of stock outstanding. Each type of security typically serves a particular function, and each has a different set of rights and features. Preferred stockholders normally have preference over common shareholders with respect to dividends and the distribution of assets in a liquidation. The right to vote usually is withheld from preferred shareholders, so preferred stock ownership normally does not convey control, regardless of the number of shares owned.

Because a subsidiary's preferred shareholders do have a claim on the net assets of the subsidiary, special attention must be given to that claim in the preparation of consolidated financial statements.

### Consolidation with Subsidiary Preferred Stock Outstanding

During preparation of consolidated financial statements, the amount of subsidiary stock-holders' equity accruing to preferred shareholders must be determined before dealing with the elimination of the intercompany common stock ownership. If the parent holds some of the subsidiary's preferred stock, its portion of the preferred stock interest must be eliminated. Any portion of the subsidiary's preferred stock interest not held by the parent is assigned to the noncontrolling interest.

As an illustration of the preparation of consolidated financial statements with sub-sidiary preferred stock outstanding, recall the following information from the example

of Peerless Products Corporation and Special Foods Incorporated used in previous chapters:

1. Peerless Products purchases 80 percent of Special Foods' common stock on January 1, 20X1, at its book value of $240,000 and accounts for the investment using the basic equity method. At the date of combination, the fair value of Special Foods' common stock held by the noncontrolling shareholders is equal to its book value of $60,000.
2. Peerless Products earns income from its own operations of $140,000 in 20X1 and declares dividends of $60,000.
3. Special Foods reports net income of $50,000 in 20X1 and declares common dividends of $30,000.

Also assume that on January 1, 20X1, immediately after the combination, Special Foods issues $100,000 of 12 percent preferred stock at par value, none of which is purchased by Peerless. The regular $12,000 preferred dividend is paid in 20X1.

### Allocation of Special Foods' Net Income

Of the total $50,000 of net income reported by Special Foods for 20X1, $12,000 ($100,000 × .12) is assigned to the preferred shareholders as their current dividend. Peerless Products records its share of the remaining amount, computed as follows:

| | |
|---|---:|
| Special Foods' net income, 20X1 | $50,000 |
| Less: Preferred dividends ($100,000 × .12) | (12,000) |
| Special Foods' income accruing to common shareholders | $38,000 |
| Peerless's proportionate share | × .80 |
| Peerless's income from Special Foods | $30,400 |

Income assigned to the noncontrolling interest for 20X1 is the total of Special Foods' preferred dividends and the noncontrolling common stockholders' 20 percent share of Special Foods' $38,000 of income remaining after preferred dividends are deducted:

| | |
|---|---:|
| Preferred dividends of Special Foods | $12,000 |
| Income assigned to Special Foods' noncontrolling common shareholders ($38,000 × .20) | 7,600 |
| Income to noncontrolling interest | $19,600 |

While consolidated net income is unaffected by preferred dividends, the amount allocated to the controlling interest is affected because the income allocated to the noncontrolling interest is deducted to arrive at the amount allocated to the controlling interest. In this example, the computation and allocation of consolidated net income is as follows:

| | |
|---|---:|
| Peerless's separate operating income | $140,000 |
| Special Foods' net income | 50,000 |
| Consolidated net income | $190,000 |
| Income to the noncontrolling interest | (19,600) |
| Income attributed to the controlling interest | $170,400 |

### Consolidation Workpaper

The workpaper to prepare consolidated financial statements at the end of 20X1 appears in Figure 9–1. The following elimination entries are included in the workpaper:

**FIGURE 9–1**  **December 31, 20X1, Consolidation Workpaper, First Year following Combination; 80 Percent Purchase at Book Value**

| Item | Peerless Products | Special Foods | Eliminations Debit | Eliminations Credit | Consolidated |
|---|---|---|---|---|---|
| Sales | 400,000 | 200,000 | | | 600,000 |
| Income from Subsidiary | 30,400 | | (1) 30,400 | | |
| Credits | 430,400 | 200,000 | | | 600,000 |
| Cost of Goods Sold | 170,000 | 115,000 | | | 285,000 |
| Depreciation and Amortization | 50,000 | 20,000 | | | 70,000 |
| Other Expenses | 40,000 | 15,000 | | | 55,000 |
| Debits | (260,000) | (150,000) | | | (410,000) |
| Consolidated Net Income | | | | | 190,000 |
| Income to Noncontrolling Interest | | | (2) 19,600 | | (19,600) |
| Income, carry forward | 170,400 | 50,000 | 50,000 | | 170,400 |
| Retained Earnings, January 1 | 300,000 | 100,000 | (3) 100,000 | | 300,000 |
| Income, from above | 170,400 | 50,000 | 50,000 | | 170,400 |
| | 470,400 | 150,000 | | | 470,400 |
| Dividends Declared: Preferred | | (12,000) | | (2) 12,000 | |
| Common | (60,000) | (30,000) | | (1) 24,000 | |
| | | | | (2) 6,000 | (60,000) |
| Retained Earnings, December 31, carry forward | 410,400 | 108,000 | 150,000 | 42,000 | 410,400 |
| Cash | 264,000 | 163,000 | | | 427,000 |
| Accounts Receivable | 75,000 | 50,000 | | | 125,000 |
| Inventory | 100,000 | 75,000 | | | 175,000 |
| Land | 175,000 | 40,000 | | | 215,000 |
| Buildings and Equipment | 800,000 | 600,000 | | | 1,400,000 |
| Investment in Special Foods Common | 246,400 | | | (1) 6,400 | |
| | | | | (3) 240,000 | |
| Debits | 1,660,400 | 928,000 | | | 2,342,000 |
| Accumulated Depreciation | 250,000 | 220,000 | | | 470,000 |
| Accounts Payable | 100,000 | 100,000 | | | 200,000 |
| Bonds Payable | 400,000 | 200,000 | | | 600,000 |
| Preferred Stock | | 100,000 | (4) 100,000 | | |
| Common Stock | 500,000 | 200,000 | (3) 200,000 | | 500,000 |
| Retained Earnings, from above | 410,400 | 108,000 | 150,000 | 42,000 | 410,400 |
| Noncontrolling Interest | | | | (2) 1,600 | |
| | | | | (3) 60,000 | |
| | | | | (4) 100,000 | 161,600 |
| Credits | 1,660,400 | 928,000 | 450,000 | 450,000 | 2,342,000 |

Elimination entries:
   (1) Eliminate income from subsidiary.
   (2) Assign income to noncontrolling interest.
   (3) Eliminate beginning investment in common stock.
   (4) Eliminate subsidiary preferred stock.

| E(1) | Income from Subsidiary | 30,400 | |
|---|---|---|---|
| | Dividends Declared—Common | | 24,000 |
| | Investment in Special Foods Common | | 6,400 |
| | Eliminate income from subsidiary. | | |

| E(2) | Income to Noncontrolling Interest | 19,600 | |
| | Dividends Declared—Preferred | | 12,000 |
| | Dividends Declared—Common | | 6,000 |
| | Noncontrolling Interest | | 1,600 |
| | Assign income to noncontrolling interest. | | |
| | | | |
| E(3) | Common Stock—Special Foods | 200,000 | |
| | Retained Earnings, January 1 | 100,000 | |
| | Investment in Special Foods Common | | 240,000 |
| | Noncontrolling Interest | | 60,000 |
| | Eliminate beginning investment in common stock. | | |
| | | | |
| E(4) | Preferred Stock—Special Foods | 100,000 | |
| | Noncontrolling Interest | | 100,000 |
| | Eliminate subsidiary preferred stock. | | |

In consolidation, the $12,000 preferred dividend is treated as income assigned to the noncontrolling interest. Because Peerless holds none of Special Foods' preferred stock, all of it is classified as part of the noncontrolling interest.

## Subsidiary Preferred Stock Held by Parent

Occasionally a parent company holds preferred stock of a subsidiary in addition to its investment in the subsidiary's common stock. Because the preferred stock held by the parent is within the consolidated entity, it must be eliminated when consolidated financial statements are prepared. Likewise, any income from the preferred stock recorded by the parent also must be eliminated.

As an illustration of the treatment of subsidiary preferred stock held by the parent, assume that Peerless Products purchases 60 percent of Special Foods' $100,000 par value, 12 percent preferred stock for $60,000 when issued on January 1, 20X1. During 20X1 dividends of $12,000 are declared on the preferred stock. Peerless recognizes $7,200 ($12,000 × .60) of dividend income from its investment in Special Foods' preferred stock, and the remaining $4,800 ($12,000 × .40) is paid to the holders of the other preferred shares.

In consolidation, the total income assigned to the noncontrolling interest includes the portion of the preferred dividend paid on the shares not held by Peerless:

| | |
|---|---|
| Noncontrolling interest's share of preferred dividends ($12,000 × .40) | $ 4,800 |
| Income assigned to Special Foods' noncontrolling common shareholders ($38,000 × .20) | 7,600 |
| Income to noncontrolling interest | $12,400 |

The eliminating entries needed in the consolidation workpaper prepared at the end of 20X1 are as follows:

| E(5) | Income from Subsidiary | 30,400 | |
| | Dividends Declared—Common | | 24,000 |
| | Investment in Special Foods Common | | 6,400 |
| | Eliminate income from subsidiary: | | |
| | $30,400 = ($50,000 − $12,000) × .80 | | |
| | | | |
| E(6) | Dividend Income—Preferred | 7,200 | |
| | Dividends Declared—Preferred | | 7,200 |
| | Eliminate dividend income from subsidiary preferred: $12,000 × .60 | | |

| E(7) | Income to Noncontrolling Interest | 12,400 | |
|---|---|---|---|
| | Dividends Declared—Preferred | | 4,800 |
| | Dividends Declared—Common | | 6,000 |
| | Noncontrolling Interest | | 1,600 |
| | Assign income to noncontrolling interest: | | |
| | $12,400 = $4,800 + $7,600 | | |
| | $4,800 = $12,000 × .40 | | |
| | | | |
| E(8) | Common Stock—Special Foods | 200,000 | |
| | Retained Earnings, January 1 | 100,000 | |
| | Investment in Special Foods Common | | 240,000 |
| | Noncontrolling Interest | | 60,000 |
| | Eliminate beginning investment in common stock. | | |
| | | | |
| E(9) | Preferred Stock—Special Foods | 100,000 | |
| | Investment in Special Foods Preferred | | 60,000 |
| | Noncontrolling Interest | | 40,000 |
| | Eliminate subsidiary preferred stock. | | |

Several points should be noted regarding these elimination entries:

1. Peerless's 60 percent share of Special Foods' preferred stock is eliminated against the preferred stock investment account. The remaining preferred stock is included in the noncontrolling interest.

2. Peerless's dividend income from its investment in Special Foods' preferred stock is eliminated against its share of Special Foods' preferred dividends declared.

3. The income assigned to the noncontrolling interest includes income of Special Foods accruing to both preferred and common shareholders other than Peerless Products. Similarly, the total noncontrolling interest includes Special Foods' stockholders' equity amounts accruing to both preferred and common stockholders other than Peerless.

## Subsidiary Preferred Stock with Special Provisions

Many different features of preferred stocks are found in practice. For example, most preferred stocks are cumulative, a few are participating, and many are callable at some price other than par value. When a subsidiary with preferred stock outstanding is consolidated, the provisions of the preferred stock agreement must be examined to determine the portion of the subsidiary's stockholders' equity to be assigned to the preferred stock interest.

A cumulative dividend provision provides some degree of protection for preferred shareholders by requiring the company to pay both current and omitted past preferred dividends before any dividend can be given to common shareholders. If a subsidiary has cumulative preferred stock outstanding, an amount of income equal to the current year's preferred dividend is assigned to the preferred stock interest in consolidation whether or not the preferred dividend is declared. When dividends are in arrears on a subsidiary's cumulative preferred stock, recognition is given in consolidation to the claim of the preferred shareholders by assigning to the preferred stock interest an amount of subsidiary retained earnings equal to the passed dividends. On the other hand, when a subsidiary's preferred stock is noncumulative, the subsidiary has no obligation to pay undeclared dividends. Consequently, no special consolidation procedures are needed with respect to undeclared dividends on noncumulative subsidiary preferred stock.

Preferred stock participation features allow the preferred stockholders to receive a share of income distribution that exceeds the preferred stock base dividend rate. Although few preferred stocks are participating, many different types of participation arrangements are possible. Once the degree of participation has been determined, the appropriate share of subsidiary income and net assets is assigned to the preferred stock interest in the consolidated financial statements.

Many preferred stocks are callable, often at prices that exceed the par value. The amount to be paid to retire a subsidiary's callable preferred stock under the preferred stock agreement is viewed as the preferred stockholders' claim on the subsidiary's assets, and that amount of subsidiary stockholders' equity is assigned to the preferred stock interest in preparing the consolidated balance sheet.

### Illustration of Subsidiary Preferred Stock with Special Features

To examine the consolidation treatment of subsidiary preferred stock with the most common special features, assume that Special Foods issues $100,000 par value 12 percent preferred stock on January 1, 20X0, and that the stock is cumulative, nonparticipating, and callable at 105. No dividends are declared on the preferred stock during 20X0. On January 1, 20X1, Peerless Products purchases 80 percent of Special Foods' common stock for $240,000, when the fair value of the noncontrolling interest in Special Foods' common stock is $60,000. Also on January 1, 20X1, Peerless purchases 60 percent of the preferred stock for $61,000. The following are the stockholders' equity accounts of Special Foods on January 1, 20X1:

| | |
|---|---|
| Preferred Stock | $100,000 |
| Common Stock | 200,000 |
| Retained Earnings | 100,000 |
| Total Stockholders' Equity | $400,000 |

The amount assigned to the preferred stock interest in the preparation of a consolidated balance sheet on January 1, 20X1, is computed as follows:

| | |
|---|---|
| Par value of Special Foods' preferred stock | $100,000 |
| Call premium | 5,000 |
| Dividends in arrears for 20X0 | 12,000 |
| Total preferred stock interest, January 1, 20X1 | $117,000 |

This amount is apportioned between Peerless and the noncontrolling shareholders:

| | |
|---|---|
| Peerless's share of preferred stock interest ($117,000 × .60) | $ 70,200 |
| Noncontrolling stockholders' share of preferred stock interest ($117,000 × .40) | 46,800 |
| Total preferred stock interest, January 1, 20X1 | $117,000 |

Because the preferred stock interest exceeds the par value of the preferred stock by $17,000, the portion of Special Foods' retained earnings accruing to the common shareholders is reduced by that amount. Therefore, Special Foods' common stockholders have a total claim on the company's net assets as follows:

| | |
|---|---|
| Common stock | $200,000 |
| Retained earnings ($100,000 − $17,000) | 83,000 |
| Total common stock interest, January 1, 20X1 | $283,000 |

Because the book value of Special Foods' common stock is only $283,000 on January 1, 20X1, a differential arises on Peerless's acquisition of Special Foods' common stock:

| | |
|---|---|
| Consideration given by Peerless Products | $240,000 |
| Fair value of noncontrolling interest in Special Foods' common stock | 60,000 |
| | $300,000 |
| Book value of Special Foods' common stock | (283,000) |
| Differential | $ 17,000 |

Eliminating entries needed in the consolidation workpaper to prepare a consolidated balance sheet as of January 1, 20X1, are as follows:

| | | | |
|---|---|---|---|
| E(10) | Common Stock—Special Foods | 200,000 | |
| | Retained Earnings | 83,000 | |
| | Differential | 17,000 | |
| |     Investment in Special Foods Common | | 240,000 |
| |     Noncontrolling Interest | | 60,000 |
| | Eliminate investment in common stock: | | |
| | $83,000 = $100,000 − $17,000 | | |
| | $17,000 = $300,000 − $283,000 | | |
| | | | |
| E(11) | Preferred Stock—Special Foods | 100,000 | |
| | Retained Earnings | 17,000 | |
| |     Investment in Special Foods Preferred | | 61,000 |
| |     Additional Paid-In Capital | | 9,200 |
| |     Noncontrolling Interest | | 46,800 |
| | Eliminate subsidiary preferred stock: | | |
| | $17,000 = $117,000 − $100,000 | | |
| | $9,200 = ($117,000 × .60) − $61,000 | | |
| | $46,800 = $117,000 × .40 | | |

The following points should be noted with respect to eliminating entries E(10) and E(11):

1. Only the $83,000 portion of Special Foods' retained earnings relating to the common stock interest is eliminated in entry E(10). The remaining $17,000 of retained earnings related to the preferred stock interest is eliminated in entry E(11).

2. Because at the date of combination the sum of the fair values of the consideration exchanged ($240,000) and the noncontrolling interest in Special Foods' common stock ($60,000) exceeds the book value of the common shares ($283,000), a differential arises. This $17,000 differential is assigned to the appropriate assets and liabilities in the workpaper.

3. The total noncontrolling interest on January 1, 20X1, consists of both preferred and common stock interests, as follows:

| | |
|---|---|
| Preferred stock interest ($117,000 × .40) | $ 46,800 |
| Common stock interest | 60,000 |
| Total noncontrolling interest, January 1, 20X1 | $106,800 |

4. The difference between the cost of Peerless's investment in Special Foods' preferred stock and the underlying claim on Special Foods' net assets is computed as follows:

| | |
|---|---|
| Claim on Special Foods' net assets ($117,000 × .60) | $70,200 |
| Cost of preferred stock investment | (61,000) |
| Difference | $ 9,200 |

From a consolidated viewpoint, Peerless's purchase of the preferred stock is considered a retirement of a noncontrolling ownership interest by the consolidated entity. Because this retirement occurred at less than book value and gains and losses are not recognized on capital transactions, this excess is considered to be additional paid-in capital of the consolidated entity and is credited to that account in entry E(11).

# CHANGES IN PARENT COMPANY OWNERSHIP

Although preceding chapters have treated the parent company's subsidiary ownership interest as remaining constant over time, in actuality ownership levels sometimes vary. Changes in ownership levels may result from either the parent's or the subsidiary's actions. The parent company can change ownership ratios by purchasing or selling shares of the subsidiary in transactions with unaffiliated companies. A subsidiary can change the parent's ownership percentage by selling additional shares to or repurchasing shares from unaffiliated parties or through stock transactions with the parent (if the subsidiary is less than wholly owned).

### Parent's Purchase of Additional Shares from Nonaffiliate

A parent company may purchase the common stock of a subsidiary at different points in time. Until control is achieved, the intercorporate investment is accounted for as discussed in Chapter 2. Once control is achieved, the entire investment is valued based on fair values at the date control is achieved, and subsequently consolidated financial statements must be presented.

Purchases of additional shares of an investee's stock were discussed in Chapters 1 and 2. Additional effects of multiple purchases of a subsidiary's stock on the consolidation process are illustrated in the following example.

Assume that on January 1, 20X0, Special Foods has $200,000 of common stock outstanding and retained earnings of $60,000. During 20X0, 20X1, and 20X2, Special Foods reports the following information:

| Period | Net Income | Dividends | Ending Book Value |
|--------|-----------|-----------|-------------------|
| 20X0 | $40,000 | -0- | $300,000 |
| 20X1 | 50,000 | $30,000 | 320,000 |
| 20X2 | 75,000 | 40,000 | 355,000 |

Peerless Products purchases its 80 percent interest in Special Foods in several blocks, as follows:

| Purchase Date | Ownership Percentage Acquired | Cost | Book Value | Differential |
|---------------|-------------------------------|------|------------|--------------|
| January 1, 20X0 | 20 | $ 56,000 | $ 52,000 | $ 4,000 |
| December 31, 20X0 | 10 | 35,000 | 30,000 | 5,000 |
| January 1, 20X2 | 50 | 185,000 | 160,000 | |
| | 80 | | | |

All of the differential relates to land held by Special Foods. Note that Peerless does not gain control of Special Foods until January 1, 20X2.

The investment account on Peerless's books includes the following amounts through 20X1:

| 20X0 | |
|---|---|
| Purchase shares (January 1) | $ 56,000 |
| Equity-method income ($40,000 × .20) | 8,000 |
| Purchase of shares (December 31) | 35,000 |
| Balance in investment account (December 31) | $ 99,000 |
| 20X1 | |
| Equity-method income ($50,000 × .30) | 15,000 |
| Dividends received ($30,000 × .30) | (9,000) |
| Balance in investment account (December 31) | $105,000 |

When Peerless gains control of Special Foods on January 1, 20X2, assume that the fair value of the 30 percent equity interest it already holds in Special Foods is $111,000, and the fair value of Special Foods' 20 percent remaining noncontrolling interest is $74,000. The book value of Special Foods as a whole on that date is $320,000. Under **FASB 141R,** the differential at the date of combination is computed as follows:

| | |
|---|---|
| Fair value of consideration exchanged | $185,000 |
| Fair value of equity interest already held | 111,000 |
| Fair value of noncontrolling interest | 74,000 |
| | $370,000 |
| Book value of Special Foods | (320,000) |
| Differential | $ 50,000 |

Because all of the differential relates to land in this example, it is not amortized or written off either on Peerless's books or for consolidation.

Under the requirements of **FASB 141R,** Peerless must remeasure the equity interest it already held in Special Foods to its fair value at the date of combination and recognize a gain or loss for the difference between the fair value and its carrying amount:

| | |
|---|---|
| Fair value of equity interest already held | $111,000 |
| Carrying amount of investment, December 31, 20X1 | (105,000) |
| Gain on increase in value of investment in Special Foods | $ 6,000 |

Peerless recognizes the $6,000 gain in income and increases the investment balance on its books by that amount. The total balance of the investment account on Peerless's books immediately after the combination is as follows:

| | |
|---|---|
| Carrying amount of investment, December 31, 20X1 | $105,000 |
| Increase in value of investment in Special Foods | 6,000 |
| Cost of January 1, 20X2, shares acquired | 185,000 |
| Peerless's total recorded amount of investment | $296,000 |

Because Peerless Products gains control of Special Foods on January 1, 20X2, consolidated statements are prepared for the year 20X2. The consolidation workpaper prepared at the end of the year includes the following elimination entries:

| E(12) | Income from Subsidiary | 60,000 | |
| | Dividends Declared | | 32,000 |
| | Investment in Special Foods Stock | | 28,000 |
| | Eliminate income from subsidiary. | | |
| | | | |
| E(13) | Income to Noncontrolling Interest | 15,000 | |
| | Dividends Declared | | 8,000 |
| | Noncontrolling Interest | | 7,000 |
| | Assign income to noncontrolling shareholders: | | |
| | $15,000 = $75,000 × .20 | | |
| | $8,000 = $40,000 × .20 | | |
| | $7,000 = $15,000 − $8,000 | | |
| | | | |
| E(14) | Common Stock—Special Foods | 200,000 | |
| | Retained Earnings, January 1 | 120,000 | |
| | Land | 50,000 | |
| | Investment in Special Foods Stock | | 296,000 |
| | Noncontrolling Interest | | 74,000 |
| | Eliminate beginning investment balance: | | |

Entry E(12) eliminates the income from Special Foods recognized by Peerless during 20X2. Entry E(13) assigns income to the noncontrolling shareholders and eliminates their share of Special Foods' dividends based on the 20 percent noncontrolling ownership interest held during 20X2. Entry E(14) eliminates the beginning stockholders' equity balances of Special Foods, establishes the noncontrolling interest as of the beginning of the year, and eliminates Peerless's beginning investment account balance. Because the business combination occurred at the beginning of the period, the amount of the noncontrolling interest at the beginning of the period is its fair value at that date. Entry E(14) also assigns the $50,000 differential at the date of combination to land.

## Parent's Sale of Subsidiary Shares to Nonaffiliate

A gain or loss normally occurs and is recorded on the seller's books when a company disposes of all or part of an investment. **APB 18** deals explicitly with sales of stock of an investee, requiring recognition of a gain or loss on the difference between the selling price and the carrying amount of the stock.[1] What happens, however, when the shares sold are those of a subsidiary and the subsidiary continues to qualify for consolidation? This question has caused difficulty in practice for many years, but the issuance of **FASB 160** has resolved the issue. When a parent sells some shares of a subsidiary but continues to hold a controlling interest, **FASB 160** makes clear that this is considered to be an equity transaction and no gain or loss may be recognized in consolidated net income. Under **FASB 160,** changes in a parent's ownership interest in a subsidiary while the parent retains control require an adjustment to the amount assigned to the noncontrolling interest to reflect its change in ownership of the subsidiary. The difference between the fair value of the consideration received or paid in the equity transaction and the adjustment to the noncontrolling interest results in an adjustment to the stockholders' equity attributable to the controlling interest.

As an illustration of the sale of subsidiary stock to a nonaffiliate, assume that on December 31, 20X0, Special Foods has 20,000 common shares outstanding with a total par value of $200,000 and retained earnings of $100,000. On that date, Peerless acquires an 80 percent interest in Special Foods by purchasing 16,000 shares of its $10 par common stock at book value of $240,000 ($300,000 × .80). The noncontrolling interest in Special Foods has a fair value equal to its book value of $60,000 at that time. Special Foods

[1]*Accounting Principles Board Opinion No. 18,* "The Equity Method of Accounting for Investments in Common Stock," March 1971, para. 19(f).

reports net income of $50,000 for 20X1 and pays dividends of $30,000. On January 1, 20X2, Peerless sells 1,000 shares of its Special Foods common stock to a nonaffiliate for $19,000, leaving it with a 75 percent interest (15,000 ÷ 20,000) in Special Foods. On the date of sale, Special Foods has total stockholders' equity of $320,000, consisting of common stock of $200,000 and retained earnings of $120,000.

### Recognition of Sale on Parent Company Books

The equity-method carrying amount of Peerless's investment in Special Foods on the date Peerless sells 1,000 shares reflects Peerless's share of Special Foods' 20X1 net income and dividends, as follows:

| | |
|---|---:|
| Cost of investment, December 31, 20X0 | $240,000 |
| Peerless's share of Special Foods' 20X1 net income ($50,000 × .80) | 40,000 |
| Peerless's share of Special Foods' 20X1 dividends ($30,000 × .80) | (24,000) |
| Investment balance, January 1, 20X2 | $256,000 |

Because no differential exists, the balance of the investment account equals 80 percent of the total stockholders' equity of Special Foods on January 1, 20X2. Likewise, the noncontrolling interest is $64,000, equal to 20 percent of Special Foods' total stockholders' equity.

In practice, companies might recognize the sale of subsidiary shares in one of two ways. Although **FASB 160** does not permit a gain or loss on the sale of the shares to be reported in consolidated net income, some parent companies might choose to recognize a gain on their separate books. Thus, Peerless might record the sale of the Special Foods stock with the following entry:

January 1, 20X2

| | | | |
|---|---|---:|---:|
| (15) | Cash | 19,000 | |
| |     Investment in Special Foods Stock | | 16,000 |
| |     Gain on Sale of Investment | | 3,000 |
| |   Record sale of investment: | | |
| |     $16,000 = $256,000 × ¹⁄₁₆ | | |

Peerless recognizes a gain of $3,000 on the sale for the difference between the $16,000 carrying amount of the shares ($256,000 × ¹⁄₁₆) and the selling price of $19,000.

On the other hand, the gain cannot be reported in the consolidated financial statements and, therefore, will have to be eliminated in consolidation. Thus, a better alternative on the parent's books may be to avoid recognizing a gain that later will have to be eliminated and instead recognize an increase in additional paid-in capital:

January 1, 20X2

| | | | |
|---|---|---:|---:|
| (15a) | Cash | 19,000 | |
| |     Investment in Special Foods Stock | | 16,000 |
| |     Additional Paid-In Capital | | 3,000 |

### Consolidation Workpaper 20X2

From a consolidated perspective, **FASB 160** requires that the difference between the proceeds received from the sale of subsidiary stock and the adjustment to the noncontrolling interest from the change in its ownership of the subsidiary be recognized in equity attributable to the parent. Upon the sale of the Special Foods stock by Peerless, the noncontrolling interest increases from $64,000 ($320,000 × .20) to $80,000 ($320,000 × .25), an increase of $16,000. The difference between the $19,000 of proceeds received and the $16,000 increase in the noncontrolling interest is $3,000, and this amount is recognized in consolidation as additional paid-in capital attributable to the parent.

If Peerless recorded on its books the sale of Special Foods shares with entry (15a), consolidated net income and additional paid-in capital in consolidated equity are correctly stated without further adjustment. However, if Peerless recorded a gain on its books with entry (15), the gain must be eliminated with the following entry in the consolidation workpaper:

| | | | |
|---|---|---|---|
| E(16) | Gain on Sale of Investment | 3,000 | |
| | Additional Paid-In Capital | | 3,000 |
| | Eliminate gain on transaction involving subsidiary stock. | | |

Entry E(16) reclassifies the gain from the parent's books so the transaction is treated from a consolidated perspective as an equity transaction, in accordance with **FASB 160.**

When consolidated financial statements are prepared at the end of 20X2, the consolidation workpaper for Peerless and Special Foods includes, in addition to entry E(16) if needed, the following eliminating entries:

| | | | |
|---|---|---|---|
| E(17) | Income from Subsidiary | 56,250 | |
| | Dividends Declared | | 30,000 |
| | Investment in Special Foods Stock | | 26,250 |
| | Eliminate income from subsidiary: | | |
| | $56,250 = $75,000 × .75 | | |
| | $30,000 = $40,000 × .75 | | |
| | $26,250 = $56,250 − $30,000 | | |
| E(18) | Income to Noncontrolling Interest | 18,750 | |
| | Dividends Declared | | 10,000 |
| | Noncontrolling Interest | | 8,750 |
| | Assign income to noncontrolling interest: | | |
| | $18,750 = $75,000 × .25 | | |
| | $10,000 = $40,000 × .25 | | |
| | $8,750 = $18,750 − $10,000 | | |
| E(19) | Common Stock—Special Foods | 200,000 | |
| | Retained Earnings, January 1 | 120,000 | |
| | Investment in Special Foods Stock | | 240,000 |
| | Noncontrolling Interest | | 80,000 |
| | Eliminate beginning investment in common stock: | | |
| | $80,000 = $320,000 × .25 | | |

Entry E(17) eliminates Peerless's 75 percent share of Special Foods' income and dividends. Entry E(18) assigns income to the noncontrolling stockholders based on their 25 percent ownership interest.

The balance in Peerless's investment account at December 31, 20X2, is $266,250. This amount is the result of the following entries in the investment account:

| **Investment in Special Foods Stock** | | | | | |
|---|---|---|---|---|---|
| Original cost | 240,000 | | | | |
| 20X1 equity accrual ($50,000 × .80) | 40,000 | | 20X1 dividends ($30,000 × .80) | 24,000 | |
| Balance, 12/31/X1 | 256,000 | | | | |
| | | (15) | Sale of 1,000 shares ($256,000 × ⅟₁₆) | 16,000 | |
| 20X2 equity accrual ($75,000 × .75) | 56,250 | | 20X2 dividends ($40,000 × .75) | 30,000 | |
| Balance, 12/31/X2 | 266,250 | | | | |

The amount of Peerless's investment eliminated in entry E(19) is the balance at the beginning of 20X2 immediately after Peerless sold the 1,000 shares; this amount equals Peerless's 75 percent share of the $320,000 beginning book value of Special Foods. Entries E(17) and E(19) together eliminate the total investment balance reported by Peerless on December 31, 20X2.

The amount assigned to the noncontrolling interest in entry E(19) is 25 percent of Special Foods' beginning book value. The total noncontrolling interest established in entries E(18) and E(19) together is $88,750, equal to 25 percent of Special Foods' $355,000 book value on December 31, 20X2.

### Consolidation Subsequent to 20X2

In preparing consolidated financial statements each year after 20X2, no special eliminating entries are needed with respect to the 20X2 sale of subsidiary shares if Peerless recorded the sale on its books with entry (15a). If, however, Peerless recorded a gain from the sale on its books in 20X2, a workpaper entry similar to E(16) is needed in subsequent workpapers to reestablish the $3,000 increase in additional paid-in capital. Because the gain recognized by Peerless in 20X2 has been closed to Retained Earnings, beginning retained earnings must be reduced to eliminate the effects of the gain. The entry included in the consolidation workpaper each year after 20X2 is as follows:

| E(20) | Retained Earnings, January 1 | 3,000 | |
|---|---|---|---|
| | Additional Paid-In Capital | | 3,000 |
| | Eliminate effects of gain on transaction involving subsidiary stock. | | |

Obviously, recording the sale of subsidiary shares as an equity transaction on the parent's books initially avoids the continued need to eliminate the effects of the gain.

## Subsidiary's Sale of Additional Shares to Nonaffiliate

Additional funds are generated for the consolidated enterprise when a subsidiary sells new shares to parties outside the economic entity. A sale of additional shares to an unaffiliated party increases the total stockholders' equity of the consolidated entity by the amount received by the subsidiary from the sale. Such a sale increases the subsidiary's total shares outstanding and, consequently, reduces the percentage ownership held by the parent company. At the same time, the dollar amount assigned to the noncontrolling interest in the consolidated financial statements increases. The resulting amounts of the controlling and noncontrolling interests are affected by two factors:

1. The number of shares sold to nonaffiliates.
2. The price at which the shares are sold to nonaffiliates.

### Difference between Book Value and Sale Price of Subsidiary Shares

If the sale price of new shares equals the book value of outstanding shares, there is no change in the existing shareholders' claim. If the subsidiary's stockholders' equity is viewed as a pie, the overall size of the pie increases. The parent's share of the pie decreases, but the size of the parent's slice remains the same because of the increase in the overall size of the pie. The eliminating entries used in consolidation simply are changed to recognize the increase in the claim of the noncontrolling shareholders and the corresponding increase in the stockholders' equity balances of the subsidiary.

Most sales, however, do not occur at book value. When the sale price and book value are not the same, all common shareholders are assigned a pro rata portion of the difference. In this situation, the book value of the subsidiary's shares held by the parent changes even though the number remains constant. The size of both the pie and the parent's share of it change; the size of the parent's slice changes because the increase in the pie's size and the decrease in the parent's share do not exactly offset one another.

The issuance of additional shares by a subsidiary to unaffiliated parties is viewed as an equity transaction from a consolidated perspective. Even though the parent is not directly involved in the transaction, the book value of its subsidiary shares changes as a result of the additional shares being issued. This change in the book value of the controlling interest in the subsidiary is recognized by the parent by adjusting the carrying amount of its investment in the subsidiary and additional paid-in capital. The parent's additional paid-in capital is then carried to the workpaper in consolidation.

From a consolidated viewpoint, a subsidiary's sale of additional shares to unaffiliated parties and a parent's sale of subsidiary shares are similar transactions: in both cases the consolidated entity sells shares to the noncontrolling interest. Because the participants in a consolidation are regarded as members of a single economic entity, the sale of subsidiary shares to the noncontrolling interest should be treated in the same way regardless of whether the parent or the subsidiary sells the shares. The recognition of a gain or loss on such a transaction is inappropriate because the sale of stock to unaffiliated parties by the consolidated entity is a capital transaction from a single-entity viewpoint.

### Illustration of Subsidiary's Sale of Stock to Nonaffiliate

To examine the sale of additional shares by a subsidiary to a nonaffiliate, assume that Peerless Products acquires an 80 percent interest in Special Foods by purchasing 16,000 shares of Special Foods' $10 par common stock on December 31, 20X0, at book value of $240,000. Special Foods has only common stock outstanding. All other information is the same as that used previously. On January 1, 20X2, Special Foods issues 5,000 additional shares of stock to nonaffiliates for $20 per share, a total of $100,000. After the sale, Special Foods has 25,000 shares outstanding, and Peerless has a 64 percent interest (16,000 ÷ 25,000) in Special Foods.

The January 1, 20X2, issuance of additional shares results in the following change in Special Foods' balance sheet:

|  | Before Sale | Following Sale |
|---|---|---|
| Common Stock, $10 par value | $200,000 | $250,000 |
| Additional Paid-In Capital |  | 50,000 |
| Retained Earnings | 120,000 | 120,000 |
| Total Stockholders' Equity | $320,000 | $420,000 |

The book value of Peerless's investment in Special Foods changes as a result of the sale of additional shares as follows:

|  | Before Sale | Following Sale |
|---|---|---|
| Special Foods' total stockholders' equity | $320,000 | $420,000 |
| Peerless's proportionate share | × .80 | × .64 |
| Book value of Peerless's investment in Special Foods | $256,000 | $268,800 |

Note that, while Peerless's ownership percentage decreases from 80 percent to 64 percent, the book value of Peerless's investment increases by $12,800. The increase in book value occurs because the $20 issue price of the additional shares exceeds the $16 ($320,000 ÷ 20,000 shares) book value of the outstanding shares before the sale:

| | |
|---|---|
| Issue price of additional shares | $ 20 |
| Book value of shares before sale ($320,000 ÷ 20,000 shares) | (16) |
| Excess of issue price over book value | $ 4 |
| Number of shares issued | × 5,000 |
| Excess book value added | $20,000 |
| Peerless's proportionate share | × .64 |
| Increase in Peerless's interest | $12,800 |

The increase in Peerless's equity in the net assets of Special Foods is recorded on Peerless's books with the following entry:

| (21) | Investment in Special Foods Stock | 12,800 | |
| | Additional Paid-In Capital | | 12,800 |
| | Record increase in equity in subsidiary resulting from subsidiary issue of shares. | | |

The investment elimination entry needed to prepare a consolidated balance sheet on January 1, 20X2, immediately after the sale of the additional shares, is as follows:

| E(22) | Common Stock—Special Foods | 250,000 | |
| | Additional Paid-In Capital—Special Foods | 50,000 | |
| | Retained Earnings, January 1 | 120,000 | |
| | Investment in Special Foods Stock | | 268,800 |
| | Noncontrolling Interest | | 151,200 |
| | Eliminate investment in common stock: | | |
| | $268,800 = $420,000 \times .64$ | | |
| | $151,200 = $420,000 \times .36$ | | |

Additional paid-in capital recorded by Special Foods from the sale of the additional shares is eliminated in the preparation of consolidated financial statements, as are all of the subsidiary's stockholders' equity accounts. The noncontrolling interest's share of the increase in the book value of Special Foods' stock resulting from the sale of additional shares is reflected in the balance of the noncontrolling interest in the consolidated balance sheet. The $151,200 balance of the noncontrolling interest is 36 percent of the $420,000 total book value of Special Foods after the sale of the additional shares. Peerless's $12,800 share of the increase in Special Foods' book value is included in the consolidated balance sheet by carrying over the additional paid-in capital recorded by Peerless in entry (21).

### *Subsidiary's Sale of Stock at Less than Book Value*

A sale of stock by a subsidiary to a nonaffiliate at less than existing book value has an effect opposite to that just illustrated. The parent company's claim is diminished as a result of selling additional shares at less than existing book value. A reduction in the book value of the shares held by the parent normally is treated as a debit to Additional Paid-In Capital and a credit to the investment account. In the absence of the Additional Paid-In Capital account, retained earnings is reduced.

## Subsidiary's Sale of Additional Shares to Parent

A sale of additional shares directly from a less-than-wholly owned subsidiary to its parent increases the parent's ownership percentage. If the sale is at a price equal to the book value of the existing shares, the increase in the parent's investment account equals the increase in the stockholders' equity of the subsidiary. The net book value assigned to the noncontrolling interest remains unchanged. In preparing consolidated financial statements, the normal elimination entries are made based on the parent's new ownership percentage.

When a parent purchases a subsidiary's shares directly from the subsidiary at an amount other than book value, it increases the carrying amount of its investment by the fair value of the consideration given. In consolidation, the amount of the noncontrolling interest must be adjusted to reflect the change in its interest in the subsidiary occasioned by the parent's purchase of additional subsidiary shares. **FASB 160** then requires an adjustment to consolidated additional paid-in capital for the difference between any consideration given or received by the consolidated entity and the amount of the adjustment to the noncontrolling interest. In the case of a parent purchasing additional shares from a less-than-wholly owned subsidiary, no consideration is given or received from a

consolidated perspective, so the amount of the adjustment to equity is equal to the change in the noncontrolling interest and total consolidated stockholders' equity is unchanged.

As an illustration of the sale of additional shares from a subsidiary to its parent, assume that in the example of Peerless Products and Special Foods, Peerless purchases in the market 16,000 shares of Special Foods $10 par common stock at book value of $240,000 on December 31, 20X0, giving Peerless an 80 percent interest. By December 31, 20X1, the equity-method carrying amount of the investment on Peerless's books is $256,000. On January 1, 20X2, Peerless purchases an additional 5,000 shares of common directly from Special Foods for $20 per share. This additional $100,000 investment gives Peerless a total ownership interest in Special Foods of 84 percent (21,000 ÷ 25,000).

The subsidiary's sale of additional shares to the parent results in the following change in Special Foods' balance sheet:

|  | Before Sale | Following Sale |
|---|---|---|
| Common Stock, $10 par value | $200,000 | $250,000 |
| Additional Paid-In Capital |  | 50,000 |
| Retained Earnings | 120,000 | 120,000 |
| Total Stockholders' Equity | $320,000 | $420,000 |

The book value of Peerless's investment in Special Foods changes as a result of the sale of additional shares, as follows:

|  | Before Sale | Following Sale |
|---|---|---|
| Special Foods' total stockholders' equity | $320,000 | $420,000 |
| Peerless's proportionate share | × .80 | × .84 |
| Book value of Peerless's investment in Special Foods | $256,000 | $352,800 |

If Special Foods' stockholders' equity is viewed as a pie, the size of both the pie and Peerless's percentage share of it increases. The size of Peerless's slice of the pie increases by $96,800 ($352,800 − $256,000).

The new book value per share of Special Foods' stock is $16.80 ($420,000 ÷ 25,000 shares) as compared with the $16.00 ($320,000 ÷ 20,000 shares) book value before the sale of additional shares. The book value is higher because the price Peerless paid for the additional shares is more than the stock's previous book value. The excess of the amount paid by Peerless for Special Foods' stock ($100,000) over the increase in the book value of the shares held by Peerless ($96,800) is $3,200.

The book value of the shares held by the noncontrolling interest, which is only 16 percent following Peerless's purchase, also increases, as follows:

| | |
|---|---|
| Noncontrolling interest after sale of additional shares to Peerless ($420,000 × .16) | $67,200 |
| Noncontrolling interest before sale of additional shares to Peerless ($320,000 × .20) | (64,000) |
| Increase in book value of noncontrolling interest | $ 3,200 |

From a consolidated perspective, **FASB 160** requires an adjustment to equity attributable to the parent (consolidated additional paid-in capital) for the amount of the difference between the consideration paid or received by the consolidated entity and the change in the noncontrolling interest. Because no consideration was paid or received by the consolidated entity overall, the required decrease in equity attributable to the parent is equal to the amount of change in the noncontrolling interest, $3,200.

The investment elimination entry needed to prepare a consolidated balance sheet immediately following the sale of additional shares to Peerless on January 1, 20X2, is as follows:

| E(23) | Common Stock—Special Foods | 250,000 | |
|---|---|---|---|
| | Additional Paid-In Capital | 53,200 | |
| | Retained Earnings, January 1 | 120,000 | |
| | Investment in Special Foods Stock | | 356,000 |
| | Noncontrolling Interest | | 67,200 |
| | Eliminate investment in common stock: | | |
| | $53,200 = $50,000 + $3,200 | | |
| | $356,000 = $256,000 + $100,000 | | |
| | $67,200 = $420,000 × .16 | | |

The balance eliminated from Peerless's investment account equals the previous balance of $256,000 plus the $100,000 cost of the additional shares. The amount of the noncontrolling interest is established at 16 percent of the $420,000 book value of Special Foods. The debit to Additional Paid-In Capital is equal to the $50,000 of additional paid-in capital on Special Foods' books from the sale of additional shares to Peerless plus the $3,200 adjustment to equity resulting from the sale.

## Subsidiary's Purchase of Shares from Nonaffiliate

Sometimes a subsidiary purchases treasury shares from noncontrolling shareholders. Noncontrolling shareholders frequently find they have little opportunity for input into the subsidiary's activities and operations and often are willing sellers. The parent company may prefer not to be concerned with outside shareholders and may direct the subsidiary to reacquire any noncontrolling shares that become available.

Although the parent is not a direct participant when a subsidiary purchases treasury stock from noncontrolling shareholders, the parent's equity in the net assets of the subsidiary may change as a result of the transaction. When this occurs, the amount of the change must be recognized in preparing the consolidated statements.

For example, assume that Peerless Products owns 80 percent of Special Foods' 20,000 shares of $10 par common stock, which it purchased on January 1, 20X1, at book value of $240,000. On January 1, 20X2, Special Foods purchases 1,000 treasury shares from a nonaffiliate for $20 per share. Peerless's interest in Special Foods increases to 84.21 percent (16,000 ÷ 19,000) as a result of Special Foods' reacquisition of shares, and the noncontrolling interest decreases to 15.79 percent (3,000 ÷ 19,000). The stockholders' equity of Special Foods before and after the reacquisition of shares is as follows:

| | Before Purchase | Following Purchase |
|---|---|---|
| Common Stock, $10 par value | $200,000 | $200,000 |
| Retained Earnings | 120,000 | 120,000 |
| Total | $320,000 | $320,000 |
| Less: Treasury Stock | | (20,000) |
| Total Stockholders' Equity | $320,000 | $300,000 |

The underlying book value of Special Foods' shares held by Peerless changes as a result of the stock reacquisition, as follows:

| | Before Purchase | Following Purchase |
|---|---|---|
| Special Foods' total stockholders' equity | $320,000 | $300,000 |
| Peerless's proportionate share | ×    .80 | × .8421 |
| Book value of Peerless's investment in Special Foods | $256,000 | $252,630 |

The reacquisition of shares by Special Foods at an amount higher than book value results in a decrease in the book value of Peerless's investment of $3,370 ($256,000 − $252,630). Peerless recognizes the decrease with the following entry:

| (24) | Retained Earnings | 3,370 | |
|---|---|---|---|
| | Investment in Special Foods Stock | | 3,370 |
| | Record decrease in equity in subsidiary from subsidiary stock reacquisition. | | |

Because Peerless's equity in Special Foods decreases as a result of the transaction between Special Foods and the noncontrolling shareholders, Peerless recognizes that decrease in equity through entry (24). Peerless reduces its retained earnings because it has no additional paid-in capital on its books.

From a consolidated perspective, the acquisition of treasury shares by the subsidiary is considered an equity transaction with the noncontrolling shareholders. **FASB 160** requires that equity attributable to the parent be adjusted for the difference between the consideration paid or received by the consolidated entity and the change in the noncontrolling interest. In this case, the stock repurchase by Special Foods reduces the noncontrolling interest as follows:

| | |
|---|---|
| Noncontrolling interest before repurchase of shares by Special Foods ($320,000 × .20) | $64,000 |
| Noncontrolling interest after repurchase of shares by Special Foods ($300,000 × .1579) | (47,370) |
| Decrease in book value of noncontrolling interest | $16,630 |

The difference between the $20,000 consideration given by Special Foods to repurchase its shares and the $16,630 decrease in the noncontrolling interest is $3,370, and equity attributable to the parent must be reduced by this amount in the consolidated balance sheet. This effect has been accomplished on Peerless's separate books with entry (24) and will carry over to the consolidated financial statements.

The investment elimination entry needed in a consolidation workpaper prepared immediately after the stock reacquisition on January 1, 20X2, is as follows:

| E(25) | Common Stock—Special Foods | 200,000 | |
|---|---|---|---|
| | Retained Earnings, January 1 | 120,000 | |
| | Treasury Stock | | 20,000 |
| | Investment in Special Foods Stock | | 252,630 |
| | Noncontrolling Interest | | 47,370 |
| | Eliminate investment in common stock: | | |
| | $252,630 = $256,000 − $3,370 | | |
| | $47,370 = $300,000 × .1579 | | |

Note that this entry eliminates all of the common stockholders' equity balances of the subsidiary, including the treasury stock. An eliminating entry is not needed to reduce equity by the $3,370 change resulting from the repurchase because entry (24) accomplished that on Peerless's books and Peerless's retained earnings amount carries over to the consolidation workpaper.

## Subsidiary's Purchase of Shares from Parent

A subsidiary can reduce the number of shares it has outstanding through purchases from the parent as well as from noncontrolling shareholders. In practice, stock repurchases from the parent occur infrequently. A parent reducing its ownership interest in a subsidiary usually does so by selling some of its holdings to nonaffiliates to generate additional funds.

When a subsidiary reacquires some of its shares from its parent, the parent has traditionally recognized a gain or loss on the difference between the selling price and the change in the carrying amount of its investment. Some question exists as to whether a transaction of this type between a parent and its subsidiary can be regarded as arm's length; consequently, reporting the gain or loss in the parent's income statement can be questioned. From a consolidated viewpoint, when a subsidiary reacquires its shares from the parent, the transaction represents an internal transfer and does not give rise to a gain or loss. Because recognizing a gain or loss on the parent's books is questionable and the gain or loss would have to be eliminated in consolidation anyway, a better approach is for the parent to adjust additional paid-in capital rather than record a gain or loss on the transaction.

As an example of the reacquisition of a subsidiary's shares from its parent, assume that Peerless Products purchases in the market 16,000 of Special Foods' 20,000 shares of $10 par common stock on December 31, 20X0, at book value of $240,000. On January 1, 20X2, Special Foods repurchases 4,000 shares from Peerless at $20 per share, leaving Peerless with a 75 percent interest (12,000 ÷ 16,000) in Special Foods. The stockholders' equity of Special Foods before and after the reacquisition of shares is as follows:

|  | Before Purchase | Following Purchase |
| --- | --- | --- |
| Common Stock, $10 par value | $200,000 | $200,000 |
| Retained Earnings | 120,000 | 120,000 |
| Total | $320,000 | $320,000 |
| Less: Treasury Stock |  | (80,000) |
| Total Stockholders' Equity | $320,000 | $240,000 |

The carrying amount of Peerless's investment in Special Foods' stock equals the underlying book value of the shares in this example. The book value of the shares changes as a result of the reacquisition, as follows:

|  | Before Purchase | Following Purchase |
| --- | --- | --- |
| Special Foods' total stockholders' equity | $320,000 | $240,000 |
| Peerless's proportionate share | × .80 | × .75 |
| Book value of Peerless's investment in Special Foods | $256,000 | $180,000 |

Peerless records the sale of 25 percent (4,000 ÷ 16,000) of its investment in Special Foods with the following entry:

| January 1, 20X2 | | | |
| --- | --- | --- | --- |
| (26) | Cash | 80,000 | |
|  | Investment in Special Foods Stock | | 76,000 |
|  | Additional Paid-In Capital | | 4,000 |
|  | Record sale of investment: | | |
|  | $80,000 = $20 × 4,000 shares | | |
|  | $76,000 = $256,000 − $180,000 | | |
|  | $4,000 = $80,000 − $76,000 | | |

The new carrying value of the investment is $180,000 ($256,000 − $76,000). Because there is no differential in this case, this amount equals 75 percent of Special Foods' total stockholders' equity of $240,000 following the reacquisition. The $76,000 decrease in the carrying value includes both the reduction resulting from the decrease in the number of shares held and the reduction in the book value of those shares still held.

The subsidiary's repurchase of shares from the parent also affects the noncontrolling interest, as follows:

| | |
|---|---:|
| Noncontrolling interest before repurchase of shares by Special Foods ($320,000 × .20) | $64,000 |
| Noncontrolling interest after repurchase of shares by Special Foods ($240,000 × .25) | (60,000) |
| Decrease in book value of noncontrolling interest | $ 4,000 |

From a consolidated perspective, **FASB 160** requires an adjustment to the equity attributable to the parent for the difference between the consideration paid or received and the change in the noncontrolling interest resulting from the subsidiary's repurchase of shares. In this example, no consideration is paid or received by the consolidated entity as a whole, so the required adjustment to equity is $4,000, the amount of the change in the noncontrolling interest. The parent's equity has already been increased for the $4,000 difference with entry (26) on the parent's books, and this amount carries into the consolidation workpaper. Thus, no other adjustments to equity are required, other than eliminating the subsidiary's stockholders' equity accounts and establishing the noncontrolling interest:

| E(27) | Common Stock—Special Foods | 200,000 | |
|---|---|---:|---:|
| | Retained Earnings, January 1 | 120,000 | |
| | Treasury Stock | | 80,000 |
| | Investment in Special Foods Stock | | 180,000 |
| | Noncontrolling Interest | | 60,000 |
| | Eliminate investment in common stock: | | |
| | $180,000 = $240,000 × .75 | | |
| | $60,000 = $240,000 × .25 | | |

# COMPLEX OWNERSHIP STRUCTURES

Current reporting standards call for preparing consolidated financial statements when one company has direct or indirect control over another. The discussion to this point has focused on a simple, direct parent–subsidiary relationship. Many companies, however, have substantially more complex organizational schemes.

Figure 9–2 shows three different types of ownership structures. A ***direct ownership*** situation of the type discussed in preceding chapters is shown in Figure 9–2(*a*); the parent has controlling interest in each of the subsidiaries. In the ***multilevel ownership*** case shown in Figure 9–2(*b*), the parent has only ***indirect control*** over the company controlled by its subsidiary. The eliminating entries used in preparing consolidated financial statements in this situation are similar to those used in a simple ownership situation, but careful attention must be given to the sequence in which the data are brought together.

Figure 9–2(*c*) reflects *reciprocal ownership* or *mutual holdings*. With reciprocal ownership, the parent owns a majority of the subsidiary's common stock and the subsidiary holds some of the parent's common shares. If mutual shareholdings are ignored in the preparation of consolidated financial statements, some reported amounts may be materially overstated.

## Multilevel Ownership and Control

In many cases, companies establish multiple corporate levels through which they carry out diversified operations. For example, a company may have a number of subsidiaries, one of which is a retailer. The retail subsidiary may in turn have a finance subsidiary, a real estate subsidiary, an insurance subsidiary, and perhaps other subsidiaries. This means

**FIGURE 9–2  Alternative Ownership Structures**

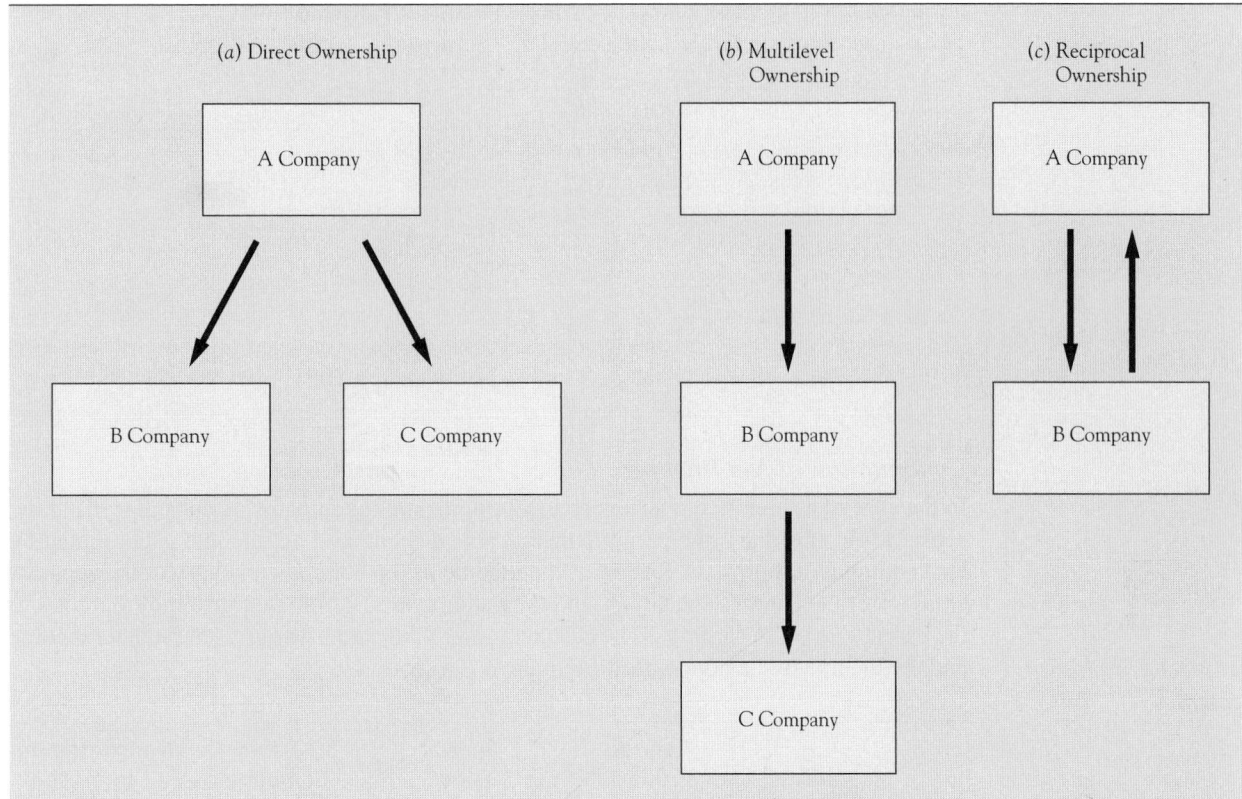

that when consolidated statements are prepared, they include companies in which the parent has only an indirect investment along with those in which it holds direct ownership.

The complexity of the consolidation process increases as additional ownership levels are included. The amount of income and net assets to be assigned to the controlling and noncontrolling shareholders, and the amount of unrealized profits and losses to be eliminated, must be determined at each level of ownership.

When a number of different levels of ownership exist, the first step normally is to consolidate the bottom, or most remote, subsidiaries with the companies at the next higher level. This sequence is continued up through the ownership structure until the subsidiaries owned directly by the parent company are consolidated with it. Income is apportioned between the controlling and noncontrolling shareholders of the companies at each level.

As an illustration of consolidation when multiple ownership levels exist, assume the following:

1. Peerless Products purchases 80 percent of Special Foods' common stock on December 31, 20X0, at book value of $240,000. On that date, Special Foods' 20 percent noncontrolling interest has a fair value of $60,000.

2. Special Foods purchases 90 percent of Bottom Company's common stock on January 1, 20X1, at book value of $162,000. At that time, Bottom Company's 10 percent noncontrolling interest has a fair value of $18,000. On the date of acquisition, Bottom has common stock of $100,000 and retained earnings of $80,000.

3. During 20X1, Bottom reports net income of $10,000 and declares dividends of $8,000; Special Foods reports separate operating income of $50,000 and declares dividends of $30,000.

All other data are the same as in the Peerless Products–Special Foods examples used throughout previous chapters. The ownership structure is as follows:

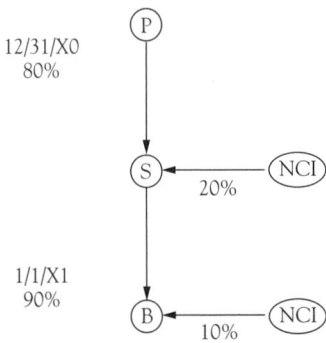

### Computation of Net Income

In the case of a three-tiered structure involving a parent company, its subsidiary, and the subsidiary's subsidiary, the parent company's equity-method net income is computed by first adding an appropriate portion of the income of the bottom subsidiary to the separate earnings of the parent's subsidiary and then adding an appropriate portion of that total to the parent's separate earnings. The computation of the parent's equity-method net income and the income to the noncontrolling interest is as follows:

| | Peerless Products | Special Foods | Bottom Company | Noncontrolling Interest |
|---|---|---|---|---|
| Operating income | $140,000 | $50,000 | $10,000 | |
| Income from: | | | | |
| Bottom Company | | 9,000 | | $ 1,000 |
| Special Foods | 47,200 | | | 11,800 |
| Net income | $187,200 | $59,000 | $10,000 | $12,800 |

The computation of consolidated net income and the allocation of that income is as follows:

| | | |
|---|---|---|
| Operating income: | | |
| Peerless Products | | $140,000 |
| Special Foods | | 50,000 |
| Bottom Company | | 10,000 |
| Consolidated net income | | $200,000 |
| Noncontrolling interest in: | | |
| Bottom Company ($10,000 × .10) | $ 1,000 | |
| Special Foods ($59,000 × .20) | 11,800 | |
| Income to noncontrolling interest | | (12,800) |
| Income to controlling interest | | $187,200 |

### Consolidation Workpaper

The 20X1 workpaper used in consolidating Peerless Products, Special Foods, and Bottom Company is shown in Figure 9–3.

**FIGURE 9–3**   **December 31, 20X1, Consolidation Workpaper, First Year following Combination; Direct and Indirect Holdings**

| Item | Peerless Products | Special Foods | Bottom Company | Eliminations Debit | Eliminations Credit | Consolidated |
|---|---|---|---|---|---|---|
| Sales | 400,000 | 200,000 | 150,000 | | | 750,000 |
| Income from Bottom Company | | 9,000 | | (28)    9,000 | | |
| Income from Special Foods | 47,200 | | | (31)  47,200 | | |
| Credits | 447,200 | 209,000 | 150,000 | | | 750,000 |
| Cost of Goods Sold | 170,000 | 115,000 | 80,000 | | | 365,000 |
| Depreciation and Amortization | 50,000 | 20,000 | 35,000 | | | 105,000 |
| Other Expenses | 40,000 | 15,000 | 25,000 | | | 80,000 |
| Debits | (260,000) | (150,000) | (140,000) | | | (550,000) |
| Consolidated Net Income | | | | | | 200,000 |
| Income to Noncontrolling Interest | | | | (29)    1,000 | | |
| | | | | (32)  11,800 | | (12,800) |
| Income, carry forward | 187,200 | 59,000 | 10,000 | 69,000 | | 187,200 |
| Retained Earnings, January 1 | 300,000 | 100,000 | 80,000 | (30)  80,000 | | |
| | | | | (33) 100,000 | | 300,000 |
| Income, from above | 187,200 | 59,000 | 10,000 | 69,000 | | 187,200 |
| | 487,200 | 159,000 | 90,000 | | | 487,200 |
| Dividends Declared | (60,000) | (30,000) | (8,000) | | (28)    7,200 | |
| | | | | | (29)       800 | |
| | | | | | (31)  24,000 | |
| | | | | | (32)    6,000 | (60,000) |
| Retained Earnings, December 31, carry forward | 427,200 | 129,000 | 82,000 | 249,000 | 38,000 | 427,200 |
| Cash | 264,000 | 20,200 | 25,000 | | | 309,200 |
| Accounts Receivable | 75,000 | 50,000 | 30,000 | | | 155,000 |
| Inventory | 100,000 | 75,000 | 40,000 | | | 215,000 |
| Land | 175,000 | 40,000 | 50,000 | | | 265,000 |
| Buildings and Equipment | 800,000 | 600,000 | 75,000 | | | 1,475,000 |
| Investment in Bottom Company Stock | | 163,800 | | | (28)    1,800 | |
| | | | | | (30) 162,000 | |
| Investment in Special Foods Stock | 263,200 | | | | (31)  23,200 | |
| | | | | | (33) 240,000 | |
| Debits | 1,677,200 | 949,000 | 220,000 | | | 2,419,200 |
| Accumulated Depreciation | 250,000 | 220,000 | 20,000 | | | 490,000 |
| Accounts Payable | 100,000 | 100,000 | 18,000 | | | 218,000 |
| Bonds Payable | 400,000 | 300,000 | | | | 700,000 |
| Common Stock | 500,000 | 200,000 | 100,000 | (30) 100,000 | | |
| | | | | (33) 200,000 | | 500,000 |
| Retained Earnings, from above | 427,200 | 129,000 | 82,000 | 249,000 | 38,000 | 427,200 |
| Noncontrolling Interest | | | | | (29)       200 | |
| | | | | | (30)  18,000 | |
| | | | | | (32)    5,800 | |
| | | | | | (33)  60,000 | 84,000 |
| Credits | 1,677,200 | 949,000 | 220,000 | 549,000 | 549,000 | 2,419,200 |

Elimination entries:
   (28)  Eliminate income from Bottom Company.
   (29)  Assign income to noncontrolling shareholders of Bottom Company.
   (30)  Eliminate investment in Bottom Company stock.
   (31)  Eliminate income from Special Foods.
   (32)  Assign income to noncontrolling shareholders of Special Foods.
   (33)  Eliminate investment in Special Foods stock.

The eliminations related to Special Foods' investment in Bottom Company are entered first:

| E(28) | Income from Bottom Company | 9,000 | |
|---|---|---|---|
| | Dividends Declared | | 7,200 |
| | Investment in Bottom Company Stock | | 1,800 |
| | Eliminate income from Bottom Company: | | |
| | $9,000 = $10,000 \times .90$ | | |
| | $7,200 = $8,000 \times .90$ | | |
| | $1,800 = $9,000 - $7,200$ | | |
| E(29) | Income to Noncontrolling Interest | 1,000 | |
| | Dividends Declared | | 800 |
| | Noncontrolling Interest | | 200 |
| | Assign income to noncontrolling shareholders of Bottom Company: | | |
| | $1,000 = $10,000 \times .10$ | | |
| | $800 = $8,000 \times .10$ | | |
| | $200 = $1,000 - $800$ | | |
| E(30) | Common Stock—Bottom Company | 100,000 | |
| | Retained Earnings, January 1 | 80,000 | |
| | Investment in Bottom Company Stock | | 162,000 |
| | Noncontrolling Interest | | 18,000 |
| | Eliminate investment in Bottom Company Stock: | | |
| | $162,000 = $180,000 \times .90$ | | |
| | $18,000 = $180,000 \times .10$ | | |

Next, the eliminations related to Peerless's investment in Special Foods are entered in the workpaper:

| E(31) | Income from Special Foods | 47,200 | |
|---|---|---|---|
| | Dividends Declared | | 24,000 |
| | Investment in Special Foods Stock | | 23,200 |
| | Eliminate income from Special Foods: | | |
| | $47,200 = $59,000 \times .80$ | | |
| | $24,000 = $30,000 \times .80$ | | |
| | $23,200 = $47,200 - $24,000$ | | |
| E(32) | Income to Noncontrolling Interest | 11,800 | |
| | Dividends Declared | | 6,000 |
| | Noncontrolling Interest | | 5,800 |
| | Assign income to noncontrolling shareholders of Special Foods: | | |
| | $11,800 = $59,000 \times .20$ | | |
| | $6,000 = $30,000 \times .20$ | | |
| | $5,800 = $11,800 - $6,000$ | | |
| E(33) | Common Stock—Special Foods | 200,000 | |
| | Retained Earnings, January 1 | 100,000 | |
| | Investment in Special Foods Stock | | 240,000 |
| | Noncontrolling Interest | | 60,000 |
| | Eliminate investment in Special Foods stock: | | |
| | $240,000 = $300,000 \times .80$ | | |
| | $60,000 = $300,000 \times .20$ | | |

*Order of Acquisition*

In the preceding example, Peerless acquired its investment in Special Foods before Special Foods acquired its investment in Bottom Company. If, however, Special Foods had already owned its interest in Bottom Company when Peerless purchased its interest in Special Foods, a portion of Bottom Company's undistributed income since its acquisition would have accrued to Special Foods. So long as Special Foods accounts for its investment in Bottom Company using the equity method, no special problems arise; the normal consolidation procedures are followed. However, if Special Foods uses the cost method in accounting for its investment in Bottom Company, a workpaper conversion to the equity method must be made so that Special Foods' retained earnings at the date of the combination includes the appropriate share of Bottom Company's earnings since acquisition and so that the differential is correctly determined.

*Unrealized Intercompany Profits*

When intercompany sales occur between multilevel affiliates, unrealized intercompany profits must be eliminated against the appropriate ownership interests. The most convenient way of doing this is to compute the amount of realized income each company contributes before apportioning income between controlling and noncontrolling interests.

For example, the realized income accruing to the ownership interests of each affiliate is computed in the following manner given the unrealized profit amounts indicated:

|  | Peerless Products | Special Foods | Bottom Company | Noncontrolling Interest |
|---|---|---|---|---|
| Operating income | $140,000 | $50,000 | $10,000 | |
| Unrealized profit | (5,000) | (10,000) | (3,000) | |
| Realized operating profit | $135,000 | $40,000 | $ 7,000 | |
| Income from: | | | | |
| Bottom Company | | 6,300 | | $ 700 |
| Special Foods | 37,040 | | | 9,260 |
| Realized net income | $172,040 | $46,300 | $ 7,000 | $9,960 |

Consolidated net income of $182,000 equals the sum of the realized incomes of each of the individual companies ($135,000 + $40,000 + $7,000). The income attributable to the controlling interest is $172,040, equal to consolidated net income less the income attributable to the noncontrolling interest ($182,000 − $9,960). The normal workpaper entries to eliminate unrealized intercompany profits, as discussed in Chapters 6 and 7, are entered in the workpaper for each company involved.

## Reciprocal or Mutual Ownership

A reciprocal relationship exists when two companies hold stock in each other. Reciprocal relationships are relatively rare in practice, and their accounting impact is often immaterial.

The method of dealing with reciprocal relationships found most often in practice is the **treasury stock method**. Under the treasury stock method, purchases of a parent's stock by a subsidiary are treated in the same way as if the parent had repurchased its own stock and was holding it in the treasury. The subsidiary normally accounts for the investment in the parent's stock using the cost method because such investments usually are small and almost never confer the ability to significantly influence the parent.

Income assigned to the noncontrolling interest in the subsidiary should be based on the subsidiary's separate income excluding the dividend income from the investment in the parent. Similarly, the parent normally bases its equity-method share of the subsidiary's income on the subsidiary's income excluding the dividend income from the parent.

As an example of the treasury stock method, assume the following:

1. Peerless Products purchases 80 percent of Special Foods' common stock on December 31, 20X0, at book value of $240,000. The fair value of the noncontrolling interest on that date is $60,000.
2. Special Foods purchases 10 percent of Peerless's common stock on January 1, 20X1, at book value of $80,000.
3. For 20X1, the two companies report the following separate operating income and dividends:

|  | Operating Income | Dividends |
|---|---|---|
| Peerless Products | $140,000 | $60,000 |
| Special Foods | 50,000 | 30,000 |
| Total operating income | $190,000 | |

The reciprocal ownership relationship between Peerless and Special Foods is as follows:

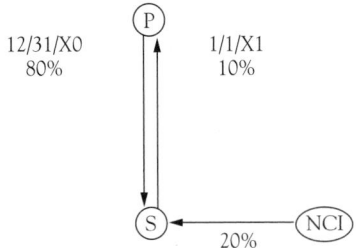

Special Foods records the purchase of its investment in Peerless's common stock with the following entry:

January 1, 20X1

| (34) | Investment in Peerless Products Stock | 80,000 | |
|---|---|---|---|
| | Cash | | 80,000 |
| | Record purchase of Peerless Products stock. | | |

Because it does not gain the ability to significantly influence Peerless, Special Foods accounts for the investment using the cost method. During 20X1, Special Foods records the receipt of dividends from Peerless with the following entry:

| (35) | Cash | 6,000 | |
|---|---|---|---|
| | Dividend Income | | 6,000 |
| | Record dividend income from Peerless: | | |
| | $60,000 × .10 | | |

The consolidation workpaper prepared at the end of 20X1, shown in Figure 9–4, includes the following eliminating entries:

| E(36) | Dividend Income | 6,000 | |
|---|---|---|---|
| | Dividends Declared | | 6,000 |
| | Eliminate dividend income from Peerless. | | |

**FIGURE 9–4**   **December 31, 20X1, Treasury Stock-Method Workpaper for First Year following Combination; 80 Percent Purchase at Book Value**

| Item | Peerless Products | Special Foods | Eliminations Debit | Eliminations Credit | Consolidated |
|---|---|---|---|---|---|
| Sales | 400,000 | 200,000 | | | 600,000 |
| Income from Subsidiary | 40,000 | | (37)   40,000 | | |
| Dividend Income | | 6,000 | (36)   6,000 | | |
| Credits | 440,000 | 206,000 | | | 600,000 |
| Cost of Goods Sold | 170,000 | 115,000 | | | 285,000 |
| Depreciation and Amortization | 50,000 | 20,000 | | | 70,000 |
| Other Expenses | 40,000 | 15,000 | | | 55,000 |
| Debits | (260,000) | (150,000) | | | (410,000) |
| Consolidated Net Income | | | | | 190,000 |
| Income to Noncontrolling Interest | | | (38)   10,000 | | (10,000) |
| Income, carry forward | 180,000 | 56,000 | 56,000 | | 180,000 |
| Retained Earnings, January 1 | 300,000 | 100,000 | (40) 100,000 | | 300,000 |
| Income, from above | 180,000 | 56,000 | 56,000 | | 180,000 |
| | 480,000 | 156,000 | | | 480,000 |
| Dividends Declared | (60,000) | (30,000) | | (36)   6,000 | |
| | | | | (37)  24,000 | |
| | | | | (38)   6,000 | (54,000) |
| Retained Earnings, December 31, carry forward | 420,000 | 126,000 | 156,000 | 36,000 | 426,000 |
| Cash | 264,000 | 1,000 | | | 265,000 |
| Accounts Receivable | 75,000 | 50,000 | | | 125,000 |
| Inventory | 100,000 | 75,000 | | | 175,000 |
| Land | 175,000 | 40,000 | | | 215,000 |
| Buildings and Equipment | 800,000 | 600,000 | | | 1,400,000 |
| Investment in Special Foods Stock | 256,000 | | | (37)  16,000 | |
| | | | | (40) 240,000 | |
| Investment in Peerless Products Stock | | 80,000 | | (39)  80,000 | |
| Debits | 1,670,000 | 846,000 | | | 2,180,000 |
| Accumulated Depreciation | 450,000 | 320,000 | | | 770,000 |
| Accounts Payable | 100,000 | 100,000 | | | 200,000 |
| Bonds Payable | 200,000 | 100,000 | | | 300,000 |
| Common Stock | 500,000 | 200,000 | (40) 200,000 | | 500,000 |
| Retained Earnings, from above | 420,000 | 126,000 | 156,000 | 36,000 | 426,000 |
| Noncontrolling Interest | | | | (38)   4,000 | |
| | | | | (40)  60,000 | 64,000 |
| Treasury Stock | | | (39)  80,000 | | (80,000) |
| Credits | 1,670,000 | 846,000 | 436,000 | 436,000 | 2,180,000 |

Elimination entries:
(36)  Eliminate dividend income from Peerless.
(37)  Eliminate income from subsidiary.
(38)  Assign income to noncontrolling interest.
(39)  Reclassify investment in Peerless stock as treasury stock.
(40)  Eliminate investment in Special Foods stock.

| E(37) | Income from Subsidiary | 40,000 | |
| | Dividends Declared | | 24,000 |
| | Investment in Special Foods Stock | | 16,000 |
| | Eliminate income from subsidiary. | | |
| | | | |
| E(38) | Income to Noncontrolling Interest | 10,000 | |
| | Dividends Declared | | 6,000 |
| | Noncontrolling Interest | | 4,000 |
| | Assign income to noncontrolling interest. | | |
| | | | |
| E(39) | Treasury Stock | 80,000 | |
| | Investment in Peerless Products Stock | | 80,000 |
| | Reclassify investment in Peerless stock as treasury stock. | | |
| | | | |
| E(40) | Common Stock—Special Foods | 200,000 | |
| | Retained Earnings, January 1 | 100,000 | |
| | Investment in Special Foods Stock | | 240,000 |
| | Noncontrolling Interest | | 60,000 |
| | Eliminate investment in Special Foods stock. | | |

Eliminating entry E(39) reclassifies Special Foods' investment in Peerless stock as if it were treasury stock. All of Peerless's common stock is shown in the consolidated balance sheet as outstanding. The treasury stock is shown at cost as an $80,000 deduction from total stockholders' equity, just as treasury stock is shown in a single company's balance sheet at cost. Note that entry E(36) reduces the amount shown in the consolidated retained earnings statement as dividends paid to those outside the consolidated entity.

The remaining entries needed in the 20X1 consolidation workpaper are the normal entries to eliminate Peerless's investment in Special Foods and income from Special Foods that Peerless recognizes. The income from Special Foods recognized by Peerless is based on Special Foods' separate income, excluding dividend income from Peerless. Therefore, the income elimination is for $40,000, Peerless's 80 percent share of Special Foods' separate operating income of $50,000.

Consolidated net income is $190,000, as can be seen in Figure 9–4. This amount can be computed and is allocated as follows:

| | | |
|---|---|---|
| Peerless's separate operating income | | $140,000 |
| Special Foods' separate operating income | | 50,000 |
| Consolidated net income | | $190,000 |
| Less income to noncontrolling interest: | | |
| Special Foods' separate income ($50,000) | $50,000 | |
| Noncontrolling stockholders' share | × .20 | |
| | | (10,000) |
| Income to controlling interest | | $180,000 |

Note that the amount of net income allocated to the noncontrolling interest is based on Special Foods' operating income of $50,000 and excludes the dividends received from Peerless. A question arises in practice as to whether the income assigned to the noncontrolling interest should be based on the subsidiary's entire net income or only the portion derived from unrelated parties. Although the noncontrolling interest certainly has a claim on its share of the entire income of the subsidiary, the approach most consistent with the FASB's entity view of consolidated financial statements is to exclude from the computation of the noncontrolling shareholders' income the dividends from the parent.

# SUBSIDIARY STOCK DIVIDENDS

Subsidiary dividends payable in shares of the subsidiary's common stock require slight changes in the elimination entries used in preparing consolidated financial statements. Because stock dividends are issued proportionally to all common stockholders, the relative interests of the controlling and noncontrolling stockholders do not change as a result of the stock dividend. The investment's carrying amount on the parent's books also is unaffected by a stock dividend. On the other hand, the stockholders' equity accounts of the subsidiary do change, although total stockholders' equity does not. The stock dividend represents a permanent capitalization of retained earnings, thus decreasing retained earnings and increasing capital stock and, perhaps, additional paid-in capital.

In the preparation of consolidated financial statements for the period in which a stock dividend is declared by the subsidiary, the stock dividend declaration must be eliminated along with the increased common stock and increased additional paid-in capital, if any. The stock dividend declared cannot appear in the consolidated retained earnings statement because only the parent's dividends are viewed as dividends of the consolidated entity.

In subsequent years, the balances in the subsidiary's stockholders' equity accounts are eliminated in the normal manner. Keep in mind that stock dividends do not change the total stockholders' equity of a company; they only realign the individual accounts within stockholders' equity. Therefore, the full balances of all the subsidiary's stockholders' equity accounts must be eliminated in consolidation, as is the usual procedure, even though amounts have been shifted from one account to another.

## Illustration of Subsidiary Stock Dividends

As an illustration of the treatment of a subsidiary's stock dividend, assume that in the Peerless Products and Special Foods example, Special Foods declares a 25 percent stock dividend in 20X1 on its $200,000 of common stock and elects to capitalize the par value of the shares. Special Foods records the stock dividend with the following entry:

| (41) | Stock Dividends Declared | 50,000 | |
|---|---|---|---|
| | Common Stock | | 50,000 |
| | Record 25 percent stock dividend: | | |
| | $200,000 × .25 | | |

The investors make only a memo entry to record the receipt of the stock dividend.

When consolidated financial statements are prepared at the end of 20X1, the normal elimination entries are made in the workpaper. If the subsidiary had declared no stock dividend, the entry for eliminating the investment account and subsidiary stockholders' equity balances at the beginning of the period would have been:

| E(42) | Common Stock—Special Foods | 200,000 | |
|---|---|---|---|
| | Retained Earnings, January 1 | 100,000 | |
| | Investment in Special Foods Stock | | 240,000 |
| | Noncontrolling Interest | | 60,000 |
| | Eliminate beginning investment balance. | | |

With the subsidiary having declared the stock dividend, all elimination entries are the same except for the investment elimination entry. Entry E(42) is altered as follows:

| E(43) | Common Stock—Special Foods | 250,000 | |
|---|---|---|---|
| | Retained Earnings, January 1 | 100,000 | |
| | Investment in Special Foods Stock | | 240,000 |
| | Noncontrolling Interest | | 60,000 |
| | Stock Dividends Declared | | 50,000 |
| | Eliminate beginning investment balance: | | |
| | $250,000 = $200,000 + $50,000 | | |
| | $50,000 = $200,000 × .25 | | |

Note that although the common stock balance has increased by the $50,000 amount of the stock dividend, the elimination of retained earnings is not changed in the year of the stock dividend because dividends declared have not been closed to retained earnings; only the beginning balance of retained earnings is eliminated. Just as with other dividends of the subsidiary, stock dividends must be eliminated because they are not viewed as dividends of the consolidated entity.

## Impact on Subsequent Periods

At the end of 20X1, the stock dividend declaration is closed into the subsidiary's Retained Earnings account and does not separately appear in the financial statements of future periods. The stock dividend results in a common stock balance $50,000 higher and a retained earnings balance $50,000 lower on the subsidiary's books than if there had been no stock dividend. The investment elimination entry in the consolidation workpaper must reflect these changed balances.

Thus, assume that the appropriate investment elimination entry on December 31, 20X2, is as follows if Special Foods declares no stock dividend:

| E(44) | Common Stock—Special Foods | 200,000 | |
|---|---|---|---|
| | Retained Earnings, January 1 | 120,000 | |
| | Investment in Special Foods Stock | | 256,000 |
| | Noncontrolling Interest | | 64,000 |
| | Eliminate beginning investment balance. | | |

The following entry would replace entry E(44) in the consolidation workpaper prepared as of December 31, 20X2, if Special Foods had declared the stock dividend during 20X1:

| E(45) | Common Stock—Special Foods | 250,000 | |
|---|---|---|---|
| | Retained Earnings, January 1 | 70,000 | |
| | Investment in Special Foods Stock | | 256,000 |
| | Noncontrolling Interest | | 64,000 |
| | Eliminate beginning investment balance. | | |

Entry E(45) is identical to entry E(44) except that the elimination of common stock is $50,000 higher and the elimination of retained earnings is $50,000 lower, reflecting the differences in the balances of those accounts due to the stock dividend.

## Summary of Key Concepts

A number of stockholders' equity issues arise in the preparation of consolidated financial statements. When subsidiaries have preferred stock outstanding, any of the preferred stock held by the parent must be eliminated because it is held within the consolidated entity. The remaining preferred stock is treated as part of the noncontrolling interest. In the assessment of the preferred shareholders' claim, consideration must be given to all the features of the preferred stock, including cumulative dividends in arrears, dividend participation features, and retirement premiums.

Transactions involving a subsidiary's common stock include purchase or sale transactions involving the parent or parties outside of the consolidated entity (noncontrolling interest). These transactions may affect the carrying amounts of both the controlling and noncontrolling interests. So long as the parent continues to maintain a controlling financial interest in the subsidiary, these transactions are viewed as equity transactions and, from a consolidated perspective, no gain or loss may be recognized. In consolidation, equity attributable to the parent is adjusted for the difference between any consideration paid or received by the consolidated entity and the change in the carrying amount of the noncontrolling interest resulting from the transaction.

The organizational structure of some consolidated entities may be more complex than just a parent and one or more subsidiaries. In some cases, subsidiaries hold controlling interests in other companies, thus giving the parent an indirect controlling interest. Consolidation proceeds from the lowest level to the highest in these cases. In a relatively few cases, a subsidiary may own common shares of its parent. Those common shares are treated as treasury stock in consolidated financial statements.

Stock dividends declared by a subsidiary result in only minor changes in the eliminations needed to prepare consolidated financial statements. In the year the stock dividend is declared, the stock dividend declaration and the higher balance of the common stock must be eliminated in preparing consolidated statements. In subsequent years, the investment elimination entry reflects the higher amount of the subsidiary's common stock and the lower amount of retained earnings.

## Key Terms

| | | |
|---|---|---|
| direct ownership, *438* | multilevel ownership, *438* | reciprocal ownership, *438* |
| indirect control, *438* | mutual holdings, *438* | treasury stock method, *443* |

## Questions

**Q9-1**  How does the consolidation process deal with preferred stock of a subsidiary?

**Q9-2**  What portion of subsidiary preferred stock outstanding is reported as part of the noncontrolling interest in the consolidated balance sheet?

**Q9-3**  Why are subsidiary preferred dividends paid to nonaffiliates normally deducted from earnings in arriving at consolidated net income? When is it not appropriate to deduct subsidiary preferred dividends in computing consolidated net income?

**Q9-4**  How does a call feature on subsidiary preferred stock affect the claim of the noncontrolling interest reported in the consolidated balance sheet?

**Q9-5**  Explain how the existence of a subsidiary's preferred shares might affect the amount of goodwill reported following the purchase of the subsidiary.

**Q9-6**  A parent company sells common shares of one of its subsidiaries to a nonaffiliate for more than their carrying value on the parent's books. How should the parent company report the sale? How should the sale be reported in the consolidated financial statements?

**Q9-7**  A subsidiary sells additional shares of its common stock to a nonaffiliate at a price that is higher than the previous book value per share. How does the sale benefit the existing shareholders?

**Q9-8**  A parent company purchases additional common shares of one of its subsidiaries from the subsidiary at $10 per share above underlying book value. Explain how this purchase is reflected in the consolidated financial statements for the year.

**Q9-9**  How are treasury shares held by a subsidiary reported in the consolidated financial statements?

**Q9-10**  What is indirect ownership? How does one company gain control of another through indirect ownership?

**Q9-11** Explain how a reciprocal ownership arrangement between two subsidiaries could lead the parent company to overstate its income if no adjustment is made for the reciprocal relationship.

**Q9-12** How will parent company shares held by a subsidiary be reflected in the consolidated balance sheet when the treasury stock method is used?

**Q9-13** Parent Company holds 80 percent ownership of Subsidiary Company, and Subsidiary Company owns 90 percent of the stock of Tiny Corporation. What effect will $100,000 of unrealized intercompany profits on Tiny's books on December 31, 20X5, have on the amounts reported as consolidated net income and income assigned to the controlling interest?

**Q9-14** Snapper Corporation holds 70 percent ownership of Bit Company, and Bit holds 60 percent ownership of Slide Company. Should Slide be consolidated with Snapper Corporation? Why?

**Q9-15** What effect will a subsidiary's 15 percent stock dividend have on the consolidated financial statements?

**Q9-16** What effect will a subsidiary's 15 percent stock dividend have on the elimination entries used in preparing a consolidated balance sheet at the end of the year in which the dividend is distributed?

**Q9-17** When multilevel affiliations exist, explain why it is generally best to prepare consolidated financial statements by completing the eliminating entries for companies furthest from parent company ownership first and completing the eliminating entries for those owned directly by the parent company last.

---

# Cases

## C9-1 Effect of Subsidiary Preferred Stock

*Analysis*

Snow Corporation issued common stock with a par value of $100,000 and preferred stock with a par value of $80,000 on January 1, 20X5, when the company was created. Klammer Corporation acquired a controlling interest in Snow on January 1, 20X6.

### Required

What does Klammer's controller need to know about the preferred stock to determine the proper allocation of consolidated net income to the controlling and noncontrolling interests?

## C9-2 Consolidated Stockholders' Equity: Theory vs. Practice

Companies sometimes employ accounting practices that are not necessarily in accordance with accounting theory or even current standards. In some cases, companies may be following industry practices rather than generally accepted practices. In other cases, the practices may be justified as expedient because the amounts may be immaterial.

*Research*
*FARS*

### Required

*a.* How has Xerox Corporation reported the sale of stock of a subsidiary in its consolidated financial statements prior to 2008? How must such sales (assuming Xerox maintains control of the subsidiary) be reported under current standards?

*b.* How does Occidental Petroleum Corporation treat subsidiary preferred stock? How should subsidiary preferred stock be reported in the consolidated financial statements?

## C9-3 Sale of Subsidiary Shares

*Research*
*FARS*

Book Corporation purchased 90,000 shares of Lance Company at underlying book value of $3 per share on June 30, 20X1. On January 1, 20X5, Lance reported its net book value as $400,000 and continued to have 100,000 shares of common stock outstanding. On that date, Book sold 30,000 shares of Lance to Triple Corporation for $5.60 per share. Book uses the equity method in accounting for its investment in Lance and recorded a gain on sale of investments of $48,000 in its consolidated income statement for 20X5.

### Required

Book's vice president of finance, Robert Reader, has asked you to prepare a memo addressed to him presenting the alternative ways to record the difference between the carrying value and sale price of the shares that are sold and your recommendations on the preferred reporting alternative. Citations to or quotations from the relevant authoritative accounting literature should be included in providing the basis of support for your recommendations.

### C9-4 Sale of Subsidiary Shares

*Analysis*

Hardcore Mining Company acquired 88 percent of the common stock of Mountain Trucking Company on January 1, 20X2, at a cost of $30 per share. On December 31, 20X7, when the book value of Mountain Trucking stock was $70 per share, Hardcore sold one-quarter of its investment in Mountain Trucking to Basic Manufacturing Company for $90 per share.

**Required**

What effect will the sale have on the 20X7 consolidated financial statements of Hardcore Mining if (*a*) Basic Manufacturing is an unrelated company or (*b*) Hardcore Mining holds 60 percent of Basic's voting shares?

### C9-5 Reciprocal Ownership

*Judgment*

Strong Manufacturing Company holds 94 percent ownership of Thorson Farm Products and 68 percent ownership of Kenwood Distributors. Thorson has excess cash at the end of 20X4 and is considering buying shares of its own stock, shares of Strong, or shares of Kenwood.

**Required**

If Thorson wishes to take the action that will be best for the consolidated entity, what factors must it consider in making its decision? How can it maximize consolidated net income?

---

**Exercises**

### E9-1 Multiple-Choice Questions on Preferred Stock Ownership

Blank Corporation prepared the following summarized balance sheet on January 1, 20X1:

| Assets | $150,000 | Liabilities | $ 20,000 |
|---|---|---|---|
| | | Preferred Stock | 30,000 |
| | | Common Stock | 40,000 |
| | | Retained Earnings | 60,000 |
| Total Assets | $150,000 | Total Liabilities and Equities | $150,000 |

Shepard Company acquires 80 percent of Blank Corporation's common stock on January 1, 20X1, for $80,000. At that date, the fair value of the common shares held by the noncontrolling interest is $20,000.

**Required**

Select the correct answer for each of the following questions.

1. The amount reported as noncontrolling interest in the consolidated balance sheet is:
   a. $20,000.
   b. $26,000.
   c. $30,000.
   d. $50,000.

2. In addition to the common shares, Shepard Company purchases 70 percent of Blank's preferred shares for $21,000. The amount reported as noncontrolling interest in Shepard's consolidated balance sheet is:
   a. $9,000.
   b. $20,000.
   c. $29,000.
   d. $50,000.

3. In addition to the common shares, Shepard Company purchases 70 percent of Blank's preferred shares for $21,000 on January 1, 20X1. If Shepard's retained earnings is $150,000 on December 31, 20X0, the consolidated retained earnings reported immediately after the stock purchases is:
   a. $48,000.
   b. $150,000.
   c. $198,000.
   d. $210,000.

4. In addition to the common shares, Shepard Company purchases 70 percent of Blank's preferred shares for $21,000 on January 1, 20X1. Shepard has no preferred shares outstanding. The amount of preferred stock reported in the consolidated balance sheet immediately after the stock purchases is:

   a. $0.

   b. $9,000.

   c. $21,000.

   d. $30,000.

### E9-2 Multiple-Choice Questions on Multilevel Ownership

Musical Corporation acquires 80 percent of Dustin Corporation's common shares on January 1, 20X2. On January 2, 20X2, Dustin acquires 60 percent of Rustic Corporation's common stock. Information on company book values on the date of purchase and operating results for 20X2 is as follows:

| Company | Book Value | Purchase Price | 20X2 Operating Income |
|---|---|---|---|
| Musical Corporation | $800,000 | | $100,000 |
| Dustin Corporation | 300,000 | $240,000 | 80,000 |
| Rustic Corporation | 200,000 | 120,000 | 50,000 |

The fair values of the noncontrolling interests of Dustin and Rustic at the dates of acquisition were $60,000 and $80,000, respectively.

### Required

Select the correct answer for each of the following questions.

1. Consolidated net income assigned to the controlling interest for 20X2 is:

   a. $180,000.

   b. $188,000.

   c. $194,000.

   d. $234,000.

2. The amount of 20X2 income assigned to the noncontrolling interest of Rustic Corporation is:

   a. $0.

   b. $20,000.

   c. $30,000.

   d. $50,000.

3. The amount of 20X2 income assigned to the noncontrolling interest of Dustin Corporation is:

   a. $10,000.

   b. $16,000.

   c. $22,000.

   d. $26,000.

4. The amount of income assigned to the noncontrolling interest in the 20X2 consolidated income statement is:

   a. $20,000.

   b. $22,000.

   c. $42,000.

   d. $46,000.

5. Assume that Dustin pays $150,000, rather than $120,000, to purchase 60 percent of Rustic's common stock, and the fair value of the noncontrolling interest is $100,000 at the date of acquisition. If the differential is amortized over 10 years, the effect on 20X2 income assigned to the controlling shareholders will be a decrease of:

   *a.* $0.

   *b.* $2,400.

   *c.* $3,000.

   *d.* $5,000.

**E9-3**  **Acquisition of Preferred Shares**

The summarized balance sheet of Separate Company on January 1, 20X3, contained the following amounts:

| | | | |
|---|---|---|---|
| Total Assets | $350,000 | Total Liabilities | $ 50,000 |
| | | Preferred Stock | 100,000 |
| | | Common Stock | 50,000 |
| | | Retained Earnings | 150,000 |
| Total Assets | $350,000 | Total Liabilities and Equities | $350,000 |

On January 1, 20X3, Joint Corporation acquired 70 percent of the common shares and 60 percent of the preferred shares of Separate Company at underlying book value. At that date, the fair value of the noncontrolling interest in Separate's common stock was equal to 30 percent of the book value of its common stock.

### Required

Give the workpaper elimination entries needed to prepare a consolidated balance sheet immediately following the purchase of shares by Joint.

**E9-4**  **Reciprocal Ownership [AICPA Adapted]**

Pride Corporation owns 80 percent of Simba Corporation's outstanding common stock. Simba, in turn, owns 10 percent of Pride's outstanding common stock.

### Required

*a.* What percent of the dividends paid by Simba is reported as dividends declared in the consolidated financial statements?

*b.* What percent of the dividends paid by Pride is reported as dividends declared in the consolidated retained earnings statement?

**E9-5**  **Subsidiary with Preferred Stock Outstanding**

Clayton Corporation purchased 75 percent of the common stock and 40 percent of the preferred stock of Topple Company on January 1, 20X6, for $270,000 and $80,000, respectively. At the time of purchase, the fair value of the common shares of Topple held by the noncontrolling interest was $90,000. Topple's balance sheet contained the following balances:

| | |
|---|---|
| Preferred Stock ($10 par value) | $200,000 |
| Common Stock ($5 par value) | 150,000 |
| Retained Earnings | 210,000 |
| Total Stockholders' Equity | $560,000 |

### Required

Give the eliminating entries needed to prepare a consolidated balance sheet immediately after Clayton purchased the Topple shares.

**E9-6**  **Subsidiary with Preferred Stock Outstanding**

Clayton Corporation purchased 75 percent of the common stock and 40 percent of the preferred stock of Topple Company on January 1, 20X6, for $270,000 and $80,000, respectively. At the time of purchase, the fair value of the common shares of Topple held by the noncontrolling interest was $90,000. Topple's balance sheet contained the following balances:

| Preferred Stock ($10 par value) | $200,000 |
|---|---|
| Common Stock ($5 par value) | 150,000 |
| Retained Earnings | 210,000 |
| Total Stockholders' Equity | $560,000 |

For the year ended December 31, 20X6, Topple reported net income of $70,000 and paid dividends of $50,000. The preferred stock is cumulative and pays an annual dividend of 8 percent.

### Required

a. Prepare the journal entries recorded by Clayton for its investments in Topple during 20X6.

b. Present the eliminating entries needed to prepare the consolidated financial statements for Clayton Corporation as of December 31, 20X6.

### E9-7 Preferred Dividends and Call Premium

On January 1, 20X2, Fischer Corporation purchased 90 percent of the common shares and 60 percent of the preferred shares of Culbertson Company at underlying book value. At that date, the fair value of the noncontrolling interest in Culbertson's common stock was equal to 10 percent of the book value of its common stock. Culbertson's balance sheet at the time of purchase contained the following balances:

| Total Assets | $860,000 | Total Liabilities | $ 80,000 |
|---|---|---|---|
| | | Preferred Stock | 100,000 |
| | | Common Stock | 300,000 |
| | | Retained Earnings | 380,000 |
| Total Assets | $860,000 | Total Liabilities and Equities | $860,000 |

The preferred shares are cumulative with regard to dividends. The shares have a 12 percent annual dividend rate and are five years in arrears on January 1, 20X2. All of the $10 par value preferred shares are callable at $12 per share after December 31, 20X0. During 20X2, Culbertson reported net income of $70,000 and paid no dividends.

### Required

a. Compute Culbertson's contribution to consolidated net income for 20X2.

b. Compute the amount of income to be assigned to the noncontrolling interest in the 20X2 consolidated income statement.

c. Compute the portion of Culbertson's retained earnings assignable to its preferred shareholders on January 1, 20X2.

d. Compute the book value of the common stock on January 1, 20X2.

e. Compute the amount to be reported as the noncontrolling interest in the consolidated balance sheet on January 1, 20X2.

### E9-8 Multilevel Ownership

Grasper Corporation owns 70 percent of Latent Corporation's common stock and 25 percent of Dally Corporation's common stock. In addition, Latent owns 40 percent of Dally's stock. In 20X6, Grasper, Latent, and Dally reported operating income of $90,000, $60,000, and $40,000 and paid dividends of $45,000, $30,000, and $10,000, respectively.

### Required

a. What amount of consolidated net income will Grasper report for 20X6?

b. What amount of income will be assigned to the noncontrolling interest in the 20X6 consolidated income statement?

c. What amount of income will be assigned to the controlling interest in the 20X6 income statement?

d. What amount will be reported as dividends declared in Grasper's 20X6 consolidated retained earnings statement?

**E9-9** **Eliminating Entries for Multilevel Ownership**

Promise Enterprises acquired 90 percent of Brown Corporation's voting common stock on January 1, 20X3, for $315,000. At that date, the fair value of the noncontrolling interest of Brown Corporation was $35,000. Immediately after Promise acquired its ownership, Brown purchased 60 percent of Tann Company's stock for $120,000. The fair value of the noncontrolling interest of Tann Company was $80,000 at that date. During 20X3, Promise reported operating income of $200,000 and paid dividends of $80,000. Brown reported operating income of $120,000 and paid dividends of $50,000. Tann reported net income of $40,000 and paid dividends of $15,000. At January 1, 20X3, the stockholders' equity sections of the balance sheets of the companies were as follows:

|  | Promise Enterprises | Brown Corporation | Tann Company |
|---|---|---|---|
| Common Stock | $200,000 | $150,000 | $100,000 |
| Additional Paid-In Capital | 160,000 | 60,000 | 60,000 |
| Retained Earnings | 360,000 | 140,000 | 40,000 |
| Total Stockholders' Equity | $720,000 | $350,000 | $200,000 |

*Required*

*a.* Prepare the journal entries recorded by Brown for its investment in Tann during 20X3.

*b.* Prepare the journal entries recorded by Promise for its investment in Brown during 20X3.

*c.* Prepare the eliminating entries related to Brown's investment in Tann and Promise's investment in Brown that are needed in preparing consolidated financial statements for Promise and its subsidiaries at December 31, 20X3.

**E9-10** **Reciprocal Ownership**

Grower Supply Corporation holds 85 percent of Schultz Company's voting common stock. At the end of 20X4, Schultz purchased 30 percent of Grower Supply's stock. Schultz records dividends received from Grower Supply as nonoperating income. In 20X5, Grower Supply and Schultz reported operating income of $112,000 and $50,000 and paid dividends of $70,000 and $30,000, respectively.

*Required*

Compute the amounts reported as consolidated net income and income assigned to the controlling interest for 20X5 under the treasury stock method.

**E9-11** **Consolidated Balance Sheet with Reciprocal Ownership**

Talbott Company purchased 80 percent of Short Company's stock on January 1, 20X8, at underlying book value. At that date, the fair value of the noncontrolling interest was equal to 20 percent of the book value of Short Company. On December 31, 20X9, Short purchased 10 percent of Talbott's stock. Balance sheets for the two companies on December 31, 20X9, are as follows:

**TALBOTT COMPANY**
**Condensed Balance Sheet**
**December 31, 20X9**

| | | | |
|---|---|---|---|
| Cash | $ 78,000 | Accounts Payable | $ 90,000 |
| Accounts Receivable | 120,000 | Bonds Payable | 400,000 |
| Inventory | 150,000 | Common Stock | 300,000 |
| Buildings and Equipment (net) | 400,000 | Retained Earnings | 310,000 |
| Investment in Short Company | | | |
| Common Stock | 352,000 | | |
| Total Assets | $1,100,000 | Total Liabilities and Equities | $1,100,000 |

### SHORT COMPANY
### Condensed Balance Sheet
### December 31, 20X9

| | | | |
|---|---:|---|---:|
| Cash | $ 39,000 | Accounts Payable | $ 60,000 |
| Accounts Receivable | 80,000 | Bonds Payable | 100,000 |
| Inventory | 120,000 | Common Stock | 200,000 |
| Buildings and Equipment (net) | 300,000 | Retained Earnings | 240,000 |
| Investment in Talbott Company | | | |
|    Common Stock | 61,000 | | |
| Total Assets | $600,000 | Total Liabilities and Equities | $600,000 |

### Required

Assuming that the treasury stock method is used in reporting Talbott's shares held by Short, prepare a consolidated balance sheet workpaper and consolidated balance sheet for December 31, 20X9.

**E9-12   Subsidiary Stock Dividend**

Lake Company reported the following summarized balance sheet data as of December 31, 20X2:

| | | | |
|---|---:|---|---:|
| Cash | $ 30,000 | Accounts Payable | $ 50,000 |
| Accounts Receivable | 80,000 | Common Stock | 100,000 |
| Inventory | 90,000 | Retained Earnings | 200,000 |
| Buildings and Equipment | 270,000 | | |
| Less: Accumulated Depreciation | (120,000) | | |
| Total Assets | $350,000 | Total Liabilities and Equities | $350,000 |

Lake issues 4,000 additional shares of its $10 par value stock to its shareholders as a stock dividend on April 20, 20X3. The market price of Lake's shares at the time of the stock dividend is $40. Lake reports net income of $25,000 and pays a $10,000 cash dividend in 20X3. Lindale Company acquired 70 percent of Lake's common shares at book value on January 1, 20X1. At that date, the fair value of the noncontrolling interest was equal to 30 percent of the book value of Lake Company. Lindale uses the basic equity method in accounting for its investment in Lake.

### Required

a. Give the journal entries recorded by Lake and Lindale at the time the stock dividend is declared and distributed.

b. Give the workpaper elimination entries needed to prepare consolidated financial statements for 20X3.

c. Give the workpaper elimination entry needed to prepare a consolidated balance sheet on January 1, 20X4.

**E9-13   Sale of Subsidiary Shares by Parent**

Stable Home Builders Inc. acquired 80 percent of the stock of Acme Concrete Works on January 1, 20X3, for $360,000. At that date, the fair value of the noncontrolling interest was $90,000. Acme Concrete's balance sheet contained the following amounts at the time of the combination:

| | | | |
|---|---:|---|---:|
| Cash | $ 30,000 | Accounts Payable | $ 50,000 |
| Accounts Receivable | 65,000 | Bonds Payable | 300,000 |
| Inventory | 15,000 | Common Stock | 200,000 |
| Construction Work in Progress | 470,000 | Retained Earnings | 250,000 |
| Other Assets (net) | 220,000 | | |
| Total Assets | $800,000 | Total Liabilities and Equities | $800,000 |

During each of the next three years, Acme Concrete reported net income of $50,000 and paid dividends of $20,000. On January 1, 20X5, Stable sold 4,000 of the Acme $10 par value shares for $120,000 in cash. Stable used the basic equity method in accounting for its ownership of Acme.

### Required

a. Compute the balance in the investment account reported by Stable on January 1, 20X5, before its sale of shares.

b. Prepare the entry recorded by Stable when it sold the Acme shares, assuming Stable records the excess of the sale price over the carrying value of the shares as an increase in additional paid-in capital.

c. Prepare the appropriate elimination entries to complete a full consolidation workpaper for 20X5.

**E9-14**  **Purchase of Additional Shares from Nonaffiliate**

Weal Corporation purchased 60 percent of Modern Products Company's shares on December 31, 20X7, for $210,000. At that date, the fair value of the noncontrolling interest was $140,000. On January 1, 20X9, Weal purchased an additional 20 percent of Modern's common stock for $96,000. Summarized balance sheets for Modern on the dates indicated are as follows:

|  | December 31 | | |
|---|---|---|---|
|  | **20X7** | **20X8** | **20X9** |
| Cash | $ 40,000 | $ 70,000 | $ 90,000 |
| Accounts Receivable | 50,000 | 90,000 | 120,000 |
| Inventory | 70,000 | 100,000 | 160,000 |
| Buildings and Equipment (net) | 340,000 | 320,000 | 300,000 |
| Total Assets | $500,000 | $580,000 | $670,000 |
| Accounts Payable | $ 50,000 | $100,000 | $140,000 |
| Bonds Payable | 100,000 | 100,000 | 100,000 |
| Common Stock | 150,000 | 150,000 | 150,000 |
| Retained Earnings | 200,000 | 230,000 | 280,000 |
| Total Liabilities and Equities | $500,000 | $580,000 | $670,000 |

Modern paid dividends of $20,000 in each of the three years. Weal uses the basic equity method in accounting for its investment in Modern and amortizes all differentials over 10 years against the related investment income. All differentials are assigned to patents in the consolidated financial statements.

### Required

a. Compute the balance in Weal's Investment in Modern Products Company Stock account on December 31, 20X8.

b. Compute the balance in Weal's Investment in Modern Products Company Stock account on December 31, 20X9.

c. Prepare the eliminating entries needed as of December 31, 20X9, to complete a three-part consolidation workpaper.

**E9-15**  **Repurchase of Shares by Subsidiary from Nonaffiliate**

Blatant Advertising Corporation acquired 60 percent of Quinn Manufacturing Company's shares on December 31, 20X1, at underlying book value of $180,000. At that date, the fair value of the noncontrolling interest was equal to 40 percent of the book value of Quinn Manufacturing. Quinn's balance sheet on January 1, 20X7, contained the following balances:

| | | | |
|---|---|---|---|
| Cash | $ 80,000 | Accounts Payable | $ 60,000 |
| Accounts Receivable | 100,000 | Bonds Payable | 240,000 |
| Inventory | 160,000 | Common Stock | 100,000 |
| Buildings and Equipment | 700,000 | Additional Paid-In Capital | 150,000 |
| Less: Accumulated Depreciation | (240,000) | Retained Earnings | 250,000 |
| Total Assets | $800,000 | Total Liabilities and Equities | $800,000 |

On January 1, 20X7, Quinn purchased 2,000 of its own $10 par value common shares from Non-affiliated Corporation for $42 per share.

### Required

*a.* Compute the change in the book value of the equity attributable to the parent as a result of the repurchase of shares by Quinn Manufacturing.

*b.* Give the entry to be recorded on Blatant Advertising's books to recognize the change in the book value of the shares it holds.

*c.* Give the eliminating entry needed in preparing a consolidated balance sheet immediately following the purchase of shares by Quinn.

**E9-16**     ### Sale of Shares by Subsidiary to Nonaffiliate

Browne Corporation purchased 11,000 shares of Schroeder Corporation on January 1, 20X3, at book value. At that date, the fair value of the noncontrolling interest was equal to 26.7 percent of the book value of Schroeder Corporation. On December 31, 20X8, Schroeder reported these balance sheet amounts:

| | | | |
|---|---|---|---|
| Cash | $ 80,000 | Accounts Payable | $ 50,000 |
| Accounts Receivable | 120,000 | Bonds Payable | 100,000 |
| Inventory | 200,000 | Common Stock | 150,000 |
| Buildings and Equipment | 600,000 | Additional Paid-In Capital | 50,000 |
| Less: Accumulated Depreciation | (250,000) | Retained Earnings | 400,000 |
| Total Assets | $750,000 | Total Liabilities and Equities | $750,000 |

On January 1, 20X9, Schroeder issued an additional 5,000 shares of its $10 par value common stock to Nonaffiliated Company for $80 per share.

### Required

*a.* Compute the change in book value of the shares held by Browne as a result of Schroeder's issuance of additional shares.

*b.* Give the entry to be recorded on Browne's books to recognize the change in book value of the shares it holds, assuming the change in book value is to be treated as an adjustment to additional paid-in capital.

*c.* Record the eliminating entry needed to prepare a consolidated balance sheet immediately after Schroeder's issuance of additional shares.

---

**Problems**     **P9-17**     ### Multiple-Choice Questions on Preferred Stock Ownership

Stacey Corporation owns 80 percent of the common shares and 70 percent of the preferred shares of Upland Company, all purchased at underlying book value on January 1, 20X2. At that date, the fair value of the noncontrolling interest in Upland's common stock was equal to 20 percent of the book value of its common stock. The balance sheets of Stacey and Upland immediately after the acquisition contained these balances:

| | Stacey Corporation | Upland Company |
|---|---|---|
| Cash and Receivables | $150,000 | $ 80,000 |
| Inventory | 200,000 | 100,000 |
| Buildings and Equipment (net) | 250,000 | 220,000 |
| Investment in Upland Preferred Stock | 70,000 | |
| Investment in Upland Common Stock | 200,000 | |
| Total Assets | $870,000 | $400,000 |
| Liabilities | $220,000 | $ 50,000 |
| Preferred Stock | | 100,000 |
| Common Stock | 300,000 | 200,000 |
| Retained Earnings | 350,000 | 50,000 |
| Total Liabilities and Equities | $870,000 | $400,000 |

The preferred stock issued by Upland pays a 10 percent dividend and is cumulative. For 20X2 Upland reports net income of $30,000 and pays no dividends. Stacey reports income from its separate operations of $100,000 and pays dividends of $40,000 during 20X2.

### Required

Select the correct answer for each of the following questions.

1. Total noncontrolling interest reported in the consolidated balance sheet as of January 1, 20X2, is:

   a. $30,000.
   b. $50,000.
   c. $70,000.
   d. $80,000.

2. Income assigned to the noncontrolling interest in the 20X2 consolidated income statement is:

   a. $6,000.
   b. $7,000.
   c. $9,000.
   d. $14,000.

3. What amount of income is attributable to the controlling interest for 20X2?

   a. $116,000.
   b. $123,000.
   c. $124,000.
   d. $130,000.

4. Total stockholders' equity reported in the consolidated balance sheet as of January 1, 20X2, is:

   a. $650,000.
   b. $700,000.
   c. $730,000.
   d. $1,000,000.

5. Preferred stock outstanding reported in the consolidated balance sheet as of January 1, 20X2, is:

   a. $0.
   b. $30,000.
   c. $70,000.
   d. $100,000.

**P9-18    Multilevel Ownership with Differential**

Purple Corporation owns 80 percent of Corn Corporation's common stock. It purchased the shares on January 1, 20X1, for $520,000. At the date of acquisition, the fair value of the noncontrolling interest was $130,000, and Corn reported common stock outstanding of $400,000 and retained earnings of $200,000. The differential is assigned to a trademark with a life of five years. Each year since acquisition, Corn has reported income from operations of $60,000 and paid dividends of $25,000.

Corn purchased 70 percent ownership of Bark Company on January 1, 20X3, for $406,000. At that date, the fair value of the noncontrolling interest was $174,000, and Bark reported common stock outstanding of $250,000 and retained earnings of $300,000. In 20X3, Bark reported net income of $30,000 and paid dividends of $20,000. The differential is assigned to buildings and equipment with an economic life of 10 years at the date of acquisition.

### Required

a. Prepare the journal entries recorded by Corn for its investment in Bark during 20X3.
b. Prepare the journal entries recorded by Purple for its investment in Corn during 20X3.
c. Prepare the eliminating entries related to Corn's investment in Bark and Purple's investment in Corn needed to prepare consolidated financial statements for Purple and its subsidiaries at December 31, 20X3.

**P9-19    Subsidiary Stock Dividend**

Pound Manufacturing Corporation prepared the following balance sheet as of January 1, 20X8:

| Cash | $ 40,000 | Accounts Payable | $ 50,000 |
|---|---|---|---|
| Accounts Receivable | 90,000 | Bonds Payable | 200,000 |
| Inventory | 180,000 | Common Stock | 100,000 |
| Buildings and Equipment | 500,000 | Additional Paid-In Capital | 70,000 |
| Less: Accumulated Depreciation | (110,000) | Retained Earnings | 280,000 |
| Total Assets | $700,000 | Total Liabilities and Equities | $700,000 |

The company is considering a 2-for-1 stock split, a stock dividend of 4,000 shares, or a stock dividend of 1,500 shares on its $10 par value common stock. The current market price per share of Pound stock on January 1, 20X8, is $50. Quick Sales Corporation acquired 68 percent of Pound's common shares on January 1, 20X4, at underlying book value. At that date, the fair value of the noncontrolling interest was equal to 32 percent of the book value of Pound Manufacturing.

### Required

Give the investment elimination entry required to prepare a consolidated balance sheet at the close of business on January 1, 20X8, for each of the alternative transactions under consideration by Pound Manufacturing.

**P9-20** **Subsidiary Preferred Stock Outstanding**

Emerald Corporation acquired 10,500 shares of the common stock and 800 shares of the 8 percent preferred stock of Pert Company on December 31, 20X4, at underlying book value. At that date, the fair value of the noncontrolling interest in Pert's common stock was equal to 30 percent of the book value of its common stock. Pert reported the following balance sheet amounts on January 1, 20X5:

| Cash | $ 30,000 | Accounts Payable | $ 20,000 |
|---|---|---|---|
| Accounts Receivable | 70,000 | Bonds Payable | 100,000 |
| Inventory | 120,000 | Preferred Stock | 200,000 |
| Buildings and Equipment | 600,000 | Common Stock | 150,000 |
| Less: Accumulated Depreciation | (150,000) | Retained Earnings | 200,000 |
| Total Assets | $670,000 | Total Liabilities and Equities | $670,000 |

Pert's preferred stock is $100 par value, and its common stock is $10 par value. The preferred dividends are cumulative and are two years in arrears on January 1, 20X5. Pert reports net income of $34,000 for 20X5 and pays no dividends.

### Required

a. Present the workpaper eliminating entries needed to prepare a consolidated balance sheet on January 1, 20X5.

b. Assuming that Emerald reported income from its separate operations of $80,000 in 20X5, compute the amount of consolidated net income and the amount of income to be assigned to the controlling shareholders in the 20X5 consolidated income statement.

**P9-21** **Ownership of Subsidiary Preferred Stock**

Presley Pools Inc. acquired 60 percent of the common stock of Jacobs Jacuzzi Company on December 31, 20X6, for $1,800,000. At that date, the fair value of the noncontrolling interest was $1,200,000. The full amount of the differential was assigned to goodwill. On December 31, 20X7, the management of Presley Pools reviewed the amount attributed to goodwill and concluded an impairment loss of $26,000 should be recognized in 20X7. On January 2, 20X7, Presley purchased 20 percent of the outstanding preferred shares of Jacobs for $42,000.

In its 20X6 annual report, Jacobs reported the following stockholders' equity balances at the end of the year:

| Preferred Stock (10 percent, $100 par) | $ 200,000 |
|---|---|
| Premium on Preferred Stock | 5,000 |
| Common Stock | 500,000 |
| Additional Paid-In Capital—Common | 800,000 |
| Retained Earnings | 1,650,000 |
| Total Stockholders' Equity | $3,155,000 |

The preferred stock is cumulative and has a liquidation value equal to its call price of $101 per share. Because of cash flow problems, Jacobs declared no dividends during 20X6, the first time it had missed a preferred dividend. With the improvement in operations during 20X7, Jacobs declared the current stated preferred dividend as well as preferred dividends in arrears; Jacobs also declared a common dividend for 20X7 of $10,000. Jacobs's reported net income for 20X7 was $280,000.

### Required

a. Compute the amount of the preferred stockholders' claim on Jacobs Jacuzzi's assets on December 31, 20X6.

b. Compute the December 31, 20X6, book value of the Jacobs common shares purchased by Presley.

c. Compute the amount of goodwill associated with Presley's acquisition of Jacobs common stock.

d. Compute the amount of income that should be assigned to the noncontrolling interest in the 20X7 consolidated income statement.

e. Compute the amount of income from its subsidiary that Presley should have recorded during 20X7 using the basic equity method.

f. Compute the total amount that should be reported as noncontrolling interest in the December 31, 20X7, consolidated balance sheet.

g. Present all elimination entries that should appear in a consolidation workpaper to prepare a complete set of 20X7 consolidated financial statements for Presley Pools and its subsidiary.

**P9-22 Consolidation Workpaper with Subsidiary Preferred Stock**

Brown Company owns 90 percent of the common stock and 60 percent of the preferred stock of White Corporation, both acquired at underlying book value on January 1, 20X1. At that date, the fair value of the noncontrolling interest in White Corporation's common stock was equal to 10 percent of the book value of its common stock. Trial balances for the companies on December 31, 20X6, are as follows:

|  | Brown Company Debit | Brown Company Credit | White Corporation Debit | White Corporation Credit |
|---|---|---|---|---|
| Cash | $ 58,000 | | $100,000 | |
| Accounts Receivable | 80,000 | | 120,000 | |
| Dividends Receivable | 9,000 | | | |
| Inventory | 100,000 | | 200,000 | |
| Buildings and Equipment (net) | 360,000 | | 270,000 | |
| Investment in White Corporation: | | | | |
| Preferred Stock | 120,000 | | | |
| Common Stock | 364,500 | | | |
| Cost of Goods Sold | 280,000 | | 170,000 | |
| Depreciation and Amortization | 40,000 | | 30,000 | |
| Other Expenses | 131,000 | | 20,000 | |
| Dividends Declared: | | | | |
| Preferred Stock | | | 15,000 | |
| Common Stock | 60,000 | | 10,000 | |
| Accounts Payable | | $ 100,000 | | $ 70,000 |
| Bonds Payable | | 300,000 | | |
| Dividends Payable | | | | 15,000 |
| Preferred Stock | | | | 200,000 |
| Common Stock | | 200,000 | | 100,000 |
| Retained Earnings | | 435,000 | | 250,000 |
| Sales | | 500,000 | | 300,000 |
| Dividend Income | | 9,000 | | |
| Income from Subsidiary | | 58,500 | | |
| Total | $1,602,500 | $1,602,500 | $935,000 | $935,000 |

White Corporation's preferred shares pay a 7.5 percent annual dividend and are cumulative. Preferred dividends for 20X6 were declared on December 31, 20X6, and are to be paid January 1, 20X7.

### Required

*a.* Prepare the eliminating entries needed to complete a full consolidation workpaper for 20X6.

*b.* Prepare a consolidation workpaper as of December 31, 20X6.

**P9-23**  **Subsidiary Stock Transactions**

Apex Corporation acquired 75 percent of Beta Company's common stock on May 15, 20X3, at underlying book value. Beta's balance sheet on December 31, 20X6, contained these amounts:

| | | | |
|---|---|---|---|
| Cash | $ 75,000 | Accounts Payable | $ 30,000 |
| Accounts Receivable | 50,000 | Bonds Payable | 200,000 |
| Inventory | 125,000 | Common Stock ($10 par) | 100,000 |
| Buildings and Equipment | 700,000 | Additional Paid-In Capital | 80,000 |
| Less: Accumulated Depreciation | (220,000) | Retained Earnings | 320,000 |
| Total Assets | $730,000 | Total Liabilities and Equities | $730,000 |

During 20X7, Apex earned operating income of $90,000, and Beta reported net income of $45,000. Neither company declared any dividends during 20X7.

Beta is considering repurchasing 1,000 of its outstanding shares as treasury stock for $68 each.

### Required

*a.* Assuming Beta purchases the shares from Nonaffiliated Company on January 1, 20X7:

  (1) Compute the effect on the book value of the shares held by Apex.

  (2) Give the entry on Apex's books to record the change in the book value of its investment in Beta's shares.

  (3) Prepare the eliminating entries needed on December 31, 20X7, to complete a consolidation workpaper.

*b.* Assuming Beta purchases the shares directly from Apex on January 1, 20X7:

  (1) Compute the effect on the book value of the shares held by Apex.

  (2) Give the entry on Apex's books to record its sale of Beta shares to Beta.

  (3) Prepare the eliminating entries needed on December 31, 20X7, to complete a consolidation workpaper.

**P9-24**  **Sale of Subsidiary Shares**

Penn Corporation purchased 80 percent ownership of ENC Company on January 1, 20X2, at underlying book value. At that date, the fair value of the noncontrolling interest was equal to 20 percent of the book value of ENC. On January 1, 20X4, Penn sold 2,000 shares of ENC's stock for $60,000 to American School Products and recorded a $10,000 gain. Trial balances for the companies on December 31, 20X4, contain the following data:

| | Penn Corporation | | ENC Company | |
|---|---|---|---|---|
| | **Debit** | **Credit** | **Debit** | **Credit** |
| Cash | $ 30,000 | | $ 35,000 | |
| Accounts Receivable | 70,000 | | 50,000 | |
| Inventory | 120,000 | | 100,000 | |
| Buildings and Equipment | 650,000 | | 230,000 | |
| Investment in ENC Company | 162,000 | | | |
| Cost of Goods Sold | 210,000 | | 100,000 | |
| Depreciation Expense | 20,000 | | 15,000 | |
| Other Expenses | 21,000 | | 25,000 | |
| Dividends Declared | 15,000 | | 10,000 | |

*(continued)*

| | | | |
|---|---:|---:|---:|
| Accumulated Depreciation | | $ 170,000 | $ 95,000 |
| Accounts Payable | | 50,000 | 20,000 |
| Bonds Payable | | 200,000 | 30,000 |
| Common Stock ($10 par) | | 200,000 | 100,000 |
| Additional Paid-In Capital | | 50,000 | 20,000 |
| Retained Earnings | | 320,000 | 130,000 |
| Sales | | 280,000 | 170,000 |
| Gain on Sale of ENC Company Stock | | 10,000 | |
| Income from Subsidiary | | 18,000 | |
| Total | $1,298,000 | $1,298,000 | $565,000 $565,000 |

ENC's net income was earned evenly throughout the year. Both companies declared and paid their dividends on December 31, 20X4. Penn uses the basic equity method in accounting for its investment in ENC.

### Required

*a.* Prepare the elimination entries needed to complete a full consolidation workpaper for 20X4.

*b.* Prepare a consolidation workpaper for 20X4.

**P9-25**  **Sale of Shares by Subsidiary to Nonaffiliate**

Craft Corporation held 80 percent of Delta Corporation's outstanding common shares on December 31, 20X2, which it had acquired at underlying book value. When the shares were acquired, the fair value of the noncontrolling interest was equal to 20 percent of the book value of Delta Corporation. Balance sheets for the two companies on that date follow:

**CRAFT CORPORATION**
**Balance Sheet**
**December 31, 20X2**

| | | | |
|---|---:|---|---:|
| Cash | $ 50,000 | Accounts Payable | $ 70,000 |
| Accounts Receivable | 90,000 | Mortgages Payable | 250,000 |
| Inventory | 180,000 | Common Stock | 300,000 |
| Buildings and Equipment | 700,000 | Additional Paid-In Capital | 180,000 |
| Less: Accumulated Depreciation | (200,000) | Retained Earnings | 500,000 |
| Investment in Delta Corporation | 480,000 | | |
| Total Assets | $1,300,000 | Total Liabilities and Equities | $1,300,000 |

**DELTA CORPORATION**
**Balance Sheet**
**December 31, 20X2**

| | | | |
|---|---:|---|---:|
| Cash | $ 50,000 | Accounts Payable | $ 70,000 |
| Accounts Receivable | 120,000 | Taxes Payable | 80,000 |
| Inventory | 200,000 | Common Stock | 200,000 |
| Buildings and Equipment | 600,000 | Additional Paid-In Capital | 50,000 |
| Less: Accumulated Depreciation | (220,000) | Retained Earnings | 350,000 |
| Total Assets | $750,000 | Total Liabilities and Equities | $750,000 |

On January 1, 20X3, Delta issued 4,000 additional shares of its $10 par value common stock to Nonaffiliated Corporation for $45 per share. Craft recorded the change in the book value of its Delta shares as an adjustment to its investment in Delta and an adjustment to its additional paid-in capital.

### Required

*a.* Give the workpaper elimination entry needed in preparing a consolidated balance sheet as of January 1, 20X3, immediately following the sale of shares by Delta.

b. Prepare a consolidated balance sheet workpaper as of the close of business on January 1, 20X3.

c. Prepare a consolidated balance sheet as of the close of business on January 1, 20X3.

**P9-26    Sale of Additional Shares to Parent**

Lane Manufacturing Company acquired 75 percent of the stock of Tin Corporation at underlying book value. At the date of acquisition, the fair value of the noncontrolling interest was equal to 25 percent of the book value of Tin Corporation. The balance sheets of the two companies for January 1, 20X1, are as follows:

**LANE MANUFACTURING COMPANY**
**Balance Sheet**
**January 1, 20X1**

| | | | |
|---|---|---|---|
| Cash | $ 227,500 | Accounts Payable | $ 50,000 |
| Accounts Receivable | 60,000 | Bonds Payable | 400,000 |
| Inventory | 100,000 | Common Stock | 200,000 |
| Buildings and Equipment | 600,000 | Additional Paid-In Capital | 50,000 |
| Less: Accumulated Depreciation | (150,000) | Retained Earnings | 400,000 |
| Investment in Tin Products | 262,500 | | |
| Total Assets | $1,100,000 | Total Liabilities and Equities | $1,100,000 |

**TIN CORPORATION**
**Balance Sheet**
**January 1, 20X1**

| | | | |
|---|---|---|---|
| Cash | $ 60,000 | Accounts Payable | $ 50,000 |
| Accounts Receivable | 100,000 | Bonds Payable | 300,000 |
| Inventory | 180,000 | Common Stock ($10 par) | 100,000 |
| Buildings and Equipment | 600,000 | Additional Paid-In Capital | 50,000 |
| Less: Accumulated Depreciation | (240,000) | Retained Earnings | 200,000 |
| Total Assets | $700,000 | Total Liabilities and Equities | $700,000 |

On January 2, 20X1, Lane purchased an additional 2,500 shares of common stock directly from Tin for $150,000. Any purchase differential is assigned to buildings and equipment.

*Required*

a. Prepare the eliminating entry needed to complete a consolidated balance sheet workpaper immediately following the issuance of additional shares to Lane.

b. Prepare a consolidated balance sheet workpaper immediately following the issuance of additional shares to Lane.

**P9-27    Complex Ownership Structure**

First Boston Corporation acquired 80 percent of the common stock of Gulfside Corporation on January 1, 20X5. Gulfside holds 60 percent of the voting shares of Paddock Company, and Paddock owns 10 percent of the stock of First Boston. All acquisitions were made at underlying book value. The fair value of the noncontrolling interest in Gulfside was equal to 20 percent of the book value of Gulfside when acquired by First Boston, and the fair value of the noncontrolling interest in Paddock was equal to 40 percent of its book value when control was acquired by Gulfside. During 20X7, income from the separate operations of First Boston, Gulfside, and Paddock was $44,000, $34,000, and $50,000, respectively, and dividends of $30,000, $20,000, and $10,000, respectively, were paid. The companies use the cost method of accounting for intercorporate investments and, accordingly, record dividends received as other (nonoperating) income.

*Required*

Compute the amount of consolidated net income and the income to be assigned to the noncontrolling shareholders of Gulfside and Paddock for 20X7 using the treasury stock method.

# Additional Consolidation Reporting Issues

The financial statements of a consolidated entity must be prepared in conformity with generally accepted accounting principles in the same manner as for any individual enterprise. Standards of reporting and presentation are no different for a consolidated entity than for a single-corporate entity. This chapter discusses the following general financial reporting topics as they relate to consolidated financial statements:

1. The consolidated statement of cash flows.
2. Consolidation following an interim acquisition.
3. Consolidation tax considerations.
4. Consolidated earnings per share.

## CONSOLIDATED STATEMENT OF CASH FLOWS

Consolidated entities, as with individual companies, must present a *statement of cash flows* when they issue a complete set of financial statements. A consolidated statement of cash flows is similar to a statement of cash flows prepared for a single-corporate entity and is prepared in basically the same manner.

### Preparation of a Consolidated Cash Flow Statement

A consolidated statement of cash flows is typically prepared after the consolidated income statement, retained earnings statement, and balance sheet. Rather than being included in the three-part consolidation workpaper, the consolidated cash flow statement is prepared from the information in the other three statements. When an indirect approach is used in preparing the statement, with consolidated net income as the starting point, consolidated net income must be adjusted for all items that affect consolidated net income and the cash of the consolidated entity differently. Preparation of a consolidated statement of cash flows requires only a few adjustments (such as those for depreciation and amortization resulting from the write-off of a differential) beyond those used in preparing a cash flow statement for an individual company.

As in the other consolidated financial statements, all transfers between affiliates should be eliminated in preparing the consolidated statement of cash flows. Although the sale or purchase of assets is a source or use of cash to an individual company, if such activities occur entirely within the consolidated entity, they should not be included in the statement of cash flows. Unrealized profits on intercompany transfers are eliminated in preparing the consolidated balance sheet and income statement, and therefore no additional elimination of unrealized intercompany profits is needed in preparing the statement of cash flows.

The existence of a noncontrolling interest typically does not cause any special problems. In and of itself, the noncontrolling interest neither generates nor uses cash. Receipts from and payments to noncontrolling shareholders usually are included in the consolidated cash flow statement as cash flows related to financing activities. For example, dividend payments to noncontrolling shareholders normally are included along with dividend payments to parent company shareholders as a use of cash. A sale of additional shares to noncontrolling shareholders or a repurchase of shares from them is considered to be a transaction with a nonaffiliate and is reported as a source or use of cash.

## Consolidated Cash Flow Statement Illustrated

As an example of the preparation of a consolidated cash flow statement, assume the following:

1. Peerless Products purchases 80 percent of Special Foods common stock on December 31, 20X0, for $66,000 above book value. At the date of acquisition, the noncontrolling interest has a fair value $16,500 in excess of its book value. The total differential at the date of acquisition is $82,500 ($66,000 + $16,500).

2. Of the $82,500 total differential, $10,000 is assigned to land, $60,000 to equipment with a 10-year remaining life, and $12,500 to goodwill. Management determines that the goodwill is impaired and writes it down by $3,125 at the end of 20X1; the value of the goodwill remains constant thereafter.

3. During 20X2, Peerless pays dividends of $60,000; Special Foods reports net income of $75,000 and pays dividends of $40,000.

4. During 20X2, Peerless sells land that it had purchased in 20X1 for $40,000 to a non-affiliate for $70,000.

5. Special Foods purchases additional equipment from an unrelated company at the end of 20X2 for $100,000.

Consolidated balance sheet information as of December 31, 20X1 and 20X2, follows:

|  | December 31 | |
| --- | --- | --- |
|  | **20X1** | **20X2** |
| Cash | $ 269,000 | $ 276,000 |
| Accounts Receivable | 125,000 | 230,000 |
| Inventories | 175,000 | 270,000 |
| Land | 225,000 | 185,000 |
| Buildings and Equipment | 1,460,000 | 1,560,000 |
| Goodwill | 9,375 | 9,375 |
| Total Debits | $2,263,375 | $2,530,375 |
| Accumulated Depreciation | $ 776,000 | $ 852,000 |
| Accounts Payable | 200,000 | 230,000 |
| Bonds Payable | 300,000 | 300,000 |
| Common Stock | 500,000 | 500,000 |
| Retained Earnings | 408,700 | 563,900 |
| Noncontrolling Interest | 78,675 | 84,475 |
| Total Credits | $2,263,375 | $2,530,375 |

The consolidated income statement for 20X2 is as follows:

| | | |
| --- | --- | --- |
| Sales | | $720,000 |
| Gain on Sale of Land | | 30,000 |
| | | $750,000 |
| Less: Cost of Goods Sold | $340,000 | |
| Depreciation Expense | 76,000 | |
| Other Expenses | 105,000 | (521,000) |
| Consolidated Net Income | | $229,000 |
| Income to Noncontrolling Interest | | (13,800) |
| Income to Controlling Interest | | $215,200 |

**FIGURE 10–1** Workpaper for Peerless Products and Subsidiary Consolidated Statement of Cash Flows, 20X2

| Item | Balance 1/1/X2 | Debits | Credits | Balance 12/31/X2 |
|---|---|---|---|---|
| Cash | 269,000 | 7,000 (*a*) | | 276,000 |
| Accounts Receivable | 125,000 | 105,000 (*b*) | | 230,000 |
| Inventory | 175,000 | 95,000 (*c*) | | 270,000 |
| Land | 225,000 | | 40,000 (*d*) | 185,000 |
| Buildings and Equipment | 1,460,000 | 100,000 (*e*) | | 1,560,000 |
| Goodwill | 9,375 | | | 9,375 |
| | 2,263,375 | | | 2,530,375 |
| | | | | |
| Accumulated Depreciation | 776,000 | | 76,000 (*f*) | 852,000 |
| Accounts Payable | 200,000 | | 30,000 (*g*) | 230,000 |
| Bonds Payable | 300,000 | | | 300,000 |
| Common Stock | 500,000 | | | 500,000 |
| Retained Earnings | 408,700 | 60,000 (*h*) | 215,200 (*i*) | 563,900 |
| Noncontrolling Interest | 78,675 | 8,000 (*j*) | 13,800 (*i*) | 84,475 |
| | 2,263,375 | 375,000 | 375,000 | 2,530,375 |
| | | | | |
| Cash Flows from Operating Activities: | | | | |
| Consolidated Net Income | | 229,000 (*i*) | | |
| Depreciation Expense | | 76,000 (*f*) | | |
| Gain on Sale of Land | | | 30,000 (*d*) | |
| Increase in Accounts Receivable | | | 105,000 (*b*) | |
| Increase in Inventory | | | 95,000 (*c*) | |
| Increase in Accounts Payable | | 30,000 (*g*) | | |
| Cash Flows from Investing Activities: | | | | |
| Acquisition of Equipment | | | 100,000 (*e*) | |
| Sale of Land | | 70,000 (*d*) | | |
| Cash Flows from Financing Activities: | | | | |
| Dividends to Parent Company Shareholders | | | 60,000 (*h*) | |
| Dividends to Noncontrolling Shareholders | | | 8,000 (*j*) | |
| Increase in Cash | | | 7,000 (*a*) | |
| | | 405,000 | 405,000 | |

(*a*) Increase in cash balance.
(*b*) Increase in accounts receivable.
(*c*) Increase in inventory.
(*d*) Sale of land.
(*e*) Purchase of buildings and equipment.
(*f*) Depreciation charges for 20X2.
(*g*) Increase in accounts payable.
(*h*) Peerless dividends, $60,000.
(*i*) Consolidated net income, $229,000.
(*j*) Special Foods dividends to noncontrolling interest ($40,000 × .20).

A workpaper to prepare a consolidated statement of cash flows is presented in Figure 10–1. Although a number of different workpaper formats may be used in preparing statements of cash flows, the workpaper for preparing a consolidated statement of cash flows is no different from that used for a single-corporate entity. The essential workpaper entries can be seen in Figure 10–1. The consolidated statement of cash flows is prepared from the bottom portion of the workpaper.

Peerless's consolidated statement of cash flows for 20X2 is shown in Figure 10–2. The statement is similar to one that would be prepared for a single company. The only item that is different from what would be found in the cash flow statement of a single company relates to subsidiary dividends. The dividends paid to subsidiary noncontrolling shareholders result in an outflow of cash from the consolidated entity even though they are not shown as dividends declared in the consolidated retained earnings statement. Although not viewed as distributions of consolidated retained earnings, dividends to the noncontrolling shareholders use cash in reducing the noncontrolling interest.

**FIGURE 10–2**
Consolidated
Statement of Cash
Flows for the Year
Ended December 31,
20X2

| PEERLESS PRODUCTS CORPORATION AND SUBSIDIARY Consolidated Statement of Cash Flows For the Year Ended December 31, 20X2 | | |
|---|---|---|
| Cash Flows from Operating Activities: | | |
| Consolidated Net Income | | $ 229,000 |
| Noncash Expenses, Revenues, Losses, and Gains included in Income: | | |
| Depreciation Expense | | 76,000 |
| Gain on Sale of Land | | (30,000) |
| Increase in Accounts Receivable | | (105,000) |
| Increase in Inventory | | (95,000) |
| Increase in Accounts Payable | | 30,000 |
| Net Cash Provided by Operating Activities | | $105,000 |
| Cash Flows from Investing Activities: | | |
| Acquisition of Equipment | $(100,000) | |
| Sale of Land | 70,000 | |
| Net Cash Used in Investing Activities | | (30,000) |
| Cash Flows from Financing Activities: | | |
| Dividends Paid: | | |
| To Parent Company Shareholders | $ (60,000) | |
| To Noncontrolling Shareholders | (8,000) | |
| Net Cash Used in Financing Activities | | (68,000) |
| Net Increase in Cash | | $   7,000 |
| Cash at Beginning of Year | | 269,000 |
| Cash at End of Year | | $276,000 |

## Consolidated Cash Flow Statement—Direct Method

Although nearly all major companies use the indirect method of presenting a cash flow statement, as illustrated in the previous example, critics have argued that the direct method is less confusing and more useful. Authoritative bodies have generally expressed a preference for the direct method even though they have not required its use.

Using the same information as in the illustration of the indirect method, Figure 10–3 shows a workpaper for the preparation of a consolidated cash flow statement using the direct method. The only section of the cash flow statement affected by the difference in approaches is the operating activities section. Under the indirect approach, as in Figure 10–2, the operating activities section starts with net income and, to derive cash provided by operating activities, adjusts for all items affecting cash and net income differently. Under the direct approach in Figure 10–3, the operating activities section of the statement shows the actual cash flows. In this example, the only cash flows related to operations are as follows:

| Cash Flows from Operating Activities: | |
|---|---|
| Cash Received from Customers | $615,000 |
| Cash Paid to Suppliers | (510,000) |
| Net Cash Provided by Operating Activities | $105,000 |

The final number in this section is the same under both approaches, but this method provides a clearer picture of cash flows related to operations than does the indirect approach. Cash received from customers equals the sales revenue ($720,000) from the consolidated income statement minus the increase in accounts receivable ($105,000). Cash paid to suppliers equals cost of goods sold ($340,000), plus other expenses ($105,000), plus the increase in inventory ($95,000), minus the increase in accounts payable ($30,000).

**FIGURE 10–3** **Workpaper for Peerless Products and Subsidiary Consolidated Statement of Cash Flows—Direct Method, 20X2**

| Item | Balance 1/1/X2 | Debits | Credits | Balance 12/31/X2 |
|---|---|---|---|---|
| Cash | 269,000 | 7,000 (a) | | 276,000 |
| Accounts Receivable | 125,000 | 105,000 (b) | | 230,000 |
| Inventory | 175,000 | 95,000 (c) | | 270,000 |
| Land | 225,000 | | 40,000 (d) | 185,000 |
| Buildings and Equipment | 1,460,000 | 100,000 (e) | | 1,560,000 |
| Goodwill | 9,375 | | | 9,375 |
| | 2,263,375 | | | 2,530,375 |
| | | | | |
| Accumulated Depreciation | 776,000 | | 76,000 (f) | 852,000 |
| Accounts Payable | 200,000 | | 30,000 (c) | 230,000 |
| Bonds Payable | 300,000 | | | 300,000 |
| Common Stock | 500,000 | | | 500,000 |
| Retained Earnings | 408,700 | 60,000 (g) | 215,200 (h) | 563,900 |
| Noncontrolling Interest | 78,675 | 8,000 (i) | 13,800 (h) | 84,475 |
| | 2,263,375 | 375,000 | 375,000 | 2,530,375 |
| | | | | |
| Sales | 720,000 | | 720,000 (b) | |
| Gain on Sale of Land | 30,000 | | 30,000 (d) | |
| | 750,000 | | | |
| Cost of Goods Sold | 340,000 | 340,000 (c) | | |
| Depreciation Expense | 76,000 | 76,000 (f) | | |
| Other Expenses | 105,000 | 105,000 (c) | | |
| | 521,000 | | | |
| Consolidated Net Income | 229,000 | 229,000 (h) | | |
| | | 750,000 | 750,000 | |

| | | | | |
|---|---|---|---|---|
| Cash Flows from Operating Activities: | | | | |
| Cash Received from Customers | | 615,000 (b) | | |
| Cash Paid to Suppliers | | | 510,000 (c) | |
| Cash Flows from Investing Activities: | | | | |
| Acquisition of Equipment | | | 100,000 (e) | |
| Sale of Land | | 70,000 (d) | | |
| Cash Flows from Financing Activities: | | | | |
| Dividends to Parent Company Shareholders | | | 60,000 (g) | |
| Dividends to Noncontrolling Shareholders | | | 8,000 (i) | |
| Increase in Cash | | | 7,000 (a) | |
| | | 685,000 | 685,000 | |

(*a*) Increase in cash balance.
(*b*) Payments received from customers.
(*c*) Payments to suppliers.
(*d*) Sale of land.
(*e*) Acquisition of equipment.
(*f*) Depreciation charges for 20X2.
(*g*) Peerless dividends, $60,000.
(*h*) Consolidated net income, $229,000.
(*i*) Special Foods dividends to noncontrolling interest ($40,000 × .20).

The remainder of the cash flow statement is the same under both approaches except that a separate reconciliation of operating cash flows and net income is required under the direct approach.

# CONSOLIDATION FOLLOWING AN INTERIM ACQUISITION

When one company purchases another company's common stock, the subsidiary is viewed as being part of the consolidated entity only from the time the stock is acquired. Consequently, when a subsidiary is acquired during a fiscal period rather than at the beginning or end, the results of the subsidiary's operations are included in the consolidated statements only for the portion of the year that the stock is owned by the parent. The subsidiary's revenues, expenses, gains, and losses for the portion of the fiscal period prior to the time at which the parent acquired its controlling financial interest in the subsidiary must be excluded from the consolidated financial statements.

To better understand consolidation following an interim acquisition, assume that on July 1, 20X1, Peerless Products purchases 80 percent of Special Foods' common stock for its underlying book value of $246,400. At the time of acquisition, the $61,600 fair value of Special Foods' noncontrolling interest is equal to its book value.

For the year 20X1, Special Foods reports the following items:

| | Before Combination (January 1 to June 30) | After Combination (July 1 to December 31) |
|---|---|---|
| Sales | $80,000 | $120,000 |
| Cost of Goods Sold | 46,000 | 69,000 |
| Depreciation and Amortization | 8,000 | 12,000 |
| Other Expenses | 6,000 | 9,000 |
| Net Income | 20,000 | 30,000 |
| Dividends | 12,000 | 18,000 |

The book value of Special Foods' stock acquired by Peerless on July 1, 20X1, is computed as follows:

| | |
|---|---|
| Book value of Special Foods on January 1, 20X1: | |
| Common stock | $200,000 |
| Retained earnings | 100,000 |
| | $300,000 |
| Net income, January 1 to June 30, 20X1 | 20,000 |
| Dividends, January 1 to June 30, 20X1 | (12,000) |
| Book value of Special Foods on July 1, 20X1 | $308,000 |
| Peerless's ownership interest | × .80 |
| Book value on July 1, 20X1, of shares acquired by Peerless | $246,400 |

The ownership situation on July 1, 20X1, is as follows:

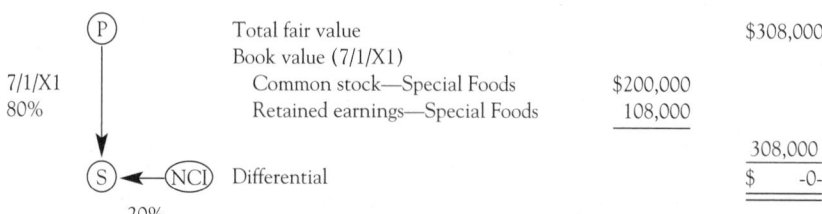

| | | |
|---|---|---|
| Total fair value | | $308,000 |
| Book value (7/1/X1) | | |
| Common stock—Special Foods | $200,000 | |
| Retained earnings—Special Foods | 108,000 | |
| | | 308,000 |
| Differential | | $ -0- |

## Parent Company Entries

Peerless records the purchase of Special Foods stock with the following entry:

July 1, 20X1

| | | | |
|---|---|---:|---:|
| (1) | Investment in Special Foods Stock | 246,400 | |
| | Cash | | 246,400 |
| | Record purchase of Special Foods stock. | | |

During the second half of 20X1, Peerless records its share of Special Foods' income and dividends under the equity method:

| | | | |
|---|---|---:|---:|
| (2) | Cash | 14,400 | |
| | Investment in Special Foods Stock | | 14,400 |
| | Record dividends from Special Foods: | | |
| | $18,000 × .80 | | |
| | | | |
| (3) | Investment in Special Foods Stock | 24,000 | |
| | Income from Subsidiary | | 24,000 |
| | Record equity-method income: | | |
| | $30,000 × .80 | | |

## Consolidation Workpaper

The consolidation workpaper reflecting the interim acquisition of Special Foods stock during 20X1 is presented in Figure 10–4. The trial balance of Special Foods for 20X1 is the same as used previously in Figure 5–5. The trial balance for Peerless is the same as in Figure 5–5 except that the amount of Peerless's cash reflects the interim purchase, as does the income from Special Foods recognized by Peerless.

The elimination entries in the consolidation workpaper prepared as of December 31, 20X1, are as follows:

| | | | |
|---|---|---:|---:|
| E(4) | Income from Subsidiary | 24,000 | |
| | Dividends Declared | | 14,400 |
| | Investment in Special Foods Stock | | 9,600 |
| | Eliminate income from subsidiary. | | |
| | | | |
| E(5) | Income to Noncontrolling Interest | 6,000 | |
| | Dividends Declared | | 3,600 |
| | Noncontrolling Interest | | 2,400 |
| | Assign income to noncontrolling interest, from July 1: | | |
| | $6,000 = $30,000 × .20 | | |
| | $3,600 = $18,000 × .20 | | |
| | | | |
| E(6) | Common Stock—Special Foods | 200,000 | |
| | Retained Earnings, January 1 | 100,000 | |
| | Sales | 80,000 | |
| | Cost of Goods Sold | | 46,000 |
| | Depreciation and Amortization | | 8,000 |
| | Other Expenses | | 6,000 |
| | Dividends Declared | | 12,000 |
| | Investment in Special Foods Stock | | 246,400 |
| | Noncontrolling Interest | | 61,600 |
| | Eliminate investment balance, subsidiary stockholders' equity, and subsidiary preacquisition income and dividends. | | |

**FIGURE 10–4** December 31, 20X1, Equity-Method Workpaper for Consolidated Financial Statements, Year of Combination; 80 Percent Purchase at Book Value; Interim Acquisition

| Item | Peerless Products | Special Foods | Eliminations Debit | Eliminations Credit | Consolidated |
|---|---|---|---|---|---|
| Sales | 400,000 | 200,000 | (6) 80,000 | | 520,000 |
| Income from Subsidiary | 24,000 | | (4) 24,000 | | |
| Credits | 424,000 | 200,000 | | | 520,000 |
| Cost of Goods Sold | 170,000 | 115,000 | | (6) 46,000 | 239,000 |
| Depreciation and Amortization | 50,000 | 20,000 | | (6) 8,000 | 62,000 |
| Other Expenses | 40,000 | 15,000 | | (6) 6,000 | 49,000 |
| Debits | (260,000) | (150,000) | | | (350,000) |
| Consolidated Net Income | | | | | 170,000 |
| Income to Noncontrolling Interest | | | (5) 6,000 | | (6,000) |
| Income, carry forward | 164,000 | 50,000 | 110,000 | 60,000 | 164,000 |
| Retained Earnings, January 1 | 300,000 | 100,000 | (6) 100,000 | | 300,000 |
| Income, from above | 164,000 | 50,000 | 110,000 | 60,000 | 164,000 |
| | 464,000 | 150,000 | | | 464,000 |
| Dividends Declared | (60,000) | (30,000) | | (4) 14,400 | |
| | | | | (5) 3,600 | |
| | | | | (6) 12,000 | (60,000) |
| Retained Earnings, December 31, carry forward | 404,000 | 120,000 | 210,000 | 90,000 | 404,000 |
| Cash | 248,000 | 75,000 | | | 323,000 |
| Accounts Receivable | 75,000 | 50,000 | | | 125,000 |
| Inventory | 100,000 | 75,000 | | | 175,000 |
| Land | 175,000 | 40,000 | | | 215,000 |
| Buildings and Equipment | 800,000 | 600,000 | | | 1,400,000 |
| Investment in Special Foods Stock | 256,000 | | | (4) 9,600 | |
| | | | | (6) 246,400 | |
| Debits | 1,654,000 | 840,000 | | | 2,238,000 |
| Accumulated Depreciation | 450,000 | 320,000 | | | 770,000 |
| Accounts Payable | 100,000 | 100,000 | | | 200,000 |
| Bonds Payable | 200,000 | 100,000 | | | 300,000 |
| Common Stock | 500,000 | 200,000 | (6) 200,000 | | 500,000 |
| Retained Earnings, from above | 404,000 | 120,000 | 210,000 | 90,000 | 404,000 |
| Noncontrolling Interest | | | | (5) 2,400 | |
| | | | | (6) 61,600 | 64,000 |
| Credits | 1,654,000 | 840,000 | 410,000 | 410,000 | 2,238,000 |

Elimination entries:
(4) Eliminate income from subsidiary.
(5) Assign income to noncontrolling interest, from July 1.
(6) Eliminate investment balance, subsidiary stockholders' equity, subsidiary preacquisition income and dividends.

Entry E(4) eliminates the income from Special Foods that Peerless has recognized since the date of combination ($30,000 × .80), Peerless's share of Special Foods' dividends declared since the date of combination ($18,000 × .80), and the change in Peerless's investment account since the date of combination. Entry E(5) assigns the noncontrolling interest's share of Special Foods' postacquisition income to the noncontrolling interest and eliminates the noncontrolling shareholders' portion of the dividends declared by Special Foods subsequent to acquisition. Entry E(6) eliminates Special Foods' stockholders' equity accounts as of the beginning of the year. It also eliminates the parent's investment account as of the date of acquisition (July 1) and establishes the noncontrolling interest in the workpaper at its fair value on that date. In the current example, the fair value of the noncontrolling interest on the date of combination is equal to its book value. If the fair value of the noncontrolling interest and the consideration given by the parent in the combination had been in excess of book value, those amounts would be included in this entry and a differential would be recorded.

Entry E(6) also eliminates the dividends declared by Special Foods prior to acquisition, completing, together with entries E(4) and E(5), the elimination of all of Special Foods' 20X1 dividends. Finally, entry E(6) eliminates Special Foods' revenues earned and expenses incurred before Special Foods became part of the consolidated entity.

The consolidated income statement prepared for the year of the interim acquisition reflects the inclusion of Special Foods in the consolidated entity only from July 1, the date of acquisition. All of Special Foods' revenues and expenses prior to the date of acquisition are excluded, and the statement appears as follows:

---

**PEERLESS PRODUCTS CORPORATION AND SUBSIDIARY**
**Consolidated Income Statement**
**For the Year Ended December 31, 20X1**

| | | |
|---|---:|---:|
| Sales | | $520,000 |
| Cost of Goods Sold | | (239,000) |
| Gross Margin | | $281,000 |
| Expenses: | | |
| Depreciation and Amortization | $62,000 | |
| Other Expenses | 49,000 | |
| Total Expenses | | (111,000) |
| Consolidated Net Income | | $170,000 |
| Income Attributable to the Noncontrolling Interest | | (6,000) |
| Income Attributable to the Controlling Interest | | $164,000 |

---

Consolidated net income is the same following the procedures illustrated as if Special Foods' books had been closed immediately before the combination and a new fiscal period started on the date of combination.

# CONSOLIDATION INCOME TAX ISSUES

A parent company and its subsidiaries may file a ***consolidated income tax return,*** or they may choose to file separate returns. For a subsidiary to be eligible to be included in a consolidated tax return, at least 80 percent of its stock must be held by the parent company or another company included in the consolidated return.

A major advantage of filing a consolidated return is the ability to offset the losses of one company against the profits of another. In addition, dividends and other transfers between the affiliated companies are not taxed. Thus, tax payments on profits from intercompany transfers can be delayed until the intercompany profits are realized through transactions with nonaffiliates. When separate returns are filed, the selling company is required to pay tax on the intercompany profits it has recognized, whether or not the profits are realized from a consolidated viewpoint. Filing a consolidated return also may make it possible to avoid limits on the use of certain items such as foreign tax credits and charitable contributions.

An election to file a consolidated income tax return carries with it some limitations. Once an election is made to include a subsidiary in the consolidated return, the company cannot file separate tax returns in the future unless it receives approval from the Internal Revenue Service. The subsidiary's tax year also must be brought into conformity with the parent's tax year. In addition, preparing a consolidated tax return can become quite difficult when numerous companies are involved and complex ownership arrangements exist between the companies.

The income tax aspects associated with equity-method reporting for unconsolidated investees were discussed in Chapter 2. Two consolidation financial reporting issues relating to income taxes are discussed in this chapter:

1. Allocation of income tax amounts from a consolidated tax return to the individual companies.
2. Tax effects of unrealized intercompany profit eliminations.

## Allocation of Tax Expense When a Consolidated Return Is Filed

A consolidated tax return portrays the companies included in the return as if they actually were a single legal entity. All intercorporate transfers of goods and services and intercompany dividends are eliminated and a single income tax figure is assessed when a consolidated return is prepared.

Consolidated companies sometimes need to prepare separate financial statements for noncontrolling shareholders and creditors. Because only a single income tax amount is determined for the consolidated entity when a consolidated tax return is filed, income tax expense must be assigned to the individual companies included in the return in some manner. The way in which the consolidated income tax amount is allocated to the individual companies can affect the amounts reported in the income statements of both the separate companies and the consolidated entity. When a subsidiary is less than 100 percent owned by the parent, income tax expense assigned to the subsidiary reduces proportionately the income assigned to the parent and the noncontrolling interest. However, the more tax expense assigned to the subsidiary, the less is assigned to the parent; the income attributed to the controlling interest then becomes greater.

Although no authoritative pronouncements specify the assignment of consolidated income tax expense to the individual companies included in the consolidated tax return, a reasonable approach is to allocate consolidated income tax expense among the companies on the basis of their relative contributions to income before taxes. As an example, assume that Peerless Products owns 80 percent of the stock of Special Foods, purchased at book value, and the two companies elect to file a consolidated tax return for 20X1. Peerless Products reports operating earnings before taxes of $140,000, excluding income from Special Foods, and Special Foods reports income before taxes of $50,000. If the corporate tax rate is 40 percent, consolidated income taxes are $76,000 ($190,000 × .40). Tax expense of $56,000 is assigned to Peerless Products, and $20,000 is assigned to Special Foods, determined as follows:

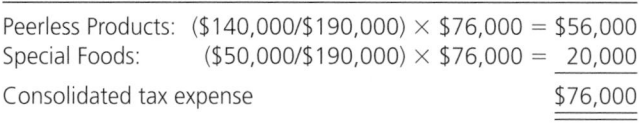

| | |
|---|---|
| Peerless Products: ($140,000/$190,000) × $76,000 = | $56,000 |
| Special Foods: ($50,000/$190,000) × $76,000 = | 20,000 |
| Consolidated tax expense | $76,000 |

Income assigned to the noncontrolling interest is computed as follows:

| | |
|---|---|
| Special Foods' income before tax | $50,000 |
| Income tax expense assigned to Special Foods | (20,000) |
| Special Foods' net income | $30,000 |
| Noncontrolling stockholders' proportionate share | × .20 |
| Income assigned to noncontrolling interest | $ 6,000 |

The consolidated income statement for 20X1 shows the following amounts:

| | |
|---|---|
| Consolidated Operating Income | $190,000 |
| Less: Income Tax Expense | (76,000) |
| Consolidated Net Income | $114,000 |
| Income Attributed to Noncontrolling Interest | (6,000) |
| Income Attributed to Controlling Interest | $108,000 |

Other allocation bases may be preferred when affiliates have significantly different tax characteristics, such as when only one of the companies qualifies for special tax exemptions or credits.

## Tax Effects of Unrealized Intercompany Profit Eliminations

The income tax effects of unrealized intercompany profit eliminations depend on whether the companies within the consolidated entity file a consolidated tax return or separate tax returns.

### *Unrealized Profits When a Consolidated Return Is Filed*

Intercompany transfers are eliminated in computing both consolidated net income and taxable income when a consolidated tax return is filed. Only sales outside the consolidated entity are recognized both for tax and for financial reporting purposes. Because profits are taxed in the same period they are recognized for financial reporting purposes, no *temporary differences* arise, and no additional tax accruals are needed in preparing the consolidated financial statements.

### *Unrealized Profits When Separate Returns Are Filed*

When each company within a consolidated entity files a separate income tax return, that company is taxed individually on the profits from intercompany sales. The focus in separate tax returns is on the transactions of the separate companies, and no consideration is given to whether the intercompany profits are realized from a consolidated viewpoint. Thus, the profit from an intercompany sale is taxed when the intercompany transfer occurs, without waiting for confirmation through sale to a nonaffiliate. For consolidated financial reporting purposes, however, unrealized intercompany profits must be eliminated. While the separate company may pay income taxes on the unrealized intercompany profit, the tax expense must be eliminated when the unrealized intercompany profit is eliminated in the preparation of consolidated financial statements. This difference in the timing of the income tax expense recognition results in the recording of *deferred income taxes.*

For example, if Special Foods sells inventory costing $23,000 to Peerless Products for $28,000, and none is resold before year-end, the entry to eliminate the intercorporate transfer when consolidated statements are prepared is:

| E(7) | Sales | 28,000 | |
|---|---|---|---|
| | Cost of Goods Sold | | 23,000 |
| | Inventory | | 5,000 |
| | Eliminate intercompany upstream sale of inventory. | | |

Income assigned to Special Foods' shareholders is reduced by $5,000 as a result of entry E(7). An adjustment to tax expense also is required in preparing consolidated statements if Special Foods files a separate tax return. With a 40 percent corporate income tax rate, eliminating entry E(8) adjusts income tax expense of the consolidated entity downward by $2,000 ($5,000 × .40) to reflect the reduction of reported profits:

| E(8) | Deferred Tax Asset | 2,000 | |
|---|---|---|---|
| | Income Tax Expense | | 2,000 |
| | Eliminate tax expense on unrealized intercompany profit. | | |

The debit to the deferred tax asset in entry E(8) reflects the tax effect of a temporary difference between the income reported in the consolidated income statement and that reported in the separate tax returns of the companies within the consolidated entity. Consistent with the treatment accorded other temporary differences, this tax effect normally is carried to the consolidated balance sheet as an asset. If the intercompany profit is expected to be recognized in the consolidated income statement in the next year, the deferred taxes are classified as current.

### *Unrealized Profit in Separate Tax Return Illustrated*

For purposes of illustrating the treatment of income taxes when Peerless and Special Foods file separate tax returns, assume the following information:

1. Peerless owns 80 percent of Special Foods' common stock, purchased at book value.
2. During 20X1, Special Foods purchases inventory for $23,000 and sells it to Peerless for $28,000. Peerless continues to hold all of the inventory at the end of 20X1.
3. The effective combined federal and state tax rate for both Peerless and Special Foods is 40 percent.

Although Special Foods' trial balance includes $50,000 of income before taxes and tax expense of $20,000 ($50,000 × .40), consolidated net income and income assigned to the controlling and noncontrolling shareholders are based on realized net income of $27,000, computed as follows:

| | |
|---|---:|
| Special Foods' net income | $30,000 |
| Add back income tax expense | 20,000 |
| Special Foods' income before taxes | $50,000 |
| Unrealized profit on upstream sale | (5,000) |
| Special Foods' realized income before taxes | $45,000 |
| Income taxes on realized income (40%) | (18,000) |
| Special Foods' realized net income | $27,000 |
| | |
| Special Foods' realized net income assigned to: | |
| Controlling interest ($27,000 × .80) | $21,600 |
| Noncontrolling interest ($27,000 × .20) | 5,400 |
| Special Foods' realized net income | $27,000 |

If Peerless accounts for its investment in Special Foods using the basic equity method, the eliminating entries needed for the preparation of a consolidation workpaper as of December 31, 20X1, are as follows:

| | | | |
|---|---|---:|---:|
| E(9) | Income from Subsidiary | 24,000 | |
| |     Dividends Declared | | 24,000 |
| | Eliminate income from subsidiary: | | |
| | $30,000 × .80 | | |
| | | | |
| E(10) | Income to Noncontrolling Interest | 5,400 | |
| | Noncontrolling Interest | 600 | |
| |     Dividends Declared | | 6,000 |
| | Assign income to noncontrolling interest: | | |
| | $5,400 = $27,000 × .20 | | |
| | $600 = $6,000 − $5,400 | | |
| | $6,000 = $30,000 × .20 | | |
| | | | |
| E(11) | Common Stock—Special Foods | 200,000 | |
| | Retained Earnings, January 1 | 100,000 | |
| |     Investment in Special Foods Stock | | 240,000 |
| |     Noncontrolling Interest | | 60,000 |
| | Eliminate beginning investment balance. | | |
| | | | |
| E(12) | Sales | 28,000 | |
| |     Cost of Goods Sold | | 23,000 |
| |     Inventory | | 5,000 |
| | Eliminate intercompany upstream sale of inventory. | | |

| E(13) | Deferred Tax Asset | 2,000 | |
|---|---|---|---|
| | Income Tax Expense | | 2,000 |
| | Eliminate tax expense on unrealized intercompany profit: | | |
| | $5,000 × .40 | | |

Entries E(9), E(10), and E(11) are the normal entries to eliminate the dividends declared and beginning stockholders' equity accounts of the subsidiary, the parent's investment account, and income from the subsidiary recognized by the parent and to establish the noncontrolling interest. As entry E(9) indicates, Special Foods distributed its entire 20X1 reported net income as dividends. Thus, the balance of the investment account remains at the original cost. Because the realized net income of Special Foods ($27,000) was less than dividends paid ($30,000), entry E(10) contains a debit to noncontrolling interest indicating a reduction in the claim of the noncontrolling shareholders during the period. Entries E(12) and E(13) eliminate the effects of the intercompany transaction, establish the tax effects of the temporary difference, and reduce consolidated net income by the unrealized intercompany profit net of taxes.

Another temporary difference normally would be included in the consolidated balance sheet and in the computation of consolidated income tax expense. In addition to temporary differences arising from unrealized profits, differences normally exist between subsidiary net income and dividend distributions. Peerless pays income taxes for the period based on its reported dividends from Special Foods but includes in consolidated net income for financial reporting its proportionate share of Special Foods' realized net income. This difference between the amount of income reported in the consolidated income statement and the amount reported in the tax return is considered a temporary difference, and deferred taxes normally must be recognized on this difference. In this example, Special Foods distributes all of its income as dividends, and the only temporary difference relates to the unrealized intercompany profit.

### Subsequent Profit Realization When Separate Returns Are Filed

When unrealized intercompany profits at the end of one period subsequently are recognized in another period, the tax effects of the temporary difference must again be considered.

If income taxes were ignored, eliminating entry E(14) would be used in preparing consolidated statements as of December 31, 20X2, assuming that Special Foods had $5,000 of unrealized inventory profit on its books on January 1, 20X2, and the inventory was resold in 20X2:

| E(14) | Retained Earnings, January 1 | 4,000 | |
|---|---|---|---|
| | Noncontrolling Interest | 1,000 | |
| | Cost of Goods Sold | | 5,000 |
| | Eliminate beginning inventory profit. | | |

On the other hand, if the 40 percent tax rate is considered, eliminating entry E(15) is used in place of entry E(14):

| E(15) | Retained Earnings, January 1 | 2,400 | |
|---|---|---|---|
| | Noncontrolling Interest | 600 | |
| | Income Tax Expense | 2,000 | |
| | Cost of Goods Sold | | 5,000 |
| | Eliminate beginning inventory profit: | | |
| | $2,400 = ($5,000 − $2,000) × .80 | | |
| | $600 = ($5,000 − $2,000) × .20 | | |
| | $2,000 = $5,000 × .40 | | |

Unrealized profit of $3,000 rather than $5,000 is apportioned between the controlling and noncontrolling shareholders in this case. Tax expense of $2,000 is recognized for financial reporting purposes in 20X2 even though the $5,000 of intercompany profit was reported on Special Foods' separate tax return and the $2,000 of taxes was paid on the profit in 20X1. Entry E(15) recognizes the tax expense in the consolidated income statement in the same year as the income is recognized from a consolidated viewpoint. No workpaper adjustment to the Deferred Tax Asset account is needed at the end of 20X2 because the deferred tax asset was entered only in the consolidation workpaper at the end of 20X1, but not on the books of either company; it does not carry over to 20X2.

# CONSOLIDATED EARNINGS PER SHARE

In general, *consolidated earnings per share* is calculated in the same way as earnings per share is calculated for a single corporation. Consolidated earnings per share is based on the income attributable to the controlling interest and available to the parent's common stockholders. Basic consolidated EPS is calculated by deducting income to the noncontrolling interest and any preferred dividend requirement of the parent company from consolidated net income. The resulting amount is then divided by the weighted-average number of the parent's common shares outstanding during the period.

Note that, while consolidated net income is viewed from an entity perspective, consolidated earnings per share follows a parent company approach and clearly is aimed at the stockholders of the parent company. The FASB noted this inconsistency, but decided that usefulness was increased by following this approach.

The computation of diluted consolidated EPS is more complicated. A subsidiary's contribution to the diluted EPS number may be different from its contribution to consolidated net income because of different underlying assumptions. Both the percentage of ownership held within the consolidated entity and the total amount of subsidiary income available to common shareholders may be different. In the computation of EPS, the parent's percentage of ownership frequently is changed when a subsidiary's convertible bonds and preferred stock are treated as common stock and the subsidiary's options and warrants are treated as if they had been exercised. In addition, income available to common shareholders of the subsidiary changes when bonds and preferred stock are treated as common stock for purposes of computing EPS. Interest expense or preferred dividends, if already deducted, must be added back in computing income available to common shareholders when the securities are considered to be common stock.

## Computation of Diluted Consolidated Earnings per Share

The parent's share of consolidated net income normally is the starting point in the computation of diluted consolidated EPS. It then is adjusted for the effects of parent and subsidiary dilutive securities. The following formulation can be used in computing diluted consolidated EPS:

$$
\text{Diluted consolidated EPS} = \frac{\left(\begin{array}{c}\text{Parent's share of} \\ \text{consolidated} \\ \text{net income}\end{array} \pm \begin{array}{c}\text{Adjustment} \\ \text{for parent} \\ \text{securities}\end{array}\right) - \left(\begin{array}{c}\text{Percent} \\ \text{ownership} \\ \text{held by} \\ \text{parent}\end{array} \times \begin{array}{c}\text{Income} \\ \text{available to} \\ \text{common} \\ \text{shareholders} \\ \text{of} \\ \text{subsidiary}\end{array}\right) + \left(\begin{array}{c}\text{Shares} \\ \text{held} \\ \text{by} \\ \text{parent}\end{array} \times \begin{array}{c}\text{Subsidiary} \\ \text{diluted} \\ \text{EPS}\end{array}\right)}{\begin{array}{c}\text{Weighted average of} \\ \text{parent company shares} \\ \text{outstanding}\end{array} + \begin{array}{c}\text{Shares of parent to be} \\ \text{issued if dilutive} \\ \text{securities are converted} \\ \text{and options exercised}\end{array}}
$$

This formula shows the adjustments to the parent's share of consolidated net income and the parent's common shares outstanding that are needed in computing diluted consolidated

EPS. In general, securities of the parent company that are convertible or exercisable into parent company shares must be included as shares outstanding if they are dilutive. When convertible bonds are treated as common stock and the additional shares are added in the denominator, the after-tax interest savings must be added back into the numerator. Dividends on preferred stock that continues to be classified as preferred stock are deducted from the numerator, and no deduction is made for dividends on preferred stock considered to be common stock.

The two other adjustments in the numerator relate to the amount of subsidiary income to be included in computing diluted consolidated EPS. First, the parent's portion of the subsidiary's income available to common shareholders is deducted so that an adjusted income number can be substituted. The amount deducted is computed by multiplying the parent's ownership percentage of subsidiary common shares outstanding times the subsidiary's income after preferred dividends have been deducted. The subsidiary's contribution to diluted consolidated EPS is determined by multiplying the subsidiary's number of shares held by the parent and other affiliates (or the number of shares that would be held after exercise or conversion of other subsidiary securities held) times the diluted EPS computed for the subsidiary. In this way, the effect of the subsidiary's dilutive securities is considered in computing diluted consolidated EPS.

Occasionally, a subsidiary is permitted to issue rights, warrants, or options to purchase the parent's common stock or to issue a security convertible into the parent's common stock. Such rights, warrants, and options of the subsidiary are treated in the same way as if the parent had issued them.

Subsidiary bonds or preferred stock convertible into the parent's common stock are treated in a slightly different manner. If the securities are treated as if converted, income available to common shareholders of the subsidiary is increased as a result of the reduction in interest expense, net of tax, or preferred dividends. The parent's portion of the earnings increase is included in the diluted consolidated EPS computation through the subsidiary EPS component. The number of parent company shares into which the security is convertible is added to the denominator of the diluted consolidated EPS computation.

## Computation of Consolidated Earnings per Share Illustrated

As an illustration of the computation of consolidated earnings per share for Peerless Products and Special Foods, assume the following:

1. Peerless Products purchases 80 percent of the stock of Special Foods on December 31, 20X0, at book value. On the date of acquisition, the fair value of Special Foods' noncontrolling interest is equal to its book value.

2. Both Special Foods and Peerless Products have effective income tax rates of 40 percent and file a consolidated tax return.

3. Special Foods has 20X1 income before taxes of $50,000, an allocated share of consolidated income taxes of $20,000, and net income of $30,000.

4. Consolidated net income for 20X1 is computed and allocated as follows:

| | |
|---|---|
| Peerless's separate operating income | $140,000 |
| Special Foods' income before taxes | 50,000 |
| Consolidated income before taxes | $190,000 |
| Consolidated income taxes (40%) | (76,000) |
| Consolidated net income | $114,000 |
| Income to noncontrolling shareholders ($30,000 × .20) | (6,000) |
| Income to controlling interest | $108,000 |

5. Peerless's capital structure consists of 100,000 shares of $5 par value common stock and 10,000 shares of $10 par 10 percent convertible preferred stock. The preferred stock is convertible into 25,000 shares of Peerless's common.

6. Special Foods has 20,000 shares of $10 par value common stock and $100,000 of 6 percent convertible bonds outstanding. The bonds, issued at par, are convertible into 4,000 shares of Special Foods' common stock.

7. On January 1, 20X1, Special Foods grants its officers options to purchase 9,000 shares of common stock of Peerless Products at $26 per share at any time during the five years following the date of the grant. None is exercised during 20X1. The average market price of Peerless's common stock during 20X1 is $29 per share.

### Special Foods' Earnings per Share

Before consolidated EPS can be calculated, the EPS total for each subsidiary must be computed. Basic and diluted EPS for Special Foods for 20X1 differ because Special Foods has dilutive convertible bonds outstanding.

Basic and diluted EPS for Special Foods for 20X1 are computed as follows:

|  | Basic | Diluted |
|---|---|---|
| Special Foods' net income | $30,000 | $30,000 |
| Interest effect of assumed conversion of bonds, net of taxes ($100,000 × .06) × (1 − .40) |  | 3,600 |
| Income accruing to common shares | $30,000 | $33,600 |
| Weighted-average common shares outstanding in 20X1 | 20,000 | 20,000 |
| Additional shares from assumed bond conversion |  | 4,000 |
| Weighted-average shares and share equivalents | 20,000 | 24,000 |
| Earnings per share: |  |  |
| $30,000 / 20,000 shares | $    1.50 |  |
| $33,600 / 24,000 shares |  | $    1.40 |

The assumed conversion of the bonds reduces Special Foods' diluted EPS from $1.50 to 1.40.

### Consolidated Earnings per Share

Consolidated earnings per share for 20X1 is $.98 based on weighted-average common shares outstanding and $.84 assuming full dilution. The computations are shown in Figure 10–5, with diluted EPS based on the formula presented earlier.

For diluted EPS, the parent's $108,000 share of consolidated net income is reduced by Peerless's $24,000 ($30,000 × .80) proportionate share of Special Foods' net income. Special Foods' contribution to diluted earnings per share is then added back. A total of $22,400 ($1.40 × 16,000 shares) is added for diluted EPS. If Peerless also had purchased a portion of Special Foods' convertible bonds, an equivalent number of shares would be added to Peerless's holdings in computing the amount added back for diluted EPS. The amount of subsidiary earnings added back into the numerator also can be computed by multiplying the revised ownership ratio times the revised earnings contribution. Earnings available to Special Foods' common shareholders in computing diluted EPS increases to $33,600 ($30,000 + $3,600) with the assumed bond conversion, and the number of shares outstanding increases by 4,000. As a result, the revised ownership ratio is reduced to 66⅔ percent (16,000 shares ÷ 24,000 shares). The earnings contribution computed in this manner is $22,400 (33,600 × .66⅔).

Peerless's preferred stock is treated as preferred stock in computing basic EPS, and preferred dividends are deducted in determining the income accruing to common shareholders in the numerator. In computing diluted EPS, the preferred stock is treated as common stock outstanding because it is convertible and dilutive. Therefore, no dividends are deducted in the numerator, and 25,000 shares of common stock are added into the denominator.

**FIGURE 10–5**
**Computation of Peerless Products and Subsidiary Consolidated Earnings per Share for 20X1**

| | Basic Earnings per Share | Diluted Earnings per Share |
|---|---|---|
| **Numerator** | | |
| Consolidated net income attributable to parent | $108,000 | $108,000 |
| Less: Peerless's share of Special Foods' net income ($30,000 × .80) | | (24,000) |
| Add: Peerless's share of Special Foods' income based on EPS ($1.40 × 16,000 shares) | | 22,400 |
| Less: Preferred dividends | (10,000) | |
| Total | $ 98,000 | $106,400 |
| **Denominator** | | |
| Weighted-average shares outstanding | 100,000 | 100,000 |
| Assumed exercise of stock options[a] | | 931 |
| Preferred stock assumed converted | | 25,000 |
| Total | 100,000 | 125,931 |
| **Earnings per Share** | | |
| $98,000 / 100,000 shares | $.98 | |
| $106,400 / 125,931 shares | | $.84 |

[a]Treasury stock method of assuming exercise of stock options:

| | | |
|---|---|---|
| Shares issued | | 9,000 |
| Shares repurchased: | | |
| Proceeds from issuing shares (9,000 shares × $26) | $234,000 | |
| Repurchase price per share | ÷ $29 | |
| Shares repurchased | | (8,069) |
| Increase in shares outstanding | | 931 |

Stock options for 9,000 shares of parent company stock can be exercised at any time and must be reflected in the computation of diluted EPS. As computed in Figure 10–5 using the treasury stock method, an additional 931 shares are added to the denominator in computing diluted EPS.

## Summary of Key Concepts

In addition to an income statement, balance sheet, and statement of retained earnings, a full set of consolidated financial statements must include a consolidated statement of cash flows. The consolidated statement of cash flows is prepared from the other three consolidated statements in the same way as the statement of cash flows is prepared for a single company. A small number of additional adjustments might be needed, such as for amortization or write-off of a differential. Also, dividends to noncontrolling shareholders must be included as a financing use of cash because they do require the use of cash even though they are not viewed as dividends of the consolidated entity.

When a subsidiary is purchased at an interim date during the year, the consolidation procedures must ensure that the subsidiary's operating results are included in the consolidated financial statements for only that portion of the year during which the parent held a controlling financial interest in the subsidiary. All of the subsidiary's revenues, expenses, gains, and losses for the portion of the year prior to the subsidiary's entry into the consolidated entity must be excluded, along with its dividends declared before acquisition.

Two major financial reporting issues related to income taxes arise in consolidation. The first is concerned with how to allocate income tax expense to individual companies included in a consolidated income tax return. One approach is to allocate the total tax based on the contributions of the individual companies to the total entity income. The issue is important because the allocation impacts the separate financial statements and the amounts assigned to the noncontrolling interests in the consolidated statements. The second tax issue involves the income tax effects of intercorporate transactions. For consolidating companies filing separate tax returns, income tax expense is recognized in the consolidated income statement when the associated transaction is recognized by the consolidated entity, not necessarily when it is reported by an individual company. If an intercompany gain or loss is included in an individual company's tax return in a different period from the one in which it is included in the consolidated income statement, deferred income taxes should be recognized on the temporary difference.

Consolidated earnings per share is calculated largely in the same way as for a single company. The numerator of the basic EPS computation is based on earnings available to the holders of the parent's common stock, and the denominator is the weighted-average number of the parent's common shares outstanding during the period. Diluted consolidated EPS assumes both the parent's and subsidiary's dilutive securities are converted, and special adjustments to income may be needed to reflect the effect of the assumed conversion on the amount of subsidiary income to include in the EPS numerator.

| Key Terms | consolidated earnings per share, *478* | deferred income taxes, *475* | temporary differences, *475* |
| --- | --- | --- | --- |
| | consolidated income tax return, *473* | statement of cash flows, *465* | |

## Questions

**Q10-1**  Why not simply add a fourth part to the three-part consolidation workpaper to permit preparation of a consolidated cash flow statement?

**Q10-2**  Why are dividend payments to noncontrolling shareholders treated as an outflow of cash in the consolidated cash flow statement but not included as dividends paid in the consolidated retained earnings statement?

**Q10-3**  Why are payments to suppliers not shown in the statement of cash flows when the indirect method is used in presenting cash flows from operating activities?

**Q10-4**  Why are changes in inventory balances not shown in the statement of cash flows when the direct method is used in presenting the cash flows from operating activities?

**Q10-5**  Are sales included in the consolidation workpaper in computing cash flows from operating activities when the indirect method or direct method is used?

**Q10-6**  How is an increase in inventory included in the amounts reported as cash flows from operating activities under (*a*) the indirect method and (*b*) the direct method?

**Q10-7**  What portion of the sales of an acquired company is included in the consolidated income statement following a midyear acquisition?

**Q10-8**  How are dividends declared by an acquired company prior to the date of a midyear acquisition treated in the consolidated financial statements?

**Q10-9**  How do the eliminating entries at the end of the year change when an acquisition occurs at midyear rather than at the beginning of the year?

**Q10-10**  Why do companies that file consolidated tax returns often choose to allocate tax expense to the individual affiliates?

**Q10-11**  How do unrealized profits on intercompany transfers affect the amount reported as income tax expense in the consolidated financial statements?

**Q10-12**  How do interperiod income tax allocation procedures affect consolidation eliminating entries in the period in which unrealized intercompany profits arise?

**Q10-13**  How do interperiod income tax allocation procedures affect consolidation eliminating entries in the period in which intercompany profits unrealized as of the beginning of the period are realized?

**Q10-14**  How does the use of interperiod tax allocation procedures affect the amount of income assigned to noncontrolling shareholders in the period in which unrealized intercompany profits are recorded by the subsidiary?

**Q10-15**  Why is it not possible simply to add together the separately computed earnings per share amounts of individual affiliates in deriving consolidated earnings per share?

**Q10-16**  How are dividends that are paid to the parent's preferred shareholders and to the subsidiary's preferred shareholders treated in computing consolidated earnings per share?

**Q10-17**  What factors may cause a subsidiary's income contribution to consolidated earnings per share to be different from its contribution to consolidated net income?

**Q10-18** When a convertible bond of a subsidiary is treated as common stock in computing the subsidiary's diluted earnings per share, how is the interest on the bond treated in the computation of diluted consolidated earnings per share?

**Q10-19** How are rights, warrants, and options of subsidiary companies treated in the computation of consolidated earnings per share?

**Q10-20** What effect does the presence of a noncontrolling interest have on the computation of consolidated earnings per share?

## Cases

**C10-1**
*Judgment*

### The Effect of Security Type on Earnings per Share

Stage Corporation has both convertible preferred stock and convertible debentures outstanding at the end of 20X3. The annual cash payment to the preferred shareholders and to the bondholders is the same, and the two issues convert into the same number of common shares.

#### Required

*a.* If both issues are dilutive and are converted into common stock, which issue will cause the larger reduction in basic earnings per share when converted? Why?

*b.* If both issues are converted into common stock, which issue will cause the larger increase in consolidated net income when converted?

*c.* If the preferred shares remain outstanding, what conditions must exist for them to be excluded entirely from the computation of basic earnings per share?

*d.* Stage is a subsidiary of Prop Company. How will these securities affect the earnings per share reported for the consolidated enterprise?

**C10-2**

*Research*
*FARS*

### Evaluating Consolidated Statements

Cowl Company has been reporting losses for the last three years and has been unable to pay its bills from cash generated from its operations. On December 31, 20X4, Cowl's president instructed its treasurer to transfer a large amount of cash to Cowl from Plum Corporation, which is 80 percent owned by Cowl. It appears Cowl will not return to profitability in the near future and may never be able to repay Plum. Cowl's treasurer is concerned that, although cash will appear to be unchanged in the consolidated financial statements, the subsidiary has much less cash than it previously held and Plum's noncontrolling shareholders might learn about the transfer and initiate a lawsuit or other action against Cowl's management.

#### Required

As a member of Cowl's accounting department, you have been asked to determine whether information on the transfer will be shown in the consolidated cash flow statement or other financial statements and to search the FASB's pronouncements and those of other authoritative bodies to see whether information germane to the noncontrolling shareholders of a subsidiary must be disclosed in cases such as this. Prepare a memo indicating your findings, and include citations to or quotations from relevant authoritative pronouncements.

**C10-3**

*Understanding*

### Income Tax Expense

Johnson Corporation purchased 100 percent ownership of Freelance Company at book value on March 3, 20X2. Johnson, which makes frequent inventory purchases from Freelance, uses the equity method in accounting for its investment in Freelance. Both companies are subject to 40 percent income tax rates and file separate tax returns.

#### Required

*a.* When will an inventory transfer cause consolidated income tax expense to be higher than the amount paid?

*b.* When tax payments are higher than tax expense, how is the overpayment reported in the consolidated financial statements?

*c.* What types of transfers other than inventory transfers will cause consolidated income tax expense to be less than income taxes paid?

*d.* What types of transfers other than inventory transfers will cause consolidated income tax expense to be more than income taxes paid?

**C10-4** **Consolidated Cash Flows**

*Analysis*

The consolidated cash flows from operations of Jones Corporation and its subsidiary Short Manufacturing for 20X2 decreased quite substantially from 20X1 despite the fact that consolidated net income increased slightly in 20X2.

#### Required

a. What factors included in the computation of consolidated net income may explain this difference between cash flows from operations and net income?

b. How might a change in credit terms extended by Short Manufacturing explain a part of the difference?

c. How would an inventory write-off affect cash flows from operations?

d. How would a write-off of uncollectible accounts receivable affect cash flows from operations?

e. How does the preparation of a statement of cash flows differ for a consolidated entity compared with a single corporate entity?

**Exercises**  **E10-1** **Analysis of Cash Flows**

In its consolidated cash flow statement for the year ended December 31, 20X2, Lamb Corporation reported operating cash inflows of $284,000, financing cash outflows of $230,000 and $80,000 for investing cash outflows, and an ending cash balance of $57,000. Lamb purchased 70 percent of Mint Company's common stock on March 12, 20X1, at book value. Mint reported net income of $30,000, paid dividends of $10,000 in 20X2, and is included in Lamb's consolidated statements. Lamb paid dividends of $45,000 in 20X2. The indirect method is used in computing cash flow from operations.

#### Required

a. What was the consolidated cash balance at January 1, 20X2?

b. What amount was reported as dividends paid in the cash flow from financing activities section of the statement of cash flows?

c. If the other adjustments to reconcile consolidated net income and cash provided by operations resulted in an increase of $77,000, what amount was reported as consolidated net income for 20X2?

**E10-2** **Statement of Cash Flows**

Becon Corporation's controller has just finished preparing a consolidated balance sheet, income statement, and statement of changes in retained earnings for the year ended December 31, 20X4. Becon owns 60 percent of Handy Corporation's stock, which it acquired at underlying book value on May 7, 20X1. At that date, the fair value of the noncontrolling interest was equal to 40 percent of Handy Corporation's book value. You have been provided with the following information:

Consolidated net income for 20X4 was $271,000.

Handy reported net income of $70,000 for 20X4.

Becon paid dividends of $25,000 in 20X4.

Handy paid dividends of $15,000 in 20X4.

Becon issued common stock on April 7, 20X4, for a total of $150,000.

Consolidated wages payable increased by $7,000 in 20X4.

Consolidated depreciation expense for the year was $21,000.

Consolidated accounts receivable decreased by $32,000 in 20X4.

Bonds payable of Becon with a book value of $204,000 were retired for $200,000 on December 31, 20X4.

Consolidated amortization expense on patents was $13,000 for 20X4.

Becon sold land that it had purchased for $142,000 to a nonaffiliate for $134,000 on June 10, 20X4.

Consolidated accounts payable decreased by $12,000 during 20X4.

Total purchases of equipment by Becon and Handy during 20X4 were $295,000.

Consolidated inventory increased by $16,000 during 20X4.

There were no intercompany transfers between Becon and Handy in 20X4 or prior years except for Handy's payment of dividends. Becon uses the indirect method in preparing its cash flow statement.

### Required

*a.* What amount of dividends was paid to the noncontrolling interest during 20X4?

*b.* What amount will be reported as net cash provided by operating activities for 20X4?

*c.* What amount will be reported as net cash used in investing activities for 20X4?

*d.* What amount will be reported as net cash used in financing activities for 20X4?

*e.* What was the change in cash balance for the consolidated entity for 20X4?

**E10-3** ### Computation of Operating Cash Flows

Toggle Company reported sales of $310,000 and cost of goods sold of $180,000 for 20X2. During 20X2, Toggle's accounts receivable increased by $17,000, inventory decreased by $8,000, and accounts payable decreased by $21,000.

### Required

Compute the amounts to be reported by Toggle as cash received from customers, cash payments to suppliers, and cash flows from operating activities for 20X2.

**E10-4** ### Consolidated Operating Cash Flows

Power Corporation owns 75 percent of Turk Company's stock; no intercompany purchases or sales were made in 20X4. For the year, Power and Turk reported sales of $300,000 and $200,000 and cost of goods sold of $160,000 and $95,000, respectively. Power's inventory increased by $35,000, but Turk's decreased by $15,000. Power's accounts receivable increased by $28,000 and its accounts payable decreased by $17,000 during 20X4. Turk's accounts receivable decreased by $10,000 and its accounts payable increased by $4,000.

### Required

Using the direct method of computing cash flows from operating activities, compute the following:

*a.* Cash received from customers.

*b.* Cash payments to suppliers.

*c.* Cash flows from operating activities.

**E10-5** ### Preparation of Statement of Cash Flows

The accountant for Consolidated Enterprises Inc. has just finished preparing a consolidated balance sheet, income statement, and statement of changes in retained earnings for 20X3. The accountant has asked for assistance in preparing a statement of cash flows for the consolidated entity. Consolidated Enterprises holds 80 percent of the stock of Separate Way Manufacturing. The following items are proposed for inclusion in the consolidated cash flow statement:

| | |
|---|---:|
| Decrease in accounts receivable | $ 23,000 |
| Increase in accounts payable | 5,000 |
| Increase in inventory | 15,000 |
| Increase in bonds payable | 120,000 |
| Equipment purchased | 380,000 |
| Common stock repurchased | 35,000 |
| Depreciation reported for current period | 73,000 |
| Gain recorded on sale of equipment | 8,000 |
| Book value of equipment sold | 37,000 |
| Goodwill impairment loss | 3,000 |
| Sales | 900,000 |
| Cost of goods sold | 368,000 |
| Dividends paid by parent | 60,000 |
| Dividends paid by subsidiary | 30,000 |
| Consolidated net income for the year | 464,000 |
| Income assigned to the noncontrolling interest | 14,000 |

### Required

Prepare in good form a statement of cash flows for Consolidated Enterprises Inc. using the indirect method of computing cash flows from operations.

**E10-6**  **Direct Method Cash Flow Statement**

Using the data presented in E10-5, prepare a statement of cash flows for Consolidated Enterprises Inc. using the direct method of computing cash flows from operating activities.

**E10-7**  **Analysis of Consolidated Cash Flow Statement**

The following 20X2 consolidated statement of cash flows is presented for Acme Printing Company and its subsidiary, Jones Delivery:

---

**ACME PRINTING COMPANY AND SUBSIDIARY**
**Consolidated Statement of Cash Flows**
**For the Year Ended December 31, 20X2**

| | | |
|---|---:|---:|
| Cash Flows from Operating Activities: | | |
| Consolidated Net Income | $ 130,000 | |
| Noncash Items Included in Income: | | |
| Depreciation Expense | 45,000 | |
| Amortization of Patents | 1,000 | |
| Amortization of Bond Premium | (2,000) | |
| Loss on Sale of Equipment | 23,000 | |
| Decrease in Inventory | 20,000 | |
| Increase in Accounts Receivable | (12,000) | |
| Net Cash Provided by Operating Activities | | $205,000 |
| Cash Flows from Investing Activities: | | |
| Purchase of Buildings | $(150,000) | |
| Sale of Equipment | 60,000 | |
| Net Cash Used in Investing Activities | | (90,000) |
| Cash Flows from Financing Activities: | | |
| Dividends Paid: | | |
| To Acme Printing Shareholders | $ (50,000) | |
| To Noncontrolling Shareholders | (6,000) | |
| Sale of Bonds | 100,000 | |
| Repurchase of Acme Printing Stock | (120,000) | |
| Net Cash Used in Financing Activities | | (76,000) |
| Net Increase in Cash | | $ 39,000 |

---

Acme Printing acquired 60 percent of the voting shares of Jones in 20X1 at underlying book value. At that date, the fair value of the noncontrolling interest was equal to 40 percent of the book value of Jones Delivery.

### Required

a.  Determine the amount of dividends paid by Jones in 20X2.

b.  Explain why the amortization of bond premium is treated as a deduction from net income in arriving at net cash flows from operating activities.

c.  Explain why an increase in accounts receivable is treated as a deduction from net income in arriving at net cash flows from operating activities.

d.  Explain why dividends to noncontrolling stockholders are not shown as a dividend payment in the retained earnings statement but are shown as a distribution of cash in the consolidated cash flow statement.

e.  Did the loss on the sale of equipment included in the consolidated statement of cash flows result from a sale to an affiliate or a nonaffiliate? How do you know?

**E10-8**  **Midyear Acquisition**

Yarn Manufacturing Corporation issued stock with a par value of $67,000 and a market value of $503,500 to acquire 95 percent of Spencer Corporation's common stock on August 30, 20X1. At that date, the fair value of the noncontrolling interest was $26,500. On January 1, 20X1, Spencer reported the following stockholders' equity balances:

| Common Stock ($10 par value) | $150,000 |
|---|---|
| Additional Paid-In Capital | 50,000 |
| Retained Earnings | 300,000 |
| Total Stockholders' Equity | $500,000 |

Spencer reported net income of $60,000 in 20X1, earned uniformly throughout the year, and declared and paid dividends of $10,000 on June 30 and $25,000 on December 31, 20X1. Yarn accounts for its investment in Spencer Corporation using the basic equity method.

Yarn reported retained earnings of $400,000 on January 1, 20X1, and had 20X1 income of $140,000 from its separate operations. Yarn paid dividends of $80,000 on December 31, 20X1.

### Required

a. Compute consolidated retained earnings as of January 1, 20X1, as it would appear in comparative consolidated financial statements presented at the end of 20X1.

b. Compute consolidated net income and income to the controlling interest for 20X1.

c. Compute consolidated retained earnings as of December 31, 20X1.

d. Give the December 31, 20X1, balance of Yarn Manufacturing's investment in Spencer Corporation.

### E10-9 Purchase of Shares at Midyear

Highbeam Corporation paid $319,500 to acquire 90 percent ownership of Copper Company on April 1, 20X2. At that date, the fair value of the noncontrolling interest was $35,500. On January 1, 20X2, Copper reported these stockholders' equity balances:

| Common Stock | $160,000 |
|---|---|
| Additional Paid-In Capital | 40,000 |
| Retained Earnings | 150,000 |
| Total Stockholders' Equity | $350,000 |

Copper's operating results and dividend payments for 20X2 were as follows:

| | January 1 to March 31 | April 1 to December 31 |
|---|---|---|
| Sales | $90,000 | $250,000 |
| Total expenses | (80,000) | (220,000) |
| Net income | $10,000 | $ 30,000 |
| Dividends paid | $ 5,000 | $ 15,000 |

Highbeam uses the equity method in recording its investment in Copper.

### Required

a. Prepare the journal entries that Highbeam recorded in 20X2 for its investment in Copper.

b. Give the workpaper eliminating entries needed at December 31, 20X2, to prepare consolidated financial statements.

### E10-10 Tax Deferral on Gains and Losses

Springdale Corporation holds 75 percent of the voting shares of Holiday Services Company. During 20X7 Springdale sold inventory costing $60,000 to Holiday Services for $90,000, and Holiday Services resold one-third of the inventory in 20X7. Also in 20X7, Holiday Services sold land with a book value of $140,000 to Springdale for $240,000, and Springdale continues to hold the land. The companies file separate tax returns and are subject to a 40 percent tax rate.

### Required

Give the eliminating entries relating to the intercorporate sale of inventories and land to be entered in the consolidation workpaper prepared at the end of 20X7.

**E10-11** **Unrealized Profits in Prior Year**

Springdale Corporation holds 75 percent of the voting shares of Holiday Services Company. During 20X7 Springdale sold inventory costing $60,000 to Holiday Services for $90,000, and Holiday Services resold one-third of the inventory in 20X7. The remaining inventory was resold in 20X8. Also in 20X7, Holiday Services sold land with a book value of $140,000 to Springdale for $240,000. Springdale continues to hold the land at the end of 20X8. The companies file separate tax returns and are subject to a 40 percent tax rate.

### Required

Give the eliminating entries relating to the intercorporate sale of inventories and land needed in the consolidation workpaper at the end of 20X8. Assume that Springdale uses the basic equity method in accounting for its investment in Holiday Services.

**E10-12** **Allocation of Income Tax Expense**

Winter Corporation owns 80 percent of Ray Guard Corporation's stock and 90 percent of Block Company's stock. The companies file a consolidated tax return each year and in 20X5 paid a total tax of $80,000. Each company is involved in a number of intercompany inventory transfers each period. Information on the companies' activities for 20X5 is as follows:

| Company | 20X5 Reported Operating Income | 20X4 Intercompany Profit Realized in 20X5 | 20X5 Intercompany Profit Not Realized in 20X5 |
|---|---|---|---|
| Winter Corporation | $100,000 | $40,000 | $10,000 |
| Ray Guard Corporation | 50,000 | | 20,000 |
| Block Company | 30,000 | 20,000 | 10,000 |

### Required

*a.* Determine the amount of income tax expense that should be assigned to each company.

*b.* Compute consolidated net income and income to the controlling interest for 20X5. (*Note:* Winter Corporation does not record income tax expense on income from subsidiaries because a consolidated tax return is filed.)

**E10-13** **Effect of Preferred Stock on Earnings per Share**

Amber Corporation holds 70 percent of Newtop Company's voting common shares but none of its preferred shares. Summary balance sheets for the companies on December 31, 20X1, are as follows:

| | Amber Corporation | Newtop Company |
|---|---|---|
| Cash | $ 14,000 | $ 30,000 |
| Accounts Receivable | 40,000 | 50,000 |
| Inventory | 110,000 | 80,000 |
| Buildings and Equipment | 280,000 | 200,000 |
| Less: Accumulated Depreciation | (130,000) | (60,000) |
| Investment in Newtop Company | 126,000 | |
| Total Assets | $440,000 | $300,000 |
| Accounts Payable | $ 70,000 | $ 70,000 |
| Wages Payable | 40,000 | |
| Preferred Stock | 100,000 | 50,000 |
| Common Stock ($10 par value) | 120,000 | 100,000 |
| Retained Earnings | 110,000 | 80,000 |
| Total Liabilities and Owners' Equity | $440,000 | $300,000 |

Neither of the preferred issues is convertible. Amber's preferred pays a 9 percent annual dividend, and Newtop's preferred pays a 10 percent dividend. Newtop reported net income of $45,000 and paid a total of $20,000 of dividends in 20X1. Amber reported income from its separate operations of $59,000 and paid total dividends of $45,000 in 20X1.

### Required

Compute 20X1 consolidated earnings per share. Ignore any tax consequences.

**E10-14**  **Effect of Convertible Bonds on Earnings per Share**

Crystal Corporation owns 60 percent of Evans Company's common shares. Balance sheet data for the companies on December 31, 20X2, are as follows:

|  | Crystal Corporation | Evans Company |
|---|---|---|
| Cash | $ 85,000 | $ 30,000 |
| Accounts Receivable | 80,000 | 50,000 |
| Inventory | 120,000 | 100,000 |
| Buildings and Equipment | 700,000 | 400,000 |
| Less: Accumulated Depreciation | (240,000) | (80,000) |
| Investment in Evans Company Stock | 150,000 | |
| Total Assets | $895,000 | $500,000 |
| Accounts Payable | $145,000 | $ 50,000 |
| Bonds Payable | 250,000 | 200,000 |
| Common Stock ($10 par value) | 300,000 | 100,000 |
| Retained Earnings | 200,000 | 150,000 |
| Total Liabilities and Owners' Equity | $895,000 | $500,000 |

The bonds of Crystal Corporation and Evans Company pay annual interest of 8 percent and 10 percent, respectively. Crystal's bonds are not convertible. Evans's bonds can be converted into 10,000 shares of its company stock any time after January 1, 20X1. An income tax rate of 40 percent is applicable to both companies. Evans reports net income of $30,000 for 20X2 and pays dividends of $15,000. Crystal reports income from its separate operations of $45,000 and pays dividends of $25,000.

### Required

Compute basic and diluted earnings per share for the consolidated entity for 20X2.

**E10-15**  **Effect of Convertible Preferred Stock on Earnings per Share**

Eagle Corporation holds 80 percent of Standard Company's common shares. The companies report the following balance sheet data for December 31, 20X1:

|  | Eagle Corporation | Standard Company |
|---|---|---|
| Cash | $ 50,000 | $ 40,000 |
| Accounts Receivable | 80,000 | 60,000 |
| Inventory | 140,000 | 90,000 |
| Buildings and Equipment | 700,000 | 300,000 |
| Less: Accumulated Depreciation | (280,000) | (140,000) |
| Investment in Standard Company Stock | 160,000 | |
| Total Assets | $850,000 | $350,000 |
| Accounts Payable | $120,000 | $ 50,000 |
| Taxes Payable | 80,000 | |
| Preferred Stock ($10 par value) | 200,000 | 100,000 |
| Common Stock: | | |
| $10 par value | 100,000 | |
| $5 par value | | 50,000 |
| Retained Earnings | 350,000 | 150,000 |
| Total Liabilities and Owners' Equity | $850,000 | $350,000 |

An 8 percent annual dividend is paid on the Eagle preferred stock and a 12 percent dividend is paid on the Standard preferred stock. The preferred shares of Eagle are not convertible. Standard's preferred shares can be converted into 15,000 shares of common stock at any time. For 20X1, Standard reports net income of $45,000 and pays total dividends of $20,000, and Eagle reports income from its separate operations of $60,000 and pays total dividends of $35,000.

### Required

Compute basic and diluted earnings per share for the consolidated entity for 20X1.

---

## Problems

### P10-16 Direct Method Computation of Cash Flows

Car Corporation owns 70 percent of the voting common stock of Bus Company. At December 31, 20X1, the companies reported the following:

| | Car Corporation | Bus Company |
|---|---|---|
| Sales, 20X1 | $400,000 | $240,000 |
| Cost of goods sold, 20X1 | 235,000 | 105,000 |
| Increase (decrease) in 20X1: | | |
| Inventory | (22,000) | 16,000 |
| Accounts receivable | 9,000 | (2,000) |
| Accounts payable | (31,000) | 15,000 |

During 20X1 Bus sold inventory costing $70,000 to Car for $100,000, and Car resold 40 percent of the inventory prior to December 31, 20X1. No intercompany inventory transactions occurred prior to 20X1, nor did intercompany receivables and payables exist at December 31, 20X1.

### Required

Using the direct method, prepare the cash flows from operating activities section of the consolidated statement of cash flows for 20X1 in good form.

### P10-17 Preparing a Statement of Cash Flows

Metal Corporation acquired 75 percent ownership of Ocean Company on January 1, 20X1, at underlying book value. At that date, the fair value of the noncontrolling interest was equal to 25 percent of the book value of Ocean Company. Consolidated balance sheets at January 1, 20X3, and December 31, 20X3, are as follows:

| Item | Jan. 1, 20X3 | Dec. 31, 20X3 |
|---|---|---|
| Cash | $ 68,500 | $ 100,500 |
| Accounts Receivable | 82,000 | 97,000 |
| Inventory | 115,000 | 123,000 |
| Land | 45,000 | 55,000 |
| Buildings and Equipment | 515,000 | 550,000 |
| Less: Accumulated Depreciation | (186,500) | (223,000) |
| Patents | 5,000 | 4,000 |
| | $644,000 | $ 706,500 |
| | | |
| Accounts Payable | $ 61,000 | $ 66,000 |
| Wages Payable | 26,000 | 20,000 |
| Notes Payable | 250,000 | 265,000 |
| Common Stock ($10 par value) | 150,000 | 150,000 |
| Retained Earnings | 130,000 | 174,500 |
| Noncontrolling Interest | 27,000 | 31,000 |
| | $644,000 | $ 706,500 |

The consolidated income statement for 20X3 contained the following amounts:

| | | |
|---|---:|---:|
| Sales | | $490,000 |
| Cost of Goods Sold | $259,000 | |
| Wage Expense | 55,000 | |
| Depreciation Expense | 36,500 | |
| Interest Expense | 16,000 | |
| Amortization Expense | 1,000 | |
| Other Expenses | 39,000 | (406,500) |
| Consolidated Net Income | | $ 83,500 |
| Income to Noncontrolling Interest | | (9,000) |
| Income to Controlling Interest | | $ 74,500 |

Metal and Ocean paid dividends of $30,000 and $20,000, respectively, in 20X3.

### Required

a. Prepare a workpaper to develop a consolidated statement of cash flows for 20X3 using the indirect method of computing cash flows from operations.

b. Prepare a consolidated statement of cash flows for 20X3.

**P10-18**   **Preparing a Statement of Cash Flows—Direct Method**

### Required

Using the data presented in P10-17:

a. Prepare a workpaper to develop a consolidated statement of cash flows for 20X3 using the direct method of computing cash flows from operations.

b. Prepare a consolidated statement of cash flows for 20X3.

**P10-19**   **Consolidated Statement of Cash Flows**

Traper Company holds 80 percent ownership of Arrow Company. The consolidated balance sheets as of December 31, 20X3, and December 31, 20X4, are as follows:

| | Dec. 31, 20X3 | Dec. 31, 20X4 |
|---|---:|---:|
| Cash | $    83,000 | $   181,000 |
| Accounts Receivable | 210,000 | 175,000 |
| Inventory | 320,000 | 370,000 |
| Land | 190,000 | 160,000 |
| Buildings and Equipment | 850,000 | 980,000 |
| Less: Accumulated Depreciation | (280,000) | (325,000) |
| Goodwill | 40,000 | 28,000 |
| Total Assets | $1,413,000 | $1,569,000 |
| Accounts Payable | $    52,000 | $    74,000 |
| Interest Payable | 45,000 | 30,000 |
| Bonds Payable | 400,000 | 500,000 |
| Bond Premium | 18,000 | 16,000 |
| Noncontrolling Interest | 40,000 | 44,000 |
| Common Stock | 300,000 | 300,000 |
| Additional Paid-In Capital | 70,000 | 70,000 |
| Retained Earnings | 488,000 | 535,000 |
| Total Liabilities and Owners' Equity | $1,413,000 | $1,569,000 |

The 20X4 consolidated income statement contained the following amounts:

| | | |
|---|---:|---:|
| Sales | | $600,000 |
| Cost of Goods Sold | $375,000 | |
| Depreciation Expense | 45,000 | |
| Interest Expense | 69,000 | |
| Loss on Sale of Land | 20,000 | |
| Goodwill Impairment Loss | 12,000 | (521,000) |
| Consolidated Net Income | | $ 79,000 |
| Income to Noncontrolling Interest | | (7,000) |
| Income to Controlling Interest | | $ 72,000 |

Traper acquired its investment in Arrow on January 1, 20X2, for $176,000. At that date, the fair value of the noncontrolling interest was $44,000, and Arrow reported net assets of $150,000. A total of $40,000 of the differential was assigned to goodwill. The remainder of the differential was assigned to equipment with a remaining life of 20 years from the date of combination.

Traper sold $100,000 of bonds on December 31, 20X4, to assist in generating additional funds. Arrow reported net income of $35,000 for 20X4 and paid dividends of $15,000. Traper reported 20X4 equity-method net income of $80,000 and paid dividends of $25,000.

### Required

a. Prepare a workpaper to develop a consolidated statement of cash flows for 20X4 using the indirect method of computing cash flows from operations.

b. Prepare a consolidated statement of cash flows for 20X4.

**P10-20** ### Consolidated Statement of Cash Flows—Direct Method

### Required
Using the data presented in P10-19:

a. Prepare a workpaper to develop a consolidated statement of cash flows for 20X4 using the direct method of computing cash flows from operations.

b. Prepare a consolidated statement of cash flows for 20X4.

**P10-21** ### Consolidated Statement of Cash Flows
Sun Corporation was created on January 1, 20X2, and quickly became successful. On January 1, 20X6, its owner sold 80 percent of the stock to Weatherbee Company at underlying book value. At the date of that sale, the fair value of the remaining shares was equal to 20 percent of the book value of Weatherbee. Weatherbee continued to operate the subsidiary as a separate legal entity and used the equity method in accounting for its investment in Sun. The following consolidated financial statements have been prepared:

**WEATHERBEE COMPANY AND SUBSIDIARY**
**Consolidated Balance Sheets**

| | *January 1, 20X6* | *December 31, 20X6* |
|---|---:|---:|
| Cash | $ 54,000 | $ 75,000 |
| Accounts Receivable | 121,000 | 111,000 |
| Inventory | 230,000 | 360,000 |
| Land | 95,000 | 100,000 |
| Buildings and Equipment | 800,000 | 650,000 |
| Less: Accumulated Depreciation | (290,000) | (230,000) |
| Total Assets | $1,010,000 | $1,066,000 |
| Accounts Payable | $ 90,000 | $ 105,000 |
| Bonds Payable | 300,000 | 250,000 |
| Noncontrolling Interest | 30,000 | 38,000 |
| Common Stock | 300,000 | 300,000 |
| Retained Earnings | 290,000 | 373,000 |
| Total Liabilities and Owners' Equity | $1,010,000 | $1,066,000 |

**WEATHERBEE COMPANY AND SUBSIDIARY**
**Consolidated Income Statement**
**Year Ended December 31, 20X6**

| | |
|---|---|
| Sales | $1,070,000 |
| Gain on Sale of Equipment | 30,000 |
| | $1,100,000 |
| Cost of Goods Sold | $ 750,000 |
| Depreciation Expense | 40,000 |
| Other Expenses | 150,000 |
| Total Expenses | $ (940,000) |
| Consolidated Net Income | $ 160,000 |
| Income to Noncontrolling Interest | (12,000) |
| Income to Controlling Interest | $ 148,000 |

**WEATHERBEE COMPANY AND SUBSIDIARY**
**Consolidated Retained Earnings Statement**
**Year Ended December 31, 20X6**

| | |
|---|---|
| Balance, January 1, 20X6 | $290,000 |
| Income to Controlling Interest | 148,000 |
| | $438,000 |
| Dividends Declared, 20X6 | (65,000) |
| Balance, December 31, 20X6 | $373,000 |

During 20X6, Sun reported net income of $60,000 and paid dividends of $20,000; Weatherbee reported net income of $148,000 and paid dividends of $65,000. There were no intercompany transfers during the period.

### Required
Prepare a workpaper for a consolidated statement of cash flows for 20X6 using the indirect method of computing cash flows from operations.

**P10-22**  **Consolidated Statement of Cash Flows—Direct Method**

### Required
Using the data presented in P10-21, prepare a workpaper to develop a consolidated statement of cash flows using the direct method for computing cash flows from operations.

**P10-23**  **Consolidated Statement of Cash Flows [AICPA Adapted]**

Following are the consolidated balance sheet accounts of Brimer Inc. and its subsidiary, Dore Corporation, as of December 31, 20X6 and 20X5.

| | 20X6 | 20X5 | Net Increase (Decrease) |
|---|---|---|---|
| **Assets** | | | |
| Cash | $ 313,000 | $ 195,000 | $118,000 |
| Marketable Equity Securities, at cost | 175,000 | 175,000 | -0- |
| Allowance to Reduce Marketable | | | |
| Equity Securities to Market | (13,000) | (24,000) | 11,000 |
| Accounts Receivable, net | 418,000 | 440,000 | (22,000) |
| Inventories | 595,000 | 525,000 | 70,000 |
| Land | 385,000 | 170,000 | 215,000 |
| Plant and Equipment | 755,000 | 690,000 | 65,000 |
| Accumulated Depreciation | (199,000) | (145,000) | (54,000) |
| Goodwill, net | 57,000 | 60,000 | (3,000) |
| Total Assets | $2,486,000 | $2,086,000 | $400,000 |

*(continued)*

*(continued)*

| | 20X6 | 20X5 | Net Increase (Decrease) |
|---|---|---|---|
| **Liabilities and Stockholders' Equity** | | | |
| Current Portion of Long-Term Note | $ 150,000 | $ 150,000 | $ -0- |
| Accounts Payable and Accrued Liabilities | 595,000 | 474,000 | 121,000 |
| Note Payable, Long-Term | 300,000 | 450,000 | (150,000) |
| Deferred Income Taxes | 44,000 | 32,000 | 12,000 |
| Minority Interest in Net Assets of Subsidiary | 179,000 | 161,000 | 18,000 |
| Common Stock, par $10 | 580,000 | 480,000 | 100,000 |
| Additional Paid-In Capital | 303,000 | 180,000 | 123,000 |
| Retained Earnings | 335,000 | 195,000 | 140,000 |
| Treasury Stock, at cost | -0- | (36,000) | 36,000 |
| Total Liabilities and Stockholders' Equity | $2,486,000 | $2,086,000 | $400,000 |

### Additional Information

1. On January 20, 20X6, Brimer issued 10,000 shares of its common stock for land having a fair value of $215,000.

2. On February 5, 20X6, Brimer reissued all of its treasury stock for $44,000.

3. On May 15, 20X6, Brimer paid a $58,000 cash dividend on its common stock.

4. On August 8, 20X6, equipment was purchased for $127,000.

5. On September 30, 20X6, equipment was sold for $40,000. The equipment cost $62,000 and had a carrying amount of $34,000 on the date of sale.

6. On December 15, 20X6, Dore paid a cash dividend of $50,000 on its common stock.

7. A goodwill impairment loss of $3,000 was recognized in 20X6.

8. Deferred income taxes represent temporary differences relating to the use of accelerated depreciation methods for income tax reporting and the straight-line method for financial reporting.

9. Net income for 20X6 was as follows:

| | |
|---|---|
| Consolidated net income | $231,000 |
| Dore Corporation | 110,000 |

10. Brimer owns 70 percent of its subsidiary, Dore. There was no change in the ownership interest in Dore during 20X5 and 20X6. There were no intercompany transactions other than the dividend paid to Brimer Inc. by its subsidiary.

### Required

Prepare a consolidated statement of cash flows for Brimer Inc. and its subsidiary for the year ended December 31, 20X6, using the indirect method.

**P10-24** **Statement of Cash Flows Prepared from Consolidation Workpaper**

Detecto Corporation purchased 60 percent of Strand Company's outstanding shares on January 1, 20X1, for $24,000 more than book value. At that date, the fair value of the noncontrolling interest was $16,000 more than 40 percent of the book value of Strand. The full amount of the differential is considered related to patents and is being amortized over an eight-year period. In 20X1, Strand purchased a piece of land for $35,000 and later in the year sold it to Detecto for $45,000. Detecto is still holding the land as an investment. During 20X3, Detecto bonds with a value of $100,000 were exchanged for equipment valued at $100,000.

On January 1, 20X3, Detecto held inventory purchased previously from Strand for $48,000. During 20X3, Detecto purchased an additional $90,000 of goods from Strand and held $54,000 of this inventory on December 31, 20X3. Strand sells merchandise to the parent at cost plus a 20 percent markup.

Strand also purchases inventory items from Detecto. On January 1, 20X3, Strand held inventory it had previously purchased from Detecto for $14,000, and on December 31, 20X3, it held goods it purchased from Detecto for $7,000 during 20X3. Strand's total purchases from Detecto in 20X3 were $22,000. Detecto sells inventory to Strand at cost plus a 40 percent markup.

The consolidated balance sheet at December 31, 20X2, contained the following amounts:

|  | Debit | Credit |
|---|---|---|
| Cash | $ 92,000 |  |
| Accounts Receivable | 135,000 |  |
| Inventory | 140,000 |  |
| Land | 75,000 |  |
| Buildings and Equipment | 400,000 |  |
| Patents | 18,000 |  |
| Accumulated Depreciation |  | $210,000 |
| Accounts Payable |  | 114,200 |
| Bonds Payable |  | 90,000 |
| Noncontrolling Interest |  | 72,800 |
| Common Stock |  | 100,000 |
| Retained Earnings |  | 273,000 |
| Totals | $860,000 | $860,000 |

The consolidation workpaper below was prepared on December 31, 20X3. All eliminating entries and adjustments have been entered properly in the workpaper. Detecto accounts for its investment in Strand using the basic equity method.

### Required

*a.* Prepare a workpaper for a consolidated statement of cash flows for 20X3 using the indirect method.

*b.* Prepare a consolidated statement of cash flows for 20X3.

### DETECTO CORPORATION AND STRAND COMPANY
#### Consolidation Workpaper
#### December 31, 20X3

| Item | Detecto Corporation | Strand Company | Eliminations Debit | Eliminations Credit | Consolidated |
|---|---|---|---|---|---|
| Sales | 400,000 | 200,000 | (8)  22,000<br>(9)  90,000 |  | 488,000 |
| Income from Subsidiary | 18,000 |  | (1)  18,000 |  |  |
| Credits | 418,000 | 200,000 |  |  | 488,000 |
| Cost of Goods Sold | 280,000 | 120,000 |  | (6)  4,000<br>(7)  8,000<br>(8)  20,000<br>(9)  81,000 | 287,000 |
| Amortization Expense |  |  | (4)  5,000 |  | 5,000 |
| Depreciation Expense | 25,000 | 15,000 |  |  | 40,000 |
| Other Expenses | 35,000 | 30,000 |  |  | 65,000 |
| Debits | (340,000) | (165,000) |  |  | (397,000) |
| Consolidated Net Income |  |  |  |  | 91,000 |
| Income to Noncontrolling Interest |  |  | (2)  11,600 |  | (11,600) |
| Income, carry forward | 78,000 | 35,000 | 146,600 | 113,000 | 79,400 |

(*continued*)

*(continued)*

| Item | Detecto Corporation | Strand Company | Eliminations Debit | Eliminations Credit | Consolidated |
|---|---|---|---|---|---|
| Retained Earnings, January 1 | 287,800 | 150,000 | (3) 150,000 | | |
| | | | (5) 6,000 | | |
| | | | (6) 4,000 | | |
| | | | (7) 4,800 | | 273,000 |
| Income, from above | 78,000 | 35,000 | 146,600 | 113,000 | 79,400 |
| | 365,800 | 185,000 | | | 352,400 |
| Dividends Declared | (50,000) | (20,000) | | (1) 12,000 | |
| | | | | (2) 8,000 | (50,000) |
| Retained Earnings, December 31, carry forward | 315,800 | 165,000 | 311,400 | 133,000 | 302,400 |
| Cash | 26,800 | 35,000 | | | 61,800 |
| Accounts Receivable | 80,000 | 40,000 | | | 120,000 |
| Inventory | 120,000 | 90,000 | | (8) 2,000 | |
| | | | | (9) 9,000 | 199,000 |
| Land | 70,000 | 20,000 | | (5) 10,000 | 80,000 |
| Buildings and Equipment | 340,000 | 200,000 | | | 540,000 |
| Investment in Strand Company Stock | 144,000 | | | (1) 6,000 | |
| | | | | (3) 138,000 | |
| Differential | | | (3) 30,000 | (4) 30,000 | |
| Patents | | | (4) 25,000 | | 25,000 |
| Debits | 780,800 | 385,000 | | | 1,025,800 |
| Accumulated Depreciation | 165,000 | 85,000 | | | 250,000 |
| Accounts Payable | 80,000 | 15,000 | | | 95,000 |
| Bonds Payable | 120,000 | 70,000 | | | 190,000 |
| Common Stock | 100,000 | 50,000 | (3) 50,000 | | 100,000 |
| Retained Earnings, from above | 315,800 | 165,000 | 311,400 | 133,000 | 302,400 |
| Noncontrolling interest | | | (5) 4,000 | (2) 3,600 | |
| | | | (7) 3,200 | (3) 92,000 | 88,400 |
| Credits | 780,800 | 385,000 | 423,600 | 423,600 | 1,025,800 |

## P10-25 Midyear Purchase of Controlling Interest

Blase Company operates on a calendar-year basis, reporting its results of operations quarterly. For the first quarter of 20X1, Blase reported sales of $240,000 and operating expenses of $180,000, and paid dividends of $10,000. On April 1, 20X1, Mega Theaters Inc. acquired 85 percent of Blase's common stock for $765,000. At that date, the fair value of the noncontrolling interest was $135,000, and Blase had 100,000 shares of $1 par common stock outstanding, originally issued at $6 per share. The differential is related to goodwill. On December 31, 20X1, the management of Mega Theaters reviewed the amount attributed to goodwill as a result of its purchase of Blase common stock and concluded that goodwill was not impaired.

Blase's retained earnings statement for the full year 20X1 appears as follows:

| | |
|---|---|
| Retained Earnings, January 1, 20X1 | $150,000 |
| Net Income | 175,000 |
| Dividends | (40,000) |
| Retained Earnings, December 31, 20X1 | $285,000 |

Mega Theaters accounts for its investment in Blase using the equity method.

### Required

a. Present all entries that Mega Theaters would have recorded in accounting for its investment in Blase during 20X1.

b. Present all eliminating entries needed in a workpaper to prepare a complete set of consolidated financial statements for the year 20X1.

**P10-26** **Consolidation Involving a Midyear Purchase**

Famous Products Corporation acquired 90 percent ownership of Sanford Company on October 20, 20X2, through an exchange of voting shares. Famous Products issued 8,000 shares of its $10 par stock to acquire 27,000 shares of Sanford's $5 par stock. The market value of shares issued by Famous Products was $247,500. At that date, the fair value of the noncontrolling interest was $27,500. Trial balances of the two companies on December 31, 20X2, are as follows:

|  | Famous Products Corporation | | Sanford Company | |
|---|---|---|---|---|
|  | **Debit** | **Credit** | **Debit** | **Credit** |
| Cash | $ 85,000 | | $ 50,000 | |
| Accounts Receivable | 100,000 | | 60,000 | |
| Inventory | 150,000 | | 100,000 | |
| Buildings and Equipment | 400,000 | | 340,000 | |
| Investment in Sanford Stock | 252,000 | | | |
| Cost of Goods Sold | 305,000 | | 145,000 | |
| Depreciation Expense | 25,000 | | 20,000 | |
| Other Expense | 14,000 | | 25,000 | |
| Dividends Declared | 40,000 | | 30,000 | |
| Accumulated Depreciation | | $ 105,000 | | $ 65,000 |
| Accounts Payable | | 40,000 | | 50,000 |
| Taxes Payable | | 70,000 | | 55,000 |
| Bonds Payable | | 250,000 | | 100,000 |
| Common Stock | | 200,000 | | 150,000 |
| Additional Paid-In Capital | | 167,500 | | |
| Retained Earnings | | 135,000 | | 100,000 |
| Sales | | 390,000 | | 250,000 |
| Income from Subsidiary | | 13,500 | | |
| Totals | $1,371,000 | $1,371,000 | $770,000 | $770,000 |

For 20X2, before acquisition, Sanford reported sales of $205,000, cost of goods sold of $126,000, depreciation of $16,000, and other expenses of $18,000. Sanford paid dividends of $20,000 in April and $10,000 in November of 20X2. Famous Products paid dividends of $40,000 in 20X2. Famous Products uses the equity method in accounting for its investment in Sanford.

### Required

a. Give all journal entries recorded by Famous Products during 20X2 that relate to its investment in Sanford.

b. Give the workpaper elimination entries needed on December 31, 20X2, to prepare consolidated financial statements.

c. Prepare a three-part consolidation workpaper as of December 31, 20X2.

**P10-27** **Tax Allocation in Consolidated Balance Sheet**

Acme Powder Corporation acquired 70 percent of Brown Company's stock on December 31, 20X7, at underlying book value. At that date, the fair value of the noncontrolling interest was equal to 30 percent of the book value of Brown Company. The two companies' balance sheets on December 31, 20X9, are as follows:

### ACME POWDER CORPORATION AND BROWN COMPANY
### Balance Sheets
### December 31, 20X9

|  | Acme Powder Corporation | Brown Company |
|---|---|---|
| Cash | $ 44,400 | $ 20,000 |
| Accounts Receivable | 120,000 | 60,000 |
| Inventory | 170,000 | 120,000 |
| Land | 90,000 | 30,000 |
| Buildings and Equipment | 500,000 | 300,000 |
| Less: Accumulated Depreciation | (180,000) | (80,000) |
| Investment in Brown Company Stock | 280,000 |  |
| Total Assets | $1,024,400 | $450,000 |
| Accounts Payable | $ 70,000 | $ 20,000 |
| Wages Payable | 80,000 | 30,000 |
| Bonds Payable | 200,000 |  |
| Common Stock | 100,000 | 150,000 |
| Retained Earnings | 574,400 | 250,000 |
| Total Liabilities and Equities | $1,024,400 | $450,000 |

On December 31, 20X9, Acme Powder holds inventory purchased from Brown for $70,000. Brown's cost of producing the merchandise was $50,000. Brown also had purchased inventory from Acme. Brown's ending inventory contains $85,000 of purchases that had cost Acme Powder $60,000 to produce.

On December 30, 20X9, Brown sold equipment to Acme Powder for $90,000. Brown had purchased the equipment for $120,000 several years earlier. At the time of sale to Acme, the equipment had a book value of $40,000. The two companies file separate tax returns and are subject to a 40 percent tax rate. Acme Powder does not record tax expense on its share of Brown's undistributed earnings.

### Required

*a.* Complete a consolidated balance sheet workpaper as of December 31, 20X9.

*b.* Prepare a consolidated balance sheet as of December 31, 20X9.

**P10-28** **Computations Involving Tax Allocation**

Broom Manufacturing used cash to acquire 75 percent of the voting stock of Satellite Industries on January 1, 20X3, at underlying book value. At that date, the fair value of the noncontrolling interest was equal to 25 percent of the book value of Satellite Industries. Broom accounts for its investment in Satellite using the basic equity method.

Broom had no inventory on hand on January 1, 20X5. During 20X5 Broom purchased $300,000 of goods from Satellite and had $100,000 remaining on hand at the end of 20X5. Satellite normally prices its items so that their cost is 70 percent of sale price. On January 1, 20X5, Satellite held inventory that it purchased from Broom for $50,000. Broom's cost of producing the items was $30,000. Satellite sold all of the merchandise in 20X5 and made no inventory purchases from Broom during 20X5.

On July 15, 20X5, Satellite sold land that it had purchased for $240,000 to Broom for $360,000. The companies file separate tax returns and have a 40 percent income tax rate. Broom does not record tax expense on its portion of the undistributed earnings of Satellite. Tax expense recorded by Broom in 20X5 with regard to its investment in Satellite is based on dividends received from Satellite in 20X5. In computing taxable income, 80 percent of intercorporate dividend payments are exempt from tax.

Satellite reported net income of $190,000 for 20X5 and net assets of $900,000 on December 31, 20X5. Broom's reported income before investment income from Satellite and income tax expense was $700,000 for 20X5. Satellite and Broom paid dividends of $150,000 and $400,000, respectively, in 20X5.

### Required

a. Give the journal entries recorded on Broom's books during 20X5 to reflect its ownership of Satellite.

b. Compute the income assigned to the noncontrolling interests in the 20X5 consolidated income statement.

c. Compute consolidated net income and income to the controlling interest for 20X5.

d. Compute the amount assigned to the noncontrolling interest in the consolidated balance sheet prepared as of December 31, 20X5.

**P10-29 Workpaper Involving Tax Allocation**

Hardtack Bread Company holds 70 percent of the common shares of Custom Pizza Corporation. Trial balances for the two companies on December 31, 20X7, are as follows:

| Item | Hardtack Bread Company Debit | Credit | Custom Pizza Corporation Debit | Credit |
|---|---|---|---|---|
| Cash | $ 35,800 | | $ 56,000 | |
| Accounts Receivable | 130,000 | | 40,000 | |
| Inventory | 220,000 | | 60,000 | |
| Land | 60,000 | | 20,000 | |
| Buildings and Equipment | 450,000 | | 400,000 | |
| Patents | 70,000 | | | |
| Investment in Custom Pizza Common Stock | 158,200 | | | |
| Cost of Goods Sold | 435,000 | | 210,000 | |
| Depreciation and Amortization | 40,000 | | 20,000 | |
| Tax Expense | 44,000 | | 24,000 | |
| Other Expenses | 11,400 | | 10,000 | |
| Dividends Declared | 20,000 | | 10,000 | |
| Accumulated Depreciation | | $ 150,000 | | $160,000 |
| Accounts Payable | | 40,000 | | 30,000 |
| Wages Payable | | 70,000 | | 20,000 |
| Bonds Payable | | 200,000 | | 100,000 |
| Deferred Income Taxes | | 120,000 | | 40,000 |
| Common Stock ($10 par value) | | 100,000 | | 50,000 |
| Retained Earnings | | 374,200 | | 150,000 |
| Sales | | 580,000 | | 300,000 |
| Income from Subsidiary | | 25,200 | | |
| Gain on Sale of Equipment | | 15,000 | | |
| Total | $1,674,400 | $1,674,400 | $850,000 | $850,000 |

At the beginning of 20X7, Hardtack held inventory purchased from Custom Pizza containing unrealized profits of $10,000. During 20X7, Hardtack purchased $120,000 of inventory from Custom Pizza and on December 31, 20X7, had goods on hand containing $25,000 of unrealized intercompany profit. On December 31, 20X7, Hardtack sold equipment to Custom Pizza for $65,000. Hardtack had purchased the equipment for $150,000 and had accumulated depreciation of $100,000 on it at the time of sale. The companies file separate tax returns and are subject to a 40 percent income tax rate on all taxable income. Intercompany dividends are 80 percent exempt from taxation.

### Required

a. Prepare all eliminating entries needed as of December 31, 20X7, to prepare consolidated financial statements for Hardtack Bread Company and its subsidiary.

b. Prepare a three-part consolidation workpaper for 20X7.

**P10-30** **Earnings per Share with Convertible Securities**

Branch Manufacturing Corporation owns 80 percent of the common shares of Short Retail Stores. The companies' balance sheets as of December 31, 20X4, were as follows:

| | Branch Manufacturing Corporation | Short Retail Stores |
|---|---|---|
| Cash | $ 50,000 | $ 30,000 |
| Accounts Receivable | 100,000 | 80,000 |
| Inventory | 260,000 | 120,000 |
| Land | 90,000 | 60,000 |
| Buildings and Equipment | 500,000 | 300,000 |
| Less: Accumulated Depreciation | (220,000) | (120,000) |
| Investment in Short Retail Stores Stock | 120,000 | |
| Total Assets | $900,000 | $470,000 |
| | | |
| Accounts Payable | $ 40,000 | $ 20,000 |
| Bonds Payable | 300,000 | 200,000 |
| Preferred Stock ($10 par value) | 200,000 | 100,000 |
| Common Stock: | | |
| $10 par value | 150,000 | |
| $5 par value | | 100,000 |
| Retained Earnings | 210,000 | 50,000 |
| Total Liabilities and Equity | $900,000 | $470,000 |

The 8 percent preferred stock of Short Retail is convertible into 12,000 shares of common stock, and Short's 10 percent bonds are convertible into 8,000 shares of common stock. Short Retail reported net income of $49,200 for 20X4 and paid dividends of $30,000.

Branch Manufacturing has 11 percent preferred stock and 12 percent bonds outstanding, neither of which is convertible. Branch Manufacturing reported after-tax income, excluding investment income from Short Retail, of $100,000 in 20X4 and paid dividends of $60,000. The companies file separate tax returns and are subject to a 40 percent income tax.

*Required*

Compute basic and diluted earnings per share for the consolidated entity.

**P10-31** **Comprehensive Earnings per Share**

Mighty Corporation holds 80 percent of Longfellow Company's common stock. The following balance sheet data are presented for December 31, 20X7:

| | Mighty Corporation | Longfellow Company |
|---|---|---|
| Cash | $ 100,000 | $ 90,000 |
| Accounts Receivable | 150,000 | 220,000 |
| Inventory | 300,000 | 300,000 |
| Land | 100,000 | 290,000 |
| Buildings and Equipment | 2,250,000 | 900,000 |
| Less: Accumulated Depreciation | (850,000) | (250,000) |
| Investment in Longfellow Company Stock | 600,000 | |
| Total Assets | $2,650,000 | $1,550,000 |
| | | |
| Accounts Payable | $ 200,000 | $ 100,000 |
| Bonds Payable | 800,000 | 500,000 |
| Preferred Stock ($100 par value) | | 200,000 |
| Common Stock ($10 par value) | 1,000,000 | 400,000 |
| Retained Earnings | 650,000 | 350,000 |
| Total Liabilities and Equities | $2,650,000 | $1,550,000 |

Longfellow reported net income of $115,000 in 20X7 and paid dividends of $60,000. Its bonds have an annual interest rate of 8 percent and are convertible into 30,000 common shares. Its preferred shares pay an 11 percent annual dividend and convert into 20,000 shares of common stock. In addition, Longfellow has warrants outstanding for 10,000 shares of common stock at $8 per share. The 20X7 average price of Longfellow common shares was $40.

Mighty reported income of $300,000 from its own operations for 20X7 and paid dividends of $200,000. Its 10 percent bonds convert into 25,000 shares of its common stock. The companies file separate tax returns and are subject to income taxes of 40 percent.

### Required

Compute basic and diluted earnings per share for the consolidated entity for 20X7.

# Multinational Accounting: Foreign Currency Transactions and Financial Instruments

Many companies, large and small, depend on international markets for supplies of goods and for sales of their products and services. Every day the business press carries stories about the effects of export and import activity on the U.S. economy and the large flows of capital among the world's major countries. Also reported are changes in the exchange rates of the major currencies of the world, such as, "The dollar weakened today against the yen." This chapter and Chapter 12 discuss the accounting issues associated with companies that operate internationally.

A company operating in international markets is subject to normal business risks such as lack of demand for its products in the foreign marketplace, labor strikes, and transportation delays in getting its products to the foreign customer. In addition, the U.S. entity may incur foreign currency risks whenever it conducts transactions in other currencies. For example, if a U.S. company acquires a machine on credit from a Swiss manufacturer, the Swiss company may require payment in Swiss francs (SFr). This means the U.S. company must eventually use a foreign currency broker or a bank to exchange U.S. dollars for Swiss francs to pay for the machine. In the process, the U.S. company may experience foreign currency gains or losses from fluctuations in the value of the U.S. dollar relative to the Swiss franc.

The topic of foreign exchange markets is one of the most important and often misunderstood subjects in international business. It provides the framework for international business and influences both the form and the content of international business activities. Multinational enterprises (MNEs) entering into international transactions must agree on which currency will be used. Factors that affect this decision include familiarity with the foreign currency, the potential for gains and losses from changes in exchange rates, nationalistic pride, and practicality.

MNEs transact in a variety of currencies as a result of their export and import activities. There are approximately 150 different currencies around the world, but most international trade has been settled in six major currencies that have shown stability and general acceptance over time: the U.S. dollar, the British pound, the Canadian dollar, the Japanese yen, the Swiss franc, and the European euro.

The European euro (symbol €) is a relatively new currency introduced in 1999 to members of the European Union (EU) that wished to participate in a common currency.

By 2002, euro notes and coins were introduced to be used in everyday trade. The EU is an organization of democratic member states from the European continent. The Union has grown over time and as of 2008 is composed of 27 member countries: Belgium, France, Germany, Italy, Luxembourg, the Netherlands, Denmark, Ireland, the United Kingdom, Greece, Portugal, Spain, Austria, Finland, Sweden, Cyprus, Czech Republic, Estonia, Hungary, Latvia, Lithuania, Malta, Poland, Slovakia, Slovenia, Bulgaria, and Romania. In addition, Croatia, Turkey, and Macedonia have applied for accession. The EU is a dominant economic force, rivaling the United States, and the euro is now as familiar to companies doing international business as the U.S. dollar.

The EU is one of several regional groupings, and these groupings are becoming increasingly important. The North American Free Trade Agreement (NAFTA) was approved by the U.S. Congress in 1993 and created a free-trade area of Canada, the United States, and Mexico, a market that exceeds 420 million people. Over time, the agreement will result in the elimination of tariffs (taxes) on goods shipped between these three countries. The Agreement on the South Asian Free Trade Area, or SAFTA, was created on January 1, 2006, and will be operational following ratification of the agreement by seven governments. SAFTA creates a framework for the creation of a free-trade zone covering 1.4 billion people in India, Pakistan, Nepal, Sri Lanka, Bangladesh, Bhutan, and the Maldives. The Association of Southeast Asian nations (ASEAN) created the ASEAN Free Trade Area (AFTA), which is a trade bloc agreement. The goal of AFTA is to increase ASEAN's competitive edge as a production base in the world market through the elimination, within ASEAN, of tariffs and nontariff barriers. AFTA currently is composed of Brunei, Indonesia, Malaysia, Philippines, Singapore, Thailand, Laos, Vietnam, Myanmar, and Cambodia. In January 2005, the Greater Arab Free Trade Area (also referred to as GAFTA) came into existence. GAFTA is a pact made by the Arab League to achieve a complete Arab economic bloc that can compete internationally. GAFTA is relatively similar to ASEAN.

Currency names and symbols often reflect a country's nationalistic pride and history. For example, the U.S. dollar receives its name from a variation of the German word *Taler,* the name of a silver piece that was first minted in 1518 and became the chief coin of Europe and the New World. Some historians argue that the dollar symbol ($) is derived from a capital letter *U* superimposed over a capital letter *S.* The greenback as we know it today was first printed in 1862, in the midst of the Civil War, and now is issued by the 12 Federal Reserve banks scattered across the United States. The U.S. dollar can be identified in virtually every corner of the world because it has become one of the most widely traded currencies.

# THE ACCOUNTING ISSUES

Accountants must be able to record and report transactions involving exchanges of U.S. dollars and foreign currencies. *Foreign currency transactions* of a U.S. company include sales, purchases, and other transactions giving rise to a transfer of foreign currency or the recording of receivables or payables that are *denominated*—that is, numerically specified to be settled—in a foreign currency. Because financial statements of virtually all U.S. companies are prepared using the U.S. dollar as the reporting currency, transactions denominated in other currencies must be restated to their U.S. dollar equivalents before they can be recorded in the U.S. company's books and included in its financial statements. This process of restating foreign currency transactions to their U.S. dollar equivalent values is termed *translation.*

In addition, many large U.S. corporations have multinational operations, such as foreign-based subsidiaries or branches. For example, a U.S. auto manufacturer may have manufacturing subsidiaries in Canada, Mexico, Spain, and Great Britain. The foreign subsidiaries prepare their financial statements in the currency of their countries; for example, the Mexican subsidiary reports its operations in pesos. The foreign currency amounts in the financial statements of these subsidiaries have to be translated, that is, restated, into their U.S. dollar equivalents, before they can be consolidated with the financial statements of the U.S. parent company that uses the U.S. dollar as its reporting currency unit.

This chapter presents the accounting procedures for recording and reporting foreign transactions. Chapter 12 presents the procedures for combining or consolidating a foreign entity with a U.S. parent company. **FASB Statement No. 52,** "Foreign Currency Translation" (FASB 52), issued in 1981, serves as the primary guide for accounting for accounts receivable and accounts payable foreign currency–denominated transactions that require payment or receipt of foreign currency. **FASB Statement No. 133,** "Accounting for Derivative Instruments and Hedging Activities" (FASB 133), issued in 1998, guides the accounting for financial instruments specified as derivatives for the purpose of hedging certain items.

# FOREIGN CURRENCY EXCHANGE RATES

Before 1972, most major currencies were valued on the basis of a gold standard whereby their international values were fixed per ounce of gold. However, in 1972, most countries signed an agreement to permit the values of their currencies to "float" based on the supply and demand for them. The resulting *foreign currency exchange rates* between currencies are established daily by foreign exchange brokers who serve as agents for individuals or countries wishing to deal in foreign currencies. Some countries, such as China, maintain an official fixed rate of currency exchange and have established fixed exchange rates for dividends remitted outside the country. These official rates may be changed at any time, and companies doing business abroad should contact the foreign country's government to ensure that the companies are in compliance with any currency exchange restrictions.

## The Determination of Exchange Rates

A country's currency is much like any other commodity, and exchange rates change because of a number of economic factors affecting the supply of and demand for a nation's currency. For example, if a nation is experiencing high levels of inflation, the purchasing power of its currency decreases. This reduction in the value of a currency is reflected by a decrease in the positioning of that country's currency relative to other nations' currencies. Other factors causing exchange rate fluctuations are a nation's balance of payments, changes in a country's interest rate and investment levels, and the stability and process of governance. For example, if the United States had a higher average interest rate than that in Great Britain, the international investment community might seek to invest in the United States, thus increasing the demand for U.S. dollars relative to British pounds. The dollar would increase in value relative to the pound because of the increased demand. Exchange rates are determined daily and published in several sources, including *The Wall Street Journal.* Figure 11–1 presents an example of a typical daily business press report for selected foreign exchange rates. The rates illustrated in the table are current as of February 2008. Updated exchange rates may be obtained from most business publications and from many metropolitan newspapers.

## Direct versus Indirect Exchange Rates

As indicated in Figure 11–1, the relative value of one currency to another may be expressed in two different ways: either *directly* or *indirectly.*

### Direct Exchange Rate

The direct exchange rate (DER) is the number of **local currency units (LCUs)** needed to acquire one **foreign currency unit (FCU)**. From the viewpoint of a U.S. entity, the direct exchange rate can be viewed as the U.S. dollar cost of one foreign currency unit. The direct exchange rate ratio is expressed as follows, with the LCU, the U.S. dollar, in the numerator:

$$\text{DER} = \frac{\text{U.S. dollar−equivalent value}}{1\,\text{FCU}}$$

**FIGURE 11–1**   **Foreign Exchange Rates for Selected Major Currencies as of February 2008**

| Country | Currency | Direct Exchange Rate (U.S. dollar equivalent) | Indirect Exchange Rate (currency per U.S. dollar) |
|---|---|---|---|
| Argentina | peso | 0.3119 | 3.1209 |
| Australia | dollar | 0.8951 | 1.1160 |
| Bahrain | dinar | 2.6439 | 0.3745 |
| Brazil | real | 0.5656 | 1.7588 |
| Canada | dollar | 1.0006 | 0.9984 |
| Chile | peso | 0.002119 | 471.600 |
| China | yuan renminbi | 0.1389 | 7.1796 |
| Colombia | peso | 0.0005108 | 1888.70 |
| Czech Republic | koruna | 0.05629 | 17.6650 |
| Denmark | krone | 0.1947 | 5.1344 |
| Egypt | pound | 0.1788 | 5.4891 |
| Hong Kong | dollar | 0.1282 | 7.7998 |
| India | rupee | 0.02522 | 39.6450 |
| Indonesia | rupiah | 0.0001082 | 9226.50 |
| Israel | new shekel | 0.2738 | 3.6434 |
| Japan | yen | 0.009313 | 107.283 |
|   1-month forward | | 0.009330 | 107.132 |
|   3-month forward | | 0.009350 | 106.935 |
|   6-month forward | | 0.00937 | 106.298 |
| Malaysia | ringgit | 0.3094 | 3.2285 |
| Mexico | peso | 0.09275 | 10.7426 |
| Philippines | peso | 0.02458 | 40.4783 |
| Russia | ruble | 0.04037 | 24.7635 |
| South Korea | won | 0.001060 | 939.800 |
| Sweden | krona | 0.1540 | 6.4889 |
| Switzerland | franc | 0.9061 | 1.1026 |
| Taiwan | dollar | 0.03122 | 32.0131 |
| Thailand | bhat | 0.03160 | 31.1469 |
| United Kingdom | pound | 1.9473 | 0.513532 |
|   1-month forward | | 1.94230 | 0.54485 |
|   3-month forward | | 1.93793 | 0.51602 |
|   6-month forward | | 1.93415 | 0.51702 |
| Venezuela | bolivar | 0.0004654 | 2145.80 |
| Euro | | 1.4501 | 0.6891 |
|   1-month forward | | 1.4529 | 0.68875 |
|   3-month forward | | 1.454 | 0.68950 |
|   6-month forward | | 1.4559 | 0.69022 |
| SDR | | 1.57435 | 0.635812 |

The direct exchange rate is used most often in accounting for foreign operations and transactions because the foreign currency–denominated accounts must be translated to their U.S. dollar equivalent values. For example, if $1.20 can acquire €1 (1 European euro), the direct exchange rate of the dollar versus the European euro is $1.20, as follows:

$$\frac{\$1.20}{€1} = \$1.20$$

### Indirect Exchange Rate

The indirect exchange rate (IER) is the reciprocal of the direct exchange rate. From the viewpoint of a U.S. entity, the indirect exchange rate is:

$$IER = \frac{1\,FCU}{U.S.\ dollar-equivalent\ value}$$

For the European euro example, the indirect exchange rate is:

$$\frac{€1}{\$1.20} = €0.8333$$

Another way to express this is:

$$IER = \frac{\text{Number of foreign currency units}}{\$1}$$

$$= \frac{€0.8333}{\$1}$$

Thus, the indirect exchange rate of €0.8333 = \$1 shows the number of foreign currency units that may be obtained for 1 U.S. dollar. The business press and people who travel outside the United States often use the indirect exchange rate.

Note that the direct and indirect rates are inversely related and that both state the same economic relationships between two currencies. For example, if the indirect exchange rate is given, the direct exchange rate may be computed by simply inverting the indirect exchange rate. If given the indirect exchange rate of €0.8333 (€0.8333 / \$1), the direct exchange rate can be computed as (\$1 / €0.8333) = \$1.20. If given the direct exchange rate of \$1.20, the indirect exchange rate can be computed as (€1 / \$1.20) = €0.8333. Again, the currency in the numerator identifies the direction of the exchange rate. In practice, a slight difference might exist in the inverse relationship because of brokers' commissions or small differences in demand for the two currencies.

Some persons identify the direct exchange rate as *American terms* to indicate that it is U.S. dollar–based and represents an exchange rate quote from the perspective of a person in the United States. The indirect exchange rate is sometimes identified as *European terms* to indicate the direct exchange rate from the perspective of a person in Europe, which means the exchange rate shows the number of units of the European's local currency units per one U.S. dollar. A guide to help remember the difference in exchange rates is to note that the U.S. dollar is the numerator for the direct rate or American terms (the foreign currency unit is in the denominator), and the foreign currency unit is in the numerator for the indirect rate or European terms (with the U.S. dollar in the denominator). The *terms currency* is the numerator and the *base currency* is the denominator in the exchange rate ratio. The numerator is the key to the identification of the rate.

## Changes in Exchange Rates

A change in an exchange rate is referred to as a *strengthening* or *weakening* of one currency against another. During the first decade of the new century the relationship between the dollar and the euro was often volatile. For example, the exchange rate of the U.S. dollar versus the euro changed as follows during 2005 and 2006:

|  | January 2005 | July 2005 | January 2006 | July 2006 |
| --- | --- | --- | --- | --- |
| Direct exchange rate (U.S. dollar–equivalent of 1 euro) | \$1.35 | \$1.20 | \$1.18 | \$1.28 |
| Indirect exchange rate (Euro per 1 U.S. dollar) | €0.74 | €0.83 | €0.85 | €0.78 |

### *Strengthening of the U.S. Dollar—Direct Exchange Rate Decreases*

Between January 1, 2005, and July 1, 2005, the direct exchange rate decreased from \$1.35 = €1 to \$1.20 = €1, indicating that it took less U.S. currency (\$) to acquire 1 European euro (€). In other words, the cost of 1 euro was \$1.35 on January 1 but decreased to \$1.20 on July 1. This means that the value of the U.S. currency rose relative to the euro. This is termed a *strengthening* of the dollar versus the euro. Alternatively, looking at the indirect exchange rate, 1 U.S. dollar could acquire 0.74 European euros on January 1, but it could acquire more euros, 0.83, on July 1. Thus, the relative value of the dollar versus the euro was greater on July 1 than on January 1.

Think of the strengthening of the U.S. dollar as:

- Taking less U.S. currency to acquire one foreign currency unit.
- One U.S. dollar acquiring more foreign currency units.

Imports from Europe were less expensive for U.S. consumers on July 1 than on January 1 because of the strengthening of the dollar. For example, assume that a European manufacturer is selling a German-made automobile for €25,000. To determine the U.S. dollar–equivalent value of the €25,000 on January 1, the following equation is used:

$$
\begin{array}{ccccc}
\textbf{U.S. dollar–} & = & \textbf{Foreign currency} & \times & \textbf{Direct exchange} \\
\textbf{equivalent value} & & \textbf{units} & & \textbf{rate} \\
\$33,750 & = & €25,000 & \times & \$1.35
\end{array}
$$

Between January 1 and July 1, the direct exchange rate decreased as the dollar strengthened relative to the euro. On July 1, the U.S. dollar equivalent value of the €25,000 is:

$$
\begin{array}{ccccc}
\textbf{U.S. dollar–} & = & \textbf{Foreign currency} & \times & \textbf{Direct exchange} \\
\textbf{equivalent value} & & \textbf{units} & & \textbf{rate} \\
\$30,000 & = & €25,000 & \times & \$1.20
\end{array}
$$

Although a strengthening of the dollar is favorable for U.S. companies purchasing goods from another country, it adversely affects U.S. companies selling products in that country. Following a strengthening of the dollar, U.S. exports to Europe are more expensive for European customers. For example, assume a U.S. manufacturer is selling a U.S.-made machine for $10,000. To determine the foreign currency (euro) equivalent value of the $10,000 on January 1, the following equation is used:

$$
\begin{array}{ccccc}
\textbf{Foreign currency} & = & \textbf{U.S. dollar} & \times & \textbf{Indirect exchange} \\
\textbf{equivalent value} & & \textbf{units} & & \textbf{rate} \\
€7,400 & = & \$10,000 & \times & €0.74
\end{array}
$$

On July 1, after a strengthening of the dollar, the machine would cost the European customer €8,300, as follows:

$$
\begin{array}{ccccc}
\textbf{Foreign currency} & = & \textbf{U.S. dollar} & \times & \textbf{Indirect exchange} \\
\textbf{equivalent value} & & \textbf{units} & & \textbf{rate} \\
€8,300 & = & \$10,000 & \times & €0.83
\end{array}
$$

This substantial increase in cost could lead the European customer to decide not to acquire the machine from the U.S. company. Thus, a U.S. company's international sales can be seriously affected by changes in foreign currency exchange rates.

### Weakening of the U.S. Dollar—Direct Exchange Rate Increases

Between July 1, 2005, and July 1, 2006, the direct exchange rate increased from $1.20 = €1 to $1.28 = €1, indicating that it took more U.S. currency to acquire 1 euro. On July 1, 2005, a euro cost $1.20, but on July 1, 2006, the relative cost for 1 euro increased to $1.28. This means that the value of the U.S. currency dropped relative to the euro, termed a *weakening* of the dollar against the euro. Another way to view this change is to note that the indirect exchange rate decreased, indicating that on July 1, 2006, 1 dollar acquired fewer euros than it did on July 1, 2005. On July 1, 2005, 1 U.S. dollar could acquire 0.83 euros, but on July 1, 2006, 1 U.S. dollar could acquire fewer euros, 0.78, indicating that the relative value of the dollar dropped between July 1, 2005, and July 1, 2006.

|  | January, 2005 | July, 2005 | July, 2006 |
| --- | --- | --- | --- |
| Direct exchange rate ($ / €) | $1.35 | $1.20 | $1.28 |
| Indirect exchange rate (€ / $) | €0.74 | €0.83 | €0.78 |

Between January 1, 2005, and July 1, 2005—strengthening of the U.S. dollar:
  Direct rate decreases
    Dollar strengthens (takes less U.S. currency to acquire 1 euro)
  Indirect rate increases
    Euro weakens (takes more euros to acquire 1 U.S. dollar)
  Imports into U.S. normally increase in quantity
    Foreign goods imported into U.S. less expensive in dollars ($1 can acquire more)
  Exports from U.S. normally decrease in quantity
    U.S.-made exports more expensive (takes more euros to acquire goods)

Between July 1, 2005, and July 1, 2006—weakening of the U.S. dollar:
  Direct rate increases
    Dollar weakens (takes more U.S. currency to acquire 1 euro)
  Indirect rate decreases
    Euro strengthens (takes fewer euros to acquire 1 U.S. dollar)
  Imports into U.S. normally decrease in quantity
    Foreign goods imported into U.S. more expensive in dollars
  Exports from U.S. normally increase in quantity
    U.S.-made exports less expensive in euros

Think of the weakening of the U.S. dollar as:

- Taking more U.S. currency to acquire one foreign currency unit.
- One U.S. dollar acquiring fewer foreign currency units.

The relationships between currencies, imports, and exports is summarized in Figure 11–2.

During the latter part of the 1970s, the dollar consistently weakened against other major currencies because of several factors, including the high inflation the United States experienced. This weakening did help the U.S. balance of trade because it reduced the quantity of then more expensive imports, while making U.S.-made goods less expensive in other countries. In the first half of the 1980s, the dollar consistently strengthened relative to other currencies. Not only was the U.S. economy strong and producing goods more efficiently but also high interest rates attracted large foreign investment in the U.S. capital markets. A stronger dollar added to the foreign trade deficit by making imports less expensive and U.S.-made goods more expensive on the world market. Beginning in 1986 and continuing through the early 1990s, the dollar again weakened relative to the major international currencies. In the latter 1990s, the dollar generally strengthened because of the robustness of the U.S. economy, but in the early 2000s, the dollar again weakened because of the high trade deficit and the sluggish U.S. economy.

These changes in the international value of the dollar affect any consumer acquiring imported goods. A weakening dollar means that imports become more expensive while a strengthening dollar means that imports become less expensive. One reason the U.S. government may let the dollar weaken is to reduce the trade deficits. U.S. exporters can sell their goods more easily overseas, thus boosting their profitability. Imports should decrease because of the higher relative prices of the foreign-made goods, thus enhancing the demand for domestic-made goods within the United States. If the dollar weakens too far, overseas investors reduce their demand for dollar-dominated U.S. assets such as U.S. stocks and bonds. The reduced investment demand may require an increase in bond interest rates to offset overseas investors' reduction in bond returns caused by the weakening dollar. An increase in interest rates may reduce economic investment within the United States. Finally a weakening dollar means that foreign travel becomes more expensive because of the reduction in the dollar's purchasing power. Thus, the U.S. government's management of the value of the dollar is a balancing act to achieve the needs of both U.S. businesses and U.S. consumers.

## Spot Rates versus Current Rates

**FASB 52** refers to the use of both spot rates and current rates for measuring the currency used in international transactions. The *spot rate* is the exchange rate for immediate delivery of currencies. The *current rate* is defined simply as the spot rate on the entity's balance sheet date.

## Forward Exchange Rates

A third exchange rate is the rate on future, or forward, exchanges of currencies. Figure 11–1 shows these exchange rates for the major international currencies for one month, three months, and six months forward. Active dealer markets in *forward exchange contracts* are maintained for companies wishing to either receive or deliver major international currencies. The forward rate on a given date is not the same as the spot rate on the same date. Expectations about the relative value of currencies are built into the forward rate. The difference between the forward rate and the spot rate on a given date is called the *spread*. The spread gives information about the perceived strengths or weaknesses of currencies. For instance, assume the spot rate for the French franc is $0.1486 and the 30-day forward rate is $0.1387. The spread is the difference between these two numbers, or $0.0099. Because the forward rate is less than the spot rate, the expectation is that the dollar will strengthen against the franc in the next 30 days. The actual spot rate when the contract is due in 30 days may be higher or lower than the forward rate. By entering into the forward contract, the U.S. company gives up the chance of receiving a better exchange rate but also avoids the possibility of an exchange rate loss. This reduces the risk for the U.S. company.

For example, a U.S. company may have a liability in British pounds due in 30 days. Rather than wait 30 days to buy the pounds and risk having the dollar weaken in value relative to the pound, the company can go to a foreign exchange dealer and enter into a one-month forward exchange contract at the forward exchange rate in effect on the contract date. The United States has approximately 2,000 foreign exchange dealer institutions of which about 200 are market making, large banks such as Citibank, Chase Manhattan Bank, and Bank of America, which do the greatest volume of foreign exchange activity. The contract enables the buyer to receive British pounds from an exchange broker 30 days from the contract date at a price fixed now by the contract.

The next section of the chapter presents the accounting for import and export transactions and for forward exchange contracts.

# FOREIGN CURRENCY TRANSACTIONS

As defined earlier, foreign currency transactions are economic activities denominated in a currency other than the entity's recording currency. These transactions include the following:

1. Purchases or sales of goods or services (imports or exports), the prices of which are stated in a foreign currency.
2. Loans payable or receivable in a foreign currency.
3. Purchase or sale of foreign currency forward exchange contracts.
4. Purchase or sale of foreign currency units.

One party in a foreign exchange transaction must exchange its own currency for another country's currency. Some persons use a shorthand to refer to foreign exchange transactions by using just the letters FX. This book uses the longer, more generally used description, which is *foreign exchange.*

For financial statement purposes, transactions denominated in a foreign currency must be translated into the currency the reporting company uses. Additionally, at each balance sheet date—interim as well as annual—account balances denominated in a currency other than the entity's reporting currency must be adjusted to reflect changes in exchange rates during the period since the last balance sheet date or since the foreign currency transaction date if it occurred during the period. This adjustment restates the foreign currency–denominated accounts to their U.S. dollar–equivalent values as of the balance sheet date. The adjustment in equivalent U.S. dollar values is a ***foreign currency transaction gain or loss*** for the entity when exchange rates have changed. For example, assume that a U.S. company acquires €5,000 from its bank on January 1, 20X1, for use in future purchases from German companies. The direct exchange rate is $1.20 = €1; thus the company pays the bank $6,000 for €5,000, as follows:

**U.S. dollar– equivalent value = Foreign currency units × Direct exchange rate**

$$\$6,000 \qquad = \qquad €5,000 \qquad \times \qquad \$1.20$$

The following entry records this exchange of currencies:

January 1, 20X1
| | | | |
|---|---|---|---|
| (1) | Foreign Currency Units (€) | 6,000 | |
| | Cash | | 6,000 |

The parenthetical notation (€) is used here after the debit account to indicate that the asset is European euros, but for accounting purposes it is recorded and reported at its U.S. dollar–equivalent value. This translation to the U.S. equivalent value is required in order to add the value of the foreign currency units to all of the company's other accounts that are reported in dollars.

On July 1, 20X1, the exchange rate is $1.100 = €1 as represented in the following time line:

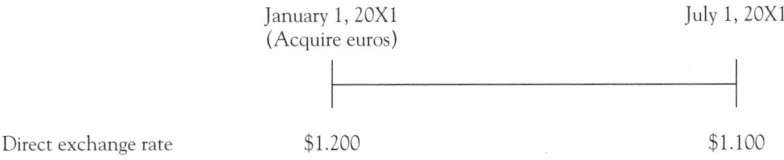

The direct exchange rate has decreased, reflecting that the U.S. dollar has strengthened. On July 1, it takes less U.S. currency to acquire 1 euro than it did on January 1. If the dollar has strengthened, the euro has weakened. By holding the euros during a weakening of the euro relative to the dollar, the company experiences a foreign currency transaction loss, as follows:

| | |
|---|---|
| Equivalent dollar value of €5.000 on January 1: | |
| €5.000 × $1.200 | $6,000 |
| Equivalent dollar value of €5.000 on July 1: | |
| €5.000 × $1.100 | 5,500 |
| Foreign currency transaction loss | $ 500 |

If the U.S. company prepares financial statements on July 1, the following adjusting entry is required:

July 1, 20X1
| | | | |
|---|---|---|---|
| (2) | Foreign Currency Transaction Loss | 500 | |
| | Foreign Currency Units (€) | | 500 |

The foreign currency transaction loss is the result of a foreign currency transaction and is included in this period's income statement, usually as a separate item under "Other

Income or Loss." Some accountants use the account title Exchange Loss instead of the longer title Foreign Currency Transaction Loss. In this book, the longer, more descriptive account title is used to communicate fully the source of the loss. The Foreign Currency Units account is reported on the balance sheet at a value of $5,500, its equivalent U.S. dollar value on that date.

In the previous examples, the U.S. company used the U.S. dollar as its primary currency for performing its major financial and operating functions, that is, as its ***functional currency***. Also, the U.S. company prepared its financial statements in U.S. dollars, its ***reporting currency***. Any transactions denominated in currencies other than the U.S. dollar require translation to their equivalent U.S. dollar values. Generally, the majority of a business's cash transactions take place in the ***local currency*** of the country in which the entity operates. The U.S. dollar is the functional currency for virtually all companies based in the United States. A company operating in Germany would probably use the euro as its functional currency. *In this chapter, the local currency is assumed to be the entity's functional and reporting currency.* The few exceptions to this general case are discussed in Chapter 12.

Illustrations of various types of foreign currency transactions are given in the sections that follow. Note that different exchange rates are used to value selected foreign currency transactions, depending on a number of factors such as management's reason for entering the foreign currency transaction, the nature of the transaction, and the timing of the transaction.

## Foreign Currency Import and Export Transactions

Payables and receivables that arise from transactions with foreign-based entities and that are denominated in a foreign currency must be measured and recorded by the U.S. entity in the currency used for its accounting records—the U.S. dollar. The relevant exchange rate for settlement of a transaction denominated in a foreign currency is the spot exchange rate on the date of settlement. At the time the transaction is settled, payables or receivables denominated in foreign currency units must be adjusted to their current U.S. dollar–equivalent value. If financial statements are prepared before the foreign currency payables or receivables are settled, their account balances must be adjusted to their U.S. dollar–equivalent values as of the balance sheet date, using the current rate on the balance sheet date.

An overview of the required accounting for an import or export transaction denominated in a foreign currency, assuming the company does *not* use forward contracts, is as follows:

1. *Transaction date.* Record the purchase or sale transaction at the U.S. dollar–equivalent value using the spot direct exchange rate on this date.
2. *Balance sheet date.* Adjust the payable or receivable to its U.S. dollar–equivalent, end-of-period value using the current direct exchange rate. Recognize any exchange gain or loss for the change in rates between the transaction and balance sheet dates.
3. *Settlement date.* First adjust the foreign currency payable or receivable for any changes in the exchange rate between the balance sheet date (or transaction date if transaction occurs after the balance sheet date) and the settlement date, recording any exchange gain or loss as required. Then record the settlement of the foreign currency payable or receivable.

This adjustment process is required because the FASB adopted what is called the *two transaction approach,* which views the purchase or sale of an item as a separate transaction from the foreign currency commitment. By adopting the two-transaction approach to foreign currency transactions, the FASB established the general rule that foreign currency exchange gains or losses resulting from the revaluation of assets or liabilities denominated in a foreign currency must be recognized currently in the income statement of the period in which the exchange rate changes. A few exceptions to this general rule are allowed and are discussed later in this chapter.

**FIGURE 11–3**   **Comparative U.S. Company Journal Entries for Foreign Purchase Transaction Denominated in Dollars versus Foreign Currency Units**

| If Denominated in U.S. Dollars | | | If Denominated in Japanese Yen | | |
|---|---|---|---|---|---|
| **October 1, 20X1 (Date of Purchase)** | | | | | |
| Inventory | 14,000 | | Inventory | 14,000 | |
|    Accounts Payable | | 14,000 |    Accounts Payable (¥) | | 14,000 |
| | | |    $14,000 = ¥2,000,000 × $.0070 spot rate | | |
| **December 31, 20X1 (Balance Sheet Date)** | | | | | |
| No entry | | | Foreign Currency Transaction Loss | 2,000 | |
| | | |    Accounts Payable (¥) | | 2,000 |
| | | | Adjust payable denominated in foreign currency to current U.S. dollar equivalent and recognize exchange loss: | | |
| | | |    $ 16,000 = ¥2,000,000 × $.0080 Dec. 31 spot rate | | |
| | | |    −14,000 = ¥2,000,000 × $.0070 Oct. 1 spot rate | | |
| | | |    $  2,000 = ¥2,000,000 × ($.0080 − $.0070) | | |
| **April 1, 20X2 (Settlement Date)** | | | | | |
| | | | Accounts Payable (¥) | 800 | |
| | | |    Foreign Currency Transaction Gain | | 800 |
| | | | Adjust payable denominated in foreign currency to current U.S. dollar equivalent and recognize exchange gain: | | |
| | | |    $ 15,200 = ¥2,000,000 × $.0076 Apr. 1 spot rate | | |
| | | |    −16,000 = ¥2,000,000 × $.0080 Dec. 31 spot rate | | |
| | | |    $   800 = ¥2,000,000 × ($.0076 − $.0080) | | |
| | | | Foreign Currency Units (¥) | 15,200 | |
| | | |    Cash | | 15,200 |
| | | | Acquire FCU to settle debt: | | |
| | | |    $15,200 = ¥2,000,000 × $.0076 April 1 spot rate | | |
| Accounts Payable | 14,000 | | Accounts Payable (¥) | 15,200 | |
|    Cash | | 14,000 |    Foreign Currency Units (¥) | | 15,200 |

### Illustration of Foreign Purchase Transaction

Figure 11–3 illustrates the journal entries used to measure and record a purchase of goods from a foreign supplier denominated either in the entity's local currency or in a foreign currency. On the left side of Figure 11–3, the transaction is denominated in U.S. dollars, the recording and reporting currency of the U.S. company; on the right side, the transaction is denominated in Japanese yen (¥). The U.S. company is subject to a foreign currency transaction gain or loss only if the transaction is denominated in the foreign currency. If the foreign transaction is denominated in U.S. dollars, no special accounting problems exist and no currency rate adjustments are necessary.

The following information describes the case:

1. On October 1, 20X1, Peerless Products, a U.S. company, acquired goods on account from Tokyo Industries, a Japanese company, for $14,000, or 2,000,000 yen.

2. Peerless Products prepared financial statements at its year-end of December 31, 20X1.

3. Settlement of the payable was made on April 1, 20X2.

The direct spot exchange rates of the U.S. dollar–equivalent value of 1 yen were as follows:

| Date | Direct Exchange Rate |
|---|---|
| October 1, 20X1 (transaction date) | $.0070 |
| December 31, 20X1 (balance sheet date) | .0080 |
| April 1, 20X2 (settlement date) | .0076 |

A time line may help to clarify the relationships between the dates and the economic events, as follows:

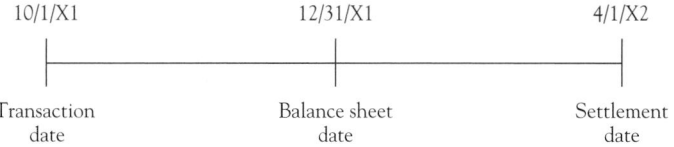

| 10/1/X1 | 12/31/X1 | 4/1/X2 |
|---|---|---|
| Transaction date | Balance sheet date | Settlement date |

Accounts relating to transactions denominated in yen are noted by the parenthetical symbol for the yen (¥) after the account title. As you proceed through the example, you should especially note the assets and liabilities denominated in the foreign currency and the adjustment needed to reflect their current values by use of the U.S. dollar–equivalent rate of exchange.

### Key Observations from Illustration

If the purchase contract is denominated in dollars, the foreign entity (Tokyo Industries) bears the foreign currency exchange risk. If the transaction is denominated in yen, the U.S. company (Peerless Products Corporation) is exposed to exchange rate gains and losses. The accounts relating to liabilities denominated in foreign currency units must be valued at the spot rate, with any foreign currency transaction gain or loss recognized in the period's income. The purchase contract includes specification of the denominated currency as the two parties agreed.

On October 1, 20X1, the purchase is recorded on the books of Peerless Products. The U.S. dollar–equivalent value of 2,000,000 yen on this date is $14,000 (¥ 2,000,000 × $.0070).

On December 31, 20X1, the balance sheet date, the payable denominated in foreign currency units must be adjusted to its current U.S. dollar–equivalent value. The direct exchange rate has increased since the date of purchase, indicating that the U.S. dollar has weakened relative to the yen. Therefore, on December 31, 20X1, $16,000 is required to acquire 2,000,000 yen (¥ 2,000,000 × $.0080), whereas, on October 1, 20X1, only $14,000 was required to obtain 2,000,000 yen (¥ 2,000,000 × $.0070). This increase in the exchange rate requires the recognition of a $2,000 foreign currency transaction loss if the transaction is denominated in yen, the foreign currency unit. No entry is made if the transaction is denominated in U.S. dollars because Peerless has a liability for $14,000 regardless of the changes in exchange rates.

The payable is settled on April 1, 20X2. If the payable is denominated in U.S. dollars, no adjustment is necessary and the liability is extinguished by payment of $14,000. However, assets and liabilities denominated in foreign currency units must again be adjusted to their present U.S. dollar–equivalent values. The dollar has strengthened between December 31, 20X1, and April 1, 20X2, as shown by the decrease in the direct exchange rate. In other words, fewer dollars are needed to acquire 2,000,000 yen on April 1, 20X2, than on December 31, 20X1. Accounts Payable is adjusted to its current dollar value, and an $800 foreign currency transaction gain [¥ 2,000,000 × ($.0076 − $.0080)] is recognized for the change in rates since the balance sheet date. Peerless acquires 2,000,000 yen, paying an exchange broker the spot exchange rate of $15,200 (¥ 2,000,000 × $.0076). Finally, Peerless extinguishes its liability denominated in yen by paying Tokyo Industries the 2,000,000 yen.

Understanding the revaluations may be easier by viewing the process within the perspective of a T-account. The following T-account posts the entries in Figure 11–3:

| Accounts Payable (¥) | |
|---|---|
| | **20X1** |
| | Oct. 1    14,000 (¥2,000,000 × $.0070) |
| | Dec. 31    2,000 [¥2,000,000 × ($.0080 − $.0070)] |
| | Dec. 31    16,000 Balance (¥2,000,000 × $.0080) |
| **20X2** | |
| **Apr. 1** | |
| [¥2,000,000 × ($.0076 − $.0080)]        800 | |
| Apr. 1 settlement | |
| (¥2,000,000 × $.0076)        15,200 | |
| | Apr. 2        -0-        Balance |

Some accountants combine the revaluation and settlement entries into one entry. Under this alternative approach, the following entries would be made on April 1, 20X2, the settlement date, instead of the entries presented for that date in Figure 11–3:

April 1, 20X2

| (3) | Foreign Currency Units (¥) | 15,200 | |
|---|---|---|---|
| | Cash | | 15,200 |
| | Acquire foreign currency. | | |

| (4) | Accounts Payable (¥) | 16,000 | |
|---|---|---|---|
| | Foreign Currency Transaction Gain | | 800 |
| | Foreign Currency Units (¥) | | 15,200 |
| | Settle foreign currency payable and recognize gain from change in exchange rates since December 31, 20X1. | | |

The final account balances resulting from the preceding one-entry approach and the two-entry approach used in Figure 11–3 are the same.

In summary, if the transaction is denominated in U.S. dollars, Peerless Products has no foreign currency exchange exposure; Tokyo Industries bears the risk of foreign currency exposure. If the transaction is denominated in yen, however, Peerless has a foreign currency exchange risk. The assets and liabilities denominated in foreign currency units must be valued at their U.S. dollar–equivalent values and a foreign currency transaction gain or loss must be recognized on that period's income statement.

# MANAGING INTERNATIONAL CURRENCY RISK WITH FOREIGN CURRENCY FORWARD EXCHANGE FINANCIAL INSTRUMENTS

Companies need to manage business risks. Derivative instruments are an important tool in managing risk. Companies operating internationally are subject not only to normal business risks but also to additional risks from changes in currency exchange rates. Therefore, multinational enterprises (MNEs) often use derivative instruments, including foreign currency–denominated forward exchange contracts, foreign currency options, and foreign currency futures, to manage risk associated with foreign currency transactions.

The accounting for derivatives and hedging activities is guided by three standards. **FASB Statement No. 133,** "Accounting for Derivative Instruments and Hedging Activities" (FASB 133), defined derivatives and established the general rule of recognizing all derivatives as either assets or liabilities in the balance sheet and measuring those financial instruments at fair value. **FASB Statement No. 138,** "Accounting for Certain Derivative Instruments and Certain Hedging Activities" (FASB 138), provided several amendments of importance to multinational entities. **FASB Statement No. 149,** "Amendment of Statement 133 on Derivative Instruments and Hedging Activities" (FASB 149), considered a number of specific implementation issues.

A *financial instrument* is cash, evidence of ownership, or a contract that both (1) imposes on one entity a contractual obligation to deliver cash or another instrument and (2) conveys to the second entity that contractual right to receive cash or another financial instrument. Examples include cash, stock, notes payable and receivable, and many financial contracts.

A *derivative* is a financial instrument or other contract whose value is "derived from" some other item that has a variable value over time. An example of a derivative is a foreign currency forward exchange contract whose value is derived from changes in the foreign currency exchange rate over the contract's term. Note that not all financial instruments are derivatives.

The specific definition of a derivative is a financial instrument or contract possessing all of the following characteristics:

1. The financial instrument must contain one or more underlyings and one or more notional amounts, which specify the terms of the financial instrument.
    *a.* An ***underlying*** is any financial or physical variable that has observable or objectively verifiable changes. Currency exchange rates, commodity prices, index of prices or rates, days of winter warming, or other variables including the occurrence or nonoccurrence of a specified event such as the scheduled payment under a contract are examples of an underlying.
    *b.* A ***notional amount*** is the number of currency units, shares, bushels, pounds, or other units specified in the financial instrument.
2. The financial instrument or other contract requires no initial net investment or an initial net investment that is smaller than required for other types of contracts expected to have a similar response to changes in market factors. Many derivative instruments require no initial net investment or only a small investment for the time value of the contract (as discussed later in this chapter).
3. The contract terms: (*a*) require or permit net settlement, (*b*) provide for the delivery of an asset that puts the recipient in an economic position not substantially different from net settlement, or (*c*) allow for the contract to be readily settled net by a market or other mechanism outside the contract. For example, a forward contract requires the delivery of a specified number of shares of stock, but there is an option market mechanism that offers a ready opportunity to sell the contract or to enter into an offsetting contract.

Occasionally, a financial instrument may have an embedded derivative that must be separated, or bifurcated, from its host contract. An example of an embedded derivative is a company's issuing debt that includes regular interest as well as a potential premium payment based on the future price of a commodity such as crude oil. In this case, the contingent payment feature is a derivative. Another example is the debt agreement that specifies a principal, but whose interest rate is based on the U.S. LIBOR (London Interbank Offered Rate), which is a variable rate. In this case, the interest is the embedded derivative because its value, which is derived from the market, is variable.

## Derivatives Designated as Hedges

Derivatives may be designated to hedge or reduce risks. Some companies obtain derivatives that are not designated as hedges but as speculative financial instruments. For example, a company may enter into a forward exchange contract that does not have any offsetting intent. In this case, the gain or loss on the derivative is recorded in periodic earnings.

**FASB 133** provided specific requirements for classifying a derivative as a hedge. Hedge accounting offsets the gain (loss) on the hedged item with the loss (gain) on the hedging instrument. Hedges are applicable to (1) foreign currency exchange risk in which currency exchange rates change over time, (2) interest rate risks, particularly for companies owing variable rate debt instruments, and (3) commodity risks whose future commodity prices may be quite different from spot prices.

For a derivative instrument to qualify as a hedging instrument, the following two criteria must be met:

1. Sufficient documentation must be provided at the beginning of the hedge term to identify the objective and strategy of the hedge, the hedging instrument and the hedged item, and how the hedge's effectiveness will be assessed on an ongoing basis.

2. The hedge must be highly effective throughout its term. Effectiveness is measured by evaluating the hedging instrument's ability to generate changes in fair value that offset the changes in value of the hedged item. This effectiveness must be tested at the time the hedge is entered into, every three months thereafter, and each time financial statements are prepared. Effectiveness is viewed as the derivative instrument's ability to offset changes in the fair value or cash flows of the hedged item within the range between 80 and 125 percent of the change in value of the hedged item.

Derivatives that meet the requirements for a hedge and are designated as such by the company's management are accounted for in accordance with **FASB 133** and **FASB 138,** as follows:

1. ***Fair value hedges*** are designated to hedge the exposure to potential changes in the fair value of (*a*) a recognized asset or liability such as available-for-sale investments or (*b*) an unrecognized firm commitment for which a binding agreement exists, such as to buy or sell inventory. The net gains and losses on the hedged asset or liability and the hedging instrument are recognized in current earnings on the statement of income. An example of a fair value hedge is presented in Appendix 11B using an option contract to hedge available-for-sale securities.

2. ***Cash flow hedges*** are designated to hedge the exposure to potential changes in the anticipated cash flows, either into or out of the company, for (*a*) a recognized asset or liability such as future interest payments on variable-interest debt or (*b*) a forecasted cash transaction such as a forecasted purchase or sale. A forecasted cash transaction is a transaction that is expected to occur but for which there is not yet a firm commitment. Thus, a forecasted transaction has no present rights to future benefits or a present liability for future obligations. **FASB 133** specifies that a derivative must be valued at its current fair market value. For cash flow hedges, changes in the fair market value of a derivative are separated into an effective portion and an ineffective portion. The net gain or loss on the effective portion of the hedging instrument should be reported in other comprehensive income. The gain or loss on the ineffective portion is reported in current earnings on the statement of income.

   The effective portion is defined as the part of the gain (or loss) on the hedging instrument that offsets a loss (or gain) on the hedged item. This portion of the change in the derivative's fair market value is related to the intrinsic value from changes in the underlying. Any remaining gain (or loss) on the hedging instrument is defined as the ineffective portion. This portion of the change in the derivative's fair market value is related to the time value of the derivative and reduces to zero at the derivative's expiration date. An example of determining the effective versus the ineffective portion of a change in value of a derivative is presented in Appendix 11B with regard to a cash flow hedge using an option to hedge an anticipated purchase of inventory.

3. ***Foreign currency hedges*** are hedges in which the hedged item is denominated in a foreign currency. Note that the incremental risk being hedged in a foreign currency hedge is the change in fair value or the change in cash flows attributable to the changes

in the foreign currency exchange rates. The following types of hedges of foreign currency risk may be designated by the entity:

a. A *fair value hedge* of a firm commitment to enter into a foreign currency transaction, such as a binding agreement to purchase equipment from a foreign manufacturer with the payable due in the foreign currency or a recognized foreign currency–denominated asset or liability (including an available-for-sale security). Just as with hedge accounting for firm commitments not involving foreign currency commitments in item (1) above, the gain or loss on the foreign currency hedging derivative and the offsetting loss or gain on the foreign currency–hedged item are recognized currently in earnings on the statement of income.

b. A *cash flow hedge* of a forecasted foreign currency transaction, such as a probable future foreign currency sale, the forecasted functional currency–equivalent cash flows associated with a recognized asset or liability, or a forecasted intercompany transaction. Just as with accounting for hedges of forecasted transactions not involving foreign currency commitments in item (2) above, the effective portion of the gain or loss on the foreign currency hedging derivative instrument is recognized as a component of other comprehensive income. The ineffective portion of the gain or loss is recognized currently in earnings.

Cash flow hedges are used when all variability in the hedged item's functional currency–equivalent cash flows are eliminated by the effect of the hedge. Cash flow hedges with a derivative based only on changes in the exchange rates cannot be designated, for example, for a variable-rate foreign currency–denominated asset or liability because some of the cash flow variability is not covered with that specific hedge. However, foreign currency–denominated forward contracts can be used as cash flow hedges of foreign currency–denominated assets or liabilities that are fixed in terms of the number of foreign currency units.

c. A hedge of a net investment in a foreign operation. A derivative designated as hedging this type of foreign currency exposure has its gain or loss reported in other comprehensive income as part of the cumulative translation adjustment, as will be discussed in Chapter 12.

## Forward Exchange Contracts

For the reporting year ended October 2005, the Foreign Exchange Committee of the New York Federal Reserve Board reported that the average daily volume in foreign exchange instruments totaled $440 billion, and the average daily volume in over-the-counter foreign exchange options totaled $37 billion.[1] The Chicago Mercantile Exchange (CME) is the world's largest and most diverse regulated foreign exchange trading market. The CME is an international marketplace that brings together buyers and sellers on its CME Globex electronic trading platform and on its trading floors. In 2005, over 84 million foreign exchange contracts with a notional value of $10.2 trillion traded at the CME.[2] In May 2006, CME foreign exchange products averaged a record 501,000 contracts per day, up 69 percent from the year earlier; electronic foreign exchange products set a monthly record of 451,000 contracts per day, an increase of 90 percent from the previous year.[3]

Companies operating internationally often enter into forward exchange contracts with foreign currency brokers for the exchange of different currencies at specified future dates at specified rates. Forward exchange contracts are acquired from foreign currency brokers. Typically, these contracts are written for one of the major international currencies. They are available for virtually any time period up to 12 months forward, but most are for relatively shorter time periods, usually between 30 and 180 days. Forward exchange contracts can be entered into to receive foreign currency or to deliver foreign currency

[1] http://www.newyorkfed.org/fxc/2006/fxc012306.pdf, accessed July 11, 2006.
[2] http://cme.mediaroom.com/file.php/60/FXfactq206.pdf, accessed July 11, 2006.
[3] http://www.cme.com/about/press/cn/06-76May06Volume18770.html, accessed July 11, 2006.

at a specified date in the future (the expiration date). The forward exchange rate differs from the spot rate because of the different economic factors involved in determining a future versus spot rate of exchange. For hedging transactions, if the forward rate is more than the spot rate, the difference between the forward and spot rate is termed *premium on the forward exchange contract;* that is, the foreign currency is selling at a premium in the forward market. If the forward rate is less than the spot rate, the difference is a *discount on the forward exchange contract;* that is, the foreign currency is selling at a discount in the forward market.

**FASB 133** establishes a basic rule of fair value for accounting for forward exchange contracts. Changes in the fair value are recognized in the accounts, but the specific accounting for the change depends on the purpose of the hedge. For forward exchange contracts, the basic rule is to use the forward exchange rate to value the forward contract.

Multinational entities often use foreign currency forward contract derivatives. These contracts may be designated as hedging instruments or may not fulfill all the requirements for a hedge and would thus not be hedging instruments. The cases discussed in the next sections of this chapter illustrate the following:

*Case 1:* This case presents the most common use of foreign currency forward contracts, which is to manage a part of the foreign currency exposure from accounts payable or accounts receivable denominated in a foreign currency. Note that the company has entered into a foreign currency forward contract but that the contract does not qualify for or the company does not designate the forward contract as a hedging instrument. Thus, the forward contract is not a designated hedge but can offset most, if not all, foreign currency risks. The forward contract is valued using the forward rate, and changes in the market value of the forward contract are recognized currently in earnings on the statement of income. The foreign currency account payable or account receivable is revalued using the spot rate in accordance with **FASB 52.**

*Case 2:* This case presents the accounting for an unrecognized firm commitment to enter into a foreign currency transaction, which is accounted for as a fair value hedge. A firm commitment exists because of a binding agreement for the future transaction that meets all requirements for a firm commitment. The hedge is against the possible changes in fair value of the firm commitment (e.g., the inventory to be purchased or the equipment to be acquired) from changes in the foreign currency exchange rates.

*Case 3:* This case presents the accounting for a forecasted foreign currency–denominated transaction, which is accounted for as a cash flow hedge of the possible changes in future cash flows. The forecasted transaction is *probable* but not a *firm* commitment. Thus, the transaction has not yet occurred nor is it assured; the company is *anticipating* a *possible* future foreign currency transaction. Because the foreign currency hedge is against the impact of changes in the foreign currency exchange rates used to predict the possible future foreign currency–denominated cash flows, it is accounted for as a cash flow hedge. **FASB 138** allows for the continuation of a cash flow hedge after the purchase or sale transaction occurs until settlement of the foreign currency–denominated account payable or receivable arising from the transaction. Alternatively, at the time the company enters into a binding agreement for the transaction that had been forecasted, the hedge can be changed to a fair value hedge, but any other comprehensive income recognized on the cash flow hedge to that date is not reclassified until the earnings process is completed.

*Case 4:* This case presents the accounting for foreign currency forward contracts used to speculate in foreign currency markets. These transactions are not hedging transactions. The foreign currency forward contract is revalued periodically to its fair value using the forward exchange rate for the remainder of the contract term. The gain or loss on the revaluation is recognized currently in earnings on the statement of income.

A time line of the possible points at which a company uses foreign currency contracts follows. Note that a company may use just one foreign currency forward contract during the time between each event and the final settlement of the foreign currency payable or receivable or may use more than one foreign currency forward contract during the time span presented. For example, a company could use one forward contract between the time of the forecast of the future transaction and the time it signs a binding agreement, or it could just continue with one forward contract the entire time between the date of the forecast and the final settlement.

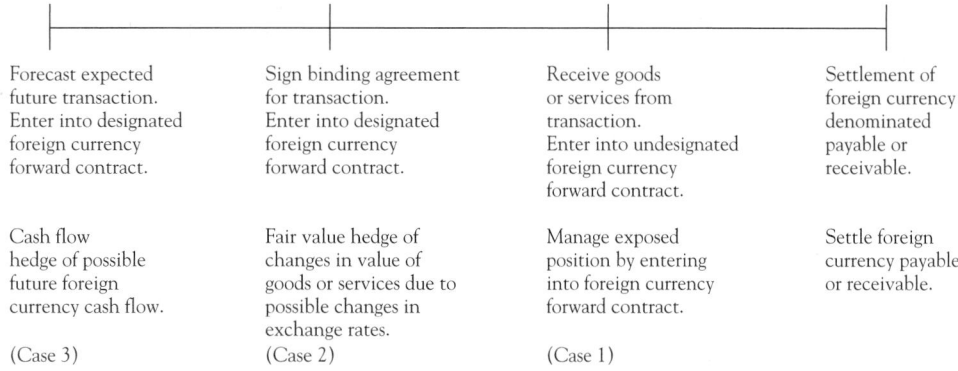

| | | | |
|---|---|---|---|
| Forecast expected future transaction. Enter into designated foreign currency forward contract. | Sign binding agreement for transaction. Enter into designated foreign currency forward contract. | Receive goods or services from transaction. Enter into undesignated foreign currency forward contract. | Settlement of foreign currency denominated payable or receivable. |
| Cash flow hedge of possible future foreign currency cash flow. | Fair value hedge of changes in value of goods or services due to possible changes in exchange rates. | Manage exposed position by entering into foreign currency forward contract. | Settle foreign currency payable or receivable. |
| (Case 3) | (Case 2) | (Case 1) | |

Thus, the accounting for the hedge is based on the purpose for which the hedge, in this case a foreign currency forward contract, is entered into.

The following four cases illustrate the accounting for the major uses of forward exchange contracts.

### Case 1: Managing an Exposed Foreign Currency Net Asset or Liability Position: Not a Designated Hedging Instrument

A company that has more trade receivables or other assets denominated in a foreign currency than liabilities denominated in that currency incurs a foreign currency risk from its *exposed net asset position.* Alternatively, the company has an *exposed net liability position* if liabilities denominated in a foreign currency exceed receivables denominated in that currency.

The most common use of forward exchange contracts is for ***managing an exposed foreign currency position, either a net asset or a net liability position***. Entering into a foreign currency forward contract balances a foreign exchange payable with a receivable in the same foreign currency, thus offsetting the risk of foreign exchange fluctuations. For example, a U.S. company acquiring goods from a Swiss company may be required to make payment in Swiss francs. If the transaction is denominated in Swiss francs, the U.S. company is exposed to the effects of changes in exchange rates between the dollar and the Swiss franc. To protect itself from fluctuations in the value of the Swiss franc, the U.S. company can enter into a forward exchange contract to receive francs at the future settlement date. The U.S. company then uses these francs to settle its foreign currency commitment arising from the foreign purchase transaction.

Alternatively, a U.S. company could have a receivable denominated in a foreign currency that it could also manage with a forward exchange contract. In this case, the U.S. company contracts to *deliver* foreign currency units to the forward exchange broker at a future date in exchange for U.S. dollars.

**FASB 133** specifies the general rule that the relevant exchange rate for measuring the fair value of a forward exchange contract is the *forward exchange rate* at each valuation date. Note that **FASB 52** specifies that the foreign currency–denominated account receivable or account payable from the exchange transaction is valued by using the *spot rate* at the valuation date. Forward contracts must be adjusted for changes in the fair value of the forward contract. Because of the two different currency exchange rates used—the spot and the forward—a difference normally exists between the amount of gain and loss. This difference should not be large but does create some volatility in the income stream.

### Time Value of Future Cash Flows from Forward Contracts

One other item of note is that **FASB 133** requires the recognition of an interest factor if interest is significant. Thus, when interest is significant, companies should use the *present value* of the expected future net cash flows to value the forward contract. By using the present value, the company explicitly recognizes the time value of money. For the examples that follow and to focus on the main points of accounting for the hedges, interest was not considered to be significant. A comprehensive example using the time value of money to value a forward contract is presented in Appendix 11A.

### Illustration of Managing an Exposed Net Liability Position

The following example shows the accounting for the management of an exposed foreign currency position with a forward exchange contract. For purposes of this example, assume the following:

1. On October 1, 20X1, Peerless Products purchases goods on account from Tokyo Industries in the amount of 2,000,000 yen.
2. This transaction is denominated in yen, and Peerless Products offsets its exposed foreign currency liability with a forward exchange contract for the receipt of 2,000,000 yen from a foreign exchange broker.
3. The term of the forward exchange contract equals the six-month credit period extended by Tokyo Industries.
4. December 31 is the year-end of Peerless Products, and the payable is settled on April 1, 20X2.

The relevant direct exchange rates are as follows:

| | U.S. Dollar–Equivalent Value of 1 Yen | |
|---|---|---|
| Date | Spot Rate | Forward Exchange Rate |
| October 1, 20X1 (transaction date) | $.0070 | $.0075 (180 days) |
| December 31, 20X1 (balance sheet date) | .0080 | .0077 (90 days) |
| April 1, 20X2 (settlement date) | .0076 | |

A time line for these transactions is as follows:

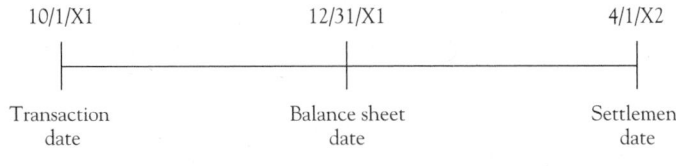

The following entries record the events for this illustration.

October 1, 20X1

| | | | | |
|---|---|---|---|---|
| (5) | Inventory | | 14,000 | |
| | Accounts Payable (¥) | | | 14,000 |
| | Purchase inventory on account | | | |
| | $14,000 = ¥2,000,000 × $.0070 Oct. 1 spot rate | | | |
| | | | | |
| (6) | Foreign Currency Receivable from Exchange Broker (¥) | | 15,000 | |
| | Dollars Payable to Exchange Broker ($) | | | 15,000 |
| | Purchase forward contract to receive 2,000,000 yen: | | | |
| | $15,000 = ¥2,000,000 × $.0075 forward rate | | | |

**FIGURE 11–4**
**T-Accounts for the Illustration of the Management of an Exposed Net Liability**

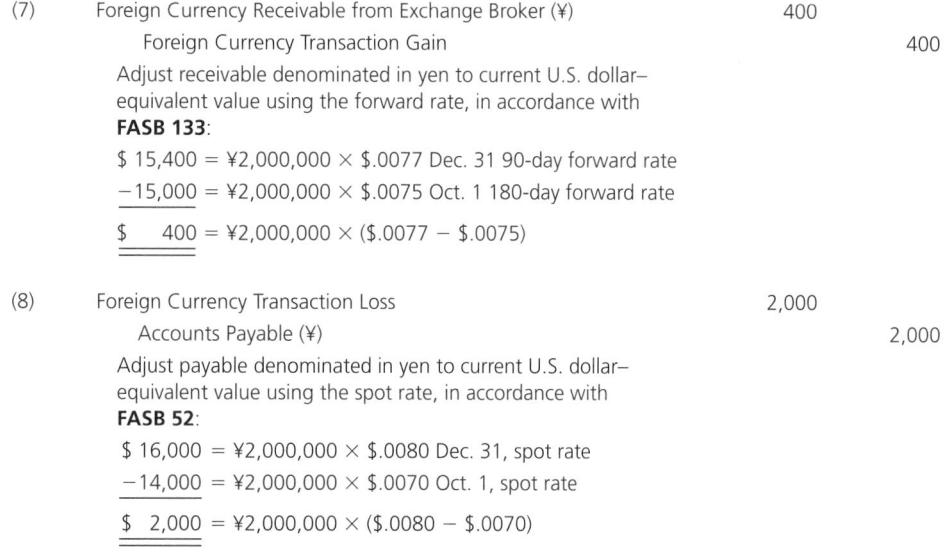

These entries record the purchase of inventory on credit, which is denominated in yen, and the signing of a six-month forward exchange contract to receive 2,000,000 yen in exchange for $15,000 (¥2,000,000 × $.0075 forward rate). The amount payable to the exchange broker is denominated in U.S. dollars, whereas the receivable from the broker is denominated in yen. The entries for the transaction, the adjusting journal entries for the balance sheet date valuations, and the settlements of the forward contract and the accounts payable are posted to T-accounts in Figure 11–4.

The required adjusting entries on December 31, 20X1, Peerless's fiscal year-end, are:

| | | | |
|---|---|---|---|
| (7) | Foreign Currency Receivable from Exchange Broker (¥) | 400 | |
| | Foreign Currency Transaction Gain | | 400 |

Adjust receivable denominated in yen to current U.S. dollar–equivalent value using the forward rate, in accordance with **FASB 133**:

$ 15,400 = ¥2,000,000 × $.0077 Dec. 31 90-day forward rate

−15,000 = ¥2,000,000 × $.0075 Oct. 1 180-day forward rate

$ _____400_ = ¥2,000,000 × ($.0077 − $.0075)

| | | | |
|---|---|---|---|
| (8) | Foreign Currency Transaction Loss | 2,000 | |
| | Accounts Payable (¥) | | 2,000 |

Adjust payable denominated in yen to current U.S. dollar–equivalent value using the spot rate, in accordance with **FASB 52**:

$ 16,000 = ¥2,000,000 × $.0080 Dec. 31, spot rate

−14,000 = ¥2,000,000 × $.0070 Oct. 1, spot rate

$ _2,000_ = ¥2,000,000 × ($.0080 − $.0070)

Note that the foreign currency–denominated account payable is valued by using the spot rate. This is the valuation requirement specified in **FASB 52.** The forward exchange contract is valued using the forward exchange rate for the remainder of the forward contract. This valuation basis is required by **FASB 133.** The direct exchange spot rate has increased between October 1, 20X1, the date of the foreign currency transaction, and December 31, 20X1, the balance sheet date. As previously illustrated, this means that the U.S. dollar has weakened relative to the yen because it takes more U.S. currency to acquire 1 yen at year-end (¥1 = $.0080) than at the initial date of the purchase transaction (¥1 = $.0070), and a U.S. company with a liability in yen experiences an exchange loss. The U.S. dollar–equivalent values of the foreign currency–denominated accounts at October 1, 20X1, and December 31, 20X1, follow:

| Accounts | U.S. Dollar–Equivalent Values of Foreign Currency–Denominated Accounts | | Foreign Currency Transaction Gain (Loss) |
| | October 1, 20X1 (Transaction Date) | December 31, 20X1 (Balance Sheet Date) | |
| --- | --- | --- | --- |
| Foreign Currency Receivable from Exchange Broker (¥) | $15,000 *(a)* | $15,400 *(b)* | $ 400 |
| Accounts Payable (¥) | 14,000 *(c)* | 16,000 *(d)* | (2,000) |

*(a)* ¥2,000,000 × $.0075 October 1, 180-day forward rate
*(b)* ¥2,000,000 × $.0077 December 31, 90-day forward rate
*(c)* ¥2,000,000 × $.0070 October 1, spot rate
*(d)* ¥2,000,000 × $.0080 December 31, spot rate

On October 1, the U.S. dollar–equivalent value of the foreign currency receivable from the broker is $15,000. Because of the increase in the forward exchange rate of the yen relative to the dollar (i.e., the weakening of the dollar versus the yen), the U.S. dollar–equivalent value of the foreign currency receivable on December 31, 20X1, increases to $15,400, resulting in a foreign currency transaction gain of $400. For the U.S. company, the U.S. dollar–equivalent value of the liability has increased to $16,000, resulting in a $2,000 foreign currency transaction loss. Because of the differing valuation requirements of the forward contract and the exposed liability, the exchange gain of the accounts payable (¥) is not necessarily an exact offset of the exchange loss on the foreign currency receivable (¥).

The required entries on April 1, 20X2, the settlement date, are:

| | | | | |
| --- | --- | --- | --- | --- |
| (9) | Foreign Currency Transaction Loss | | 200 | |
| | Foreign Currency Receivable from Exchange Broker (¥) | | | 200 |
| | Adjust receivable to spot rate on settlement date: | | | |
| | $ 15,200 = ¥2,000,000 × $.0076 Apr. 1, 20X2, spot rate | | | |
| | −15,400 = ¥2,000,000 × $.0077 Dec. 31, 20X1, 90-day forward rate | | | |
| | $ 200 = ¥2,000,000 yen × ($.0076 − $.0077) | | | |

| | | | | |
| --- | --- | --- | --- | --- |
| (10) | Accounts Payable (¥) | | 800 | |
| | Foreign Currency Transaction Gain | | | 800 |
| | Adjust payable denominated in yen to spot rate on settlement date: | | | |
| | ¥2,000,000 × ($.0076 − $.0080) | | | |

| | | | | |
| --- | --- | --- | --- | --- |
| (11) | Dollars Payable to Exchange Broker ($) | | 15,000 | |
| | Cash | | | 15,000 |
| | Deliver U.S. dollars to currency broker as specified in forward contract. | | | |

| | | | | |
| --- | --- | --- | --- | --- |
| (12) | Foreign Currency Units (¥) | | 15,200 | |
| | Foreign Currency Receivable from Exchange Broker (¥) | | | 15,200 |
| | Receive ¥2,000,000 from exchange broker; valued at Apr. 1, 20X2, spot rate: | | | |
| | $15,200 = ¥2,000,000 × $.0076 | | | |

| | | | | |
| --- | --- | --- | --- | --- |
| (13) | Accounts Payable (¥) | | 15,200 | |
| | Foreign Currency Units (¥) | | | 15,200 |
| | Pay 2,000,000 yen to Tokyo Industries, Inc., in settlement of liability denominated in yen. | | | |

The direct exchange spot rate has decreased from the $.0080 rate on the balance sheet date to $.0076 on April 1, 20X2, the settlement date, indicating that the U.S. dollar has strengthened relative to the yen. Fewer dollars are needed to acquire the same number of yen on the settlement date than were needed on the balance sheet date. The forward exchange contract becomes due on April 1, 20X2, and is now valued at the current spot rate. The difference between the 90-day forward rate on December 31, 20X1, and the spot rate at the date of the completion of the forward rate results in the loss of $200. The U.S. dollar equivalent values of the foreign currency–denominated accounts on December 31, 20X1, and April 1, 20X2, follow:

| | U.S. Dollar–Equivalent Values of Foreign Currency–Denominated Accounts | | Foreign Currency Transaction Gain (Loss) |
| --- | --- | --- | --- |
| **Accounts** | **December 31, 20X1 (Balance Sheet Date)** | **April 1, 20X2 (Settlement Date)** | |
| Foreign Currency Receivable from Exchange Broker (¥) | $15,400 (a) | $15,200 (b) | $(200) |
| Accounts Payable (¥) | 16,000 (c) | 15,200 (d) | 800 |

(a) ¥2,000,000 yen × $.0077 December 31, 90-day forward rate
(b) ¥2,000,000 yen × $.0076 April 1, 20X2, spot rate
(c) ¥2,000,000 yen × $.0080 December 31, spot rate
(d) ¥2,000,000 yen × $.0076 April 1, 20X2 spot rate

On December 31, 20X1, the U.S. dollar–equivalent value of the foreign currency receivable from the broker is $15,400. Because the yen weakened relative to the dollar, the foreign currency receivable on April 1, 20X2, is lower in U.S. dollar–equivalent value, and an exchange loss of $200 is recognized. The U.S. dollar–equivalent value of the foreign currency account payable is $16,000 on December 31, 20X1, but because the yen weakened (i.e., the dollar strengthened) during the period from December 31, 20X1, to April 1, 20X2, the U.S. dollar–equivalent value of the payable decreases to $15,200 on April 1, 20X2. This results in an $800 foreign currency transaction gain during this period.

Note that the total net foreign exchange transactions loss for the two years combined is $1,000 [20X1: $(2,000) plus $400; 20X2: $800 less $(200)]. This is the effect of the forward contract premium on October 1, 20X1, being taken into the earnings stream. Note the premium was for the difference between the forward rate ($.0075) and the spot rate ($.0070) at the date the forward contract was signed. At the April 1, 20X2, completion date, both of the foreign currency–denominated accounts are valued at the spot rate. Thus, the ¥2,000,000 × ($.0070 − $.0075) premium is the net effect on earnings over the term of the forward contract. The two accounts denominated in foreign currency start at different valuations but end using the same spot rate at the end of the term of the forward contract.

The forward exchange contract offsets the foreign currency liability position. On April 1, 20X2, Peerless pays the $15,000 forward contract price to the exchange broker and receives the 2,000,000 yen, which it then uses to extinguish its account payable to Tokyo Industries. Note that after settlement, all account balances in Figure 11–4 are reduced to zero.

If Peerless Products had a foreign currency receivable, it could also manage its exposed net asset position by acquiring a forward exchange contract to deliver foreign currency to the exchange broker. In this case, the forward currency payable to the exchange broker is denominated in the foreign currency. The forward exchange contract is settled when Peerless gives the broker the foreign currency units it has received from its customer. The foreign currency is then exchanged for U.S. dollars at the agreed-upon contractual rate from the forward exchange contract. The assets and liabilities denominated in foreign currency units must be revalued to their U.S. dollar–equivalent values in the same manner as for the import illustration. Recall that, for valuation purposes, **FASB 133** requires the use of the forward exchange rate for forward contracts, and **FASB 52** requires the use of spot rates for exposed net asset or liability accounts arising from foreign currency transactions.

### *Formal Balance Sheets Reporting Net Amounts for Forward Exchange Contracts*

**FASB 133** requires the recognition of all derivatives in the statement of financial position (the balance sheet) at net fair value. This means that the balance sheet presents the net of the forward contract receivable from the exchange broker against the dollars payable to the exchange broker. Some companies account for the forward exchange contract with only memorandum entries, using the philosophy that the contract is simply for the exchange of one currency for another. The underlying exposed accounts receivable or accounts payable denominated in foreign currency units are still presented. For example, a formal balance sheet prepared on October 1, 20X1, after the transactions recorded in entries (5) and (6), reports the following net amounts:

| Assets | | Liabilities | |
|---|---|---|---|
| Inventory | $14,000 | Accounts Payable (¥) | $14,000 |

Under the net method of reporting the forward exchange contract, the gain or loss on the change in the value of the forward exchange contract must be recorded and reported in the balance sheet. The balance sheet prepared on December 31, 20X1, after posting entries (7) and (8) includes the following:

| Assets | | Liabilities and Equity | |
|---|---|---|---|
| Forward Exchange Contract (¥) (at net fair value) | $400 | Accounts Payable (¥) | $16,000 |
| | | Retained Earnings (for net exchange loss) | (1,600) |

Note that under the net approach to reporting, the forward exchange contract is valued at net fair value. The $2,000 foreign currency transaction loss on the account payable denominated in yen is partially offset with the $400 foreign currency transaction gain for the forward contract receivable in yen.

The net balance sheet presented on April 1, 20X2, immediately after entry (10) but before the settlement of the forward exchange contract and the accounts payable is:

| Assets | | Liabilities and Equity | |
|---|---|---|---|
| Forward Exchange Contract (¥) (at net fair value) | $200 | Accounts Payable (¥) | $15,200 |
| | | Retained Earnings (for amount of the premium) | (1,000) |

The forward exchange contract is then settled by paying the exchange broker the $15,000 in U.S. dollars as initially contracted for in the forward exchange contract, receiving the 2,000,000 yen now valued at $15,200, and closing the net forward exchange contract for the difference of the $200.

The net approach is required for reporting derivative forward exchange contracts on the balance sheet. Nevertheless, we believe that recording both sides of the forward exchange contracts in the account maintains a full record of each side of the transaction.

## Case 2: Hedging an Unrecognized Foreign Currency Firm Commitment: A Foreign Currency Fair Value Hedge

A company may expose itself to foreign currency risk *before* a purchase or sale transaction occurs. For example, a company may sign a noncancelable order to purchase goods from a foreign entity in the future to be paid for in the foreign currency. By agreeing to a purchase price in the present for a future purchase, the company has accepted an *identifiable foreign currency commitment* although the purchase has not yet occurred; that is, the purchase contract is still executory (unrecognized). The company will not have a liability obligation until after delivery of the goods, but it is exposed to changes in currency exchange rates before the transaction date (the date of delivery of the goods).

**FASB 133** specified the accounting requirements for the use of forward exchange contracts *hedging unrecognized foreign currency firm commitments*. The company can separate the commitment into its financial instrument (the obligation to pay yen) and nonfinancial asset (the right to receive inventory) aspects. The forward contract taken out is then a hedge of the changes in the fair value of the firm commitment for the foreign currency risk being hedged. A hedge of a firm commitment comes under the accounting for fair value hedges, and the forward contract is to be valued at its fair value.

It is interesting to note the different accounting treatment of a hedge of a forecasted transaction (cash flow hedge) versus that for a hedge of an unrecognized foreign currency firm commitment (fair value hedge). A *forecasted* transaction is *anticipated* but not *guaranteed*. The forecasted transaction may actually occur as anticipated, but a hedge of a forecasted transaction is accounted for as a cash flow hedge with the effective portion of the change in the hedge's fair value recognized in other comprehensive income. On the other hand, a firm commitment is an agreement with an unrelated party that is binding and usually legally enforceable. The agreement has the following characteristics:

1. The agreement specifies all significant terms such as the quantity, the fixed price, and the timing of the transaction. The price may be denominated in either the entity's functional currency or in a foreign currency.

2. The agreement must contain a penalty provision sufficiently large to make performance of the agreement probable.

A forecasted transaction may become a firm commitment if an agreement having these listed characteristics is made between the parties. Any cash flow hedge of the forecasted transaction may be changed to a fair value hedge when the firm commitment agreement is made. However, any amounts recorded in other comprehensive income under the cash flow hedge are not reclassified into earnings until the initially forecasted transaction impacts earnings.

**FASB 131** provides for management of an enterprise to select the basis by which the effectiveness of the hedge will be measured. Management may select the forward exchange rate, the spot rate, or the intrinsic value for measuring effectiveness. The examples used in this chapter use the forward rate, which is consistent with the general rule of valuing forward exchange contracts as specified in **FASB 133.** The measure of the change in fair value of the forward contract uses the forward exchange rate for the remainder of the term and then, if interest is significant, the change in the forward rates is discounted to reflect the time value of money. The entries for a hedge of an identifiable foreign currency commitment are presented in the following illustration.

### *Illustration of Hedging an Unrecognized Foreign Currency Firm Commitment*

For illustration purposes, the import transaction between Peerless Products and Tokyo Industries used throughout this chapter is extended with the following information:

1. On August 1, 20X1, Peerless contracts to purchase special-order goods from Tokyo Industries. Their manufacture and delivery will take place in 60 days (on October 1, 20X1). The contract price is 2,000,000 yen, to be paid by April 1, 20X2, which is 180 days after delivery.

2. On August 1, Peerless hedges its foreign currency payable commitment with a forward exchange contract to receive 2,000,000 yen in 240 days (the 60 days until delivery plus 180 days of credit period). The future rate for a 240-day forward contract is $.0073 to 1 yen. The purpose of this 240-day forward exchange contract is twofold. First, for the 60 days from August 1, 20X1, until October 1, 20X1, the forward exchange contract is a hedge of an identifiable foreign currency commitment. For the 180-day period from October 1, 20X1, until April 1, 20X2, the forward exchange contract is a hedge of a foreign currency exposed net liability position.

The relevant exchange rates for this example are as follows:

| | U.S. Dollar–Equivalent Value of 1 Yen | |
|---|---|---|
| **Date** | **Spot Rate** | **Forward Exchange Rate** |
| August 1, 20X1 | $.0065 | $.0073 (240 days) |
| October 1, 20X1 | .0070 | .0075 (180 days) |

A time line for the transactions follows:

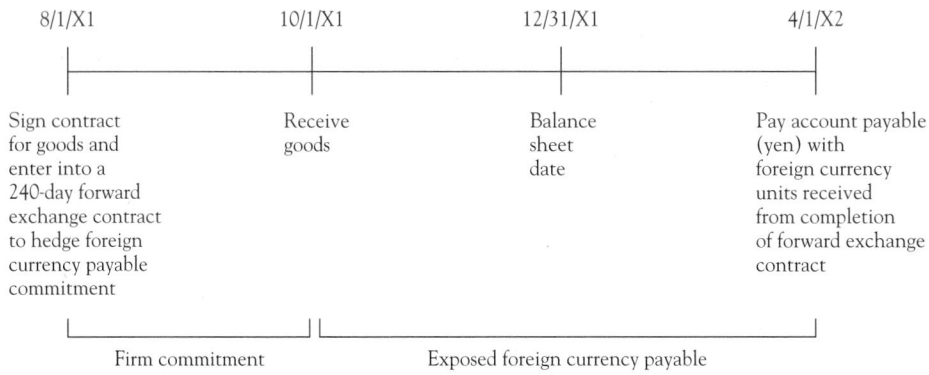

| 8/1/X1 | 10/1/X1 | 12/31/X1 | 4/1/X2 |
|---|---|---|---|
| Sign contract for goods and enter into a 240-day forward exchange contract to hedge foreign currency payable commitment | Receive goods | Balance sheet date | Pay account payable (yen) with foreign currency units received from completion of forward exchange contract |

Firm commitment     Exposed foreign currency payable

On August 1, 20X1, the company determines the value of its commitment to pay yen for the future accounts payable using the forward exchange rate. However, the payable is not recorded on August 1 because the exchange transaction has not yet occurred; the payable is maintained in memorandum form only. The forward exchange contract must be valued at its fair value. At the time the company enters into the forward exchange contract, the contract has no net fair value because the $14,600 foreign currency receivable equals the $14,600 dollars payable under the contract. The subsequent changes in the fair value of the forward contract are measured using the forward rate and then, if interest is significant, discounted to reflect the time value of money. For purposes of this illustration, we assume that interest is not significant and that hedge effectiveness is measured with reference to the change in the forward exchange rates.

August 1, 20X1

(14)   Foreign Currency Receivable from Exchange Broker (¥)        14,600
     Dollars Payable to Exchange Broker ($)        14,600
    Sign forward exchange contract for receipt of
    2,000,000 yen in 240 days:
    $14,600 = ¥2,000,000 × $.0073 Aug. 1, 240-day forward rate

On October 1, 20X1, the forward exchange contract is revalued to its fair value in accordance with **FASB 133.** The accounts payable in yen are recorded at the time the inventory is received.

October 1, 20X1

(15)   Foreign Currency Receivable from Exchange Broker (¥)        400
    Foreign Currency Transaction Gain        400
    Adjust forward contract to fair value, using
    the forward rate at this date, and recognize gain:
    $ 15,000 = ¥2,000,000 × $.0075 Oct. 1, 180-day forward rate
    −14,600 = ¥2,000,000 × $.0073 Aug. 1, 240-day forward rate
    $   400 = ¥2,000,000 × $($.0075 − $.0073)

(16)    Foreign Currency Transaction Loss                                    400
          Firm Commitment                                                              400

          To record the loss on the financial instrument
          aspect of the firm commitment:

          $ 15,000 = ¥2,000,000 × $.0075 Oct. 1, 180-day forward rate

          −14,600 = ¥2,000,000 × $.0073 Aug. 1, 240-day forward rate

          $    400 = ¥2,000,000 × $($.0075 − $.0073)

The Firm Commitment account is a temporary account for the term of the unrecognized firm commitment. If it has a debit balance, it is shown in the assets section of the balance sheet; when it has a credit balance, as in this example, it is shown in the liability section of the balance sheet:

| Assets | | Liabilities and Equity | |
|---|---|---|---|
| Forward Exchange Contract (¥) (at net fair value) | $400 | Firm Commitment | $400 |

Note that the $400 foreign currency transaction gain is offset against the $400 foreign currency transaction loss, resulting in no net effect on earnings.

The next entry records the receipt of the inventory and the recognition of the accounts payable in yen. Note that the temporary account, Firm Commitment, is closed against the purchase price of the inventory. The accounts payable are valued at the spot exchange rate in accordance with **FASB 52.**

(17)    Inventory                                                     13,600
          Firm Commitment                                          400
              Accounts Payable(¥)                                              14,000

          Record accounts payable at spot rate
          and record inventory purchase:

          $14,000 = ¥2,000,000 × $.0070 Oct. 1, spot rate

### *Key Observations from Illustration*

The August 1, 20X1, entry records the signing of the forward exchange contract that is used to hedge the identifiable foreign currency commitment arising from the noncancelable purchase agreement. In entries (15) and (16), the forward contract and the underlying hedged foreign currency payable commitment are both revalued to their current value, and the $400 gain on the forward contract offsets the $400 loss on the foreign currency payable commitment. Entry (17) records the accounts payable in yen at the current spot rate and records the $400 inventory net that resulted from the recognition of the $400 loss on the financial instrument aspect of the firm commitment in entry (16).

At this point, the company has an exposed net liability position, which is hedged with a forward exchange contract, and the subsequent accounting follows the accounting for an exposed foreign currency liability position as presented previously in Case 1. Figure 11–5 presents a side-by-side comparison of the journal entries for the forward contract and the unrecognized firm commitment, which are valued at the forward exchange rates. The exposed foreign currency–denominated account payable is recognized at the time the company receives the inventory and is valued using the spot exchange rate.

## Case 3: Hedging a Forecasted Foreign Currency Transaction: A Foreign Currency Cash Flow Hedge

It is interesting to note the different accounting treatment of a hedge of a forecasted transaction as a cash flow hedge versus that of an identifiable foreign currency commitment as a fair value hedge. A forecasted transaction is anticipated but not guaranteed.

**FIGURE 11–5** **Comparison of Journal Entries: Hedge of an Unrecognized Firm Commitment**

| Forward Exchange Contract (Use forward exchange rate) | | Hedge of an Unrecognized Firm Commitment (Use forward exchange rate) | |
|---|---|---|---|

**August 1, 20X1.** Recognize forward exchange contract valued at forward rate.

| | | | | |
|---|---|---|---|---|
| (14) Foreign Currency Receivable (¥) | 14,600 | | | |
| Dollars Payable to Exchange Broker | | 14,600 | | |

**October 1, 20X1.** Revalue foreign currency receivable and firm commitment hedge using forward rate.

| | | | | |
|---|---|---|---|---|
| (15) Foreign Currency Receivable (¥) | 400 | | (16) Foreign Currency Transaction Loss | 400 | |
| Foreign Currency Transaction Gain | | 400 | Firm Commitment | | 400 |

| | | | |
|---|---|---|---|
| | | Economic Management of an Exposed Foreign Currency Payable (Use spot exchange rate) | |

**October 1, 20X1.** Receive inventory, close firm commitment, and recognize foreign currency accounts payable.

| | | |
|---|---|---|
| (17) Inventory | 13,600 | |
| Firm Commitment | 400 | |
| Accounts Payable (¥) | | 14,000 |

**December 31, 20X1.** Revalue forward contract using forward rate, and accounts payable in yen using spot rate.

| | | | | |
|---|---|---|---|---|
| (7) Foreign Currency Receivable (¥) | 400 | | (8) Foreign Currency Transaction Loss | 2,000 | |
| Foreign Currency Transaction Gain | | 400 | Accounts Payable (¥) | | 2,000 |

**April 1, 20X2.** Revalue forward contract at its termination to spot rate, and accounts payable in yen to spot rate.

| | | | | |
|---|---|---|---|---|
| (9) Foreign Currency Transaction Loss | 200 | | (10) Accounts Payable (¥) | 800 | |
| Foreign Currency Receivable (¥) | | 200 | Foreign Currency Transaction Gain | | 800 |

**April 1, 20X2.** Deliver $14,600 in U.S. dollars to exchange broker, receiving yen. Use yen to settle accounts payable.

| | | | | |
|---|---|---|---|---|
| (11) Dollars Payable to Exchange Broker | 14,600 | | | |
| Cash | | 14,600 | | |
| (12) Foreign Currency Units (¥) | 15,200 | | (13) Accounts Payable (¥) | 15,200 | |
| Foreign Currency Receivable (¥) | | 15,200 | Foreign Currency Units (¥) | | 15,200 |

The forecasted transaction may actually occur as anticipated, but a hedge of a forecasted transaction is accounted for as a cash flow hedge with the effective portion of the change in fair value of the hedging instrument recognized in other comprehensive income. This type of hedge is against the changes in possible future cash flow that may result from changes in the foreign currency exchange rate. A forecasted transaction may become a firm commitment if the parties make a binding agreement. Prior to **FASB 138,** an entity could designate a forward foreign currency contract as a cash flow hedge if the purpose of the contract was offsetting forecasted cash flows, including transactions such as forecasted purchases or sales. Changes in the fair value of the cash flow hedge would be recognized as part of other comprehensive income. When the forecasted transaction became a firm commitment, the forward contract would be redesignated as a fair value hedge, and changes in the fair value of the contract would then be recognized in earnings. Any amount recorded in other comprehensive income under the cash flow hedge would not be reclassified into earnings until the initially forecasted transaction impacted earnings. If the forecasted foreign currency transaction did not occur and was not expected to occur in the future, the amount recorded in other comprehensive income would be reclassified into earnings. The forward rate was used to value the forward contract and the spot rate was used to value the account receivable or payable resulting from the transaction.

**FASB 138** allows management the additional option of designating the forward contract as a cash flow hedge from the time the contract is initially made until the final settlement of the payable or receivable, rather than requiring that the contract be redesignated as a fair value hedge when the forecasted transaction becomes a firm commitment. Changes in the value of the forward contract are measured using the forward exchange rate, while changes in the account payable or receivable are measured using the spot exchange rate. However, **FASB 138** requires that other comprehensive income from the forward contract revaluation be offset for any foreign exchange gain or loss on the account receivable or payable. Any remaining component of other comprehensive income is taken into the earnings stream only on final completion of the earnings process. Note that the forward contract must meet the requirements of a hedging instrument under the provisions of **FASB 133,** including the designation and tests of effectiveness.

**FASB 138** allows management to: (1) designate the forward contract as a cash flow hedge while it is a forecasted transaction and then redesignate it as a fair value hedge for the remainder of the contract, or (2) designate the forward contract as a cash flow hedge for the entire period of time from the initial forecasting of the transaction through the eventual settlement of the receivable or payable. However, most companies regularly hedge their foreign currency receivables and payables and are likely to declare the forward contract as a continuing cash flow hedge in order to fully offset any gains or losses on changes in the fair value of the forward contract.

The following example is based on the data in Case 2 but adds the following assumption: the purchase of inventory is forecasted in August, but there is not a binding agreement for this purchase. Peerless Products Corporation enters into the 240-day forward exchange contract as a designated hedge against the future cash flows from the forecasted transaction, including the foreign currency–denominated accounts payable that would result from the purchase. Figure 11–6 presents the entries for this case, assuming that the hedge is designated as a cash flow hedge when the transaction is forecasted and then redesignated as a fair value hedge when the transaction occurs and the inventory is

**FIGURE 11–6**  Journal Entries for Cash Flow Hedge Redesignated as Fair Value Hedge When a Forecasted Transaction Becomes a Transaction

| Entries for Forward Contract (Use forward exchange rate) | | Entries for Foreign Currency Account Payable (Use spot rate) | |
|---|---|---|---|

**August 1, 20X1.** Acquire forward exchange contract valued at forward rate.

| (14) Foreign Currency Receivable (¥) | 14,600 | | |
| Dollars Payable to Exchange Broker | | 14,600 | |

**October 1, 20X1.** Receive inventory that was a forecasted transaction and recognize the foreign currency accounts payable at the spot rate. Change designation from a cash flow hedge to a fair value hedge; bring the forward contract to fair value as of this date.

| (15C) Foreign Currency Receivable (¥) | 400 | (17C) Inventory | 14,000 |
| Other Comprehensive Income | 400 | Accounts Payable (¥) | 14,000 |
| ¥2,000,000 × ($.0075 − $.0073) | | | |

**December 31, 20X1.** Revalue the forward contract to year-end fair values using the change in the forward rate since October 1 and recognize gain or loss in net income. Revalue accounts payable in yen using the spot rate.

| (7) Foreign Currency Receivable (¥) | 400 | (8) Foreign Currency Transaction Loss | 2,000 |
| Foreign Currency Transaction Gain | 400 | Accounts Payable (¥) | 2,000 |
| ¥2,000,000 × ($.0077 − $.0075) | | | |

**April 1, 20X2.** Revalue the forward contract using the spot rate at the termination of the contract and accounts payable in yen using the spot rate. Offset transaction gain on payable against other comprehensive income.

| (9) Foreign Currency Transaction Loss | 200 | (10) Accounts Payable (¥) | 800 |
| Foreign Currency Receivable (¥) | 200 | Foreign Currency Transaction Gain | 800 |
| ¥2,000,000 × ($.0076 − $.0077) | | | |

**April 1, 20X2.** Deliver $14,600 in U.S. dollars to the exchange broker and receive yen. Use yen to settle accounts payable.

| (11) Dollars Payable to Exchange Broker | 14,600 | | |
| Cash | | 14,600 | |
| (12) Foreign Currency Units (¥) | 15,200 | (13) Accounts Payable (¥) | 15,200 |
| Foreign Currency Receivable | | 15,200 | Foreign Currency Units (¥) | 15,200 |

**FIGURE 11–7** **Journal Entries for Cash Flow Hedge of a Forecasted Transaction**

| **Entries for Forward Contract**<br>(Use forward exchange rate) | | **Entries for Foreign Currency Account Payable**<br>(Use spot rate) | |
|---|---|---|---|

**August 1, 20X1.** Acquire forward exchange contract valued at forward rate.

| (14) Foreign Currency Receivable (¥) | 14,600 | | |
|---|---|---|---|
| Dollars Payable to Exchange Broker | | 14,600 | |

**October 1, 20X1.** Receive inventory that was a forecasted transaction and recognize the foreign currency accounts payable at the spot rate.

| (No revaluation of foreign currency receivable required at this date) | | (17C) Inventory | 14,000 |
|---|---|---|---|
| | | Accounts Payable (¥) | 14,000 |

**December 31, 20X1.** Revalue the forward contract to year-end fair value using the change in the forward rate since August 1 and recognize the effective portion of the change in value as other comprehensive income. Revalue accounts payable in yen using the spot rate. Then, in accordance with **FASB 133**, reclassify a portion of the other comprehensive income to equally offset the foreign currency transaction loss recognized on the foreign currency payable that was remeasured using the spot exchange rate in accordance with **FASB 52**.

| (7C) Foreign Currency Receivable (¥) | 800 | | (8) Foreign Currency Transaction Loss | 2,000 | |
|---|---|---|---|---|---|
| Other Comprehensive Income | | 800 | Accounts Payable (¥) | | 2,000 |
| (¥2,000,000 × ($.0077 − $.0073)) | | | | | |
| (C) Other Comprehensive Income | 2,000 | | | | |
| Foreign Currency Transaction Gain | | 2,000 | | | |
| To offset loss on account payable. | | | | | |

**April 1, 20X2.** Revalue the forward contract at its termination using the spot rate and accounts payable in yen using the spot rate. Offset transaction gain on payable against other comprehensive income.

| 9(C) Other Comprehensive Income | 200 | | (10) Accounts Payable (¥) | 800 | |
|---|---|---|---|---|---|
| Foreign Currency Receivable (¥) | | 200 | Foreign Currency Transaction Gain | | 800 |
| (C) Foreign Currency Transaction Loss | 800 | | | | |
| Other Comprehensive Income | | 800 | | | |
| To offset gain on account payable. | | | | | |

**April 1, 20X2.** Deliver $14,600 in U.S. dollars to the exchange broker and receive yen. Use yen to settle accounts payable.

| (11) Dollars Payable to Exchange Broker | 14,600 | | | | |
|---|---|---|---|---|---|
| Cash | | 14,600 | | | |
| (12) Foreign Currency Units (¥) | 15,200 | | (13) Accounts Payable (¥) | 15,200 | |
| Foreign Currency Receivable (¥) | | 15,200 | Foreign Currency Units (¥) | | 15,200 |

Assumed sale of inventory and culmination of earnings process of other comprehensive income from forward contract.

| Cost of Goods Sold | 600 | | Cost of Goods Sold | 14,000 | |
|---|---|---|---|---|---|
| Other Comprehensive Income | | 600 | Inventory | | 14,000 |

purchased. Figure 11–6 presents the entries for this case by bringing into the illustration Case 1 entries that would not change and noting the entries that would change with a *C* behind the entry number. Note that the entry on October 1 records the effect of the change in value of the forward contract as a component of Other Comprehensive Income.

Figure 11–7 presents the entries for this case assuming the hedge is designated as a cash flow hedge and remains as such between inception in August and final settlement in April. Figure 11–7 presents the entries for this case by bringing into the illustration Case 1 entries that would not change and noting the entries that would change with a letter *C* behind the entry number. Note the major differences in accounting for the forward contract as a cash flow hedge here versus as a fair value hedge in Case 2 are (1) the effective portion of the revaluation of the forward exchange contract is recorded in Other Comprehensive Income, (2) no firm commitment account exists under a forecasted transaction, (3) no revaluation of the forward contract receivable is required on October 1 and the inventory is recorded at its equivalent U.S. dollar cost determined at the spot rate, (4) there is an offset against Other Comprehensive Income to fully match the foreign currency transaction gain or loss recognized on the exposed foreign currency account payable, and (5) the $600 remaining balance in Other Comprehensive Income after the foreign currency payable is paid on April 1, 20X2, is finally reclassified into cost of goods sold at the time the inventory is sold, which is the culmination of the earnings process related to the cash flow hedge.

## Case 4: Speculation in Foreign Currency Markets

An entity may also decide to speculate in foreign currency as with any other commodity. For example, a U.S. company expects that the dollar will strengthen against the Swiss franc, that is, that the direct exchange rate will decrease. In this case, the U.S. company might *speculate with a forward exchange contract* to sell francs for future delivery, expecting to be able to purchase them at a lower price at the time of delivery.

The economic substance of this foreign currency speculation is to expose the investor to foreign exchange risk for which the investor expects to earn a profit. The exchange rate for valuing accounts related to speculative foreign exchange contracts is the forward rate for the remaining term of the forward contract. The gain or loss on a speculative forward contract is computed by determining the difference between the forward exchange rate on the date of contract (or on the date of a previous valuation) and the forward exchange rate available for the remaining term of the contract. The forward exchange rate is used to value the forward contract.

### *Illustration of Speculation with Forward Contract*

The following example illustrates the accounting for a U.S. company entering into a speculative forward exchange contract in Swiss francs (SFr), a currency in which the company has no receivables, payables, or commitments.

1. On October 1, 20X1, Peerless Products entered into a 180-day forward exchange contract to deliver SFr 4,000 at a forward rate of $.74 = SFr 1, when the spot rate was $.73 = SFr 1. Thus, the forward contract was to deliver SFr 4,000 and receive $2,960 (SFr 4,000 × $.74).

2. On December 31, 20X1, the balance sheet date, the forward rate for a 90-day forward contract was $.78 = SFr 1, and the spot rate for francs was $.75 = SFr 1.

3. On April 1, 20X2, the company acquired SFr 4,000 in the open market and delivered the francs to the broker, receiving the agreed-upon forward contract price of $2,960. At this date, the spot rate was $.77 = SFr 1.

A summary of the direct exchange rates for this illustration follows.

| | U.S. Dollar–Equivalent of 1 Franc | |
| --- | --- | --- |
| Date | Spot Rate | Forward Rate |
| October 1, 20X1 | $.73 | $.74 (180 days) |
| December 31, 20X1 | .75 | .78 (90 days) |
| April 1, 20X2 | .77 | |

A time line of the economic events is as follows:

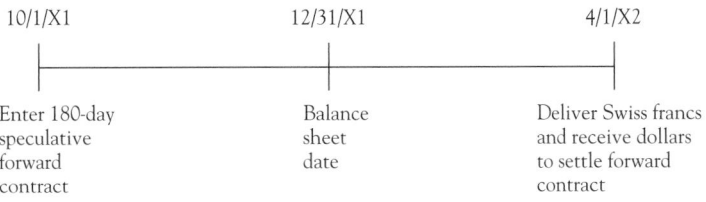

| 10/1/X1 | 12/31/X1 | 4/1/X2 |
| --- | --- | --- |
| Enter 180-day speculative forward contract | Balance sheet date | Deliver Swiss francs and receive dollars to settle forward contract |

The entries for these transactions are as follows:

October 1, 20X1

(18)    Dollars Receivable from Exchange Broker ($)                                2,960
        Foreign Currency Payable to Exchange Broker (SFr)                          2,960
        Enter into speculative forward exchange contract:
        $2,960 = SFr 4,000 × $.74, the 180-day forward rate

December 31, 20X1

(19)    Foreign Currency Transaction Loss                                         160
        Foreign Currency Payable to Exchange Broker (SFr)                            160
        Recognize speculation loss on forward contract
        for difference between initial 180-day forward
        rate and forward rate for remaining term
        to maturity of contract of 90 days:
        $160 = SFr 4,000 × ($.78 − $.74)

April 1, 20X2

(20)    Foreign Currency Payable to Exchange Broker (SFr)                          40
        Foreign Currency Transaction Gain                                            40
        Revalue foreign currency payable to spot rate
        at end of term of forward contract:
        $40 = SFr 4,000 × ($.78 − $.77)

(21)    Foreign Currency Units (SFr)                                              3,080
        Cash                                                                        3,080
        Acquire foreign currency units (SFr) in
        open market when spot rate is $.77 = SFr1:
        $3,080 = SFr 4,000 × $.77 spot rate

(22)    Foreign Currency Payable to Exchange Broker (SFr)                          3,080
        Foreign Currency Units (SFr)                                                3,080
        Deliver foreign currency units to exchange
        broker in settlement of forward contract:
        $3,080 = SFr 4,000 × $.77 spot rate

(23)    Cash                                                                      2,960
        Dollars Receivable from Exchange Broker ($)                                 2,960
        Receive U.S. dollars from exchange broker as contracted.

### Key Observations from Illustration

The October 1 entry records the forward contract payable of 4,000 Swiss francs to the exchange broker. The payable is denominated in a foreign currency but must be translated into U.S. dollars used as the reporting currency of Peerless Products. For speculative contracts, the forward exchange contract accounts are valued to fair value by using the forward exchange rate for the remaining contract term.

The December 31 entry adjusts the payable denominated in foreign currency to its appropriate balance at the balance sheet date. The payable, Foreign Currency Payable to Exchange Broker, is adjusted for the increase in the forward exchange rate from October 1, 20X1. The foreign currency transaction loss is reported on the income statement, usually under "Other Income (Loss)."

Entry (20), the first April 1 entry, revalues the foreign currency payable to its current U.S. dollar–equivalent value using the spot rate of exchange and recognizes the speculation gain. Entry (21) shows the acquisition of the 4,000 francs in the open market at the spot rate of $.77 = SFr 1. These francs will be used to settle the foreign currency payable to the exchange broker. The next two entries on this date, (22) and (23), recognize the settlement of the forward contract with the delivery of the 4,000 francs to the exchange broker and the receipt of the $2,960 agreed to when the contract was signed on October 1, 20X1. The $40 foreign currency transaction gain is the difference between the value of the foreign currency contract on December 31 using the forward rate and the value of the foreign currency units on April 1 using the spot rate.

Note that the company has speculated and lost because the dollar actually weakened against the Swiss franc. The net loss on the speculative forward contract was $120, which is the difference between the $160 loss recognized in 20X1 and the $40 gain recognized in 20X2.

Although this example shows a delivery of foreign currency units with a forward exchange contract, a company may also arrange a future contract for the receipt of foreign currency units. In this case, the October 1 entry is as follows:

October 1, 20X1

| | | | |
|---|---|---|---|
| (24) | Foreign Currency Receivable from Exchange Broker (SFr) | 2,960 | |
| | Dollars Payable to Exchange Broker ($) | | 2,960 |
| | Sign forward exchange contract for future receipt of foreign currency units: | | |
| | $2,960 = SFr 4,000 × $.74 | | |

The remainder of the accounting is similar to that of a delivery contract except that the company records an exchange gain on December 31 because it has a receivable denominated in a foreign currency that has now strengthened relative to the dollar.

### Foreign Exchange Matrix

The relationships between changes in exchange rates and the resulting exchange gains and losses are summarized in Figure 11–8. For example, if a company has an account receivable denominated in a foreign currency, the exposed net monetary asset position results in the recognition of an exchange gain if the direct exchange rate increases but an exchange loss if the exchange rate decreases. If a company offsets an asset denominated in a foreign currency with a liability also denominated in that currency, the company has protected itself from any changes in the exchange rate because any gain is offset by an equal exchange loss.

## ADDITIONAL CONSIDERATIONS

### A Note on Measuring Hedge Effectiveness

**FASB 133** states that, at the beginning of each hedging transaction, a company must define the method it will use to measure the effectiveness of the hedge. *Effectiveness* means that there will be an approximate offset, within the range of 80 to 125 percent,

**FIGURE 11–8** **Foreign Exchange Matrix**

| Transactions or Accounts Denominated in Foreign Currency Units | Direct Exchange Rate Changes | |
|---|---|---|
| | Exchange Rate Increases (dollar has weakened) | Exchange Rate Decreases (dollar has strengthened) |
| Net monetary asset position, for example:<br>(1) Foreign Currency Units<br>(2) Accounts Receivable<br>(3) Foreign Currency Receivable from Exchange Broker | EXCHANGE GAIN | EXCHANGE LOSS |
| Net monetary liability position, for example:<br>(1) Accounts Payable<br>(2) Bonds Payable<br>(3) Foreign Currency Payable to Exchange Broker | EXCHANGE LOSS | EXCHANGE GAIN |

of the changes in the fair value of the cash flows or changes in fair value to the risk being hedged. Effectiveness must be assessed at least every three months and when the company reports financial statements or earnings. A company may elect to choose from several different measures for assessing hedge effectiveness. The examples to this point in the chapter use the change in forward rates, but a company may use the change in spot prices or change in intrinsic value. The ***intrinsic value of a derivative*** is the value related to the changes in value of the underlying item. The ***time value of a derivative*** is related to the value assigned to the opportunity to hold the derivative open for a period of time. The time value expires over the term of the derivative and is zero at the derivative's maturity date. If the company uses spot prices for measuring hedge effectiveness, any difference between the spot price and the forward price is excluded from the assessment of hedge effectiveness and is included currently in earnings.

### Interperiod Tax Allocation for Foreign Currency Gains (Losses)

Temporary differences in the recognition of foreign currency gains or losses between tax accounting and GAAP accounting require interperiod tax allocation. Generally, the accrual method of recognizing the effects of changes in exchange rates in the period of change differs from the general election for recognizing exchange gains for tax purposes in the period of actual conversion of the foreign currency–denominated item. The temporary difference is recognized in accordance with **FASB Statement No. 109**, "Accounting for Income Taxes" (FASB 109).

### Hedges of a Net Investment in a Foreign Entity

In the earlier discussions of the use of forward exchange contracts as a hedging instrument, the exchange risks from transactions denominated in a foreign currency could be offset. This same concept is applied by U.S. companies that view a net investment in a foreign entity as a long-term commitment that exposes them to foreign currency risk. A number of balance sheet management tools are available for a U.S. company to hedge its net investment in a foreign affiliate. Management may use forward exchange contracts, other foreign currency commitments, or certain intercompany financing arrangements, including intercompany transactions. For example, a U.S. parent company could borrow 10,000 British pounds to hedge against an equivalent net asset position of its British subsidiary. Any effects of exchange rate fluctuations between the pound and the dollar would be offset by the investment in the British subsidiary and the loan payable.

    **FASB 133** specifies that for derivative financial instruments designated as a hedge of the foreign currency exposure of a net investment in a foreign operation, the portion of the change in fair value equivalent to a foreign currency transaction gain or loss should be reported in other comprehensive income. That part of other comprehensive income resulting from a hedge of a net investment in a foreign operation then becomes part of the cumulative translation adjustment in accumulated other comprehensive income. Chapter 12 presents both the translation adjustment portion of other comprehensive income and accumulated other comprehensive income.

## Summary of Key Concepts

Virtually all companies have foreign transactions. The general rule is that accounts resulting from transactions denominated in foreign currency units must be valued and reported at their equivalent U.S. dollar values. Forward exchange contracts typically use the forward rate for determining current fair value. These accounts must be adjusted to recognize the effects of changes in the exchange rates. For fair value hedges, the gain or loss is taken into current earnings. For cash flow hedges, the gain or loss is taken to other comprehensive income for the period.

## Key Terms

cash flow hedges, *516*
current rate, *509*
derivative, *515*
fair value hedges, *516*

financial instrument, *515*
foreign currency exchange
  rate, *504*
foreign currency hedges, *516*

foreign currency transaction
  gain or loss, *510*
foreign currency
  transactions, *503*

## Appendix 11A  Illustration of Valuing Forward Exchange Contracts with Recognition for the Time Value of Money

This illustration uses the exmple of a hedge of an identifiable, unrecognized foreign currency commitment from the chapter to illustrate the present value of the forward exchange contract and hedge.

1. On August 1, 20X1, Peerless Products Corporation contracts to purchase special-order goods from Tokyo Industries. The manufacture and delivery of the goods will take place in 60 days (on October 1, 20X1). The contract price is 2,000,000 yen to be paid by April 1, 20X2, which is 180 days after delivery.

2. On August 1, 20X1, Peerless Products hedges its foreign currency payable commitment with a forward exchange contract to receive 2,000,000 yen in 240 days (the 60 days until delivery plus 180 days of credit period). The future rate for a 240-day forward contract is $.0073 to 1 yen. The purpose of this 240-day forward exchange contract is twofold. First, for the 60 days from August 1, 20X1, until October 1, 20X1, the forward exchange contract is a hedge of an identifiable foreign currency commitment. For the 180-day period from October 1, 20X1, until April 1, 20X2, the forward exchange contract is a hedge of a foreign currency–exposed net liability position.

3. Peerless uses a discount interest rate of 10 percent to present value the expected future cash flows from forward exchange contracts.

4. Peerless measures the effectiveness of hedges of identifiable, unrecognized firm commitments based on changes in the forward exchange rate.

The relevant exchange rates for this example are as follows:

| Date | U.S. Dollar–Equivalent Value of 1 Yen | |
|---|---|---|
| | **Spot Rate** | **Forward Exchange Rate** |
| August 1, 20X1 | $.0065 | $.0073 (240 days) |
| October 1, 20X1 | .0070 | .0075 (180 days) |
| December 31, 20X1 (balance sheet date) | .0080 | .0077 (90 days) |
| April 1, 20X2 (settlement date) | .0076 | |

A time line for transactions follows.

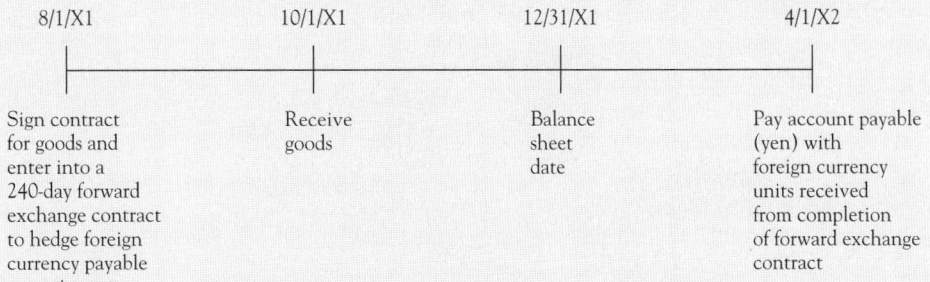

| 8/1/X1 | 10/1/X1 | 12/31/X1 | 4/1/X2 |
|---|---|---|---|
| Sign contract for goods and enter into a 240-day forward exchange contract to hedge foreign currency payable commitment | Receive goods | Balance sheet date | Pay account payable (yen) with foreign currency units received from completion of forward exchange contract |

The computation of hedge effectiveness is performed using the changes in the forward exchange rate in accordance with the general requirements of **FASB 133** and the company's specific policies regarding measurement of effectiveness of the hedge by using the forward exchange rates.

| | **Change in the Fair Value of** | | |
| | **Forward Contract Based on Changes in Forward Rate Gain (Loss)** | **Firm Commitment Based on Changes in Forward Rate Gain (Loss)** | **Effectiveness Ratio for the Period** |
| --- | --- | --- | --- |
| October 1, 20X1 | $380(a) | $(380) | 1.00 |
| December 31, 20X1 | 400(b) | No longer applicable because firm commitment was completed on October 1, 20X1. | |
| April 1, 20X2 | (180)(c) | | |

(a) $380 = [($.0075 − $.0073) × ¥2,000,000] for the $400 cumulative, undiscounted gain from the change in the forward rates and then discounted at a 10 percent annual rate for the six-month period from October 1, 20X1, to April 1, 20X2, the completion date of the forward contract: NPV (.05, 400) = $380.95, rounded.

(b) $400 = [($.0077 − $.0073) × ¥2,000,000] for the $800 cumulative, undiscounted gain from the change in the forward rates since entering the forward contract and then (1) discounted at a 10 percent annual rate for the three-month period from December 31, 20X1, to April 1, 20X2, NPV (.025,800) = $780.49, rounded; and then (2) subtract prior recognition of $380 reported for October 1, 20X1, in (a).

(c) $(180) = [($.0076 − $.0073) × ¥2,000,000] for the $600 cumulative gain from the change in the forward rate since entering the forward contract on August 1, 20X1, to the spot rate on April 1, 20X2, the completion of the forward contract; then subtract the prior recognition of $780 gain recognized previously in (a) and (b). This results in a loss of $(180) in the current period.

The amounts in the following entry on August 1, 20X1, are not present valued because the entry is a memorandum-type entry and because the interest factor will be taken into earnings through the changes in the fair value of the forward contract. Note that at the date of signing the forward contract, the net fair value of the forward contract is zero because the receivable and payable are equal to each other.

August 1, 20X1

| (25) | Foreign Currency Receivable from Exchange Broker (¥) | 14,600 | |
| --- | --- | --- | --- |
| | Dollars Payable to Exchange Broker ($) | | 14,600 |
| | Sign forward exchange contract for receipt of 2,000,000 yen in 240 days: $14,600 = ¥2,000,000 × $.0073 Aug. 1, 240-day forward rate | | |

On October 1, 20X1, the forward exchange contract will be revalued to its net fair value, recognizing the time value of money by using the present value of the expected future net cash flow from the forward contract. The temporary liability account, Firm Commitment, is also recorded at this time. Net present values can easily be computed using an electronic spreadsheet such as Excel and the Net Present Value (NPV) function.

October 1, 20X1

| (26) | Foreign Currency Receivable from Exchange Broker (¥) | 380 | |
| --- | --- | --- | --- |
| | Foreign Currency Transaction Gain | | 380 |
| | Adjust forward contract to net fair value, using the present value of the change in the forward rates. [Item (a) in the hedge effectiveness illustration.] | | |

| (27) | Foreign Currency Transaction Loss | 380 | |
| --- | --- | --- | --- |
| | Firm Commitment | | 380 |
| | To record the loss on the financial instrument aspect of the firm commitment, using the present value of the change in the forward exchange rates. [Same amount as item (a) for this example because the effectiveness of the hedge on the firm commitment is assessed using the change in the forward exchange rates.] | | |

On October 1, 20X1, the discounted net fair value of the forward contract is $380.

The next entry is to record the receipt of the inventory and the recognition of the accounts payable in yen. Note that the temporary account, Firm Commitment, is closed against the purchase price of the inventory.

| (28) | Inventory | 13,620 | |
| | Firm Commitment | 380 | |
| | Accounts Payable (¥) | | 14,000 |
| | Record accounts payable at spot rate and the inventory purchase, closing the temporary liability account: $14,000 = ¥2,000,000 × $.0070 Oct. 1 spot rate | | |

The required adjusting entries on December 31, 20X1, Peerless's fiscal year-end, are:

| (29) | Foreign Currency Receivable from Exchange Broker (¥) | 400 | |
| | Foreign Currency Transaction Gain | | 400 |
| | Adjust forward contract to net fair value, using the present value of the change in the forward rates. [Item (b) in the hedge effectiveness illustration.] | | |

| (30) | Foreign Currency Transaction Loss | 2,000 | |
| | Accounts Payable (¥) | | 2,000 |
| | Adjust payable denominated in yen to current U.S. dollar–equivalent value: $2,000 = ¥2,000,000 × ($.0080 − $.0070). No interest factor is used for this revaluation; thus, no present value computation is made. | | |

On December 31, 20X1, the discounted net fair value of the forward contract is $780.

The first required entry on April 1, 20X2, the settlement date, is:

| (31) | Foreign Currency Transaction Loss | 180 | |
| | Foreign Currency Receivable from Exchange Broker (¥) | | 180 |
| | Adjust forward contract for the change in the forward rate to the spot rate on settlement date: [Item (c) in the hedge effectiveness illustration.] | | |

$$\begin{array}{ll} \$ \phantom{0}.0076 & \text{spot rate on 4/1/X2, the end of the forward contract} \\ \underline{-.0073} & \text{forward rate on 8/1/X1, the beginning of the forward contract} \\ \underline{\$ \phantom{0}.0003} \times ¥2,000,000 = \$ \phantom{0}600 & \text{cumulative change from 8/1/X1} \\ \phantom{xxxxxxxxxxx} \underline{-780} & \text{gains previously recognized} \\ \phantom{xxxxxxxxxxx} \underline{\underline{\$(180)}} & \text{reduction (loss) this period} \end{array}$$

Note that at this point, the net foreign currency transaction gain on just the forward contract is $600. This is the difference between the time value of the forward contract (the $1,600 premium on the forward contract—$.0073 forward rate less $.0065 spot rate—when the forward contract was signed on August 1, 20X1, which is taken into earnings over the term of the forward contract) and the intrinsic value of the forward contract (the $2,200 difference between the spot rate of $.0065 on August 1, 20X1, and the spot rate of $.0076 on the forward contract completion date of April 1, 20X2). Another way to compute the net gain over the term of the forward contract is to compare the forward rate at the date the contract is signed ($.0073) and the spot rate at the date the contract is completed ($.0076). The net gain is $600 [¥2,000,000 × ($.0073 − $.0076)].

The following April 1, 20X2, entries complete the forward contract and the payment of the accounts payable that was denominated as ¥2,000,000.

| (32) | Accounts Payable (¥) | 800 | |
| | Foreign Currency Transaction Gain | | 800 |
| | Adjust payable denominated in yen to spot rate on settlement date. No interest factor for this item. $800 = ¥2,000,000 × ($.0076 − $.0080) | | |

| (33) | Dollars Payable to Exchange Broker ($) | 14,600 | |
| | Cash | | 14,600 |
| | Deliver U.S. dollars to currency broker as specified in forward contract. | | |

| (34) | Foreign Currency Units (¥) | 15,200 | |
| | Foreign Currency Receivable from Exchange Broker (¥) | | 15,200 |
| | Receive ¥2,000,000 from exchange broker; valued at Apr. 1, 20X2, spot rate: $15,200 = ¥2,000,000 × $.0076 | | |

| (35) | Accounts Payable (¥) | 15,200 | |
| | Foreign Currency Units (¥) | | 15,200 |
| | Pay 2,000,000 yen to Tokyo Industries, Inc., in settlement of liability denominated in yen. | | |

## Appendix 11B  Use of Other Financial Instruments by Multinational Companies

This chapter detailed the accounting for forward exchange contracts that were used to hedge exposed asset or liability positions or to hedge foreign currency commitments, or that were entered into for speculative purposes. Many multinational enterprises (MNEs) typically use financial instruments other than forward contracts to manage the risks associated with international transactions. A general definition of a financial instrument is that it is cash, stock, or a contract that imposes a contractual obligation to deliver or receive cash or another financial instrument to another entity. Examples of financial instruments are receivables/payables, bonds, shares of stock, foreign currency forward contracts, futures contracts, options, and financial swaps. A derivative financial instrument is when the value of a financial instrument is derived from some other item such as a contract valued on an index of stock values or futures contracts in which the value is determined by contemporary and predicted economic events. The other derivative financial instruments most often used by MNEs are futures, options, and swaps.

Accounting standard setters have had the daunting task of obtaining a consensus on the accounting, reporting, and disclosing of financial instruments. The FASB first placed the financial instrument project on its agenda in 1986 and has since continued to work on this project. Along the way, it issued **FASB Statement No. 105,** "Disclosure of Information about Financial Instruments with Off-Balance Sheet Risk" (FASB 105), **FASB Statement No. 107,** "Disclosures about Fair Value of Financial Instruments" (FASB 107), and **FASB Statement No. 119,** "Disclosure about Derivative Financial Instruments and Fair Value of Financial Instruments" (FASB 119). In 1998, the FASB issued **FASB Statement No. 133,** "Accounting for Derivative Instruments and Hedging Activities" (FASB 133). **FASB 133** supersedes **FASB Statement No. 80,** "Accounting for Future Contracts" (FASB 80), **FASB 105,** and **FASB 119.** In 1999, the FASB issued **FASB 137,** which delayed the implementation date of **FASB 133** for one year, until June 15, 2000, but **FASB 137** did not change any of **FASB 133**'s requirements.

**FASB 133** specified four major decisions underlying the logic of the standard: (1) derivatives are assets or liabilities and should be reported in the financial statements, (2) fair value is the most relevant measure for financial instruments and the only relevant measure for derivatives, and adjustment to the carrying amount of hedged items should reflect offsetting changes in their fair value while the hedge is in effect, (3) only items that are assets or liabilities should be reported as such in the financial statements, and (4) special accounting for items designated as being hedged should be provided only for qualifying transactions, and an aspect of qualification should be an assessment of offsetting changes in fair values or cash flows. Thus, **FASB 133** has a general rule of fair value, requires the recognition of gains and losses for the changes in fair value, and limits the applications of hedge accounting. It defines *fair value* as the amount at which an asset (liability) could be bought (incurred) or sold (settled) in a current transaction between willing parties. Quoted market prices are typically the best evidence of fair value. In addition, **FASB 133** amended **FASB 107** to include specific disclosures about concentrations of credit risk of all financial instruments and encouraged disclosure about the market risk of all financial instruments. *Credit risk* is the loss that might occur if a party to the contract involving the entity fails to perform. *Market risk* is the loss that might occur from future changes in market prices that would impair the value of the financial instrument.

**FASB Statement No. 138,** "Accounting for Certain Derivative Instruments and Certain Hedging Activities: An Amendment of FASB Statement No. 133" (FASB 138), issued in 2000, amended four smaller items in **FASB 133** in response to technical concerns raised by practitioners and preparers of the financial statements: (1) it broadened the application of the normal purchases and sales exception so that fewer of these contracts requiring delivery of nonfinancial assets would need to be accounted for as derivatives, (2) it redefined the interest rate risk to permit a benchmark risk-free interest rate to be the hedged risk, (3) it permitted hedging recognized foreign currency–denominated assets or liabilities with either cash flow or fair value hedges but still requires the foreign currency–denominated asset or liability to be valued according to the provisions of **FASB 52,** and (4) it broadened the ability to hedge with intercompany derivatives.

**FASB Statement No. 149,** "Amendment of Statement 133 on Derivative Instruments and Hedging Activities" (FASB 149), issued in 2003, presented a series of modifications resulting from implementation issues related to the definition of a derivative. **FASB 149** clarified several definitional issues but did not change the basic concepts presented in **FASB 133.**

This appendix supplements the chapter by presenting a brief overview of futures, options, and swaps. It first gives brief definitions and descriptions. Next, it presents several examples of accounting for a hedge with a futures contract, a hedge with an option contract, and an interest-rate swap. Finally, it presents a description of the disclosure requirements that currently apply. A discussion of the detailed mechanics and risk ramifications of transactions that utilize these instruments is beyond the coverage of an advanced financial accounting textbook.

# DEFINITIONS AND DESCRIPTIONS

A *derivative financial instrument* is an instrument whose value is based on or "derived from" the value of something else (an underlying). That underlying can be the value of another financial instrument, a commodity, an index, an asset, or a debt instrument. Because the derivative financial instrument has a value that is linked to the underlying, it makes the derivative a useful hedging instrument to offset the change in value of the hedged item. Examples of derivative financial instruments include futures, forward, swap, and option contracts; interest-rate caps; and fixed-rate loan commitments.

## Forward and Futures Contracts

A forward contract is an agreement between a buyer and a seller that requires the delivery of some commodity at a specified future date at a price agreed to today (the exercise price). As presented in the chapter, foreign currency forward contracts are typically made with dealers of foreign exchange, and the contract is fulfilled at the end of the contract term by the exchanges of the currencies between the company and the dealer. Changes in the underlying market value of the foreign currency are recognized by the company holding the forward contract. The net fair value of a forward contract when it is written is zero because neither party pays anything and neither party receives anything. The contract is executory at this point. During the term of the forward contract, the net fair value changes based on the difference between a newly written forward contract for the remaining term and the original forward contract. At expiration, the forward contract's net fair value is the difference between the spot price and the original forward rate.

Futures are very similar to forward contracts except futures have standardized contract terms, they are traded on organized exchanges, and traders must realize any losses or gains on each and every trading day. Futures are contracts between two parties—a buyer and a seller—to buy or sell something at a specified future date, which is termed the *expiration date.* The contract trades on a futures exchange such as the Chicago Board of Trade (CBOT) or the Chicago Mercantile Exchange (CME). Futures contracts are actively traded in a number of commodities including grains and oilseeds, livestock and meat, food and fiber, and metals and energy. It is even possible to enter into futures contracts on foreign currencies. Companies trading in futures contracts are normally required to place cash in their margin accounts held by the brokerage exchange or a *clearing house,* and the gain (loss) on the futures contract is then added (subtracted) from the company's margin account. This margin account is settled daily for the changes in contract value. Margin accounts are maintained at some percentage (typically 2 to 5 percent) of the contract amount. Most investors do not expect to actually exchange the futures contract for the optioned item—the futures contract is simply an investment vehicle to ride the value curve of the optioned item—and they use a *closing transaction* to settle the future contract. If a company is the purchaser of a futures contract, it is said to "go long" in a position. If a company contracts to sell with a futures contract, it is said to "go short." Futures contracts are sometimes referred to as *liquid forward contracts* because futures trade separately. The accounting for futures contracts is quite similar to accounting for foreign currency forward contracts.

Both futures and forward contracts are obligations to deliver a specified amount at a specified point in time. There is a potential for a gain under favorable circumstances and a potential for a loss under unfavorable circumstances. As presented in Chapter 11, not only the losses but also the gains are minimized by using foreign currency forward contracts. Forward contracts are commonly used for hedging foreign currency transactions because the forward contracts can be customized as to duration and amounts. Futures contracts are standardized as to duration and amount but are more readily accessible because of their wide acceptance in a futures exchange arena.

### Option Contracts

An option contract between two parties—the buyer and the seller—gives the buyer (option holder) the right, but not the obligation, to purchase from or sell something to the option seller (option writer) at a date in the future at a price agreed to at the time the option contract is exchanged. Options can be written on a large variety of commodities such as grains, food and fibers, petroleum, livestock, metals, interest rates, and various foreign currencies. The option buyer pays the seller some amount of money, typically termed the "premium," for this right. An option to buy something is referred to as a "call"; an option to sell something is called a "put." Options trade on organized markets similar to the stock market. Exchanges on which options trade are the Chicago Board Options Exchange (CBOE), the Philadelphia Stock Exchange (PHLX), the American Stock Exchange (AMEX), and the Pacific Stock Exchange (PSE).

An option contract can give the buyer future control over a large number of shares or other items at the nominal cost of the option. This ability of the option for future control is the *time value* of the option. Over the option's term, the time value decreases to zero at the option's expiration date. Changes in the time value of the option are always taken to current earnings. The party selling the right is the writer; the party buying the right is the holder. The option holder has the right to exercise or not exercise the option. The holder of the option would not exercise the right embedded in the option if by doing so it would result in a loss. The option writer, however, is subject to risk because the option holder could exercise the option, forcing the writer to deliver under terms that are not favorable to the writer. An option's *intrinsic value* is directly related to the change in underlying value of the hedged item. The change in intrinsic value of a fair value hedge is taken to current earnings. The change in the effective portion of intrinsic value of a cash flow hedge is taken to other comprehensive income. An example of an option used as a hedge is presented later in this appendix.

The option is sold with a *strike price,* the price at which the holder has the option to buy or sell the item. If an investor holds a call option to purchase one share of Peerless Products stock for $5 a share from the writer, the holder may exercise that option when the market share price exceeds the strike price. If the market price is $6 a share, the holder will save $1 by exercising the option and purchasing the stock for $5. If the holder wishes to turn the savings into a cash profit, the investor would sell the share of stock, purchased for $5, on the market for $6. Alternatively, the holder of the option could directly sell the option for $1, its intrinsic value. When the market price is more than the strike price, the option to buy is "in the money." When the market price is less than the strike price, the option to buy is "out of the money."

If an investor is the holder of a put option to sell one share of Peerless Products for $5 a share to the writer, the holder will exercise that option when the share price is below the strike price. If the market price is $4 a share, the holder will make $1 by exercising the sell option at $5 per share rather than selling the share on the open market at $4 per share. When the market price is less than the option price, the option to sell is "in the money."

For the Peerless Products stock example, a summary of the relationship between the option type and the term used to describe the difference between the current market price of the underlying and the option's strike price is as follows:

| Option | Current Market Price Equals the Option's Strike Price ($5 = $5) | Current Market Price Is More than the Option's Strike Price ($6 > $5) | Current Market Price Is Less than the Option's Strike Price ($4 < $5) |
| --- | --- | --- | --- |
| Call (buy) | At the money | In the money | Out of the money |
| Put (sell) | At the money | Out of the money | In the money |

**FIGURE 11–9**
**Features of Forwards, Futures, and Options**

| Type of Derivative | Features |
|---|---|
| Forwards | • Contracted through a dealer, usually a bank<br>• Possibly customized to meet contracting company's terms and needs<br>• Typically no margin deposit required<br>• Must be completed either with the underlying's future delivery or net cash settlement |
| Futures | • Traded on an exchange and acquired through an exchange broker<br>• Cannot be customized; for a specific amount at a specific date<br>• Often company required to open a margin account with a small deposit so daily changes in futures value can be posted to the account<br>• Usually settled with a net cash amount prior to maturity date; not expected to be completed by the underlying's future delivery |
| Options | • Traded on a variety of exchanges<br>• Acquired on a large variety of commodities and major foreign currencies<br>• Issued in two types, put (sell) and call (buy)<br>• Option premium (fee) paid by the option holder to the writer (counterparty) for that right<br>• Taker's or holder's loss limited to a maximum of the premium paid but virtually unlimited potential profit if underlying market moves in the option holder's desired direction<br>• Grantor (counterparty or writer) offered potential to earn a maximum of the option premium and to lose a virtually unlimited amount if underlying market moves in the opposite direction than desired |

Options are typically purchased for a fee that is usually a small percentage of the optioned item's current value (e.g., 1 to 7 percent). The option's terms stipulate whether the option can be exercised at any time during the option period or only at the end of the exercise period. The minimum value of a put option is zero because a put option need not be exercised. Therefore, a put option can never have a negative value, and the maximum loss of the holder of a put option is the premium initially paid for the option.

Figure 11–9 presents an overview of the major features of forwards, futures, and options.

## Swaps

A *swap* is an arrangement by which two parties exchange cash flows over a period of time. Swaps can be designed to swap currencies, interest rates, or commodities. The two most common types of financial swaps used by companies are (1) currency swaps and (2) interest rate swaps. An example of a currency swap is Peerless Products Corporation's sale of products in Great Britain for which it receives pounds sterling. Another company located in London, England, sells products in the United States for which it receives U.S. dollars. A currency swap would occur, for example, if Peerless (a U.S. company) agrees that the periodic currency flows in pounds sterling from its Great Britain operations will be forwarded to its counterparty in Great Britain, and the dollar sales in the United States by the London company will be forwarded to Peerless, the U.S. company. At the end of each period, the two companies agree to settle up for any differences in the notional amount of the swap at the end of the period. Thus, both parties to this currency swap avoid dealing in other than their local currencies and avoid foreign currency exchange costs.

Another example of a swap is an interest-rate swap in which two parties agree to exchange the interest payments on a stated amount of principal (also called the "notional amount"). Typically, the swap is an exchange of a variable (floating) rate interest and a fixed-rate interest. For example, Peerless may issue variable-rate debt but wish to fix its interest rates because it believes the variable rate may increase. Peerless may enter into a contract with a counterparty who has a fixed-rate bond but who is looking for a variable-rate interest because that company assumes the interest rates may decrease. Often the contract includes a financial intermediary to which net settlement payments are made and which charges a nominal fee for its services. Sometimes the counterparty is a dealer, which is a bank or an investment banking firm, that makes a market in swaps and other interest-rate derivatives. The notional amount (principal) is specified as the same for both parties,

**FIGURE 11–10**   **Overview of Three Types of Hedges**

| Type of Hedge | Basic Criteria | Recognition and Measurement |
|---|---|---|
| Fair value hedge | A hedge of the derivative instrument's exposure to changes in the fair value of an asset or liability, or of an unrecognized firm commitment. | Gain or loss on the hedging instrument, as well as the related loss or gain on the hedged item, should be recognized currently in earnings. |
| Cash flow hedge | Hedge the derivative instrument's exposure to variability in expected future cash flows of a recognized asset or liability, or of a forecasted transaction, that is attributable to a particular risk. | Gain or loss on the effective portion of hedge (e.g., the intrinsic value) is deferred and reported as a component of other comprehensive income. Any gain or loss on the derivative that is not offset by cash flow losses and gains on the hedged forecasted transaction (i.e., ineffective, including the time value of the option) is recognized currently in earnings. |
| Foreign currency hedge | A hedge of the foreign currency exposure of:<br>1. An unrecognized firm commitment<br>2. An available-for-sale security<br>3. A forecasted transaction<br>4. A net investment in a foreign operation | The recognition and measurement differ by type of hedge:<br>1. This is a foreign currency fair value hedge.<br>2. This is a foreign currency fair value hedge.<br>3. This is a foreign currency cash flow hedge.<br>4. The gain or loss on the effective portion of the hedging derivative on a net investment in a foreign operative shall be reported as part of the translation adjustment component of other comprehensive income. |

and Peerless fixes the interest rate on its notional amount while the counterparty obtains the variable rate it was seeking. Note that the debt is not being extinguished and any fees paid to arrange the swap should be treated as debt issuance costs that are amortized over the term of the debt. Each company is still responsible for its actual interest payment to its creditor. The swap is merely an agreement for the net periodic settlement of the difference between the two interest rates and is done solely between the two companies that contracted for the interest swap. The simple swap of fixed- versus variable-interest rates is sometimes referred to as a *plain vanilla swap* or a *generic swap*. An interest rate swap is presented later in this appendix.

An overview of the accounting for the three major types of hedges is presented in Figure 11–10. Review this figure before proceeding to the examples.

## EXAMPLE OF THE USE OF AN OPTION TO HEDGE AN ANTICIPATED PURCHASE OF INVENTORY: A CASH FLOW HEDGE

Assume that Peerless Products plans in 90 days to purchase 30,000 bushels of wheat that currently have a value of $75,000 (30,000 bushels × $2.50 spot price per bushel). Also assume that Peerless wants to lock in the value of the anticipated future purchase.

Peerless purchases a call option on wheat futures to hedge against a price change in the anticipated purchase of the inventory. If the price of wheat increases, the profit on the purchased call option will offset the higher price that Peerless would have to pay for the wheat. If the price of wheat decreases, Peerless loses the premium it paid for the call option but can then buy the wheat at a lower price.

On November 1, 20X1, Peerless purchases call options for a February 1, 20X2, call (90 days in the future) at a call price of $2.50. Peerless pays a premium of $.05 per bushel, for a total cost of $1,500 (30,000 bushels × $.05). The call options are for a notional amount of 30,000 bushels of wheat. Peerless specifies that the derivative qualifies for cash flow hedge accounting. It is a cash flow hedge because the option is hedging a forecasted, or planned, future transaction involving cash flows. Note that this example shows the entire $1,500 as the time value of the option; in other words, it sets a futures price equal to the current market price. This type of contract is sometimes termed "at the money," meaning it specifies the futures price of the underlying at the current market price. Thus, the value of the contract when it is signed is only with regard to the *time value* of the expectation that the actual future price of the commodity will differ from the current market price.

An overview of this hedge follows:

| | |
|---|---|
| Hedging instrument | Call option on wheat futures |
| Hedged item | Forecasted purchase of wheat |
| Type of hedge | Cash flow hedge |
| Underlying | Price of a bushel of wheat |
| Notional amount | 30,000 bushels of wheat |
| Time value at origin of hedge | $1,500, at the money |
| Valuation of call option | Fair value |
| If underlying increases in value | Call option increases in value |
| If underlying decreases in value | Call option decreases in value |

Gain or loss on hedge:

| | |
|---|---|
| Effective portion | To Other Comprehensive Income; related to change in intrinsic value of hedge |
| Ineffective portion | To current earnings; related to change in time value of hedge |

The entry to record the purchase of the call options is as follows:

November 1, 20X1

| | | | |
|---|---|---|---|
| (36) | Purchased Call Options | 1,500 | |
| | Cash | | 1,500 |
| | To record the purchase of call options for 30,000 bushels of wheat at $2.50 per bushel in 90 days. The options are at the money; therefore, the $1,500 is all time value. | | |

The fair market information for this example follows:

| **Fair Value Computations** | | | |
|---|---|---|---|
| | **November 1, 20X1** | **December 31, 20X1** | **February 1, 20X2** |
| Bushel of wheat | $ 2.50 | $ 2.60 | $ 2.58 |
| Total: 30,000 bushels | | | |
| Call Option: | | | |
| Option market value (from market information) | $1,500 | $3,700 | $2,400 |
| Less: Intrinsic value: [Number of bushels × (Market price − Strike price)] | | | |
| [30,000 bushels × ($2.50 − $2.50)] | -0- | | |
| [30,000 bushels × ($2.60 − $2.50)] | | (3,000) | |
| [30,000 bushels × ($2.58 − $2.50)] | | | (2,400) |
| Time value remaining | $1,500 | $ 700 | $ -0- |

Note that for a cash flow hedge, the change in the intrinsic value (effective portion) is recognized in Other Comprehensive Income, and the change in the time value (ineffective portion) is recognized in current earnings.

At December 31, 20X1, the price of wheat increases to $2.60 per bushel. The *intrinsic value* is the change in value of the options due to the change in market value of the underlying. For cash flow hedges, the change in a derivative's intrinsic value is recorded in other comprehensive income. On December 31, the intrinsic value of the options is $3,000 (30,000 bushels × $.10 increase).

**FASB 133** requires that hedging instruments be revalued to fair value at each balance sheet date. The change in value of the options is due to two factors: the change in the intrinsic value and the reduction of the time value. An option's time value decreases over its term and is zero when the options expire. At December 31, 20X1, the fair market value of the options is $3,700, meaning that the option's remaining time value is valued by the market at $700 ($3,700 fair value less $3,000 intrinsic value). **FASB 133** specifies that the $800 ($1,500 initial amount − $700 remaining) reduction in the time value portion of a derivative is recognized as part of current earnings. Entry (37) records the change in the value of the options to value them at their fair value at the balance sheet date.

December 31, 20X1

| | | | |
|---|---|---|---|
| (37) | Purchased Call Options | 2,200 | |
| | Loss on Hedge Activity | 800 | |
| | Other Comprehensive Income | | 3,000 |

To revalue the options to their fair market value,
recognizing the reduction in time value and
the increase in intrinsic value:

$2,200 = $3,700 current fair value of options less $1,500 balance on November 1

$800 = ($1,500 − $700 remaining) reduction in time value of options

$3,000 = 30,000 bushels × $.10 increase in intrinsic value

Note that the increase in intrinsic value is recorded in Other Comprehensive Income pending the completion of the forecasted inventory transaction. The Other Comprehensive Income account is used to "store" the intrinsic value gains or losses on cash flow hedges until they are reclassified into earnings when the hedged transaction affects earnings.

At February 1, 20X2, the end of the 90 days, the price of wheat is $2.58 per bushel. The decrease in the intrinsic value of the call options is recorded as follows:

February 1, 20X2

| | | | |
|---|---|---|---|
| (38) | Other Comprehensive Income | 600 | |
| | Purchased Call Options | | 600 |

To record the other comprehensive income,
deferring the earning recognition of the
loss on the purchased call options:
$600 = 30,000 bushels × ($2.58 − $2.60)

The next entry (39) recognizes the expiration of the remaining amount ($700) of the time value of the purchased call option because the option has now expired. **FASB 133** specifies that the change in the time value portion of a derivative be recognized in current earnings.

February 1, 20X2

| | | | |
|---|---|---|---|
| (39) | Loss on Hedge Activity | 700 | |
| | Purchased Call Options | | 700 |

To recognize the loss of the $700 remaining
time value of the purchased call options
that have now expired.

Peerless now decides to sell the contracts for their intrinsic value of $2,400 [30,000 bushels × ($2.58 − $2.50 call price)]. In addition, Peerless acquires the 30,000 bushels of wheat at the current market price of $2.58 per bushel. The next entry records the sale of the purchased call options at their current market price.

February 1, 20X2

| | | | |
|---|---|---|---|
| (40) | Cash | 2,400 | |
| | Purchased Call Options | | 2,400 |

To record the sale of the call options.

Peerless now purchases the 30,000 bushels of wheat at the current market price of $2.58 per bushel.

February 1, 20X2

| | | | |
|---|---|---|---|
| (41) | Wheat Inventory | 77,400 | |
| | Cash | | 77,400 |

Finally, Peerless later sells the wheat at a price of $100,000 and records the sale as well as the reclassification of the other comprehensive income resulting from the purchased call options. Note that the other comprehensive income is taken into income only when the underlying item enters the income stream.

| (42) | Cash | 100,000 | |
| | Sale | | 100,000 |
| | To record the sale of the 30,000 bushels of wheat. | | |

| (43) | Cost of Goods Sold | 77,400 | |
| | Wheat Inventory | | 77,400 |
| | To recognize the cost of the wheat sold. | | |

| (44) | Other Comprehensive Income—Reclassification | 2,400 | |
| | Cost of Goods Sold. | | 2,400 |
| | To reclassify into earnings the other comprehensive income from the cash flow hedge. | | |

The reduction of the cost of goods sold increases net income for the period. The earning process for the other comprehensive income was the sale of the wheat. The hedge was successful. Peerless has a gain of $2,400 less the $1,500 it paid for the time value of the call options.

# EXAMPLE OF AN OPTION CONTRACT TO HEDGE AVAILABLE-FOR-SALE SECURITIES: A FAIR VALUE HEDGE

Assume that on January 1, 20X1, Peerless purchases 100 shares of Special Foods stock at a cost of $25 per share. The company classifies these as available-for-sale securities because it does not intend to sell them in the near term. To protect itself from a decrease in the value of the investment, on December 31, 20X1, the company purchases, for a $300 premium, an at-the-money put option (i.e., option price is current market price), which gives it the right but not the obligation to sell 100 shares of Special Foods at $30 per share. The option expires on December 31, 20X3. The fair value of the investment and the option follow:

| **Fair Value Computations** | | | |
|---|---|---|---|
| | **December 31** | | |
| | **20X1** | **20X2** | **20X3** |
| Special Foods shares: | | | |
| Per share | $   30 | $   29 | $   26 |
| Total (100 shares) | 3,000 | 2,900 | 2,600 |
| Put option: | | | |
| Market value (*a*) | $ 300 | $ 340 | $ 400 |
| Less: Intrinsic value (*b*) | (-0-) | (100) | (400) |
| Time value (*c*) | $ 300 | $ 240 | $   -0- |

(a) Market value is obtained from the current market price. There is a variety of option pricing models, such as the Black-Scholes model, to estimate the value of these options.
(b) Intrinsic value is the difference between the current market price and the option price times the number of shares. It is easy to compute at any point in the life of the option. For example, the intrinsic value on December 31, 20X2, is ($30 option price − $29 current market price) × 100 shares.
(c) The time value of the option reflects the effect of discounting the expected future cash flows and a portion for the expected volatility in the price of the underlying asset. A simple way to compute the value is that it is the difference between the option's market value and its intrinsic value.

Note that the time value at December 31, 20X1, is for the entire option price because the option was purchased for the current market price. The time value decreases to zero at the end of the option because no time element remains at that expiration point and the market value of the option is then based solely on its intrinsic value. Peerless exercises the option just before its expiration on December 31, 20X3, and delivers the Special Foods shares to the option writer.

Peerless determines the hedge effectiveness based on the changes in the option's intrinsic value. This is an acceptable method for determining effectiveness using options because of the ultimate value of the option being based on the price of the underlying asset in this example, the stock of Special Foods.

| | Hedge Effectiveness Analysis | | |
|---|---|---|---|
| **Date** | **Change in Option's Intrinsic Value (Gain) Loss** | **Change in Value of Special Foods Shares (Gain) Loss** | **Effectiveness Ratio for Period** |
| December 31, 20X2 | $(100) | $100 | 1.00 |
| December 31, 20X3 | $(300) | $300 | 1.00 |

An overview of this hedge is:

| | |
|---|---|
| Hedging instrument | Put option on Special Foods stock |
| Hedged item | 100 shares of Special Foods stock |
| Type of hedge | Fair value hedge |
| Underlying | Price of a share of Special Foods stock |
| Notional amount | 100 shares of Special Foods stock |
| Time value at origin of hedge | $300, at the money |
| Valuation of put option | Fair value |
| If underlying increases in value | Put option decreases in value |
| If underlying decreases in value | Put option increases in value |

Gain or loss on hedge:

| | |
|---|---|
| Effective portion | To current earnings; related to change in intrinsic value of hedge |
| Ineffective portion | To current earnings; related to change in time value of hedge |

The entries for this example follow:

January 1, 20X1

| (45) | Available-for-Sale Securities | 2,500 | |
|---|---|---|---|
| | Cash | | 2,500 |
| | Acquire 100 shares of Special Foods stock at a price of $25 per share. | | |

December 31, 20X1

| (46) | Available-for-Sale Securities | 500 | |
|---|---|---|---|
| | Other Comprehensive Income | | 500 |
| | Mark to market of $30 the Special Foods stock and recognize the other comprehensive income in accordance with **FASB 115**: $500 = ($30 − $25) × 100 shares | | |

| (47) | Put Option | 300 | |
|---|---|---|---|
| | Cash | | 300 |
| | Purchase put option, at the money, to sell 100 shares of Special Foods at $30. This $300 is the time value of the option. | | |

Note that **FASB 133** amends **FASB 115** and requires the gain or loss on an available-for-sale security designated as a hedged item to be recognized in current earnings during the period. In entry (46), the marked-to-market value for the available-for-sale securities was recognized in other comprehensive income, in accordance with **FASB 115**. As can be seen in entry (48), once available-for-sale securities are hedged in a fair value hedge, the gain or loss on marking to market must be taken to earnings for the period.

| (48) | Loss on Hedge Activity | 100 | |
| | Available-for-Sale Securities | | 100 |

Record decrease in fair value for the Special Foods
stock in accordance with **FASB 133**:
$100 = ($30 − $29) × 100 shares

**FASB 133** specifies that the change in intrinsic value of fair value hedges be recognized currently in net earnings of the period. This is different from cash flow hedges in which the changes in intrinsic value were taken to other comprehensive income. Therefore, entry (49) recognizes the increase in the intrinsic value of this fair value hedge as a gain that will be closed to Retained Earnings.

December 31, 20X2

| (49) | Put Option | 100 | |
| | Gain on Hedge Activity | | 100 |

Record increase in the intrinsic value of the put option.

| (50) | Loss on Hedge Activity | 60 | |
| | Put Option | | 60 |

To record in earnings the ineffective portion of the change in
the fair value of the put options (i.e., the change in the time value).
$60 = $300 initial time value − $240 remaining time value

The entries for December 31, 20X3, continue the valuation process.

December 31, 20X3

| (51) | Loss on Hedge Activity | 300 | |
| | Available-for-Sale Securities | | 300 |

Mark to market of $26 the Special Foods
stock and recognize the loss in earnings:
$300 = ($26 − $29) × 100 shares

| (52) | Put Option | 300 | |
| | Gain on Hedge Activity | | 300 |

Record the increase in the intrinsic value of the put option.

| (53) | Loss on Hedge Activity | 240 | |
| | Put Option | | 240 |

Record in earnings the ineffective portion of
the change in fair value of the put option
(i.e., the change in the time value).

Entry (53) eliminates the remainder of the option's time value, which was initially $300. Entry (50) took $60 of the time value of the option against earnings of 20X2. Entry (53) takes the remainder into earnings of 20X3 because at the end of the option period, no time value remains. The only value of the put option at its term date is its intrinsic value.

| (54) | Cash | 3,000 | |
| | Put Option | | 400 |
| | Available-for-Sale Securities | | 2,600 |

Exercise the put option and delivery of the securities
at a price of $30 per share.

| (55) | Other Comprehensive Income | 500 | |
| | Realized Gain on Sale of Securities | | 500 |

Reclassify the other comprehensive income on Special Foods
stock that was recorded on Dec. 31, 20X1, to earnings
because the securities have now been sold.
$100 = ($30 − 2 $29) × 100 shares

It is also important to note that **FASB 133** does not permit hedge accounting for hedges of trading securities. **FASB 115** requires that trading securities be marked to market with the gain or loss reported in net earnings for the period. Therefore, any gains or losses on financial instruments

**FIGURE 11–11**   Journal Entries for a Fair Value Hedge of Available-for-Sale Securities

| Entries for Available-for-Sale Securities (hedged item) | | Entries for Put Option Contract (hedging instrument) | |
|---|---|---|---|

**January 1, 20X1.** Acquire 100 shares of Special Foods stock as available-for-sale security.

| (45) Available-for-Sale Securities | 2,500 | | |
|---|---|---|---|
| Cash | | 2,500 | |

**December 31, 20X1.** Revalue available-for-sale securities to market value in accordance with **FASB 115** and purchase put option for current market price of underlying.

| (46) Available-for-Sale Securities | 500 | (47) Put Option | 300 | |
|---|---|---|---|---|
| Other Comprehensive Income | | 500 | Cash | | 300 |

**December 31, 20X2.** Revalue available-for-sale securities in accordance with **FASB 133** and adjust put option to current market value for increases in $100 intrinsic value and $60 reduction in time value of option.

| (48) Loss on Hedge Activity | 100 | (49) Put Option | 100 | |
|---|---|---|---|---|
| Available-for-Sale Securities | | 100 | Gain on Hedge Activity | | 100 |
| | | (50) Loss on Hedge Activity | 60 | |
| | | Put Option | | 60 |

**December 31, 20X3.** Revalue available-for-sale securities and adjust put option to current market value for the $300 increase in intrinsic value and the $240 reduction in time value of the option.

| (51) Loss on Hedge Activity | 300 | (52) Put Option | 300 | |
|---|---|---|---|---|
| Available-for-Sale Securities | | 300 | Gain on Hedge Activity | | 300 |
| | | (53) Loss on Hedge Activity | 240 | |
| | | Put Option | | 240 |

**December 31, 20X3.** Exercise put option and deliver 100 shares of stock at a $30 per share price. Reclassify other comprehensive income recognized in (46) on available-for-sale securities now sold.

| (54) Cash | 3,000 | |
|---|---|---|
| Put Option | | 400 |
| Available-for-Sale Securities | | 2,600 |
| (55) Other Comprehensive Income | 500 | |
| Realized Gain on Sale of Securities | | 500 |

that are planned to hedge the risks of holding trading securities are always taken to net earnings for the period.

An overview of the journal entries made for the hedged available-for-sale securities and for the hedging put option is presented in Figure 11–11.

## EXAMPLE OF AN INTEREST-RATE SWAP TO HEDGE VARIABLE-RATE DEBT: A CASH FLOW HEDGE

Assume that on June 30, 20X1, Peerless borrows $5,000,000 of three-year, variable-rate debt with interest payments equal to the six-month U.S.$LIBOR (London Interbank Offered Rate) for the prior six months. The debt is not prepayable. The company then enters into a three-year interest-rate swap with First Bank to convert the debt's variable rate to a fixed rate. The swap agreement specifies that Peerless will pay interest at a fixed rate of 7.5 percent and receive interest at a variable rate equal to the six-month U.S.$LIBOR rate based on the notional amount of $5,000,000. Both the debt and the swap require interest to be paid semiannually on June 30 and December 31. Peerless specifies the swap as a cash flow hedge. A schematic of the swap relationships is presented in Figure 11–12.

The six-month U.S.$LIBOR rate and the market value of the swap agreement, as determined by a swap broker, follow for the first year of the swap agreement:

| Date | Six-Month U.S. $LIBOR Rate | Swap Agreement Fair Value Asset (Liability) |
|---|---|---|
| June 30, 20X1 | 6.0% | $    -0- |
| December 31, 20X1 | 7.0 | 165,000 |
| June 30, 20X2 | 5.5 | (70,000) |

**FIGURE 11–12**
**Fixed for Variable Interest-Rate Swap on $5,000,000 Notional Amount**

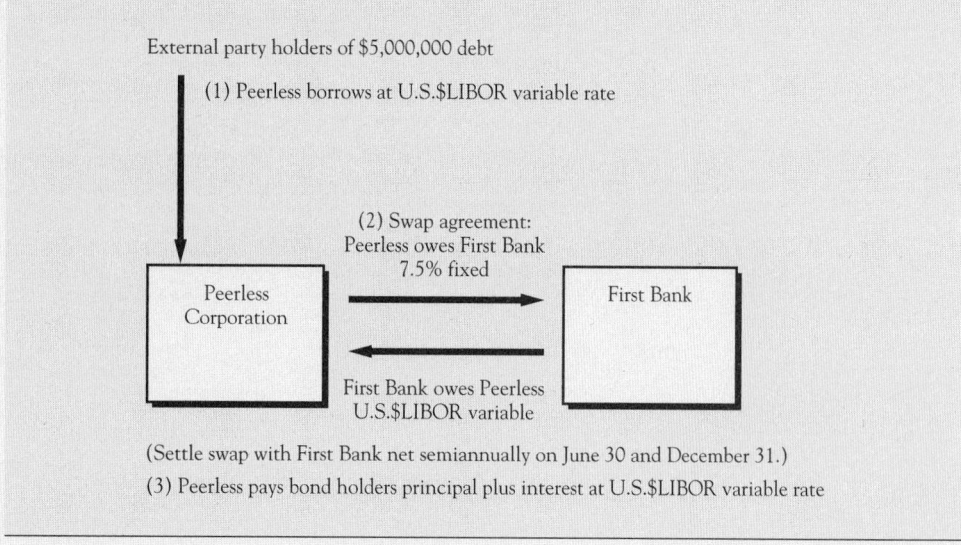

External party holders of $5,000,000 debt

(1) Peerless borrows at U.S.$LIBOR variable rate

(2) Swap agreement: Peerless owes First Bank 7.5% fixed

Peerless Corporation

First Bank

First Bank owes Peerless U.S.$LIBOR variable

(Settle swap with First Bank net semiannually on June 30 and December 31.)

(3) Peerless pays bond holders principal plus interest at U.S.$LIBOR variable rate

Note that Peerless must still pay the variable interest to the holders of the $5,000,000 debt. The interest-rate swap is just between Peerless and First Bank. The estimate of the fair value of the swap agreement was obtained from a broker-dealer of interest-rate swap agreements. Note that the value of the swap agreement to Peerless is positive if it believes that the variable rate will rise to higher than the fixed rate, but the swap agreement's value to Peerless is negative if it believes that the variable rate will remain lower than the fixed rate. Peerless's payments on the variable-rate debt and the net payments to First Bank on the interest-rate swap agreement are presented for the initial two semiannual periods:

|  | **Interest Payments** | |
|---|---|---|
|  | **December 31, 20X1** | **June 30, 20X2** |
| Variable-rate interest payment | $150,000 (a) | $175,000 (b) |
| Interest-rate swap net payment | 37,500 (c) | 12,500 |
| Total cash payment | $187,500 (d) | $187,500 |

(a) $150,000 = $5,000,000 × .06 × 6/12 months
(b) $175,000 = $5,000,000 × .07 × 6/12 months
(c) $37,500 = net payment required to First Bank for difference between variable and fixed interest rates
(d) $187,500 = $5,000,000 × .075 fixed rate × 6/12 months

Peerless recognizes interest expense based on the two factors of the variable rate plus the net payment or receipt from the swap agreement. In essence, Peerless has an interest expense equal to 7.5 percent of the notional amount of $5,000,000.

The entries to account for the first year of the interest-rate swap follow:

June 30, 20X1
| (56) | Cash | 5,000,000 | |
| | Debt Payable | | 5,000,000 |
| | Issue variable-rate debt. | | |

December 31, 20X1
| (57) | Interest Expense | 150,000 | |
| | Cash | | 150,000 |
| | Pay debt holders semiannual interest at a variable rate of 6.0 percent (from [a] in preceding table). | | |

| (58) | Interest Expense | 37,500 | |
| | Cash | | 37,500 |
| | Payment to First Bank for semiannual net settlement of swap agreement (from [c] in preceding table). | | |

| | | | |
|---|---|---|---|
| (59) | Swap Agreement | 165,000 | |
| |     Other Comprehensive Income | | 165,000 |
| |     Recognize change in fair value of swap agreement | | |
| |     to other comprehensive income because the | | |
| |     swap is a cash flow hedge. | | |

June 30, 20X2

| | | | |
|---|---|---|---|
| (60) | Interest Expense | 175,000 | |
| |     Cash | | 175,000 |
| |     Pay debt holders semiannual interest at a | | |
| |     variable rate of 7.0 percent (from [b] in preceding table). | | |
| | | | |
| (61) | Interest Expense | 12,500 | |
| |     Cash | | 12,500 |
| |     Payment to First Bank for semiannual | | |
| |     net settlement of swap agreement | | |
| | | | |
| (62) | Other Comprehensive Income | 235,000 | |
| |     Swap Agreement | | 235,000 |
| |     Recognize decrease in fair value of swap agreement | | |
| |     from $165,000 asset to $(70,000) liability to | | |
| |     Other Comprehensive Income because the | | |
| |     swap is a cash flow hedge. | | |

The swap agreement is reported on the balance sheet at its fair value. The amounts accumulated in Other Comprehensive Income are indirectly recognized in Peerless's earnings as periodic settlements of the payments required under the swap agreement are made, and the fair value of the swap agreement reaches zero at the end of the term of the agreement.

# REPORTING AND DISCLOSURE REQUIREMENTS: DISCLOSURES ABOUT FAIR VALUE OF FINANCIAL INSTRUMENTS

**FASB Statement No. 107,** "Disclosures about Fair Value of Financial Instruments" (FASB 107), required disclosure of information pertaining to all financial instruments. This standard is the first to require information with respect to the current fair value of the financial instruments. Estimating fair value is of great practical difficulty because many financial instruments do not have a readily traded market from which to determine their value. Estimation methods are permitted, but if no estimation can be made, the reasons for the impracticality must be disclosed.

**FASB 107** does not permit the fair values of derivatives to be netted or aggregated with nonderivative financial instruments. The required disclosures are as follows:

1. The fair value based on quoted market prices. If fair value is not quoted, then a practical estimation is allowed.
2. Information relevant to the fair value such as carrying value, effective interest rate, maturity, and reasons why it is not practical to estimate, if such is the case.
3. Distinction between instruments held for trading or nontrading purposes.

**FASB 133** added a number of disclosures regarding derivatives and financial instruments. The company holding or issuing derivatives must disclose both its objectives for holding or issuing the instruments and the face or contract amount of the derivatives. The company must also distinguish between derivatives designated as fair value hedges, as cash flow hedges, as hedges of the foreign currency exposure of a net investment in a foreign operation, and all other derivatives. Specific disclosures are required for each type of hedge, but generally the company must disclose the purpose of the activity, the amount of any gains or losses recognized during the period (either in earnings or in other comprehensive income), and where those gains or losses and related assets and liabilities are reported in the statement of income and statement of financial position.

Companies operating internationally have increased risks when transacting in more than one currency. For that reason, a number of financial instruments are used in order to manage the increased risk. Chapter 11 presented the most commonly used financial instrument, the foreign currency forward exchange contract. This appendix briefly discussed several of the other major financial instruments used by multinational companies. It is certain that increased sophistication of the types of risk management tools will continue to occur in the business arena, and accountants must continue their efforts to understand and account for these instruments.

| | | |
|---|---|---|
| **Questions** | **Q11-1** | Explain the difference between indirect and direct exchange rates. |
| | **Q11-2** | What is the direct exchange rate if a U.S. company receives $1.3623 in Canadian currency in exchange for $1.00 in U.S. currency? |
| | **Q11-3** | The U.S. dollar strengthened against the European euro. Will imports from Europe into the United States be more expensive or less expensive in U.S. dollars? Explain. |
| | **Q11-4** | Differentiate between a foreign transaction and a foreign currency transaction. Give an example of each. |
| | **Q11-5** | What types of economic factors affect currency exchange rates? Give an example of a change in an economic factor that results in a weakening of the local currency unit versus a foreign currency unit. |
| | **Q11-6** | How are assets and liabilities denominated in a foreign currency measured on the transaction date? On the balance sheet date? |
| | **Q11-7** | When are foreign currency transaction gains or losses recognized in the financial statements? Where are these gains or losses reported in the financial statements? |
| | **Q11-8** | Sun Company, a U.S. corporation, has an account payable of $200,000 denominated in Canadian dollars. If the direct exchange rate increases, will Sun experience a foreign currency transaction gain or loss on this payable? |
| | **Q11-9** | What are some ways a U.S. company can manage the risk of changes in the exchange rates for foreign currencies? |
| | **Q11-10** | Distinguish between an exposed net asset position and an exposed net liability position. |
| | **Q11-11** | Explain why a difference usually exists between a currency's spot rate and forward rate. Give two reasons this difference is usually positive when a company enters into a contract to receive foreign currency at a future date. |
| | **Q11-12** | A forward exchange contract may be used (*a*) to manage an exposed foreign currency position, (*b*) to hedge an identifiable foreign currency commitment, (*c*) to hedge a forecasted foreign currency transaction, or (*d*) to speculate in foreign currency markets. What are the main differences in accounting for these four uses? |
| | **Q11-13** | How—if at all—should the following items be reported on the financial statements? |

*a.* Foreign Currency Receivable from Broker

*b.* Foreign Currency Transaction Loss

*c.* Foreign Currency Transaction Gain

*d.* Dollars Payable to Exchange Broker

*e.* Premium on Forward Contract

*f.* Foreign Currency Units

*g.* Accounts Payable (denominated in a foreign currency)

| | | |
|---|---|---|
| **Cases** | **C11-1** | **Effects of Changing Exchange Rates** |
| | | Since the early 1970s, the U.S. dollar has both increased and decreased in value against other currencies such as the Japanese yen, the Swiss franc, and the British pound. The value of the U.S. dollar, as well as the value of currencies of other countries, is determined by the balance between the demand |
| | *Analysis* | for and the supply of the currency on the foreign exchange markets. A drop in the value of the U.S. dollar has a widespread impact not only on consumers and businesses that deal with their counterparts overseas but also on consumers and businesses that operate solely within the United States. |

### Required

a. Identify the factors that influence the demand for and supply of the U.S. dollar on the foreign exchange markets.

b. Explain the effect a drop in value of the U.S. dollar in relation to other currencies on the foreign exchange markets has on:

(1) The sales of a U.S. business firm that exports part of its output to foreign countries.

(2) The costs of a U.S. business firm that imports from foreign countries part of the inputs used in the manufacture of its products.

c. Explain why and how consumers and business firms that operate solely within the United States are affected by the drop in value of the U.S. dollar in relation to other currencies on the foreign exchange markets.

**C11-2** **Reporting a Foreign Currency Transaction on the Financial Statements [AICPA Adapted]**

*Judgment*

On November 30, 20X5, Bow Company received goods with a cost denominated in pounds. During December 20X5, the dollar's value declined relative to the pound. Bow believes that the original exchange rate will be restored by the time payment is due in 20X6.

### Required

a. State how Bow should report the impact, if any, of the changes in the exchange rate of the dollar and the pound on its 20X5 financial statements.

b. Explain why the reporting is appropriate.

**C11-3** **Changing Exchange Rates**

*Research*

Using the library or electronic resources, obtain and or prepare charts of the monthly average direct exchange rates for the past two years for the U.S. dollar versus (1) the Japanese yen, (2) the European euro, (3) the British pound, and (4) the Mexican peso. Your four charts should each have time on the horizontal axis and the direct exchange rate on the horizontal axis.

### Questions for Discussion

a. Has the dollar strengthened or weakened during this time against each of the currencies?

b. What major economic or political factors could have caused the changes in the four foreign currencies' exchange rates versus the U.S. dollar?

c. Select one major factor from part (*b*) for each currency and present an argument showing how a change in that factor could cause the change in the exchange rate.

**C11-4** **Accounting for Foreign Currency–Denominated Accounts Payable**

Mardi Gras Corporation operates a group of specialty shops throughout the southeastern United States. The shops have traditionally stocked and sold kitchen and bath products manufactured in the United States. This year, Mardi Gras has established a business relationship with a manufacturing company in Lucerne, Switzerland, to purchase a line of luxury bath products to sell in its shops. As part of the business arrangement, payments by Mardi Gras are due 30 days after receipt

*Research*
*FARS*

of the merchandise, whose cost is quoted and payable in Swiss francs.

Mardi Gras records the purchases in inventory when it receives the merchandise and records a liability to the Swiss company, using the exchange rate for Swiss francs on the date the inventory purchase is recorded. When payment is made, Mardi Gras debits or credits to inventory any difference between the liability previously recorded and the dollar amount required to settle the liability in Swiss francs. Mardi Gras uses a perpetual inventory system and the FIFO method of inventory costing and can easily trace these adjustments to the specific inventory purchased.

### Required

Obtain the most current accounting standards on accounting for foreign currency transactions. You can obtain access to accounting standards through the Financial Accounting Research System (FARS), from your library, or from some other source. As a staff accountant with the public accounting firm that audits Mardi Gras' annual financial statements, write a memo to Marie Lamont, the manager in charge of the audit, discussing the client's accounting for its transactions with the Swiss company. Support any recommendations with citations and quotations from the authoritative financial reporting standards.

**C11-5**  **Accounting for Foreign Currency Forward Contracts**

Avanti Corporation is a small Midwestern company that manufactures wooden furniture. Tim Martin, Avanti's president, has decided to expand operations significantly and has entered into a contract with a German company to purchase specialty equipment for the expansion in manufacturing capacity. The contract fixes the price of the equipment at 4.5 million euros, and the equipment will be delivered in five months with payment due 30 days after delivery.

*Research*
*FARS*

Tim is concerned that the value of the euro versus the U.S. dollar could increase during the six months between the date of the contract and the date of payment, thus increasing the effective price of the equipment to Avanti. Lindsay Williams, Avanti's treasurer, has suggested that the company enter into a forward contract to purchase 4.5 million euros in six months, thereby locking in an exchange rate for euros. Tim likes the idea of eliminating the uncertainty over the exchange rate for euros but is concerned about the effects of the forward contract on Avanti's financial statements. Because Avanti has not had previous experience with foreign currency transactions, Lindsay is unsure of what the financial statement effects are.

### Required

Obtain the most current accounting standards on accounting for foreign currency forward contracts. You can obtain access to accounting standards through the Financial Accounting Research System (FARS), from your library, or from some other source. Lindsay has asked you, as her assistant, to research the accounting for a foreign currency forward contract. Write a memo to her reporting on the results of your research. Support your recommendations with citations and quotations from the authoritative financial reporting standards.

**C11-6**  **Accounting for Hedges of Available-for-Sale Securities**

Rainy Day Insurance Company maintains an extensive portfolio of bond investments classified as available-for-sale securities under FASB 115. The bond investments have a variety of fixed interest rates and have maturity dates ranging from 1 to 15 years. Rainy Day acquired the bonds with the expectation that it could hold them until maturity or sell them any time that funds are required for unusually high insurance claims.

*Research*
*FARS*

Because of the large dollar amount invested, Rainy Day is concerned about fluctuations in interest rates that affect the fair value of its bond portfolio. One of Rainy Day's investment professionals has proposed that the company invest in an interest rate futures contract to hedge its exposure to interest rate changes. Changes in the fair value of the futures contract would offset changes in the bond portfolio's fair value. If Rainy Day applies hedge accounting under FASB 133, the income statement effect of changes in the fair value of the derivative would be offset by recording in earnings the changes in the fair value of the bond portfolio attributable to the hedged (interest rate) risk.

### Required

Obtain the most current accounting standards on accounting for hedges of available-for-sale securities. You can obtain access to accounting standards through the Financial Accounting Research System (FARS), from your library, or from some other source. Rainy Day's CFO, Mark Becker, has asked you, as an accountant in Rainy Day's investment division, to determine whether hedge accounting can be used in the scenario proposed. Write a memo to Mark, reporting on the results of your research. Support your recommendations with citations and quotations from the authoritative financial reporting standards.

---

**Exercises**  **E11-1**  **Exchange Rates**

Suppose the direct foreign exchange rates in U.S. dollars are:

1 British pound = $1.60
1 Canadian dollar = $.74

### Required

a.  What are the indirect exchange rates for the British pound and the Canadian dollar?

b.  How many pounds must a British company pay to purchase goods costing $8,000 from a U.S. company?

c.  How many U.S. dollars must be paid for a purchase costing 4,000 Canadian dollars?

**E11-2** **Changes in Exchange Rates**

Upon arrival at the international airport in the country of Canteberry, Charles Alt exchanged $200 of U.S. currency into 1,000 florins, the local currency unit. Upon departure from Canteberry's international airport on completion of his business, he exchanged his remaining 100 florins into $15 of U.S. currency.

***Required***

*a.* Determine the currency exchange rates for each of the cells in the following matrix for Charles Alt's business trip to Canteberry.

*b.* Discuss and illustrate whether the U.S. dollar strengthened or weakened relative to the florin during Charles's stay in Canteberry.

*c.* Did Charles experience a foreign currency transaction gain or a loss on the 100 florins he held during his visit to Canteberry and converted to U.S. dollars at the departure date? Explain your answer.

|  | Arrival Date | Departure Date |
|---|---|---|
| Direct exchange rate |  |  |
| Indirect exchange rate |  |  |

**E11-3** **Basic Understanding of Foreign Exposure**

The Hi-Stakes Company has a number of importing and exporting transactions. Importing activities result in payables, and exporting activities result in receivables. (LCU represents the local currency unit of the foreign entity.)

***Required***

*a.* If the direct exchange rate increases, does the dollar weaken or strengthen relative to the other currency? If the indirect exchange rate increases, does the dollar weaken or strengthen relative to the other currency?

*b.* Indicate in the following table whether Hi-Stakes will have a foreign currency transaction gain (G), loss (L), or not be affected (NA) by changes in the direct or indirect exchange rates for each of the four situations presented.

| Transaction | Settlement Currency | Direct Exchange Rate | | Indirect Exchange Rate | |
|---|---|---|---|---|---|
| | | Increases | Decreases | Increases | Decreases |
| Importing | Dollar | _____ | _____ | _____ | _____ |
| Importing | LCU | _____ | _____ | _____ | _____ |
| Exporting | Dollar | _____ | _____ | _____ | _____ |
| Exporting | LCU | _____ | _____ | _____ | _____ |

**E11-4** **Account Balances**

Merchant Company had the following foreign currency transactions:

1. On November 1, 20X6, Merchant sold goods to a company located in Munich, Germany. The receivable was to be settled in European euros on February 1, 20X7, with the receipt of €250,000 by Merchant Company.

2. On November 1, 20X6, Merchant purchased machine parts from a company located in Berlin, Germany. Merchant is to pay €125,000 on February 1, 20X7.

The direct exchange rates are as follows:

| | |
|---|---|
| November 1, 20X6 | €1 = $.60 |
| December 31, 20X6 | €1 = $.62 |
| February 1, 20X7 | €1 = $.58 |

### Required

a. Prepare T-accounts for the following five accounts related to these transactions: Foreign Currency Units (€), Accounts Receivable (€), Accounts Payable (€), Foreign Currency Transaction Loss, and Foreign Currency Transaction Gain.

b. Within the T-accounts you have prepared, appropriately record the following items:

1. The November 1, 20X6, export transaction (sale).
2. The November 1, 20X6, import transaction (purchase).
3. The December 31, 20X6, year-end adjustment required of the foreign currency–denominated receivable of €250,000.
4. The December 31, 20X6, year-end adjustment required of the foreign currency–denominated payable of €125,000.
5. The February 1, 20X7, adjusting entry to determine the U.S. dollar–equivalent value of the foreign currency receivable on that date.
6. The February 1, 20X7, adjusting entry to determine the U.S. dollar–equivalent value of the foreign currency payable on that date.
7. The February 1, 20X7, settlement of the foreign currency receivable.
8. The February 1, 20X7, settlement of the foreign currency payable.

**E11-5** ### Determining Year-End Account Balances for Import and Export Transactions

Delaney Inc. has several transactions with foreign entities. Each transaction is denominated in the local currency unit of the country in which the foreign entity is located. For each of the following independent cases, determine the December 31, 20X2, year-end balance in the appropriate accounts for the case. Write "NA" for "not applicable" in the space provided in the following chart if that account is not relevant to the specific case.

**Case 1.** On November 12, 20X2, Delaney purchased goods from a foreign company at a price of LCU 40,000 when the direct exchange rate was 1 LCU = $.45. The account has not been settled as of December 31, 20X2, when the exchange rate has decreased to 1 LCU = $.40.

**Case 2.** On November 28, 20X2, Delaney sold goods to a foreign entity at a price of LCU 20,000 when the direct exchange rate was 1 LCU = $1.80. The account has not been settled as of December 31, 20X2, when the exchange rate has increased to 1 LCU = $1.90.

**Case 3.** On December 2, 20X2, Delaney purchased goods from a foreign company at a price of LCU 30,000 when the direct exchange rate was 1 LCU = $.80. The account has not been settled as of December 31, 20X2, when the exchange rate has increased to 1 LCU = $.90.

**Case 4.** On December 12, 20X2, Delaney sold goods to a foreign entity at a price of LCU 2,500,000 when the direct exchange rate was 1 LCU = $.003. The account has not been settled as of December 31, 20X2, when the exchange rate has decreased to 1 LCU = $.0025.

### Required

Provide the December 31, 20X2, year-end balances on Delaney's records for each of the following applicable items:

| | Accounts Receivable | Accounts Payable | Foreign Currency Transaction Exchange Loss | Foreign Currency Transaction Exchange Gain |
|---|---|---|---|---|
| Case 1 | _____ | _____ | _____ | _____ |
| Case 2 | _____ | _____ | _____ | _____ |
| Case 3 | _____ | _____ | _____ | _____ |
| Case 4 | _____ | _____ | _____ | _____ |

**E11-6    Transactions with Foreign Companies**

Harris Inc. had the following transactions:

1. On May 1, Harris purchased parts from a Japanese company for a U.S. dollar equivalent value of $8,400 to be paid on June 20. The exchange rates were:

| | |
|---|---|
| May 1 | 1 yen = $.0070 |
| June 20 | 1 yen =   .0075 |

2. On July 1, Harris sold products to a Brazilian customer for a U.S. dollar equivalent of $10,000, to be received on August 10. Brazil's local currency unit is the real. The exchange rates were:

| | |
|---|---|
| July 1 | 1 real = $.20 |
| August 10 | 1 real =   .22 |

### Required

*a.* Assume that the two transactions are denominated in U.S. dollars. Prepare the entries required for the dates of the transactions and their settlement in U.S. dollars.

*b.* Assume that the two transactions are denominated in the applicable local currency units of the foreign entities. Prepare the entries required for the dates of the transactions and their settlement in the local currency units of the Japanese company (yen) and the Brazilian customer (real).

**E11-7    Foreign Purchase Transaction**

On December 1, 20X1, Rone Imports, a U.S. company, purchased clocks from Switzerland for 15,000 francs (SFr), to be paid on January 15, 20X2. Rone's fiscal year ends on December 31, and its reporting currency is the U.S. dollar. The exchange rates are:

| | |
|---|---|
| December 1, 20X1 | 1 SFr = $.70 |
| December 31, 20X1 | 1 SFr =   .66 |
| January 15, 20X2 | 1 SFr =   .68 |

### Required

*a.* In which currency is the transaction denominated?

*b.* Prepare journal entries for Rone to record the purchase, the adjustment on December 31, and the settlement.

**E11-8    Adjusting Entries for Foreign Currency Balances**

Chocolate De-lites imports and exports chocolate delicacies. Some transactions are denominated in U.S. dollars and others in foreign currencies. A summary of accounts receivable and accounts payable on December 31, 20X6, before adjustments for the effects of changes in exchange rates during 20X6, follows:

| | |
|---|---|
| Accounts receivable: | |
| In U.S. dollars | $164,000 |
| In 475,000 Egyptian pounds (E£) | $ 73,600 |
| Accounts payable: | |
| In U.S. dollars | $ 86,000 |
| In 21,000,000 yen (¥) | $175,300 |

The spot rates on December 31, 20X6, were:

E£1 = $.176

¥1 = $.0081

The average exchange rates during the collection and payment period in 20X7 are:

E£1 = $.18

¥1 = $.0078

### Required

a. Prepare the adjusting entries on December 31, 20X6.

b. Record the collection of the accounts receivable in 20X7.

c. Record the payment of the accounts payable in 20X7.

d. What was the foreign currency gain or loss on the accounts receivable transaction denominated in E£ for the year ended December 31, 20X6? For the year ended December 31, 20X7? Overall for this transaction?

e. What was the foreign currency gain or loss on the accounts receivable transaction denominated in ¥? For the year ended December 31, 20X6? For the year ended December 31, 20X7? Overall for this transaction?

f. What was the combined foreign currency gain or loss for both transactions? What could Chocolate De-lites have done to reduce the risk associated with the transactions denominated in foreign currencies?

**E11-9** **Purchase with Forward Exchange Contract**

Merit & Family purchased engines from Canada for 30,000 Canadian dollars on March 10, with payment due on June 8. Also, on March 10, Merit acquired a 90-day forward contract to purchase 30,000 Canadian dollars of C$1 = $.58. The forward contract was acquired to manage Merit & Family's exposed net liability position in Canadian dollars, but it was not designated as a hedge. The spot rates were:

| | |
|---|---|
| March 10 | C$1 = $.57 |
| June 8 | C$1 = $.60 |

### Required

Prepare journal entries for Merit & Family to record the purchase of the engines, entries associated with the forward contract, and entries for the payment of the foreign currency payable.

**E11-10** **Purchase with Forward Exchange Contract and Intervening Fiscal Year-End**

Pumped Up Company purchased equipment from Switzerland for 140,000 francs on December 16, 20X7, with payment due on February 14, 20X8. On December 16, 20X7, Pumped Up also acquired a 60-day forward contract to purchase francs at a forward rate of SFr 1 = $.67. On December 31, 20X7, the forward rate for an exchange on February 14, 20X8, is SFr 1 = $.695. The spot rates were:

| | |
|---|---|
| December 16, 20X7 | 1 SFr = $.68 |
| December 31, 20X7 | 1 SFr = .70 |
| February 14, 20X8 | 1 SFr = .69 |

### Part I

Assume that the forward contract is not designated as a hedge but is entered into to manage the company's foreign currency–exposed accounts payable.

a. Prepare journal entries for Pumped Up to record the purchase of equipment, all entries associated with the forward contract, the adjusting entries on December 31, 20X7, and entries to record the revaluations and payment on February 14, 20X8.

b. What was the effect on the statement of income of the foreign currency transactions, including both the accounts payable and the forward contract, for the year ended December 31, 20X7?

c. What was the overall effect on the statement of income of these transactions from December 16, 20X7, to February 14, 20X8?

### Part II

Now assume the forward contract is designated as a cash flow hedge of the variability of the future cash flows from the foreign currency account payable. The company uses the forward exchange rate to assess effectiveness.

### Required

Prepare journal entries for Pumped Up to record the purchase of equipment, all entries associated with the forward contract, the adjusting and reclassification entries on December 31, 20X7, and entries to record the revaluations and payment on February 14, 20X8.

**E11-11   Foreign Currency Transactions [AICPA Adapted]**

Select the correct answer for each of the following questions.

1. Dale Inc., a U.S. company, bought machine parts from a German company on March 1, 20X1, for 30,000 euros, when the spot rate for euros was $.4895. Dale's year-end was March 31, when the spot rate was $.4845. On April 20, 20X1, Dale paid the liability with 30,000 euros acquired at a rate of $.4945. Dale's income statements should report a foreign exchange gain or loss for the years ended March 31, 20X1 and 20X2 of:

|    | 20X1 | 20X2 |
|----|------|------|
| a. | $0 | $0 |
| b. | $0 | $150 loss |
| c. | $150 loss | $0 |
| d. | $150 gain | $300 loss |

2. Marvin Company's receivable from a foreign customer is denominated in the customer's local currency. This receivable of 900,000 local currency units (LCU) has been translated into $315,000 on Marvin's December 31, 20X5, balance sheet. On January 15, 20X6, the receivable was collected in full when the exchange rate was 3 LCU to $1. The journal entry Marvin should make to record the collection of this receivable is:

|    |  | Debit | Credit |
|----|----|-------|--------|
| a. | Foreign Currency Units | 300,000 | |
|    |    Accounts Receivable | | 300,000 |
| b. | Foreign Currency Units | 300,000 | |
|    | Exchange Loss | 15,000 | |
|    |    Accounts Receivable | | 315,000 |
| c. | Foreign Currency Units | 300,000 | |
|    | Deferred Exchange Loss | 15,000 | |
|    |    Accounts Receivable | | 315,000 |
| d. | Foreign Currency Units | 315,000 | |
|    |    Accounts Receivable | | 315,000 |

3. On July 1, 20X1, Black Company lent $120,000 to a foreign supplier, evidenced by an interest-bearing note due on July 1, 20X2. The note is denominated in the borrower's currency and was equivalent to 840,000 local currency units (LCU) on the loan date. The note principal was appropriately included at $140,000 in the receivables section of Black's December 31, 20X1, balance sheet. The note principal was repaid to Black on the July 1, 20X2, due date when the exchange rate was 8 LCU to $1. In its income statement for the year ended December 31, 20X2, what amount should Black include as a foreign currency transaction gain or loss on the note principal?

   a. $0.

   b. $15,000 loss.

   c. $15,000 gain.

   d. $35,000 loss.

4. If 1 Canadian dollar can be exchanged for 90 cents of U.S. currency, what fraction should be used to compute the indirect quotation of the exchange rate expressed in Canadian dollars?

   a. 1.10/1.

   b. 1/1.10.

   c. 1/.90.

   d. .90/1.

5. On July 1, 20X4, Bay Company borrowed 1,680,000 local currency units (LCU) from a foreign lender evidenced by an interest-bearing note due on July 1, 20X5, which is denominated in the currency of the lender. The U.S. dollar equivalent of the note principal was as follows:

| Date | Amount |
|------|--------|
| 7/1/X4 (date borrowed) | $210,000 |
| 12/31/X4 (Bay's year-end) | 240,000 |
| 7/1/X5 (date repaid) | 280,000 |

In its income statement for 20X5, what amount should Bay include as a foreign exchange gain or loss on the note principal?

 *a.* $70,000 gain.

 *b.* $70,000 loss.

 *c.* $40,000 gain.

 *d.* $40,000 loss.

6. An entity denominated a sale of goods in a currency other than its functional currency. The sale resulted in a receivable fixed in terms of the amount of foreign currency to be received. The exchange rate between the functional currency and the currency in which the transaction was denominated changed. The effect of the change should be included as a:

 *a.* Separate component of stockholders' equity whether the change results in a gain or a loss.

 *b.* Separate component of stockholders' equity if the change results in a gain, and as a component of income if the change results in a loss.

 *c.* Component of income if the change results in a gain, and as a separate component of stockholders' equity if the change results in a loss.

 *d.* Component of income whether the change results in a gain or a loss.

7. An entity denominated a December 15, 20X6, purchase of goods in a currency other than its functional currency. The transaction resulted in a payable fixed in terms of the amount of foreign currency, and was paid on the settlement date, January 20, 20X7. The exchange rates between the functional currency and the currency in which the transaction was denominated changed at December 31, 20X6, resulting in a loss that should:

 *a.* Not be reported until January 20, 20X7, the settlement date.

 *b.* Be included as a separate component of stockholders' equity at December 31, 20X6.

 *c.* Be included as a deferred charge at December 31, 20X6.

 *d.* Be included as a component of income from continuing operations for 20X6.

**E11-12  Sale in Foreign Currency**

Marko Company sold spray paint equipment to Spain for 5,000,000 pesetas (P) on October 1, with payment due in six months. The exchange rates were:

| | |
|---|---|
| October 1, 20X6 | 1 peseta = $.0068 |
| December 31, 20X6 | 1 peseta = .0078 |
| April 1, 20X7 | 1 peseta = .0076 |

*Required*

 *a.* Did the dollar strengthen or weaken relative to the peseta during the period from October 1 to December 31? Did it strengthen or weaken between January 1 and April 1 of the next year?

 *b.* Prepare all required journal entries for Marko as a result of the sale and settlement of the foreign transaction, assuming that its fiscal year ends on December 31.

 *c.* Did Marko have an overall net gain or net loss from its foreign currency exposure?

**E11-13  Sale with Forward Exchange Contract**

Alman Company sold pharmaceuticals to a Swedish company for 200,000 kronor (SKr) on April 20, with settlement to be in 60 days. On the same date, Alman entered into a 60-day forward contract to sell 200,000 SKr at a forward rate of 1 SKr = $.167 in order to manage its exposed foreign currency receivable. The forward contract is not designated as a hedge. The spot rates were:

| | |
|---|---|
| April 20 | SKr 1 = $.170 |
| June 19 | SKr 1 = .165 |

### Required

a. Record all necessary entries related to the foreign transaction and the forward contract.

b. Compare the effects on net income of Alman's use of the forward exchange contract versus the effects if Alman had not used a forward exchange contract.

**E11-14    Foreign Currency Transactions [AICPA Adapted]**

Choose the correct answer for each of the following questions.

1. On November 15, 20X3, Chow Inc., a U.S. company, ordered merchandise FOB shipping point from a German company for 200,000 euros. The merchandise was shipped and invoiced on December 10, 20X3. Chow paid the invoice on January 10, 20X4. The spot rates for euros on the respective dates were:

   | | |
   |---|---|
   | November 15, 20X3 | $.4955 |
   | December 10, 20X3 | .4875 |
   | December 31, 20X3 | .4675 |
   | January 10, 20X4 | .4475 |

   In Chow's December 31, 20X3, income statement, the foreign exchange gain is:

   a. $9,600.

   b. $8,000.

   c. $4,000.

   d. $1,600.

2. Stees Corporation had the following foreign currency transactions during 20X2. First, it purchased merchandise from a foreign supplier on January 20, 20X2, for the U.S. dollar equivalent of $90,000. The invoice was paid on March 20, 20X2, at the U.S. dollar equivalent of $96,000. Second, on July 1, 20X2, Stees borrowed the U.S. dollar equivalent of $500,000 evidenced by a note that was payable in the lender's local currency on July 1, 20X4. On December 31, 20X2, the U.S. dollar equivalents of the principal amount and accrued interest were $520,000 and $26,000, respectively. Interest on the note is 10 percent per annum. In Stees's 20X2 income statement, what amount should be included as a foreign exchange loss?

   a. $0.

   b. $6,000.

   c. $21,000.

   d. $27,000.

3. On September 1, 20X1, Cott Corporation received an order for equipment from a foreign customer for 300,000 local currency units (LCU) when the U.S. dollar equivalent was $96,000. Cott shipped the equipment on October 15, 20X1, and billed the customer for 300,000 LCU when the U.S. dollar equivalent was $100,000. Cott received the customer's remittance in full on November 16, 20X1, and sold the 300,000 LCU for $105,000. In its income statement for the year ended December 31, 20X1, Cott should report a foreign exchange gain of:

   a. $0.

   b. $4,000.

   c. $5,000.

   d. $9,000.

4. On April 8, 20X3, Trul Corporation purchased merchandise from an unaffiliated foreign company for 10,000 units of the foreign company's local currency. Trul paid the bill in full on March 1, 20X4, when the spot rate was $.45. The spot rate was $.60 on April 8, 20X3, and was $.55 on December 31, 20X3. For the year ended December 31, 20X4, Trul should report a transaction gain of:

   a. $1,500.

   b. $1,000.

   c. $500.

   d. $0.

5. On October 1, 20X5, Stevens Company, a U.S. company, contracted to purchase foreign goods requiring payment in pesos one month after their receipt in Stevens's factory. Title to the goods passed on December 15, 20X5. The goods were still in transit on December 31, 20X5. Exchange rates were 1 dollar to 22 pesos, 20 pesos, and 21 pesos on October 1, December 15, and December 31, 20X5, respectively. Stevens should account for the exchange rate fluctuations in 20X5 as

   *a.* A loss included in net income before extraordinary items.

   *b.* A gain included in net income before extraordinary items.

   *c.* An extraordinary gain.

   *d.* An extraordinary loss.

6. On October 2, 20X5, Louis Co., a U.S. company, purchased machinery from Stroup, a German company, with payment due on April 1, 20X6. If Louis's 20X5 operating income included no foreign exchange gain or loss, then the transaction could have

   *a.* Resulted in an extraordinary gain.

   *b.* Been denominated in U.S. dollars.

   *c.* Caused a foreign currency gain to be reported as a contra account against machinery.

   *d.* Caused a foreign currency translation gain to be reported as a separate component of stockholders' equity.

7. Cobb Co. purchased merchandise for 300,000 pounds from a vendor in London on November 30, 20X5. Payment in British pounds was due on January 30, 20X6. The exchange rates to purchase 1 pound were as follows:

| | November 30, 20X5 | December 31, 20X5 |
|---|---|---|
| Spot rate | $1.65 | $1.62 |
| 30-day rate | 1.64 | 1.59 |
| 60-day rate | 1.63 | 1.56 |

   In its December 31, 20X5, income statement, what amount should Cobb report as a foreign exchange gain?

   *a.* $12,000.

   *b.* $9,000.

   *c.* $6,000.

   *d.* $0.

**E11-15    Sale with Forward Contract and Fiscal Year-End**

Jerber Electronics Inc. sold electrical equipment to a Dutch company for 50,000 guilders (G) on May 14, with collection due in 60 days. On the same day, Jerber entered into a 60-day forward contract to sell 50,000 guilders at a forward rate of G1 = $.541. The forward contract is not designated as a hedge. Jerber's fiscal year ends on June 30. The forward rate on June 30 for an exchange on July 13 is G1 = $.530. The spot rates follow:

| | |
|---|---|
| May 14 | G1 = $.530 |
| June 30 | G1 = .534 |
| July 13 | G1 = .525 |

***Required***

*a.* Prepare journal entries for Jerber to record (1) the sale of equipment, (2) the forward contract, (3) the adjusting entries on June 30, (4) the July 13 collection of the receivable, and (5) the July settlement of the forward contract.

*b.* What was the effect on the income statement in the fiscal year ending June 30?

*c.* What was the overall effect on the income statement from this transaction?

*d.* What would have been the overall effect on income if the forward contract had not been acquired?

**E11-16A**  **Hedge of a Purchase (Commitment without and with Time Value of Money Considerations)**

On November 1, 20X6, Smith Imports Inc. contracted to purchase teacups from England for 30,000 pounds (£). The teacups were to be delivered on January 30, 20X7, with payment due on March 1, 20X7. On November 1, 20X6, Smith entered into a 120-day forward contract to receive 30,000 pounds at a forward rate of £1 = $1.59. The forward contract was acquired to hedge the financial component of the foreign currency commitment.

### Additional Information for the Exchange Rate

1. Assume the company uses the forward rate in measuring the forward exchange contract and for measuring hedge effectiveness.
2. Spot and exchange rates follow:

| Date | Spot Rate | Forward Rate for March 1, 20X7 |
|---|---|---|
| November 1, 20X6 | £1 = $1.61 | £1 = $1.59 |
| December 31, 20X6 | £1 = 1.65 | £1 = 1.62 |
| January 30, 20X7 | £1 = 1.59 | £1 = 1.60 |
| March 1, 20X7 | £1 = 1.585 | |

### Required

a. What is Smith's net exposure to changes in the exchange rate of pounds for dollars between November 1, 20X6, and March 1, 20X7?

b. Prepare all journal entries from November 1, 20X6, through March 1, 20X7, for the purchase of the subassemblies, the forward exchange contract, and the foreign currency transaction. Assume Smith's fiscal year ends on December 31, 20X6.

*Note:* Requirement (*c*) requires information from Appendix 11A.

c. Assume that interest is significant and the time value of money is considered in valuing the forward contract and hedged commitment. Use a 12 percent annual interest rate. Prepare all journal entries from November 1, 20X6, through March 1, 20X7, for the purchase of the subassemblies, the forward exchange contract, and the foreign currency transaction. Assume Smith's fiscal year ends on December 31, 20X7.

**E11-17**  **Gain or Loss on Speculative Forward Exchange Contract**

On December 1, 20X1, Sycamore Company acquired a 90-day speculative forward contract to sell 120,000 European euros (€) at a forward rate of €1 = $.58. The rates are as follows:

| Date | Spot Rate | Forward Rate for March 1 |
|---|---|---|
| December 1, 20X1 | €1 = $.60 | €1 = $.58 |
| December 31, 20X1 | €1 = .59 | €1 = .56 |
| March 1, 20X2 | €1 = .57 | |

### Required

a. Prepare a schedule showing the effects of this speculation on 20X1 income before income taxes.

b. Prepare a schedule showing the effects of this speculation on 20X2 income before income taxes.

**E11-18**  **Speculation in a Foreign Currency**

Nick Andros of Streamline Company suggested that the company speculate in foreign currency as a partial hedge against its operations in the cattle market, which fluctuates like a commodity market. On October 1, 20X1, Streamline bought a 180-day forward contract to purchase 50,000,000 yen (¥) at a forward rate of ¥1 = $.0075 when the spot rate was $.0070. Other exchange rates were as follows:

"A" indicates that the item relates to "Appendix A."

| Date | Spot Rate | Forward Rate for March 31, 20X2 |
|------|-----------|--------------------------------|
| December 31, 20X1 | $.0073 | $.0076 |
| March 31, 20X2 | .0072 | |

### Required

a. Prepare all journal entries related to Streamline Company's foreign currency speculation from October 1, 20X1, through March 31, 20X2, assuming the fiscal year ends on December 31, 20X1.

b. Did Streamline Company gain or lose on its purchase of the forward contract? Explain.

**E11-19    Forward Exchange Transactions [AICPA Adapted]**

Select the correct answer for each of the following questions.

1. The following information applies to Denton Inc.'s sale of 10,000 foreign currency units under a forward contract dated November 1, 20X5, for delivery on January 31, 20X6:

| | 11/1/X5 | 12/31/X5 |
|---|---------|----------|
| Spot rates | $0.80 | $0.83 |
| 30-day forward rate | 0.79 | 0.82 |
| 90-day forward rate | 0.78 | 0.81 |

Denton entered into the forward contract to speculate in the foreign currency. In its income statement for the year ended December 31, 20X5, what amount of loss should Denton report from this forward contract?

a. $400.

b. $300.

c. $200.

d. $0.

2. On September 1, 20X5, Johnson Inc. entered into a foreign exchange contract for speculative purposes by purchasing 50,000 European euros for delivery in 60 days. The rates to exchange U.S. dollars for euros follow:

| | 9/1/X5 | 9/30/X5 |
|---|--------|---------|
| Spot rate | $.75 | $.70 |
| 30-day forward rate | .73 | .72 |
| 90-day forward rate | .74 | .73 |

In its September 30, 20X5, income statement, what amount should Johnson report as foreign exchange loss?

a. $2,500.

b. $1,500.

c. $1,000.

d. $500.

*Note:* Items 3 through 5 are based on the following:

On December 12, 20X5, Dahl Company entered into three forward exchange contracts, each to purchase 100,000 francs in 90 days. The relevant exchange rates are as follows:

| | Spot Rate | Forward Rate for March 12, 20X6 |
|---|-----------|--------------------------------|
| December 12, 20X5 | $.88 | $.90 |
| March 31, 20X2 | .98 | .93 |

3. Dahl entered into the first forward contract to manage the foreign currency risk from a purchase of inventory in November 20X5, payable in March 20X6. The forward contract is not designated as a hedge. At December 31, 20X5, what amount of foreign currency transaction gain should Dahl include in income from this forward contract?

   a. $0.

   b. $3,000.

   c. $5,000.

   d. $10,000.

4. Dahl entered into the second forward contract to hedge a commitment to purchase equipment being manufactured to Dahl's specifications. At December 31, 20X5, what amount of foreign currency transaction gain should Dahl include in income from this forward contract?

   a. $0.

   b. $3,000.

   c. $5,000.

   d. $10,000.

5. Dahl entered into the third forward contract for speculation. At December 31, 20X5, what amount of foreign currency transaction gain should Dahl include in income from this forward contract?

   a. $0.

   b. $3,000.

   c. $5,000.

   d. $10,000.

## Problems    P11-20    Multiple-Choice Questions on Foreign Currency Transactions

Jon-Jan Restaurants purchased green rice, a special variety of rice, from China for 100,000 renminbi on November 1, 20X8. Payment is due on January 30, 20X9. On November 1, 20X8, the company also entered into a 90-day forward contract to purchase 100,000 renminbi. The forward contract is not designated as a hedge. The rates were as follows:

| Date | Spot Rate | Forward Rate |
|------|-----------|--------------|
| November 1, 20X8 | $.120 | $.126 (90 days) |
| December 31, 20X8 | .124 | .129 (30 days) |
| January 30, 20X9 | .127 | |

### Required

Select the correct answer for each of the following questions.

1. The entry on November 1, 20X8, to record the forward contract includes a:

   a. Debit to Foreign Currency Receivable from Exchange Broker, 100,000 renminbi.

   b. Debit to Foreign Currency Receivable from Exchange Broker, $12,600.

   c. Credit to Premium on Forward Contract, $600.

   d. Credit to Dollars Payable to Exchange Broker, $12,600.

2. The entries on December 31, 20X8, include a:

   a. Debit to Financial Expense, $300.

   b. Credit to Foreign Currency Payable to Exchange Broker, $300.

   c. Debit to Foreign Currency Receivable from Exchange Broker, $300.

   d. Debit to Foreign Currency Receivable from Exchange Broker, $12,600.

3. The entries on January 30, 20X9, include a:

   a. Debit to Dollars Payable to Exchange Broker, $12,000.

   b. Credit to Cash, $12,600.

   c. Credit to Premium on Forward Contract, $600.

   d. Credit to Foreign Currency Receivable from Exchange Broker, $12,600.

4. The entries on January 30, 20X9, include a:

   *a.* Debit to Financial Expense, $400.

   *b.* Debit to Dollars Payable to Exchange Broker, $12,600.

   *c.* Credit to Foreign Currency Units (renminbi), $12,600.

   *d.* Debit to Foreign Currency Payable to Exchange Broker, $12,700.

5. The entries on January 30, 20X9, include a:

   *a.* Debit to Foreign Currency Units (renminbi), $12,700.

   *b.* Debit to Dollars Payable to Exchange Broker, $12,700.

   *c.* Credit to Foreign Currency Transaction Gain, $100.

   *d.* Credit to Foreign Currency Receivable from Exchange Broker, $12,600.

**P11-21  Foreign Sales**

Tex Hardware sells many of its products overseas. The following are some selected transactions.

1. Tex sold electronic subassemblies to a firm in Denmark for 120,000 Danish krones (Dkr) on June 6, when the exchange rate was Dkr 1 = $.1750. Collection was made on July 3, when the rate was Dkr 1 = $.1753.

2. On July 22, Tex sold copper fittings to a company in London for 30,000 pounds (£), with payment due on September 20. Also, on July 22, Tex entered into a 60-day forward contract to sell 30,000 pounds at a forward rate of £1 = $1.630. The spot rates follow:

   | | |
   |---|---|
   | July 22 | £1 = $1.580 |
   | September 20 | £1 = $1.612 |

3. Tex sold storage devices to a Canadian firm for C$70,000 (Canadian dollars) on October 11, with payment due on November 10. On October 11, Tex entered into a 30-day forward contract to sell Canadian dollars at a forward rate of C$1 = $.730. The forward contract is not designated as a hedge. The spot rates were as follows:

   | | |
   |---|---|
   | October 11 | C$1 = $.7350 |
   | November 10 | C$1 = $.7320 |

*Required*

Prepare journal entries to record Tex's foreign sales of its products, use of forward contracts, and settlements of the receivables.

**P11-22  Foreign Currency Transactions**

Globe Shipping, a U.S. company, is an importer and exporter. The following are some transactions with foreign companies.

1. Globe sold blue jeans to a South Korean importer on January 15 for $7,400, when the exchange rate was KRW1 = $.185. Collection, in dollars, was made on March 15, when the exchange rate was $.180.

2. On March 8, Globe purchased woolen goods from Ireland for 7,000 pounds (IR£). The exchange rate was IR£1 = $1.68 on March 8, but the rate was $1.66 when payment was made on May 1.

3. On May 12, Globe signed a contract to purchase toys made in Taiwan for 80,000 Taiwan dollars (NT$). The toys were to be delivered 80 days later on August 1, and payment was due on September 9, which was 40 days after delivery. On May 12, Globe also entered into a 120-day undesignated forward contract to buy 80,000 Taiwan dollars at a forward rate of NT$1 = $.0376. On August 1, the forward rate for a September 9 exchange is NT$1 = $.0378. The spot rates were as follows:

   | | |
   |---|---|
   | May 12 | NT$1 = $.0370 |
   | August 1 | NT$1 = .0375 |
   | September 9 | NT$1 = .0372 |

4. Globe sold microcomputers to a German enterprise on June 6 for 150,000 euros. Payment was due in 90 days, on September 4. On July 6, Globe entered into a 60-day undesignated forward contract to sell 150,000 euros at a forward rate of €1 = $.580. The spot rates follow:

| | |
|---|---|
| June 6 | €1 = $.600 |
| July 6 | €1 = .590 |
| September 4 | €1 = .585 |

### Required

Prepare all necessary journal entries for Globe to account for the foreign transactions, including the sales and purchases of inventory, forward contracts, and settlements.

**P11-23A** **Comprehensive Problem: Four Uses of Forward Exchange Contracts without and with Time Value of Money Considerations**

On December 1, 20X1, Micro World, Inc., entered into a 120-day forward contract to purchase 100,000 Australian dollars (A$). Micro World's fiscal year ends on December 31. The direct exchange rates follow:

| Date | Spot Rate | Forward Rate for March 31, 20X2 |
|---|---|---|
| December 1, 20X1 | $.600 | $.609 |
| December 31, 20X1 | .610 | .612 |
| January 30, 20X2 | .608 | .605 |
| March 31, 20X2 | .602 | |

### Required

Prepare all journal entries for Micro World, Inc., for the following *independent* situations:

a. The forward contract was to manage the foreign currency risks from the purchase of furniture for 100,000 Australian dollars on December 1, 20X1, with payment due on March 31, 20X2. The forward contract is not designated as a hedge.

b. The forward contract was to hedge a firm commitment agreement made on December 1, 20X1, to purchase furniture on January 30, with payment due on March 31, 20X2. The derivative is designated as a fair value hedge.

c. The forward contract was to hedge an anticipated purchase of furniture on January 30. The purchase took place on January 30, with payment due on March 31, 20X2. The derivative is designated as a cash flow hedge. The company uses the forward exchange rate to measure hedge effectiveness.

d. The forward contract was for speculative purposes only.

*Note:* Requirement (*e*) uses the material in Appendix 11A.

e. Assume that interest is significant and the time value of money is considered in valuing the forward contract. Use a 12 percent annual interest rate. Prepare all journal entries required if, as in requirement (*a*), the forward contract was to manage the foreign currency–denominated payable from the purchase of furniture for 100,000 Australian dollars on December 1, 20X1, with payment due on March 31, 20X2.

**P11-24** **Foreign Purchases and Sales Transactions and Hedging**
**Part I**

Maple Company had the following export and import transactions during 20X5:

1. On March 1, Maple sold goods to a Canadian company for 30,000 Canadian dollars (C$), receivable on May 30. The spot rates for marks were C$1 = $.65 on March 1 and C$1 = $.68 on May 30.

2. On July 1, Maple signed a contract to purchase equipment from a Japanese company for 500,000 yen. The equipment was manufactured in Japan during August and was delivered to Maple on August 30, with payment due in 60 days on October 29. The spot rates for yen were ¥1 = $.102 on July 1, ¥1 = $.104 on August 30, and ¥1 = $.106 on October 29. The 60-day forward exchange rate on August 30, 20X5, was ¥1 = $.1055.

3. On November 16, Maple purchased inventory from a London company for 10,000 pounds, payable on January 15, 20X6. The spot rates for pounds were £1 = $1.65 on November 16, £1 = $1.63 on December 31, and £1 = $1.64 on January 15, 20X6. The forward rate on December 31, 20X5, for a January 15, 20X6, exchange was £1 = $1.645.

### Required

a. Prepare journal entries to record Maple's import and export transactions during 20X5 and 20X6.

b. What amount of foreign currency transaction gain or loss would Maple report on its income statement for 20X5?

### Part II

Assume that Maple used forward contracts to manage the foreign currency risks of all of its export and import transactions during 20X5.

1. On March 1, 20X5, Maple, anticipating a weaker Canadian dollar on the May 30, 20X5, settlement date, entered into a 90-day forward contract to sell 30,000 Canadian dollars at a forward exchange rate of C$1 = $.64. The forward contract was not designated as a hedge.

2. On July 1, 20X5, Maple, anticipating a strengthening of the yen on the October 29, 20X5, settlement date, entered into a 120-day forward contract to purchase 500,000 yen at a forward exchange rate of ¥1 = $.105. The forward contract was designated as a fair value hedge of a firm commitment.

3. On November 16, 20X5, Maple, anticipating a strengthening of the pound on the January 15, 20X6, settlement date, entered into a 60-day undesignated forward exchange contract to purchase 10,000 pounds at a forward exchange rate of £1 = $1.67.

### Required

a. Prepare journal entries to record Maple's foreign currency activities during 20X5 and 20X6.

b. What amount of foreign currency transaction gain or loss would Maple report on its income statement for 20X5, if Parts I and II of this problem were combined?

c. What amount of foreign currency transaction gain or loss would Maple report on its statement of income for 20X6, if Parts I and II of this problem were combined?

**P11-25  Understanding Foreign Currency Transactions**

Dexter Inc. had the following items in its unadjusted and adjusted trial balances at December 31, 20X5:

| | Trial Balances | |
| --- | --- | --- |
| | **Unadjusted** | **Adjusted** |
| Accounts Receivable (denominated in Australian dollars) | $42,000 | $41,700 |
| Dollars Receivable from Exchange Broker | 40,600 | ? |
| Foreign Currency Receivable from Exchange Broker | 82,000 | 81,000 |
| Accounts Payable (denominated in South Korean wons) | 80,000 | ? |
| Dollars Payable to Exchange Broker | ? | ? |
| Foreign Currency Payable to Exchange Broker | 40,600 | ? |

### Additional Information

1. On December 1, 20X5, Dexter sold goods to a company in Australia for 70,000 Australian dollars. Payment in Australian dollars is due on January 30, 20X6. On the transaction date, Dexter entered into a 60-day forward contract to sell 70,000 Australian dollars on January 30, 20X6. The 30-day forward rate on December 31, 20X5, was A$1 = $.57.

2. On October 2, 20X5, Dexter purchased equipment from a South Korean company for 400,000 South Korean wons (KRW), payable on January 30, 20X6. On the transaction date, Dexter entered into a 120-day forward contract to purchase 400,000 South Korean wons on January 30, 20X6. On December 31, 20X5, the spot rate was KRW1 = $.2020.

### Required

Using the information contained in the trial balances, answer each of the following questions:

*a.* What was the indirect exchange rate for Australian dollars on December 1, 20X5? What was the indirect exchange rate on December 31, 20X5?

*b.* What is the balance in the account Foreign Currency Payable to Exchange Broker in the adjusted trial balance?

*c.* When Dexter entered into the 60-day forward contract to sell 70,000 Australian dollars, what was the direct exchange rate for the 60-day forward contract?

*d.* What is the amount of Dollars Receivable from Exchange Broker in the adjusted trial balance?

*e.* What was the indirect exchange rate for South Korean wons on October 2, 20X5? What was the indirect exchange rate on December 31, 20X5?

*f.* What is the balance in the account Dollars Payable to Exchange Broker in both the unadjusted and the adjusted trial balance columns?

*g.* When Dexter entered into the 120-day forward contract to purchase 400,000 South Korean wons, what was the direct exchange rate for the 120-day forward contract?

*h.* What was the Accounts Payable balance at December 31, 20X5?

**P11-26** **Matching Key Terms**

Match the items in the left-hand column with the descriptions/explanations in the right-hand column.

| Items | Descriptions/Explanations |
|---|---|
| 1. Direct exchange rate | A. Exchange rate for immediate delivery of currencies. |
| 2. Indirect exchange rate | B. Imports and exports whose prices are stated in a foreign currency. |
| 3. Managing an exposed net asset position | C. The primary currency used by a company for performing its major financial and operating functions. |
| 4. Spot rates | D. U.S. companies prepare their financial statements in U.S. dollars. |
| 5. Current rates | E. 1 European euro equals $.65. |
| 6. Foreign currency transaction gain | F. A forward contract is entered into when receivables denominated in European euros exceed payables denominated in that currency. |
| 7. Foreign currency transaction loss | G. Accounts that are fixed in terms of foreign currency units. |
| 8. Foreign currency transactions | H. 1 U.S. dollar equals 99 Japanese yen. |
| 9. Hedging a firm commitment | I. Spot rate on the entity's balance sheet date. |
| 10. Functional currency | J. In an export or import transaction, the date that foreign currency units are received or paid, respectively. |
| 11. Speculating in a foreign currency | K. A forward contract is entered into when payables denominated in British pounds exceeds receivables denominated in that currency. |
| 12. Managing an exposed net liability position | L. Reported when receivables are denominated in European euros and the euro strengthens compared to the U.S. dollar. |
| 13. Settlement date | M. A forward contract is entered into on May 1 that hedges an import transaction to occur on July 1. |
| 14. Denominated | N. Forward contract in which no hedging is intended. |
| 15. Reporting currency | O. Reported when payables are denominated in Swiss francs and the franc strengthens compared to the U.S. dollar. |

**P11-27B** **Multiple-Choice Questions on Derivatives and Hedging Activities**

Select the correct answer for each of the following questions.

1. According to FASB 133, which of the following is *not* an underlying?

   *a.* A security price.

   *b.* A monthly average temperature.

   *c.* The price of a barrel of oil.

   *d.* The number of foreign currency units.

2. The intrinsic value of a cash flow hedge has increased since the last balance sheet date. Which of the following accounting treatments is appropriate for this increase in value?

"B" indicates that the item relates to "Appendix B."

   *a.* Do not record the increase in the value because it has not been realized in an exchange transaction.

   *b.* Record the increase in value to current earnings.

   *c.* Record the increase to Other Comprehensive Income.

   *d.* Record the increase in a deferred income account.

3. The requirements for a derivative instrument include all but which of the following?

   *a.* Has one or more underlyings.

   *b.* Has one or more notional amounts.

   *c.* Requires an initial net investment equal to that required for other types of contracts that would be expected to have a similar response to changes in market factors.

   *d.* Requires or permits net settlement.

4. A decrease in the intrinsic value of a fair value hedge is accounted for as:

   *a.* A decrease of current earnings.

   *b.* Not recorded because the exchange transaction has not yet occurred.

   *c.* A decrease of other comprehensive income.

   *d.* A liability to be offset with subsequent increases in the fair value of the hedge.

5. Changes in the fair value of the effective portion of a hedging financial instrument are recognized as a part of current earnings of the period for which of the following:

| | Cash Flow Hedge | Fair Value Hedge |
|---|---|---|
| *a.* | Yes | Yes |
| *b.* | No | Yes |
| *c.* | Yes | No |
| *d.* | No | No |

6. According to FASB 133, for which of the following is hedge accounting not allowed?

   *a.* A forecasted purchase or sale.

   *b.* Available-for-sale securities.

   *c.* Trading securities.

   *d.* An unrecognized firm commitment.

**P11-28B**    **A Cash Flow Hedge: Use of an Option to Hedge an Anticipated Purchase**

Mega Company believes the price of oil will increase in the coming months. Therefore, it decides to purchase call options on oil as a price-risk-hedging device to hedge the expected increase in prices on an anticipated purchase of oil.

On November 30, 20X1, Mega purchases call options for 10,000 barrels of oil at $30 per barrel at a premium of $2 per barrel, with a March 1, 20X2, call date. The following is the pricing information for the term of the call:

| Date | Spot Price | Futures Price (for March 1, 20X2, delivery) |
|---|---|---|
| November 30, 20X1 | $30 | $31 |
| December 31, 20X1 | 31 | 32 |
| March 1, 20X2 | 33 | |

The information for the change in the fair value of the options follows:

| Date | Time Value | Intrinsic Value | Total Value |
|---|---|---|---|
| November 30, 20X1 | $20,000 | $ -0- | $20,000 |
| December 31, 20X1 | 6,000 | 10,000 | 16,000 |
| March 1, 20X2 | | 30,000 | 30,000 |

On March 1, 20X2, Mega sells the options at their value on that date and acquires 10,000 barrels of oil at the spot price. On June 1, 20X2, Mega sells the oil for $34 per barrel.

### Required

a. Prepare the journal entry required on November 30, 20X1, to record the purchase of the call options.

b. Prepare the adjusting journal entry required on December 31, 20X1, to record the change in time and intrinsic value of the options.

c. Prepare the entries required on March 1, 20X2, to record the expiration of the time value of the options, the sale of the options, and the purchase of the 10,000 barrels of oil.

d. Prepare the entries required on June 1, 20X2, to record the sale of the oil and any other entries required as a result of the option.

**P11-29B**  **A Fair Value Hedge: Use of an Option to Hedge Available-for-Sale Securities**

On November 3, 20X2, PRD Corporation acquired 100 shares of JRS Company at a cost of $12 per share. PRD classifies them as available-for-sale securities. On this same date, PRD decides to hedge against a possible decline in the value of the securities by purchasing, at a cost of $100, an at-the-money put option to sell the 100 shares at $12 per share. The option expires on March 3, 20X3. The fair values of the investment and the options follow:

| | November 3, 20X2 | December 31, 20X2 | March 3, 20X3 |
|---|---|---|---|
| JRS Company shares | | | |
| Per share: | $ 12 | $ 11 | $ 10.50 |
| Put Option (100 shares) | | | |
| Market value | $100 | $140 | $150 |
| Intrinsic value | -0- | 100 | 150 |
| Time value | $100 | $ 40 | $ -0- |

### Required

a. Prepare the entries required on November 3, 20X2, to record the purchase of the JRS stock and the put options.

b. Prepare the entries required on December 31, 20X2, to record the change in intrinsic value and time value of the options, as well as the revaluation of the available-for-sale securities.

c. Prepare the entries required on March 3, 20X3, to record the exercise of the put option and the sale of the securities at that date.

**P11-30B**  **Matching Key Terms—Hedging and Derivatives**

Match the items in the left-hand column with the descriptions/explanations in the right-hand column.

| Items | Descriptions/Explanations |
|---|---|
| 1. Put option | A. Hedge of the exposure to changes in the fair value of a recognized asset or liability or an unrecognized firm commitment. |
| 2. Notional amount | |
| 3. Intrinsic value | |
| 4. Underlying | B. Hedge of the exposure to variable cash flows of a forecasted transaction. |
| 5. Gains or losses on cash flow hedges | |
| | C. Derivative instrument that is part of a host contract. |
| 6. Foreign currency hedge | D. Specified interest rate, security price, or other variable. |
| | E. Number of currency units, shares, bushels, or other units specified in the contract. |
| 7. Fair value hedge | |
| 8. Call option | F. Recognized in current earnings in the period of the change in value. |

(continued)

9. Effectiveness
10. Time value
11. Gains or losses on fair value hedges
12. Cash flow hedge
13. Interest rate swap
14. Bifurcation
15. Embedded derivative

G. Recognized in Other Comprehensive Income in the period of the change in value.
H. Measure of the extent to which the derivative offsets the changes in the fair values or cash flows of the hedged item.
I. Hedge of the net investment in foreign operations.
J. Conversion of a company's fixed-rate debt to a variable-rate debt.
K. Option that provides the right to acquire an underlying at an exercise or strike price.
L. Option that provides the right to sell an underlying at an exercise or strike price.
M. Value of an option due to the spread between the current market price of the hedged item and the option's strike price.
N. Value of an option due to the opportunity to exercise the option over the term of the option period.
O. Process of separating the value of an embedded derivative from its host contract.

**P11-31   Determining Financial Statement Amounts**

Kiwi Painting Company engages in a number of foreign currency transactions in euros (€). For each of the following independent transactions, determine the dollar amount to be reported in the December 31, 2004, financial statements for the items presented in the following requirements. The relevant direct exchange rates for the euro follow:

| | September 1, 2004 | November 30, 2004 | December 31, 2004 |
|---|---|---|---|
| Spot rate | $0.95 | $1.05 | $0.98 |
| Forward rate for exchange on | | | |
| February 1, 2005 | 0.97 | 1.03 | 1.01 |

These are the independent transactions:

1. Kiwi entered into a forward exchange contract on September 1, 2004, to be settled on February 1, 2005, to hedge a firm foreign currency commitment to purchase inventory on November 30, 2004, with payment due on February 1, 2005. The forward contract was for 20,000 euros, the agreed-upon cost of the inventory. The derivative is designated as a fair value hedge of the firm commitment.

2. Kiwi entered into a forward exchange contract on September 1, 2004, to be settled on February 1, 2005, to hedge a forecasted purchase of inventory on November 30, 2004. The inventory was purchased on November 30 with payment due on February 1, 2005. The forward contract was for 20,000 euros, the expected cost of the inventory. The derivative is designated as a cash flow hedge to be continued through to payment of the euro-denominated account payable.

3. Kiwi entered into a forward contract on November 30, 2004, to be settled on February 1, 2005, to manage the financial currency exposure of a euro-denominated accounts payable in the amount of 20,000 euros from the purchase of inventory on that date. The payable is due on February 1, 2005. The forward contract is not designated as a hedge.

4. Kiwi entered into a forward contract on September 1, 2004, to speculate on the possible changes in exchange rates between the euro and the U.S. dollar between September 1, 2004, and February 1, 2005. The forward contract is for speculation purposes and is not a hedge.

### *Required*

Enter the dollar amount that would be shown for each of the following items as of December 31, 2004. Compute the statement amounts net. For example, if the transaction generated both a foreign currency exchange gain and a loss, specify just the net amount that would be reported in the financial statements. If no amount would be reported for an item, enter NA for Not Applicable in the space.

| | Transaction | | | |
|---|---|---|---|---|
| | 1 | 2 | 3 | 4 |
| Forward contract receivable | _____ | _____ | _____ | _____ |
| Inventory | _____ | _____ | _____ | _____ |
| Accounts payable (€) | _____ | _____ | _____ | _____ |
| Foreign currency exchange gain (loss), net | _____ | _____ | _____ | _____ |
| Other comprehensive income gain (loss), net | _____ | _____ | _____ | _____ |

# Multinational Accounting: Issues in Financial Reporting and Translation of Foreign Entity Statements

When a U.S. multinational company prepares its financial statements for reporting to its stockholders, it must prepare the statements according to U.S. GAAP and measured in U.S. dollars. These foreign operations may be subsidiaries, branches, or investments of the U.S. company. This chapter presents the current efforts to develop a global set of high-quality accounting standards and the translation of the financial statements of a foreign business entity into U.S. dollars.

Differences in accounting standards across countries and jurisdictions can cause significant difficulties for multinational firms. Some of the challenges multinational companies face include the preparation of financial statements according to the differing standards in countries where their subsidiaries are located and subsequent consolidation of the financial statements. These and significant other problems that result from differences in accounting standards are generating significant interest in the potential to converge accounting standards globally.

Accountants preparing financial statements must consider both the differences in accounting principles and the differences in currencies used to measure the foreign entity's operations. Restatement into U.S. dollars is necessary before the statements can be combined or consolidated with the U.S. company statements, which are already reported in dollars. For example, a British subsidiary of a U.S. company provides the parent statements measured in British pounds sterling, using the British system of accounting. The U.S. parent company must typically perform the following steps in the translation and consolidation of the British subsidiary:

1. Receive the British subsidiary's financial statements, which are reported in pounds sterling.
2. Restate the statements to conform to U.S. GAAP.

3. Translate the statements measured in pounds sterling into their equivalent U.S. dollar amounts. Each foreign entity account balance must be individually translated into its U.S. dollar equivalent, as follows:

$$
\begin{array}{ccc}
\text{Account measured} & \text{Appropriate} & \text{Account measured} \\
\text{in foreign} \quad \times & \text{exchange} \quad = & \text{in U.S. dollar--} \\
\text{currency units} & \text{rate} & \text{equivalent value}
\end{array}
$$

4. Consolidate the translated subsidiary's accounts, which are now measured in dollars, with the parent company's accounts.

# DIFFERENCES IN ACCOUNTING PRINCIPLES

Methods used to measure economic activity differ around the world. A country's economic, legal, educational, and political systems; stages of technological development or sophistication; culture and tradition; and various other socioeconomic factors all influence the development of accounting standards and the accounting profession in that nation. These differences have led to significant diversity in accounting standards from one nation to another. The lack of a uniform set of accounting standards creates problems for companies, preparers, and users. Some countries develop their accounting principles based on the information needs of the taxing authorities. Other countries have accounting principles designed to meet the needs of the central government economic planners. U.S. accounting standards focus on the information needs of the common stockholder or the creditors.

Arthur Levitt, former chairman of the Securities and Exchange Commission (SEC), noted in 1999 that the world economy was in a period of profound change as the notion of distance as a barrier was no longer a relevant impediment to business growth and development. Levitt noted that the flow of capital is a critical factor in global economic development, which had created a compelling need for a common business reporting language. Indeed, Levitt stated that "new business opportunities demand financial reporting standards that supersede national borders and cultural customs. These standards are not merely an ideal for a better global marketplace—they are fundamental to its very existence."[1]

Important benefits could be realized from the adoption of a single set of globally accepted accounting standards. Expected benefits include continued expansion of capital markets across national borders. Countries where accounting principles do not currently focus on the needs of investors could more quickly achieve stable, liquid capital markets, which in turn would be expected to drive economic growth, if they adopted a set of standards that have already gained a high degree of investor understanding and confidence. Use of a single set of accounting standards should help investors to better evaluate opportunities across national borders, which would also facilitate a more efficient use of global capital. A set of global standards would also reduce reporting costs that corporations currently incur if they attempt to access capital in markets outside their home country because corporations would no longer need to produce multiple sets of financial statements using different sets of accounting standards. Financial statement users are likely to have more confidence in financial reporting if it conforms to standards that have gained wide global acceptance.

A major financial reporting model that has the potential to become globally accepted is being developed by the International Accounting Standards Board (IASB). The IASB is an independent, privately funded accounting standards-setting body based in London. The mission of the IASB is to develop a single set of high-quality, understandable, and

---

[1] Arthur Levitt, Speech by SEC Chairman, "Remarks to the American Council on Germany: Corporate Governance in a Global Arena," October 7, 1999, http://www.sec.gov/news/speech/speecharchive/1999/spch302.htm.

enforceable global accounting standards. Standards published by the IASB are called *International Financial Reporting Standards (IFRS).* The IASB is composed of 14 members who each serve a five-year term subject to one reappointment. Members are required to sever all employment relationships that might compromise their independent judgment in setting accounting standards. The IASB solicits input from the public when evaluating potential standards and publishes a discussion paper and/or an exposure draft which are subject to comment before issuing a final standard. The IASB also has an advisory council, the Standards Advisory Council, that is composed of approximately 40 individuals from geographically diverse countries and draws members from both countries that have adopted IFRS and those that have not. The IASB has a mandate from the International Organization of Securities Commissions (IOSCO) to develop a high-quality set of international financial reporting standards, and this effort has the support of the U.S. regulators and standard setters.

There is already widespread acceptance of IFRS, and these standards are mandated or permitted in over 100 countries around the world. Beginning in 2005, the European Union mandated the use of IFRS for companies listing on stock exchanges in the EU, although the EU continues to accept statements prepared according to U.S. GAAP. The increasing use of IFRS is already significant for U.S. stock exchanges. According to the SEC there has been a significant increase in the number of foreign private issuers who file within the United States from a relative few companies in 2005 to approximately 110 in 2006.[2] These companies prepare financial statements that comply with IFRS as published by the IASB. Further, the Commission expects to see this number continue to increase in the future, particularly as Canada will adopt IFRS beginning in 2011; there currently are approximately 500 foreign private issuers from Canada. This movement to IFRS also has begun to affect U.S. issuers, in particular those with a significant global footprint. For instance, certain U.S. issuers may compete for capital globally in industry sectors in which a critical mass of non-U.S. companies report under IFRS. Also, U.S. issuers with subsidiaries located in jurisdictions that have moved to IFRS may prepare those subsidiaries' financial statements according to IFRS for purposes of local regulatory or statutory filings.

The FASB is working with the IASB to improve the quality of reporting standards and to "converge" their two sets of standards. In September 2002, the FASB issued the "Norwalk Agreement" in which both the FASB and the IASB pledged to work together both to improve the quality of their financial reporting standards and to converge the standards by working to minimize the differences between them. The convergence effort focuses on both the evaluation of existing standards and guidance for implementing current standards and new standards as they are developed. PricewaterhouseCoopers offers a publication on its Web site entitled "Similarities and Differences—A Comparison of IFRS and U.S. GAAP" that provides a topic-based comparison. This publication can be accessed on the Web at http://www.pwc.com/extweb/pwcpublications.nsf/docid/74d6c09e0a4ee610802569a1003354c8.

Until 2007, the SEC required foreign issuers that do use U.S. GAAP to reconcile their financial statements to U.S. GAAP and to file this reconciliation with the SEC on a Form 20-F. On January 4, 2008, the SEC issued new rules that allow foreign private issuers to file statements prepared in accordance with IFRS as issued by the IASB without reconciliation to U.S. GAAP.[3] Removing the Form 20-F requirement reduces costs to foreign

---

[2] Securities and Exchange Commission, 17 CFR Parts 210, 228, 229, 239, 240, and 249. Release Nos. 33-8831; 34-56217; IC-27924; File No. S7-20-07. RIN 3235-AJ93. "Concept Release on Allowing U.S. Issuers to Prepare Financial Statements in Accordance with International Financial Reporting Standards," p. 6, http://www.sec.gov/rules/concept/2007/33-8831.pdf.

[3] Federal Register, vol. 73, no. 3, January 4, 2008. 17 CFR Parts 210, 230, 239, and 249. Release Nos. 33-8870, 34-57206; International Series Release No. 1306; File No. S7-13-07. RIN 3235-AJ90. "Acceptance from Foreign Private Issuers of Financial Statements Prepared in Accordance with International Financial Reporting Standards without Reconciliation to U.S. GAAP." Agency: Securities and Exchange Commission. Action: Final Rule. http://www.sec.gov/rules/final/2008/33-8879fr.pdf.

private issuers and encourages their continued participation in the U.S. public capital market, which is a benefit to investors by increasing investment possibilities and furthering the efficient allocation of capital.

In December 2007, the SEC held roundtable discussions with representatives from public companies, audit firms, investor groups, academia, rating agencies, the legal community, and government agencies to obtain feedback on whether public companies in the United States should be permitted or required to file their consolidated financial statements using IFRS as published by the IASB instead of U.S. GAAP. Among this group, there was overwhelming support for the use of a single set of global standards, and the majority of the panelists agreed that IFRS ultimately will be the standard. There was general agreement among roundtable participants that the SEC should specify a date by which U.S. issuers would be required to prepare financial statements in accordance with IFRS. The target date most often mentioned should conversion be required is 2011, to coincide with the adoption of IFRS by a number of other countries including Canada and India.[4]

In general, panelists at the SEC roundtable felt that U.S. corporations could be more competitive globally if they were permitted to use IFRS for financial reporting. Benefits expected to accrue to U.S. firms included the following:

- Increase the quality of information available to investors.

- Reduce costs of compliance for companies that are currently using multiple reporting frameworks.

- Enhance global capital markets.

- Companies would have easier access to raising capital in the global markets.

- Because SEC now permits foreign private issuers to file their financial reports using IFRS without reconciliation, not allowing U.S. companies to report under IFRS could result in U.S. companies bearing costs not incurred by foreign private issuers.

- Enhance comparability across companies for users. SEC Chairman Cox noted that two-thirds of U.S. investors own securities of foreign companies, a 30 percent increase in the last five years.

Some observers fear that the United States could even become marginalized if more countries move to IFRS but the United States does not. Not only are U.S. investors divesting themselves of U.S. holdings and investing in non-U.S. holdings, but more companies are electing to raise capital on non-U.S. exchanges. As recently as 2000, nine out of every 10 dollars raised for foreign companies through new stock offerings were done in New York. However, by 2005, nine out of every 10 dollars were raised through new company listings in London or Luxembourg.[5]

There are still significant issues that must be addressed before a decision about adoption of IFRS by U.S. corporations can be made. Extensive training for professionals, users, and even regulators may be necessary. Still, many believe that convergence to a single set of international standards is key to economic development. Among 143 worldwide leaders of the accounting profession representing 91 countries who responded to a survey conducted by the International Federation of Accountants, 89 percent indicated that convergence to international financial reporting standards was either important or very important for economic growth in their countries, and only 1 percent said it was not important.[6]

---

[4] Ernst and Young's Professional Practice Group, December 21, 2007, "Hot Topic: IFRS in the U.S.— December 2007 Roundtable's Overwhelming Support Expressed for IFRS in the U.S."
[5] Craig Karmin and Aaron Lucchetti, "New York Loses Edge in Snagging Foreign Listings," *The Wall Street Journal* (Eastern Edition), January 26, 2006, p. C1.
[6] For a summary of the survey findings, along with responses to the full survey, visit www.ifac.org/ globalsurvey.

# DETERMINING THE FUNCTIONAL CURRENCY

Imagine that you received 100 British pounds sterling in payment on an account in your London subsidiary on December 31, 20X1, and deposited it in a London bank. Assume that at the end of 20X1 the exchange rate is $1.80. To report the deposit on your 20X1 balance sheet stated in dollars, you would translate the deposit at the current rate and you would report an asset of $180. At the end of 20X2, assume you still have the 100 pounds sterling in the bank, but now the exchange rate is $1.70. To report the deposit on your 20X2 balance sheet, if you use the exchange rate at the end of 20X2, this amount would now translate into $170 and you would have an imbalance, also referred to as a *translation adjustment,* of $10 to deal with. If you translated at the historical rate, you would still translate into $180 and there would be no imbalance. Which is the correct exchange rate to use?

| Date | Currency on Deposit | Current Exchange Rate | Dollar Equivalent |
|------|---------------------|-----------------------|-------------------|
| 12/31/20X1 | £100 | $1.80 | $180 |
| 12/31/20X2 | 100 | 1.70 | 170 |

Two major issues that must be addressed when financial statements are translated from a foreign currency into U.S. dollars are:

1. Which exchange rate should be used to translate foreign currency balances to domestic currency?
2. How should translation gains and losses be accounted for? Should they be included in income?

There are three possible exchange rates that may be used in converting foreign currency values to the U.S. dollar. The ***current rate*** is the exchange rate at the end of the trading day on the balance sheet date. The ***historical rate*** is the exchange rate that existed when an initial transaction took place, such as the exchange rate on the date an asset was acquired or a liability was incurred. The ***average rate*** for the period is usually a simple average for a period of time and is usually the exchange rate used to measure revenues and expenses. Translation methods may employ a single rate or multiple rates. The translation adjustment created by the application of these exchange rates also must be reflected in the financial statements, either as a component of net income or a component of comprehensive income. The disposition of the translation adjustment will be discussed later in this chapter.

**FASB Statement No. 52,** "Foreign Currency Translation" (FASB 52), provides specific guidelines for translating a foreign currency into U.S. dollars to allow preparation of consolidated financial statements measured, or denominated, in dollars. The purpose of **FASB 52** is to present results that are directionally sympathetic to the real economic effects of exchange rate movements. Additionally, **FASB 52** seeks to preserve financial results and relationships in the foreign financial statements through the translation process. For instance, if the gross margin on sales is positive when measured in the foreign currency, it should still be positive when sales and cost of goods sold are translated into dollars. The FASB adopted the concept of the ***functional currency,*** which is defined as "the currency of the primary economic environment in which the entity operates; normally that is the currency of the environment in which an entity primarily generates and receives cash."[7] The functional currency is used to differentiate between two types of foreign operations, those that are self-contained and integrated into a local environment, and those that are an extension of the parent and integrated with the parent. A U.S. company may have foreign affiliates in many different countries. Each affiliate must be analyzed to determine its individual functional currency.

---

[7] *Financial Accounting Standards Board Statement No. 52,* "Foreign Currency Translation," 1981, para. 5.

**FIGURE 12–1** **Functional Currency Indicators**

| Indicator | Factors Indicating Foreign Currency (Local Currency) Is the Functional Currency | Factors Indicating U.S. Dollar (Parent's Currency) Is the Functional Currency |
|---|---|---|
| Cash flows | Primarily in foreign currency and do not affect parent's cash flows | Directly impact the parent's current cash flows and are readily available to the parent company |
| Sales prices | Primarily determined by local competition or local government regulation; not generally responsive to changes in exchange rates | Responsive to short-term changes in exchange rates and worldwide competition |
| Sales markets | Active local sales markets for company's products; possibly, significant amounts of exports | Sales markets mostly in parent's country, or sales contracts are denominated in parent's currency |
| Expenses | Labor, materials, and other costs are primarily local costs | Production components generally obtained from the parent company's country |
| Financing | Primarily obtained from, and denominated in, local currency units; entity's operations generate funds sufficient to service financing needs | Primarily from the parent, or other dollar-denominated financing |
| Intercompany transactions and arrangements | Few intercompany transactions with parent | Frequent intercompany transactions with parent, or foreign entity is an investment or financing arm for the parent |

Figure 12–1 presents the six indicators that must be assessed to determine an entity's functional currency: cash flows, sales prices, sales markets, expenses, financing, and intercompany transactions. If a foreign affiliate uses the local currency for most of its transactions, and if the cash generated is not regularly physically returned to the parent in the United States, the local currency is usually the functional currency. Also, the foreign affiliate usually has active sales markets in its own country and obtains financing from local sources.

Some foreign-based entities, however, use a functional currency different from the local currency. For example, a U.S. company subsidiary in Venezuela may conduct virtually all of its business in Brazil, or a branch or a subsidiary of a U.S. company operating in Britain may well use the U.S. dollar as its major currency although it maintains its accounting records in British pounds sterling. The following factors indicate that the U.S. dollar is the functional currency for the British subsidiary: Most of its cash transactions are in U.S. dollars; its major sales markets are in the United States; production components are generally obtained from the United States; and the U.S. parent is primarily responsible for financing the British subsidiary.

The FASB adopted the functional currency approach after considering the following objectives of the translation process:

a. Provide information that is generally compatible with the expected economic effects of a rate change on an enterprise's cash flows and equity.

b. Reflect in consolidated statements the financial results and relationships of the individual consolidated entities as measured in their functional currencies in conformity with U.S. generally accepted accounting principles.[8]

The functional currency approach requires the foreign entity to translate all of its transactions into its functional currency. If an entity has transactions denominated in other than its functional currency, the foreign transactions must be adjusted to their equivalent functional currency value before the company may prepare financial statements.

[8] *FASB 52,* para. 4.

## Functional Currency Designation in Highly Inflationary Economies

An exception to the criteria for selecting a functional currency is specified when the foreign entity is located in countries such as Argentina and Peru, which have experienced severe inflation. Severe inflation is defined as inflation exceeding 100 percent over a three-year period.[9] The FASB concluded that the volatility of hyperinflationary currencies distorts the financial statements if the local currency is used as the foreign entity's functional currency. Therefore, in cases of operations located in highly inflationary economies, the reporting currency of the U.S. parent—the U.S. dollar—should be used as the foreign entity's functional currency. This exception prevents unrealistic asset values and income statement charges if the hyperinflation is ignored and normal translation procedures are used. For example, assume that a foreign subsidiary constructed a building that cost 1,000,000 pesos when the exchange rate was $.05 = 1 peso. Further assume that because of hyperinflation in the foreign subsidiary's country, the exchange rate becomes $.00005 = 1 peso. The translated values of the building at the time it was constructed and after the hyperinflation follow:

| Amount (pesos) | Date of Construction | | After Hyperinflation | |
| --- | --- | --- | --- | --- |
| | Rate | Translated Amount | Rate | Translated Amount |
| 1,000,000 | $.05 | $50,000 | $.00005 | $50 |

The translated values after the hyperinflation do not reflect the building's market value or historical cost. Thus, the FASB required the use of the U.S. dollar as the functional currency in cases of hyperinflation to give some stability to the financial statements.

Once a foreign affiliate's functional currency is chosen, it should be used consistently. However, if changes in economic circumstances necessitate a change in the designation of the foreign affiliate's functional currency, the accounting change should be treated as a change in estimate: current and prospective treatment only, no restatement of prior periods.

# TRANSLATION VERSUS REMEASUREMENT OF FOREIGN FINANCIAL STATEMENTS

Two different methods are used to restate foreign entity statements to U.S. dollars: (1) the *translation* of the foreign entity's functional currency statements into U.S. dollars and (2) the *remeasurement* of the foreign entity's statements into the functional currency of the entity. After remeasurement, the statements must then be translated if the functional currency is *not* the U.S. dollar. No additional work is needed if the functional currency is the U.S. dollar.

*Translation* is the most common method used and is applied when the local currency is the foreign entity's functional currency. This is the normal case in which, for example, a U.S. company's French subsidiary uses the euro as its recording and functional currency. The subsidiary's statements must be translated from euros into U.S. dollars. To translate the financial statements, the company will use the current rate, which is the exchange rate on the balance sheet date, to convert the local currency balance sheet account balances into U.S. dollars. Any translation adjustment that occurs is a component of comprehensive income. Because revenues and expenses are assumed to occur uniformly over the period, revenues and expenses on the income statement are translated using the average rate for the reporting period. This translation method is called the ***current rate method.***

[9] *FASB 52,* para. 11.

*Remeasurement* is the restatement of the foreign entity's financial statements from the local currency that the entity used into the foreign entity's functional currency. Remeasurement is required only when the functional currency is different from the currency used to maintain the books and records of the foreign entity. For example, a relatively self-contained Canadian sales branch of a U.S. company may use the U.S. dollar as its functional currency but may select the Canadian dollar as its recording and reporting currency. Of course, if the Canadian branch uses the U.S. dollar for both its functional and reporting currency, no translation or remeasurement is necessary: Its statements are already measured in U.S. dollars and are ready to be combined with the U.S. home office statements.

The method used to remeasure the financial statements from the local currency to the functional currency is called the ***temporal method.*** Monetary assets and liabilities are those that represent rights to receive or obligations to pay a fixed number of foreign currency units in the future. Under the temporal method, the current rate is usually used to translate these monetary amounts to the functional currency. Nonmonetary items include fixed assets, long-term investments, and inventories. These items are usually translated at the historical rate that existed when the assets were originally purchased or the liability originally was incurred. Revenues and expenses on the income statement are translated using the average rate for the reporting period. Any imbalance that occurs because of the application of the temporal method is included in the calculation of net income on the income statement.

The application of the temporal method converts a foreign currency to the functional currency. If the functional currency is the U.S. dollar, no additional adjustments are needed. If the functional currency is something other than the U.S. dollar, the current rate method must be applied to restate the financial information in U.S. dollars.

One application of remeasurement is for affiliates located in countries experiencing hyperinflation. For example, an Argentinian subsidiary of a U.S. parent records and reports its financial statements in the local currency, the Argentine peso. However, because the Argentine economy experiences inflation exceeding 100 percent over a three-year period, the U.S. dollar is specified as the functional currency for reporting purposes and the subsidiary's statements must then be remeasured from Argentine pesos into U.S. dollars.

The following table presents an overview of the methods a U.S. company would use to restate a foreign affiliate's financial statements in U.S. dollars.

| Currency in Which the Foreign Affiliate's Books and Records Are Maintained | Functional Currency | Restatement Method |
|---|---|---|
| Local currency (i.e., currency of the country in which the foreign entity is located) | Local currency | Translate to U.S. dollars using current exchange rates |
| Local currency | U.S. dollar (such as required in hyperinflationary economies) | Remeasure from local currency to U.S. dollar |
| Local currency | Third country's currency (Not LCU or U.S. dollar) | First, remeasure from the local currency into the functional currency, then translate from functional currency to U.S. dollars |
| U.S. dollar | U.S. dollar | No restatement is necessary; already in U.S. dollars |

The conceptual reasons for the two different methods, translation and remeasurement, come from a consideration of the primary objective of the translation process: to provide information that shows the expected impact of exchange rate changes on the U.S. company's cash flows and equity. Foreign affiliates fall into two groups. Those in the first group are relatively self-contained entities that generate and spend local currency units. The local currency is the functional currency for this group of entities. These foreign affiliates may reinvest the currency they generate or may distribute funds to their home office or parent company in the form of dividends. Exchange rate changes do not directly affect the U.S. parent company's cash flows. Rather, the rate changes affect the foreign affiliate's net assets (assets minus liabilities) and, therefore, the U.S. parent company's net investment in the entity.

The second group of foreign affiliates is made up of entities that are an extension of the U.S. company. These affiliates operate in a foreign country but are directly affected by changes in exchange rates because they depend on the U.S. economy for sales markets, production components, or financing. For this group, the U.S. dollar is the functional currency. There is a presumption that the effect of exchange rate changes on the foreign affiliate's net assets will directly affect the U.S. parent company's cash flows, so the exchange rate adjustments are reported in the U.S. parent's income.

Translation and remeasurement include different adjustment procedures and may result in significantly different consolidated financial statements. Both methods are illustrated in this chapter.

# TRANSLATION OF FUNCTIONAL CURRENCY STATEMENTS INTO THE REPORTING CURRENCY OF THE U.S. COMPANY

Most business entities transact and record business activities in the local currency. Therefore, the local currency of the foreign entity is its functional currency. The translation of the foreign entity's statement into U.S. dollars is a relatively straightforward process.

The FASB believes that the underlying economic relationships presented in the foreign entity's financial statements should not be distorted or changed during the translation process from the foreign entity's functional currency into the currency of the U.S. parent. For example, if the foreign entity's functional currency statements report a current ratio of 2:1 and a gross margin of 60 percent of sales, these relationships should pass through the translation process into the U.S. parent's reporting currency. It is important to be able to evaluate the performance of the foreign entity's management with the same economic measures used to operate the foreign entity. To maintain the economic relationships in the functional currency statements, the account balances must be translated by a comparable exchange rate.

The translation is made by using the current exchange rate for *all* assets and liabilities. This rate is the spot rate on the balance sheet date. The income statement items—revenue, expenses, gains, and losses—should be translated at the exchange rate on the dates on which the underlying transactions occurred, although for practical purposes an average exchange rate for the period may be used for these items with the assumption that revenues and expenses are recognized evenly over the period. However, if a material gain or loss results from a specific event, the exchange rate on the date of the event rather than the average exchange rate should be used to translate the transaction results.

The stockholders' equity accounts, other than retained earnings, are translated at historical exchange rates. The appropriate historical rate is the rate on the latter of the date the parent company acquired the investment in the foreign entity or the date the subsidiary had the stockholders' equity transaction. This is necessary to complete the elimination of the parent company's investment account against the foreign subsidiary's capital accounts in the consolidation process. The subsidiary's translated retained earnings are carried forward from the previous period with additions for this period's income and deductions for dividends declared during the period. Dividends are translated at the exchange rate on the date of declaration. It is interesting to observe that if the foreign entity has not paid its declared dividend by the end of its fiscal period, it has a dividends payable account that is translated at the current rate. Nevertheless, the dividend deduction from Retained Earnings is translated using the exchange rate on the date of dividend declaration.

In summary, the translation of the foreign entity's financial statements from its functional currency into the reporting currency of the U.S. company is made as follows:

| | |
|---|---|
| Income statement accounts: | |
| Revenue and expenses | Generally, average exchange rate for period covered by statement |
| Balance sheet accounts: | |
| Assets and liabilities | Current exchange rate on balance sheet date |
| Stockholders' equity | Historical exchange rates |

Because various rates are used to translate the foreign entity's individual accounts, the trial balance debits and credits after translation generally are not equal. The balancing item to make the translated trial balance debits equal the credits is called the ***translation adjustment.***

## Financial Statement Presentation of Translation Adjustment

The translation adjustment resulting from the translation process is part of the entity's comprehensive income for the period. **FASB Statement No. 130,** "Reporting Comprehensive Income" (FASB 130), issued in June 1997, defined comprehensive income to include all changes in equity during a period except those resulting from investments by owners and distributions to owners. ***Comprehensive income*** includes net income and ***"other comprehensive income"*** items that are part of the changes in the net assets of a business enterprise from nonowner sources (e.g., not additional capital investments and dividends) during a period. **FASB 130** requires the reporting of comprehensive income as part of the primary financial statements of the entity. The major items comprising the other comprehensive income items are the changes during the period in foreign currency translation adjustments, unrealized gains or losses on available-for-sale securities, revaluation of cash flow hedges, and adjustments in the minimum pension liability item.

**FASB 130** allows for several alternative presentation formats for comprehensive income. The single-statement, combined income approach first presents the items composing net income and then has a section presenting the other comprehensive income items. An alternative, two-statement presentation first presents the computation of net income on one statement and then a related statement that begins with net income and reconciles to comprehensive income by reporting the other comprehensive income items separately. A third alternative, used by many companies, is just to present the items composing other comprehensive income in a schedule of accumulated other comprehensive income in the consolidated statement of shareholders' equity. An entity may present the components of other comprehensive income items net of tax or show the aggregate tax effects related to the total other comprehensive income items as one amount.

Each period's other comprehensive income (OCI) is closed to accumulated other comprehensive income (AOCI), which is displayed separately from other stockholders' equity items (e.g., capital stock, additional paid-in capital, and retained earnings). An appropriate title, such as ***"Accumulated Other Comprehensive Income,"*** is used to describe this stockholders' equity item. The statement of changes in stockholders' equity opens with the accumulated balance of the other comprehensive income items at the beginning of the period, then includes the change in the translation adjustment and the additional other comprehensive income items during the period that were included in the period's comprehensive income, and ends with the accumulated other comprehensive income balance at the end of the period. The accumulated ending balance of the other comprehensive income items is then reported in the entity's balance sheet as part of the stockholders' equity section, usually after retained earnings. The discussion of the disclosure requirements presented later in this chapter demonstrates the financial statements for the Peerless Products Corporation example presented in the chapter.

**FIGURE 12–2**
Balance Sheet Accounts for the Two Companies on January 1, 20X1 (Immediately before Acquisition of 100 percent of German Company's Stock by Peerless Products, a U.S. Company)

| | Peerless Products | German Company |
|---|---|---|
| Cash | $ 350,000 | € 2,500 |
| Receivables | 75,000 | 10,000 |
| Inventory | 100,000 | 7,500 |
| Land | 175,000 | -0- |
| Plant and Equipment | 800,000 | 50,000 |
| Total Debits | $1,500,000 | €70,000 |
| Accumulated Depreciation | $ 400,000 | € 5,000 |
| Accounts Payable | 100,000 | 2,500 |
| Bonds Payable | 200,000 | 12,500 |
| Common Stock | 500,000 | 40,000 |
| Retained Earnings, 12/31/X0 | 300,000 | 10,000 |
| Total Credits | $1,500,000 | €70,000 |

## Illustration of Translation and Consolidation of a Foreign Subsidiary

In Chapter 11, the examples illustrated the effects of a dollar that was strengthening against the euro during 20X1. In the examples for the remainder of this chapter, the dollar weakens against the euro during 20X1. Thus, in Chapters 11 and 12, changes in exchange rates in both directions will have been illustrated.

To examine the consolidation of a foreign subsidiary, assume the following facts:

1. On January 1, 20X1, Peerless, a U.S. company, purchased 100 percent of the outstanding capital stock of German Company, a firm located in Berlin, Germany, for $66,000, which is $6,000 above book value. (The proof of the differential is shown at the end of the next section of the chapter.) The excess of cost over book value is attributable to a patent amortizable over 10 years. Balance sheet accounts in a trial balance format for both companies immediately *before* the acquisition are presented in Figure 12–2.

2. The local currency for German Company is the euro (€), which is also its functional currency.

3. On October 1, 20X1, the subsidiary declared and paid dividends of €6,250.

4. The subsidiary received $4,200 in a sales transaction with a U.S. company when the exchange rate was $1.20 = €1. The subsidiary still has this foreign currency on December 31, 20X1.

5. Relevant direct spot exchange rates ($/€1) are:

| Date | Rate |
|---|---|
| January 1, 20X1 | $1.20 |
| October 1, 20X1 | 1.36 |
| December 31, 20X1 | 1.40 |
| 20X1 average | 1.30 |

### Date-of-Acquisition Translation Workpaper

Figure 12–3 presents the translation of German Company's trial balance on January 1, 20X1. This illustration assumes that the subsidiary's books and records are maintained in European euros, the subsidiary's functional currency.

The translation of the subsidiary's trial balance from the functional currency (€) into dollars, the U.S. parent's reporting currency, is made using the *current rate method.* Under purchase accounting, the subsidiary's stockholders' equity accounts are translated using the current rate on the date of the parent company's purchase of the subsidiary's stock.

**FIGURE 12–3**
**Workpaper to Translate Foreign Subsidiary on January 1, 20X1 (Date of Acquisition)** Functional Currency Is the European Euro

| Item | Trial Balance, € | Exchange Rate, $/€ | Trial Balance, $ |
|---|---|---|---|
| Cash | 2,500 | 1.20 | 3,000 |
| Receivables | 10,000 | 1.20 | 12,000 |
| Inventory | 7,500 | 1.20 | 9,000 |
| Plant and Equipment | 50,000 | 1.20 | 60,000 |
| Total Debits | 70,000 | | 84,000 |
| Accumulated Depreciation | 5,000 | 1.20 | 6,000 |
| Accounts Payable | 2,500 | 1.20 | 3,000 |
| Bonds Payable | 12,500 | 1.20 | 15,000 |
| Common Stock | 40,000 | 1.20 | 48,000 |
| Retained Earnings | 10,000 | 1.20 | 12,000 |
| Total Credits | 70,000 | | 84,000 |

*Note:* $1.20 is direct exchange rate on January 1, 20X1.

The entry made by Peerless Products to record the purchase of 100 percent of German Company's stock is:

January 1, 20X1

| (1) | Investment in German Company Stock | 66,000 | |
|---|---|---|---|
| | Cash | | 66,000 |
| | Purchase of German Company stock. | | |

The differential on January 1, 20X1, the date of acquisition, is computed as follows:

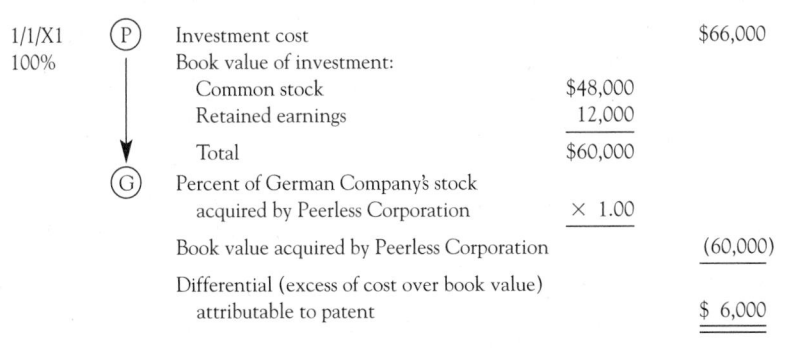

1/1/X1 (P) 100%

| Investment cost | | $66,000 |
|---|---|---|
| Book value of investment: | | |
| Common stock | $48,000 | |
| Retained earnings | 12,000 | |
| Total | $60,000 | |
| (G) Percent of German Company's stock acquired by Peerless Corporation | × 1.00 | |
| Book value acquired by Peerless Corporation | | (60,000) |
| Differential (excess of cost over book value) attributable to patent | | $ 6,000 |

A graphic representation of the acquisition is as follows:

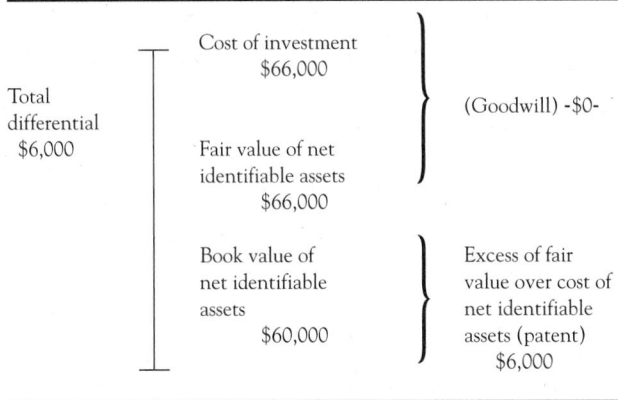

**FIGURE 12–4** **January 1, 20X1, Workpaper for Consolidated Balance Sheet, Date of Acquisition**
100 Percent Purchase at More than Book Value

| | Peerless Products | German Company | Eliminations Debit | Eliminations Credit | Consolidated |
|---|---|---|---|---|---|
| Cash | $ 284,000 | $ 3,000 | | | $ 287,000 |
| Receivables | 75,000 | 12,000 | | | 87,000 |
| Inventory | 100,000 | 9,000 | | | 109,000 |
| Land | 175,000 | | | | 175,000 |
| Plant and Equipment | 800,000 | 60,000 | | | 860,000 |
| Investment in German Co. Stock | 66,000 | | | (2) 66,000 | |
| Differential | | | (2) 6,000 | (3) 6,000 | |
| Patent | | | (3) 6,000 | | 6,000 |
| Total Debits | $1,500,000 | $84,000 | | | $1,524,000 |
| Accumulated Depreciation | 400,000 | 6,000 | | | 406,000 |
| Accounts Payable | 100,000 | 3,000 | | | 103,000 |
| Bonds Payable | 200,000 | 15,000 | | | 215,000 |
| Common Stock | 500,000 | 48,000 | (2) 48,000 | | 500,000 |
| Retained Earnings | 300,000 | 12,000 | (2) 12,000 | | 300,000 |
| Total Credits | $1,500,000 | $84,000 | 72,000 | 72,000 | $1,524,000 |

### Date-of-Acquisition Consolidated Balance Sheet

The consolidated balance sheet workpaper for Peerless Products and its German subsidiary on January 1, 20X1, is presented in Figure 12–4. The consolidation process is identical to the date-of-acquisition consolidations presented in Chapter 4. The eliminating entries are as follows:

| | | | |
|---|---|---|---|
| E(2) | Common Stock—German Company | 48,000 | |
| | Retained Earnings | 12,000 | |
| | Differential | 6,000 | |
| | Investment in German Company Stock | | 66,000 |
| | Eliminate investment balance. | | |
| E(3) | Patent | 6,000 | |
| | Differential | | 6,000 |
| | Assign differential. | | |

### Subsequent to Date of Acquisition

The accounting subsequent to the date of acquisition is very similar to the accounting used for domestic subsidiaries. The major differences are due to the effects of changes in the exchange rates of the foreign currency.

***Translation of Foreign Subsidiary's Postacquisition Trial Balance*** Figure 12–5 illustrates the translation of German Company's December 31, 20X1, trial balance.

Note the account Foreign Currency Units in the trial balance of the German subsidiary. This account represents the $4,200 of U.S. dollars held by the subsidiary. Because this account is denominated in a currency other than the subsidiary's reporting currency, German Company made an adjusting journal entry to revalue the account from the amount originally recorded using the exchange rate on the date the company received the currency to that amount's equivalent exchange value at the end of the year.

The subsidiary made the following entry on its books when it received the U.S. dollars:

**FIGURE 12–5**
**December 31, 20X1,**
**Translation of**
**Foreign Subsidiary's**
**Trial Balance**
European Euro Is the
Functional Currency

| Item | Balance, € | Exchange Rate | Balance, $ |
|---|---|---|---|
| Cash | 10,750 | 1.40 | 15,050 |
| Foreign Currency Units | 3,000 | 1.40 | 4,200 |
| Receivables | 10,500 | 1.40 | 14,700 |
| Inventory | 5,000 | 1.40 | 7,000 |
| Plant and Equipment | 50,000 | 1.40 | 70,000 |
| Cost of Goods Sold | 22,500 | 1.30 | 29,250 |
| Operating Expenses | 14,500 | 1.30 | 18,850 |
| Foreign Currency Transaction Loss | 500 | 1.30 | 650 |
| Dividends Paid | 6,250 | 1.36 | 8,500 |
| Total Debits | 123,000 | | 168,200 |
| Accumulated Depreciation | 7,500 | 1.40 | 10,500 |
| Accounts Payable | 3,000 | 1.40 | 4,200 |
| Bonds Payable | 12,500 | 1.40 | 17,500 |
| Common Stock | 40,000 | 1.20 | 48,000 |
| Retained Earnings (1/1) | 10,000 | (a) | 12,000 |
| Sales | 50,000 | 1.30 | 65,000 |
| Total | 123,000 | | 157,200 |
| Accumulated Other Comprehensive Income—Translation Adjustment | | | 11,000 |
| Total Credits | | | 168,200 |

(a) From the January 1, 20X1, translation workpaper.

| (4) | Foreign Currency Units ($) | | €3,500 |
|---|---|---|---|
| | Sales | | | €3,500 |
| | Record sales and receipt of 4,200 U.S. dollars at spot exchange rate on date of receipt: €3,500 = $4,200/$1.20 exchange rate | | | |

At the end of the period, the subsidiary adjusted the foreign currency units (the U.S. dollars) to the current exchange rate ($1.40 = €1) by making the following entry:

| (5) | Foreign Currency Transaction Loss | | €500 | |
|---|---|---|---|---|
| | Foreign Currency Units ($) | | | €500 |
| | Adjust account denominated in foreign currency units to current exchange rate: | | | |
| | $4,200/$1.40 | | €3,000 | |
| | Less: Preadjusted balance | | (3,500) | |
| | Foreign currency transaction loss | | € (500) | |

The foreign currency transaction loss is a component of the subsidiary's net income, and the Foreign Currency Units account is classified as a current asset on the subsidiary's balance sheet. The subsidiary's net income consists of the following elements:

| | |
|---|---|
| Sales | €50,000 |
| Cost of Goods Sold | (22,500) |
| Operating Expenses | (14,500) |
| Foreign Currency Transaction Loss | (500) |
| Net Income | €12,500 |

Because the European euro is the foreign entity's functional currency, the subsidiary's statements must be translated into U.S. dollars using the current rate method. The assets and liabilities are translated using the current exchange rate at the balance sheet date ($1.40), the income statement accounts are translated using the average rate for the period ($1.30), and the stockholders' equity accounts are translated using the appropriate historical exchange rates ($1.20 and $1.36). The dividends are translated at the October 1 rate ($1.36), which was the exchange rate on the date the dividends were declared. The example assumes the dividends were paid on October 1, the same day they were declared. If the dividends had not been paid by the end of the year, the liability dividends payable would be translated at the current exchange rate of $1.40 = €1.

One of the analytical features provided by the current rate method is that many of the ratios management uses to manage the foreign subsidiary are the same in U.S. dollars as they are in the foreign currency unit. This relationship is true for the assets and liabilities of the balance sheet and the revenue and expenses of the income statement because the translation for these accounts uses the same exchange rate—the current rate for the assets and liabilities, and the average exchange rate for the income statement accounts. Thus, the *scale* of these accounts has changed but not their *relative amounts* within their respective statements. This relationship is not true when the ratio includes numbers from both the income statement and the balance sheet or when a stockholders' equity account is included with an asset or liability. The following table illustrates the relative relationships within the financial statements using the data in Figure 12–5:

|  | Measured in € | Measured in U.S. Dollars |
|---|---|---|
| Current ratio: |  |  |
| Current assets | €29,250 | $40,950 |
| Current liabilities | €  3,000 | $ 4,200 |
| Current ratio | 9.75 | 9.75 |
| Cost of goods sold as a percentage of sales: |  |  |
| Cost of goods sold | €22,500 | $29,250 |
| Sales | €50,000 | $65,000 |
| Percent | 45% | 45% |

The translation adjustment in Figure 12–5 arises because the investee's assets and liabilities are translated at the current rate, whereas other rates are used for the stockholders' equity and income statement account balances. Although the translation adjustment may be thought of as a balancing item to make the trial balance debits equal the credits, the effects of changes in the exchange rates during the period should be calculated to prove the accuracy of the translation process. This proof for 20X1, the acquisition year, is provided in Figure 12–6.

The proof begins with determination of the effect of changes in the exchange rate on the beginning investment and on the elements that alter the beginning investment. Note that only events affecting the stockholders' equity accounts will change the net assets investment. In this example, the changes to the investment account occurred from income of €12,500 and dividends of €6,250. No changes occurred in the stock outstanding during the year. The beginning net investment is translated using the exchange rate at the beginning of the year. The income and dividends are translated using the exchange rate at the date the transactions occurred. The income was earned evenly over the year; thus the average exchange rate for the period is used to translate income. The ending net assets position is translated using the exchange rate at the end of the year. The cumulative translation adjustment at the beginning of the year is zero in this example because the subsidiary was acquired on January 1, 20X1.

The Accumulated Other Comprehensive Income—Translation Adjustment account has a credit balance because the spot exchange rate at the end of the first period of ownership is higher than the exchange rate at the beginning of the period or the average for the period. If the exchange rate had decreased during the period, the translation adjustment

**FIGURE 12–6**
**Proof of Translation Adjustment as of December 31, 20X1**
European Euro Is the Functional Currency

| PEERLESS PRODUCTS AND SUBSIDIARY | | | |
|---|---|---|---|
| **Proof of Translation Adjustment** | | | |
| **Year Ended December 31, 20X1** | | | |
| | | **Translation** | |
| | **€** | **Rate** | **$** |
| Net assets at beginning of year | 50,000 | 1.20 | 60,000 |
| Adjustment for changes in net assets position during year: | | | |
| Net income for year | 12,500 | 1.30 | 16,250 |
| Dividends paid | (6,250) | 1.36 | (8,500) |
| Net assets translated at: | | | |
| Rates during year | | | 67,750 |
| Rates at end of year | 56,250 | 1.40 | 78,750 |
| Change in other comprehensive income—translation adjustment during year (net increase) | | | 11,000 |
| Accumulated other comprehensive income—translation adjustment, 1/1 | | | -0- |
| Accumulated other comprehensive income—translation adjustment, 12/31 (credit) | | | 11,000 |

would have had a debit balance. Another way of determining whether the accumulated translation adjustment has a debit or credit balance is to use balance sheet logic. For example, the subsidiary's translated balance sheet at the beginning of the year would be:

| **Translated Balance Sheet, 1/1/X1** | | | |
|---|---|---|---|
| Net assets | $60,000 | Common stock | $60,000 |

The translated balance sheet at the end of the year would be:

| **Translated Balance Sheet, 12/31/X1** | | | |
|---|---|---|---|
| Net assets | $78,750 | Common stock | $60,000 |
| | | Retained earnings (net income less dividends) | 7,750 |
| | | Accumulated other comprehensive income—translation adjustment | 11,000 |
| Total | $78,750 | Total | $78,750 |

Note that the $11,000 is a credit balance in order to make the balance sheet "balance."

***Entries on Parent Company's Books*** Entries on the parent company's books are made to recognize the dollar equivalent values of the parent's share of the subsidiary's income, amortization of the excess of cost over book value, a cumulative translation adjustment for the parent's differential, and the dividends received from the foreign subsidiary. In addition, the parent company must recognize its share of the translation adjustment arising from the translation of the subsidiary's financial statements. The periodic change in the parent company's translation adjustment from the foreign investment is reported as a component of the parent company's other comprehensive income.

The entries that Peerless Products makes to account for its investment in German Company follow. Peerless Products received the dividend on October 1, 20X1, and immediately converted it to U.S. dollars as follows:

October 1, 20X1

| (6) | Cash | 8,500 | |
| | Investment in German Company Stock | | 8,500 |

Dividend received from foreign subsidiary:
€6,250 × $1.36 exchange rate

December 31, 20X1

| (7) | Investment in German Company Stock | 16,250 | |
| | Income from Subsidiary | | 16,250 |

Equity in net income of foreign subsidiary:
€12,500 × $1.30 average exchange rate

| (8) | Investment in German Company Stock | 11,000 | |
| | Other Comprehensive Income—Translation Adjustment | | 11,000 |

Parent's share of change in translation adjustment from
translation of subsidiary's accounts: $11,000 × 1.00

If some time passed between the declaration and payment of dividends, the parent company would record dividends receivable from the foreign subsidiary on the declaration date. This account would be denominated in a foreign currency and would be adjusted to its current exchange rate on the balance sheet date and on the payment date, just like any other account denominated in a foreign currency. Any foreign transaction gain or loss resulting from the adjustment procedure would be included in the parent's income for the period.

***The Differential*** The allocation and amortization of the excess of cost over book value require special attention in the translation of a foreign entity's financial statements. The differential does not exist on the foreign subsidiary's books; it is part of the parent's investment account. However, the translated book value of the foreign subsidiary is a major component of the investment account on the parent's books and is directly related to a foreign-based asset. **FASB 52** requires that the allocation and amortization of the difference between the investment cost and its book value be made in terms of the functional currency of the foreign subsidiary and that these amounts then be translated at the appropriate exchange rates on the workpaper balance sheet date. The periodic amortization affects the income statement and is therefore measured at the average exchange rate used to translate other income statement accounts. On the other hand, the remaining unamortized balance of the differential is reported in the balance sheet and is translated at the current exchange rate used for balance sheet accounts. The effect of this difference in rates is shown in the parent company's translation adjustment as a revision of part of the parent's original investment in the subsidiary.

Peerless Products amortizes the patent over a 10-year period. The patent amortization follows.

| | European Euros | Translation Rate | U.S. Dollars |
|---|---|---|---|
| **Income Statement** | | | |
| Differential at beginning of year | €5,000 | 1.20 | $6,000 |
| Amortization this period (€5,000/10 years) | (500) | 1.30 | (650) |
| Remaining balances | €4,500 | | $5,350 |
| **Balance Sheet** | | | |
| Remaining balance on | | | |
| 12/31/X1 translated at year-end exchange rates | €4,500 | 1.40 | $6,300 |
| Difference to other comprehensive income— | | | |
| translation adjustment (credit) | | | $ 950 |

Another way to view the differential adjustment of $950 is that it adjusts the parent company's differential, which is currently part of the investment account, to the amount necessary to prepare the consolidated balance sheet. In this example, if no differential adjustment is made, the patent on the consolidated balance sheet would be $5,350, which is incorrect. Because the balance sheet must report the patent translated at the end-of-period exchange rate of $6,300, the differential adjustment is made to properly report the amount in the consolidated balance sheet. Thus, the adjustment may be thought of as an adjustment necessary to obtain the correct amount of the differential to prepare the consolidated balance sheet. Depending on the direction of the changes in the exchange rate, the differential adjustment could be a debit or credit amount. In this case, the differential must be increased from $5,350 to $6,300, necessitating a debit of $950 to the investment account and a corresponding credit to the Other Comprehensive Income—Translation Adjustment account.

Entry (9) recognizes the amortization of the patent for the period. Entry (10) records the portion of the translation adjustment on the increase in the differential for the investment in the foreign subsidiary.

| | | | |
|---|---|---|---|
| (9) | Income from Subsidiary | 650 | |
| |     Investment in German Company Stock | | 650 |
| |     Amortization of patent: | | |
| |     $650 = €500 × $1.30 average exchange rate | | |
| (10) | Investment in German Company Stock | 950 | |
| |     Other Comprehensive Income—Translation Adjustment | | 950 |
| |     Recognize translation adjustment on increase in differential. | | |

It is important to note that the $950 translation adjustment from the differential is attributed solely to the parent company. Noncontrolling Interest is not assigned any portion of this translation adjustment. This $950 translation adjustment is attributable to the excess of cost paid over the book value of the assets and therefore is added to the differential, which is a component of the investment in the foreign subsidiary, thereby resulting in a debit to the investment account on the parent company's books.

The December 31, 20X1, balance in the Investment in German Company Stock account is $85,050, as shown in the following T-account. The numbers in parentheses are the corresponding journal entry numbers from the text.

| Investment in German Company Stock | | | | |
|---|---|---|---|---|
| (1) | Purchase price | 66,000 | | |
| | | | (6) Dividends | 8,500 |
| (7) | Equity income | 16,250 | | |
| (8) | Share of subsidiary's translation adjustment | 11,000 | | |
| | | | (9) Amortization of differential | 650 |
| (10) | Translation adjustment on differential | 950 | | |
| | Balance, 12/31/X1 | 85,050 | | |

Note that the $11,950 Other Comprehensive Income—Translation Adjustment account balance in the parent company's books is composed of its share of the translation adjustment from translating the subsidiary's trial balance ($11,000) plus the parent company's adjustment ($950) due to the differential it paid for the investment.

During the parent company's closing entries process, the following two entries would be included to separately close net income from the subsidiary and the other comprehensive income arising from its investment in the subsidiary.

| | | | |
|---|---|---:|---:|
| (11) | Income from Subsidiary | 15,600 | |
| | Retained Earnings | | 15,600 |
| | To close net income from subsidiary: | | |
| | $15,600 = $16,250 − $650 | | |

| | | | |
|---|---|---:|---:|
| (12) | Other Comprehensive Income—Translation Adjustment | 11,950 | |
| | Accumulated Other Comprehensive Income— | | |
| | Translation Adjustment | | 11,950 |
| | To close other comprehensive income resulting from the investment in the German subsidiary: | | |
| | $11,950 = $11,000 + $950 | | |

***Subsequent Consolidation Workpaper***   The consolidation workpaper is prepared after the translation process is completed. The process of consolidation is the same as for a domestic subsidiary, except for two major differences: (1) The parent company will record its share of the translation adjustment arising from the translation of the foreign subsidiary's accounts; as presented in entry (8) for this example, the parent owns 100 percent of the subsidiary, but, in cases of a less-than-wholly owned subsidiary, the noncontrolling interest would be assigned its percentage share of the translation adjustment, and (2) as shown previously, the patent amortization for the period is translated at the income statement rate (average for the period), whereas the ending patent balance is translated at the balance sheet rate (current exchange rate). As shown in entry (10), a translation adjustment must be computed on the differential and assigned as part of the parent company's investment in the foreign subsidiary.

The workpaper is presented in Figure 12–7. The trial balance for German Company is obtained from the translated amounts computed earlier in Figure 12–5. The workpaper entries follow in journal entry form. These entries are *not* made on either company's books; they are only in the workpaper elimination columns.

| | | | |
|---|---|---:|---:|
| E(13) | Income from Subsidiary | 15,600 | |
| | Dividends Declared | | 8,500 |
| | Investment in German Company Stock | | 7,100 |
| | Eliminate income from subsidiary: | | |
| | $15,600 = $16,250 equity share − $650 amortization | | |
| | | | |
| E(14) | Other Comprehensive Income—Translation Adjustment | 11,000 | |
| | Investment in German Co. Stock | | 11,000 |
| | To eliminate the other comprehensive income from the subsidiary that had been recorded by the parent. | | |
| | | | |
| E(15) | Common Stock—German Co. | 48,000 | |
| | Retained Earnings, January 1, 20X1 | 12,000 | |
| | Accumulated Other Comprehensive Income, January 1, 20X1 | 0 | |
| | Differential | 6,000 | |
| | Investment in German Co. Stock | | 66,000 |
| | Eliminate beginning-of-period investment balance. | | |
| | | | |
| E(16) | Differential | 950 | |
| | Investment in German Co. Stock | | 950 |
| | Eliminate end-of-period differential adjustment that was recorded in investment account. | | |
| | | | |
| E(17) | Patent | 6,950 | |
| | Differential | | 6,950 |
| | Assign differential, including periodic adjustment of $950, to patent: | | |
| | $6,950 = $6,000 + $950 differential adjustment | | |

**FIGURE 12–7** December 31, 20X1, Consolidation Workpaper, Prepared after Translation of Foreign Statements

| Item | Peerless Products | German Company | Eliminations Debit | Eliminations Credit | Consolidated |
|---|---|---|---|---|---|
| Sales | 400,000 | 65,000 | | | 465,000 |
| Income from Subsidiary | 15,600 | | (13) 15,600 | | |
| Credits | 415,600 | 65,000 | | | 465,000 |
| Cost of Goods Sold | 170,000 | 29,250 | | | 199,250 |
| Operating Expenses | 90,000 | 18,850 | (18)    650 | | 109,500 |
| Foreign Currency Transaction Loss | | 650 | | | 650 |
| Debits | (260,000) | (48,750) | | | (309,400) |
| Net Income, carry forward | 155,600 | 16,250 | 16,250 | | 155,600 |
| Retained Earnings, 1/1 | 300,000 | 12,000 | (15) 12,000 | | 300,000 |
| Net Income, from above | 155,600 | 16,250 | 16,250 | | 155,600 |
| | 455,600 | 28,250 | | | 455,600 |
| Dividends Declared | (60,000) | (8,500) | | (13)   8,500 | (60,000) |
| Retained Earnings, 12/31 | 395,600 | 19,750 | 28,250 | 8,500 | 395,600 |
| Cash | 422,500 | 15,050 | | | 437,550 |
| Dollars Held by Subsidiary | | 4,200 | | | 4,200 |
| Receivables | 75,000 | 14,700 | | | 89,700 |
| Inventory | 100,000 | 7,000 | | | 107,000 |
| Land | 175,000 | | | | 175,000 |
| Plant and Equipment | 800,000 | 70,000 | | | 870,000 |
| Investment in German Co. Stock | 85,050 | | | (13)   7,100 | |
| | | | | (14) 11,000 | |
| | | | | (15) 66,000 | |
| | | | | (16)    950 | |
| Differential | | | (15)   6,000 | (17)   6,950 | |
| | | | (16)    950 | | |
| Patent | | | (17)   6,950 | (18)    650 | 6,300 |
| Debits | 1,657,550 | 110,950 | | | 1,689,750 |
| Accumulated Depreciation | 450,000 | 10,500 | | | 460,500 |
| Accounts Payable | 100,000 | 4,200 | | | 104,200 |
| Bonds Payable | 200,000 | 17,500 | | | 217,500 |
| Common Stock | 500,000 | 48,000 | (15) 48,000 | | 500,000 |
| Retained Earnings, from above | 395,600 | 19,750 | 28,250 | 8,500 | 395,600 |
| Accumulated Other Comprehensive Income, from below | 11,950 | 11,000 | 11,000 | | 11,950 |
| Credits | 1,657,550 | 110,950 | 101,150 | 101,150 | 1,689,750 |
| Accumulated Other Comp. Income, 1/1 | 0 | 0 | (15)      0 | | 0 |
| Other Comp. Income— Translation Adj. | 11,950 | 11,000 | (14) 11,000 | | 11,950 |
| Accumulated Other Comp. Income, 12/31, (credit) carry up | 11,950 | 11,000 | 11,000 | 0 | 11,950 |

Key to eliminations:

(13) Eliminate net income from subsidiary.

(14) Eliminate parent company's share of other comprehensive income from change in translation adjustment.

(15) Eliminate beginning investment account balance.

(16) Eliminate translation adjustment to differential.

(17) Assign differential to patent.

(18) Amortize patent.

| E(18) | Operating Expenses—Amortization of Patent | 650 | |
| | Patent | | 650 |
| | Amortize patent: | | |
| | $650 = €500 × $1.30 | | |

When the parent company uses the equity method and no intercompany revenue transactions occur, the parent's net income and retained earnings equal the consolidated net income and consolidated retained earnings. This makes it possible to verify the amounts reported on the consolidated financial statements.

### Noncontrolling Interest of a Foreign Subsidiary

Most U.S. companies prefer to own 100 percent of their foreign subsidiaries. Doing so provides for more efficient management of the subsidiary and no requirement to prepare separate financial statements of the subsidiary for a noncontrolling interest. If a foreign subsidiary was less-than-wholly owned, however, the noncontrolling interest would be computed and accounted for just as it was beginning in Chapter 4 of this text. The only difference is the allocation of the translation adjustment that arises from the translation of the foreign subsidiary's trial balance accounts. Thus, for example, if Peerless had an 80 percent interest in German Company and another investor owned a 20 percent noncontrolling interest, the noncontrolling interest would be allocated its percentage share of the translation adjustment through the elimination entry process. The noncontrolling interest on the consolidated balance sheet at year-end would include its share of the accumulated other comprehensive income from the translation adjustment, as follows:

| | | |
|---|---:|---:|
| Common stock ($48,000 × .20) | | $ 9,600 |
| Retained earnings: | | |
| Beginning retained earnings ($12,000 × .20) | $2,400 | |
| Add: Net income ($16,250 × .20) | 3,250 | |
| Less: Dividends ($8,500 × .20) | (1,700) | |
| Total retained earnings | | 3,950 |
| Accumulated other comprehensive income— | | |
| translation adjustment ($11,000 × .20) | | 2,200 |
| Total noncontrolling interest | | $15,750 |

## REMEASUREMENT OF THE BOOKS OF RECORD INTO THE FUNCTIONAL CURRENCY

A second method of restating foreign affiliates' financial statements in U.S. dollars is remeasurement. Although remeasurement is not as commonly used as translation, some situations in which the functional currency of the foreign affiliate is not its local currency exist. Remeasurement is similar to translation in that its goal is to obtain equivalent U.S. dollar values for the foreign affiliate's accounts so they may be combined or consolidated with the U.S. company's statements. The exchange rates used for remeasurement, however, are different from those used for translation, resulting in different dollar values for the foreign affiliate's accounts.

The FASB provided examples of several situations requiring remeasurement:[10]

1. A foreign sales branch or subsidiary of a U.S. manufacturer that primarily takes orders from foreign customers for U.S.-manufactured goods, that bills and collects from

---

[10] These examples were provided in the exposure draft of **FASB 52** but were not included in its final draft. The FASB did not want the examples to limit remeasurement to those cases in which the U.S. dollar is the functional currency.

foreign customers, and that might have a warehouse to provide for timely delivery of the product to those foreign customers. In substance, this foreign operation may be the same as the export sales department of a U.S. manufacturer.

2. A foreign division, branch, or subsidiary that primarily manufactures a subassembly shipped to a U.S. plant for inclusion in a product that is sold to customers located in the United States or in different parts of the world.

3. A foreign shipping subsidiary that primarily transports ore from a U.S. company's foreign mines to the United States for processing in a U.S. company's smelting plants.

4. A foreign subsidiary that is primarily a conduit for euro borrowings to finance operations in the United States.

In most cases, the foreign affiliate may be thought of as a direct production or sales arm of the U.S. company, but it uses the local currency to record and report its operations. In addition, foreign entities located in highly inflationary economies, defined as economies having a cumulative three-year inflation rate exceeding 100 percent, must use the dollar as their functional currency, and their statements are remeasured into U.S. dollars. Many South American countries have experienced hyperinflation, with some countries having annual inflation rates in excess of 100 percent. If the foreign affiliate uses the U.S. dollar as both its functional and its reporting currency, no remeasurement is necessary because its operations are already reported in U.S. dollars.

The remeasurement process should produce the same end result as if the foreign entity's transactions had been initially recorded in dollars. For this reason, certain transactions and account balances are restated to their U.S. dollar equivalents using a historical exchange rate, the spot exchange rate at the time the transaction originally occurred. The remeasurement process divides the balance sheet into monetary and nonmonetary accounts. Monetary assets and liabilities, such as cash, short-term or long-term receivables, and short-term or long-term payables, have their amounts fixed in terms of the units of currency. These accounts are subject to gains or losses from changes in exchange rates. Nonmonetary assets are accounts such as inventories and plant and equipment, which are not fixed in relation to monetary units.

The monetary accounts are remeasured using the current exchange rate. The appropriate historical exchange rate is used to remeasure nonmonetary balance sheet account balances and related revenue, expense, gain, and loss account balances. A list of the accounts to be remeasured with the appropriate historical exchange rate is provided in Figure 12–8.[11]

Because of the variety of rates used to remeasure the foreign currency trial balance, the debits and credits of the U.S. dollar–equivalent trial balance will probably not be equal. In this case, the balancing item is a ***remeasurement gain or loss,*** which is included in the period's income statement.

### Statement Presentation of Remeasurement Gain or Loss

Any exchange gain or loss arising from the remeasurement process is included in the current period income statement, usually under "Other Income." Various account titles are used, such as Foreign Exchange Gain (Loss), Currency Gain (Loss), Exchange Gain (Loss), or Remeasurement Gain (Loss). The title Remeasurement Gain (Loss) is used here because it is most descriptive of the source of the item. The remeasurement gain or loss is included in the period's income because if the transactions had originally been recorded in U.S. dollars, the exchange gains and losses would have been recognized this period as part of the adjustments required for valuation of foreign transactions denominated in a foreign currency. Upon completion of the remeasurement process, the foreign entity's financial statements are presented as they would have been had the U.S. dollar been used to record the transactions in the local currency as they occurred.

[11] *FASB 52,* para. 48.

**FIGURE 12–8**
**Accounts to Be Remeasured Using Historical Exchange Rates**

Source: *FASB 52*, para. 48.

Marketable securities:
  Equity securities
  Debt securities not intended to be held until maturity
Inventories
Prepaid expenses such as insurance, advertising, and rent
Property, plant, and equipment
Accumulated depreciation on property, plant, and equipment
Patents, trademarks, licenses, and formulas
Goodwill
Other intangible assets
Deferred charges and credits, except deferred income taxes and policy acquisition costs for
  life insurance companies
Deferred income
Common stock
Preferred stock carried at issuance price
Revenue and expenses related to nonmonetary items, for example:
  Cost of goods sold
  Depreciation of property, plant, and equipment
  Amortization of intangible items such as patents, licenses, etc.
  Amortization of deferred charges or credits, except deferred income taxes and policy
    acquisition costs for life insurance companies

## Illustration of Remeasurement of a Foreign Subsidiary

German Company again is used, this time to present remeasurement of financial statements. The only difference between the previous example of translation and the current example is that the foreign subsidiary's functional currency is now assumed to be the U.S. dollar rather than the European euro. German Company maintains its books and records in euros to provide required reports to the German government. Because the dollar is the functional currency, German Company's financial statements will be remeasured into dollars. Once the foreign affiliate's statements are remeasured, the consolidation process is the same as for a domestic subsidiary.

### Remeasurement of Foreign Subsidiary's Postacquisition Trial Balance

The subsidiary's trial balance must be remeasured from the European euro into the U.S. dollar as shown in Figure 12–9. The current exchange rate is used to remeasure the monetary accounts, and the appropriate historical exchange rates are used for each of the nonmonetary accounts.

Three items need special attention. First, the plant and equipment is remeasured using the historical rate on the date the parent company acquired the foreign subsidiary. If the subsidiary purchases any additional plant or equipment after the parent has acquired the subsidiary's stock, the additional plant or equipment will be remeasured using the exchange rate on the date of the purchase of the additional plant. The same cautionary note is applicable for the other nonmonetary items. It is important to maintain a record of the subsidiary's acquisition or disposition of nonmonetary assets and equities after the foreign subsidiary's stock is acquired to ensure use of the proper exchange rates to remeasure these items. Recall that the business combination was accounted for as a purchase; therefore, the appropriate historical rate is the spot rate on the date the parent purchased the foreign subsidiary's stock. If the combination had been accounted for as a pooling, the appropriate historical spot rates would be the rates on the dates the subsidiary originally issued the stock and acquired the nonmonetary assets, not the later date on which the parent company acquired the subsidiary's stock.

Second, the cost of goods sold consists of transactions that occurred at various exchange rates. The beginning inventory was acquired when the rate was $1.20 = €1. Inventory purchases were made at different times during the year, so the average rate of $1.30 was used for the remeasurement exchange rate. For purposes of illustration, the

**FIGURE 12–9**
**December 31, 20X1, Remeasurement of the Foreign Subsidiary's Trial Balance**
U.S. Dollar Is the Functional Currency

| Item | Balance, € | Exchange Rate | Balance, $ |
|---|---|---|---|
| Cash | 10,750 | 1.40 | 15,050 |
| Foreign Currency Units | 3,000 | 1.40 | 4,200 |
| Receivables | 10,500 | 1.40 | 14,700 |
| Inventory | 5,000 | 1.38 | 6,900 |
| Plant and Equipment | 50,000 | 1.20 | 60,000 |
| Cost of Goods Sold | 22,500 | (a) | 28,100 |
| Operating Expenses | 14,500 | (b) | 18,600 |
| Foreign Currency Transaction Loss | 500 | 1.30 | 650 |
| Dividends Paid | 6,250 | 1.36 | 8,500 |
| Total Debits | 123,000 | | 156,700 |
| Accumulated Depreciation | 7,500 | 1.20 | 9,000 |
| Accounts Payable | 3,000 | 1.40 | 4,200 |
| Bonds Payable | 12,500 | 1.40 | 17,500 |
| Common Stock | 40,000 | 1.20 | 48,000 |
| Retained Earnings | 10,000 | (c) | 12,000 |
| Sales | 50,000 | 1.30 | 65,000 |
| Total | 123,000 | | 155,700 |
| Remeasurement Gain | | | 1,000 |
| Total Credits | | | 156,700 |

|  | In Euros | Exchange Rate | In Dollars |
|---|---|---|---|
| (a) Cost of Goods Sold: | | | |
| Beginning Inventory | 7,500 | 1.20 | 9,000 |
| Purchases | 20,000 | 1.35 | 26,000 |
| Goods Available | 27,500 | | 35,000 |
| Less: Ending Inventory | (5,000) | 1.38 | (6,900) |
| Cost of Goods Sold | 22,500 | | 28,100 |
| (b) Operating Expenses: | | | |
| Cash Expenses | 12,000 | 1.35 | 15,600 |
| Depreciation Expense | 2,500 | 1.20 | 3,000 |
| | 14,500 | | 18,600 |

(c) Carry forward from January 1, 20X1, workpaper.

example assumes that ending inventory was acquired when the direct exchange rate was $1.38 = €1 and the FIFO inventory method is used.

Third, the operating expenses are also incurred at different exchange rates. The depreciation expense is remeasured at $1.20 = €1 because it is associated with a nonmonetary account, Plant and Equipment, which is remeasured at the historical exchange rate of $1.20 = €1. The average exchange rate is used to remeasure the remaining operating expenses because they are assumed to be incurred evenly throughout the period.

The remeasurement gain is recognized in this period's income statement. The remeasurement exchange gain is a balancing item to make total debits and total credits equal, but it can be proved by analyzing changes in the monetary items during the period. The subsequent consolidation workpaper and the proof of the remeasurement exchange gain are shown in the "Additional Considerations" section later in this chapter.

## Summary of Translation versus Remeasurement

When the functional currency is the dollar, the nonmonetary items on the balance sheet are remeasured using historical exchange rates. In this example, the direct exchange rate has increased during the period; therefore, the nonmonetary accounts are lower when remeasured than when translated. A summary of the differences between the translation and remeasurement methods is presented in Figure 12–10.

**FIGURE 12–10** **Summary of the Translation and Remeasurement Processes**

| Item | Translation Process | Remeasurement Process |
|---|---|---|
| Foreign entity's functional currency | Local currency unit | U.S. dollar |
| Method used | Current rate method | Monetary-nonmonetary method |
| Income statement accounts: | | |
|   Revenue | Weighted-average exchange rate | Weighted-average exchange rate, except revenue related to nonmonetary items (historical exchange rate) |
|   Expenses | Weighted-average exchange rate | Weighted-average exchange rate, except costs related to nonmonetary items (historical exchange rate) |
| Balance sheet accounts: | | |
|   Monetary accounts | Current exchange rate | Current exchange rate |
|   Nonmonetary accounts | Current exchange rate | Historical exchange rate |
|   Stockholders' equity capital accounts | Historical exchange rate | Historical exchange rate |
|   Retained earnings | Prior-period balance plus income less dividends | Prior-period balance plus income less dividends |
| Exchange rate adjustments arising in process | Translation adjustment accumulated in stockholders' equity | Remeasurement gain or loss included in period's income statement |

# FOREIGN INVESTMENTS AND UNCONSOLIDATED SUBSIDIARIES

Most companies consolidate their foreign subsidiaries in conformity with **FASB Statement No. 94,** "Consolidation of All Majority-Owned Subsidiaries" (FASB 94). In some cases these operations are not consolidated, because of criteria that apply to foreign subsidiaries. Generally, a parent company consolidates a foreign subsidiary, except when one of the following conditions becomes so severe that the U.S. company owning a foreign company may not be able to exercise the necessary level of economic control over the foreign subsidiary's resources and financial operations to warrant consolidation:

1. Restrictions on foreign exchange in the foreign country.
2. Restrictions on transfers of property in the foreign country.
3. Other governmentally imposed uncertainties.

An unconsolidated foreign subsidiary is reported as an investment on the U.S. parent company's balance sheet. The U.S. investor company must use the equity method if it has the ability to exercise "significant influence" over the investee's financial and operating policies. If the equity method cannot be applied, the cost method is used to account for the foreign investment, recognizing income only as dividends are received.

When the equity method is used for an unconsolidated foreign subsidiary, the investee's financial statements are either remeasured or translated, depending on the determination of the functional currency. If remeasurement is used, the foreign entity's statements are remeasured in dollars and the investor records its percentage of the investee's income and makes necessary amortizations or impairments of any differential. A shortcut approach is available for translation: Multiply the foreign affiliate's net income measured in foreign currency units by the average exchange rate during the period and then recognize the parent company's percentage share of the translated net income. In addition, the investor must recognize its share of the translation adjustment arising from the translation of the foreign entity's financial statements. The investor's share of the translation adjustment from its foreign investees is reported on the investor's balance sheet as a separate component of stockholders' equity and as an adjustment of the carrying value of the investment account. The entries on the investor's books are the same under the equity method whether the subsidiary is consolidated or reported as an unconsolidated investment.

### Liquidation of a Foreign Investment

The translation adjustment account is directly related to a company's investment in a foreign entity. If the investor sells a substantial portion of its stock investment, **FASB Interpretation No. 37,** "Accounting for Translation Adjustments upon Sale of Part of an Investment in a Foreign Entity" (FIN 37), requires that the pro rata portion of the accumulated translation adjustment account attributable to that investment be included in computing the gain or loss on the disposition of the investment. For example, if the parent company sold off 30 percent of its investment in a foreign subsidiary, 30 percent of the related cumulative translation adjustment would be removed from the translation adjustment account and included in determining the gain or loss on the disposition of the foreign investment.

## HEDGE OF A NET INVESTMENT IN A FOREIGN SUBSIDIARY

**FASB 133** permits hedging of a net investment in foreign subsidiaries. For example, Peerless has a net investment of €50,000 in its German subsidiary for which it paid $66,000. Peerless could decide to hedge all, some, or none of this investment by accepting a liability in euros. Peerless could hedge its net asset investment by contracting for a forward exchange contract to sell euros, or the company could incur a euro-based liability. **FASB 133** states that the gain or loss on the effective portion of a hedge of a net investment is taken to other comprehensive income as part of the translation adjustment. However, the amount of offset to comprehensive income is limited to the translation adjustment for the net investment. For example, if the forward exchange rate is used to measure effectiveness, the amount of offset is limited to the change in spot rates during the period. Any excess on the ineffective portion of the hedge must be recognized currently in earnings.

For example, on January 1, 20X1, Peerless decides to hedge the portion of its investment that it just made in German Company that is related to the book value of German Company's net assets. Peerless is unsure whether the direct exchange rate for euros will increase or decrease for the year and wishes to hedge its net asset investment. On January 1, 20X1, Peerless's 100 percent ownership share of German Company's net assets is equal to €50,000 (€40,000 capital stock plus €10,000 retained earnings). Peerless borrows €50,000, at a 5 percent rate of interest to hedge its equity investment in German Company, and the principal and interest are due and payable on January 1, 20X2.

The entries on Peerless's books to account for this hedge of a net investment follow:

January 1, 20X1

| | | | |
|---|---|---|---|
| (19) | Cash | 60,000 | |
| |     Loan Payable (€) | | 60,000 |
| | Borrow a euro-denominated loan to hedge | | |
| | net investment in German subsidiary: | | |
| | $60,000 = €50,000 × $1.20 spot rate | | |

December 31, 20X1

| | | | |
|---|---|---|---|
| (20) | Other Comprehensive Income | 10,000 | |
| |     Loan Payable (€) | | 10,000 |
| | Revalue foreign currency–denominated | | |
| | payable to end-of-period spot rate: | | |
| | $10,000 = €50,000 × ($1.40 − $1.20) | | |
| (21) | Interest Expense | 3,250 | |
| | Foreign Currency Transaction Loss | 250 | |
| |     Interest Payable (€) | | 3,500 |
| | Accrue interest expense and payable on euro loan: | | |
| | $3,250 = €50,000 × .05 interest × $1.30 average exchange rate | | |
| | $3,500 = €50,000 × .05 interest × $1.40 ending spot rate | | |

| (22) | Accumulated Other Comprehensive Income— | | |
|---|---|---|---|
| | Translation Adjustment | 10,000 | |
| | Profit and Loss Summary (or Retained Earnings) | 250 | |
| | Foreign Currency Transaction Loss | | 250 |
| | Other Comprehensive Income | | 10,000 |
| | Close nominal accounts related to hedge of net investment in foreign subsidiary. | | |

Then, when the principal and interest are paid on January 1, 20X2, the following entry is made:

January 1, 20X2

| (23) | Interest Payable (€) | 3,500 | |
|---|---|---|---|
| | Loan Payable (€) | 70,000 | |
| | Cash | | 73,500 |
| | Pay principal and interest due on euro-denominated hedge: $70,000 = $60,000 + $10,000 | | |

During 20X1, Peerless hedged a portion of its net asset investment in the foreign subsidiary. The dollar weakened against the euro (the direct exchange rate increased) and Peerless recognized a gain on a net asset investment in euros and a loss on a liability payable in euros. Without this hedge of the net investment, Peerless would have reported a $11,950 credit balance in the cumulative translation portion of accumulated other comprehensive income ($11,950 = $11,000 + $950 differential adjustment). With the hedge of its net investment, Peerless will report just $1,950 ($11,950 − $10,000 effect of hedge) as its change in the cumulative translation adjustment for 20X1. Thus, Peerless has balanced a portion of its net exposure on its January 1, 20X1, net asset investment in German Company.

Note also that the amount of the offset to other comprehensive income is limited to the effective portion of the hedge based on the revaluation of the net assets. Any excess, in this case the $250 loss on the revaluation of the interest payable in entry (21), is taken directly to current earnings on the income statement.

# DISCLOSURE REQUIREMENTS

**FASB 52** requires the aggregate foreign transaction gain or loss included in income to be separately disclosed in the income statement or in an accompanying note. This includes gains or losses recognized from foreign currency transactions, forward exchange contracts, and any remeasurement gain or loss. If not disclosed as a one-line item on the income statement, this disclosure is usually a one-sentence footnote summarizing the company's foreign operations.

Under the translation method, the periodic change in the translation adjustment is reported as an element of other comprehensive income, as required by **FASB 130.** Figure 12–11 presents the two-statement approach to displaying comprehensive income. The consolidated statement of comprehensive income presents the detail of the parent's other comprehensive income of $11,950. Figure 12–12 presents the statement of changes in equity that reconciles all of the elements of stockholders' equity. The balance sheet would then display the capital stock, retained earnings, and accumulated other comprehensive income in the stockholders' equity section. In addition, **FASB 52** requires footnote disclosure of exchange rate changes that occur after the balance sheet date and their effect on unsettled foreign currency transactions, if significant.

# ADDITIONAL CONSIDERATIONS IN ACCOUNTING FOR FOREIGN OPERATIONS AND ENTITIES

This section covers special topics in accounting for multinational enterprises. Although many of these additional considerations are very technical, study of this section will complement your understanding of the many issues of accounting for foreign entities.

**FIGURE 12–11** Two-Statement Approach to Display Comprehensive Income

| PEERLESS PRODUCTS AND SUBSIDIARY<br>Consolidated Statement of Income<br>Year Ended December 31, 20X1 | |
| --- | --- |
| Sales | $465,000 |
| Cost of Goods Sold | (199,250) |
| Gross Profit | 265,750 |
| Operating Expenses | (109,500) |
| Foreign Currency Transaction Loss | (650) |
| Consolidated Net Income to Controlling Interest | $155,600 |

| PEERLESS PRODUCTS AND SUBSIDIARY<br>Consolidated Statement of Comprehensive Income<br>Year Ended December 31, 20X1 | |
| --- | --- |
| Consolidated Net Income to Controlling Interest | $155,600 |
| Other Comprehensive Income: | |
| Foreign Currency Translation Adjustment | $ 11,950 |
| Comprehensive Income to Controlling Interest | $167,550 |

## Remeasurement Case: Subsequent Consolidation Workpaper

The consolidation workpaper for the remeasurement case is presented in Figure 12–13. The accounts for German Company are obtained from the remeasured accounts computed in Figure 12–9. The remeasurement gain is included in the German subsidiary's trial balance because the source of this account is the remeasurement of the subsidiary's accounts.

The Income from Subsidiary account can be proved as follows:

| Income from Subsidiary | | | |
| --- | --- | --- | --- |
| | | Parent's share of subsidiary<br>income: ($18,650 × 1.00) | 18,650 |
| Amortization of patent<br>($6,000 / 10 years) | 600 | | |
| | | Balance, 12/31/X1 | 18,050 |

**FIGURE 12–12** Consolidated Statement of Changes in Stockholders' Equity

| PEERLESS PRODUCTS AND SUBSIDIARY<br>Consolidated Statement of Changes in Equity<br>Year Ended December 31, 20X1 | | | | | |
| --- | --- | --- | --- | --- | --- |
| | Total | Comprehensive<br>Income | Retained<br>Earnings | Accumulated<br>Other<br>Comprehensive<br>Income | Capital<br>Stock |
| Beginning Balance | $800,000 | | $300,000 | $    -0- | $500,000 |
| Comprehensive Income: | | | | | |
| Net Income | 155,600 | $155,600 | 155,600 | | |
| Other Comprehensive Income: | | | | | |
| Foreign Currency Translation Adjustment | 11,950 | 11,950 | | 11,950 | |
| Comprehensive Income | | $167,550 | | | |
| Dividends Declared on Common Stock | (60,000) | | (60,000) | | |
| Ending Balance | $907,550 | | $395,600 | $11,950 | $500,000 |

**FIGURE 12–13** December 31, 20X1, Consolidation Workpaper, Prepared after Remeasurement of Foreign Statements

| Item | Peerless Products | German Company | Eliminations Debit | Eliminations Credit | Consolidated |
|---|---|---|---|---|---|
| Sales | 400,000 | 65,000 | | | 465,000 |
| Remeasurement Gain | | 1,000 | | | 1,000 |
| Income from Subsidiary | 18,050 | | (24) 18,050 | | |
| Credits | 418,050 | 66,000 | | | 466,000 |
| Cost of Goods Sold | 170,000 | 28,100 | | | 198,100 |
| Operating Expenses | 90,000 | 18,600 | (27) 600 | | 109,200 |
| Foreign Currency Transaction Loss | | 650 | | | 650 |
| Debits | (260,000) | (47,350) | | | (307,950) |
| Net Income, carry forward | 158,050 | 18,650 | 18,650 | | 158,050 |
| Retained Earnings, 1/1 | 300,000 | 12,000 | (25) 12,000 | | 300,000 |
| Net Income, from above | 158,050 | 18,650 | 18,650 | | 158,050 |
| | 458,050 | 30,650 | | | 458,050 |
| Dividends Declared | (60,000) | (8,500) | | (24) 8,500 | (60,000) |
| Retained Earnings, 12/31 | 398,050 | 22,150 | 30,650 | 8,500 | 398,050 |
| Cash | 422,500 | 15,050 | | | 437,550 |
| Dollars Held by Subsidiary | | 4,200 | | | 4,200 |
| Receivables | 75,000 | 14,700 | | | 89,700 |
| Inventory | 100,000 | 6,900 | | | 106,900 |
| Land | 175,000 | | | | 175,000 |
| Plant and Equipment | 800,000 | 60,000 | | | 860,000 |
| Investment in German Co. Stock | 75,550 | | | (24) 9,550 | |
| | | | | (25) 66,000 | |
| Differential | | | (25) 6,000 | (26) 6,000 | |
| Patent | | | (26) 6,000 | (27) 600 | 5,400 |
| Debits | 1,648,050 | 100,850 | | | 1,678,750 |
| Accumulated Depreciation | 450,000 | 9,000 | | | 459,000 |
| Accounts Payable | 100,000 | 4,200 | | | 104,200 |
| Bonds Payable | 200,000 | 17,500 | | | 217,500 |
| Common Stock | 500,000 | 48,000 | (25) 48,000 | | 500,000 |
| Retained Earnings, from above | 398,050 | 22,150 | 30,650 | 8,500 | 398,050 |
| Credits | 1,648,050 | 100,850 | 90,650 | 90,650 | 1,678,050 |

Elimination entries:
(24) Eliminate income and dividends from subsidiary.
(25) Eliminate beginning investment account balance.
(26) Assign beginning differential to patent.
(27) Amortize patent.

In the consolidated income statement, the Remeasurement Gain account is usually offset against the foreign currency transaction loss account, generating, in this example, a net gain of $350 ($1,000 − $650). This gain is reported in the other income section of the income statement.

The remaining consolidation process is identical to the process for a domestic subsidiary. Note that the $5,400 patent shown on the consolidated balance sheet is the unamortized portion of the initial $6,000 amount ($5,400 = $6,000 − $600). No special adjustments are required for the patent when using the remeasurement process.

The eliminating entries are as follows:

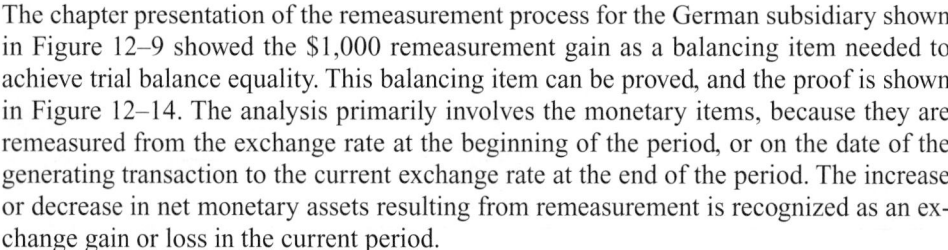

| E(24) | Income from Subsidiary | 18,050 | |
| | Dividends Declared | | 8,500 |
| | Investment in German Co. Stock | | 9,550 |
| | Eliminate income from subsidiary. | | |
| | | | |
| E(25) | Common Stock—German Co. | 48,000 | |
| | Retained Earnings, January 1, 20X1 | 12,000 | |
| | Differential | 6,000 | |
| | Investment in German Co. Stock | | 66,000 |
| | Eliminate beginning-of-period investment balance. | | |
| | | | |
| E(26) | Patent | 6,000 | |
| | Differential | | 6,000 |
| | Assign differential to patent. | | |
| | | | |
| E(27) | Operating Expenses—Amortization of Patent | 600 | |
| | Patent | | 600 |
| | Amortize patent. | | |

A comparison of Figures 12–7 and 12–13 shows that the foreign subsidiary's reported income differs between translation and remeasurement. The primary reason that subsidiary income is approximately 15 percent higher when the dollar is the functional currency ($18,650 versus $16,250 under translation) is that the U.S. dollar weakened against the European euro during the year. This results in a remeasurement gain for the subsidiary because it was transacting in the stronger currency (the euro) during the period. Furthermore, the subsidiary's cost of goods sold and operating expenses are remeasured at a lower exchange rate, resulting in a higher income.

### Proof of Remeasurement Exchange Gain

The chapter presentation of the remeasurement process for the German subsidiary shown in Figure 12–9 showed the $1,000 remeasurement gain as a balancing item needed to achieve trial balance equality. This balancing item can be proved, and the proof is shown in Figure 12–14. The analysis primarily involves the monetary items, because they are remeasured from the exchange rate at the beginning of the period, or on the date of the generating transaction to the current exchange rate at the end of the period. The increase or decrease in net monetary assets resulting from remeasurement is recognized as an exchange gain or loss in the current period.

Schedule 1 presents the net monetary positions at the beginning and end of the year. The €11,250 change in the net monetary position is the change from a net liability opening balance of €2,500 to a net monetary asset position ending balance of €8,750. Schedule 2 presents the detailed effects of exchange rate changes on the foreign entity's net monetary position during this period. The beginning net monetary position is included using the exchange rate at the beginning of the year. Then all increases and decreases in the net monetary accounts are added or deducted using the exchange rates at the time the transactions occurred. Other sources of increases or decreases in the monetary accounts would include financing and investing transactions such as purchases of plant or equipment, issuance of long-term debt, or selling stock. The computed net monetary position at the end of the year using the transaction date exchange rates ($11,250) is then compared with the year-end net monetary position using the year-end exchange rate ($12,250). Because of the increasing exchange rate, the net asset position at the year-end was higher when remeasured using the December 31, 20X1, exchange rate of $1.40. This means that the U.S. dollar–equivalent value of the net monetary assets at the end of the year increased from $11,250 to $12,250 and that a remeasurement gain of $1,000 should be recognized. If the U.S. dollar–equivalent value of the December 31, 20X1, exposed net monetary

**FIGURE 12–14**
**Proof of the Remeasurement Exchange Gain for the Year Ended December 31, 20X1**
Functional Currency Is the U.S. Dollar

| Proof of Remeasurement Gain |
| Remeasurement of German Company |
| For Year Ended December 31, 20X1 |

**Schedule 1**
**Statement of Net Monetary Positions**

|  | End of Year | Beginning of Year |
| --- | --- | --- |
| Monetary assets: |  |  |
| Cash | €10,750 | € 2,500 |
| Foreign currency units | 3,000 | -0- |
| Receivables | 10,500 | 10,000 |
| Total | €24,250 | €12,500 |
| Less: Monetary equities: |  |  |
| Accounts payable | € 3,000 | € 2,500 |
| Bonds payable | 12,500 | 12,500 |
| Total | €15,500 | €15,000 |
| Net monetary liabilities |  | €(2,500) |
| Net monetary assets | € 8,750 |  |
| Increase in net monetary assets during year | €11,250 |  |

**Schedule 2**
**Analysis of Changes in Monetary Accounts**

|  | € | Exchange Rate | U.S. $ |
| --- | --- | --- | --- |
| Exposed net monetary liability position, 1/1 | (2,500) | 1.20 | (3,000) |
| Adjustments for changes in net monetary position during year: |  |  |  |
| Increases: |  |  |  |
| From operations: |  |  |  |
| Sales | 50,000 | 1.30 | 65,000 |
| From other sources | -0- |  | -0- |
| Decreases: |  |  |  |
| From operations: |  |  |  |
| Purchases | (20,000) | 1.30 | (26,000) |
| Cash expenses | (12,000) | 1.30 | (15,600) |
| Foreign currency transaction loss | (500) | 1.30 | (650) |
| From dividends | (6,250) | 1.36 | (8,500) |
| From other uses | -0- |  | -0- |
| Net monetary position prior to remeasurementat year-end rates |  |  | 11,250 |
| Exposed net monetary asset position, 12/31 | 8,750 | 1.40 | 12,250 |
| Remeasurement gain |  |  | 1,000 |

assets position, as remeasured with the December 31 exchange rate, would have been lower than the computed value of $11,250, then a remeasurement loss would have been recognized for the reduction in the U.S. dollar–equivalent value of the net assets.

## Statement of Cash Flows

The statement of cash flows is a link between two balance sheets. Individual companies have some latitude and flexibility in preparing the statement of cash flows. A general rule is that accounts reported in the statement of cash flows should be restated in U.S. dollars using the same rates as used for balance sheet and income statement purposes. Because the average exchange rate is used in the income statement and the ending spot exchange rate (current rate) is used in the balance sheet, a balancing item for the differences in exchange rates appears in the statement of cash flows. This balancing item can be analyzed and traced to the specific accounts that generate the difference, but it does not affect the net change in the cash flow for the period.

## Lower-of-Cost-or-Market Inventory Valuation under Remeasurement

The application of the lower-of-cost-or-market rule to inventories requires special treatment when the recording currency is not the entity's functional currency and, therefore, the foreign entity's financial statements must be remeasured into the functional currency. The historical cost of inventories must first be remeasured using historical exchange rates to determine the functional currency historical cost value. Then these remeasured costs are compared with the market value of the inventories translated using the current rate. The final step is to compare the cost and market, now both in the functional currency, and to recognize any appropriate write-downs to market. The comparison is made in functional currency values, not local or recording currency values; therefore, it is possible to have a write-down appear in the functional currency statements but not on the subsidiary's books, or on the subsidiary's books but not in the consolidated statements.

To illustrate the application of the lower-of-cost-or-market method, assume that a German subsidiary acquired €5,000 of inventory when the direct exchange rate was $1.38 = €1. At the end of the year, the direct exchange rate had decreased to $1.20 = €1. The estimated net realizable value of the inventory (ceiling) is €5,500; its replacement cost is €5,000; and the net realizable value less a normal profit margin (floor) is €4,000. The valuation of the inventory is first specified in the local currency unit (euro), and then evaluated after remeasurement into its functional currency, the U.S. dollar, using the end-of-period exchange rate, as follows:

| | € | Exchange | U.S. $ |
|---|---|---|---|
| Historical cost | €5,000 | $1.38 | $6,900 |
| Net realizable value (ceiling) | €5,500 | $1.20 | $6,600 |
| Replacement cost | 5,000 | 1.20 | 6,000 |
| Net realizable value less normal profit (floor) | 4,000 | 1.20 | 4,800 |

The market value of the inventory is €5,000, or $6,000 in U.S. dollars. Note that the subsidiary recorded no write-down because the historical cost of the inventory was the same as market. However, the comparison in functional currency (U.S. dollar) values shows that the U.S. parent requires a $900 write-down to write the inventory down from its functional currency historical cost of $6,900 to its functional currency market value of $6,000.

## Intercompany Transactions

A U.S. parent or home office may have many intercompany sales or purchases transactions with its foreign affiliate that create intercompany receivables or payables. The process of translating receivables or payables denominated in a foreign currency was discussed in Chapter 11. For example, assume that a U.S. company has a foreign currency–denominated receivable from its foreign subsidiary. The U.S. company would first revalue the foreign currency–denominated receivable to its U.S. dollar equivalent value as of the date of the financial statements. After the foreign affiliate's statements have been translated or remeasured, depending on the foreign affiliate's functional currency, the intercompany payable and receivable should be at the same U.S. dollar value and can be eliminated.

**FASB 52** provides an exception when the intercompany foreign currency transactions will not be settled within the foreseeable future. These intercompany transactions may be considered part of the net investment in the foreign entity. The translation adjustments on these long-term receivables or payables are deferred and accumulated as part of the cumulative translation account. For example, a U.S. parent company may loan its German subsidiary $10,000 for which the parent does not expect repayment for the foreseeable future. Under the translation method, the dollar-denominated loan payable account of the subsidiary would first be adjusted for the effects of any changes in exchange rates during the period. Any exchange gain or loss adjustment relating to this intercompany note should be classified as part of the cumulative translation adjustment account in stockholders' equity, not in the subsidiary's net income for the period. The same result would occur whether the long-term intercompany financing was denominated in U.S. dollars or the local currency—in our example, the euro. Thus, where financing is regarded as part of the long-term investment in the foreign entity, any exchange gain or loss adjustments on that financing are accumulated in the cumulative translation adjustment account in stockholders' equity.

A particularly interesting problem arises when unrealized intercompany profits occur from transactions between the parent and foreign subsidiary. The problem is how to eliminate the profit across currencies that are changing in value relative to each other. For example, assume that the parent, Peerless Products Corporation, made a downstream sale of inventory to its German subsidiary. The goods cost the parent $10,000 but were sold to the subsidiary for €10,000 when the exchange rate was $1.30 = €1, resulting in an intercompany profit of $3,000 ($13,000 − $10,000). The goods are still in the subsidiary's inventory at the end of the year when the current exchange rate is $1.40 = €1. The relevant facts are summarized as follows:

| | Measured in U.S. Dollars | Measured in European Euros |
|---|---|---|
| Initial inventory transfer date ($1.30 = €1): | | |
|   Selling price (€10,000 × $1.30) | $13,000 | €10,000 |
|   Cost to parent | (10,000) | |
| Intercompany profit | $ 3,000 | |
| Balance sheet date ($1.40 = €1): | | |
|   Inventory translation ($14,000 = €10,000 × $1.40) | $14,000 | €10,000 |

There are two issues here:

1. At what amount should the ending inventory be shown on the consolidated balance sheet—the original intercompany transfer price of $13,000 (€10,000 × $1.30), the present equivalent exchange value of $14,000 (€10,000 × $1.40 current exchange rate), or some other amount?

2. What amount should be eliminated for the unrealized intercompany gain—the original intercompany profit of $3,000 or the balance sheet date exchange equivalent of the intercompany profit of $4,000 ($14,000 present exchange value less $10,000 original cost to parent)?

**FASB 52** provides the following guidance to answer these questions.[12]

> The elimination of intercompany profits that are attributable to sales or other transfers between entities that are consolidated, combined, or accounted for by the equity method in the enterprise's financial statements shall be based on the exchange rates at the dates of the sales or transfers. The use of reasonable approximations or averages is permitted.

[12] *FASB 52*, para. 25.

Therefore, for the example, the eliminating entry for the intercompany profit is:

| E(28) | Cost of Goods Sold | 3,000 | |
|---|---|---|---|
| | Ending Inventory | | 3,000 |
| | Elimination of unrealized intercompany | | |
| | profit based on exchange rates of date of transfer. | | |

The inventory is shown on the consolidated balance sheet at $11,000, which is a $1,000 increase over the initial cost to the parent company. This increase will result in a corresponding increase in a credit to the translation adjustment component of stockholders' equity. The FASB has stated that changes in exchange rates occurring *after* the date of the intercompany transaction are independent of the initial inventory transfer.

## Income Taxes

Interperiod tax allocation is required whenever temporary differences exist in the recognition of revenue and expenses for income statement purposes and for tax purposes. Exchange gains and losses from foreign currency transactions require the recognition of a deferred tax if they are included in income but not recognized for tax purposes in the same period.

A deferral is required for the portion of the translation adjustment related to the subsidiary's undistributed earnings that are included in the parent's income. **APB Opinion No. 23,** "Accounting for Income Taxes—Special Areas" (APB 23), presumes that a temporary difference exists for the undistributed earnings of a subsidiary unless the earnings are indefinitely reinvested in it. Deferred taxes need not be recognized if the undistributed earnings will be indefinitely reinvested in the subsidiary. However, if the parent expects eventually to receive the presently undistributed earnings of a foreign subsidiary, deferred tax recognition is required, and the tax entry recorded by the parent should include a debit to Other Comprehensive Income rather than to additional income tax, as follows:

| (29) | Other Comprehensive Income—Translation Adjustment | X,XXX | |
|---|---|---|---|
| | Deferred Taxes Payable | | X,XXX |

## Translation When a Third Currency Is the Functional Currency

There may be a few cases in which the foreign subsidiary maintains its books and records in the local currency unit but has a third currency as its functional currency. For example, assume that our subsidiary, German Company, maintains its records in its local currency, the euro. If the subsidiary conducts many of its business activities in the Swiss franc, management may conclude that the Swiss franc is the subsidiary's functional currency. If the entity's books and records are *not* expressed in its functional currency, the following two-step process must be used:

1. Remeasure the subsidiary's financial statements into the functional currency. In our example, the financial statements expressed in euros would be remeasured into Swiss francs. The remeasurement process would be the same as illustrated earlier in the chapter. The statements would now be expressed in the entity's functional currency, the Swiss franc.

2. The statements expressed in Swiss francs are then translated into U.S. dollars using the translation process illustrated in the chapter.

As indicated, this occurrence is not common in practice but is a consideration for foreign subsidiaries that have very significant business activities in a currency other than the currency of the country in which the subsidiary is physically located. This discussion indicates that it is important first to determine the foreign entity's functional currency before beginning the translation process.

## Summary of Key Concepts

The restatement of a foreign affiliate's financial statements in U.S. dollars may be made using the translation or remeasurement method, depending on the foreign entity's functional currency. Most foreign affiliates' statements are translated using the current rate method because the local currency unit is typically the functional currency. If the U.S. dollar is the functional currency, remeasurement is used to convert the foreign entity's statements from the local currency into dollars. The choice of functional currency affects the valuations of the foreign entity's accounts reported on the consolidated financial statements.

Because translation or remeasurement is performed with different exchange rates applied to balance sheet and income statement accounts, a balancing item called a "translation adjustment" or "remeasurement gain or loss" is created in the process. The translation adjustment is proportionally divided between the parent company and the noncontrolling interest. The parent company's share, adjusted for the effects from the differential paid for the investment, is reported as a component of other comprehensive income and then accumulated in the stockholders' equity section of the consolidated balance sheet. The noncontrolling interest's share is a direct adjustment to noncontrolling interest reported in the consolidated balance sheet. The remeasurement gain or loss is reported in the consolidated statement of income.

## Key Terms

| | | |
|---|---|---|
| Accumulated Other Comprehensive Income, *582* | functional currency, *577* | remeasurement, *579* |
| average rate, *577* | historical rate, *577* | remeasurement gain or loss, *594* |
| comprehensive income, *582* | International Financial Reporting Standards (IFRS) *575* | temporal method, *580* |
| current rate, *577* | other comprehensive income, *582* | translation, *579* |
| current rate method, *579* | | translation adjustment, *582* |

## Questions

**Q12-1** Why is there increasing interest in the adoption of a single set of high-quality accounting standards?

**Q12-2** Briefly discuss the International Accounting Standards Board (IASB). What is its mission? What is the composition of the membership of the Board and how long do members serve? Where is the IASB located?

**Q12-3** The IASB promulgates International Financial Reporting Standards (IFRS). Briefly describe the standard-setting process used by the IASB.

**Q12-4** How widely used are IFRS? Can IFRS be used for listings on U.S. stock exchanges?

**Q12-5** What is the attitude toward the possible use of IFRS in the United States?

**Q12-6** What potential benefits might be achieved if U.S. firms are allowed to use IFRS?

**Q12-7** Define the following terms: (*a*) local currency unit, (*b*) recording currency, and (*c*) reporting currency.

**Q12-8** What factors are used to determine a reporting entity's functional currency? Provide at least one example for which a company's local currency may not be its functional currency.

**Q12-9** Some accountants are seeking to harmonize international accounting standards. What is meant by the term *harmonize?* How might harmonization result in better financial reporting for a U.S. parent company with many foreign investments?

**Q12-10** A Canadian-based subsidiary of a U.S. parent uses the Canadian dollar as its functional currency. Describe the methodology for translating the subsidiary's financial statements into the parent's reporting currency.

**Q12-11** A U.S. company has a foreign sales branch located in Spain. The Spanish branch has selected the U.S. dollar for its functional currency. Describe the methodology for remeasuring the branch's financial statements into the U.S. company's reporting currency.

**Q12-12** Discuss the accounting treatment and disclosure of translation adjustments. When does the translation adjustment account have a debit balance? When does it have a credit balance?

**Q12-13** Where is the remeasurement gain or loss shown in the consolidated financial statements?

**Q12-14** When the functional currency is the foreign affiliate's local currency, why are the stockholders' equity accounts translated at historical exchange rates? How is retained earnings computed?

**Q12-15** Comment on the following statement: "The use of the current exchange rate method of translating a foreign affiliate's financial statements allows for an assessment of foreign management by the same ratio criteria used to manage the foreign affiliate."

**Q12-16** A U.S. company paid more than book value in acquiring a foreign affiliate. How is this excess reported in the consolidated balance sheet and income statement in subsequent periods when the functional currency is the local currency unit of the foreign affiliate?

**Q12-17** What is the logic behind the parent company's recognizing on its books its share of the translation adjustment arising from the translation of its foreign subsidiary?

**Q12-18** Are all foreign subsidiaries consolidated? Why or why not?

**Q12-19** Describe the accounting for a foreign investment that is not consolidated with the U.S. company.

**Q12-20** Describe the basic problem of eliminating intercompany transactions with a foreign affiliate.

---

# Cases

### C12-1 Comparison of U.S. GAAP and IFRS

*Research*

PricewaterhouseCoopers offers a publication on its Web site entitled "Similarities and Differences—A Comparison of IFRS and U.S. GAAP" that provides a topic-based comparison. Access this publication on the Web at http://www.pwc.com/extweb/pwcpublications.nsf/docid/74d6c 09e0a4ee610802569a1003354c8. On pages 4–11 of this publication, there is a table of differences between U.S GAAP and IFRS by reporting issue. There is also a reference to the pages in the document where each of these items is explained in more detail. Select any three of the items and read about the nature of the differences. Prepare a short paper approximately 2–3 pages long that defines the nature of the differences and discusses what you have found.

### C12-2 Structure of the IASB

*Research*

The IASB Web site can be found at www.iasb.org. At the top of the page, click on the link "About Us." Briefly describe the structure of the IASB.

### C12-3 IASB Deliberations

*Research*

The IASB Web site can be found at www.iasb.org. Access the Web site and click on the link at the top of the page for Current Projects. On the Current Projects page, click on the IASB link. You may also access this page by going directly to http://www.iasb.org/Current+Projects/IASB+ Projects/IASB+Work+Plan.htm. What are three projects currently on the active agenda that are being addressed by the IASB? What is the timetable identified for milestones on each of the projects? What is the status of the Conceptual Framework project?

### C12-4 Determining a Functional Currency

Following are descriptions of several independent situations.

*Judgment*

1. Rockford Company has a subsidiary in Argentina. The subsidiary does not have much debt because of the high interest costs resulting from the average annual inflation rate exceeding 100 percent. Most of its sales and expense transactions are denominated in Argentinian pesos, and the subsidiary attempts to minimize its receivables and payables. Although the subsidiary owns a warehouse, the primary asset is inventory that it receives from Rockford. The Argentinian government requires all companies located in Argentina to provide the central government with a financial report using the Argentinian system of accounts and government-mandated forms for financial statements.

2. JRB International located in Dallas, Texas, is the world's largest manufacturer of electronic stirrups. The company acquires the raw materials for its products from around the world and begins the assembly process in Dallas. It then sends the partially completed units to its subsidiary in Mexico for assembly completion. Mexico has been able to hold its inflation rate under 100 percent over the last three years. The subsidiary is required to pay its employees and local vendors in Mexican pesos. The parent company provides all financing for the Mexican subsidiary, and the subsidiary sends all of its production back to the warehouse in Dallas, from which it is shipped as orders are received. The subsidiary provides the Mexican government with financial statements.

3. Huskie Inc. maintains a branch office in Great Britain. The branch office is fairly autonomous because it must find its own financing, set its own local marketing policies, and control its own costs. The branch receives weekly shipments from Huskie Inc., which it then conveys to its customers. The pound sterling is used to pay the subsidiary's employees and to pay for the weekly shipments.

4. Hola Company has a foreign subsidiary located in a rural area of Switzerland, right next to the Swiss–French border. The subsidiary hires virtually all its employees from France and makes most of its sales to companies in France. The majority of its cash transactions are maintained in the European euro. However, it is required to pay local property taxes and sales taxes in Swiss francs and to provide annual financial statements to the Swiss government.

### Required

For each of these independent cases, determine:

*a.* The foreign entity's reporting currency in which its books and records are maintained.

*b.* The foreign entity's functional currency.

*c.* The process to be used to restate the foreign entity's financial statements into the reporting currency of the U.S.-based parent company.

**C12-5**   **Principles of Consolidating and Translating Foreign Accounts [AICPA Adapted]**

Petie Products Company was incorporated in Wisconsin in 20X0 as a manufacturer of dairy supplies and equipment. Since incorporating, Petie has doubled in size about every three years and is now considered one of the leading dairy supply companies in the country.

*Understanding*   During January 20X4, Petie established a subsidiary, Cream Ltd., in the emerging nation of Kolay. Petie owns 90 percent of the outstanding capital stock of Cream; Kolay citizens hold the remaining 10 percent of Cream's outstanding capital stock, as Kolay law requires. The investment in Cream, accounted for by Petie using the equity method, represents about 18 percent of Petie's total assets at December 31, 20X7, the close of the accounting period for both companies.

### Required

*a.* What criteria should Petie use in determining whether it would be appropriate to prepare consolidated financial statements with Cream Ltd. for the year ended December 31, 20X7? Explain.

*b.* Independent of your answer to part *a,* assume it has been appropriate for Petie and Cream to prepare consolidated financial statements for each year, 20X4 through 20X7. Before they can be prepared, the individual account balances in Cream's December 31, 20X7, adjusted trial balance must be translated into dollars. The kola (K) is the subsidiary's functional currency. For each of the following 10 accounts, taken from Cream's adjusted trial balance, specify what exchange rate (e.g., average exchange rate for 20X7, current exchange rate on December 31, 20X7) should be used to translate the account balance into dollars and explain why that rate is appropriate. Number your answers to correspond with these accounts.

(1) Cash in Kolay National Bank.

(2) Trade Accounts Receivable (all from 20X7 revenue).

(3) Supplies Inventory (all purchased during the last quarter of 20X7).

(4) Land purchased in 20X4.

(5) Short-Term Note Payable to Kolay National Bank.

(6) Capital Stock (no par or stated value and all issued in January 20X4).

(7) Retained Earnings, January 1, 20X7.

(8) Sales Revenue.

(9) Depreciation Expense (on buildings).

(10) Salaries Expense.

**C12-6**   **Translating and Remeasuring Financial Statements of Foreign Subsidiaries [AICPA Adapted]**

*Communication*   Wahl Company's 20X5 consolidated financial statements include two wholly owned subsidiaries, Wahl Company of Australia (Wahl A) and Wahl Company of France (Wahl F). Functional currencies are the U.S. dollar for Wahl A and the European euro for Wahl F.

### Required

*a.* What are the objectives of translating a foreign subsidiary's financial statements?

*b.* How are gains and losses arising from the translation or remeasurement of each subsidiary's financial statements measured and reported in Wahl's consolidated financial statements?

*c.* FASB Statement No. 52 identifies several economic indicators to be considered both individually and collectively in determining the functional currency for a consolidated subsidiary. List three of these indicators.

*d.* What exchange rate is used to incorporate each subsidiary's equipment cost, accumulated depreciation, and depreciation expense in Wahl's consolidated financial statements?

**C12-7** **Translation Adjustment and Comprehensive Income**

*Analysis*

Dundee Company owns 100 percent of a subsidiary located in Ireland. The parent company uses the Irish pound as the subsidiary's functional currency. At the beginning of the year, the debit balance in Accumulated Other Comprehensive Income—Translation Adjustment account, which was the only item in accumulated other comprehensive income, was $80,000. The subsidiary's translated trial balance at the end of the year is as follows:

| | Debit | Credit |
|---|---|---|
| Cash | $ 50,000 | |
| Receivables | 24,700 | |
| Inventories | 60,300 | |
| Property, Plant, and Equipment (net) | 328,000 | |
| Cost of Sales | 285,000 | |
| Operating Expenses (including depreciation) | 140,000 | |
| Dividends | 12,000 | |
| Current Payables | | $ 16,000 |
| Long-Term Payables | | 181,000 |
| Capital Stock | | 100,000 |
| Retained Earnings (1/1 balance) | | 135,000 |
| Sales | | 560,000 |
| Accumulated Other Comprehensive Income—Translation Adjustment | 92,000 | |
| | $992,000 | $992,000 |

### Required

*a.* Prepare the subsidiary's statement of income, ending in net income, for the year.

*b.* Prepare the subsidiary's statement of comprehensive income for the year.

*c.* Prepare a year-end balance sheet for the subsidiary.

*d.* FASB 130 allows for alternative operating statement displays of the other comprehensive income items. Discuss the major differences between the one-statement format of the Statement of Income and Comprehensive Income versus the two-statement format of the Statement of Income with a separate Statement of Comprehensive Income.

**C12-8** **Changes in the Cumulative Translation Adjustment Account**

The following footnote was abstracted from a recent annual report of Johnson & Johnson Company:

Footnote 7: Foreign Currency Translation
For translation of its international currencies, the Company has determined that the local currencies of its international subsidiaries are the functional currencies except those in highly inflationary economies, which are defined as those which have had compound cumulative rates of inflation of 100% or more during the last three years.

*Understanding*

In consolidating international subsidiaries, balance sheet currency effects are recorded as a separate component of stockholders' equity. This equity account includes the results of translating all balance sheet assets and liabilities at current exchange rates, except those located in highly inflationary economies, principally Brazil, which are reflected in operating results. These translation adjustments do not exist in terms of functional cash flows; such adjustments are not reported as part of operating results since realization is remote unless the international businesses were sold or liquidated.

An analysis of the changes during 20X3 and 20X2 in the separate component of stockholders' equity for foreign currency translation adjustments follows (with debit amounts in parentheses):

| (Dollars in Millions) | 20X3 | 20X2 |
|---|---|---|
| Balance at beginning of year | $(146) | $ 134 |
| Change in translation adjustments | (192) | (280) |
| Balance at end of year | $(338) | $(146) |

### Required

*a.* What is the main point of the footnote?

*b.* How is the footnote related to the concepts covered in the chapter?

*c.* List some possible reasons the company's translation adjustment decreased from a $134 million credit balance at the end of 20X1 to a $338 million debit balance at the end of 20X3.

*d.* Assume that the translated stockholders' equities of the foreign subsidiaries, other than the cumulative translation adjustment, remained constant from 20X1 through 20X3 at a balance of $500 million. What were the translated balances in the net assets (assets minus liabilities) of the foreign subsidiaries in each of the three years? What factors might cause the changes in the balances of the net assets over the three-year period?

*e.* How would changes in the local currency unit's exchange rate in the countries in which the company has subsidiaries affect the cumulative translation adjustment?

*f.* How could you verify the actual causal factors for the changes in the cumulative translation adjustment of Johnson & Johnson Company for the years presented? Be specific!

**C12-9**   **Pros and Cons of Foreign Investment**

Many larger U.S. companies have significant investments in foreign operations. For example, McDonald's Corporation, the food service company, obtains 47 percent of its consolidated revenues and 44 percent of its operating income from, and has 45 percent of its invested assets in, non-U.S. locations. Unisys, the information systems company, obtains 51 percent of its consolidated revenues and 65 percent of its operating income from, and has 40 percent of its invested assets in, non-U.S. locations. Foreign operations impose additional types of operating risks to companies, including the risks from changes in the exchange rates for currencies, statutory acts by the foreign governments, and producing and marketing goods in an environment outside the United States.

*Judgment*

With the passage of the North American Free Trade Agreement (NAFTA), more companies are confronted with the decision of whether or not to expand their production and marketing investments to Canada and Mexico.

### Required

Using NAFTA as a discussion focus, address the following questions:

*a.* Explain why a U.S. company might find it advantageous to increase its production capacity of its subsidiaries in Mexico. Describe some circumstances under which it would be disadvantageous for a U.S. company to increase its investment in production subsidiaries located in Mexico.

*b.* In your opinion, would an increase in U.S. companies' investments in Mexico and Canada be good or bad for U.S. consumers?

*c.* What are some possible solutions to the possible problem of an increase in the U.S. unemployment rate if U.S. companies shift their production facilities to non-U.S. locations? Select one and discuss the pros and cons of that possible solution.

*d.* What conclusion can you draw from the attempts of the U.S. government to decrease barriers to international trade and investment? In your opinion, is this a good effort on the part of the government, or do you feel this effort should be changed?

**C12-10**   **Determining an Entity's Functional Currency**

Maxima Corporation, a U.S. company, manufactures lighting fixtures and ceiling fans. Eight years ago, it set up a subsidiary in Mexico to manufacture three of its most popular ceiling fan models. When the subsidiary, Luz Maxima, was set up, it did business exclusively with Maxima, receiving shipments of materials from U.S. suppliers selected by Maxima and selling all of its production to Maxima. Maxima's management made a determination that its subsidiary's functional currency was the U.S. dollar.

During the past five years changes in Luz Maxima's operations have occurred. The subsidiary has developed relationships with suppliers within Mexico and is obtaining a significant percentage of its materials requirements from these suppliers. In addition, Luz Maxima has expanded its production by introducing a new product line marketed within Mexico and Central America. These products now make up a substantial percentage of the subsidiary's sales. Luz Maxima obtained long-term debt financing and a line of credit from several Mexican banks to expand its operations.

Prior to the preparation of Maxima's consolidated financial statements for the current year, Luz Maxima's financial statements, reported in Mexican pesos, must be converted into U.S. dollars. Maxima's CFO, Garry Parise, is concerned that Luz Maxima's functional currency may no longer be the U.S. dollar and that remeasurement of its financial statements may not be appropriate.

***Research
FARS***

### Required

Obtain the most current accounting standards on determining an entity's functional currency. You can obtain access to accounting standards through the Financial Accounting Research System (FARS), from your library, or from some other source. Garry has asked you, as an accountant in the controller's department, to research the functional currency issue. Write a memo to him, reporting on the results of your research. Support your recommendations with citations and quotations from the authoritative financial reporting standards.

**C12-11** ### Accounting for the Translation Adjustment

Sonoma Company has owned 100 percent of the outstanding common stock of Valencia Corporation, a Spanish subsidiary, for the past 15 years. The Spanish company's functional currency is the peso, and its financial statements are translated into U.S. dollars prior to consolidation.

In the current year, Sonoma has sold 30 percent of Valencia's voting common stock to a nonaffiliated company. Sonoma's controller, Renee Voll, has calculated a gain on the sale of this portion of its investment in Valencia. The consolidated balance sheet at the end of last year contained a debit balance cumulative translation adjustment related to the Spanish subsidiary. Voll believes that the decrease in Sonoma's share of Valencia's translation adjustment will be automatically included in other comprehensive income as the year-end translation adjustment is calculated and that Sonoma's share is included in the consolidated financial statements. However, she has asked you, as an accountant in her department, to research the accounting for the translation adjustment as a result of the sale of a part of the investment in the Spanish subsidiary.

***Research
FARS***

### Required

Obtain the most current accounting standards on accounting for the translation adjustment resulting from translating the trial balance of a foreign affiliate. You can obtain access to accounting standards through the Financial Accounting Research System (FARS), from your library, or from some other source. Write a memo to Renee reporting on the results of your research. Support your recommendations with citations and quotations from the authoritative financial reporting standards.

## Exercises

**E12-1** ### Multiple-Choice Questions on Translation and Remeasurement [AICPA Adapted]

For each of the seven cases presented below, work the case twice and select the best answer. First assume that the foreign currency is the functional currency; then assume that the U.S. dollar is the functional currency.

1. Certain balance sheet accounts in a foreign subsidiary of Shaw Company on December 31, 20X1, have been restated in United States dollars as follows:

| | Restated at | |
|---|---|---|
| | **Current Rates** | **Historical Rates** |
| Accounts Receivable, Current | $100,000 | $110,000 |
| Accounts Receivable, Long-Term | 50,000 | 55,000 |
| Prepaid Insurance | 25,000 | 30,000 |
| Patents | 40,000 | 45,000 |
| Total | $215,000 | $240,000 |

What total should be included in Shaw's balance sheet for December 31, 20X1, for the above items?

a. $215,000.

b. $225,000.

c. $230,000.

d. $240,000.

2. A wholly owned foreign subsidiary of Nick Inc. has certain expense accounts for the year ended December 31, 20X4, stated in local currency units (LCU) as follows:

| | LCU |
|---|---|
| Depreciation of Equipment (related assets were purchased January 1, 20X2) | 120,000 |
| Provision for Uncollectible Accounts | 80,000 |
| Rent | 200,000 |

The exchange rates at various dates were as follows:

| | Dollar Equivalent of 1 LCU |
|---|---|
| January 1, 20X2 | $.50 |
| December 31, 20X4 | .40 |
| Average, 20X4 | .44 |

What total dollar amount should be included in Nick's statement of income to reflect the preceding expenses for the year ended December 31, 20X4?

a. $160,000.

b. $168,000.

c. $176,000.

d. $183,200.

3. Linser Corporation owns a foreign subsidiary with 2,600,000 local currency units (LCU) of property, plant, and equipment before accumulated depreciation on December 31, 20X4. Of this amount, 1,700,000 LCU were acquired in 20X2 when the rate of exchange was 1.5 LCU = $1, and 900,000 LCU were acquired in 20X3 when the rate of exchange was 1.6 LCU = $1. The rate of exchange in effect on December 31, 20X4, was 1.9 LCU = $1. The weighted average of exchange rates that were in effect during 20X4 was 1.8 LCU = $1. Assuming that the property, plant, and equipment are depreciated using the straight-line method over a 10-year period with no salvage value, how much depreciation expense relating to the foreign subsidiary's property, plant, and equipment should be charged in Linser's statement of income for 20X4?

a. $144,444.

b. $162,000.

c. $169,583.

d. $173,333.

4. On January 1, 20X1, Pat Company formed a foreign subsidiary. On February 15, 20X1, Pat's subsidiary purchased 100,000 local currency units (LCU) of inventory. Of the original inventory purchased on February 15, 20X1, 25,000 LCU made up the entire inventory on December 31, 20X1. The exchange rates were 2.2 LCU = $1 from January 1, 20X1, to June 30, 20X1, and 2 LCU = $1 from July 1, 20X1, to December 31, 20X1. The December 31, 20X1, inventory balance for Pat's foreign subsidiary should be restated in U.S. dollars in the amount of:

a. $10,500.

b. $11,364.

c. $11,905.

d. $12,500.

5. At what rates should the following balance sheet accounts in the foreign currency financial statements be restated into U.S. dollars?

| | Equipment | Accumulated Depreciation of Equipment |
|---|---|---|
| a. | Current | Current |
| b. | Current | Average for year |
| c. | Historical | Current |
| d. | Historical | Historical |

6. A credit-balancing item resulting from the process of restating a foreign entity's financial statement from the local currency unit to U.S. dollars should be included as a (an):

 a. Separate component of stockholders' equity.

 b. Deferred credit.

 c. Component of income from continuing operations.

 d. Extraordinary item.

7. A foreign subsidiary of the Bart Corporation has certain balance sheet accounts on December 31, 20X2. Information relating to these accounts in U.S. dollars is as follows:

| | Restated at | |
|---|---|---|
| | Current Rates | Historical Rates |
| Marketable Securities | $ 75,000 | $ 85,000 |
| Inventories, carried at average cost | 600,000 | 700,000 |
| Refundable Deposits | 25,000 | 30,000 |
| Goodwill | 55,000 | 70,000 |
| | $755,000 | $885,000 |

What total should be included in Bart's balance sheet on December 31, 20X2, as a result of the preceding information?

 a. $755,000.

 b. $780,000.

 c. $870,000.

 d. $880,000.

**E12-2** **Multiple-Choice Questions on Translation and Foreign Currency Transactions [AICPA Adapted]**

The following information should be used for questions 1, 2, and 3: Select the best answers under each of two alternative assumptions: (a) the LCU is the functional currency and the translation method is appropriate or (b) the U.S. dollar is the functional currency and the remeasurement method is appropriate.

1. Refer to the preceding requirements. Gate Inc. had a credit adjustment of $30,000 for the year ended December 31, 20X2, from restating its foreign subsidiary's accounts from their local currency units into U.S. dollars. Additionally, Gate had a receivable from a foreign customer payable in the customer's local currency. On December 31, 20X1, this receivable for 200,000 local currency units (LCU) was correctly included in Gate's balance sheet at $110,000. When the receivable was collected on February 15, 20X2, the U.S. dollar equivalent was $120,000. In Gate's 20X2 consolidated statement of income, how much should be reported as foreign exchange gain in computing net income?

 a. $0.

 b. $10,000.

 c. $30,000.

 d. $40,000.

2. Refer to the preceding requirements. Bar Corporation had a realized foreign exchange loss of $13,000 for the year ended December 31, 20X2, and must also determine whether the following items will require year-end adjustment:

(1) Bar had a $7,000 credit resulting from the restatement in dollars of the accounts of its wholly owned foreign subsidiary for the year ended December 31, 20X2.

(2) Bar had an account payable to an unrelated foreign supplier payable in the supplier's local currency. The U.S. dollar–equivalent of the payable was $60,000 on the October 31, 20X2, invoice date and $64,000 on December 31, 20X2. The invoice is payable on January 30, 20X3.

What amount of the net foreign exchange loss in computing net income should be reported in Bar's 20X2 consolidated statement of income?

   *a.* $6,000.
   *b.* $10,000.
   *c.* $13,000.
   *d.* $17,000.

3. Refer to the preceding requirements. The balance in Simpson Corp.'s foreign exchange loss account was $15,000 on December 31, 20X2, before any necessary year-end adjustment relating to the following:

(1) Simpson had a $20,000 debit resulting from the restatement in dollars of the accounts of its wholly owned foreign subsidiary for the year ended December 31, 20X2.

(2) Simpson had an account payable to an unrelated foreign supplier, payable in the supplier's local currency on January 27, 20X3. The U.S. dollar–equivalent of the payable was $100,000 on the November 28, 20X2, invoice date, and $106,000 on December 31, 20X2.

In Simpson's 20X2 consolidated income statement, what amount should be included as foreign exchange loss in computing net income?

   *a.* $41,000.
   *b.* $35,000.
   *c.* $21,000.
   *d.* $15,000.

4. When remeasuring foreign currency financial statements into the functional currency, which of the following items would be remeasured using a historical exchange rate?

   *a.* Inventories carried at cost.
   *b.* Trading securities carried at market values.
   *c.* Bonds payable.
   *d.* Accrued liabilities.

5. A foreign subsidiary's functional currency is its local currency, which has not experienced significant inflation. The weighted-average exchange rate for the current year would be the appropriate exchange rate for translating:

|      | Sales to Customers | Wages Expense |
|------|--------------------|---------------|
| *a.* | No                 | No            |
| *b.* | Yes                | Yes           |
| *c.* | No                 | Yes           |
| *d.* | Yes                | No            |

6. The functional currency of Dahl Inc.'s subsidiary is the European euro. Dahl borrowed euros as a partial hedge of its investment in the subsidiary. In preparing consolidated financial statements, Dahl's debit balance of its translation adjustment exceeded its exchange gain on the borrowing. How should the translation adjustment and the exchange gain be reported in Dahl's consolidated financial statements?

   *a.* The translation adjustment should be netted against the exchange gain, and the excess translation adjustment should be reported in the stockholders' equity section of the balance sheet.
   *b.* The translation adjustment should be netted against the exchange gain, and the excess translation adjustment should be reported in the statement of income in computing net income.

    *c.* The translation adjustment is reported as a component of other comprehensive income and then accumulated in the stockholders' equity section of the balance sheet, and the exchange gain should be reported in the statement of income in computing net income.

    *d.* The translation adjustment should be reported in the statement of income, and the exchange gain should be reported separately in the stockholders' equity section of the balance sheet.

**E12-3**   **Matching Key Terms**

Match the descriptions of terms on the left with the terms on the right. Some terms may be used once, more than once, or not at all.

| Descriptions of Terms | Terms |
|---|---|
| 1. The group that has attempted to harmonize the world's many different accounting methods. | A. Financial Accounting Standards Board |
| 2. The currency of the primary economic environment in which the entity operates. | B. Remeasurement gain or loss |
| 3. The functional currency for a U.S. subsidiary located in a country with > 100 percent inflation over the last three years. | C. Translation adjustment |
| 4. Translation of all assets and liabilities of a foreign subsidiary using the foreign exchange rate at the balance sheet date. | D. Current rate method |
| 5. Restatement of the fixed assets and inventories of a foreign subsidiary into U.S. dollars using historical exchange rates. | E. Remeasurement method |
| 6. Inclusion of this gain or loss on the U.S. company's statement of income as part of net income. | F. U.S. dollar |
| 7. The item that balances the debits and credits of the foreign subsidiary's adjusted trial balance in U.S. dollars, assuming the functional currency is the currency of the foreign subsidiary's country. | G. Functional currency |
| 8. The item that balances the debits and credits of the foreign subsidiary's adjusted trial balance in U.S. dollars, assuming the functional currency is the U.S. dollar. | H. International Accounting Standards Board |
| 9. Translation of the statement of income accounts of a foreign subsidiary using the average exchange rate for the year. | I. International Managerial Accounting Society |
| 10. Restatement of depreciation expense and cost of goods sold of a foreign subsidiary using historical exchange rates. | J. Functional currency indicators |
| 11. An analysis of a foreign subsidiary's cash flows, sales prices, sales markets, expenses, and financing. | K. Historical rate method |
| 12. The periodic change in this item reported as a component of other comprehensive income. | L. Cumulative transaction gain or loss |

**E12-4**   **Multiple-Choice Questions on Translation and Remeasurement**

Use the following information for questions 1, 2, and 3.

Bartell Inc., a U.S. company, acquired 90 percent of the common stock of a Malaysian company on January 1, 20X5, for $160,000. The net assets of the Malaysian subsidiary amounted to 680,000 ringitts (RM) on the date of acquisition. On January 1, 20X5, the book values of the Malaysian subsidiary's identifiable assets and liabilities approximated their fair values. Exchange rates at various dates during 20X5 follow:

| | |
|---|---|
| January 1 | RM 1 = $.21 |
| December 31 | RM 1 = $.24 |
| Average for 20X5 | RM 1 = $.22 |

1. Refer to the preceding information. On January 1, 20X5, how much goodwill was acquired by Bartell?

    *a.* $17,200.

    *b.* $31,480.

    *c.* $11,400.

    *d.* $25,360.

2. Refer to the preceding information. Assume that Bartell acquired $10,500 of goodwill on January 1, 20X5, and the goodwill suffered a 10 percent impairment loss in 20X5. If the functional currency is the Malaysian ringgit, how much goodwill impairment loss should be reported on Bartell's consolidated statement of income for 20X5?

   a. $1,050.

   b. $1,200.

   c. $1,100.

   d. $1,175.

3. Refer to the preceding information but now assume that the U.S. dollar is the functional currency. How much goodwill impairment loss should be reported on Bartell's consolidated statement of income in this situation?

   a. $1,050.

   b. $1,200.

   c. $1,100.

   d. $1,175.

Use the following information for questions 4, 5, 6, and 7.

Mondell Inc., a U.S. company, acquired 100 percent of the common stock of a German company on January 1, 20X5, for $402,000. The German subsidiary's net assets amounted to 300,000 euros on the date of acquisition. On January 1, 20X5, the book values of its identifiable assets and liabilities approximated their fair values. As a result of an analysis of functional currency indicators, Mondell determined that the euro was the functional currency. On December 31, 20X5, the German subsidiary's adjusted trial balance, translated into U.S. dollars, contained $12,000 more debits than credits. The German subsidiary reported income of 25,000 euros for 20X5 and paid a cash dividend of 5,000 euros on November 30, 20X5. Included on the German subsidiary's income statement was depreciation expense of 2,500 euros. Mondell uses the basic equity method of accounting for its investment in the German subsidiary and determined that goodwill in the first year had an impairment loss of 10 percent of its initial amount. Exchange rates at various dates during 20X5 follow:

| | |
|---|---|
| January 1 | €1 = $1.20 |
| November 30 | €1 = 1.30 |
| December 31 | €1 = 1.32 |
| Average for 20X5 | €1 = 1.24 |

4. Refer to the preceding information. What amount should Mondell record as "income from subsidiary" based on the German subsidiary's reported net income?

   a. $31,000.

   b. $31,100.

   c. $33,000.

   d. $30,000.

5. Refer to the preceding information. The receipt of the dividend will result in:

   a. A credit to the investment account for $6,200.

   b. A debit to the income from subsidiary account for $6,600.

   c. A credit to the investment account for $6,600.

   d. A credit to the investment account for $6,500.

6. Refer to the preceding information. On Mondell's consolidated balance sheet at December 31, 20X5, what amount should be reported for the goodwill acquired on January 1, 20X5?

   a. $37,660.

   b. $37,800.

   c. $41,580.

   d. $39,880.

7. Refer to the preceding information. In the stockholders' equity section of Mondell's consolidated balance sheet at December 31, 20X5, Mondell should report the translation adjustment as a component of other comprehensive income of:

   a. $12,000.

   b. $15,920.

   c. $13,400.

   d. $8,080.

### E12-5 Translation

On January 1, 20X1, Popular Creek Corporation organized RoadTime Company as a subsidiary in Switzerland with an initial investment cost of Swiss francs (SFr) 60,000. RoadTime's December 31, 20X1, trial balance in SFr is as follows:

| | Debit | Credit |
|---|---|---|
| Cash | SFr 7,000 | |
| Accounts Receivable (net) | 20,000 | |
| Receivable from Popular Creek | 5,000 | |
| Inventory | 25,000 | |
| Plant and Equipment | 100,000 | |
| Accumulated Depreciation | | SFr 10,000 |
| Accounts Payable | | 12,000 |
| Bonds Payable | | 50,000 |
| Common Stock | | 60,000 |
| Sales | | 150,000 |
| Cost of Goods Sold | 70,000 | |
| Depreciation Expense | 10,000 | |
| Operating Expense | 30,000 | |
| Dividends Paid | 15,000 | |
| Total | SFr 282,000 | SFr 282,000 |

### Additional Information

1. The receivable from Popular Creek is denominated in Swiss francs. Popular Creek's books show a $4,000 payable to RoadTime.

2. Purchases of inventory goods are made evenly during the year. Items in the ending inventory were purchased November 1.

3. Equipment is depreciated by the straight-line method with a 10-year life and no residual value. A full year's depreciation is taken in the year of acquisition. The equipment was acquired on March 1.

4. The dividends were declared and paid on November 1.

5. Exchange rates were as follows:

   | | |
   |---|---|
   | January 1 | SFr1 = $.73 |
   | March 1 | SFr1 = .74 |
   | November 1 | SFr1 = .77 |
   | December 31 | SFr1 = .80 |
   | 20X1 Average | SFr1 = .75 |

6. The Swiss franc is the functional currency.

### Required

Prepare a schedule translating the December 31, 20X1, trial balance from Swiss francs to dollars.

### E12-6 Proof of Translation Adjustment

Refer to the data in Exercise E12-5.

### Required

*a.* Prepare a proof of the translation adjustment computed in Exercise E12-5.

*b.* Where is the translation adjustment reported on Popular Creek's consolidated financial statements and its foreign subsidiary?

### E12-7  Remeasurement

Refer to the data in Exercise E12-5, but assume that the dollar is the functional currency for the foreign subsidiary.

### Required

Prepare a schedule remeasuring the December 31, 20X1, trial balance from Swiss francs to dollars.

### E12-8*  Proof of Remeasurement Gain (Loss)

Refer to the data in Exercises E12-5 and E12-7.

### Required

*a.* Prepare a proof of the remeasurement gain or loss computed in Exercise E12-7.

*b.* How should this remeasurement gain or loss be reported on Popular Creek's consolidated financial statements and the financial statements of its foreign subsidiary?

### E12-9  Translation with Strengthening U.S. Dollar

Refer to the data in Exercise E12-5, but now assume that the exchange rates were as follows:

| | |
|---|---|
| January 1 | SFr1 = $.80 |
| March 1 | SFr1 =  .77 |
| November 1 | SFr1 =  .74 |
| December 31 | SFr1 =  .73 |
| 20X1 Average | SFr1 =  .75 |

The receivable from Popular Creek Corporation is denominated in Swiss francs. Popular Creek's books show a $3,650 payable to RoadTime.

Assume the Swiss franc is the functional currency.

### Required

*a.* Prepare a schedule translating the December 31, 20X1, trial balance from Swiss francs to dollars.

*b.* Compare the results of Exercise E12-5, in which the dollar is weakening against the Swiss franc during 20X1, with the results in this exercise (E12-9), in which the dollar is strengthening against the Swiss franc during 20X1.

### E12-10  Remeasurement with Strengthening U.S. Dollar

Refer to the data in Exercise E12-5, but now assume that the exchange rates were as follows:

| | |
|---|---|
| January 1 | SFr1 = $.80 |
| March 1 | SFr1 =  .77 |
| November 1 | SFr1 =  .74 |
| December 31 | SFr1 =  .73 |
| 20X1 Average | SFr1 =  .75 |

The receivable from Popular Creek is denominated in Swiss francs. Its books show a $3,650 payable to RoadTime.

Assume that the U.S. dollar is the functional currency.

*Indicates that the item relates to "Additional Considerations."

### Required

a. Prepare a schedule remeasuring the December 31, 20X1, trial balance from Swiss francs to dollars.

b. Compare the results of Exercise E12-7, in which the dollar weakens against the Swiss franc during 20X1, with the results in this exercise (E12-10), in which the dollar strengthened against the Swiss franc during 20X1.

### E12-11 Remeasurement and Translation of Cost of Goods Sold

Duff Company is a subsidiary of Rand Corporation and is located in Madrid, Spain, where the currency is the Spanish peseta (P). Data on Duff 's inventory and purchases are as follows:

| | |
|---|---|
| Inventory, January 1, 20X7 | P220,000 |
| Purchases during 20X7 | P846,000 |
| Inventory, December 31, 20X7 | P180,000 |

The beginning inventory was acquired during the fourth quarter of 20X6, and the ending inventory was acquired during the fourth quarter of 20X7. Purchases were made evenly over the year. Exchange rates were as follows:

| | |
|---|---|
| Fourth quarter of 20X6 | P1 = $0.0070 |
| January 1, 20X7 | P1 = $0.0075 |
| Average during 20X7 | P1 = $0.0080 |
| Fourth quarter of 20X7 | P1 = $0.0082 |
| December 31, 20X7 | P1 = $0.0085 |

### Required

a. Show the remeasurement of cost of goods sold for 20X7, assuming that the U.S. dollar is the functional currency.

b. Show the translation of cost of goods sold for 20X7, assuming that the Spanish peseta is the functional currency.

### E12-12 Equity-Method Entries for a Foreign Subsidiary

Thames Company is located in London, England. The local currency is the British pound (£). On January 1, 20X8, Dek Company purchased an 80 percent interest in Thames for $400,000, which resulted in an excess of cost-over-book value of $48,000 due solely to a trademark having a remaining life of 10 years. Dek uses the equity method to account for its investment.

Dek's December 31, 20X8, trial balance has been translated into U.S. dollars, requiring a translation adjustment debit of $6,400. Thames's net income translated into U.S. dollars is $60,000. It declared and paid a £15,000 dividend on May 1, 20X8.

Relevant exchange rates are as follows:

| | |
|---|---|
| January 1, 20X8 | £1 = $1.60 |
| Average for 20X8 | £1 = $1.63 |
| May 1, 20X8 | £1 = $1.64 |
| December 31, 20X8 | £1 = $1.65 |

### Required

a. Record the dividend received by Dek from Thames.

b. Prepare the entries to record Dek's equity in the net income of Thames and the parent's share of the translation adjustment.

c. Show a calculation of the differential reported on the consolidated balance sheet of December 31, 20X8, and the translation adjustment from differential.

d. Record the amortization of the trademark on Dek's books.

e. Calculate the amount of the translation adjustment reported on the statement of comprehensive income as an element of other comprehensive income.

### E12-13 Effects of a Change in the Exchange Rate—Translation and Other Comprehensive Income

Bentley Company owns a subsidiary in India whose balance sheets in rupees (R) for the last two years follow:

|  | December 31, 20X6 | December 31, 20X7 |
|---|---|---|
| **Assets:** | | |
| Cash | R 100,000 | R 80,000 |
| Receivables | 450,000 | 550,000 |
| Inventory | 680,000 | 720,000 |
| Fixed Assets, net | 1,000,000 | 900,000 |
| Total Assets | R2,230,000 | R2,250,000 |
| **Equities:** | | |
| Current Payables | R 260,000 | R 340,000 |
| Long-Term Debt | 1,250,000 | 1,100,000 |
| Common Stock | 500,000 | 500,000 |
| Retained Earnings | 220,000 | 310,000 |
| Total Equities | R2,230,000 | R2,250,000 |

Bentley formed the subsidiary on January 1, 20X6, when the exchange rate was 30 rupees for 1 U.S. dollar. The exchange rate for 1 U.S. dollar on December 31, 20X6, and December 31, 2007, had increased to 35 rupees and 40 rupees, respectively. Income is earned evenly over the year, and the subsidiary declared no dividends during its first two years of existence.

#### Required

a. Present both the direct and the indirect exchange rate for the rupees for the three dates of (1) January 1, 20X6, (2) December 31, 20X6, and (3) December 31, 20X7. Did the dollar strengthen or weaken in 20X6 and in 20X7?

b. Prepare the subsidiary's translated balance sheet as of December 31, 20X6, assuming the rupee is the subsidiary's functional currency.

c. Prepare the subsidiary's translated balance sheet as of December 31, 20X7, assuming the rupee is the subsidiary's functional currency.

d. Compute the amount that 20X7's other comprehensive income would include as a result of the translation.

### E12-14 Computation of Gain or Loss on Sale of Asset by Foreign Subsidiary

On December 31, 20X2, your company's Mexican subsidiary sold land at a selling price of 3,000,000 pesos. The land had been purchased for 2,000,000 pesos on January 1, 20X1, when the exchange rate was 10 pesos to 1 U.S. dollar. The exchange rate for 1 U.S. dollar was 11 pesos on December 31, 20X1, and 12 pesos on December 31, 20X2. Assume that the subsidiary had no other assets and no liabilities during the two years that it owned the land.

#### Required

a. Prepare all entries regarding the purchase and sale of the land that would be made on the books of the Mexican subsidiary whose reporting currency is the Mexican peso.

b. Determine the amount of the gain or loss on the transaction that would be reported on the subsidiary's remeasured statement of income in U.S. dollars, assuming the U.S. dollar is the functional currency. Determine the amount of the remeasurement gain or loss that would be reported on the remeasured statement of income in U.S. dollars.

c. Determine the amount of the gain or loss on the transaction that would be reported on the subsidiary's translated statement of income in U.S. dollars, assuming the Mexican peso is the functional currency. Determine the amount of the other comprehensive income that would be reported on the consolidated statement of other comprehensive income for 20X2.

### E12-15*   Intercompany Transactions

Hawk Company sold inventory to United Ltd., an English subsidiary. The goods cost Hawk $8,000 and were sold to United for $12,000 on November 27, payable in British pounds. The goods are still on hand at the end of the year on December 31. The British pound (£) is the functional currency of the English subsidiary. The exchange rates follow:

| | |
|---|---|
| November 27 | £1 = $1.60 |
| December 31 | £1 =   1.70 |

#### Required

a. At what dollar amount is the ending inventory shown in the trial balance of the consolidated workpaper?

b. What amount is eliminated for the unrealized intercompany gross profit, and at what amount is the inventory shown on the consolidated balance sheet?

## Problems

### P12-16   Parent Company Journal Entries and Translation

On January 1, 20X1, Par Company purchased all the outstanding stock of North Bay Company, located in Canada, for $120,000. On January 1, 20X1, the direct exchange rate for the Canadian dollar (C$) was C$1 = $.80. North Bay's book value on January 1, 20X1, was C$90,000. The fair value of North Bay's plant and equipment was C$10,000 more than book value, and the plant and equipment is being depreciated over 10 years, with no salvage value. The remainder of the differential is attributable to a trademark, which will be amortized over 10 years.

During 20X1, North Bay earned C$20,000 in income and declared and paid C$8,000 in dividends. The dividends were declared and paid in Canadian dollars when the exchange rate was C$1 = $.75. On December 31, 20X1, Par continues to hold the Canadian currency received from the dividend. On December 31, 20X1, the direct exchange rate is C$1 = $.70. The average exchange rate during 20X1 was C$1 = $.75. Management has determined that the Canadian dollar is the appropriate functional currency for North Bay Company.

#### Required

a. Prepare a schedule showing the differential allocation and amortization for 20X1. The schedule should present both Canadian dollars and U.S. dollars.

b. Par uses the basic equity method to account for its investment. Provide the entries that it would record in 20X1 for its investment in North Bay for the following items:

   (1) Purchase of investment in North Bay.

   (2) Equity accrual for Par's share of North Bay's income.

   (3) Recognition of dividend declared and paid by North Bay.

   (4) Amortization of differential.

   (5) Recognition of translation adjustment on differential.

c. Prepare a schedule showing the proof of the translation adjustment for North Bay as a result of the translation of the subsidiary's accounts from Canadian dollars to U.S. dollars. Then provide the entry that Par would record for its share of the translation adjustment resulting from the translation of the subsidiary's accounts.

d. Provide the entry required by Par to restate the C$8,000 in the Foreign Currency Units account into its year-end U.S. dollar equivalent value.

### P12-17   Translation, Journal Entries, Consolidated Comprehensive Income, and Stockholders' Equity

On January 1, 20X5, Taft Company acquired all of the outstanding stock of Vikix, Inc., a Norwegian company, at a cost of $151,200. Vikix's net assets on the date of acquisition were 700,000 kroner (NKr). On January 1, 20X5, the book and fair values of the Norwegian subsidiary's identifiable assets and liabilities approximated their fair values except for property, plant, and equipment and patents acquired. The fair value of Vikix's property, plant, and equipment exceeded its book value by $18,000. The remaining useful life of Vikix's equipment at January 1, 20X5 was 10 years.

The remainder of the differential was attributable to a patent having an estimated useful life of 5 years. Vikix's trial balance on December 31, 20X5, in kroner, follows:

|  | Debits | Credits |
|---|---|---|
| Cash | NKr 150,000 | |
| Accounts Receivable (net) | 200,000 | |
| Inventory | 270,000 | |
| Property, Plant, and Equipment | 600,000 | |
| Accumulated Depreciation | | NKr 150,000 |
| Accounts Payable | | 90,000 |
| Notes Payable | | 190,000 |
| Common Stock | | 450,000 |
| Retained Earnings | | 250,000 |
| Sales | | 690,000 |
| Cost of Goods Sold | 410,000 | |
| Operating Expenses | 100,000 | |
| Depreciation Expense | 50,000 | |
| Dividends Paid | 40,000 | |
| Total | NKr1,820,000 | NKr1,820,000 |

### Additional Information

1. Vikix uses the FIFO method for its inventory. The beginning inventory was acquired on December 31, 20X4, and ending inventory was acquired on December 15, 20X5. Purchases of NKr420,000 were made evenly throughout 20X5.
2. Vikix acquired all of its property, plant, and equipment on July 1, 20X3, and uses straight-line depreciation.
3. Vikix's sales were made evenly throughout 20X5, and its operating expenses were incurred evenly throughout 20X5.
4. The dividends were declared and paid on July 1, 20X5.
5. Taft's income from its own operations was $275,000 for 20X5, and its total stockholders' equity on January 1, 20X5, was $3,500,000. Taft declared $100,000 of dividends during 20X5.
6. Exchange rates were as follows:

| | |
|---|---|
| July 1, 20X3 | NKr1 = $.15 |
| December 30, 20X4 | NKr1 = $.18 |
| January 1, 20X5 | NKr1 = $.18 |
| July 1, 20X5 | NKr1 = $.19 |
| December 15, 20X5 | NKr1 = $.205 |
| December 31, 20X5 | NKr1 = $.21 |
| Average for 20X5 | NKr1 = $.20 |

### Required

*a.* Prepare a schedule translating the trial balance from Norwegian kroner into U.S. dollars. Assume the kroner is the functional currency.

*b.* Assume that Taft uses the basic equity method. Record all journal entries that relate to its investment in the Norwegian subsidiary during 20X5. Provide the necessary documentation and support for the amounts in the journal entries, including a schedule of the translation adjustment related to the differential.

*c.* Prepare a schedule that determines Taft's consolidated comprehensive income for 20X5.

*d.* Compute Taft's total consolidated stockholders' equity at December 31, 20X5.

**P12-18  Remeasurement, Journal Entries, Consolidated Net Income, and Stockholders' Equity**

Refer to the information in Problem P12-17. Assume the U.S. dollar is the functional currency, not the kroner.

### Required

a. Prepare a schedule remeasuring the trial balance from Norwegian kroner into U.S. dollars.

b. Assume that Taft uses the basic equity method. Record all journal entries that relate to its investment in the Norwegian subsidiary during 20X5. Provide the necessary documentation and support for the amounts in the journal entries.

c. Prepare a schedule that determines Taft's consolidated net income for 20X5.

d. Compute Taft's total consolidated stockholders' equity at December 31, 20X5.

**P12-19   Proof of Translation Adjustment**

Refer to the information presented in Problem P12-17 and your answer to part *a* of Problem P12-17.

### Required

Prepare a schedule providing a proof of the translation adjustment.

**P12-20\*   Remeasurement Gain or Loss**

Refer to the information given in Problem P12-17 and your answer to part *a* of Problem P12-18.

### Required

Prepare a schedule providing a proof of the remeasurement gain or loss. For this part of the problem, assume that the Norwegian subsidiary had the following monetary assets and liabilities at January 1, 20X5:

| Monetary Assets | |
| --- | --- |
| Cash | NKr 10,000 |
| Accounts Receivable (net) | 140,000 |

| Monetary Liabilities | |
| --- | --- |
| Accounts Payable | NKr 70,000 |
| Notes Payable | 140,000 |

On January 1, 20X5, the Norwegian subsidiary has a net monetary liability position of NKr60,000.

**P12-21   Translation and Calculation of Translation Adjustment**

On January 1, 20X4, Alum Corporation acquired DaSilva Company, a Brazilian subsidiary, by purchasing all the common stock at book value. DaSilva's trial balances on January 1, 20X4, and December 31, 20X4, expressed in Brazilian reals (BRL), follow:

| | January 1, 20X4 | | December 31, 20X4 | |
| --- | --- | --- | --- | --- |
| | **Debit** | **Credit** | **Debit** | **Credit** |
| Cash | BRL 62,000 | | BRL 57,700 | |
| Accounts Receivable (net) | 83,900 | | 82,000 | |
| Inventories | 95,000 | | 95,000 | |
| Prepaid Insurance | 5,600 | | 2,400 | |
| Plant and Equipment | 250,000 | | 350,000 | |
| Accumulated Depreciation | | BRL 67,500 | | BRL 100,000 |
| Intangible Assets | 42,000 | | 30,000 | |
| Accounts Payable | | 20,000 | | 24,000 |
| Income Taxes Payable | | 30,000 | | 27,000 |
| Interest Payable | | 1,000 | | 1,100 |
| Notes Payable | | 20,000 | | 20,000 |
| Bonds Payable | | 120,000 | | 120,000 |
| Common Stock | | 80,000 | | 80,000 |
| Additional Paid-In Capital | | 150,000 | | 150,000 |
| Retained Earnings | | 50,000 | | 50,000 |
| Sales | | | | 500,000 |

*(continued)*

| | | | | |
|---|---|---|---|---|
| Cost of Goods Sold | | | 230,000 | |
| Insurance Expense | | | 3,200 | |
| Depreciation Expense | | | 32,500 | |
| Amortization Expense | | | 12,000 | |
| Operating Expense | | | 152,300 | |
| Dividends Paid | | | 25,000 | |
| Total | BRL538,500 | BRL538,500 | BRL1,072,100 | BRL1,072,100 |

### Additional Information

1. DaSilva uses FIFO inventory valuation. Purchases were made uniformly during 20X4. Ending inventory for 20X4 is composed of units purchased when the exchange rate was $.25.
2. The insurance premium for a two-year policy was paid on October 1, 20X3.
3. Plant and equipment were acquired as follows:

| Date | Cost |
|---|---|
| January 1, 20X1 | BRL 200,000 |
| July 10, 20X2 | 50,000 |
| April 7, 20X4 | 100,000 |

4. Plant and equipment are depreciated using the straight-line method and a 10-year life, with no residual value. A full month's depreciation is taken in the month of acquisition.
5. The intangible assets are patents acquired on July 10, 20X2, at a cost of BRL60,000. The estimated life is five years.
6. The common stock was issued on January 1, 20X1.
7. Dividends of BRL 10,000 were declared and paid on April 7. On October 9, BRL15,000 of dividends were declared and paid.
8. Exchange rates were as follows:

| | |
|---|---|
| January 1, 20X1 | BRL1 = $.45 |
| July 10, 20X2 | BRL1 = .40 |
| October 1, 20X3 | BRL1 = .34 |
| January 1, 20X4 | BRL1 = .30 |
| April 7, 20X4 | BRL1 = .28 |
| October 9, 20X4 | BRL1 = .23 |
| December 31, 20X4 | BRL1 = .20 |
| 20X4 average | BRL1 = .25 |

### Required

*a.* Prepare a schedule translating the December 31, 20X4, trial balance of DaSilva from reals to dollars.

*b.* Prepare a schedule calculating the translation adjustment as of the end of 20X4. The net assets on January 1, 20X4, were BRL 280,000.

**P12-22\*** **Remeasurement and Proof of Remeasurement Gain or Loss**

Refer to the information in Problem P12-21. Assume that the dollar is the functional currency.

### Required

*a.* Prepare a schedule remeasuring the December 31, 20X4, trial balance of DaSilva Company from reals to dollars.

*b.* Prepare a schedule providing a proof of the remeasurement gain or loss.

**P12-23** **Translation**

Alamo Inc. purchased 80 percent of the outstanding stock of Western Ranching Company, located in Australia, on January 1, 20X3. The purchase price in Australian dollars (A$) was A$200,000, and A$40,000 of the differential was allocated to plant and equipment, which is amortized over a

10-year period. The remainder of the differential was attributable to a patent. Alamo Inc. amortizes the patent over 10 years. Western Ranching's trial balance on December 31, 20X3, in Australian dollars is as follows:

|  | Debits | Credits |
|---|---|---|
| Cash | A$ 44,100 | |
| Accounts Receivable (net) | 72,000 | |
| Inventory | 86,000 | |
| Plant and Equipment | 240,000 | |
| Accumulated Depreciation | | A$ 60,000 |
| Accounts Payable | | 53,800 |
| Payable to Alamo Inc. | | 10,800 |
| Interest Payable | | 3,000 |
| 12% Bonds Payable | | 100,000 |
| Premium on Bonds | | 5,700 |
| Common Stock | | 90,000 |
| Retained Earnings | | 40,000 |
| Sales | | 579,000 |
| Cost of Goods Sold | 330,000 | |
| Depreciation Expense | 24,000 | |
| Operating Expenses | 131,500 | |
| Interest Expense | 5,700 | |
| Dividends Paid | 9,000 | |
| Total | A$942,300 | A$942,300 |

## Additional Information

1. Western Ranching uses average cost for cost of goods sold. Inventory increased by A$20,000 during the year. Purchases were made uniformly during 20X3. The ending inventory was acquired at the average exchange rate for the year.

2. Plant and equipment were acquired as follows:

| Date | Cost |
|---|---|
| January 20X1 | A$180,000 |
| January 1, 20X3 | 60,000 |

3. Plant and equipment are depreciated using the straight-line method and a 10-year life, with no residual value.

4. The payable to Alamo is in Australian dollars. Alamo's books show a receivable from Western Ranching of $6,480.

5. The 10-year bonds were issued on July 1, 20X3, for A$106,000. The premium is amortized on a straight-line basis. The interest is paid on April 1 and October 1.

6. The dividends were declared and paid on April 1.

7. Exchange rates were as follows:

| | |
|---|---|
| January 20X1 | A$1 = $.93 |
| August 20X1 | A$1 = $.88 |
| January 1, 20X3 | A$1 = $.70 |
| April 1, 20X3 | A$1 = $.67 |
| July 1, 20X3 | A$1 = $.64 |
| December 31, 20X3 | A$1 = $.60 |
| 20X3 average | A$1 = $.65 |

### Required

a. Prepare a schedule translating the December 31, 20X3, trial balance of Western Ranching from Australian dollars to U.S. dollars.

b. Prepare a schedule providing a proof of the translation adjustment.

## P12-24   Parent Company Journal Entries and Translation

Refer to the information given in Problem P12-23 for Alamo and its subsidiary, Western Ranching. Assume that the Australian dollar (A$) is the functional currency and that Alamo uses the basic equity method for accounting for its investment in Western Ranching.

### Required

a. Prepare the entries that Alamo would record in 20X3 for its investment in Western Ranching. Your entries should include the following:

(1) Record the initial investment on January 1, 20X3.

(2) Record the dividend received by the parent company.

(3) Recognize the parent company's share of the equity income of the subsidiary.

(4) Record the amortizations of the differential.

(5) Recognize the translation adjustment required by the parent from the adjustment of the differential.

(6) Recognize the parent company's share of the translation adjustment resulting from the translation of the subsidiary's accounts.

b. Provide the necessary documentation and support for the amounts recorded in the journal entries, including a schedule of the translation adjustment related to the differential.

## P12-25   Consolidation Workpaper after Translation

Refer to the information given in Problems P12-23 and P12-24 for Alamo and its subsidiary, Western Ranching. Assume that the Australian dollar (A$) is the functional currency and that Alamo uses the basic equity method for accounting for its investment in Western Ranching. A December 31, 20X3, trial balance for Alamo Inc. follows. Use this translated trial balance for completing this problem.

| Item | Debit | Credit |
|---|---|---|
| Cash | $    38,000 | |
| Accounts Receivable (net) | 140,000 | |
| Receivable from Western Ranching | 6,480 | |
| Inventory | 128,000 | |
| Plant and Equipment | 500,000 | |
| Investment in Western Ranching | 152,064 | |
| Cost of Goods Sold | 600,000 | |
| Depreciation Expense | 28,000 | |
| Operating Expenses | 204,000 | |
| Interest Expense | 2,000 | |
| Dividends Declared | 50,000 | |
| Translation Adjustment | 22,528 | |
| Accumulated Depreciation | | $    90,000 |
| Accounts Payable | | 60,000 |
| Interest Payable | | 2,000 |
| Common Stock | | 500,000 |
| Retained Earnings, January 1, 20X3 | | 179,656 |
| Sales | | 1,000,000 |
| Income from Subsidiary | | 39,416 |
| Total | $1,871,072 | $1,871,072 |

### Required

a. Prepare a set of eliminating entries, in general journal form, for the entries required to prepare a comprehensive consolidation workpaper (including other comprehensive income) as of December 31, 20X3.

b. Prepare a comprehensive consolidation workpaper as of December 31, 20X3.

**P12-26***  **Remeasurement**

Refer to the information in Problem P12-23. Assume the U.S. dollar is the functional currency.

### Required

a. Prepare a schedule remeasuring the December 31, 20X3, trial balance of Western Ranching from Australian dollars to U.S. dollars.

b. Prepare a schedule providing a proof of the remeasurement gain or loss. The subsidiary's net monetary liability position on January 1, 20X3, was A$80,000.

**P12-27**  **Parent Company Journal Entries and Remeasurement**

Refer to the information given in Problems P12-23 and P12-26* for Alamo and its subsidiary, Western Ranching. Assume that the U.S. dollar is the functional currency and that Alamo uses the basic equity method for accounting for its investment in Western Ranching.

### Required

a. Prepare the entries that Alamo would record in 20X3 for its investment in Western Ranching. Your entries should do the following:

  (1) Record the initial investment on January 1, 20X3.

  (2) Record the dividend received by the parent company.

  (3) Recognize the parent company's share of the equity income from the subsidiary.

  (4) Record the amortizations of the differential.

b. Provide the necessary documentation and support for the amounts recorded in the journal entries.

**P12-28***  **Consolidation Workpaper after Remeasurement**

Refer to the information given in Problems P12-23 and P12-27 for Alamo and its subsidiary, Western Ranching. Assume that the U.S. dollar is the functional currency and that Alamo uses the basic equity method for accounting for its investment in Western Ranching. A December 31, 20X3, trial balance for Alamo follows. Use this remeasured trial balance for completing this problem.

| Item | Debit | Credit |
|---|---|---|
| Cash | $ 38,000 | |
| Accounts Receivable (net) | 140,000 | |
| Receivable from Western Ranching | 6,480 | |
| Inventory | 128,000 | |
| Plant and Equipment | 500,000 | |
| Investment in Western Ranching | 178,544 | |
| Cost of Goods Sold | 600,000 | |
| Depreciation Expense | 28,000 | |
| Operating Expenses | 204,000 | |
| Interest Expense | 2,000 | |
| Dividends Declared | 50,000 | |
| Accumulated Depreciation | | $ 90,000 |
| Accounts Payable | | 60,000 |
| Interest Payable | | 2,000 |
| Common Stock | | 500,000 |
| Retained Earnings, January 1, 20X3 | | 179,656 |
| Sales | | 1,000,000 |
| Income from Subsidiary | | 43,368 |
| Total | $1,875,024 | $1,875,024 |

### Required

*a.* Prepare a set of eliminating entries, in general journal form, for the entries required to prepare a three-part consolidation workpaper as of December 31, 20X3.

*b.* Prepare a three-part consolidation workpaper as of December 31, 20X3.

**P12-29** ### Foreign Currency Remeasurement [AICPA Adapted]

On January 1, 20X1, Kiner Company formed a foreign subsidiary that issued all of its currently outstanding common stock on that date. Selected accounts from the balance sheets, all of which are shown in local currency units, are as follows:

|  | December 31 | |
|---|---|---|
|  | **20X2** | **20X1** |
| Accounts Receivable (net of allowance for uncollectible accounts of 2,200 LCU on December 31, 20X2, and 2,000 LCU on December 31, 20X1) | LCU 40,000 | LCU 35,000 |
| Inventories, at cost | 80,000 | 75,000 |
| Property, Plant, and Equipment (net of allowance for accumulated depreciation of 31,000 LCU on December 31, 20X2, and 14,000 LCU on December 31, 20X1) | 163,000 | 150,000 |
| Long-Term Debt | 100,000 | 120,000 |
| Common Stock, authorized 10,000 shares, par value 10 LCU per share; issued and outstanding, 5,000 shares on December 31, 20X2, and December 31, 20X1 | 50,000 | 50,000 |

### Additional Information

1. Exchange rates are as follows:

| | |
|---|---|
| January 1, 20X1–July 31, 20X1 | 2 LCU = $1 |
| August 1, 20X1–October 31, 20X1 | 1.8 LCU = $1 |
| November 1, 20X1–June 30, 20X2 | 1.7 LCU = $1 |
| July 1, 20X2–December 31, 20X2 | 1.5 LCU = $1 |
| Average monthly rate for 20X1 | 1.9 LCU = $1 |
| Average monthly rate for 20X2 | 1.6 LCU = $1 |

2. An analysis of the accounts receivable balance is as follows:

|  | **20X2** | **20X1** |
|---|---|---|
| Accounts Receivable: | | |
| Balance at beginning of year | LCU 37,000 | |
| Sales (36,000 LCU per month in 20X2 and 31,000 LCU per month in 20X1) | 432,000 | LCU 372,000 |
| Collections | (423,600) | (334,000) |
| Write-offs (May 20X2 and December 20X1) | (3,200) | (1,000) |
| Balance at end of year | LCU 42,200 | LCU 37,000 |

|  | **20X2** | **20X1** |
|---|---|---|
| Allowance for Uncollectible Accounts: | | |
| Balance at beginning of year | LCU 2,000 | |
| Provision for uncollectible accounts | 3,400 | LCU 3,000 |
| Write-offs (May 20X2 and December 20X1) | (3,200) | (1,000) |
| Balance at end of year | LCU 2,200 | LCU 2,000 |

3. An analysis of inventories, for which the first-in, first-out inventory method is used, follows:

| | 20X2 | 20X1 |
|---|---|---|
| Inventory at beginning of year | LCU 75,000 | |
| Purchases (June 20X2 and June 20X1) | 335,000 | LCU375,000 |
| Goods available for sale | LCU410,000 | LCU375,000 |
| Inventory at end of year | (80,000) | (75,000) |
| Cost of goods sold | LCU330,000 | LCU300,000 |

4. On January 1, 20X1, Kiner's foreign subsidiary purchased land for 24,000 LCU and plant and equipment for 140,000 LCU. On July 4, 20X2, additional equipment was purchased for 30,000 LCU. Plant and equipment is being depreciated on a straight-line basis over a 10-year period, with no residual value. A full year's depreciation is taken in the year of purchase.

5. On January 15, 20X1, 7 percent bonds with a face value of 120,000 LCU were issued. These bonds mature on January 15, 20X7, and the interest is paid semiannually on July 15 and January 15. The first interest payment was made on July 15, 20X1.

### Required

Prepare a schedule remeasuring the selected accounts into U.S. dollars for December 31, 20X1, and December 31, 20X2, respectively, assuming the U.S. dollar is the functional currency for the foreign subsidiary. The schedule should be prepared using the following form:

| Item | Balance in LCU | Appropriate Exchange Rate | Remeasured into U.S. Dollars |
|---|---|---|---|
| December 31, 20X1: | | | |
|   Accounts Receivable (net) | | | |
|   Inventories | | | |
|   Property, Plant, and Equipment (net) | | | |
|   Long-Term Debt | | | |
|   Common Stock | | | |
| December 31, 20X2: | | | |
|   Accounts Receivable (net) | | | |
|   Inventories | | | |
|   Property, Plant, and Equipment (net) | | | |
|   Long-Term Debt | | | |
|   Common Stock | | | |

**P12-30** ### Foreign Currency Translation

Refer to the information in Problem P12-29 for Kiner Company and its foreign subsidiary.

### Required

Prepare a schedule translating the selected accounts into U.S. dollars as of December 31, 20X1, and December 31, 20X2, respectively, assuming that the local currency unit is the foreign subsidiary's functional currency.

**P12-31** ### Matching Key Terms

Match the items in the left-hand column with the descriptions/explanations in the right-hand column.

| Items | Descriptions/Explanations |
|---|---|
| 1. Current exchange rate | A. Method used to restate a foreign entity's financial statement when the local currency unit is the functional currency. |
| 2. Foreign entity goodwill under translation | |
| 3. Increase in the translation adjustment for the year | |
| 4. Other comprehensive income—translation adjustment | B. Method used to restate a foreign entity's financial statements when the U.S. dollar is the functional currency. |
| 5. Translation | C. Currency of the environment in which an entity primarily generates and expends cash. |
| 6. Historical exchange rate | |

*(continued)*

7. Foreign entity goodwill under remeasurement
8. Remeasurement
9. A decrease in the translation adjustment for the year
10. Functional currency

D. Is always the local currency unit of the foreign entity.
E. Exchange rate at the end of the period.
F. Exchange rate at the date of the asset acquisition or at the date of dividend declaration.
G. Average exchange rate during the period.
H. Periodic change in the cumulative translation adjustment.
I. Method under which goodwill must be adjusted to the current exchange rate at the balance sheet date.
J. Method under which goodwill is restated using the historical exchange rate.
K. Increase of the exchange rate during the year.
L. Decrease of the exchange rate during the year.

**P12-32** **Translation Choices**

The U.S. parent company is preparing its consolidated financial statements for December 31, 20X4. The foreign company's local currency (LCU) is the functional currency. Information is presented in Data Set A and Data Set B.

*Data Set A:*

| | Exchange Rate | Date |
|---|---|---|
| 1. | LCU .74 | June 16, 20X1: date foreign company purchased |
| 2. | LCU .80 | January 1, 20X4: beginning of current year |
| 3. | LCU .87 | March 31, 20X4 |
| 4. | LCU .86 | June 12, 20X4 |
| 5. | LCU .85 | Average for year 20X4 |
| 6. | LCU .84 | November 1, 20X4 |
| 7. | LCU .83 | December 31, 20X4: end of current year |
| 8. | No translation rate is applied | |

*Data Set B:*

a. Accounts receivable outstanding from sales on March 31, 20X4.
b. Sales revenue earned during year.
c. Dividends declared on November 1, 20X4.
d. Ending inventory balance from acquisitions through the year.
e. Equipment purchased on March 31, 20X4.
f. Depreciation expense on equipment.
g. Common stock outstanding.
h. Dividends payable from dividends declared on June 12, 20X4.
i. Accumulated Other Comprehensive Income balance from prior fiscal year.
j. Bond payable issued January 1, 20X4.
k. Interest expense on the bond payable.

*Required*

a. Select the appropriate exchange rate from the amounts presented in Data Set A to prepare the translation worksheet for each of the accounts presented in Data Set B.
b. Determine the direct exchange rate for January 1, 20X4.
c. Determine whether the U.S. dollar strengthened or weakened during 20X4.

## P12-33   Proof of Translation Adjustment

MaMi Co. Ltd. located in Mexico City is a wholly owned subsidiary of Special Foods, a U.S. company. At the beginning of the year, MaMi's condensed balance sheet was reported in Mexican pesos (MXP) as follows:

| Assets | 3,425,000 | Liabilities | 2,850,000 |
|---|---|---|---|
| | | Stockholders' Equity | 575,000 |

During the year, the company earned income of MXP270,000 and on November 1 declared dividends of MXP150,000. The Mexican peso is the functional currency. Relevant exchange rates between the peso and the U.S. dollar follow:

| | |
|---|---|
| January 1 (beginning of year) | $.0870 |
| Average for year | .0900 |
| November 1 | .0915 |
| December 31 (end of year) | .0930 |

### Required

a. Prepare a proof of the translation adjustment, assuming that the beginning credit balance of the accumulated other comprehensive income—translation adjustment was $3,250.

b. Did the U.S. dollar strengthen or weaken against the Mexican peso during the year?

---

## Kaplan CPA Review

SCHWESER

Please visit the text Web site for the online CPA Simulation: www.mhhe.com/baker8e.
**Situation:** The Texas Corporation located in San Antonio has transactions both in the United States and in Mexico. The U.S. dollar is its functional currency. In addition, this company has a wholly owned subsidiary (Mexico, Inc.) located in Mexico. Consolidated financial statements are being prepared for year 1. The currency exchange rates are as follows for the current year (year 1M):

| | |
|---|---|
| January 1, year 1 | 1 peso equals $0.088 |
| Average for year 1 | 1 peso equals $0.090 |
| November 1, year 1 | 1 peso equals $0.092 |
| December 31, year 1 | 1 peso equals $0.094 |
| December 31, year 1 | 1 peso equals $0.095 |
| January 31, year 2 | 1 peso equals $0.098 |

Topics to be covered in simulation:

- Sale to an unrelated company in Mexico.
- Purchase of equipment from an unrelated company in Mexico.
- Impact of the designation of the functional currency as the dollar or the peso.
- Translation of expenses from the peso to the dollar, assuming the peso is the functional currency.
- Translation of expenses from the peso to the dollar, assuming the dollar is the functional currency.
- Translation of fixed assets.
- Translation of liabilities.
- Translation adjustment.
- Functional currency.
- Forward exchange contracts.

# Segment and Interim Reporting

## REPORTING FOR SEGMENTS

Diversification into new products and multinational markets during the 1960s and early 1970s created the need for disaggregated information about the individual segments or components of an enterprise. This information need was addressed by the Accounting Principles Board, the Financial Executives Institute, the Institute of Management Accountants, the Securities and Exchange Commission, and, finally, the Financial Accounting Standards Board.

Large, diversified companies can be viewed as a portfolio of assets operated as divisions or subsidiaries, often multinational in scope. The various components of a large company may have different profit rates, different degrees and types of risk, and different opportunities for growth. A major issue for accountants is how to develop and disclose the information necessary to reflect these essential differences. The following discussion presents the accounting standards for reporting an entity's operating components, foreign operations, and major customers.

## SEGMENT REPORTING ACCOUNTING ISSUES

In 1967, the APB issued **APB Statement No. 2,** "Disclosure of Supplemental Financial Information by Diversified Companies" (APB 2), which recommended voluntary disclosure of segment information. In 1969, the SEC required line-of-business reporting in registration statements of new stock issues and in 1970 extended this requirement to Form 10-K, the report filed annually by all publicly held companies. Using extensive research reports prepared by the Institute of Management Accountants[1] and the Financial Executives Institute,[2] the FASB issued **FASB Statement No. 14,** "Financial Reporting for Segments of a Business Enterprise" (FASB 14), in December 1976. This pronouncement required the supplemental disclosure of revenue, profits, assets, and other information for selected industry segments of an entity as well as disclosures about its foreign operations.

Preparers of financial statements believed that **FASB 14** required significant additional accounting costs because companies had to analyze their financial operations by industrial lines of business, although that was not how most businesses were organized. Furthermore, financial analysts and other financial statement users stated that, although information about segments was essential for full analysis of a company, the standards in **FASB 14** were inadequate.

---

[1] M. Backer and R. McFarland, *External Reporting for Segments of a Business,* Institute of Management Accountants (New York, 1968).

[2] R. Mautz, *Financial Reporting by Diversified Companies,* Financial Executives Research Foundation (New York, 1968).

The FASB joined with the Canadian Institute of Chartered Accountants (CICA) to study the information needs for disaggregated disclosures. Also, the AICPA formed the Special Committee on Financial Reporting ("The Jenkins Committee," named after its chairman, Ed Jenkins), which recommended in 1994 that the FASB assign its highest priority to improving segment reporting. In June 1997, the FASB published **FASB Statement No. 131,** "Disclosures about Segments of an Enterprise and Related Information" (FASB 131). Although some aspects of the disclosure criteria from **FASB 14** were continued, **FASB 131** took a ***management approach*** to the definition of segments. The standard focuses on financial information that an enterprise's financial decision makers use to evaluate the entity's operating segments. Thus, **FASB 131** required that financial information be provided about segments that correspond to the internal organization structure of the entity as used by the company's chief operating decision maker in deciding how to allocate resources and assessing performance. These components are termed *operating segments.* Thus, the financial statements report disaggregated information on the same organizational basis as the company's internal decision makers use.

**FASB 131** defines an operating segment as having three characteristics:

1. The component unit's business activities generate revenue and incur expenses, including any revenue or expenses in transactions with other business units of the company.
2. The component unit's operating results are regularly reviewed by the entity's chief operating decision maker, who then determines the resources to be assigned to the segment and evaluates its performance.
3. Separate financial information is available for the component unit.

Generally, the corporate headquarters is not a separate operating segment. Also, the company may choose to aggregate several individual operating segments that have very similar economic characteristics (i.e., products and services, production processes, type or class of customer, methods used to distribute products or provide for services). Management may also believe that the aggregation will provide more meaningful information to the users of the financial statements.

Whenever the issue of defining the income for a segment of an enterprise arises, one problem is the allocation of costs to specific segments. For example, should a segment's income include directly traceable costs only, or should it also include an allocation of common costs, such as companywide advertising or a central purchasing department? One accounting researcher has stated that all allocations are arbitrary, that is, not completely verifiable with empirical evidence, and therefore, net income after deducting any allocated costs is arbitrary.[3] In **FASB 131,** the FASB stated that the allocations of revenues and costs should be included for a reported segment only if they are included in the segment's profit or loss that the chief operating decision maker uses. Also, only those assets included in the measure of the segment's assets that the chief operating decision maker uses shall be reported for that segment. Thus, the FASB again is striving to align the segments' external financial disclosures with the internal reporting used by the company's management to make resource allocations and other decisions regarding the operating segments.

### International Financial Reporting Standards for Operating Segments

Segment reporting has been specified in **International Financial Reporting Standard No. 8,** "Operating Segments" (IFRS 8). This standard requires disclosure of information about an entity's reportable operating segments both in its annual and its interim financial statements. The international standards are similar to those of U.S. GAAP although there are several differences, including the following: IFRS requires disclosures for both business segments and geographical segments; two different bases of segmentation are used, a primary basis and a secondary basis, for which more disclosure is required for primary segments; and the amounts disclosed under IFRS are based on the same accounting policies as the amounts recognized in the financial statements, not based on amounts reported to the chief operating decision maker as under U.S. GAAP.

---

[3] A. Thomas, *The Allocation Problem: Part Two,* American Accounting Association (Sarasota, FL, 1974).

# INFORMATION ABOUT OPERATING SEGMENTS

Many entities are diversified across several lines of business. Each line may be subject to unique competitive factors and may react differently to changes in the economic environment. For example, a large company such as Johnson & Johnson operates in several major lines: consumer, pharmaceutical, and professional. Its products include disposable contact lenses, baby products, surgical products, antibody therapies, and cold and flu medications. A conglomerate may operate in several consumer markets, each with different characteristics. In addition, a company is exposed to different risks in each of the markets in which it acquires its factors of production. Consolidated statements present all of these heterogeneous factors in a single-entity context. The purpose of segment reporting is to allow financial statement users to look behind the consolidated totals to the individual components that constitute the entity.

## Defining Reportable Segments

The process of determining separately ***reportable operating segments,*** that is, segments for which separate supplemental disclosures must be made, is based on management's specification of those operating segments that are used internally for evaluating the enterprise's financial position and operating performance.

### *10 Percent Quantitative Thresholds*

The FASB specified three ***10 percent significance rules*** to determine which of the operating segments shall have separately reported information. The separate disclosures are required for segments meeting at least one of the following tests:

1. The segment's revenue, including both external sales and intersegment sales or transfers, is 10 percent or more of the total revenues from external sales plus intersegment transactions of all operating segments.
2. The absolute value of the segment's profit or loss is 10 percent or more of the greater, in absolute value, of (*a*) the total profit of all operating segments that did not report a loss, or (*b*) the total loss of all operating segments that did report a loss.
3. The segment's assets are 10 percent or more of the total assets of all operating segments.

Note that the revenue test includes intersegment sales or transfers. The FASB found that the full impact of a particular segment on the entire enterprise should be measured. Also, the FASB believed that the definition of an operating segment should include components of an enterprise that sell primarily or exclusively to other components of the enterprise. Information about these "vertically integrated" operations provide insight into the production and operations of the enterprise.

**FASB 131** states that the segment disclosure should include the reportable segments' measures of profit or loss. Thus, the report shall be the same as used for internal decision-making purposes. Some companies may allocate operating expenses arising from shared facilities such as a common warehouse. Other companies may allocate items such as interest costs, income taxes, or income from equity investments to specific segments. Whatever is used for internal decision-making purposes to measure the operating segment's profit or loss shall be reported in the external disclosure.

Although an enterprise is required to report the assets of the separately reportable operating segments, **FASB 131** also allows companies to report their segments' liabilities if the company finds that the fuller disclosure would be meaningful. The assets to be reported are those used by the chief operating decision maker in making decisions about the segment and might include intangible assets such as goodwill or other intangibles. If commonly used assets are allocated to the segments, then these should be included in the reported amounts. The assets might also include financing items such as investments in equity securities or intersegment loans. The key point is that the revenues, profit or loss, and assets should be reported on the same basis as used for internal decision-making purposes.

**FIGURE 13–1**
**Consolidated Financial Statements for Peerless Products Corporation and Subsidiary**

| PEERLESS PRODUCTS CORPORATION AND SUBSIDIARY | |
|---|---|
| **Consolidated Statement of Income and Retained Earnings** | |
| **Year Ended December 31, 20X1** | |
| Revenues: | |
| Sales | $572,000 |
| Income from Investment in Barclay | 32,000 |
| Expenses and Deductions: | |
| Cost of Goods Sold | (267,000) |
| Depreciation and Amortization | (70,000) |
| Other Expenses | (15,000) |
| Interest Expense | (30,000) |
| Income to Noncontrolling Interest | (10,000) |
| Income Taxes | (62,000) |
| Net Income | $150,000 |
| Retained Earnings, January 1 | 300,000 |
| Less: Dividends | (60,000) |
| Retained Earnings, December 31 | $390,000 |

| PEERLESS PRODUCTS CORPORATION AND SUBSIDIARY | | |
|---|---|---|
| **Consolidated Balance Sheet** | | |
| **December 31, 20X1** | | |
| Cash | | $ 131,000 |
| Accounts Receivable | | 125,000 |
| Inventory | | 165,000 |
| Investment in Barclay Stock | | 184,000 |
| Land | | 215,000 |
| Building and Equipment | $1,400,000 | |
| Less: Accumulated Depreciation | (770,000) | 630,000 |
| Total Assets | | $1,450,000 |
| Accounts Payable | | $ 200,000 |
| Bonds Payable | | 300,000 |
| Noncontrolling Interest | | 60,000 |
| Common Stock | | 500,000 |
| Retained Earnings | | 390,000 |
| Total Liabilities and Stockholders' Equity | | $1,450,000 |

If the total external revenue of the separately reportable operating segments is less than 75 percent of the total consolidated revenue, then management must select and disclose information about additional operating segments until at least 75 percent of consolidated revenue is included in reportable segments. The choice of which additional operating segments to report is left to management.

Information about the operating segments that are not separately reportable is combined and disclosed in an "All Other" category. The sources of the revenue in the All Other category must be described, but the level of disclosure for this category is significantly less than for the separately reportable segments. Again, note that the corporate headquarters (or corporate administration) is not typically included as an operating segment of an enterprise.

### Illustration of 10 Percent Tests

Figure 13–1 represents the consolidated financial statements for Peerless Products Corporation and Special Foods Inc. Information for the example is as follows:

1. Peerless owns 80 percent of Special Foods' common stock. Special Foods reports a profit of $50,000 for 20X1 and pays dividends of $30,000. The December 31, 20X1, balances in Special Foods' stockholders' equity accounts total $300,000, of which the noncontrolling interest is 20 percent.

2. Peerless acquires 40 percent of Barclay Company stock on January 1, 20X1, for a cost of $160,000, which is equal to the book value of the stock on that date. The equity method is used to account for this investment. Barclay Company earns $80,000 in profit during 20X1 and pays $20,000 in dividends. This investment is managed by the corporate office and is not assigned to any operating segment.

Segment disclosure provides a breakdown of the consolidated totals into their constituent parts. The items that appear in the consolidated statements and must be disaggregated are sales of $572,000 and total assets of $1,450,000. In the segment analysis, segment profit is also used; however, this figure is not usually presented directly on the consolidated income statement and is computed separately.

Figure 13–2 is a workpaper used to perform the disaggregation from the consolidated totals into the various operating segments. Figure 13–2 also includes additional data necessary for preparing the annual report footnote disclosure presented later in this chapter.

Additional information for this illustration is as follows:

1. The consolidated entity of Peerless Products and Special Foods comprises five different operating segments as well as a central corporate administration. The operating segments are defined by management as Food Products, Plastic and Packaging, Consumer and Commercial, Health and Scientific, and Chemicals.

2. On January 1, 20X1, the Food Products segment of Special Foods issues a $100,000, 12 percent note payable to the Plastic and Packaging segment of Peerless Products. The intercompany interest is $12,000 for the year and is properly eliminated from the consolidated statements.

3. Each operating segment makes sales to unaffiliated customers. In addition, $28,000 of intersegment sales are made during the year by the Food Products, the Plastic and Packaging, and the Consumer and Commercial segments. The cost of these intersegment sales is $18,000. These goods are still in the ending inventories of the purchasing operating segments, and the unrealized inventory profit of $10,000 must be eliminated from both cost of goods sold and inventories in preparing the consolidated financials. Specific revenue information is presented in Figure 13–2.

4. Figure 13–2 also presents the profit and loss information for each segment as it is defined by the entity. The entity uses a concept it terms "controllable earnings" to measure segment performance. As defined by the company, controllable earnings includes interest revenue and interest expense in the entity's definition of segment profit or loss. Therefore, interest is reported on a segment basis. Depreciation is separately reported because if depreciation, depletion, or amortization expenses are included in the measure of segment profit or loss, **FASB 131** requires that these cost elements be disclosed separately to provide information to financial statement users to approximate the cash flow for each segment.

5. A computer costing $30,000 is acquired during the year. The computer is used for production scheduling and control and is being depreciated by the straight-line method over a period of three years ($30,000 ÷ 3 years = $10,000 per year). The annual expense of this computer is allocated on the basis of use, which the computer itself monitors. These allocated costs are shown in Figure 13–2 immediately below the other costs for each operating segment.

6. The intersegment interest expense from the intercompany note is attributable to the Food Products segment, and the intercompany interest income is earned by the Plastic and Packaging segment.

7. The company's policy on determining segment performance does not include income from the investment in any of its operating segment's profit or loss. Rather, this item is

# FIGURE 13–2  Workpaper to Analyze Peerless Products and Subsidiary's Operating Segments

## PEERLESS PRODUCTS CORPORATION AND SPECIAL FOODS INC.
### Segmental Disclosure Workpaper

| Item | Operating Segments | | | | | Corporate Administration | Combined | Intersegment Eliminations | Consolidated |
| --- | --- | --- | --- | --- | --- | --- | --- | --- | --- |
| | Food Products | Plastic and Packaging | Consumer and Commercial | Health and Scientific | Chemicals | | | | |
| **Revenue:** | | | | | | | | | |
| Sales to unaffiliated customers | 317,000 | 95,000 | 41,000 | 86,000 | 33,000 | | 572,000 | | 572,000 |
| Intersegment sales | 6,000 | 18,000 | 4,000 | | | | 28,000 | (28,000) | |
| Total revenue | 323,000 | 113,000 | 45,000 | 86,000 | 33,000 | | 600,000 | (28,000) | 572,000 |
| **Profit:** | | | | | | | | | |
| Directly traceable operating costs | (103,000) | (31,000) | (63,000) | (55,000) | (37,000) | | (289,000) | 18,000 | (271,000) |
| Depreciation of segment's assets | (7,000) | (4,000) | (5,000) | (6,000) | (4,000) | | (26,000) | | (26,000) |
| Allocated depreciation | (3,000) | (1,000) | (2,000) | (3,000) | (1,000) | | (10,000) | | (10,000) |
| Other items: | | | | | | | | | |
| Interest revenue—intersegment | | 12,000 | | | | | 12,000 | (12,000) | |
| Interest expense—to unaffiliates | | (30,000) | | | | | (30,000) | | (30,000) |
| Interest expense—intersegment | (12,000) | | | | | | (12,000) | 12,000 | |
| Segment profit (loss) | 198,000 | 59,000 | (25,000) | 22,000 | (9,000) | | 245,000 | (10,000) | 235,000 |
| General corporate expenses | | | | | | (45,000) | (45,000) | | (45,000) |
| Income from equity investment | | | | | | 32,000 | 32,000 | | 32,000 |
| Income from continuing operations, before taxes | 198,000 | 59,000 | (25,000) | 22,000 | (9,000) | (13,000) | 232,000 | (10,000) | 222,000 |
| **Assets:** | | | | | | | | | |
| Operating segments: | | | | | | | | | |
| Segment (other than intersegment) | 411,000 | 275,000 | 100,000 | 310,000 | 80,000 | | 1,176,000 | (10,000) | 1,166,000 |
| Intersegment notes | | 100,000 | | | | | 100,000 | (100,000) | |
| Total of operating segments | 411,000 | 375,000 | 100,000 | 310,000 | 80,000 | | 1,276,000 | (110,000) | 1,166,000 |
| General corporate | | | | | | 100,000 | 100,000 | | 100,000 |
| Equity investments | | | | | | 184,000 | 184,000 | | 184,000 |
| Total assets | 411,000 | 375,000 | 100,000 | 310,000 | 80,000 | 284,000 | 1,560,000 | (110,000) | 1,450,000 |
| Total expenditures made during year for long-term assets | 48,000 | 21,000 | 10,000 | 29,000 | 12,000 | | 120,000 | | |

assigned to corporate administration. This information is collected in the workpaper to reconcile the consolidated totals.

8. The assets section of Figure 13–2 presents the assets for the operating segments as well as for the corporate administration center. Included in the segments' assets is an allocation of the $20,000 book value ($30,000 less $10,000 of accumulated depreciation) of the production computer. Note also that the intersegment notes are assigned to a specific segment for internal decision-making purposes, but these notes are eliminated in the preparation of the consolidated financials.

The specific significance tests that Peerless Products and its subsidiary must use to determine separately reportable operating segments are as follows:

*10 Percent Revenue Test* The first 10 percent test is applied to each operating segment's total revenue as a percentage of the combined revenue of all segments before elimination of intersegment transfers and sales. If an operating segment's total revenue is 10 percent or more of the combined revenue of all segments, then the segment is separately reportable and supplementary disclosures must be provided for it in the annual report.

The 10 percent revenue tests are applied as follows:

| Segment | Segment Revenue | Percent of Combined Revenue of $600,000 | Reportable Segment |
|---|---|---|---|
| Food Products | $323,000 | 53.8% | Yes |
| Plastic and Packaging | 113,000 | 18.8 | Yes |
| Consumer and Commercial | 45,000 | 7.5 | No |
| Health and Scientific | 86,000 | 14.3 | Yes |
| Chemicals | 33,000 | 5.5 | No |
| Total | $600,000 | 100.0%* | |

*Unrounded percents for segments total to 100 percent.

The revenue test shows that the following operating segments are separately reportable: Food Products, Plastic and Packaging, and Health and Scientific. A common shortcut is to compute 10 percent of the denominator of the test (for Peerless and its subsidiary, $600,000 × .10) and then compare each segment's total revenue with that fraction. In this case, reportable segments are those with $60,000 or more in total revenue.

*10 Percent Profit (Loss) Test* The profit or loss test is the second test to determine which operating segments are separately reportable. The test is to determine whether a segment's profit or loss is equal to or greater than 10 percent of the absolute value of either the combined operating profits or the combined operating losses of the segments, whichever is greater.

Because two segments had operating losses for the year, separate tabulations are made, as follows:

| Segment | Segment Profits | Segment Losses |
|---|---|---|
| Food Products | $198,000 | |
| Plastic and Packaging | 59,000 | |
| Consumer and Commercial | | $(25,000) |
| Health and Scientific | 22,000 | |
| Chemicals | | (9,000) |
| Total | $279,000 | $(34,000) |

The greater absolute total is the $279,000 of profits. This amount becomes the denominator for the 10 percent operating profit or loss test. Because this test is based on absolute amounts, all numbers are treated as positive numbers. The test data follow:

| Segment | Profit (Loss) | Percent of Test Amount of $279,000 | Separately Reportable |
|---|---|---|---|
| Food Products | $198,000 | 71.0% | Yes |
| Plastic and Packaging | 59,000 | 21.1 | Yes |
| Consumer and Commercial | (25,000) | 9.0 | No |
| Health and Scientific | 22,000 | 7.9 | No |
| Chemicals | (9,000) | 3.2 | No |

The Food Products and Plastic and Packaging segments are separately reportable using the profit or loss test.

***10 Percent Assets Test***   The last of the tests to determine whether a segment is separately reportable is the 10 percent assets test. Note that the items composing each segment's assets are defined by management, as used for internal decision-making purposes. Management may include intangibles, receivables, and even intercompany items, as defined by the management. Assume that Peerless's management defines the segment assets to include intercompany items such as the intercompany notes. Recognize that it really is up to the management to define what is, and what is not, included in each of the definitions of segment profit or loss and the segment assets.

The combined assets of all operating segments ($1,276,000) are used for this test. The difference of $110,000 between the combined assets of the operating segments ($1,276,000) and the amount included ($1,166,000) in the consolidated assets is due to (*a*) the $10,000 unrealized intercompany profit from intersegment inventory transactions that has not been realized in sales to third parties, and (*b*) the $100,000 of intersegment notes. These intercompany amounts must be eliminated in the consolidation process.

The 10 percent significance rule is applied to segment assets as follows:

| Segment | Segment Assets | Percent of Test Amount of $1,276,000 | Separately Reportable |
|---|---|---|---|
| Food Products | $ 411,000 | 32.2% | Yes |
| Plastic and Packaging | 375,000 | 29.4 | Yes |
| Consumer and Commercial | 100,000 | 7.8 | No |
| Health and Scientific | 310,000 | 24.3 | Yes |
| Chemicals | 80,000 | 6.3 | No |
| Total | $1,276,000 | 100.0% | |

The Food Products, Plastic and Packaging, and Health and Scientific operating segments are separately reportable using the 10 percent assets test; that is, their assets are equal to or greater than 10 percent of the combined assets of the operating segments ($127,600 = $1,276,000 × .10).

Figure 13–3 summarizes the results of the three tests. Recall that a segment is separately reportable if it meets any one of the three 10 percent tests. The following segments are separately reportable under the three tests: Food Products, Plastic and Packaging, and Health and Scientific. The remaining segments, Consumer and Commercial and Chemicals, are not separately reportable under any of the three tests. Specific segment information must therefore be reported in the annual report for the three separately reportable segments, and summary information for the remaining two nonreportable segments must be combined under the heading "All Other."

**FIGURE 13–3**
Summary of
Reportable Industry
Segments: 10 Percent
Tests

| | Food Products | Plastic and Packaging | Consumer and Commercial | Health and Scientific | Chemicals |
|---|---|---|---|---|---|
| Revenue test | Yes | Yes | No | Yes | No |
| Operating profit (loss) test | Yes | Yes | No | No | No |
| Assets test | Yes | Yes | No | Yes | No |

## Comprehensive Disclosure Test

After determining which of the segments is reportable under any of the three 10 percent tests, the company must apply a comprehensive test. The comprehensive test is the **75 percent consolidated revenue test.**

### 75 Percent Consolidated Revenue Test

The total revenue from external sources by all separately reportable operating segments must equal at least 75 percent of the total consolidated revenue. The reporting company must identify additional operating segments as reportable until this test is met. Peerless Products and Special Foods, with three reportable segments, compute the 75 percent test as follows:

| | | |
|---|---|---|
| Sales to unaffiliated customers by reportable segments: | | |
| Food Products | $317,000 | |
| Plastic and Packaging | 95,000 | |
| Health and Scientific | 86,000 | |
| Total of reportable segments | | $498,000 |
| Consolidated revenue | | $572,000 |
| Reportable segments' percentage of consolidated revenue ($498,000 ÷ $572,000) | | 87.1% |

Because this percentage is equal to or greater than 75 percent, no further operating segments must be separately reported. Had the percentage been less than 75 percent, additional individual operating segments would have been required to be treated as reportable until the 75 percent test was met.

### *Other Considerations*

A practical limit of about 10 segments is used as an upper limit on the number of reportable segments because above that number, the supplemental information may become overly detailed. A company having more than about 10 reportable segments should consider aggregating the most closely related segments. Peerless Products and Special Foods have just three reportable segments.

In addition, companies must exercise judgment to determine the individual segments to be reported. For example, a segment may meet or fail a specific test because of some unusual situation, such as an abnormally high profit or loss on a one-time contract. The concept of interperiod comparability should be followed in deciding whether or not the segment should be disclosed in the current period. Companies should separately report segments that have been reported in prior years but fail the current period's significance tests because of abnormal occurrences. Similarly, companies need not separately report a segment that has met a 10 percent test on a one-time basis only because of abnormal circumstances. A company is required, however, to indicate why a reportable segment is not disclosed.

Finally, if a segment becomes reportable in the current period but has not been reported separately in earlier periods, the prior years' comparative segment disclosures, which are included in the current year's annual report, should be restated to obtain comparability of financial data.

## Reporting Segment Information

The specific disclosures required for each reportable segment are defined in **FASB 131.** In segment reporting, the following quantitative and descriptive information must be disclosed for *each* segment determined to be separately reportable:

1. *General information.* Information must be disclosed regarding: (*a*) how the company identifies each separately reportable segment, including information about the company's organizational structure (i.e., whether the company organizes along product lines, geographic areas, or some other organizational factor), and (*b*) the types of products or services from which each reportable segment earns its revenues.

2. *Amounts for each separately reportable segment.* Segment disclosures must include amounts for: (*a*) each segment's profit or loss and the measurement procedures used to determine the profit or loss, including how the company accounts for intersegment transactions, and (*b*) each segment's assets.

3. *Measures of segment profit or loss.* Each of the following must be disclosed if it is used to measure the segment profit or loss reviewed by the company's chief operating decision maker: (*a*) revenues from external sales, (*b*) revenues from transactions with other operating segments of the company, (*c*) interest revenue, (*d*) interest expense, (*e*) depreciation and amortization expense, (*f*) equity in the income of investees accounted for by the equity method, (*g*) income tax expense or benefit, (*h*) extraordinary items, and (*i*) other significant noncash items.

4. *Segment assets.* The following information on each separately reportable segment's assets must be disclosed if it is included in the computation of segment assets reviewed by the company's chief operating decision maker: (*a*) the amount of investment in equity-method investees, and (*b*) the total expenditures for increases to long-term productive assets through the capital budget, since these expenditures often indicate which segments the company is building for the future.

5. *Reconciliations to consolidated totals.* Finally, the segment disclosures must include reconciliations between the reportable segments' total revenues, total profits or losses, and total assets and the related consolidated totals for those items. If the company decides to disclose liabilities for each reportable segment, a reconciliation is also required between the reportable segments' total liabilities and the consolidated total liabilities.

Companies are allowed to present these disclosures in separate schedules or in the footnotes. Most companies present footnote disclosures with accompanying schedules. An example of a commonly used disclosure format is presented in Figure 13–4 for Peerless Products and Special Foods. The figure presents the information on the operating segments used in the example and only the current year's data. In practice, however, companies provide comparative data for at least two prior fiscal periods together with the current period's information.

**FASB 131** specified that segment disclosures must also be made in interim statements such as the quarterly financial statements. The interim reports must disclose the following about each reportable segment: (1) revenues from external customers, (2) intersegment revenues, (3) a measure of segment profit or loss, (4) total assets for which there has been a material change from the most recent annual report, (5) any differences from the most recent annual report in the definition of operating segments or in how segment profit or loss is computed, and (6) a reconciliation of the total of segment profit or loss to the entity's consolidated totals.

**FIGURE 13–4** **Required Footnote Disclosures for Peerless Products Corporation and Subsidiary's Operating Segments**

**Footnote X**
**Information about the Company's Operations in Different Operating Segments**

| Item | Food Products | Plastics and Packaging | Health and Scientific | All Others | Combined |
|---|---|---|---|---|---|
| Revenue to unaffiliated customers | 317,000 | 95,000 | 86,000 | 74,000 | 572,000 |
| Intersegment revenue | 6,000 | 18,000 | | 4,000 | 28,000 |
| Interest revenue—-intersegment | | 12,000 | | | 12,000 |
| Interest expense—unaffiliated | | 30.000 | | | 30,000 |
| Interest expense—intersegment | 12,000 | | | | 12,000 |
| Depreciation | 10,000 | 5,000 | 9,000 | 12,000 | 36,000 |
| Segment profit (loss) | 198,000 | 59,000 | 22,000 | (34,000) | 245,000 |
| Segment assets | 411,000 | 375,000 | 310,000 | 180,000 | 1,276,000 |
| Expenditures for segment assets | 48,000 | 21,000 | 29,000 | 22,000 | 120,000 |

Reconciliation of Reportable Segment Revenue to Consolidated Revenue

| | |
|---|---|
| Total revenues for reportable segments | $  522,000 |
| Other revenues | 78,000 |
| Elimination of intersegment revenues | (28,000) |
| Total consolidated revenues | $  572,000 |

Reconciliation of Reportable Segment Profit and Loss to Consolidated Profit or Loss

| | |
|---|---|
| Total profit and loss for reportable segments | $  279,000 |
| Other profits or loss | (34,000) |
| Elimination of intersegment profit | (10,000) |
| General corporate expense | (45,000) |
| Income from equity investment | 32,000 |
| Income before income taxes and extraordinary items | $  222,000 |

Reconciliation of Reportable Segment Assets to Consolidated Assets

| | |
|---|---|
| Total assets for reportable segments | $1,096,000 |
| Other assets | 180,000 |
| Elimination of intersegment profits in assets | (10,000) |
| Intersegment notes | (100,000) |
| General corporate assets | 100,000 |
| Equity investments | 184,000 |
| Consolidated total assets | $1,450,000 |

# ENTERPRISEWIDE DISCLOSURES

The focus in **FASB 131** is to provide financial statement users with information by which they may determine the risks and potential returns of an entity, using the same basis of information aggregation as used by the company's management. Certainly, the risks of doing business in one country may be quite different from the risks of doing business in another country. Today's large multinational entities have operations in many countries and foreign markets. In addition, a company that obtains a significant percentage of its revenue from just one customer has a different risk profile than a company that has many smaller customers. Thus, **FASB 131** established what it termed *enterprisewide disclosure* standards to provide users more information about the risks of the company. These enterprisewide disclosures are typically made in a footnote to the financial statements.

## Information about Products and Services

Three categories of required information are included under enterprisewide disclosures. The first is that the company is required to report the revenues from external customers for each major product and service, or each group of similar products and services, unless it is impracticable for it to do so. The reason for this requirement is that the company may have organized its operating segments on a basis different from its product lines. However, if the company does establish its operating segments by product line, then the segment disclosures discussed earlier in this chapter meet this first, enterprisewide disclosure requirement.

## Information about Geographic Areas

The second category is information about the geographic areas in which the company operates. The company must report the following unless it is impracticable for it to do so:

1. Revenues from external customers attributed to the company's home country of domicile (the United States for U.S. firms) and the revenue from external customers attributed to all foreign countries in which the enterprise generates revenues. If revenues from external customers generated in an individual country are material, then the revenues for that country shall also be separately disclosed.

2. Long-lived productive assets located in the entity's home country of domicile and the total assets located in all foreign countries in which the entity holds assets. As with revenue, if assets in an individual foreign country are material, then the amount of assets held in that specific country shall also be disclosed separately.

**FASB 131** defines the long-term assets as excluding financial instruments, long-term customer relationships of a financial institution, mortgage or other servicing rights, deferred policy acquisition costs, and deferred tax assets. The FASB believes that companies typically maintain accounting records on a country-by-country basis because of the political, economic, and other specific factors that differ across countries. Thus, if the company generates a material amount of revenue in a specific country or has made a material long-lived asset investment in a specific country, this information should be readily available for management to include in the enterprisewide disclosures. Although **FASB 131** specified no materiality threshold for specific country disclosures, the 10 percent guideline for disaggregated disclosures seems to have gained acceptance.

Note that the revenues for the geographic information are those only to unaffiliated, external customers. Intersegment revenues are not included. The assets are only those long-lived, productive assets and exclude current assets and several types of noncurrent assets as specified by **FASB 131.** All companies must disclose domestic versus total foreign revenues and long-lived assets unless it is impracticable to do so. For purposes of the following disclosure, assume that $840,000 of the total consolidated assets of $1,450,000 are determined to be long-lived, productive assets meeting the specifications of **FASB 131.** Separate country disclosures would be provided for material amounts. Assume that Peerless uses a 10 percent materiality threshold for assessing its foreign operations. Therefore, separate disclosure is presented for any country having greater than or equal to 10 percent of the consolidated revenue or the total long-lived assets. An example of the footnote disclosure that could be made by Peerless Products follows:

| Geographic Information | | |
| --- | --- | --- |
| | **Revenue** | **Long-Lived Asset** |
| United States | $380,000 | $471,000 |
| Total Foreign | 192,000 | 369,000 |
| Total | $572,000 | $840,000 |
| Significant Countries: | | |
| Canada | $116,000 | $220,000 |
| Mexico | 28,000 | 102,000 |

The company must also disclose the basis for attributing revenues from external customers to the individual countries. For example, one method may be to assign revenues based on the location of the customer.

### Information about Major Customers

The third and final category of enterprisewide disclosures required by **FASB 131** is information about major customers. An important issue is how to define an individual customer. For applying the disclosure test, each of the following is considered to be an individual customer: any single customer (including a group of customers or companies under common control), the federal government, a state government, a local government, or a foreign government. Materiality is not defined for this disclosure, but again, the 10 percent guideline seems to have gained the support of practice. The disclosures include the amount of revenue from each significant customer and the identity of the segment or segments reporting the revenues. The names of the individual customers need not be disclosed. The following is an example of the type of footnote disclosure that Peerless Products could use:

> Revenues from one customer of the Food Products segment represent approximately $64,000 of the company's consolidated revenues.

This concludes the discussion of segment reporting. The remainder of the chapter presents another major area of financial disclosure: interim financial reporting.

## INTERIM FINANCIAL REPORTING

*Interim reports,* which cover a time period of less than one year, provide timely information on the operating progress of the entity throughout the year. Interim reports can be for a week, a month, a quarter, or for several quarters. Many companies prepare monthly financial statements for internal management purposes. Publicly held companies are required to publish quarterly reports and the rapid stock market reaction to the public release of quarterly information indicates that investors and other financial statement users look closely at these reports. The quarterly report is, in many ways, a smaller version of the annual report. It includes an abbreviated statement of income, balance sheet, statement of cash flows, and selected footnotes and other disclosures for the quarter being reported, as well as comparative data for prior quarters.

Form 10-Q is the SEC's quarterly report and, for most companies, this quarterly report must be filed within 35 days after the end of each of the first three quarters. The annual report may be used in place of the interim report for the fourth quarter. The 35-day requirement is for publicly owned companies classified as "accelerated filers," which are companies with at least $75 million in aggregate market value that have been subject to the periodic and annual reporting requirements for at least one year, including the filing of at least one annual report. Most companies traded on the major stock exchanges are in the accelerated filers category. Those companies not meeting the accelerated filers criteria have 45 days after the end of each of the first three quarters to file their quarterly reports.

The SEC does not require quarterly financial statements to be audited, but selected quarterly financial data must be reported in a footnote in the annual financial report. This annual disclosure requirement means that the independent registered public accounting firm performing the company's annual audit must review the company's quarterly reports made during the fiscal year and note any errors or restatements. Because of the wide use of interim reports, including monthly and quarterly reports, accountants must be aware of the principles and procedures used in preparing these reports.

## THE FORMAT OF THE QUARTERLY FINANCIAL REPORT

Quarterly financial reports generally contain the following items:

1. An income statement for the most recent quarter of the current fiscal period and a comparative income statement for the same quarter for the prior fiscal year.

2. Income statements for the cumulative year-to-date time period and for the corresponding period of the prior fiscal year.

3. A condensed balance sheet at the end of the current quarter and a condensed balance sheet at the end of the prior fiscal year. However, companies should include the balance sheet as of the end of the corresponding interim period of the previous year if it is necessary for an understanding of the impact of seasonal fluctuations on the company's financial condition.

4. A statement of cash flows as of the end of the current cumulative year-to-date period and for the same time span for the prior year.

5. Footnotes that update those in the last annual report. These interim footnotes include summaries of material changes in measurement or major economic events that have occurred since the end of the most recent fiscal year.

6. A report by management analyzing and discussing the results for the latest interim period.

# ACCOUNTING ISSUES

Interim reporting presents accountants with several technical and conceptual measurement issues. Most of these center on the accounting concept of periodicity and the division of the annual period into interim periods. Note that interim reporting includes financial statements for any period less than one year, including monthly reports, quarterly reports, or any other portion of an annual period.

The use of quarterly reports to provide timely information is a fairly recent development. Many firms began publishing quarterly reports voluntarily in the late 1940s. These early reports raised substantive accounting issues because no standards existed to guide their presentation. Some firms' first three quarterly reports suggested a significant profit for the year, and then arbitrary and questionable fourth-quarter adjustments reconciled to an actual loss for the year. The lack of established guidelines led to experimentation with a variety of cost allocations among periods, resulting in unrealistic patterns of quarterly income. It was not until 1973, when the Accounting Principles Board issued **APB Opinion No. 28,** "Interim Financial Reporting" (APB 28), that guidelines were finally standardized.

## Discrete versus Integral View of Interim Reporting

Two divergent views of interim reporting were held before the release of **APB 28.** The *discrete theory of interim reporting* views each interim period as a basic accounting period to be evaluated as if it were an annual accounting period. Any end-of-period adjustments and deferrals are determined using the same accounting principles used for the annual report.

The *integral theory of interim reporting* views an interim period as an installment of an annual period. Under this view, recognition and adjustment of certain income or expense items may be affected by judgments about the expected results of the entire year's operations. For example, expenses that normally would be charged to operations in one period for annual accounting purposes could be deferred and expensed in several interim periods based on an allocation using sales volume, production levels, or some other basis.

To examine the differences between these two theories, assume that Peerless Products Corporation incurred a $20,000 cost at the beginning of the second quarter of its fiscal year for an advertising campaign intended to generate sales revenue for the remainder of the year. Under the discrete view, the entire $20,000 must be charged against income in the second quarter. Under the integral view, however, the advertising cost could initially be recorded as a deferred cost and expensed over the second, third, and fourth interim periods. The allocation to the individual periods could be made on the basis of the sales volume generated or some other appropriate basis. Under the integral view, one interim period would not bear the entire expense that benefits more than one interim period.

Both views were applied in practice, and it was up to the Accounting Principles Board to settle the conflict. The integral view was selected as the primary theory for interim reporting, although some modifications of this theory were made so that reports would conform closely to the results of operations for the year.

## Accounting Pronouncements on Interim Reporting

**APB 28** standardized the preparation and reporting of interim income statements. The opinion defines the income elements and the measurement of costs on an interim basis. The opinion also provides guidance for the annual report footnote summarizing the published interim disclosures and explaining any adjustments required to make the interim figures total the annual figures. This conformance to the annual report increases the reliability of the published interim statements and brings interim reporting under the view of the external auditors who review the footnotes in the annual report as part of the audit.

**FASB Statement No. 154,** "Accounting Changes and Error Corrections" (FASB 154), issued in 2005, replaced **APB Opinion No. 20,** "Accounting Changes" (APB 20), and **FASB Statement No. 3,** "Reporting Accounting Changes in Interim Financial Statements" (FASB 3). **FASB 154** specifies that a change in an accounting principle made in an interim period is reported using the retrospective application to the prechange interim periods for the direct effects of the change. The financial statements for the earliest period presented, either annual or interim, are adjusted for the effects of the change at that point in time and all subsequent financial statements, again both annual and interim, are adjusted for the newly adopted accounting principle. A change in estimate in an interim period is reported currently and prospectively, and no prior periods are restated. A change in entity in an interim period requires retrospective application.

**FASB Interpretation No. 18,** "Accounting for Income Taxes in Interim Periods" (FIN 18), amended **APB 28.** This interpretation tackles the difficult problems of measuring the tax provision for interim reports when the actual tax expense is based on annual income. The interpretation allows estimates and judgments in order to obtain a reasonable relationship between the reported interim operating income and the related income tax provision. Examples of accounting for taxes in interim statements are presented later in this chapter.

## International Financial Reporting Standards for Interim Reporting

The minimum content for an interim financial report to be in accordance with IFRS is defined in **International Accounting Standard 34,** "Interim Financial Reporting" (IAS 34). The international standards for interims are very similar to those of U.S. GAAP and explicitly recognize that more estimates may be used in determining interim amounts than for measurements of annual financial data. Materiality tests for interim reporting are made based on the relation to the interim period data, not on an estimate of annual data. **IAS 34** requires year-to-date disclosures in addition to the specific interim period disclosures, just as required by U.S. GAAP.

# REPORTING STANDARDS FOR INTERIM INCOME STATEMENTS

The form of the interim income statement is the same as the form of the annual income statement. Some differences exist in the measurement of specific components of income because of the shorter time period. In general, the accounting standards used for interim statements are the same as those used for the annual statements, although **APB 28** provides an abundance of technical assistance to measure and report on an interim basis. Figure 13–5 presents an overview of the major accounting principles used for the interim income statement. The technical requirements relevant to interim reporting are discussed in the following sections.

**FIGURE 13–5**  **Overview of Interim Income Statement Accounting Principles**

| | |
|---|---|
| Revenue | Recognize as earned during an interim period on same basis as used for annual reporting. |
| Cost of goods sold | Product costs for interim period recognized on same basis as used for annual reporting, except for interims: |
| | • Estimated gross profit rates may be used to determine interim cost of goods sold. |
| | • Temporary liquidations of LIFO-base inventories are charged to cost of goods sold using expected replacement cost of the items. |
| | • Lower-of-cost-or-market valuation method allows for loss recoveries for increases in market prices in later interim periods of the same fiscal year. |
| | • Standard cost systems should use same procedures as for annual reporting except that price variances or volume or capacity variances expected to be absorbed by end of the year should be deferred. |
| All other costs and expenses | Expense as incurred or allocated among interim periods' expenses based on benefits received or other systematic and rational basis. |
| Income taxes | Based on estimated annual effective tax rate, with recognition of tax benefits of an operating loss if benefits are assured beyond a reasonable doubt; second and subsequent quarters are based on changes in cumulative amount of tax computed, including changes in estimates. |
| Disposal of a component of the entity, or extraordinary, unusual, infrequently occurring, and contingent items | Recognize in interim period in which they occur. |
| Accounting changes: | |
| 1. Change in accounting principle | Retrospective application to all prechange interim periods reported. |
| 2. Change in an accounting estimate | Apply to current and prospective interim periods only. |
| 3. Change in a reporting entity | Retrospective application to all prechange interim periods reported. |

## Revenue

One of the most significant elements of the interim income statement is revenue from sales. Investors wish to assess the entity's revenue-generating capability, so they compare revenue of the current interim period with revenue of the corresponding interim period of prior years. The measurement basis used to determine revenue earned in an interim period should be the same as that used for the full fiscal year.

Thus, revenue must be recognized and reported in the period in which earned and cannot be deferred to other periods to present a more stable revenue stream. Revenue from seasonal businesses, such as in agriculture, food products, wholesale or retail outlets, and amusements, cannot be manipulated to eliminate seasonal trends.

The APB considered the issue of seasonality to be very important. Businesses that experience material seasonal variations in their revenue are encouraged to supplement their interim reports with information for 12-month periods ending at the interim date for the current and preceding years. Such disclosures reduce the possibility that users of the reports might make unwarranted inferences about the annual results from an interim report with material seasonal variation.

## Cost of Goods Sold and Inventory

Cost of goods sold is generally the largest single expense on the interim statement of income. A general rule is that interim cost of goods sold should be computed with the direct and allocated cost elements on the same basis as used to compute the annual cost of goods sold. However, **APB 28** does permit the following practical modifications to this general rule:

1. *Use estimated gross profit rates.* Estimated gross profit rates may be used to compute the interim cost of goods sold. Thus, a physical inventory count does not need to be made in each interim period.

2. *LIFO temporary liquidations.* Due to seasonality and other factors, companies using the LIFO method of inventory valuation sometimes have temporary liquidations of the LIFO-base inventory during one or more interim periods. These temporary liquidations are expected to be replenished by the end of the fiscal year. In these cases, the interim cost of goods sold is charged for the expected replacement cost of the liquidated inventory, not the LIFO historical cost of the inventory. If, by the end of the year, the LIFO inventory base is not replaced, then the liquidated inventory is charged to cost of goods sold at its LIFO cost base.

3. *Lower-of-cost-or-market valuations.* Inventory losses from decreases in market value below cost are recognized in the period of the decline. Recoveries of market price in subsequent interim periods should be recognized in the period of recovery as recoveries of losses that were recognized in prior interim periods of that fiscal year. No gains are recognized for increases of market value above cost. Temporary market price declines that are expected to be reversed by the end of the fiscal year do not have to be recognized in the interim period because no loss is expected for the full fiscal year.

4. *Standard cost systems.* Manufacturers that use standard cost systems to compute cost of goods sold and ending inventory should use the same procedures for determining variances for an interim period as are used for the fiscal year. However, variances that are anticipated to be absorbed by the end of the fiscal year are usually not included in computing interim income.

### Illustration of Temporary LIFO Liquidation

The reason that the interim treatment of LIFO inventory liquidations differs from the annual treatment of LIFO liquidations is that the inventory is expected to be replaced by the end of the fiscal year. Interim income for the period of the temporary liquidation would be overstated if cost of goods sold were charged with the lower LIFO inventory costs in a time of rising prices. The following example illustrates this point.

1. During the third quarter of its fiscal year, Special Foods experienced a temporary liquidation of 2,000 units in its LIFO base owing to seasonal fluctuations. The LIFO unit cost is $25. The liquidation is normal, and the company plans to replace the liquidated inventory during the early part of the next (fourth) interim period.

2. The estimated replacement cost of the inventory is $35 per unit.

   The entry in the third interim period to account for the temporary inventory liquidation is:

| (1) | Cost of Goods Sold | 70,000 | |
|---|---|---|---|
| | Inventory | | 50,000 |
| | Excess of Replacement Cost over LIFO | | |
| | Cost of Inventory Liquidated | | 20,000 |
| | Record temporary LIFO inventory liquidation: | | |
| | $70,000 = 2,000 units × $35 | | |
| | $50,000 = 2,000 units × $25 LIFO cost | | |

The interim income statement presents cost of goods sold at the expected replacement cost. The Excess of Replacement Cost over LIFO Cost of Inventory Liquidated should be shown as a current liability on the interim balance sheet, although some accountants net this against the inventory reported on the interim balance sheet.

When the inventory is replaced at $36 per unit during the fourth quarter, the following entry is made:

| (2) | Cost of Goods Sold | 2,000 | |
| | Inventory | 50,000 | |
| | Excess of Replacement Cost over | | |
| |   LIFO Cost of Inventory Liquidated | 20,000 | |
| |     Accounts Payable | | 72,000 |
| |   Record replacement of LIFO inventory liquidation: | | |
| |     $50,000 = 2,000 \times \$25$ LIFO cost | | |
| |     $72,000 = 2,000 \times \$36$ | | |

The actual replacement price of $36 is different from the estimated replacement price of $35. The difference is an adjustment to cost of goods sold in the replacement period. The third quarter's interim report is not retroactively restated. If the liquidated inventory is not replaced by the end of the fiscal year, the liability account is written off to Cost of Goods Sold, decreasing the reported annual cost of goods sold to its correct amount.

### Illustration of Market Write-Down and Recovery

The following example illustrates the use of the lower-of-cost-or-market (LCM) method for interim reports:

1. At the beginning of its fiscal year, Peerless Products has 10,000 units of inventory on hand with a FIFO cost of $10 each.

2. No additional purchases are made during the year.

3. The sales and market values at the end of each quarter during the fiscal year are as follows:

| Quarter | Units Sold in Quarter | Unit Market Values at End of Quarter |
|---------|-----------------------|--------------------------------------|
| 1 | 2,000 | $ 7 |
| 2 | 2,000 | 6 |
| 3 | 2,000 | 7 |
| 4 | 2,000 | 11 |

Peerless is not certain of the causes of the reductions in market value and considers them to be permanent; therefore, it recognizes the reductions in the quarters in which they occur. *No recognition is required* if the reductions are anticipated to be temporary, with recovery by year-end.

Figure 13–6 presents the calculations needed to adjust Peerless's inventory account to the lower of cost or market. At the end of the first quarter, the ending inventory of the quarter is written down by $24,000, and a loss is recognized on the interim income statement. Many companies report this write-down as part of their cost of goods sold because it is associated with inventory. By the end of the second quarter, a write-down of $6,000 of the ending inventory is required. The third-quarter interim report shows a loss recovery of $4,000 due to an increase in inventory replacement costs. Note that this is a recovery of valuation losses recognized in prior quarters. In quarter 4, the $11 market price is $1 higher than the initial cost of the inventory. A $6,000 loss recovery on the fourth-quarter ending inventory of the 2,000 units is recognized to bring the inventory valuation from $7 per unit to its original cost of $10 per unit. Note that the inventory may not be valued at an amount in excess of cost.

A graphical representation of the market prices during the year is presented in Figure 13–7. Note that after decreasing during the first two quarters, the market price increases during the third and fourth quarters. At year-end, the price is $11 per unit, which is above the initial cost for the inventory.

**FIGURE 13–6**
**Interim Lower-of-Cost-or-Market Analysis of the Inventory Account of Peerless Products Corporation**

| | | Inventory | | |
|---|---|---|---|---|
| Quarter | Item | Units | Unit Price | Dollars |
| | Balance, beginning of year | 10,000 | $10 | $100,000 |
| 1 | Inventory sold, first quarter | (2,000) | $10 | (20,000) |
| | Adjustment to market: [8,000 units × ($10 − $7)] | 8,000 | (3) | (24,000) |
| | Balance, end of first quarter | 8,000 | $ 7 | $ 56,000 |
| 2 | Inventory sold, second quarter | (2,000) | $ 7 | (14,000) |
| | Adjustment to market: [6,000 units × ($7 − $6)] | 6,000 | (1) | (6,000) |
| | Balance, end of second quarter | 6,000 | $ 6 | $ 36,000 |
| 3 | Inventory sold, third quarter | (2,000) | $ 6 | (12,000) |
| | Market price recovery: [4,000 units × ($6 − $7)] | 4,000 | 1 | 4,000 |
| | Balance, end of third quarter | 4,000 | $ 7 | $ 28,000 |
| 4 | Inventory sold, fourth quarter | (2,000) | $ 7 | (14,000) |
| | Market price recovery: [2,000 units × ($7 − $10)] | 2,000 | 3 | 6,000 |
| | Balance, end of fourth quarter | 2,000 | $10(a) | $ 20,000 |

(*a*) Note that although market value is $11, inventory valuation cannot exceed cost.

Another way to view the effects of the write-downs is to compute the amount that would be reported in each quarter's cost of goods sold. This amount would include the costs assigned to the goods sold during the quarter plus the effects of any inventory write-downs and less the effects of any recoveries of losses recognized in prior interim periods. These market adjustments are normally treated as adjustments of cost of goods sold to represent all the product costs in one location on the income statement. The following table shows the computation of cost of goods sold for each quarter:

**FIGURE 13–7**
**Graph of Market Prices of Inventory**

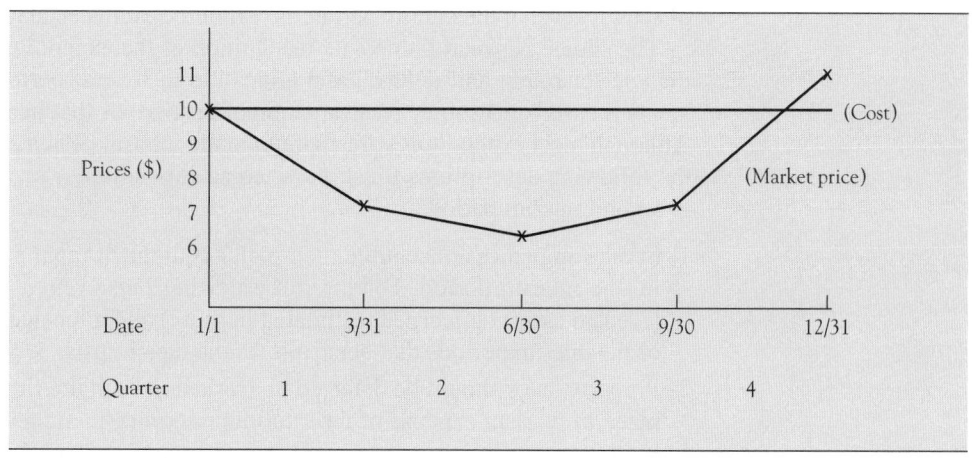

| Quarter | Costs Assigned to Goods Sold | Ending Inventory Write-Down to Market (or Loss Recovery) | Total |
|---|---|---|---|
| 1 | 2,000 units × $10 | 8,000 units × $3 | $44,000 |
| 2 | 2,000 units × $7 | 6,000 units × $1 | 20,000 |
| 3 | 2,000 units × $6 | (4,000 units × $1) | 8,000 |
| 4 | 2,000 units × $7 | (2,000 units × $3) | 8,000 |

If the reductions in market value in quarters 1 and 2 were considered temporary, no write-downs would need to be recognized and therefore no loss recoveries would be recognized in quarters 3 and 4. The total of the cost of goods sold reported for the interims must reconcile to the amount reported on the annual financial statements. Note that the year-end market price ($11) is higher than the market price at the beginning of the year ($10). On the annual statement:

$$8,000 \text{ units} \times \$10 \text{ unit price} = \$80,000$$

On the interim statements:

| | |
|---|---|
| Quarter 1 | $44,000 |
| Quarter 2 | 20,000 |
| Quarter 3 | 8,000 |
| Quarter 4 | 8,000 |
| Total | $80,000 |

To be able to focus on the main points of the example, it was assumed that no additional inventory was acquired during the year. Of course, in actual practice, most companies make continuous inventory acquisitions. These purchases would be added to inventory at whatever cost flow method the company uses. The lower-of-cost-or-market valuation method would be applied at the end of each quarter in the same manner as in the example, and the losses or loss recoveries would be recognized.

## All Other Costs and Expenses

The integral view adopted by the APB is evident when dealing with interim period costs. The general principle is that costs and expenses should be charged to interim income in the interim period in which they are incurred. Some costs and expenses however, are allocated among the interim periods based on an estimate of time used, benefit received, or activity level of the interim period, as part of the estimated amount for the full fiscal year.

The choice between immediate recognition of the expenditure on the interim period's income statement and deferral and allocation to several periods' interim income statements is based on a subjective evaluation of the periods that benefit from the expenditure. Although most expenditures are charged to the interim period in which they are incurred, the following descriptions illustrate when an expenditure may be deferred and allocated to several interim periods:

1. Some companies concentrate their major equipment repairs in a plant shut-down time in one interim period. For interim reporting these repair costs should be deferred (prepaid asset) or accrued (estimated liability) and allocated to repair expense in each of the interim periods that benefit from the repair costs.

2. Property taxes should be deferred or accrued in each interim period rather than recognized fully as an expense of the interim period in which they are paid.

3. Major advertising campaign costs should be allocated to the interim periods that benefit from them rather than recognized solely in the interim period in which they are incurred. A typical allocation procedure is to estimate the anticipated sales volume for

each of the interim periods that will benefit from the advertising campaign. Generally, the total advertising costs are expensed for determining annual income and no deferral is made beyond the fiscal year-end.

Note that a company can accrue probable and estimable costs in earlier interim periods than the period in which the cash is paid. For example, Peerless has a management policy of closing its main production plant each August for a two-week painting and repairs period. On January 1 the company estimates that a total of $60,000 will be incurred for this plant rehabilitation effort and that it will benefit all four quarters of the year. The company will allocate this cost to each quarter, even the two quarters preceding the actual shutdown. In this case, an accrual for the repair expense will be made in the first and second quarters. When the actual cost is incurred in the third quarter, the accrual liability will be eliminated, but the repair expense will still be shown for each quarter. The remaining repair expense for the year will then be allocated to the third and fourth quarters. The key point is that the repair expense can be allocated to each quarter that benefits, even though the cash flow for the item does not occur until a late quarter in the fiscal year. Accruals (estimated liabilities) and deferrals (prepaid assets) are used for these applications.

### Illustration of Deferral and Allocation of Advertising Costs

On April 1, the beginning of the second quarter of Peerless Products and Subsidiary's consolidated fiscal year, a $20,000 cost was incurred for an advertising campaign expected to benefit the last three quarters of the current year. Consolidated sales for the second, third, and fourth quarters are expected to total $400,000. In this case, Peerless determined that the advertising campaign would not benefit the first quarter; therefore, no advertising expense was accrued in the first quarter ending March 31, and the only advertising expenditure during the year is the $20,000 incurred on April 1.

The $20,000 cost is recorded as a prepaid asset when incurred and then charged to Advertising Expense in each of the interim periods benefited, as shown in Figure 13–8. The allocation base selected is the quarterly sales in the periods benefited as a percentage of the estimated total sales for the period of benefit.

At the beginning of the third quarter (July 1), $15,000 of advertising cost remains in Prepaid Advertising. If actual quarterly sales differ from the estimated amounts, the allocation procedure is revised for the change in estimate. For example, if on September 30, management determines the consolidated sales for the third quarter, ending on September 30, to be $120,000 and estimates that fourth-quarter sales will be $180,000, then the remaining balance of $15,000 in Prepaid Advertising is allocated to the third quarter as follows:

$$\$6,000 = \frac{\$120,000}{\$300,000} \times \$15,000$$

The fourth quarter is charged for any remaining balance in the Prepaid Advertising account.

**FIGURE 13–8**
**Accounting for Advertising Costs That Benefit More than One Interim Period**

| Date | Quarterly Sales | Debit Advertising Expense | Credit Prepaid Advertising | Balance in Prepaid Advertising |
|---|---|---|---|---|
| April 1 | | | | $20,000 |
| June 30 | $100,000 | $ 5,000(a) | $ 5,000 | 15,000(b) |
| September 30 | 100,000 | 5,000 | 5,000 | 10,000 |
| December 31 | 200,000 | 10,000 | 10,000 | -0- |
| Totals | $400,000 | $20,000 | $20,000 | |

(*a*) $5,000 = ($100,000 / $400,000) × $20,000.
(*b*) $15,000 = $20,000 − $5,000.

## Accounting for Income Taxes in Interim Periods

The *interim income tax* computation poses a particularly troublesome problem for accountants because the actual tax burden is computed on income for the entire fiscal year. In addition, temporary differences between tax accounting and GAAP accounting require the recognition of deferred taxes. Nevertheless, the interim tax provision is a significant item and requires estimates and a number of subjective evaluations based on the anticipated annual tax. The first step is to determine the effective annual tax rate for use in computing the interim income tax provision.

### *Estimating the Effective Annual Tax Rate*

Estimates are a normal part of the accounting cycle, and the interim income tax provision is based on an estimate of the effective annual tax rate on income from continuing operations. The estimated annual tax rate includes all anticipated tax credits, state income taxes, foreign income taxes, capital gains taxes, and other tax planning efforts that are expected for the full fiscal period. The estimate is updated each interim period and the interim tax provision or benefit is then determined.

Items such as unusual or infrequent events, discontinued operations, and extraordinary items are not included in the estimate because the statement of income reports these separately along with their related net-of-tax effects. Also, extraordinary items often have specific tax treatments different from operating income. For example, a fire loss of a building may involve depreciation recapture and other capital loss tax considerations.

**Differences between Book and Tax Income** There typically will be differences between the amount of operating income computed for financial statement (book) purposes and the operating income computed for tax purposes. The two major categories of differences are discussed in **FASB Statement 109,** "Accounting for Income Taxes" (FASB 109), and are often covered extensively in intermediate financial accounting classes.

The first category is most often referred to as "permanent" or nontemporary differences. Permanent differences are not included in determining the amount of taxable income for a period. Examples of these permanent differences include:

1. Life insurance premiums paid by the company on executive policies for which the company is the beneficiary (not tax deductible).
2. Proceeds of life insurance collected (not tax includible).
3. Dividends received deduction on dividends received from U.S. corporation stock investments (not tax includible).
4. Interest income received on state or local government bonds that is classified as not taxable (not tax includible).
5. Certain types of fines or court penalties designated as not tax deductible.

These items are included in the determination of financial statement income (book), but they are not included in the computation of taxable income. Thus, book income is adjusted for these items in order to determine the taxable income for the interim period.

The second category of differences is usually referred to as "temporary" differences. Temporary differences between the recognition of a transaction for book versus tax income result in deferred taxes. For example, a revenue may be recognized for tax either before or after the period in which it is recognized for book purposes. Or, an expense may be recognized for tax purposes in a period different from that used for book purposes. Examples of temporary differences include:

1. Rent collected in advance (reported on tax return in period collected but as revenue on books in period earned).
2. Estimated expenses and losses (reported on books at time of accrual but on tax return in period paid).
3. Accelerated depreciation on tax return and straight-line depreciation on the income statement (difference of depreciation expense on books versus tax).

**FIGURE 13–9**
Estimation of
Effective Annual
Tax Rate

| | Estimated Annual Amounts |
|---|---|
| Income from continuing operations | $225,000 |
| Adjust for permanent differences: | |
|    Add premiums on key officers' life insurance | 2,000 |
|    Deduct dividends received exclusion | (27,000) |
| Estimated annual taxable income | $200,000 |
| Combined federal and state income taxes | × 38% |
| Estimated annual taxes before tax credits | $ 76,000 |
| Deduct business tax credit | (22,000) |
| Estimated income taxes for year | $ 54,000 |
| Divide by estimated annual income from continuing operations | $225,000 |
| Estimated effective annual tax rate on continuing operations ($54,000 ÷ $225,000) | 24% |

4. Revaluing inventory to lower-of-cost-or-market on financial statements (loss shown on books in period of write-down but on tax return in period sold).

The deferred tax asset or deferred tax liability created by these temporary differences is reported on the balance sheet. The income tax expense shown on the income statement is the sum of the income tax actually payable in the period plus (or minus for a deferred tax asset) the amount of the tax deferral for the period.

The reporting process is illustrated next.

### Illustration of Estimating Effective Annual Tax Rate

Figure 13–9 illustrates the computation of the tax rate. While proceeding through the example, note the adjustments, such as the differences between tax accounting and GAAP accounting, necessary to determine the annual rate. Following are data for the illustration:

1. Peerless Products and its subsidiary expect to earn $225,000 consolidated income from continuing operations for the 20X1 fiscal year.
2. Permanent differences between accounting income and tax income are expected to be $2,000 for premiums paid for life insurance carried by the company on key officers (company is beneficiary) and an exclusion of $27,000 for dividends received from investments in stocks of other companies.
3. The combined federal and state income tax rate is estimated to be 38 percent (30 percent federal and 8 percent state), and the company expects to be eligible for a $22,000 business tax credit related to new job development expenditures and employee retraining costs.

The estimated effective tax rate of 24 percent computed in Figure 13–9 is used to determine the income tax provision for the first quarter. Assuming that the first-quarter earnings were $20,000, the following entry records the tax provision:

| | | | |
|---|---|---|---|
| (3) | Income Tax Expense | 4,800 | |
| |    Income Taxes Payable | | 4,800 |
| |    Record first-quarter tax provision: | | |
| |     $4,800 = $20,000 × .24 effective tax rate | | |

### Updating the Estimated Annual Rate in Subsequent Interim Periods

Assume that second-quarter actual earnings are $25,000, for a cumulative total for the year to date of $45,000 ($20,000 + $25,000). The consolidated entity must first recompute its estimate of its effective annual tax rate based on the updated information it has at the end of the second quarter, such as additional differences between taxable and accounting income or a better estimate of projected annual earnings. Assuming the new estimated effective annual tax rate is 34 percent because of changes in the estimated amount of the available business tax credit and other changes in estimates, this rate replaces the 24 percent rate used at the end of the first quarter.

The new estimated tax rate is used to compute the estimated year-to-date income tax provision at the end of the second interim period, as follows:

| | |
|---|---:|
| Actual cumulative income for first two quarters ($20,000 + $25,000) | $45,000 |
| Updated estimated effective annual tax rate | × 34% |
| Cumulative income tax provision (expense) | $15,300 |
| Less: Income tax provision made in first quarter | (4,800) |
| Income tax provision required in second quarter | $10,500 |

Peerless Products and its subsidiary report an income tax expense of $10,500 on the second-quarter consolidated income statement. The tax provision is cumulative, and the first-quarter provision is *not* retroactively restated for the change in the estimate of the annual tax rate.

The example does not include any temporary differences between accounting income and taxable income that result in deferred taxes. Temporary differences generally do not affect the estimate of the tax provision. Instead, the recognition of any temporary difference is normally made in the entry to record the tax provision and associated tax liability. For example, if $2,000 of the second-quarter income of $25,000 is due to a temporary difference in which accounting income is higher than tax income, the following entry is made to recognize the provision and deferral:

| | | | |
|---|---|---:|---:|
| (4) | Income Tax Expense | 10,500 | |
| | Deferred Tax Liability | | 680 |
| | Income Taxes Payable | | 9,820 |
| | Record second-quarter tax provision: | | |
| | $10,500 = Income taxes payable plus deferred tax liability | | |
| | $   680 = Computation of deferred tax liability effect from temporary difference between tax and book income | | |

### Losses and Operating Loss Carrybacks and Carryforwards

Accountants face an interesting problem when a company has a year-to-date loss as of the end of an interim period. Normally, an operating loss creates a tax benefit (that is, reduces tax payable) because the loss can be carried back against the operating income shown in previous years and the company may file a claim for a refund of taxes paid in prior years. After the carryback portion of an operating loss is depleted, any remaining operating loss is carried forward against future operating income. These carryback and carryforward provisions, however, apply only to annual results, not to interim results.

These and other special tax problems are discussed in **FIN 18.** The first part of the interpretation deals with the numerous alternative income trends possible, such as an operating loss for year to date but income anticipated for the year, or operating income for year to date but loss expected for the year. The possible combinations of interim and annual results are too numerous to show here, but one special case is covered. This special case is the determination of the tax benefit for a company with a year-to-date operating loss but with the expectation of an annual income. The issue is how to determine and report the income tax for the interim periods.

**FASB Statement No. 109,** "Accounting for Income Taxes" (FASB 109), also addresses the issue of accounting for income taxes in an interim period. **FASB 109** affirms the general rule that the realization of a tax benefit must be assured beyond a reasonable doubt before the benefit may be recognized in the financial statements. For interim

**FIGURE 13–10**
Interim Analysis
When Tax Benefit
of Operating Loss
Is Assured

| Reporting Period | Continuing Income (Loss) before Taxes | | Estimated Effective Annual Tax Rate, % | Tax (Benefit) | | |
|---|---|---|---|---|---|---|
| | Reporting Period | Year to Date | | Year to Date (a) | Less Previously Provided | Reported in Period |
| First quarter | $ (40,000) | $ (40,000) | 24.0% | $ (9,600) | | $ (9,600) |
| Second quarter | $ 20,000 | (20,000) | 34.0 | (6,800) | $ (9,600) | 2,800 |
| Third quarter | 80,000 | 60,000 | 34.0 | 20,400 | (6,800) | 27,200 |
| Fourth quarter | 162,000 | 222,000 | 27.9(b) | 62,000 | 20,400 | 41,600 |
| Fiscal year | $222,000 | | | | | $62,000 |

(a) Year to date: Year-to-date continuing income (loss) × Updated estimated effective annual tax rate.

(b) Rounded off.

reporting purposes, the most common reason for allowing the recognition of a tax benefit for a company with a year-to-date operating loss is that the company has had consistent seasonal trends in income during the year. Thus, the company has generally had income in the later interim periods that has offset the losses in the earlier interim periods. **FASB Interpretation No. 48,** "Accounting for Uncertainty in Income Taxes: An Interpretation of FASB Statement No. 109" (FIN 48), established a more-likely-than-not criterion of having a likelihood of more than 50 percent as the threshold for beyond a reasonable doubt. Therefore, a company with an operating loss in the early interim periods, with consistent experience of seasonality and income for the year, can recognize a tax benefit of a to-date operating loss in the early interim periods. If the realization of a tax benefit of an interim operating loss is not assured by the end of the fiscal period, the company cannot show any tax benefit on the interim statements.

### *Illustration of Interim Operating Loss*

Figure 13–10 presents the computation of the tax or benefit that should be shown on the interim statements if a company experiences a year-to-date loss but anticipates an annual income. For example, assume that the consolidated entity of Peerless Products Corporation and Special Foods Inc. has an actual first-quarter loss of $40,000 but expects an annual income of $2,22,000. The estimated annual tax rate is 24 percent. The consolidated entity has a normal seasonal variation of losses in the first quarter followed by profits in subsequent quarters. Therefore, the tax benefit of the operating loss of $9,600 ($40,000 × .24) is assured beyond a reasonable doubt, and the tax benefit is shown in the loss quarter.

A partial income statement for the first quarter follows. Note how the tax benefit reduces the reported net loss:

**PEERLESS PRODUCTS AND SPECIAL FOODS**
**Partial Interim Consolidated Income Statement**
**First Quarter Ended March 31, 20X1**

| | |
|---|---|
| Operating Loss before Income Tax Effect | $(40,000) |
| Less: Tax Benefit of Operating Loss | 9,600 |
| Net Loss | $(30,400) |

At the end of 20X1, Peerless Products and Subsidiary computed its actual annual income tax provision for 20X1 as $62,000. The year-to-date tax provision in the fourth quarter should equal the total actual annual provision, and the amount of tax reported in the fourth quarter is the balance necessary to reach the amount of the annual provision. Therefore, the actual annual income tax rate on continuing income for 20X1 was 27.9 percent ($62,000 annual tax provision ÷ $222,000 annual income from continuing operations before the deduction for income to noncontrolling interest).

**FIGURE 13–11**
**Interim Analysis When Operating Loss Benefit Is Not Assured**

| Reporting Period | Continuing Income (Loss) before Taxes | | Estimated Effective Annual Tax Rate, % | Tax (Benefit) | | |
| | Reporting Period | Year to Date | | Year to Date (a) | Less Previously Provided | Reported in Period |
|---|---|---|---|---|---|---|
| First quarter | $ (40,000) | $ (40,000) | 24.0% | $    -0- | | $    -0- |
| Second quarter | $  20,000 | (20,000) | 34.0 | $    -0- | $    -0- | $    -0- |
| Third quarter | 80,000 | 60,000 | 34.0 | 20,400 | $    -0- | 20,400 |
| Fourth quarter | 162,000 | 222,000 | 27.9 | 62,000 | 20,400 | 41,600 |
| Fiscal year | $222,000 | | | | | $62,000 |

(*a*) Year to date: Year-to-date continuing income (loss) × Updated estimated effective annual tax rate.

If the realizability of the tax benefit from the operating loss is not assured beyond a reasonable doubt, no tax benefit should be shown. This case is presented in Figure 13–11. Note that the actual annual provisions are identical; the differences are in the interim presentations.

### Disposal of a Component of the Entity or Extraordinary, Unusual, Infrequently Occurring, and Contingent Items

**APB 28** requires the measurement and reporting of major nonoperating items on the same bases as used to prepare the annual report. Extraordinary items, discontinued operations, and unusual and infrequently occurring items should be reported in the interim period in which they occur and not allocated to the other interim periods of the year. The materiality test for extraordinary items should be based on the estimate of income for the entire fiscal year. The materiality test for discontinued operations and unusual and infrequent transactions should be based on the operating income of the interim period in which the discontinued operations are first reported.

Contingencies or other major uncertainties that could affect the company also must be disclosed on the same basis as that used in the annual report. This disclosure is required to provide information on items that might affect the fairness of the interim report. The procedures for measuring and reporting contingencies in both interim and annual reports are presented in **FASB Statement No. 5,** "Accounting for Contingencies" (FASB 5).

## ACCOUNTING CHANGES IN INTERIM PERIODS

**FASB Statement No. 154,** "Accounting Changes and Error Corrections" (FASB 154), specified three categories of accounting changes, as follows: (*a*) change in an accounting principle, (*b*) change in an accounting estimate, and (*c*) change in a reporting entity. The statement noted that a correction of an error in previously issued financial statements is not an accounting change and the entity must restate all prior financial statements presented to correct the error(s) in those financials. The standard does not alter the transition provisions presented in existing pronouncements for applying changes in specific accounting requirements covered in an existing standard.

### Change in an Accounting Principle (Retrospective Application)

A change in accounting principle may be made by an entity only if the change is required by a new accounting standard, or if the company can justify that the new accounting principle is preferable to the old accounting principle. A change from a generally accepted accounting principle to another generally accepted accounting principle for measurement or valuation purposes requires that the *retrospective application* process be applied to all prior periods' financial statements, including the financial statements for interim periods. Only the direct effects of the change in accounting principle, including any related tax effects, are included in the retrospective application to the prior periods.

A change from an accounting principle *not* generally accepted to a generally accepted accounting principle is a correction of an error, requiring restatement of all prior financial statements. However, accounting for changes in the method of depreciation, amortization, or depletion for long-lived, nonfinancial assets, such as from the straight-line to the accelerated method of depreciation for equipment, are accounted for as a change in estimate effected by a change in accounting principle. Changes in accounting estimates are discussed in the next section of this chapter.

### *Retrospective Application*

Direct effects are those adjustments necessary to make the change in accounting principle in the immediately affected assets or liabilities. Indirect effects are those affecting current or future cash flows that result from making the change in accounting principle. These indirect effects are reported in the period the change is made. An adjusted balance sheet to reflect the retrospective application of the new accounting principle is provided for the earliest period presented. All financial statements for each subsequent annual and interim period are adjusted for the effects of the change in accounting principle. For example, if a company makes a change from the weighted-average method to the FIFO method of accounting for inventories in the current year, the company would retrospectively apply the FIFO method to all prior periods for which financial statements are provided. The beginning inventory amount for the earliest period presented would be adjusted to reflect the new accounting principle, with a corresponding adjustment to retained earnings, and the new method would be reflected in all subsequent financial statements presented.

If the cumulative amount of the effect of the change can be determined, but it is impracticable to determine its period-by-period effects, the company should report the cumulative amount of the change on the financial statements as of the beginning of the earliest period practicable and then revise the subsequent financial statements presented. However, if a company wishes to make an accounting change in principle in an interim period and the entity is not able to determine the effects of the change on the previous interim periods of the current fiscal year, the entity must wait until the beginning of a subsequent fiscal year to make the change in accounting principle.

## Change in an Accounting Estimate (Current and Prospective Application)

Changes in accounting estimates are the result of new information that becomes available to the entity. These changes are reported on a current and prospective basis only; that is, the changes are reported only in the current period in which the change is made and in the future periods affected by the change. Previously issued financial statements are *not* adjusted. An example of a change in accounting estimate is a change in the method of computing the allowance for uncollectibles of accounts receivable because more recent information indicates the prior provisions were inadequate.

### *Changes in Depreciation, Amortization, or Depletion*

**FASB 154** requires a change in the method of depreciation, amortization, or depletion of long-lived, nonfinancial assets because of new information, such as current usage patterns that differ from expectations, to be accounted for as a change in accounting estimate effected by a change in accounting principle. The current and prospective application is used to report this change and prior financial statements are not restated.

## Change in a Reporting Entity (Retrospective Application)

A change in reporting entity requires a retrospective application to all prior periods presented to reflect the new reporting entity. The primary examples of changes in reporting entity are: (*a*) presenting consolidated or combined financial statements rather than individual statements for the separate entities, (*b*) changing the specific subsidiaries that comprise the consolidated entity for which consolidated financials are presented, and (*c*) changing the entities that are included in combined financial statements.

An entity making an accounting change is also required to make a number of disclosures in the period of the change. Included in these disclosures are the effect of the change on income from continuing operations and net income. In the case of a change in accounting principle, the entity must also disclose the nature and justification for the change and the cumulative effect of the change on retained earnings or other components of equity as of the beginning of the earliest period presented.

### International Financial Reporting Standards for Accounting Changes

**International Accounting Standard No. 8,** "Accounting Policies, Changes in Accounting Estimates and Errors," (IAS 8), provides the accounting treatment and disclosures for changes in accounting policies, changes in accounting estimates, and corrections of errors. The international standards for these changes are very similar to U.S. GAAP. **IAS 8** specifies that changes in accounting policy are applied retrospectively unless the change was made in initial application of a standard, in which case the specific transitional provisions presented in that standard will be applied. Changes in accounting estimates are recognized in the period of the change and future periods (prospectively). Prior period errors are included in the international standard and are accounted for retrospectively, just as in U.S. GAAP.

| | |
|---|---|
| **Summary of Key Concepts** | Segment disclosures about an entity's components' operations and foreign areas in which an entity operates provide information about the different risks and profitability of each of the individual components that the entity comprises. These additional disclosures are useful in assessing past performance and prospects of future performance. A critical issue is the definition of a segment. The FASB allows management the flexibility it needs to disaggregate its operations but imposes several significance tests to determine which segments are separately reportable.<br><br>Interim reports must be issued by publicly held corporations so users of the information can assess corporate performance and make predictions about results for the annual fiscal period. The major issues are the measurement and disclosure problems of breaking down the annual reporting period into smaller parts. The FASB has selected the integral theory of interim reporting, which views an interim period as an integral part of an annual period. Many of the technical problems revolve around cost of goods sold and income taxes. Estimates based on expected annual results are allowed when determining both of these costs. Even with the estimation and measurement problems, interim reports are primary disclosure vehicles that are quickly and carefully evaluated by investors and other users of financial statements. |

**Key Terms**

discrete theory of interim reporting, *646*
enterprisewide disclosure, *643*
integral theory of interim reporting, *646*

interim income tax, *654*
interim reports, *645*
management approach, *634*
reportable operating segments, *635*

75 percent consolidated revenue test, *641*
10 percent significance rules, *635*

**Questions**

**Q13-1** How might information on a company's operations in different industries be helpful to investors?

**Q13-2** What is the relationship between the FASB's requirements for segment-based disclosures and a company's profit centers?

**Q13-3** What are the three 10 percent significance tests used to determine reportable segments under FASB 131? Give the numerator and denominator for each of the tests.

**Q13-4** Specifically, what items are in the determination of a segment's profit or loss?

**Q13-5** A company has 10 industry segments, of which the largest five account for 80 percent of the combined revenues of the company. What considerations are important in determining the number of segments that are separately reportable? How are the remaining segments reported?

**Q13-6**   Only two materiality tests are used to determine separately reportable foreign operations. What are these two tests? Why isn't the third test, the profit or loss test, used to assess foreign operations?

**Q13-7**   What information must be disclosed about a company's major customers? Are the names of customers disclosed?

**Q13-8**   How can interim reports be used by investors to identify a company's seasonal trends?

**Q13-9**   Distinguish between the discrete and integral views of interim reporting. Which view is used in APB Opinion No. 28?

**Q13-10**   How is revenue recognized on an interim basis?

**Q13-11**   Describe the basic rules for computing cost of goods sold and inventory on an interim basis. In what circumstances are estimates permitted to determine costs?

**Q13-12**   How does the application of the lower-of-cost-or-market valuation method for inventories differ between interim statements and annual statements?

**Q13-13**   How might the accounting for an advertising campaign expenditure of $200,000 in the first quarter of a company's fiscal year differ between the integral theory and the discrete theory of interim reporting?

**Q13-14**   Describe the process of updating the estimate of the effective annual tax rate in the second quarter of a company's fiscal year.

**Q13-15**   How is the tax benefit of an interim period's operating loss treated if the future realizability of the tax benefit is *not* assured beyond a reasonable doubt?

**Q13-16**   How are extraordinary items reported on an interim basis?

**Q13-17**   The Maness Company made a change in accounting for its inventories during the third quarter of its fiscal year. The company switched from the LIFO method to the average cost method. Describe the reporting of this accounting change on prior interim financial statements and on the third quarter's interim financial statements.

---

# Cases

### C13-1   Segment Disclosures [CMA Adapted]

Chemax Inc. manufactures a wide variety of pharmaceuticals, medical instruments, and other related medical supplies. Eighteen months ago the company developed and began to market a new product line of antihistamine drugs under various trade names. Sales and profitability of this product line during the current fiscal year greatly exceeded management's expectations. The new product line will account for 10 percent of the company's total sales and 12 percent of the company's operating income for the fiscal year ending June 30, 20X0. Management believes sales and profits will be significant for several years.

*Judgment*

Chemax is concerned that its market share and competitive position may suffer if it discloses the volume and profitability of its new product line in its annual financial statements. Management is not sure how FASB 131 applies in this case.

#### Required

*a.* What is the purpose of requiring segment information in financial statements?

*b.* Identify and explain the factors that should be considered when attempting to decide how products should be grouped to determine a single business segment.

*c.* What options, if any, does Chemax Inc. have with the disclosure of its new antihistamine product line? Explain your answer.

### C13-2   Matching Revenue and Expenses for Interim Periods

*Understanding*

Periodic reporting adds complexity to accounting by requiring estimates, accruals, deferrals, and allocations. Interim reporting creates even greater difficulties in matching revenue and expenses.

#### Required

*a.* Explain how revenue, product costs, gains, and losses should be recognized for interim periods.

*b.* Explain how determination of cost of goods sold and inventory differs for interim period reports versus annual reports.

*c.* Explain the interim accounting treatment of period costs such as depreciation.

d. Explain the treatment of the following items for interim financial statements:

(1) Long-term contracts

(2) Advertising

(3) Seasonal revenue

(4) Flood loss

(5) Annual major repairs and maintenance to plant and equipment during the last two weeks in December

### C13-3 Segment Disclosures in the Financial Statements [CMA Adapted]

*Analysis*

Bennett Inc. is a publicly held corporation whose diversified operations have been separated into five industry segments. Bennett is in the process of preparing its annual financial statements for the year ended December 31, 20X5. The following information has been collected for the preparation of the segment reports required by FASB 131.

**BENNETT INC.**
**Selected Data**
**For the Year Ended December 31, 20X5**
**(in thousands)**

| Item | Power Tools | Fastening Systems | Household Products | Plumbing Products | Security Systems |
|---|---|---|---|---|---|
| Sales to Unaffiliated Customers | $32,000 | $ 4,500 | $ 4,800 | $3,000 | $2,000 |
| Intersegment Sales | 10,000 | 5,500 | 200 | 1,000 | — |
| Total Revenue | 42,000 | 10,000 | 5,000 | 4,000 | 2,000 |
| Cost of Goods Sold | 30,000 | 8,000 | 4,500 | 3,100 | 1,700 |
| Operating Profit | 4,500 | 1,000 | (600) | 700 | (100) |
| Net Income | 2,600 | 800 | (750) | (100) | (200) |
| Segment Assets | 50,000 | 23,000 | 17,000 | 6,000 | 4,000 |

### Required

a. Determine which of the operating segments are reportable segments for Bennett. Your determination should include all required tests and the results of those tests for each of Bennett's five segments.

b. The reportable segments determined in (a) must represent a substantial portion of Bennett's total operations when taken together. Describe how to determine whether a substantial portion of Bennett's operations are explained by its segment information.

### C13-4 Determining Industry and Geographic Segments

*Research*

A major producer of cereal breakfast foods had been reporting in its annual reports just one dominant product line (cereals) in only the U.S. domestic geographic area. The company had no other separately reportable segments. For several years, the U.S. company had a Canadian subsidiary that produced a variety of pasta. In 20X5, one brand of pasta, "Healthcare," suddenly became very popular with the health-conscious public in both the United States and Canada, and the Canadian subsidiary more than tripled its sales and profits within the year.

The management of the U.S. parent company did not want to disclose to its competitors how profitable the Canadian subsidiary was because the company wanted to maintain its strong economic position without more competition.

You have been able to determine the following (in millions):

| | Cereal Products | Pasta Products |
|---|---|---|
| Net sales | $3,885 | $834 |
| Operating profit | 445 | 151 |
| Segment assets | 1,565 | 147 |

All cereal product operations are located in the United States, and all pasta product operations are located in Canada. The Standard Industrial Classification (SIC) number is 2043 for cereal products, and 2098 for the Canadian subsidiary's pasta products. (The Standard Industrial Classification Index is prepared by the U.S. Office of Management and Budget and is used widely to define a company's major industrial groups.)

### Required

*a.* Why would management be reluctant to disclose information about very successful—and very unsuccessful—operations in the segmental disclosure footnote in the annual report?

*b.* Present both theoretical and applied arguments for including the pasta products segment with the cereal products segment as one internal operating segment, thus not requiring separate disclosure under FASB 131. How does the fact that the pasta products have suddenly become popular affect the disclosure requirements under FASB 131?

*c.* Present the requirements under FASB 131 for reporting the cereal products and pasta products by geographic area. Must the Canadian operations be disclosed separately in a geographic disclosure footnote?

**C13-5    Segment Reporting**

*Research*

The manager you work for has asked you to perform some research to determine what types of information public companies are providing on their Internet home pages. The public company you work for is considering establishing its own home page. In particular, the manager wants you to note how these companies describe their products and services on their home pages. After researching the home pages, the manager wants you to review each company's Form 10-K by using the Electronic Data Gathering, Analysis, and Retrieval Database (EDGAR). While looking at the Form 10-Ks, the manager wants you to observe how the companies describe the segments of their business. For example, are the segments as described in the Form 10-K similar to the products and services mentioned on the same company's home page?

### Required

*a.* Using an Internet search engine, find a home page of a *public company*. (*Hint:* A helpful search term is "Company Home Pages.") Then write a brief summary about what you find on the company's home page discussing the following:

    (1) What type of information is provided related to the company's products or services?

    (2) What other information is listed on the home page?

*b.* Using the EDGAR database, locate the most recent Form 10-K for the company you selected. (*Note:* The Electronic Data Gathering, Analysis, and Retrieval Database [EDGAR] collects and maintains the forms that are required to be filed by public companies to the U.S. Securities and Exchange Commission [SEC].) (*Hint:* The Internet URL for the EDGAR Database is http://www.sec.gov/edgarhp.htm.)

    (1) Review the Form 10-K and locate the segment disclosure information. Print off this segment information.

    (2) Write a brief report summarizing what you find in the company's Form 10-K regarding segment disclosures. Include the following information:

        (a) Describe the company's segments as displayed in the Form 10-K. Discuss on what basis the segments are presented.

        (b) Discuss which segment(s) has (have) the highest revenues, is (are) the most profitable, and has (have) the most assets.

**C13-6    Interim Reporting**

*Research*

The company you work for is considering going public. Your current position is within the external financial reporting group. The manager you work for wants you to review some public company quarterly reports, Form 10-Qs, to see what type of information is disclosed. The manager does not want you to perform technical research to determine what the exact reporting requirements are for the Form 10-Q but to understand generally what information other companies seem to be supplying in their Form 10-Qs.

### Required

*a.* Determine the name of two public companies you would like to use in your review of Form 10-Qs. (*Hint:* There are various ways to determine the public companies you want to research. For example, you could use an Internet search engine to find a home page of a *public* company. A helpful search term is "Company Home Pages." Another method would be to select public companies you already know of or you find through the use of a newspaper or periodical.)

*b.* Using the EDGAR database, locate the most recent Form 10-Qs for the two companies you selected. (*Hint:* The Internet URL for the SEC's home page is http://www.sec.gov/. The SEC provides a company search engine for its EDGAR database. Alternatively, some persons prefer to use Edgarscan at http://edgarscan.pwcglobal.com to access and use the SEC's EDGAR database.) In addition, for one of these companies, locate the Form 10-Q for the same period in the prior year. Prepare a one- to two-page summary after performing the following analysis:

(1) Take one company's recent Form 10-Q and write a brief summary of the contents of the Form 10-Q. Discuss how the Form 10-Q information compares with the information you know is included in a Form 10-K, which is the annual report to the SEC.

(2) Review the same company's Form 10-Q from the previous year and discuss the similarities and differences you notice in the Form 10-Qs for different time periods.

(3) Review the other company's Form 10-Q from the current year and provide a discussion of the similarities and differences you notice in the Form 10-Qs for different companies.

### C13-7 Defining Segments for Disclosure

Randy Rivera, CFO of Stanford Corporation, a manufacturer of packaged retail food products, has reviewed the company's segment disclosures for the current year. In the first draft of the disclosures, the company reports information about four segments: cheese, snacks and crackers, pizza, and desserts and confectionery. He has suggested that the segment disclosures be expanded to include additional segments.

Randy notes that the cereals segment, included in the segment disclosures last year, is not included in the current year. Although the cereals segment reported a loss for the current year and suffered a significant decline in revenues as a result of a prolonged labor dispute, he believes that Stanford should continue to provide information about this segment. In addition, Stanford recently

*Research FARS* introduced a new product line, sports beverages. This operating segment is expected to expand rapidly and is highly profitable. Randy believes that shareholders would view this profitability positively if the sports beverage segment were included in the segment disclosures.

The accountant who prepared the segment information has reviewed the segment data with Randy. Revenues of the cereals segment and the sports beverage segment account for 9 percent and 6 percent of combined revenues of all segments, respectively. Each segment's assets are approximately 8 percent of the combined assets of all segments. The cereals segment was the only segment to record a loss, which amounted to 5 percent of the combined profit of all segments reporting profits. The sports beverage segment profit was 9 percent of this total.

After reviewing the data, Randy still believes that the inclusion of the two segments would improve the segment disclosures and has asked you to research the appropriateness of his suggestion.

### Required

Obtain the most current accounting standards on accounting for segments. You can obtain access to accounting standards through the Financial Accounting Research System (FARS), from your library, or from some other source. Write a memo to Randy responding to his suggestion that the segment disclosures be expanded to include the cereals and sports beverage segments. Support your recommendations with citations and quotations from the authoritative financial reporting standards.

### C13-8 Income Tax Provision in Interim Periods

Andrea Meyers, a supervisor in the controller's department at Vanderbilt Company, is reviewing the calculation of the income tax provision to be included in the financial statements for the first quarter of 20X5. She is questioning the estimate of the effective tax rate expected to be applicable for fiscal year 20X5 because this estimated rate is significantly lower than Vanderbilt's actual effective tax rate for 20X4.

*Research*
*FARS*
Bob Graber, who prepared the income tax calculation, explains to Andrea that the estimate of the effective annual tax rate reflects the anticipated enactment of a new business energy tax credit that will provide substantial tax benefits to Vanderbilt. This energy tax credit has the approval of the president, has been passed by the House of Representatives, and is under consideration in the Senate. It is expected to be enacted no later than the third quarter of 20X5, and its benefits should be available beginning with 20X5 tax returns.

### Required

Obtain the most current accounting standards for interim reporting. You can obtain access to accounting standards through the Financial Accounting Research System (FARS), from your library, or from some other source. Andrea has asked you, an accountant in the controller's department, to research the computation of the estimated effective annual tax rate for interim reporting. Write a memo to her reporting on the results of your research. Support your recommendations with citations and quotations from the authoritative financial reporting standards.

**C13-9   Questions about Interim Reporting**

### Required

*Application*
Prepare a brief answer to each of the following questions about interim reporting, assuming the company is preparing its Form 10-Q for the third quarter of its fiscal year.

1. How many different income statements would the company present? Describe the reporting periods presented in the income statements.

2. How would the company report a change in accounting principle for depreciation of its building that was made effective the first day of the third quarter? The change was made as a result of an accounting study that concluded that the estimated future benefits from the equipment will be different from those previously expected.

3. How many different balance sheets would the company present? What is the balance sheet date (as of what date) for each balance sheet?

4. Must interim financial statements filed with the SEC be audited by an independent public accountant who would provide an audit opinion on those statements? Explain your answer.

5. Is a company required to present segment information in the interim report? If yes, are the interim segment disclosures different from the annual segment disclosures? Explain your answers.

6. Within what period of time after the end of the quarter must a Form 10-Q be filed with the SEC?

7. May a company use one accounting method for computing interim total revenues and a different accounting method for computing its annual total revenues?

8. Is the company required to physically count its ending inventory each quarter so that it can accurately determine its ending inventory for the balance sheet and its cost of goods sold for the income statement? Explain how ending inventory is computed for interim reporting.

9. The company shuts down each year for two weeks during its third quarter in order to retool its manufacturing lines for the next year's products. Can the company allocate the costs of retooling incurred in its third quarter to the other three quarters (I, II, and IV) during the year? If yes, explain how this allocation would be made.

10. How would the company report a change in accounting principle from the completed contract method of revenue recognition to the percentage-of-completion method of revenue recognition on its long-term construction contracts? The change was made on the last day of the third quarter.

11. The company had assumed during the first two quarters of the year that it would receive a material income tax credit from the federal government. However, during the third quarter the company was informed that it would not be receiving the expected tax credit this year. The company had included the estimated tax credit in the computation of its income tax rate for the first two quarters of the year. Should the company retroactively restate the first two quarters of tax expense because of the change in information received in the third quarter? Explain your answer.

# Exercises

## E13-1 Reportable Segments

Amalgamated Products has seven operating segments. Data on the segments are as follows:

| Segments | Revenues | Segment Profit (Loss) | Segment Assets |
|---|---|---|---|
| Electronics | $ 42,000 | $ (8,600) | $ 73,000 |
| Bicycles | 105,000 | 30,400 | 207,000 |
| Sporting Goods | 53,000 | (4,900) | 68,000 |
| Home Appliances | 147,000 | 23,000 | 232,000 |
| Gas and Oil Equipment | 186,000 | 11,700 | 315,000 |
| Glassware | 64,000 | (19,100) | 96,000 |
| Hardware | 178,000 | 38,600 | 194,000 |
| Total | $775,000 | $71,100 | $1,185,000 |

Included in the $105,000 revenue of the Bicycles segment are sales of $25,000 made to the Sporting Goods segment.

### Required

*a.* Which segments are separately reportable?

*b.* Do the separately reportable segments include a sufficient portion of total revenue? Explain.

## E13-2 Multiple-Choice Questions on Segment Reporting [AICPA Adapted]

Select the correct answer for each of the following questions.

1. Barbee Corporation discloses supplementary operating segment information for its two reportable segments. Data for 20X5 are available as follows:

| | Segment E | Segment W |
|---|---|---|
| Sales | $750,000 | $250,000 |
| Traceable operating expenses | 325,000 | 130,000 |

Additional 20X5 expenses are as follows:

| | |
|---|---|
| Indirect operating expenses | $120,000 |

Appropriately selected common indirect operating expenses are allocated to segments based on the ratio of each segment's sales to total sales. The 20X5 operating profit for Segment E was:

*a.* $260,000.

*b.* $335,000.

*c.* $395,000.

*d.* $425,000.

2. The viewpoint used to determine segmental disclosures in annual reports is called the:

*a.* Segment approach.

*b.* Portfolio approach.

*c.* Economic entity approach.

*d.* Management approach.

3. Dutko Company has three lines of business, each of which is a significant industry segment. Company sales aggregated $1,800,000 in 20X6, of which Segment 3 contributed 60 percent. Traceable costs were $600,000 for Segment 3 from a total of $1,200,000 for the company as a whole. In addition, $350,000 of common costs are allocated in the ratio of a segment's income

before common costs to the total income before common costs. For Segment 3 Dutko should report a 20X6 segment profit of:

*a.* $200,000.

*b.* $270,000.

*c.* $280,000.

*d.* $480,000.

*e.* None of the above.

4. Stein Company is a diversified company that discloses supplemental financial information on its industry segments. The following information is available for 20X2:

|  | Sales | Traceable Costs | Allocable Costs |
|---|---|---|---|
| Segment A | $400,000 | $225,000 | |
| Segment B | 300,000 | 240,000 | |
| Segment C | 200,000 | 135,000 | |
| Totals | $900,000 | $600,000 | $150,000 |

Allocable costs are assigned based on the ratio of a segment's income before allocable costs to total income before allocable costs. This is an appropriate method of allocation. The segment profit for Segment B for 20X2 is:

*a.* $0.

*b.* $10,000.

*c.* $30,000.

*d.* $50,000.

*e.* None of the above.

5. Selected data for a segment of a business enterprise are to be reported separately in accordance with FASB 131 when the revenue of the segment exceeds 10 percent of the:

*a.* Combined net income of all segments reporting profits.

*b.* Total revenue obtained in transactions with outsiders.

*c.* Total revenue of all the enterprise's industry segments.

*d.* Total combined revenue of all segments reporting profits.

6. Kimber Company operates in four different industries, each of which is appropriately regarded as a reportable segment. Total sales for 20X2 for all segments combined were $1,000,000. Sales for Segment 2 were $400,000, and the traceable costs were $150,000. Total common costs for all segments combined were $500,000. Kimber allocates common costs based on the ratio of a segment's sales to total sales, an appropriate method of allocation. The segment profit to be reported for Segment 2 for 20X2 is:

*a.* $50,000.

*b.* $125,000.

*c.* $200,000.

*d.* $250,000.

*e.* None of the above.

7. The following information pertains to Reding Corporation for the year ended December 31, 20X6.

| | |
|---|---|
| Sales to unaffiliated customers | $2,000,000 |
| Intersegment sales of products similar to those sold to unaffiliated customers | 600,000 |

All of Reding's segments are engaged solely in manufacturing operations. Reding has a reportable segment if that segment's revenue exceeds:

a. $264,000.

b. $260,000.

c. $204,000.

d. $200,000.

8. Snow Corporation's revenue for the year ended December 31, 20X2, was as follows:

| | |
|---|---:|
| Consolidated revenue per income statement | $1,200,000 |
| Intersegment sales | 180,000 |
| Intersegment transfers | 60,000 |
| Combined revenue of all industry segments | $1,440,000 |

Snow has a reportable operating segment if that segment's revenue exceeds:

a. $6,000.

b. $24,000.

c. $120,000.

d. $144,000.

9. Porter Corporation is engaged solely in manufacturing operations. The following data (consistent with prior years' data) pertain to the industries in which operations were conducted for the year ended December 31, 20X5:

| Industry Segment | Total Revenue | Segment Profit | Assets at 12/31/X5 |
|:---:|---:|---:|---:|
| A | $10,000,000 | $1,750,000 | $20,000,000 |
| B | 8,000,000 | 1,400,000 | 17,500,000 |
| C | 6,000,000 | 1,200,000 | 12,500,000 |
| D | 3,000,000 | 550,000 | 7,500,000 |
| E | 4,250,000 | 675,000 | 7,000,000 |
| F | 1,500,000 | 225,000 | 3,000,000 |
| Totals | $32,750,000 | $5,800,000 | $67,500,000 |

In its segment information for 20X5, how many reportable segments does Porter have?

a. Three.

b. Four.

c. Five.

d. Six.

10. Boecker is a multidivisional corporation that has both intersegment sales and sales to unaffiliated customers. Boecker should report segment financial information for each segment meeting which of the following criteria?

a. Segment profit or loss is 10 percent or more of consolidated profit or loss.

b. Segment profit or loss is 10 percent or more of combined profit or loss of all company segments.

c. Segment revenue is 10 percent or more of combined revenue of all company segments.

d. Segment revenue is 10 percent or more of consolidated revenue.

*Note:* Use the following information for questions 11 and 12.

Ward Corporation, a publicly owned corporation, is subject to the requirements for segment reporting. In its income statement for the year ending December 31, 20X5, Ward reported revenues of $50,000,000, operating expenses of $47,000,000, and net income of $3,000,000. Operating expenses included payroll costs of $15,000,000. Ward's combined assets of all industry segments at December 31, 20X5, were $40,000,000.

11. In its 20X5 financial statements, Ward should disclose major customer data if sales to any single customer amount to at least:

    a. $300,000.

    b. $1,500,000.

    c. $4,000,000.

    d. $5,000,000.

12. In its 20X5 financial statements, Ward should disclose foreign revenues in a specific country if revenues from foreign operations in that country are at least:

    a. $5,000,000.

    b. $4,700,000.

    c. $4,000,000.

    d. $1,500,000.

**E13-3    Multiple-Choice Questions on Interim Reporting [AICPA Adapted]**

Select the correct answer for each of the following questions.

1. In considering interim financial reporting, how did the Accounting Principles Board conclude that such reporting should be viewed?

    a. As a "special" type of reporting that need not follow generally accepted accounting principles.

    b. As useful only if activity is evenly spread throughout the year so that estimates are unnecessary.

    c. As reporting for a basic accounting period.

    d. As reporting for an integral part of an annual period.

2. Which of the following is an inherent difficulty in determining the results of operations on an interim basis?

    a. Cost of sales reflects only the amount of product expense allocable to revenue recognized as of the interim date.

    b. Depreciation on an interim basis is a partial estimate of the actual annual amount.

    c. Costs expensed in one interim period may benefit other periods.

    d. Revenue from long-term construction contracts accounted for by the percentage-of-completion method is based on annual completion, and interim estimates may be incorrect.

3. Which of the following reporting practices is permissible for interim financial reporting?

    a. Use of the gross profit method for interim inventory pricing.

    b. Use of the direct costing method for determining manufacturing inventories.

    c. Deferral of unplanned variances under a standard cost system until the following year.

    d. Deferral of nontemporary inventory market declines until year-end.

4. On January 1, 20X2, Harris Inc. paid $40,000 property taxes on its plant for the calendar year 20X2. In March 20X2, Harris made $120,000 annual major repairs to its machinery. These repairs will benefit the entire calendar year's operations. How should these expenses be reflected in Harris's quarterly income statements?

|  | **Three Months Ended** | | | |
|  | **March 31, 20X2** | **June 30, 20X2** | **September 30, 20X2** | **December 31, 20X2** |
|---|---|---|---|---|
| a. | $ 22,000 | $46,000 | $46,000 | $46,000 |
| b. | 40,000 | 40,000 | 40,000 | 40,000 |
| c. | 70,000 | 30,000 | 30,000 | 30,000 |
| d. | 160,000 | -0- | -0- | -0- |

5. Wenger Company experienced an inventory loss from market decline of $420,000 in April 20X2. The company recorded this loss in April 20X2 after its March 31, 20X2, quarterly report was issued. None of this loss was recovered by the end of the year. How should this loss be reflected in Wenger's quarterly income statements?

| | March 31, 20X2 | June 30, 20X2 | September 30, 20X2 | December 31, 20X2 |
|---|---|---|---|---|
| | **Three Months Ended** | | | |
| *a.* | $    -0- | $    -0- | $    -0- | $420,000 |
| *b.* | -0- | 140,000 | 140,000 | 140,000 |
| *c.* | -0- | 420,000 | -0- | -0- |
| *d.* | 105,000 | 105,000 | 105,000 | 105,000 |

6. A company that uses the last-in, first-out (LIFO) method of inventory costing finds, at an interim reporting date, that there has been a partial liquidation of the base-period inventory level. The decline is considered temporary, and the base inventory will be replaced before year-end. The amount shown as inventory on the interim reporting date should:

   *a.* Not consider the LIFO liquidation, and cost of sales for the interim reporting period should include the expected cost of replacement of the liquidated LIFO base.

   *b.* Be shown at the actual level, and cost of sales for the interim reporting period should reflect the decrease in LIFO base-period inventory level.

   *c.* Not consider the LIFO liquidations, and cost of sales for the interim reporting period should reflect the decrease in LIFO base-period inventory level.

   *d.* Be shown at the actual level, and the decrease in inventory level should not be reflected in the cost of sales for the interim reporting period.

7. During the second quarter of 20X5, Camerton Company sold a piece of equipment at a $12,000 gain. What portion of the gain should Camerton report in its income statement for the second quarter of 20X5?

   *a.* $12,000.

   *b.* $6,000.

   *c.* $4,000.

   *d.* $0.

8. On March 15, 20X1, Burge Company paid property taxes of $180,000 on its factory building for calendar year 20X1. On April 1, 20X1, Burge made $300,000 in unanticipated repairs to its plant equipment. The repairs will benefit operations for the remainder of the calendar year. What total amount of these expenses should be included in Burge's quarterly income statement for the three months ended June 30, 20X1?

   *a.* $75,000.

   *b.* $145,000.

   *c.* $195,000.

   *d.* $345,000.

9. SRB Company had an inventory loss from a market price decline that occurred in the first quarter. The loss was not expected to be restored in the fiscal year. However, in the third quarter the inventory had a market price recovery that exceeded the first-quarter decline. For interim financial reporting, the dollar amount of net inventory should:

   *a.* Decrease in the first quarter by the amount of the market price decline and increase in the third quarter by the amount of the market price recovery.

   *b.* Decrease in the first quarter by the amount of the market price decline and increase in the third quarter by the amount of the decrease in the first quarter.

   *c.* Not be affected in the first quarter and increase in the third quarter by the amount of the market price recovery that exceeded the amount of the market price decline.

   *d.* Not be affected in either the first quarter or the third quarter.

10. For external reporting purposes, it is appropriate to use estimated gross profit rates to determine the cost of goods sold for:

| | Interim Financial Reporting | Year-End Financial Reporting |
|---|---|---|
| *a.* | Yes | Yes |
| *b.* | Yes | No |
| *c.* | No | Yes |
| *d.* | No | No |

11. On June 30, 20X5, Park Corporation incurred a $100,000 net loss from disposal of a business component. Also, on June 30, 20X5, Park paid $40,000 for property taxes assessed for the calendar year 20X5. What amount of the preceding items should be included in the determination of Park's net income or loss for the six-month interim period ended June 30, 20X5?

    *a.* $140,000.

    *b.* $120,000.

    *c.* $90,000.

    *d.* $70,000.

**E13-4  LIFO Liquidation**

During July, Laesch Company, which uses a perpetual inventory system, sold 1,240 units from its LIFO-base inventory, which had originally cost $18 per unit. The replacement cost is expected to be $27 per unit.

*Required*

Please respond to the following two independent scenarios as requested.

    *a. Case 1:* In July, the company is planning to reduce its inventory and expects to replace only 900 of these units by December 31, the end of its fiscal year.

      (1) Prepare the entry in July to record the sale of the 1,240 units.

      (2) Discuss the proper financial statement presentation of the valuation account related to the 1,240 units sold.

      (3) Prepare the entry for the replacement of the 900 units in September at an actual cost of $31 per unit.

    *b. Case 2:* In July, the company is planning to reduce its inventory and expects to replace only 300 of its units by December 31, the end of its fiscal year.

      (1) Prepare the entry in July to record the sale of the 1,240 units.

      (2) In December, the company decided not to replace any of the 1,240 units. Prepare the entry required on December 31 to eliminate any valuation accounts related to the inventory that will not be replaced.

**E13-5  Inventory Write-Down and Recovery**

Cub Company, a calendar-year entity, had 2,100 geo-thermal heating pumps in its beginning inventory for 20X1. On December 31, 20X0, the heating pumps had been adjusted down to $850 per unit from an actual cost of $920 per unit. It was the lower of cost or market. No additional units were purchased during 20X1. The following additional information is provided for 20X1:

| Quarter | Date | Inventory (units) | Unit Market Value |
|---|---|---|---|
| 1 | March 31, 20X1 | 1,700 | $845 |
| 2 | June 30, 20X1 | 1,400 | 860 |
| 3 | September 30, 20X1 | 1,300 | 830 |
| 4 | December 31, 20X1 | 900 | 840 |

### Required

Please respond to the following two independent scenarios as requested.

a. *Case 1:* The company does not have sufficient experience with the seasonal market for geo-thermal pumps and assumes that any reductions in market value during the year will be permanent.

(1) Determine the cost of goods sold for each quarter.

(2) Verify the total cost of goods sold by computing annual cost of goods sold on a lower-of-cost-or-market basis.

b. *Case 2:* The company has prior experience with the seasonal market for geo-thermal pumps and expects that any reductions in market value during the year will be only temporary and will recover by year-end.

(1) Determine the cost of goods sold for each quarter.

(2) Verify the total cost of goods sold by computing annual cost of goods sold on a lower-of-cost-or-market basis.

**E13-6** **Multiple-Choice Questions on Income Taxes at Interim Dates [AICPA Adapted]**

Select the correct answer for each of the following questions.

1. According to APB Opinion No. 28, "Interim Financial Reporting," income tax expense in an income statement for the first interim period of an enterprise's fiscal year should be computed by:

a. Applying the estimated income tax rate for the full fiscal year to the pretax accounting income for the interim period.

b. Applying the estimated income tax rate for the full fiscal year to the taxable income for the interim period.

c. Applying the statutory income tax rate to the pretax accounting income for the interim period.

d. Applying the statutory income tax rate to the taxable income for the interim period.

2. Neil Company, which has a fiscal year ending January 31, had the following pretax accounting income and estimated effective annual income tax rates for the first three quarters of the year ended January 31, 20X2:

| Quarter | Pretax Accounting Income | Estimated Effective Annual Income Tax Rate at End of Quarter, % |
|---------|--------------------------|----------------------------------------------------------------|
| First   | $60,000                  | 40%                                                            |
| Second  | 70,000                   | 40                                                             |
| Third   | 40,000                   | 45                                                             |

Neil's income tax expenses in its interim income statement for the third quarter are:

a. $18,000.

b. $24,500.

c. $25,500.

d. $76,500.

e. None of the above.

3. Beckett Corporation expects to sustain an operating loss of $100,000 for the full year ending December 31, 20X3. Beckett operates entirely in one jurisdiction, where the tax rate is 40 percent. Anticipated tax credits for 20X3 total $10,000. No permanent differences are expected. Realization of the full tax benefit of the expected operating loss and realization of anticipated tax credits are assured beyond any reasonable doubt because they will be carried back. For the first quarter ended March 31, 20X3, Beckett reported an operating loss of $20,000. How much of a tax benefit should Beckett report for the interim period ended March 31, 20X3?

a. $0.

b. $8,000.

c. $10,000.

d. $12,500.

e. None of the above.

4. The computation of a company's third-quarter provision for income taxes should be based on earnings:

   *a.* For the quarter at an expected effective annual income tax rate.

   *b.* For the quarter at the statutory rate.

   *c.* To date at an expected effective annual income tax rate less prior quarters' provisions.

   *d.* To date at the statutory rate less prior quarters' provisions.

5. During the first quarter of 20X5, Stahl Company had income before taxes of $200,000, and its effective income tax rate was 15 percent. Stahl's 20X4 effective annual income tax rate was 30 percent, but Stahl expects its 20X5 effective annual income tax rate to be 25 percent. In its first-quarter interim income statement, what amount of income tax expense should Stahl report?

   *a.* $0.

   *b.* $30,000.

   *c.* $50,000.

   *d.* $60,000.

6. Which of the following items will result in the recognition of a deferred tax asset or liability in the second quarter of 2007 for Nelson Company:

   *a.* The portion of dividends received this quarter on an investment in stock of a U.S. corporation that qualifies for the dividend exclusion.

   *b.* A provision of an expected loss from a lawsuit that is finally settled in 2008.

   *c.* Expenses related to the acquisition of a municipal bond whose income is not taxable for income tax purposes.

   *d.* Life insurance payments made on policies for executives for which the company is the beneficiary.

## E13-7  Significant Foreign Operations

Information about the domestic and foreign operations of Radon Inc. is as follows:

| | Geographic Area | | | | | |
| --- | --- | --- | --- | --- | --- | --- |
| | **United States** | **Britain** | **Brazil** | **Israel** | **Australia** | **Total** |
| Sales to unaffiliated customers | $364,000 | $252,000 | $72,000 | $58,000 | $47,000 | $ 793,000 |
| Interarea sales between affiliates | 38,000 | 19,000 | 6,000 | | | 63,000 |
| Total revenue | $402,000 | $271,000 | $78,000 | $58,000 | $47,000 | $ 856,000 |
| Profit | 34,500 | 22,500 | 11,300 | 3,200 | 4,500 | 76,000 |
| Long-lived assets | 509,000 | 439,000 | 93,000 | 66,000 | 75,000 | 1,182,000 |

### Required

Prepare schedules showing appropriate tests to determine which countries are material, using a 10 percent materiality threshold.

## E13-8  Major Customers

Sales by Knight Inc. to major customers are as follows:

| Customer | Sales | Reporting Segment |
| --- | --- | --- |
| State of Illinois | $2,700,000 | Computer hardware |
| Cook County, Illinois | 3,500,000 | Computer software |
| U.S. Treasury Department | 3,900,000 | Service contract |
| U.S. Department of Defense | 2,200,000 | Service contract |
| Bank of England | 4,650,000 | Computer software |
| Philips NV | 2,850,000 | Computer hardware |
| Honda | 5,400,000 | Computer hardware |

### Required

If worldwide sales total $43,000,000 for the year, which of Knight's customers should be disclosed as major customers?

### E13-9 Estimated Annual Tax Rate

Supra, Inc., estimates total federal and state tax rates to be 40 percent. Expected annual pretax earnings from continuing operations are $1,200,000. Differences between tax income and financial statement income are expected to be the following:

| | |
|---|---:|
| Dividend exclusion for dividends received on the company's stock investments | $70,000 |
| Tax exempt income received | 20,000 |
| Premiums for life insurance on officers for which the company is the beneficiary | 12,000 |

A business tax credit of $40,000 should be available.

Supra's first quarter pretax earnings are $170,000, which includes an extraordinary loss of $30,000 before any tax effect of the extraordinary loss.

### Required

*a.* Estimate Supra's effective combined federal and state tax rate on income from continuing operations for the year.

*b.* Prepare the entry to record the tax provision for the income from continuing operations for the first quarter.

### E13-10 Operating Loss Tax Benefits

Tem Technology has a first-quarter operating loss of $100,000 and expects the following income for the other three quarters:

| | |
|---|---:|
| Second quarter | $ 80,000 |
| Third quarter | 160,000 |
| Fourth quarter | 400,000 |

Tem estimated the effective annual tax rate at 40 percent at the end of the first quarter and changed it to 45 percent at the end of the third quarter. The company has a normal seasonal pattern of losses in the first quarter and income in the other quarters.

### Required

Prepare a schedule computing the tax or tax benefits that should be shown on the interim statements.

### E13-11 Industry Segment and Geographic Area Revenue Tests

Symbiotic Chemical Company has four major industry segments and operates both in the U.S. domestic market and in several foreign markets. Information about its revenue from the specific industry segments and its foreign activities for the year 20X2 is as follows:

| Sales to Unaffiliated Customers (in thousands) | | | |
|---|---|---|---|
| **Industry Segment** | **Domestic** | **Foreign** | **Total** |
| Ethical Drugs | $300 | | $300 |
| Nonprescription Drugs | 325 | $100 | 425 |
| Generic Drugs | 125 | 245 | 370 |
| Industrial Chemicals | 70 | | 70 |

| Sales to Affiliated Customers (in thousands) | | | |
|---|---|---|---|
| **Industry Segment** | **Domestic** | **Foreign** | **Total** |
| Ethical Drugs | $20 | | $ 20 |
| Nonprescription Drugs | 50 | $40 | 90 |
| Generic Drugs | 40 | 60 | 100 |
| Industrial Chemicals | 10 | | 10 |

All of the foreign revenues of the Nonprescription Drugs segment, both to unaffiliated and inter-segment customers, were attributable to a Taiwanese division of the company. This division operated exclusively in Taiwan except for a $10,000 sale from the division to a U.S. subsidiary of the company. All other foreign operations of the company take place exclusively within the country of Mexico.

### Required

*a.* Determine which of the company's operating segments are separately reportable under the revenue test for segment reporting.

*b.* Determine which of the foreign countries are separately reportable under the revenue test for reporting foreign operations using a 10 percent materiality threshold.

*c.* Prepare a schedule for disclosing the company's revenue by industry segment for 20X2.

*d.* Prepare a schedule for disclosing the company's revenue by geographic area for 20X2.

**E13-12  Different Reporting Methods for Interim Reports [CMA Adapted]**

Following are seven independent cases on how accounting facts might be reported on an individual company's interim financial reports.

1. Bean Company was reasonably certain it would have an employee strike in the third quarter. As a result, the company shipped heavily during the second quarter but plans to defer the recognition of the sales in excess of the normal sales volume. The deferred sales will be recognized as sales in the third quarter when the strike is in progress. Bean management thinks this is more nearly representative of normal second- and third-quarter operations.

2. Green Inc. takes a physical inventory at year-end for annual financial statement purposes. Inventory and cost of sales reported in the interim quarterly statements are based on estimated gross profit rates because a physical inventory would result in a cessation of operations.

3. ER Company is planning to report one-fourth of its annual pension expense each quarter.

4. Fair Corporation wrote down inventory to reflect the lower of cost or market in the first quarter of 20X1. At year-end, the market price exceeds the original acquisition cost of this inventory. Consequently, management plans to write the inventory back up to its original cost as a year-end adjustment.

5. Carson Company realized a large gain on the sale of investments at the beginning of the second quarter. The company wants to report one-third of the gain in each of the remaining quarters.

6. Ring Corporation has estimated its annual audit fee. Management plans to prorate this expense equally over all four quarters.

7. Mega Corporation made a change in the depreciation of its warehouse building during the third quarter of 20X1. The change was from the accelerated method to the straight-line method to better match the depreciation expense to the current levels of usage of the warehouse. The company plans to use the cumulative effect approach to present the effects of the change as of the beginning of the third quarter.

### Required

For the seven cases, state whether the method proposed for interim reporting is acceptable under generally accepted accounting principles applicable to interim financial data. Support each answer with a brief explanation.

## Problems

### P13-13 Segment Reporting Workpaper and Schedules

West Corporation reported the following consolidated data for 20X2:

| | |
|---|---:|
| Sales | $ 810,000 |
| Consolidated income before taxes | 128,000 |
| Total assets | 1,200,000 |

Data reported for West's four operating divisions are as follows:

| | Division A | Division B | Division C | Division D |
|---|---|---|---|---|
| Sales to outsiders | $280,000 | $130,000 | $340,000 | $60,000 |
| Intersegment sales | 60,000 | | 18,000 | 12,000 |
| Traceable costs | 245,000 | 90,000 | 290,000 | 82,000 |
| Assets | 400,000 | 105,000 | 500,000 | 75,000 |

Intersegment sales are priced at cost, and all goods have been subsequently sold to nonaffiliates. Some joint production costs are allocated to the divisions based on total sales. These joint costs were $45,000 in 20X2. The company's corporate center had $20,000 of general corporate expenses and $120,000 of assets that the chief operating decision maker did not use in decision making regarding the operating segments.

#### Required

Each of the following items is unrelated to the others.

a. The divisions are industry segments.

 (1) Prepare a segmental disclosure worksheet for the company.

 (2) Prepare schedules showing which segments are reportable.

b. Assume that each division operates in an individual geographic area and Division A is in the domestic area and the other divisions each operate in a separate foreign country. Assume that one-half of the assets in each geographic area represent long-lived, productive assets as defined in FASB 131. Prepare schedules showing which geographic areas are reportable using a 10 percent materiality threshold.

c. Determine the amount of sales to an outside customer that would cause that outside customer to be classified as a major customer under the criteria of FASB 131.

### P13-14 Segment Reporting Workpaper and Schedules

Calvin Inc. has operating segments in five different industries: apparel, building, chemical, furniture, and machinery. Data for the five segments for 20X1 are as follows:

| | Apparel | Building | Chemical | Furniture | Machinery |
|---|---|---|---|---|---|
| Sales to nonaffiliates | $870,000 | $750,000 | $55,000 | $95,000 | $180,000 |
| Intersegment sales | | | 5,000 | 15,000 | 140,000 |
| Cost of goods sold | 480,000 | 450,000 | 42,000 | 78,000 | 150,000 |
| Selling expenses | 160,000 | 40,000 | 10,000 | 20,000 | 30,000 |
| Other traceable expenses | 40,000 | 30,000 | 6,000 | 12,000 | 18,000 |
| Allocated general corporate expenses | 80,000 | 75,000 | 7,000 | 13,000 | 25,000 |
| Other information: | | | | | |
| Segment assets | 610,000 | 560,000 | 80,000 | 90,000 | 140,000 |
| Depreciation expense | 60,000 | 50,000 | 10,000 | 11,000 | 25,000 |
| Capital expenditures | 20,000 | 30,000 | | | 15,000 |

## Additional Information

1. The corporate headquarters had general corporate expenses totaling $235,000. For internal reporting purposes, $200,000 of these expenses were allocated to the divisions based on their cost of goods sold. The other corporate expenses are not used in segmental decision making by the chief operating decision maker.

2. The company has an intercorporate transfer pricing policy that all intersegment sales shall be priced at cost. All intersegment sales were sold to outsiders by December 31, 20X1.

3. Corporate headquarters had assets of $125,000 that were not used in segmental decision making by the chief operating decision maker.

4. The depreciation expense (listed in the section titled, "Other information") has already been added into cost of goods sold in accordance with the company's cost measurement policies.

## Required

a. Prepare a segmental disclosure workpaper for Calvin Inc.

b. Prepare schedules to show which segments are separately reportable.

c. Prepare the information about the company's operations in different industry segments as required by FASB 131.

d. Would there be any differences in the specification of reportable segments if the building segment had $460,000 in assets instead of $560,000, and the furniture segment had $190,000 in assets instead of $90,000? Justify your answer by preparing a schedule showing the percentages for each of the three 10 percent segment tests for each of the five segments using these new amounts for segment assets.

**P13-15**  **Interim Income Statement**

Chris Inc. has accumulated the following information for its second-quarter income statement for 20X2:

| | |
|---|---|
| Sales | $850,000 |
| Cost of goods sold | 420,000 |
| Operating expenses | 230,000 |

## Additional Information

1. First-quarter income before taxes was $100,000, and the estimated effective annual tax rate was 40 percent. At the end of the second quarter, expected annual income is $600,000, and a dividend exclusion of $30,000 and a business tax credit of $15,000 are anticipated. The combined state and federal tax rate is 50 percent.

2. The $420,000 cost of goods sold is determined by the LIFO method and includes 7,500 units from the base layer at a cost of $12 per unit. However, you have determined that these units are expected to be replaced at a cost of $26 per unit.

3. The operating expenses of $230,000 include a $60,000 factory rearrangement cost incurred in April. You have determined that the second quarter will receive about 25 percent of the benefits from this project, with the remainder benefiting the third and fourth quarters.

## Required

a. Calculate the expected effective annual tax rate at the end of the second quarter for Chris Inc.

b. Prepare the income statement for the second quarter of 20X2. Your solution should include a computation of income tax (or benefit) with the following headings:

| | Operating Income (Loss before Taxes) | | Estimated Effective Annual Tax Rate | Tax (Benefit) | | |
|---|---|---|---|---|---|---|
| Interim Period | Current Period | Year to Date | | Year to Date | Less Previously Provided | Reported in This Period |

**P13-16** **Interim Income Statement**

At the end of the second quarter of 20X1, Malta Corporation assembled the following information:

1. The first quarter resulted in a $90,000 loss before taxes. During the second quarter, sales were $1,200,000; purchases were $650,000; and operating expenses were $320,000.

2. Cost of goods sold is determined by the FIFO method. The inventory at the end of the first quarter was reduced by $4,000 to a lower-of-cost-or-market figure of $78,000. During the second quarter, replacement costs recovered, and by the end of the period, market value exceeded the ending inventory cost by $1,250.

3. The ending inventory is estimated by the gross profit method. The estimated gross profit rate is 46 percent.

4. At the end of the first quarter, the effective annual tax rate was estimated at 45 percent. At the end of the second quarter, expected annual income is $600,000. An investment tax credit of $15,000 and dividends received deduction of $75,000 are expected for the year. The combined state and federal tax rate is 40 percent.

5. The tax benefits from operating losses are assured beyond a reasonable doubt. Prior years' income totaling $50,000 is available for operating loss carrybacks.

### Required

a. Calculate the expected effective annual tax rate at the end of the second quarter for Malta Corporation.

b. Prepare the income statement for the second quarter of 20X1. Your solution should include a computation of income tax (or benefit) for the first and second quarters.

**P13-17** **Evaluating Foreign Operations**

For many years, Clark Company operated exclusively in the United States, but recently it expanded its operations to the Pacific Rim countries of New Zealand, Singapore, and Australia. After a modest beginning in these countries, recent successes have resulted in an increased level of operations in each country. Operating information (in thousands of U.S. dollars) for the company's domestic and foreign operations follows.

|  | **United States** | **New Zealand** | **Singapore** | **Australia** |
|---|---|---|---|---|
| Sales to unaffiliated | $2,500 | $320 | $ 60 | $120 |
| Interarea sales | 100 |  | 10 |  |
| Operating expenses | 1,820 | 290 | 70 | 30 |
| Long-lived assets | 2,200 | 280 | 140 | 80 |

In addition, common costs of $120,000 are to be allocated to operations on the basis of the ratio of an area's sales to nonaffiliates to total company sales to nonaffiliates.

### Required

a. Determine the profit or loss for each geographic segment.

b. Discuss the general reporting requirements related to the company's geographic areas.

c. Determine which, if any, of the three individual foreign geographic segments is separately reportable, using a 10 percent materiality threshold.

**P13-18** **Interim Accounting Changes**

During the third quarter of its 20X7 fiscal year, Press Company is considering the different methods of reporting accounting changes on its interim segments. Preliminary data are available for the third quarter of 20X7, ending on September 30, 20X7, prior to any adjustments required for any accounting changes. The company's tax rate is 40 percent of income. Selected interim data for the company, in thousands of dollars, follow:

| Quarter Ended | Net Sales | Gross Profit | Earnings from Operations, Before Tax | Net Earnings |
|---|---|---|---|---|
| 20X7: | | | | |
| March 31 | $388 | $133 | $27 | $16.2 |
| June 30 | 406 | 135 | 30 | 18.0 |
| September 30 (preliminary) | 428 | 151 | 32 | 19.2 |
| 20X6: | | | | |
| March 31 | 394 | 139 | 27 | 16.2 |
| June 30 | 416 | 151 | 32 | 19.2 |
| September 30 | 403 | 148 | 31 | 18.6 |
| December 31 | 385 | 134 | 31 | 18.6 |

### Required

For each of the following *independent* cases, present the interim financial data for the company for the three quarters of 20X7 and the comparative data for 20X6, assuming that in a meeting on the last day of the third quarter of 20X7, the company decides to make the specified accounting change.

a. The company decides to change from the FIFO method of accounting for inventory to the LIFO method. The accounting department has prepared the following schedule of data, in thousands of dollars, showing the cost of goods sold each quarter under the LIFO method. The selected interim data presented above are based on the FIFO method. The accounting department has determined that there will be no difference in cost of goods sold prior to January 1, 20X6.

| Quarter Ended | LIFO |
|---|---|
| 20X7: | |
| March 31 | $265 |
| June 30 | 283 |
| September 30 | 291 |
| 20X6: | |
| March 31 | 267 |
| June 30 | 278 |
| September 30 | 280 |
| December 31 | 260 |

b. The company decides to switch from the straight-line method of depreciation to the accelerated method of depreciation because of a change in the estimated future benefits from the asset. The company has determined that the accumulated depreciation would have been $42,000 higher as of January 1, 20X6, if the accelerated method had been used. The depreciation expense determined under the two methods is presented below:

| Quarter Ended | Depreciation Expense— Accelerated Method | Depreciation Expense— Straight-Line Method |
|---|---|---|
| 20X7: | | |
| March 31 | $45 | $45 |
| June 30 | 44 | 45 |
| September 30 | 42 | 45 |
| 20X6: | | |
| March 31 | 50 | 40 |
| June 30 | 48 | 40 |
| September 30 | 47 | 40 |
| December 31 | 45 | 40 |

c. The company decides to change its method of accounting for recognizing sales revenue on its long-term contracts. The company had been using the completed contract method, but changed to the percentage-of-completion method. The accounting department has prepared an analysis of the sales and gross profit recognition under each of the two methods, in thousands of dollars, as follows:

| Quarter Ended | Completed Contract Sales | Completed Contract Gross Profit | Percentage-of-Completion Sales | Percentage-of-Completion Gross Profit |
|---|---|---|---|---|
| 20X7: | | | | |
| March 31 | $ 80 | $ 20 | $60 | $30 |
| June 30 | -0- | -0- | 55 | 30 |
| September 30 | 100 | 50 | 70 | 40 |
| 20X6: | | | | |
| March 31 | -0- | -0- | 60 | 40 |
| June 30 | 150 | 100 | 40 | 20 |
| September 30 | -0- | -0- | 50 | 30 |
| December 31 | 60 | 40 | 50 | 30 |

**P13-19 Segment Disclosures in the Financial Statements**

Multiplex Inc., a public company whose stock is traded on a national stock exchange, reported the following information on its consolidated financial statements for 20X5:

| | |
|---|---|
| From the consolidated income statement: | |
| Sales revenues | $564,000,000 |
| Rental revenues | 34,000,000 |
| Income before income taxes | 65,000,000 |
| Income taxes | 20,000,000 |
| From the consolidated balance sheet: | |
| Total assets | $475,000,000 |

Multiplex management determined that it had the following operating segments during 20X5: (1) car rental, (2) aerospace, (3) communications, (4) health and fitness products, and (5) heavy equipment manufacturing. The company assembled the following information for these industry segments for 20X5 (dollar amounts stated in millions):

| Item | Car Rental | Aerospace | Communications | Health/ Fitness | Heavy Equipment |
|---|---|---|---|---|---|
| Sales | | $204 | $60 | $50 | $250 |
| Rentals | $34 | | | | |
| Intersegment sales | 5 | | | | 25 |
| Cost of goods sold | | 141 | | | 177 |
| Selling expenses | 16 | 42 | 29 | 23 | 37 |
| Other traceable expenses | 4 | 8 | 11 | 5 | 10 |
| Allocation of common costs | 2 | 7 | 2 | 2 | 7 |
| Assets | 20 | 107 | 70 | 80 | 195 |
| Other information: | | | | | |
| Depreciation expense (included above) | 4 | 15 | 4 | 5 | 25 |
| Capital expenditures | 3 | 30 | | 15 | 40 |

### Additional Information

1. The corporate headquarters had general corporate expenses totaling $33,000,000 and assets of $25,000,000 (the chief operating decision maker used neither piece of information in defining operating segment performance).

2. The $5,000,000 of intersegment sales of the car rental segment consisted of car rentals to the aerospace ($2,000,000) and communications ($3,000,000) segments. The intersegment sales of $25,000,000 of the heavy equipment segment were made to the aerospace segment. The aerospace segment is using the equipment in its manufacturing operations. The heavy equipment segment realized a profit of $8,000,000 from this sale. At December 31, 20X5, $7,000,000 of this profit was unrealized from a consolidated viewpoint.

3. At December 31, 20X5, there were no intercompany receivables or payables related to the intersegment car rentals. However, the heavy equipment segment had a $15,000,000 receivable from the intersegment sale to the aerospace segment. The company's policy is to include intersegment receivables in a segment's assets for purposes of evaluating segment performance.

### Required

a. Prepare schedules for each of the three 10 percent tests: (1) the revenue test, (2) the profit or loss test, and (3) the assets test. Each schedule should indicate which of Multiplex's industry segments are reportable segments for 20X5.

b. Indicate whether Multiplex's reportable segments meet the 75 percent revenue test.

c. Prepare the information about the company's operations in different industry segments as required by FASB 131.

## P13-20 Reporting Operations in Different Countries

Watson Inc., a multinational company, has operating divisions in France, Mexico, and Japan as well as in the United States. The company reported the following information on its consolidated financial statements for 20X5:

| | |
|---|---|
| From the consolidated income statement: | |
| Sales revenues | $856,000,000 |
| Net income | 60,000,000 |
| From the consolidated balance sheet: | |
| Total assets | $750,000,000 |

The following additional information was assembled for Watson's domestic and international operations for 20X5 (dollars stated in millions):

| Item | Domestic | France | Mexico | Japan |
|---|---|---|---|---|
| Sales to unaffiliated customers | $430 | $300 | $36 | $90 |
| Intracompany sales between geographic areas | 50 | | | 10 |
| Operating profit | 7 | 40 | 2 | 18 |
| General corporate expenses | 30 | | | |
| Long-lived assets | 235 | 160 | 29 | 81 |

### Additional Information

1. The domestic intracompany sales of $50,000,000 were made to Watson's French division. A total gross profit of $20,000,000 was realized by Watson's domestic operations on these sales. At December 31, 20X5, $10,000,000 of the total gross profit was unrealized from a consolidated viewpoint. At December 31, 20X5, Watson's French division owed domestic $15,000,000 related to these sales.

2. The intracompany sales made by Watson's Japanese division were made to Watson's Mexican division. The Japanese division realized a gross profit of $2,000,000 on the sales. At December 31,

20X5, all of the goods sold to the Mexican division remained in its inventory. At December 31, 20X5, the Japanese division had an $8,000,000 receivable related to these sales.

### Required

a. Determine whether Watson Inc. must separately report its foreign operations.

b. Determine which of the three individual foreign geographic segments is separately reportable, using a 10 percent materiality threshold.

c. Prepare the information about the company's domestic and foreign operations as required by FASB 131.

**P13-21** **Matching Key Terms**

Match the terms on the left side with the descriptions on the right. A description may be used once, more than once, or not at all.

| Terms | Descriptions of Terms |
|---|---|
| 1. Management approach | A. Based on all assets used by management to assess that business unit's performance. |
| 2. Reportable operating segment | B. Not computed until tax is paid. |
| 3. 10 percent revenue test for segments | C. Each interim period viewed as an installment of an annual period. |
| 4. Revenue test for material foreign country disclosure | D. Includes intercorporate sales and transfers. |
| 5. Asset test for reportable operating segments | E. Annual statutory tax rate. |
| 6. Asset test for material foreign country disclosure | F. Based on long-lived assets used in that business unit only. |
| 7. Comprehensive segment disclosure test | G. Values cost of goods sold at the LIFO cost of the goods sold. |
| 8. Enterprisewide disclosures | H. Values cost of goods sold at the expected costs of replacements. |
| 9. Discrete theory of interim reporting | I. Requires sales to unaffiliated units for separately disclosed segments to be greater than or equal to 75 percent of total consolidated revenue. |
| 10. Integral theory of interim reporting | |
| 11. Recovery of prior write-down for interim inventory valuations | J. Segment that must meet each of the three 10 percent segment significance tests. |
| 12. Interim LIFO liquidations to be replaced by year-end | K. Product revenues, geographic areas, and information about major customers. |
| 13. Effective annual tax rate | L. Basis of defining segments for financial statements. |
| | M. Views each interim period as a basic accounting period, similar to an annual accounting period. |
| | N. Recovery allowed by APB 28. |
| | O. Based on sales to unaffiliated entities only. |
| | P. Not permitted under APB 28. |
| | Q. Estimate of the income tax that will actually be paid for the year. |
| | R. Segment that has met at least one of the three 10 percent segment significance tests. |

*Supplemental Problems* for this chapter are available as part of the *Online Learning Center* on the textbook's Web site (URL: www.mhhe.com/baker8e).

# SEC Reporting

Since its creation in 1934, the Securities and Exchange Commission (SEC) has had a significant impact on the capital formation process by which companies obtain capital from investors. The SEC is an independent federal agency responsible for regulating securities markets in which stocks and bonds of the major companies trade and for the "full and fair disclosure" of financial information so investors may make informed investment decisions. The ability of companies to raise capital in the stock markets and the hundreds of millions of shares that are traded daily both indicate the SEC's success in maintaining an effective marketplace for companies issuing securities and for investors seeking capital investments.

If our example company, Peerless Products Corporation, decides to issue securities on a stock exchange (i.e., go public), the process begins with the company filing a registration statement, usually a Form S-1, with the Securities and Exchange Commission. Once approved by the SEC, Peerless would then make an initial public offering (IPO) of its securities. To remain publicly traded, Peerless would be required to meet a number of SEC filing requirements, including annual and interim reports to the SEC. This chapter presents an overview of the SEC and the laws and regulations that a publicly held company must follow.

## HISTORY OF SECURITIES REGULATION

The need for regulation has gone hand in hand with the offering of securities to the general public. In the thirteenth century, King Edward I of England established a Court of Aldermen to regulate security trades in London. In the latter part of the eighteenth century, England's Parliament passed several acts, termed the Bubble Acts, to control questionable security schemes that had become popular. In 1790, the New York Stock Exchange was created to serve as a clearinghouse for securities trades between members of the exchange. The need for additional sources of capital paralleled the advent of the industrial revolution and the growth of commerce in the United States. Some individuals took advantage of this situation and offered securities of fictitious companies for sale to the general public or used financial reports that were not factual about the offering company's financial picture. In 1911, because of the lack of any federal security regulatory laws, several states began passing what were called "blue sky laws" to regulate the offering of securities by companies made up only of "blue sky," that is, which did not have a sound financial base.

The era of the 1920s was one of heavy stock speculation by many individuals. Business executives, cab drivers, and assembly-line workers all wanted to participate in the many stock opportunities that existed at that time. Unfortunately, a number of abuses were occurring in the marketplace. For example, certain speculators sought to manipulate selected stock prices by issuing untrue press releases about companies' operations or managements. Companies were not required to be audited, and some of them issued false and misleading financial statements. Investors were using excessive amounts of margin; that is, they were borrowing heavily to invest in stocks. Some employees of companies were using inside information—information that had not been released to the public—to purchase or sell their company's stock for personal advantage.

The month of October 1929 is often viewed as the beginning of the Great Depression. Stock prices plunged to record lows within just a few weeks as panic took over the market. It became obvious that some form of federal regulation was necessary to restore confidence in the stock market. The Federal Securities Acts of 1933 and 1934 were part of President Franklin D. Roosevelt's New Deal legislation. The Securities Act of 1933 regulated the initial distribution of security issues by requiring companies to make "full and fair" disclosure of their financial affairs before their securities could be offered to the public. The Securities Exchange Act of 1934 required all companies whose stocks were traded on a stock exchange to periodically update their financial information. In addition, the 1934 act created the Securities and Exchange Commission and assigned it the responsibility of administering both the 1933 and 1934 acts.

The SEC has the legal responsibility to regulate trades of securities and to determine the types of financial disclosures that a publicly held company must make. Although the SEC has the ultimate legal authority to establish the disclosure requirements, it has worked closely with the accounting profession to prescribe the accounting principles and standards used to measure and report companies' financial conditions and results of operations. The SEC's role is to ensure full and fair disclosure; it does not guarantee the investment merits of any security. Stock markets still operate on a *caveat emptor* ("Let the buyer beware") basis. The SEC has consistently taken the position that investors must have the necessary information to make their own assessments of the risk and return attributes of a security.

The present role of the SEC is particularly complex. In 1935, its first year of full activity, only 284 new securities were registered for sale to the general public. Now the number of new securities being registered for sale is more than 5,000 per year. The SEC also regulates more than 10,000 securities brokers and dealers and must monitor stock exchange volumes often surpassing a billion shares a day.

# ELECTRONIC DATA GATHERING, ANALYSIS, AND RETRIEVAL (EDGAR) SYSTEM

The SEC continues to work to facilitate the registration and filing process and has developed an electronic filing system known as EDGAR (Electronic Data Gathering, Analysis, and Retrieval). Under this system, firms electronically file directly by using computers, facilitating the data transfer and making public data more quickly available. EDGAR filings may be found on the World Wide Web, under the SEC's home page (www.sec.gov) within 24 hours of filing. All public companies are now required to use EDGAR, although some hardship exemptions are allowed for smaller firms.

The SEC believes that EDGAR is accomplishing its primary purpose of increasing the efficiency and fairness of the securities markets by expediting the receipt, acceptance, dissemination, and analysis of time-sensitive data filed with the SEC. Any individual with access to the World Wide Web can easily download and print the documents from EDGAR, which has become an important data source for corporate researchers, investors, and all other participants in the securities markets.

# INTERNATIONAL HARMONIZATION OF ACCOUNTING STANDARDS FOR PUBLIC OFFERINGS

The global economy has a number of major securities exchanges in which business entities can seek equity or debt capital. The SEC wants to preserve the international prestige of the U.S. capital markets by providing financial markets for multinational and non-U.S. companies. With the encouragement of the SEC and the International Organization of Securities Commissions (IOSCO), the International Accounting Standards Board (IASB) is working with the Financial Accounting Standards Board (FASB) to converge on a uniform set of accounting and financial reporting standards that can be used by all companies seeking financing through any of the world's major stock markets, including those of the United States.

In 2007, the SEC took two actions on their roadmap toward a uniform global set of financial reporting standards. In its first action, the SEC published **Securities Act Release No. 33-8879,** "Acceptance From Foreign Private Issuers of Financial Statements Prepared in Accordance with International Financial Reporting Standards without Reconciliation to U.S. GAAP," under which financial statements from foreign private issuers[1] will be accepted by the SEC without reconciliation to U.S. GAAP, if they are prepared using International Financial Reporting Standards (IFRSs) as issued by the IASB. Previously, foreign companies using IFRSs in their SEC filings were required to present a reconciliation schedule that reconciled foreign financial statement items to U.S. GAAP. This schedule, Form 20-F, had been a cause of concern for a number of foreign companies that felt it was an unnecessary requirement and an indirect criticism of the IFRSs. By removing the requirement for the reconciliation schedule, the SEC felt that it would show support for the IASB-approved version of IFRSs and encourage the development to IFRSs as a uniform global standard, not as a divergent set of standards that can be applied differently in each county. This new rule is applicable to financial statements for fiscal years ending after November 15, 2007, and to interim financial statements within those years. Furthermore, the SEC hopes this new rule will encourage more foreign businesses to list their securities on U.S. stock exchanges.

The second action taken by the SEC to support the use of IFRSs in U.S. capital markets was the issuance of **Securities Act Release No. 33-8831,** "Concept Release on Allowing U.S. Issuers to Prepare Financial Statements in Accordance with International Financial Reporting Standards." A Concept Release is not a final rule, but is a strong signal of the position of the SEC on the subject of the release. If U.S. issuers are allowed to use IFRSs in their filings with the SEC, multinational U.S. companies operating in several countries could use just one set of accounting and financial reporting standards for all of their global operations. The SEC acknowledges that many publicly held U.S. companies may not have extensive experience with the IFRSs, and this is one reason that the SEC provides that these companies may elect to use IFRSs or U.S. GAAP in their SEC filings. The SEC also recognizes that educational institutions preparing accountants for careers in accounting will have to substantially increase curricular coverage of international financial accounting standards. Despite these challenges, the SEC is pushing toward the acceptance of a single set of worldwide, principles-based accounting standards for use in the U.S. securities markets.

# SECURITIES AND EXCHANGE COMMISSION

## Organizational Structure of the Commission

The SEC's five commissioners are appointed by the president of the United States with the advice and consent of the Senate. Figure 14–1 is an organizational chart of the Commission showing the four separate divisions and the major offices of the 18 that must report directly to the Commission. The four divisions, and their primary responsibilities, are as follows:

1. *Division of Corporation Finance.* Develops and administers the disclosure requirements for the securities acts and reviews all registration statements and other issue-oriented disclosures. This is the division with which accountants are most familiar because all registration forms are submitted to it.

---

[1] A foreign private issuer (FPI) is defined by Rule 205 of the Securities Act of 1933, as any foreign issuer, other than a foreign government, *except* an issuer that meets the following conditions: (1) more than 50 percent of its outstanding voting securities are directly or indirectly owned by residents of the United States and (2) any of the following: (a) the majority of its executive officers or directors are United States citizens or residents; (b) more than 50 percent of the assets of the issuer are located in the United States; or (c) the business of the issuer is administered principally in the United States.

**FIGURE 14–1**
Organizational
Structure of
the Securities
and Exchange
Commission

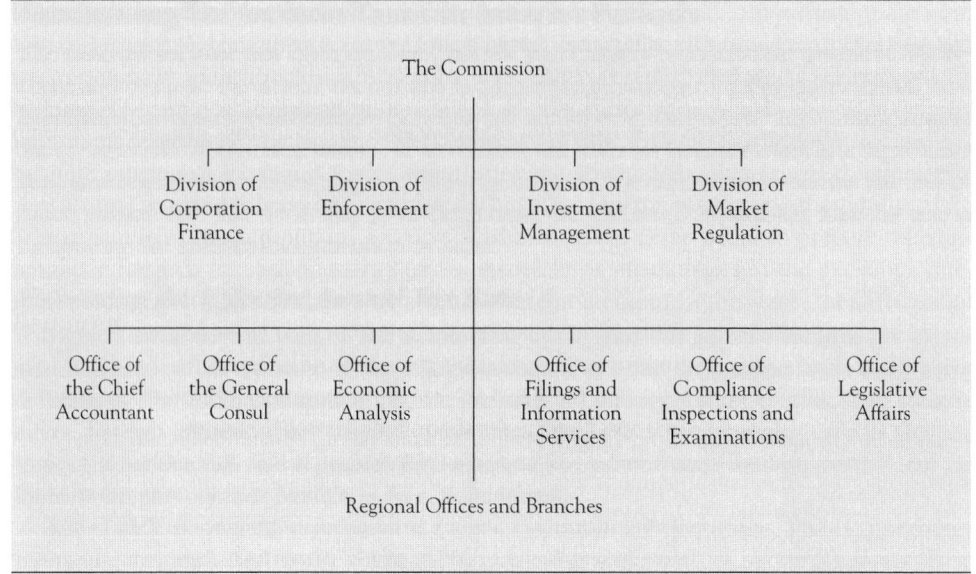

2. *Division of Enforcement.* Directs the SEC's enforcement actions. This division has several options for enforcement ranging from persuasion to administrative proceedings to litigation. An administrative proceeding often is used to gather evidence and present findings on a specific issue, such as a significant shareholder not filing proper reports with the SEC. Many of the administrative proceedings result in a consent action by a registrant, stock market participant, or professional practicing before the SEC in which the party accepts the judgment of the SEC. Litigation is used for serious infractions of the laws administered by the SEC, such as when a securities broker engages in the fraudulent sale of securities. Litigation can result in injunctions to discontinue actions as well as civil or criminal sanctions.

3. *Division of Investment Management.* Regulates investment advisers and investment companies.

4. *Division of Market Regulation.* Regulates national securities exchanges, brokers, and dealers of securities.

Several offices support these divisions, of which one of the most important for accountants is the Office of the Chief Accountant. This office assists the Commission by studying current accounting issues and preparing position papers for the SEC to consider. The other major offices listed offer the Commission advice on a variety of economic and regulatory matters.

## Laws Administered by the SEC

In addition to the Securities Acts of 1933 and 1934, the SEC is responsible for administering other laws established to regulate companies or individuals involved with the securities markets. The laws are as follows:

1. *Public Utility Holding Company Act of 1935.* This prohibits artificial pyramids of capital in public utilities and allows the SEC to restructure those "holding companies" whose only purpose is to concentrate the stock voting power in a few individuals.

2. *Trust Indenture Act of 1939.* This requires a trustee to be appointed for sales of bonds, debentures, and other debt securities of public corporations, thus bringing in a bonded expert to administer the debt.

3. *Investment Company Act of 1940.* This controls companies such as mutual funds that invest funds for the public. These companies must be audited annually, with the auditor reporting directly to the SEC.

4. *Investment Advisors Act of 1940.* This requires complete disclosure of information about investment advisers, including their backgrounds, business affiliations, and bases for compensation.

5. *Securities Investor Protection Act of 1970.* This created the Securities Investor Protection Corporation (SIPC), an entity responsible for insuring investors from possible losses if an investment house enters bankruptcy. A small fee is added to the cost of each stock trade to cover the costs of the SIPC.

6. *Sarbanes-Oxley Act of 2002.* This created the Public Company Accounting Oversight Board (PCAOB) and created a number of responsibilities for audit committees of publicly held companies and for public accounting firms.

The SEC is often asked for assistance in the administration of two other major laws, as follows:

7. *Foreign Corrupt Practices Act of 1977.* This amended the 1934 Securities Exchange Act. It requires accurate and fair recording of financial activities and requires management to maintain an adequate system of internal control.

8. *Federal Bankruptcy Acts.* The SEC provides assistance to the courts when a publicly held company declares bankruptcy. The SEC's primary concern in these cases is the protection of security holders.

## The Regulatory Structure

Many people beginning a study of the regulatory structure of the SEC are overwhelmed by the myriad of regulations, acts, guides, and releases the SEC uses to perform its tasks. It is easier to understand how the SEC operates after obtaining a basic understanding of these public documents and the nature of the SEC's pronouncements. Figure 14–2, which will be referenced throughout the chapter, presents an overview of this regulatory structure.

The Securities Act of 1933 and the Securities Exchange Act of 1934 are broken down into rules, regulations, forms, guides, and releases. The rules generally provide specific definitions for complying with the acts. The regulations establish compliance requirements; for example, the regulations of the 1933 act detail specific reporting requirements for special cases such as small companies. The forms specify the format of the reports to be made under each of the acts. The guides provide specified additional disclosure requirements for selected industries such as oil and gas, and banks. The releases are used for amendments or adoptions of new requirements under the acts.

Two major regulations, **Regulation S-X** and **Regulation S-K,** govern the preparation of financial statements and associated disclosures made in reports to the SEC. Specifically, Regulation S-X presents the rules for preparing financial statements, footnotes, and the auditor's report. Regulation S-K covers all nonfinancial items, such as management's discussion and analysis of the company's operations and financial position.

The SEC needed some reporting vehicle to inform accountants about changes made in disclosure requirements, regulatory changes in the auditor–client relationship, and the results of enforcement actions taken against participants in the financial disclosure or securities trading process. Before 1982, the SEC used Accounting Series Releases (ASRs) for this purpose and had issued 307 ASRs covering a wide range of topics. In 1982, these ASRs were classified as covering either financial accounting topics or enforcement actions. Regulatory actions of the SEC are now provided on the SEC's Web site. Those governing reporting and financial accounting requirements are identified by a release number that begins with the number of the securities act being changed or amended (e.g., Release No. 33-8545, Release No. 34-51293, and so on).

The ***Accounting and Auditing Enforcement Releases (AAERs)*** present the results of enforcement actions taken against accountants, brokers, and other participants in the filing process. Most of these actions result from the filing of a false or misleading statement. The SEC can use administrative proceedings, in which case the hearings take place before an administrative law judge (ALJ) who is independent of the Commission. Both

**FIGURE 14–2** **The Regulatory Structure**

| Item | Contents |
|---|---|
| Securities Act of 1933 | Statute regulating initial registration and sale of securities. |
| Securities Act rules | Basic definitions of Securities Act terms such as *offers, distribution, participation,* and *accredited investor.* |
| Securities Act regulations | Detailed requirements of registration. At the present time there are six regulations (Regulations A, B, C, D, E, F), of which two (A and D) specify exemptions from registration requirements for small or private stock offerings. |
| Securities Act forms | Content of registration forms. The most frequently used forms are Form 1-A for small offerings of securities and Forms S-1, S-2, and S-3, which are general registration forms. |
| Securities Act industry guides | Specifications of additional disclosures required in registration statements of companies in special industries such as oil and gas, banking, and real estate. |
| Securities Act releases (SRs) | Announcements amending or adopting new rules, guides, forms, or policies under the 1933 act. Approximately 6,000 releases have been published. These are noted with a prefix; for example, for release number 6,000, Release 33-6000. |
| Securities Exchange Act of 1934 | Regulation of security trading and requirements for periodic reports by publicly held companies. |
| Exchange Act rules | Specific reporting requirements of over-the-counter securities, special reports required by stockholders who own 5 percent or more of a company's outstanding stock, and prohibition of manipulative and deceptive devices or contrivances. |
| Exchange Act forms | Specification of the content of periodic reports. The most commonly used forms are Form 10-K (annual report), Form 10-Q (quarterly report), and Form 8-K (current events report). |
| Exchange Act industry guides | Additional periodic reporting requirements of companies in specialized industries such as electric and gas utilities, oil and gas, and banking. |
| Securities Exchange Act releases (SRs) | Announcements of amendments or adoptions of new rules, guides, forms, or policy statements pertaining to the 1934 act. More than 15,000 have been issued, identified with a prefix; for example, for number 15,000, Release 34-15000. |
| Regulation S-X (Reg. S-X) | Articles specifying the form and content of financial disclosures: financial statements, schedules, footnotes, reports of accountants, and pro forma disclosures. |
| Regulation S-K (Reg. S-K) | Articles specifying disclosure rules of nonfinancial items to be included in registration statements, annual reports, and proxy statements. Major items are descriptions of business, management's discussion and analysis, disagreements with accountants, and required information about new stock issues. |
| Accounting and Auditing Enforcement Releases (AAERs) | Announcements of enforcement actions involving accountants practicing before the SEC. Includes discussion of the findings and opinions (including sanctions against the accountants involved) of enforcement hearings held by the Commission. *AAER No. 1* is a codification of all enforcement topics previously included in the Accounting Series Releases. |
| Staff Accounting Bulletins (SABs) | New or revised administrative practices and interpretations used by the Commission's staff in reviewing financial statements. |

the SEC and the defendant are allowed to present evidence. The administrative law judge then issues a report which includes the findings of fact and a recommended sanction, such as barring a person from further participation in auditing publicly traded companies or from employment as a broker or a member of management of a publicly traded company. In more serious cases, the SEC may file a complaint with a federal court seeking injunctions prohibiting illegal acts or practices, or other court orders seeking civil monetary penalties or other forms of sanctions.

An interesting example of a civil action is presented in Litigation Release No. 17588, on June 27, 2002. It is also identified as Accounting and Auditing Release No. 1585. The title of the release is, "SEC Charges WorldCom with $3.8 Billion Fraud. Commission Action Seeks Injunction, Money Penalties, Prohibitions on Destroying Documents and Making Extraordinary Payments to WorldCom Affiliates, and the Appointment of a Corporate Monitor." This litigation release presents the initial SEC action against WorldCom for its massive accounting fraud in which the company capitalized and deferred, rather than properly expensing, approximately $3.8 billion of costs. This fraud eventually led to the bankruptcy of WorldCom and the indictments of several of the company's top management.

The ***Staff Accounting Bulletins (SABs)*** allow the Commission's staff to make announcements on technical issues with which it is concerned as a result of reviews of SEC filings. The SABs are not formal actions of the Commission; nevertheless, most preparers do follow these bulletins because they represent the views of the staff that will be reviewing their companies' filings.

An example of a Staff Accounting Bulletin is SAB No. 101, "Revenue Recognition in Financial Statements," issued in 1999. SAB No. 101 focused on the several revenue recognition procedures the SEC staff found inconsistently applied by registrants. One special item was the discussion of revenue recognition by the "New Economy" Internet firms. These companies focus on revenue growth, and many do not report any positive income. Analysts and stock market investors gauge these companies based on their revenue growth. For example, Company A, an Internet company, may offer another company's products (Company T) on Company A's Web site. Customers place their orders and provide a credit card number to A's Internet site. Company A then forwards the order to Company T, which ships the goods to the customer. The goods normally cost $200, for which Company A receives $20 for facilitating the sale. The question is this: Can Company A record the entire $200 gross sale and a $180 cost of goods sold to report its profit of $20, or should Company A record just the net $20 sales commission as its revenue? SAB No. 101 states that the revenue should be reported on the net basis, not the gross basis that the SEC staff believes inflates both the reported revenue and cost of goods sold. As viewed by the SEC staff, Company A did not take title to the goods, did not incur the risks and rewards of ownership of the goods, and was only an agent or broker for Company T for which it received a commission or fee.

The 1933 and 1934 securities acts provided the SEC with broad regulatory powers to determine the accounting and reporting standards for publicly traded companies. The SEC has generally relied on the accounting profession to establish accounting standards through creation and support for a standard-making body, for example, the APB and the FASB. The cooperation between the SEC and the FASB has worked with varying levels of success. The FASB is sensitive to the changes in the business world and attempts to react quickly to these changes by promulgating new accounting standards when needed. The SEC, however, continues to fulfill its responsibility by issuing releases on subjects that it believes must be addressed.

# ISSUING SECURITIES: THE REGISTRATION PROCESS

Companies wishing to sell debt or stock securities in interstate offerings to the general public are generally required by the Securities Act of 1933 to register those securities with the SEC. The registration process requires extensive disclosure about the company, its management, and the intended use of the proceeds from the issue. The registrant must also provide audited financial statements. The basic financial statements required in the annual report are: (1) two years of balance sheets, (2) three years of statements of income, (3) three years of statements of cash flows, and (4) three years of statements of shareholders' equity. Prior years' statements are presented on a comparative basis with those for the current period. In addition, the SEC requires at least five years of selected financial information presenting key numbers from the four basic financial statements.

A number of types of securities and securities transactions are exempt from the need to be registered under the 1933 act. Although the SEC may exempt these from full registration requirements, the antifraud provisions of the securities acts still apply to all offerings. The exempt securities are commercial paper (i.e., notes) with a maturity of nine months or less; intrastate issues in which the securities are offered and sold only within one state; securities exchanged by an issuer exclusively with its existing shareholders with no commission charged (e.g., a stock split or a stock dividend issued by a corporation); issuances of securities by governments, banks, savings and loan associations, farmers, co-ops, and common carriers regulated by the Interstate Commerce Commission; and securities of nonprofit religious, educational, or charitable organizations. Small issues under the SEC's **Regulation A** for issuances up to $5,000,000 within a 12-month period can be exempt if there is a notice filed with the SEC and an "offering circular" containing financial and other information provided to the persons to whom the offer is made (the financial statements in the offering circular do not have to be audited). Thus, some required disclosures of financial statements and other financial information fall under Regulation A.

**Regulation D** of the SEC presents three important exemptions from full registration requirements for private placements (i.e., not offered to the general public) of securities, as follows:

1. Rule 504 of Regulation D exempts small issuances up to $1,000,000 within a 12-month period to any number of investors. No specific disclosures are required, but the offerer must send a notice of the offering to the SEC within 15 days of the first sale of the securities.

2. Rule 505 of Regulation D exempts issuances up to $5,000,000 within a 12-month period. The sales can be made to up to 35 "unaccredited investors" and to an unlimited number of "accredited investors." Accredited investors include banks, credit unions, insurance companies, partnerships and corporations, and individuals having a net worth exceeding $1,000,000 or individual income of $200,000 for the two most recent years. Unaccredited investors are persons who do not meet the income or net worth requirements. An unaccredited investor who purchases the securities must be supplied with audited balance sheets along with other financial statements. If the sales are only to accredited investors, no disclosures are required. Under Rule 505, the SEC must be notified within 15 days of the first sale, and the issuer must restrict the purchasers' rights to resell the securities, generally for a period of two years. The securities typically state the nature of their restriction and that they have not been registered with the SEC.

3. Rule 506 of Regulation D allows private placements of an unlimited amount of securities and applies, in general, the same rules of Rule 505 except the maximum of 35 unaccredited investors must be sophisticated investors who have knowledge and experience in financial affairs.

The offering process usually begins with the selection of an investment banker, also called an "underwriter," who assists the company in the registration process by providing marketing information and ultimately directing the distribution of the securities. The underwriting agreement is a contract between the company and the underwriter and specifies such items as the underwriter's responsibilities and the final disposition of any unsold securities remaining at the end of the public offering. In some cases, the underwriter agrees to purchase any remaining securities; in others, the company is required to withdraw any unsold securities. An offering team includes the company, the underwriter, the company's independent accountant, the company's legal counsel, and experts such as appraisers or engineers who may be required. Typically, the underwriter requires a "comfort letter" from the accountant to indicate that the company has fulfilled all the accounting requirements in the registration process.

## The Registration Statement

The process of public offerings of securities begins with the preparation of the registration statement. The company must select one from among approximately 20 different forms the SEC currently has for registering securities. The most common are ***Form S-1, Form S-2,*** and ***Form S-3.*** Others are required when registering stock option plans, foreign issues, limited issuances under Regulation D, and special types of offerings. Form S-1 is the most comprehensive registration statement; Form S-2 is an abbreviated form for present registrants who have other publicly traded stock; Form S-3 is a brief form available for large, established registrants whose stock has been trading for several years.

Form S-1 has two different levels of disclosure. Part I, often referred to as the "prospectus," is intended primarily for investors and includes the basic information package as well as information about the intended use of the proceeds, a description of the securities being offered, and the plan of distribution, including the name of the principal underwriter. Filings for bond issues must include summary information about the ratio of earnings to fixed charges so investors are informed about some of the financial risk the new bond issue adds to the company. Part II of Form S-1 includes more detailed information, such as a list of the expenses of issuing and distributing the new security, additional information about directors and officers, and additional financial statement schedules. The registration statement must be signed by the principal executive, financial, and accounting officers, as well as a majority of the company's board of directors. The company then submits its registration statement to an SEC review by the Division of Corporation Finance.

## SEC Review and Public Offering

The SEC seeks to provide potential investors full and fair disclosure of all material information necessary for assessing the securities' risk and return expectations. The SEC does not, however, guarantee the value of the stock or bond security.

Most first-time registrants receive a "customary review," which is a thorough examination by the SEC that may result in acceptance, or, alternatively, a ***comment letter*** specifying the deficiencies that must be corrected before the securities may be offered for sale. Established companies that already have stock widely traded generally are subject to a summary review or a cursory review. Once the registration statement becomes effective, the company may begin selling securities to the public. This review period is 20 days unless the company receives a comment letter from the SEC.

Between the time the registration statement is presented to the SEC and its effective date, the company may issue a ***preliminary prospectus,*** referred to as a *red herring prospectus,* which provides tentative information to investors about an upcoming issue. The name "red herring" comes from the red ink used on the cover of this preliminary prospectus, indicating that it is not an offering statement and that the securities being discussed are not yet available for sale. In addition, the company generally prepares a "tombstone ad" in the business press to inform investors of the upcoming offering. These ads are bordered in black ink, hence the title.

The time period between the initial decision to offer securities and the actual sale may not exceed 120 days. In the interim, many factors can affect the stock market and decrease the company's ability to obtain capital. In 1982, the SEC devised the ***shelf registration*** rule for large, established companies with other issues of stock already actively traded. These companies may file a registration statement with the SEC for a stock issue that may be "brought off the shelf" and, with the aid of an underwriter, updated within a very short time, usually two to three days. A shelf registration is limited to 10 percent of the company's currently outstanding stock but allows large companies to select the optimal time to sell their stock.

## Accountants' Legal Liability in the Registration Process

Accountants play a key role in the preparation of the registration statement. The company's own accountants prepare the initial financial disclosures, which are then audited by the company's independent accountants. The 1933 act created a very broad legal liability for all participants in the registration process, and this legal exposure is particularly high for accountants because financial disclosures make up the majority of the registration statement. Under section 11 of the 1933 act, accountants are liable for any materially false or misleading information *to the effective date* of the registration statement. The underwriters handling the sale of the securities often require a "comfort letter" from the registrant's public accountants for the period between the filing date and the effective date. This comfort letter provides additional evidence that the public accountant has not found any adverse financial changes since the filing date. Plaintiffs suing the accountant are not required to show they relied on the registration statement, only that the statement was wrong at the effective date! Accountants have a "due diligence" defense, the result of interpretations by the courts as to what is generally required in a reasonable investigation of the company's financial position; however, the broad legal exposure causes many anxieties for accountants involved with the offering of securities.

# PERIODIC REPORTING REQUIREMENTS

The Securities Exchange Act of 1934 regulates the trading of securities and imposes reporting requirements on companies whose securities trade on one of the stock exchanges. Companies with more than $10 million in assets and whose securities are held by more than 500 persons must file annual and other periodic reports as updates on their economic activities. The three basic forms used for this updating are Form 10-K, Form 10-Q, and Form 8-K.

*Form 10-K* is the annual filing to the SEC. In 2002, the SEC changed the filing deadlines of the Form 10-K for "accelerated filers," which are defined as those companies having at least $75 million in aggregate market value that have been subject to the periodic and annual reporting requirements for at least one year, including the filing of at least one annual report. Accelerated filers must file their Form 10-K within 60 days after the end of the company's fiscal year. Small businesses, and others who do not meet the requirements for an accelerated filer, have until 90 days after the end of their fiscal years.

Form 10-K has four parts and the general format is similar to the company's annual report to shareholders (ARS). Parts I, II, and III include the management's discussion and analysis, the audited financial statements and footnotes, the report by management on the internal control structure and the assessment of the effectiveness of those controls, the auditor's opinion, and at least five years of condensed financial information disclosures. Some of this information is sometimes "incorporated by reference" to other annual reports to shareholders (ARS) or other filings made to the SEC. Also included must be a statement signed by the CEO and CFO that certifies that the financials and disclosures contained in the report are appropriate and that those financial statements and disclosures fairly present, in all material respects, the operations and the financial condition of the issuer.

Part IV of the Form 10-K contains additional schedules and exhibits. Form 10-K differs from the annual report to shareholders by providing specific information relevant to the security holders, such as descriptions of any matters submitted to a vote of security holders; discussion of any disagreements with external auditors; management compensation and major ownership blocks; and schedules detailing selected asset and liability accounts, including accounts receivable, property, plant, and equipment, the company's investments in other enterprises, and indebtedness of the company and its affiliates. The SEC also requires disclosure in the annual report as to where investors can obtain access to a company's SEC periodic filings, including whether the company provides access to its filings on its Web site, free of charge, as soon as possible after the filings are made to the SEC.

*Form 10-Q* is the quarterly report to the SEC. Accelerated filers must file a Form 10-Q within 35 days after the end of each of their first three quarters. No Form 10-Q is filed for the fourth quarter because that is when the Form 10-K is filed. Those companies not classified as accelerated filers must file within 45 days after the end of each of their first three quarters.

Part I of Form 10-Q includes comparative financial statements prepared in accordance with **APB 28;** these interim statements need not be audited. Essentially, the company provides financial statements for the most recent quarter, cumulative statements from the beginning of the fiscal period, and comparative statements for the equivalent quarters in the preceding fiscal year. Selected data from the interim statements must also be disclosed in a footnote in the company's annual report, and the independent auditors do, on an ex post basis, review the previously issued interims for the year as part of the year-end, annual audit.

Part II of Form 10-Q is an update on significant matters occurring since the last quarter. These include new legal proceedings, changes in the rights of securities, defaults on senior securities, increases or decreases in the number of securities outstanding, and other materially important events affecting security holders.

***Form 8-K*** is used to disclose unscheduled material events. In 2004, the SEC issued final rules that increased the number of reportable items to be disclosed by Form 8-K filings and also accelerated the timing of the filing requirement. Companies must file a Form 8-K within four business days of the occurrence of a "triggering event." Many of the 19 triggering events involve the company's board of directors, or an authorizing officer of the company, making a commitment or conclusion regarding one or more of the reportable items. A number of these events involve accountants and it is important that accountants understand which events require a Form 8-K filing. Because of the expansion of the number of reportable items, the SEC reorganized Form 8-K items into nine topical sections, each with a subnumbering system used for specific items in that section.

1. *Registrant's Business and Operations.* The three reportable events in this section are: (1.01) entry into a material agreement; (1.02) termination of a material agreement; and (1.03) the bankruptcy or receivership of the company.

2. *Financial Information.* This section contains the following six items: (2.01) the completion of the acquisition or disposition of assets; (2.02) the public announcement of material results of operations and financial condition; (2.03) the creation of a direct financial obligation under an off-balance sheet arrangement; (2.04) an event that accelerates or increases a direct financial obligation under an off-balance sheet arrangement; (2.05) costs associated with exit or disposal activities when the board commits the company to an exit or disposal of a material part of the business; and (2.06) material impairments of a company's assets.

3. *Securities and Trading Markets.* The three items in this section are: (3.01) notice of delisting or failure to satisfy a continuing listing rule; (3.02) an unregistered sale of equity securities; and (3.03) material modifications to the rights of security holders.

4. *Matters Related to Accountants and Financial Statements.* The two items in this section are: (4.01) changes in the registrant's certifying accountant; and (4.02) nonreliance on previously issued financial statements or a related audit report.

5. *Corporate Governance and Management.* The six items in this section are: (5.01) changes in control of the registrant; (5.02) the departure of directors or principal officers, or the election or appointment of principal officers; (5.03) amendments to the articles of incorporation or bylaws, including any change in the registrant's fiscal year; (5.04) the temporary suspension of trading under the registrant's employee benefit plans; (5.05) amendments to the registrant's code of ethics, or waiver of a provision of the code of ethics; and (5.06) a change in shell company status. A shell company has very limited operations and holds only minor amounts of assets. The company is essentially a legal shell under which other companies operate.

6. *Asset-based Securities.* This section requires disclosure of material items related to asset-backed securities such as a bond issue. Disclosures are required for a change of servicer or trustee of the security; a change in the credit enhancement or other external support for the securities; or a failure to make a distribution required by the security agreement.

7. *Regulation FD.* (Item 7.01) This section requires filing a Form 8-K to broadly report material information that is being provided to securities analysts, selected institutional investors, or others. Regulation FD seeks to eliminate the informational advantages of having access to officers or other management members through public channels. For example, if the CEO of a registrant spoke to a group of financial analysts at a lunch meeting during which the general future of the company and its industry was discussed, the company would file a Form 8-K disclosing the meeting and include major informational items presented by the CEO.

8. *Other Events.* (Item 8.01) This section is unstructured and flexible to allow management to disclose items it believes may be of material importance to security holders.

9. *Financial Statements and Exhibits.* (Item 9.01) This section includes a listing of the financial statements, pro forma financial information, and exhibits required to be filed as part of Form 8-K.

For changes in the registrant's certifying accountant (Item 4.01), Form 8-K must include the following: the date the former auditor resigned or was dismissed, a statement describing and fully discussing any material disagreements with the former auditors over accounting or auditing standards over the past 24 months, a statement stating whether the former auditor's opinion was qualified in any way for the past two years and describing the nature of any qualification, and a letter from the former auditor as an exhibit to Form 8-K that states whether the former auditor agrees or disagrees with the facts as stated in the Form 8-K, as presented by the registrant.

**Schedule 13D** is filed by any person or group of persons who acquire a beneficial ownership of more than 5 percent of a class of registered equity securities and must be filed within 10 days after such an acquisition. *Beneficial ownership* is defined as directly or indirectly having the power to vote the shares or investment power to sell the security. In addition, any time there are material changes in the facts set forth in the schedule, the investor must file an amendment on Schedule 13D. Thus, any investor making an acquisition of 5 percent or more of any class of equity securities of a publicly held company must promptly report the investment to the SEC.

**Proxy statements** are materials submitted to shareholders for votes on corporate matters such as the election of directors, changes in the corporate charter, issuance of new securities or modification of outstanding securities, or plans for a major business combination. In many cases, voting on these matters takes place at the annual meeting but it may also occur at a special meeting. A proxy card soliciting the shareholder's vote is often in the form of a checkoff ballot that management encourages the shareholder to return to be voted at the meeting. The proxy solicitation materials must include the specific proposals being presented to the shareholders, accompanied by supporting statements of facts and circumstances to explain the proposals. The materials also include information about the committees of the board of directors and executive compensation and share ownership. If there will be an election of directors, the SEC also requires that the registrant's annual report to shareholders be included with the proxy materials. An increasing number of companies are using the Internet to provide their proxy materials, annual report, and proxy cards to shareholders who request the electronic form. The company must send out printed materials to all other shareholders. A copy of a registrant's proxy statement is available on the SEC's EDGAR database of filings for that company under the title "DEF 14A" to identify it as the definitive, or final, proxy statement filed under Section 14A of the Securities Exchange Act of 1934.

Individual shareholders or a group of shareholders may sometimes use proxy solicitations for proposals that are opposed by management. Rule 14-8 of the Securities Exchange Act of 1934 presents detailed rules and regulations that must be met in order to have these shareholder proposals included on a company's proxy card and included along with any supporting statements in the proxy statement. The rules are quite specific with regard to who is eligible to submit a proposal, the content and subject matter of a proposal, and deadlines for submitting a proposal. At times, the business press carries news of proxy battles between management and non-management groups, in which each side is soliciting shareholders' support.

### Accountants' Legal Liability in Periodic Reporting

The 1934 Securities Exchange Act provides for a limited level of legal exposure from involvement in the preparation and filing of periodic reports. Civil liability is imposed for filing materially false or misleading statements. The accountant's liability for registration statements under the 1933 act extends to the date the registration becomes effective. Plaintiffs suing accountants under the 1934 act must show that a periodic report contains a misleading material fact and that they suffered a loss because they relied on that report. Accountants are provided with due diligence defenses to combat any lawsuits brought under the 1934 act.

## FOREIGN CORRUPT PRACTICES ACT OF 1977

In the mid-1970s, Congress held a number of public hearings that brought to light the payment of millions of dollars in bribes to high government officials of other countries by U.S.-based companies seeking to win defense or consumer product contracts. Alarmed by the size and scope of these activities, Congress passed the *Foreign Corrupt Practices Act of 1977 (FCPA)* as a major amendment to the Securities Exchange Act of 1934. The FCPA has two major sections: Part I prohibits foreign bribes, and Part II requires publicly held companies to maintain an adequate system of internal control and accurate records.

Under Part I, individuals associated with U.S. companies are prohibited from bribing foreign governmental or political officials for the purpose of securing a contract or otherwise increasing the company's business. Small compensating or agents' fees to lower-level civil servants are allowed if the purpose of these fees is to facilitate a transaction that is already in process, such as to obtain shipping permits or to acquire local licenses in a foreign country. Both civil and criminal sanctions can be imposed on individuals making foreign bribes.

Part II of the FCPA has had a significant impact on both corporate accountants and independent auditors. This part requires all public companies, whether operating internationally or not, to keep detailed records that accurately and fairly reflect their financial transactions and to develop and maintain an adequate internal control system. An internal control system should ensure that all major transactions are fully authorized, that transactions are properly recorded and reported, that the company's assets are safeguarded, and that management's policies are properly carried out.

Although the FCPA was not specific about the types of internal controls necessary, it defined the following as important aspects of a good internal control system: (1) strong budgetary controls, (2) an objective internal audit function that helps develop, document, and then monitor the control system, (3) an active audit committee of nonmanagement members of the company's board of directors, and (4) a review of the internal control system by the independent auditors. The FCPA allows for the development of "tailored" control procedures that best serve the company. In addition, the FCPA indicated that the cost of an internal control procedure should not outweigh its benefit to the firm.

The FCPA also had a significant effect on independent auditors by requiring them to evaluate a company's internal controls and to communicate any material weaknesses in those controls to the company's top management and board of directors. The total impact of the FCPA is still unclear. Subsequent proposals offered by the SEC itself have somewhat softened the foreign bribery section of the act; however, Part II of the FCPA, dealing with internal control, certainly increased the interest of companies in maintaining strong internal control systems.

## SARBANES-OXLEY ACT OF 2002

A major law affecting auditors and publicly traded companies was signed into law on July 30, 2002. The proposed law gained impetus after the revelations about accounting and financial mismanagement at Enron, WorldCom, and others. Named after its two sponsors, Senator Paul Sarbanes and Congressman Michael Oxley, the *Sarbanes-Oxley Act* (broadly known as SOX) has a number of major implications for accountants.

Its supporters hoped that the act would minimize corporate governance accounting and financial reporting abuses and help restore investor confidence in the financial reports of publicly traded companies. The following discussion summarizes the major sections of the Sarbanes-Oxley Act.

## Title I: Public Company Accounting Oversight Board

Section 101 of Title I of the act established a new accounting oversight board to regulate accounting firms and be responsible for establishing or modifying auditing and attestation standards. The ***Public Company Accounting Oversight Board (PCAOB)*** is administered by the SEC, which is responsible for appointing its five full-time members. Many accountants use the shorthand of "Peek-A-Boo" to refer to the PCAOB. Two board members must be or must have been CPAs; however, the other three cannot have been CPAs. The PCAOB chair may be a CPA but that person must not have practiced accounting during the five years prior to being appointed as chair. The board's funding includes mandatory fees from public companies. Accounting firms with publicly held audit clients must be registered with the PCAOB and are subject to continuing quality inspections for compliance to the requirements of the act.

The PCAOB has the authority to establish or to adopt standards for audit firm quality controls. The range of its authority includes auditing and related attestation standards, quality control, ethics, independence, and other areas necessary to protect the public interest. The board also manages the regular inspection of the registered accounting firms' operations and auditing processes. Any accounting firm that does not cooperate can be prohibited from auditing public companies. If the PCAOB finds any violations of its standards, that accounting firm can be referred to the SEC and possibly to the Department of Justice for prosecution.

## Title II: Auditor Independence

A major change brought about by the Sarbanes-Oxley Act prohibits auditors from offering certain nonaudit services to their audit clients. These services include information systems design and implementations, appraisals or valuation services, internal audits, human resources services, legal or expert services not related to audit services, and bookkeeping services. Tax services provided by an auditor for a publicly held company require preapproval of the company's audit committee. Thus, accounting firms must determine whether they wish to provide a company with audit or nonaudit services; they cannot provide both to the same company.

Title II requires that both the lead audit partner and the audit review partner for publicly held companies be rotated at least every five years. To avoid a conflict of interest, the company's CEO, controller, CFO, chief accounting officer, or person in an equivalent position cannot have been employed by the company's audit firm during the one-year period preceding the audit.

## Title III: Corporate Responsibility

Title III specifies that ***audit committees*** be composed of nonmangement members of a company's board of directors. Generally, the chair of the audit committee has financial experience. The Sarbanes-Oxley Act requires the auditor to report directly to, and have its work overseen by, the company's audit committee, not the company's management. The audit committee is responsible for the appointment, compensation, and oversight of the work of the public accounting firm employed by the company. Furthermore, the audit committee must approve all services provided by the auditor, and the auditor must report the following additional information to the audit committee: critical accounting policies and practices, alternative treatments within GAAP that have been discussed with the company's management, accounting disagreements between the auditor and management, and any other important issues arising between the auditor and management.

Section 302 of the act requires both the CEO and the CFO of each publicly traded company to provide a signed statement to accompany each annual and quarterly financial report. These two officers are required to certify that the financial statements and disclosures fairly present, in all material respects, the operations and conditions of the issuer. Furthermore, their signed statement must include declarations that they are responsible for establishing and maintaining internal controls and that these controls have been evaluated as to their effectiveness within 90 days prior to the report.

In the case of accounting restatements due to the material noncompliance of the issuer, the CEO and CFO must forfeit bonuses and incentive compensation provided on the basis of the incorrect accounting information.

## Title IV: Enhanced Financial Disclosures

Financial reports filed with the SEC must reflect all material correcting adjustments that have been identified by the registered accounting firm and also all material off-balance sheet transactions and relationships that may have a material effect on the financial status of the issuer. Section 402 prohibits a company from making personal loans to any director or executive officer. However, consumer credit companies may make home improvement and consumer credit loans to its officers if these loans are made on the same terms as those made to the general public.

A major requirement of the Sarbanes-Oxley Act is specified in Section 404, which requires that each annual filing of a stock issuer must contain an ***internal control report*** by management that reports on the existence and effectiveness of the company's internal control over financial reporting. A company's internal control over financial reporting is a process designed to provide reasonable assurance of the reliability of the financial reporting and preparation of financial statements for external purposes in accordance with generally accepted accounting principles. In May 2003, the SEC released rules (Release No. 33-8238) that established specific requirements for the content of this report. Management's internal control report must include the following items: (*a*) a statement that management is responsible for establishing and maintaining an adequate system; (*b*) the identification of the framework used to evaluate the internal controls; (*c*) a statement as to whether or not the internal control is effective as of year-end; (*d*) the disclosure of any material weaknesses in the internal control system; and (*e*) a statement that the company's external auditors have issued an audit report on management's assessment of its internal controls. The independent auditors also must report on the reliability of management's assessment of internal controls over financial reporting.

In May 2005, the Securities and Exchange Commission released a statement on the first year's implementation of Section 404 suggesting that there were significant start-up costs from this new requirement. However, the SEC feels that benefits have been produced from Section 404's requirements and that the Section 404 implementation process will become more efficient over time. The annual filings of publicly held companies now include both the management report on internal control over financial reporting and the expanded independent auditor's report on its assessment of that internal control system. The auditor's report must include a statement attesting to the assessment made by management on the company's internal control structures, including specific notes about any significant defects or material noncompliance found on the basis of that testing.

## Title V: Analyst Conflicts of Interest

Research analysts and brokers and dealers must report if they hold securities in any company for which they prepare a research report, if any compensation was received from the company that was the subject of a research report, and if a company that is the subject of a research report was a client of the broker or dealer.

## Title VI: Commission Resources and Authority

Title VI increased the funding for the SEC and also increased the SEC's disciplinary and litigation authority over auditors, attorneys, brokers and dealers, and others who practice in the securities markets and who have engaged in illegal, unethical, or improper professional conduct.

### Title VII: Studies and Reports

The GAO and SEC are charged with conducting various studies, including of the factors leading to the consolidation of public accounting firms since 1989 and the impacts of that consolidation, the role of credit rating agencies in the securities markets, and whether investment banks and financial advisers assisted public companies in earnings manipulation and obfuscation of financial conditions.

### Title VIII: Corporate and Criminal Fraud Accountability

The act established severe penalties for anyone who destroys records, commits securities fraud, or fails to report fraud. The penalty for willfully failing to maintain all audit or review workpapers for at least five years is a felony punishable by up to 10 years. Section 802 of the act specifies that persons destroying documents in a federal or bankruptcy investigation are punishable by up to 20 years. The criminal penalty for securities fraud was increased to 25 years.

The statute of limitations for the discovery of fraud was increased to two years from the date of discovery and five years after the actual fraud. Previously, it had been only one year from the date of discovery and three years after the actual fraud. Section 806 provides "whistleblower protection" to employees of the company or the accounting firm who lawfully assist in an investigation of fraud or other criminal conduct by federal regulators, Congress, or supervisors.

### Title IX: White-Collar Crime Penalty Enhancements

This title increases the minimum penalty for mail and wire fraud from 5 to 10 years, makes it a crime to tamper with a record or impede any official proceeding, and allows the SEC to prohibit anyone convicted of securities fraud from being an officer or director of any publicly traded company. In addition, this section of SOX includes criminal liability up to five years for corporate officers who fail to certify financial reports or who willfully certify financial statements knowing they do not comply with the act.

### Title X: Sense of Congress Regarding Corporate Tax Returns

Congress felt that the federal income tax return of a corporation should be signed by the chief executive officer.

### Title XI: Corporate Fraud and Accountability

This section increased the penalties for persons using deceptive devices, engaging in fraudulent transactions, or otherwise acting to impede an official proceeding. It also increased the penalties for violations of the Securities Exchange Act of 1934 up to $25 million and up to 20 years in prison.

The Sarbanes-Oxley Act will have a significant impact on financial reporting, auditing, and corporate governance. The SEC continues to develop the implementation guidelines for various sections of the act, and, therefore, the daily business and accounting press will have continued coverage of the act. The complete act is linked to on the SEC's Web site (www.sec.gov).

## DISCLOSURE REQUIREMENTS

Virtually every SEC accounting release reminds registrants of the commitment to full and fair disclosure of financial information needed by investors. The SEC has taken the lead in requiring management to provide its analysis of the company's operations.

### Management Discussion and Analysis

The ***management discussion and analysis (MD&A)*** of a company's financial condition and results of operations is part of the basic information package (BIP) required in all major filings with the SEC. The SEC has taken the leadership role in requiring management to analyze and discuss the financial statements for investors, and this discussion often extends to four or more pages of the annual report. The financial statements are, after all, management's expressions of the economic consequences of their decisions made during the period. Management has the clearest picture of the company's financial environment. A key element in the MD&A is a view that looks both historically and forward at the company's liquidity and solvency. The SEC recognizes that investors are particularly concerned with a company's ability to generate adequate amounts of cash to meet short-term and long-term cash needs.

The MD&A is continually being monitored by the SEC because the Commission believes the information presented in the MD&A is important for investors. In response to the requirement in section 401 of the Sarbanes-Oxley Act and new section 13(j) of the Securities Exchange Act of 1934, the SEC examined the items listed in its MD&A rules. With Release No. 33-8182, the SEC revised the list of required items in the MD&A, effective April 7, 2003. The items now required in the MD&A are:

1. *Liquidity.* Identify trends, commitments, events, or uncertainties that are reasonably likely to materially change the registrant's liquidity. Indicate the course of action that is proposed to remedy any deficiency identified. Also, identify and describe the internal and external sources of liquidity, with a brief discussion of any material unused sources of liquid assets.

2. *Capital resources.* Discuss material commitments for capital expenditures, their general purposes, and the expected sources of funds to fulfill those commitments. Also discuss trends and expected material changes in the mix of equity, debt, and any off-balance sheet financing arrangements.

3. *Results of operations.* Describe and discuss unusual or infrequent events or transactions affecting revenues, expenses, and the reported income from continuing operations. Discuss trends or expectations of material impacts on future revenues and expenses. For material increases in net sales, discuss the impact of an increase in price versus the impact of an increase in volume and discuss the impact of the introduction of new products. Then, for each of the most recent three years, discuss the impact of inflation and changing prices on net sales and revenue and on income from continuing operations.

4. *Off-balance sheet arrangements.* A separately identified section that includes discussion of off-balance sheet arrangements that have or are likely to have a material effect on the company's financial condition, changes in financial condition, results of operations, liquidity, capital expenditures, or capital resources. Required disclosures for these off-balance sheet arrangements include the nature and business purpose of the arrangements, the impact of the arrangements on revenues, expenses, and cash flows, and a description of events or other items that would materially change the benefits of the arrangement and the actions the company has taken or would take if those circumstances were to occur.

5. *Tabular disclosure of contractual obligations.* A table in the following format shall be provided, listing the aggregated amount of each type of contractual obligations, (if present):

| Contractual Obligations | Payments Due by Period | | | | |
|---|---|---|---|---|---|
| | Total | Less than 1 Year | 1–3 Years | 3–5 Years | More than 5 Years |
| Long-term debt obligations | | | | | |
| Capital lease obligations | | | | | |
| Operating lease obligations | | | | | |
| Purchase obligations for goods or services | | | | | |
| Other long-term liabilities reflected on the registrant's balance sheet under GAAP | | | | | |
| Total | | | | | |

The MD&A should cover the financial statements and other statistical data for the most recent three-year time span and make year-to-year comparisons of material changes in the line items. Management should attempt to explain the cause(s) of the material changes. Section 401 of the Sarbanes-Oxley Act specifies the required disclosure of material off-balance sheet transactions, arrangements, and obligations in each annual and each quarterly report. The MD&A in the quarterly reports should be viewed as updating the annual information. Thus, the MD&A in quarterly reports is generally much shorter than that in the annual report.

## Pro Forma Disclosures

*Pro forma disclosures* are essentially "what-if" financial presentations often taking the form of summarized financial statements. Pro forma statements are used to show the effects of major transactions that occur after the end of the fiscal period or that have occurred during the year but are not fully reflected in the company's historical cost financial statements. The SEC requires these to be presented whenever the company has made a significant business combination or disposition, a corporate reorganization, an unusual asset exchange, or a restructuring of existing indebtedness. A pro forma condensed income statement presented in the footnotes shows the impact of the transaction on the company's income from continuing operations, thereby helping investors to focus on the specific effects of the major transaction. The pro forma balance sheet includes all adjustments reflecting the full impact of the transaction. Investors therefore have (1) the historical cost primary financial statements, and (2) the pro forma statements, which more fully present and illustrate the effects of the transaction on the company's financial condition.

## Summary of Key Concepts

Since its creation in 1934, the SEC has played a significant role in the development of financial disclosures necessary for investor confidence in the capital formation process. The Commission has consistently worked for full and fair disclosure of information it considers necessary so investors can assess the risks and returns of companies wishing to offer their securities to the public. The SEC has taken the leadership in a myriad of reporting issues, predominantly in reporting liquidity and solvency measures, thereby ensuring that investors have access to a management narrative of the company's performance.

Although the SEC has the statutory responsibility to develop and maintain accounting principles used for financial reporting, it has permitted the rule-making bodies of the accounting profession to take the initiative in establishing accounting principles and reporting standards. The cooperation has worked with varying success over the years. The SEC has shown its willingness and capacity to assume the lead in those areas in which it feels the private sector is not moving rapidly enough. It is expected that this arrangement will continue in the future.

## Key Terms

Accounting and Auditing Enforcement Releases (AAERs), *687*
audit committees, *696*
comment letter, *691*
Foreign Corrupt Practices Act of 1977 (FCPA), *695*
internal control report, *697*
management discussion and analysis (MD&A), *698*
periodic reporting forms: Form 10-K, Form 10-Q, Form 8-K, *692–693*

preliminary prospectus, *691*
pro forma disclosures, *700*
proxy statements, *694*
Public Company Accounting Oversight Board (PCAOB), *696*
registration statements: Form S-1, Form S-2, Form S-3, *691*
Regulation A, *690*
Regulation D, *690*
Regulation S-K, *687*
Regulation S-X, *687*

Sarbanes-Oxley Act, *695*
Schedule 13D, *694*
shelf registration, *691*
Staff Accounting Bulletins (SABs), *689*

| Questions | | |
|---|---|---|
| **Q14-1** | What is the basis of the SEC's legal authority to regulate accounting principles? | |

**Q14-2**  Which securities act—1933 or 1934—regulates the initial registration of securities? Which regulates the periodic reporting of publicly traded companies?

**Q14-3**  Which division of the SEC receives the registration statements of companies wishing to make public offerings of securities? Which division investigates individuals or firms that may be in violation of a security act?

**Q14-4**  Which law requires that companies maintain accurate accounting records and an adequate system of internal control? What is meant by an "adequate system of internal control"?

**Q14-5**  What does Regulation S-X cover? What is included in Regulation S-K?

**Q14-6**  What types of public offerings of securities are exempted from the comprehensive registration requirements of the SEC?

**Q14-7**  When must a company use a Form S-1 registration form? In what circumstances may a company use a Form S-3 registration form?

**Q14-8**  Define the following terms, which are part of the SEC terminology: (*a*) customary review, (*b*) comment letter, (*c*) red herring prospectus, (*d*) shelf registration.

**Q14-9**  What is included in Form 10-K? When must a 10-K be filed with the SEC?

**Q14-10**  Must interim reports submitted to the SEC be audited? What is the role of the public accountant in the preparation of Form 10-Q?

**Q14-11**  What types of items that specifically involve the accounting function are reported on Form 8-K?

**Q14-12**  What is a proxy? What must be included in the proxy material submitted to security holders?

**Q14-13**  Describe Parts I and II of the Foreign Corrupt Practices Act. What is the impact of this act on companies and public accountants?

**Q14-14**  What types of information must be disclosed in the management discussion and analysis?

**Q14-15**  Describe the major requirements of the Sarbanes-Oxley Act of 2002.

## Cases

### C14-1  Objectives of Securities Acts [CMA Adapted]

*Research*

During the late 1920s, approximately 55 percent of all personal savings in the United States was used to purchase securities. Public confidence in the business community was extremely high as stock values doubled and tripled in short periods of time. The road to wealth was believed to be through the stock market, and everyone who was able to participate. Thus, the public was severely affected when the Dow Jones Industrial Average fell 89 percent between 1929 and 1933. The public outcry arising from this decline in stock prices motivated the passage of major federal laws regulating the securities industry.

#### Required

*a.* Describe the investment practices of the 1920s that contributed to the erosion of the stock market.

*b.* Explain the basic objectives of each of the following:

    (1)  Securities Act of 1933.

    (2)  Securities Exchange Act of 1934.

*c.* More legislation has resulted from abuses in the securities industry. Explain the provisions of the Foreign Corrupt Practices Act of 1977.

### C14-2  Roles of SEC and FASB [CMA Adapted]

*Understanding*

The development of accounting theory and practice has been influenced directly and indirectly by many organizations and institutions. Two of the most important institutions have been the Financial Accounting Standards Board (FASB) and the Securities and Exchange Commission (SEC).

The FASB is an independent body established in 1972. It is composed of seven persons who represent public accounting and fields other than public accounting.

The SEC is a governmental regulatory agency created in 1934 to administer the Securities Act of 1933 and the Securities Exchange Act of 1934. These acts and the creation of the SEC resulted from the widespread collapse of business and the securities markets in the early 1930s.

*Required*

a. What official role does the SEC have in the development of financial accounting theory and practice?

b. What is the interrelationship between the FASB and the SEC with respect to the development and establishment of financial accounting theory and practice?

### C14-3 Information Content of Proxy

*Application*

The proxy contains an abundance of information believed by the SEC to be necessary for stock-holders to make an informed vote on the items the company presents for their voting consideration. This case provides opportunities to analyze the proxy of a publicly held company and to survey the types of information presented in the proxy.

*Required*

Using EDGAR or another source, obtain the most recent proxy for Caterpillar Inc. or a different company specified by your instructor. Answer the following questions regarding the information presented in the proxy.

a. Summarize the proposals that are being placed before the shareholders for their voting consideration and state the board of directors' recommendation on each proposal.

b. List and briefly describe the duties of each of the standing committees of the board of directors.

c. For the most recent year presented in your proxy, what was the total annual compensation received by the chairman and CEO of the company?

### C14-4 Form 10-K Disclosures

*Application*

Form 10-K is the annual filing required of publicly traded entities. The form contains the financial information for the year, but also includes a number of other disclosures required by the SEC.

*Required*

Using EDGAR or another source, obtain the most recent Form 10-K (the annual report) for Caterpillar Inc. or a different company specified by your instructor. Answer the following questions regarding information presented in the Form 10-K.

a. Identify the categories and major information presented in Management's Discussion and Analysis.

b. Summarize the information presented in Management's Report on Internal Control over Financial Reporting.

c. What does the Report of Independent Registered Public Accounting Firm include with regard to its evaluation of the company's internal control over financial reporting?

d. Who has to sign the Section 302 Certifications? What does this Certification include with regard to the company's internal control over financial reporting?

### C14-5 Registration Process [CMA Adapted]

Bandex Inc. has been in business for 15 years. The company has compiled a record of steady but not spectacular growth. Bandex's engineers have recently perfected a product that has an application in the small computer market. Initial orders have exceeded the company's capacity and the decision has been made to expand.

Bandex has financed past growth from internally generated funds, and since the initial stock offering 15 years ago, no further shares have been sold. Bandex's finance committee has been discussing methods of financing the proposed expansion. Both short-term and long-term notes were

*Research*

ruled out because of high interest rates. Mel Greene, the chief financial officer, said, "It boils down to either bonds, preferred stock, or additional common stock." Alice Dexter, a consultant employed to help in the financing decision, stated, "Regardless of your choice, you will have to file a registration statement with the SEC."

Bob Schultz, Bandex's chief accountant for the past five years, stated, "I've coordinated the filing of all the periodic reports required by the SEC—10-Ks, 10-Qs, and 8-Ks. I see no reason I can't prepare a registration statement also."

*Required*

a. Identify the circumstances under which a firm must file a registration statement with the Securities and Exchange Commission (SEC).

b. Explain the objectives of the registration process required by the Securities Act of 1933.

c. Identify and explain the SEC publications that Bob Schultz would use to guide him in preparing the registration statement.

*Communication*

### C14-6   Change in Auditors and Form 8-K [CMA Adapted]

Jerford Company is a well-known manufacturing company with several wholly owned subsidiaries. The company's stock is traded on the New York Stock Exchange, and the company files all appropriate reports with the Securities and Exchange Commission. Jerford's financial statements are audited by a public accounting firm. Jerford Company changed independent auditors during 20X6. Consequently, the financial statements were certified by a different public accounting firm in 20X6 than in 20X5.

#### Required

a. What information is Jerford responsible for filing with the SEC with respect to this change in auditors? Explain your answer completely. (*Hint:* Item 304 of Regulation S-K provides guidance on reporting a change in auditor.)

b. Identify a company that has made a change in its auditor during the last two years. Summarize the reason(s) for the change, the major items reported in its Form 8-K regarding the change, and then compare those items with the requirements listed in Item 304 of Regulation S-K.

### C14-7   Form 8-K [CMA Adapted]

The purpose of the Securities Act of 1933 is to regulate the initial offering of a firm's securities by ensuring that investors are given full and fair disclosure of all pertinent information about the firm. The Securities Exchange Act of 1934 was passed to regulate the trading of securities on secondary markets and to eliminate abuses in the trading of securities after their initial distribution. To accomplish these objectives, the 1934 act created the Securities and Exchange Commission. Under the auspices of the SEC, public companies must not only register their securities but also periodically prepare and file Forms 8-K, 10-K, and 10-Q.

*Understanding*

#### Required

a. With regard to Form 8-K, discuss:

   (1) The purpose of the report.

   (2) The timing of the report.

   (3) The format of the report.

   (4) The role of financial statements in the filing of the report.

b. Identify five circumstances under which the SEC requires the filing of Form 8-K.

### C14-8   Audit Committees [CMA Adapted]

An early event leading to the establishment of audit committees as a regular subcommittee of boards of directors occurred in 1940 as part of the consent decree relative to the McKesson-Robbins scandal. (A consent decree is the formal statement issued in an enforcement action when a person agrees to terms of a disciplinary nature without admitting to the allegations in the complaint.) An audit committee composed of outside directors was required as part of the consent decree.

*Understanding*

Title III of the Sarbanes-Oxley Act of 2002 specifies requirements for the membership of the audit committee and its authority. The Sarbanes-Oxley Act must be followed by all publicly traded firms.

#### Required

a. Explain the role of the audit committee, as specified by the Sarbanes-Oxley Act, with regard to the annual audit conducted by the company's external auditors.

b. Discuss the relationship that should exist between the audit committee and a company's internal audit staff.

c. Explain why the members of the audit committee should be outside (independent of management) board members.

**C14-9** **SEC**

The company that employs you is a U.S. publicly traded corporation that manufactures chemicals. You are in the external financial reporting department, and your position requires that you keep current on all the new accounting requirements. While you realize that Staff Accounting Bulletins (SABs) are not formal SEC actions, periodically you like to review the new SABs to see if any are relevant to your company.

*Research*     Today you decided to perform some research and ascertain if any new SABs have been issued. In addition, your boss, the manager in charge of the department, recently mentioned something to you about the SEC's Division of Enforcement. You do not know a lot about this particular division; however, because you will be doing some SEC research today anyway, you have decided you will find out more about the SEC's Division of Enforcement.

### Required

*a.* Prepare a one-page memo summarizing a recent SAB.

*b.* Research the SEC's Division of Enforcement. Answer or perform the following:

   (1) What year was the division formed?

   (2) Discuss various actions the division may take.

   (3) Prepare a one-paragraph summary of a recent litigation proceeding.

   (4) Prepare a one-paragraph summary of a recent administrative proceeding.

**C14-10** **EDGAR Database**

Currently, you are an experienced senior working at a public accounting firm. For the upcoming busy season you received a new client, a publicly traded corporation. The manager on this client is someone you have not worked with before. You hope to impress this manager because you hear that she strongly supports those seniors who work for her if she considers them to be excellent employees. At the end of this busy season, you will be up for promotion to manager and would like her support.

*Research*     Next week you have an internal planning meeting with the manager. Today you will be working in the office, and you have decided to devote the day to performing some background reading to become acquainted with this client. When you get to the office today, you learn that the manager is at a client location and unreachable. Since you will not be able to get any background information on your client from her today, you decide you will get information alternatively using the Internet.

### Required

*a.* Using the SEC's browser, select a company from the EDGAR database with a name beginning with the first letter of your last name. The company selected will be your new client as discussed above.

*b.* Prepare a one- to two-page summary listing the types of reports made to the SEC by your client over the last year. Include a brief description of the contents of each of these reports. Select one of the reports and print the first page of that report.

**C14-11** **Discovery Case**

This case provides learning opportunities using available databases and/or the Internet to obtain contemporary information about the topics in advanced financial accounting. Note that the Internet is dynamic and any specific Web site listed may change its address. In that case, use a good *Research* search engine to locate the current address for the Web site.

### Required

Find two recent articles on the Sarbanes-Oxley Act of 2002. Then review and summarize the major information items reported in the articles. Prepare a one- to two-page report presenting your summary.

One search process could be to use a good search engine to search the Internet for the two articles. Another search process could be to access a business articles index such as that for *The Wall Street Journal*. Locate your two articles and then obtain the articles through your library. A third search process could be to use a database of business articles such as ABI/INFORM® or LEXIS-NEXIS® to find your two articles.

# Exercises

## E14-1   Organization Structure and Regulatory Authority of the SEC [CMA Adapted]

Select the correct answer for each of the following questions.

1. Two interesting and important topics concerning the SEC are the role it plays in the development of accounting principles and the impact it has had and will continue to have on the accounting profession and business in general. Which of the following statements about the SEC's authority on accounting practice is *false?*

   a. The SEC has the statutory authority to regulate and to prescribe the form and content of financial statements and other reports it receives.

   b. Regulation S-X of the SEC is the principal source of the form and content of financial statements to be included in registration statements and financial reports filed with the Commission.

   c. The SEC has little if any authority over disclosures in corporate annual reports mailed to shareholders with proxy solicitations. The type of information disclosed and the format to be used are left to the discretion of management.

   d. If the Commission disagrees with some presentation in the registrant's financial statements but the principles used by the registrant have substantial authoritative support, the SEC often accepts footnotes to the statements in lieu of correcting the statements to the SEC view, provided the SEC has not previously expressed its opinion on the matter in published material.

2. The Securities and Exchange Commission was established in 1934 to help regulate the U.S. securities market. Which of the following statements is *true* about the SEC?

   a. The SEC prohibits the sale of speculative securities.

   b. The SEC regulates securities offered for public sale.

   c. Registration with the SEC guarantees the accuracy of the registrant's prospectus.

   d. The SEC's initial influences and authority have diminished in recent years as the stock exchanges have become more organized and better able to police themselves.

   e. The SEC's powers are broad with respect to enforcement of its reporting requirements as established in the 1933 and 1934 acts but narrow with respect to new reporting requirements because these require confirmation by Congress.

3. The Securities and Exchange Commission is organized into several divisions and principal offices. The organization unit that reviews registration statements, annual reports, and proxy statements filed with the Commission is:

   a. The Office of the Chief Accountant.

   b. The Division of Corporation Finance.

   c. The Division of Enforcement.

   d. The Division of Market Regulation.

   e. The Office of the Comptroller.

4. Regulation S-X:

   a. Specifies the information that can be incorporated by reference from the annual report into the registration statement filed with the SEC.

   b. Specifies the regulation and reporting requirements of proxy solicitations.

   c. Provides the basis for generally accepted accounting principles.

   d. Specifies the general form and content requirements of financial statements filed with the SEC.

   e. Provides explanations and clarifications of changes in accounting or auditing procedures used in reports filed with the SEC.

5. Which of the following is not a purpose of the Securities Exchange Act of 1934?

   a. To establish federal regulation over securities exchanges and markets.

   b. To prevent unfair practices on securities exchanges and markets.

   c. To discourage and prevent the use of credit in financing excessive speculation in securities.

   d. To approve the securities of corporations which are to be traded publicly.

   e. To control unfair use of information by corporate insiders.

6. Regulation S-K disclosure requirements of the SEC deal with the company's business, properties, and legal proceedings; selected five-year summary financial data; management's discussion and analysis of financial condition and results of operations; and:

   a. The form and content of the required financial statements.

   b. The requirements for filing interim financial statements.

   c. Unofficial interpretations and practices regarding securities laws disclosure requirements.

   d. Supplementary financial information such as quarterly financial data and information on the effects of changing prices.

   e. The determination of the proper registration statement form to be used in any specific public offering of securities.

### E14-2 Registration of New Securities [CMA Adapted]

Select the correct answer for each of the following questions.

1. In the registration and sales of new securities issues, the SEC:

   a. Endorses the investment merit of a security by allowing its registration to "go effective."

   b. Provides a rating of the investment quality of the security.

   c. May not allow the registration to "go effective" if it judges the security's investment risk to be too great.

   d. Allows all registrations to "go effective" if the issuing company's external accountant is satisfied that disclosures and representations are not misleading.

   e. Does not make any guarantees regarding the material accuracy of the registration statement.

2. The 1933 Securities Act provides for a 20-day waiting period between the filing and the effective date of the registration. During this waiting period the registrant is prohibited from:

   a. Preparing any amendments to the registration statement.

   b. Announcing the prospective issue of the securities being registered.

   c. Accepting offers to purchase the securities being registered from potential investors.

   d. Placing an advertisement indicating by whom orders for the securities being registered will be accepted.

   e. Issuing a prospectus in preliminary form.

3. Before turning over the proceeds of a securities offering to a registrant, the underwriters frequently require a "comfort letter" from the public accountant. The purpose of the comfort letter is:

   a. To remove the public distrust of a red herring by converting the letter into a prospectus.

   b. To find out if the public accountant found any adverse financial change between the date of audit and the effective date of the securities offering.

   c. To gain comfort from the public accountant's audit of the stub-period financial statements contained in the registration statement.

   d. To meet SEC regulations requiring the public accountant to give an opinion as an expert on the financial statements of the registrant.

   e. To conform to New York Stock Exchange (NYSE) member requirements that a comfort letter from a public accountant be obtained before public sale of securities.

### E14-3 Reporting Requirements of the SEC [CMA Adapted]

Select the correct answer for each of the following questions.

1. Form 10-K is filed with the SEC to update the information a company supplied when filing a registration statement under the Securities and Exchange Act of 1934. Form 10-K is a report that is filed:

   a. Annually within 60 days of the end of a company's fiscal year.

   b. Semiannually within 30 days of the end of a company's second and fourth fiscal quarters.

   c. Quarterly within 45 days of the end of each quarter.

   d. Monthly within two weeks of the end of each month.

   e. Within 15 days of the occurrence of significant events.

2. Regulation S-X disclosure requirements of the SEC deal with:

   a. Changes in and disagreements with accountants on accounting and financial disclosure.

   b. Management's discussion and analysis of the financial condition and the results of operations.

   c. The requirements for filing interim financial statements and pro forma financial information.

   d. Summary information, risk factors, and the ratio of earnings to fixed charges.

   e. Information concerning recent sales of unregistered securities.

3. Form 10-Q is filed with the SEC to keep both investors and experts apprised of a company's operations and financial position. Form 10-Q is a report that is filed within:

   a. 90 days after the end of the fiscal year covered by the report.

   b. 35 days after the end of each of the first three quarters of each fiscal year.

   c. 90 days after the end of an employee stock purchase plan fiscal year.

   d. 15 days after the occurrence of a significant event.

   e. 60 days after the end of the fiscal year covered by the report.

4. A significant event affecting a company registered under the Securities and Exchange Act of 1934 should be reported on:

   a. Form 10-K.

   b. Form 10-Q.

   c. Form S-1.

   d. Form 8-K.

   e. Form 11-K.

5. Within four days after the occurrence of any event that is of material importance to the stockholders, a company must file a Form 8-K information report with the SEC to disclose the event. An example of the type of event required to be disclosed is:

   a. A salary increase to the officers.

   b. A contract to continue to employ the same certified public accounting firm as in the prior year.

   c. A change in projected earnings per share from $12.00 to $12.11 per share.

   d. The purchase of bank certificates of deposit.

   e. The acquisition of a large subsidiary other than in the ordinary course of business.

6. Form 8-K must generally be submitted to the SEC within four days after the occurrence of a significant event. Which one of the following is not an event that would be reported by Form 8-K?

   a. The replacement of the registrant company's external auditor.

   b. A change in accounting principle.

   c. The resignation of one of the directors of the registrant company.

   d. A significant acquisition or disposition of assets.

   e. A change in control of the registrant company.

7. Which one of the following items is *not* required to be included in a company's periodic 8-K report filed with the SEC when significant events occur?

   a. Acquisition or disposition of a significant amount of assets.

   b. Instigation or termination of material legal proceedings other than routine litigation incidental to the business.

   c. Change in certifying public accountant.

   d. Election of new vice president of finance to replace the retiring incumbent.

   e. Default in the payment of principal, interest, or sinking fund installment.

**E14-4   Corporate Governance [CMA Adapted]**

Select the correct answer for each of the following questions.

1. A major impact of the Foreign Corrupt Practices Act of 1977 is that registrants subject to the Securities Exchange Act of 1934 are required to:

   a. Keep records that reflect the transactions and dispositions of assets and maintain a system of internal accounting controls.

    *b.* Provide access to records by authorized agencies of the federal government.

    *c.* Record all correspondence with foreign nations.

    *d.* Prepare financial statements in accordance with international accounting standards.

    *e.* Produce full, fair, and accurate periodic reports on foreign commerce, foreign political party affiliations, or both.

2. The requirement of the Foreign Corrupt Practices Act of 1977 to devise and maintain an adequate system of internal accounting control is assigned in the act to the:

    *a.* Chief financial officer.

    *b.* Board of directors.

    *c.* Director of internal auditing.

    *d.* Company's external auditor.

    *e.* Company as a whole with no designation of specific persons or positions.

3. Shareholders may ask or allow others to enter their vote at a shareholders' meeting that they are unable to attend. The document furnished to shareholders to provide background information for their vote is a:

    *a.* Registration statement.

    *b.* Proxy statement.

    *c.* 10-K report.

    *d.* Prospectus.

4. Formation and meaningful utilization of an audit committee of the board of directors is required of publicly traded companies that are subject to the rules of the:

    *a.* Securities and Exchange Commission.

    *b.* Financial Accounting Standards Board.

    *c.* National Association of Securities Dealers.

    *d.* American Institute of Certified Public Accountants.

5. An external auditor's involvement with a Form 10-Q that is being prepared for filing with the SEC would most likely consist of:

    *a.* An audit of the financial statements included in Form 10-Q.

    *b.* A compilation report on the financial statements included in Form 10-Q.

    *c.* Issuing a comfort letter that covers stub-period financial data.

    *d.* Issuing an opinion on the internal controls under which the Form 10-Q data were developed.

    *e.* A review of the interim financial statements included in Form 10-Q.

**E14-5  Application of Securities Act of 1933 [AICPA Adapted]**

Various Enterprises Corporation is a medium-size conglomerate listed on the American Stock Exchange. It is constantly in the process of acquiring small corporations and invariably needs additional money. Among its diversified holdings is a citrus grove that it purchased eight years ago as an investment. The grove's current fair market value is in excess of $2 million. Various also owns 800,000 shares of Resistance Corporation, which it acquired in the open market over a period of years. These shares represent a 17 percent minority interest in Resistance and are worth approximately $2.5 million. Various does its short-term financing with a consortium of banking institutions. Several of these loans are maturing; in addition to renewing these loans, it wishes to increase its short-term debt from $3 to $4 million.

Because of these factors, Various is considering resorting to one or all of the following alternatives to raise additional working capital.

1. An offering of 500 citrus grove units at $5,000 per unit. Each unit would give the purchaser a 0.2 percent ownership interest in the citrus grove development. Various would furnish management and operation services for a fee under a management contract, and net proceeds would be paid to the unit purchasers. The offering would be confined almost exclusively to the state in which the groves are located or in the adjacent state in which Various is incorporated.

2. An increase in the short-term borrowing by $1 million from the banking institution that currently provides short-term funds. The existing debt would be consolidated, extended, and

increased to $4 million and would mature over a nine-month period. This would be evidenced by a short-term note.

3. Sale of the 17 percent minority interest in Resistance in the open market through its brokers over a period of time and in such a way as to minimize decreasing the value of the stock. The stock is to be sold in an orderly manner in the ordinary course of the broker's business.

### Required

In separate paragraphs discuss the impact of the registration requirements of the Securities Act of 1933 on each of the proposed alternatives.

**E14-6   Federal Securities Acts [AICPA Adapted]**

Select the correct answer for each of the following questions.

1. Which of the following statements concerning the prospectus required by the Securities Act of 1933 is correct?

   *a.* The prospectus is a part of the registration statement.

   *b.* The prospectus should enable the SEC to pass on the merits of the securities.

   *c.* The prospectus must be filed after an offer to sell.

   *d.* The prospectus is prohibited from being distributed to the public until the SEC approves the accuracy of the facts embodied therein.

2. Which of the following securities would be regulated by the provisions of the Securities Act of 1933?

   *a.* Securities issued by not-for-profit, charitable organizations.

   *b.* Securities guaranteed by domestic governmental organizations.

   *c.* Securities issued by savings and loan associations.

   *d.* Securities issued by insurance companies.

3. Which of the following securities is exempt from registration under the Securities Act of 1933?

   *a.* Shares of nonvoting common stock, provided their par value is less than $1.

   *b.* A class of stock given in exchange for another class by the issuer to its existing stockholders without the issuer paying a commission.

   *c.* Limited partnership interests sold for the purpose of acquiring funds to invest in bonds issued by the United States.

   *d.* Corporate debentures that were previously subject to an effective registration statement, provided they are convertible into shares of common stock.

4. Pix Corp. is making a $6,000,000 stock offering. Pix wants the offering exempt from registration under the Securities Act of 1933. Which of the following provisions of the act would Pix have to comply with for the offering to be exempt?

   *a.* Regulation A.

   *b.* Regulation D, Rule 504.

   *c.* Regulation D, Rule 505.

   *d.* Regulation D, Rule 506.

5. An offering made under the provisions of Regulation A of the Securities Act of 1933 requires that the issuer:

   *a.* File an offering circular with the SEC.

   *b.* Sell only to accredited investors.

   *c.* Provide investors with the prior four years' audited financial statements.

   *d.* Provide investors with a proxy registration statement.

6. Integral Corp. has assets in excess of $4 million, has 350 stockholders, and has issued common and preferred stock. Integral is subject to the reporting provisions of the Securities Exchange Act of 1934. For its 2000 fiscal year, Integral filed the following with the SEC: quarterly reports, an annual report, and a periodic report listing newly appointed officers of the corporation. Integral did not notify the SEC of stockholder "short swing" profits; did not report that a competitor made a tender offer to Integral's stockholders; and did not report changes in the

price of its stock as sold on the New York Stock Exchange. Under SEC reporting requirements, which of the following was Integral required to do?

a. Report the tender offer to the SEC.

b. Notify the SEC of stockholder "short swing" profits.

c. File the periodic report listing newly appointed officers.

d. Report the changes in the market price of its stock.

7. Which of the following factors, by itself, requires a corporation to comply with the reporting requirements of the Securities Exchange Act of 1934?

a. 600 employees.

b. Shares listed on a national securities exchange.

c. Total assets of $2 million.

d. 400 holders of equity securities.

8. Which of the following persons is *not* an insider of a corporation subject to the Securities Exchange Act of 1934 registration and reporting requirements?

a. An attorney for the corporation.

b. An owner of 5 percent of the corporation's outstanding debentures.

c. A member of the board of directors.

d. A stockholder who owns 10 percent of the outstanding common stock.

# Partnerships: Formation, Operation, and Changes in Membership

The number of partnerships in the United States has been estimated to be between 1.5 and 2.0 million, second only to sole proprietorships, which number in excess of 15 million businesses. In contrast, there are about 1 million corporations in the United States. Accountants are often called on to aid in the formation and operation of partnerships to ensure proper measurement and valuation of the partnership's transactions. This chapter focuses on the formation and operation of partnerships, including accounting for the addition of new partners and the retirement of a present partner. Chapter 16 presents the accounting for the termination and liquidation of partnerships.

Partnerships are a popular form of business because they are easy to form and they allow several individuals to combine their talents and skills in a particular business venture. In addition, partnerships provide a means of obtaining more equity capital than a single individual can obtain and allow the sharing of risks for rapidly growing businesses.

Accounting for partnerships requires recognition of several important factors. First, from an accounting viewpoint, the partnership is a separate business entity. The Internal Revenue Code, however, views the partnership form as a conduit only, not separable from the business interests of the individual partners. Therefore, several differences exist between tax and financial accounting for specific events, such as the value assigned to assets contributed in the formation of the partnership. This chapter presents the generally accepted accounting principles of partnership accounting. A brief discussion of the tax aspects of a partnership is presented in Appendix 15A to this chapter.

Second, although many partnerships account for their operations using accrual accounting, some partnerships use the cash basis or modified cash basis of accounting. These alternatives are allowed because the partnership records are maintained for the partners and must reflect their information needs. The partnership's financial statements are usually prepared only for the partners but occasionally for the partnership's creditors. Unlike publicly traded corporations, most partnerships are not required to have annual audits of their financial statements. Although many partnerships adhere to generally accepted accounting principles (GAAP), deviations from GAAP are found in practice. The specific needs of the partners should be the primary criteria for determining the accounting policies to be used for a specific partnership.

## NATURE OF PARTNERSHIP ENTITY

The partnership form of business has several unique elements because of its legal and accounting status. The following section describes the major characteristics that distinguish the partnership form of organization.

## Legal Regulation of Partnerships

Each state regulates the partnerships that are formed in it. Accountants advising partnerships must be familiar with partnership laws because these laws describe many of the rights of each partner and of creditors during the creation, operation, and liquidation of the partnership. Each state tends to begin with a uniform or model act and then modifies it to fit that state's business culture and history. The Uniform Partnership Act of 1914 served for many years as the model for defining the rights and responsibilities of the partners to each other and to the creditors of the partnership. In 1994 the National Conference of Commissioners on Uniform State Laws (NCCUSL) approved the first major revision of the model act to better reflect current business practices while also retaining many of the valuable provisions of the original act. This 1994 revision was titled the Revised Uniform Partnership Act (RUPA). During the next three years the NCCUSL continued to make small revisions of the model act and in 1997 it approved the final model as the ***Uniform Partnership Act of 1997 (UPA 1997).*** Most states have now adopted the UPA 1997 model partnership act because, although the UPA 1997 contains many of the features of the Uniform Partnership Act of 1914, the UPA 1997 reflects today's more complex partnership events and transactions, and stresses the fiduciary responsibilities of the partners to each other. The UPA 1997 will be used for discussion and illustration in this and the next chapter on partnerships.

## Definition of a Partnership

Section 202 of the UPA 1997 states that, ". . . the association of two or more persons to carry on as co-owners of a business for profit forms a partnership . . ." This definition encompasses three distinct factors:

1. *Association of two or more persons.* The "persons" are usually individuals; however, they may also be corporations or other partnerships.
2. *To carry on as co-owners.* This means that each partner has the apparent authority, unless restricted by the partnership agreement, to act as an agent of the partnership for transactions in the ordinary course of business of the kind carried on by the partnership. These transactions can legally bind the partnership to third parties.
3. *Business for profit.* A partnership may be formed to perform any legal business, trade, profession, or other service. However, the partnership must attempt to make a profit; therefore, not-for-profit entities, such as fraternal groups, may not organize as partnerships.

## Formation of a Partnership

A primary advantage of the partnership form of entity is ease of formation. The agreement to form a partnership may be as informal as a handshake or as formal as a many-paged partnership agreement. Each partner must agree to the formation agreement, and partners are strongly advised to have a formal written agreement to avoid potential problems that may arise during the operation of the business. It is usually true that if the potential partners cannot agree on the various operating aspects before a partnership is formed, many future disputes may arise that could cause severe management problems and that might seriously imperil the operations of the partnership.

The partnership agreement should include the following items:

1. The name of the partnership and the names of the partners.
2. The type of business to be conducted by the partnership and the duration of the partnership agreement.
3. The initial capital contribution of each partner and the method by which to account for future capital contributions.
4. A complete specification of the profit or loss distribution, including salaries, interest on capital balances, bonuses, limits on withdrawals in anticipation of profits, and the percentages used to distribute any residual profit or loss.

5. Procedures used for changes in the partnership, such as admission of new partners and the retirement of a partner.

6. Other aspects of operations the partners decide on, such as the management rights of each partner, election procedures, and accounting methods.

Each partner should sign the partnership agreement to indicate acceptance of the terms. A carefully prepared partnership agreement can eliminate many of the more common types of problems and disputes that may arise in the partnership's future operations.

## Other Major Characteristics of Partnerships

After a state adopts the provisions of the UPA 1997, all partnerships formed in that state are regulated by the act. For partnerships that do not have a formal partnership agreement, the act provides the legal framework that governs the relationships among the partners and the rights of creditors of the partnership; in essence, the UPA 1997 becomes the partnership agreement for those partnerships that do not have one. The following presents the sections of the UPA 1997 applicable to the formation and operation of a partnership. Chapter 16 will present the sections of the UPA 1997 applicable to the dissolution and liquidation of a partnership.

1. *Partnership agreement.* The UPA 1997 governs in those partnership relations that are not specifically presented in the partnership agreement; thus, the UPA 1997 is used by the courts when there is no partnership agreement. There are several provisions of the UPA 1997 that are not waivable by partnership agreement. For example, a partnership may not restrict a partner's rights of access to the partnership's books and records, eliminate the obligations of partners for good faith and fair dealing with the other partners and the partnership, restrict any rights of third parties under the act, or reduce any legal rights of individual partners.

2. *Partnership as a separate entity.* A partnership is a separate business entity distinct from its partners. This **entity concept** means that a partnership can sue or be sued and that partnership property belongs to the partnership and not to any individual partner. Thus, there is no new partnership entity when there is a membership change in the partners (a new partner is admitted or a partner leaves the partnership).

3. *Partner is an agent of the partnership.* Each partner is an agent of the partnership for transactions of the kind carried on in the ordinary course of the partnership business, unless the partner did not have the authority to act for the partnership in that specific matter and the third party knew or had received a notification that the partner lacked authority. This agency relationship among the partners is very important. If the partnership determines that only specific partners shall have the authority for specific business transactions, then the partnership must make third parties aware of the limitations of authority of other partners. This notice should be in a public form either as a formal filing of a statement of partnership authority (discussed in the next point) or in direct communications with third parties. Otherwise, third parties may presume a partner has the authority to act as an agent for the partnership in those normal business transactions of the type engaged in for the business in which the partnership operates.

4. *Statement of partnership authority.* A **Statement of Partnership Authority** describes the partnership and identifies the specific authority of partners to transact specific types of business on behalf of the partnership. This voluntary statement is filed with the secretary of the state. The statement is a notice of any limitations on the rights of specific partners to enter into specific types of transactions. Partnerships should file these statements particularly for partnership transactions in real estate. The act states that a filed statement of partnership authority is sufficient constructive notice to third parties for partnership real estate transactions, but it is not necessarily sufficient notice for other types of partnership transactions.

5. *Partner's liability is joint and several.* All partners are liable jointly and severally for all obligations of the partnership unless otherwise provided by law. In the event

a partnership fails and its assets are not sufficient to pay its obligations, partners are required to make contributions to the partnership in the proportion to which they share partnership losses. If a partner fails to make a contribution of the amount required, then all other partners must contribute in the proportion to which those partners share partnership losses. Partnership creditors must first be satisfied from partnership assets and additional partner contributions are classified as partnership assets. However, a partner is liable for partnership liabilities incurred prior to that partner's admission into the partnership only to the extent of the partner's capital credit. A new partner is not personally liable for partnership debts incurred prior to that partner's admission into the partnership. If a partnership creditor takes legal action against an individual partner for a partnership obligation, the partnership creditor does not have any superior rights to the partner's individual assets. In this case, the partnership creditor joins with the other personal creditors.

6. *Partner's rights and duties.* Each partner is to have a capital account presenting the amount of that partner's contributions to the partnership, net of any liabilities, and the partner's share of the partnership profits or losses, less any distributions. The partner is entitled to an equal share of the profits or losses unless otherwise agreed to in the partnership agreement. New partners can be admitted only with the consent of all of the partners. Each partner has a right of access to the partnership's books and records, and each partner has a duty to act for the partnership in good faith and fair dealing.

7. *Partner's transferable interest in the partnership.* Under the entity approach to a partnership stated in the act, a partner is not a co-owner of any partnership property. This means that the only **transferable interest** of a partner is the partner's share of the profits and losses of the partnership and the right to receive distributions, including any liquidating distribution. A partner may not transfer any rights of management or authority to transact any of the partnership's business operations. Thus the partner's individual creditors may not attach any of the partnership's assets but a partner's personal creditor may obtain a legal judgment for attachment of the partner's transferable interest.

8. *Partner's dissociation.* A **partner's dissociation** means that the partner can no longer act on behalf of the partnership. A partner is dissociated from a partnership when any of the following events occurs: (*a*) the partner gives notice to the partnership of the partner's express will to withdraw as a partner; (*b*) the partner is expelled from the partnership in accordance with the partnership agreement, typically because the partner has violated some part of the partnership agreement or it becomes unlawful for the partnership to continue business with that partner; (*c*) one of several judicial determinations occurs (such as the partner committing a material breach of the partnership agreement, or the partner engaging in serious conduct that materially and adversely affects the partnership); (*d*) the partner becomes a debtor in bankruptcy; or (*e*) the partner dies.

### Types of Limited Partnerships

Many persons view the possibility of personal liability for a partnership's obligations as a major disadvantage of the general partnership form of business. For this reason, sometimes people become limited partners in one of the several limited partnership forms. A limited partnership (LP) is different from a limited liability partnership (LLP), or a limited liability limited partnership (LLLP). The variations are based on the degree of liability shield provided to the partners.

**Limited Partnerships (LP)** In a limited partnership (LP), there is at least one general partner and one or more limited partners. The general partner is personally liable for the obligations of the partnership and has management responsibility. Limited partners are liable only to the extent of their capital contribution but do not have any management authority. The Uniform Limited Partnership Act of 2001 (ULPA 2001) is the model legal act used to regulate limited partnerships and has been adopted in many states. Accounting for the investment in a limited partnership is based on an evaluation of control.

Typically, the general partner has the necessary elements of operational control of the limited partnership and will consolidate the investment on the general partner's books. The limited partners typically use the equity method to account for their investments. However, in 2005, the Emerging Issues Task Force (EITF) reached consensus in **EITF Issue No. 04-05,** "Determining Whether a General Partner, or the General Partners as a Group, Controls a Limited Partnership or Similar Entity When the Limited Partners Have Certain Rights" (EITF 04-05). The EITF examined cases in which the limited partners have either (*a*) the ability to dissolve the limited partnership or to remove the general partners without cause (the so-called "kick-out right"), or (*b*) have substantive participating rights to be actively engaged in the significant decisions of the limited partnership's business. In these two cases, the presumption of control by the general partners could be overcome and then each of the general partners would account for its investment in the limited partnership using the equity method of accounting. The identifier, LP or Limited Partnership, must be included in the name or identification of the limited partnership.

***Limited Liability Partnerships (LLP)***   A limited liability partnership (LLP) is one in which each partner has some degree of liability shield. There are no general or limited partners in an LLP; thus each partner has the rights and duties of a general partner, but limited legal liability. A partner in a limited liability partnership is not personally liable for a partnership obligation. However, several states have defined that each partner in an LLP is fully liable for the obligations of the partnership, though not for acts of professional negligence or malpractice committed by other partners. Some legal support for the LLP came as a result of the fact that most professional service partnerships, such as accounting firms, have significant amounts of insurance to cover judgments in lawsuits and other losses from offering services. A limited liability partnership must identify itself as such by adding the LLP letters behind the name of the partnership in all correspondence or other means of identification of the firm. Virtually all large public accounting firms are LLPs. This designation has not changed the nature of accounting services provided to clients and has been generally accepted in the business market.

***Limited Liability Limited Partnership (LLLP)***   In most states, a limited partnership may elect to become a limited liability limited partnership. In an LLLP, each partner is liable only for the business obligations of the partnership, and not for acts of malpractice or other wrongdealing by the other partners in the normal course of the partnership's business. The ULPA 2001 includes the regulatory guidance for LLLPs. The advantage of an LLLP is that general partners, even though responsible for management of the partnership, have no personal liability for partnership obligations, similar to the shield provided to limited partners. The identifier "LLLP" or the phrase "limited liability limited partnership" must be included in the name or identification of the entity.

## Accounting and Financial Reporting Requirements for Partnerships

Most partnerships are small or medium-sized entities, although there are some large partnership entities. Partnerships do not issue stock and thus the information needs of a partnership are typically different from those of corporations that have stockholders. A partnership has much more flexibility to select specific accounting measurement and recognition methods and specific financial reporting formats.

If a partnership wishes to issue general-purpose financial statements for external users such as credit grantors, vendors, or others, then the partnership should use generally accepted accounting principles as promulgated by the FASB and other standard-setting bodies, and the independent auditor can issue an opinion that the statements are in accordance with generally accepted accounting principles. The FASB created the Private Company Financial Reporting Committee in June 2006 to provide input to the FASB on proposed, and existing, accounting standards as to their impact on nonpublic business entities. Thus, the FASB has a vehicle by which GAAP standards can be adapted to meet the cost/benefit perspective of nonpublic entities.

If a partnership has only internal reporting needs, then the accounting and financial reporting should meet those internal information needs of the partners. In this case, the partnership may use non-GAAP accounting methods and have financial reports in a format different from those required under GAAP. For example, some partnerships use the accounting methods prescribed by tax laws, thereby generating tax-based financial reports. Some partnerships use the cash-based accounting system, often with some adjustments, so the financial reports provide specific cash flow and cash positions. And other partnerships may use accounting methods that are proximate to GAAP, with some adjustments that fit the information needs of the partners, such as recognizing increases in the fair value of nonfinancial assets at the time of admission of a new partner. In these cases, if the financial statements are presented to users external to the partnership, such as banks, vendors or regulatory bodies, it should be clearly identified on the statements what specific accounting methods were used by the entity so that the users are informed that the information presented in the financial statements does not conform to GAAP. An independent accountant's opinion on these financial statements would also have to disclose the specific accounting methods used or the deviations from GAAP that affected the amounts reported in the financial statements. It is up to the partners to determine their financial information needs and then the partnership accountant applies the necessary accounting measurement, recognition, and reporting methods that meet the partners' financial information needs.

### International Financial Reporting Standards for Small and Medium-Sized Entities

In 2007, the International Accounting Standards Board issued an Exposure Draft, "International Financial Reporting Standard for Small and Medium-sized Entities," more commonly known as IFRS for SMEs. SMEs are defined as those entities that (*a*) do not have public accountability (i.e., do not have stock or issue bonds in a public capital market) and (*b*) publish general-purpose financial statements for external users. The exposure draft presents the definitions of items and accounting concepts that are quite similar to those already in the international financial accounting and reporting standards, except that less detail and fewer disclosures are mandated and more flexibility is provided for the formats of the financial statements. Thus, the IASB is addressing the specific accounting and financial reporting requirements for SMEs that are required to provide general-purpose financial statements to external users. But these standards would not apply to partnerships that do *not* have public accountability *and* do *not* issue general-purpose financial statements to external users.

## ACCOUNTING FOR THE FORMATION OF A PARTNERSHIP

At the formation of a partnership, it is necessary to assign a proper value to the noncash assets and liabilities contributed by the partners. Section 201 of the UPA 1997 specifies that a partnership is an entity distinct from its partners. Thus, an item contributed by a partner becomes partnership property. The partnership must clearly distinguish between capital contributions and loans made to the partnership by individual partners. Loan arrangements should be evidenced by promissory notes or other legal documents necessary to show that a loan arrangement exists between the partnership and an individual partner. Also, it is important to clearly distinguish between tangible assets that are owned by the partnership and those specific assets that are owned by individual partners but are used by the partnership. Accurate records of the partnership's tangible assets must be maintained.

**FASB Statement No. 157,** "Fair Value Measurements" (FASB 157), continues the long-held accounting concept that the contributed assets should be valued at their fair values, which may require appraisals or other valuation techniques. Liabilities assumed by the partnership should be valued at the present value of the remaining cash flows.

The individual partners must agree to the percentage of equity that each will have in the net assets of the partnership. Generally, the capital balance is determined by the proportionate share of each partner's capital contribution. For example, if A contributes 70 percent of the net assets in a partnership with B, then A will have a 70 percent capital share and B will have a 30 percent capital share. In recognition of intangible factors, such as a partner's special expertise or necessary business connections, however, partners may agree to any proportional division of capital. Therefore, before recording the initial capital contribution, all partners must agree on the valuation of the net assets and on each partner's capital share.

## Illustration of Accounting for Partnership Formation

The following illustration is used as the basis for the remaining discussion in this chapter. Alt, a sole proprietor, has been developing software for several types of computers. The business has the following account balances as of December 31, 20X0:

| | | | |
|---|---|---|---|
| Cash | $ 3,000 | Liabilities | $10,000 |
| Inventory | 7,000 | Alt, Capital | 15,000 |
| Equipment | 20,000 | | |
| Less Accumulated | | | |
| Depreciation | (5,000) | | |
| Total Assets | $25,000 | Total Liabilities and Capital | $25,000 |

Alt needs additional technical assistance to meet the increasing sales and offers Blue an interest in the business. Alt and Blue agree to form a partnership. Alt's business is audited, and its net assets are appraised. The audit and appraisal disclose that $1,000 of liabilities has not been recorded, inventory has a market value of $9,000, and the equipment has a fair value of $19,000.

Alt and Blue prepare and sign a partnership agreement that includes all significant operating policies. Blue will contribute $10,000 cash for a one-third capital interest. The AB Partnership is to acquire all of Alt's business and assume its debts.

The entry to record the initial capital contribution on the partnership's books is:

January 1, 20X1
| | | | |
|---|---|---|---|
| (1) | Cash | 13,000 | |
| | Inventory | 9,000 | |
| | Equipment | 19,000 | |
| |     Liabilities | | 11,000 |
| |     Alt, Capital | | 20,000 |
| |     Blue, Capital | | 10,000 |

Formation of AB Partnership by capital contributions of Alt and Blue.

### *Key Observations from Illustration*

Note that the partnership is an accounting entity separate from each of the partners and that the assets and liabilities are recorded at their market values at the time of contribution. No accumulated depreciation is carried forward from the sole proprietorship to the partnership. All liabilities are recognized and recorded.

The partnership's capital is $30,000. This is the sum of the individual partners' capital accounts and is the value of the partnership's assets less liabilities. The fundamental accounting equation—assets less liabilities equals capital—is used often in partnership accounting. Blue is to receive a one-third capital interest in the partnership with a contribution of $10,000. In this case, his capital interest equals his capital contribution.

Each partner's capital amount recorded does not necessarily have to equal his or her capital contribution. The partners could decide to divide the total capital equally regardless of the source of the contribution. For example, although Alt contributed $20,000 of the $30,000 partnership capital, he could agree to $15,000 as his initial capital balance and permit Blue the remaining $15,000 as a capital credit. On the surface this may not seem to be a reasonable action by Alt, but it is possible that Blue has some particularly important business experience needed by the partnership and Alt agrees to the additional credit to Blue in recognition of his experience and skills. The key point is that the partners may allocate the capital contributions in any manner they desire. The accountant must be sure that all partners agree to the allocation and then record it accordingly.

# ACCOUNTING FOR OPERATIONS OF A PARTNERSHIP

A partnership provides services or sells products in pursuit of profit. These transactions are recorded in the appropriate journals and ledger accounts. Many partnerships use accrual accounting and generally accepted accounting principles to maintain their books because GAAP results in better measures of income over time. Some creditors, such as banks, and some vendors, such as large suppliers to the partnership, may periodically require audited financial statements, and if GAAP are used, the financial statements can then receive a "clean" or unqualified audit opinion. Furthermore, the partners can compare their business' GAAP-based financial statements against published financial profiles, such as Moody's or many published by the U.S. government, against other companies in the same line of business so that the partners can evaluate their respective financial performance and position.

But some partnerships use alternative non-GAAP methods such as the cash-basis method, or the modified cash-basis method. These two methods have simplified record-keeping requirements and can continuously provide the partners with the current cash position of their partnership. A small number of partnerships revalue all their assets at the end of each fiscal period in order to estimate the market value of their business as a whole at year-end. Some partnerships use federal income tax rules to account for transactions so the partners can determine the effects of transactions that will be reportable on their personal income tax returns. The accountant works with the partners to determine their specific information needs regarding the partnership and then applies the appropriate accounting and financial reporting methods to meet those needs.

## Partners' Accounts

The partnership may maintain several accounts for each partner in its accounting records. These *partners' accounts* are as follows:

### Capital Accounts

The initial investment of a partner, any subsequent capital contributions, profit or loss distributions, and any withdrawals of capital by the partner are ultimately recorded in the partner's capital account. Each partner has one capital account, which usually has a credit balance. On occasion, a partner's capital account may have a debit balance, called a *deficiency* or sometimes termed a *deficit,* which occurs because the partner's share of losses and withdrawals exceeds his or her capital contribution and share of profits. A deficiency is usually eliminated by additional capital contributions. The balance in the capital account represents the partner's share of the partnership's net assets.

### Drawing Accounts

Partners generally make withdrawals of assets from the partnership during the year in anticipation of profits. A separate drawing account often is used to record the periodic withdrawals and is then closed to the partner's capital account at the end of the period. For example, the following entry is made in the AB Partnership's books for a $3,000 cash withdrawal by Blue on May 1, 20X1:

May 1, 20X1

| (2) | Blue, Drawing | 3,000 | |
| |     Cash | | 3,000 |
| |      Withdrawal of $3,000 by Blue. | | |

Noncash drawings should be valued at their market values at the date of the withdrawal. A few partnerships make an exception to the rule of market value for partners' withdrawals of inventory. They record withdrawals of inventory at cost, thereby not recording a gain or loss on these drawings.

### Loan Accounts

The partnership may look to its present partners for additional financing. Any loans between a partner and the partnership should always be accompanied by proper loan documentation such as a promissory note. A loan from a partner is shown as a payable on the partnership's books, the same as any other loan. Unless all partners agree otherwise, the partnership is obligated to pay interest on the loan to the individual partner. Note that interest is *not* required to be paid on capital investments unless the partnership agreement states that capital interest is to be paid. The partnership records interest on loans as an operating expense. Alternatively, the partnership may lend money to a partner, in which case it records a loan receivable from the partner. Again, unless all partners agree otherwise, these loans should bear interest, and the interest income should be recognized on the partnership's income statement. The following entry is made to record a $4,000, 10 percent, one-year loan from Alt to the partnership on July 1, 20X1:

July 1, 20X1

| (3) | Cash | 4,000 | |
| |     Loan Payable to Alt | | 4,000 |
| |      Sign loan agreement with partner Alt. | | |

The loan payable to Alt is reported in the partnership's balance sheet. A loan from a partner is a related-party transaction for which separate footnote disclosure is required, and it must be reported as a separate balance sheet item, not included with other liabilities.

## ALLOCATING PROFIT OR LOSS TO PARTNERS

Profit or loss is allocated to the partners at the end of each period in accordance with the partnership agreement. If no partnership agreement exists, section 401 of the UPA 1997 declares that all partners are to share profits and losses equally. Virtually all partnerships have a profit or loss allocation agreement. The agreement must be followed precisely, and if it is unclear, the accountant should make sure that all partners agree to the profit or loss distribution. Many problems and later arguments can be avoided by carefully specifying the profit or loss distribution in the articles of copartnership.

A wide range of *profit distribution plans* is found in the business world. Some partnerships have straightforward distribution plans; others have extremely complex ones. It is the accountant's responsibility to distribute the profit or loss according to the partnership agreement regardless of how simple or complex that agreement is. Profit distributions are similar to dividends for a corporation: These distributions should not be included on the partnership's income statement regardless of how the profit is distributed. Profit distributions are recorded directly into the partner's capital accounts, not treated as expense items.

Most partnerships use one or more of the following distribution methods:

1. Preselected ratio.
2. Interest on capital balances.
3. Salaries to partners.
4. Bonuses to partners.

Preselected ratios are usually the result of negotiations between the partners. Ratios for profit distributions may be based on the percentage of total partnership capital, time, and effort invested in the partnership, or a variety of other factors. Smaller partnerships often split profits evenly among the partners. In addition, some partnerships have different ratios if the firm suffers a loss rather than earns a profit. The partnership form of business allows a wide selection of profit distribution ratios to meet the partners' individual desires.

Distributing partnership income based on interest on capital balances recognizes the contribution of the partners' capital investments to the partnership's profit-generating capacity. This interest on capital is generally not an expense of the partnership; it is a distribution of profits. If one or more of the partners' services are important to the partnership, the profit distribution agreement may provide for salaries or bonuses. Again, these salaries paid to partners are generally a form of profit distribution, not an expense of the partnership. Occasionally, the distribution process may depend on the size of the profit or may differ if the partnership has a loss for the period. For example, salaries to partners might be paid only if revenue exceeds expenses by a certain amount. The accountant must carefully read the partnership agreement to determine the precise profit distribution plan for the specific circumstances at the time.

The profit or loss distribution is recorded with a closing entry at the end of each period. The revenue and expenses are closed into an income summary account or directly into the partners' capital accounts. In the following examples, an income summary account is used, the balance of which is net income or net loss after the revenue and expense accounts are closed and before the income or loss is distributed to the partners' capital accounts.

## Illustrations of Profit Allocation

During 20X1, the AB Partnership earns $45,000 of revenue and incurs $35,000 in expenses, leaving a profit of $10,000 for the year. Alt maintains a capital balance of $20,000 during the year, but Blue's capital investment varies during the year as follows:

| Date | Debit | Credit | Balance |
|------|-------|--------|---------|
| January 1 | | | $10,000 |
| May 1 | $3,000 | | 7,000 |
| September 1 | | $500 | 7,500 |
| November 1 | 1,000 | | 6,500 |
| December 31 | | | 6,500 |

The debits of $3,000 and $1,000 are recorded in Blue's drawing account; the additional investment is credited to his capital account.

### *Arbitrary Profit Sharing Ratio*

Alt and Blue could agree to share profits in a ratio unrelated to their capital balances or to any other operating feature of the partnership. For example, the partners might agree to share profits or losses in the ratio of 60 percent to Alt and 40 percent to Blue. Some partnership agreements specify this ratio as 3:2. The following schedule illustrates how the net income is distributed using a 3:2 profit sharing ratio:

| | Alt | Blue | Total |
|------|------|------|-------|
| Profit sharing percentage | 60% | 40% | 100% |
| Net income | | | $10,000 |
| Allocate 60:40 | $6,000 | $4,000 | (10,000) |
| Total | $6,000 | $4,000 | $   -0- |

This schedule shows how net income is distributed to the partners' capital accounts. The actual distribution is accomplished by closing the Income Summary account. In addition, the drawing accounts are closed to the capital accounts at the end of the period.

December 31, 20X1

| (4) | Blue, Capital | 4,000 | |
| |     Blue, Drawing | | 4,000 |
| |       Close Blue's drawing account. | | |

| (5) | Revenue | 45,000 | |
| |     Expenses | | 35,000 |
| |     Income Summary | | 10,000 |
| |       Close revenue and expenses. | | |

| (6) | Income Summary | 10,000 | |
| |     Alt, Capital | | 6,000 |
| |     Blue, Capital | | 4,000 |
| |       Distribute profit in accordance with partnership agreement. | | |

### Interest on Capital Balances

The partnership agreement may provide for interest to be credited on the partners' capital balances as part of the distribution of profits. The rate of interest is often a stated percentage, but some partnerships use an interest rate that is determined by reference to current U.S. Treasury rates or current money market rates.

As stated earlier, interest calculated on partners' capital is generally a form of profit distribution. The calculation is made after net income is determined in order to decide how to distribute the income.

Particular caution must be exercised whenever interest on capital balances is included in the profit distribution plan. For example, the amount of the distribution can be significantly different depending on whether the interest is computed on beginning capital balances, ending capital balances, or average capital balances for the period. Most provisions for interest on capital specify that a weighted-average capital should be used. This method explicitly recognizes the time span for which each capital level is maintained during the period. For example, Blue's weighted-average capital balance for 20X1 is computed as follows:

| Date | Debit | Credit | Balance | Months Maintained | Months Times Dollar Balance |
|------|-------|--------|---------|-------------------|------------------------------|
| January 1 | | | $10,000 | 4 | $40,000 |
| May 1 | $3,000 | | 7,000 | 4 | 28,000 |
| September 1 | | $500 | 7,500 | 2 | 15,000 |
| November 1 | 1,000 | | 6,500 | 2 | 13,000 |
| Total | | | | 12 | $96,000 |
| Average capital ($96,000 ÷ 12 months) | | | | | $ 8,000 |

If Alt and Blue agreed to allow interest of 15 percent on the weighted-average capital balances with any remaining profit to be distributed in the 60:40 ratio, the distribution of the $10,000 profit would be calculated as follows:

| | Alt | Blue | Total |
|---|-----|------|-------|
| Profit percentage | 60% | 40% | 100% |
| Average capital | $20,000 | $8,000 | |
| Net income | | | $10,000 |
| Interest on average capital (15%) | $ 3,000 | $1,200 | (4,200) |
| Residual income | | | $ 5,800 |
| Allocate 60:40 | 3,480 | 2,320 | (5,800) |
| Total | $ 6,480 | $3,520 | $   -0- |

### Salaries

Salaries to partners are generally included as part of the profit distribution plan to recognize and compensate for differing amounts of personal services partners provide to the business.

Section 401 of the UPA 1997 states that a partner is not entitled to compensation for services performed for the partnership except for reasonable compensation for services in winding up the business of the partnership. Some partnership agreements, however, do specify a management fee to be paid to a partner who provides very specific administration responsibilities.

A general precept of partnership accounting is that salaries to partners are not operating expenses but are part of the profit distribution plan. This precept is closely related to the proprietary concept of owner's equity. According to the proprietary theory, the proprietor invests capital and personal services in pursuit of income. The earnings are a result of those two investments. The same logic applies to the partnership form of organization. Some partners invest capital while others invest personal time. Those who invest capital are typically rewarded with interest on their capital balances; those who invest personal time are rewarded with salaries. However, both interest and salaries are a result of the respective investments and are used not in the determination of income but in the determination of the proportion of income to credit to each partner's capital account. An interesting question arises if the partnership experiences losses. Can salaries to the partners during the year be treated as a distribution of profits? Although any amounts actually paid to partners during the year are really drawings made in anticipation of profits, the agreed salary amounts usually are added to the loss and that total is then distributed to the partners' capital accounts. Caution should be exercised if the partnership experiences a loss during the year. Some partnership agreements specify different distributions for profit than for losses. The accountant must be especially careful to follow precisely the partnership agreement when distributing the period's profit or loss to the partners.

To examine partnership salaries, assume that the partnership agreement provides for salaries of $2,000 to Alt and $5,000 to Blue. Any remainder is to be distributed in the profit and loss–sharing ratio of 60:40 percent. The profit distribution is calculated as follows:

|  | Alt | Blue | Total |
|---|---|---|---|
| Profit percentage | 60% | 40% | 100% |
| Net income |  |  | $10,000 |
| Salary | $2,000 | $5,000 | (7,000) |
| Residual income |  |  | $ 3,000 |
| Allocate 60:40 | 1,800 | 1,200 | (3,000) |
| Total | $3,800 | $6,200 | $     -0- |

### Bonuses

Bonuses are sometimes used as a means of providing additional compensation to partners who have provided services to the partnership. Bonuses are typically stated as a percentage of income either before or after the bonus. Sometimes the partnership agreement requires a minimum income to be earned before a bonus is calculated. The bonus is easily calculated by deriving and solving an equation. For example, a bonus of 10 percent of income in excess of $5,000 is to be credited to Blue's capital account before distributing the remaining profit. In Case 1, the bonus is computed as a percentage of income *before* subtracting the bonus. In Case 2, the bonus is computed as a percentage of income *after* subtracting the bonus.

*Case 1:*

$$\text{Bonus} = X\%(\text{NI} - \text{MIN})$$

where: $X\%$ = The bonus percentage

NI = Net income before bonus

MIN = Minimum amount of income before bonus

$$\text{Bonus} = .10(\$10,000 - \$5,000) = \$500$$

*Case 2:*

$$\text{Bonus} = X\%(\text{NI} - \text{MIN} - \text{Bonus})$$
$$= .10(\$10,000 - \$5,000 - \text{Bonus})$$
$$= .10(\$5,000 - \text{Bonus})$$
$$= \$500 - .10 \text{ Bonus}$$
$$1.10 \text{ Bonus} = \$500$$
$$\text{Bonus} = \$454.55$$

The distribution of net income based on Case 2 is calculated as follows:

|  | Alt | Blue | Total |
|---|---|---|---|
| Profit percentage | 60% | 40% | 100% |
| Net income |  |  | $10,000 |
| Bonus to partner |  | $ 455 | (455) |
| Residual income |  |  | $ 9,545 |
| Allocate 60:40 | $5,727 | 3,818 | (9,545) |
| Total | $5,727 | $4,273 | $ -0- |

## Multiple Bases of Profit Allocation

A partnership agreement may describe a combination of several allocation procedures to be used to distribute profit. For example, the profit and loss agreement of the AB Partnership specifies the following allocation method:

1. Interest of 15 percent on weighted-average capital balances.
2. Salaries of $2,000 for Alt and $5,000 for Blue.
3. A bonus of 10 percent to be paid to Blue on partnership income exceeding $5,000 before subtracting the bonus, partners' salaries, and interest on capital balances.
4. Any residual to be allocated in the ratio of 60 percent to Alt and 40 percent to Blue.

The partnership agreement should also contain a provision to specify the allocation process in the event that partnership income is not sufficient to satisfy all allocation procedures. Some partnerships specify a profit distribution to be followed to whatever extent is possible. Most agreements specify that the entire process is to be completed and any remainder is to be allocated in the profit and loss ratio as illustrated in the following schedule:

|  | **Alt** | **Blue** | **Total** |
|---|---|---|---|
| Profit percentage | 60% | 40% | 100% |
| Average capital | $20,000 | $8,000 | |
| Net income: | | | $10,000 |
| Step 1: | | | |
| Interest on average capital (15 percent) | $ 3,000 | $1,200 | (4,200) |
| Remaining after step 1 | | | $ 5,800 |
| Step 2: | | | |
| Salary | 2,000 | 5,000 | (7,000) |
| Deficiency after step 2 | | | $ (1,200) |
| Step 3: | | | |
| Bonus | | 500 | (500) |
| Deficiency after step 3 | | | $ (1,700) |
| Step 4: | | | |
| Allocate 60:40 | (1,020) | (680) | 1,700 |
| Total | $ 3,980 | $6,020 | $    -0- |

In this case, the first two distribution steps created a deficiency. The AB Partnership agreement provided that the entire profit distribution process must be completed and any deficiency distributed in the profit and loss ratio. A partnership agreement could specify that the profit distribution process stop at any point in the event of an operating loss or the creation of a deficiency. Again, it is important for the accountant to have a thorough knowledge of the partnership agreement before beginning the profit distribution process.

### Special Profit Allocation Methods

Some partnerships distribute net income on the basis of other criteria. For example, most public accounting partnerships distribute profit on the basis of partnership "units." A new partner acquires a certain number of units, and additional units are assigned by a firmwide compensation committee for obtaining new clients, for providing the firm with specific areas of industrial expertise, for serving as a local office's managing partner, or for accepting a variety of other responsibilities.

Other partnerships may devise profit distribution plans that reflect the earnings of the partnership. For example, some medical or dental partnerships allocate profit on the basis of billed services. Other criteria may be number or size of clients, years of service with the firm, or the partner's position within the firm. An obvious advantage of the partnership form of organization is the flexibility it allows partners for the distribution of profits.

## PARTNERSHIP FINANCIAL STATEMENTS

A partnership is a separate reporting entity for accounting purposes, and the three financial statements—income statement, balance sheet, and statement of cash flows—typically are prepared for the partnership at the end of each reporting period. Interim statements may also be prepared to meet the partners' information needs. In addition to the three basic financial statements, a *statement of partners' capital* is usually prepared to present the changes in the partners' capital accounts for the period. The statement of partners' capital for the AB Partnership for 20X1 under the multiple-base profit distribution plan illustrated in the prior section follows:

**AB PARTNERSHIP**
**Statement of Partners' Capital**
**For the Year Ended December 31, 20X1**

|  | Alt | Blue | Total |
|---|---|---|---|
| Balance, January 1, 20X1 | $20,000 | $10,000 | $30,000 |
| Add: Additional investment |  | 500 | 500 |
| Net income distribution | 3,980 | 6,020 | 10,000 |
|  | $23,980 | $16,520 | $40,500 |
| Less: Withdrawal |  | (4,000) | (4,000) |
| Balance, December 31, 20X1 | $23,980 | $12,520 | $36,500 |

# CHANGES IN MEMBERSHIP

Changes in the membership of a partnership occur with the addition of new partners or the dissociation of present partners. New partners are often a primary source of additional capital or needed business expertise. The legal structure of a partnership requires that the ***admission of a new partner*** be subject to the unanimous approval of the present partners. Furthermore, public announcements are typically made about new partner additions so that third parties transacting business with the partnership are aware of the partnership change. Section 306 of the Uniform Partnership Act of 1997 states that a person admitted as a new partner of an existing partnership is not personally liable for any partnership obligation incurred before the new partner was admitted. Thus, a new partner can be charged only up to the amount of his or her capital contribution at the time of admission for partnership liabilities existing prior to admission.

The retirement or withdrawal of a partner from a partnership is a dissociation of that partner. A partner's dissociation does not necessarily mean a dissolution and winding up of the partnership. Many partnerships continue in business and, under section 701 of the UPA 1997, the partnership may purchase the dissociated partner's interest at a ***buyout price.*** The buyout price is the estimated amount if (1) the assets were sold for a price equal to the greater of the liquidation value or the value based on a sale of the entire business as a going concern without the dissociated partner, and (2) the partnership was wound up at that time, with payment of all the partnership's creditors and termination of the business. Partners who simply wish to leave a partnership may be liable to the partnership for damages to the partnership caused by a wrongful dissociation. A wrongful dissociation occurs when the dissociation is in breach of an express provision of the partnership agreement or, for partnerships formed for a definite term or specific undertaking, before the term or undertaking has been completed. There are also some events that require judicial dissolution and winding up of the partnership. These will be discussed in Chapter 16.

## General Concepts to Account for a Change in Membership in the Partnership

### *The Partnership as an Entity Separate from the Individual Partners and the Use of GAAP*

The Uniform Partnership Act of 1997 clearly defines a partnership as an entity separate from the individual partners. As such, the partnership entity does not change because of the addition or withdrawal of an individual partner. This is similar to the concept of the entity for the corporate form of business, in which the business is not necessarily revalued each time there is a change in stockholders.

Some partnerships choose to comply with generally accepted accounting principles (GAAP) in their accounting and financial reporting. These partnerships follow the same standards established by the FASB and other regulatory bodies as public companies. Often venture capital firms or other credit suppliers may require that the private partnership company comply with GAAP so that the partnership's financials can be compared with those of other public companies. Venture capital firms have a goal of eventually taking their investees public. Thus, if a partnership follows GAAP and is audited by external auditors, the partnership can receive an audit opinion stating that it is in conformity with generally accepted accounting principles.

A partnership following GAAP and defining its company as an entity separate from the individual partners would account for a change in membership in the same manner as a corporate entity would account for changes in its investors. Additional investments would be recognized at their fair values along with the related increase in the company's total capital.

***Recognizing Decreases in Net Asset Revaluations*** There are a few situations under GAAP for recognizing decreases in the fair value of specific nonfinancial assets that may be triggered by a change in partnership membership. For example, **FASB Statement No. 142,** "Goodwill and Other Intangible Assets" (FASB 142), presents procedures for recognizing impairments of currently held goodwill. **FASB Statement No. 144,** "Accounting for the Impairment or Disposal of Long-Lived Assets" (FASB 144), presents the accounting standards for recognizing impairment losses on long-lived assets. Net asset revaluations performed using the appropriate accounting standards are in accordance with GAAP. However, there are no GAAP standards that provide for *increases* in the value of nonfinancial assets or recognition of new goodwill, solely due to a change in partnership membership.

***Bonus Method*** The ***bonus method*** is sometimes agreed upon by the partners to record a change in the partnership membership. This method records an increase in the partnership's total capital only for the capital amount invested by the new partner, in accordance with GAAP. However, the bonus method assigns partners' capitals based on the agreement of the partners, and it is often based on the value of the new partner's investment. In some cases, the current partners assign some of their capital to a new partner; in other cases, a new partner agrees to assign a portion of his or her capital interest to the prior partners. Thus, the bonus method does not violate GAAP because partners may legally assign any or all of their transferable partnership capital interest to other partners.

### The Partnership as an Aggregate of Partners' Interests and the Use of Non-GAAP Accounting

The partners in a private company may choose to follow non-GAAP accounting methods that meet their specific information needs. These partnerships may use the transactions surrounding the change of partnership members as an opportunity for recognizing increases in the fair value of the partnership's existing nonfinancial assets or for recording previously unrecognized goodwill.

***Recognizing Increases in Net Asset Revaluations or Goodwill*** The practices of recognizing increases in a partnership's net assets using the ***net asset revaluation*** method, or recognizing previously unrecorded goodwill using the ***goodwill recognition*** method, are *not* in compliance with GAAP. Partnerships using these non-GAAP methods argue that revaluing all assets and liabilities at the time of the change in partnership membership states fully the true economic condition of the partnership at that point in time, and properly assigns the changes in asset and liability values and goodwill to the partners who have been managing the business during the time the changes in value occurred.

Partners in private companies have free choice as to how they may account for changes in partnership membership. As noted, a private partnership may use either GAAP or non-GAAP methods, based on the information needs of the partners. Because some partnerships do record increases in value by applying the net asset revaluation or goodwill recognition methods, the following sections of this chapter discuss these non-GAAP methods of accounting for the change in the partnership membership

## New Partner Purchases an Interest

An individual may acquire a partnership interest directly from one or more of the present partners. In this type of transaction, cash or other assets are exchanged outside the partnership, and the only entry necessary on the partnership's books is a reclassification of the total capital of the partnership.

A concept used with some frequency is book value. The ***book value of a partnership*** is simply the total amount of the capital, which is also the amount of net assets (total assets minus total liabilities). Book value is important because it serves as a basis for asset and liability revaluations or goodwill recognition.

For purposes of this discussion, assume that after operations and partners' withdrawals during 20X1 and 20X2, AB Partnership has a book value of $30,000 and profit percentages on January 1, 20X3, as follows:

|  | Capital Balance | Profit Percentage |
|---|---|---|
| Alt | $20,000 | 60 |
| Blue | 10,000 | 40 |
| Total | $30,000 | 100 |

The following information describes the case:

1. On January 1, 20X3, Alt and Blue invite Cha to become a partner in their business. The resulting partnership will be called the ABC Partnership.

2. Cha purchases a one-fourth interest in the partnership capital directly from Alt and Blue for a total cost of $9,000, paying $5,900 to Alt and $3,100 to Blue. Cha will have a capital credit of $7,500 ($30,000 × .25) in a proportionate reclassification from Alt and Blue's capital accounts.

3. Cha will be entitled to a 25 percent interest in the profits or losses of the partnership. The remaining 75 percent interest will be divided between Alt and Blue in their old profit ratio of 60:40 percent. The resulting profit and loss percentages after the admission of Cha follow:

| Partner | Profit Percentage |
|---|---|
| Alt | 45 (75% of .60) |
| Blue | 30 (75% of .40) |
| Cha | 25 |
| Total | 100 |

In this example, Cha's 25 percent share of partnership profits or losses is the same as her one-fourth capital interest. These two percentage shares do not have to be the same. As described earlier in the chapter, a partner's capital interest may change over time because of profit distributions, withdrawals, or additional investments in capital. Furthermore, Cha could have acquired her entire capital interest directly from either partner. It is not necessary that a new partner directly purchasing an interest do so in a proportionate reclassification from each of the prior partners.

The transaction is between Cha and the individual partners and is not reflected on the partnership's books. The only entry in this case is to reclassify the partnership capital. Both Alt and Blue provide one-fourth of their capital to Cha, as follows:

January 1, 20X3

| (7) | Alt, Capital | 5,000 | |
| | Blue, Capital | 2,500 | |
| |     Cha, Capital | | 7,500 |

     Reclassify capital to new partner:

     From Alt: $5,000 = $20,000 × .25

     From Blue: $2,500 = $10,000 × .25

In this case the capital credit to Cha is only $7,500, although $9,000 is paid for the one-fourth interest. The $9,000 payment implies that the fair value of the partnership is $36,000, calculated as follows:

$$\$9,000 = \text{Fair value} \times .25$$

$$\$36,000 = \text{Fair value}$$

The partnership's book value is $30,000 before Cha's investment. The payment of $9,000 is made directly to the individual partners, and it does not become part of the partnership's assets. The $6,000 difference between the partnership's fair value and its new book value could be due to understated assets or to unrecognized goodwill.

### Recognizing Fair Value Increases in the Partnership's Net Assets (Non-GAAP)

Up to this point, the partnership is still following GAAP because the partners may legally assign any or all of their transferable partnership capital interest to other persons or among themselves as they agree. If the partners wish to be in accordance with GAAP, then they must follow the appropriate recognition and measurement methods for the net assets as prescribed in GAAP.

Assume that Alt and Blue decide to use the evidence from Cha's investment to recognize increases in fair values of the nonfinancial long-lived assets that have taken place before the admission of Cha. The partners have been informed by the partnership's accountant that this type of revaluation is not in accordance with GAAP. For example, if the partnership has land that is undervalued by $6,000 that it sells after Cha is admitted to the partnership, Cha will share in the gain on the sale according to the profit ratio. To avoid this possible problem, some partnerships revalue the assets at the time a new partner is admitted even if the new partner purchases the partnership interest directly from the present partners. In this case, Alt and Blue could recognize the increase in the value of the land immediately before the admission of Cha and allocate the increase to their capital accounts in their 60:40 profit ratio, as follows:

| (8) | Land | 6,000 | |
| |     Alt, Capital | | 3,600 |
| |     Blue, Capital | | 2,400 |

     Revaluation of land before admission of new partner:

     To Alt: $3,600 = $6,000 × .60

     To Blue: $2,400 = $6,000 × .40

Note that the partnership's total resulting capital is $36,000 ($30,000 prior plus the $6,000 revaluation). The transfer of a one-fourth capital credit to Cha is recorded as follows:

| (9) | Alt, Capital | 5,900 | |
| | Blue, Capital | 3,100 | |
| |     Cha, Capital | | 9,000 |

     Reclassify capital to new partner:

     $5,900 = $23,600 × .25

     $3,100 = $12,400 × .25

     $9,000 = $36,000 × .25

The partnership's accountant should ensure that sufficient evidence exists for any revaluation of assets and liabilities to prevent valuation abuses. Corroborating evidence such as appraisals or an extended period of excess earnings helps support asset valuations.

## New Partner Invests in Partnership

A new partner may acquire a share of the partnership by investing in the business. In this case, the partnership receives the cash or other assets. Three cases are possible when a new partner invests in a partnership:

*Case 1.* The new partner's investment equals the new partner's proportion of the partnership's book value.

*Case 2.* The investment is for *more* than the new partner's proportion of the partnership's book value. This indicates that the partnership's prior net assets are undervalued on the books or that unrecorded goodwill exists.

*Case 3.* The investment is for *less* than the new partner's proportion of the partnership's book value. This suggests that the partnership's prior net assets are overvalued on its books or that the new partner may be contributing goodwill in addition to other assets.

The first step in determining how to account for the admission of a new partner is to compute the ***new partner's proportion of the partnership's book value*** as follows:

$$\begin{array}{c} \text{New partner's} \\ \text{proportion of} \\ \text{the partnership's} \\ \text{book value} \end{array} = \left(\begin{array}{c} \text{Prior} \\ \text{capital of} \\ \text{present} \\ \text{partners} \end{array} + \begin{array}{c} \text{Investment} \\ \text{of new} \\ \text{partner} \end{array}\right) \times \begin{array}{c} \text{Percentage} \\ \text{of capital} \\ \text{to new} \\ \text{partner} \end{array}$$

The new partner's proportion of the partnership's book value is compared with the amount of the investment the new partner made to determine the procedures to be followed in accounting for his or her admission. Figure 15–1 presents an overview of the three cases presented above. Step 1 is to compare the new partner's investment with his or her proportion of the partnership's book value. Note that this is done before any

**FIGURE 15–1  Overview of Accounting for Admission of a New Partner**

| *Step 1: Compare Proportionate Book Value and Investment of New Partner* | *Step 2: Alternative Methods to Account for Admission* | *Key Observations* |
|---|---|---|
| Investment cost > Book value (Case 2) | 1. Revalue net assets up to market value and allocate to prior partners. 2. Record unrecognized goodwill and allocate to prior partners. 3. Assign bonus to prior partners. | • Prior partners receive asset valuation increase, goodwill, or bonus indicated by the excess of new partner's investment over book value of the capital share initially assignable to new partner. • Recording asset valuation increase or prior partners' goodwill increases total resulting partnership capital. |
| Investment cost = Book value (Case 1) | 1. No revaluations, bonus, or goodwill. | • No additional allocations necessary because new partner will receive a capital share equal to the amount invested. • Total resulting partnership capital equals prior partners' capital plus investment of new partner. |
| Investment cost < Book value (Case 3) | 1. Revalue net assets down to market value and allocate to prior partners. 2. Recognize goodwill brought in by new partner. 3. Assign bonus to new partner. | • Prior partners are assigned the reduction of asset values occurring before admission of the new partner. Alternatively, new partner is assigned goodwill or bonus as part of admission incentive. • Recording asset valuation decrease reduces total resulting capital, while recording new partner's goodwill increases total resulting capital. |

revaluations or recognition of goodwill. Step 2 is to determine the specific admission method. Three different methods are available to the partnership to account for the admission of a new partner when a difference exists between the new partner's investment and his or her proportion of the partnership's book value. The three methods are: (1) revalue net assets, (2) recognize goodwill, or (3) use the bonus method. Under the revaluation of net assets and goodwill recognition methods, the historical cost bases of the partnership's net assets are adjusted during the admission of the new partner. Some partners object to this departure from historical cost and prefer to use the bonus method, which uses capital interest transfers among the partners to align the total resulting capital of the partnership. Under the bonus method, net assets remain at their historical cost bases to the partnership. The choice of method of accounting for the admission of a new partner is up to the partners.

Several parallels exist between accounting for the admission of a new partner and accounting for an investment in the stock of another company. If a new partner pays more than book value, the excess of cost over book value, that is, the positive differential, may be due to unrecognized goodwill or to undervalued assets—the same cases as in accounting for the differential for stock investments. If book value equals the investment cost, then no differential exists, indicating that the book values of the net assets equal their fair values. If the new partner's investment is less than the proportionate book value, that is, an excess of book value over cost exists, the assets of the partnership may be overvalued. A concept unique to partnership accounting is the use of the bonus method. Figure 15–1 serves as a guide through the following discussion.

The AB Partnership example presented earlier is again used to illustrate the three cases. A review of the major facts for this example follows:

1. The January 1, 20X3, capital of the AB Partnership is $30,000. Alt's balance is $20,000, and Blue's balance is $10,000. Alt and Blue share profits in the ratio of 60:40.
2. Cha is invited into the partnership. Cha will have a one-fourth capital interest and a 25 percent share of profits. Alt and Blue will share the remaining 75 percent of profits in the ratio of 60:40, resulting in Alt having a 45 percent share of any profits and Blue having a 30 percent share.

### Case 1. Investment Equals Proportion of the Partnership's Book Value

The total book value of the partnership before the admission of the new partner is $30,000, and the new partner, Cha, is buying a one-fourth capital interest for $10,000.

The amount of a new partner's investment is often the result of negotiations between the prior partners and the prospective partner. As with any acquisition or investment, the investor must determine its market value. In the case of a partnership, the prospective partner attempts to ascertain the market value and earning power of the partnership's net assets. The new partner's investment is then a function of the percentage of partnership capital being acquired. In this case, Cha must believe that the $10,000 investment required is a fair price for a one-fourth interest in the resulting partnership; otherwise, she would not make the investment.

After the amount of investment is agreed on, it is possible to calculate the new partner's proportionate book value. For a $10,000 investment, Cha will have a one-fourth interest in the partnership, as follows:

| | |
|---|---|
| Investment in partnership | $10,000 |
| New partner's proportionate book value: | |
| ($30,000 + $10,000) × .25 | (10,000) |
| Difference (Investment = Book value) | $   -0- |

Because the amount of the investment ($10,000) equals the new partner's 25 percent proportionate book value ($10,000 = $40,000 × .25), there is an implication that the net assets are fairly valued. Total resulting capital equals the prior partners' capital ($30,000) plus the new partner's tangible investment ($10,000). Note that the capital credit assigned to the new partner is her share of the total resulting capital of the partnership after her admission as partner. The entry on the partnership's books is:

January 1, 20X3

| (10) | Cash | 10,000 | |
|---|---|---|---|
| | Cha, Capital | | 10,000 |
| | Admission of Cha for one-fourth interest upon investment of $10,000. | | |

The following schedule presents the key concepts in Case 1:

| | Prior Capital | New Partner's Tangible Investment | New Partner's Proportion of Partnership's Book Value (25%) | Total Resulting Capital | New Partner's Share of Total Resulting Capital (25%) |
|---|---|---|---|---|---|
| *Case 1* | | | | | |
| New partner's investment equals proportionate book value | $30,000 | $10,000 | $10,000 | | |
| No revaluations, bonus, or goodwill | | | | $40,000 | $10,000 |

### Case 2. New Partner's Investment More than Proportion of the Partnership's Book Value

In some cases, a new partner may invest more in an existing partnership than his or her proportionate share of the partnership's book value. This means that the new partner perceives some value in the partnership that the books of account do not reflect.

For example, assume Cha invests $11,000 for a one-fourth capital interest in the ABC Partnership. The first step is to compare the new partner's investment with the new partner's proportionate book value, as follows:

| | |
|---|---|
| Investment in partnership | $11,000 |
| New partner's proportionate book value: | |
| ($30,000 + $11,000) × .25 | (10,250) |
| Difference (Investment > Book value) | $   750 |

Cha has invested $11,000 for an interest with a book value of $10,250, thus paying an excess of $750 over the present book value.

Generally, an excess of investment over the respective book value of the partnership interest indicates that the partnership's prior net assets are undervalued or that the partnership has some unrecorded goodwill. Three alternative accounting treatments exist in this case:

1. *Revalue net assets upward.* Under this alternative:
   a. Book values of net assets are increased to their market values.
   b. The prior partners' capital accounts are increased for their respective shares of the increase in the book values of the net assets.
   c. The partnership's total resulting capital reflects the prior capital balances plus the amount of asset revaluation plus the new partner's investment.
2. *Record unrecognized goodwill.* With this method:
   a. Unrecognized goodwill is recorded.

b. The prior partners' capital accounts are increased for their respective shares of the goodwill.

c. The partnership's total resulting capital reflects the prior capital balances plus the goodwill recognized plus the new partner's investment.

3. *Use bonus method.* Essentially, the bonus method is a transfer of capital balances among the partners. This method is used when the partners do not wish to record adjustments in asset and liability accounts or recognize goodwill. Under this method:

a. The prior partners' capital accounts are increased for their respective shares of the bonus paid by the new partner.

b. The partnership's total resulting capital reflects the prior capital balances plus the new partner's investment.

The partnership may use any one of the three alternatives. The decision is usually a result of negotiations between the prior partners and the prospective partner. Some accountants criticize the revaluation of net assets or recognition of goodwill because it results in a marked departure from the historical cost principle and differs from the accepted accounting principles in **FASB Statement No. 142,** "Goodwill and Other Intangible Assets" (FASB 142), which prohibits corporations from recognizing goodwill that has not been acquired by purchase. Accountants who use the goodwill or asset revaluation methods argue that the goal of partnership accounting is to state fairly the relative capital equities of the partners, and this may require different accounting procedures from those used in corporate entities.

The accountant's function is to ensure that any estimates used in the valuation process are based on the best evidence available. Subjective valuations that could impair the fairness of the presentations made in the partnership's financial statements should be avoided or minimized.

***Illustration of Revaluation of Net Assets Approach (Non-GAAP)*** Assume that Cha paid a $750 excess ($11,000 − $10,250) over her proportionate book value because the partnership owns land on which are constructed warehouse buildings. The land has a book value of $4,000 but a recent appraisal indicates the land has a market value of $7,000. The partnership expects to continue using the land for warehouse space for as long as the business operates. The prior partners have been informed by their accountant that GAAP does not allow for *increasing* the value of nonfinancial, long-lived assets held and used in the operations of the business. But these prior partners decide to use the admission of the new partner to recognize the increase in the land's value and to assign this increase to the capital accounts of the prior partners. The increase in land value is allocated to the partners' capital accounts in the profit and loss ratio that existed during the time of the increase. Alt's capital is increased by $1,800 (60 percent of the $3,000 increase), and Blue's capital is increased by $1,200 (40 percent of the $3,000). The partnership makes the following entry for the revaluation of the land:

| | | | |
|---|---|---|---|
| (11) | Land | 3,000 | |
| | Alt, Capital | | 1,800 |
| | Blue, Capital | | 1,200 |
| | Revalue partnership land to market value. | | |

Cha's $11,000 investment brings the partnership's total resulting capital to $44,000, as follows:

| | |
|---|---|
| Prior capital of AB Partnership | $30,000 |
| Revaluation of land to market value | 3,000 |
| Cha's investment | 11,000 |
| Total resulting capital of ABC Partnership | $44,000 |

Cha is acquiring a one-fourth interest in the total resulting capital of the ABC Partnership. Her capital credit, after revaluing the land, is calculated as follows:

$$\text{New partner's share of total resulting capital} = (\$30{,}000 + \$3{,}000 + \$11{,}000) \times .25 = \$11{,}000$$

The entry to record the admission of Cha into the partnership follows:

| (12) | Cash | 11,000 | |
|---|---|---|---|
| | Cha, Capital | | 11,000 |
| | Admission of Cha for one-fourth capital interest in ABC Partnership. | | |

When the land is eventually sold, Cha will participate in the gain or loss calculated on the basis of the new $7,000 book value, which is the land's market value at the time of her admission into the partnership. The entire increase in the land value before Cha's admission belongs to the prior partners.

***Illustration of Goodwill Recognition (Non-GAAP)***    An entering partner may be paying an excess because of unrecognized goodwill, indicated by the partnership's high profitability. Some partnerships use the change in membership as an opportunity to record unrecognized goodwill created by the prior partners. Recording unrecognized goodwill is used for partnership accounting to establish appropriate capital equity among the partners. As noted earlier, this is not in accordance with the rule established in **FASB 142,** but the partners' information needs and the specific purposes of the partnership's financial statements could serve to support the use of this non-GAAP method.

Generally, the amount of goodwill is determined by negotiations between the prior and prospective partners and is based on estimates of future earnings. For example, the prior and new partners may agree that, due to the prior partners' efforts, the partnership has superior earnings potential and that $3,000 of goodwill should be recorded to recognize this fact. The new partner's negotiated investment cost will be based partly on the earnings potential of the partnership. Alternatively, goodwill may be estimated from the amount of the new partner's investment. For example, in this case, Cha is investing $11,000 for a one-fourth interest; therefore, she must believe the total resulting partnership capital is $44,000 ($11,000 × 4). The estimated goodwill is $3,000:

| | |
|---|---|
| *Step 1* | |
| 25% of estimated total resulting capital | $11,000 |
| Estimated total resulting capital ($11,000 ÷ .25) | $44,000 |
| *Step 2* | |
| Estimated total resulting capital | $44,000 |
| Total net assets not including goodwill | |
| ($30,000 prior plus $11,000 invested by Cha) | (41,000) |
| Estimated goodwill | $ 3,000 |

Another way to view the creation of goodwill at the time of a new partner's admission is to use a T-account form for the partnership's balance sheet. Any additional net assets, such as recognizing goodwill, must be balanced with additional capital, as follows:

| | **Balance Sheet** | | | |
|---|---|---|---|---|
| Prior to admission of new partner Cha | Net assets | $30,000 | Partners' capital | $30,000 |
| New partner's cash investment | Cash | 11,000 | New tangible capital | 11,000 |
| Capital prior to recognizing goodwill | | $41,000 | | $41,000 |
| Estimated new goodwill | Goodwill | 3,000 | Capital from goodwill | 3,000 |
| Total resulting capital | Net assets | $44,000 | Total resulting capital | $44,000 |

Once the new ABC Partnership's total resulting capital is estimated ($44,000), the new goodwill ($3,000) is the balance sheet balancing difference between the tangible capital ($41,000), which includes the new partner's cash investment and the estimated total resulting capital of ABC Partnership ($44,000).

The unrecorded goodwill is recorded, and the prior partners' capital accounts are credited for the increase in assets. The adjustments to the capital accounts are in the profit and loss ratio that existed during the periods the goodwill was developed. This increased Alt's capital by 60 percent of the goodwill and Blue's by 40 percent. The entries to record goodwill and the admission of Cha are as follows:

| (13) | Goodwill | 3,000 | |
| | Alt, Capital | | 1,800 |
| | Blue, Capital | | 1,200 |
| | Recognize unrecorded goodwill. | | |

| (14) | Cash | 11,000 | |
| | Cha, Capital | | 11,000 |
| | Admission of Cha to partnership for a one-fourth capital interest: $44,000 × .25. | | |

Another reason for recording goodwill is that the new partner may want her capital balance to equal the amount of investment made. The investment is based on the market value of the partnership, and for this equality to occur, the partnership must restate its prior net assets to their fair values.

It is important to note that the $11,000 credit to Cha's capital account is one-fourth of the total resulting capital of ABC Partnership of $44,000 as follows:

$$\text{New partner's share of total resulting capital} = (\$30,000 + \$3,000 + \$11,000) \times .25 = \$11,000$$

In future periods, any impairment loss of goodwill will be charged against partnership earnings before net income is distributed to the partners. Consequently, Cha's future profit distribution may be affected by the goodwill recognized at the time of her admission into the partnership.

***Illustration of Bonus Method (GAAP)*** Some partnerships are averse to recognizing asset revaluations or unrecorded goodwill when a new partner is admitted. Instead, they record a portion of the new partner's investment as a bonus to the existing partners to align the capital balances properly at the time of the new partner's admission. In this case, the $750 excess paid by Cha is a bonus allocated to the prior partners in their profit and loss ratio of 60 percent to Alt and 40 percent to Blue. ABC Partnership's total resulting capital consists of $30,000 prior capital of Alt and Blue plus the $11,000 investment of Cha. No additional capital is recognized by revaluing assets. The value of the capital credit acquired by the new partner is calculated as:

$$\text{New partner's share of total resulting capital} = (\$30,000 + \$11,000) \times .25 = \$10,250$$

The entry to record the admission of Cha under the bonus method is as follows:

| (15) | Cash | 11,000 | |
| | Alt, Capital | | 450 |
| | Blue, Capital | | 300 |
| | Cha, Capital | | 10,250 |
| | Admission of Cha with bonus to Alt and Blue. | | |

Cha may dislike the bonus method because her capital balance is $750 less than her investment in the partnership. This is a disadvantage of the bonus method.

The following schedule presents the key concepts for Case 2:

| | Prior Capital | New Partner's Tangible Investment | New Partner's Proportion of Partnership's Book Value (25%) | Total Resulting Capital | New Partner's Share of Total Resulting Capital (25%) |
|---|---|---|---|---|---|
| *Case 2* | | | | | |
| New partner's investment greater than proportionate book value | $30,000 | $11,000 | $10,250 | | |
| 1. Revalue assets by increasing land $3,000 | | | | $44,000 | $11,000 |
| 2. Recognize $3,000 goodwill for prior partners | | | | $44,000 | $11,000 |
| 3. Bonus of $750 to prior partners | | | | $41,000 | $10,250 |

### Case 3. New Partner's Investment Less than Proportion of the Partnership's Book Value

It is possible that a new partner may pay less than his or her proportionate share of the partnership's book value. For example, assume Cha invests $8,000 for a one-fourth capital interest in the ABC Partnership. The first step is to compare the new partner's investment with the new partner's proportionate book value, as follows:

| | |
|---|---|
| Investment in partnership | $ 8,000 |
| New partner's proportionate book value: ($30,000 + $8,000) × .25 | (9,500) |
| Difference (Investment < Book value) | $(1,500) |

The fact that Cha's investment is less than the book value of a one-fourth interest in the partnership indicates that the partnership has overvalued net assets or the prior partners recognize that Cha is contributing additional value in the form of expertise or skills she possesses that are needed by the partnership. In this case, Cha is investing $8,000 in cash and an additional amount that may be viewed as goodwill.

As with Case 2, in which the investment is more than the book value acquired, there are three alternative approaches to account for the differential when the investment is less than the book value acquired. The three approaches are as follows:

1. *Revalue net assets downward.* Under this alternative:
   a. Book values of net assets are decreased to recognize the reduction in their values.
   b. The prior partners' capital accounts are decreased for their respective share of the decrease in the values of the net assets.
   c. The partnership's total resulting capital reflects the prior capital balances less the amount of the net asset valuation write-down plus the new partner's investment.

2. *Recognize goodwill brought in by the new partner.* In this approach:
   a. Goodwill or other intangible benefits brought in by the new partner are recorded and included in the new partner's capital account.
   b. The prior partners' capital accounts remain unchanged.
   c. The partnership's total resulting capital reflects the prior capital balances plus the new goodwill brought in plus the new partner's tangible investment.

3. *Use bonus method.*  Under the bonus method:

   a. The new partner is assigned a bonus from the prior partners' capital accounts, which are decreased for their respective shares of the bonus paid to the new partner.

   b. The partnership's total resulting capital reflects the prior capital balances plus the new partner's investment.

***Illustration of Revaluation of Net Assets Approach (GAAP)***   Almost all of an entity's assets and liabilities have one or more generally accepted accounting principles for recognizing impairment losses or write-downs to fair value. Several examples of these GAAP were noted earlier in this chapter, such as recognizing a valuation loss on inventory valued using the lower-of-cost-or-market method, impairment losses on goodwill, impairment losses on long-lived assets used in the business, and losses on financial assets such as investments. Thus, recognizing decreases in the values of many assets is allowed by GAAP. The process of admitting a new partner is a common time for evaluating the fair values of the partnership's net assets and comparing those values with the related book values.

Assume that the reason Cha paid only $8,000 for a one-fourth interest in the partnership is that equipment used in current production is recorded at a book value of $14,000 but has a fair value of only $8,000. The partners agree to recognize the impairment loss and write down the equipment to its fair value before the new partner's admission. The write-down is allocated to the prior partners in the profit and loss ratio that existed during the period of the decline in the fair value of the equipment: 60 percent to Alt and 40 percent to Blue. The write-down is recorded as follows:

| (16) | Alt, Capital | 3,600 | |
| | Blue, Capital | 2,400 | |
| | Equipment | | 6,000 |
| | Recognize impairment loss on equipment. | | |

Note that the partnership's total capital has now been reduced from $30,000 to $24,000 as a result of the $6,000 write-down. The value of Cha's share of total resulting capital of the ABC Partnership, *after the write-down,* is calculated as follows:

$$\text{New partner's share of total resulting capital} = (\$24,000 + \$8,000) \times .25 = \$8,000$$

The entry to record the admission of Cha as a partner in the ABC Partnership is:

| (17) | Cash | 8,000 | |
| | Cha, Capital | | 8,000 |
| | Admission of Cha to partnership. | | |

Cha's recorded capital credit is equal to her investment because the total partnership capital of $32,000 ($24,000 + $8,000) now represents the partnership's fair value.

***Illustration of Recording Goodwill for New Partner (Non-GAAP)***   The prior partners may offer Cha a one-fourth capital interest in the ABC Partnership for an $8,000 investment because Cha has essential business experience, skills, customer contacts, reputation, or other ingredients of goodwill that she will bring into the partnership. The amount of goodwill brought in by the new partner is usually determined through negotiations between the prior partners and the prospective partner. For example, Alt, Blue, and Cha may agree that Cha's abilities will generate excess earnings for the resulting ABC Partnership. They agree that Cha should be given $2,000 of goodwill recognition when she joins the partnership in recognition of her anticipated excess contribution to the partnership's future earnings. The negotiated goodwill is recognized and added to her tangible investment to determine the amount of capital credit.

Alternatively, the amount of goodwill brought in by the new partner may be estimated from the amount of the total capital being retained by the prior partners. In this case, the prior partners are retaining a 75 percent interest in the partnership and allowing the new partner a 25 percent capital interest. The dollar amount of the prior partners' 75 percent interest is $30,000. Cha's investment of $8,000 plus goodwill makes up the remaining 25 percent. The amount of goodwill that Cha brought into the partnership is determined as follows:

| | |
|---|---:|
| *Step 1* | |
| 75% of estimated total resulting capital | $30,000 |
| Estimated total resulting capital ($30,000 ÷ .75) | $40,000 |
| *Step 2* | |
| Estimated total resulting capital | $40,000 |
| Total net assets not including goodwill | |
| ($30,000 + $8,000) | (38,000) |
| Estimated goodwill | $ 2,000 |

Note that the goodwill estimate for the new partner is made using the information from the prior partners' interests. In Case 2, the estimate of goodwill to the prior partners was made using the information from the new partner's investment. The reason for this difference is that the best available information should be used for the goodwill estimates. If the new partner's goodwill is being estimated, it is not logical to use the new partner's tangible investment to estimate the total investment made by the new partner, including goodwill. That is circular reasoning that involves using a number to estimate itself. Furthermore, when goodwill is being assigned to the prior partners, it is not logical to use the existing capital of the prior partners to estimate their goodwill. A useful way to remember how to estimate goodwill is to use the opposite partner's information for the estimate:

Use new partner to estimate goodwill to prior partners; use prior partners to estimate goodwill to new partner.

The entry to record the admission of Cha into the ABC Partnership is:

| | | | |
|---|---|---:|---:|
| (18) | Cash | 8,000 | |
| | Goodwill | 2,000 | |
| |     Cha, Capital | | 10,000 |
| |   Admission of Cha to partnership. | | |

Note that the ABC Partnership's total resulting capital is now $40,000, with Alt and Blue together having a 75 percent interest and Cha having a 25 percent interest.

***Illustration of Bonus Method (GAAP)***   Cha's admission as a new partner with a one-fourth interest in the ABC Partnership for an investment of only $8,000 may be accounted for by recognizing a bonus given to Cha from the prior partners. The $1,500 bonus is the difference between the new partner's $9,500 book value and her $8,000 investment. The prior partners' capital accounts are reduced by $1,500 in their profit and loss ratio of 60 percent for Alt and 40 percent for Blue, and Cha's capital account is credited for $9,500, as follows:

| | | | |
|---|---|---:|---:|
| (19) | Cash | 8,000 | |
| | Alt, Capital | 900 | |
| | Blue, Capital | 600 | |
| |     Cha, Capital | | 9,500 |
| |   Admission of Cha to partnership. | | |

Note that the amount of the capital credit assigned to the new partner is her share of the total resulting capital, as follows:

$$\text{New partner's share of total resulting capital} = (\$30,000 + \$8,000) \times .25 = \$9,500$$

The following schedule presents the key concepts for Case 3:

| | Prior Capital | New Partner's Tangible Investment | New Partner's Proportion of Partnership's Book Value (25%) | Total Resulting Capital | New Partner's Share of Total Resulting Capital (25%) |
|---|---|---|---|---|---|
| *Case 3* | | | | | |
| New partner's investment less than proportionate book value | $30,000 | $8,000 | $9,500 | | |
| 1. Revalue assets by decreasing equipment by $6,000 | | | | $32,000 | $ 8,000 |
| 2. Recognize goodwill of $2,000 for new partner | | | | $40,000 | $10,000 |
| 3. Bonus of $1,500 to new partner | | | | $38,000 | $ 9,500 |

### Summary and Comparison of Accounting for Investment of New Partner

Figure 15–2 presents the entries made in each of the three cases discussed. In addition, the capital balance of each of the three partners immediately after the admission of Cha is presented to the right of the journal entries.

The following summarizes the alternative methods of accounting for the investment of a new partner:

**Case 1. New partner's investment equals *his or her proportion of the partnership's book value.***

1. The new partner's capital credit equals his or her investment.
2. This case recognizes no goodwill or bonus.

**Case 2. New partner's investment is more than *his or her proportion of the partnership's book value.***

1. The revaluation of an asset or recognition of goodwill increases the partnership's total resulting capital. The increase is allocated to the prior partners in their profit and loss ratio.
2. After recognition of the asset revaluation or unrecorded goodwill, the new partner's capital credit equals his or her investment and his or her percentage of the total resulting capital.
3. Under the bonus method, the partnership's total resulting capital is the sum of the prior partnership's capital plus the investment by the new partner. The capital credit recorded for the new partner is less than the investment but equals his or her percentage of the resulting partnership capital.

**Case 3. New partner's investment is less than *his or her proportion of the partnership's book value.***

1. Under the revaluation of assets approach, the write-down of the assets reduces the prior partners' capital in their profit and loss ratio. The new partner's capital is then credited for the amount of the investment.

**FIGURE 15–2**
**Summary of Accounting for Investment of New Partner: Journal Entries and Capital Balances after Admission of New Partner**

**Case 1: New partner's investment equals proportionate book value. Cha invests $10,000 cash for one-fourth capital interest.**

| | | | | |
|---|---|---|---|---|
| Cash | 10,000 | | Alt | $20,000 |
| Cha, Capital | | 10,000 | Blue | 10,000 |
| | | | Cha | 10,000 |
| | | | Total | $40,000 |

**Case 2: New partner's investment is greater than proportionate book value. Cha invests $11,000 cash for one-fourth capital interest.**

(a) Revalue net assets: (upward)

| | | | | |
|---|---|---|---|---|
| Land | 3,000 | | Alt | $21,800 |
| Alt, Capital | | 1,800 | Blue | 11,200 |
| Blue, Capital | | 1,200 | Cha | 11,000 |
| Cash | 11,000 | | Total | $44,000 |
| Cha, Capital | | 11,000 | | |

(b) Recognize goodwill for prior partners:

| | | | | |
|---|---|---|---|---|
| Goodwill | 3,000 | | Alt | $21,800 |
| Alt, Capital | | 1,800 | Blue | 11,200 |
| Blue, Capital | | 1,200 | Cha | 11,000 |
| Cash | 11,000 | | Total | $44,000 |
| Cha, Capital | | 11,000 | | |

(c) Bonus to prior partners:

| | | | | |
|---|---|---|---|---|
| Cash | 11,000 | | Alt | $20,450 |
| Alt, Capital | | 450 | Blue | 10,300 |
| Blue, Capital | | 300 | Cha | 10,250 |
| Cha, Capital | | 10,250 | Total | $41,000 |

**Case 3: New partner's investment is less than proportionate book value. Cha invests $8,000 cash for a one-fourth capital interest.**

(a) Revalue net assets: (downward)

| | | | | |
|---|---|---|---|---|
| Alt, Capital | 3,600 | | Alt | $16,400 |
| Blue, Capital | 2,400 | | Blue | 7,600 |
| Equipment | | 6,000 | Cha | 8,000 |
| Cash | 8,000 | | Total | $32,000 |
| Cha, Capital | | 8,000 | | |

(b) Recognize goodwill for new partner:

| | | | | |
|---|---|---|---|---|
| Cash | 8,000 | | Alt | $20,000 |
| Goodwill | 2,000 | | Blue | 10,000 |
| Cha, Capital | | 10,000 | Cha | 10,000 |
| | | | Total | $40,000 |

(c) Bonus to new partner:

| | | | | |
|---|---|---|---|---|
| Cash | 8,000 | | Alt | $19,100 |
| Alt, Capital | 900 | | Blue | 9,400 |
| Blue, Capital | 600 | | Cha | 9,500 |
| Cha, Capital | | 9,500 | Total | $38,000 |

2. Under the goodwill method, goodwill is assigned to the new partner, and the total resulting capital of the partnership is increased. The new partner's capital is credited for his or her percentage interest in the total resulting capital of the partnership.

3. The bonus method results in a transfer of capital from the prior partners to the new partner. The new partnership's total resulting capital equals the prior capital plus the new partner's investment. The new partner's capital credit is more than the investment made but equals his or her percentage of the total resulting capital.

## Determining a New Partner's Investment Cost

In the previous sections, the amount of the new partner's contribution has been provided. In some instances, accountants are asked to determine the amount of cash investment the new partner should be asked to contribute. The basic principles of partnership accounting provide the means to solve this question. For example, let's continue the basic example of partners Alt and Blue wishing to admit Cha as a new partner. The prior partnership capital was $30,000, and the partners wish to invite Cha into the partnership for a one-fourth interest.

Assume that the prior partners, Alt and Blue, agree that the partnership's assets should be revalued up by $3,000 to recognize the increase in value of the land held by the partnership. The question is how much Cha, the new partner, should be asked to invest for her one-fourth interest.

When determining the new partner's investment cost, it is important to note the total resulting capital of the partnership and the percentage of ownership interest retained by the prior partners. In this example, the prior partners retain a three-fourth interest in the resulting partnership, for which their 75 percent capital interest is $33,000, the $30,000 of prior capital plus the $3,000 from the revaluation of the land, as follows:

| | |
|---|---|
| 75% of total resulting capital | $33,000 |
| Total resulting capital (100%) | $44,000 |
| Less prior partners' capital | (33,000) |
| Cash contribution required of new partner | $11,000 |

Note that this is simply another way to evaluate the admission process as discussed in the net asset revaluation illustration under Case 2.

In some cases, the bonus amount may be determined prior to the determination of the cash contribution required from the new partner. For example, assume that Alt and Blue agree to give Cha a bonus of $1,500 for joining the partnership. The following schedule determines the amount of cash investment required of Cha, the new partner:

| | |
|---|---|
| Prior capital of Alt and Blue | $30,000 |
| Less bonus given to Cha upon admission | (1,500) |
| Capital retained by Alt and Blue (75%) | $28,500 |
| Total resulting capital ($28,500 ÷ .75) | $38,000 |
| Less prior partners' capital | (28,500) |
| Capital credit required of new partner | $ 9,500 |
| Less bonus to new partner from prior partners | (1,500) |
| Cash contribution required of new partner | $ 8,000 |

This second example is another way to view the bonus-to-new-partner method under Case 3 as presented. The key is to determine the amount of capital that the prior partners will retain for their percentage share in the partnership's total resulting capital after admitting the new partner. The new partner's cash contribution can be computed simply by determining the amount of the capital credit that will be assigned to him or her and then recognizing any bonuses that will be used to align the capital balances.

## Dissociation of a Partner from the Partnership

When a partner retires or withdraws from a partnership, that partner is dissociated from the partnership. In most cases, the partnership purchases the dissociated partner's interest in the partnership for a buyout price. Section 701 of the UPA 1997 states that the buyout price is the estimated amount if (1) the assets of the partnership were sold at a price equal to the greater of the liquidation value or the value based on a sale of the entire business as a going concern without the dissociated partner, and (2) the partnership was wound up at that time, with all partnership obligations settled. Note that goodwill may be included in the valuation. The partnership must pay interest to the dissociated partner from the date of dissociation to the date of payment. In cases of wrongful dissociation, the partnership may sue the partner for damages the wrongful dissociation causes the partnership.

In the case in which the partnership agrees to the dissociation and it is not wrongful, the accountant can aid in the computation of the buyout price. It is especially important to determine all existing liabilities on the dissociation date. The partnership agreement may include other procedures to use in the case of a partner dissociation, such as the specifics of valuation, the process of the acquisition of the dissociated partner's transferable value, and other aspects of the change in membership process.

Some partnerships have an audit performed when a change in partners is made. This audit establishes the existence of and the accuracy of the book values of the assets and liabilities. On occasion, accounting errors are found during an audit. Errors should be corrected and the partners' capital accounts adjusted based on the profit and loss ratio that existed in the period in which the errors were made. For example, if an audit disclosed that three years ago depreciation expense was charged for $4,000 less than it should have been, the error is corrected retroactively, and the partners' capital accounts are charged with their respective shares of the adjustment based on their profit and loss ratio of three years ago.

Generally, the continuing partners buy out the retiring partner either by making a direct acquisition or by having the partnership acquire the retiring partner's interest. If the continuing partners directly acquire the retiring partner's interest, the only entry on the partnership's books is to record the reclassification of capital among the partners. If the partnership acquires the retiring partner's interest, the partnership must record the reduction of total partnership capital and the corresponding reduction of assets paid to the retiring partner. Computation of the buyout price when a partner dissociates from the partnership can take the form of three possible scenarios. These are discussed next.

### 1. Buyout Price Equal to Partner's Capital Credit

Assume Alt retires from the ABC Partnership when his capital account has a balance of $55,000 after recording all increases in the partnership's net assets including income earned up to the date of the retirement. All partners agree to $55,000 as the buyout price of Alt's partnership interest. The entry made by the ABC Partnership is:

| | | | |
|---|---|---|---|
| (20) | Alt, Capital | 55,000 | |
| | Cash | | 55,000 |
| | Retirement of Alt. | | |

If the partnership is unable to pay the total of $55,000 to Alt at the time of retirement, it must recognize a liability for the remaining portion.

### 2. Buyout Price Greater than Partner's Capital Credit

Assume Alt has a capital credit of $55,000 and all the partners agree to a buyout price of $65,000. Most partnerships would account for the $10,000 payment above Alt's capital credit ($65,000 paid − $55,000) as a capital adjustment bonus to Alt from the capital accounts of the remaining partners. In this case, the $10,000 would be allocated against the capital accounts of Blue and Cha in their profit ratio. Blue has a 30 percent interest, and Cha has a 25 percent interest in the net income of the ABC Partnership. The sum of their respective shares is 55 percent (30 percent + 25 percent), and their relative profit percentages, rounded to the nearest percentage, are 55 percent for Blue and 45 percent for Cha, computed as follows:

|  | Prior Profit Percentage | Remaining Profit Percentage |
|---|---|---|
| Alt | 45 | 0 |
| Blue | 30 | 55 (30/55) |
| Cha | 25 | 45 (25/55) |
| Total | 100 | 100 |

The entry to record the retirement of Alt is:

| (21) | Alt, Capital | 55,000 | |
|---|---|---|---|
| | Blue, Capital | 5,500 | |
| | Cha, Capital | 4,500 | |
| | Cash | | 65,000 |
| | Retirement of Alt. | | |

The $10,000 bonus paid to Alt is allocated to Blue and Cha in their respective profit ratios. Blue is charged for 55 percent, and Cha is charged for the remaining 45 percent.

Occasionally, a partnership uses the retirement of a partner to record unrecognized goodwill. In this case, the partnership may record the retiring partner's share only, or it may impute the entire amount of goodwill based on the retiring partner's profit percentage. If it imputes total goodwill, the remaining partners also receive their respective shares of the total goodwill recognized. Many accountants criticize recording goodwill on the retirement of a partner on the same theoretical grounds as they criticize recording unrecognized goodwill on the admission of a new partner. Nevertheless, partnership accounting sometimes uses all the recognition of goodwill at this event.

For example, if $65,000 is paid to Alt and only Alt's share of unrecognized goodwill is to be recorded, the partnership makes the following entries at the time of Alt's retirement:

| (22) | Goodwill | 10,000 | |
|---|---|---|---|
| | Alt, Capital | | 10,0000 |
| | Recognize Alt's share of goodwill. | | |

| (23) | Alt, Capital | 65,000 | |
|---|---|---|---|
| | Cash | | 65,000 |
| | Retirement of Alt. | | |

### 3. Buyout Price Less than Partner's Capital Credit

Sometimes, the buyout price is less than a partner's capital credit. This could result if liquidation values of net assets are less than their book values or it may occur because the dissociating partner wishes to leave the partnership badly enough to accept less than his or her current capital balance. For example, Alt agrees to accept $50,000 as the buyout price for his partnership interest. The partnership should evaluate its net assets to determine if any impairments or write-downs should be recognized. If no revaluations of the net assets are necessary, then the $5,000 difference ($50,000 cash paid less $55,000 capital credit) is distributed as a capital adjustment to Blue and Cha in their respective profit and loss ratio.

**Summary of Key Concepts**

Accounting for partnerships recognizes the unique aspects of this form of business organization. Most states have enacted the major provisions of the Uniform Partnership Act of 1997 (UPA 1997). This act includes the rights and responsibilities of the partners, both with third parties and among the partners, and the rights of third parties, such as creditors, against the partnership. A partnership agreement is very important because many of the sections of the UPA 1997 can be waived with a formal partnership agreement. The partnership should also file a Statement of Partnership Authority with the secretary of the state and the clerk of the county in which the partnership business takes place. The UPA 1997 includes sections stating that the partnership is an entity distinct from its partners, that partners are agents of the partnership, that partners are personally liable for the partnership obligations that exceed the partnership's assets, that partnership profits or losses are shared equally, and that a partner may dissociate, in which case that partner no longer may share in the management of the partnership.

Partnerships use a wide variety of profit or loss distribution methods and accountants must ensure that the partnership agreement is followed closely. Most partnerships continue on in business when a partner dissociates (leaves the partnership) by purchasing the dissociated partner's interest at a buyout price based on the value of the partnership were it to wind up its business. Several methods of accounting are used to account for changes in partnership membership. Some partnerships use a net asset revaluation approach, sometimes including recognizing goodwill. The other major accounting approach used to account for changes in membership is the bonus method, which uses a reclassification of partner capital. Partnerships provide four financial statements: the statement of income, the balance sheet, the statement of cash flows, and a statement of partners' capital that presents the changes in the partners' capital accounts during the period.

## Key Terms

admission of a new partner, *725*
bonus method, *726*
book value of a partnership, *727*
buyout price, *725*
entity concept, *713*
goodwill recognition, *726*

net asset revaluation, *726*
new partner's proportion of the partnership's book value, *729*
partners' accounts, *718*
partner's dissociation, *714*
profit distribution plans, *719*

statement of partners' capital, *724*
Statement of Partnership Authority, *713*
transferable interest, *714*
Uniform Partnership Act of 1997 (UPA 1997), *712*

## Appendix 15A  Tax Aspects of a Partnership

The Internal Revenue Service views the partnership form of organization as a temporary aggregation of some of the individual partners' rights. The partnership is not a separate taxable entity. Therefore, the individual partners must report their share of the partnership income or loss on their personal tax returns, whether withdrawn or not. This sometimes creates cash flow problems for partners who leave their share of income in the partnership and permit the partnership to use the income for growth. In such cases, the partners must pay income tax on income that was not distributed to them. However, this tax conduit feature also offers special tax features to the individual partners. For example, charitable contributions made by the partnership are reported on the partners' individual tax returns. Also, any tax-exempt income earned by the partnership is passed through to the individual partners.

This pass-through benefits individual partners when the business has an operating loss. The individual partners can recognize their shares of the partnership loss on their own tax returns, thereby offsetting other taxable income. If the business is incorporated, the loss does not pass through to the stockholders.

### TAX BASIS OF ASSET INVESTMENTS

For capital investments, the accounting basis and the tax basis are computed differently. For tax purposes, a partnership must value the assets invested in the partnership at the tax basis of the individual partner who invests the assets. For example, assume that partner A contributes a building to the AB Partnership. The building originally cost $6,000 and has been depreciated $2,000, leaving a book value of $4,000. The building has a market value of $10,000. For tax purposes, the partnership records the building at $4,000, the adjusted basis of partner A.

This tax valuation differs from the amount that is recognized under generally accepted accounting principles. A basic concept in GAAP is to value asset transfers between separate reporting entities at their respective fair market values. In this case, the partnership records the building at its $10,000 fair value for accounting purposes. Most partnerships maintain their accounting records and financial statements using GAAP, and they use a separate adjusting schedule at the end of each period to report the results for tax purposes on Form 1065, the partnership tax information form.

In addition to asset transfers, a partnership may also assume the liabilities associated with an asset. For example, if the building was subject to a $2,000 mortgage, which the AB Partnership assumed with the building, partner A benefits because the other partners have assumed a portion of the mortgage that A originally owed entirely.

A partner's tax basis in a partnership is the sum of the following:

The partner's tax basis of any assets contributed to the partnership.

Plus the partner's share of other partners' liabilities assumed by the partnership.

Less the amount of the partner's liabilities assumed by the other partners.

To illustrate, A contributes the building discussed, which has an adjusted tax basis of $4,000 ($6,000 cost less $2,000 depreciation) and is subject to a mortgage of $2,000. The building's market value is $10,000. B contributes machinery that has a book value of $15,000 and a market value of $20,000 and is subject to a note payable of $5,000. The partners agree to share equally in the liabilities assumed by the AB Partnership. The tax basis of each partner in the partnership is calculated as follows:

|  | Partner A | Partner B |
|---|---|---|
| Tax basis of assets contributed | $4,000 | $15,000 |
| Partner's share of other partner's liabilities assumed by partnership: | | |
| Partner A: (1/2 of $5,000) | 2,500 | |
| Partner B: (1/2 of $2,000) | | 1,000 |
| Partner's liabilities assumed by other partners: | | |
| Partner A: (1/2 of $2,000) | (1,000) | |
| Partner B: (1/2 of $5,000) | | (2,500) |
| Tax basis of partner's interest | $5,500 | $13,500 |

The tax basis of each partner is used for tax recognition of gains or losses on subsequent disposals of the partner's investment in the partnership.

For GAAP purposes, each partner's investment is based on the fair value of the assets less liabilities assumed. Thus, in the preceding case, partner A's accounting basis is $8,000 ($10,000 market value of the building less $2,000 mortgage), and partner B's accounting basis is $15,000 ($20,000 market value of the equipment less $5,000 note payable). Any asset disposal gain or loss in the accounting financial statements is based on the valuations made using GAAP. A separate schedule of tax bases for each of the partners is typically maintained in case the information is required for a partner's individual tax return.

## S CORPORATIONS

An S corporation is a corporate entity that elects to be taxed in the same manner as a partnership, with the shareholders including their share of corporate income or loss in their personal returns, whether or not the income has been distributed as dividends. This eliminates the double taxation of corporate income: first, as taxable income to the corporation, and second, as taxable dividend income to the shareholder. The S corporation form provides the shareholders with the liability limitation of an investment in a corporation. The Internal Revenue Service has certain qualifying criteria for S corporation status: (1) a maximum of 75 shareholders, all of whom must be either U.S. citizens or permanent resident aliens, is permitted; (2) only one class of stock may be issued; and (3) no more than 25 percent of the corporation's gross income can be derived from passive investment activities.

A limited liability company (LLC) is a relatively new form of corporate entity governed by the laws of the state in which it is formed. The LLC provides liability protection to its investors as well as the pass-through taxation benefits of partnerships and S corporations. However, each state has its own distinct set of laws governing LLCs, while the IRS has just one set of definitions for an S corporation. Over time, the LLC form of entity may gain in use.

# Appendix **15B**   Joint Ventures

A joint venture usually is a business entity owned and operated by a small group of investors as a separate and specific business project organized for the mutual benefit of the ownership group. Many joint ventures are short-term associations of two or more parties to fulfill a specific project, such as the development of real estate, joint oil or gas drilling efforts, the financing of a joint production center, or the financing of a motion picture effort. Many international efforts to expand production or markets involve joint ventures either with foreign-based companies or with foreign governments. A recent phenomenon is the formation of research joint ventures in which two or more corporations agree to share the costs and eventual research accomplishments of a separate research laboratory. The venturers might not have equal ownership interests; a venturer's share could be as low as 5 or 10 percent or as high as 90 or 95 percent. Many joint ventures of only two venturers, called 50 percent–owned ventures, divide the ownership share equally.

A joint venture may be organized as a corporation, partnership, or undivided interest. A corporate joint venture is usually formed for long-term projects such as the development and sharing of technical knowledge among a small group of companies. The incorporation of the joint venture formalizes the legal relationships between the venturers and limits each investor's liability to the amount of the investment in the venture. The venture's stock is not traded publicly, and the venturers usually have other business transactions between them. Accounting for a corporate joint venture is guided by **APB Opinion No. 18,** "The Equity Method of Accounting for Investments in Common Stock" (APB 18), which requires that investors use the equity method to account for their investments in the common stock of corporate joint ventures.

When one corporation has control over another, the controlled corporation is considered a subsidiary rather than a corporate joint venture, even if it has a small number of other owners. A subsidiary should be consolidated by the controlling owner, and a noncontrolling interest recognized for the interests of other owners.

A partnership joint venture is accounted for as any other partnership. All facets of partnership accounting presented in the chapter apply to these partnerships, each of which has its own accounting records. Some joint ventures are accounted for on the books of one of the venturers; however, this combined accounting does not fully reflect the fact that the joint venture is a separate reporting entity. Each partner, or venturer, maintains an investment account on its books for its share of the partnership venture capital. The investment in the partnership account is debited for the initial investment and for the investor's share of subsequent profits. Withdrawals and shares of losses are credited to the investment account. The balance in the investment account should correspond to the balance in the partner's capital account shown on the joint venture partnership's statements.

In 1971, the AICPA issued **Accounting Interpretation No. 2,** "Investments in Partnerships and Ventures" (AIN 2 of APB 18), which stated that many of the provisions of **APB 18** are appropriate for accounting for investments in partnerships and unincorporated joint ventures. In particular, intercompany profits should be eliminated and the investor-partners should record their shares of the venture's income or loss in the same manner as with the equity method. For financial reporting purposes, if one of the investor-venturers in fact controls the joint venture, that venturer should consolidate the joint venture into its financial statements. If all investor-venturers maintain joint control, then the one-line equity method should be used to report the investment in the joint venture.

Accounting for unincorporated joint ventures that are undivided interests usually follows the method of accounting used by partnerships. An *undivided interest* exists when each investor-venturer owns a proportionate share of each asset and is proportionately liable for its share of each liability. Some established industry practices, especially in oil and gas venture accounting, provide for a pro rata recognition of a venture's assets, liabilities, revenue, and expenses. For example, assume that both A Company and B Company are 50 percent investors in a joint venture, called JTV, for the purposes of oil exploration. The JTV venture has plant assets of $500,000 and long-term liabilities of $200,000. Therefore, both A Company and B Company have an investment of $150,000 ($300,000 × .50). Under the equity method, the investment is reported in A and B companies' balance sheets as a $150,000 investment in joint venture.

**International Accounting Standard No. 31,** "Interests in Joint Ventures" (IAS 31), specified the reporting of joint ventures under international accounting financial reporting standards. **IAS 31** identified three types of joint ventures: (*a*) *jointly controlled operations,* for which each venturer recognizes the assets that it controls and the liabilities it incurs and the expenses it incurs and its share of the joint venture's income; (*b*) *jointly controlled assets,* for which each venturer recognizes its share of the jointly controlled assets, any liabilities it has incurred plus its share of any liabilities incurred by the joint venture, and its share of the income together with its share of the expenses incurred from the operations of the joint venture plus any expenses that the individual venturer has incurred from its interest in the joint venture; and (*c*) *jointly controlled entities,* for which each venturer recognizes its interest in the joint venture using proportionate consolidation or the equity method.

Under the proportionate consolidation method, each venturer recognizes a pro rata share of the assets, liabilities, income, and expenses of the jointly controlled entity. This approach is illustrated in the JTV example. In this case, assets of \$250,000 (\$500,000 $\times$ .50) and liabilities of \$100,000 (\$200,000 $\times$ .50) are added to the present assets and liabilities of each investor-venturer. The proportionate share of the assets and liabilities should be added to similar items in the investor's financial statements. The same pro rata method is also used for the joint venture's revenue and expenses. A comparison of the equity method and the proportionate consolidation for venturer A Company is presented in Figure 15–3.

Joint ventures provide flexibility to their investors as to management, operations, and the division of profits or losses. However, companies need to be aware of **FASB Interpretation No. 46,** "Consolidation of Variable Interest Entities: An Interpretation of ARB No. 51" (FIN 46), which was issued in 2003. In situations in which an investor does not have a majority stock ownership, there may exist contractual or other agreements specifying allocation of the entity's profits or losses. **FIN 46** specifies that consolidation of a variable interest entity (VIE) is required if an investor will absorb a majority of the entity's expected losses or receive a majority of the entity's expected return. Therefore, an equity investor not having a controlling financial interest may be determined to be the primary beneficiary of the VIE and thus be required to fully consolidate that entity.

Real estate development is often carried out through joint ventures. Accounting for noncontrolling interests in real estate joint ventures is guided by the AICPA's **Statement of Position 78-9,** "Accounting for Investments in Real Estate Ventures" (SOP 78-9). **SOP 78-9** recommends that the equity method be used to account for noncontrolling investments in corporate or noncorporate real estate ventures.

A joint venture also makes additional footnote disclosures to present additional details about the joint venture's formation and operation, the methods of accounting it uses, and a summary of its financial position and earnings.

Another form of business association is the syndicate. Syndicates are usually short term and have a defined single purpose, such as developing a financing proposal for a corporation. Syndicates are typically very informal; nevertheless, the legal relationships between the parties should be clearly specified before beginning the project.

**FIGURE 15–3**
**Comparative Balance Sheets for Reporting a Joint Venture**

| | **Balance Sheets of A Company** | | |
|---|---|---|---|
| | **Before Joint Venture** | **Equity Method** | **Proportionate Consolidation** |
| Current Assets | \$250 | \$100 | \$100 |
| Property, Plant, and Equipment | 400 | 400 | 650 |
| Investment in Joint Venture | -0- | 150 | -0- |
| Total | \$650 | \$650 | \$750 |
| Current Liabilities | \$100 | \$100 | \$100 |
| Long-Term Debt | 300 | 300 | 400 |
| Stockholders' Equity | 250 | 250 | 250 |
| Total | \$650 | \$650 | \$750 |

| Questions | Q15-1 | Why is the partnership form of business organization sometimes preferred over the corporate or sole proprietorship forms? |
|---|---|---|
| | Q15-2 | What is the Uniform Partnership Act of 1997 and what is its relevance to partnership accounting? |
| | Q15-3 | What types of items are typically included in the partnership agreement? |
| | Q15-4 | Define the following features of a partnership: (*a*) separate business entity, (*b*) agency relationship, and (*c*) partner's joint and several liability. |
| | Q15-5 | Under what circumstances would a partner's capital account have a debit, or deficiency, balance? How is the deficiency usually eliminated? |
| | Q15-6 | A partnership agreement specifies that profits will be shared in the ratio of 4:6:5. What percentage of profits will each partner receive? Allocate a profit of $60,000 to each of the three partners. |
| | Q15-7 | The Good-Nite partnership agreement includes a profit distribution provision for interest on capital balances. Unfortunately, the provision does not state the specific capital balance to be used in computing the profit share. What choices of capital balances are available to the partners? What is the preferred capital balance to be used in an interest allocation? Why? |
| | Q15-8 | Are salaries to partners a partnership expense? Why or why not? |
| | Q15-9 | Does a partner leaving the partnership require the partnership to dissolve and wind up its business? Explain how the partnership may purchase the dissociated partner's interest in the partnership. |
| | Q15-10 | What is the book value of a partnership? Does book value also represent the partnership's market value? |
| | Q15-11 | Present the arguments for and against the bonus method of recognizing the admission of a new partner. |
| | Q15-12 | In which cases of admission of a new partner does the new partner's capital credit equal the investment made? In which cases of admission of a new partner is the new partner's capital credit less than or more than the amount of the investment? |
| | Q15-13 | Aabel, a partner in the ABC Partnership, receives a bonus of 15 percent of income. If income for the period is $20,000, what is Aabel's bonus, assuming the bonus is computed as a percentage of income before the bonus? What is the bonus if it is computed as a percentage of income *after* deducting the bonus? |
| | Q15-14 | Caine, a new partner in the ABC Partnership, has invested $12,000 for a one-third interest in a partnership with a prior capital of $21,000. What is the ABC Partnership's implied fair value? If the partners agree to recognize goodwill for the difference between the book value and fair value, present the entries the ABC Partnership should make upon Caine's admission. |
| | Q15-15A | S. Horton contributes assets with a book value of $5,000 to a partnership. The assets have a market value of $10,000 and a remaining liability of $2,000 that the partnership assumes. If the liability is shared equally with the other three partners, what is the basis of Horton's contribution for tax purposes? For GAAP purposes? |
| | Q15-16B | What is a joint venture? How are corporate joint ventures accounted for on the books of the investor companies? |

## Cases

### C15-1  Partnership Agreement

*Judgment*

J. Nitty and G. Gritty are considering the formation of a partnership to operate a crafts and hobbies store. They have come to you to obtain information about the basic elements of a partnership agreement. Partnership agreements usually specify an income and loss–sharing ratio. The agreements may also provide for such additional income and loss–sharing features as salaries, bonuses, and interest allowances on invested capital.

#### Required

*a.* Discuss why a partnership agreement may need features in addition to the income and loss–sharing ratio.

b. Discuss the arguments in favor of recording salary and bonus allowances to partners as expenses included in computing net income.

c. What are the arguments against recording salary and bonus allowances to partners as partnership expenses?

d. Some partnership agreements contain a provision for interest on invested capital in distributing income to the individual partners. List the additional provisions that should be included in the partnership agreement so the interest amounts can be computed.

**C15-2** **Comparisons of Bonus, Goodwill, and Asset Revaluation Methods**

*Communication*

Bill, George, and Anne are partners in the BGA Partnership. A difference of opinion exists among the partners as to how to account for the admission of Newt, a new partner. The three present partners have the following positions:

> Bill wants to use the bonus method.
>
> George believes the goodwill method is best.
>
> Anne wants to revalue the existing tangible assets.

You have been called in to advise the three partners.

### Required

Prepare a memo discussing the three different methods of accounting for the admission of a new partner, including consideration of the effects on partnership capital in the year Newt is admitted, and the effects on the capital balances in future years.

**C15-3** **Uniform Partnership Act Issues**

(*Note:* Obtain a copy of the Uniform Partnership Act of 1997 [UPA 1997] for answering this case question. The UPA 1997 can be obtained from your university's general library, law library, or the Internet.)

*Research*

You are in a group that is considering forming a partnership for the purpose of purchasing a coffee shop located near your campus. The coffee shop offers freshly brewed coffee and rolls in the morning and soup and sandwiches the remainder of the day. During your preliminary discussions, several issues have emerged for which your group needs additional information.

### Required

Research and provide a written summary for the following:

a. Does, in fact, every partner have the right to serve as an agent of the partnership and bind the partnership by that individual partner's actions in carrying out the partnership business?

b. If a new partner is admitted after the partnership operates for a time, what is the new partner's liability for partnership obligations arising before his or her admission? What is the new partner's liability for obligations of the partnership incurred after his or her admission?

c. Should all partners be able to examine the accounting records (the partnership's books) at any time?

d. What happens if the term of the partnership is set at one year and the partners decide to continue doing business? Is a new partnership agreement necessary at that time?

e. What happens if an individual partner wishes to leave the partnership? Can that person just announce to the other partners that he or she no longer wishes to be in the partnership and will not be liable for any future partnership obligations? What are the rights of the other partners in this matter?

f. What items do you believe should be in the partnership agreement that would be prepared before actually agreeing to form the partnership?

**C15-4** **Reviewing the Annual Report of a Limited Partnership**

Although few partnerships provide publicly available financial reports, some limited partnerships do provide their financial reports. These limited partnerships usually have a general partner or other major affiliate that has offered securities to the public, such as those offered by a real estate investment trust.

Using the SEC's EDGAR (www.sec.gov), obtain the annual report for Riverside Park Associates LP for the most recent year available. The form the entity filed is a 10-KSB, which is the small business annual filing.

### Required

Answer each of the following questions from the information you obtain by analyzing the annual report of Riverside Park Associates LP.

a. Describe the business in which the limited partnership is engaged.

b. Identify the general partner of the limited partnership and describe the business relationships between the general partner and its major affiliates.

c. What percentage of the total number of outstanding units is owned by the general partner and its affiliates at the end of the year?

d. What amounts are presented for the net balances in the partners' capital accounts as presented on the year-end balance sheet? Discuss how a partnership can have deficit balances for its partnership capital.

e. Who provides management and administrative services for the limited partnership? What is the total amount of these charges for the year of your 10-KSB and the prior year? How much of these costs are charged in the determination of partnership income/loss? Where are the other costs charged to? Explain.

f. What is the profit allocation ratio between the general partner and the limited partners?

### C15-5  Defining Partners' Authority

*Understanding*

Adam, Bob, and Cathy are planning to form a partnership to create a business that will retail cell phones in a new shopping center just completed in their city. They have been able to reach agreement on many issues, but Cathy is still concerned that Adam might become a little irresponsible and use his position as a partner, and the partnership's name, in business transactions that Cathy would not approve of for the partnership. Cathy feels that Adam has superb marketing skills that will benefit the business, but she wonders what Adam may do in regard to transactions with third parties on behalf of the partnership.

#### Required

Prepare a memo to Cathy discussing the rights of each partner to engage in transactions on behalf of the partnership and how a partnership can restrict a partner's authority to engage in specific types of transactions.

### C15-6  Preferences for Using GAAP for Partnership Accounting

*Understanding*

You are providing accounting services for the JR Company partnership. The two partners, Jason and Richard, are thinking of adding a third partner to their business, and they have several questions regarding the use of generally accepted accounting principles (GAAP) for their partnership.

#### Required

Prepare a memo for the partners addressing each of the following questions from the partners.

a. Why are salaries to partners not shown on the partnership's Statement of Income prepared using GAAP?

b. Why should the partnership use GAAP to account for the admission of a new partner? Why is it not preferable for the partnership to recognize holding gains on its long-lived assets at the time of admitting the third partner? (The two partners argue that recognizing these gains now would allocate them to the partners who were growing the business prior to the admission of a new partner.)

c. Why should the partners and the partnership go through all the work of fully analyzing all the partnership's liabilities to ensure that there are no unrecognized liabilities at the time the new partner is admitted? (The two partners feel this is an unnecessary cost because if a supplier is not paid, then the supplier will simply send another bill in the future.)

### C15-7  Comparison of UPA 1997 with UPA 1914

*Understanding*

One of the partners of the partnership for which you are the accountant asks you to compare the major features of the Revised Uniform Partnership Act of 1997 with those of the original Uniform Partnership Act of 1914.

#### Required

Using an Internet search engine or other database, do some research and provide a two- to three-page report comparing UPA 1997 and UPA 1914. Consider the following:

a. Determine whether the state in which your college or university is located has adopted the UPA 1997. (*Hint:* The National Conference of Commissioners on Uniform State Laws maintains a Web site with a few facts about the UPA 1997.)

b. Locate two articles that compare or contrast the UPA 1997 with the UPA 1914 and summarize the major differences in the two acts as discussed in the articles.

# Exercises

## E15-1 Multiple-Choice on Initial Investment [AICPA Adapted]

Select the correct answer for each of the following questions.

1. On May 1, 20X1, Cathy and Mort formed a partnership and agreed to share profits and losses in the ratio of 3:7, respectively. Cathy contributed a parcel of land that cost her $10,000. Mort contributed $40,000 cash. The land was sold for $18,000 immediately after formation of the partnership. What amount should be recorded in Cathy's capital account on formation of the partnership?

   a. $18,000.

   b. $17,400.

   c. $15,000.

   d. $10,000.

2. On July 1, 20X1, James and Short formed a partnership. James contributed cash. Short, previously a sole proprietor, contributed property other than cash, including realty subject to a mortgage, which the partnership assumed. Short's capital account at July 1, 20X1, should be recorded at:

   a. Short's book value of the property at July 1, 20X1.

   b. Short's book value of the property less the mortgage payable at July 1, 20X1.

   c. The fair value of the property less the mortgage payable at July 1, 20X1.

   d. The fair value of the property at July 1, 20X1.

3. A partnership is formed by two individuals who were previously sole proprietors. Property other than cash that is part of the initial investment in the partnership is recorded for financial accounting purposes at the:

   a. Proprietors' book values or the fair value of the property at the date of the investment, whichever is higher.

   b. Proprietors' book values or the fair value of the property at the date of the investment, whichever is lower.

   c. Proprietors' book values of the property at the date of the investment.

   d. Fair value of the property at the date of the investment.

4. Mutt and Jeff formed a partnership on April 1 and contributed the following assets:

   |  | Mutt | Jeff |
   |---|---|---|
   | Cash | $150,000 | $ 50,000 |
   | Land |  | 310,000 |

   The land was subject to a $30,000 mortgage, which the partnership assumed. Under the partnership agreement, Mutt and Jeff will share profit and loss in the ratio of one-third and two-thirds, respectively. Jeff's capital account at April 1 should be:

   a. $300,000.

   b. $330,000.

   c. $340,000.

   d. $360,000.

5. On July 1, Mabel and Pierre formed a partnership, agreeing to share profits and losses in the ratio of 4:6, respectively. Mabel contributed a parcel of land that cost her $25,000. Pierre contributed $50,000 cash. The land was sold for $50,000 on July 1, four hours after formation of the partnership. How much should be recorded in Mabel's capital account on the partnership formation?

   a. $10,000.

   b. $20,000.

   c. $25,000.

   d. $50,000.

**E15-2** **Division of Income—Multiple Bases**

The partnership agreement of Angela and Dawn has the following provisions:

1. The partners are to earn 10 percent on the average capital.

2. Angela and Dawn are to earn salaries of $25,000 and $15,000, respectively.

3. Any remaining income or loss is to be divided between Angela and Dawn using a 70:30 ratio.

Angela's average capital is $50,000 and Dawn's is $30,000.

### Required

Prepare an income distribution schedule assuming the income of the partnership is (*a*) $80,000, and (*b*) $20,000. If no partnership agreement exists, what does the UPA 1997 prescribe as the profit or loss distribution percentages?

**E15-3** **Division of Income—Interest on Capital Balances**

Left and Right are partners. Their capital accounts during 20X1 were as follows:

| | Left, Capital | | | | Right, Capital | |
|---|---|---|---|---|---|---|
| 8/23 | 6,000 | 1/1 | 30,000 | 3/5 | 9,000 | 1/1 | 50,000 |
| | | 4/3 | 8,000 | | | 7/6 | 7,000 |
| | | 10/31 | 6,000 | | | 10/7 | 5,000 |

Partnership net income is $50,000 for the year. The partnership agreement provides for the division of income as follows:

1. Each partner is to be credited 8 percent interest on his or her average capital.

2. Any remaining income or loss is to be divided equally.

### Required

Prepare an income distribution schedule.

**E15-4** **Distribution of Partnership Income and Preparation of a Statement of Partners' Capital**

The income statement for the Apple-Jack Partnership for the year ended December 31, 20X5, follows:

---

**APPLE-JACK PARTNERSHIP**
**Income Statement**
**For the Year Ended December 31, 20X5**

| | |
|---|---|
| Net Sales | $300,000 |
| Cost of Goods Sold | (190,000) |
| Gross Margin | $110,000 |
| Operating Expenses | (30,000) |
| Net Income | $ 80,000 |

---

### Additional Information for 20X5

1. Apple began the year with a capital balance of $40,800.

2. Jack began the year with a capital balance of $112,000.

3. On April 1, Apple invested an additional $15,000 into the partnership.

4. On August 1, Jack invested an additional $20,000 into the partnership.

5. Throughout 20X5, each partner withdrew $400 per week in anticipation of partnership net income. The partners agreed that these withdrawals are not to be included in the computation of average capital balances for purposes of income distributions.

Apple and Jack have agreed to distribute partnership net income according to the following plan:

|  | Apple | Jack |
|---|---|---|
| 1. Interest on average capital balances | 6% | 6% |
| 2. Bonus on net income before the bonus but after interest on average capital balances | 10% | |
| 3. Salaries | $25,000 | $30,000 |
| 4. Residual (if positive) | 70% | 30% |
| Residual (if negative) | 50% | 50% |

### Required

*a.* Prepare a schedule that discloses the distribution of partnership net income for 20X5. Show supporting computations in good form. Round to the nearest dollar.

*b.* Prepare the statement of partners' capital at December 31, 20X5.

*c.* How would your answer to part *a* change if all of the provisions of the income distribution plan were the same except that the salaries were $30,000 to Apple and $35,000 to Jack?

**E15-5   Matching Partnership Terms with Their Descriptions**
### Required
Match the descriptions of terms on the left with the terms on the right. A term may be used once, more than once, or not at all.

| Descriptions of Terms | Terms |
|---|---|
| 1. Item that occurs when the new partner's investment exceeds the new partner's capital credit. | A. General partner |
| 2. Partner who cannot actively participate in the management of the partnership. | B. Note payable to a partner |
| 3. The allocation of partnership profits and losses when nothing is stated in the partnership agreement. | C. Recognition of neither bonus nor goodwill |
| 4. Item that occurs when the new partner's investment equals the new partner's capital credit and no change occurs in the old partners' capital balances. | D. Drawing account<br>E. Limited partner<br>F. Bonus to old partners |
| 5. Cost not deducted to determine the partnership's net income for the period. | G. Interest on capital accounts |
| 6. Partner who actively participates in the partnership management and who is personally liable for the partnership's debts. | H. Partnership income or loss shared equally |
| 7. Item that occurs when the new partner's capital credit exceeds the new partner's investment and no change occurs in the old partners' capital balances. | I. New partner's goodwill recognized<br>J. Old partners' goodwill recognized |
| 8. Account that increases when a partner takes assets out of the partnership in anticipation of partnership net income. | K. Partnership agreement<br>L. Bonus to new partner<br>M. Capital account |
| 9. Account that increases for the fair value of noncash assets invested by a partner. | |
| 10. Related-party transaction that must be disclosed in the notes to the financial statements. | |
| 11. Item that occurs when the new partner's investment equals the new partner's capital credit and an increase occurs in the old partners' capital balances. | |
| 12. Item that occurs when the new partner's capital credit exceeds the new partner's investment and a decrease occurs in the old partners' capital balances. | |
| 13. Recognition of an intangible asset upon a new partner's admission to the partnership that results in increases in the old partners' capital balances. | |
| 14. Account closed to the capital account at year-end. | |
| 15. Deduction of interest expense on this payable to determine the partnership's net income. | |

**E15-6    Admission of a Partner**

In the GMP partnership (to which Elan seeks admittance), the capital balances of Mary, Gene, and Pat, who share income in the ratio of 6:3:1, are:

| | |
|---|---|
| Mary | $240,000 |
| Gene | 120,000 |
| Pat | 40,000 |

### Required

a. If no goodwill or bonus is recorded, how much must Elan invest for a one-third interest?

b. Prepare journal entries for the admission of Elan if she invests $80,000 for a one-fifth interest and goodwill is recorded.

c. Prepare journal entries for the admission of Elan if she invests $200,000 for a 20 percent interest. Total capital will be $600,000.

d. Elan is concerned that she may be held liable for the partnership liabilities existing on the day she is admitted to the GMP partnership. She found nothing in the partnership agreement on this item. What does the UPA 1997 state with regard to the liability of a new partner for partnership obligations incurred prior to admission?

**E15-7    Admission of a Partner**

Pam and John are partners in the PJ's partnership, having capital balances of $120,000 and $40,000, respectively, and share income in a ratio of 3:1. Gerry is to be admitted into the partnership with a 20 percent interest in the business.

### Required

For each of the following independent situations, first, record Gerry's admission into the partnership; and second, specify and briefly explain why the accounting method used in that situation is GAAP or non-GAAP.

a. Gerry invests $50,000, and goodwill is to be recorded.

b. Gerry invests $50,000. Total capital is to be $210,000.

c. Gerry purchases the 20 percent interest by directly paying Pam $50,000. Gerry is assigned 20 percent interest in the partnership solely from Pam's capital account.

d. Gerry invests $35,000. Total capital is to be $195,000.

e. Gerry invests $35,000, and goodwill is to be recorded.

f. Gerry invests $35,000. During the valuation process made as part of admitting the new partner, it is determined that the partnership's inventory is overvalued by $20,000 because of obsolescence. PJ's partnership uses the lower-of-cost-or-market value method for inventories.

**E15-8    Multiple-Choice Questions on the Admission of a Partner**

Select the correct answer for each of the following questions.

*Note:* The following balance sheet is for the partnership of Alex, Betty, and Claire in questions 1 and 2:

| | |
|---|---|
| Cash | $ 20,000 |
| Other Assets | 180,000 |
| | $200,000 |
| | |
| Liabilities | $ 50,000 |
| Alex, Capital (40%) | 37,000 |
| Betty, Capital (40%) | 65,000 |
| Claire, Capital (20%) | 48,000 |
| Total Liabilities and Capital | $200,000 |

(*Note:* Figures shown parenthetically reflect agreed profit and loss–sharing percentages.)

1. If the assets are fairly valued on this balance sheet and the partnership wishes to admit Denise as a new one-sixth-interest partner without recording goodwill or bonus, Denise should contribute cash or other assets of:

a. $40,000.

b. $36,000.

    *c.* $33,333.

    *d.* $30,000.

2. If assets on the initial balance sheet are fairly valued, Alex and Betty give their consent, and Denise pays Claire $51,000 for her interest, the revised capital balances of the partners would be:

    *a.* Alex, $38,000; Betty, $66,500; Denise, $51,000.

    *b.* Alex, $38,500; Betty, $66,500; Denise, $48,000.

    *c.* Alex, $37,000; Betty, $65,000; Denise, $51,000.

    *d.* Alex, $37,000; Betty, $65,000; Denise, $48,000.

3. On December 31, 20X4, Alan and Dave are partners with capital balances of $80,000 and $40,000, and they share profit and losses in the ratio of 2:1, respectively. On this date Scott invests $36,000 cash for a one-fifth interest in the capital and profit of the new partnership. The partners agree that the implied partnership goodwill is to be recorded simultaneously with the admission of Scott. The total implied goodwill of the firm is:

    *a.* $4,800.

    *b.* $6,000.

    *c.* $24,000.

    *d.* $30,000.

4. Boris and Richard are partners who share profits and losses in the ratio of 6:4. On May 1, 20X9, their respective capital accounts were as follows:

| | |
|---|---|
| Boris | $60,000 |
| Richard | 50,000 |

On that date, Lisa was admitted as a partner with a one-third interest in capital and profits for an investment of $40,000. The new partnership began with a total capital of $150,000. Immediately after Lisa's admission, Boris's capital should be:

    *a.* $50,000.

    *b.* $54,000.

    *c.* $56,667.

    *d.* $60,000.

5. At December 31, Rod and Sheri are partners with capital balances of $40,000 and $20,000, and they share profits and losses in the ratio of 2:1, respectively. On this date, Pete invests $17,000 in cash for a one-fifth interest in the capital and profit of the new partnership. Assuming that the bonus method is used, how much should be credited to Pete's capital account on December 31?

    *a.* $12,000.

    *b.* $15,000.

    *c.* $15,400.

    *d.* $17,000.

6. The capital accounts of the partnership of Ella, Nick, and Brandon follow with their respective profit and loss ratios:

| | | |
|---|---|---|
| Ella | $139,000 | (.500) |
| Nick | 209,000 | (.333) |
| Brandon | 96,000 | (.167) |

Tony was admitted to the partnership when he purchased directly, for $132,000, a proportionate interest from Ella and Nick in the net assets and profits of the partnership. As a result, Tony acquired a one-fifth interest in the net assets and profits of the firm. Assuming that implied goodwill is not to be recorded, what is the combined gain realized by Ella and Nick upon the sale of a portion of their interests in the partnership to Tony?

    *a.* $0.

    *b.* $43,200.

    *c.* $62,400.

    *d.* $82,000.

7. Fred and Ralph are partners who share profits and losses in the ratio of 7:3, respectively. Their respective capital accounts are as follows:

| | |
|---|---|
| Fred | $35,000 |
| Ralph | 30,000 |

They agreed to admit Lute as a partner with a one-third interest in the capital and profits and losses, upon an investment of $25,000. The new partnership will begin with total capital of $90,000. Immediately after Lute's admission, what are the capital balances of Fred, Ralph, and Lute, respectively?

a. $30,000, $30,000, $30,000.

b. $31,500, $28,500, $30,000.

c. $31,667, $28,333, $30,000.

d. $35,000, $30,000, $25,000.

8. If $A$ is the total capital of a partnership before the admission of a new partner, $B$ is the total capital of the partnership after the investment of a new partner, $C$ is the amount of the new partner's investment, and $D$ is the amount of capital credit to the new partner, then there is:

a. A bonus to the new partner if $B = A + C$ and $D < C$.

b. Goodwill to the old partners if $B > (A + C)$ and $D = C$.

c. Neither bonus nor goodwill if $B = A - C$ and $D > C$.

d. Goodwill to the new partner if $B > (A + C)$ and $D < C$.

### E15-9 Withdrawal of a Partner

In the LMK partnership, Luis's capital is $40,000, Marty's is $50,000, and Karl's is $30,000. They share income in a 4:1:1 ratio, respectively. Karl is retiring from the partnership.

#### Required

Prepare journal entries to record Karl's withdrawal according to each of the following independent assumptions:

a. Karl is paid $38,000, and no goodwill is recorded.

b. Karl is paid $42,000, and only his share of the goodwill is recorded.

c. Karl is paid $35,000, and all implied goodwill is recorded.

d. Prepare a one-paragraph note summarizing the guidance the UPA 1997 offers on computing the buyout price for a partner who is retiring from the partnership.

### E15-10 Retirement of a Partner

On January 1, 20X1, Eddy decides to retire from the partnership of Cobb, Davis, and Eddy. The partners share profits and losses in the ratio of 3:2:1, respectively. The following condensed balance sheets present the account balances immediately before and, for six independent cases, after Eddy's retirement.

| | Balances prior to Eddy's Retirement | Balances after Eddy's Retirement | | | | | |
|---|---|---|---|---|---|---|---|
| **Accounts** | | **Case 1** | **Case 2** | **Case 3** | **Case 4** | **Case 5** | **Case 6** |
| Assets: | | | | | | | |
| Cash | $ 90,000 | $ 10,000 | $ 16,000 | $ 25,000 | $ 16,000 | $ 50,000 | $ 90,000 |
| Other Assets | 200,000 | 200,000 | 200,000 | 200,000 | 200,000 | 220,000 | 200,000 |
| Goodwill | 10,000 | 10,000 | 14,000 | 10,000 | 34,000 | 10,000 | 10,000 |
| Total Assets | $300,000 | $220,000 | $230,000 | $235,000 | $250,000 | $280,000 | $300,000 |
| Liabilities and Capital: | | | | | | | |
| Liabilities | $ 60,000 | $ 60,000 | $ 60,000 | $ 60,000 | $ 60,000 | $ 60,000 | $ 60,000 |
| Cobb, Capital | 80,000 | 74,000 | 80,000 | 83,000 | 92,000 | 110,000 | 80,000 |
| Davis, Capital | 90,000 | 86,000 | 90,000 | 92,000 | 98,000 | 110,000 | 160,000 |
| Eddy, Capital | 70,000 | -0- | -0- | -0- | -0- | -0- | -0- |
| Total Liabilities and Capital | $300,000 | $220,000 | $230,000 | $235,000 | $250,000 | $280,000 | $300,000 |

### Required
Prepare the necessary journal entries to record Eddy's retirement from the partnership for each of the six independent cases.

## Problems

### P15-11 Admission of a Partner

Debra and Merina sell electronic equipment and supplies through their partnership. They wish to expand their computer lines and decide to admit Wayne to the partnership. Debra's capital is $200,000, Merina's capital is $160,000, and they share income in a ratio of 3:2, respectively.

### Required

Record Wayne's admission for each of the following independent situations:

a. Wayne directly purchases half of Merina's investment in the partnership for $90,000.

b. Wayne invests the amount needed to give him a one-third interest in the capital of the partnership if no goodwill or bonus is recorded.

c. Wayne invests $110,000 for a one-fourth interest. Goodwill is to be recorded.

d. Debra and Merina agree that some of the inventory is obsolete. The inventory account is decreased before Wayne is admitted. Wayne invests $100,000 for a one-fourth interest.

e. Wayne directly purchases a one-fourth interest by paying Debra $80,000 and Merina $60,000. The land account is increased before Wayne is admitted.

f. Wayne invests $80,000 for a one-fifth interest in the total capital of $440,000.

g. Wayne invests $100,000 for a one-fifth interest. Goodwill is to be recorded.

### P15-12 Division of Income

C. Eastwood, A. North, and M. West are manufacturers' representatives in the architecture business. Their capital accounts in the ENW partnership for 20X1 were as follows:

| C. Eastwood, Capital | | | | A. North, Capital | | | | M. West, Capital | | | |
|---|---|---|---|---|---|---|---|---|---|---|---|
| 9/1 | 8,000 | 1/1 | 30,000 | 3/1 | 9,000 | 1/1 | 40,000 | 8/1 | 12,000 | 1/1 | 50,000 |
| | | 5/1 | 6,000 | | | 7/1 | 5,000 | | | 4/1 | 7,000 |
| | | | | | | 9/1 | 4,000 | | | 6/1 | 3,000 |

### Required

For each of the following independent income-sharing agreements, prepare an income distribution schedule.

a. Salaries are $15,000 to Eastwood, $20,000 to North, and $18,000 to West. Eastwood receives a bonus of 5 percent of net income after deducting his bonus. Interest is 10 percent of ending capital balances. Eastwood, North, and West divide any remainder in a 3:3:4 ratio, respectively. Net income was $78,960.

b. Interest is 10 percent of weighted-average capital balances. Salaries are $24,000 to Eastwood, $21,000 to North, and $25,000 to West. North receives a bonus of 10 percent of net income after deducting the bonus and her salary. Any remainder is divided equally. Net income was $68,080.

c. West receives a bonus of 20 percent of net income after deducting the bonus and the salaries. Salaries are $21,000 to Eastwood, $18,000 to North, and $15,000 to West. Interest is 10 percent of beginning capital balances. Eastwood, North, and West divide any remainder in an 8:7:5 ratio, respectively. Net income was $92,940.

### P15-13 Determining a New Partner's Investment Cost

The following condensed balance sheet is presented for the partnership of Der, Egan, and Oprins, who share profits and losses in the ratio of 4:3:3, respectively.

| | | | |
|---|---|---|---|
| Cash | $ 40,000 | Accounts Payable | $150,000 |
| Other Assets | 710,000 | Der, Capital | 260,000 |
| | | Egan, Capital | 180,000 |
| | | Oprins, Capital | 160,000 |
| Total Assets | $750,000 | Total Liabilities and Capital | $750,000 |

Assume that the partnership decides to admit Snider as a new partner with a one-fourth interest.

### Required

For each of the following independent cases, determine the amount that Snider must contribute in cash or other assets.

a. No goodwill or bonus is to be recorded.

b. Goodwill of $30,000 is to be recorded and allocated to the prior partners.

c. A bonus of $24,000 is to be paid by Snider and allocated to the prior partners.

d. The prior partners, Der, Egan, and Oprins, agree to give Snider $10,000 of goodwill upon admission to the partnership.

e. Other assets are revalued for an increase of $20,000, and goodwill of $40,000 is recognized and allocated to the prior partners at the time of the admission of Snider.

f. The partners agree that total resulting capital should be $820,000 and no goodwill should be recognized.

g. Other assets are revalued down by $20,000 and a bonus of $40,000 is paid to Snider at the time of admission.

**P15-14**  **Division of Income**

Champion Play Company is a partnership that sells sporting goods. The partnership agreement provides for 10 percent interest on invested capital, salaries of $24,000 to Luc and $28,000 to Dennis, and a bonus for Luc. The 20X3 capital accounts were as follows:

| Luc, Capital | | | | | Dennis, Capital | | | |
|---|---|---|---|---|---|---|---|---|
| 8/1 | 15,000 | 1/1 | 50,000 | | 7/1 | 10,000 | 1/1 | 70,000 |
| | | 4/1 | 5,000 | | | | 9/1 | 22,500 |

### Required

For each of the following independent situations, prepare an income distribution schedule.

a. Interest is based on weighted-average capital balances. The bonus is 5 percent and is calculated on net income after deducting the bonus. In 20X3, net income was $64,260. Any remainder is divided between Luc and Dennis in a 3:2 ratio, respectively.

b. Interest is based on ending capital balances after deducting salaries, which the partners normally withdraw during the year. The bonus is 8 percent and is calculated on net income after deducting the bonus and salaries. Net income was $108,700. Any remainder is divided equally.

c. Interest is based on beginning capital balances. The bonus is 12.5 percent and is calculated on net income after deducting the bonus. Net income was $76,950. Any remainder is divided between Luc and Dennis in a 4:2 ratio, respectively.

**P15-15**  **Withdrawal of a Partner under Various Alternatives**

The partnership of Ace, Jack, and Spade has been in business for 25 years. On December 31, 20X5, Spade decided to retire from the partnership. The partnership balance sheet reported the following capital balances for each partner at December 31, 20X5:

| | |
|---|---|
| Ace, Capital | $150,000 |
| Jack, Capital | 200,000 |
| Spade, Capital | 120,000 |

The partners allocate partnership income and loss in the ratio 20:30:50.

### Required

Record Spade's withdrawal under each of the following independent situations.

a. Jack acquired Spade's capital interest for $150,000 in a personal transaction. Partnership assets were not revalued, and partnership goodwill was not recognized.

b. Assume the same facts as in part a except that partnership goodwill applicable to the entire business was recognized by the partnership.

c. Spade received $180,000 of partnership cash upon retirement. Capital of the partnership after Spade's retirement was $290,000.

d. Spade received $60,000 of cash and partnership land with a fair value of $120,000. The carrying amount of the land on the partnership books was $100,000. Capital of the partnership after Spade's retirement was $310,000.

e. Spade received $150,000 of partnership cash upon retirement. The partnership recorded the portion of goodwill attributable to Spade.

f. Assume the same facts as in part *e* except that partnership goodwill attributable to all the partners was recorded.

g. Because of limited cash in the partnership, Spade received land with a fair value of $100,000 and a note payable for $50,000. The carrying amount of the land on the partnership books was $60,000. Capital of the partnership after Spade's retirement was $360,000.

**P15-16 Multiple-Choice Questions—Initial Investments, Division of Income, Admission and Retirement of a Partner [AICPA Adapted]**

Select the correct answer for each of the following questions.

1. When property other than cash is invested in a partnership, at what amount should the noncash property be credited to the contributing partner's capital account?

   a. Contributing partner's tax basis.

   b. Contributing partner's original cost.

   c. Assessed valuation for property tax purposes.

   d. Fair value at the date of contribution.

2. William and Martha drafted a partnership agreement that lists the following assets contributed at the partnership's formation:

|  | Contributed by | |
|---|---|---|
|  | **William** | **Martha** |
| Cash | $20,000 | $30,000 |
| Inventory |  | 15,000 |
| Building |  | 40,000 |
| Furniture and Equipment | 15,000 |  |

The building is subject to a $10,000 mortgage, which the partnership has assumed. The partnership agreement also specifies that profits and losses are to be distributed evenly. What amounts should be recorded as capital for William and Martha at the formation of the partnership?

|  | **William** | **Martha** |
|---|---|---|
| a. | $35,000 | $85,000 |
| b. | $35,000 | $75,000 |
| c. | $55,000 | $55,000 |
| d. | $60,000 | $60,000 |

3. Smith and Duncan are partners with capital balances of $60,000 and $20,000, respectively. Profits and losses are divided in the ratio of 60:40. Smith and Duncan decided to form a new partnership with Johnson, who invested land valued at $15,000 for a 20 percent capital interest in the new partnership. Johnson's cost of the land was $12,000. The partnership elected to use the bonus method to record the admission of Johnson into the partnership. Johnson's capital account should be credited for:

   a. $12,000.

   b. $15,000.

   c. $16,000.

   d. $19,000.

4. On April 30, 20X5, Apple, Blue, and Crown formed a partnership by combining their separate business proprietorships. Apple contributed $50,000 cash. Blue contributed property with a $36,000 carrying amount, a $40,000 original cost, and $80,000 fair value. The partnership

accepted responsibility for the $35,000 mortgage attached to the property. Crown contributed equipment with a $30,000 carrying amount, a $75,000 original cost, and $55,000 fair value. The partnership agreement specifies that profits and losses are to be shared equally but is silent regarding capital contributions. Which partner has the largest April 30, 20X5, capital account balance?

a. Apple.

b. Blue.

c. Crown.

d. All capital account balances are equal.

*Note:* The following information is for questions 5 and 6:

The Moon-Norbert Partnership was formed on January 2, 20X5. Under the partnership agreement, each partner has an equal initial capital balance accounted for under the goodwill method. Partnership net income or loss is allocated 60 percent to Moon and 40 percent to Norbert. To form the partnership, Moon originally contributed assets costing $30,000 with a fair value of $60,000 on January 2, 20X5, and Norbert contributed $20,000 in cash. Partners' drawings during 20X5 totaled $3,000 by Moon and $9,000 by Norbert. Moon-Norbert's net income for 20X5 was $25,000.

5. Norbert's initial capital balance in Moon-Norbert is:

a. $20,000.

b. $25,000.

c. $40,000.

d. $60,000.

6. Moon's share of Moon-Norbert's net income is:

a. $15,000.

b. $12,500.

c. $12,000.

d. $7,800.

7. In the Crowe-Dagwood partnership, Crowe and Dagwood had a capital ratio of 3:1 and a profit and loss ratio of 2:1. They used the bonus method to record Elman's admittance as a new partner. What ratio should be used to allocate, to Crowe and Dagwood, the excess of Elman's contribution over the amount credited to Elman's capital account?

a. Crowe and Dagwood's new relative capital ratio.

b. Crowe and Dagwood's new relative profit and loss ratio.

c. Crowe and Dagwood's old capital ratio.

d. Crowe and Dagwood's old profit and loss ratio.

8. Blue and Green formed a partnership in 20X4. The partnership agreement provides for annual salary allowances of $55,000 for Blue and $45,000 for Green. The partners share profits equally and losses in a 60:40 ratio. The partnership had earnings of $80,000 for 20X5 before any allowance to partners. What amount of these earnings should be credited to each partner's capital account?

|    | Blue | Green |
|----|------|-------|
| a. | $40,000 | $40,000 |
| b. | $43,000 | $37,000 |
| c. | $44,000 | $36,000 |
| d. | $45,000 | $35,000 |

9. When Jill retired from the partnership of Jill, Bill, and Hill, the final settlement of her interest exceeded her capital balance. Under the bonus method, the excess:

a. Was recorded as goodwill.

b. Was recorded as an expense.

c. Reduced the capital balances of Bill and Hill.

d. Had no effect on the capital balances of Bill and Hill.

**P15-17** **Partnership Formation, Operation, and Changes in Ownership**

The partnership of Jordan and O'Neal began business on January 1, 20X7. Each partner contributed the following assets (the noncash assets are stated at their fair values on January 1, 20X7):

|  | Jordan | O'Neal |
|---|---|---|
| Cash | $ 60,000 | $ 50,000 |
| Inventories | 80,000 | -0- |
| Land | -0- | 130,000 |
| Equipment | 100,000 | -0- |

The land was subject to a $50,000 mortgage, which the partnership assumed on January 1, 20X7. The equipment was subject to an installment note payable that had an unpaid principal amount of $20,000 on January 1, 20X7. The partnership also assumed this note payable. Jordan and O'Neal agreed to share partnership income and losses in the following manner:

|  | Jordan | O'Neal |
|---|---|---|
| Interest on beginning capital balances | 3% | 3% |
| Salaries | $12,000 | $12,000 |
| Remainder | 60% | 40% |

During 20X7, the following events occurred:

1. Inventory was acquired at a cost of $30,000. At December 31, 20X7, the partnership owed $6,000 to its suppliers.
2. Principal of $5,000 was paid on the mortgage. Interest expense incurred on the mortgage was $2,000, all of which was paid by December 31, 20X7.
3. Principal of $3,500 was paid on the installment note. Interest expense incurred on the installment note was $2,000, all of which was paid by December 31, 20X7.
4. Sales on account amounted to $155,000. At December 31, 20X7, customers owed the partnership $21,000.
5. Selling and general expenses, excluding depreciation, amounted to $34,000. At December 31, 20X7, the partnership owed $6,200 of accrued expenses. Depreciation expense was $6,000.
6. Each partner withdrew $200 each week in anticipation of partnership profits.
7. The partnership's inventory at December 31, 20X7, was $20,000.
8. The partners allocated the net income for 20X7 and closed the accounts.

### Additional Information

On January 1, 20X8, the partnership decided to admit Hill to the partnership. On that date, Hill invested $99,800 of cash into the partnership for a 20 percent capital interest. Total partnership capital after Hill was admitted totaled $450,000.

### Required

a. Prepare journal entries to record the formation of the partnership on January 1, 20X7, and to record the events that occurred during 20X7.

b. Prepare the income statement for the Jordan-O'Neal Partnership for the year ended December 31, 20X7.

c. Prepare a balance sheet for the Jordon-O'Neal Partnership at December 31, 20X7.

d. Prepare the journal entry for the admission of Hill on January 1, 20X8.

**P15-18A** **Initial Investments and Tax Bases [AICPA Adapted]**

The DELS partnership was formed by combining individual accounting practices on May 10, 20X1. The initial investments were as follows:

|  | Current Value | Tax Basis |
|---|---|---|
| Delaney: | | |
| Cash | $ 8,000 | $ 8,000 |
| Building | 60,000 | 32,000 |
| Mortgage payable, assumed by DELS | 36,000 | 36,000 |
| Engstrom: | | |
| Cash | 9,000 | 9,000 |
| Office furniture | 23,000 | 17,000 |
| Note payable, assumed by DELS | 10,000 | 10,000 |
| Lahey: | | |
| Cash | 12,000 | 12,000 |
| Computers and printers | 18,000 | 21,000 |
| Note payable, assumed by DELS | 15,000 | 15,000 |
| Simon: | | |
| Cash | 21,000 | 21,000 |
| Library (books and periodicals) | 7,000 | 5,000 |

### Required

*a.* Prepare the journal entry to record the initial investments, using GAAP accounting.

*b.* Calculate the tax basis of each partner's capital if Delaney, Engstrom, Lahey, and Simon agree to assume equal amounts for the payables.

**P15-19**  **Formation of a Partnership and Allocation of Profit and Loss**

Haskins and Sells formed a partnership on January 2, 20X3. Each had been a sole proprietor before forming their partnership.

### Part I

Each partner's contributions follow. The amounts under the cost column represent the amounts reported on the books of each sole proprietorship immediately before the formation of the partnership.

|  | Cost | Fair Value |
|---|---|---|
| Haskins: | | |
| Cash | $ 45,000 | $ 45,000 |
| Inventories (FIFO) | 48,000 | 49,000 |
| Trade accounts receivable | 40,000 | 40,000 |
| Allowance for uncollectible accounts | (1,500) | (2,000) |
| Building | 550,000 | 600,000 |
| Accumulated depreciation | (200,000) | (230,000) |
| Mortgage on building assumed by partnership | (175,000) | (175,000) |
| Sells: | | |
| Cash | $ 10,000 | $ 10,000 |
| Trade accounts receivable | 30,000 | 30,000 |
| Allowance for uncollectible accounts | (2,000) | (2,500) |
| Inventories (FIFO) | 15,000 | 13,500 |
| Note receivable due in 6 months | 50,000 | 50,000 |
| Temporary Investments | 100,000 | 81,500 |
| Customer lists | -0- | 60,000 |

### Required

Using the preceding information, prepare a classified balance sheet as of January 2, 20X3, for the Haskins and Sells Partnership. Assume that $25,000 of the mortgage is due in 20X3 and that the customer lists are accounted for as an intangible asset to be amortized over a five-year period.

### Part II

During 20X3, the Haskins and Sells Partnership reported the following information:

| | |
|---|---:|
| Revenues | $650,000 |
| Cost of goods sold | 320,000 |
| Selling, general, and administrative expenses | 70,000 |
| Salaries paid to each partner (not included in selling, general, and administrative expenses): | |
| Haskins | 90,000 |
| Sells | 70,000 |
| Bonus paid to Haskins (not included in selling, general, and adinistrative expenses) | 10% of net income |
| Withdrawals made during the year in addition to salaries: | |
| Haskins | 10,000 |
| Sells | 5,000 |
| Residual profit and loss–sharing ratio: | |
| Haskins | 20% |
| Sells | 80% |

### Required

a. Prepare an income statement for the Haskins and Sells Partnership for the year ended December 31, 20X3.

b. Prepare a schedule that shows how to allocate the partnership net income for 20X3.

c. What are the partners' capital balances that will appear on the December 31, 20X3, balance sheet?

d. Assume that the distribution of partnership net income remains the same (i.e., Haskins will continue to receive a 10 percent bonus and salaries will continue to be $90,000 and $70,000 to Haskins and Sells, respectively) and that the residual profit and loss–sharing ratio will continue to be 20:80. What would partnership net income have to be for each partner to receive the same amount of income?

*Supplemental Problems* for this chapter are available as part of the *Online Learning Center* on the textbook's Web site (URL: www.mhhe.com/baker8e).

# Partnerships: Liquidation

Because of the normal risks of doing business, the majority of partnerships begun in any one year fail within three years and require dissolution and liquidation. The ending of a partnership's business is often an emotional event for the partners. The partners may have had high expectations and invested a large amount of personal resources and time in the business. The end of the partnership often is the end of those business dreams. Accountants usually assist in the winding down and liquidation process and must recognize the legitimate rights of and any amounts due to the many parties involved in the partnership: individual partners, creditors of the partnership, customers, and others doing business with the partnership.

The Uniform Partnership Act of 1997 has 71 sections, 7 of which deal specifically with the dissolution and winding up of a partnership. Several sections discuss the specific rights of creditors of the partnership. Creditors have first claim to the partnership's assets. After the creditors are fully satisfied, any remaining assets are distributed to the partners based on the balances in their capital accounts. This chapter presents the concepts that accountants must know if they offer professional services to partnerships undergoing winding down and liquidation.

## OVERVIEW OF PARTNERSHIP LIQUIDATIONS

The major provisions of the Uniform Partnership Act of 1997 (UPA 1997) have been adopted by most states and that act is used for the illustrations in this chapter. The chapter first presents the UPA 1997's major provisions regarding events and processes associated with partnership liquidations. After this overview, the chapter illustrates the winding up process in both a lump-sum liquidation and an installment liquidation.

### Dissociation, Dissolution, Winding Up, and Liquidation of a Partnership

#### Dissociation

*Dissociation* is the legal description of the withdrawal of a partner, including the following:

1. A partner's death.
2. A partner's voluntary withdrawal (i.e., a retirement).
3. A judicial determination, including: (*a*) the partner engaged in wrongful conduct that materially and negatively affected the partnership, (*b*) the partner willfully committed a material breach of the partnership agreement, (*c*) the partner became a debtor in bankruptcy, and (*d*) an individual partner has become incapable of performing his or her duties under the partnership agreement.

Not all dissociations result in a partnership liquidation. Many partner dissociations involve only a buyout of the withdrawing partner's interest rather than a winding up and liquidation of the partnership's business.

### Dissolution

***Dissolution*** is the dissolving of a partnership. Events that cause dissolution and winding up of the partnership business are presented in section 801 of the UPA 1997, as follows:

1. In a partnership at will, a partner's express notice to leave the partnership. An at will partnership is one in which there is, at most, only an oral understanding among the partners, and there is no definite term or specific task undertaking. A partnership agreement can eliminate this event as a cause for partnership dissolution by including, for example, a provision for a buyout of that partner's interest in the partnership.

2. In a partnership for a definite term or specific undertaking, dissolution takes place: (*a*) when after a partner's death or wrongful dissociation, at least half of the remaining partners decide to wind up the partnership business, (*b*) when all of the partners agree to wind up the partnership business, or (*c*) when the term or specific undertaking has expired or been completed.

3 An event that makes it unlawful to carry on a substantial part of the partnership business.

4. A judicial determination that: (*a*) the economic purpose of the partnership is unlikely to be achieved, (*b*) a partner has engaged in conduct relating to the partnership business that makes it impracticable to carry on the partnership business, or (*c*) it is not reasonably practicable to carry on the partnership business in conformity with the partnership agreement.

On dissolution, the partnership begins the winding up of the partnership's business.

### Winding Up and Liquidation

Winding up and liquidation of the partnership begins after the dissolution of the partnership. The partnership continues for the limited purpose of winding up the business and completing work in process. The winding up process includes the transactions necessary to liquidate the partnership, such as the collection of receivables, including any receivables from partners, conversion of the noncash assets to cash, payment of the partnership's obligations, and the distribution of any remaining net balance to the partners, in cash, according to their capital interests. If the partnership agreement does not provide for a special liquidation ratio, then profits or losses during the liquidation process are distributed in the normal profit and loss ratio that was used during the operation of the partnership.

Some terminating partnerships change to the liquidation basis of accounting once they no longer consider the business to be a going concern. At the point at which the liquidation basis of accounting is adopted, the partnership's assets are valued at their estimated net realizable liquidation values and liabilities at their estimated settlement amounts. Because of the apparent uncertainties in practice of specifically defining the point at which an entity is no longer a going concern, the FASB, in the second quarter of 2007, added to its agenda a project on *Going Concern and Liquidation Basis of Accounting*. However, after further staff research and an evaluation of the FASB's agenda, the Board decided late in the third quarter of 2007 to remove the project from its agenda and include the project with the Board's ongoing codification project. The points raised in the Board's consideration of these two issues were, first, it was felt that the existing accounting and auditing guidance did not provide sufficient guidance to management for making their going-concern assessment. Second, the accounting and auditing guidance did not sufficiently define when the financial statements should be presented using the liquidation basis of accounting and what should be the form and content of those liquidation-basis financial statements.

***Loans with Partners*** Under the UPA 1997, liabilities to partners for loans the partners made to the partnership have the same status as liabilities to the partnerships' third party creditors. Loans from partners have no priority for payment. Under the UPA 1997, there is no offset of liabilities to partners with the partners' capital accounts. These partnership obligations to the individual partners must be paid during the winding up of the partnership on the same proportional basis as the other liabilities of the partnership.

Receivables from partners for loans or other advances made by the partnership to partners have the same status as other assets of the partnership. The partnership has a claim to a partner's personal net assets for amounts not paid by the individual partner for outstanding loans from the partnership. There is no offset of loans receivable from individual partners with the partners' capital accounts.

***Deficits in Partners' Capital Accounts***   As part of the liquidation process, each partner with a deficit in his or her capital account must make a contribution to the partnership to remedy that capital deficit. The partnership makes a liquidating distribution, in cash, to each partner with a capital credit balance. The UPA 1997 specifies cash for these liquidating distributions. If a partner fails to make a required contribution to remedy his or her capital deficit, all other partners must contribute, in the proportion to which those partners share partnership losses, the additional amount necessary to pay the partnership's obligations.

### Statement of Partnership Realization and Liquidation

To guide and summarize the partnership liquidation process, a ***statement of partnership realization and liquidation*** may be prepared. The statement, often called a "statement of liquidation," is the basis of the journal entries made to record the liquidation. It presents, in workpaper form, the effects of the liquidation on the balance sheet accounts of the partnership. The statement shows the conversion of assets into cash, the allocation of any gains or losses to the partners, and the distribution of cash to creditors and partners. This statement is a basic feature of accounting for a partnership liquidation and is presented and illustrated in the remainder of the chapter.

# LUMP-SUM LIQUIDATIONS

A ***lump-sum liquidation*** of a partnership is one in which all assets are converted into cash within a very short time, creditors are paid, and a single, lump-sum payment is made to the partners for their capital interests. Although most partnership liquidations take place over an extended period, as illustrated later, the lump-sum liquidation is an excellent focal point for presenting the major concepts of partnership liquidation.

## Realization of Assets

Typically, a partnership experiences losses on the disposal of its assets. A partnership may have a "Going out of Business" sale in which its inventory is marked down well below normal selling price to encourage immediate sale. Often, the remaining inventory may be sold to companies that specialize in acquiring assets of liquidating businesses. The partnership's furniture, fixtures, and equipment may also be offered at a reduced price or sold to liquidators. Any goodwill on the partnership's books is generally written off at the time the partnership begins a liquidation because the entity is no longer a going concern.

The partnership attempts to collect its accounts receivable. Sometimes the partnership offers a large cash discount for the prompt payment of any remaining receivables whose collection may otherwise delay terminating the partnership. Alternatively, the receivables may be sold to a *factor,* a business that specializes in acquiring accounts receivables and immediately paying cash to the seller of the receivables. The partnership records the sale of the receivables as it would any other asset. Typically, the factor acquires only the best of a business's receivables at a price below face value, but some factors are willing to buy all receivables and pay a significantly lower price than face value.

The assets of the partnership, including any receivables from the partners and any contributions required of partners to remedy their capital deficits, are applied to pay the partnership's creditors. The UPA 1997 specifies that liabilities to individual partners, for example, liabilities resulting from loans made to the partnership from a partner, have the same status as liabilities to third party creditors; outside creditors do not have any priority over a partner who has made a loan to the partnership. It is very important that loans between the partnership and partners are fully documented, such as with promissory notes, to indicate clearly that the transaction is a loan and not a capital contribution or withdrawal. These loans carry interest until paid unless otherwise agreed to by the partnership and the individual partner. Loans to or from partners must be settled during the winding up process. Any remaining amount is then paid, in cash, to the partners in accordance with their rights to liquidating distributions. Section 807 of the UPA 1997 states that the liquidating distributions to the partners are to be made in cash.

## Expenses of Liquidation

The liquidation process usually begins with scheduling the partnership's known assets and liabilities. The names and addresses of creditors and the amounts owed to each are specified. As diligent as the effort usually is, additional, unscheduled creditors may become known during the liquidation process. The liquidation process also involves some expenses, such as additional legal and accounting costs. The partnership may also incur costs of disposing of the business, such as special advertising and costs of locating specialized equipment dealers. These expenses are allocated to partners' capital accounts in the profit and loss distribution ratio.

## Illustration of Lump-Sum Liquidation

The following illustration presents the liquidation of the ABC Partnership, whose partners, Alt, Blue, and Cha, decide to terminate the business on May 1, 20X5. The AB Partnership was formed on January 1, 20X1. Cha was admitted into the partnership on January 1, 20X3, and the name of the business was changed to the ABC Partnership. For purposes of this illustration, assume that Alt remained in the partnership and, in 20X4, the partners agreed to a realignment of their profit and loss–sharing percentages to more closely conform with each partner's efforts. The profit and loss–sharing percentages after realignment in 20X4 were as follows: Alt, 40 percent, Blue, 40 percent, and Cha, 20 percent. A condensed trial balance of the company on May 1, 20X5, the day the partners decide to liquidate the business, follows:

| ABC PARTNERSHIP Trial Balance May 1, 20X5 | | |
|---|---|---|
| Cash | $ 10,000 | |
| Noncash Assets | 90,000 | |
| Liabilities | | $ 42,000 |
| Alt, Capital (40%) | | 34,000 |
| Blue, Capital (40%) | | 10,000 |
| Cha, Capital (20%) | | 14,000 |
| Total | $100,000 | $100,000 |

The basic accounting equation, Assets − Liabilities = Owners' equity, applies to partnership accounting. In this case, owners' equity is the sum of the partners' capital accounts, as follows:

$$\text{Assets} - \text{Liabilities} = \text{Owners' equity}$$
$$\$100,000 - \$42,000 = \$58,000$$

The following three cases illustrate the partnership liquidation concepts used most commonly. Each case begins with the May 1, 20X5, trial balance of the ABC Partnership. The amount of cash realized from the disposal of the noncash assets is different for each of the three cases, and the effects of the different realizations are shown in the statement of partnership realization and liquidation presented for each case.

**FIGURE 16–1**  Case 1. Partnership Solvent; No Deficits in Partners' Capital Accounts

| | | | | Capital Balance | | |
|---|---|---|---|---|---|---|
| | Cash | Noncash Assets | Liabilities | Alt, 40% | Blue, 40% | Cha, 20% |
| **ABC PARTNERSHIP** Statement of Partnership Realization and Liquidation Lump-Sum Liquidation | | | | | | |
| Preliquidation balances, May 1 | 10,000 | 90,000 | (42,000) | (34,000) | (10,000) | (14,000) |
| Sales of assets and distribution of $10,000 loss | 80,000 | (90,000) | | 4,000 | 4,000 | 2,000 |
| | 90,000 | -0- | (42,000) | (30,000) | (6,000) | (12,000) |
| Payment to creditors | (42,000) | | 42,000 | | | |
| | 48,000 | -0- | -0- | (30,000) | (6,000) | (12,000) |
| Lump-sum payment to partners | (48,000) | | | 30,000 | 6,000 | 12,000 |
| Postliquidation balances | -0- | -0- | -0- | -0- | -0- | -0- |

*Note:* Parentheses indicate credit amount.

### Case 1. Partnership Solvent and No Deficits in Partners' Capital Accounts

The noncash assets are sold for $80,000 on May 15, 20X5, at a $10,000 loss. The partnership's creditors are paid their $42,000 on May 20, and the remaining $48,000 cash is distributed to the partners on May 30, 20X5.

The statement of realization and liquidation for Case 1 is presented in Figure 16–1. Note that parentheses are used to indicate credit amounts in the workpapers used throughout this chapter. The statement includes only balance sheet accounts across the columns, with all noncash assets presented together as a single total. Once a business has entered liquidation, the balance sheet accounts are the only relevant ones; the income statement is for a going concern. The liquidation process is presented in the order of occurrence in the rows of the workpaper. Thus, the workpaper includes the entire realization and liquidation process and is the basis for the journal entries to record the liquidation.

Other important observations are as follows:

1. The preliquidation balances are obtained from the May 1, 20X5, trial balance.
2. The $10,000 loss is distributed directly to the partners' capital accounts.
3. Creditors, including individual partners who have made any loans to the partnership, are paid before any cash is distributed to partners.
4. Payments to partners are made for their capital credit balances.
5. The postliquidation balances are all zero, indicating the accounts are all closed and the partnership is fully liquidated and terminated.

The statement of partnership realization and liquidation is the basis for the following journal entries to record the liquidation process:

May 15, 20X5

| | | | |
|---|---|---|---|
| (1) | Cash | 80,000 | |
| | Alt, Capital | 4,000 | |
| | Blue, Capital | 4,000 | |
| | Cha, Capital | 2,000 | |
| | Noncash Assets | | 90,000 |

Realization of all noncash assets of the ABC Partnership and distribution of $10,000 loss using profit and loss ratio.

May 20, 20X5

| (2) | Liabilities | 42,000 | |
| | Cash | | 42,000 |
| | Pay creditors. | | |

May 30, 20X5

| (3) | Alt, Capital | 30,000 | |
| | Blue, Capital | 6,000 | |
| | Cha, Capital | 12,000 | |
| | Cash | | 48,000 |
| | Lump-sum payments to partners. | | |

### Case 2. Partnership Solvent and Deficit Created in Partner's Capital Account

A deficit in a partner's capital account can occur if the credit balance of that capital account is too low to absorb his or her share of losses. A capital deficit may be created at any time in the liquidation process. Such deficits may be remedied by either of the following two means:

1. The partner invests cash or other assets to eliminate the capital deficit.
2. The partner's capital deficit is distributed to the other partners in their resulting loss-sharing ratio.

The approach used depends on the solvency of the partner with the capital deficit. A partner who is personally solvent and has sufficient net worth to eliminate the capital deficit must make an additional investment in the partnership to cover the deficit. On the other hand, if the partner is personally insolvent—that is, personal liabilities exceed personal assets—section 807 of the UPA 1997 requires the remaining partners to absorb the insolvent partner's deficit by allocating it to their capital accounts in their resulting loss-sharing ratio.

The following lump-sum distribution illustrates these points:

1. The three partners' personal financial statements are as follows:

| | Alt | Blue | Cha |
|---|---|---|---|
| Personal assets | $150,000 | $12,000 | $42,000 |
| Personal liabilities | (86,000) | (16,000) | (14,000) |
| Net worth (deficit) | $ 64,000 | $ (4,000) | $28,000 |

Blue is personally insolvent; Alt and Cha are personally solvent.

2. The partnership's noncash assets are sold for $35,000 on May 15, 20X5, and the $55,000 loss is allocated to the partners' capital accounts.
3. The partnership's creditors are paid $42,000 on May 20, 20X5.
4. Because Blue is personally insolvent, Blue's capital deficit of $12,000 is allocated to the other partners.
5. The remaining $4,000 cash is distributed as a lump-sum payment on May 30, 20X5.

The statement of partnership realization and liquidation for Case 2 is presented in Figure 16–2.

The following observations emerge from this illustration:

1. The $55,000 loss on the realization of noncash assets is allocated in the partners' loss-sharing ratio of 40 percent for Alt, 40 percent for Blue, and 20 percent for Cha. Blue's $22,000 share of the loss on disposal creates a $12,000 deficit in his capital account. Blue is personally insolvent and is unable to make an additional investment to remove the capital deficit.

**FIGURE 16–2**   Case 2. Partnership Solvent; Deficit Created in Personally Insolvent Partner's Capital Account

**ABC PARTNERSHIP**
Statement of Partnership Realization and Liquidation
Lump-Sum Liquidation

| | Cash | Noncash Assets | Liabilities | Capital Balance | | |
| --- | --- | --- | --- | --- | --- | --- |
| | | | | Alt, 40% | Blue, 40% | Cha, 20% |
| Preliquidation balances, May 1 | 10,000 | 90,000 | (42,000) | (34,000) | (10,000) | (14,000) |
| Sales of assets and distribution of $55,000 loss | 35,000 | (90,000) | | 22,000 | 22,000 | 11,000 |
| | 45,000 | -0- | (42,000) | (12,000) | 12,000 | (3,000) |
| Payment to creditors | (42,000) | | 42,000 | | | |
| | 3,000 | -0- | -0- | (12,000) | 12,000 | (3,000) |
| Distribution of deficit of insolvent partner: | | | | | (12,000) | |
| 40/60 × $12,000 | | | | 8,000 | | |
| 20/60 × $12,000 | | | | | | 4,000 |
| | 3,000 | -0- | -0- | (4,000) | -0- | 1,000 |
| Contribution by Cha to remedy capital deficit | 1,000 | | | | | (1,000) |
| | 4,000 | -0- | -0- | (4,000) | -0- | -0- |
| Lump-sum payment to partners | (4,000) | | | 4,000 | | |
| Postliquidation balances | -0- | -0- | -0- | -0- | -0- | -0- |

*Note:* Parentheses indicate credit amount.

2. The partnership's creditors are paid before any distributions are made to the partners.

3. Blue's $12,000 deficit is distributed to Alt and Cha in their resulting loss-sharing ratio. Note that the UPA 1977 specifies the loss-sharing ratio be used for this allocation. Alt absorbs two-thirds (40/60) of Blue's deficit, and Cha absorbs one-third (20/60).

4. The distribution of Blue's deficit creates a deficit in Cha's capital account. Cha must contribute $1,000 to remedy her capital deficit.

5. A lump-sum payment is made to Alt for his $4,000 capital credit.

6. All postliquidation balances are zero, indicating the completion of the liquidation process.

### Case 3. Partnership Is Insolvent and Deficit Created in Partner's Capital Account

A partnership is insolvent when existing cash and cash generated by the sale of the assets is not sufficient to pay the partnership's liabilities. In this case, the individual partners are liable for the remaining unpaid partnership liabilities. The following illustration presents an insolvent partnership and a deficit in one of the partner's capital accounts.

1. Alt and Cha are personally solvent, and Blue is personally insolvent as in Case 2.

2. The noncash assets are sold for $20,000 on May 15, 20X5.

3. The partnership's creditors are paid $42,000 on May 20, 20X5.

The statement of partnership realization and liquidation for Case 3 is presented in Figure 16–3.

The following observations are made from this illustration:

1. The $70,000 loss is allocated to the partners in their loss-sharing ratio. This allocation creates a deficit of $18,000 in Blue's capital account.

2. Because Blue is personally insolvent, his $18,000 deficit is distributed to Alt and Cha in their loss-sharing ratio of 40:60 for Alt and 20:60 for Cha. The distribution of Blue's deficit results in a $6,000 deficit for Alt and a $6,000 deficit for Cha.

**FIGURE 16–3** **Case 3. Partnership Insolvent; Deficit Created in Personally Insolvent Partner's Capital Account**

**ABC PARTNERSHIP**
**Statement of Partnership Realization and Liquidation**
**Lump-Sum Liquidation**

| | Cash | Noncash Assets | Liabilities | Capital Balance | | |
|---|---|---|---|---|---|---|
| | | | | Alt, 40% | Blue, 40% | Cha, 20% |
| Preliquidation balances, May 1 | 10,000 | 90,000 | (42,000) | (34,000) | (10,000) | (14,000) |
| Sales of assets and distribution of $70,000 loss | 20,000 | (90,000) | | 28,000 | 28,000 | 14,000 |
| | 30,000 | -0- | (42,000) | (6,000) | 18,000 | -0- |
| Distribution of deficit of insolvent partner: | | | | | (18,000) | |
| 40/60 × $18,000 | | | | 12,000 | | |
| 20/60 × $18,000 | | | | | | 6,000 |
| | 30,000 | -0- | (42,000) | 6,000 | -0- | 6,000 |
| Contribution by Alt and Cha to remedy capital deficit | 12,000 | | | (6,000) | | (6,000) |
| | 42,000 | -0- | (42,000) | -0- | -0- | -0- |
| Payment to creditors | (42,000) | | 42,000 | | | |
| Postliquidation balances | -0- | -0- | -0- | -0- | -0- | -0- |

*Note:* Parentheses indicate credit amount.

3. Alt and Cha make additional capital contributions to remedy their respective capital deficits of $6,000 and $6,000.
4. The $42,000 partnership cash now available is used to pay the partnership's creditors.
5. The postliquidation balances are zero, indicating completion of the partnership liquidation.

In Case 3, Alt and Cha each made additional capital contributions to eliminate their capital deficits. Whenever a partner must remedy another partner's capital deficit, the partner making the remedy has cause to bring suit against the failing partner. Blue's failure in the amount of $12,000 in Case 2, and $18,000 in Case 3, required Alt and Cha to remedy Blue's deficit. Alt and Cha can sue Blue and be included in the list of Blue's personal liabilities. Although Blue is personally insolvent, Alt and Cha may obtain a partial recovery of their amounts.

## INSTALLMENT LIQUIDATIONS

An *installment liquidation* typically requires several months to complete and includes periodic, or installment, payments to the partners during the liquidation period. Most partnership liquidations take place over an extended period in order to obtain the largest possible amount from the realization of the assets. The partners typically receive periodic payments during the liquidation because they require funds for personal purposes.

Some partnerships using installment liquidations prepare a Plan of Liquidation and Dissolution prior to the beginning of the liquidation. This plan sets out the intended liquidation of its assets and the winding up of its affairs. The partners discuss and perhaps modify the plan, but an agreement of the partners is expected for the plan. And some partnerships, upon obtaining the consent of the partners to proceed with the installment liquidation, adopt the liquidation basis of accounting under which assets are stated at their estimated net realizable value and liabilities, including projected costs of liquidation, are stated at their estimated settlement amounts. These partnerships may prepare a Statement of Net Assets in Liquidation and a Statement of Changes in Net Assets in Liquidation. However, those partnerships using GAAP apply **FASB 144,** "Accounting for the Impairment or Disposal of Long-Lived Assets" (FASB 144), to value their long-lived assets to be disposed of by sale. **FASB 144** states that these assets are to be classified separately and valued at the lower of carrying amount or fair value less costs to sell. And **FASB 146,** "Accounting for Costs Associated with Exit or Disposal Activities" (FASB 146), requires that costs associated with an exit activity be recognized and measured at fair value in the period in which the liability is incurred, not in earlier periods when, for example, a restructuring plan is adopted. Most partnerships use the Statement of Partnership Realization and Liquidation during the installment liquidation process and recognize gains or losses from the liquidation events.

Installment liquidations involve the distribution of cash to partners before complete liquidation of the assets occurs. The accountant must be especially cautious when distributing available cash because future events may change the amounts to be paid to each partner. For this reason, the following practical guides are used to assist the accountant in determining safe installment payments to the partners:

1. Distribute no cash to the partners until all liabilities and actual plus potential liquidation expenses have been paid or provided for by reserving the necessary cash.

2. Anticipate the worst, or most restrictive, possible case before determining the amount of cash installment each partner receives:

   *a.* Assume that all remaining noncash assets will be written off as a loss; that is, assume that nothing will be realized on asset disposals.

   *b.* Assume that deficits created in the partners' capital accounts will be distributed to the remaining partners; that is, assume that deficits will not be eliminated by additional partner capital contributions.

3. After the accountant has assumed the worst possible cases, the remaining credit balances in capital accounts represent safe distributions of cash that may be distributed to partners in those amounts.

## Illustration of Installment Liquidation

The same illustration used in the lump-sum liquidation of the ABC Partnership is now used to illustrate liquidation in installments. Alt, Blue, and Cha decide to liquidate their business over a period of time and to receive installment distributions of available cash during the liquidation process.

ABC Partnership's condensed trial balance on May 1, 20X5, the day the partners decide to liquidate the business, follows. Each partner's profit and loss–sharing percentage is also shown.

|  | **ABC PARTNERSHIP**<br>**Trial Balance**<br>**May 1, 20X5** |  |
| --- | --- | --- |
| Cash | $ 10,000 |  |
| Noncash Assets | 90,000 |  |
| Liabilities |  | $ 42,000 |
| Alt, Capital (40%) |  | 34,000 |
| Blue, Capital (40%) |  | 10,000 |
| Cha, Capital (20%) |  | 14,000 |
| Total | $100,000 | $100,000 |

The following describes this case.

1. The partners' net worth statements on May 1, 20X5, are as follows:

|  | Alt | Blue | Cha |
|---|---|---|---|
| Personal assets | $150,000 | $12,000 | $42,000 |
| Personal liabilities | (86,000) | (16,000) | (14,000) |
| Net worth (deficit) | $ 64,000 | $ (4,000) | $28,000 |

Blue is personally insolvent; Alt and Cha are personally solvent.

2. The noncash assets are sold as follows:

| Date | Book Value | Proceeds | Loss |
|---|---|---|---|
| 5/15/X5 | $55,000 | $45,000 | $10,000 |
| 6/15/X5 | 30,000 | 15,000 | 15,000 |
| 7/15/X5 | 5,000 | 5,000 |  |

3. The creditors are paid $42,000 on May 20.

4. The partners agree to maintain a $10,000 cash reserve during the liquidation process to pay for any liquidation expenses.

5. The partners agree to distribute the available cash at the end of each month; that is, installment liquidations will be made on May 31 and June 30. The final cash distributions to partners will be made on July 31, 20X5, the end of the liquidation process.

Figure 16–4 presents the statement of partnership realization and liquidation for the installment liquidation of the ABC Partnership.

### Transactions during May 20X5

The events during May 20X5 result in a distribution of $5,000 to the partners. The procedure to arrive at this amount is as follows:

1. The sale of $55,000 of assets results in a loss of $10,000, which is distributed to the three partners in their loss-sharing ratio.

2. Payments of $42,000 are made to the partnership's creditors for the known liabilities.

3. Available cash is distributed to the partners on May 31, 20X5.

To determine the safe payment of cash to be distributed to partners, the accountant must make some assumptions about the future liquidation of the remaining assets. Under the assumption of the worst possible situation, the remaining $35,000 of assets will result in a total loss. Before making a cash distribution to the partners, the accountant prepares a *schedule of safe payments to partners* using the worst-case assumptions. Figure 16–5 presents the schedule of safe payments to partners as of May 31, 20X5.

The schedule of safe payments begins with the partners' capital balances as of May 31. The logic of using just the capital accounts comes from the accounting equation: Assets − Liabilities = Partners' capital balances. Thus, for example, if there was an increase in a liability that reduced the net assets, the equality of the accounting equation would also result in a decrease in the total of partners' capital balances. Because the partners' capital accounts are the focus of the payments to partners, it is unnecessary to include the assets and liabilities in the schedule of safe payments to partners. The schedule includes all the information necessary for partners to know how much cash they will receive at each cash distribution date.

Alt, Blue, and Cha agree to withhold $10,000 for possible liquidation expenses. In addition, the noncash assets have a remaining balance of $35,000 on May 31. A worst-case assumption is a complete loss on the noncash assets and $10,000 of liquidation expenses,

**FIGURE 16–4** **Installment Liquidation Workpaper**

| | | | | **Capital Balance** | | |
|---|---|---|---|---|---|---|
| | Cash | Noncash Assets | Liabilities | Alt, 40% | Blue, 40% | Cha, 20% |
| **ABC PARTNERSHIP** Statement of Partnership Realization and Liquidation Installment Liquidation | | | | | | |
| Preliquidation balances, May 1 | 10,000 | 90,000 | (42,000) | (34,000) | (10,000) | (14,000) |
| *May 20X5:* | | | | | | |
| Sale of assets and distribution of $10,000 loss | 45,000 | (55,000) | | 4,000 | 4,000 | 2,000 |
| | 55,000 | 35,000 | (42,000) | (30,000) | (6,000) | (12,000) |
| Payment to creditors | (42,000) | | 42,000 | | | |
| | 13,000 | 35,000 | -0- | (30,000) | (6,000) | (12,000) |
| Payment to partners (Schedule 1, Figure 16–5) | (3,000) | | | 3,000 | | |
| | 10,000 | 35,000 | -0- | (27,000) | (6,000) | (12,000) |
| *June 20X5:* | | | | | | |
| Sale of assets and distribution of $15,000 loss | 15,000 | (30,000) | | 6,000 | 6,000 | 3,000 |
| | 25,000 | 5,000 | -0- | (21,000) | -0- | (9,000) |
| Payment to partners (Schedule 2, Figure 16–5) | (15,000) | | | 11,000 | | 4,000 |
| | 10,000 | 5,000 | -0- | (10,000) | -0- | (5,000) |
| *July 20X5:* | | | | | | |
| Sale of assets at book value | 5,000 | (5,000) | | | | |
| | 15,000 | -0- | -0- | (10,000) | -0- | (5,000) |
| Payment of $7,500 in liquidation costs | (7,500) | | | 3,000 | 3,000 | 1,500 |
| | 7,500 | -0- | -0- | (7,000) | 3,000 | (3,500) |
| Distribution of deficit of insolvent partner: | | | | | (3,000) | |
| 40/60 × $3,000 | | | | 2,000 | | |
| 20/60 × $3,000 | | | | | | 1,000 |
| | 7,500 | -0- | -0- | (5,000) | -0- | (2,500) |
| Payment to partners | (7,500) | | | 5,000 | | 2,500 |
| Postliquidation balances, July 31 | -0- | -0- | -0- | -0- | -0- | -0- |

*Note*: Parentheses indicate credit amount.

totaling $45,000 of charges to be distributed to the partners' capital accounts. The capital accounts of Alt, Blue, and Cha would be charged for $18,000, $18,000, and $9,000, respectively, for their shares of the $45,000 assumed loss. These assumptions result in a pro forma deficit in Blue's capital account. This is not an actual deficit that must be remedied! It is merely the result of applying the worst-case assumptions.

Continuing such worst-case planning, the accountant assumes that Blue is insolvent (which happens to be true in this example) and distributes the pro forma deficit in Blue's capital account to Alt and Cha in their *loss-sharing ratio* of 40:60 to Alt and 20:60 to Cha. The resulting credit balances indicate the amount of cash that may be safely distributed to the partners. The May 31 cash distribution is shown in Figure 16–4. The available cash of $3,000 is distributed to Alt. The ending balances should satisfy the equality of assets and equities of the accounting equation. If the equality has been destroyed, an error has occurred that must be corrected before proceeding further. As of May 31, after the installment distribution, the accounting equation is:

$$\text{Assets} - \text{Liabilities} = \text{Owners' equity}$$
$$\$45,000 - \$0 = \$45,000$$

**FIGURE 16–5** Schedule of Safe Payment to Partners for an Installment Liquidation

| | Partner | | |
|---|---|---|---|
| **ABC PARTNERSHIP**<br>**Schedule of Safe Payment to Partners** | **Alt**<br>**40%** | **Blue**<br>**40%** | **Cha**<br>**20%** |
| **Schedule 1, May 31, 20X5** | | | |
| Computation of distribution of cash available on May 31, 20X5: | | | |
| Capital balances, May 31, before cash distribution | (30,000) | (6,000) | (12,000) |
| Assume full loss of $35,000 on remaining noncash assets and $10,000 | | | |
| in possible future liquidation expenses | 18,000 | 18,000 | 9,000 |
| | (12,000) | 12,000 | (3,000) |
| Assume Blue's potential deficit must be absorbed by Alt and Cha: | | (12,000) | |
| 40/60 × $12,000 | 8,000 | | |
| 20/60 × $12,000 | | | 4,000 |
| | (4,000) | -0- | 1,000 |
| Assume Cha's potential deficit must be absorbed by Alt | 1,000 | | (1,000) |
| Safe payment to partners, May 31 | (3,000) | -0- | -0- |
| **Schedule 2, June 30, 20X5** | | | |
| Computation of distribution of cash available on June 30, 20X5: | | | |
| Capital balances, June 30, before cash distribution | (21,000) | -0- | (9,000) |
| Assume full loss of $5,000 on remaining noncash assets and $10,000 in | | | |
| possible future liquidation expenses | 6,000 | 6,000 | 3,000 |
| | (15,000) | 6,000 | (6,000) |
| Assume Blue's potential deficit must be absorbed by Alt and Cha: | | (6,000) | |
| 40/60 × $6,000 | 4,000 | | |
| 20/60 × $6,000 | | | 2,000 |
| Safe payment to partners, June 30 | (11,000) | -0- | (4,000) |

*Note:* Parentheses indicate credit amount.

### Transactions during June 20X5

Figure 16–4 continues with transactions for June 20X5, as follows:

1. Noncash assets of $30,000 are sold on June 15 for a $15,000 loss, which is distributed to the partners in their loss-sharing ratio, resulting in a zero capital balance for Blue.
2. On June 30, 20X5, available cash is distributed as an installment payment to the partners.

The schedule of safe payments to partners as of June 30, 20X5, in Figure 16–5 shows how the amounts of distribution are calculated. A worst-case plan assumes that the remaining noncash assets of $5,000 must be written off as a loss and that the $10,000 cash in reserve will be completely used for liquidation expenses. This $15,000 pro forma loss is allocated to the partners in their loss-sharing ratio, which creates a $6,000 deficit in Blue's capital account. Continuing the worst-case scenario, it is assumed Blue will not eliminate this debit balance. Therefore, the $6,000 potential deficit is allocated to Alt and Cha in their resulting loss-sharing ratio of 40:60 to Alt and 20:60 to Cha. The resulting credit balances in the partners' capital accounts show the amount of cash that can be distributed safely. Only $15,000 of the available cash is distributed to Alt and Cha on June 30, as shown in Figure 16–4.

### Transactions during July 20X5

The last part of Figure 16–4 shows the completion of the liquidation transactions during July 20X5:

1. The remaining assets are sold at their book value of $5,000.

2. Actual liquidation costs of $7,500 are paid and allocated to the partners in their loss-sharing ratio, creating a deficit of $3,000 in Blue's capital account. The remaining $2,500 of the $10,000 reserved for the expenses is released for distribution to the partners.

3. Because Blue is personally insolvent and cannot contribute to the partnership, the $3,000 deficit is distributed to Alt and Cha in their loss-sharing ratio. Note that this is an actual deficit, not a pro forma deficit.

4. The $7,500 of remaining cash is paid to Alt and Cha to the extent of their capital balances. After this last distribution, all account balances are zero, indicating the completion of the liquidation process.

## Cash Distribution Plan

At the beginning of the liquidation process, accountants commonly prepare a ***cash distribution plan,*** which gives the partners an idea of the installment cash payments each will receive as cash becomes available to the partnership. The actual installment distributions are determined using the statement of realization and liquidation, supplemented with the schedule of safe payments to partners as presented in the preceding section of the chapter. The cash distribution plan is a pro forma projection of the application of cash as it becomes available.

### Loss Absorption Power

A basic concept of the cash distribution plan at the beginning of the liquidation process is ***loss absorption power (LAP).*** An individual partner's LAP is defined as the maximum loss that the partnership can realize before that partner's capital account balance is extinguished. The loss absorption power is a function of two elements, as follows:

$$LAP = \frac{\text{Partner's capital account balance}}{\text{Partner's loss share}}$$

For example, on May 1, 2005, Alt has a capital account credit balance of $34,000 and a 40 percent share in the losses of ABC Partnership. Alt's LAP is

$$LAP = \frac{\$34,000}{.40} = \$85,000$$

This means that $85,000 in losses on disposing of noncash assets or from additional liquidation expenses would eliminate the credit balance in Alt's capital account, as follows:

$$\$85,000 \times .40 = \$34,000$$

### Illustration of Cash Distribution Plan

The following illustration is based on the ABC Partnership example. A trial balance of its balance sheet accounts on May 1, 20X5, the day the partners decide to liquidate the business, is prepared.

|  | **ABC PARTNERSHIP** Trial Balance May 1, 20X5 | |
| --- | --- | --- |
| Cash | $ 10,000 | |
| Noncash Assets | 90,000 | |
| Liabilities | | $ 42,000 |
| Alt, Capital (40%) | | 34,000 |
| Blue, Capital (40%) | | 10,000 |
| Cha, Capital (20%) | | 14,000 |
| Total | $100,000 | $100,000 |

**FIGURE 16–6**  **Cash Distribution Plan for Liquidating Partnership**

**ABC PARTNERSHIP**
**Cash Distribution Plan**
**May 1, 20X5**

| | Loss Absorption Power | | | Capital Balance | | |
|---|---|---|---|---|---|---|
| | **Alt** | **Blue** | **Cha** | **Alt** | **Blue** | **Cha** |
| Loss-sharing percentages | | | | 40% | 40% | 20% |
| Preliquidation capital balances, May 1, 20X5 | | | | (34,000) | (10,000) | (14,000) |
| Loss absorption power (LAP) | | | | | | |
| (Capital balance / Loss ratio) | (85,000) | (25,000) | (70,000) | | | |
| Decrease highest LAP to next-highest LAP: | | | | | | |
| Decrease Alt by $15,000 | | | | | | |
| (cash distribution: $15,000 × .40 = $6,000) | 15,000 | | | 6,000 | | |
| | (70,000) | (25,000) | (70,000) | (28,000) | (10,000) | (14,000) |
| Decrease LAPs to next-highest level: | | | | | | |
| Decrease Alt by $45,000 | | | | | | |
| (cash distribution: $45,000 × .40 = $18,000) | 45,000 | | | 18,000 | | |
| Decrease Cha by $45,000 | | | | | | |
| (cash distribution: $45,000 × .20 = $9,000) | | | 45,000 | | | 9,000 |
| | (25,000) | (25,000) | (25,000) | (10,000) | (10,000) | (5,000) |
| Decrease LAPs by distributing cash in the | | | | | | |
| loss-sharing percentages | 40% | 40% | 20% | | | |

**Summary of Cash Distribution Plan**

| | | | | | | |
|---|---|---|---|---|---|---|
| Step 1: First $42,000 to creditors | | | | | | |
| Step 2: Next $10,000 to liquidation expenses | | | | | | |
| Step 3: Next $6,000 to Alt | | | | 6,000 | | |
| Step 4: Next $45,000 to Alt and Cha in their respective | | | | | | |
| loss ratios ($27,000 now available) | | | | 18,000 | | 9,000 |
| Step 5: Any additional distributions in the partners' | | | | | | |
| loss-sharing ratios | | | | 40% | 40% | 20% |

*Note:* Parentheses indicate credit amount.

The partners ask for a cash distribution plan as of May 1, 20X5, to determine the distributions of cash as it becomes available during the liquidation process. Such a plan always provides for payment to the partnership's creditors before any distributions may be made to the partners. Figure 16–6 presents the cash distribution plan as of May 1, the beginning date of the liquidation process.

The important observations from this illustration are as follows:

1. Each partner's loss absorption power is computed as the partner's capital balance divided by that partner's *loss-sharing percentage.* Alt has the highest LAP ($85,000), Cha has the next highest ($70,000), and Blue has the lowest ($25,000). Each partner's LAP is the amount of loss that would completely eliminate his or her net capital credit balance. Alt is the least vulnerable to a loss, and Blue is the most vulnerable.

2. The least vulnerable partner is the first to receive any cash distributions after providing for creditors. Alt is the only partner to receive cash until his LAP is decreased to the level of the next highest partner, Cha. To decrease Alt's LAP by $15,000 requires the payment of $6,000 ($15,000 × .40) to Alt. After payment of $6,000 to Alt, his new loss absorption power will be the same as Cha's, calculated as Alt's remaining capital balance of $28,000 divided by his loss-sharing percentage of 40 percent ($28,000 ÷ .40 = $70,000).

3. Alt's and Cha's LAPs are now equal, and they will receive cash distributions until the LAP of each decreases to the next highest level, the $25,000 of Blue. Multiplying the loss absorption power of $45,000 ($70,000 − $25,000) by the two partners' loss-sharing ratios shows how much of the next available cash can be safely paid to

**FIGURE 16–7**
Confirmation of Cash
Distribution Plan

| | ABC PARTNERSHIP Capital Account Balances May 1, 20X5, through July 31, 20X5 | | |
| --- | --- | --- | --- |
| | | Partner | |
| | Alt 40% | Blue 40% | Cha 20% |
| Preliquidation balances, May 1 | (34,000) | (10,000) | (14,000) |
| May loss of $10,000 on disposal of assets | 4,000 | 4,000 | 2,000 |
| | (30,000) | (6,000) | (12,000) |
| May 31 distribution of $3,000 available cash to partners: | | | |
| First $3,000 (of $6,000 priority to Alt) | 3,000 | | |
| | (27,000) | (6,000) | (12,000) |
| June loss of $15,000 on disposal of assets | 6,000 | 6,000 | 3,000 |
| | (21,000) | -0- | (9,000) |
| June 30 distribution of $15,000 available cash to partners: | | | |
| Next $3,000 (to complete Alt's $6,000 priority) | 3,000 | | |
| Remaining $12,000: | | | |
| 40/60 to Alt | 8,000 | | |
| 20/60 to Cha | | | 4,000 |
| | (10,000) | -0- | (5,000) |
| Liquidation cost of $7,500 | 3,000 | 3,000 | 1,500 |
| | (7,000) | 3,000 | (3,500) |
| Distribution of Blue's actual deficit | 2,000 | (3,000) | 1,000 |
| | (5,000) | -0- | (2,500) |
| Final payment of $7,500 to partners on July 31, 20X5: | | | |
| 40/60 to Alt | 5,000 | | |
| 20/60 to Cha | | | 2,500 |
| Postliquidation balances, July 31 | -0- | -0- | -0- |

*Note:* Parentheses indicate credit amount.

each partner. Alt and Cha will receive cash distributions according to their loss-sharing ratios. As the next $27,000 of cash becomes available, it will be distributed to Alt and Cha in the ratio of 40:60 to Alt and 20:60 to Cha.

4. Finally, when all three partners have the same LAPs, any remaining cash is distributed according to their loss-sharing ratios.

The summary of the cash distribution plan on the bottom of Figure 16–6 is provided to the partners. From this summary, partners are able to determine the relative amounts each will receive as cash becomes available to the partnership.

Figure 16–7 presents the capital balances for each of the partners in the ABC Partnership during the installment liquidation period from May 1, 20X5, through July 31, 20X5. The installment payments to partners are computed on the statement of partnership realization and liquidation (Figure 16–4) using a schedule of safe distributions to partners (Figure 16–5). Figure 16–7 shows that the actual distributions of available cash conform to the cash distribution plan prepared at the beginning of the liquidation process, with adjustment because of the actual deficit of Blue absorbed by Alt and Cha.

# ADDITIONAL CONSIDERATIONS

## Incorporation of a Partnership

As a partnership continues to grow, the partners may decide to incorporate the business to have access to additional equity financing, to limit their personal liability, to obtain selected tax advantages, or to achieve other sound business purposes. At the incorporation, the partnership is terminated, and the assets and liabilities are revalued to their fair values. The gain or loss on revaluation is allocated to the partners' capital accounts in the profit and loss–sharing ratio.

Capital stock in the new corporation is then distributed in proportion to the partners' capital accounts. The separate business entity of the partnership should now close its accounting records and the corporation, as a new business entity, should open its own new accounting records to record the issuance of its capital stock to the prior partners of the partnership.

The ABC Partnership's trial balance on May 1, 20X5, as shown previously, is used to illustrate incorporation of a partnership. Instead of liquidating the partnership as shown throughout the chapter, assume the partners agree to incorporate it.

The new corporation is to be called the Peerless Products Corporation. At the time of conversion from a partnership to a corporation, all assets and liabilities should be appraised and valued at their fair values. Any gain or loss must be distributed to the partners in their profit and loss–sharing ratios. Assume that the noncash assets have an $80,000 fair value. The $10,000 loss to fair value is allocated to the partners' capital accounts before the incorporation, as follows:

| (4) | Alt, Capital | 4,000 | |
| | Blue, Capital | 4,000 | |
| | Cha, Capital | 2,000 | |
| | Noncash Assets | | 10,000 |
| | Recognize loss on reduction of assets to fair values. | | |

Of course, in practice, specific asset accounts are used instead of the general classification of noncash assets. Gains on asset revaluations also may occur when a successful partnership elects to incorporate.

The partnership's net assets have a fair value of $48,000 ($90,000 of assets less $42,000 of liabilities). The corporation issues 4,600 shares of $1 par common stock in exchange for the assets and liabilities of the ABC Partnership. The entry made by the Peerless Products Corporation to acquire the partnership's assets and liabilities in exchange for the issuance of the 4,600 shares of stock is:

| (5) | Cash | 10,000 | |
| | Noncash Assets | 80,000 | |
| | Liabilities | | 42,000 |
| | Common Stock | | 4,600 |
| | Paid-In Capital in Excess of Par | | 43,400 |
| | Issuance of stock for partnership's assets and liabilities. | | |

The partners make the following entry on the partnership's books:

| (6) | Investment in Peerless Products Stock | 48,000 | |
| | Liabilities | 42,000 | |
| | Cash | | 10,000 |
| | Noncash Assets | | 80,000 |
| | Receipt of stock in Peerless Products in exchange for partnership's net assets. | | |

Recall that the noncash assets were reduced to their fair values in entry (4). To distribute the stock to the partners and close the partnership's books, the final entry is as follows:

| (7) | Alt, Capital | 30,000 | |
| | Blue, Capital | 6,000 | |
| | Cha, Capital | 12,000 | |
| | Investment in Peerless Products Stock | | 48,000 |
| | Distribution of Peerless Products stock to partners. | | |

## Summary of Key Concepts

The process of terminating and liquidating a partnership is often a traumatic time for partners. The Uniform Partnership Act of 1997 provides guidance for the liquidation process and specifies the legal rights of the partners and of partnership creditors.

Dissociation of a partner is his or her withdrawal, either voluntarily or involuntarily, from the partnership. Dissolution is the dissolving of a partnership. Not all dissociations and dissolutions require termination, which is the cessation of normal business functions, or liquidation, with the disposal of assets, payment of liabilities, and distribution of remaining cash to the partners. UPA 1997 defines a partnership as a legal entity apart from the individual partners. Therefore, unless required by judicial determination, termination and liquidation often can be avoided by carefully preparing the partnership agreement to allow continuation of the business when a partner retires or leaves the partnership. The most common reasons for involuntary liquidation are court decrees or the bankruptcy of the partnership.

Liquidation can involve a single lump-sum payment to partners. Most liquidations, however, take several months and involve installment payments to partners during the liquidation process. Liquidations are facilitated by the preparation of the statement of partnership realization and liquidation, a workpaper summarizing the liquidation process and serving as a basis for the journal entries to record the events. Installment payments to partners are determined on a worst-case basis using a schedule of safe payments to partners, which assumes that all noncash assets will be written off and that partners with debit balances in their capital accounts will not be able to remedy the deficiencies.

A cash distribution plan provides information to partners about the installment payments they will receive as cash becomes available to the partnership. The plan is prepared at the beginning of the liquidation process. Actual cash distributions during the liquidation process are determined with the statement of partnership realization and liquidation. The concept of loss absorption power (LAP) is central to the development of the cash distribution plan. Loss absorption power is the amount of partnership loss required to eliminate a given partner's capital credit balance. The loss absorption power is determined by dividing a partner's net capital credit balance by his or her loss-sharing percentage.

## Key Terms

cash distribution plan, *775*
dissociation (of a partner), *763*
dissolution (of a partnership), *764*

installment liquidation, *770*
loss absorption power (LAP), *775*
lump-sum liquidation, *765*

schedule of safe payments to partners, *772*
statement of partnership realization and liquidation, *765*

## Appendix **16A**  Partners' Personal Financial Statements

At the beginning of the liquidation process, partners are usually asked for personal financial statements to determine each partner's personal solvency. Guidelines for preparing personal financial statements are found in **Statement of Position 82-1,** "Personal Financial Statements" (SOP 82-1).[1] Personal financial statements consist of the following:

1. Statement of financial condition, or personal balance sheet, which presents the person's assets and liabilities at a point in time.
2. Statement of changes in net worth, or personal income statement, which presents the primary sources of changes in the person's net worth.

In addition to presenting a person's assets and liabilities, the statement of financial condition should include an estimate of the income taxes incurred as if all the assets were converted and the liabilities extinguished. The person's net worth would then be computed as assets less liabilities less estimated taxes (see Figure 16–8). In general, the accrual basis of accounting should be used to determine the person's assets and liabilities, and comparative statements are usually provided. However, unlike a balance sheet of a business that is based on historical cost, the assets in the personal statement of financial condition are stated at their estimated current values. The liabilities are stated at the lower of the discounted value of future cash payments or the current cash settlement

[1] *Accounting Standards Division of AICPA (Statement of Position 82-1),* "Accounting and Financial Reporting for Personal Financial Statements" (New York: AICPA, 1982).

**FIGURE 16–8**
Personal Statement of
Financial Condition

**C. ALT**
**Statement of Financial Condition**
**May 1, 20X5 and 20X4**

| | Year | |
| --- | --- | --- |
| | **20X5** | **20X4** |
| **Assets** | | |
| Cash | $ 4,000 | $ 2,500 |
| Receivables | 3,500 | 4,000 |
| Investments: | | |
| Marketable securities | 5,000 | 4,000 |
| ABC Partnership | 34,000 | 26,000 |
| Cash surrender value of life insurance | 3,100 | 3,000 |
| Residence | 84,000 | 76,000 |
| Personal effects | 16,400 | 12,500 |
| Total assets | $150,000 | $128,000 |
| **Liabilities and Net Worth** | | |
| Charge accounts | $ 2,000 | $ 3,000 |
| Income taxes—current-year balance | 1,200 | 800 |
| 10 percent note payable | 6,000 | 10,000 |
| Mortgage payable | 60,000 | 62,000 |
| Estimated income taxes on the difference between the estimated current values of assets and liabilities and their tax bases | 16,800 | 12,200 |
| Net worth | 64,000 | 40,000 |
| Total liabilities and net worth | $150,000 | $128,000 |

amount. Included immediately below the liabilities are the estimated taxes that would be paid if all the assets were converted to cash and all the liabilities were paid.

Assets and liabilities are presented in their order of liquidity and maturity, not as current and noncurrent. **SOP 82-1** provides guidelines for determining the current value of a person's assets and liabilities. The primary valuation methods are discounted value of future cash flows, current market prices of marketable securities or other investments, and appraisals of properties. An investment in a separate business entity (e.g., a partnership) should be reported as a one-line, combined amount valued at the net investment's market value. The liabilities are stated at their discounted cash flow value or current liquidation value. The accountant uses applicable tax laws, carryover provisions, and other regulations to compute the estimated tax liability from the assumed conversion of assets and the assumed extinguishment of liabilities.

The statement of changes in net worth presents the major sources of income. It recognizes both realized and unrealized income. A commercial business's income statement may not recognize holding gains on some marketable securities, but such gains are recognized on an individual's statement of changes in net worth.

# ILLUSTRATION OF PERSONAL FINANCIAL STATEMENTS

The following illustration presents Alt's personal financial condition as of May 1, 20X5, the day the partners decide to liquidate the ABC Partnership. Alt's net worth on this date is as follows:

| | |
| --- | --- |
| Personal assets | $150,000 |
| Personal liabilities | (86,000) |
| Net worth | $ 64,000 |

## Statement of Financial Condition

Alt's statement of financial condition on May 1, 20X5, is presented in Figure 16–8 along with the prior year's statement. The 20X5 statement illustrates the following:

1.  Receivables due to Alt from other people have a present value of $3,500.
2.  Alt has two investments, one of which is his interest in the ABC Partnership, valued at estimated current market value, which in this case also equals its book value of $34,000. The marketable security investments are shown at market value.
3.  The cash surrender value of life insurance is presented net of any loans payable on the policies.
4.  Alt's residence and personal effects are presented at their appraised values.
5.  Liabilities are presented at their estimated current liquidation value or the discounted value of the future cash flows.
6.  The estimated income taxes on the difference between the estimated current values of assets and liabilities and their tax bases represent the amount of income tax Alt would be liable for if all assets were converted to cash and all liabilities were paid.
7.  Net worth is the difference between the estimated current value of Alt's assets and liabilities, including estimated tax.

## Statement of Changes in Net Worth

Alt's statement of changes in net worth, shown in Figure 16–9, illustrates the following:

1.  The statement separates the realized and unrealized changes in net worth. Realized changes are cash flows to or from Alt that have already taken place. Unrealized changes are equivalent to holding gains or losses. They have not yet been converted to cash. For example, Alt received

**FIGURE 16–9**
**Personal Statement of Changes in Net Worth**

| C. ALT<br>Statement of Changes in Net Worth<br>For the Years Ended May 1, 20X5 and 20X4 | | |
|---|---|---|
| | **Year Ended May 1** | |
| | **20X5** | **20X4** |
| Realized increases in net worth: | | |
| Salary | $ 36,900 | $ 34,900 |
| Dividends and interest income | 800 | 400 |
| Distribution from ABC Partnership | 3,000 | 1,000 |
| Cash surrender value of life insurance | 100 | 100 |
| Gains on sales of marketable securities | 1,400 | 1,200 |
| | $ 42,200 | $ 37,600 |
| Realized decreases in net worth: | | |
| Income taxes | $ 8,200 | $ 7,800 |
| Interest expense | 1,400 | 700 |
| Real estate taxes | 2,400 | 2,200 |
| Insurance payments (including $100 for increase in<br>  cash surrender value of life insurance) | 400 | 300 |
| Personal expenditures | 18,800 | 18,600 |
| | $(31,200) | $(29,600) |
| Net realized increase in net worth | $ 11,000 | $ 8,000 |
| Unrealized increases in net worth: | | |
| Marketable securities | $ 1,600 | $ 400 |
| ABC Partnership | 8,000 | 5,000 |
| Residence | 8,000 | 4,000 |
| | $ 17,600 | $ 9,400 |
| Unrealized decreases in net worth: | | |
| Increase in estimated income taxes on the difference<br>  between the estimated current values of assets and<br>  liabilities and their tax bases | (4,600) | (4,400) |
| Net unrealized increase in net worth | $ 13,000 | $ 5,000 |
| Net increase in net worth: | | |
| Realized and unrealized | $ 24,000 | $ 13,000 |
| Net worth at beginning of period | 40,000 | 27,000 |
| Net worth at end of period | $ 64,000 | $ 40,000 |

$3,000 from the ABC Partnership during the year ended May 1, 20X5. In addition, Alt's partnership interest increased by $8,000 during the year.

2. Alt had $42,200 of realized increases in net worth during the year ended May 1, 20X5. The primary source was a salary of $36,900 from full-time employment outside the ABC Partnership.

3. The major realized decrease in net worth during the year ended May 1, 20X5, was for personal expenditures of $18,800.

4. Unrealized increases of $17,600 during the year were primarily from an increase in the value of Alt's personal residence ($8,000) and an increase in the investment value of his partnership interest in the ABC Partnership ($8,000). Unrealized holding gains of $1,600 are available in Alt's investments in marketable securities.

5. The change in the estimated tax liability is an unrealized decrease because this amount is due only if Alt converts these assets to cash.

6. The net unrealized changes in net worth are added to the net realized changes in net worth to obtain the total change in Alt's net worth for each year. Alt's net worth increased by $13,000 during the year ended May 1, 20X4, and by $24,000 during the year ended May 1, 20X5.

## Footnote Disclosures

Sufficient footnote disclosures should accompany the two personal financial statements. The footnotes should describe the following:

1. The methods used to value the major assets.

2. The names and the nature of businesses in which the person has major investments.

3. The methods and assumptions used to compute the estimated tax bases and a statement that the tax provision in an actual liquidation will probably differ from the estimate because the actual tax burden will then be based on actual realizations determined by market values at the point of liquidation.

4. Maturities, interest rates, and other details of any receivables and debt.

5. Any other information needed to present fully the person's net worth.

---

## Questions

**Q16-1**  What are the major causes of a dissolution? What are the accounting implications of a dissolution?

**Q16-2**  During a partnership liquidation, do a partnership's liabilities to individual partners have a lower priority than the partnership's obligations to other, third party creditors? Explain.

**Q16-3**  X, Y, and Z are partners. The partnership is liquidating, and Partner Z is personally insolvent. What implications may this have for Partners X and Y?

**Q16-4**  May an individual partner simply decide to leave a partnership? Does the partnership have any legal recourse against that partner? Explain.

**Q16-5**  Contrast a lump-sum liquidation with an installment liquidation.

**Q16-6**  How is a deficit in a partner's capital account eliminated if he or she is personally insolvent?

**Q16-7**  The DEF Partnership has total assets of $55,000. Partner D has a capital credit of $6,000, Partner E has a capital deficit of $20,000, and Partner F has a capital credit of $8,000. Is the DEF Partnership solvent or insolvent?

**Q16-8**  Assume that, because of a new law recently passed, the types of significant transactions in which a partnership engages are no longer lawful. Two of the five partners wish to have a winding up and termination of the partnership. Can these two partners require the partnership to terminate? Explain.

**Q16-9**  How are a partner's personal payments to partnership creditors accounted for on the partnership's books?

**Q16-10**  What is the purpose of the schedule of safe payments to partners?

**Q16-11**  In what ratio are losses during liquidation assigned to the partners' capital accounts? Is this ratio used in all instances?

**Q16-12**  The installment liquidation process uses a worst-case assumption in computing the payments to partners. What does this *worst-case assumption* mean?

**Q16-13**  Define *loss absorption power* and explain its importance in the determination of cash distributions to partners.

**Q16-14**  Partner A has a capital credit of $25,000. Partner B's capital credit is also $25,000. Partners A and B share profits and losses in a 60:40 ratio. Which partner will receive the first payment of cash in an installment liquidation?

**Q16-15***  Explain the process of incorporating a partnership.

---

# Cases

### C16-1  Cash Distributions to Partners

*Analysis*

The partnership of A. Bull and T. Bear is in the process of termination. The partners have disagreed on virtually every decision and have decided to liquidate the present business, with each partner taking his own clients from the partnership. Bull wants cash distributed as it becomes available; Bear wants no cash distributed until all assets are sold and all liabilities are settled. You are called in to aid in the termination and liquidation process.

#### Required
How would you respond to each of the partners' requests?

### C16-2  Cash Distributions to Partners

*Analysis*

Adam and Bard agreed to liquidate their partnership. You have been asked to assist them in this process, and you prepare the following balance sheet for the date of the beginning of the liquidation. The loss-sharing percentages are in parentheses next to the capital account balances.

| | |
|---|---:|
| Cash | $ 40,000 |
| Loan Receivable from Adam | 10,000 |
| Other Assets | 200,000 |
| Total | $250,000 |
| | |
| Accounts Payable | $ 30,000 |
| Loan Payable to Bard | 100,000 |
| Adam, Capital (50%) | 80,000 |
| Bard, Capital (50%) | 40,000 |
| Total | $250,000 |

Bard is demanding that the loan from him be paid before any cash is distributed to Adam. Adam believes the available cash should be paid to him until his capital account is reduced to $40,000, the same as Bard's. Adam will then pay the loan receivable to the partnership with the cash received. You have been asked to reconcile the argument.

#### Required
How would you advise in this case?

### C16-3*  Incorporation of a Partnership

*Judgment*

After successfully operating a partnership for several years, the partners have proposed to incorporate the business and admit another investor. The original partners will purchase at par an amount of preferred stock equal to the book values of their capital interests in the partnership and common stock for the amount of the market value, including unrecognized goodwill, of the business that exceeds book value. The new investor will make an investment, at a 5 percent premium over par value, in both preferred and common stock equal to one-third of the total number of shares purchased by the original partners. The corporation will acquire all the partnership's assets, assume the liabilities, and employ the original partners and the new investor.

#### Required

a. Discuss the differences in accounts used and valuations expected in comparing the balance sheets of the proposed corporation and the partnership.

*Indicates that the item relates to "Additional Considerations."

*b.* Discuss the differences that would be expected in a comparison of the income statements of the proposed corporation and the partnership.

### C16-4 Sharing Losses during Liquidation

*Research*

Hiller, Luna, and Welsh are attempting to form a partnership to operate a travel agency. They have agreed to share profits in a ratio of 4:3:2 but cannot agree on the terms of the partnership agreement relating to possible liquidation. Hiller believes that it is best not to get into any arguments about potential liquidation at this time because the partnership will be a success and it is not necessary to think negatively at this point in time. Luna believes that in the event of liquidation, any losses should be shared equally because each partner would have worked equally for the partnership's success, or lack thereof. Welsh believes that any losses during liquidation should be distributed in the ratio of capital balances at the beginning of any liquidation because then the losses will be distributed based on a capital ability to bear the losses.

You have been asked to help resolve the differences and to prepare a memo to the three individuals including the following items.

#### Required

*a.* Specify the procedures for allocating losses among partners stated in the Uniform Partnership Act of 1997 to be used if no partnership agreement terms are agreed upon regarding liquidation. (You may wish to access a copy of the Uniform Partnership Act of 1997 for this requirement.)

*b.* Critically assess each partner's viewpoint, discussing the pros and cons of each.

*c.* Specify another option for allocating potential liquidation losses not included in the positions currently taken by the three individuals. Critically assess the pros and cons of your alternative.

### C16-5 Analysis of a Court Decision on a Partnership Liquidation

*Application*

The *Mattfield v. Kramer Brothers* court case presents a number of the interesting legal issues that often arise from the dissolution of a partnership. The case was heard in the Supreme Court of the State of Montana in 2005 and decided on May 31, 2005, as Case 03-796. The decision of the court includes a summary of the disputes and lower court decisions.

The Montana State Supreme Court's decision is available at the FindLaw site. The easiest way to obtain the script of the decision is to Google the search term "Mattfield v. Kramer Brothers" and then follow the link to the Court's 2005 decision. The legal briefs from each side that were presented to the Supreme Court may be obtained at the State Law Library of Montana site by making a Google search using "State of Montana Law Library" or use the URL: http://courts.mt.gov/library, click on Cases, and then search using case number 03-796, or a text term such as Mattfield. The briefs will then be made available.

#### Required

Obtain a copy of the Montana Supreme Court decision in the *Mattfield v. Kramer Brothers* case. Then answer each of the following questions regarding the case.

*a.* Prepare a short summary of the history of the Kramer Brothers Co-Partnership from formation through the appeal to the Montana Supreme Court.

*b.* What type of partnership agreement existed? Recommend several provisions that you feel should have been included in a formal, written partnership agreement of the partnership.

*c.* At the time the case was appealed to the Supreme Court, did Bill Kramer still have an economic interest in the partnership? Explain.

*d.* What legal recourse did the other partners have at the time Don Kramer dissociated from the partnership in 1994?

*e.* In February 1997, why did Don Kramer's attorney, Floyd Brower, request copies of Ray Kramer's and Doug Kramer's personal tax returns?

*f.* Select and discuss two key points regarding partnership liquidations that are illustrated by this case and that you feel are important.

### C16-6 Reviewing the Liquidation Process of a Limited Partnership

*Application*

Some limited partnerships have SEC filing requirements because of selling partnership units or debt securities to the public. One such partnership was Fairfield Inn By Marriott Limited Partnership, which had a series of filings from January 1998 to May 2006. Using the SEC's EDGAR (www.sec.gov), obtain the annual report for this limited partnership for the year ended December 31, 2003, which was filed on May 14, 2004.

### Required

Answer each of the following questions from the information you obtain by analyzing the 10-K of Fairfield Inn By Marriott Limited Partnership.

*a.* Describe the formation of the partnership, including the date of formation and the purpose for the limited partnership.

*b.* Who was the initial general partner? What was the general partner's initial percentage interest in the partnership? And who was general partner as of December 31, 2003?

*c.* What was the general partner's profit percentage? What economic reasons might the general partner have had for investing in this partnership?

*d.* What were the major elements of the Restructuring Plan approved in 2001 by the limited partners?

*e.* What were the major elements of the Plan of Liquidation that was initiated in 2003?

*f.* The partnership adopted the liquidation basis of accounting beginning on September 30, 2003. Briefly describe the liquidation basis of accounting the partnership used.

*g.* Compare the partnership's financial statements before and then after the September 30, 2003, adoption of the liquidation basis of accounting.

*h.* The partnership filed a Form 15-12G on May 1, 2006. Obtain this filing. What is the purpose of this form that is required by the SEC?

---

## Exercises

**E16-1**

### Multiple-Choice Questions on Partnership Liquidations

Select the correct answer for each of the following questions.

*Note:* The following information is for questions 1, 2, and 3.

The balance sheet for the partnership of Joan, Charles, and Thomas, whose shares of profits and losses are 40, 50, and 10 percent, is as follows:

| Cash | $ 50,000 | Accounts Payable | $150,000 |
|---|---|---|---|
| Inventory | 360,000 | Joan, Capital | 160,000 |
| | | Charles, Capital | 45,000 |
| | | Thomas, Capital | 55,000 |
| Total Assets | $410,000 | Total Liabilities and Equities | $410,000 |

1. If the inventory is sold for $300,000, how much should Joan receive upon liquidation of the partnership?

   *a.* $48,000.

   *b.* $100,000.

   *c.* $136,000.

   *d.* $160,000.

2. If the inventory is sold for $180,000, how much should Thomas receive upon liquidation of the partnership?

   *a.* $28,000.

   *b.* $32,500.

   *c.* $37,000.

   *d.* $55,000.

3. The partnership will be liquidated in installments. As cash becomes available, it will be distributed to the partners. If inventory costing $200,000 is sold for $140,000, how much cash should be distributed to each partner at this time?

| | Joan | Charles | Thomas |
|---|---|---|---|
| *a.* | $56,000 | $70,000 | $14,000 |
| *b.* | $16,000 | $20,000 | $ 4,000 |
| *c.* | $32,000 | $ -0- | $ 8,000 |
| *d.* | $20,000 | $ -0- | $20,000 |

4. In accounting for partnership liquidation, cash payments to partners after all creditors' claims have been satisfied, but before the final cash distribution, should be according to:

   a. The partners' relative profit and loss–sharing ratios.

   b. The final balances in partner capital accounts.

   c. The partners' relative share of the gain or loss on liquidations.

   d. Safe payments computations.

5. After all noncash assets have been converted into cash in the liquidation of the Adam and Kay Partnership, the ledger contains the following account balances:

   |  | Debit | Credit |
   |---|---|---|
   | Cash | $47,000 | |
   | Accounts Payable | | $32,000 |
   | Loan Payable to Adam | | 15,000 |
   | Adam, Capital | 7,000 | |
   | Kay, Capital | | 7,000 |

   Available cash should be distributed with $32,000 going to accounts payable and then:

   a. $15,000 to the loan payable to Adam.

   b. $7,500 each to Adam and Kay.

   c. $8,000 to Adam and $7,000 to Kay.

   d. $7,000 to Adam and $8,000 to Kay.

*Note:* The following information is for questions 6 and 7.

F, A, S, and B are partners sharing profits and losses equally. The partnership is insolvent and is to be liquidated. The status of the partnership and each partner is as follows:

| | Partnership Capital Balance | Personal Assets (exclusive of partnership interest) | Personal Liabilities (exclusive of partnership interest) |
|---|---|---|---|
| F | $(15,000) | $100,000 | $40,000 |
| A | (10,000) | 30,000 | 60,000 |
| S | 20,000[a] | 80,000 | 5,000 |
| B | 30,000[a] | 1,000 | 28,000 |
| Total | $ 25,000[a] | | |

[a]Deficit

6. The partnership creditors:

   a. Must first seek recovery against S because she is personally solvent and has a negative capital balance.

   b. Will *not* be paid in full regardless of how they proceed legally because the partnership assets are less than the partnership liabilities.

   c. Will have to share A's interest in the partnership on a pro rata basis with A's personal creditors.

   d. Have first claim to the partnership assets before any partner's personal creditors have rights to the partnership assets.

7. The partnership creditors should seek recovery of their claims:

   a. From the partnership, including additional contributions from F and S.

   b. From the personal assets of either F or A.

   c. From the personal assets of either S or B.

   d. From the personal assets of any of the partners for all or some of their claims.

**E16-2** **Multiple-Choice Questions on Partnership Liquidation [AICPA Adapted]**

Select the correct answer for each of the following questions.

1. On January 1, 20X7, the partners of Casey, Dithers, and Edwards, who share profits and losses in the ratio of 5:3:2, decided to liquidate their partnership. On this date the partnership condensed balance sheet was as follows:

| Assets | | Liabilities and Capital | |
|---|---|---|---|
| Cash | $ 50,000 | Liabilities | $ 60,000 |
| Other Assets | 250,000 | Casey, Capital | 80,000 |
| | | Dithers, Capital | 90,000 |
| | | Edwards, Capital | 70,000 |
| Total | $300,000 | Total | $300,000 |

On January 15, 20X7, the first cash sale of other assets with a carrying amount of $150,000 realized $120,000. Safe installment payments to the partners were made on the same date. How much cash should be distributed to each partner?

| | Casey | Dithers | Edwards |
|---|---|---|---|
| a. | $15,000 | $51,000 | $44,000 |
| b. | $40,000 | $45,000 | $35,000 |
| c. | $55,000 | $33,000 | $22,000 |
| d. | $60,000 | $36,000 | $24,000 |

2. In a partnership liquidation, the final cash distribution to the partners should be made in accordance with the:

a. Partners' profit and loss–sharing ratio.

b. Balances of the partners' capital accounts.

c. Ratio of the capital contributions by the partners.

d. Ratio of capital contributions less withdrawals by the partners.

*Note:* The following information is for questions 3 through 5.

The balance sheet for the Art, Blythe, and Cooper Partnership is as follows. Figures shown parenthetically reflect agreed profit and loss–sharing percentages.

| Assets | | Liabilities and Capital | |
|---|---|---|---|
| Cash | $ 20,000 | Liabilities | $ 50,000 |
| Other Assets | 180,000 | Art, Capital (40%) | 37,000 |
| | | Blythe, Capital (40%) | 65,000 |
| | | Cooper, Capital (20%) | 48,000 |
| Total | $200,000 | Total | $200,000 |

3. If the firm, as shown on the balance sheet, is dissolved and liquidated by selling assets in installments and if the first sale of noncash assets having a book value of $90,000 realizes $50,000 and all cash available after settlement with creditors is distributed, the respective partners would receive (to the nearest dollar):

| | Art | Blythe | Cooper |
|---|---|---|---|
| a. | $8,000 | $ 8,000 | $ 4,000 |
| b. | $6,667 | $ 6,667 | $ 6,666 |
| c. | $  -0- | $13,333 | $ 6,667 |
| d. | $  -0- | $ 3,000 | $17,000 |

4. If the facts are as in question 3 except that $3,000 cash is to be withheld, the respective partners would then receive (to the nearest dollar):

|     | Art | Blythe | Cooper |
| --- | --- | --- | --- |
| a. | $6,800 | $ 6,800 | $ 3,400 |
| b. | $5,667 | $ 5,667 | $ 5,666 |
| c. | $  -0- | $11,333 | $ 5,667 |
| d. | $  -0- | $ 1,000 | $16,000 |

5. If each partner properly received some cash in the distribution after the second sale, if the cash to be distributed amounts to $12,000 from the third sale, and if unsold assets with an $8,000 book value remain, ignoring questions 3 and 4, the respective partners would receive:

|     | Art | Blythe | Cooper |
| --- | --- | --- | --- |
| a. | $ 4,800 | $ 4,800 | $ 2,400 |
| b. | $ 4,000 | $ 4,000 | $ 4,000 |
| c. | 37/150 | 65/150 | 48/150 |
|    | of | of | of |
|    | $12,000 | $12,000 | $12,000 |
| d. | $   -0- | $ 8,000 | $ 4,000 |

6. The following condensed balance sheet is presented for the partnership of Arnie, Bart, and Kurt, who share profits and losses in the ratio of 4:3:3, respectively:

| Assets | | Liabilities and Capital | |
| --- | --- | --- | --- |
| Cash | $100,000 | Liabilities | $150,000 |
| Other Assets | 300,000 | Arnie, Capital | 40,000 |
|  |  | Bart, Capital | 180,000 |
|  |  | Kurt, Capital | 30,000 |
| Total | $400,000 | Total | $400,000 |

The partners agreed to dissolve the partnership after selling the other assets for $200,000. On dissolution of the partnership, Arnie should receive:

a. $0.

b. $40,000.

c. $60,000.

d. $70,000.

### E16-3 Computing Alternative Cash Distributions to Partners

Bracken, Louden, and Menser, who share profits and losses in a ratio of 4:3:3, are partners in a home decorating business that has not been able to generate the type of income hoped for by the partners. They have decided to liquidate the business and have sold all the assets except for their decorating equipment. All partnership liabilities have been settled and all the partners are personally insolvent. The decorating equipment has a book value of $40,000, and the partners have capital account balances as follows:

| Bracken, capital | $25,000 |
| --- | --- |
| Louden, capital | 5,000 |
| Menser, capital | 10,000 |

### Required

Determine the amount of cash each partner will receive as a liquidating distribution if the decorating equipment is sold for the amount stated in each of the following independent cases:

## Skype

rob.hoskin1
callin1

A+    4.3
A     4.0
A-    3.2
B+    3.3
B     3.0

3.85

Grade Dist

At    3.3
A     56.7
A-    31.7
B+    6.7
B     1.7

17    10:15 AM
May 14
15    9:00 AM
# 245

263
958
428
―――――
1,848,000

Skype

friction, don
calling

LA 2 — 3/24, 25
25, 26
7/14, 15
15, 16
9/22, 23

LA 3

April 27 – 5/1

Oct 5 – 9

9
24
28
―――
61

*a.* $30,000.

*b.* $21,000.

*c.* $7,000.

### E16-4 Lump-Sum Liquidation

Matthews, Mitchell, and Michaels are partners in the BG Land Development Company and share losses in a 5:3:2 ratio. The balance sheet on June 30, 20X1, when they decide to liquidate the business, is as follows:

| Assets | | Liabilities and Equities | |
|---|---|---|---|
| Cash | $ 20,000 | Accounts Payable | $ 30,000 |
| Noncash Assets | 150,000 | Mitchell, Loan | 10,000 |
| | | Matthews, Capital | 80,000 |
| | | Mitchell, Capital | 36,000 |
| | | Michaels, Capital | 14,000 |
| Total Assets | $170,000 | Total Liabilities and Equities | $170,000 |

The noncash assets are sold for $110,000.

#### Required

*a.* Prepare a statement of partnership realization and liquidation.

*b.* Prepare the required journal entries to account for the liquidation of the BG Land Development Company.

### E16-5 Schedule of Safe Payments

After working for the In the Kitchen remodeling business for several years, Terry and Phyllis decided to go into business for themselves and formed the Kitchens Just for You partnership. Three years ago, they admitted Connie as a partner and recognized goodwill at that time because of her good client list for planned kitchen makeovers. However, they were not able to gain a sufficient market for new customers and on September 1, 20X9, they agreed to dissolve and liquidate the business. They decided on an installment liquidation in order to complete the projects already initiated. The balance sheet, with profit and loss–sharing percentages at the beginning of liquidation, is as follows:

| **KITCHENS JUST FOR YOU** | | | |
|---|---|---|---|
| **Balance Sheet** | | | |
| **September 1, 20X9** | | | |
| Assets | | Liabilities and Equities | |
| Cash | $ 12,000 | Accounts Payable | $ 43,000 |
| Receivables | 63,000 | Connie, Loan | 15,000 |
| Terry, Loan | 9,000 | Terry, Capital (30%) | 12,000 |
| Inventory | 48,000 | Phyllis, Capital (50%) | 36,000 |
| Goodwill | 28,000 | Connie, Capital (20%) | 54,000 |
| Total Assets | $160,000 | Total Liabilities and Equities | $160,000 |

Connie's loan was for working capital; the loan to Terry was for his unexpected personal medical bills.

During September 20X9, the first month of liquidation, the partnership collected $41,000 in receivables and decided to write off $12,000 of the remaining receivables. Sales of one-half of the book value of the inventory realized a loss of $4,000. The partners estimate that the costs of liquidating the business such as newspaper ads, signs, etc., are expected to be $6,000 for the remainder of the liquidation process.

#### Required

Prepare a schedule of safe payments to partners as of September 30, 20X9, to show how the available cash should be distributed to the partners.

**E16-6 Schedule of Safe Payments to Partners**

Partners Maness and Joiner have decided to liquidate their business. The ledger shows the following account balances:

| | | | |
|---|---|---|---|
| Cash | $ 25,000 | Accounts Payable | $15,000 |
| Inventory | 120,000 | Maness, Capital | 65,000 |
| | | Joiner, Capital | 65,000 |

Maness and Joiner share profits and losses in an 8:2 ratio. During the first month of liquidation, half the inventory is sold for $40,000, and $10,000 of the accounts payable is paid. During the second month, the rest of the inventory is sold for $30,000, and the remaining accounts payable are paid. Cash is distributed at the end of each month, and the liquidation is completed at the end of the second month.

### Required

Prepare a statement of partnership realization and liquidation with a schedule of safe payments for the two-month liquidation period.

**E16-7 Alternative Profit and Loss–Sharing Ratios in a Partnership Liquidation**

Nelson, Osman, Peters, and Quincy have decided to terminate their partnership because of recurrent arguments among the partners. The partnership's balance sheet at the time they decide to wind up is as follows:

| | | | |
|---|---|---|---|
| Cash | $ 17,000 | Accounts Payable | $ 12,000 |
| Noncash Assets | 190,000 | Nelson, Capital | 15,000 |
| | | Osman, Capital | 75,000 |
| | | Peters, Capital | 75,000 |
| | | Quincy, Capital | 30,000 |
| Total Assets | $207,000 | Total Liabilities and Equities | $207,000 |

During the winding up of the partnership, the other assets are sold for $100,000 and the accounts payable are paid. Osman and Peters are personally solvent, but Nelson and Quincy are personally insolvent.

### Required

Determine the amount of cash each partner will receive from the final distributions of the partnership for each of the following independent cases of profit and loss ratios for Nelson, Osman, Peters, and Quincy.

*a.* The partners share profits and losses in the ratio of 3:3:2:2.

*b.* The partners share profits and losses in the ratio of 3:1:3:3.

*c.* The partners share profits and losses in the ratio of 3:1:2:4.

**E16-8 Cash Distribution Plan**

Adams, Peters, and Blake share profits and losses for their APB Partnership in a ratio of 2:3:5. When they decide to liquidate, the balance sheet is as follows:

| **Assets** | | **Liabilities and Equities** | |
|---|---|---|---|
| Cash | $ 40,000 | Liabilities | $ 50,000 |
| Adams, Loan | 10,000 | Adams, Capital | 55,000 |
| Other Assets | 200,000 | Peters, Capital | 75,000 |
| | | Blake, Capital | 70,000 |
| Total Assets | $250,000 | Total Liabilities and Equities | $250,000 |

Liquidation expenses are expected to be negligible. No interest accrues on loans with partners after termination of the business.

### Required

Prepare a cash distribution plan for the APB Partnership.

### E16-9 Confirmation of Cash Distribution Plan

Refer to the data in Exercise E16-8. During the liquidation process for the APB Partnership, the following events occurred:

1. During the first month of liquidation, noncash assets with a book value of $85,000 were sold for $65,000, and $21,000 of the liabilities were paid.
2. During the second month, the remaining noncash assets were sold for $79,000. The loan receivable from Adams was collected, and the rest of the creditors were paid.
3. Cash is distributed to partners at the end of each month.

### Required

Prepare a statement of partnership realization and liquidation with a schedule of safe payments to partners for the liquidation period.

### E16-10* Incorporation of a Partnership

When Alice and Betty decided to incorporate their partnership, the trial balance was as follows:

|  | Debit | Credit |
| --- | --- | --- |
| Cash | $ 8,000 | |
| Accounts Receivable (net) | 22,400 | |
| Inventory | 36,000 | |
| Equipment (net) | 47,200 | |
| Accounts Payable | | $ 17,200 |
| Alice, Capital (60%) | | 62,400 |
| Betty, Capital (40%) | | 34,000 |
| Total | $113,600 | $113,600 |

The partnership's books will be closed, and new books will be used for A & B Corporation. The following additional information is available:

1. The estimated fair values of the assets follow:

| | |
| --- | --- |
| Accounts Receivable | $21,600 |
| Inventory | 32,800 |
| Equipment | 40,000 |

2. All assets and liabilities are transferred to the corporation.
3. The common stock is $10 par. Alice and Betty receive a total of 7,100 shares.
4. The partners' profit and loss–sharing ratio is shown in the trial balance.

### Required

a. Prepare the entries on the partnership's books to record (1) the revaluation of assets, (2) the transfer of the assets to the A & B Corporation and the receipt of the common stock, and (3) the closing of the books.

b. Prepare the entries on A & B Corporation's books to record the assets and the issuance of the common stock.

### E16-11A Multiple-Choice on Personal Financial Statements [AICPA Adapted]

Select the correct answer for each of the following questions.

1. On December 31, 20X7, Judy is a fully vested participant in a company-sponsored pension plan. According to the plan's administrator, Judy has at that date the nonforfeitable right to receive a lump sum of $100,000 on December 28, 20X8. The discounted amount of $100,000

is $90,000 at December 31, 20X7. The right is not contingent on Judy's life expectancy and requires no future performance on Judy's part. In Judy's December 31, 20X7, personal statement of financial condition, the vested interest in the pension plan should be reported at:

a. $0.

b. $90,000.

c. $95,000.

d. $100,000.

2. On December 31, 20X7, Mr. and Mrs. McManus owned a parcel of land held as an investment. The land was purchased for $95,000 in 20X0, and was encumbered by a mortgage with a principal balance of $60,000 at December 31, 20X7. On this date the fair value of the land was $150,000. In the McManuses' December 31, 20X7, personal statement of financial condition, at what amount should the land investment and mortgage payable be reported?

|     | Land Investment | Mortgage Payable |
| --- | --- | --- |
| a. | $150,000 | $60,000 |
| b. | $ 95,000 | $60,000 |
| c. | $ 90,000 | $   -0- |
| d. | $ 35,000 | $   -0- |

3. Rich Drennen's personal statement of financial condition at December 31, 20X6, shows net worth of $400,000 before consideration of employee stock options owned on that date. Information relating to the stock options is as follows:

• Options are to purchase 10,000 shares of Oglesby Corporation stock.

• Options exercise price is $10 a share.

• Options expire on June 30, 20X7.

• Market price of the stock is $25 a share on December 31, 20X6.

• Assume that exercise of the options in 20X7 would result in ordinary income taxable at 35 percent.

After giving effect to the stock options, Drennen's net worth at December 31, 20X6, would be:

a. $497,500.

b. $550,000.

c. $562,500.

d. $650,000.

4. Nancy Emerson owns 50 percent of the common stock of Marks Corporation. She paid $25,000 for this stock in 20X3. At December 31, 20X8, it was ascertained that her 50 percent stock ownership in Marks had a current value of $185,000. Marks's cumulative net income and cash dividends declared for the five years ended December 31, 20X8, were $300,000 and $30,000 respectively. In Nancy's personal statement of financial condition at December 31, 20X8, what amount should be reported as her net investment in Marks?

a. $25,000.

b. $160,000.

c. $175,000.

d. $185,000.

5. In a personal statement of financial condition, which of the following should be reported at estimated current values?

|     | Investments in Closely Held Business | Investments in Leaseholds |
| --- | --- | --- |
| a. | Yes | Yes |
| b. | Yes | No |
| c. | No | No |
| d. | No | Yes |

6. Personal financial statements should include which of the following statements?

| | Financial Condition | Changes in Net Worth | Cash Flows |
|---|---|---|---|
| *a.* | No | Yes | Yes |
| *b.* | Yes | No | No |
| *c.* | Yes | Yes | No |
| *d.* | Yes | Yes | Yes |

7. A business interest that constitutes a large part of an individual's total assets should be presented in a personal statement of financial condition as:

   *a.* A single amount equal to the proprietorship equity.

   *b.* A single amount equal to the estimated current value of the business interest.

   *c.* A separate list of the individual assets and liabilities, at cost.

   *d.* Separate line items of both total assets and total liabilities, at cost.

8. Personal financial statements should report assets and liabilities at:

   *a.* Historical cost.

   *b.* Historical cost and, as additional information, at estimated current values at the date of the financial statements.

   *c.* Estimated current values at the date of the financial statements.

   *d.* Estimated current values at the date of the financial statements and, as additional information, at historical cost.

9. The following information pertains to marketable equity securities owned by Kent:

| | Fair Value at December 31 | | |
|---|---|---|---|
| Stock | 20X3 | 20X2 | Cost in 20X0 |
| City Manufacturing Inc. | $95,500 | $93,000 | $89,900 |
| Tri Corporation | 3,400 | 5,600 | 3,600 |
| Zee Inc. | | 10,300 | 15,000 |

The Zee stock was sold in January 20X3 for $10,200. In Kent's personal statement of financial condition at December 31, 20X3, what amount should be reported for marketable equity securities?

   *a.* $93,300.

   *b.* $93,500.

   *c.* $94,100.

   *d.* $98,900.

10. Personal financial statements should report an investment in life insurance at the:

   *a.* Face amount of the policy less the amount of premiums paid.

   *b.* Cash value of the policy less the amount of any loans against it.

   *c.* Cash value of the policy less the amount of premiums paid.

   *d.* Face amount of the policy less the amount of any loans against it.

11. Mrs. Taft owns a $150,000 insurance policy on her husband's life. The cash value of the policy is $125,000, and there is a $50,000 loan against the policy. In the Tafts' personal statement of financial condition at December 31, 20X3, what amount should be shown as an investment in life insurance?

   *a.* $150,000.

   *b.* $125,000.

   *c.* $100,000.

   *d.* $75,000.

### E16-12A  Personal Financial Statements

Leonard and Michelle have asked you to prepare their statement of changes in net worth for the year ended August 31, 20X3. They have prepared the following comparative statement of financial condition based on estimated current values as required by SOP 82-1:

### LEONARD AND MICHELLE
### Statement of Financial Condition
### August 31, 20X3 and 20X2

| | | 20X3 | | 20X2 |
|---|---|---|---|---|
| **Assets** | | | | |
| Cash | | $ 3,600 | | $ 6,700 |
| Marketable securities | | 4,900 | | 16,300 |
| Residence | | 94,800 | | 87,500 |
| Personal effects | | 10,000 | | 10,000 |
| Cash surrender value of life insurance | | 3,200 | | 5,600 |
| Investment in farm business: | | | | |
| Farm land | $ 42,000 | | $32,100 | |
| Farm equipment | 22,400 | | 9,000 | |
| Note payable on farm equipment | (10,000) | | -0- | |
| Net investment in farm | | 54,400 | | 41,100 |
| Total assets | | $170,900 | | $167,200 |
| **Liabilities and Net Worth** | | | | |
| Credit card | | $ 2,400 | | $ 1,500 |
| Income taxes payable | | 11,400 | | 12,400 |
| Mortgage payable on residence | | 71,000 | | 76,000 |
| Estimated income taxes on the difference between the estimated current values of assets and liabilities and their tax bases | | 19,700 | | 16,500 |
| Net worth | | 66,400 | | 60,800 |
| Total liabilities and net worth | | $170,900 | | $167,200 |

### Additional Information

1. Leonard and Michelle's total salaries during the fiscal year ended August 31, 20X3, were $44,300; farm income was $6,700; personal expenditures were $43,500; and interest and dividends received were $1,400.

2. Marketable securities purchased in 20X1 at a cost of $11,000 and with a current market value of $11,000 on August 31, 20X2, were sold on March 1, 20X3, for $10,700. No additional marketable securities were purchased or sold during the fiscal year.

3. The values of the residence and farm land are based on year-end appraisals.

4. On August 31, 20X3, Leonard purchased a used combine at a cost of $14,000. He made a $4,000 down payment and signed a five-year, 10 percent note payable for the $10,000 balance owed. No other farm equipment was purchased or sold during the fiscal year.

5. The cash surrender value of the life insurance policy increased during the fiscal year by $1,600. However, Leonard borrowed $4,000 against the policy on September 1, 20X2. Interest at 15 percent for the first year of this loan was paid when due on August 31, 20X3.

6. Federal income taxes of $12,400 were paid during the 20X3 fiscal year.

7. Mortgage payments made during the year totaled $9,000, which included payments of principal and interest.

### Required

Using the comparative statement of financial condition and additional information provided, prepare the statement of changes in net worth for the year ended August 31, 20X3. (*Hint:* It will be helpful to use T-accounts to determine several realized and unrealized amounts. An analysis of the cash, personal effects, and credit card accounts should not be required to properly complete the statement.)

# Problems

## P16-13   Lump-Sum Liquidation

The Carlos, Dan, and Gail (CDG) Partnership has decided to liquidate as of December 1, 20X6. A balance sheet as of December 1, 20X6, appears below:

**CDG PARTNERSHIP**
**Balance Sheet**
**At December 1, 20X6**

**Assets**

| | |
|---|---:|
| Cash | $ 25,000 |
| Accounts Receivable (net) | 75,000 |
| Inventories | 100,000 |
| Property, Plant, and Equipment (net) | 300,000 |
| Total Assets | $500,000 |

**Liabilities and Capital**

Liabilities:

| | | |
|---|---:|---:|
| Accounts Payable | | $270,000 |
| Capital: | | |
| Carlos, Capital | $120,000 | |
| Dan, Capital | 50,000 | |
| Gail, Capital | 60,000 | |
| Total Capital | | 230,000 |
| Total Liabilities and Capital | | $500,000 |

### Additional Information

1. The personal assets (excluding partnership capital interests) and personal liabilities of each partner as of December 1, 20X6, follow:

| | Carlos | Dan | Gail |
|---|---:|---:|---:|
| Personal assets | $250,000 | $300,000 | $350,000 |
| Personal liabilities | (230,000) | (240,000) | (325,000) |
| Personal net worth | $ 20,000 | $ 60,000 | $ 25,000 |

2. Carlos, Dan, and Gail share profits and losses in the ratio 20:40:40.
3. All of the noncash assets were sold on December 10, 20X6, for $260,000.

### Required

a. Prepare a statement of realization and liquidation for the CDG Partnership on December 10, 20X6.

b. Prepare a schedule of the net worth of each of the three partners as of December 10, 2006, after the liquidation of the partnership is completed.

## P16-14   Installment Liquidation [AICPA Adapted]

On January 1, 20X1, partners Art, Bru, and Chou, who share profits and losses in the ratio of 5:3:2, decide to liquidate their partnership. The partnership trial balance at this date is as follows:

| | Debit | Credit |
|---|---:|---:|
| Cash | $ 18,000 | |
| Accounts Receivable | 66,000 | |
| Inventory | 52,000 | |
| Machinery and Equipment (net) | 189,000 | |
| Accounts Payable | | $ 53,000 |
| Art, Capital | | 88,000 |
| Bru, Capital | | 110,000 |
| Chou, Capital | | 74,000 |
| Total | $325,000 | $325,000 |

The partners plan a program of piecemeal conversion of assets to minimize liquidation losses. All available cash, less an amount retained to provide for future expenses, is to be distributed to the partners at the end of each month. A summary of the liquidation transactions is as follows:

### January 20X1

1. $51,000 was collected on accounts receivable; the balance is uncollectible.
2. $38,000 was received for the entire inventory.
3. $2,000 liquidation expenses were paid.
4. $50,000 was paid to creditors, after offset of a $3,000 credit memorandum received on January 11, 20X1.
5. $10,000 cash was retained in the business at the end of the month for potential unrecorded liabilities and anticipated expenses.

### February 20X1

6. $4,000 liquidation expenses were paid.
7. $6,000 cash was retained in the business at the end of the month for potential unrecorded liabilities and anticipated expenses.

### March 20X1

8. $146,000 was received on sale of all items of machinery and equipment.
9. $5,000 liquidation expenses were paid.
10. No cash was retained in the business.

### Required

Prepare a statement of partnership liquidation for the partnership with schedules of safe payments to partners.

**P16-15**  **Cash Distribution Plan**

The partnership of Pen, Evan, and Torves has asked you to assist in winding up its business affairs. You compile the following information.

1. The trial balance of the partnership on June 30, 20X1, is:

|  | Debit | Credit |
|---|---|---|
| Cash | $ 6,000 | |
| Accounts Receivable (net) | 22,000 | |
| Inventory | 14,000 | |
| Plant and Equipment (net) | 99,000 | |
| Accounts Payable | | $ 17,000 |
| Pen, Capital | | 55,000 |
| Evan, Capital | | 45,000 |
| Torves, Capital | | 24,000 |
| Total | $141,000 | $141,000 |

2. The partners share profits and losses as follows: Pen, 50 percent; Evan, 30 percent; and Torves, 20 percent.
3. The partners are considering an offer of $100,000 for the accounts receivable, inventory, and plant and equipment as of June 30. The $100,000 will be paid to creditors and the partners in installments, the number and amounts of which are to be negotiated.

### Required

Prepare a cash distribution plan as of June 30, 20X1, showing how much cash each partner will receive if the offer to sell the assets is accepted.

### P16-16 Installment Liquidation

Refer to the facts in Problem 16-15. The partners have decided to liquidate their partnership by installments instead of accepting the offer of $100,000. Cash is distributed to the partners at the end of each month. A summary of the liquidation transactions follows:

#### July

1. $16,500 collected on accounts receivable; balance is uncollectible.
2. $10,000 received for the entire inventory.
3. $1,000 liquidation expense paid.
4. $17,000 paid to creditors.
5. $8,000 cash retained in the business at the end of the month.

#### August

6. $1,500 in liquidation expenses paid.
7. As part payment of his capital, Torves accepted an item of special equipment that he developed, which had a book value of $4,000. The partners agreed that a value of $10,000 should be placed on this item for liquidation purposes.
8. $2,500 cash retained in the business at the end of the month.

#### September

9. $75,000 received on sale of remaining plant and equipment.
10. $1,000 liquidation expenses paid. No cash retained in the business.

#### Required

Prepare a statement of partnership realization and liquidation with supporting schedules of safe payments to partners.

### P16-17 Installment Liquidation

The DSV Partnership decided to liquidate the partnership as of June 30, 20X5. The balance sheet of the partnership as of this date is presented as follows:

**DSV PARTNERSHIP**
**Balance Sheet**
**At June 30, 20X5**

**Assets**

| | |
|---|---|
| Cash | $ 50,000 |
| Accounts Receivable (net) | 95,000 |
| Inventories | 75,000 |
| Property, Plant, and Equipment (net) | 500,000 |
| Total Assets | $720,000 |

**Liabilities and Partners' Capitals**

| | | |
|---|---|---|
| Liabilities: | | |
| Accounts Payable | | $405,000 |
| Partners' Capitals: | | |
| D, Capital | $100,000 | |
| S, Capital | 140,000 | |
| V, Capital | 75,000 | |
| Total Capital | | 315,000 |
| Total Liabilities and Capital | | $720,000 |

#### Additional Information

1. The personal assets (excluding partnership loan and capital interests) and personal liabilities of each partner as of June 30, 20X5, follow:

|  | D | S | V |
|---|---|---|---|
| Personal assets | $250,000 | $450,000 | $300,000 |
| Personal liabilities | (270,000) | (420,000) | (240,000) |
| Personal net worth | $ (20,000) | $ 30,000 | $ 60,000 |

The DSV Partnership was liquidated during the months of July, August, and September. The assets sold and the amounts realized follow:

| Month | Assets Sold | Carrying Amount | Amount Realized |
|---|---|---|---|
| July | Inventories | $ 50,000 | $ 45,000 |
|  | Accounts receivable (net) | 60,000 | 40,000 |
|  | Property, plant, and equipment | 400,000 | 305,000 |
| August | Inventories | $ 25,000 | $ 18,000 |
|  | Accounts receivable (net) | 10,000 | 4,000 |
| September | Accounts receivable (net) | $ 25,000 | $ 10,000 |
|  | Property, plant, and equipment | 100,000 | 45,000 |

### Required

Prepare a statement of partnership realization and liquidation for the DSV Partnership for the three-month period ended September 30, 20X5. D, S, and V share profits and losses in the ratio 50:30:20. The partners wish to distribute available cash at the end of each month after reserving $10,000 of cash at the end of July and August to meet unexpected liquidation expenses. Actual liquidation expenses incurred and paid each month amounted to $2,500. Support each cash distribution to the partners with a schedule of safe installment payments.

**P16-18** **Cash Distribution Plan**

Refer to the information contained in Problem 16-17. Assume the following amounts of cash were received during the months of July, August, and September from the sale of DSV Partnership's noncash assets:

| | |
|---|---|
| July | $390,000 |
| August | 22,000 |
| September | 55,000 |

The partnership wishes to keep $10,000 of cash on hand at the end of July and August to pay for unexpected liquidation expenses.

It paid liquidation expenses of $2,500 at the end of each month, July, August, and September.

### Required

a. Prepare a statement, as of June 30, 20X5, showing how cash will be distributed among partners as it becomes available.

b. Prepare schedules showing how cash is distributed at the end of July, August, and September, 20X5.

**P16-19** **Matching**

Match the terms on the left with the descriptions on the right. Each description may be used only once (or not at all).

| Terms | Descriptions of Terms |
|---|---|
| 1. Dissolution | A. Sale of the partnership assets, payment of the partnership creditors, and the distribution of any remaining assets to partners. |
| 2. Partner's loss absorption power | |
| 3. Liquidation | B. Allocation to other partners in their profit and loss–sharing ratio if the partner is personally insolvent. |
| 4. Statement of partnership realization and liquidation | C. Schedule that shows how cash is to be distributed as it becomes available during liquidation process. |
| 5. Installment liquidation | D. Computed by dividing a partner's capital balance by that partner's loss-sharing ratio. |
| 6. Cash distribution plan | |
| 7. Incorporation of a partnership | E. Revaluation of a partnership's assets and liabilities to their market values. |
| 8. Partner's deficit in capital | F. Change in the legal relationship between partners. |
| | G. End of the normal business function of the partnership. |
| 9. Lump-sum liquidation | H. Liquidation in which all assets are converted into cash over a short time period, enabling all creditors to be paid, with any remaining cash being distributed according to the partner's capital balance. |
| 10. Safe payments to partners | |
| | I. Cash payments to partners computed on the assumption that all noncash assets will be sold for nothing. |
| | J. Presents, in workpaper form, the effects of the liquidation process on the balance sheet accounts of the partnership. |
| | K. Liquidation in which cash is periodically distributed to partners during the liquidation process. |

**P16-20**  **Partnership Agreement Issues [AICPA Adapted]**

A partnership involves an association between two or more persons to carry on a business as co-owners for profit. Items 1 through 10 relate to partnership agreements.

The statement of facts for Parts A and B are followed by numbered sentences that state legal conclusions relating to those facts. Determine whether each legal conclusion is correct or not and mark it with the letter Y for yes, correct, or N for no, not correct.

### Part A

Adams, Webster, and Coke were partners in the construction business. Coke decided to retire and found Black, who agreed to purchase his interest. Black was willing to pay Coke $20,000 and promised to assume Coke's share of all firm obligations.

### Required (Use Y for yes and N for no)

1. Unless the partners agree to admit Black as a partner, she could not become a member of the firm.
2. The retirement of Coke would cause a dissolution of the firm.
3. The firm's creditors are third party beneficiaries of Black's promise to Coke.
4. Coke would be released from all liability for the firm's debts if Black purchased his interest and promised to pay Coke's share of firm debts.
5. If the other partners refused to accept Black as a partner, Coke could retire, thereby causing a dissolution.

### Part B

Carson, Crocket, and Kitt were partners in the importing business. They needed additional capital to expand and located an investor named White, who agreed to purchase a one-quarter interest in the partnership by contributing $50,000 in capital to the partnership. Before White became a partner, several large creditors had previously loaned money to the partnership. The partnership subsequently failed, and the creditors are now attempting to assert personal liability against White.

### Required (Use Y for yes and N for no)

6. White is personally liable on all of the firm's debts contracted subsequent to his entry into the firm.

7. Creditors of the partnership prior to the admission of a new partner automatically continue to be creditors of the partnership after the admission of the new partner.

8. Creditors of the partnership that existed prior to White's entry can assert rights against his capital contribution.

9. White has personal liability for firm debts existing prior to his entry into the firm.

10. White must remain in the partnership for at least one year to be subject to personal liability.

*Supplemental Problems* for this chapter are available as part of the *Online Learning Center* on the textbook's Web site (URL: www.mhhe.com/baker8e).

# Governmental Entities: Introduction and General Fund Accounting

In the early 2000s, the combined annual spending of federal, state, and local governments exceeded $4.0 trillion. Governmental purchases of goods and services constitute approximately 20 percent of the total gross national product of the United States.[1]

The first part of this chapter introduces the accounting and reporting requirements for state and local governmental units. The major concepts of governmental accounting are discussed and illustrated first. The last part of this chapter presents a comprehensive illustration of accounting for the general fund of a city. The comprehensive illustration reviews and integrates the concepts presented in the first part of the chapter. Chapter 18 continues the comprehensive illustration to complete the discussion on state and local governmental accounting and reporting.

Each of the 50 states follows relatively uniform accounting standards; however, some states have unique statutory provisions for selected items. Local governments are political subdivisions of state government. The 87,000-plus local governmental units in the United States are classified as (1) general-purpose local governments, such as counties, cities, towns, villages, and townships; (2) special-purpose local governments, such as soil conservation districts; and (3) authorities and agencies, such as the New York Port Authority and local housing authorities. Authorities and agencies differ from other governmental units because they typically do not have taxing power and may sell only revenue bonds, not general obligation bonds.

Governmental entities have operating objectives different from those of commercial entities; therefore, governmental accounting is different from accounting for commercial enterprises. The major differences between governmental and for-profit entities are as follows:

1. Governmental accounting must recognize that governmental units collect resources and make expenditures to fulfill societal needs. Society expects governmental units to develop and maintain an infrastructure of highways, streets, and sewer and sanitation systems, as well as to provide public protection, recreation, and cultural services.

2. Except for some proprietary activities such as utilities, governmental entities do not have a general profit motive. Police and fire departments do not have a profit motive; instead these units must be evaluated on their abilities to provide for society's needs.

3. Governmental operations have legal authorization for their existence, conduct revenue-raising through the power of taxation, and have mandated expenditures they must make to provide their services. The governmental accounting system must make it possible to determine and demonstrate compliance with finance-related legal and contractual

[1] Annual reports of the national income and product accounts, including aggregate revenues and expenditures of governmental entities, are presented in the *Survey of Current Business,* published periodically by the U.S. Department of Commerce.

provisions. Governmental units are subject to extensive regulatory oversight through laws, grant restrictions, bond indentures, and a variety of other legal constraints.

4. Governmental entities use comprehensive budgetary accounting, which serves as a significant control mechanism and provides the basis for comparing actual operations against budgeted amounts. The budget is a legally established statutory control vehicle.

5. The primary emphasis in governmental fund accounting is to measure and report on management's stewardship of the financial resources committed to the objectives of the governmental unit. Accountability for the flow of financial resources is a chief objective of governmental accounting. The managers of the governmental unit must be able to show that they are in compliance with the many legal regulations governing its operations.

6. Governmental entities typically are required to establish separate funds to carry out their various missions. Each fund is an independent accounting and fiscal entity and is responsible for using its own resources to accomplish its specific responsibilities.

7. Many fund entities do not record fixed assets or long-term debt in their funds. These fund entities record the purchase of assets such as equipment and buildings as expenditures of the period. A separate record of the fixed assets and long-term debt is maintained within the governmental unit.

8. An important objective of governmental financial reporting is accountability. Governments must be able to explain and justify to citizens and to other governments the raising and using of public resources. A key element of accountability is *interperiod equity* in which it is determined if current-year revenues are sufficient to pay for services provided during that year, or if future taxpayers will be required to assume burdens for services previously provided or deficits created in prior years.

# HISTORY OF GOVERNMENTAL ACCOUNTING

Before 1984, the development of accounting principles for local governmental units was directed by the Municipal Finance Officers Association (MFOA). In 1934, the National Committee on Municipal Accounting, a committee of the MFOA, published the first statement on local governmental accounting. The report was entitled *A Tentative Outline—Principles of Municipal Accounting.* In 1968, the National Committee on Governmental Accounting, the successor committee, published *Governmental Accounting, Auditing, and Financial Reporting (GAAFR).* Some governmental accountants call it the "blue book" after the color of its cover. The GAAFR is periodically updated to include the most recent governmental financial reporting standards.

In 1974, the American Institute of Certified Public Accountants (AICPA) published an industry audit guide, *Audits of State and Local Governmental Units,* in which it stated that "except as modified in this guide, they [GAAFR] constitute generally accepted accounting principles."[2] In March 1979, the National Council on Governmental Accounting (NCGA) issued its **Statement No. 1,** "Governmental Accounting and Financial Reporting Principles" (NCGA 1), which established a set of accounting principles for governmental reporting.

In 1984, the Financial Accounting Foundation created a companion group to the Financial Accounting Standards Board. The Governmental Accounting Standards Board (GASB) is now responsible for maintaining and developing accounting and reporting standards for state and local governmental entities. In **GASB Statement No. 1,** "Authoritative Status of NCGA Pronouncements and AICPA Industry Audit Guide" (GASB 1), released in July 1984, the GASB stated that all NCGA statements and interpretations issued and in effect on that date were accepted as generally accepted accounting principles for governmental accounting. In 1985, the GASB published a codification of the existing GAAP for state

---

[2] Committee on Governmental Accounting and Auditing, *Audits of State and Local Governmental Units,* American Institute of Certified Public Accountants, New York, 1974, pp. 8–9.

and local governments entitled *Codification of Governmental Accounting and Financial Reporting Standards.* The first section of the codification is virtually identical to **NCGA 1** as amended by subsequent NCGA statements. Section 2 presents the financial reporting issues for governmental entities. Sections 3 and 4 present specific balance sheet and operating statement topics. The GASB continues to publish updated codifications periodically. The codification is an authoritative source for accounting and financial reporting principles for governmental units.

A very significant change in the governmental reporting model for governmental units was required by **GASB Statement 34,** "Basic Financial Statements—and Management's Discussion and Analysis—for State and Local Governments" (GASB 34), issued in 1999. **GASB 34** established government-wide financial statements to be prepared on the accrual basis of accounting and an array of fund-based financial statements. This standard also required several new footnote and schedule disclosures that increase the transparency of governmental reporting. The GASB continues to issue new standards to meet the information needs of citizens, creditors, and other users of the financial reports of governmental units.

Accounting for governmental entities is given the general name of *fund accounting* to distinguish it from accounting for commercial entities. This chapter first presents an overview of fund accounting, including accounting for typical transactions and providing required financial statements for a governmental entity. After introducing the major concepts of governmental accounting, a comprehensive illustration is presented of accounting and financial reporting for the general fund, typically the most important fund of most governmental entities. Chapter 18 presents the accounting for the remaining funds of a governmental entity and the required financial statements for a governmental entity. The comprehensive illustration provides integrated examples of the governmental accounting and financial reporting concepts that are discussed in the first part of Chapter 17. Some students may initially find governmental accounting to be quite different from the financial accounting learned in earlier accounting courses. However, after studying the concepts and working through the comprehensive illustration, the reasons and logic for fund accounting, and the content and form of the governmental financial statements, become more focused.

# MAJOR CONCEPTS OF GOVERNMENTAL ACCOUNTING

Governmental accounting is different from commercial accounting. Governmental entities use a fund-based accounting system in which some of the funds use a modified-accrual accounting method as opposed to the accrual method used by commercial entities. Also, the financial statements of governmental entities have a foundation in the individual funds but aggregate to a government-wide level. The following section discusses the major concepts for governmental accounting.

## Elements of Financial Statements

In 2007, the GASB published **Concepts Statement No. 4,** "Elements of Financial Statements" (G CON 4), that defined each of the seven elements of financial statements of state and local governments. Each definition uses the central focus of a *resource,* which is an item having a present capacity to provide, directly or indirectly, services for the governmental entity. This present service capacity may be in the form of direct provision of services as well as those items having the ability to affect cash flows in the future.

The *five elements of a statement of financial condition* are:

1. *Assets* are resources with present service capacity that the entity presently controls.
2. *Liabilities* are present obligations to sacrifice resources that the entity has little or no discretion to avoid.
3. A *deferred outflow of resources* is a consumption of net assets that is applicable to a future reporting period.

4. A *deferred inflow of resources* is an acquisition of net assets that is applicable to a future reporting period.

5. *Net position* is the residual of all other elements presented in a statement of financial condition.

The *two elements of the resource flows statements* are:

6. An *outflow of resources* is a consumption of net assets that is applicable to the current reporting period.

7. An *inflow of resources* is an acquisition of net assets that is applicable to the current reporting period.

The central focus of present service capacity for defining the elements of governmental financial statements is different from the focus used by the FASB in its **Statement of Financial Accounting Concepts No. 6,** "Elements of Financial Statements," (CON 6). The FASB developed its definitions of the elements of financial statements based on the usefulness of financial reporting information to investors and creditors in making economic decisions for allocating scarce resources among alternative uses.

The GASB felt that its concepts statement provides a framework that will enhance consistency in setting future governmental accounting standards and serve as guidance for preparers and auditors when evaluating transactions that are not explicitly included in existing governmental accounting standards.

## Expendability of Resources versus Capital Maintenance Objectives

The major differences between commercial and governmental accounting and reporting stem from the objectives of the entities. In commercial, profit-seeking enterprises, the measurement focus is on the flow of *all economic resources* of the firm. The accrual method of accounting is used to match the revenues and expenses during a period, with the purpose of measuring profitability. The company's balance sheet contains both current and noncurrent assets and liabilities, and the change in retained earnings reflects the company's ability to maintain its capital investment.

In contrast, the measurement focus for the governmental funds of a government entity is on changes in *current financial resources* available to provide services to the public in accordance with the government entity's legally adopted budget. The modified accrual method of accounting is used to measure the revenues that are available to finance current expenditures and the expenditures made during the period. The balance sheet reports only current assets, current liabilities, and a fund balance. Operating authorization for a fiscal period's transactions is initiated by the passage of a budget by the legislative governing body. Managers of governmental units must be fiscally accountable to show that resources are expended in compliance with the legal and financial restrictions placed on the governmental entity by its legislative body.

In 2006, the Governmental Accounting Standards Board (GASB) published a White Paper that identified a number of key differences between financial reporting for governments and for-profit businesses.[3] The White Paper made the argument that users of governmental financial reports and users of business financial reports require substantially different financial and economic information in order to evaluate fiscal and operational performance. The White Paper expands on the differences stated in the list above and presents the GASB's perspective on the need for separate governmental accounting and financial reporting standards.

## Definitions and Types of Funds

Fund accounting must recognize the unique aspects of governmental operations. Governmental units must provide a large range of services, such as fire and police protection, water and sewerage, legal courts, and construction of public buildings and other facilities.

[3] Governmental Accounting Standards Board, *Why Governmental Accounting and Financial Reporting Is—And Should Be—Different,* GASB, Norwalk, CT, 2006.

In addition, governmental units receive their resources from many different sources and must make expenditures in accordance with legal restrictions.

The operations of a governmental unit must also be broken down into periodic reporting intervals of fiscal years because the management of these public operations may change as a result of elections or new appointments. Thus, governmental accounting must recognize the many different purposes, the different sources of revenue, the mandated expenditures, and the fiscal periodicity of the governmental unit. To accomplish the objectives of the governmental unit, the unit establishes a variety of *funds* as fiscal and accounting entities of the governmental unit. A fund is a separate accounting group with accounts to record the transactions and prepare the financial statements of a defined part of the governmental entity that is responsible for specific activities or objectives. Each fund records those transactions affecting its assets, related liabilities, and residual fund balance.

Different funds are established for the specific functions that a government must provide. Most funds obtain resources from taxes on property, income, or commercial sales; they also may obtain resources as grants from other governmental agencies, from fines or licenses, and from charges for services. Each fund must make its expenditures in accordance with its specified purposes. For example, a fund established for fire protection cannot be used to provide school buses for the local school. The fire department may make expenditures only as directly related to its function of providing fire protection.

Each governmental fund has its own asset and liability accounts and its own revenue and expenditures accounts. The term *expenditures* refers to decreases in net financial resources available under the current financial resources measurement focus. Expenditures are made in accordance with the budget established by the government unit's governing body, and the internal control structure of a vouchers payable system is generally used prior to payments to external vendors. Upon receipt and acceptance of the goods or services from the external vendor, the journal entry to recognize the approved expenditure is a debit to expenditures and a credit to vouchers payable. The increase in the payables decreases the net financial resources available. The payment of the vouchers payable must then be approved by the government's governing body.

Separate fund-based financial statements must be prepared for each fiscal period. In this manner, governing bodies or other interested parties may assess the fiscal and operating performance of each fund in fulfillment of the specific purposes for which each fund was established.

Governmental accounting systems are established on a fund basis in three major categories: governmental, proprietary, and fiduciary. Figure 17–1 presents an overview of each of the funds and provides a brief description of the types of activities accounted for in each fund.

### Governmental Funds

Five types of *governmental funds* are used to provide basic governmental services to the public. These are: (1) general fund, (2) special revenue funds, (3) capital projects funds, (4) debt service funds, and (5) permanent funds (see Figure 17–1). The number of governmental funds maintained by the governmental entity is based on its legal and operating requirements. Each governmental entity creates only one general fund, but it may create more than one of each of the other types of governmental funds based on the entity's specific needs. For example, some governmental entities establish a separate capital projects fund for each major capital project.

### Proprietary Funds

Some activities of a governmental unit, such as the operation of a public swimming pool or a municipal water system, are similar to those of commercial enterprises. The objective of the governmental unit is to recover its costs in these operations through a system of user charges. The two types of *proprietary funds* typically used by governmental entities are (6) enterprise funds and (7) internal service funds (see Figure 17–1). Accounting and

**FIGURE 17–1** **Fund Structure**

### Governmental Fund Types

1. General fund — Accounts for all financial resources except for those accounted for in another fund. Includes transactions for general governmental services provided by the executive, legislative, and judicial operations of the governmental entity.

2. Special revenue fund — Accounts for the proceeds of specific revenue sources that are restricted for specified purposes. Includes resources and expenditures for operations, such as public libraries, when a separate tax is levied for their support.

3. Capital projects fund — Accounts for financial resources for the acquisition or construction of major capital facilities that benefit many citizens, such as parks and municipal buildings. This fund is in existence only during the acquisition or construction of the facilities and is closed once the project is completed.

4. Debt service fund — Accounts for the accumulation of resources for, and the payment of, general long-term debt principal and interest. This fund is used for servicing the long-term debt of the government.

5. Permanent fund — Accounts for resources that are restricted such that only earnings, but not principal, may be used in support of governmental programs that benefit the government or its citizenry.

### Proprietary Fund Types

6. Enterprise fund — Accounts for operations of governmental units that charge for services provided to the general public. Includes those activities financed in a manner similar to private business enterprises where the intent of the governing body is to recover the costs of providing goods or services to the general public on a continuing basis through user charges. Also includes those operations that the governing body intends to operate at a profit. Examples include sports arenas, municipal electric utilities, and municipal bus companies.

7. Internal service fund — Accounts for the financing of goods or services provided by one department or agency to other departments or agencies of the governmental unit. The services are usually provided on a cost-reimbursement basis and are offered only to other governmental agencies, not the general public. Examples are municipal motor vehicle pools, city print shops, and central purchasing operations.

### Fiduciary Fund Types and Similar Component Units

8. Pension (and other employee benefit) trust fund — Accounts for resources required to be held in trust for the members and beneficiaries of pension plans, other post-employment benefit plans, or other employee benefit plans.

9. Investment trust fund — Accounts for the external portion of investment pools reported by the sponsoring government.

10. Private-purpose trust fund — Accounts for all other trust arrangements under which the fund's resources are to be used to benefit specific individuals, private organizations, or other governments, as specified in the trust agreement.

11. Agency fund — Accounts for assets held by a governmental unit in an agency capacity for employees or for other governmental units. An example is the city employees' payroll withholding for health insurance premiums.

reporting for a proprietary fund are similar to accounting for a commercial operation. The balance sheet of each proprietary fund reports all assets, including long-term capital assets, and all liabilities, including long-term liabilities. Chapter 18 presents a complete discussion of proprietary funds.

### Fiduciary Funds

Four types of *fiduciary funds* are provided for a governmental unit. Three are trust funds that account for financial resources maintained in trust by the government. These three are (8) pension and other employee benefit trust funds, (9) investment trust funds, and (10) private-purpose trust funds. The fourth fiduciary fund, (11) agency funds, is used to account for resources held by the government solely in a custodial capacity (see Figure 17–1). Note that the permanent fund, which is a governmental fund, includes resources that are legally restricted so that the governmental entity must maintain the principal and can use only the earnings from the fund's resources to benefit the government's programs for all of its citizens. The private-purpose trust funds include trusts under which the principal may or may not be expendable but for which the trust agreement specifies the principal, if expendable, and the earnings may be used only for the benefit of specific individuals, organizations, or other governments. Examples of fiduciary funds are presented in Chapter 18.

# FINANCIAL REPORTING OF GOVERNMENTAL ENTITIES

A governmental unit may have a variety of boards, commissions, authorities, or other component units under its control. The financial statements of a governmental entity are presented for the ***reporting entity,*** which consists of:

1. The *primary government* such as a state government, a general-purpose local government, or a special-purpose local government that has a separately elected government body.
2. *Component units* which are legally separate organizations for which the primary unit has financial accountability.
3. Other organizations that have a significant relationship with the primary government and need to be included in the primary government's financial statements to avoid misleading or incomplete financial representations. (More on these "other organizations" will be presented in Chapter 18.)

**GASB Statement No. 14,** "The Financial Reporting Entity" (GASB 14), states that financial accountability exists for those component units if the primary government unit appoints a majority of an organization's governing body and

(*a*) is able to impose its will on the organization, or

(*b*) possesses a financial benefit or assumes a financial burden for the organization.

The ***governmental financial reporting model*** is specified in **GASB Statement No. 34,** "Basic Financial Statements—and Management's Discussion and Analysis—for State and Local Governments" (GASB 34). Figure 17–2 presents the names of the financial statements and the other major information specified by **GASB 34.** The reporting model has two integrated levels of financial statements.

1. The first level is the ***fund-based financial statements*** because governments continue to use fund-based accounting to record transactions in accordance with the legal or budgetary requirements established by their governing body. These fund-based financial statements demonstrate fiscal accountability of the management of each of the funds.
2. The second level is the ***government-wide financial statements.*** After preparing the fund-based financial statements, the government prepares reconciliation schedules to go from the governmental fund financial statements to the government-wide financial statements. In addition to the governmental funds, the reporting entity includes other funds in the government-wide financial statements. The government entity's capital assets, such as buildings and equipment, and long-term debt are also included in the government-wide financial statements. The government-wide financial statements demonstrate the operational accountability of the management of the governmental unit as a whole.

This chapter and the first part of Chapter 18 focus on the fund-based financial statements. After completing our discussion of each fund type in Chapter 18, the government-wide financial statements are presented.

**FIGURE 17–2**
**The Government**
**Reporting Model**

1. Independent auditors' report
2. Management's Discussion and Analysis (required supplementary information)
3. Government-wide financial statements
   a. Statement of Net Assets
   b. Statement of Activities
4. Fund-based financial statements
   a. Governmental funds
      (1) Balance Sheet
      (2) Statement of Revenues, Expenditures, and Changes in Fund Balances
      (3) Reconciliation Schedules (of each of the two governmental fund-based statements to their related government-wide financial statements, either at the bottom of each of the two fund-based financial statements or in an accompanying schedule)
   b. Proprietary funds
      (1) Statement of Net Assets
      (2) Statement of Revenues, Expenses, and Changes in Fund Net Assets
      (3) Statement of Cash Flows
   c. Fiduciary funds
      (1) Statement of Fiduciary Net Assets
      (2) Statement of Changes in Fiduciary Net Assets
5. Notes to the financial statements
6. Required Supplementary Information (RSI) (in addition to the MD&A)
   a. Budgetary Comparison Schedules
   b. Information about Infrastructure Assets
   c. Information about Pensions

## Fund-Based Financial Statements: Governmental Funds

Two financial statements are required for the governmental funds: (1) balance sheet and (2) statement of revenues, expenditures and changes in fund balance.

### *Balance Sheet for Governmental Funds*

The format of the balance sheet, with added parenthetical guidance for learning assistance, for each of the governmental funds is:

| Balance Sheet for Governmental Funds | | |
|---|---|---|
| Assets (financial resources available for current use; presented in order of liquidity) | | $X,XXX |
| Total Assets | | $X,XXX |
| Liabilities and Fund Balances | | |
| Liabilities (due and expected to be paid from current financial resources; presented in order of due date) | | $ XXX |
| Fund Balances | | |
| Reserved (not available for appropriation for expenditures) | $ X | |
| Unreserved (amount of net current financial resources available for expenditure) | XX | XX |
| Total Liabilities and Fund Balances | | $X,XXX |

The five governmental funds use the ***current financial resources measurement focus.*** Under this method, the asset section of the balance sheet reports only financial assets such as cash or other assets that will convert into cash (e.g., receivables) in the normal course of operations over the near future. Some governments report inventories or other prepayments because these save the entity from the incurrence of future outflows of current financial resources. Long-term capital items such as equipment or buildings are not reported on the fund-based balance sheet because these amounts are no longer currently available for expenditure. However, the long-term capital assets of the governmental entity are scheduled and reported in the government-wide financial statements, as illustrated in Chapter 18.

The liability section of the balance sheet reports only those liabilities that have become due and that will require current financial resources to liquidate, such as vouchers payable or the current portion of long-term debt. A short-term debt often used in governmental funds is tax-anticipation notes. These notes represent loans obtained using future taxes as collateral for the notes. Most states restrict these borrowings to those taxes that have been levied but not yet collected. These notes payable are paid from the first tax collections of the tax levy to which the notes are related. The principal of long-term debt not due within the next year is not reported on the balance sheet because it will not be settled in the near term with current financial resources. However, the governmental unit's long-term debt is scheduled and is reported in the government-wide financial statements.

The third section of the balance sheet for the five governmental funds reports the net fund balance, which is the amount of the difference between reported assets and reported liabilities. **GASB 34** specified that the fund balances for the governmental funds should be segregated into two categories: *(a)* Reserved, which is the portion of the fund balance that is not available, such as resources already used to acquire ending inventory or for encumbrances for purchase commitments, and *(b)* Unreserved, which is the amount of current financial resources still available for expenditure.

### *Proposed Standard for Fund Balance Reporting*

In February 2008, the GASB published an exposure draft (ED) of a proposed statement entitled "Fund Balance Reporting and Governmental Fund Type Definitions." This ED modifies the definitions of some of the governmental funds to make the definitions consistent across all government units. Furthermore, the ED establishes a fund balance classification system for the governmental fund types. Note that this proposed statement applies only to the governmental fund types, not to proprietary or fiduciary fund types. The governmental fund balance classification system uses a hierarchy based on the extent to which a government is required to comply with constraints placed upon the use of resources reported in governmental funds. The hierarchy separates the fund balance between nonspendable and spendable resources.

1. *Nonspendable fund balances* represent amounts that are *(a)* not in spendable form, such as amounts related to inventories and prepaid items, or *(b)* are required by legal or contractual provisions to be maintained intact, such as the principal of a permanent fund.

2. *Spendable fund balances* represent amounts that are available for spending. Amounts in this portion of the fund balance would be further classified as *(a)* restricted, *(b)* limited, *(c)* assigned, or *(d)* unassigned. The classification would be based on an examination of requirements imposed by legal or contractual provisions and then of any constraints established by the governing body of the government entity.

Because of the extensive study and background work for this Exposure Draft, it is anticipated that it will become a GASB standard. The major points of this ED will be presented in the additional considerations section of chapter 17. The ED proposes an effective date for implementation in financial statements for periods beginning after June 15, 2010, with earlier application encouraged. The comprehensive illustration presented later in this chapter, and continued in chapter 18, will present the fund balance in the financial statements of the governmental fund types as required under **GASB 34.** However, because of the expectation that the proposed statement will be adopted, the fund balance disclosures required by the proposed statement will be illustrated at the conclusion of the discussion of governmental funds in Chapter 18. Note that the accounting is not changed by the proposed statement, only the presentation of the fund balances for the governmental funds.

### Statement of Revenues, Expenditures, and Changes in Fund Balance for Governmental Funds

This is often called the *operating statement* of the governmental funds, but the financial statements for the governmental funds use the full title. The statement of revenues, expenditures, and changes in fund balance has four major sections:

1. *Operating section.* The top section includes the revenues less expenditures for the period, with the difference shown as the excess (or deficiency) of revenues over expenditures.

2. *Other financing sources or uses.* This section includes nonrevenue items such as bond issue proceeds and interfund transfers. (Note that issuance of bonds and debt refundings of governmental long-term debt are shown in the other financing sources and uses section although the long-term debt is not shown on the fund's balance sheet.)

3. *Special and extraordinary items.* This section presents extraordinary items that are both unusual and infrequent, such as losses due to a hurricane. Special items are transactions or events within the control of management that are either unusual or infrequent in occurrence. An example of a special item would be the one-time sale of county park land.

4. *Fund balance.* The bottom portion presents both the beginning and the ending fund balance.

The format of the statement of revenues, expenditures, and changes in fund balance, with added parenthetical guidance, is:

| Statement of Revenues, Expenditures, and Changes in Fund Balance | |
| --- | --- |
| Revenues (recognized when both measurable and available; presented by source of revenue) | $XX,XXX |
| Expenditures (approved decreases in net financial resources; presented by function and character) | X,XXX |
| Excess of Revenues over Expenditures | $   XXX |
| Other Financing Sources or Uses (other increases or decreases in net financial resources available, such as bond issue proceeds and interfund transfers) | XX |
| Special Items and Extraordinary Items | (X) |
| Net Change in Fund Balance | $   XX |
| Fund Balance—Beginning | XXX |
| Fund Balance—Ending (reconciles to total fund balance on balance sheet) | $   XXX |

Under the current financial resources measurement focus, revenues are recognized when they become both measurable and available to finance expenditures of the fiscal period. Profit-seeking businesses measure revenue by the accrual basis as it is earned, but the current financial resources measurement focus requires that the expected timing of the revenue-related inflow be evaluated. Availability means that the transaction will result in financial resources collectible within the current period or soon thereafter in order to be used to pay liabilities of the current period.

The expenditure portion of the operating statement reports reductions in available current financial assets. Expenditures are recognized when approved services or goods are received by the governmental entity. Vouchers Payable or some other payable is credited when the expenditure is recognized. The increase in liabilities decreases the net financial resources still available for spending to meet the public purposes established by the governing body. Expenditures also include amounts to purchase capital assets such as trucks or buildings. These are expenditures because they result in a net outflow of current financial assets. Note that once the expenditure has been made for a capital asset, that amount is no longer currently available to spend. Thus, although an expenditure is recognized for the purchase of a capital asset, the capital asset (e.g., truck) is not reported on the governmental fund's balance sheet.

Other financing sources and uses, the second section of the operating statement under the current financial resources measurement focus, reports changes in current financial resources from nonrevenue items, such as sales of bonds or interfund transfers with other funds of the governmental entity. Note that under the current financial resources focus the proceeds from a sale of bonds are reported in the operating statement, but the long-term bond payable is not reported in the liabilities on the governmental fund's balance sheet. Interfund transfers are discussed in depth later in this chapter.

The special items section presents unusual or infrequent items that affect the fund balance but are not revenue or expenditure items. Finally, the fund balance section presents the change in the fund balance to obtain the ending fund balance. The ending fund balance amount should reconcile to the total fund balance shown on the balance sheet.

After each governmental fund prepares its financial statements, a combined balance sheet and a combined operating statement are prepared. These combined statements include all the governmental funds. The format for the combined government funds statements is multicolumnar, with a separate column for each of the major governmental funds and a separate column for the aggregated nonmajor (small) governmental funds. The columns are then added together horizontally and a total column for each line item in the governmental funds is presented. This will be illustrated in Chapter 18.

# MEASUREMENT FOCUS AND BASIS OF ACCOUNTING (MFBA)

Because the concepts of *measurement focus* and *basis of accounting* are so important in understanding accounting for the various funds of state and local governments, a brief review of these two concepts is presented first. Then, coverage is provided of the accounting measurement and recognition requirements applicable to revenues and expenditures in the governmental funds.

The **basis of accounting** refers to the timing of recognizing a transaction for financial reporting purposes. For example, the cash basis recognizes revenue or expenditures when cash is received or paid. The accrual basis recognizes revenue or expenditures when the transaction or event takes place. The **modified accrual basis** is a hybrid system that includes some aspects of accrual accounting and some aspects of cash basis accounting. The modified accrual basis is used in funds that have a flow of *current financial resources measurement focus.* This measurement focus is on the flow of current financial resources and the proper expendability of the resources for designated purposes and determination of the available resources remaining to be expended. Expenditures recognized under the modified accrual basis are the amounts that would normally be liquidated with expendable available financial resources. The five governmental funds have this focus.

The accrual basis is used in funds that have a flow of **economic resources measurement focus.** This measurement focus is concerned with all economic resources available to a fund during a particular time period, thereby allowing for a comparison of revenues and expenses and a focus on maintenance of capital. The proprietary funds and fiduciary funds have this focus.

In addition, as is presented in Chapter 18, the government-wide financial statements are based on the accrual basis. This necessitates a reconciliation schedule for those items accounted for under the modified accrual basis for governmental fund accounting to obtain the accrual basis amount that is reported on the government-wide financials. The reconciliation schedule is discussed in more detail in Chapter 18.

## Basis of Accounting—Governmental Funds

The current financial resources measurement focus and the modified accrual basis of accounting are used for the governmental funds financial statements. The modified accrual basis is applied as follows:

1. *Revenue* is recorded in the accounting period in which it is both measurable and available to finance expenditures made during the current fiscal period.

2. *Expenditures* are recognized in the period in which the liabilities are both measurable and incurred and are payable out of current financial resources.

*Measurable* means that the amount of the revenue or expenditure can be objectively determined. *Available* means due or past due and receivable within the current period and collected within the current period or expected to be collected soon enough thereafter to be used to pay current-period liabilities. The definition of "soon enough thereafter" has been stated for property taxes as a period of not more than 60 days after the end of the current fiscal period.

### Recognition of Revenue

The accrual method of accounting recognizes revenues from exchange transactions (sales of goods or services) and from nonexchange transactions in which the government gives or receives value without directly receiving or giving equal value in exchange. In **GASB Statement 33,** "Accounting and Financial Reporting for Nonexchange Transactions" (GASB 33), issued in 1998, the GASB classified nonexchange transactions into four categories. **GASB 33** was written from the viewpoint of the accrual basis, and modifications are required to this statement when using the modified accrual basis of accounting. How revenues are recognized depends on the category. The four categories are discussed next.

1. *Derived tax revenues,* resulting from assessments on exchange transactions. Examples are income taxes and sales taxes.

    a. The *asset (cash or receivable) is recognized* when the underlying transaction occurs or resources are received, whichever comes first.

    b. *Revenue recognition* depends on the accounting basis used to measure the transaction. Under accrual accounting (proprietary and fiduciary funds), revenue is recognized when the underlying exchange transaction occurs. Under modified accrual accounting (governmental funds), revenue is recognized when the underlying exchange has occurred and the resources are available.

Resources received prior to the exchange transaction would be reported as deferred revenue (reported as a liability) until the revenue recognition requirement is met for the fund receiving the resources.

2. *Imposed nonexchange revenues,* resulting from assessments on nongovernmental entities, including individuals. Examples include property taxes and fines.

    a. The *asset (cash or receivable) is recognized* when the government has an enforceable legal claim to the resources or the resources are received, whichever comes first.

    b. *Revenue recognition* is made in the period when use of the resources for current expenditures is first permitted or required, or at the time the asset is recorded if no time restriction on the fund's use of the resources exists.

Resources received or recorded as receivables prior to the period in which they can be recognized as revenue should be reported as deferred revenues.

The next two categories have additional eligibility requirements that the providers of financial resources often impose. These eligibility requirements must be met before the transaction can be completed, that is, before the receiving governmental unit can recognize an asset and the associated revenue. The four types of eligibility requirements are typically (1) required characteristics of the recipient as specified by the provider of the financial resources (e.g., the receiving entity must be a school district), (2) time requirements for expending the resources (e.g., the resources must all be expended within a specific fiscal period), (3) reimbursements for only those costs determined to be allowable and incurred in conformity with a program's requirements, and (4) contingencies in which the recipient has met all actions required by the provider. If the recipient has met all of the eligibility requirements imposed by the provider, then the provider should recognize the liability (or decrease in assets) and expense, and the recipient should recognize the receivable (or increase in assets) and revenue at the time the eligibility requirements have been met. The two categories are as follows:

3. *Government-mandated nonexchange transactions,* resulting from one governmental unit's provision of resources to a governmental unit at another level and the requirement that the recipient use the resources for a specific purpose. An example of this type is federal programs that state or local governments are required to perform.

4. *Voluntary nonexchange transactions,* resulting from legislative or contractual agreements, other than exchanges. Examples include certain grants and private donations.

**GASB Statement No. 36,** "Recipient Reporting for Certain Shared Nonexchange Revenues" (GASB 36), issued in 2000, amended **GASB 33** for government-mandated and voluntary nonexchange situations in which a providing government provides part of its own derived tax units to recipients. Typically, the providing government provides the recipients with a periodic report of the amount of shared revenues the recipients should anticipate. **GASB 36** states that if the notification from the providing government is not available in a timely manner, the recipient governments should use a reasonable estimate of the amount to be accrued and not wait until the actual receipt of the cash resources.

The following examples present the accounting, under the modified accrual basis of accounting, as used in preparing the governmental funds financial statements.

1. *Property taxes.* Property taxes involve a series of steps that guide the recognition of the property tax asset and the property tax revenue. A typical process is as follows:

Year 1:

    Step 1:    Levy filed for enforceable claims to property taxes for year 1.

    Step 2:    Assessment notice presenting assessed value as of levy date is mailed to each property owner and any appeals are heard.

    Step 3:    Property tax bills for year 1 mailed to each property owner. (Property tax on each property based on assessed value multiplied by the tax rate. The tax rate is determined based on the requirements specified in the levy request filed by each unit of government within the taxing district.)

Year 2:

    Step 4:    First installment of property taxes for year 1 are due.

    Step 5:    Second (and last) installment of property taxes for year 1 are due.

The levy creates an enforceable claim to the future collection of property taxes and a property tax receivable should be recorded at that date along with a deferred property tax revenue credit. As presented above, the property tax bill is mailed to each property owner in one fiscal period and the property taxes applicable to that fiscal period are then collected in the next fiscal period. There normally is a legally imposed time restriction on the use of the property tax resources until, in this example, year 2 at which time the resources become available for expenditure. In this example, property tax revenue would not be recognized until year 2 when the time restriction is extinguished. The year 2 entry would include a debit to deferred property tax revenue and a credit to property tax revenue. While this example presents the levy date in year 1 and the collection in year 2, some governmental entities do make the levy and the collection within the same fiscal period. The key to the timing of recognizing revenue from property taxes is to determine the fiscal period in which the use of the resources for current expenditures is permitted, not necessarily when the property taxes are levied or collected.

**NCGA Interpretation No. 3,** "Revenue Recognition—Property Taxes" (NCGA 3), specifies that property taxes must be collectible within a maximum of 60 days after the end of the current fiscal period in order to be recognized as revenue in the current period. Taxes collectible 60 days or more after the current period ends are recorded as deferred revenue for the current period and then accounted for as next period's revenue.

Revenue from another governmental unit or tax-exempt entity in lieu of taxes, such as a payment by a university to a city for police and fire protection, should be accrued and recorded as revenue when it becomes billable.

Revenue from property taxes should be recorded *net* of any uncollectibles or abatements. The Property Taxes Receivable account is debited for the full amount of the taxes levied, with estimated uncollectibles recorded separately in an allowance account reported as a contra account to the receivable.

2. *Interest on investments and delinquent taxes.* Interest on investments or delinquent property taxes is accrued in the period in which the interest is earned and available to finance expenditures in the period. The governmental funds may temporarily invest available cash in interest-generating financial instruments such as certificates of deposit and federal or state securities. Governmental entities should carefully determine the credit risks and market risks of possible investments to minimize their potential loss. Governmental funds report their own current and long-term financial investments and any accrued interest receivable as assets of the funds.

3. *Income taxes and sales taxes.* These derived tax revenues are recognized as assets under the modified accrual basis of accounting in the period in which the tax is imposed or when the resources are received, whichever comes first. These taxes must be available to finance expenditures made during the current fiscal period before recognition as revenue for the period. Income tax revenue should be reported net of any anticipated refunds to taxpayers. Sales taxes collected by another governmental unit (e.g., the state government) but not yet distributed should be accrued prior to receipt by the governmental unit to which they will be distributed (e.g., a city) if the taxes are both measurable and available for expenditure. Measurability in this case is based on an estimate of the sales taxes to be received, and availability is based on the ability of the governing entity (the city) to obtain current resources through credit by using future sales tax collections as collateral for the loan.

4. *Miscellaneous revenue.* Miscellaneous revenues such as license fees, fines, parking meter revenue, and charges for services are generally recorded when the cash is received because these cannot be predicted accurately. Often states take custody of private property when its legal owner cannot be found, as with unclaimed estates or abandoned bank accounts. The property is said to *escheat* (or revert) to the state government. The government should record the property as revenue at its fair market value less a liability for any anticipated claims from possible heirs or other claimants. States generally record the net revenue in the general fund, but some states prefer to account for these resources in a separate, private-purpose trust fund.

5. *Grants, entitlements, and shared revenue.* These are resources received from other governmental units. *Grants* are contributions from another governmental unit to be used for a specified purpose, activity, or facility. *Entitlements* are payments local governments are entitled to receive as determined by the federal government. *Shared revenue* is levied by one governmental unit but shared with others on some predetermined basis (e.g., revenue from taxes on the retail sale of gasoline collected by the state). Grants are recognized as revenue in the period in which all eligibility requirements have been met. This may be at the point the grant is authorized, but, in practice, some governmental units wait until the cash is received because the grant may be withdrawn by the grantor. Some grants are made to reimburse a governmental unit for expenditures made in accordance with legal requirements. The revenue from such grants should be recognized only when the expenditure is made and all other eligibility requirements have been met. For example, a state government might agree to provide a grant for a local government's purchase of fire-fighting vehicles. Typically, the local government must meet all the requirements of the grant before it receives the monies from the state government. In these cases, the local government would record the grant revenue at the time it is received. In a few cases, such as a state grant of reimbursement for the purchase of the firefighting vehicles, the local government may receive grant monies before all the steps of the required expenditure are completed. In those few cases, the local government may be required to record the receipt of the grant monies as an unearned revenue (liability) until all the requirements have been met and the grant is expendable—at which time the unearned revenue is reclassified as earned revenue.

Proceeds from the sale of bonds are not revenue! These proceeds are reported as other financing sources on the statement of revenues, expenditures, and changes in fund balance. Although bond sales do increase the resources available for expenditure, bonds must be repaid, whereas revenue of the governmental unit does not need to be repaid.

### *Recognition of Expenditures*

Under the modified accrual basis of accounting, expenditures are recorded in the period in which the related liability is both measurable and incurred. Specific examples are as follows:

1. Costs for personal services, such as wages and salaries, are generally recorded in the period paid because they are normal, recurring expenditures of a governmental unit.
2. Goods and services obtained from outside the governmental entity are recorded as expenditures in the period in which they are received.
3. Capital outlays for equipment, buildings, and other long-term facilities are recorded as expenditures in the period of acquisition.
4. Interest on long-term debt is recorded in the period in which it is legally payable.

## Basis of Accounting—Proprietary Funds

The two major proprietary funds are the internal service fund and the enterprise fund. Proprietary funds are established for governmental operations that have a management focus of income determination and capital maintenance; therefore, the accrual method as used by profit–seeking corporate entities is used to account for these funds. Proprietary funds record their own long-term assets, and depreciation is recognized on these assets. Long-term debt is recorded and interest is accrued as it is for commercial operations.

## Basis of Accounting—Fiduciary Funds

The accrual basis of accounting is used for all fiduciary funds. Agency funds are for those resources for which the governing unit is the temporary custodian. Agency funds have only assets and liabilities; no fund equity, revenue, or expenditures are used. An example of an agency fund is a county's billing and collecting taxes on behalf of other governmental entities, such as a city and a school district. After collection is completed on the "tax roll," the county properly distributes the taxes in accordance with each governmental entity's approved levy.

For fiduciary trust funds, the economic resources measurement focus and the accrual basis of accounting are used. Note that the fiduciary trust funds include those funds in which both the principal and income may be used for the benefit of specific individuals, organizations, or other governments, in accordance with the terms under which the trust fund was established. Agency and trust funds are discussed in depth in Chapter 18.

# BUDGETARY ASPECTS OF GOVERNMENTAL OPERATIONS

*Budgets* are used in governmental accounting to assist in management control and to provide the legal authority to levy taxes, collect revenue, and make expenditures in accordance with the budget. Budgets establish the objectives and priorities of governing units.

For state governments, budgets are proposed by governors and debated by the legislative bodies. After passage, the budget usually becomes part of the fiscal period's state law. For local governments, the mayor or the major administrator may propose the budget. Public hearings and discussions of the budget are then held by governing boards such as the city council, county board, or township board prior to the adoption of the final budget.

A governmental unit may have several types of budgets, including the following:

1. *Operating budgets.* Operating budgets specify expected revenue from the various sources provided by law. The operating budget includes expected expenditures for

various line items, such as payrolls of employees, supplies, and goods and services to be obtained from outside the governing unit. Operating budgets are used in the general fund, special revenue funds, and sometimes the debt service funds.

2. *Capital budgets.* A capital budget is prepared to provide information about proposed construction projects such as new buildings or street projects. Capital budgets are used in the capital projects funds.

Although budgets may be prepared for proprietary funds, these budgets do not serve as a primary control vehicle. Budgets in the proprietary funds are advisory in much the same way budgets are used in commercial entities.

## Recording the Operating Budget

Budgets are such an important control vehicle that those governmental funds with legally adopted annual operating budgets should enter their budgets into the formal accounting records, although capital budgets are not normally entered. Recording the operating budgets permits better management control and facilitates a year-end comparison of budgeted and actual amounts. This comparison is part of the required supplementary information for the government reporting model for the funds that must have operating budgets. A budget-to-actual comparison provides an assessment of management's stewardship of the governmental entity and allows citizens and others to determine whether the governmental entity remained within its operating budgetary limits.

To help understand the process of accounting for operating budgets, this text uses the technique illustrated in *Governmental Accounting, Auditing, and Financial Reporting* (GAAFR),[4] in which the budgetary accounts are identified with all capital letters. Capitalization of the budgetary accounts clearly separates the budgetary nominal accounts from the operating accounts of the governmental unit. Although budgetary accounts are not capitalized in actual practice, this convention is helpful in learning the following material.

The recording of the operating budget for the general fund is shown with the following example. Assume that at January 1, 20X1, the first day of the new fiscal period, the city council of Barb City approves the operating budget for the general fund, providing for $900,000 in revenue and $850,000 in expenditures. Approval of the budget provides the legal authority to levy the local property taxes and to appropriate resources for the expenditures. The term ***appropriation*** is the legal description of the authority to expend resources. The entry made in the general fund's accounting records on this date is as follows:

January 1, 20X1

| | | | |
|---|---|---|---|
| (1) | ESTIMATED REVENUES CONTROL | 900,000 | |
| | APPROPRIATIONS CONTROL | | 850,000 |
| | BUDGETARY FUND BALANCE—UNRESERVED | | 50,000 |
| | Record general fund budget for year. | | |

Note the word CONTROL used as part of the account titles. In governmental accounting, control accounts often are used in the major journals, with subsidiary accounts recording the detail behind each control account. This method is similar to a commercial entity's using a control account for its accounts receivable and then using subsidiary ledgers for the specific customer transactions. Throughout this chapter, the control account level is illustrated to focus on the major issues. In practice, detailed accounting is maintained for each separate classification of revenue and appropriation, either in the major journal or in a subsidiary ledger. The AICPA uses both control-level accounts and budgetary accounts on the Uniform CPA Examination, although it does not capitalize the letters of the budgetary accounts used in the exam.

The ESTIMATED REVENUES CONTROL account is an *anticipatory asset;* that is, the governmental unit anticipates receiving resources from the revenue sources listed

---

[4] *Governmental Accounting, Auditing, and Financial Reporting* is updated periodically by the Government Finance Officers Association (Chicago).

in the budget. The APPROPRIATIONS CONTROL account is an *anticipatory liability;* that is, the governmental unit anticipates incurring expenditures and liabilities for the budgeted amount. The excess of estimated revenues over anticipated expenditures is the budget surplus and is recorded to BUDGETARY FUND BALANCE—UNRESERVED. Some approved budgets have budget deficits in which expected expenditures exceed anticipated revenue. These budgets are recorded with a debit to BUDGETARY FUND BALANCE—UNRESERVED.

Recording the budget in the governmental entity's books makes the budget a formal accounting control mechanism for the fiscal period. In addition, having the budget in the accounting records provides the necessary information for the budgetary comparison schedules that are part of the required supplementary information (RSI) footnotes required by the government reporting model in **GASB 34.** At the end of the year, after the appropriate financial statements have been prepared, all the budgetary accounts are closed.

# ACCOUNTING FOR EXPENDITURES

The governmental funds use a variety of controls over expenditures to ensure that each expenditure is made in accordance with any legal restrictions on the fund.

## The Expenditure Process

The expenditure process in governmental accounting comprises the following sequential steps: appropriation, encumbrance, expenditure, and disbursement.

### Step 1. Appropriation

The budget provides the appropriating authority to make future expenditures. Operating budgets are prepared for the general, special revenue, and often the debt service funds. The capital projects fund prepares capital budgets.

The appropriation was recorded in the budget entry made previously in entry (1) for the general fund of Barb City. Recall that a total of $850,000 in anticipated expenditures was approved in the budget.

### Step 2. Encumbrance

An *encumbrance* is a reservation of part of the budgetary appropriation and is recognized at the time an order is placed for goods or services. Encumbrances are a unique element of governmental accounting. Their purpose is to ensure that the expenditures within a period do not exceed the budgeted appropriations. The appropriation level was established by the approved budget and sets the legal maximum that may be expended for each budgeted item. The managers of the governmental unit must be sure that they do not exceed this budgetary authority. Thus, encumbrances provide a control system and safeguard for governmental unit administrators.

When an order is placed for goods or services to be received from outside the governmental unit, the budgeted appropriation is encumbered for the estimated cost of the order. Encumbrances are of greatest use when an order is placed and a period of time expires before delivery. Payroll costs, immaterial costs, and costs for goods acquired from within the governmental entity typically are not encumbered because these are normal and recurring and the managers of the governmental unit are able to predict these costs based on past experiences and other administrative controls, such as employment agreements.

A sensible approach should be used with an encumbrance system. For example, it is not necessary to establish an individual encumbrance when an employee orders a pad of paper. Rather, a blanket purchase order with a maximum dollar amount, for example, a total of $500, should be prepared and encumbered, and then it can serve as the control for small, routine supply purchases. Encumbrances provide the unit administrators an important accounting control to fulfill their responsibilities to manage within an approved budget.

To illustrate encumbrance accounting, assume that on August 1, 20X1, Barb City completed a purchase order (PO) from an outside vendor for goods that are estimated to cost $15,000. The entry to record this application of part of the budgeted appropriation authority for the period is as follows:

August 1, 20X1

| | | | |
|---|---|---|---|
| (2) | ENCUMBRANCES | 15,000 | |
| |     BUDGETARY FUND BALANCE—RESERVED FOR ENCUMBRANCES | | 15,000 |
| |     Record order for goods estimated to cost $15,000. | | |

Note that the ENCUMBRANCES account is a budgetary account that is reserving part of the appropriation authority of the budget. For detailed accounting, governmental entities often maintain a subsidiary ledger including accounts for specific types of encumbrances to correspond to each specific type of appropriation. For purposes of this illustration, the single title ENCUMBRANCES is used to indicate a control-level account to focus attention on the major aspects of governmental accounting. In practice, very detailed account titles and classification numbers are used to fully account for each type of transaction. It is important to note that the BUDGETARY FUND BALANCE—RESERVED FOR ENCUMBRANCES is a *reservation (or restriction) of the budgetary fund balance,* not an actual liability.

### Step 3. Expenditure

An expenditure and a corresponding liability are recorded when the governmental entity receives the goods or services ordered in step 2. When the goods are received, the encumbrance entry is reversed for the amount encumbered and the expenditure is recorded for the actual cost to the governmental entity. Although the actual cost is typically very close to the encumbered amount, some differences may exist because of partially completed orders, less expensive replacements, or unforeseen costs. Assume that the goods are received on September 20, 20X1, at an actual cost of $14,000. The entries to reverse the encumbrance for the goods and to record the actual expenditures are as follows:

September 20, 20X1

| | | | |
|---|---|---|---|
| (3) | BUDGETARY FUND BALANCE—RESERVED FOR ENCUMBRANCES | 15,000 | |
| |     ENCUMBRANCES | | 15,000 |
| |     Reverse encumbrances for goods received. | | |
| (4) | Expenditures | 14,000 | |
| |     Vouchers Payable | | 14,000 |
| |     Receive goods at cost of $14,000. | | |

At any time, the remaining appropriating authority available to the fund managers can be determined by the following equation:

$$\text{Appropriating authority remaining available} = \text{APPROPRIATIONS} - (\text{ENCUMBRANCES} + \text{Expenditures})$$

### Step 4. Disbursement

A *disbursement* is the payment of cash for expenditures. Disbursements usually must be approved by the governing board or council as an additional level of control over expenditures.

Virtually all governmental entities use a comprehensive voucher system to control cash outflows. The governing board receives a schedule of vouchers to be approved for payment by vote of the board. This is usually one of the early agenda items in any board or council meeting as a vote is taken to "pay all bills." Checks are then written and delivered to the supplier of the goods. If the Barb City council approved the voucher at its October 8 meeting and a check was prepared in the amount of $14,000 and mailed on October 15, 20X1, the following entry records the disbursement:

October 15, 20X1

| | | | |
|---|---|---|---|
| (5) | Vouchers Payable | 14,000 | |
| | Cash | | 14,000 |
| | Payment of voucher for goods received. | | |

## Classification of Expenditure Transactions and Accounts

Governmental accounting places many controls over expenditures, and much of the financial reporting focuses on the various aspects of an expenditure. Expenditures should be classified by fund, character, function (or program), organizational unit, activity, and principal classes of objects. Figure 17–3 describes the major expenditure classifications.

Many governmental units have a comprehensive chart of accounts with specific coding digits that provide the basis for classifying each expenditure. For example, an expenditure journal entry might specify the expenditure account to be charged as number 421.23-110. The chart of accounts shows that the 421.23 account is for public safety: police—crime control and investigation—patrol, as follows:

420. Public safety
    421. Police
        421.2    Crime control and investigation
        421.23    Patrol

The -110 suffix indicates that this expenditure is for personal services in the form of salaries and wages for regular employees. It is not unusual for some accounting systems to have 11- to 14-digit accounts classifying each individual transaction. The level of specificity in the chart of accounts depends on the particular governing entity's information needs. Classifying information with such specificity allows the governing entity to maintain complete database control over the expenditure information, which it can use at any time in aggregate or relational analysis. For the examples in this chapter, only the expenditure control level is presented; in practice, a complete specification of the expenditure is made.

## Outstanding Encumbrances at the End of the Fiscal Period

In the previous Barb City example, the goods were received within the same fiscal period in which they were ordered. What happens if the goods are ordered in one fiscal year and received in the next year? In this case, the encumbrance is not reversed before the end of the fiscal period.

Accounting for these outstanding encumbrances depends on the governmental unit's policy. The government may allow outstanding encumbrances to lapse; that is, the governmental unit is not required to honor these encumbrances carried over to the new year, and the new year's budget must rebudget them. In virtually all cases, the encumbrances will be rebudgeted and honored; however, this policy specifically recognizes the legal authority of the new governing board to determine its own expenditures. A second method is to carry over the encumbrances as nonlapsing spending authority. This method recognizes the practical aspects of encumbrances outstanding at the end of a fiscal period. Either method may be used in governmental accounting.

To illustrate the differences between the lapsing and nonlapsing methods of accounting for encumbrances, assume the following:

1. On August 1, 20X1, $15,000 of goods are ordered and an appropriate entry is made to record the encumbrance.
2. The goods have not been received on December 31, 20X1, the end of the fiscal period.
3. The goods are received on February 1, 20X2, at an actual cost of $14,000.

**FIGURE 17–3**
**Major Expenditure**
**Classifications for**
**Governmental Funds**

| Classification | Description |
| --- | --- |
| Fund | The fund is identified to show the specific source of the expenditure. For example, the general fund would be noted for expenditures from that fund. |
| Character | Character classifications are based primarily on the period the expenditures are anticipated to benefit. Four major character classifications are current, capital outlay, debt service, and intergovernmental. |
| Function (or program) | Functions are group-related activities directed at accomplishing a major service or regulatory responsibility. Standard classifications of function include general governmental; public safety; highway and streets; sanitation; health and welfare; culture and recreation; and education. |
| Organizational unit | Classifying by organization unit maintains accountability by each unit director. The organization unit is determined by the governmental unit's organization chart. For example, public safety could be broken down into police, fire, corrections, protective inspection (such as plumbing and electrical code inspections), and other protection (such as flood control, traffic engineering, and examination of licensed occupations). |
| Activity | Activities within a function are recorded to maintain a record of the efficiency of each activity. For example, the police function could be broken down into the following activities: police administration, crime control and investigation, traffic control, police training, support service (such as communication services and ambulance services), special detail services, and police station and building maintenance. Each of these activities could be broken down further, if desired. |
| Object class | Object class is a grouping of types of items purchased or services obtained. For example, operating expenditures include personal services, purchased and contractual services, and commodities. Each of these objects could be further broken down, depending on the information needs of the governing entity. For example, purchased services could include utility services, cleaning services (such as custodial, lawn care, and snow plowing), repair and maintenance services, rentals, construction services, and other purchased services, such as insurance or printing. |

Figure 17–4 presents a comparison of the journal entries that would be required under each of the two methods of accounting for unfilled encumbrances at year-end.

### Outstanding Encumbrances Lapse at Year-End

The closing entries on December 31, 20X1, close the remaining budgetary encumbrances and establish a reserve of the actual fund balance on the December 31, 20X1, balance sheet. Although the GAAFR recommends that a reserve for lapsing encumbrances be reported on the balance sheet, the GASB's codification allows the alternative of only footnote disclosure of lapsing orders at year-end that are expected to be honored in the next fiscal period. If only footnote disclosure is used, the governmental entity would have only the first closing entry on December 31, 20X1, to close out the budgetary accounts related to the encumbrance. No balance sheet reserve is established if the footnote disclosure alternative is used.

Normal procedure for many governmental entities is for the next year's governing board to meet after elections or appointments for the next year take place. This meeting is generally held shortly before the beginning of the next fiscal year so that the budget is effective beginning on January 1 of the next year. Thus, the incoming governing board will typically make a decision during the budget process as to whether or not year-end

**FIGURE 17–4**  Comparison of Accounting for Lapsing and Nonlapsing Encumbrances at Year-End

| Item | Outstanding Encumbrances Lapse at Year-End | | Outstanding Encumbrances Nonlapsing at Year-End | |
|---|---|---|---|---|
| **December 31, 20X1** | | | | |
| Close remaining budgetary encumbrances | BUDGETARY FUND BALANCE—RESERVED FOR ENCUMBRANCES     15,000 | | BUDGETARY FUND BALANCE—RESERVED FOR ENCUMBRANCES     15,000 | |
| | ENCUMBRANCES | 15,000 | ENCUMBRANCES | 15,000 |
| Reserve actual fund balance for outstanding encumbrances at end of 20X1 expected to be honored in 20X2 | Fund Balance—Unreserved     15,000 | | Fund Balance—Unreserved     15,000 | |
| | Fund Balance—Reserved for Encumbrances | 15,000 | Fund Balance—Reserved for Encumbrances | 15,000 |
| **January 1, 20X2** | | | | |
| Reverse prior year encumbrance reserve | Fund Balance—Reserved for Encumbrances     15,000 | | | |
| | Fund Balance—Unreserved | 15,000 | | |
| Establish budgetary control over encumbrances renewed from prior period | ENCUMBRANCES     15,000 | | | |
| | BUDGETARY FUND BALANCE—RESERVED FOR ENCUMBRANCES | 15,000 | | |
| Reclassify reserve from prior year | | | Fund Balance—Reserved for Encumbrances     15,000 | |
| | | | Fund Balance—Reserved for Encumbrances—20X1 | 15,000 |
| **February 1, 20X2** | | | | |
| Receive goods and remove budgetary reserve for encumbrances | BUDGETARY FUND BALANCE—RESERVED FOR ENCUMBRANCES     15,000 | | | |
| | ENCUMBRANCES | 15,000 | | |
| Record actual expenditure for goods received | Expenditures     14,000 | | Expenditures—20X1     14,000 | |
| | Vouchers Payable | 14,000 | Vouchers Payable | 14,000 |
| **December 31, 20X2** | | | | |
| Close expenditures account | Fund Balance—Unreserved     14,000 | | Fund Balance—Reserved for Encumbrances—20X1     15,000 | |
| | Expenditures | 14,000 | Expenditures—20X1 | 14,000 |
| | | | Fund Balance—Unreserved | 1,000 |

outstanding encumbrances will be honored in the next fiscal period. If the new governing board decides not to honor the 20X1 year-end outstanding encumbrances, then only the closing entry to close the remaining budgetary encumbrances would be made on December 31, 20X1. If the governmental entity uses the footnote disclosure alternative, no footnote disclosure in the 20X1 financial statements would be made for those outstanding encumbrances not expected to be renewed in the next fiscal year.

If the new governing board decides to honor the outstanding encumbrances from 20X1, then the outstanding encumbrances must be included in the 20X2 budgeted appropriations. An entry is made as of January 1, 20X2, to establish budgetary control over the expected expenditure. A "fresh start," new spending authority is established, and the sequence of entries continues as if this is a new purchase order effective for 20X2.

In the unusual case that the new governing board makes a decision as of January 1, 20X2, not to honor the outstanding encumbrances, and the December 31, 20X1, entry had already been recorded, then the following entry would be made as of January 1, 20X2, to record the cancellation of the outstanding encumbrance from 20X1:

January 1, 20X2

| | | | |
|---|---|---|---|
| (6) | Fund Balance—Reserved for Encumbrances | 15,000 | |
| | Fund Balance—Unreserved | | 15,000 |
| | Eliminate reserve for outstanding encumbrances not being renewed. | | |

If the January 1, 20X2, entries had already been made, and the governing board later decides not to honor the outstanding encumbrance from 20X1, reversing entries would be made to eliminate the actual fund balance reserve and the budgetary fund balance reserve that had been created on January 1, 20X2. If the governmental entity used only footnote disclosure in its 20X1 financial statements for the year-end outstanding encumbrances expected to be honored, then only a reversing entry would be required to reverse the January 1, 20X2, entry that had established the budgetary encumbrances and budgetary fund balance reserve. The governmental entity then simply cancels the order with the external vendor.

### Outstanding Encumbrances Are Nonlapsing at Year-End

Some governing entities carry over the prior year appropriations authority as nonlapsing encumbrances. In this case, the budget for the second fiscal period does not show these carryovers because they arose from the appropriations authority of the prior year. The non-lapsing encumbrances are dated for the prior year to indicate they arose from that year's appropriating authority. Some governmental accountants believe this method is realistic for many situations in which orders placed with outside vendors cannot easily be canceled.

The 20X1 year-end closing entries presented in Figure 17–4 show the required reservation of the actual fund balance. Note that these are the same two entries made under the lapsing method with balance sheet recognition of the reserve of the fund balance. The differences between the two methods become apparent during the second fiscal period. Under the nonlapsing method, it is important to identify separately expenditures made from spending authority carried over from prior periods. Typically this is done in a reclassification entry on the first day of the second fiscal period, which dates the Fund Balance—Reserved for Encumbrances. No budgetary entry is made in the second year because the appropriation authority comes from the first year's budget. When the goods are received, the expenditures account is also dated to indicate that the expenditure authority emanated from 20X1.

At the end of 20X2, the Expenditures—20X1 account is closed directly to the Fund Balance—Reserved for Encumbrances—20X1. Note that the $1,000 difference between the actual $14,000 cost and the $15,000 reserved amount is closed to Fund Balance—Unreserved because the actual cost is less than the amount encumbered from the prior year's appropriation authority. If the actual cost is more than the reserve, the difference must be approved as part of the appropriation authority for 20X2.

### Key Observations from the Illustrations

As a practical matter, almost all outstanding encumbrances at year-end are honored and completed in the next fiscal period. The method of accounting for open encumbrances at year-end is based on the governmental unit's budgetary policy which may be affected by legal statutes controlling carryover of appropriating ability from one fiscal period to the next. Both methods are used in practice. It is important to note that, in this example, the 20X1 statement of revenues, expenditures, and changes in fund balance will report no expenditures relating to this item. In 20X2, $14,000 of expenditures will be recognized. Under the nonlapsing method, expenditures made in 20X2 but carried over from 20X1 encumbrances are dated to note they arose from 20X1's appropriations. The comprehensive illustration presented later in this chapter uses the lapsing method because of its widespread use.

### *Reporting of Encumbrances under the Proposed Standard on Fund Balance Reporting*

The proposed standard does not report any reserves of fund balance on the balance sheet. Rather, the amount of encumbrances is included as part of the spendable fund balance, usually in the assigned category. Only footnote disclosure would be used to report the aggregate amount of encumbrances, along with the required disclosures about other significant commitments. It is expected that governments will continue to use encumbrance accounting because of the control and management information an encumbrance system provides. The proposed standard does not restrict the accounting systems used by governments.

## Expenditures for Inventory

Most governmental units maintain a small amount of inventory in office supplies. A first issue is to determine which of two methods should be followed to account for the expenditure of inventories. The first method recognizes the entire expenditure for inventory in the period the supplies are acquired. This is called the *purchase* method. The second method is the *consumption* method; it recognizes expenditures for only the amount of inventory used in the period. The specific method to follow depends on the governing unit's policy and how inventory expenditures are included in the budget.

A second issue is whether to show inventory as an asset on the balance sheet of the governmental funds. Inventory is not an expendable asset; that is, it may not be spent as the governing entity wishes. **NCGA 1** states that inventory should be shown on the balance sheets for governmental funds if the amount of inventory is material. Immaterial inventories need not be shown on the balance sheet. If the inventory is material, it is presented as an asset on the balance sheet; an amount equal to the inventory also should be shown as a reservation of the fund balance, indicating that that amount is no longer expendable.

Figure 17–5 presents the entries to account for inventories under both the purchase method and the consumption method. The illustration assumes that Barb City acquires $2,000 of inventory on November 1, 20X1, having held no inventory previously. On December 31, 20X1, the end of Barb City's fiscal year, a physical count shows $1,400 still in stock. During 20X2, $900 of this inventory is used, resulting in a $500 remaining balance of supplies on December 31, 20X2.

**FIGURE 17–5** **Comparison of Accounting for Inventories—Purchase versus Consumption Method**

| Item | Purchase Method of Accounting | | Consumption Method of Accounting | |
|---|---|---|---|---|
| **November 1, 20X1** | | | | |
| Record acquisition of $2,000 of inventory. | Expenditures 2,000 | | Expenditures 2,000 | |
| | Vouchers Payable | 2,000 | Vouchers Payable | 2,000 |
| **December 31, 20X1** | | | | |
| Recognize ending inventory of $1,400. | Inventory of Supplies 1,400 | | Inventory of Supplies 1,400 | |
| | Fund Balance—Reserved for Inventories | 1,400 | Expenditures | 1,400 |
| | | | Fund Balance—Unreserved 1,400 | |
| | | | Fund Balance—Reserved for Inventories | 1,400 |
| **December 31, 20X2** | | | | |
| Record remaining inventory of $500, with $900 of supplies having been consumed during 20X2. | Fund Balance—Reserved for Inventories 900 | | Expenditures 900 | |
| | Inventory of Supplies | 900 | Inventory of Supplies | 900 |
| | | | Fund Balance—Reserved for Inventories 900 | |
| | | | Fund Balance—Unreserved | 900 |

### *Purchase Method of Accounting for Inventories*

Under the purchase method, the entire amount of inventory acquired is charged to Expenditures in the period acquired. On December 31, 20X1, the end of the fiscal year, an adjusting entry is made to recognize the $1,400 remaining inventory as an asset and to restrict the fund balance for the nonexpendable portion applicable to inventories.

The expenditure of $2,000 is closed into Fund Balance—Unreserved for 20X1 in a closing entry made at the end of the fiscal year. The December 31, 20X1, balance sheet includes the inventory of supplies as an asset in the amount of $1,400, and Fund Balance—Reserved for Inventories is shown as a fund balance reserve for $1,400. The 20X1 operating statement shows a $2,000 expenditure for supplies.

At the end of 20X2, an adjusting entry is made to recognize the use of the $900 of supplies of the $1,400 remaining from the 20X1 purchase. This entry reduces the reservation of the fund balance and decreases inventory. At the end of 20X2, Inventory of Supplies is $500, and Fund Balance—Reserved for Inventories is $500, for the remaining unused supplies.

In summary, the $2,000 expenditure is recognized in the period in which the supplies are purchased. No expenditures are recognized in subsequent periods although some of the supplies are used in those periods.

### *Consumption Method of Accounting for Inventories*

Under the consumption method, expenditures for a period are reported only for the amount consumed. In this case, the budget for the period should be based on the expected amount of use so the budgeted and actual amounts compared at the end of the year are on the same basis.

A net expenditure of $600 ($2,000 − $1,400) for supplies used is reported in 20X1, the year the supplies were acquired. With $500 of inventory remaining at the end of 20X2, an expenditure of $900 is reported in the 20X2 operating statement to show the amount of supplies consumed during 20X2. The consumption method relates the expenditures with the use of the inventory.

A comparison of selected account balances under the purchase method and consumption method shows the different amounts reported under these two methods:

|  | **Purchase Method** | **Consumption Method** |
| --- | :---: | :---: |
| 20X1: |  |  |
| Expenditures | $2,000 | $  600 |
| Inventory of Supplies | 1,400 | 1,400 |
| 20X2: |  |  |
| Expenditures | -0- | 900 |
| Inventory of Supplies | 500 | 500 |

Note that the choice of methods has no effect on the balance sheet amounts; the only effect is on the period in which the expenditures for inventory are reported.

Both inventory methods are used in practice. The method used by a specific governmental unit depends on its budgeting policy. If the governmental unit includes all inventory acquisitions in its appropriations for the period, the purchase method should be used. If the governmental unit includes only the expected amount of inventory to be used during a period in that period's appropriations, the consumption method should be used.

### *Reporting of Inventory under the Proposed Standard on Fund Balance Reporting*

Inventories, if they are material in amount, are reported as an asset on the balance sheet. Under the proposed standard, reserves of fund balance are not reported on the face of the balance sheet. But the fund balance associated with inventories is reported in the nonspendable fund balance category.

## Accounting for Fixed Assets

Governmental entities may acquire equipment that has an economic life of more than one year. Accounting for this acquisition depends on which fund expends the resources for the acquisition. The governmental funds are concerned with the expendability and control over available resources and account for the acquisitions of equipment as expenditures. In the governmental funds, the entire amount of the cost of the acquisition of equipment and other capital assets is recognized as an expenditure in the year the asset is acquired. No capital assets are recorded in the general fund; they are treated as expenditures of the period.

The proprietary funds are concerned with capital maintenance and account for acquisitions of capital assets in the same manner as commercial entities. Thus, the accounting for the purchase of a capital asset differs in the five governmental funds from the accounting used in the proprietary funds.

For example, assume that Barb City acquires a truck. The acquisition is made from the resources of, and is accounted for in, the general fund. The encumbrance is $12,000, but the actual cost is $12,500 because of minor modifications required by the city.

The general fund makes the following entries to account for the acquisition of the truck:

| | | | |
|---|---|---|---|
| (7) | ENCUMBRANCES | 12,000 | |
| |   BUDGETARY FUND BALANCE—RESERVED | | |
| |     FOR ENCUMBRANCES | | 12,000 |
| |   Order truck at estimated cost of $12,000. | | |
| | | | |
| (8) | BUDGETARY FUND BALANCE—RESERVED | | |
| |   FOR ENCUMBRANCES | 12,000 | |
| |     ENCUMBRANCES | | 12,000 |
| |   Cancel reserve for truck received. | | |
| | | | |
| (9) | Expenditures | 12,500 | |
| |   Vouchers Payable | | 12,500 |
| |   Receive truck at actual cost of $12,500. | | |

The truck is not recorded as an asset in the general fund; it is an expenditure in this fund. Sales of capital assets are recorded as a debit to Cash (or receivable) and a credit to Other Financing Sources—Sales of General Capital Assets for the amount received from the sale. If the amount from the sale is immaterial, the government entity may elect to record the credit to other revenues. A schedule of the acquisition or sale of capital assets by any governmental fund should be maintained, but that record is only for the government-wide financial statements, which do report the assets of a government unit.

### *Works of Art and Historical Treasures*

For the purposes of government-wide financial statements, governments should capitalize works of art, historical treasures, and similar types of assets at their historical costs at acquisition or at their fair values at the date of the contribution. For example, if the general fund expended $10,000 for a work of art, it reports an expenditure for that amount. However, when preparing the government-wide financial statements, the cost of the work of art is reported as an asset of the government. If the assets are donated, contribution revenue is recognized in the government-wide financial statements.

The GASB provided practical guidance to the general rule of capitalizing works of art and historical treasures. For example, many collections have a very large number of items collected over long periods of time, and it is virtually impossible to determine the cost or fair value at the times of acquisition. A provision in **GASB 34** states that the government is not required but is still encouraged to capitalize a collection of art or historical treasures if the government meets all three of the following provisions: (1) holds the collection for public exhibition, education, or research, (2) protects and preserves the collection, and (3) has an organizational policy that requires the proceeds from sales of collection items to be used to acquire other items for collections. If contributed items are not capitalized, the government-wide financial statements report both a program expense and a contribution revenue for the fair market value of the item at the time of its donation.

Capitalized collections that are exhaustible, such as displays of works whose useful lives are reduced due to display, or used for education or research, should be depreciated over their estimated useful lives. Collections or individual items whose lives are inexhaustible are not depreciated.

## Long-Term Debt and Capital Leases

Commercial, profit-seeking businesses recognize long-term debt and capital leases as noncurrent liabilities. The debt or capital lease is entered into to earn income, and the liability is recognized under the flow of economic resources measurement focus model. However, accounting for long-term liabilities in governmental funds is directly affected by the flow of current financial resources measurement focus model.

The governmental funds, which include the general fund, record the proceeds from a bond issue as a debit to Cash and a credit to Bond Issue Proceeds, an other-financing source. Bond issue proceeds are not revenue because the bonds must be repaid. Other financing sources are shown in the middle section of the statement of revenues, expenditures, and other changes in fund balances. Bonds are not reported on the governmental funds' balance sheets but only on the government-wide financial statements.

Capital leases are accounted for in a manner similar to long-term debt. If a proprietary fund (e.g., internal service or enterprise fund) enters into a capital lease, the lease is accounted for using methods similar to those used by commercial, profit-seeking entities, with the recording of an asset and a lease liability. However, if a governmental fund (e.g., general fund) enters into a capital lease, the capital lease is accounted for in a manner similar to a bond's accounting.

## Investments

Some governmental entities maintain investments in stock or bond securities. The purpose of these investments typically is to obtain an investment return on available resources. **GASB Statement No. 31,** "Accounting and Financial Reporting for Certain Investments and for External Investment Pools" (GASB 31), established a general rule of fair market valuation for investments held by a government entity. The following investments are to be valued at fair value, if determinable, in the asset section of the balance sheet for the governmental entity: (1) investments in debt securities; (2) investments in equity securities (other than those accounted for under the equity method as provided for in **APB 18**),[5] including option contracts, stock warrants, and stock rights; (3) investments in open-end mutual funds; (4) investment pools in which a governmental entity combines with other investors; and (5) interest-earning investment contracts in which the value is affected by market (interest rate) changes. **GASB Statement No. 52,** "Land and Other Real Estate Held as Investments by Endowments" (GASB 52), extended the general rule of using fair value to real estate investments by endowments. The periodic changes in the fair value of all the types of investments included in **GASB 31** and **GASB 52** should be recognized as an element of investment income in the operating statement (or statement of activities) of each fund making the investment. In the case of an internal investment pool that combines the resources of several of the governmental entity's funds, for financial reporting purposes the pool's assets and its income are allocated to each individual fund based on its percentage of the total invested.

Many state and local governments have deposits and make investments that are open to a variety of risks. **GASB Statement No. 40,** "Deposit and Investment Risk Disclosures" (GASB 40), established detailed note disclosure requirements related to the following types of investment risks: credit risk, (including concentrations of credit risk),

---

[5] *APB Opinion No. 18,* "The Equity Method of Accounting for Investments in Common Stock," March 1971.

interest rate risk, and foreign currency risk, as well as for deposit risks of custodial credit risk and foreign currency risk. The main objective of **GASB 40** is to require footnote disclosures of the policies and the profiles of the government's investment portfolios such as the credit quality ratings of investments in debt securities and other fixed-income securities, and the terms of investments whose fair value is highly sensitive to changes in the interest rate.

# INTERFUND ACTIVITIES

A basic concept in governmental accounting is that each fund is a separate entity and has separate sources of resources, sometimes including the power to levy and collect taxes. The revenues of each fund must then be expended in accordance with the budget and restrictions established by law. Because a single governmental entity has a number of separate funds, it sometimes becomes necessary to transfer resources from one fund to another. *Interfund activities* are resource flows between fund entities. In a consolidated financial statement for a commercial entity, intercompany transactions are eliminated to report only the effect of transactions with external entities. Governmental accounting, on the other hand, requires the separate maintenance and reporting of interfund items. The governing body must approve any interfund transfers and transactions to provide a public record and to prevent distortion of fund uses. Many governmental entities include interfund activities anticipated during a fiscal year in the operating budgets for the year. Budgetary entries for interfund activities are illustrated in the comprehensive example of Sol City presented later in this chapter. Interfund transfers must be accounted for carefully to ensure that the legal and budgetary restrictions are followed and that resources intended for one fund are not used in another.

**GASB 34** established four types of interfund activities, as follows: (1) interfund loans, (2) interfund services provided and used, (3) interfund transfers, and (4) interfund reimbursements. A discussion of the four interfund items follows; they are illustrated in Figure 17–6.

**FIGURE 17–6**  **Interfund Transactions and Transfers**

| Item | Entry in General Fund | | | Entry in Other Fund | | |
|---|---|---|---|---|---|---|
| | | | | **INTERNAL SERVICE FUND:** | | |
| 1. Interfund loan | Due from Internal Service Fund | 4,000 | | Cash | 4,000 | |
| | Cash | | 4,000 | Due to General Fund | | 4,000 |
| | Cash | 4,000 | | Due to General Fund | 4,000 | |
| | Due from Internal Service Fund | | 4,000 | Cash | | 4,000 |
| | | | | **INTERNAL SERVICE FUND:** | | |
| 2. Interfund service provided and used | Expenditures | 100 | | Due from General Fund | 100 | |
| | Due to Internal Service Fund | | 100 | Charge for Services | | 100 |
| | Due to Internal Service Fund | 100 | | Cash | 100 | |
| | Cash | | 100 | Due from General Fund | | 100 |
| | | | | **CAPITAL PROJECTS FUND:** | | |
| 3. Interfund transfer | Other Financing Uses—Transfer Out to Capital Projects Fund | 10,000 | | Cash | 10,000 | |
| | Cash | | 10,000 | Other Financing Sources—Transfer In from General Fund | | 10,000 |
| | | | | **CAPITAL PROJECTS FUND:** | | |
| 4. Interfund reimbursement | Cash | 3,000 | | Expenditures | 3,000 | |
| | Expenditures | | 3,000 | Cash | | 3,000 |

## (1) Interfund Loans

State law may allow lending or borrowing activities between funds. The loans must be repaid, usually within one year or before the end of the fiscal period. Loans and advances are not shown on a fund's statement of revenues, expenditures, and changes in fund balance; however, all outstanding loans or advances must be shown on the balance sheet as payables or receivables. Interest usually is not charged on interfund financing arrangements. If interest is charged, it is accounted for in the funds in the same manner as for other interest income or expense.

Some governmental entities distinguish between short-term and long-term financing arrangements by using the term "Advances to (or from)" to denote a long-term agreement and "Due to (or from)" for a short-term agreement.

The illustration of an interfund financing transaction in Figure 17–6 assumes that Barb City's general fund loans the internal service fund $4,000 for two months. The general fund reports a receivable for the amount of the loan until the loan is repaid.

## (2) Interfund Services Provided and Used

These interfund activities are transactions that would be treated as revenue, expenditures, or expenses if they involved parties external to the governmental unit. These interfund activities are still reported as revenue, expenditures, or expenses but are different because they are entirely within the governmental unit. These interfund activities are often normal and recurring items, usually involving at least one proprietary fund. Three examples are as follows:

1. The general fund purchases goods or services from an internal service or enterprise fund.
2. Payments are made to the general fund from the enterprise fund for fire and police protection.
3. A transfer of resources from the general fund to the pension trust fund is made to pay for the city's cost of pension benefits for its employees. This is a cost associated with employee services provided to the city and is therefore an expenditure of the general fund.

Usually these transfers involve the recognition of a receivable or payable because of the time lag between the purchase of the services and the disbursement of funds. A "Due to (or from)" account is used for short-term interfund receivables and payables rather than a formal Vouchers Payable account.

The illustration of this type of interfund activity in Figure 17–6 assumes that Barb City's general fund uses an auto from the city motor pool. The motor pool operates as an internal service fund. The general fund is billed $100 based on mileage and pays the bill 30 days later.

## (3) Interfund Transfers

The general fund often transfers resources into another fund to be used by the receiving fund for its own operations; occasionally, the general fund receives resources from other funds. These interfund transfers are not expected to be repaid. Such transfers are not fund revenues or expenditures but are instead called "interfund transfers." These transfers are classified under "Other Financing Sources or Uses" in the operating financial statements of the funds. The reason that the receiving fund does not recognize these transfers as revenue is that the issuing fund has already properly recognized these resources as revenue. Thus, the recording of these transfers as other financing sources eliminates the possibility of double counting the same resources as revenue in two different funds of the combined governmental entity. Examples include the following:

1. A transfer of resources, such as cash or other assets, is made from the general fund to an enterprise fund or internal service fund that has an operating deficit that must be eliminated.

2. A transfer of resources from the general fund to a capital projects fund is made to help finance new construction.

3. A transfer of resources from the general fund to the debt service fund is made to pay principal and interest.

The illustration of an interfund transfer in Figure 17–6 assumes that the general fund of Barb City agrees to provide $10,000 to the capital projects fund toward the construction of a new library. The Transfer Out account in the general fund is closed to its Unreserved Fund Balance at the end of the fiscal period. The capital projects fund also closes its Transfer In account at the end of the fiscal period to its Unreserved Fund Balance. These interfund transfers are not expected to be repaid.

### (4) Interfund Reimbursements

A reimbursement transaction is for the reimbursement of a fund's expenditure or expense that was initially made from the fund but that is properly chargeable to another fund. These initial payments are sometimes made either because of improper classification to the wrong fund or for expediency within the governmental entity. The reimbursement from one fund to another is recorded as a reduction of the expenditure in the fund initially recording the expenditure and a recording of the expenditure in the proper fund for the appropriate amount. Two examples are as follows:

1. An expenditure properly chargeable to the special revenue fund is initially recorded and paid by the general fund, and the general fund subsequently is reimbursed by the special revenue fund.

2. The general fund records and pays for an expenditure to provide preliminary architectural work on the planning for a new sports arena. The sports arena enterprise fund later reimburses the general fund.

The illustration of an interfund reimbursement in Figure 17–6 assumes that the general fund of Barb City recorded a $3,000 expenditure for a bill from outside consultants that is later discovered to be properly chargeable to the capital projects fund. Upon notification, the capital projects fund reimbursed the general fund and properly recorded the expenditure in its fund.

## OVERVIEW OF ACCOUNTING AND FINANCIAL REPORTING FOR THE GENERAL FUND

Figure 17–7 presents an overview of the accounting for the general fund, including accounting for the interfund activities on the general fund's operating statement, the statement of revenues, expenditures, and changes in fund balance. Note that the interfund loans are reported only on the fund's balance sheet.

The illustration uses the financial reporting requirements under **GASB 34.** The highlights of the proposed statement for fund balance reporting are covered in the additional considerations section of this chapter. Chapter 18 presents an example of the fund balance reporting for the governmental fund types under the proposed statement.

## COMPREHENSIVE ILLUSTRATION OF ACCOUNTING FOR THE GENERAL FUND

The following example illustrates the accounting for the general fund of Sol City for the January 1, 20X2, to December 31, 20X2, fiscal year. The entries are presented by topic, not necessarily in chronological order. The balance sheet for the general fund as of December 31, 20X1, presented in Figure 17–8, represents the opening balances for fiscal 20X2.

**FIGURE 17–7**
**Overview of**
**General Fund**

| Item | Description |
|---|---|
| Measurement focus | Flow of current financial resources—expendability. |
| Accounting basis | Modified accrual. |
| Budgetary basis | Operating budget. |
| Financial statements | 1. Balance sheet. |
| | 2. Statement of revenues, expenditures, and changes in fund balance. |
| **Balance Sheet** | |
| Current assets | Includes current financial resources such as cash, certificates of deposit, accrued property taxes receivable and estimated allowance for uncollectible taxes. Interfund loans receivable are included as assets. Material inventories reported. |
| Long-term productive assets (buildings, etc.) | Fixed assets not reported in general fund. |
| Current liabilities | Vouchers payable is primary current liability. Interfund loans payable also included as liabilities. |
| Long-term debt | Governmental unit long-term debt not reported in general fund. |
| Fund balance | Unreserved fund balance and reservations of fund balance (e.g., encumbrances and inventories). |
| **Statement of Revenues, Expenditures, and Changes in Fund Balance** | |
| Revenue | Recorded when measurable and available under the modified accrual basis of accounting. Interfund services provided and used also included in revenues (or expenditures). |
| Expenditures | Recognized in period when measurable and fund liability arises. |
| Other financing sources and uses | Includes bond issue proceeds and interfund transfers. |
| Changes in fund balance | Reconciles changes in fund balance during period, including changes in reservations of fund balance. |

**FIGURE 17–8**
**General Fund**
**Balance Sheet at the**
**Beginning of 20X2**

**SOL CITY**
**General Fund Balance Sheet**
**December 31, 20X1**

| | | |
|---|---:|---:|
| Assets: | | |
| Cash | | $ 50,000 |
| Property Taxes Receivable—Delinquent | $100,000 | |
| Less: Allowance for Uncollectibles—Delinquent | (5,000) | 95,000 |
| Inventory of Supplies | | 14,000 |
| Total Assets | | $159,000 |
| | | |
| Liabilities and Fund Balance: | | |
| Vouchers Payable | | $ 30,000 |
| Fund Balance: | | |
| Reserved for Encumbrances | $ 11,000 | |
| Reserved for Inventories | 14,000 | |
| Unreserved | 104,000 | 129,000 |
| Total Liabilities and Fund Balance | | $159,000 |

**FIGURE 17–9**
**General Fund Operating Budget for Fiscal 20X2**

| SOL CITY General Fund Operating Budget For Period of January 1, 20X2, to December 31, 20X2 | | |
|---|---|---|
| Estimated Revenue: | | |
| Property Taxes | $775,000 | |
| Grants | 55,000 | |
| Sales Taxes | 25,000 | |
| Miscellaneous | 20,000 | |
| Total Estimated Revenue | | $875,000 |
| Appropriations: | | |
| General Government | $200,000 | |
| Streets and Highways | 75,000 | |
| Public Safety | 400,000 | |
| Sanitation | 150,000 | |
| Total Appropriations | | (825,000) |
| Excess of Estimated Revenue over Appropriations | | $ 50,000 |
| Other Financing Uses: | | |
| Transfer out to Capital Projects Fund | $ (20,000) | |
| Transfer out to Initiate Internal Service Fund | (10,000) | |
| Total Other Financing Uses | | (30,000) |
| Excess of Estimated Revenue and Interfund Transfers over Appropriations and Interfund Transfers | | $ 20,000 |

## Adoption of the Budget

The city council adopts the budget for fiscal 20X2 as presented in Figure 17–9. Charles Alt, an alderman of Sol City, voted in favor of adopting the budget. The budget summarizes the four major functions of the city: general government, streets and highways, public safety (fire and police), and sanitation. In the complete budget used by the city council, the expenditures in each of the four functions are broken down into the following categories: personal services, supplies, other services and charges, and capital outlay. The public safety budget includes a budgeted capital outlay of $50,000 for a new fire truck.

Among the city's accounting policies are the following:

1. *Consumption method for inventories.* The city budgets the supplies inventory on the consumption method, including only the costs of expected inventory use during the year.

2. *Lapsing method of accounting for encumbrances.* The city uses the lapsing method for accounting for any encumbrances outstanding at the end of fiscal periods. The APPROPRIATIONS CONTROL for fiscal 20X2 includes a reappropriation of the $11,000 of outstanding encumbrances as of December 31, 20X1.

3. *Use of control accounts.* The city uses a comprehensive system of control accounts for its major journals. The following accounts have extensive subsidiary ledgers that correspond to the entries made in the journal: ESTIMATED REVENUES CONTROL, APPROPRIATIONS CONTROL, ENCUMBRANCES, and Expenditures. The specific details supporting each of these control accounts are maintained in the subsidiary records. For purposes of focusing on the major aspects of governmental accounting, the Sol City illustration includes the control-level entries only.

4. *Budgeted interfund activities.* The city includes in the budget all anticipated interfund activities during the fiscal year. The general fund is expected to have the following interfund transfers:

| OTHER FINANCING USES: | |
|---|---|
| Transfer Out to Capital Projects Fund | $20,000 |
| Transfer Out to Internal Service Fund | 10,000 |

The interfund transfer out to the capital projects fund is to pay for the city's share of a municipal courthouse addition project, and the transfer out to the internal service fund is to initiate the internal service fund.

The following entries are made to record the budget and to renew the lapsing encumbrances from the prior period:

January 1, 20X2

| | | | |
|---|---|---|---|
| (10) | ESTIMATED REVENUES CONTROL | 875,000 | |
| | APPROPRIATIONS CONTROL | | 825,000 |
| | ESTIMATED OTHER FINANCING USES—TRANSFER OUT TO CAPITAL PROJECTS | | 20,000 |
| | ESTIMATED OTHER FINANCING USES—TRANSFER OUT TO INTERNAL SERVICE | | 10,000 |
| | BUDGETARY FUND BALANCE—UNRESERVED | | 20,000 |
| | Record budget for fiscal 20X2. | | |
| | | | |
| (11) | Fund Balance—Reserved for Encumbrances | 11,000 | |
| | Fund Balance—Unreserved | | 11,000 |
| | Reverse prior-year encumbrances reserve. | | |
| | | | |
| (12) | ENCUMBRANCES | 11,000 | |
| | BUDGETARY FUND BALANCE—RESERVED FOR ENCUMBRANCES | | 11,000 |
| | Renew encumbrances from prior period as included in budgeted appropriations in 20X2. | | |

(*Note:* The technique of capitalizing the account titles of all budgetary accounts continues through the comprehensive illustration. This technique is used in the text to assist differentiation of the budgetary from the operating accounts. In practice, the budgetary accounts are not capitalized.)

## Property Tax Levy and Collection

Most municipalities obtain resources from property taxes, which should be recorded as a receivable when an enforceable legal claim arises. Revenue is recorded if the property taxes are measurable and available for current expenditures. Recall that the 60-day rule for property taxes allows the recognition of revenue for the current fiscal period if the property taxes are expected to be collected within 60 days of the end of the current fiscal period. A deferred revenue account is credited if the property taxes are not available for current expenditures. For Sol City, the property taxes are due and available for use within the fiscal period and therefore are recorded as revenue as of the levy date. Note that a provision for uncollectibles must be recorded, and this provision is a reduction of property tax revenue, not a bad debts expense as in commercial accounting. Governmental funds have no such account as bad debts expense. The receivables are classified as current, collectible within this period, or delinquent, for past-due accounts.

The entries in Sol City's general fund for the transactions relating to property taxes are as follows:

| | | | |
|---|---|---|---|
| (13) | Property Taxes Receivable—Current | 785,000 | |
| | Allowance for Uncollectible Taxes—Current | | 10,000 |
| | Revenue—Property Tax | | 775,000 |
| | Property taxes levied for this fiscal year with a reduction from revenues for the estimated uncollectibles. | | |
| | | | |
| (14) | Cash | 791,000 | |
| | Property Taxes Receivable—Current | | 695,000 |
| | Property Taxes Receivable—Delinquent | | 96,000 |
| | Collect portion of property taxes including $96,000 of past due accounts. | | |

| (15) | Allowance for Uncollectible Taxes—Delinquent | 4,000 | |
| | Property Taxes Receivable—Delinquent | | 4,000 |
| | Write off remaining $4,000 of delinquent property taxes. | | |

| (16) | Allowance for Uncollectible Taxes—Delinquent | 1,000 | |
| | Allowance for Uncollectible Taxes—Current | 5,000 | |
| | Revenues—Property Tax | | 6,000 |
| | Revise estimate of uncollectibles from $10,000 to $5,000 and close remaining $1,000 balance of allowance account for delinquent accounts. | | |

| (17) | Property Taxes Receivable—Delinquent | 90,000 | |
| | Allowance for Uncollectible Taxes—Current | 5,000 | |
| | Property Taxes Receivable—Current | | 90,000 |
| | Allowance for Uncollectible Taxes—Delinquent | | 5,000 |
| | Reclassify remaining receivables and allowance account from current to delinquent. | | |

## Other Revenue

Other sources of income are grants from other governmental units, a portion of the sales tax collected on retail sales made within the city, and miscellaneous revenue from parking meters, fines, and licenses. Grants from other governmental units should be recognized as revenue when the grants become available and measurable. The city's policy is to recognize these grants as the monies are received because the grants may be withdrawn by the grantor at any time up to the actual transmittal of the monies. In our example, the city receives only 60 percent of the expected grant that had been budgeted at $55,000. Sales tax revenue may be accrued if the city can make a good estimate of the amount to be received and if the sales tax revenue is available for current expenditures. The city's policy is to recognize the sales taxes when received. Miscellaneous revenue is recognized as received.

The entries to record the other sources of income are as follows:

| (18) | Cash | 33,000 | |
| | Revenue—Grant | | 33,000 |
| | Receive only 60 percent of expected grant. | | |

| (19) | Cash | 32,000 | |
| | Revenue—Sales Tax | | 32,000 |
| | Receive sales tax revenue from state. | | |

| (20) | Cash | 18,000 | |
| | Revenue—Miscellaneous | | 18,000 |
| | Receive miscellaneous revenue from fines, license fees, minor disposals of equipment, and other sources. | | |

## Expenditures

The appropriations were recorded in the budget entry [entry (10)] with a renewal of the encumbrances carried over from the prior period under the lapsing method of accounting for encumbrances [entries (11) and (12)]. Orders for goods and services from outside vendors are encumbered, and a voucher system is used. Recall that a governmental entity typically does not encumber internal payroll.

The entries for the encumbrances, expenditures, and disbursements made in Sol City's general fund during the year are as follows:

| (21) | ENCUMBRANCES | 210,000 | |
| | BUDGETARY FUND BALANCE—RESERVED FOR ENCUMBRANCES | | 210,000 |
| | Encumber for purchase orders for goods and services ordered from outside vendors. | | |

(22)    BUDGETARY FUND BALANCE—RESERVED FOR ENCUMBRANCES                5,000
       ENCUMBRANCES                                                                        5,000
       Reverse encumbrance for portion of order that is not deliverable
       because item has been discontinued.

(23)    BUDGETARY FUND BALANCE—RESERVED FOR ENCUMBRANCES              190,000
       ENCUMBRANCES                                                                      190,000
       Reverse reserve for partial order of goods received.

(24)    Expenditures                                                  196,000
       Vouchers Payable                                                                  196,000
       Receive goods at actual cost of $196,000 that had been
       encumbered for $190,000. Difference due to increase in cost of
       items. Includes supplies for inventory.

(25)    BUDGETARY FUND BALANCE—RESERVED FOR ENCUMBRANCES               11,000
       ENCUMBRANCES                                                                       11,000
       Reverse reserve for goods received that were ordered in prior year.

(26)    Expenditures                                                    9,000
       Vouchers Payable                                                                    9,000
       Receive goods ordered in prior year. Actual cost is $9,000 on
       encumbered amount of $11,000. Difference due to price
       reduction as part of special sale.

(27)    Expenditures                                                  550,000
       Vouchers Payable                                                                  550,000
       Payroll costs to employees for period.

(28)    Vouchers Payable                                              730,000
       Cash                                                                              730,000
       Vouchers approved by city council and paid during period.

## Acquisition of Capital Asset

The budget for the fire department includes $50,000 for a new fire truck. This capital outlay is accounted for as any other expenditure of available resources. The resources for the fire truck are encumbered when the order is placed with the truck manufacturer. The entries in the general fund for the fire truck acquisition are as follows:

(29)    ENCUMBRANCES                                                   50,000
       BUDGETARY FUND BALANCE—RESERVED
         FOR ENCUMBRANCES                                                               50,000
       Order fire truck at estimated cost of $50,000.

(30)    BUDGETARY FUND BALANCE—RESERVED FOR ENCUMBRANCES               50,000
       ENCUMBRANCES                                                                       50,000
       Reverse reserve for fire truck received.

(31)    Expenditures                                                   58,000
       Vouchers Payable                                                                   58,000
       Receive fire truck at actual cost of $58,000 due to approved
       additional items required to meet new fire code.

(32)    Vouchers Payable                                               58,000
       Cash                                                                               58,000
       Voucher approved and disbursement made for fire truck.

## Interfund Activities

The anticipated interfund items are included in the budget for the fiscal period. They include the estimated transfer out of $10,000 to initiate the internal service fund and the estimated transfer out of $20,000 for capital improvements to a capital projects fund. In addition to these transfers, the general fund also has an interfund transaction with the internal service fund for services received in the amount of $1,000, and it lends the enterprise fund $3,000.

The following entries in the general fund record the general fund's side of the interfund activities during the year. Chapter 18 continues the comprehensive example of Sol City and presents the entries for these interfund transactions and transfers in each of the related funds so that both sides of accounting for interfund items are illustrated for the Sol City example:

| | | | | |
|---|---|---|---|---|
| (33) | Other Financing Uses—Transfer Out to Internal Service Fund | | 10,000 | |
| | Due to Internal Service Fund | | | 10,000 |
| | Recognize the transfer out and associated liability to the internal service fund as included in the budget. | | | |
| (34) | Other Financing Uses—Transfer Out to Capital Projects Fund | | 20,000 | |
| | Due to Capital Projects Fund | | | 20,000 |
| | Recognize the transfer out and associated liability to the capital projects fund as included in the budget. | | | |
| (35) | Due to Internal Service Fund | | 10,000 | |
| | Cash | | | 10,000 |
| | Pay cash to internal service fund for payable from interfund transfer out previously recognized. | | | |
| (36) | Due to Capital Projects Fund | | 20,000 | |
| | Cash | | | 20,000 |
| | Pay cash to capital projects fund for payable from interfund transfer out previously recognized. | | | |
| (37) | Expenditures | | 1,000 | |
| | Due to Internal Service Fund | | | 1,000 |
| | Recognize payable for interfund supplies provided and used (received from the internal service fund). | | | |
| (38) | Due to Internal Service Fund | | 1,000 | |
| | Cash | | | 1,000 |
| | Pay cash to eliminate payable. | | | |
| (39) | Due from Enterprise Fund | | 3,000 | |
| | Cash | | | 3,000 |
| | City Council approves loan to enterprise fund to be repaid in 90 days. | | | |

## Adjusting Entries

Certain adjusting entries are required to state correctly the balance sheet items for the year. Assume that a physical count of the inventory shows an ending balance of $17,000 on December 31, 20X2. This is a net increase of $3,000 from the beginning balance of $14,000.

The policy of the general fund is to recognize inventory as an asset and to report a reserve against fund balance for the ending balance. Recall that the city is using the consumption method of accounting for inventories. The entries required to adjust the ending balance of the supplies inventory are as follows:

| | | | | |
|---|---|---|---|---|
| (40) | Inventory of Supplies | | 3,000 | |
| | Expenditures | | | 3,000 |
| | Adjust ending inventory to $17,000 and reduce expenditures to net amount consumed during the period. | | | |

| (41) | Fund Balance—Unreserved | 3,000 | |
| | Fund Balance—Reserved for Inventories | | 3,000 |
| | Adjust the reserve for inventories from beginning balance of $14,000 to its ending balance of $17,000. | | |

## Closing Entries

The final set of entries closes the nominal accounts. The format presented first reverses the budget entry and then closes the operating revenues and expenditures. Some governmental entities close the accounts in a slightly different order by closing budgeted revenue against actual revenue and budgeted appropriations against actual expenditures. The specific order of closing the accounts has no impact on the final effect; all budgetary accounts and nominal operating accounts must be closed at year-end.

A preclosing trial balance is presented in Figure 17–10. Recall that the city is using the lapsing method of accounting for encumbrances open at the end of the fiscal year. The closing entries for the general fund of Sol City for fiscal 20X2 follow:

December 31, 20X2

| (42) | APPROPRIATIONS CONTROL | 825,000 | |
| | ESTIMATED OTHER FINANCING USES— TRANSFER OUT TO CAPITAL PROJECTS | 20,000 | |
| | ESTIMATED OTHER FINANCING USES— TRANSFER OUT TO INTERNAL SERVICES | 10,000 | |
| | BUDGETARY FUND BALANCE—UNRESERVED | 20,000 | |
| | ESTIMATED REVENUES CONTROL | | 875,000 |
| | Close budgetary accounts. | | |
| (43) | BUDGETARY FUND BALANCE—RESERVED FOR ENCUMBRANCES | 15,000 | |
| | ENCUMBRANCES | | 15,000 |
| | Close remaining encumbrances by reversing remaining budgetary balance. | | |
| (44) | Fund Balance—Unreserved | 15,000 | |
| | Fund Balance—Reserved for Encumbrances | | 15,000 |
| | Reservation of fund balance for encumbrances that lapse but are expected to be honored in 20X3. | | |
| (45) | Revenue—Property Tax | 781,000 | |
| | Revenue—Grant | 33,000 | |
| | Revenue—Sales Tax | 32,000 | |
| | Revenue—Miscellaneous | 18,000 | |
| | Expenditures | | 811,000 |
| | Other Financing Uses—Transfer Out to Capital Projects Fund | | 20,000 |
| | Other Financing Uses—Transfer Out to Internal Service Fund | | 10,000 |
| | Fund Balance—Unreserved | | 23,000 |
| | Close operating statement accounts. | | |

A reconciliation of the Fund Balance—Unreserved account is used to determine its ending balance of $120,000, as follows:

| **Fund Balance—Unreserved** | | | |
|---|---|---|---|
| | | Bal. 1/1/X2 | 104,000 |
| (41) | 3,000 | (11) | 11,000 |
| | | Bal. Preclosing | 112,000 |
| (44) | 15,000 | (45) | 23,000 |
| | | Bal. 12/31/X2 | 120,000 |

**FIGURE 17–10**
Preclosing Trial
Balance for General
Fund

| | Debit | Credit |
|---|---|---|
| **SOL CITY** | | |
| **General Fund** | | |
| **Preclosing Trial Balance** | | |
| **December 31, 20X2** | | |
| Cash | $ 102,000 | |
| Property Taxes Receivable—Delinquent | 90,000 | |
| Allowance for Uncollectible Taxes—Delinquent | | $ 5,000 |
| Due from Enterprise Fund | 3,000 | |
| Inventory of Supplies | 17,000 | |
| Vouchers Payable | | 55,000 |
| Fund Balance—Reserved for Inventories | | 17,000 |
| Fund Balance—Unreserved | | 112,000 |
| Revenue—Property Tax | | 781,000 |
| Revenue—Grant | | 33,000 |
| Revenue—Sales Tax | | 32,000 |
| Revenue—Miscellaneous | | 18,000 |
| Expenditures | 811,000 | |
| Other Financing Uses—Transfer Out to Capital Projects Fund | 20,000 | |
| Other Financing Uses—Transfer Out to Internal Service Fund | 10,000 | |
| ESTIMATED REVENUES CONTROL | 875,000 | |
| APPROPRIATIONS CONTROL | | 825,000 |
| ESTIMATED OTHER FINANCING USES— TRANSFER OUT TO CAPITAL PROJECTS | | 20,000 |
| ESTIMATED OTHER FINANCING USES— TRANSFER OUT TO INTERNAL SERVICE | | 10,000 |
| ENCUMBRANCES | 15,000 | |
| BUDGETARY FUND BALANCE—RESERVED FOR ENCUMBRANCES | | 15,000 |
| BUDGETARY FUND BALANCE—UNRESERVED | | 20,000 |
| Total | $1,943,000 | $1,943,000 |

## General Fund Financial Statement Information

The general fund is always specified as a major governmental fund type. The two required statements for a major governmental fund are *(a)* the balance sheet, and *(b)* the statement of revenues, expenditures, and changes in fund balance. For purposes of illustration, the two financial statements for the general fund are provided, applying the requirements of **GASB 34,** and then a presentation is made of the fund balance section of the balance sheet under the proposed governmental accounting statement on fund balance reporting and governmental fund type definitions.

### *The Balance Sheet*

The balance sheet required under **GASB 34** is presented in Figure 17–11. This balance sheet includes the supplies inventory for $17,000 and the associated reservation of fund balance, reflecting that the portion of the fund balance already applied to inventory is not expendable. The $3,000 receivable from the interfund loan transaction with the enterprise fund is shown as a current asset. The outstanding encumbrances of $15,000 are a reservation of fund balance indicating that a portion of the year's appropriation has been used but that the ordered goods or services have not yet been received.

### *The General Fund's Balance Sheet under the Proposed Statement*

The proposed statement on fund balance reporting and governmental fund type definitions does not change the reporting of assets or liabilities. It affects only the reporting of the fund balance for governmental fund types which includes the general fund. The fund

**FIGURE 17–11**
General Fund
Balance Sheet
Information at the
End of the Fiscal
Period

| SOL CITY<br>General Fund<br>Balance Sheet Information<br>December 31, 20X2 | | |
|---|---:|---:|
| Assets: | | |
| Cash | | $102,000 |
| Property Taxes Receivable—Delinquent | $ 90,000 | |
| Less: Allowance for Uncollectibles—Delinquent | (5,000) | 85,000 |
| Due from Enterprise Fund | | 3,000 |
| Inventory of Supplies | | 17,000 |
| Total Assets | | $207,000 |
| | | |
| Liabilities and Fund Balance: | | |
| Vouchers Payable | | $ 55,000 |
| Fund Balance: | | |
| Reserved for Encumbrances | $ 15,000 | |
| Reserved for Inventories | 17,000 | |
| Unreserved | 120,000 | 152,000 |
| Total Liabilities and Fund Balance | | $207,000 |

balance section of the balance sheet could report only aggregate amounts for the non-spendable and spendable categories with detail presented in the footnotes. Alternatively, the balance sheet can report the detailed items within each category of the general fund balance. The nonspendable category includes the two classifications of amounts not in spendable form, such as inventories, or amounts that are legally or contractually required to be maintained. The spendable category includes resources that are in spendable form and are considered to be available for spending, such as fund balance related to cash, investments, and receivables. Amounts in the spendable fund balance category can then be classified as restricted, limited, assigned, or unassigned based on a hierarchy of the level of control over the spending of the resources.

Under the proposed statement, no reserves are reported on the balance sheet; rather, the amount of encumbrances would be reported in the footnotes along with other commitments. The Sol City government has no restricted or limited spendable fund balances, but does have an assigned amount for the amount of resources intended by the government to be used for the specific purpose of paying currently outstanding encumbrances from goods and services ordered to be used for general government functions. Under the proposed statement, a detailed presentation of the fund balance of the general fund would be as follows:

| | |
|---|---:|
| Fund Balances: | |
| Nonspendable: | |
| Inventory of Supplies | $ 17,000 |
| Spendable: | |
| Assigned to: | |
| General Government Services | 15,000 |
| Unassigned: | 120,000 |
| Total Fund Balance | $152,000 |

### The Statement of Revenues, Expenditures, and Changes in Fund Balance

This required statement is presented in Figure 17–12 and has the following sections:

1. *Operating section.* Revenues less expenditures, resulting in an excess of revenues over expenditures for the period. Expenditures include the interfund services provided and used, and separate reporting of outlays for capital assets.

**FIGURE 17–12**
General Fund
Statement
of Revenues,
Expenditures and
Changes in Fund
Balance Information
for Fiscal 20X2

| SOL CITY |
|---|
| Statement of Revenues, Expenditures, and Changes in Fund Balance Information |
| General Fund |
| For the Year Ended December 31, 20X2 |

| | | |
|---|---:|---:|
| Revenues: | | |
| Property Taxes | $781,000 | |
| Grants | 33,000 | |
| Sales Taxes | 32,000 | |
| Miscellaneous | 18,000 | |
| Total Revenues | | $864,000 |
| Expenditures: | | |
| General Government | $206,000 | |
| Streets and Highways | 71,000 | |
| Public Safety | 335,000 | |
| Sanitation | 141,000 | |
| Capital Outlay: | | |
| Public Safety | 58,000 | |
| Total Expenditures | | 811,000 |
| Excess of Revenues Over Expenditures | | $ 53,000 |
| Other Financing Sources (Uses): | | |
| Transfer Out to Capital Projects Fund | $ (20,000) | |
| Transfer Out to Internal Service Fund | (10,000) | |
| Total Other Financing Sources (Uses) | | (30,000) |
| Net Change in Fund Balances | | $ 23,000 |
| Fund Balance, January 1 | | 129,000 |
| Fund Balance, December 31 | | $152,000 |

2. *Other financing sources (uses).* This section includes interfund transfers and non-revenue proceeds such as bond issues.
3. *Reconciliation of fund balance.* The ending balance in fund balances, including both reserved and unreserved, is reconciled for (*a*) the results of operations, (*b*) other financing sources or uses, and (*c*) special or extraordinary items in the period.

Revenues should be classified by major sources, and expenditures by character and major functions. Although the entries presented in the illustrations for Sol City did not break down the expenditures by function (general government, streets and highways, public safety, and sanitation), this breakdown is done in the actual governmental accounting process so each expenditure can be classified by both function and object (personal services, supplies, and other services and charges). The amounts presented in the expenditures section in Figure 17–12 are the assumed amounts from a comprehensive accounting system. Total expenditures do reconcile to the expenditures recorded in the Sol City illustration.

The statement of revenues, expenditures, and changes in fund balance presents the total fund balance, including both reserved and unreserved. Note that in this example, Sol City reported no extraordinary items or special items. Special items would include significant transactions or other events within the control of management that were either unusual in nature or infrequent in occurrence. An example of a special item could be a one-time sale of some city park land. If the city did have a special item or extraordinary item, it would be reported below the other financing sources (uses) section.

### The General Fund's Statement of Revenues, Expenditures, and Changes in Fund Balance under the Proposed Statement

The proposed GASB statement on governmental fund type balances does not require any changes in the statement of revenues, expenditures, and changes in fund balance. The reconciliation in this financial statement is to total fund balance, not to a specific classification of the fund balance. Therefore, this financial statement will be the same under the proposed GASB statement as currently required under **GASB 34.**

# ADDITIONAL CONSIDERATIONS

As stated earlier in the chapter, in February 2008, the GASB published an exposure draft (ED) of a proposed statement entitled "Fund Balance Reporting and Governmental Fund Type Definitions." The following presents highlights of this proposed statement.

## Proposed Statement of the GASB: Fund Balance Reporting and Governmental Fund Type Definitions

It is important to note that the proposed statement applies only to the five governmental fund types.

1. If the proposed statement is adopted, the effective date is scheduled for periods beginning after June 15, 2010. Earlier implementation is encouraged.

2. Fund balance classifications are based on a hierarchy of the extent the government must observe constraints on the use of the resources. These constraints may be imposed externally to the government or internally within the government.

3. The first evaluation of a fund balance separates the amounts that are considered *nonspendable,* such as the fund balance related to inventories, from those considered *spendable,* such as the fund balance related to cash, investments, and receivables.

4. The nonspendable fund balance represents amounts that cannot be spent because they *(a)* are not in spendable form, such as inventories, or *(b)* are legally or contractually required to be maintained.

5. The *spendable fund balance* is further categorized by the degree of constraints over how the specific amounts may be spent. The hierarchy goes from most constrained to least constrained, as follows:

   a. *Restricted fund balance.* These are amounts restricted to specific purposes because of externally imposed constraints from creditors, grantors, contributors, or other governments; or legally imposed constraints such as enabling legislation. Note the external sourcing of these restrictions.

   b. *Limited fund balance.* These are amounts committed for specific purposes by formal decisions of the government's decision-making authority. These amounts are not legally enforceable like the restricted fund balance; but these amounts cannot be used for other purposes unless the government changes the limitation in the same manner as it was imposed.

   c. *Assigned fund balance.* These amounts are intended to be used for specific purposes, but are not restricted or limited. The intent can be established by the governing body, or by a high-level official or group that has the authority to assign amounts to be used for specific purposes. Amounts encumbered can be placed into this category.

   d. *Unassigned fund balance.* These are the residual amounts that are not assigned to other funds and have not been restricted, limited, or assigned within the general fund. Only the general fund may have an unassigned fund balance. The four other governmental fund types may not report any unassigned fund balance.

6. Governments may choose to report only the aggregate amount for each classification and then present the detail in the notes to the financial statements. Alternatively, the government may choose to report the detail on the face of the balance sheet or in a related schedule.

7. The reserved categories of fund balance are not displayed on the face of the balance sheet; instead, they are reported in the notes along with other commitments. The amounts that are required to be reported as a reserve of fund balance under **GASB 34**

would be classified into one of the categories of fund balance based on the nature of the constraint of the encumbrance. Governments may still use an encumbrance accounting system; the proposed statement applies only to the financial statement reporting for the fund balances of the governmental fund types.

8. Stabilization (rainy-day) amounts that are set aside by formal arrangements to stabilize revenue, working capital needs, contingencies, or emergencies are reported as restricted or limited based on the nature of the constraint.

9. The definition of each of the five governmental funds is clarified and made consistent across all government entities. The definitions are based on the current classification schema with relatively minor modifications.

Chapter 18 will present the fund display for the governmental funds under **GASB 34,** which established our funds display standards currently used. Then the fund balance reporting for the governmental funds that would be required under the proposed statement will be presented.

## Summary of Key Concepts

Accounting for state and local governmental units requires the use of fund accounting to recognize properly the variety of services and objectives of the governmental unit. Funds are separate fiscal and accounting entities established to segregate, control, and account for resource flows. Three types of funds are used by governmental units: governmental funds, of which the general fund is usually the most important; proprietary funds; and fiduciary funds. The basis of accounting for each fund depends on the fund's objective. The current financial resources measurement focus and the modified accrual basis of accounting are used for the governmental fund financial statements. The economic resources measurement focus and accrual basis of accounting are used for the government-wide statements, the proprietary fund statements, and the fiduciary fund statements.

Under the modified accrual basis, revenue is recognized when it is both measurable and available for financing expenditures of the period. A major source of revenue is property tax levies, but other sources may include sales taxes; grants from other governmental units; and fines, licenses, or permits. Note that in the five governmental funds, the estimated uncollectible property taxes are a reduction of the property tax revenue, not an expense as in commercial accounting. Expenditures are recognized in the period in which the related liability is both measurable and incurred. The expenditure process usually begins with a budget, which establishes the spending authority for the fund. Encumbrances are used for purchases outside the governmental entity to recognize the use of a portion of the spending authority for the period and to avoid overspending the expenditure authority. Under current GAAFR, encumbrances outstanding at the end of a fiscal period are reported as a reserve of the fund balance and may be accounted for as lapsing or nonlapsing. Another type of fund balance reserve is a reserve for inventories, which is used if the amount of inventory is material.

The general fund is responsible for offering many of the usual services of governmental units. Fire and police protection, the local government's administrative and legislative functions, and many other basic governmental services are administered through the general fund. The general fund will provide balance sheet information and statement of revenues, expenditures, and changes in fund balances information to the governmental funds financial statements.

The government reporting model, as established by GASB 34, specifies that both fund-based financial statements and government-wide financial statements must be presented. The general fund uses the modified accrual basis of accounting to recognize revenue and expenditure transactions. Furthermore, no long-term capital assets or general long-term debt is recorded in the general fund. However, a reconciliation schedule will be required to go from the governmental fund types financial statements to the government-wide financial statements. The government-wide financial statements use the accrual basis of accounting and report all capital assets and all long-term debt. Government-wide financial statements are presented in Chapter 18 after the conclusion of that chapter's discussion of the remaining funds.

Interfund activities must be evaluated carefully to ensure that the legal and budgetary controls of the governmental unit are not violated. Four types of interfund activities exist: (1) interfund loans, (2) interfund services provided and used, (3) interfund transfers, and (4) interfund reimbursements. Outstanding interfund loans are presented as receivables or payables on the fund's balance sheet information. Interfund services provided and used are reported as part of the revenues and expenditures on the operating statements. Interfund transfers are reported separately in the other financing sources (uses) section of the operating statement. Interfund reimbursements are not reported separately on the fund's financial statements.

## Key Terms

appropriation, *816*
basis of accounting, *811*
budgets, *815*
current financial resources
   measurement focus, *808*
disbursement, *818*
economic resources
   measurement focus, *811*
encumbrance, *817*
expenditure, *805*

fiduciary funds, *806*
fund-based financial
   statements, *807*
funds, *805*
governmental financial
   reporting model, *807*
governmental funds, *805*
government-wide financial
   statements, *807*
interfund activities, *827*

modified accrual basis, *811*
proprietary funds, *805*
reporting entity, *807*
reservation (or restriction)
   of the budgetary fund
   balance, *818*

## Questions

**Q17-1**  What is a fund? How does a fund receive resources?

**Q17-2**  What are the 11 funds generally used by local and state governments? Briefly state the purpose of each fund.

**Q17-3**  Compare the modified accrual basis with the accrual accounting basis.

**Q17-4**  Which of the two, the modified accrual basis or the accrual basis, is used for funds for which expendability is the concern? Why?

**Q17-5**  When are property taxes recognized as revenue in the general fund?

**Q17-6**  How are taxpayer-assessed income and sales taxes recognized in the general fund? Why?

**Q17-7**  What is meant by "budgetary accounting"? Explain the accounting for expected revenue and anticipated expenditures.

**Q17-8**  Are all expenditures encumbered?

**Q17-9**  Why do some governmental units not report small amounts of supply inventories in their balance sheets?

**Q17-10**  What are the main differences between the lapsing and nonlapsing methods of accounting for encumbrances outstanding at the end of the fiscal year? What are the differences in accounting between the lapsing and nonlapsing methods when accounting for the actual expenditure in the subsequent year?

**Q17-11**  When is the expenditure for inventories recognized under the purchase method? Under the consumption method?

**Q17-12**  Explain the difference between an interfund services provided and used and an interfund transfer. Give examples of each.

**Q17-13**  Where is an interfund transfer reported on the general fund's financial statements?

**Q17-14**  The general fund agrees to lend the enterprise fund $2,000 for three months. How is this interfund loan reported on the financial statements of the general fund?

**Q17-15**  Explain how an expenditure may be classified by (1) function, (2) activity, and (3) object within the financial statements of a governmental unit.

## Cases

**C17-1**

*Understanding*

### Budget Theory

Governmental accounting gives substantial recognition to budgets, with budgets being recorded in the accounts of the governmental unit.

**Required**

*a.* What is the purpose of a governmental accounting system, and why is the budget recorded in the accounts of a governmental unit? Include in your discussion the purpose and significance of appropriations.

*b.* Describe when and how a governmental unit (1) records its budget and (2) closes out the budgetary accounts.

**C17-2** **Municipal versus Financial Accounting**

*Judgment*

Wilma Bates is executive vice president of Mavis Industries Inc., a publicly held industrial corporation. She has just been elected to the city council of Gotham City. Before assuming office, she asks you to explain the major differences that exist in accounting and financial reporting for a large city when compared to accounting and reporting for a large industrial corporation.

**Required**

*a.* Describe the major differences that exist in the purpose of accounting and financial reporting and in the type of financial reports of a large city when compared to a large industrial corporation.

*b.* Why are inventories often ignored in accounting for local governmental units? Explain.

**C17-3** **Revenue Issues**

*Communication*

The bookkeeper for the community of Spring Valley has asked for your assistance on the following items.

**Required**

Prepare a memo discussing the proper accounting and financial reporting in the general fund for each of the following items.

*a.* Property taxes receivable are recognized at the levy date. One percent of the levy is not expected to be collected.

*b.* Property taxes are collected in advance of the year in which they are expendable.

*c.* Sales tax revenues are received from the state but the city is still owed another $15,000 by the state that will not be received until the next month.

*d.* An unexpected state grant is received to finance the purchase of fire prevention equipment. One-half of the grant is expended in this fiscal period, and the remainder is expected to be expended in the next fiscal period.

*e.* Interest is earned on short-term investments made from the general fund's resources.

*f.* A gift from a local citizen was given to be used for a new city park once the park has been completed. If the park is not constructed within two years, the gift must be returned to the grantor. It is expected that the park will be completed in the next fiscal period.

**C17-4** **Summarizing the Requirements of GASB 34**

*Research*

You have a friend who was just elected to the County Board for your county. One of the first items of business for the County Board is to prepare a budget for the new fiscal period. Your friend does not understand the county governmental entity financial reporting requirements so you volunteer to assist by preparing a report on the financial statements and the management's discussion and analysis (MD&A) of the county government.

**Required**

Obtain the preface and summary of GASB Statement 34, "Basic Financial Statements—And Management's Discussion and Analysis—For State and Local Governments" (GASB 34). You may obtain these from the GASB's Web site (www.gasb.org), from your library, or the GASB's Governmental Accounting Research System (GARS), a computer-based database sold by the GASB. Then answer the following questions.

*a.* GASB established the requirement for government annual reports to include a management's discussion and analysis (MD&A). Describe the purposes of the MD&A in a government's annual report.

*b.* GASB 34 discusses both fund financial statements and government-wide financial statements.

(1) Discuss the major contents of the fund financial statements and why those statements are necessary in the government's annual report.

(2) Discuss the major contents of the government-wide financial statements and why those statements are necessary in the government's annual report.

**C17-5**

*Analysis*

**Examining the General Fund Disclosures in a Comprehensive Annual Financial Report (CAFR)**

This case focuses on the general fund of a governmental unit.

**Required**

Using the Comprehensive Annual Financial Report (CAFR) for a governmental entity chosen by your instructor, answer the following questions that relate to the overall government and the governmental funds:

*a.* Find the budgetary comparison schedules for the general fund. Using these schedules, what were the estimated revenues and appropriations for the most recent fiscal year?

*b.* Using the same information as in question (*a*), list the amounts of any transfers in and transfers out that were budgeted for the most recent year.

*c.* Based on the notes following the financial statements, what is the policy of the general fund with respect to outstanding encumbrances at the end of the fiscal year?

*d.* On the balance sheet of the general fund at the end of the most recent fiscal year, what is the total amount reported for assets and for fund balance? Of the total amount reported for fund balance, how much is unreserved?

*e.* On the balance sheet of the general fund at the end of the most recent fiscal year, what is the amount reported for inventories? If inventories are reported, does the government use the purchase method or the consumption method?

*f.* Based on the notes following the financial statements, what is the government's revenue recognition policy with respect to property taxes in the general fund? What percentage of the property tax levy is estimated to be uncollectible?

*g.* Read the section of the CAFR that contains management's discussion and analysis. What reasons were given for the increase or decrease in general fund revenues for the most recent year?

*h.* Examine the statement of revenues, expenditures, and changes in fund balance for the most recent year. Compare the change in fund balance for the general fund with the amount of change in fund balance that was budgeted for the year. Were the government's general fund actual results better or worse than expected?

*i.* After revenue from taxes, what was the next most significant source of revenue for the general fund for the most recent year?

*j.* Has the general fund engaged in any interfund loans and advances? If yes, show the amounts that are owed to or by the general fund as of the end of the most recent year.

**C17-6**

*Discovery*

**Examining Deposit and Investment Risk Disclosures of a Governmental Entity**

The financial reports of governmental entities must provide footnote disclosure of the deposit and investment risks faced by the entity. GASB Statement No. 40, "Deposit and Investment Risk Disclosures" (GASB 40), amended GASB Statement No. 3, "Deposits with Financial Institutions, Investments (including Repurchase Agreements) and Reverse Repurchase Agreements" (GASB 3).

The GASB requires disclosures of (*a*) the natures of the deposits and investment risks the governmental entity faces, (*b*) the policies of the governmental entity regarding each of those risks, and (*c*) specific disclosures such as credit ratings of investments in fixed income securities along with a schedule of maturity dates and fair values of these fixed income securities; the types of other investment securities held along with the amounts and fair values of those other investment securities; any concentrations of investments, other than those in U.S. government securities or in mutual or pooled investment funds, comprising 5 percent or more of total investments; and discussion of the risks from changing interest rates and changing foreign exchange rates.

**Required**

First, go to the GASB's web site (www.gasb.org) and obtain the summaries of GASB 40 and GASB 3 (the GASB does not provide online access to their complete publications). Second, using an online search engine such as Google, locate the most recent annual report of a local government near your college or university. Then provide answers to the following questions.

*a.* List the types of deposit and investment risks addressed in GASB 3 and GASB 40.

*b.* Explain why disclosures of information about these risks are important to the users of the government's financial statements.

The following questions should be answered using the footnote information for Deposits and Investments from your local government's most recent annual report.

*c.* Describe the types of deposit and investment risks of your local government.

*d.* Describe the policies your local government has for each type of risk identified.

*e.* Describe the types of specific disclosures of information for each type of risk identified.

---

**Exercises**  **E17-1**  **Multiple-Choice Questions on the General Fund [AICPA Adapted]**

Select the correct answer for each of the following questions.

1. One of the differences between accounting for a governmental (not-for-profit) unit and a commercial (for profit) enterprise is that a governmental unit should:

   *a.* *Not* record depreciation expense in any of its funds.

   *b.* Always establish and maintain complete self-balancing accounts for each fund.

   *c.* Use only the cash basis of accounting.

   *d.* Use only the modified accrual basis of accounting.

2. Belle Valley incurred $100,000 of salaries and wages for the month ended March 31, 20X2. How should this be recorded on that date?

|  | Debit | Credit |
|---|---|---|
| *a.* Expenditures—Salaries and Wages | 100,000 | |
|     Vouchers Payable | | 100,000 |
| *b.* Salaries and Wages Expense | 100,000 | |
|     Vouchers Payable | | 100,000 |
| *c.* Encumbrances—Salaries and Wages | 100,000 | |
|     Vouchers Payable | | 100,000 |
| *d.* Fund Balance | 100,000 | |
|     Vouchers Payable | | 100,000 |

3. Which of the following expenditures is normally recorded on the accrual basis in the general fund?

   *a.* Interest.

   *b.* Personal services.

   *c.* Inventory items.

   *d.* Prepaid expenses.

4. Which of the following accounts of a governmental unit is credited when taxpayers are billed for property taxes?

   *a.* Estimated Revenue.

   *b.* Revenue.

   *c.* Appropriations.

   *d.* Fund Balance—Reserved for Encumbrances.

5. Fixed assets purchased from general fund revenue were received. What account, if any, should have been debited in the general fund?

   *a.* No journal entry should have been made in the general fund.

   *b.* Fixed Assets.

   *c.* Expenditures.

   *d.* Fund Balance—Unreserved.

6. The initial transfer of cash from the general fund in order to establish an internal service fund would require the general fund to credit Cash and debit:

   *a.* Accounts Receivable—Internal Service Fund.

   *b.* Transfers Out.

   *c.* Budgetary Fund Balance—Reserved for Encumbrances.

   *d.* Expenditures.

**E17-2   Matching for General Fund Transactions [AICPA Adapted]**

For each general fund transaction listed in items 1 through 12, select the appropriate recording for the transaction listed next to letters A through O. A letter may be selected once, more than once, or not at all.

| Transactions | Recording of Transactions |
|---|---|
| 1. An interfund transfer out was made to the capital projects fund. | A. Credit Revenues |
| 2. Approved purchase orders were issued for supplies. | B. Debit Expenditures |
| 3. The above-mentioned supplies were received and the related invoices were approved. | C. Debit Encumbrances |
| | D. Debit Inventories |
| | E. Debit Interfund Services Provided and Used |
| 4. Salaries and wages were incurred. | F. Credit Budgetary Fund Balance—Unreserved |
| 5. Cash was transferred to establish an internal service fund. | G. Debit Appropriations Control |
| 6. The property tax levy was passed by the city council and tax bills were sent to property owners. | H. Credit Property Taxes Receivable—Current |
| | I. Credit Appropriations Control |
| | J. Credit Residual Equity Transfer Out |
| 7. Property taxes for the current year were collected. | K. Debit Interfund Transfer Out |
| 8. Appropriations were recorded on adoption of the budget. | L. Credit Interfund Transfer Out |
| | M. Debit Estimated Revenues Control |
| 9. Estimated revenues were recorded on adoption of the budget. | N. Debit Budgetary Fund Balance—Unreserved |
| 10. There was an excess of estimated inflows over estimated outflows. | O. Debit Computer Equipment |
| 11. Invoices for computer equipment were received. | |
| 12. Received billing from water and sewer fund (enterprise fund) for using city water and sewer. | |

**E17-3   Multiple-Choice Questions on Budgets, Expenditures, and Revenue [AICPA Adapted]**

Select the correct answer for each of the following questions.

1. Which of the following steps in the acquisition of goods and services occurs first?

   a. Appropriation.

   b. Encumbrance.

   c. Budget.

   d. Expenditure.

2. What account is used to earmark the fund balance to recognize the contingent obligations of goods ordered but not yet received?

   a. Appropriations.

   b. Encumbrances.

   c. Obligations.

   d. Fund Balance—Reserved for Encumbrances.

3. When the Estimated Revenues Control account of a governmental unit is closed out at the end of the fiscal year, the excess of estimated revenues over estimated appropriations is:

   a. Debited to Fund Balance—Unreserved.

   b. Debited to Fund Balance—Reserved for Encumbrances.

   c. Debited to Budgetary Fund Balance—Unreserved.

   d. Credited to Fund Balance—Reserved for Encumbrances.

4. The Carson City general fund issued purchase orders of $630,000 to vendors and supplies. Which of the following entries should be made to record this transaction?

| | Debit | Credit |
|---|---|---|
| *a.* Encumbrances | 630,000 | |
|     Budgetary Fund Balance—Reserved for Encumbrances | | 630,000 |
| *b.* Expenditures | 630,000 | |
|     Vouchers Payable | | 630,000 |
| *c.* Expenses | 630,000 | |
|     Accounts Payable | | 630,000 |
| *d.* Budgetary Fund Balance—Reserved for Encumbrances | 630,000 | |
|     Encumbrances | | 630,000 |

5. The following balances are included in the subsidiary records of Dogwood's Parks and Recreation Department on March 31, 20X2:

| | |
|---|---|
| Appropriations—Supplies | $7,500 |
| Expenditures—Supplies | 4,500 |
| Encumbrances—Supply Orders | 750 |

How much does the department have available for additional purchases of supplies?

   *a.* $0.

   *b.* $2,250.

   *c.* $3,000.

   *d.* $6,750.

6. The board of commissioners of the City of Elgin adopted its budget for the year ending July 31, 20X2, which indicated revenue of $1,000,000 and appropriations of $900,000. If the budget is formally integrated into the accounting records, what is the required journal entry?

   *a.* Memorandum entry only

| *b.* Appropriations Control | 900,000 | |
|---|---|---|
|     Budgetary Fund Balance—Unreserved | 100,000 | |
|         Estimated Revenues Control | | 1,000,000 |
| *c.* Estimated Revenues Control | 1,000,000 | |
|     Appropriations Control | | 900,000 |
|     Budgetary Fund Balance—Unreserved | | 100,000 |
| *d.* Revenue Receivable | 1,000,000 | |
|     Expenditures Payable | | 900,000 |
|     Budgetary Fund Balance—Unreserved | | 100,000 |

7. Which of the following accounts of a governmental unit is credited when the budget is recorded?

   *a.* Encumbrances.

   *b.* Budgetary Fund Balance—Reserved for Encumbrances.

   *c.* Estimated Revenue Control.

   *d.* Appropriations Control.

8. Which of the following accounts of a governmental unit is debited when supplies previously ordered are received?

   *a.* Encumbrances.

   *b.* Budgetary Fund Balance—Reserved for Encumbrances.

   *c.* Vouchers Payable.

   *d.* Appropriations Control.

9. Which of the following situations will increase the fund balance of a governmental unit at the end of the fiscal year?

   *a.* Appropriations are less than expenditures and budgetary fund balance is reserved for encumbrances.

   *b.* Appropriations are less than expenditures and encumbrances.

   *c.* Appropriations are more than expenditures and encumbrances.

   *d.* Appropriations are more than estimated revenue.

10. Which of the following accounts of a governmental unit is credited to close it out at the end of the fiscal year?

    a. Appropriations Control.

    b. Revenue—Property Tax.

    c. Budgetary Fund Balance—Reserved for Encumbrances.

    d. Encumbrances.

**E17-4    Multiple-Choice Questions on the General Fund**

Select the correct answer for each of the following questions.

1. The primary focus in accounting and reporting for governmental funds is on:

    a. Income determination.

    b. Flow of financial resources.

    c. Capital maintenance.

    d. Transfers relating to proprietary activities.

2. The governmental fund measurement focus is on the determination of:

|     | Income | Financial Position | Flow of Financial Resources |
|-----|--------|--------------------|------------------------------|
| a.  | Yes    | Yes                | No                           |
| b.  | No     | Yes                | No                           |
| c.  | No     | No                 | Yes                          |
| d.  | No     | Yes                | Yes                          |

3. A Budgetary Fund Balance—Reserved for Encumbrances in excess of a balance of Encumbrances Control indicates:

    a. An excess of vouchers payable over encumbrances.

    b. An excess of purchase orders over invoices received.

    c. A recording error.

    d. An excess of appropriations over encumbrances.

4. The Encumbrances Control account of a governmental unit is debited when:

    a. Goods are received.

    b. A voucher payable is recorded.

    c. A purchase order is approved.

    d. The budget is recorded.

5. The following pertains to property taxes levied by Cedar City for the calendar year 20X6:

| | |
|---|---:|
| Expected collections during 20X6 | $500,000 |
| Expected collections during the first 60 days of 20X7 | 100,000 |
| Expected collections during the remainder of 20X7 | 60,000 |
| Expected collections during January 20X8 | 30,000 |
| Estimated to be uncollectible (3/1/X7 through 1/1/X8) | 10,000 |
| Total levy | $700,000 |

   What amount should Cedar report for 20X6 as revenues from property taxes?

    a. $700,000.

    b. $600,000.

    c. $690,000.

    d. $500,000.

6. Oak City issued a purchase order for supplies with an estimated cost of $5,000. When the supplies were received, the accompanying invoice indicated an actual price of $4,950. What amount should Oak debit (credit) to Budgetary Fund Balance—Reserved for Encumbrances after the supplies and invoice are received?

a. $5,000.

b. $(50).

c. $4,950.

d. $50.

7. For the budgetary year ending December 31, 20X6, Johnson City's general fund expects the following inflows of resources:

| | |
|---|---|
| Property taxes, licenses, and fines | $9,000,000 |
| Transfer in from internal service fund | 500,000 |
| Transfer in from debt service fund | 1,000,000 |

In the budgetary entry, what amount should Johnson record for estimated revenues?

a. $9,000,000.

b. $9,500,000.

c. $10,500,000.

d. $10,000,000.

8. Encumbrances outstanding at year-end in a state's general fund should be reported as a:

a. Liability in the general fund.

b. Fund balance designation in the general fund.

c. Fund balance reserve in the general fund.

d. Liability in the general long-term debt account group.

9. Interperiod equity is an objective of financial reporting for governmental entities. According to the Governmental Accounting Standards Board, is interperiod equity fundamental to public administration? Is it a component of accountability?

| | **Fundamental to Public Administration** | **Component of Accountability** |
|---|---|---|
| a. | Yes | Yes |
| b. | No | No |
| c. | Yes | No |
| d. | No | Yes |

10. Which of the following statements is correct regarding comparability of governmental financial reports?

a. Comparability is not relevant in governmental financial reporting.

b. Differences between financial reports should be due to substantive differences in underlying transactions or the governmental structure.

c. Selection of different alternatives in accounting procedures or practices account for the differences between financial reports.

d. Similarly designated governments perform the same functions.

**E17-5**  **Encumbrances at Year-End**

The City of Batavia ordered new computer equipment for $21,000 on November 3, 20X2. The equipment had not been received by December 31, 20X2, the end of Batavia's fiscal year.

### Required

a. Assume that the city has a policy that outstanding encumbrances lapse at year-end.

(1) Prepare the entry to record the encumbrance on November 3, 20X2.

(2) Prepare the entries required on December 31, 20X2.

(3) Assuming that the city council accepts outstanding encumbrances in its budget for the next fiscal period (20X3), prepare entries on January 1, 20X3.

(4) Prepare entries on January 18, 20X3, when the equipment was received with an invoice cost of $21,800 and accepted by the city.

(5) Prepare the closing entry on December 31, 20X3, to close the expenditures account.

> b. Assume the city's policy is that outstanding encumbrances are nonlapsing.
>
>> (1) Prepare the entry to record the encumbrance on November 3, 20X2.
>>
>> (2) Prepare the entries required on December 31, 20X2.
>>
>> (3) Prepare the entry on January 1, 20X3, to classify the expenditure with 20X2, the year the encumbrance was initiated.
>>
>> (4) Prepare the entry on January 18, 20X3, when the equipment was received for $21,800. The City Council approved the additional cost of $800 for the equipment as an addition to 20X3's expenditures.
>>
>> (5) Prepare the closing entries on December 31, 20X3, to close the expenditures accounts.
>
> c. Now assume the city has a policy that outstanding encumbrances are nonlapsing, but the 20X3 City Council decided, during its budget hearings for 20X3, not to accept the encumbrance for the computer equipment that had been ordered on November 3, 20X2.
>
>> (1) Prepare the entry required on January 1, 20X3, to cancel the encumbrance reserve for the equipment ordered on November 3, 20X2.

### E17-6 Accounting for Inventories of Office Supplies

Georgetown purchased supplies on August 8, 20X2, for $3,600. At the fiscal year-end on September 30, the inventory of supplies was $2,800.

#### Required

> a. Assume that Georgetown uses the consumption method of accounting for inventories.
>
>> (1) Prepare the entry for the purchase on August 8, 20X2.
>>
>> (2) Prepare the entries required on September 30, 20X2, including the closing of the Expenditures account.
>>
>> (3) Assuming the supplies were used during 20X3, prepare the entries on September 30, 20X3.
>
> b. Assume that Georgetown uses the purchase method of accounting for inventories.
>
>> (1) Prepare the entry for the purchase on August 8, 20X2.
>>
>> (2) Prepare the entries required on September 30, 20X2, including the closing of the Expenditures account.
>>
>> (3) Assuming the supplies were used during 20X3, prepare the entry on September 30, 20X3.

### E17-7 Accounting for Prepayments and Capital Assets

#### Required

Prepare journal entries for the Iron City general fund for the following, including any adjusting and closing entries on December 31, 20X1:

> a. Acquired a three-year fire insurance policy for $5,400 on September 1, 20X1.
>
> b. Ordered new furniture for the city council meeting room on September 17, 20X1, at an estimated cost of $15,600. The furniture was delivered on October 1, its actual cost was $15,200, its estimated life is 10 years, and it has no residual value.
>
> c. Acquired supplies on November 4, 20X1, for $1,800. Iron City uses the consumption method of accounting. Supplies on hand on December 31, 20X1, were $1,120.

### E17-8 Computation of Revenues Reported on the Statement of Revenues, Expenditures, and Changes in Fund Balance for the General Fund

Gilbert City had the following transactions involving resource inflows into its general fund for the year ended June 30, 20X8:

> 1. The general fund levied $2,000,000 of property taxes in July 20X7. The city estimated that 2 percent of the levy would be uncollectible and that $100,000 of the levy would not be collected until after August 31, 20X8.
>
> 2. On April 1, 20X8, the general fund received $50,000 repayment of an advance made to internal service fund. Interest on the advance of $1,500 was also received.

3. During the year ended June 30, 20X8, the general fund received $1,800,000 of the property taxes levied in transaction (1).

4. The general fund received $250,000 in grant monies from the state to be used solely for the acquisition of computer equipment. During March 20X8, the general fund acquired computer equipment using $235,000 of the grant. The city has not yet determined the use of the remainder of the grant.

5. During the year ended June 30, 20X8, the general fund received $125,000 from the state as its portion of the sales tax. At June 30, 20X8, the state owed the general fund an additional $25,000 of sales taxes. The general fund does not expect to have the $25,000 available until early August 20X8.

6. In July 20X7, the general fund borrowed $800,000 from a local bank using the property tax levy as collateral. The loan was repaid in September 20X7, with the proceeds of property tax collections.

7. In February 20X8, a terminated debt service fund transferred $30,000 to the general fund. The $30,000 represented excess resources left in the debt service fund after a general long-term debt obligation had been paid in full.

8. On July 1, 20X7, the general fund estimated that it would receive $75,000 from the sale of liquor licenses during the fiscal year ended June 30, 20X8. For the year ended June 30, 20X8, $66,000 was received from liquor license sales.

9. The general fund received $15,000 in October 20X7, from one of the city's special revenue funds. The amount received represented a reimbursement for an expenditure of the special revenue fund that was paid by the city's general fund.

10. In July 20X7, the general fund collected $80,000 of delinquent property taxes. These property taxes were classified as delinquent on June 30, 20X7. In the entry to record the property tax levy in July 20X6, the general fund estimated that it would collect all property tax revenues by July 31, 20X7.

### Required

Prepare a schedule showing the amount of revenue that should be reported by Gilbert's general fund on the statement of revenues, expenditures, and changes in fund balance for the year ended June 30, 20X8.

**E17-9** **Computation of Expenditures Reported on the Statement of Revenues, Expenditures, and Changes in Fund Balance for the General Fund**

Benson City had the following transactions involving resource outflows involving its general fund for the year ended June 30, 20X8:

1. During March 20X8, the general fund transferred $150,000 to a capital projects fund to help pay for the construction of a new police station.

2. During August 20X7, the general fund ordered computer equipment at an estimated cost of $200,000. The equipment was received in September 20X7, and an invoice for $202,000 was paid.

3. In November 20X7, the city authorized the establishment of an internal service fund for the maintenance of city owned vehicles. The general fund was authorized to transfer $500,000 to the internal service fund in late November. Of this amount, $200,000 will be repaid by the internal service fund in two years with interest at 6 percent; the remaining $300,000 represents a permanent transfer to the internal service fund.

4. In May 20X8, the general fund made a $15,000 payment to one of the city's special revenue funds. The amount paid represented a reimbursement to the special revenue fund for expending $15,000 of its resources on behalf of the general fund.

5. During the year ended June 30, 20X8, the general fund received bills from the city's water department totaling $12,000. Of this amount, the general fund paid all but $500 by June 30, 20X8.

6. During the year ended June 30, 20X8, the general fund acquired supplies costing $35,000 and paid the salaries and wages of its employees totaling $900,000. The general fund uses the purchase method of accounting for its supplies. At June 30, 20X8, unused supplies in the general fund amounted to $5,000.

7. At June 30, 20X8, outstanding encumbrances for goods ordered in the general fund amounted to $25,000. Outstanding encumbrances do not lapse at the end of the fiscal year.

8. On March 15, 20X8, the general fund repaid a loan to a local bank. The amount paid was $265,000, of which $250,000 represented the principal borrowed. The general fund borrowed the money in July 20X7 and used collections of the property tax levy to repay the loan.

9. For the year ended June 30, 20X8, the general fund transferred $95,000 to the city's pension trust fund. The amount transferred represented the employer's contribution to the pension trust on behalf of the employees of the general fund.

10. During May 20X8, the general fund decided to lease several copying machines instead of purchasing them. The lease arrangement was properly accounted for as an operating lease. By June 30, 20X8, the general fund had made lease payments of $10,000 to the owner of the machines.

### Required

Prepare a schedule showing the amount of expenditures that should be reported by Benson's general fund on the statement of revenues, expenditures, and changes in fund balance for the year ended June 30, 20X8.

### E17-10    Closing Entries and Balance Sheet

The preclosing trial balance at December 31, 20X1, for Lone Wolf's general fund follows.

| | Debit | Credit |
|---|---|---|
| Cash | $ 90,000 | |
| Property Taxes Receivable—Delinquent | 100,000 | |
| Allowance for Uncollectibles—Delinquent | | $ 7,200 |
| Due from Other Funds | 14,600 | |
| Vouchers Payable | | 65,000 |
| Due to Other Funds | | 8,400 |
| Fund Balance—Unreserved | | 119,000 |
| Property Tax Revenue | | 1,130,000 |
| Miscellaneous Revenue | | 40,000 |
| Expenditures | 1,140,000 | |
| Other Financing Uses—Transfer Out | 25,000 | |
| Estimated Revenues Control | 1,200,000 | |
| Appropriations Control | | 1,145,000 |
| Estimated Other Financing Uses—Transfer Out | | 25,000 |
| Encumbrances | 32,000 | |
| Budgetary Fund Balance—Reserved for Encumbrances | | 32,000 |
| Budgetary Fund Balance—Unreserved | | 30,000 |
| Total | $2,601,600 | $2,601,600 |

Lone Wolf uses the purchase method of accounting for inventories and the lapsing method of accounting for encumbrances.

### Required

*a.* Prepare the closing entries for the general fund.

*b.* Prepare a general fund–only balance sheet at December 31, 20X1.

### E17-11    Statement of Revenues, Expenditures, and Changes in Fund Balance

Refer to the preclosing trial balance in Exercise 17-10. Assume that the balances on December 31, 20X0, were as follows:

| | |
|---|---|
| Fund Balance—Reserved for Encumbrances | $28,000 |
| Fund Balance—Unreserved | 91,000 |

### Required

Prepare a general fund–only statement of revenues, expenditures, and changes in fund balance for fiscal 20X1.

### E17-12 Matching Questions Involving Interfund Transactions and Transfers in the General Fund

The general fund of Mattville had several interfund activities during the fiscal year ended June 30, 20X9. These interfund activities are presented in the left-hand column of the following table. A list of the types of interfund activities that occur in state and local governmental accounting is provided on the right. For each general fund transaction/transfer, select a letter from the list on the right that best describes the interfund activity.

| General Fund Transactions and Transfers | Type of Interfund Transactions and Transfers |
|---|---|
| 1. Received bills from an internal service fund for using city-owned vehicles. | A. Interfund loan |
| 2. Transferred cash to start an enterprise fund. The enterprise fund does not have to return the cash to the general fund. | B. Interfund service provided and used |
| 3. Received cash from a special revenue fund that was discontinued. | C. Interfund transfer |
| 4. Transferred cash to a capital projects fund to help construct a building. | D. Interfund reimbursement |
| 5. Transferred cash to a debt service fund to pay interest and principal of general long-term debt. | |
| 6. Transferred cash to the pension trust fund representing the employer's contribution toward the pension of general fund employees. | |
| 7. Transferred resources to an enterprise fund. It is expected that these resources will be repaid with interest. | |
| 8. Transferred cash to a special revenue fund. The special revenue fund incurred and paid expenditures on behalf of the general fund. | |
| 9. Received cash from an internal service fund. The cash received represented repayment of an advance made during the previous year. | |
| 10. Received bills from an enterprise fund for using public parking facilities. | |

## Problems

### P17-13 General Fund Entries [AICPA Adapted]

The following information was abstracted from the accounts of the general fund of the City of Noble after the books had been closed for the fiscal year ended June 30, 20X2.

| | Postclosing Trial Balance, June 30, 20X1 | Transactions July 1, 20X1–June 30, 20X2 Debit | Transactions July 1, 20X1–June 30, 20X2 Credit | Postclosing Trial Balance, June 30, 20X2 |
|---|---|---|---|---|
| Cash | $700,000 | $1,820,000 | $1,852,000 | $668,000 |
| Taxes Receivable | 40,000 | 1,870,000 | 1,828,000 | 82,000 |
| Total | $740,000 | | | $750,000 |
| Allowance for Uncollectible Taxes | $ 8,000 | 8,000 | 10,000 | $ 10,000 |
| Vouchers Payable | 132,000 | 1,852,000 | 1,840,000 | 120,000 |
| Fund Balance: | | | | |
| Reserved for Encumbrances | | | 70,000 | 70,000 |
| Unreserved | 600,000 | 70,000 | 20,000 | 550,000 |
| Total | $740,000 | | | $750,000 |

### Additional Information

The budget for the fiscal year ended June 30, 20X2, provided for estimated revenue of $2,000,000 and appropriations of $1,940,000. Encumbrances of $1,070,000 were made during the year.

### Required

Prepare proper journal entries to record the budgeted and actual transactions for the fiscal year ended June 30, 20X2. Include closing entries.

**P17-14**   **General Fund Entries [AICPA Adapted]**

The following trial balances were taken from the accounts of Omega City's general fund before the books had been closed for the fiscal year ended June 30, 20X2:

| | Trial Balance July 1, 20X1 | Trial Balance June 30, 20X2 |
|---|---|---|
| Cash | $400,000 | $ 700,000 |
| Taxes Receivable | 150,000 | 170,000 |
| Allowance for Uncollectible Taxes | (40,000) | (70,000) |
| Estimated Revenues Control | — | 3,000,000 |
| Expenditures | — | 2,900,000 |
| Encumbrances | — | 91,000 |
| Total | $510,000 | $6,791,000 |
| Vouchers Payable | $ 80,000 | $ 408,000 |
| Due to Other Funds | 210,000 | 142,000 |
| Fund Balance—Reserved for Encumbrances | 60,000 | — |
| Fund Balance—Unreserved | 160,000 | 220,000 |
| Revenue from Taxes | — | 2,800,000 |
| Miscellaneous Revenues | — | 130,000 |
| Appropriations Control | — | 2,980,000 |
| Budgetary Fund Balance—Reserved for Encumbrances | — | 91,000 |
| Budgetary Fund Balance—Unreserved | — | 20,000 |
| Total | $510,000 | $6,791,000 |

### Additional Information

1. The estimated taxes receivable for the year ended June 30, 20X2, were $2,870,000, and the taxes collected during the year totaled $2,810,000. Miscellaneous revenue of $130,000 was also collected during the year.
2. Encumbrances in the amount of $2,700,000 were recorded. In addition, the $60,000 of lapsed encumbrances from the 20X1 fiscal year was renewed.
3. During the year, the general fund was billed $142,000 for services performed on its behalf by other city funds (debit Expenditures).
4. An analysis of the transactions in the Vouchers Payable account for the year ended June 30, 20X2, is as follows:

| | Debit (Credit) |
|---|---|
| Current expenditures (liquidating all encumbrances to date except for renewed 20X1 commitment) | $(2,700,000) |
| Expenditures applicable to previous year | (58,000) |
| Vouchers for payments to other funds | (210,000) |
| Cash payments during year | 2,640,000 |
| Net change | $ (328,000) |

5. On May 10, 20X2, encumbrances were recorded for the purchase of next year's supplies at an estimated cost of $91,000.

### Required

On the basis of the data presented, reconstruct the original detailed journal entries that were required to record all transactions for the fiscal year ended June 30, 20X2, including the recording of the current year's budget. Do not prepare closing entries for June 30, 20X2.

**P17-15   General Fund Entries and Statements**

The postclosing trial balance of the general fund of the town of Pine Ridge on December 31, 20X1, is as follows:

|  | Debit | Credit |
|---|---|---|
| Cash | $111,000 | |
| Property Taxes Receivable—Delinquent | 90,000 | |
| Allowance for Uncollectibles—Delinquent | | $  9,000 |
| Vouchers Payable | | 31,000 |
| Fund Balance—Reserved for Encumbrances | | 21,000 |
| Fund Balance—Unreserved | | 140,000 |
| Total | $201,000 | $201,000 |

### Additional Information Related to 20X2

1. Estimated revenue: property taxes, $1,584,000 from a tax levy of $1,600,000 of which 1 percent was estimated uncollectible; sales taxes, $250,000; and miscellaneous, $43,000. Appropriations totaled $1,840,000; and estimated transfers out $37,000. Appropriations included outstanding purchase orders from 20X1 of $21,000. Pine Ridge uses the lapsing method for outstanding encumbrances.

2. Cash receipts: property taxes, $1,590,000, including $83,000 from 20X1; sales taxes, $284,000; licenses and fees, $39,000; and a loan from the motor pool, $10,000. The remaining property taxes from 20X1 were written off, and those remaining from 20X2 were reclassified.

3. Orders were issued for $1,800,000 in addition to the acceptance of the $21,000 outstanding purchase orders from 20X1. A total of $48,000 of purchase orders still was outstanding at the end of 20X2. Actual expenditures were $1,788,000, including $42,000 for office furniture. Vouchers paid totaled $1,793,000.

4. Other cash payments and transfers were as follows:

| Loan to central stores | $13,000 |
|---|---|
| Transfer out | 37,000 |

### Required

a. Prepare entries to summarize the general fund budget and transactions for 20X2.

b. Prepare a preclosing trial balance.

c. Prepare closing entries for the general fund.

d. Prepare a balance sheet for the general fund as of December 31, 20X2.

e. Prepare a statement of revenues, expenditures, and changes in fund balance for 20X2 for the general fund.

**P17-16   Matching Governmental Terms with Descriptions**

Match the terms on the left with the descriptions on the right. A description may be used once or not at all.

| Terms | Descriptions of Terms |
|---|---|
| 1. Proprietary funds | A. Trust and agency funds. |
| 2. Modified accrual method | B. Fiscal and accounting entities of a government. |
| | C. Basis of accounting used by proprietary funds. |
| 3. Estimated revenues | D. Example of this transaction when the general fund uses the services of an internal service fund. |
| 4. Appropriations | |
| 5. Encumbrances | E. Expenditures for inventories representing the amount of inventories consumed during the period. |
| 6. Expenditures | |
| 7. Budgetary fund balance—unreserved | F. General, special revenue, debt service, capital projects funds, and permanent funds. |
| 8. Consumption method for supplies inventories | G. Legal authority to make expenditures. |
| | H. Budgeted resource inflows. |
| | I. Revenues recognized when they are both measurable and available to finance expenditures made during the current period. |
| 9. Nonlapsing encumbrances | |
| | J. Internal service and enterprise funds. |
| 10. Interfund services provided or used | K. Expenditures for inventories representing the amount of inventories acquired during the current period. |
| 11. Governmental funds | L. Reports government unit's infrastructure assets. |
| 12. Interfund transfers | M. Recorded when the general fund orders goods and services. |
| 13. Fiduciary funds | N. Appropriation authority that carries over to the next fiscal year for these orders. |
| 14. Funds | |
| 15. Government-wide financials | O. Appropriation authority that does not carry over to the next fiscal year for these orders. |
| 16. Accrual method | P. Type of transaction that occurs when the general fund makes a cash transfer to establish an internal service fund. |
| | Q. Account debited in the general fund when an invoice is received for computer equipment. |
| | R. Account that would indicate a budget surplus or deficit in the general fund. |

**P17-17    Identification of Governmental Accounting Terms**

For each of the following numbered statements, give the term(s) that is (are) described in the statement.

1. This is the set of financial statements that presents the governmental unit's infrastructure assets and long-term debt.

2. At the present time, this body has the authority to prescribe generally accepted accounting principles for state and local governmental entities.

3. This is a fiscal and an accounting entity with a self-balancing set of accounts recording cash and other financial resources with all related liabilities and residual equities or balances and changes therein that are segregated for the purpose of carrying on specific activities or attaining certain objectives in accordance with special regulations, restrictions, or limitations.

4. This type of interfund activity is accounted for as an expenditure or revenue.

5. These are the proprietary funds.

6. These are assets of the governmental unit and include roads, municipal buildings, sewer systems, sidewalks, and so forth.

7. These are the fiduciary funds.

8. This basis is used in funds that have a flow of financial resources measurement focus.

9. This is the measurement focus of government-wide financials.

10. This gives the governmental entity the legal right to collect property taxes.

11. These are the governmental funds.

12. This is subtracted from Property Taxes Receivable—Current to get the revenue from property taxes for the year.

13. This account is credited in the budget entry for the general fund if expected resource inflows exceed expected resource outflows.

14. This account is debited when the general fund records a purchase order for goods or services.

15. This method of accounting for supplies inventories in the general fund reports expenditures for supplies for only the amount used during the year.

16. This account is debited in the general fund when a transfer out is made to another fund.

17. This account is debited in the general fund when it records a billing from another fund for services that were provided to the general fund.

18. This is reported on the general fund balance sheet when assets exceed liabilities and reserved fund balance.

19. This account is debited in the general fund when fixed assets are acquired. Assume that a purchase order to acquire the fixed assets was not recorded.

20. This is the legal term that allows the general fund to make expenditures.

21. Under this method of accounting for encumbrances outstanding at year-end, expenditures are dated in the following year when the orders are received.

## P17-18 Questions on General Fund Entries [AICPA Adapted]

The DeKalb City Council approved and adopted its budget for 20X2. The budget contained the following amounts:

| | |
|---|---|
| Estimated revenues | $700,000 |
| Appropriations | 660,000 |
| Authorized transfer out to the library debt service fund | 30,000 |

During 20X2, various transactions and events occurred that affected the general fund.

### Required

For items 1 through 39, indicate whether the item should be debited (D) or credited (C) or it is not affected (N).

Items 1 through 5 involve recording the adopted budget in the general fund.

1. Estimated Revenues.
2. Budgetary Fund Balance.
3. Appropriations.
4. Estimated Transfer Out.
5. Expenditures.

Items 6 through 10 involve recording the 20X2 property tax levy in the general fund. It was estimated that $5,000 would be uncollectible.

6. Property Tax Receivable.
7. Bad Debts Expense.
8. Allowance for Uncollectibles—Current.
9. Revenues.
10. Estimated Revenues.

Items 11 through 15 involve recording, in the general fund, encumbrances at the time purchase orders are issued.

11. Encumbrances.
12. Budgetary Fund Balance—Reserved for Encumbrances.
13. Expenditures.
14. Vouchers Payable.
15. Purchases.

Items 16 through 20 involve recording, in the general fund, expenditures that had been previously encumbered in the current year.

16. Encumbrances.
17. Budgetary Fund Balance—Reserved for Encumbrances.
18. Expenditures.

19. Vouchers Payable.

20. Purchases.

Items 21 through 25 involve recording, in the general fund, the transfer out of $30,000 made to the library debt service fund. (No previous entries were made regarding this transaction.)

21. Interfund Services Provided and Used.

22. Due from Library Debt Service Fund.

23. Cash.

24. Other Financing Uses—Transfer Out.

25. Encumbrances.

Items 26 through 35 involve recording, in the general fund, the closing entries (other than encumbrances) for 20X2.

26. Estimated Revenues.

27. Budgetary Fund Balance.

28. Appropriations.

29. Estimated Transfer Out.

30. Expenditures.

31. Revenues.

32. Other Financing Uses—Transfer Out.

33. Allowance for Uncollectibles—Current.

34. Bad Debt Expense.

35. Depreciation Expense.

Items 36 through 39 involve recording, in the general fund, the closing entry relating to the $12,000 of outstanding encumbrances at the end of 20X2 and an adjusting entry to reflect the intent to honor these commitments in 20X3.

36. Encumbrances.

37. Budgetary Fund Balance—Reserved for Encumbrances.

38. Fund Balance—Unreserved.

39. Fund Balance—Reserved for Encumbrances.

**P17-19    Questions on Fund Items [AICPA Adapted]**

The following information relates to actual results from Central Town's general fund for the year ended December 31, 20X1:

|  | Revenues | Expenditures and Transfers |
|---|---|---|
| Property tax collections: |  |  |
| Current year taxes collected | $630,000 |  |
| Prior year taxes due 12/1/X0, collected 2/1/X1 | 50,000 |  |
| Current year taxes due 12/1/X1, collection expected by 2/15/X2 | 70,000 |  |
| Other cash receipts | 190,000 |  |
| General government expenditures: |  |  |
| Salaries and wages |  | $160,000 |
| Other |  | 100,000 |
| Public safety and welfare expenditures: |  |  |
| Salaries and wages |  | 350,000 |
| Other |  | 150,000 |
| Capital outlay |  | 140,000 |
| Transfer out to debt service fund |  | 30,000 |

- Other cash receipts include a county grant of $100,000 for a specified purpose, of which $80,000 was expended; $50,000 in fines; and $40,000 in fees.

- General Government Expenditures—Other includes employer contributions to the pension plan and $20,000 in annual capital lease payments for computers over three years; the fair value and present value at lease inception is $50,000.

- Capital outlay is for police vehicles.
- Debt service represents annual interest payments due December 15 of each year on $500,000 face value, 6 percent, 20-year term bonds.

### Capital Projects Fund

Central's council approved $750,000 for construction of a fire station to be financed by $600,000 in general obligation bonds and a $150,000 state grant. Construction began during 20X1, but the fire station was not completed until April 20X2. During 20X1, the following transactions were recorded:

| | |
|---|---|
| State grant | $150,000 |
| Bond proceeds | 610,000 |
| Expenditures | 500,000 |
| Unpaid invoices at year-end | 30,000 |
| Outstanding encumbrances at year-end, which do not lapse and are to be honored the following year | 25,000 |

The unreserved fund balance in the capital projects fund at January 1, 20X1, was $110,000.

### Required

For questions *a* through *i,* determine the December 31, 20X1, year-end amounts to be recognized in the particular fund. If the item is not reported in a particular fund but is reported on the government-wide financial statements, then specify the amount that would be reported on the government-wide financials. Select your answer from the list of amounts below the questions. An amount may be selected once, more than once, or not at all.

a. What amount was recorded for property tax revenues in the general fund?

b. What amount was recorded for other revenues in the general fund?

c. What amount was reported for capital leases of computers in the government-wide statement of net assets?

d. What amount was reported for the new police vehicles in the government-wide statement of net assets?

e. What amount was reported for the debt service interest payment in the debt service fund?

f. What was the total amount recorded for function expenditures in the general fund?

g. What amount was recorded for revenues in the capital projects fund?

h. What amount was reported for construction in progress in the government-wide statement of net assets?

i. What amount was reported as the Fund Balance—Unreserved at December 31, 20X1, in the capital projects fund?

| Amounts |
|---|
| 1. $0 |
| 2. $30,000 |
| 3. $50,000 |
| 4. $55,000 |
| 5. $60,000 |
| 6. $140,000 |
| 7. $150,000 |
| 8. $170,000 |
| 9. $190,000 |
| 10. $315,000 |
| 11. $345,000 |
| 12. $370,000 |
| 13. $500,000 |
| 14. $525,000 |
| 15. $630,000 |
| 16. $700,000 |
| 17. $710,000 |
| 18. $760,000 |

**P17-20**   **Identifying Types of Revenue Transactions**

*Required*

Using the requirements of GASB Statement No. 33, "Accounting and Financial Reporting for Nonexchange Transactions," classify each of the following independent transactions for the community of Fair Lake into the proper category of revenue as presented in the right-hand column.

| Transactions | Types of Revenue |
|---|---|
| 1. Property taxes were levied by the general fund. | A. Derived tax revenue |
| 2. The electric utility (enterprise) fund billed the general fund for power usage. | B. Imposed nonexchange revenue |
| 3. The city received a state grant for training its police force in additional security measures of public property. | C. Government-mandated nonexchange transaction |
| 4. The city estimated its share of locally generated sales taxes that it expects to receive within the next month. | D. Voluntary nonexchange transaction |
| 5. The city collected various fines it imposed during the period. | E. None of the above |
| 6. The city sold excess office equipment from its municipal headquarters. | |
| 7. The city received resources from the state that must be used to pay for local welfare costs. | |
| 8. The city received a bequest from a local citizen to buy children's recreational items for the city park. | |
| 9. The city collects its share of the local hotel taxes for which the proceeds are legislatively required to be used for a new community convention center. | |
| 10. The state reimburses the city for specific costs related to extra security training of the city's fire department employees. | |
| 11. The city receives its share of funds for environmental improvement resources under a state-required program. | |
| 12. The city receives resources from the federal government to acquire new fire-prevention equipment. The equipment has not yet been acquired. | |
| 13. The city receives grant monies under a state program encouraging cities to make their infrastructure assets wheelchair-accessible. | |
| 14. A company that manufactures road-repaving materials gives the city a grant for the company to conduct a research project on the durability of various types of road repair materials. | |

*Supplemental Problems* for this chapter are available as part of the *Online Learning Center* on the textbook's Web site (URL: www.mhhe.com/baker8e).

# Governmental Entities: Special Funds and Government-wide Financial Statements

In addition to the general fund, discussed in Chapter 17, governments have a number of other funds. This chapter presents the accounting and financial reporting requirements for (1) the four remaining governmental fund types, (2) the two proprietary fund types and (3) the four fiduciary fund types. The typical fund organization for a local government is presented in Figure 18–1. In practice, the funds are often identified with the acronyms from the first letters of their titles, as follows:

**Governmental Fund Types**

GF      General fund
SRF     Special revenue funds
DSF     Debt service funds
CPF     Capital projects funds
PF      Permanent funds

**Proprietary Fund Types**

EF      Enterprise funds
ISF     Internal service funds

**Fiduciary Fund Types**

PTF      Pension trust funds
ITF      Investment trust funds
P-PTF    Private-purpose trust funds
AF       Agency funds

A government should establish those funds required by law and the specific operating and management needs of the government entity. Unnecessary, additional funds add unneeded complexity and do not enhance the operational efficiency of the government. A general rule followed in many governmental entities is that all activities should be accounted for in the general fund unless specifically required by law or the different measurement focus used for proprietary and fiduciary funds. This rule does not prohibit the creation of additional funds but places a reasonable restraint on the proliferation of additional funds. The structure of funds discussed in this chapter is the typical one used in most state and local governmental systems.

One event may require entries in several funds. For example, the construction of a new municipal building through the issuance of general obligation bonds may require entries in both a capital project fund and a debt service fund. In addition, interfund activities require entries in two or more funds.

**FIGURE 18–1**
**Funds for a Governmental Entity**

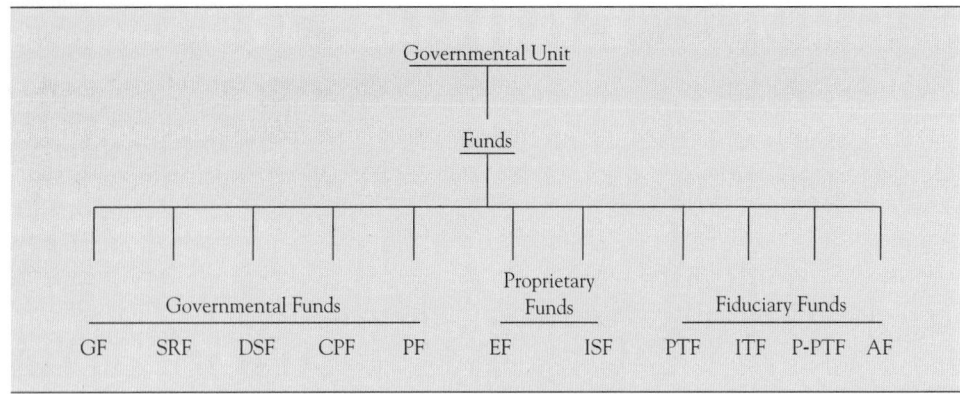

The governmental funds use the modified accrual basis of accounting, and the proprietary and fiduciary funds use the accrual basis of accounting. Governmental entities recognize estimated uncollectible amounts as a reduction of revenue, not as an expense. The five governmental funds do not report long-term assets or long-term debt, but the government-wide statements do report them. Investments are reported in the appropriate funds and are valued at their fair market values at each balance sheet date. The government entity's financial report includes both fund-based and government-wide financial statements. The government-wide statements are prepared using the accrual basis of accounting. Reconciliation schedules are required to show the differences between the amounts reported in the governmental funds financial statements, presented using the modified accrual basis of accounting, and the amounts reported in the government-wide financial statements, presented using the accrual basis of accounting.

Some governmental units have pension trust funds for their employees. Accounting and reporting for pension trust funds is quite complex and beyond the scope of an advanced financial accounting course. Pension trust funds are covered briefly in the "Additional Considerations" section of this chapter.

This chapter continues the example of Sol City started in Chapter 17 where the entries and financial reports for the general fund were presented for 20X2. Sol City uses the lapsing method of accounting for encumbrances and the consumption method for inventories and records all expected budgetary accounts including anticipated interfund transactions. The techniques of capitalizing all budgetary accounts and recording journal entries at the control level are continued from Chapter 17. The financial statements for the illustration are prepared using the requirements of **GASB 34.** Many of the numbers for the Sol City example are assumed in order to focus on the main concepts of accounting and financial reporting for a governmental entity. Thus, some of the numbers cannot be computed from the data given. Instead, focus on the concepts being discussed. The fund balance reporting for the governmental funds that would be required under the proposed statement is provided after the governmental funds balance sheet which is presented at the conclusion of the discussion of the governmental funds. The final section of this chapter presents the government-wide financial statements for Sol City.

Figure 18–2 presents an overview of the major accounting and financial standards for the individual funds. This figure can be used as a continual reference point during study of Chapter 18.

## GOVERNMENTAL FUNDS WORKSHEETS

Each of the five governmental funds will report two *fund-based financial statements:* the balance sheet and the statement of revenues, expenditures, and changes in fund balance. Rather than present each of the separate governmental funds' financial statements in the chapter, worksheets for the preparation of the governmental funds' financial statements are presented. Figure 18–3 presents the individual fund information that will be used to prepare the governmental funds' balance sheet. Figure 18–4 presents the

**FIGURE 18–2** Overview of Accounting and Financial Reporting for Governments

| | Governmental Funds | | | | | Proprietary Funds | | Fiduciary Funds | | Government-wide Financials |
| --- | --- | --- | --- | --- | --- | --- | --- | --- | --- | --- |
| | General Fund | Special Revenue Funds | Capital Projects Funds | Debt Service Funds | Permanent Funds | Enterprise Funds | Internal Service Funds | Trust Funds | Agency Funds | |
| **Basis of accounting** | Modified accrual | Modified accrual | Modified accrual | Modified accrual | Modified accrual | Accrual | Accrual | Accrual | Accrual | Accrual |
| Budgetary basis recorded: (Budgetary accounts are typically used when a legally adopted annual operating budget is passed) | Operating budget often recorded | Operating budget often recorded | Capital budget usually not recorded | Not required | Not required | No | No | No | | |
| Long-term productive assets (buildings, equipment, etc.) reported | No | No | No | No | No | Yes | Yes | Yes | No | Yes |
| Long-term debt reported | No | No | No | No | No | Yes | Yes | Yes | No | Yes |
| Encumbrances recorded | Yes | Yes | Possibly | Possibly | Possibly | No | No | No | No | |
| **Financial Statements** | | | | | | | | | | |
| Balance sheet | X | X | X | X | X | | | | | |
| Statement of net assets | | | | | | X | X | | | X |
| Statement of revenues, expenditures, and changes in fund balance | X | X | X | X | X | | | | | |
| Statement of revenues, expenses, and changes in fund net assets | | | | | | X | X | | | |
| Statement of activities | | | | | | | | | | X |
| Statement of cash flows | | | | | | X | X | | | |
| Statement of fiduciary net assets | | | | | | | | X | X | |
| Statement of changes in fiduciary net assets | | | | | | | | X | X | |

863

**FIGURE 18–3**  Worksheet for the Balance Sheet for the Governmental Funds

| | General | Special Revenue | Capital Projects | Debt Service | Permanent | Total Governmental Funds | Enterprise Fund | Total Governmental and Enterprise |
|---|---|---|---|---|---|---|---|---|
| **Assets** | | | | | | | | |
| Current | | | | | | | | |
|   Cash | 102,000 | 15,000 | 16,000 | 2,000 | 13,000 | | | |
|   Property Taxes (net of allowances) | 85,000 | 1,000 | | 3,000 | | | | |
|   Due From Enterprise Fund | 3,000 | | | | | | | |
|   Inventory of Supplies | 17,000 | | | | | | | |
| Noncurrent | | | | | | | | |
|   Investment in Government Bonds | | | | | 90,000 | | | |
| **Total Assets** | 207,000 | 16,000 | 16,000 | 5,000 | 103,000 | 347,000 | 140,000 | 487,000 |
| **Liabilities and Fund Balances** | | | | | | | | |
| Vouchers Payable | 55,000 | 3,000 | | | | | | |
| Contract Payable—Retainage | | | 10,000 | | | | | |
| **Total Liabilities** | 55,000 | 3,000 | 10,000 | -0- | -0- | 68,000 | 112,000 | 180,000 |
| Fund Balances | | | | | | | | |
| Reserved for: | | | | | | | | |
|   Encumbrances | 15,000 | 6,000 | | | | | | |
|   Inventories | 17,000 | | | | | | | |
|   Debt Service | | | | 5,000 | | | | |
|   Permanent Fund | | | | | 103,000 | | | |
| Unreserved, reported in: | | | | | | | | |
|   General Fund | 120,000 | | | | | | | |
|   Special Revenue Fund | | 7,000 | | | | | | |
|   Capital Projects Fund | | | 6,000 | | | | | |
| **Total Fund Balances** | 152,000 | 13,000 | 6,000 | 5,000 | 103,000 | 279,000 | | |
| **Total Liabilities and Fund Balances** | 207,000 | 16,000 | 16,000 | 5,000 | 103,000 | 347,000 | | |
| **Major Fund Tests on Total Assets:** | | | | | | | | |
| 10% Test of Total Governmental or Enterprise | | 4.61% | 4.61% | 1.44% | 29.68% | | 100.00% | |
| 5% Test of Governmental Plus Enterprise | | 3.29% | 3.29% | 1.03% | 21.15% | | 28.75% | |
| Major Fund Test (Yes or No) | Yes | No | No | No | Yes | | Yes | |
| **Major Fund Tests on Total Liabilities:** | | | | | | | | |
| 10% Test of Total Governmental or Enterprise | | 4.41% | 14.71% | 0.00% | 0.00% | | 100.00% | |
| 5% Test of Governmental Plus Enterprise | | 1.67% | 5.56% | 0.00% | 0.00% | | 62.22% | |
| Major Fund Test (Yes or No) | Yes | No | Yes | No | No | | Yes | |

**FIGURE 18–4** Worksheet for the Statement of Revenues, Expenditures, and Changes in Fund Balances for the Governmental Funds

| | Governmental Funds | | | | | Total Governmental Funds | Enterprise Fund | Total Governmental and Enterprise |
|---|---|---|---|---|---|---|---|---|
| | General | Special Revenue | Capital Projects | Debt Service | Permanent | | | |
| **Revenues** | | | | | | | | |
| Property Taxes | 781,000 | 62,000 | | 33,000 | | | | |
| Sales Taxes | 32,000 | | | | | | | |
| Grants | 33,000 | | 10,000 | | | | | |
| Miscellaneous | 18,000 | | | | 8,000 | | | |
| Total Revenues | 864,000 | 62,000 | 10,000 | 33,000 | 8,000 | 977,000 | 37,000 | 1,014,000 |
| **Expenditures** | | | | | | | | |
| Current | | | | | | | | |
| General Government | 206,000 | | | | | | | |
| Streets and Highways | 71,000 | | | | | | | |
| Public Safety | 335,000 | | | | | | | |
| Sanitation | 141,000 | | | | | | | |
| Culture and Recreation | | 49,000 | | | | | | |
| Miscellaneous | | | | | 5,000 | | | |
| Debt Service | | | | | | | | |
| Principal Retirement | | | | 20,000 | | | | |
| Interest Charges | | | | 10,000 | | | | |
| Capital Outlay | 58,000 | | 124,000 | | | | | |
| Total Expenditures/Expenses | 811,000 | 49,000 | 124,000 | 30,000 | 5,000 | 1,019,000 | 35,000 | 1,054,000 |
| Excess (deficiency) of Revenues over Expenditures | 53,000 | 13,000 | (114,000) | 3,000 | 3,000 | (42,000) | | |
| **Other Financing Sources (Uses)** | | | | | | | | |
| Proceeds of Bond Issue | | | 102,000 | | | | | |
| Transfers In | | | 20,000 | 2,000 | | | | |
| Transfers Out | (30,000) | | (2,000) | | | | | |
| Total Other Financing Sources and Uses | (30,000) | -0- | 120,000 | 2,000 | -0- | 92,000 | | |
| **Special Item** | | | | | | | | |
| Contribution | | | | | 100,000 | 100,000 | | |
| Net Change in Fund Balances | 23,000 | 13,000 | 6,000 | 5,000 | 103,000 | 150,000 | | |
| Fund Balances—Beginning | 129,000 | -0- | -0- | -0- | -0- | 129,000 | | |
| Fund Balances—Ending | 152,000 | 13,000 | 6,000 | 5,000 | 103,000 | 279,000 | | |
| **Major Fund Tests on Total Revenues:** | | | | | | | | |
| 10% Test of Total Governmental or Enterprise | | 6.35% | 1.02% | 3.38% | 0.82% | | 100.00% | |
| 5% Test of Governmental and Enterprise | | 6.11% | 0.99% | 3.25% | 0.79% | | 3.65% | |
| Major Fund Test (Yes or No) | Yes | No | No | No | No | | No | |
| **Major Fund Tests on Total Expenditures/Expenses:** | | | | | | | | |
| 10% Test of Total Governmental or Enterprise | | 4.81% | 12.17% | 2.94% | 0.49% | | 100.00% | |
| 5% Test of Governmental and Enterprise | | 4.65% | 11.76% | 2.85% | 0.47% | | 3.32% | |
| Major Fund Test (Yes or No) | Yes | No | Yes | No | No | | No | |

individual governmental funds information that will be used to prepare the governmental funds' statement of revenues, expenditures, and changes in fund balance. The amounts for the general fund are taken from the information in Chapter 17. The amounts for the other funds will be developed throughout this chapter. These two worksheets are used throughout the discussion of the governmental funds and are the basis for preparing the governmental funds' financial statements that will be presented later in the chapter. The worksheets also include major funds tests that will be discussed later in the chapter. Thus, the two worksheets will be developed through the following discussions in this chapter.

# SPECIAL REVENUE FUNDS

Current governmental resources may be restricted to expenditure for specific purposes, such as development of the state highway system, maintenance of public parks, or operation of the public school system, city libraries, and museums. The necessary revenue often comes from special tax levies or federal or state governmental grants. Some minor revenue may be earned through user charges, but these charges are usually not sufficient to fully fund the service. *Special revenue funds* are used to account for such restricted resources. The governmental entity usually has a separate special revenue fund for each different activity of this type. Thus, a city may have several special revenue funds.

Accounting for special revenue funds is the same as for the general fund. The modified accrual basis of accounting is used, no fixed assets or depreciation are recorded, the operating budget is typically recorded in the accounts, and no long-term debt is recorded.

Special revenue fund accounting is not illustrated in the chapter because the principles for the special revenue fund are the same as those for the general fund as covered in Chapter 17. For purposes of the governmental funds statements, assume that $62,000 of property taxes were collected for the special revenue fund and that $49,000 was expended for the designated culture and recreation purposes for which the special revenue fund was established. The focus of this chapter is on the unique or interesting aspects of governmental accounting and financial reporting. Figure 18–3 presents the assumed numbers for the special revenue fund's balance sheet, and Figure 18–4 presents the revenues ($62,000) and expenditures ($49,000) assumed for the special revenue fund.

# CAPITAL PROJECTS FUNDS

*Capital projects funds* account for financial resources that are specified for the acquisition or construction of major capital facilities or improvements that benefit the public. Examples are the construction of libraries, civic centers, fire stations, courthouses, bridges, major streets, and city municipal buildings. A separate capital projects fund is created at the time the project is approved and ceases at its completion. Each project or group of related projects usually is accounted for in a separate capital projects fund.

Accounting for capital projects funds is similar to accounting for the general fund. The modified accrual basis of accounting is used, no fixed assets or depreciation are recorded in the capital projects funds, and no long-term debt is recorded in these funds. Capital projects funds, however, typically do not have annual operating budgets. A capital budget is prepared as a basis for selling bonds to finance a project, and the capital budget is the control mechanism for the length of the project. The capital budget for the project may, or may not, be formally recorded in the accounts. Theoretically, encumbrances are part of the budgetary system and should flow from the appropriating authority of the budget. However, encumbrances may be recorded even if the capital project budget is not recorded. Encumbrances maintain an ongoing accounting record of the expenditure commitments that have been made on a project and Sol City has a policy to use encumbrances in its capital projects funds. Sol City chose not to formally enter the project budget into the accounts.

The capital projects fund records capital outlays as expenditures. Thus, no fixed assets are recorded in this fund. A record of the construction in progress, however, may be maintained in memorandum format.

## Illustration of Transactions

On January 1, 20X2, Sol City establishes a capital projects fund to account for a capital addition to the municipal courthouse. The expected cost of the addition is $120,000. A $100,000, 10 percent general obligation bond issue is sold at 102 for total proceeds of $102,000. The bond is a five-year serial bond with equal amounts of $20,000 to be paid each year, beginning on December 31, 20X2, until the debt is extinguished. The bond proceeds are not revenue to the capital projects fund; they are reported in the other financing sources section of the fund's statement of revenues, expenditures, and changes in fund balance. Any debt issue costs such as underwriting fees or attorney fees are recognized as expenditures when the liabilities are both measurable and incurred, and are payable out of current financial resources.

The capital projects fund is not entitled to the $2,000 premium on the sale of bonds. This premium is transferred as a transfer out to the debt service fund immediately upon receipt. The debt service fund records the receipt of the transfer as a transfer in (see entry [15] later in this chapter). The premium is viewed as an adjustment of the interest rate, not as a part of the funds expendable by the capital projects fund. If bonds are sold at a discount, either the amount expended for the improvement must be decreased or the general fund must make up the difference to the face value of the bonds.

In addition, a federal grant for $10,000 is received as financial support for part of the capital addition, and the capital projects fund receives an interfund transfer in of $20,000 from the city's general fund. Recall that an interfund transfer is an interfund transaction in which resources are moved from one fund, usually from the general fund, to another fund to be used for the operations of the receiving fund. The general fund records this transfer of $20,000 as an interfund transfer out (see entry [34] in Chapter 17). The following entries are recorded for the 20X2 fiscal year.

### *Capital Projects Revenue and Bond Proceeds*

The sale of the bonds and receipt of the federal grant and operating transfer in are recorded as follows:

| | | | |
|---|---|---:|---:|
| (1) | Cash | 102,000 | |
| | Other Financing Sources—Bond Issue | | 100,000 |
| | Other Financing Sources—Bond Premium | | 2,000 |
| | Issue $100,000 of bonds at 102. | | |
| (2) | Other Financing Uses—Transfer Out to Debt Service Fund | 2,000 | |
| | Cash | | 2,000 |
| | Forward bond premium to debt service fund. | | |
| (3) | Cash | 10,000 | |
| | Revenue—Federal Grant | | 10,000 |
| | Receive federal grant to be applied to courthouse addition. | | |
| (4) | Due from General Fund | 20,000 | |
| | Other Financing Sources—Transfer In from General Fund | | 20,000 |
| | Establish receivable for interfund transfer in from general fund. | | |
| (5) | Cash | 20,000 | |
| | Due from General Fund | | 20,000 |
| | Receive transferred resources from general fund. | | |

Entry (3) recognizes the $10,000 grant from the federal government as revenue when the grant is received. Some grants from the federal government are termed "expenditure-driven" grants, for which revenue can be recognized only as expenditures are incurred in conformity with the grant agreement. For these expenditure-driven grants, the local governmental entity recognizes revenue only after the eligibility requirements for the government-mandated nonexchange transaction have been met: that is, the allowable expenditures have been made.

### Capital Projects Fund Expenditures

The following encumbrances, expenditures, and disbursements are recorded in 20X2.

| | | | | |
|---|---|---|---|---|
| (6) | ENCUMBRANCES | | 110,000 | |
| | BUDGETARY FUND BALANCE—RESERVED FOR ENCUMBRANCES | | | 110,000 |
| | Issue construction contract for $110,000. | | | |
| | | | | |
| (7) | BUDGETARY FUND BALANCE—RESERVED FOR ENCUMBRANCES | | 110,000 | |
| | ENCUMBRANCES | | | 110,000 |
| | Project is completed. Reverse reserve for encumbrances. | | | |
| | | | | |
| (8) | Expenditures | | 118,000 | |
| | Contract Payable | | | 108,000 |
| | Contract Payable—Retained Percentage | | | 10,000 |
| | Actual construction cost of courthouse addition is $118,000. | | | |
| | Additional cost is approved. Contract terms include retained percentage of $10,000 until full and final acceptance of project. | | | |
| | | | | |
| (9) | Expenditures | | 6,000 | |
| | Vouchers Payable | | | 6,000 |
| | Additional items for courthouse addition. | | | |
| | | | | |
| (10) | Vouchers Payable | | 6,000 | |
| | Contract Payable | | 108,000 | |
| | Cash | | | 114,000 |
| | Pay current portion of construction contract and vouchers. | | | |

In entry (8), Contract Payable is credited for $108,000 for the current portion due, and Contract Payable—Retained Percentage is credited for $10,000. In entry (10), the $108,000 current portion of the contract liability is paid in full. A normal practice of governmental units is to have a retained percentage of the total amount due under a construction contract held back to ensure that the contractor fully completes the project to the satisfaction of the governmental unit. For example, a city may stipulate that 10 percent of the total contract price is retained until the project is fully completed and accepted. This retainage payable is released and paid upon final acceptance of the project by the governmental unit.

### Closing Entries in the Capital Projects Fund

The nominal accounts are closed with the following entries:

| | | | | |
|---|---|---|---|---|
| (11) | Revenue—Federal Grant | | 10,000 | |
| | Fund Balance—Unreserved | | 114,000 | |
| | Expenditures | | | 124,000 |
| | Close operating accounts of revenue and expenditures. | | | |
| | | | | |
| (12) | Other Financing Sources—Bond Issue | | 100,000 | |
| | Other Financing Sources—Bond Premium | | 2,000 | |
| | Fund Balance—Unreserved | | | 102,000 |
| | Close other financing sources. | | | |

| (13) | Other Financing Sources—Transfer In from General Fund | 20,000 | |
| | Other Financing Uses—Transfer Out to Debt Service Fund | | 2,000 |
| | Fund Balance—Unreserved | | 18,000 |
| | Close interfund transfers. | | |

No encumbrances are outstanding as of the end of the fiscal year. At this point, the Fund Balance—Unreserved account has a credit balance of $6,000. Upon completion and final approval of a capital project, the remaining fund balance is transferred either to the general fund or to the debt service fund, depending on the policy of the governmental unit. The transfer is a transfer out for the capital projects fund and a transfer in for the receiving fund because it involves the one-time transfer of the remaining resources in the capital projects fund. In the preceding example, Sol City decided that the fund should remain open through the first part of the next fiscal year in case any minor modifications of the new courthouse addition are required. If no further modifications are required, and the courthouse addition project is officially accepted, the $10,000 in the Contract Payable—Retained Percentage account is paid to the contractor. Any remaining resources in the capital projects fund are then transferred and the capital projects fund is closed.

### Financial Statement Information for the Capital Projects Fund

The financial statement information for the capital projects funds is presented in Figure 18–3 for the balance sheet and in Figure 18–4 for the statement of revenues, expenditures, and changes in fund balances. The Sol City capital projects fund was created on January 1, 20X2, the date the capital addition was approved and the serial bonds were sold. Figure 18–3 shows that the only asset remaining in this fund on December 31, 20X2, is $16,000 of cash, which includes the $10,000 for the contract payable–retainage. Figure 18–4 for the capital projects fund column presents the $102,000 of proceeds from the bond issue, which is reported among other financing sources, with a reduction for the transfer out of the $2,000 premium to the debt service fund, and the transfer in of $20,000, netting against the large excess of expenditures over revenue in the amount of $114,000. The statement of revenues, expenditures, and changes in fund balance reconciles to the $6,000 fund balance at the end of the fiscal period.

## DEBT SERVICE FUNDS

*Debt service funds* account for the accumulation and use of resources for the payment of general long-term debt principal and interest. A government may have several types of general long-term debt obligations, as follows:

1. *Serial bonds.* The most common form of debt issued by governments is in the form of serial bonds. The bonds are repaid in installments over the life of the debt. A serial bond is called "regular" if the installments are equal and "irregular" if they are not equal.

2. *Term bonds.* This form of debt is less frequent now than in the past. The entire principal of the debt is due at the maturity date.

3. *Special assessment bonds.* Special assessment bonds are secured by tax liens on the property located within the special assessment tax district. The governmental unit may also become obligated in some manner to assume the payment of the debt in the event of default by the property owners. Special assessment bonds may be used to finance capital projects, or to acquire other assets, such as ambulances or fire engines, necessary to operate the governmental unit. Special assessment bonds sold to acquire enterprise fund assets, however, should be accounted for within the enterprise fund. The special assessment feature simply states the source of financing and means of repayment.

4. *Notes and warrants.* These consist of debt typically issued for one or two years. These debts are usually secured by specific tax revenue, which must first be used to repay the debt. Property tax anticipation warrants are an example.

5. *Capital leases.* Governmental entities must record capital leases in accordance with generally accepted accounting principles. These leases then become long-term liabilities of the governmental unit.

Some governmental entities service long-term debt directly from the general fund, thereby eliminating the need for a debt service fund as a separate fiscal, accounting, and reporting entity. However, if a governmental entity has several long-term general obligations outstanding, it may be required by bond indentures or other regulations to establish a separate debt service fund for each obligation to account for the proper servicing of each debt obligation.

The accounting and financial reporting for debt service funds are the same as for the general fund. The modified accrual basis of accounting is used, and only that portion of the long-term debt that has matured and is currently payable is recorded in the debt service funds.

Interest payable on long-term debt is not accrued; interest is recognized as a liability only when it comes due and payable. The "when due" recognition of interest matches the debt service expenditures with the resources accumulated to repay the debt. This approach prevents an understatement of the debt service fund balance. For example, if interest is accrued before it is actually due, the fund balance may show a deficit because of the excess of liabilities over assets. The function of the debt service fund is to accumulate resources to pay debt principal and interest as they become due. Thus, the when-due recognition of interest is consistent with the fund's objectives.

## Illustration of Transactions

Sol City establishes a debt service fund to service the $100,000, five-year, 10 percent serial bond issued on January 1, 20X2, to finance the capital project courthouse addition. The bond initially sold at a premium of $2,000. The resources to pay the bond principal and interest as they become due will be obtained from a property tax levy specifically for debt service.

### *Adoption of Debt Service Fund Budget*

Debt service funds are not required to adopt annual operating budgets because the fund's expenditures are generally mandated by bond agreements and an operating budget may be viewed as unnecessarily redundant. Nevertheless, there is no restriction against having an operating budget for the debt service fund as part of a comprehensive budgeting system for a governmental entity, as illustrated here.

The annual operating budget for the debt service fund is adopted at the time the fund is created to service the serial bonds sold for the courthouse addition. Appropriations of $30,000 are budgeted to pay $20,000 of maturing principal and $10,000 of interest for the year. Sol City budgets all expected interfund transactions, and the anticipated interfund transfer in of the $2,000 premium on the serial bonds sold is part of the entry to record the budget:

| | | | |
|---|---|---:|---:|
| (14) | ESTIMATED REVENUES CONTROL | 30,000 | |
| | ESTIMATED OTHER FINANCING SOURCES—TRANSFER IN | 2,000 | |
| | APPROPRIATIONS CONTROL | | 30,000 |
| | BUDGETARY FUND BALANCE | | 2,000 |
| | Adopt budget for 20X2. | | |

The budgetary accounts ESTIMATED REVENUES CONTROL and APPROPRIATIONS CONTROL are used to account for servicing serial bonds.

### *Debt Service Fund Revenue and Other Financing Sources*

In this example, the debt service fund obtains revenue from a specified property tax levy. The bond premium received from the capital projects fund is recognized as a transfer in.

Note that the capital projects fund records this transfer as an interfund transfer out (see entry [2] earlier in this chapter). The entries to record the receipt of the bond premium and the levy and collection of taxes are as follows:

| (15) | Cash | 2,000 | |
| |     Other Financing Sources—Transfer In from Capital Projects Fund | | 2,000 |
| | Receive bond premium from capital projects fund. | | |

| (16) | Property Taxes Receivable | 35,000 | |
| |     Allowance for Uncollectible Taxes | | 5,000 |
| |     Revenue—Property Tax | | 30,000 |
| | Levy property taxes and provide for allowance for uncollectible taxes. Estimated uncollectible property taxes reduce Revenue. | | |

| (17) | Cash | 30,000 | |
| |     Property Taxes Receivable | | 30,000 |
| | Receive portion of property taxes. | | |

| (18) | Property Taxes Receivable—Delinquent | 5,000 | |
| | Allowance for Uncollectible Taxes | 5,000 | |
| |     Property Taxes Receivable | | 5,000 |
| |     Revenue—Property Tax | | 3,000 |
| |     Allowance for Uncollectible Taxes—Delinquent | | 2,000 |
| | Reclassify remaining property taxes as delinquent and reduce allowance for uncollectible taxes from $5,000 to $2,000. | | |

### Debt Service Fund Expenditures

The primary expenditures of the debt service fund are for the first annual payment of principal and for interest on the serial bonds payable. An encumbrance system is typically not used for matured principal and interest because the debt agreement serves as the expenditure control mechanism:

| (19) | Expenditures—Principal | 20,000 | |
| |     Matured Bonds Payable | | 20,000 |
| | Recognize matured portion of serial bond: | | |
| |     $100,000 \div 5$ years | | |

| (20) | Expenditures—Interest | 10,000 | |
| |     Matured Interest Payable | | 10,000 |
| | Recognize interest due this period: | | |
| |     $100,000 \times .10 \times 1$ year | | |

| (21) | Matured Bonds Payable | 20,000 | |
| | Matured Interest Payable | 10,000 | |
| |     Cash | | 30,000 |
| | Pay first year's installment plus interest on bond. | | |

### Closing Entries in the Debt Service Fund

The nominal accounts are closed as follows:

| (22) | APPROPRIATIONS CONTROL | 30,000 | |
| | BUDGETARY FUND BALANCE | 2,000 | |
| |     ESTIMATED REVENUES CONTROL | | 30,000 |
| |     ESTIMATED OTHER FINANCING SOURCES—TRANSFER IN | | 2,000 |
| | Close budgetary accounts. | | |

| (23) | Revenue—Property Tax | 33,000 | |
|---|---|---|---|
| | Expenditures—Principal | | 20,000 |
| | Expenditures—Interest | | 10,000 |
| | Fund Balance—Reserved for Debt Service | | 3,000 |
| | Close operating revenue and expenditures. | | |

| (24) | Other Financing Sources—Transfer In from Capital Projects Fund | 2,000 | |
|---|---|---|---|
| | Fund Balance—Reserved for Debt Service | | 2,000 |
| | Close interfund transfer. | | |

If the debt service fund services term bonds, a different budgetary account system is used. The following budgetary entry would be made for term bonds for the periods prior to the maturity date:

| | | |
|---|---|---|
| REQUIRED CONTRIBUTIONS | XXX | |
| REQUIRED EARNINGS | X | |
| BUDGETARY FUND BALANCE | | XXX |

The budgetary amounts are determined based on a computation of the contributions needed each period to be invested, earning a given return to accumulate to the amount required for the payment of the bonds. The debt service fund may then receive resources from the general fund or from a tax levy, which it would invest until the term bonds became due. In the period the term bonds reach maturity, the debt service fund pays the matured principal and interest from its available resources. The debt service fund may make temporary investments of excess cash in order to maximize the return from its resources. These investments are reported as an asset of the debt service fund. Most temporary investments are made in low-risk U.S. Treasury securities or in certificates of deposit from larger banks. Interest income is accrued as earned. The investments are valued in accordance with **GASB Statement No. 31,** "Accounting for Financial Reporting for Certain Investments and for External Investment Pools" (GASB 31). The general valuation standard in **GASB 31** is fair value for most investments made by a governmental entity. However, an exception is allowed for governmental entities other than external investment pools, so that market investments may be reported at amortized cost, provided the investment has a remaining maturity of one year or less from the date of purchase. Unrealized gains or losses on investments are combined with realized gains or losses and are reported on the governmental entity's operating statements as net investment income or loss.

### Financial Statement Information for the Debt Service Fund

The financial statement information for the debt service fund for the governmental funds is presented in Figure 18–3 for the balance sheet and in Figure 18–4 for the governmental funds statement of revenues, expenditures, and changes in fund balance.

## PERMANENT FUNDS

*Permanent funds* are established in those cases in which there is a donor restriction that the fund principal must be preserved but the income from these permanent funds is required to be used to benefit the government's programs or its general citizenry. The donor-restricted donation may be from individuals, estates, and public or private organizations. Permanent funds are classified in the governmental funds category because the income resources in these funds are to be used toward the government's programs and services for its general citizenry. The modified accrual basis of accounting is used in this fund and the financial statements for the permanent funds are the same as for all other governmental funds.

## Illustration of Transactions

On January 1, 20X2, Sol City receives a $100,000 bequest from a long-term city resident. The will stipulates that the $100,000 be invested and the income be used to provide for maintenance and improvement of the city park. Note that a private-purpose fund, which would be a fiduciary fund, is one in which the government is required to use the principal or earnings for the benefit of specific individuals, private organizations, or other designated governments, as stated in the trust agreement. This bequest is for the benefit of the general citizenry, however, and is established as a permanent fund that is a governmental fund type. The entries in this permanent fund during 20X2 are as follows:

| (25) | Cash | 100,000 | |
|------|------|---------|---|
| | Contributions | | 100,000 |
| | Accept permanent fund resources. | | |

This contribution will be reported as a special item, after other financing sources and uses, toward the bottom of the statement of revenues, expenditures, and changes in fund balance.

### *Investment and Interest*

The fund's resources are used to acquire $100,000 face value, high-grade, 8 percent governmental securities at 90 to yield an effective interest rate of 10 percent. Interest income is accrued under the modified accrual method, which means that the revenue recognition may be for only that amount of interest that is both measurable and available to finance expenditures made during the current fiscal period. Therefore, only the $8,000 of accrued interest receivable is available for expenditures this period, and the discount amortization would not be shown in the modified accrual basis financial statements.

| (26) | Investment in Bonds | 90,000 | |
|------|---------------------|--------|---|
| | Cash | | 90,000 |
| | Acquire $100,000 face value government securities at 90. | | |

| (27) | Accrued Interest Receivable | 8,000 | |
|------|-----------------------------|-------|---|
| | Interest Revenue | | 8,000 |
| | Accrue interest: | | |
| | $8,000 = $100,000 × .08, nominal (coupon) rate | | |

| (28) | Cash | 8,000 | |
|------|------|-------|---|
| | Accrued Interest Receivable | | 8,000 |
| | Collect accrued interest on securities. | | |

### *Expenditures*

The permanent trust fund expends $5,000 during the period for maintenance of the city park and recognizes the following entry:

| (29) | Expenditures | 5,000 | |
|------|--------------|-------|---|
| | Cash | | 5,000 |
| | Expenditures made for maintenance of the city park. | | |

The balance sheet information for the permanent fund as of December 31, 20X2, is presented in Figure 18–3. The entire amount of the fund balance for the permanent fund is classified as reserved because the principal must be preserved and the income in this fund is required to be used for specified purposes. The information for the statement of revenues, expenditures, and changes in fund balance for the permanent fund is presented in Figure 18–4. Note that the $100,000 contribution is not part of operations but is reported at the bottom of the operating statement.

**FIGURE 18–5** Governmental Funds Balance Sheet

**SOL CITY**
**Balance Sheet**
**Governmental Funds**
**December 31, 20X2**

| | General | Capital Projects | Permanent | Other Governmental Funds | Total Governmental Funds |
|---|---|---|---|---|---|
| Assets | | | | | |
| Current | | | | | |
| Cash | $102,000 | $16,000 | $ 13,000 | $17,000 | $148,000 |
| Property Taxes (net of allowances) | 85,000 | | | 4,000 | 89,000 |
| Due from Enterprise Fund | 3,000 | | | | 3,000 |
| Inventory of Supplies | 17,000 | | | | 17,000 |
| Noncurrent | | | | | |
| Investment in Government Bonds | | | 90,000 | | 90,000 |
| Total Assets | $207,000 | $16,000 | $103,000 | $21,000 | $347,000 |
| | | | | | |
| Liabilities and Fund Balances | | | | | |
| Vouchers Payable | 55,000 | | | 3,000 | $ 58,000 |
| Contract Payable—Retainage | | $10,000 | | | 10,000 |
| Total Liabilities | $ 55,000 | $10,000 | | $ 3,000 | $ 68,000 |
| | | | | | |
| Fund Balances | | | | | |
| Reserved for: | | | | | |
| Encumbrances | $ 15,000 | | | $ 6,000 | $ 21,000 |
| Inventories | 17,000 | | | | 17,000 |
| Debt Service | | | | 5,000 | 5,000 |
| Permanent Fund | | | $103,000 | | 103,000 |
| Unreserved, reported in: | | | | | |
| General Fund | 120,000 | | | | 120,000 |
| Special Revenue Fund | | | | 7,000 | 7,000 |
| Capital Projects Fund | | $ 6,000 | | | 6,000 |
| Total Fund Balances | $152,000 | $ 6,000 | $103,000 | $18,000 | $279,000 |
| | | | | | |
| Total Liabilities and Fund Balances | $207,000 | $16,000 | $103,000 | $21,000 | $347,000 |

# GOVERNMENTAL FUNDS FINANCIAL STATEMENTS

**GASB Statement No. 34,** "Basic Financial Statements—and Management's Discussion and Analysis—for State and Local Governments" (GASB 34), requires two financial statements for the governmental funds. The first is the governmental funds balance sheet presented in Figure 18–5, and the second is the governmental statement of revenues, expenditures, and changes in fund balance presented in Figure 18–6. The worksheets in Figures 18–3 and 18–4 are the basis for preparing these two financial statements. In practice, the two financial statements will be prepared for each individual governmental fund and these individual fund statements are the foundation for the financial statements prepared for the governmental entity. But the fund-based financial statements for the governmental entity's annual report separately report only major governmental funds, not necessarily individually each of the five governmental funds. **GASB 34** specifies that the general fund is always a major fund. But some of the other governmental funds may not be determined to be major funds, and these nonmajor funds are aggregated and reported in a single column as other governmental funds. **GASB 34** establishes criteria that also encompass the enterprise funds. To determine which of the other governmental or specific enterprise funds are major, **GASB 34** specifies that *both* of the following criteria must be met:

**FIGURE 18–6**  **Governmental Funds Statement of Revenues, Expenditures, and Changes in Fund Balance**

**SOL CITY**
**Statement of Revenues, Expenditures, and Changes in Fund Balance**
**Governmental Funds**
**For the Year Ended December 31, 20X2**

| | General | Capital Projects | Permanent | Other Governmental Funds | Total Governmental Funds |
|---|---|---|---|---|---|
| **Revenues** | | | | | |
| Property Taxes | $781,000 | | | $95,000 | $ 876,000 |
| Sales Taxes | 32,000 | | | | 32,000 |
| Grants | 33,000 | $ 10,000 | | | 43,000 |
| Miscellaneous | 18,000 | | $ 8,000 | | 26,000 |
| Total Revenues | $864,000 | $ 10,000 | $ 8,000 | $95,000 | $ 977,000 |
| **Expenditures** | | | | | |
| Current | | | | | |
| General Government | $206,000 | | | | $ 206,000 |
| Streets and Highways | 71,000 | | | | 71,000 |
| Public Safety | 335,000 | | | | 335,000 |
| Sanitation | 141,000 | | | | 141,000 |
| Culture and Recreation | | | $ 5,000 | $49,000 | 54,000 |
| Debt Service | | | | | |
| Principal Retirement | | | | 20,000 | 20,000 |
| Interest Charges | | | | 10,000 | 10,000 |
| Capital Outlay | 58,000 | $ 124,000 | | | 182,000 |
| Total Expenditures | $811,000 | $ 124,000 | $ 5,000 | $79,000 | $1,019,000 |
| **Excess (deficiency) of** | | | | | |
| Revenues over Expenditures | $ 53,000 | $(114,000) | $ 3,000 | $16,000 | $ (42,000) |
| **Other Financing Sources (Uses)** | | | | | |
| Proceeds of Bond Issue | | $ 102,000 | | | $ 102,000 |
| Transfers In | | 20,000 | | $ 2,000 | 22,000 |
| Transfers Out | $(30,000) | (2,000) | | | (32,000) |
| **Total Other Financing** | | | | | |
| Sources and Uses | $(30,000) | $ 120,000 | $ -0- | $ 2,000 | $ 92,000 |
| **Contributions, Special Items and Extraordinary Items:** | | | | | |
| Contribution | | | $100,000 | | $ 100,000 |
| Net Change in Fund Balances | $ 23,000 | $ 6,000 | $103,000 | $18,000 | $ 150,000 |
| Fund Balances—Beginning | 129,000 | -0- | -0- | -0- | 129,000 |
| Fund Balances—Ending | $152,000 | $ 6,000 | $103,000 | $18,000 | $ 279,000 |

1. *10 percent criterion:* Total assets, liabilities, revenues, or expenditures/expenses of that individual governmental or enterprise fund are at least 10 percent of the corresponding total (assets, liabilities, revenues, or expenditures/expenses) for all funds of that category or type (i.e., total governmental funds or total enterprise funds).

2. *5 percent criterion:* Total assets, liabilities, revenues, or expenditures/expenses of the individual governmental fund or enterprise fund are at least 5 percent of the corresponding total for all governmental *plus* enterprise funds combined.

Note that the major fund reporting requirements apply to a governmental or enterprise fund only if the same element (e.g., assets, liabilities, revenues, or expenditures/expenses) exceeds both the 10 percent and the 5 percent criteria. These major funds tests are presented at the bottom of Figure 18–3 and Figure 18–4. To prepare the tests, information is also required for the enterprise funds. The underlying transactions for Sol City's enterprise fund are presented in the next section of this chapter. The information for the total assets, liabilities, revenues, and expenses of Sol City's enterprise fund is taken from the enterprise fund's financial statement information. For right now, the information for the enterprise fund is presented solely to discuss the major funds tests. More detail on the enterprise fund will be presented immediately after the following discussion of the two major funds tests.

### 10 Percent Criterion Tests

To compute the 10 percent criterion tests for the five governmental funds, the denominators of the four tests (assets, liabilities, revenues, and expenditures) are the totals from the five governmental funds. For example, Figure 18–3 shows the total assets of the governmental funds as $347,000. Note again that the general fund is always a major fund, so no percentages need be computed for that fund. The 10 percent asset test shows that the permanent fund meets the 10 percent criterion for total assets (29.68% = $103,000 ÷ $347,000). Continuing down to the liabilities, only the capital projects fund meets the 10 percent criterion for total liabilities (14.71% = $10,000 ÷ $68,000). Information in Figure 18–4 indicates that none of the nongeneral governmental funds meets the 10 percent criterion for revenues. For expenditures, the capital projects fund meets the 10 percent criterion for total expenditures (12.17% = $124,000 ÷ $1,019,000). Thus, the only two nongeneral governmental funds that meet the 10 percent criterion tests for a major fund are (1) the permanent fund (for total assets) and (2) the capital projects fund (for both total liabilities and for total expenditures).

### 5 Percent Criterion Tests

To compute the 5 percent criterion tests, the second group of major fund tests, the GASB specifies that the denominator of each of the four tests (assets, liabilities, revenues, and expenditures/expenses) is the combined total of each of these items for the five governmental funds *plus* the enterprise funds. For example, Figure 18–3 shows the combined total assets for the 5 percent asset test is $487,000 ($347,000 from the governmental funds plus $140,000 from the enterprise fund). For the nongeneral governmental funds, the permanent fund is the only one that meets the 5 percent criterion for total assets (21.15% = $103,000 ÷ $487,000). For total liabilities, the capital projects fund meets the 5 percent criterion (5.56% = $10,000 ÷ $180,000). Figure 18–4 shows that for revenues, the special revenue fund meets the 5 percent criterion (6.11% = $62,000 ÷ $1,014,000). For expenditures/expenses, only the capital projects fund meets the 5 percent criterion (11.76% = $124,000 ÷ $1,054,000).

Note that a governmental fund other than the general fund must meet *both* the 10 percent and the 5 percent criterion tests for at least one of the four financial statement items to be classified as a major fund. Thus, the following governmental funds are classified as major funds: (1) the general fund—always a major fund, (2) the capital projects fund (for liabilities and expenditures), and (3) the permanent fund (for assets). As shown in Figures 18–5 and 18–6, the governmental funds financial statements present details on these three funds. The two nonmajor funds, special revenue and debt service, are combined into a single Other Governmental Funds column. However, management of the governmental unit may elect to provide separate disclosure on any nonmajor fund that it believes is important for users of the financial statements to fully understand. **GASB 34** requires that a total for all governmental funds be provided. Note that enterprise funds are not governmental-type funds.

Governmental units are permitted to disclose, on the governmental funds' balance sheet, designations of unreserved funds. A designation is not a legal reservation or restriction but is similar to an appropriation of retained earnings for a commercial entity. The designation represents management's plans for the intended use of the resources and is a communication to users of the financial statements. However, designations are not permitted to be reported on the government-wide financial statements.

**FIGURE 18–7** Fund Balance Reporting for Governmental Fund Types as Specified by Proposed GASB Statement

| | General Fund | Capital Projects Fund | Permanent Fund | Other Governmental Funds | Total Governmental Funds |
|---|---|---|---|---|---|
| **SOL CITY** Fund Balance Reporting under Proposed GASB Statement Governmental Funds December 31, 20X2 | | | | | |
| Fund Balances: | | | | | |
| Nonspendable: | | | | | |
| Inventory | $ 17,000 | | | | $ 17,000 |
| Permanent Fund Principal | | | $100,000 | | 100,000 |
| Spendable: | | | | | |
| Restricted for: | | | | | |
| Maintain City Park | | | 3,000 | | 3,000 |
| Limited to: | | | | | |
| Culture & Recreation | | | | $13,000 | 13,000 |
| Assigned to: | | | | | |
| General Government | 15,000 | | | | 15,000 |
| Courthouse Project | | $ 6,000 | | | 6,000 |
| Debt Service | | | | 5,000 | 5,000 |
| Unassigned: | 120,000 | — | — | — | 120,000 |
| Total Fund Balances | $152,000 | $ 6,000 | $103,000 | $18,000 | $279,000 |

**GASB 34** requires a reconciliation schedule to the government-wide financial statements to be presented either at the bottom of each of the two fund financial statements or in accompanying schedules. These two schedules reconcile the modified accrual basis of accounting used for the governmental funds to the accrual basis of accounting used for reporting in the two government-wide financial statements. The reconciliation schedules are presented later in this chapter within the discussion of presenting the government-wide financial statements.

### *Fund Balance Reporting for Governmental Fund Types under Proposed Statement of the GASB*

The display specifications in the proposed statement affect only the balance sheet reporting of the fund balances of the governmental fund types. Figure 18–5 presented the reporting as required by **GASB 34.** Figure 18–7 presents the fund balance section of the governmental funds balance sheet as specified in the proposed statement on fund balance reporting and governmental fund type definitions.

The nonspendable fund balance is the amount spent for inventory and the grantor-imposed restriction on the principal of the permanent fund. The spendable fund balances would be classified based on an examination of the degree of constraints that control how specific amounts can be spent. Note that only the general fund has an unassigned portion of fund balance and that the total fund balances reported under the proposed GASB statement are the same as reported under **GASB 34.**

## ENTERPRISE FUNDS

Governments sometimes offer goods or services for sale to the public. The amounts charged to customers are intended to recover all or most of the cost of these goods or services. For example, a city may operate electric, gas, and water utilities; transportation systems such as buses, trains, and subways; airports; sports arenas; parking lots and garages; and public housing. Such operations are accounted for in ***enterprise funds,*** which differ from special revenue funds in that the costs of enterprise fund activities are recovered by user charges. Therefore, the primary difference between establishing a special revenue fund and an enterprise fund is the source of revenue.

Enterprise funds are one of the two proprietary fund types and have a measurement focus of all economic resources and use the accrual basis of accounting. Proprietary funds report fixed assets, which are depreciated, and long-term debt, if issued, and they focus on income determination and capital maintenance, the same as for commercial entities. The financial statements for proprietary funds are very similar to those for commercial entities: (1) the statement of net assets (balance sheet), (2) the statement of revenues, expenses, and changes in fund net assets (income statement), and (3) the statement of cash flows.

Budgeting in the proprietary funds also has the same role as in commercial entities. A budget may be prepared for management planning purposes; however, the budget is normally not entered into the accounts.

## Illustration of Transactions

Sol City has a municipal water utility that it operates as an enterprise fund. The trial balance of the water utility as of January 1, 20X2, the first day of the 20X2 fiscal year, is presented here:

| SOL CITY Trial Balance for Water Utility Enterprise Fund January 1, 20X2 | | |
|---|---|---|
| Cash | $ 9,000 | |
| Machinery and Equipment | 94,000 | |
| Buildings | 40,000 | |
| Accumulated Depreciation—Machinery and Equipment | | $ 15,000 |
| Accumulated Depreciation—Buildings | | 2,000 |
| Bonds Payable, 5% | | 100,000 |
| Net Assets: | | |
|   Invested in Capital Assets, Net of Related Debt | | 17,000 |
|   Unrestricted | | 9,000 |
| Totals | $143,000 | $143,000 |

One difference between balance sheet accounts for commercial entities and those for proprietary funds is the absence of a stockholders' equity section in governmental accounting. The general public is the theoretical owner of all governmental assets. Furthermore, no stock certificates are issued; therefore, a net assets section is used instead of common stock and additional paid-in capital. **GASB 34** requires the separate disclosure of the net assets invested in capital assets, net of related debt, which reports the book value (cost basis less accumulated depreciation) invested in capital assets such as land, buildings, machinery, equipment, and other tangible and intangible assets having expected useful lives exceeding one year. These resources are not readily available for other, unrestricted uses as are the current assets. The related debt is that directly associated with the capital assets and is typically long-term in nature. For our example, assume the $100,000 of bonds payable is related to the $117,000 of net capital assets ($134,000 cost less $17,000 of accumulated depreciation). Other interesting differences are the large relative amounts of fixed assets and long-term debt because enterprise funds typically require large investments in productive assets in order to provide the necessary level of service to the public, and these investments are usually financed by long-term revenue bonds.

The water utility sells its product to the residents of Sol City based on a user charge. In addition to water revenue, the water utility receives a $3,000 short-term interfund loan from the general fund and obtains its office supplies from the city's centralized purchasing operation, which is accounted for as an internal service fund. During the year, the water utility acquires a new pump costing $6,000.

### Enterprise Fund Revenues

The water utility provides service during the period and bills its customers for the amount of water used. The utility estimates that 7.5 percent of its billings will not be collected. Note that revenues are reported net of uncollectibles. These transactions are recorded as follows:

| | | | |
|---|---|---:|---:|
| (30) | Accounts Receivable | 40,000 | |
| | Allowance for Uncollectibles | | 3,000 |
| | Revenue—Water Sales | | 37,000 |
| | Bill customers for water used as indicated by meter readings. | | |
| | Estimate $3,000 of billings will be uncollectible. | | |
| | | | |
| (31) | Cash | 32,000 | |
| | Accounts Receivable | | 32,000 |
| | Collect portion of accounts receivable. | | |

### Capital Asset Acquisition

The water utility acquires a new pump during the year.

| | | | |
|---|---|---:|---:|
| (32) | Equipment | 6,000 | |
| | Vouchers Payable | | 6,000 |
| | Receive new pump for wellhouse. | | |
| | | | |
| (33) | Vouchers Payable | 6,000 | |
| | Cash | | 6,000 |
| | Pay voucher for new pump. | | |

### Interfund Activities

Several interfund transactions occur during the year. First, in an interfund financing transaction, the water utility receives $3,000 from the general fund as a short-term loan to be repaid within 90 days. The general fund records this as a short-term receivable, Due from Enterprise Fund (see entry [39] in Chapter 17). Second, the utility acquires its office supplies from the internal service fund in an interfund services provided and used transaction. The internal service fund reports this as a revenue transaction (see entry [48] later in this chapter):

| | | | |
|---|---|---:|---:|
| (34) | Cash | 3,000 | |
| | Due to General Fund | | 3,000 |
| | Recognize payable for loan from general fund. | | |
| | | | |
| (35) | Supplies Inventory | 3,000 | |
| | Due to Internal Service Fund | | 3,000 |
| | Receive office supplies from centralized purchasing department at a cost of $3,000. | | |
| | | | |
| (36) | Due to Internal Service Fund | 2,000 | |
| | Cash | | 2,000 |
| | Approve payment of $2,000 to centralized purchasing department for supplies received. | | |

### Enterprise Fund Expenses

The water utility fund incurs $9,000 of operating expenses during the period. In addition, several adjusting journal entries are required at the end of the fiscal year to recognize additional expenses. Note that these adjusting entries are similar to those of a commercial entity:

| (37) | General Operating Expenses | 9,000 | |
| | Vouchers Payable | | 9,000 |
| | Incur operating expenses during year. | | |

| (38) | Vouchers Payable | 6,000 | |
| | Cash | | 6,000 |
| | Pay approved vouchers for operating expenses. | | |

| (39) | General Operating Expenses | 3,000 | |
| | Supplies Inventory | | 3,000 |
| | Adjust for $3,000 of supplies consumed. | | |

| (40) | Depreciation Expense | 18,000 | |
| | Accumulated Depreciation—Buildings | | 3,000 |
| | Accumulated Depreciation—Machinery and Equipment | | 15,000 |
| | Recognize depreciation expense for year. | | |

| (41) | Interest Expense | 5,000 | |
| | Accrued Interest Payable | | 5,000 |
| | Accrue interest on bond payable: $100,000 \times .05 \times 1$ year | | |

## Closing and Reclassification Entries in the Enterprise Fund

The nominal accounts are closed, the period's profit or loss is determined, and, at the close of the fiscal year, the government reclassifies the various components of net assets based on the year-end amount of net assets invested in capital assets, net of related debt:

| (42) | Revenue—Water Sales | 37,000 | |
| | General Operating Expenses | | 12,000 |
| | Depreciation Expense | | 18,000 |
| | Interest Expense | | 5,000 |
| | Profit and Loss Summary | | 2,000 |
| | Close nominal accounts into profit and loss summary. | | |

| (43) | Profit and Loss Summary | 2,000 | |
| | Net Assets—Unrestricted | | 2,000 |
| | Close profit and loss summary into net assets. | | |

| (44) | Net Assets—Invested in Capital Assets, Net of Related Debt | 12,000 | |
| | Net Assets—Unrestricted | | 12,000 |
| | To reclassify net assets as of end of fiscal period: | | |

12/31/X1 balance: $ 5,000 = $105,000 capital assets − $100,000 of related debt
1/1/X1 balance: 17,000 = $117,000 capital assets − $100,000 of related debt

$12,000 = Decrease during period in net assets
invested in capital assets, net of related debt

## Financial Statements for the Proprietary Funds

Three financial statements are required for the proprietary funds. If a governmental entity has more than one enterprise fund, each must be individually assessed by both the 10 percent criterion and the 5 percent criterion tests to determine whether it is a major fund. Sol City has only one enterprise fund. Figure 18–8 presents the statement of net assets for the enterprise proprietary fund and for the internal service proprietary fund that will be discussed in the next section of this chapter. Figure 18–9 presents the statement of revenues, expenses, and changes in fund net assets for Sol City's two proprietary funds. Figure 18–10 presents the statement of cash flows for these two proprietary funds.

The statement of net assets in Figure 18–8 is similar to that required for commercial entities. Proprietary funds report their own fixed assets, investments, and long-term liabilities. **GASB 34** specifies that the net assets section for the proprietary funds, which

**FIGURE 18–8**
**Proprietary Funds
Statement of Net
Assets**

| | SOL CITY Statement of Net Assets Proprietary Funds December 31, 20X2 | |
|---|---|---|
| | Enterprise Fund | Internal Service Fund |
| Assets: | | |
| Current Assets: | | |
| Cash | $ 30,000 | $ 4,000 |
| Accounts Receivable (net) | 5,000 | |
| Due from Other Funds | | 1,000 |
| Inventory of Supplies | | 6,000 |
| Total Current Assets | $ 35,000 | $11,000 |
| Noncurrent Assets: | | |
| Capital Assets: | | |
| Machinery and Equipment | $100,000 | $ 3,000 |
| Less Accumulated Depreciation | (30,000) | (1,000) |
| Buildings | 40,000 | |
| Less Accumulated Depreciation | (5,000) | |
| Total Noncurrent Assets | $105,000 | $ 2,000 |
| Total Assets | $140,000 | $ 13,000 |
| Liabilities: | | |
| Current Liabilities: | | |
| Vouchers Payable | $ 3,000 | $ 6,000 |
| Accrued Interest Payable | 5,000 | |
| Due to Other Funds | 4,000 | |
| Total Current Liabilities | $ 12,000 | $ 6,000 |
| Noncurrent Liabilities: | | |
| Bonds Payable, 5% | 100,000 | |
| Total Liabilities | $112,000 | $ 6,000 |
| Net Assets: | | |
| Invested in Capital Assets, Net of Related Debt | $ 5,000 | $ 2,000 |
| Unrestricted | 23,000 | 5,000 |
| Total Net Assets | $ 28,000 | $ 7,000 |

is presented below liabilities, be separated into three components: (1) invested in capital assets, net of related debt; (2) restricted because of restrictions beyond the government's control, such as externally imposed restrictions or legal requirements; and (3) unrestricted. **GASB Statement 46,** "Net Assets Restricted by Enabling Legislation" (GASB 46), issued in 2004, amended **GASB 34** with regard to net assets restricted by legally enforceable actions such as enabling legislation, which specifies that a government use resources only for the purposes as specified in the enabling legislation. **GASB 46** provides guidance for reporting the net assets so restricted and accounting for changes when new enabling legislation replaces the prior legislation. The key point is that **GASB 46** confirms the **GASB 34** requirement for separate disclosure of net assets restricted by legal requirements. For our example, there are no externally imposed or legal restrictions on net assets. The amount of the net assets invested in capital assets, net of related debt, is computed as capital assets less accumulated depreciation, less outstanding principal of related debt. For purposes of this example, assume that the information in Figure 18–8 shows that the enterprise fund has $5,000 of net assets invested in capital assets, net of related debt ($105,000 − $100,000), and the internal service fund has $2,000 invested in capital assets, net of related debt ($2,000 − $0).

**FIGURE 18–9**
Proprietary Funds
Statement of
Revenues, Expenses,
and Changes in
Fund Net Assets

| | SOL CITY<br>Statement of Revenues, Expenses, and Changes in Fund Net Assets<br>Proprietary Funds<br>For the Year Ended December 31, 20X2 | |
| --- | --- | --- |
| | **Enterprise Fund** | **Internal Service Fund** |
| Operating Revenues: | | |
|   Charges for Services | $37,000 | $ 4,000 |
| Total Operating Revenues | $37,000 | $ 4,000 |
| Operating Expenses: | | |
|   General Operating | $12,000 | $ 4,000 |
|   Cost of Goods Sold | | 2,000 |
|   Depreciation | 18,000 | 1,000 |
| Total Operating Expenses | $30,000 | $ 7,000 |
| Nonoperating Revenue (Expenses): | | |
|   Interest Expense | $ (5,000) | |
| Total Nonoperating Expense | $ 5,000 | |
| Income (Loss) before Contributions and Transfers | $ 2,000 | $(3,000) |
|   Transfer In | | 10,000 |
| Change in Net Assets | $ 2,000 | $ 7,000 |
| Net Assets—Beginning | 26,000 | -0- |
| Net Assets—Ending | $28,000 | $ 7,000 |

The statement of revenues, expenses, and changes in fund net assets is similar to the income statement for commercial entities. A separation of operating and nonoperating revenues and expenses is made to provide more information value regarding the operations of the proprietary funds. Contributions and transfers in or out are reported below the income (loss) line in the statement of revenues, expenses, and changes in fund net assets. Contributions would include any capital asset transfers from a governmental fund to a proprietary fund. For example, the general fund may transfer equipment to an enterprise fund. Note that the governmental funds describe the interfund transfers as other financing sources or uses, but the proprietary funds use only the terms *transfer in* or *transfer out* to describe these nonoperating interfund transactions. And both interest income and interest expense are reported as nonoperating items.

The statement of cash flows for enterprise funds is specified by **GASB Statement No. 9,** "Reporting Cash Flows of Proprietary and Nonexpendable Trust Funds and Governmental Entities that Use Proprietary Fund Accounting" (GASB 9). This standard provides a format that differs somewhat from the three-section format of the statement of cash flows for commercial entities. Because of the large number of capital asset acquisition and financing transactions in proprietary funds, the GASB specified four sections of the statement of cash flows, as follows:

1. *Cash flows from operating activities.* This first section includes all transactions from providing services and delivering goods. **GASB 34** requires the use of the direct method of computing cash flows from operating activities. It includes cash flows from interfund operating transactions and reimbursements from other funds.

2. *Cash flows from noncapital financing activities.* This second section includes activities such as borrowing or repaying money for purposes other than to acquire, construct, or improve capital assets. It includes cash for financing activities received from, or paid to, other funds except that which is specifically specified for capital asset use.

3. *Cash flows from capital and related financing activities.* This third section includes all activities clearly related to, or attributable to, the acquisition, disposition, construction, or improvement of capital assets. This section also includes the interest paid on borrowings for capital assets.

**FIGURE 18–10** **Proprietary Funds Statement of Cash Flows**

**SOL CITY**
**Statement of Cash Flows**
**Proprietary Funds**
**For the Year Ended December 31, 20X2**

| | Enterprise Fund | Internal Service Fund |
|---|---|---|
| Cash Flows from Operating Activities: | | |
| Receipts from Customers | $32,000 | $ 3,000 |
| Cash Payments for Goods and Services | (6,000) | (6,000) |
| Cash Paid to Internal Service Fund for Supplies | (2,000) | |
| Net Cash Provided (Used) by Operating Activities | $24,000 | $(3,000) |
| Cash Flows from Noncapital Financing Activities: | | |
| Cash Received from General Fund for Noncapital Loan | $ 3,000 | $ 7,000 |
| Net Cash Provided by Noncapital Financing Activities | $ 3,000 | $ 7,000 |
| Cash Flows from Capital and Related Financing Activities: | | |
| Acquisition of Capital Asset | $ (6,000) | $(3,000) |
| Cash Received from General Fund for Capital Activity | | 3,000 |
| Net Cash Provided (Used) for Capital Financing Activities | $ (6,000) | $ -0- |
| Cash Flows from Investing Activities | $ -0- | $ -0- |
| Net Increase in Cash | $21,000 | $ 4,000 |
| Balances—Beginning of Year | 9,000 | -0- |
| Balances—End of Year | $30,000 | $ 4,000 |
| Reconciliation of Operating Income to Net Cash Provided by Operating Activities: | | |
| Operating Income | $ 7,000 | $(3,000) |
| Adjustments to Reconcile Operating Income to Net Cash Provided (Used) by Operating Activities: | | |
| Depreciation | 18,000 | 1,000 |
| Change in Assets and Liabilities: | | |
| Increase in Net Accounts Receivable | (5,000) | |
| Increase in Due from Other Funds from Billings | | (1,000) |
| Increase in Inventory of Supplies | | (6,000) |
| Increase in Vouchers Payable | 3,000 | 6,000 |
| Increase in Due to Internal Service Fund | 1,000 | |
| Net Cash Provided (Used) by Operating Activities | $24,000 | $(3,000) |

4. *Cash flows from investing activities.* This fourth section includes all investing activities, interest and dividend revenue, and acquisition and disposition of debt or equity instruments.

In addition to the statement of cash flows, proprietary funds are also required to provide a supplementary schedule that reconciles the cash flow from operating activities with the operating income or loss reported on the statement of revenues, expenses, and changes in fund net assets.

# INTERNAL SERVICE FUNDS

***Internal service funds*** account for the financing of goods or services provided by one department or agency to other departments or agencies on a cost-reimbursement basis. These services are not available to the general public, making the internal service fund different from the enterprise fund. Examples are motor vehicle pools, central computer facilities, printing shops, and centralized purchasing and storage facilities. Separate internal service funds are established for each of these functions maintained by the local governmental unit.

Accounting and financial reporting for internal service funds are the same as for enterprise funds or for commercial entities. The accrual basis is used to measure revenue and expenses, and the balance sheet may include fixed assets, which are depreciated, and long-term debt, if issued. The statement of revenue, expenses, and changes in fund net assets reports the fund's income for the period. The statement of cash flows is also required.

## Illustration of Transactions

Sol City decides to establish a centralized purchasing and storage function as an internal service fund. This centralized purchasing department provides office supplies to all other funds of the local government on a user-charge basis. After acquiring the necessary supplies, the centralized purchasing department makes the following sales:

| Buying Fund | Selling Price | Cost to Internal Service Fund |
|---|---|---|
| General fund | $1,000 | $ 500 |
| Enterprise fund | 3,000 | 1,500 |

The following entries are made during the year to record the activities of the centralized purchasing and storage department.

### *Establishment of Internal Service Fund and Acquisition of Inventories*

The fund is started with a transfer in from the general fund in the amount of $10,000, which the internal service fund then uses to acquire inventory and equipment. The general fund records this interfund transfer as a transfer out (see entry [33] in Chapter 17):

| | | | | |
|---|---|---|---|---|
| (45) | Cash | | 10,000 | |
| |     Transfer In | | | 10,000 |
| |     Receive interfund transfer in from general fund | | | |
| |        to initiate centralized purchasing and storage function. | | | |
| | | | | |
| (46) | Inventory | | 8,000 | |
| |     Vouchers Payable | | | 8,000 |
| |     Acquire inventory of supplies. | | | |
| | | | | |
| (47) | Machinery and Equipment | | 3,000 | |
| |     Vouchers Payable | | | 3,000 |
| |     Acquire equipment. | | | |

### *Internal Service Fund Revenue*

The revenue of the internal service fund is earned by selling supplies to other funds and billing them for the value of the supplies. The billing rate is typically established at more than the operating costs of the internal service fund so that the fund may acquire replacement assets or new assets:

| | | | | |
|---|---|---|---|---|
| (48) | Due from General Fund | | 1,000 | |
| | Due from Enterprise Fund | | 3,000 | |
| |     Charges for Services | | | 4,000 |
| |     Recognize revenue from providing supplies | | | |
| |        to general fund and enterprise fund. | | | |
| | | | | |
| (49) | Cash | | 3,000 | |
| |     Due from General Fund | | | 1,000 |
| |     Due from Enterprise Fund | | | 2,000 |
| |     Collect portion of receivables. | | | |

The general fund records the $1,000 for supplies as an interfund expenditures transaction (see entry [37] in Chapter 17). The enterprise fund records the $3,000 as an interfund inventory purchase transaction (see entry [35] earlier in this chapter).

### Internal Service Fund Expenses

The internal service fund incurs $4,000 of operating expenses, including payroll, during the period. In addition, cost of goods sold of $2,000 and $1,000 of depreciation expense are recognized in adjusting entries. The $9,000 of vouchers paid include a voucher in the amount of $3,000 for the equipment acquired in entry (47) above:

| | | | |
|---|---|---:|---:|
| (50) | General Operating Expenses | 4,000 | |
| |     Vouchers Payable | | 4,000 |
| |     Incur operating expenses. | | |
| (51) | Vouchers Payable | 9,000 | |
| |     Cash | | 9,000 |
| |     Pay approved vouchers. | | |
| (52) | Cost of Goods Sold | 2,000 | |
| |     Inventory | | 2,000 |
| |     Recognize cost of supplies sold. | | |
| (53) | Depreciation Expense | 1,000 | |
| |     Accumulated Depreciation | | 1,000 |
| |     Depreciation of equipment. | | |

### Closing Entries in the Internal Service Fund

The closing and reclassifying entries for the internal service fund follow. "Profit and Loss Summary" is used here in the closing process; however, some governmental units use the account called Excess of Net Revenues over Costs to perform the same function.

| | | | |
|---|---|---:|---:|
| (54) | Charges for Services | 4,000 | |
| | Profit and Loss Summary | 3,000 | |
| |     Cost of Goods Sold | | 2,000 |
| |     General Operating Expenses | | 4,000 |
| |     Depreciation Expense | | 1,000 |
| |     Close revenue and expenses. | | |
| (55) | Transfer In | 10,000 | |
| |     Profit and Loss Summary | | 3,000 |
| |     Net Assets—Unrestricted | | 7,000 |
| |     Close profit and loss summary and transfer in to net assets. | | |
| (56) | Net Assets—Unrestricted | 2,000 | |
| |     Net Assets—Invested in Capital Assets, Net of Related Debt | | 2,000 |
| |     To reclassify net assets as of end of fiscal period: | | |
| |     $2,000 = $2,000 net capital assets − $0 related debt | | |

## Financial Statements for Internal Service Funds

The financial statements required for internal service funds are the same as those required for the enterprise fund. Figure 18–8 presents the statement of net assets, and Figure 18–9 presents the statement of revenues, expenses, and changes in fund net assets for the internal service fund. Figure 18–10 presents the statement of cash flows for the internal service fund.

**FIGURE 18–11**
**Fiduciary Funds**
**Statement of**
**Fiduciary Net Assets**

| SOL CITY<br>Statement of Fiduciary Net Assets<br>Fiduciary Funds<br>December 31, 20X2 | | |
| --- | --- | --- |
| | **Private-Purpose Funds** | **Agency Funds** |
| Assets: | | |
| Cash | $ 1,600 | $1,000 |
| Investments, at Fair Value: | | |
| Municipal Bonds | 26,200 | |
| Total Assets | $27,800 | $1,000 |
| Liabilities: | | |
| Due to Insurance Company | | $1,000 |
| Total Liabilities | $ -0- | $1,000 |
| Net Assets Held in Trust | $27,800 | |

# TRUST FUNDS

*Trust funds* are a fiduciary fund type that accounts for resources held by a government unit in a trustee capacity. The governmental unit acts as a fiduciary for monies or properties held on behalf of individuals, employees, or other governmental agencies. The three main types of fiduciary trust funds are: (1) pension and other employee benefit trust funds, (2) investment trust funds, and (3) private-purpose trust funds.

The accrual basis of accounting is used for the fiduciary funds, and the financial statements required for fiduciary funds are the statement of fiduciary net assets (Figure 18–11), and the statement of changes in fiduciary net assets (Figure 18–12). The statement of fiduciary net assets includes all trusts and agency funds. The statement of changes in fiduciary net assets includes only the trust funds because agency funds do not have a net asset balance; their assets must equal their liabilities. Agency funds are discussed after trust funds.

**FIGURE 18–12**
**Fiduciary Funds**
**Statement of Changes**
**in Fiduciary Net Assets**

| SOL CITY<br>Statement of Changes in Fiduciary Net Assets<br>Fiduciary Funds<br>For the Year Ended December 31, 20X2<br>Private-Purpose Fund | | |
| --- | --- | --- |
| Additions: | | |
| Contributions | | $50,000 |
| Investment Earnings: | | |
| Increase in Fair Value of Investments | $1,200 | |
| Interest | 600 | |
| Total Investment Earnings | | 1,800 |
| Total Additions | | $51,800 |
| Deductions: | | |
| Benefits | | $23,000 |
| Administrative Costs | | 1,000 |
| Total Deductions | | $24,000 |
| Change in Net Assets | | $27,800 |
| Net Assets—Beginning of Year | | -0- |
| Net Assets—End of Year | | $27,800 |

Private-purpose trust funds account for trust agreements for which the principal and/ or income benefits specific individuals, private organizations, or other governments. Note that the benefit is limited to private, rather than general public, purposes. The trust agreement may require the principal to be preserved (i.e., nonexpendable principal), in which case an endowment is created. In other trust agreements, both the principal and income may be used for the specific purposes for which the trust was created. The governmental entity does not have to accept the donation if it is not consistent with the government's objectives. However, there are many cases in which a governmental entity accepts the donation and agrees to its provisions because of the benefits that can be achieved with the resources. For example, a citizen group may donate money to a city to be used for award recognition for businesses located in the downtown area that update and improve the appearances of their storefronts. The governmental entity is typically allowed to charge the private-purpose trust fund a fee for managing the trust's resources, which would include investing the resources and making the allowed expenditures from the resources.

An example of a private-purpose trust fund is illustrated in the next section of this chapter. Public employee pension funds are discussed in the "Additional Considerations" section later in the chapter.

## Illustration of Private-Purpose Trust Fund

On January 1, 20X2, Sol City receives a $50,000 donation from Charles Alt, a citizen of Sol City. The terms of the trust agreement specify that the city is to use about $25,000 each year for the next two years to help alleviate the cost of transporting senior citizens to and from the senior citizens' center. The city accepts the donation and, as allowed by the trust agreement, invests $25,000 in highly rated bonds. The remaining $25,000 is deposited in a bank account that earns 4 percent interest. The terms of the trust agreement allow the city to deduct $1,000 per year for its administrative costs of managing the trust and the transportation services. During the first year, 20X2, $23,000 is paid out of the fund for transportation services. The fund pays out the remaining resources in 20X3.

| | | | |
|---|---|---:|---:|
| (57) | Cash | 50,000 | |
| |     Additions—Contributions | | 50,000 |
| |     The city accepts a private-purpose trust fund of $50,000. | | |
| | | | |
| (58) | Investment in Bonds | 25,000 | |
| |     Cash | | 25,000 |
| |     The city invests half of the trust funds, as allowed<br>    by the trust agreement. | | |
| | | | |
| (59) | Cash | 600 | |
| |     Additions—Interest | | 600 |
| |     Interest earned during the year on the monies deposited<br>    in the bank is recognized from bank statements. | | |
| | | | |
| (60) | Deductions—Transportation Benefits | 23,000 | |
| |     Cash | | 23,000 |
| |     Transportation costs during the year are paid. | | |
| | | | |
| (61) | Deductions—Administration Costs | 1,000 | |
| |     Cash | | 1,000 |
| |     The $1,000 of administrative costs allowed to the<br>    city are recognized and paid. | | |

An adjusting journal entry is made on December 31, 20X2, to revalue the investment in bonds to their fair values, as follows:

| (62) | Investment in Bonds | 1,200 | |
| | Additions—Investment Revalued | | 1,200 |
| | The fair value of the investment in bonds increased by $1,200 by the end of the year. | | |

Note that this private-purpose trust fund had an expendable principal as well as earnings. The requirement for a private-purpose trust fund is that its resources may be used only for specific individuals, organizations, or other governmental units as specified by the donor. Some private-purpose trust funds specify that the principal is nonexpendable and that only the earnings may be used for the private purpose. A private-purpose trust fund is differentiated from a permanent fund, which is part of the governmental funds, in the following manner. A permanent fund must maintain its principal, but the earnings are used to support the government's programs that benefit all citizens. A private-purpose trust fund must be used only for the specific purposes specified by the donor or grantor of the trust fund and is not available to support the government's general programs.

Figure 18–11 reports the statement of fiduciary net assets for the fiduciary funds for Sol City, including the private-purpose fund and agency fund. Figure 18–12 presents the statement of changes in fiduciary net assets for the private-purpose trust fund. Agency funds are presented in the next section of the chapter.

# AGENCY FUNDS

*Agency funds* are a fiduciary fund type that accounts for resources held by a governmental unit as a custodial agent for individuals, private organizations, other funds, or other governmental units. Examples are tax collection funds that collect property taxes and then distribute them to local governmental units and employee benefit funds for such items as dental insurance or charitable contributions that employees authorize as withholdings from their paychecks.

The accrual basis of accounting is used to account for agency funds. Because agency funds are custodial in nature, assets always equal liabilities and there is no fund equity. The financial statement for agency funds is the statement of fiduciary net assets as presented in Figure 18–10. Note that there cannot be any net asset balance for agency funds; therefore, no statement of changes in fiduciary net assets is required for agency funds.

## Illustration of Transactions in an Agency Fund

Sol City has established an agency fund to account for employees' share of health insurance, which is deducted from the employees' monthly paychecks and then forwarded to the insurance company on a quarterly basis. For purposes of this example, a total of $9,000 was deducted from the employees' paychecks, and $8,000 was paid to the insurance company in 20X2. The remaining $1,000 will be paid to the insurance company in the first quarter of 20X3.

### Agency Fund Receipts and Disbursements

The receipts and disbursements in the agency fund during 20X2 are as follows:

| (63) | Cash | 9,000 | |
| | Due to Insurance Company | | 9,000 |
| | Employees' contributory share of health insurance deducted from payroll checks. | | |

| (64) | Due to Insurance Company | 8,000 | |
| | Cash | | 8,000 |
| | Pay liability to insurance company for employees' share of insurance cost. | | |

# THE GOVERNMENT REPORTING MODEL

**GASB 34** specifies the reporting model for governmental entities. All general-purpose units such as states, counties, and municipalities must provide all financial statements required in **GASB 34.** These statements are both the fund-based financial statements presented earlier in this chapter plus the government-wide financial statements that will be discussed in a following section of this chapter. Some special-purpose government units such as cemetery associations that are engaged in a single governmental activity are not required to provide the government-wide financial statements but still must provide fund-based financial statements.

## Four Major Issues

### Issue 1: What Organizations Comprise the Reporting Entity?

The first issue to address is the determination of the **reporting entity** for which the statements will be provided. The primary government is part of the reporting entity, but this issue concerns what other boards, commissions, agencies, or authorities should be included with the reporting entity. **GASB 34** defines the reporting entity as (*a*) the primary government, such as a city, county, or state, (*b*) a component unit for which the primary government is financially accountable, and (*c*) any organization that has a significant relationship with the primary government and should be included to avoid misleading or incomplete financial statements.

### Issue 2: What Constitutes Financial Accountability?

**GASB Statement No. 14,** "The Financial Reporting Entity" (GASB 14), states that financial accountability of the primary government for the component organization is evidenced by either *board appointment* or *fiscal dependence.* Financial accountability is evidenced when the primary government appoints a majority of the organization's governing board. Thus, the primary government has effective control over the organization, which in turn may provide specific benefits to, or may impose specific financial burdens on, the primary government. Financial accountability may also exist if the organization has a separately elected or appointed board but fiscally depends on the primary government for the financial resources required to operate.

The primary government's ability to impose its will on an organization is evidenced by such things as its ability (1) to remove appointed members of the organization's governing board, (2) to approve or modify the organization's budget or approve rates or fee changes, (3) to veto or overrule the decisions of the organization's governing body, or (4) to appoint, hire, reassign, or dismiss those persons responsible for the organization's day-to-day operations. The potential for an organization to impose specific burdens on the primary government is evidenced by such things as the primary government's legal obligation or its assumption of the obligation to finance the deficits, or otherwise provide financial support to, the organization, or the primary government's obligation in some manner for the debt of the organization. These criteria indicate that when the primary governmental unit is financially accountable for legally separate organizations, those organizations should be included in the primary government's financial statements as **component units.**

### Issue 3: What Other Organizations Should Be Included in the Reporting Entity?

**GASB 14** specifies a third category of organizations to be evaluated to determine if they are part of the reporting entity with the primary government. These are legally separate, tax-exempt entities for which the primary government is *not* financially accountable. **GASB Statement No. 39,** "Determining Whether Certain Organizations Are Component Units" (GASB 39), amended parts of **GASB 14** to more fully define what other organizations should be included in a government's reporting entity. In general, a legally separate, tax-exempt organization is reported as a component unit of the primary government if *all three* of the following characteristics are met:

1. The resources of the separate organization are held for the benefit of the primary government, its component units, or the persons served by the primary government or its component units.

2. The primary government, or its component units, is entitled to, or can use, a majority of the economic resources of the separate organization.

3. The economic resources that the primary government, or its component units, can use are significant to the primary government.

Examples of other organizations that should be included in the reporting entity include university foundations and university alumni associations.

### Issue 4: How Should the Financial Results of the Component Units Be Reported?

The fourth issue is how to report the financial results of component units. A choice between two methods must be made: (1) *discrete presentation* in a separate column of the primary government's financial statements, or (2) *blended presentation* by combining the organization's results into the primary government's financial results.

Most component units are discretely presented; however, the blending method should be used when the component unit is so intertwined with the primary government that, in essence, they are the same governmental unit. Blending should be used when either (1) the component unit's governing body is substantively the same as the primary government's governing body or (2) the component unit provides services entirely, or almost entirely, to the primary government or almost exclusively benefits the primary government. Some of these organizations are similar to the internal services fund. Component units may use governmental fund accounting or proprietary fund accounting, depending on their types of activities. Neither discretely presenting nor blending should change the measurement basis of the type of accounting used by the component unit; however, a general fund of a blended component unit should be reported as a special revenue fund for the primary government.

For purposes of the Sol City example, assume that the city has a separate library board responsible for managing the city library. The mayor appoints the library board, which must have its budget and tax levy approved by the mayor and council. In this case, the library is a component unit that will be discretely presented in a separate column of Sol City's two government-wide financial statements.

## Government Financial Reports

The annual report of a governmental entity is termed the ***comprehensive annual financial report*** (CAFR). Figure 18–13 presents the components of the CAFR along with parenthetical information noting the figure number in the text, or the number of the GASB standard providing guidance on the information to be included in that item.

The GASB has continued to develop the reporting standards for the statistical section to make it more useful and comparative for users of the annual report. In 2004, the GASB issued **GASB Statement 44,** "Economic Condition Reporting: The Statistical Section—An Amendment of NCGA Statement 1" (GASB 44), which specifies the types of information that should be reported in each of the five sections of the statistical section: (1) financial trends information, (2) revenue capacity information, (3) debt capacity information, (4) demographic and economic information, and (5) operating information. The intent of this statement is to further improve the understandability and usefulness of this section by also requiring the governmental unit to add information about the sources of the data and the major assumptions used and expand explanations for any unusual information presented. Thus, the statistical section is an important part of the CAFR.

The fund-based financial statements were discussed previously in the chapter. The following discussion centers on the government-wide financials and the required supplementary information (RSI).

**FIGURE 18–13** **The Comprehensive Annual Financial Report (CAFR)**

*Section 1: Introductory Section* This section contains organizational information and other preliminary items.

*Section 2: Financial Section* The financial section contains the following items:

1. Independent auditors report.
2. Management's discussion and analysis (required supplementary information) (**GASB 34**).
3. Government-wide financial statements.
   a. Statement of net assets (Figure 18–14).
   b. Statement of activities (Figure 18–15).
4. Fund-based financial statements.
   a. Governmental funds.
      (1) Balance sheet (Figure 18–5).
      (2) Statement of revenues, expenditures, and changes in fund balances (Figure 18–6).
      (3) Reconciliation schedules (Figures 18–16 and 18–17).
   b. Proprietary funds.
      (1) Statement of net assets (Figure 18–8).
      (2) Statement of revenues, expenses, and changes in fund net assets (Figure 18–9).
      (3) Statement of cash flows (Figure 18–10).
   c. Fiduciary funds.
      (1) Statement of fiduciary net assets (Figure 18–11).
      (2) Statement of changes in fiduciary net assets (Figure 18–12).
5. Notes to the financial statements (**GASB 34 and 38**).
6. Required supplementary information (RSI).
   a. Budgetary comparison schedules (Figure 18–18) (**GASB 41**).
   b. Information about infrastructure assets (**GASB 34** for modified approach).
   c. Information about pension funding progress and employer contributions to retirement and pension funds (**GASB 25, 27, 43, 45, and 50**).

*Section 3: Combining and Individual Fund Financial Statements* This section contains the financial statements of each individual fund as well as financial statements showing the combining of individual funds together as a fund type (e.g., combining all individual special projects fund into one fund).

*Section 4: Statistical Section* This section presents the economic condition reporting required by **GASB 44** to be presented in the statistical section of the annual report.

## Government-wide Financial Statements

The ***government-wide financial statements*** include (1) the statement of net assets and (2) the statement of activities. **GASB 34** requires that government-wide financial statements be prepared on the *economic resources measurement focus* with the accrual basis of accounting. *Note:* The fiduciary funds (e.g., private-purpose trust funds and agency funds) are *not* included in the two government-wide financial statements because fiduciary funds are not available to support government programs.

### *Statement of Net Assets*

Figure 18–14 presents the statement of net assets for Sol City. Some important points regarding this statement of net assets follow:

1. *Format.* The format of the statement is Assets − Liabilities = Net assets. This focuses attention on the net assets of the government entity.

2. *Columnar presentation.* A columnar presentation is used because it emphasizes that the primary government has two different categories of activities, each needing a net asset base to support that category's activities, and the reporting entity's component units have their own net asset base. *Note:* **GASB 34** requires the following presentation for the statement of net assets:

**FIGURE 18–14** **Government-wide Statement of Net Assets**

| | Primary Government | | | |
| | Governmental Activities | Business-type Activities | Total | Component Unit |
|---|---|---|---|---|
| **Assets:** | | | | |
| Cash and Cash Equivalents | $ 152,000 | $ 30,000 | $ 182,000 | $ 3,000 |
| Receivables, Net | 89,000 | 5,000 | 94,000 | |
| Internal Balances | 4,000 | (4,000) | -0- | |
| Inventories | 23,000 | | 23,000 | 1,000 |
| Investment in Government Bonds | 91,000 | | 91,000 | |
| Capital Assets: | | | | |
| Land and Infrastructure | 3,000,000 | | 3,000,000 | |
| Depreciable Assets, Net | 1,202,000 | 105,000 | 1,307,000 | 870,000 |
| Total Assets | $4,561,000 | $136,000 | $4,697,000 | $874,000 |
| **Liabilities:** | | | | |
| Vouchers Payable | $ 64,000 | $ 3,000 | $ 67,000 | |
| Accrued Interest Payable | | 5,000 | 5,000 | |
| Contract Payable—Retainage | 10,000 | | 10,000 | |
| Noncurrent Liabilities: | | | | |
| Due in More Than 1 Year | 80,000 | 100,000 | 180,000 | $120,000 |
| Total Liabilities | $ 154,000 | $108,000 | $ 262,000 | $120,000 |
| **Net Assets:** | | | | |
| Invested in Capital Assets, Net of Related Debt | $4,122,000 | $ 5,000 | $4,127,000 | $750,000 |
| Restricted for: | | | | |
| Debt Service | 5,000 | | 5,000 | |
| Permanent Funds | 103,000 | | 103,000 | |
| Unrestricted | 177,000 | 23,000 | 200,000 | 4,000 |
| Total Net Assets | $4,407,000 | $ 28,000 | $4,435,000 | $754,000 |

*Table title (header):*

**SOL CITY**
**Statement of Net Assets**
**December 20X2**

a. The primary government's activities are assigned to either governmental activities or business-type activities.

b. The internal service funds are included as part of the governmental activities. This is because internal service funds provide service only to the governmental entity, not to external parties.

c. The enterprise funds are presented as business-type activities of the primary government. This is because the enterprise funds offer services to the public, and thus they are more business oriented.

3. *Assets.* Reported assets include all types of assets of the governmental entity, including infrastructure such as roads, sewers, and so on. These capital assets are not reported in the governmental funds that, under the current financial resources measurement focus, record costs of capital assets as expenditures of the period. **GASB 34** requires that all capital and infrastructure assets be reported on the government-wide financial statements. Capital assets, such as buildings and equipment, will be depreciated and that depreciation will be presented as an expense on the government-wide statement of activities. Infrastructure assets are, by their definition, long-lived assets that can be maintained for a much longer time than capital assets. Roads can be paved over, bridges can be repaired, and water and sewer systems can be maintained.

Because of the difficulty in determining any reasonable estimated useful life for the infrastructure assets, **GASB 34** provides for two methods to account for the depreciating attribute of these infrastructure assets.

    *a. Report estimated depreciation expense.* The first method requires governments to estimate depreciation expense and report that estimated expense on the government-wide statement of activities.

    *b. Modified approach.* The second approach allows governments to avoid the requirement to estimate depreciation expense on infrastructure assets that are part of a network or subsystem of a network as long as the government manages those assets using an asset management system and the government can document that the assets are preserved approximately at, or above, a condition level established by the government. Under the modified approach, the government entity annually expenses actual repair and renewal costs associated with the infrastructure assets. Additions and improvements are added to the cost basis of the infrastructure asset. Required footnote disclosures include: (1) an estimate of the amount required to maintain or preserve the infrastructure assets, along with the actual costs for each of the last five years, and (2) the presentation of condition assessments of the infrastructure assets for the last three years to show that these assets are indeed being maintained.

Many governments use the modified approach rather than the estimated depreciation expense method. Regardless of the method used for the depreciation element, the government must report the infrastructure assets in the asset section of the government-wide statement of net assets.

Note that Sol City distinguishes between its infrastructure assets and its buildings and equipment. Sol City has chosen to use the modified approach in recognizing the depreciating factors in its infrastructure assets. Thus, the depreciation expense reported on the statement of activities is only from the Depreciable Assets category, which includes items such as buildings and equipment. The asset, Internal Balances, represents interfund receivables/payables between the governmental activities and the business-type activities. In the Sol City example, the enterprise fund owes a total of $4,000 to other funds: $3,000 to the general fund for a loan, and $1,000 to the internal fund for supplies purchases. Note again that the internal fund is considered a governmental activity because the internal fund provides services and supplies only to other entities within the government's reporting entity.

The asset, Internal Balances, represents interfund receivables/payables between the primary government's funds comprising the governmental activities (governmental funds plus internal service funds) and the funds comprising the business-type activities (the enterprise funds). These internal balances cancel out each other for the total column. **GASB Statement No. 37,** "Basic Financial Statements—and Management's Discussion and Analysis—for State and Local Governments: Omnibus" (GASB 37), issued in 2001, eliminated the requirement for capitalizing construction-period interest on capital assets used in governmental activities. Thus, on the government-wide financial statements, this interest is now shown as an indirect expense of the period in which it is incurred.

    4. *Categories of net assets.* Net assets are separated into three categories, as follows:

      *a.* Invested in capital assets, net of related debt.

      *b.* Restricted (by external requirements of creditors, grantors, contributors, or other governmental entities).

      *c.* Unrestricted.

Note that restricted and unrestricted do not mean the same things as reserved and unreserved as used for the fund-based statements.

### Statement of Activities

The statement of activities for Sol City is presented in Figure 18–15. Important observations regarding this statement of activities follow:

    1. *Accrual basis.* The full accrual basis of accounting is used to measure revenues and expenses for the government-wide statements. A reconciliation between the modified accrual basis of accounting for the governmental funds and the accrual basis of the government-wide statements is required.

**FIGURE 18–15**  Government-wide Statement of Activities

| Functions/Programs | Expenses | Program Revenues | | | Net (Expenses) Revenue and Changes in Net Assets | | | |
| | | Charges for Services | Operating Grants and Contributions | Capital Grants and Contributions | Primary Government | | Total | Component Unit |
| | | | | | Governmental Activities | Business-Type Activities | | |
|---|---|---|---|---|---|---|---|---|
| **Primary Government** | | | | | | | | |
| Governmental Activities: | | | | | | | | |
| General Government | $212,000 | $ 4,000 | $23,000 | $20,000 | $ (165,000) | | $ (165,000) | |
| Streets and Highways | 71,000 | | | | (71,000) | | (71,000) | |
| Public Safety | 335,000 | | | | (335,000) | | (335,000) | |
| Sanitation | 141,000 | | | | (141,000) | | (141,000) | |
| Culture and Recreation | 54,000 | | | | (54,000) | | (54,000) | |
| Depreciation of Capital Assets | 120,000 | | | | (120,000) | | (120,000) | |
| Interest on Long-term Debt | 10,000 | | | | (10,000) | | (10,000) | |
| Total Government Activities | $943,000 | $ 4,000 | $23,000 | $20,000 | $ (896,000) | | $ (896,000) | |
| Business-Type Activities: | | | | | | | | |
| Water | $ 38,000 | $40,000 | | | | $ 2,000 | $ 2,000 | |
| Total Business-Type Activities | $ 38,000 | $40,000 | | | | $ 2,000 | $ 2,000 | |
| Total Primary Government | $981,000 | $44,000 | $23,000 | $20,000 | $ (896,000) | $ 2,000 | $ (894,000) | |
| Component Unit: | | | | | | | | |
| Library | $ 6,000 | $ -0- | | | | | | $ (6,000) |
| Total Component Unit | $ 6,000 | $ -0- | | | | | | $ (6,000) |
| General Revenues: | | | | | | | | |
| Taxes: | | | | | | | | |
| Property Taxes, Levied for General Purposes | | | | | $ 781,000 | | $1,035,000 | |
| Property Taxes, Levied for Special Purposes | | | | | 62,000 | | | |
| Property Taxes, Levied for Debt Service | | | | | 33,000 | | | |
| Sales Taxes | | | | | 32,000 | | | |
| Investment Earnings | | | | | 9,000 | | | |
| Miscellaneous Revenues | | | | | 18,000 | | | |
| Contribution | | | | | 100,000 | | | |
| Transfers between Governmental and Business-Type Funds | | | | | -0- | | | $ 12,000 |
| Total General Revenues, Special Items, and Transfers | | | | | $1,035,000 | | $1,035,000 | |
| Change in Net Assets | | | | | $ 139,000 | $ 2,000 | $ 141,000 | $ 6,000 |
| Net Assets—Beginning | | | | | 4,268,000 | 26,000 | 4,294,000 | 748,000 |
| Net Assets—Ending | | | | | $4,407,000 | $28,000 | $4,435,000 | $754,000 |

894

2. *Format.* The format of the statement of activities is based on the functions or programs of the government entity.

  a. Program revenues are categorized by type, and the net expenses (revenues) are shown separately for each of the governmental and business-type activities.

  b. The internal service fund is blended into the Governmental Activities because this fund provides service solely within the governmental entity.

  c. The enterprise funds are presented in the Business-Type Activities column because this fund includes resources obtained by user charges to the public.

  d. Fiduciary funds are not reported on the statement of activities because these funds are not available to be used for providing governmental services.

  e. Note that the component unit, the city library, is discretely presented in its own column.

3. *Expenses.* The expenses include depreciation of the capital assets and expenses for any infrastructure assets. However, the expenses would not include any expenditures in the governmental funds that were made for long-term capital assets. For government-wide statements, these expenditures must be included as increases to long-term capital assets on the balance sheet.

4. *General revenues.* General revenues are reported separately on the bottom of the statement. These are revenues that are not directly tied to any specific program. **GASB 34** requires that contributions to permanent endowments, special items, and extraordinary items be reported in this section for the government-wide statements. Special items are events within the control of management that are either unusual in nature or infrequent in occurrence. Sol City has no special or extraordinary items, and the only contribution to a permanent endowment was the $100,000 contribution received by the permanent fund. Note that the amount of ending net assets reported in this statement articulates with the amount of ending net assets presented on the statement of net assets.

## Reconciliation Schedules

**GASB 34** requires that two *reconciliation schedules* be presented to reconcile the net change in the total amounts reported on the governmental funds statements with the amounts reported on the government-wide statements. These reconciliation schedules may be presented as part of the governmental funds statements or in an accompanying schedule on the page immediately following the governmental fund financial statement it supports. The two required reconciliation schedules are as follows:

1. *Reconciliation schedule for Statement of Net Assets.* The first reconciliation schedule, the reconciliation between the fund balances reported for the governmental funds to the net assets for the government-wide financials, is presented in Figure 18–16. This schedule describes the adjustments necessary to move from the modified accrual basis used in the governmental funds to the accrual basis used for the government-wide statements. For example, the balance sheets of the government funds do not include infrastructure and capital assets. These costs are recognized as expenditures in the periods in which they are made. However, the government-wide statement of net assets must report the balance sheet date cost less depreciation of these infrastructure and capital assets. In addition, the government-wide statements must include the accounts of the internal service funds, which are separately reported from the governmental funds in the fund-based financial statements.

2. *Reconciliation schedule for Statement of Activities.* The second reconciliation schedule, the reconciliation between the net change in fund balances reported in the governmental funds' statement of revenues, expenditures, and changes in fund balance to the change in net assets reported in the government-wide financials, is presented in Figure 18–17. For example, interest revenue on the investment in bonds in the permanent fund was presented in that fund under the modified accrual basis for the amount of $8,000. However, under the accrual basis, the interest revenue would be computed based on the effective interest rate, with amortization of the discount, in the amount of $9,000

**FIGURE 18–16**
Reconciliation
Schedule for the
Statement of Net
Assets

| SOL CITY<br>Reconciliation of the Balance Sheet of<br>Governmental Funds to the Statement of Net Assets<br>December 31, 20X2 | |
| --- | --- |
| Fund balances reported in the governmental funds | $ 279,000 |
| Amounts reported for the governmental activities in the statement of net assets are different because: | |
| Capital assets used in governmental activities are not financial resources and therefore are not reported in the governmental funds. | 4,200,000 |
| Internal service funds are used by management to charge the costs of certain activities, such as centralized purchasing and storage functions, to individual funds. The assets and liabilities of the internal service fund are included in governmental activities in the statement of net assets. | 7,000 |
| Long-term liabilities, including bonds payable, are not due and payable in the current period and therefore are not reported in the funds. | (80,000) |
| Interest on bonds in the permanent fund is recognized in that fund under the modified accrual basis, but must be adjusted to the accrual basis for the government-wide financial statements. | 1,000 |
| Net assets of governmental activities | $4,407,000 |

($90,000 × .10). The difference of $1,000 is an adjustment both to the change in net assets and to the net assets.

## Budgetary Comparison Schedule

**GASB 34** requires that a *budgetary comparison schedule* be presented as required supplementary information for the general fund and for each special revenue fund that has a legally adopted annual budget. This schedule may be presented as a separate financial statement after the governmental funds financials or in the footnotes of the annual report. The budgetary comparison schedule for Sol City's general fund is presented in Figure 18–18.

**FIGURE 18–17**
Reconciliation
Schedule for the
Statement of Revenues,
Expenditures, and
Changes in Fund
Balances

| SOL CITY<br>Reconciliation of the Statement of Revenues, Expenditures, and Changes<br>in Fund Balances of Governmental Funds to the<br>Statement of Activities For the Year Ended December 31, 20X2 | |
| --- | --- |
| Net change in fund balances—governmental funds | $150,000 |
| Governmental funds report capital outlays as expenditures. However, in the statement of activities, the costs of those assets are capitalized and depreciated over their estimated useful lives. This is the amount by which capital outlays in the governmental funds ($182,000) exceeded depreciation of the governmental assets ($119,000). | 63,000 |
| Bond proceeds provide current financial resources for the governmental funds. However, the issuance of debt increases long-term liabilities in the statement of net assets. Repayment of debt principal is an expenditure in the governmental funds, but the repayment reduces the long-term liabilities in the statement of net assets. This is the amount by which bond proceeds ($102,000) exceeded the net repayments of principal ($20,000). | (82,000) |
| Revenues in the statement of activities are recorded on the accrual basis. Interest revenue in the governmental funds is recorded on the modified accrual basis. This is the amount that accrual interest exceeded the interest recognized in the permanent funds. | 1,000 |
| Internal service funds are used by management to charge the costs of certain services, such as a centralized purchasing function, to individual funds. The net revenue (expense) of the internal service funds is reported with governmental activities. | 7,000 |
| Change in net assets of governmental activities | $139,000 |

**FIGURE 18–18**   Budgetary Comparison Schedule

**SOL CITY**
**Budgetary Comparison Schedule**
**General Fund**
**For the Year Ended December 31, 20X2**

| | Budgeted Amount | | Actual Amounts (Budgetary Basis) | Variance with Final Budget Positive (Negative) |
|---|---|---|---|---|
| | Original | Final | | |
| Budgetary fund balance, January 1 | $ 129,000 | $129,000 | $ 129,000 | $      -0- |
| Resources (inflows): | | | | |
| Property taxes | 775,000 | 775,000 | 781,000 | 6,000 |
| Grants | 55,000 | 55,000 | 33,000 | (22,000) |
| Sales taxes | 25,000 | 25,000 | 32,000 | 7,000 |
| Miscellaneous | 20,000 | 20,000 | 18,000 | (2,000) |
| Amounts available for appropriation | $ 875,000 | $875,000 | $ 864,000 | $ (11,000) |
| Charges to appropriations (outflows): | | | | |
| General government | $ 200,000 | $200,000 | $ 206,000 | $   (6,000) |
| Streets and highways | 75,000 | 75,000 | 71,000 | 4,000 |
| Public safety | 400,000 | 400,000 | 393,000 | 7,000 |
| Sanitation | 150,000 | 150,000 | 141,000 | 9,000 |
| Nondepartmental: | | | | |
| Transfers out to other funds | 30,000 | 30,000 | 30,000 | -0- |
| Total charges to appropriations | $ 855,000 | $855,000 | $ 841,000 | $ 14,000 |
| Budgetary fund balance, December 31 | $ 149,000 | $149,000 | $ 152,000 | $   3,000 |

Important observations regarding the budgetary comparison schedule follow:

1. **GASB 34** requires that both the original budget and the final budget be presented. The original budget is the first budget for the fiscal period adopted by the government entity. Through the year, many government entities will modify the original budget because of new events or changes in expectations. These changes must go through the legislative process of the government, such as the city council. For our example, no changes were made to the formal budget during the year.

2. The budgetary comparison schedule should be presented on the same format with the same terminology and classifications as the original budget.

3. A separate column for the variance between the final budget and the actual amounts is encouraged but not required. It is presented here to provide a complete presentation of the possible disclosures of a governmental entity.

**GASB Statement No. 41,** "Budgetary Comparison Schedules—Perspective Differences" (GASB 41), amended **GASB 34** for state and local governments that have significantly different structures for budgetary purposes from the fund structures in **GASB 34.** These differences are termed perspective differences. A government with significant budgetary perspective differences such that the government cannot provide budgetary comparisons for the fund structure of the general fund and each special revenue fund is then required to present a budgetary comparison schedule in its required supplementary information based on the fund, program, or organizational structure that government uses for its legally adopted budget.

## Management's Discussion and Analysis

**GASB 34** specifies that the Management's Discussion and Analysis (MD&A) be included in the ***required supplementary information*** (RSI) of the government-wide financial statements. The MD&A is presented before the financial statements and provides an analytical overview of the government's financial and operating activities.

The MD&A discusses current-period operations and financial position and then compares those with the prior-periods. The purpose of this RSI item is to provide users of the financial statements an objective discussion of whether the government's financial position has improved or deteriorated during the year. **GASB 37** states that the MDA should be limited to the items specified in **GASB 34** rather than be used to present an abundance of other topics not specifically required. The GASB believes that additional discussions beyond those required might result in information that is not objective and cannot be directly analyzed. Governments that wish to provide additional information may do so in other supplementary information such as footnotes or transmittal letters.

## Notes to the Government-wide Financial Statements

**GASB Statement No. 34,** "Basic Financial Statements—and Management's Discussion and Analysis—for State and Local Governments" (GASB 34), specified a number of required note disclosures in the government-wide financial statements that include the following:

1. Accounting and measurement policies used in the primary governmental entity.
2. Information about capital assets, including beginning and ending balances, along with capital acquisitions and sales during the year; and depreciation expense and accumulated depreciation.
3. For collections not capitalized, disclosures describing the collection, along with the reasons for not capitalizing these collections.
4. Note disclosures about long-term liabilities include a schedule of the beginning and ending balances along with increases or decreases during the year, for each long-term debt item; the current portion of each long-term item; and the amount of annual debt service required.
5. Disclosures about donor-restricted endowments should include net increases in investments for which the income is available for expenditure, and the policy for spending investment income.
6. Segment information is to be provided for the enterprise funds included in the government-wide financial statements.

**GASB Statement No. 38,** "Certain Financial Statement Note Disclosures" (GASB 38), was issued in June 2001 and stated that the required footnotes should be modified for the following:

1. In the summary of significant accounting policies, provide descriptions of the activities accounted for in the major funds, internal service fund type, and fiduciary fund types. This change is a result of **GASB 34**'s focus on major funds rather than all funds.
2. Delete the requirement to disclose the accounting policy for encumbrances in the summary of significant accounting policies (i.e., the lapsing or nonlapsing method).
3. Disclose the period of availability used for recording revenues in governmental funds.
4. Disclose debt service requirements to maturity, separately identifying principal and interest for each of the subsequent five years and in five-year increments thereafter and changes in variable-rate debt. In addition, governments should disclose the future minimum payments for each of the five succeeding years for capital and noncancelable operating leases.
5. Provide a schedule of changes in short-term debt during the year along with the purposes for which the debt was issued.
6. Add a disclosure of actions taken to address any significant violations of finance-related legal or contractual provisions to the footnote describing these significant violations.
7. Disclose details of the payable and receivable amounts for interfund balances and the purposes of the interfund transfers. In addition, disclosures should be made regarding the amounts of interfund transfers during the period along with a description and amount of significant transfers that are not expected to occur on a routine basis.

8. Provide details of the components of accounts payable so that the financial statement users can understand the timeliness and payment priorities of payables.

9. Provide details about significant individual accounts when their nature is obscured by aggregation. For example, more disclosure could be made for receivables that contain a myriad of different credit risks or liquidity attributes.

## Other Financial Report Items

Governments may choose to provide additional information beyond that required as discussed previously. For example, some government entities present comprehensive annual financial reports (CAFRs), which include additional statistical information about the sources of revenues, property tax levies and property values, demographic statistics, and other miscellaneous statistics that management of the governmental entity believes will aid users of the financial report. Some governmental entities may additionally disclose financial statements for individual funds or combined by fund type. Some governments may go beyond the required footnote disclosures and provide additional schedules and information. As with commercial enterprises, it is up to the management of the governmental entity to determine how much additional disclosure it wishes to provide in its annual report.

## Interim Reporting

Governmental entities generally are not required to publish interim reports, although many prepare monthly or quarterly reports to determine the current progress of compliance with legal and budgetary limitations and to plan for changes in events or developments that were not foreseen when the annual budget was prepared. Interim reports are a valuable internal management control instrument; they typically are not made available to the general public.

## Auditing Governmental Entities

Most governmental entities are audited annually because of state or federal requirements or because long-term creditors demand audited statements as part of the debt agreements. The audit of a governmental entity is different from the audit of a commercial entity. The auditor not only must express an opinion on the fairness of the audited entity's financial statements in conformity with applicable accounting principles but also must assess the audited entity's compliance with legal or contractual provisions of state law, debt covenants, terms of grants from other governmental entities, and other restrictions on the governmental entity. The AICPA publishes the "State and Local Governments—Audit and Accounting Guide" that provides guidance relevant to audits of state and local governments. The guide includes planning the audit under the Risk Assessment Statements of Auditing Standards (SAS) in eight recent standards, number 104 through number 111. In addition, the guide defines internal control deficiencies for state and local governments.

The Single Audit Act of 1984 is a federal law specifying the audit requirements for all state and local governments receiving federal financial assistance. The audit act requires auditors to determine whether (1) the financial statements fairly present the government's financial condition, (2) the governmental entity has an internal control system to provide reasonable assurance that it is managing federal financial assistance programs in compliance with applicable laws and regulations, and (3) the governmental entity has complied with laws and regulations that may have a material effect on each federal program. The auditors issue not only the standard audit report but also special reports on items (2) and (3) above.

The Single Audit Act does not apply to all governmental entities receiving federal assistance. For fiscal years ending after December 31, 2003, governmental entities that expend $500,000 or more in federal awards in a year must have either a single or a program-specific audit for that year. A governmental entity is eligible for a program-specific audit only if the federal award is expended under a single federal program and that federal program's laws, regulations or grant agreements do not require the governmental entity to have a financial statement audit. Otherwise a single audit is required. Governmental entities that expend less that $500,000 in federal awards in a year are exempt from the single audit requirement for that year. However, their records must be available for review or audit by officials from the federal agency, the pass-through entity providing the award, or the Government Accountability Office (GAO).

# ADDITIONAL CONSIDERATIONS

## Special-Purpose Governmental Entities

The accounting and financial reporting standards for general-purpose governments such as states, counties, and municipalities are discussed in this chapter and Chapter 17. However, a number of governments are *special-purpose governments,* which are legally separate entities. They may be component units of a general-purpose government or stand-alone governments apart from a general-purpose government. Special-purpose governments include governmental entities such as cemetery districts, levee districts, park districts, tollway authorities, and school districts. Some of these special-purpose government entities may be engaged in governmental activities that generally are financed through taxes, intergovernmental revenues, and other nonexchange revenues. These activities are usually reported in governmental or internal service funds. Some of these entities are engaged in business-type activities that are financed by fees charged for goods or services. These activities are usually reported in enterprise funds. **GASB 34** establishes specific reporting requirements for each of the following types of special-purpose governments:

1. Engaged in more than one governmental program or in both governmental and business-type activities: These governmental entities must provide both fund financial statements and government-wide financial statements as presented earlier in this chapter and in Chapter 17.
2. Engaged in a single governmental program (such as cemetery districts or drainage districts): These governmental entities may present a simplified set of government-wide and fund-based financial statements, often combining these two statements.
3. Engaged in only business-type activities: These governmental entities must present only the financial statements required for enterprise funds. Many public universities and public hospitals will be included in this category.
4. Engaged in only fiduciary-type activities: These governmental entities are not required to present the government-wide financials but must provide only the financial statements required for fiduciary funds. This category includes special-purpose governments responsible for managing pension funds.

Regardless of the category of special-purpose government entity, all governments must include in their financial reports the Management's Discussion and Analysis, the footnotes, and any required supplementary information.

## Financial Reporting for Pensions and OPEB Plans

Most states and many local governments provide a variety of pensions and other postemployment benefits (OPEB) to their employees. OPEBs include postemployment health care, life insurance, and other nonpension benefits for persons after retirement from the governmental unit. The GASB has a series of standards that prescribe the employer's accounting for these costs and the financial reporting by the entity that maintains the plans. In some cases, the governmental unit administers its own plans, such as a state-based pension plan covering all state employees in a specific employment category, while in other cases the governmental unit uses a multi-employer plan, such as a firefighter's retirement plan that includes fire-fighters from a number of cities.

Two GASB statements present the accounting and financial reporting requirements for the entity that administers the plan's assets and for the employer of the employees covered by the plans. The first is **GASB Statement No. 25,** "Financial Reporting for

Defined Benefit Pension Plans and Note Disclosures for Defined Contribution Plans" (GASB 25), which established the financial reporting requirements for pension plans. For defined benefit plans, the payout to the retirees is based on work-related factors such as number of years worked and is not related to the amount in the plan. For defined contribution plans, the payout is based on the amount accumulated for each employee. Some plans are contributory, in which the employees must make contributions, and some plans are noncontributory, in which the employer makes all the contributions. The second standard is **GASB Statement No. 43,** "Financial Reporting for Postemployment Benefits Plans Other than Pension Plans" (GASB 43), which provided financial reporting standards for OPEB plans. The general principles in these two standards are similar. The entity that administers the plan must provide two categories of information in its financial reporting: *(a)* current financial information about plan assets and funding activities, and *(b)* information about the funded position of the plan and the plan's progress in accumulating sufficient financial resources to provide benefits when due. The two financial statements required for pension plans and other postemployment benefits plans are: *(a)* a statement of plan net assets that provides information about the fair value and composition of the plan's assets and information about the plan's liabilities; and *(b)* a statement of changes in plan net assets that provides information on the period's changes in the net assets of the plans. If a pension or OPEB plan is included within the reporting entity, that is, the governmental entity administers the plans, then the information for these two statements will be included with the other fiduciary funds in that fund's financial statements. The accrual method of accounting is required and informative footnotes must be provided.

### Employer Accounting for Pensions and OPEB Plan Benefits

Two GASB statements present the standards for the employer's measurement and display of accounting for the expenditures/expenses for the benefits and any related liabilities (or assets) for the difference between the expenditure/expenses recognition and the amount funded by the employer. The first is **GASB Statement No. 27,** "Accounting for Pensions by State and Local Governmental Employers" (GASB 27), which presents the standards for pensions. The second is **GASB Statement No. 45,** "Accounting and Financial Reporting by Employers for Postemployment Benefits Other than Pensions" (GASB 45). The general principles for measurement, recognition, and display in these two standards are similar. The accrual method of accounting is typically used for the government-wide financial statements to measure the expenses of the employer for pension costs for its employees and for the costs of other postemployment benefits for its employees. Actuarial assumptions are required under the accrual method. The state and local government employers must report the expense/expenditures and related liabilities (or assets) for both their pension benefits and for their OPEBs.

Although **GASB 27** and **GASB 45** have many of the same measurement and display standards, there are some differences due to the differences in the nature of the specific benefits given by the employer. Accountants responsible for accounting for these two sets of postemployment benefits readily acknowledge that some plans and benefits can be quite complex and require detailed study of the specific requirements in the related GASB statements.

**GASB Statement No. 50,** "Pension Disclosures—an amendment of GASB Statement No. 25 and No. 27" (GASB 50), requires additional disclosures for defined benefit plans and disclosures by the employers. The plans and the employers must present the following in their financial statements: *(a)* notes disclosing the funded status of the plan along with any actuarial methods and significant assumptions used to make the most recent actuarial valuation, *(b)* as RSI, a schedule of funding progress of defined benefit plans for which the annual required contribution of the employer is based on the aggregate actuarial cost method, *(c)* notes disclosing legal or contractual maximum contribution rates, and *(d)* notes disclosing changes in actuarial assumptions for successive years.

### Accounting for Termination Benefits

Finally, termination benefits are sometimes offered by governmental entities when an employee is involuntarily terminated (i.e., fired or laid off) or voluntarily terminates in order to accept early-retirement benefits. These termination benefits may include health care–related programs, job transition costs, early retirement incentives, and other similar types of items. The accounting and reporting requirements for these benefits are presented in **GASB Statement No. 47,** "Accounting for Termination Benefits" (GASB 47). In the case of employees who voluntarily terminate, the employer recognizes a liability and expense when the employee accepts the offer and the amount can be estimated. The general measurement principle is that the dollar amount recognized should be the discounted present value of the estimated future payments.

Governmental entities may develop a plan for a reduction in their work force that involves the involuntary termination of some employees. A liability and an expense should be recognized when the plan of termination is approved by the governing body, the plan has been communicated to the employees, and the amount can be estimated. For the government-wide financial statements, the accrual method is used to recognize the discounted present value of the estimated future payments.

Governmental entities have found that they must offer employees benefits similar to those offered in the private sector in order to attract and employ persons who would otherwise seek employment with business firms in the private sector. Thus, as the private sector changes what it offers employees, governmental entities will have to adjust what they offer to their employees.

## Summary of Key Concepts

This chapter completes the discussion of accounting and financial reporting principles used by local and state governments. Governments may use five governmental fund types, two proprietary fund types, and four fiduciary fund types (including agency funds). The governmental funds use the modified accrual basis of accounting; the other funds use the accrual basis of accounting.

The government reporting model is currently specified in **GASB 34.** Both fund-based financial statements and government-wide financial statements are required. The government-wide statements are based on the accrual basis and present both long-term capital assets, including infrastructure assets, and long-term debt. Government entities must include required supplementary information (RSI) in their annual financial reports as specified by **GASB 34.** This RSI includes reconciliation schedules and a budgetary comparison schedule. A proposed GASB statement specifies changes for fund balance reporting in the governmental fund types.

## Key Terms

agency funds, *888*
blended presentation, *890*
budgetary comparison schedule, *896*
capital projects funds, *866*
component units, *889*
comprehensive annual financial report, *890*
debt service funds, *869*

discrete presentation, *890*
enterprise funds, *877*
fund-based financial statements, *862*
government-wide financial statements, *891*
internal service funds, *883*
permanent funds, *872*
reconciliation schedules, *895*

reporting entity, *889*
required supplementary information (RSI), *897*
special revenue funds, *866*
special-purpose governments, *900*
trust funds, *886*

## Appendix 18A  Other Governmental Entities—Public School Systems and the Federal Government

In addition to local and state governmental entities, two other governmental entities—public schools and the federal government—have pervasive influences on the lives of citizens. This appendix presents a brief overview of the basic accounting and financial reporting requirements for these two governmental entities.

# PUBLIC SCHOOL SYSTEMS

In the United States today, more than 50 million students attend approximately 14,000 public elementary and secondary school systems employing about 2.5 million teachers and expending more than $100 billion annually. Many others attend one of the myriad of private schools formed by religious or other groups.

## Accounting and Financial Reporting for Public School Systems

Accounting for public schools is similar to accounting for local or state governments. The modified accrual basis of accounting is used for most funds, and the financial statements for a school district are similar to those of a local government. More than half of school district revenue is obtained from local property taxes; the remaining sources are fees for services, state education aid, and federal grants to education. Most school districts have an elected school board that serves as a public policy-making body for the school system.

The fund structure for a school district is similar to the fund structure for a local or state government. School district funds include the general fund, special revenue funds, capital projects funds, debt service funds, enterprise funds, internal service funds, and trust and agency funds.

The school district's general fund resources are expended for costs directly associated with the education process: teachers' salaries, books and supplies, and other costs. Special revenue funds may include specific funds for operations, building, and maintenance (OBM) of the physical facilities of the school district, as well as the transportation special revenue fund, which is responsible for acquiring and maintaining the buses for transporting children to and from the schools.

Public school systems have a public hearing on the annual budget, which is then approved by the school board or other governing body. The budget specifies the revenue from the three basic sources: local property taxes and fees, state school aid, and federal sources. The expenditures are broken down into the following three dimensions: *program,* such as gifted, vocational, elementary, secondary, and adult/continuing education; *function,* such as guidance counselors, instructional staff, school administration, and student transportation; and *object,* such as salaries, employee benefits, purchased services, and supplies and materials.

The department of education of each state receives the annual reports from that state's school districts. Typically these financial statements must be audited by independent auditors. Many school districts are legally separate, fiscally independent, special-purpose government entities engaged in both governmental and business-type activities. These school districts have their own legally mandated budget process and tax levy authority, and they do not depend financially on another government entity. In these cases, school districts present their financial statements in accordance with **GASB 34,** which requires government-wide financial statements as well as fund financial statements. **GASB 34** also requires management's discussion and analysis, footnotes, and required supplementary information. School districts that are fiscally dependent and component units of a primary government entity, such as the city government in which the school is located, present their financial information within the primary government's financial statements, usually discretely presented in a column separate from the financial data of the primary government. Other statements required are the same as for other governmental units. In addition, the comprehensive annual financial report for a school district includes a variety of other disclosures relevant to the school district, such as the cost per student, the debt capacity of the district, and the assessed valuation of all property included in the school district.

## Federal Government Accounting

An accounting structure for the federal government has been part of the U.S. statutes since 1789. The following individuals or entities have significant roles in the federal budgeting and expending process:

| Executive Branch | Legislative Branch |
| --- | --- |
| President | Congress |
| Office of Management and Budget (OMB) | Government Accountability Office (GAO) |
| Secretary of the Treasury | Congressional Budget Office (CBO) |
| Federal agencies | |

The fiscal period for the U.S. federal government is from October 1 to September 30 of the next calendar year. The President of the United States directs that the annual budget be prepared by the director of the Office of Management and Budget, who is a member of the president's staff. The director of the OMB then consults with the various federal agencies and the Secretary of the Treasury and prepares the budget that the president presents to Congress. The Congressional Budget Office then evaluates the executive budget and may propose that Congress present one of its own. After the legislative process runs its course and the budget is approved, Congress provides the authority for the executive branch to obtain revenue through taxation or other charges. The primary agency responsible for obtaining revenue is the Internal Revenue Service, which is an agency of the Department of the Treasury.

The appropriation-expenditure process is a little different for the federal government than for local government units. The federal budget provides the appropriation authority for the federal government. This appropriation authority is then allocated to the various agencies through a process of apportionments made by the Office of Management and Budget. The apportionment is then divided among the agency's programs and activities by a process of allotments. The agency then makes obligations by incurring costs for services provided. These obligations are then liquidated through the preparation of vouchers, which are submitted to the Department of the Treasury for payment.

The Federal Accounting Standards Advisory Board (FASAB) establishes the generally accepted accounting principles for federal financial reporting entities. In 1990, three federal government officials created the FASAB as a federal advisory committee. The three officials were the Secretary of the Treasury, the Director of the Office of Management and Budget, and the Comptroller General of the United States. The FASAB has issued over 30 statements and several technical releases establishing federal financial accounting standards. These standards are quite different from those for either profit-seeking entities (FASB) or state and local government entities (GASB) because of the many unique aspects of the federal government's operations.

The Department of Treasury annually issues the "Financial Report of the United States Government," which includes the auditor's report from the comptroller general of the United States. The financial report presents information on the federal government and its agencies, including a stewardship report and a statement of net cost by agency. The financial report is available on the Department of Treasury's Web site.

## Audits of Federal Agencies

The comptroller general of the United States is the head of the Government Accountability Office (GAO). The GAO is an agency of the legislative branch of the federal government and works with the Department of the Treasury, an executive department, to develop and maintain the federal government's accounting system. The GAO reviews the accounting systems of each executive agency each year from both a financial and a compliance perspective. The compliance part of the audit ensures that the agency fulfilled all legal and budgetary restrictions. Exceptions are reported to Congress, which then communicates them to the executive branch, thus completing the cycle that began when the executive branch first proposed the annual budget to Congress.

---

**Questions**

**Q18-1** In what circumstances would a governmental unit use a special revenue fund rather than a general fund?

**Q18-2** Which governmental funds use operating budgets? Which use capital budgets?

**Q18-3** How is interest on long-term debt accounted for in the debt service fund?

**Q18-4** What are the major differences between a special revenue fund and an enterprise fund?

**Q18-5** What is the basis of accounting in the proprietary funds? Why?

**Q18-6** What financial statements must be prepared for the governmental funds? For the enterprise funds?

**Q18-7** How are the proceeds from a bond issue accounted for in governmental funds? Where are these proceeds reported on the governmental funds' statement of revenues, expenditures, and changes in fund balance?

**Q18-8** What are the primary differences between a permanent fund (governmental) and a private-purpose trust fund (fiduciary)?

**Q18-9** Not all governmental funds need to be separately presented on the governmental funds financial statements. What are the two tests for determining major governmental funds for which separate disclosure is required?

**Q18-10**   How are contributions to governmental funds as well as special or extraordinary items reported on the governmental funds' statement of revenues, expenditures, and changes in fund balance?

**Q18-11**   Do agency funds have a net fund balance? Why or why not?

**Q18-12**   What are component units of a government, and how are these component units reported on the government-wide financial statements?

**Q18-13**   Reconciliation schedules are a required disclosure in the government-wide financial statements. What are the purpose and content of these reconciliation schedules?

**Q18-14**   GASB 34 requires a budgetary comparison schedule for each governmental fund that has a legally adopted budget. Briefly describe this budgetary comparison schedule.

**Q18-15**   How are infrastructure and other long-term assets as well as general long-term debt reported on the government-wide financial statements?

---

# Cases

### C18-1   Basis of Accounting and Reporting Issues

*Judgment*   The accounting system of Barb City is organized and operated on a fund basis. Among the types of funds used are a general fund, a special revenue fund, and an enterprise fund.

#### Required

*a.* Explain the basic differences in revenue recognition between the accrual basis of accounting and the modified accrual basis of accounting in relation to governmental accounting.

*b.* What basis of accounting should be used for each of the following funds: (1) general fund, (2) special revenue fund, and (3) enterprise fund?

### C18-2   Capital Projects, Debt Service, and Internal Service Funds

*Understanding*   The funds of Lake City include a debt service fund, a capital projects fund, and an internal service fund.

#### Required

*a.* Explain the use of capital projects funds. Include what they account for, the basis of accounting used, unusual entries and accounts, and their financial statements.

*b.* Explain the use of debt service funds. Include what they account for, the basis of accounting used, unusual entries and accounts, and their financial statements.

*c.* Explain the use of internal service funds. Include what they account for, the basis of accounting used, unusual entries and accounts, and their financial statements.

### C18-3   Discovery

This case provides learning opportunities using available databases and/or the Internet to obtain contemporary information about the topics in advanced financial accounting. Note that the Internet *Research* is dynamic and the specific Web site listed may change addresses. In that case, use a good search engine to locate the current address for the Web site.

#### Required

Access the Department of Treasury's Web site and scroll through until you locate the most recent "Financial Report of the United States Government" (http://fms.treas.gov/fr/index.html). Look over the report, especially the comptroller general's statement and the auditor's report, and then prepare a one- to two-page memo summarizing the major information items reported in the Financial Report of the United States Government.

### C18-4   Becoming Familiar with a Local Government's Comprehensive Annual Financial Report (CAFR)

*Analysis*   Using the Internet, find the comprehensive annual financial report (CAFR) of a local government selected by your instructor. At a minimum, a CAFR will include (1) management's discussion and analysis (MDA), (2) the basic financial statements—government-wide and fund-based financial statements, (3) notes to the basic financial statements, (4) other required supplementary information (RSI), and (5) the external auditor's opinion on the basic financial statements.

#### Required

Using the CAFR chosen by your instructor, answer the following questions that relate to the overall government and to the governmental funds:

a. Read the section of the report that contains management's discussion and analysis. Is your government a general purpose government? If yes, what types of services does your government provide?

b. What type of opinion was given by the external auditor on the basic financial statements? What responsibility did the auditor take with regard to MDA and the other RSI?

c. Examine the financial statements for the funds. List the fund types used by your government.

d. From reading the notes that follow the government-wide and fund-based financial statements, what is the measurement focus and basis of accounting used by the governmental funds?

e. List the financial statements of the government that use the economic resources measurement focus and the accrual basis of accounting.

f. In addition to the general fund, list your government's other major governmental and proprietary funds.

g. Examine the government-wide financial statements. List any component units over which your government has fiscal accountability.

h. Examine the balance sheet of the governmental funds. What are the total assets and the total fund balance as of the most recent balance sheet date? How much of the total fund balance is reserved?

i. Examine the statement of revenues, expenditures, and changes in fund balance for the most recent year. How much of the total revenue came from taxes?

j. Examine the statement of revenues, expenditures, and changes in fund balance for the most recent year. How are expenditures classified?

k. Examine the statement of revenues, expenditures, and changes in fund balance for the most recent year. How much of the other financing sources resulted from transfers in?

l. Examine the statement of revenues, expenditures, and changes in fund balance for the most recent year. List any special items reported. What was the increase or decrease in fund balance for the year?

### C18-5 The GASB's Decision-Making Process

The Statements of Governmental Accounting Standards are the final step in the GASB's decision-making process. Standard setting has a number of specific steps, with open and thorough study of the issues, and with public participation and input encouraged throughout the process.

#### Required

*Discovery*

Access the GASB's Web site at www.gasb.org; scroll down through the GASB Facts until reaching the Web page entitled "An Open Decision-Making Process." Then read through the process and prepare a one-page memorandum summarizing the steps the GASB takes before adopting a new governmental accounting standard.

### C18-6 Summarizing a Recent GASB Exposure Draft

The Governmental Accounting Standards Board places exposure drafts (EDs) of proposed future standards on its Web site. These exposure drafts provide an early view of the consensus viewpoints of the Board on a project. Accountants wishing to remain current in governmental accounting and auditing need to be aware of proposed governmental standards and their potential impacts on the accounting and reporting of the governmental entities with which the accountant is associated.

*Discovery*

#### Required

Access the GASB's Web site at www.gasb.org; locate the most recent exposure draft of a proposed Statement. Read through the Summary presented at the front of the exposure draft and then prepare a one-page memorandum on what issues the proposed Statement is addressing; why the GASB feels the proposed Statement is needed; and the key provisions of the proposed Statement. Toward the bottom of your memorandum, place the expected effective date of the proposed Statement and, if included in the ED, the proposed transition implementation from current standards to the new standard.

---

**Exercises**   **E18-1**   **Multiple-Choice Questions on Government Financial Reporting**

Select the correct answer for each of the following questions.

1. The government-wide financial statements use the:

   a. Economic resources measurement focus and the accrual basis of accounting.

   b. Current financial resources measurement focus and the accrual basis of accounting.

   *c.* Economic resources measurement focus and the modified accrual basis of accounting.

   *d.* Current financial resources measurement focus and the modified accrual basis of accounting.

2. The financial statements for the governmental funds use the:

   *a.* Economic resources measurement focus and the accrual basis of accounting.

   *b.* Current financial resources measurement focus and the accrual basis of accounting.

   *c.* Economic resources measurement focus and the modified accrual basis of accounting.

   *d.* Current financial resources measurement focus and the modified accrual basis of accounting.

3. According to GASB Statement No. 34, infrastructure fixed assets:

   *a.* Must be capitalized and depreciated.

   *b.* Must be capitalized but governments do *not* have to depreciate them.

   *c.* May be capitalized and depreciated.

   *d.* Must be reported using the modified approach.

4. On which of the following government-wide financial statements would you find all liabilities of a state or local government?

   *a.* Statement of net assets.

   *b.* Statement of financial condition.

   *c.* Statement of activities.

   *d.* Statement of financial position.

5. On which of the following financial statements would you find all of the capital assets of a local government?

   *a.* Statement of net assets.

   *b.* Statement of financial condition.

   *c.* Statement of activities.

   *d.* Statement of financial position.

6. For which fund category is a statement of cash flows prepared?

   *a.* Governmental.

   *b.* Proprietary.

   *c.* Fiduciary.

   *d.* None of the above.

*Note:* Use the information below to answer questions 7 through 9.

The Village of Hampton reported the following data for its governmental activities for the year ended June 30, 20X5:

| Item | Amount |
|------|--------|
| Cash and cash equivalents | $ 1,880,000 |
| Receivables | 459,000 |
| Capital assets | 14,250,000 |
| Accumulated depreciation | 1,750,000 |
| Accounts payable | 650,000 |
| Long-term liabilities | 5,350,000 |

Additional data:
   All of the long-term debt was used to acquire capital assets.
   Cash of $654,000 is restricted for debt service.

7. On the statement of net assets prepared at June 30, 20X5, what amount should be reported for total net assets?

   *a.* $8,839,000.

   *b.* $7,804,000.

   *c.* $7,150,000.

   *d.* $8,189,000.

8. On the statement of net assets prepared at June 30, 20X5, what amount should be reported for net assets, invested in capital assets net of related debt?

    *a.* $8,839,000.

    *b.* $7,804,000.

    *c.* $7,150,000.

    *d.* $8,189,000.

9. On the statement of net assets prepared at June 30, 20X5, what amount should be reported for net assets, unrestricted?

    *a.* $1,685,000.

    *b.* $1,689,000.

    *c.* $1,035,000.

    *d.* $1,031,000.

10. Which of the following funds can be major funds assuming the appropriate tests are met?

    *a.* The parking meter special revenue fund and the water utility enterprise fund.

    *b.* The fire station capital projects fund and a property tax agency fund.

    *c.* The fire station bonds debt service fund and the city teachers pension trust fund.

    *d.* The local symphony permanent fund and the Edwina Williams private-purpose trust fund.

11. Where in the basic financial statements would you find a description of the measurement focus and the basis of accounting used in the government-wide financial statements?

    *a.* In the statement of net assets.

    *b.* In the statement of activities.

    *c.* In management's discussion and analysis.

    *d.* In the notes to the financial statements.

12. Where in the financial section of a CAFR would you find an analysis of the balances and transactions of individual funds?

    *a.* In the government-wide financial statements.

    *b.* In the fund financial statements.

    *c.* In management's discussion and analysis.

    *d.* In the notes to the financial statements.

**E18-2**  **Multiple-Choice Questions on Governmental Funds [AICPA Adapted]**

Select the correct answer for each of the following questions.

1. On December 31, 20X1, Tiffin Township paid a contractor $2,000,000 for the total cost of a new firehouse built in 20X1 on township-owned land. Financing was by means of a $1,500,000 general obligation bond issue sold at face amount on December 31, 20X1, with the remaining $500,000 transferred from the general fund. What should be reported on Tiffin's financial statements for the capital projects fund?

    *a.* Revenue, $1,500,000; Expenditures, $1,500,000.

    *b.* Revenue, $1,500,000; Other Financing Sources, $500,000; Expenditures, $2,000,000.

    *c.* Revenue, $2,000,000; Expenditures, $2,000,000.

    *d.* Other Financing Sources, $2,000,000; Expenditures, $2,000,000.

2. A debt service fund of a municipality is an example of which of the following types of funds?

    *a.* Fiduciary.

    *b.* Governmental.

    *c.* Proprietary.

    *d.* Internal service.

3. Revenue of a special revenue fund of a governmental unit should be recognized in the period in which the:

    *a.* Revenue becomes available and measurable.

    *b.* Revenue becomes available for appropriation.

    *c.* Revenue is billable.

    *d.* Cash is received.

4. Taxes collected and held by a municipality for a school district would be accounted for in a(n):

    *a.* Enterprise fund.

    *b.* Intragovernmental (internal) service fund.

    *c.* Agency fund.

    *d.* Special revenue fund.

5. Interest expense on bonds payable should be recorded in a debt service fund:

    *a.* At the end of the fiscal period if the interest due date does not coincide with the end of the fiscal period.

    *b.* When bonds are issued.

    *c.* When legally payable.

    *d.* When paid.

6. Which of the following funds does *not* have a fund balance?

    *a.* General fund.

    *b.* Agency fund.

    *c.* Special revenue fund.

    *d.* Capital projects fund.

**E18-3**  **Multiple-Choice Questions on Proprietary Funds [AICPA Adapted]**

Select the correct answer for each of the following questions.

1. Which of the following accounts could be included in the statement of net assets of an enterprise fund?

    |  | Reserve for Encumbrances | Revenue Bonds Payable | Net Assets |
    |---|---|---|---|
    | *a.* | No | No | Yes |
    | *b.* | No | Yes | Yes |
    | *c.* | Yes | Yes | No |
    | *d.* | No | No | No |

2. Customers' meter deposits that cannot be spent for normal operating purposes would most likely be classified as restricted cash in the balance sheet of which fund?

    *a.* Internal service.

    *b.* Private-purpose trust.

    *c.* Agency.

    *d.* Enterprise.

3. Which fund is not an expendable fund?

    *a.* Capital projects.

    *b.* General.

    *c.* Special revenue.

    *d.* Internal service.

4. If a governmental unit established a data processing center to service all agencies within the unit, the data processing center should be accounted for as a(n):

    *a.* Capital projects fund.

    *b.* Internal service fund.

    *c.* Agency fund.

    *d.* Trust fund.

5. Recreational facilities run by a governmental unit and financed on a user-charge basis would be accounted for in which fund?

    *a.* General.

    *b.* Trust.

    *c.* Enterprise.

    *d.* Capital projects.

6. The Underwood Electric Utility Fund, which is an enterprise fund, had the following during its 20X1 fiscal year, ending at December 31, 20X1:

| | |
|---|---|
| Prepaid insurance paid in December 20X1 | $ 43,000 |
| Depreciation for 20X1 | 129,000 |

What amount should be reflected in the statement of revenues, expenses, and changes in fund net assets of the Underwood Electric Utility Fund for these items?

a. $(43,000).

b. $0.

c. $129,000.

d. $172,000.

7. Which of the following funds of a governmental unit uses the same basis of accounting as an enterprise fund?

a. Special revenue.

b. Internal service.

c. Permanent trust.

d. Capital projects.

8. Fixed assets utilized in a city-owned utility are accounted for in which of the following?

| | Enterprise Fund | General Fund |
|---|---|---|
| a. | No | No |
| b. | No | Yes |
| c. | Yes | No |
| d. | Yes | Yes |

9. Which of the following funds of a governmental unit would account for long-term debt in the accounts of the fund?

a. Special revenue.

b. Capital projects.

c. Internal service.

d. General.

### E18-4 Multiple-Choice Questions on Various Funds

Use the information below to answer questions 1 and 2:

On August 1, 20X6, the City of Rockhaven received $1,000,000 from a prominent citizen to establish a private-purpose trust fund. The donor stipulated that the cash be permanently invested and that the earnings from the investments be spent to support local artists. During the year ended June 30, 20X7, $50,000 of dividends were received from stock investments and $35,000 of interest was earned from bond investments. At June 30, $5,000 of the interest earned was not yet received. During the year ended June 30, 20X7, $75,000 was spent by the trust fund to support local artists.

1. For the year ended June 30, 20X7, the trust fund should report investment earnings of:

a. $80,000.

b. $50,000.

c. $85,000.

d. $35,000.

2. For the year ended June 30, 20X7, the trust fund should report the $75,000 spent to support local artists as a(n):

a. Deduction.

b. Contra contribution.

c. Transfer out.

d. Direct adjustment from fund balance.

3. Which of the following statements is (are) correct about agency funds?

I. Agency funds should report investment earnings only when they are both measurable and available.

II. Agency funds are reported on the proprietary funds' statement of cash flows.

   *a.* I only.

   *b.* II only.

   *c.* I and II.

   *d.* Neither I nor II.

*Note:* Use the following information to answer questions 4 through 8.

On July 2, 20X6, the Village of Westbury established an internal service fund to service the data processing needs of the other village departments. The internal service fund received a transfer of $600,000 from the general fund and a $100,000 long-term advance from the water utility enterprise fund to acquire computer equipment. During July of 20X6, computer equipment costing $650,000 was acquired. The following events occurred during the year ended June 30, 20X7:

| | |
|---|---|
| Charges for services to other departments for data processing services rendered | $100,000 |
| Operating expenses (exclusive of depreciation expense) | 45,000 |
| Depreciation expense | 40,000 |
| Interest expense on the advance | 5,000 |

At June 30, 20X7, all but $7,000 of the billings were collected, and all operating expenses and the interest expense were paid except for $3,000 of operating expenses.

4. For the year ended June 30, 20X7, what was the income of Westbury's internal service fund?

   *a.* $13,000.

   *b.* $6,000.

   *c.* $3,000.

   *d.* $10,000.

5. At June 30, 20X7, what total assets amount would appear on the internal service fund balance sheet?

   *a.* $700,000.

   *b.* $710,000.

   *c.* $713,000.

   *d.* $708,000.

6. Assume that the mayor's office and the police department were billed $55,000 for data processing work during the year ended June 30, 20X7. What account should be debited in the general fund to record these billings?

   *a.* Other Financing Use—Transfers Out.

   *b.* Expenditures.

   *c.* Due to Internal Service Fund.

   *d.* Operating Expenses.

7. Assume that the water utility, an enterprise fund, was billed $25,000 for data processing work during the year ended June 30, 20X7. What account should be debited in the enterprise fund to record these billings?

   *a.* Operating expenses.

   *b.* Other Financing Use—Transfers Out.

   *c.* Expenditures.

   *d.* Due to Internal Service Fund.

8. Assume that the income for Westbury's internal service fund was $10,000 for the year ended June 30, 20X7. What net assets should be reported on the internal service fund's statement of net assets at June 30, 20X7?

   *a.* $713,000.

   *b.* $610,000.

   *c.* $710,000.

   *d.* $613,000.

**E18-5**   **Multiple-Choice Questions on Financial Reporting Issues for Government-wide and Fund-Based Financial Statements**

Select the correct answer for each of the following questions.

1. Which of the following statements is correct?

   I. In the government-wide financial statements, internal service fund activities are reported in the governmental activities column.

   II. The total fund balance for the governmental funds that is reported on the governmental funds balance sheet will not equal the total net assets of governmental activities that is reported on the government-wide statement of net assets.

   a. I only.

   b. II only.

   c. I and II.

   d. Neither I nor II.

2. For the year ended June 30, 20X5, the internal service funds of Stanton Township reported an increase in net assets of $300,000 and ending net assets at June 30, 20X5, of $4,500,000. On the reconciliation of the balance sheet of the governmental funds to the statement of net assets as of June 30, 20X5, what amount should be added?

   a. $300,000.

   b. $4,200,000.

   c. $4,500,000.

   d. $4,800,000.

3. For the year ended June 30, 20X5, the enterprise funds of Stanton Township reported an increase in net assets of $300,000 and ending net assets at June 30, 20X5, of $4,500,000. The enterprise fund also reported net assets—unrestricted of $1,200,000 at June 30, 20X5, on its statement of net assets. On the reconciliation of the balance sheet of the governmental funds to the statement of net assets as of June 30, 20X5, what amount should be added?

   a. $4,200,000.

   b. $5,700,000.

   c. $4,800,000.

   d. $0.

4. Which of the following is true regarding permanent funds?

   a. Permanent funds use modified accrual accounting.

   b. The principal of permanent funds cannot be expended.

   c. Dividend and interest income from permanent fund investments are used to benefit the government and its citizens.

   d. All of the above.

*Note:* Use the information below to answer questions 5 through 7.

A water and sewer enterprise fund provided you with the following information for the year ended June 30, 20X5:

| | |
|---|---:|
| Customer receipts | $ 500,000 |
| Dividends received from investments in common and preferred stock | 25,000 |
| Proceeds from issuance of revenue bonds (used for plant construction) | 1,000,000 |
| Proceeds of short-term notes (used to pay operating expenses) | 30,000 |
| Capital grant received from state (used for wastewater plant addition) | 300,000 |
| Paid interest on revenue bonds | 40,000 |
| Paid interest on short-term notes | 1,000 |
| Proceeds received from sale of Dell common stock | 20,000 |
| Acquired investments in corporate bonds | 8,000 |
| Made capital expenditures | 600,000 |
| Operating expenses paid | 350,000 |
| Depreciation expense for period | 50,000 |

Answer the following questions about the amounts reported on the statement of cash flows for the water and sewer enterprise fund.

5. What amount should be reported for cash flows provided by operating activities?

   a. $150,000.

   b. $175,000.

   c. $134,000.

   d. $100,000.

6. What amount should be reported for cash flows provided by investing activities?

   a. $12,000.

   b. $45,000.

   c. $17,000.

   d. $37,000.

7. What amount should be reported for cash flows provided by capital and related financing activities?

   a. $700,000.

   b. $360,000.

   c. $660,000.

   d. $400,000.

8. Mary Smith donated cash of $1,000,000 to Elizabeth City with the stipulation that the contribution be invested and that earnings from the investment be spent for salaries for the City's symphony orchestra. The contribution was received on June 30, 20X4, and the cash received was invested in bonds on July 1, 20X4. The bonds were acquired at face value and pay interest at 6 percent on January 1 and July 1. At June 30, 20X5, the fair value of the bonds was $995,000. During the year ended June 30, 20X5, $20,000 was provided to the symphony orchestra to help pay salaries. On the statement of fiduciary net assets at June 30, 20X5, what would be the amount reported for net assets held in trust for the symphony orchestra?

   a. $1,060,000.

   b. $1,055,000.

   c. $1,025,000.

   d. $1,035,000.

### E18-6 Capital Projects Fund Entries and Statement

The City of Waterman established a capital projects fund for the construction of a ramp for handicapped access from the parking garage to the city's office building. The estimated cost of the ramp is $200,000. On January 1, 20X2, a 10 percent, $150,000 bond issue was sold at 104.0 with the premium transferred to the debt service fund. At that date, the county board provided a $50,000 grant. After a period of negotiation, the city council awarded a construction contract for $182,000 on April 5, 20X2. The ramp was completed on August 8, 20X2; its actual cost was $189,000. The city council approved payment of the total actual cost of $189,000. In addition to the $189,000, the ramp was carpeted with all-weather material at a cost of $5,500. On November 3, 20X2, the city council gave the final approval to pay for the ramp and the carpeting. After all bills were paid, the remaining fund balance was transferred to the debt service fund.

#### Required

a. Prepare entries for the capital projects fund for 20X2.

b. Prepare a statement of revenues, expenditures, and changes in fund balance for 20X2 for the capital projects fund.

### E18-7 Debt Service Fund Entries and Statement

The City of Waterman established a debt service fund to account for the financial resources used to service the bonds issued to finance the ramp (see Exercise 18-6). The 10 percent, $150,000 bond issue was sold at 104.0 on January 1, 20X2. It is a 10-year serial bond issue. The resources to pay the interest and annual principal will be from a property tax levy.

#### Additional Information

1. The operating budget for 20X2 included estimated revenue of $35,000. Budgeted appropriations included $15,000 for principal, $15,000 for interest, and $4,000 for other items. The budget also included an estimated transfer in of $5,000 from the capital projects fund.

2. The property tax levy was for $40,000 and an allowance for uncollectibles of $4,000 was established. Collections totaled $35,000. The remaining taxes were reclassified as delinquent and the allowance was reduced to $1,000. The bond premium was received from the capital projects fund.

3. The current portion of the serial bonds and the interest due this year were recorded and paid. Other expenses charged to the debt service fund totaled $1,700 of which $1,200 was paid.

4. The nominal accounts were closed.

### Required

*a.* Prepare entries for the debt service fund for 20X2.

*b.* Prepare a balance sheet as of December 31, 20X2, for the debt service fund.

*c.* Prepare a statement of revenues, expenditures, and changes in fund balance for 20X2 for the debt service fund.

### E18-8    Enterprise Fund Entries and Statements

Augusta has a municipal water and gas utility district (MUD). The trial balance on January 1, 20X1, was as follows:

| | Debit | Credit |
|---|---|---|
| Cash | $ 92,000 | |
| Accounts Receivable | 25,000 | |
| Inventory of Supplies | 8,000 | |
| Land | 120,000 | |
| Plant and Equipment | 480,000 | |
| Accumulated Depreciation | | $ 80,000 |
| Vouchers Payable | | 15,000 |
| Bonds Payable, 6% | | 500,000 |
| Net Assets: | | |
| Invested in Capital Assets, Net of Related Debt | | 20,000 |
| Unrestricted | | 110,000 |
| Total | $725,000 | $725,000 |

### Additional Information for 20X1

1. Charges to customers for water and gas were $420,000; collections were $432,000.
2. A loan of $30,000 for two years was received from the general fund.
3. The water and gas lines were extended to a new development at a cost of $75,000. The contractor was paid.
4. Supplies were acquired from central stores (internal service fund) for $12,400. Operating expenses were $328,000, and interest expense was $30,000. Payment was made for the interest and the payable to central stores, and $325,000 of the vouchers were paid.
5. Adjusting entries were as follows: for estimated uncollectible accounts receivable, $6,300; depreciation expense, $32,000; supplies expense, $15,200.

### Required

*a.* Prepare entries for the MUD enterprise fund for 20X1, and prepare closing entries.

*b.* Prepare a statement of net assets for the fund for December 31, 20X1.

*c.* Prepare a statement of revenues, expenses, and changes in fund net assets for 20X1. Assume that the $500,000 of the 6 percent bonds is related to the net capital assets of land and of plant and equipment.

*d.* Prepare a statement of cash flows for 20X1.

### E18-9    Interfund Transfers and Transactions

During 20X8, the following transfers and transactions between funds took place in the City of Matthew.

1. A $12,000 transfer was made on March 1 from the general fund to establish a building maintenance internal service fund. Matthew uses transfer accounts to account for this type of transfer.
2. On April 1, the general fund made an $8,000, six-month loan to the building maintenance service fund.
3. On April 15, $2,400 was transferred from the general fund to the debt service fund to pay interest.
4. On May 5, the Matthew transportation service fund billed the general fund $825 for April services.

### Required

a. Prepare journal entries for the general fund and the other fund involved that should be recorded at the time of each transfer or transaction.

b. For each transfer or transaction, prepare the appropriate closing entries for the general fund and the other fund involved for the year ended June 30, 20X8.

**E18-10  Internal Service Fund Entries and Statements**

Bellevue City's printing shop had the following trial balance on January 1, 20X2:

|  | Debit | Credit |
|---|---|---|
| Cash | $ 24,600 | |
| Due from Other Funds | 15,600 | |
| Inventory of Supplies | 9,800 | |
| Furniture and Equipment | 260,000 | |
| Accumulated Depreciation | | $ 50,000 |
| Vouchers Payable | | 12,000 |
| Net Assets: | | |
|    Invested in Capital Assets | | |
|     (no related debt) | | 210,000 |
|    Unrestricted | | 38,000 |
| Total | $310,000 | $310,000 |

### Additional Information for 20X2

1. During 20X2, the printing shop acquired supplies for $96,000, furniture for $1,500, and a copier for $3,200.
2. Printing jobs billed to other funds amounted to $292,000; cash received from other funds, $287,300; costs of printing jobs, $204,000, including $84,000 of supplies; operating expenses, $38,000, including $8,400 of supplies; depreciation expense, $23,000; and vouchers paid, $243,000.

### Required

a. Prepare entries for the printing shop for 20X2, including closing entries.

b. Prepare a statement of net assets for the fund on December 31, 20X2. No debt is related to the year-end amount of the fund's capital assets.

c. Prepare a statement of revenues, expenses, and changes in fund net assets for 20X2.

d. Prepare a statement of cash flows for 20X2.

**E18-11  Multiple-Choice Questions on Government-wide Financial Statements**

*Note:* Items 1 and 2 are based on the following:

Mountain View City is preparing its government-wide financial statements for the year. As of the year end, the city has determined the following information for its capital assets, exclusive of its infrastructure assets:

| | |
|---|---|
| Cost of capital assets acquired by governmental funds | $1,450,000 |
| Accumulated depreciation on the capital assets | 120,000 |
| Outstanding debt related to the capital assets | 780,000 |

1. On the government-wide statement of net assets for the year-end, what amount should be reported for capital assets in the Governmental Activities column?

   a. $550,000.

   b. $780,000.

   c. $1,330,000.

   d. $1,450,000.

2. On the government-wide statement of net assets for the year-end, what amount should be reported in the net assets section for the capital assets?

   a. $550,000.

   b. $780,000.

   c. $1,330,000.

   d. $1,450,000.

3. In accordance with GASB 34, "Basic Financial Statements—and Management's Discussion and Analysis—for State and Local Governments," which of the following statements is correct regarding the reporting of internal service funds?

   I. The internal service fund should be discretely presented as part of the business-type activities of the government.

   II. The internal service fund should be blended into the governmental activities.

   a. I only.

   b. II only.

   c. I and II.

   d. Neither I nor II.

*Note:* Items 4 and 5 are based on the following:

During the year, the City of Vero Beach sold bonds in its capital projects fund. The 6 percent, $500,000 par bonds were sold for 102. The effective interest rate was 5 percent.

4. How should the bonds be reported in the reconciliation schedule for the statement of revenues, expenditures, and changes in fund balance?

   a. A decrease of $500,000 for the par value of the bonds.

   b. A decrease of $30,000 for the interest paid on the bonds.

   c. A decrease of $510,000 for the selling price of the bonds.

   d. Not shown in this reconciliation schedule.

5. How should an interest adjustment be shown in the reconciliation of the balance sheet of governmental funds to the statement of net assets for the year?

   a. A decrease of $30,000.

   b. A decrease of $25,000.

   c. A decrease of $5,000.

   d. Not shown in this reconciliation schedule.

6. For which of the following should the accrual basis of accounting be used to measure financial performance?

   |  | General Fund | Internal Service Fund | Government-wide Financial Statements |
   |---|---|---|---|
   | a. | Yes | Yes | Yes |
   | b. | Yes | No | Yes |
   | c. | No | No | No |
   | d. | No | Yes | Yes |

7. The City of Hastings has a separately elected school board that administers the city's schools. The city council must approve the school district's budget and tax levy. The school district's financial results should be reported in Hastings's financial statements in which way?

   a. Included only as schedules in the footnotes of Hastings's financial reports.

   b. Blended into Hastings's financial reports.

   *c.* Discretely presented in Hastings's financial reports.

   *d.* Not required to be presented in Hastings's financial reports.

8. Glen Valley City has properly adopted the modified approach to account for its infrastructure assets. Which of the following statements is correct about accounting for these infrastructure assets on the government-wide statement of activities?

   I. Depreciation expense should be computed based on the assets' estimated useful lives and reported under the governmental activities column of the city's statement of activities.

   II. The amount of the expenditures made for the infrastructure assets, except for additions and improvements, should be expensed in the period incurred.

   *a.* I only.

   *b.* II only.

   *c.* I and II.

   *d.* Neither I nor II.

9. A statement of cash flows is required for

| | General Fund | Enterprise Fund | Government-wide Entity |
|---|---|---|---|
| *a.* | Yes | Yes | Yes |
| *b.* | No | Yes | Yes |
| *c.* | No | Yes | No |
| *d.* | Yes | No | No |

10. Which of the following is reported as a restriction of net assets in the net assets section of the statement of net assets?

   *a.* A reservation of the fund balance in the general fund for $10,000 of encumbrances.

   *b.* A requirement in the permanent funds that the $100,000 principal of a bequest be maintained.

   *c.* A governing board decision that $15,000 of general fund resources should be reserved for planning for a city park.

   *d.* A governing board allocation of $4,000 to establish an internal services fund.

## Problems

### P18-12   Adjusting Entries for General Fund [AICPA Adapted]

On June 30, 20X2, the end of the fiscal year, the Wadsworth Park District prepared the following trial balance for the general fund:

| | Debit | Credit |
|---|---|---|
| Cash | $    47,250 | |
| Taxes Receivable—Current | 31,800 | |
| Allowance for Uncollectibles—Current | | $     1,800 |
| Temporary Investments | 11,300 | |
| Inventory of Supplies | 11,450 | |
| Buildings | 1,300,000 | |
| Estimated Revenues Control | 1,007,000 | |
| Appropriations Control | | 1,000,000 |
| Revenue—State Grants | | 300,000 |
| Bonds Payable | | 1,000,000 |
| Vouchers Payable | | 10,200 |
| Expenditures | 848,200 | |
| Debt Service from Current Funds | 130,000 | |
| Capital Outlays (Equipment) | 22,000 | |
| Revenue—Taxes | | 1,008,200 |
| Fund Balance—Unreserved | | 81,800 |
| Budgetary Fund Balance—Unreserved | | 7,000 |
| Total | $3,409,000 | $3,409,000 |

An examination of the records disclosed the following information:

1. The recorded estimate of losses for the current year taxes receivable was considered to be adequate.

2. The local governmental unit gave the park district 20 acres of land to be used for a new community park. The unrecorded estimated value of the land was $50,000. In addition, a state grant of $300,000 was received, and the full amount was used in payment of contracts pertaining to the construction of the park buildings. Purchases of playground equipment costing $22,000 were paid from general funds.

3. Five years ago, a 4 percent, 10-year sinking fund bond issue in the amount of $1,000,000 for constructing park buildings was sold; it is still outstanding. Interest on the issue is payable at maturity. Budgetary requirements of a contribution of $130,000 to the debt service fund were met. Of this amount, $100,000 represents the fifth equal contribution for principal repayment.

4. Outstanding purchase orders not recorded in the accounts at year-end totaled $2,800.

5. A physical inventory of supplies at year-end revealed $6,500 of the supplies on hand.

6. Except where indicated to the contrary, all recordings were made in the general fund.

### Required

Prepare the adjusting entries to correct the general fund records.

**P18-13** **Entries for Funds [AICPA Adapted]**

Olivia Village was recently incorporated and began financial operations on July 1, 20X2, the beginning of its fiscal year. The following transactions occurred during this first fiscal year, July 1, 20X2, to June 30, 20X3:

1. The village council adopted a budget for general operations for the fiscal year ending June 30, 20X3. Revenue was estimated at $400,000. Legal authorizations for budgeted expenditures totaled $394,000.

2. Property taxes were levied in the amount of $390,000; 2 percent of this amount was estimated to prove uncollectible. These taxes are available as of the date of levy to finance current expenditures.

3. During the year, a village resident donated marketable securities valued at $50,000 to the village under the terms of a trust agreement. Those terms stipulated that the principal amount be kept intact. The use of revenue generated by the securities is restricted to financing college scholarships for needy students. Revenue earned and received on these marketable securities amounted to $5,500 through June 30, 20X3.

4. A general fund transfer of $5,000 was made to establish an internal service fund to provide for a permanent investment in inventory.

5. The village decided to install lighting in the village park through a special assessment project authorized to do so at a cost of $75,000. The city is obligated if the property owners default on their special assessments. Special assessment bonds were issued in the amount of $72,000, and the first year's special assessment of $24,000 was levied against the village's property owners. The remaining $3,000 for the project will be contributed from the village's general fund.

6. The special assessments for the lighting project are due over a three-year period, and the first year's assessments of $24,000 were collected. The $3,000 transfer from the village's general fund was received by the lighting capital projects fund.

7. A contract for $75,000 was let for the installation of the lighting. The capital projects fund was encumbered for the contract. On June 30, 20X3, the contract was completed and the contractor was paid.

8. During the year, the internal service fund purchased various supplies at a cost of $1,900.

9. Cash collections recorded by the general fund during the year were as follows:

| | |
|---|---|
| Current property taxes | $386,000 |
| Licenses and permit fees | 7,000 |

The allowance for estimated uncollectible taxes is adjusted to $4,000.

10. The village council decided to build a village hall at an estimated cost of $500,000 to replace space occupied in rented facilities. The village does not record project authorizations. It was

decided that general obligation bonds bearing interest at 6 percent would be issued. On June 30, 20X3, the bonds were issued at face value of $500,000, payable in 20 years. No contracts have been signed for this project, and no expenditures have been made, nor has an annual operating budget been prepared.

11. A fire truck was purchased for $15,000 and the voucher was approved and paid by the general fund. This expenditure was previously encumbered for $15,000.

### Required

Prepare journal entries to record properly each of these transactions in the appropriate fund or funds of Olivia Village for the fiscal year ended June 30, 20X3.

Use the following funds: general fund, capital projects fund, internal service fund, and private-purpose trust fund. Each journal entry should be numbered to correspond to the transactions. Do not prepare closing entries for any fund. Your answer sheet should be organized using the following format:

| Fund | Journal Entry |
| --- | --- |

**P18-14** **Entries to Adjust Account Balances [AICPA Adapted]**

You have been assigned by the town of Papillion to examine its June 30, 20X1, balance sheet. You are the first CPA to be engaged by the town, and you find that acceptable methods of municipal accounting have not been employed. The town clerk stated that the books had not been closed and presented the following preclosing trial balance of the general fund as of June 30, 20X1:

| | Debit | Credit |
| --- | --- | --- |
| Cash | $150,000 | |
| Taxes Receivable—Current Year | 59,200 | |
| Allowance for Uncollectibles—Current | | $ 18,000 |
| Taxes Receivable—Delinquent | 8,000 | |
| Allowance for Uncollectibles—Delinquent | | 10,200 |
| Estimated Revenues Control | 310,000 | |
| Appropriations Control | | 348,000 |
| Donated Land | 27,000 | |
| Expenditures—Building Addition Constructed | 50,000 | |
| Expenditures—Serial Bonds Paid | 16,000 | |
| Other Expenditures | 280,000 | |
| Special Assessment Bonds Payable | | 100,000 |
| Revenue | | 354,000 |
| Accounts Payable | | 26,000 |
| Fund Balance—Unreserved | | 82,000 |
| Budgetary Fund Balance—Unreserved | 38,000 | |
| Total | $938,200 | $938,200 |

### Additional Information

1. The estimated losses of $18,000 for current-year taxes receivable were determined to be a reasonable estimate. The delinquent taxes allowance account should be adjusted to $8,000, the amount of the remaining delinquent taxes.

2. Included in the Revenue account is a credit of $27,000, representing the value of land donated by the state as a grant-in-aid for construction of a municipal park.

3. Operating supplies ordered in the prior fiscal year and chargeable to that year were received, recorded, and consumed in July 20X0. The outstanding purchase orders for these supplies, which were not recorded in the accounts on June 30, 20X0, amounted to $8,800. The vendors' invoices for these supplies totaled $9,400. Appropriations lapse one year after the end of the fiscal year for which they are made.

4. Outstanding purchase orders on June 30, 20X1, for operating supplies totaled $2,100. These purchase orders were not recorded on the books.

5. The special assessment bonds were sold in June 20X1 to finance a street-paving project. No contracts have been signed for this project, and no expenditures have been made from the capital projects fund. The city is obligated for the bonds if the property owners default.

6. The balance in the Revenue account includes credits for $20,000 for a note issued to a bank to obtain cash in anticipation of tax collections and for $1,000 for the sale of scrap iron from the town's water plant. The note was still outstanding on June 30, 20X1. The operations of the water plant are accounted for in the water fund.

7. The Expenditures—Building Addition Constructed account balance is the cost of an addition to the town hall building. This addition was constructed and completed in June 20X1. The general fund recorded the payment as authorized.

8. The Expenditures—Serial Bonds Paid account reflects the annual retirement of general obligation bonds issued to finance the construction of the town hall. Interest payments of $7,000 for the bond issue are included in other expenditures.

### Required

*a.* Prepare the formal adjusting and closing journal entries for the general fund for the fiscal year ended June 30, 20X1.

*b.* The preceding information disclosed by your examination was recorded only in the general fund even though other funds were involved. Prepare the formal adjusting journal entries for any other funds involved.

**P18-15** **Capital Projects Fund Entries and Statements**

During the fiscal year ended June 30, 20X3, West City Council authorizes construction of a new city hall building and the sale of serial bonds to finance the construction. The following transactions, related to financing and constructing the city hall, occur during fiscal 20X3:

1. On August 1, 20X2, West issues $5,000,000 of serial bonds for $5,080,000. Interest is payable annually, and the first retirement of $500,000 is due on July 31, 20X7. The premium is transferred to the debt service fund.

2. The old city hall, which had a recorded cost of $650,000, is torn down. The cost of razing the old building is $45,000, net of salvage value. This cost was included in the capital budget but was not encumbered. The cost is vouchered and paid.

3. West signs a contract with Roth Construction Company to build the city hall for $4,500,000. The contract cost is to be encumbered. Construction is to be completed during fiscal 20X4.

4. Roth Construction Company bills West $2,000,000 for construction completed during fiscal 20X3. Ten percent of the billings will be retained until final acceptance of the new city hall. The billing less the retainage was paid during the fiscal year.

### Required

*a.* For each of these transactions, prepare the necessary journal entries for all the funds involved. Indicate the fund in which the entry is made by giving its initials in the left margin: CPF (capital projects fund) or DSF (debt service fund). Give the closing entries for the capital projects fund.

*b.* Prepare a balance sheet for the capital projects fund at June 30, 20X3.

*c.* Prepare a statement of revenues, expenditures, and changes in fund balance for the capital projects fund for the fiscal year ended June 30, 20X3.

**P18-16** **Recording Entries in Various Funds [AICPA Adapted]**

The following information relates to Vane City during the year ended December 31, 20X8:

1. On October 31, 20X8, to finance the construction of a city hall annex, Vane issued 8 percent, 10-year general obligation bonds at their face value of $800,000. A contractor's bid of $750,000 was accepted for the construction of the annex. By year-end, one-third of the contract was completed at a cost of $246,000, all of which was paid on January 5, 20X9.

2. Vane collected $109,000 from hotel room taxes, restricted for tourist promotion, in a special revenue fund. The fund incurred and paid $81,000 for general promotions and $22,000

for a motor vehicle. Estimated revenues for 20X8 were $112,000, while appropriations were expected to be $108,000.

3. General fund revenues of $313,500 for 20X8 were transferred to a debt service fund and used to repay $300,000 of 9 percent, 15-year term bonds, which matured in 20X8, and to repay $13,500 of matured interest. The bond proceeds were used to construct a citizens' center.

4. At December 31, 20X8, Vane was responsible for $83,000 of outstanding encumbrances in its general fund. The city uses the nonlapsing method to account for its outstanding encumbrances.

5. Vane uses the purchases method to account for supplies in the general fund. At December 31, 20X8, an inventory indicated that the supplies inventory was $42,000. At December 31, 20X7, the supplies inventory was $45,000.

### Required

For each numbered item above, make all the journal entries for the year ended December 31, 20X8, in all funds affected. Before each journal entry, identify the fund in which the journal entry is made. *Do not make any adjusting/closing entries for items (1), (2), and (3).*

**P18-17**  **Matching Questions Involving Various Funds**

The numbered items listed on the left consist of a variety of transactions that occur in a municipality. The lettered items on the right consist of various ways to record the transactions. Select the appropriate method for recording each transaction. Some transactions have more than one correct answer. Some responses under Recording of Transactions may be used once, more than once, or not at all.

| Transactions | Recording of Transactions |
|---|---|
| 1. Term bond proceeds of $100,000 were received by the capital projects fund. | A. Debit expenditures in the general fund |
| 2. Equipment costing $50,000 was acquired by the water utility, an enterprise fund. | B. Debit general operating expenses in the general fund |
| 3. Land with a fair value of $500,000 was donated to the city to be used as a municipal park. | C. Debit equipment in the enterprise fund |
| | D. Debit equipment in the general fund |
| | E. Debit building in the capital projects fund |
| 4. Central stores, an internal service fund, received a transfer in of $750,000 from the general fund. | F. Debit general operating expenses in the enterprise fund |
| | G. Debit expenditures in the capital projects fund |
| 5. General obligation serial bonds of $250,000 matured and were paid by the debt service fund. | H. Credit building in the capital projects fund |
| | I. Debit expenditures in the debt service fund |
| 6. Expenditures of $5,000,000 were incurred by the capital projects fund to construct a new city hall annex. The project was started and completed within the fiscal year. | J. Credit revenue in the private-purpose trust fund |
| | K. Credit revenue in the capital projects fund |
| | L. Credit other financing sources in the capital projects fund |
| 7. The water utility, an enterprise fund, billed the mayor's office $200 for water usage. | M. Credit transfers in in the internal services fund |
| | N. Debit revenue in the agency fund |
| 8. The mayor's office received the billing in item 7. | O. Credit due to other governmental units in the agency fund |
| 9. The tax agency fund received $250,000 of tax revenues that are to be distributed to the school districts within the municipality. | P. Credit revenue in the agency fund |
| | Q. Credit revenue in the enterprise fund |
| 10. Salaries and wages of $25,000 were incurred by the water utility enterprise fund. | R. Reported only on the government-wide financial statements |

**P18-18**　**Questions on Fund Transactions [AICPA Adapted]**

The following information relates to Dane City during its fiscal year ended December 31, 20X2:

1. On October 31, 20X2, to finance the construction of a city hall annex, Dane issued 8 percent, 10-year general obligation bonds at their face value of $600,000. Construction expenditures during the period equaled $364,000.

2. Dane reported $109,000 from hotel room taxes, restricted for tourist promotion, in a special revenue fund. The fund paid $81,000 for general promotions and $22,000 for a motor vehicle.

3. Dane transferred 20X2 general fund revenues of $104,500 to a debt service fund and used them to repay $100,000 of 9 percent, 15-year term bonds, and to pay $4,500 of interest. The bonds were used to acquire a citizens' center.

4. At December 31, 20X2, as a consequence of past services, city firefighters had accumulated entitlements for compensated absences of $86,000. General fund resources available at December 31, 20X2, are expected to be used to settle $17,000 of this amount, and $69,000 is expected to be paid out of future general fund resources.

5. At December 31, 20X2, Dane was responsible for $83,000 of outstanding general fund encumbrances, including the $8,000 for supplies that follow.

6. Dane uses the purchases method to account for supplies. The following information relates to supplies:

| | |
|---|---:|
| Inventory—1/1/X2 | $ 39,000 |
| —12/31/X2 | 42,000 |
| Encumbrances outstanding—1/1/X2 | 6,000 |
| —12/31/X2 | 8,000 |
| Purchase orders during 20X2 | 190,000 |
| Amount credited to vouchers payable during 20X2 | 181,000 |

### Required

For items 1 through 10, determine the amounts based solely on the preceding information.

1. What is the amount of 20X2 general fund transfers out?
2. How much should be reported in 20X2 general fund liabilities from entitlements for compensated absences?
3. What is the 20X2 reserved amount of the general fund balance?
4. What is the 20X2 capital projects fund balance?
5. What is the 20X2 fund balance on the special revenue fund for tourist promotion?
6. What is the amount of 20X2 debt service fund expenditures?
7. What amount should be included in the government-wide financial statements for the cost of long-term assets acquired in 20X2?
8. What amount stemming from the 20X2 transactions and events decreased the long-term debt liabilities reported in the government-wide financial statements?
9. Using the purchases method, what is the amount of 20X2 supplies expenditures?
10. What was the total amount of 20X2 supplies encumbrances?

**P18-19**　**Matching Questions Involving the Statement of Cash Flows for a Proprietary Fund**

The numbered items on the left consist of a variety of transactions that occurred in the water utility enterprise fund of Jeffersen City for the year ended June 30, 20X9. Items A, B, C, and D on the right represent the four categories of cash flows that are reported on the statement of cash flows for proprietary funds. Item E is for transactions that are not reported on the statement of cash flows. Assume that the direct method is used for disclosing cash flows from operating activities. For each transaction, select the appropriate letter to indicate where that transaction should be disclosed on the statement of cash flows or whether that item would not be reported on the statement of cash flows.

| Transactions | Categories of Disclosure |
|---|---|
| 1. Received $5,000,000 from revenue bonds to be used for construction of water treatment plant. | A. Operating activities<br>B. Noncapital financing activities<br>C. Capital and related financing activities<br>D. Investing activities<br>E. Not reported on the statement of cash flows |
| 2. Paid $500,000 of salaries to employees of the water utility. | |
| 3. Received $1,000,000 state grant restricted for construction of water treatment plant. | |
| 4. Collected $2,500,000 of accounts receivable from households for use of city water. | |
| 5. Depreciation expense for the year amounted to $300,000. | |
| 6. Received $75,000 state grant restricted to the maintenance of fixed assets. | |
| 7. Paid $250,000 of interest on the revenue bonds issued in item 1. | |
| 8. Borrowed $125,000 from a local bank on revenue anticipation notes payable. | |
| 9. Paid $5,000 of interest on the notes payable in item 8. | |
| 10. Spent $1,200,000 of the revenue bonds for construction of the water treatment plant. | |
| 11. Paid $5,000 fire insurance premium on June 30, 20X9, for next year's insurance coverage. | |
| 12. Uncollected accounts receivable amounted to $135,000 on June 31, 20X9. | |
| 13. Acquired $250,000 of state bonds as an investment of idle funds. | |
| 14. Received $7,500 of interest on the state bonds in item 13. | |
| 15. Received a $375,000 contribution from the city's general fund to be used for the construction of water treatment plant. | |

**P18-20**  **Matching Questions Involving the Statement of Revenues, Expenditures, and Changes in Fund Balance for a Capital Projects Fund and a Debt Service Fund**

The numbered items on the left consist of a variety of transactions and events that occurred in the capital projects and debt service funds of Walton City for the year ended June 30, 20X9. Items A, B, and C on the right represent three categories that are reported of the statement of revenues, expenditures, and changes in fund balance for capital projects and debt service funds. Item D is for transactions that are not reported on the statement of revenues, expenditures, and changes in fund balance for either debt service or capital projects funds. For each transaction, select the appropriate letter to indicate where that transaction should be reported on the statement of revenues, expenditures, and changes in fund balance or whether that item would not be reported on the statement.

| Transactions/Events | Categories of Disclosure |
|---|---|
| 1. The capital projects fund received the proceeds of general obligation bonds to be used for construction of a new courthouse. | A. Revenues |
| 2. The capital projects fund accepted the lowest bid for the construction of the courthouse. | B. Expenditures |
| 3. The capital projects fund received resources from the city's general fund to be used in the construction of the courthouse. | C. Other financing sources and uses |
| 4. The bonds in item 1 were rold at a premium. The capital projects fund transferred the premium to the debt service fund. Indicate how this transaction should be reported by the capital projects fund. | D. Not reported on the statement of revenues, expenditures, and changes in fund balance |
| 5. During the year ended June 30, 20X9, courthouse construction was completed. | |
| 6. In addition to the resources provided by the general obligation bonds and the general fund, the capital projects fund also received a state grant that it used to construct the courthouse. | |
| 7. The general fund of the city transferred a portion of the property tax collections to the debt service fund to be used to pay the principal and interest of the general obligation bonds issued in item 1. | |
| 8. The debt service fund acquired investments with part of the resources provided by the general fund. | |
| 9. Interest was earned on the investments acquired in item 8. | |
| 10. The debt service fund received the bond premium from the capital projects fund. | |
| 11. The debt service fund paid semiannual interest on the general obligation bonds on March 1, 20X9. | |
| 12. The debt service fund used a local bank to be its fiscal agent with regard to the recordkeeping activities related to the general obligation bonds issued in item 1. The bank charged a fee for this service. | |
| 13. As of June 30, 20X9, unmatured interest for four months was due on the general obligation bonds issued in item 1. Resources to pay this interest will be transferred to the debt service fund in the next fiscal year. | |

**P18-21**  **Question on Fund Transactions [AICPA Adapted]**

Items 1 through 10 in the left-hand column represent various transactions pertaining to a municipality that uses encumbrance accounting. Items 11 through 20, also listed in the left-hand column, represent the funds and accounts used by the municipality. To the right of these items is a list of possible accounting and reporting methods.

### Required

a. For each of the municipality's transactions (items 1 through 10), select the appropriate method for recording the transaction. A method of recording the transactions may be selected once, more than once, or not at all.

b. For each of the municipality's funds, accounts, and other items (items 11 to 20), select the appropriate method of accounting and reporting. An accounting and reporting method may be selected once, more than once, or not at all.

| Transactions | Recording of Transactions |
|---|---|
| 1. General obligation bonds were issued at par. | A. Credit Appropriations Control |
| 2. Approved purchase orders were issued for supplies. | B. Credit Budgetary Fund Balance— Unreserved |
| 3. Supplies in item 2 were received and the related invoices were approved. | C. Credit Expenditures Control |

*(continued)*

4. General fund salaries and wages were incurred.
5. The internal service fund had interfund billings.
6. Revenues were earned from a previously awarded grant.
7. Property taxes were collected in advance.
8. Appropriations were recorded on adoption of the budget.
9. Short-term financing was received from a bank, secured by the city's taxing power.
10. There was an excess of estimated inflows over estimated outflows.

D. Credit Deferred Revenues
E. Credit Interfund Revenues
F. Credit Tax Anticipation Notes Payable
G. Credit Other Financing Sources
H. Credit Other Financing Uses
I. Debit Appropriations Control
J. Debit Deferred Revenues
K. Debit Encumbrances Control
L. Debit Expenditures Control

| Funds and Accounts | Accounting and Reporting |
|---|---|
| 11. Enterprise fund fixed assets. | A. Accounted for in a fiduciary fund |
| 12. Capital projects fund. | B. Accounted for in a proprietary fund |
| 13. Permanent fund. | C. Accounts for permanent endowments that can be used for government programs |
| 14. Infrastructure fixed assets. | D. Reported as an other financing use |
| 15. Enterprise fund cash. | E. Accounted for in a special assessment fund |
| 16. General fund. | F. Accounts for major construction activities |
| 17. Agency fund cash. | G. Accounts for property tax revenues |
| 18. Transfer out from the general fund to the internal service fund. | H. Accounts for payment of interest and principal on tax-supported debt |
| 19. Special revenue fund (a major fund). | I. Accounts for revenues from earmarked sources to finance designated activities |
| 20. Debt service fund (a major fund). | J. Reported in government-wide statements |

### P18-22 Major Fund Tests

The City of Somerset has the following fund information:

| Fund | Assets | Liabilities | Revenues | Expenditures (Expenses) |
|---|---|---|---|---|
| General | $1,320,400 | $ 878,300 | $4,620,000 | $4,550,000 |
| Special revenue | 27,000 | 19,000 | 327,000 | 328,000 |
| Capital project—library | 450,000 | 38,000 | 460,000 | 418,000 |
| Capital project—arena | 28,000 | 16,000 | 41,000 | 55,800 |
| Debt service | 41,000 | -0- | 331,000 | 290,000 |
| Permanent | 246,000 | -0- | 11,000 | 18,000 |
| Enterprise—electric | 2,640,000 | 1,800,700 | 289,000 | 245,000 |
| Enterprise—water | 1,356,000 | 1,100,000 | 329,000 | 298,000 |

### Required

Apply the criteria specified in GASB 34 to determine which of these funds meets the major fund reporting criteria.

### P18-23 Reconciliation Schedules

The City of Sycamore is preparing its financial reports for the year and has requested that you prepare the reconciliation schedules to accompany its government-wide financial statements based on the following information:

1. The fund balances reported in the five governmental funds as of the end of the fiscal year total $888,400. The fund balances in governmental funds at the beginning of the year totaled $379,000.

2. The city has estimated its depreciation on capital assets to be $187,000 for the period. The city expended a total of $287,000 in capital outlays from the governmental funds. At year-end, the capital assets, net of depreciation, totaled $4,329,000. The internal service fund reported $18,000 of net capital assets. Total accumulated depreciation at year-end was $1,208,000.

3. The internal service fund reports $178,000 in total assets and $141,000 in total liabilities. The internal service fund reported $48,000 of revenues and $39,000 of expenses during the year.

4. The debt service fund paid $40,000 in interest during the year. Bonds with a face value of $500,000 and a coupon rate of 8 percent were sold at the beginning of the year at $460,000 for an effective interest rate of 10 percent. Interest is paid annually on the last day of the fiscal year. The bonds were sold to provide current financial resources for the governmental funds.

5. The permanent fund recorded interest received of $4,000 under the modified accrual basis of measurement. If the accrual basis of measurement had been used in the fund, an additional $1,000 of interest revenue would have been earned.

### Required

a. Prepare a reconciliation schedule of the balance sheet of the governmental funds to the statement of net assets.

b. Prepare a reconciliation schedule of the statement of revenues, expenditures, and changes in fund balance of governmental funds to the statement of activities.

**P18-24**  **True/False Questions**

1. The budgetary comparison schedule in the government-wide financial statements requires only the final budget for the period and the actual amounts for the period.

2. The accrual basis of accounting is used in the government-wide financial statements.

3. A component unit of a primary government is a unit that is related to the primary government but is not financially accountable to the primary government.

4. The statement of net assets in the government-wide financial statements requires the net assets to be segregated as follows: reserved net assets (for items such as encumbrances and inventories) and unreserved net assets.

5. A major governmental fund that must be separately disclosed in the government-wide financial statements would be a fund that composed 5 percent of the total of the governmental funds.

6. Permanent governmental funds account for resources that have a principal that must be maintained and whose earnings are available for any government program that benefits all citizens.

7. The government unit's infrastructure and other fixed assets are reported on the government-wide statement of net assets.

8. The internal service fund is a proprietary fund and is not, therefore, shown in the Governmental Activities column of the government-wide statement of net assets.

9. In the reconciliation schedule for the statement of net assets, to reconcile from the net assets reported in the governmental funds to the net assets of governmental activities, capital assets used in governmental activities would be added.

10. In the reconciliation schedule for the statement of revenues, expenditures, and changes in fund balance, to reconcile from the net change in fund balances—governmental funds to the change in net assets of governmental activities, bond proceeds would be added back.

11. In the government-wide statement of activities, transfers between governmental and business-type funds must be reported as part of the change in net assets.

12. In the government-wide statement of activities, depreciation of fixed assets would equal the amount of the expenditures for assets made in the governmental funds.

13. The Management's Discussion and Analysis is a recommended but voluntary disclosure in the government-wide financial statements.

14. The government-wide statement of net assets includes the fiduciary funds of the government unit.

15. The format of the government-wide statement of activities is based on the programs of the government entity rather than the type of revenues of the government entity.

**P18-25**  **Determining Whether a Special Revenue Fund Is a Major Fund**

The City of Elmtree is preparing its financial statements for the year ended December 31, 20X2, and has asked for your assistance in determining whether its special revenue fund is a major or a nonmajor fund for the financial statements of its governmental funds. The city has provided the following information:

| Items | Totals for Governmental Funds | Totals for Governmental and Enterprise Funds |
|---|---|---|
| Assets | $50,000,000 | $80,000,000 |
| Liabilities | 22,000,000 | 37,000,000 |
| Revenues | 70,000,000 | 95,000,000 |
| Expenditures/expenses | 60,000,000 | 82,000,000 |

The special revenue fund reported the following amounts at December 31, 20X2 (assets and liabilities), and for the year ended December 31, 20X2 (revenues and expenditures):

| | |
|---|---|
| Assets | $4,100,000 |
| Liabilities | 3,900,000 |
| Revenues | 6,700,000 |
| Expenditures | 6,500,000 |

### Required
Determine whether the special revenue fund of Elmtree is a major fund for the 20X2 financial statements of the city's governmental funds.

**P18-26** **Preparation of a Statement of Net Assets for a Governmental Entity**

Gibson City reported the following items at December 31, 20X2. It has no component units and does not depreciate its infrastructure fixed assets. All bonds—general obligation bonds and revenue—were issued to acquire capital assets. As of December 31, 20X2, net assets of $25,000 were restricted for road maintenance in special revenue funds, and net assets of $30,000 were restricted for debt service. Cash of $5,000 was restricted in business-type activities for plant maintenance.

| | Governmental Activities | Business-Type Activities |
|---|---|---|
| Assets: | | |
| Cash and cash equivalents | $ 68,000 | $28,000 |
| Taxes receivable (net) | 52,000 | |
| Accounts receivable (net) | | 12,000 |
| Due from governmental activities | | 5,000 |
| Inventories | 10,000 | 7,000 |
| Investments | 25,000 | 15,000 |
| Capital assets: | | |
| Land | 100,000 | 50,000 |
| Infrastructure | 60,000 | |
| Other depreciable assets (net) | 75,000 | 45,000 |
| Liabilities: | | |
| Vouchers payable | 32,000 | 4,000 |
| Accrued interest payable | 1,500 | 2,000 |
| Due to business-type activities | 5,000 | |
| Revenue bonds payable | | 80,000 |
| General obligation bonds payable | 60,000 | |

### Required
Using the information provided, prepare in good form a statement of net assets for Gibson City at December 31, 20X2.

| Kaplan CPA Review | **Kaplan CPA Review Simulation on Governmental Accounting and Reporting** |
|---|---|

Access to the online CPA Simulation can be attained by visiting the text's Web site at www.mhhe .com/baker8e.

SCHWESER

### Situation

The City of Clarksville (Clarksville) is incorporated and has a December 31 year-end. The budget is approved by the City Council (Council) annually. For internal reporting purposes, Clarksville uses the modified accrual basis of accounting to record its general fund transactions. For external reporting purposes, Clarksville prepares a comprehensive annual financial report that includes both government-wide and fund-based financial statements.

The city has a policy that any amounts to be received within 60 days are viewed as currently being available.

At the beginning of Year One, the Council authorized the construction of a new recreation center. The estimated cost of the recreation center is $25 million. Clarksville plans to finance the construction by (1) combining bond proceeds with a state grant, and (2) making a transfer from the general fund.

### Topics Included in the Simulation

a. Assigning transactions in a proprietary fund to the appropriate classification on the statement of cash flows.

b. Evaluating the accuracy of recorded amounts in the governmental funds for recording budgets, the levy of taxes, and the collections of taxes.

c. Assigning nonexchange transactions to their correct categories of recognition.

d. Accounting for the construction of the new recreation center: issuance of the bonds, receipt of the state grant, accounting for the interfund transfer, and accounting for interest on the bonds.

e. Comparing fund-based reporting of the construction of the recreation center to that reportable on the government-wide financial statements.

f. Comparing the reporting of an acquisition of a capital asset on the fund-based financial statements with that on the government-wide financial statements.

g. Researching required disclosures in the comprehensive annual financial report for infrastructure assets under the modified approach.

*Supplemental Problems* for this chapter are available as part of the *Online Learning Center* on the textbook's Web site (URL:www.mhhe.com/baker8e).

# Not-for-Profit Entities

This chapter presents the accounting and financial reporting principles used by both governmental (public) and nongovernmental (private) colleges and universities, health care providers such as hospitals and nursing homes, voluntary health and welfare organizations such as the Red Cross and United Way, and other not-for-profit organizations such as professional or fraternal associations.

The accounting and financial reporting for governmental, nonprofit entities is controlled by the Governmental Accounting Standards Board (GASB). Accounting and financial reporting for nongovernmental, nonprofit entities is controlled by the Financial Accounting Standards Board (FASB). Thus, it is important to determine the role the government has in the organization.

## FINANCIAL REPORTING FOR PRIVATE, NOT-FOR-PROFIT ENTITIES

Private, not-for-profit entities follow the accounting and reporting standards established by the FASB. Several FASB standards and statements are particularly relevant for private, not-for-profit entities.

Private, not-for-profit entities must report their net assets in accordance with **Financial Accounting Concepts Statement No. 6,** "Elements of Financial Statements" (FAC 6). **FAC 6** specifies three mutually exclusive classes of net assets (assets less liabilities), as follows:

1. *Unrestricted net assets.* This class of net assets is not restricted by a donor. These assets are used for the entity's general operations. Unrestricted net assets include all assets and liabilities that do not have externally imposed restrictions on their use.

2. *Temporarily restricted net assets.* This net asset class reports net assets that have donor-imposed time or purpose restrictions, typically detailed in the contribution agreement between the donor and the organization. A *time restriction* means that the assets will not be available for use until after a specific time has passed. *Term endowments* that have limited lives are included in temporarily restricted net assets. A *purpose restriction* means that the resources may be used only for specified purposes. For example, the donor may specify that the contribution be used in a specific program or for specified building and equipment acquisitions.

3. *Permanently restricted net assets.* This class of net assets includes permanently restricted contributions such as regular endowments for which the principal must be preserved into perpetuity.

It is very important to properly account for, and report, each class of net assets. Some not-for-profit entities use a fund structure to account for each type of net asset class because of the accounting discipline that fund accounting provides. These entities would have funds such as the general fund, specific-purpose fund, building fund, endowment fund, and so on. Other not-for-profit entities maintain only an accounting record to show the amounts in each net asset class. The specific identification of any restricted asset must be made when the asset comes into the entity, generally by donation or bequest.

The gifting agreement must be examined fully to determine whether the gift has any donor-imposed restrictions on its principal and/or on the income generated from the principal. Revenue is recorded in only one net asset class when the contribution is made. Then, as restrictions are eliminated or met, the resources are released and transferred from the restricted net asset class to the unrestricted net asset class.

For example, if C. Alt donates $40,000 to a not-for-profit organization to be used specifically for a research program, the following entry is made in the *temporarily restricted class of net assets* because of the donor-imposed use restriction:

| | | | |
|---|---|---|---|
| (1) | Cash | 40,000 | |
| | Contribution Revenue | | 40,000 |
| | Receipt of $40,000 donor-restricted contribution for a specified research program. | | |

Note that the contribution revenue is recorded in the temporarily restricted net asset class when the restricted contribution is received.

Then, when the research program costs are approved in the unrestricted net asset class, a reclassification entry is made in the temporarily restricted net asset class to record the transfer of the resources from the temporarily restricted class to the unrestricted net asset class. Note that the reclassification entry is not an expense of the restricted class.

| | | | |
|---|---|---|---|
| (2) | Reclassification from Temporarily Restricted Net Assets—Satisfaction of Program Restriction | 40,000 | |
| | Cash | | 40,000 |
| | Reclassification of temporarily restricted resources to the unrestricted fund upon satisfaction of the use restriction. | | |

Entries are then made in the unrestricted net asset class to show the receipt of the cash and the reclassification for satisfaction of the program restriction. The reclassification is not a revenue in the unrestricted net asset class because the revenue from the contribution has already been recognized once in the temporarily restricted net asset class. A key concept is that revenue should be recognized only once and only by the appropriate receiving net asset class. The entries in the *unrestricted net asset class* follow:

| | | | |
|---|---|---|---|
| (3) | Cash | 40,000 | |
| | Reclassification into Unrestricted Net Assets—Satisfaction of Program Restriction | | 40,000 |
| | Receipt of resources from the temporarily restricted net asset class due to satisfaction of use restriction. | | |
| (4) | Expenses | 40,000 | |
| | Cash | | 40,000 |
| | Expenses for research program. | | |

Some not-for-profit entities use the terms "net assets released from restriction" instead of "reclassification." The purpose is the same; the resources are released from a restricted net asset class and assigned or transferred to another net asset class.

It is very important to note that the restricted net asset classes, either temporarily or permanently, do not report expenses on the organization's statement of activities. The restricted net asset classes (temporarily or permanently) report restricted contribution revenue and any restricted investment income/losses but cannot report any expenses. Expenses are reported *only* in the unrestricted net asset class. Thus, the reclassification entry records the transfer of the resources from a restricted net asset class to the unrestricted net asset class. The reclassification and transfer is made when appropriate evidence is provided to the restricted net asset class that the cash can be released due to the satisfaction of the temporary restriction or that the permanent restriction is no longer valid. The reclassification entry ensures that the resources are being spent by the unrestricted net asset class in accordance with the donor's wishes.

## Important FASB Standards for Not-for-Profit Entities

The FASB has issued five standards that have direct applicability to private, not-for-profit entities: **FASB 93,** which guides depreciation; **FASB 116,** which guides accounting for contributions; **FASB 117,** which establishes financial display requirements; **FASB 124,** which establishes the accounting for investments; and **FASB 136,** which guides the accounting for transfers of assets to a not-for-profit organization that raises or holds contributions for others.

**FASB Statement No. 93,** "Recognition of Depreciation by Not-for-Profit Organizations" (FASB 93), requires that private, not-for-profit entities must show depreciation. Depreciation must be recognized on long-lived tangible assets, other than works of art or historical treasures that have cultural, aesthetic, or historical value that is worth preserving perpetually and whose holders have the ability to preserve that value and are so doing. The depreciation is reported as an expense for the period. **FASB 93** requires disclosure of the following items: (1) depreciation for the period, (2) the total of each of the major classes of depreciable assets, (3) the accumulated depreciation at the balance sheet date, and (4) the method used to compute depreciation for the major classes of depreciable assets.

**FASB Statement No. 116,** "Accounting for Contributions Received and Contributions Made" (FASB 116), establishes the guidelines for private, not-for-profit entities to account for contributions. Contributions can be of cash, other assets, or a promise to give (a pledge). The general rule is that contributions received are measured at their fair value and are recognized as revenues or gains in the period received. The contributions are reported as unrestricted support or, if there are donor-imposed restrictions, as restricted support. A private, not-for-profit entity does not need to recognize contributions of works of art, historical treasures, and similar assets if the donated items are added to collections that (1) are held for public exhibition, education, or research, (2) are protected, cared for, and preserved, and (3) have an organizational policy in existence that proceeds from the sales of collection items are to be used to acquire other items for collections.

Contributions of services are recognized as a revenue, with an equivalent amount recorded as an expenditure, if the services received (1) create or enhance nonfinancial assets or (2) require specialized skills, are provided by individuals possessing those skills, and typically need to be purchased if not provided by donation. Examples of contributed services are specialized skills provided by accountants, architects, doctors, teachers, and other professionals. Some religious-based colleges record revenue, with an offsetting amount to an expense, for the fair value of contributed lay teaching services. This recognition is made to report the full cost of the teaching mission of these private colleges.

**FASB Statement No. 124,** "Accounting for Certain Investments Held by Not-for-Profit Organizations" (FASB 124), is discussed before **FASB 117,** which is presented in the next paragraph. **FASB 124** extended to not-for-profit organizations the basic standard of fair value for investments that was presented in **FASB 115** on investments. **FASB 124** specifies that fair value should be the measurement basis for investments in all debt securities and in equity securities that have readily determinable fair values (other than those equity securities that are accounted for under the equity method in accordance with **APB 18**). Note that **FASB 124** requires that debt securities be valued at fair value. Investment income for the period includes interest or dividends and the changes in fair value. Changes in the fair value of investments in temporarily restricted or permanently restricted net assets are recognized in accordance with donor restrictions as to the income. Otherwise, investment income is reported as a change in unrestricted net assets.

**FASB Statement No. 117,** "Financial Statements of Not-for-Profit Organizations" (FASB 117), specifies the financial display standards for private, not-for-profit entities. The three major financial statements are (1) a statement of financial position, (2) a statement of activities, and (3) a statement of cash flows. The unique features of the statement of financial position and the statement of activities for not-for-profit organizations are presented in greater detail in the following discussions. While some flexibility exists in the presentation of financial statements under **FASB 117,** a major feature of the statement of financial position is the combined presentation of all assets and equities in a single, simplified statement. In addition, the net assets are separated into those that are (1) unrestricted, (2) temporarily restricted, and (3) permanently restricted.

**FASB Statement No. 136,** "Transfers of Assets to a Not-for-Profit Organization or Charitable Trust that Raises or Holds Contributions for Others" (FASB 136), establishes the accounting for contributions made to foundations or other similar organizations that raise resources for not-for-profit entities. **FASB 136** defines three parties to the typical contribution process. The *donor* is the initial provider of the resources. The *recipient organization* receives the assets from the donor. The *beneficiary* is the entity that eventually receives the assets through the recipient organization, as specified by the donor.

Many not-for-profit, private colleges and universities have a foundation that is responsible for raising financial support from alumni and other donors. Typically, these foundations are institutionally related to the college or university and use its assets for the benefit of the college or university. In most cases, at the time the assets are contributed by the donor to the foundation (the recipient organization), the foundation records an increase in assets and a contribution revenue for the fair value of the donation. Usually these assets are temporarily restricted until the foundation transfers them to the college or university. When the foundation does transfer the assets to the university (the beneficiary), the foundation records an expense and a decrease in its assets. The college or university normally has an interest in the net assets of the foundation and, at the time of the donation to the foundation, the college or university will recognize the change in its interest in the university foundation, usually as a temporarily restricted net asset, unless the donor specified a permanent restriction on the donation. Then, when the college or university actually receives the assets, it increases the specific assets received and decreases its interest in the net assets of the foundation. The institutionally related foundation recognizes the contribution revenue when it receives the donation.

Some recipient organizations, such as United Way, do fund-raising that will benefit a number of not-for-profit organizations. Donors may name the specific recipient of their gifts or the donor may give to United Way without a restriction as to where the gift should be used. When the donor restricts his or her contribution to a specific beneficiary, United Way acts as an agent and recognizes an increase in its assets and records a liability to the specified beneficiary. The organization specified by the donor records an increase in its net assets, usually as a receivable, and records contribution revenue at the time of the donation. When United Way transfers the assets to the specified beneficiaries, United Way decreases its liabilities and its assets. For unrestricted donations for which United Way may determine the best uses of the resources, it records an increase in its assets and records the unrestricted gifts as contribution revenue. Then, when the assets are distributed, United Way records the expense and the decrease in its assets, and the beneficiary records contribution revenue for the fair value of the assets transferred.

Finally, **FASB 136** states that in the case of nonfinancial assets such as artwork, the recipient organization (for example, the university foundation or United Way) may choose whether or not to record the fair value of these nonfinancial assets in its books. Typically, these nonfinancial assets will be transferred to the beneficiary. However, all contributed financial assets must be recorded at their fair values when received.

### Mergers and Acquisitions of Not-for-Profit Organizations

In 2006, the FASB issued two exposure drafts discussing the Board's positions on accounting for mergers and acquisitions and accounting for goodwill and intangibles for not-for-profit organizations. These exposure drafts were necessary because **FASB Statement No. 141(R ),** "Business Combinations" [FASB 141(R)], and **FASB Statement No. 160,** "Noncontrolling Interests in Consolidated Financial Statements—an amendment of ARB No. 51" (FASB 160), specifically stated that each of those FASB statements did not apply to not-for-profit entities.

The first exposure draft, entitled "Not-for-Profit Organizations: Mergers and Acquisitions," provided guidance to not-for-profit entities for the initial accounting for a merger or acquisition of either another not-for-profit entity or a business. The proposed standard requires the recognition of identifiable assets acquired and liabilities assumed at their fair values at the date of the acquisition. Certain exceptions to the fair value approach are applied to identifiable assets or liabilities for which other GAAP methods of valuation are required: certain inexhaustible collection items; conditional promises to give; operating leases; assets held for sale; deferred taxes; and pension and other postemployment benefits. Identifiable assets include intangible assets apart from goodwill. Goodwill would be the value of the consideration transferred (if any) that exceeds the net amount assigned to identifiable assets acquired and liabilities assumed. In essence, this recognizes only the goodwill that the acquiring net-for-profit entity has paid for. Noncontrolling interest, if any, would be valued at its share of the acquisition-date values of the identifiable net assets of the acquired entity, and would not include goodwill. An exception to this general rule of no goodwill for the noncontrolling interest applies in the infrequent case of no consideration passed in the acquisition and the acquired entity's acquisition-date values of its identifiable assets being less than its liabilities (net deficit position). In this case, the noncontrolling interest is assigned a portion of the goodwill necessary to balance the financial position of the acquired entity.

The second exposure draft, entitled "Not-for-Profit Organizations: Goodwill and Other Intangible Assets Acquired in a Merger or Acquisition (an amendment of FASB Statement No. 142)," requires that intangible assets other than goodwill and goodwill be assigned to reporting units that are acquired. Intangible assets other than goodwill shall be accounted for in accordance with **FASB Statement No. 142,** "Goodwill and Other Intangible Assets" (FASB 142), that specifies that an identifiable intangible asset that has a finite useful life shall be amortized over that useful life. An identifiable intangible asset that has an indefinite useful life shall be tested at least annually for impairment by comparing its fair value with its carrying value.

Two different approaches to evaluating acquired goodwill for impairment are presented in the proposed standard:

a. *Qualitative Evaluation Method.* This method is used for those reporting units that are primarily supported by contributions and returns on investments. This qualitative evaluation would require the not-for-profit organization to first identify the reasons there was goodwill at the acquisition date and then identify specific events that would indicate that the acquired goodwill subsequently has become impaired. The second step is to determine if the identified events have occurred. If any specific identified events have occurred, the not-for-profit entity would recognize an impairment loss equal to the carrying amount of the goodwill assigned to the reporting unit that was acquired. If no specific identified events have occurred, then no goodwill impairment would be recognized.

b. *Fair-Value-Based Evaluation.* This method is applied to those reporting units that are primarily supported by resources other than contributions and returns on investments. The goodwill impairment evaluation is the same as required for business entities in **FASB 142.**

# COLLEGES AND UNIVERSITIES

There are more than 3,000 colleges and universities in the United States. Some offer two-year programs, some offer four-year programs, and others offer a wide selection of both undergraduate and graduate programs. Public and private institutions provide a large variety of liberal arts, science, and professional programs for our society. Public colleges and universities receive a significant portion of their operating resources from state governments. Private, not-for-profit colleges and universities receive most of their resources from tuition and fees.

## Special Conventions of Revenue and Expenditure Recognition

Both public and private colleges and universities follow several conventions of recognizing revenue and expenses, as follows:

1. *Tuition and fee remissions/waivers and uncollectible accounts.* Tuition and fees are important revenue sources for colleges and universities. In college and university accounting, the full amount of the standard rate for tuition and fees is recognized as revenue. The accounting for university-sponsored scholarships, fellowships, tuition and fee remissions or waivers depends on whether the recipient provides any services to the university. For example, if a student receives a university-sponsored scholarship that does not require any employment-type of work to be given to the university, the university accounts for this as a deduction from revenue. On the other hand, if the student must provide employment-type work to the university, the university accounts for the scholarship as an expense. Another example is the tuition remission (reduction) often given to graduate students who accept teaching assistantships. The university records revenue for the graduate student's tuition at the standard rate and then records the tuition remission as an expense of the year in which the graduate student is a teaching assistant.

2. *Tuition and fee reimbursements for withdrawals from coursework.* Students withdrawing from classes after the beginning of the class term may be able to collect a reimbursement or return of some of the tuition and fees paid at the beginning of the term. Colleges and universities account for these reimbursements of tuition and fees as a reduction of revenue. When the check to the student is approved, the university debits revenue from tuition and fee reimbursements and credits cash or accounts payable.

3. *Academic terms that span two fiscal periods.* Some academic terms may begin in one fiscal year of the university and be completed in another. This is often true for summer school sessions. For example, many universities end their fiscal years on June 30 of each year. The 1994 College and University Audit Guide, published by the AICPA, recommended that colleges and universities account for the tuition and fees as revenue in the fiscal year in which the term is predominantly conducted, along with all expenses incurred to finance that term. However, more recent practices by the National Association of College and University Business Officers (NACUBO) recommend the use of the accrual basis of accounting, which requires that the tuition revenue and costs be allocated proportionately to the two fiscal years based on the relative portions of the academic term. Many colleges and universities are electing to follow the NACUBO recommendation.

For example, if tuition and fees are collected at the beginning of summer school, in which two weeks are offered in the first fiscal year and the remaining six weeks are offered in the second fiscal year, the AICPA audit guide's approach would result in recording the collections as a debit to Cash and a credit to Deferred Revenue for the entire amount of the collections. The deferred revenue and any deferred expenses would then be recognized as revenue and expenses of the next fiscal period, in which most of the term is conducted. Under the NACUBO approach, revenue would be recognized in the first fiscal period for two-eighths of the tuition and fees and the remaining six-eighths of the collections would be recorded as a deferred revenue. The NACUBO method also would recognize the related expenses that correspond with the first two weeks of the summer session in the first fiscal period. The remaining six-eighths of the revenue, and the related expenses, would be recognized in the second fiscal period for the last six weeks of the summer session. NACUBO feels its approach follows the principles of accrual accounting.

## Board-Designated Funds

The governing board, sometimes termed *regents* or *trustees,* may designate unrestricted current fund resources for specific purposes in future periods. These *board-designated funds* are internal designations similar to appropriations of retained earnings for a commercial entity. The governing board may make any designations at its own volition. For example, it might designate $50,000 of future spending in the unrestricted current fund for the development of a foreign student counseling office. Such designations are usually reported in the footnotes to the financial statements, but they may also be shown as allocations of part of the fund balance in the unrestricted current fund balance sheet. However, **FASB 117** specifies that these board-designated funds may not be reported as restricted net assets because only external, donor-imposed restrictions can result in restricted net assets.

## Public Colleges and Universities

The accounting and reporting for public colleges and universities is specified by the GASB. **GASB Statement No. 35,** "Basic Financial Statements—and Management's Discussion and Analysis—for Public Colleges and Universities" (GASB 35), issued in 1999, requires that these institutions follow the standards for governmental entities as specified in **GASB 34.** Most public institutions will be special-purpose government entities engaged in only business-type activities. This is so because most public colleges and universities do not have their own taxing authority. These special-purpose governmental entities present only the financial statements required for enterprise funds and then are included as component units of the state government. However, some community colleges do have their own taxing authority, and these are special-purpose government entities engaged in both governmental and business-type activities. These community colleges provide both fund-based financial statements and government-wide financial statements.

## Private Colleges and Universities

The FASB specifies the accounting and financial reporting standards for private colleges and universities. Although many private colleges and universities are not-for-profit entities, some private colleges, such as the University of Phoenix, are profit-seeking. Accounting for profit-seeking educational entities is similar to accounting for any commercial entity and is not covered in this chapter.

The three financial statements required for private, not-for-profit colleges and universities are the (1) statement of financial position, (2) statement of activities, and (3) statement of cash flows. Private colleges and universities are free to select any account structure that best serves their management and financial reporting needs, but some choose to use fund accounting similar to that of governmental entities. Fund accounting creates an accounting discipline and provides an accounting vehicle to track revenues and expenses related to specific programs. Figure 19–1 presents an overview of the accounting and financial reporting of colleges and universities. The financial reporting for public, special-purpose governmental entities is presented in Chapters 17 and 18 of this textbook.

The statement of financial position for Sol City College, a private, not-for-profit college, is presented in Figure 19–2. This statement presents all assets and equities in a single statement. Note that the net assets are separated into three categories: (1) unrestricted, (2) temporarily restricted, and (3) permanently restricted. The unrestricted category includes all assets, including property, plant, and equipment, whose use is not restricted by the provider or donor. Temporarily restricted assets include those that the donor has designated for specific use or for use in subsequent periods. Term endowments, funds donated for support of special activities, and those donated for unrestricted (or other) use in future periods are included as temporarily restricted net assets. Permanently restricted assets typically include only the principal balance of permanent endowments.

**FIGURE 19–1** Overview of the Accounting and Reporting of Colleges and Universities

| | Public, Special-Purpose Governmental Entities | | Private Entities | |
| --- | --- | --- | --- | --- |
| | Engaged in Both Governmental and Business-Type Activities | Engaged in Only Business-Type Activities | Not-for-Profit | Profit-Seeking |
| Accounting and reporting standards | GASB | GASB | FASB | FASB |
| Accounting structure | Funds | Funds | Not required to, but many use fund-based structure | Account-based, same as for commercial businesses |
| Distinguishing features | Separate governmental entity with own taxing authority | Generally reported as a component unit of a state government | Net assets classified into three classes:<br>1. Unrestricted net assets<br>2. Temporarily restricted net assets<br>3. Permanently restricted net assets | Same as for profit-seeking businesses |
| Financial statements | Both fund-based and government-wide financial statements, as presented in Chapters 17 and 18 | Same as for an enterprise fund, as presented in Chapter 18 | Three basic financial statements:<br>1. Statement of Financial Position<br>2. Statement of Activities<br>3. Statement of Cash Flows | Same as for profit-seeking businesses |

**FIGURE 19–2**
**Statement of**
**Financial Position**
**for a Private College**

| SOL CITY COLLEGE<br>Statement of Financial Position<br>June 30, 20X2 and 20X1 | | |
|---|---|---|
| | **20X2** | **20X1** |
| Cash | $ 579,000 | $ 514,000 |
| Investments, at Fair Value | 10,763,000 | 9,536,000 |
| Deposits with Trustees | 125,000 | 122,000 |
| Accounts Receivable | 161,000 | 182,000 |
| Less: Allowance for Uncollectibles | (13,000) | (14,000) |
| Loans to Students, Faculty, and Staff | 275,000 | 190,000 |
| Inventories | 45,000 | 40,000 |
| Prepaid Expenses | 14,000 | 10,000 |
| Property, Plant, and Equipment (net) | 20,330,000 | 19,970,000 |
| Total Assets | $32,279,000 | $30,550,000 |
| Accounts Payable | $ 70,000 | $ 53,000 |
| Accrued Liabilities | 10,000 | 8,000 |
| Students' Deposits | 15,000 | 18,000 |
| Deferred Credits | 15,000 | 10,000 |
| Annuities Payable | 1,080,000 | 1,155,000 |
| Notes Payable | 50,000 | — |
| Bonds Payable | 1,300,000 | 1,200,000 |
| Mortgage Payable | 200,000 | 100,000 |
| Deposits Held in Custody | 55,000 | 45,000 |
| Total Liabilities | $ 2,795,000 | $ 2,589,000 |
| Net Assets: | | |
| Unrestricted | $20,221,000 | $20,294,000 |
| Temporarily Restricted by Donors | 5,363,000 | 4,307,000 |
| Permanently Restricted by Donors | 3,900,000 | 3,360,000 |
| Total Net Assets | $29,484,000 | $27,961,000 |
| Total Liabilities and Net Assets | $32,279,000 | $30,550,000 |

The statement of activities presented in Figure 19–3 presents separately the revenues and expenses of the unrestricted, temporarily restricted, and permanently restricted net asset categories. It also shows the transfer of assets between the three categories of net assets during the period. For example, contributions received in 20X1 and available for use in 20X2 are shown as a transfer from temporarily restricted to unrestricted net assets in the statement of activities for 20X2. Auxiliary enterprises include activities such as a student union bookstore, cafeterias, and residence halls.

The statement of cash flows presented in Figure 19–4 is similar to that used for commercial entities. Either the direct or indirect method may be used to compute cash flows from operating activities. Activities in the restricted funds are noted separately from those in the unrestricted funds.

# HEALTH CARE PROVIDERS

The health care environment is currently undergoing a revolution. Rapidly increasing costs of providing medical care are forcing hospitals to merge at an increasing rate in order to consolidate the types of services offered. The cost of new technology is also requiring health care providers to reevaluate their missions to the communities they serve.

Although the major focus of this section of the chapter is on hospitals, the accounting and financial reporting guidelines for hospitals are the same as those used by all health

**FIGURE 19–3** **Statement of Activities for a Private College**

**SOL CITY COLLEGE**
**Statement of Activities**
**For the Year Ended June 30, 20X2**

| | Unrestricted | Temporarily Restricted | Permanently Restricted | Total |
|---|---|---|---|---|
| Revenues, Gains, and Other Support: | | | | |
| Tuition and Fees | $ 1,290,000 | | | $ 1,290,000 |
| Government Appropriations | 650,000 | $ 40,000 | | 690,000 |
| Government Grants and Contracts | 20,000 | 300,000 | | 320,000 |
| Contributions | 425,000 | 1,063,000 | $ 495,000 | 1,983,000 |
| Auxiliary Enterprises | 1,100,000 | | | 1,100,000 |
| Investment Income | 265,000 | 139,000 | 15,000 | 419,000 |
| Gain on Investments | | 69,000 | 25,000 | 94,000 |
| Net Assets Transferred or Released from Restriction: | | | | |
| Program Use Restriction | 601,000 | (601,000) | | |
| Transferred to Restricted Funds | (101,000) | 101,000 | | |
| Expired Term Endowment | 50,000 | (50,000) | | |
| Transferred to Endowment | | (5,000) | 5,000 | |
| Total Revenue, Gains, and Other Support | $ 4,300,000 | $1,056,000 | $ 540,000 | $ 5,896,000 |
| Expenditures and Other Deductions: | | | | |
| Instruction | $ 1,725,000 | | | $ 1,725,000 |
| Research | 250,000 | | | 250,000 |
| Public Service | 77,000 | | | 77,000 |
| Academic Support | 125,000 | | | 125,000 |
| Student Services | 100,000 | | | 100,000 |
| Scholarships and Fellowships | 95,000 | | | 95,000 |
| Institutional Support | 275,000 | | | 275,000 |
| Operation and Maintenance | 110,000 | | | 110,000 |
| Depreciation Expense | 500,000 | | | 500,000 |
| Interest Expense | 106,000 | | | 106,000 |
| Auxiliary Enterprises | 915,000 | | | 915,000 |
| Other Operating Costs | 95,000 | | | 95,000 |
| Total Expenses | $ 4,373,000 | $ -0- | $ -0- | $ 4,373,000 |
| Change in Net Assets | $ (73,000) | $1,056,000 | $ 540,000 | $ 1,523,000 |
| Net Assets at Beginning of Year | 20,294,000 | 4,307,000 | 3,360,000 | 27,961,000 |
| Net Assets at End of Year | $20,221,000 | $5,363,000 | $3,900,000 | $29,484,000 |

care providers included within the scope of the AICPA's Audit and Accounting guide for Health Care Organizations.[1] The Audit and Accounting Guide applies to the following health care entities:

1. Clinics, medical group practices, individual practice associations, individual practitioners, emergency care facilities, laboratories, surgery centers, and other ambulatory care organizations.

2. Continuing-care retirement communities (CCRCs).

3. Health maintenance organizations (HMOs) and similar prepaid health care plans.

4. Home health agencies.

5. Hospitals.

6. Nursing homes that provide skilled, intermediate, and less intensive levels of health care.

7. Drug and alcohol rehabilitation centers and other rehabilitation facilities.

[1] The AICPA periodically revises its audit and accounting guides for specialized industries.

**FIGURE 19–4**
**Statement of Cash Flows for a Private College**

### SOL CITY COLLEGE
### Statement of Cash Flows
### For the Year Ended June 30, 20X2

| | | | |
|---|---|---|---|
| Cash flows from Operating Activities: | | | |
| Change in Net Assets | | | $1,523,000 |
| Adjustments to Reconcile Changes in Net Assets | | | |
| to Net Cash Provided by Operating Activities: | | | |
| Depreciation | $ 500,000 | | |
| Increase in Deposits with Trustees | (3,000) | | |
| Decrease in Accounts Receivable | 20,000 | | |
| Increase in Loans to Students, Faculty, and Staff | (85,000) | | |
| Increase in Inventories | (5,000) | | |
| Increase in Prepaid Expenses | (4,000) | | |
| Increase in Accounts Payable | 17,000 | | |
| Increase in Accrued Liabilities | 2,000 | | |
| Decrease in Students' Deposits | (3,000) | | |
| Increase in Deferred Credits | 5,000 | | |
| Restricted Contributions and Investment Income: | | | |
| Contributions, Grants, and Investment Income | | | |
| in Permanently Restricted Funds | $(1,611,000) | | |
| Contributions, Grants, and Investment Income | | | |
| in Temporarily Restricted Funds | (535,000) | | |
| Total Restricted Contributions and Investment Income | $(2,146,000) | (2,146,000) | |
| Total Adjustments | | $(1,702,000) | (1,702,000) |
| Net Cash Provided by Operating Activities | | | $ (179,000) |
| Cash Flows from Investing Activities: | | | |
| Acquisition of Property, Plant, and Equipment | $ (920,000) | | |
| Sale of Used Equipment | 60,000 | | |
| Net Acquisition of Investments | (65,000) | | |
| Flows Related to Restricted Items: | | | |
| Net Acquisition of Temporarily Restricted | | | |
| Investments | $ (112,000) | | |
| Net Acquisition of Permanently Restricted | | | |
| Investments | (1,050,000) | | |
| Net Cash Flow Related to Restricted Items | $(1,162,000) | (1,162,000) | |
| Net Cash Provided by Investing Activities | | | (2,087,000) |
| Cash Flows from Financing Activities: | | | |
| Decrease in Annuities Payable | $ (75,000) | | |
| Increase in Notes Payable | 50,000 | | |
| Increase in Bonds Payable | 100,000 | | |
| Increase in Mortgage Payable | 100,000 | | |
| Increase in Deposits Held in Custody | 10,000 | | |
| Flows Related to Restricted Items: | | | |
| Contributions, Grants, and Investment Income | | | |
| in Temporarily Restricted Funds | $ 1,611,000 | | |
| Contributions, Grants, and Investment Income | | | |
| in Permanently Restricted Funds | 535,000 | | |
| Cash Flows Related to Restricted Items | $ 2,146,000 | $ 185,000 | |
| Net Cash Provided by Financing Activities | | | 2,331,000 |
| Net Change in Cash | | | $ 65,000 |
| Cash at the Beginning of the Year | | | 514,000 |
| Cash at the End of the Year | | | $ 579,000 |

The AICPA audit guide serves as an important authoritative source in selecting accounting and financial reporting procedures for health care providers. The hospital financial statements illustrated in this chapter incorporate the disclosure standards of **FASB 117,** as presented and amplified in the AICPA's Audit and Accounting Guide for Health Care Organizations.

## Hospital Accounting

There are about 6,500 hospitals in the United States. Some of these are not-for-profit hospitals managed by charities. A large number of hospitals are managed by government agencies. For example, many universities operate a university-affiliated hospital. The federal government operates several hundred hospitals, including those offering health care to veterans. About 1,400 hospitals are investor-owned, for-profit companies.

1. The not-for-profit hospitals use the FASB's accounting and reporting requirements for not-for-profit organizations.
2. The governmental hospitals follow the GASB's accounting and reporting requirements.
3. The investor-owned, for-profit hospitals follow the FASB's accounting and reporting requirements the same as other profit-seeking business entities.

Investor-owned hospitals seek additional financial resources through the sale of stocks and the issuance of large amounts of debt. These profit-seeking hospitals provide the same types of financial reports as commercial entities. Not-for-profit hospitals present their financial results using a specific format required by the FASB. Not-for-profit hospitals are often affiliated with a religious group or a civic association. Governmental hospitals are managed by or affiliated with a government unit. Governmental hospitals follow the GASB's accounting and reporting requirements and are considered special-purpose entities engaged in business-type activities. As such, they present financial statements that are required for enterprise funds as presented in Chapter 18 of this textbook. Governmental hospitals then are included in the government entity's government-wide financial statements.

Two professional associations, the American Hospital Association (AHA) and the Hospital Financial Management Association (HFMA), are active in developing and improving hospital management, accounting, and financial reporting. Publications of both organizations can be useful to individuals seeking additional information on hospital accounting and reporting practices.

In this chapter, it is assumed that the hospital is a separate, not-for-profit reporting entity and is not a component unit of any government. The focus of this chapter is on not-for-profit hospitals because of the large number of such hospitals and because of their special accounting and financial reporting issues.

### *Hospital Fund Structure*

Although not required to do so, many hospitals have used a fund accounting structure for accounting purposes. In general, operating activities are carried on in the general fund, and a series of restricted funds can be used to account for assets whose use has been restricted by the donor. If separate funds are not maintained, then all transactions are recorded in the general fund, and memorandum records show restricted amounts in the general fund. The presentation of financial statement information under **FASB 117** requires a distinction between those net assets that are unrestricted, temporarily restricted, and permanently restricted. The discussion of accounting and financial reporting for hospitals that follows assumes that unrestricted net assets are accounted for in the general fund and that one or more separate funds are used to account for temporarily restricted and permanently restricted net assets.

All transactions involving the use of unrestricted net assets are recorded in the general fund. As such, the general fund is the hospital's primary operating fund. Assets that were restricted as to the period of use or that must be used for particular purposes are accounted for in restricted funds until the restriction is satisfied. When the restriction is satisfied, the assets are transferred (reclassified) from the restricted fund to the general (unrestricted) fund. Any expenses that are incurred in satisfying the restrictions are reported as expenses in the general fund.

Restricted funds account for assets received from donors or other third parties who have imposed certain restrictions on their use. The restricted funds are often termed

**FIGURE 19–5**
Overview of
Hospital Accounting
and Reporting

| | | Fund Groups | | | |
|---|---|---|---|---|---|
| | | Restricted | | | |
| | General | Specific Purpose | Time Restricted | Plant Replacement and Expansion | Endowment |
| Distinguishing features | | Resources restricted for specific operating purposes. | Resources not available until date specified by donor. | Resources restricted for additions to plant assets. | Principal preserved as specified by donor. |
| Financial statements | | Balance Sheet | | | |
| | | Statement of Operations | | | |
| | | Statement of Changes in Net Assets | | | |
| | | Statement of Cash Flows | | | |

"holding" funds because they must hold the restricted assets and transfer expendable resources to the general fund for expenditure. Figure 19–5 presents an overview of the fund structure and the typical financial reporting for hospitals.

***General Fund*** The ***general fund*** accounts for the resources received and expended in the hospital's primary health care mission. The basis of accounting is the accrual method in order to measure fully all expenses of providing services during the period. Depreciation is included in the operating expenses. Fixed assets are included in the fund based on the theory that the governing board may use these assets in any manner desired.

The governing board may establish ***board-designated resources*** within the general fund. For example, the board may designate resources for the expansion of the hospital, for retirement of debt, or for other purposes. Funds designated in this manner are considered to be part of the unrestricted funds, but this designation provides information on the intended use of the resources.

***Donor Restricted Funds*** All ***restricted funds*** account for resources whose use is restricted by the donor. For financial reporting purposes, a distinction is made between temporarily and permanently restricted funds. The major *temporarily restricted* funds are (1) specific-purpose funds, (2) time-restricted funds, and (3) plant replacement and expansion funds. *Permanently restricted funds* are assets that must be held into perpetuity and generally are included in an endowment fund. Hospitals may also have restricted loan funds and annuity and life income funds; however, few hospitals use these funds, and they are not discussed in this chapter.

*Specific-purpose funds* are restricted for ***specific operating purposes.*** For example, a donor may specify that a donation of $25,000 may be used only for maternity care. The donation is held in the specific-purpose fund until the maternity expenditure is approved in the general fund. Once approved, the specific-purpose fund transfers the resources to the general fund.

*Time-restricted funds* account for assets received or pledged by donors for use in future periods. The donor's restriction is satisfied by the passage of time. A pledge received in 20X1 to contribute a stated amount in 20X2 to be used for unrestricted purposes is included in the time-restricted fund in the balance sheet prepared at December 31, 20X1.

*Plant replacement and expansion restricted funds* account for contributions to be used only for additions to fixed assets. When the general fund approves or makes the appropriate expenditures for the fixed assets, the plant replacement and expansion fund transfers the resources to the general fund.

*Endowment funds* account for resources when the principal must be preserved. The income from these resources is usually available for either a restricted or a general purpose. Endowments may be either permanent or term. Term endowments are for limited time periods, for example, 5 or 10 years, or until a specific event occurs, such as the death of the donor. After the term expires, the governing board uses the principal of the fund in accordance with the gift agreement.

## Financial Statements for a Not-for-Profit Hospital

Separate, not-for-profit hospitals issue four basic financial statements: (1) the balance sheet, (2) the statement of operations, (3) the statement of changes in net assets, and (4) the statement of cash flows. Comparative data for prior fiscal periods are normally presented within each statement. Each of the four statements is demonstrated in the comprehensive illustration presented later in this chapter.

### Balance Sheet

The *balance sheet* presents the total assets, liabilities, and net assets of the organization as a whole.

***Receivables***   Receivables may include amounts due from patients, third party payors, other insurers of health care, pledges or grants, and interfund transactions. Receivables should be reported at the anticipated realizable amount. Thus, the realizable amounts may include reductions due to contractual agreements with third party payors or provider practices, such as allowing courtesy discounts to medical staff members and employees. An allowance for uncollectibles is recognized for estimated bad debts. Note that not-for-profit hospitals recognize estimated uncollectibles from providing services as bad debts expense. Charity care occurs when health care services are provided to a patient who has demonstrated, in accordance with the hospital's established criteria, an inability to pay. In these cases, charity care does not qualify for recognition as either receivables or revenue in the hospital's financial statements. The determination of a charity care case may not be able to be made when the patient is admitted, but at some point the hospital must be able to determine that the person does meet the necessary qualifications for charity care before reducing the amount owed. Receivables from pledges of future contributions are reported in the period the pledge is made, net of an allowance for uncollectible amounts.

***Investments***   Investments are initially recorded at cost if purchased or at fair value at the date of receipt if received as a gift. Subsequently, for investor-owned, *profit-seeking hospitals,* equity and debt securities are reported in accordance with **FASB Statement No. 115,** "Accounting for Certain Investments in Debt and Equity Securities" (FASB 115). **FASB 115** establishes three portfolios of investments: trading securities, available-for-sale securities, and hold-to-maturity debt securities. The accounting and reporting of the investment differ according to the category. For *nonprofit hospitals,* equity securities with readily determinable fair values and all investments in debt securities are measured at fair value, in accordance with **FASB Statement No. 124,** "Accounting for Certain Investments Held by Not-for-Profit Organizations" (FASB 124). The Audit and Accounting Guide for Health Care Organizations states that the investment return (including realized and unrealized gains and losses) not restricted by donors should be classified as changes in unrestricted net assets in the hospital's statement of operations. The investment return designated for current operations is included above the operation performance indicator line (Excess of Revenues, Gains, and Other Support over Expenses) reflecting operations; the investment return in excess of amounts designated for current operations is reported in the statement of operations below the operating performance indicator line. Investment returns restricted by donors or by law are reported as changes in net assets in the appropriate restricted funds. For *governmental health care entities,* **GASB Statement No. 31,** "Accounting and Financial Reporting for Certain Investments and for External Investment Pools" (GASB 31), specifies the general rule of fair value accounting for investments.

For these three types of hospitals, investments in stock accounted for under the equity method are reported in accordance with **APB Statement No. 18,** "The Equity Method of Accounting for Investments in Common Stock" (APB 18). Some hospitals receive income from trusts that donors have established with fiduciaries, such as banks. If the hospital does not own the trust or its investments, the independent trusts are not an asset of the hospital and are not reported on the hospital's balance sheet. Footnote disclosure may be made of major independent endowments or trust agreements that benefit the hospital.

*Plant Assets*   Property, plant, and equipment is reported with any accumulated depreciation. Depreciation is recorded in the general fund because the use of assets is part of the cost of providing medical services. The assets are reported in the general fund because they are available for use in any manner deemed necessary by the governing board.

*Assets Whose Use Is Limited*   Separate disclosure should be made for assets that have restrictions placed on their use by the donor or that have been designated by the board of directors for special use. Such funds may come from a variety of sources. For example, grant monies received for cancer research are reported as funds restricted for specific purposes and classified as temporarily restricted until used in support of research. Funds contributed to assist in constructing a new children's wing of the hospital are reported as restricted for plant replacement and expansion and classified as temporarily restricted until used in construction. Funds received for permanent investment in the principal of an endowment fund are reported as permanently restricted. Only those funds whose use is restricted by the donor are classified as restricted; thus, assets set aside for identified purposes by the governing board and over which the board retains control are not classified as restricted but are regarded as *assets whose use is limited.*

*Long-Term Debt*   The hospital must also account for its long-term debt and pay the principal and interest as it becomes due. The debt is shown in the balance sheet. This practice differs from that used by most governmental entities that establish a separate debt service fund to service debt.

*Net Assets*   The hospital segregates its net assets into (1) **unrestricted net assets** available for use at the discretion of the hospital staff and board of directors, (2) **temporarily restricted net assets** available for use when specific events established by the donor are satisfied, and (3) **permanently restricted net assets** that have been restricted by the donor as to their use.

### Statement of Operations

The results of not-for-profit hospitals' operations are reported in a *statement of operations,* also often termed "the statement of activities." This statement includes the revenues, expenses, gains and losses, and other transactions affecting the unrestricted net assets during the period. Note that only those transactions in the general fund are reported on the statement of operations. Transactions affecting only the restricted funds are *not* shown on the statement of operations; rather, they are reported on the statement of changes in net assets. Gains and losses from transactions that are peripheral or ancillary to the provision of health care services are reported separately from net patient service revenue. The statement of operations should report an operating *performance indicator,* which reports the results of the hospital's operating activities for the period. This performance indicator should include both operating income (loss) for the period and other income available for current operations. **FASB 117** requires that net assets released from restrictions for use in operations be included before the performance indicator line on the statement of activities, generally termed "above the line." This is so because the transfer of net assets from the restricted group of assets for use in the entity's operations in the unrestricted group of net assets can then be matched with the expenses incurred to fulfill the operating restriction. The title of the performance indicator should be descriptive, such as the "Excess of Operating Revenues, Gains, and Other Support over Operating Expenses."

Other changes in the unrestricted net assets during the period should be reported after the performance indicator, generally termed "below the line." These changes include investment return in excess of amounts designated for current operations as defined by **FASB 124.** For example, a hospital's board of directors could reserve a portion of the investment return from the revaluation of investments for use in future periods, thus making them unavailable for current operations. The AICPA's audit guide for hospitals indicates that the investment return from other than trading securities should be presented below the operating performance line, and the investment return from trading securities should be presented above the operating line. However, an audit guide is lower than a FASB standard in the hierarchy of generally accepted accounting principles. Other changes reported below the operating performance indicator line would include transfers from restricted net assets of resources used for the purchase of property and equipment. Note that the statement of operations must separately report those items related to the acquisition of property or equipment from those related to operating activities.

A separate, third statement, entitled the *statement of changes in net assets,* is used to report items affecting the temporarily restricted and permanently restricted net assets. This third statement is covered in this chapter following discussion of the statement of operations.

***Net Patient Service Revenue*** Net patient service revenue represents the hospital's revenue from inpatient and outpatient care excluding charity care and contractual adjustments. Net patient service revenue represents the billings for services provided and the earning capacity of the hospital. Many hospitals are required to perform a certain amount of charity care for which they recognize no revenue. The charity cases are imposed by terms of certain federal medical care grant programs. Charity care helps ensure that indigent persons living in the region served by the hospital may obtain adequate medical services. When charity care is provided, no revenue is recognized, but disclosure of the estimated amount of charity care is presented in the footnotes to the financial statements.

***Contractual Adjustments*** Contractual adjustments constitute a major deduction from gross patient service revenue. Contractual adjustments result from the involvement of third party payors in the medical reimbursement process. Insurance companies or government units (especially the federal government) reimburse less than the full standard rate for medical services provided to patients covered by insurance- or by government-provided services such as Medicare. These third party payors may stipulate limits on the amount of costs they will pay. A hospital may have a standard rate for a specific service but may contract with the third party payor to accept a lower amount for that service. For example, Medicare establishes specific reimbursement rates for various services, termed a "diagnosis-related group" (DRG). The hospital makes a contractual adjustment from its normal service charge, and this adjustment is a deduction from gross Patient Service Revenue.

***Income from Ancillary Programs*** Income from ancillary programs represents the income earned from nonpatient sources such as television rentals, cafeteria sales, sales in hospital-operated gift shops, parking fees, and tuition on hospital-provided educational programs. The income reported typically represents the net earnings from such operations rather than the gross receipts.

***Interfund Transfers*** It is not appropriate to hold assets in a restricted fund when the donor-specified requirements have been satisfied. For example, when contributions received to purchase plant and equipment are used to purchase new assets or when contributions received for use in educational programs are used for that purpose, the funds should be transferred from the restricted fund to the general fund. For financial reporting purposes, this transfer between funds is reported as "net assets released" in the statement of operations and is shown as an addition to the general fund. If the interfund transfer to the general fund is to be used for operations, the general fund reports it above the operating performance indicator line in the statement of operations. If the interfund transfer to the general fund is to be used for acquiring long-term assets, the general fund reports it below the performance indicator line in the statement of operations.

***General Fund Expenses***  The major expenses in the general fund are for nursing services, other professional services, depreciation, bad debts, and the general and administrative costs of the hospital. These costs are recognized on the accrual basis of accounting, similar to commercial entities. Hospitals that self-insure for malpractice costs should recognize an expense and a liability for malpractice costs in the period during which the incidents that give rise to the claims occur if it is probable that liabilities have been incurred and the amounts of the losses can be reasonably estimated. Any expenses related to fundraising should be classified separately.

***Donations***  Hospitals often receive a wide variety of services from volunteers. For example, retired physicians or pharmacists may voluntarily work part-time in their professional roles. In addition, the hospital may receive donations of supplies or equipment. The rules on accounting for donations and contributions to hospitals are as follows:

1. *Donated services.* Because it is often difficult to place a value on donated services, their values are usually not recorded. However, if the following conditions exist, the estimated value of the donated services is reported as an expense and a corresponding amount is reported as contributions. **FASB 116** specifies that a contribution of services should be recognized if the services received (*a*) create or enhance nonfinancial assets or (*b*) require specialized skills, are provided by individuals possessing those skills, and would typically need to be purchased if not provided by donations.

2. *Donated assets.* Donated assets are reported at fair market value at the date of the contribution:

   *a.* Donated assets are reported as contributions in the statement of operations, if unrestricted. For example, a donation of medical supplies is recorded as a contribution in the general fund in the period received.

   *b.* Donated assets that are restricted in use by the donor are recognized as contribution revenue in the temporarily restricted or permanently restricted fund at the time of receipt. Note that contribution revenue is recognized in the appropriate restricted fund at the time the restricted donation is received. When the restriction no longer applies, the donated assets are transferred to the general fund. For example, when the general fund purchases assets with resources that have been restricted for that purpose, the transfer is made from the restricted fund as a debit to Net Assets Released from Restriction and a credit to Cash. The general fund accounts for the transfer of cash with a debit to Cash and a credit to Net Assets Released from Restriction, which is reported in the general fund's statement of operations.

   If the hospital does not use a fund structure for restricted assets, the contribution of restricted assets is accounted for as a debit to Cash and a credit to Net Assets Restricted, which is reported on the hospital's balance sheet. However, the statement of operations of the general fund does not report the donated assets until the restriction is no longer applicable and the assets have become available for use in the general fund. At the time the assets become available for use in the general fund, the general fund reports the transfer of the assets for use in the operations of the hospital on the statement of operations for the general fund and reclassifies the assets from the restricted net asset class to the unrestricted net asset class.

Appropriate expense accounts are charged as the donated assets are consumed. For example, donated supplies such as medicines, linen, and disposable medical items are charged to an expense as used from inventory. For donated physical plant or equipment having an estimated economic life of more than one year, depreciation is charged to each period in which the plant or equipment is used.

### Statement of Changes in Net Assets

The third of the four financial statements for a not-for-profit hospital is termed the *statement of changes in net assets.* It presents the changes in all three categories of net assets: unrestricted, temporarily restricted, and permanently restricted. Donor-restricted contributions are reported in the appropriate category of restricted net assets. Net assets released from restrictions are shown as deductions from restricted net assets and as transfers to the unrestricted net assets. This release could be due to the completion of a time restriction, the fulfillment of a use restriction, or the satisfaction of any other donor-specified restriction.

### Statement of Cash Flows

The fourth, and final, financial statement for a not-for-profit hospital is the *statement of cash flows.* Its format is similar to that for commercial entities and is presented as part of the comprehensive illustration in the next section of this chapter.

## Comprehensive Illustration of Hospital Accounting and Financial Reporting

Sol City Community Hospital, a not-for-profit hospital operated by a community group, provides medical care for the region surrounding Sol City. The hospital has established the following funds: (1) general, (2) specific-purpose, (3) time-restricted, (4) plant replacement and expansion, and (5) endowment.

Entries to record transactions in each of the funds during the 20X2 fiscal year, ending December 31, 20X2, are presented in the next section of the chapter. First the financial statements for the period are presented, and then the transactions from which these statements resulted are discussed. The balance sheet for both the general and the restricted funds is presented in Figure 19–6. Note that the balance sheet is presented in what is generally termed an *aggregated style* rather than a *columnar* or *layered style* that would separately show the financial position of each fund. The selection of display formats is the choice of the hospital's governing board, but the aggregated format for the entity as a whole is more in keeping with the recommendations of **FASB 117.** An analysis of the composition of the net assets held as temporarily and permanently restricted at December 31, 20X2 and 20X1, provides the following amounts:

| | Dec. 31, 20X2 | Net Change | Dec. 31, 20X1 |
|---|---|---|---|
| Temporarily restricted: | | | |
| Plant Replacement and Expansion Fund | | | |
| Cash | $    50,000 | $(150,000) | $200,000 |
| Pledges receivable | 15,000 | (105,000) | 120,000 |
| Investments | 140,000 | 122,000 | 18,000 |
| Net assets | $  205,000 | $(133,000) | $338,000 |
| Specific-Purpose Fund | | | |
| Cash | $      3,000 | $    1,000 | $    2,000 |
| Investments | 20,000 | -0- | 20,000 |
| Net assets | $    23,000 | $    1,000 | $  22,000 |
| Time-Restricted Fund | | | |
| Cash | $      2,000 | $      -0- | $    2,000 |
| Contributions receivable | -0- | (12,000) | 12,000 |
| Investments | 196,000 | -0- | 196,000 |
| Net assets | $  198,000 | $  (12,000) | $210,000 |
| Permanently restricted: | | | |
| Endowment Fund | | | |
| Cash | $    25,000 | $  15,000 | $  10,000 |
| Investments | 1,190,000 | 400,000 | 790,000 |
| Net assets | $1,215,000 | $  415,000 | $800,000 |

The specific-purpose fund and the time-restricted fund contain resources that will be available for operations as the restrictions are met.

**FIGURE 19–6**
Balance Sheet for
a Not-for-Profit
Hospital

| SOL CITY COMMUNITY HOSPITAL | | |
|---|---|---|
| Balance Sheet | | |
| December 31, 20X2 and 20X1 | | |
| | **20X2** | **20X1** |
| **Assets** | | |
| Current: | | |
|   Cash | $ 295,000 | $ 14,000 |
|   Receivables | 460,000 | 400,000 |
|   Less: Estimated Uncollectibles | (40,000) | (30,000) |
|   Contributions and Pledges Receivable | -0- | 12,000 |
|   Inventories | 50,000 | 60,000 |
|   Prepaid Expenses | 15,000 | 20,000 |
| Total Current Assets | $ 780,000 | $ 476,000 |
| Assets Limited as to Use: | | |
|   Cash Restricted as to Use for Plant Expansion and Endowment | $ 75,000 | $ 210,000 |
|   Pledges Receivable Restricted for Plant Expansion and Replacement | 15,000 | 120,000 |
|   Investments Restricted as to Use for Plant Expansion and Endowment | 1,330,000 | 808,000 |
| Total Limited Assets | $1,420,000 | $1,138,000 |
| Investments (at fair value) | $ 681,000 | $ 716,000 |
| Property, Plant, and Equipment | $3,375,000 | $3,200,000 |
| Less: Accumulated Depreciation | (1,150,000) | (1,000,000) |
| Net Property, Plant, and Equipment | $2,225,000 | $2,200,000 |
| Total Assets | $5,106,000 | $4,530,000 |
| **Liabilities and Net Assets** | | |
| Current: | | |
|   Notes Payable to Bank | $ 65,000 | $ 70,000 |
|   Current Portion of Long-Term Debt | 50,000 | 60,000 |
|   Accounts Payable | 50,000 | 90,000 |
|   Accrued Expenses | 30,000 | 25,000 |
|   Estimated Malpractice Costs Payable | 30,000 | -0- |
|   Advances from Third Parties | 160,000 | 125,000 |
|   Deferred Revenue | 5,000 | 5,000 |
| Total Current Liabilities | $ 390,000 | $ 375,000 |
| Long-Term Debt: | | |
|   Mortgage Payable | 1,050,000 | 1,100,000 |
| Total Liabilities | $1,440,000 | $1,475,000 |
| Net Assets: | | |
|   Unrestricted | $2,025,000 | $1,685,000 |
|   Temporarily Restricted by Donors | 426,000 | 570,000 |
|   Permanently Restricted by Donors | 1,215,000 | 800,000 |
| Total Net Assets | $3,666,000 | $3,055,000 |
| Total Liabilities and Net Assets | $5,106,000 | $4,530,000 |

The statement of operations is presented in Figure 19–7, the statement of changes in net assets is presented in Figure 19–8, and the statement of cash flows is presented in Figure 19–9. Each of these statements is discussed after presentation of the journal entries for 20X2 for Sol City Community Hospital.

### General Fund

The transactions in the general fund for 20X2 are presented in accordance with their relative degree of importance in the hospital's operations. The first series of entries presented

**FIGURE 19–7**
**Statement of Operations for a Not-for-Profit Hospital**

## SOL CITY COMMUNITY HOSPITAL
### Statement of Operations
### For the Year Ended December 31, 20X2

| | |
|---|---:|
| Unrestricted Revenue, Gains, and Other Support: | |
|   Net Patient Service Revenue | $2,360,000 |
|   Ancillary Programs | 30,000 |
|   Unrestricted Gifts Used in Operations | 93,000 |
|   Disposal of Hospital Assets | 5,000 |
|   Donated Services | 10,000 |
|   Investment Income Designated for Current Operations | 10,000 |
|   Net Assets Released from Restrictions for Use in Operations | 192,000 |
| Total Revenue, Gains, and Other Support | $2,700,000 |
| Expenses: | |
|   Nursing Services | $  800,000 |
|   Other Professional Services | 630,000 |
|   General Services | 700,000 |
|   Fiscal Services | 100,000 |
|   Administrative Services | 80,000 |
|   Medical Malpractice Costs | 30,000 |
|   Bad Debts | 60,000 |
|   Depreciation | 200,000 |
| Total Expenses | $2,600,000 |
| Excess of Operating Revenues over Operating Expenses | $  100,000 |
| Other Items: | |
|   Investment Return in Excess of Amounts Designated for Current Operations | 15,000 |
|   Net Assets Released from Restrictions Used for Acquisition of Equipment | 225,000 |
| Increase in Unrestricted Net Assets | $  340,000 |

**FIGURE 19–8**
**Statement of Changes in Net Assets for a Not-for-Profit Hospital**

## SOL CITY COMMUNITY HOSPITAL
### Statement of Changes in Net Assets
### For the Year Ended December 31, 20X2

| | |
|---|---:|
| Unrestricted Net Assets: | |
|   Excess of Operating Revenues over Operating Expenses | $  100,000 |
|   Investment Return in Excess of Amounts Designated for Current Operations | 15,000 |
|   Net Assets Released from Equipment Acquisition Restrictions | 225,000 |
| Increase in Unrestricted Net Assets | $  340,000 |
| Temporarily Restricted Net Assets: | |
|   Contributions | $  200,000 |
|   Investment Gains | 73,000 |
|   Net Assets Released from: | |
|     Program Use Restrictions | (180,000) |
|     Equipment Acquisition Restrictions | (225,000) |
|     Passage of Time | (12,000) |
| Decrease in Temporarily Restricted Net Assets | $ (144,000) |
| Permanently Restricted Net Assets: | |
|   Contributions | $  415,000 |
| Increase in Permanently Restricted Net Assets | $  415,000 |
| Increase in Net Assets | $  611,000 |
| Net Assets at Beginning of Year | 3,055,000 |
| Net Assets at End of Year | $3,666,000 |

**FIGURE 19–9**  Statement of Cash Flows for a Not-for-Profit Hospital (Indirect Method)

**SOL CITY COMMUNITY HOSPITAL**
Statement of Cash Flows
For the Year Ended December 31, 20X2

| | | | |
|---|---:|---:|---:|
| Cash Flows from Operating Activities: | | | |
| Change in Total Net Assets | | | $ 611,000 |
| Adjustments to Reconcile Changes in Net Assets | | | |
| to Net Cash Provided by Operating Activities: | | | |
| Depreciation | | $ 200,000 | |
| Investment Unrealized Holding Gain (not | | | |
| available for current operations) | | (15,000) | |
| Contribution of Property, Plant, and Equipment | | (25,000) | |
| Gain on Disposal of Equipment | | (5,000) | |
| Increase in Advances from Third Parties | | 35,000 | |
| Increase in Malpractice Costs | | 30,000 | |
| Increase in Accrued Expenses | | 5,000 | |
| Decrease in Accounts Payable | | (40,000) | |
| Increase in Receivables, Net | | (50,000) | |
| Decrease in Pledges Receivable—Current | | 12,000 | |
| Decrease in Prepaid Expenses | | 5,000 | |
| Decrease in Inventories | | 10,000 | |
| Restricted Contributions and Investment Income: | | | |
| Contribution for Permanent Endowment | $(415,000) | | |
| Contributions Restricted for Plant Acquisition | (60,000) | | |
| Investment Income Restricted for Plant Acquisition | (7,000) | | |
| Total Restricted Contributions and Investment Income | | (482,000) | |
| Total Adjustments | | | (320,000) |
| Net Cash Provided by Operating Activities | | | $ 291,000 |
| Cash Flows from Investing Activities: | | | |
| Sale of Used Hospital Assets | | $ 55,000 | |
| Sale of Investments | | 50,000 | |
| Acquisition of Plant, Property, and Equipment | | (250,000) | |
| Flows Related to Restricted Items: | | | |
| Purchase of Investments in Endowment and Plant Replacement Funds | $(522,000) | | |
| Remainder of Contributions to Endowment Fund Restricted to Investing | (15,000) | | |
| Remainder of Contributions to Plant Fund Restricted to Plant Purchases | (50,000) | | |
| Cash Transferred from Plant Fund for Plant Expansion | 200,000 | | |
| Total Investing Flows Related to Restricted Items | | (387,000) | |
| Net Cash Used by Investing Activities | | | $(532,000) |
| Cash Flows from Financing Activities: | | | |
| Paid Notes Payable | | $ (5,000) | |
| Paid Current Portion of Long-Term Debt | | (60,000) | |
| Proceeds from Restricted Contributions: | | | |
| Contributions Restricted for Permanent Endowment | $ 415,000 | | |
| Contributions Restricted for Acquiring Fixed Assets | 172,000 | | |
| Total Restricted Proceeds | | 587,000 | |
| Net Cash Provided by Financing Activities | | | $ 522,000 |
| Net Increase in Cash | | | $ 281,000 |
| Cash at the Beginning of Year | | | 14,000 |
| Cash at the End of Year (unrestricted) | | | $ 295,000 |

are for the revenues generated from patient care and the associated operating expenses for the period.

***Net Patient Care Revenue***  The hospital provides patient services of $2,600,000 measured by standard rates. From this amount, $240,000 is deducted for contractual adjustments with third party payors which results in a net patient revenue of $2,360,000. Charity care is not recognized as a revenue nor as a reduction in revenue. The expenses related to charity care are recognized as operating expenses. Although charity care is not explicitly recognized on the statement of operations, footnote disclosures of the amount of charity care should be provided in the financial reports.

| | | | |
|---|---|---|---|
| (5) | Accounts Receivable | 2,600,000 | |
| |     Patient Services Revenue | | 2,600,000 |
| |   Gross charges at standard rates. | | |
| | | | |
| (6) | Patient Services Revenue | 240,000 | |
| |     Accounts Receivable | | 240,000 |
| |   Deduction from gross patient services revenue for contractual adjustments. | | |

**Revenue from Ancillary Programs**   The hospital receives income in 20X2 from providing nonpatient services that include operating a cafeteria and gift shop and from vending machine commissions.

| | | | |
|---|---|---|---|
| (7) | Cash | 30,000 | |
| |     Revenue from Cafeteria Sales | | 20,000 |
| |     Revenue from Gift Shop Sales | | 4,000 |
| |     Revenue from Vending Machine Commissions | | 6,000 |
| |   Income from ancillary services. | | |

**Operating Expenses**   The hospital incurs $2,600,000 in operating expenses for nursing and other professional care, for general and administrative expenses, for bad debts expense, and for depreciation. Not-for-profit hospitals account for estimated uncollectibles from provided services as an operating expense. Fiscal Services Expense includes interest expense on the hospital's debt. The hospital recognized $30,000 in estimated malpractice costs that are probable and reasonably estimated. Cash payments are made for $2,125,000 of the total operating expenses, and the remainder is consumption of Prepaid Assets, Allowance for Uncollectibles, Depreciation, and increases in liabilities. The hospital receives donated services valued at $10,000, which are recognized in entry (9):

| | | | |
|---|---|---|---|
| (8) | Nursing Services Expense | 800,000 | |
| | Other Professional Services Expense | 620,000 | |
| | General Services Expense | 700,000 | |
| | Fiscal Services Expense | 100,000 | |
| | Administrative Services Expense | 80,000 | |
| | Medical Malpractice Costs | 30,000 | |
| | Bad Debts Expense | 60,000 | |
| | Depreciation Expense | 200,000 | |
| |   Cash | | 2,125,000 |
| |   Allowance for Uncollectibles | | 60,000 |
| |   Inventories | | 90,000 |
| |   Prepaid Expenses | | 5,000 |
| |   Accumulated Depreciation | | 200,000 |
| |   Accounts Payable | | 50,000 |
| |   Accrued Expenses | | 30,000 |
| |   Estimated Medical Malpractice Costs Payable | | 30,000 |
| |   Record operating expenses. | | |
| | | | |
| (9) | Other Professional Services Expense | 10,000 | |
| |   Donated Services—Revenue | | 10,000 |
| |   Receive donated services. | | |

Entry (9) records the fair value of donated services both as a debit for the operating expense and as a credit for operating revenue. Therefore, donated services do not affect the bottom line of the hospital's statement of revenue and expenses, but they do affect the amounts shown for the expenses and revenue sections of the statement.

***Contribution Revenue*** During 20X2, Sol City Community Hospital received unrestricted cash gifts in the amount of $63,000 and donated medicines and medical supplies with a market value of $30,000:

| | | | |
|---|---|---|---|
| (10) | Cash | 63,000 | |
| | Contributions—Unrestricted | | 63,000 |
| | Unrestricted contributions received. | | |

| | | | |
|---|---|---|---|
| (11) | Inventory | 30,000 | |
| | Contributions—Unrestricted | | 30,000 |
| | Donated supplies received. | | |

***Other Revenues and Gains*** Also during 20X2, income of $10,000 was earned in the unrestricted fund and is available for current operations. In addition, a gain of $5,000 was realized on the sale of equipment:

| | | | |
|---|---|---|---|
| (12) | Cash | 10,000 | |
| | Investment Income—Designated for Current Operations | | 10,000 |
| | Investment earnings available for current operations. | | |

| | | | |
|---|---|---|---|
| (13) | Cash | 55,000 | |
| | Accumulated Depreciation | 50,000 | |
| | Property, Plant, and Equipment | | 100,000 |
| | Gain on Disposal of Equipment | | 5,000 |
| | Sale of hospital equipment. The cash will be used in the operations of the hospital. | | |

***Net Assets Released from Restriction*** Assets were released for unrestricted use from a variety of sources in 20X2, as follows:

| Amount | From Restricted Fund | Description |
|---|---|---|
| $120,000 | Specific-Purpose Fund | Resources for education and research |
| 60,000 | Specific-Purpose Fund | Income from endowment investment |
| 200,000 | Plant Expansion and Replacement | Resources to acquire equipment |
| 25,000 | Plant Expansion and Replacement | Donated assets placed into use |
| 12,000 | Time-Restricted Fund | Collection of pledges receivable |

Entries in the unrestricted fund to record these transactions are presented here:

| | | | |
|---|---|---|---|
| (14) | Cash | 120,000 | |
| | Net Assets Released from Program Use Restrictions | | 120,000 |
| | Record payment for reimbursement of operating expenses incurred in accordance with restricted gift. | | |

| | | | |
|---|---|---|---|
| (15) | Cash | 60,000 | |
| | Net Assets Released from Program Use Restrictions | | 60,000 |
| | Receipt of endowment earnings from specific-purpose fund upon approval and completion of specified purpose. | | |

| | | | |
|---|---|---|---|
| (16) | Cash | 200,000 | |
| | Net Assets Released from Equipment Acquisition Restriction | | 200,000 |
| | Transfer from temporarily restricted plant replacement and expansion fund for use in acquiring plant assets. | | |

| | | | |
|---|---|---|---|
| (17) | Property, Plant, and Equipment | 25,000 | |
| | Net Assets Released from Equipment Acquisition Restriction | | 25,000 |
| | Transfer from temporarily restricted plant replacement and expansion fund of donated assets placed in service. | | |

| (18) | Cash | 12,000 | |
| | Net Assets Released from Passage of Time | | 12,000 |
| | Transfer from temporarily restricted funds restricted for use in 20X2. | | |

Each of the transfers from temporarily restricted funds involves one or more journal entries in those funds. These amounts are not included among 20X2 contributions or income in the unrestricted fund because they were recorded as contributions or income at the time of receipt in the temporarily restricted or permanently restricted funds. The transfer of donated equipment initially is recorded in the temporarily restricted plant fund until the hospital begins using the asset. At the time the assets are placed in service, the value of the donated equipment is transferred to the unrestricted fund.

***Other Transactions in the General Fund***  The remaining transactions during the 20X2 fiscal year affect the balance sheet accounts. Transactions affecting only the asset accounts include collecting receivables, acquiring inventory, selling an investment, and purchasing additional physical plant assets, as follows:

| (19) | Cash | 2,250,000 | |
| | Allowance for Uncollectibles | 50,000 | |
| | Accounts Receivable | | 2,300,000 |
| | Collect some receivables and write off $50,000 as uncollectible. | | |

| (20) | Inventories | 50,000 | |
| | Cash | | 50,000 |
| | Acquire inventories. | | |

| (21) | Cash | 50,000 | |
| | Investments | | 50,000 |
| | Sell investment at cost. | | |

| (22) | Property, Plant, and Equipment | 250,000 | |
| | Cash | | 250,000 |
| | Purchase new plant with cash of $50,000 from sale of investments and $200,000 from transfer in from temporarily restricted plant replacement and expansion fund. | | |

Transactions affecting the current liability accounts include paying current liabilities and recording the receipt of cash in advance of billings from third parties. The hospital reclassified the portion of the long-term mortgage that is currently due. The hospital also revalues, to fair value, the general fund's investment securities.

**FASB 124** requires that not-for-profit organizations value their investment securities, other than those equity investments accounted for under **APB 18,** at fair value at each balance sheet date. The total investment income during a period is from dividends, interest, and realized and unrealized holding gains or losses. For a not-for-profit hospital, after the total investment income is determined, the portion of investment income designated for current operations is reported above the operating performance indicator line on the hospital's statement of activities. The investment return in excess of the amount designated for current operations is separately reported below the operating performance indicator line on the hospital's statement of activities. The not-for-profit entity's management is permitted to establish a policy as to the separation of total investment return for current operations or for other purposes. This policy should be described in the footnotes of the hospital's financial statements. For our example, assume that Sol City Community Hospital's board of directors has a policy to set aside the recognition of unrealized holding gains of unrestricted investments for possible future operations. Therefore, the entire $15,000 of unrealized holding gain recognized on the hospital's year-end revaluation of its investment securities is separated and reported below the operating performance indicator line on the hospital's statement of activities.

| | | | | |
|---|---|---|---:|---:|
| (23) | Notes Payable to Bank | | 5,000 | |
| | Current Portion of Long-Term Debt | | 60,000 | |
| | Accounts Payable | | 90,000 | |
| | Accrued Expenses | | 25,000 | |
| | Cash | | | 180,000 |
| | Pay liabilities outstanding at beginning of period. | | | |
| (24) | Cash | | 35,000 | |
| | Advances from Third Parties | | | 35,000 |
| | Increase in cash received from third parties for deposits in advance of service billings. | | | |
| (25) | Mortgage Payable | | 50,000 | |
| | Current Portion of Long-Term Debt | | | 50,000 |
| | Reclassify current portion of long-term debt. | | | |
| (26) | Investments | | 15,000 | |
| | Unrealized Holding Gain on Investment Securities | | | 15,000 |
| | Revalue securities to fair value and report as not designated for current operations. | | | |

Closing entries, required for all nominal accounts, are not presented because the focus is on other aspects of hospital accounting and because the closing process for hospitals is the same as for any other accounting entity. As presented in Figure 19–8, the statement of changes in net assets includes a reconciliation of net assets between the beginning of the year and the year-end.

The statement of cash flows (Figure 19–9) is a required statement. Either the direct or the indirect method may be used to display net cash flows from operations. Under the direct method, the specific inflows and outflows from operations are presented. Under the indirect method, the statement begins with the change in net assets as presented on the statement of changes in net assets. It then presents the adjustments necessary to reconcile the net amount shown on the statement of changes in net assets with the cash flow that is provided by operating activities. Figure 19–9 presents the indirect method because of its popularity and wide use by hospitals. The statement of cash flows is similar to that required of commercial, profit-seeking entities. The three categories of operating activities, investing activities, and financing activities are the same as for commercial entities. There is an important feature, however, for the statement of cash flows for a nonprofit hospital. A nonprofit hospital's cash flow statement reconciles to the change in cash and cash equivalents that is reported as a current asset on the hospital's balance sheet. This cash amount does not include the cash balances in the restricted accounts not available for operations (the plant fund and the endowment fund in the Sol City Community Hospital example). For example, Sol City Community Hospital received a cash contribution to the endowment fund in the amount of $415,000 in transaction (40) (presented later in this chapter). The $415,000 must first be subtracted from the change in net assets in the operating section of the statement of cash flows because the endowment fund does not constitute operating activities. The $415,000 is reported as an increase in financing activities on the statement of cash flows. Of the $415,000 received, $400,000 was used to acquire investments (transaction [41] presented later in this chapter) and this amount is included in the $522,000 as an investing activity on the statement of cash flows. The $15,000 of contributions not used to acquire investments in 20X2 is reported on the statement of cash flows as an investing activity, "Remainder of contributions to endowment fund restricted to investing." This is so because the amount of financing resources from the restricted endowment fund must equal the amount of investing resources from that restricted fund. Thus, the statement of cash flows reconciles only to the change in cash and cash equivalents shown as a current asset on the hospital's balance sheet.

In addition to the primary financial statements for the present fiscal period, with comparatives for the prior period, hospitals are required to present extensive footnotes similar to those of a commercial entity. A specific footnote disclosure is required to report the estimated value of charity care services provided by the hospital during the period.

## Temporarily Restricted Funds

Sol City Community Hospital uses three funds to account for temporarily restricted funds. The specific-purpose fund is for contributions designated for a particular use by the donor other than plant replacement and expansion. The time-restricted fund is for contributions pledged or received in advance that will be available for unrestricted use in the future. The plant replacement and expansion fund is for contributions to be used in acquiring additional land, buildings, and equipment.

### Specific-Purpose Fund

The specific-purpose fund is used to account for contributions received for which a donor-specific use has been designated. For the most part, such contributions support particular operating activities of the hospital, such as educational or research programs, or provide a particular type of service to patients. The specific-purpose fund does not directly spend the resources; it holds the restricted resources until the general fund satisfies the terms of the restriction, usually by making the appropriate operating cost or by having the restricted cost approved by the governing board, upon which the resources are transferred from the specific-purpose fund to the general fund to pay for the operating cost.

The specific-purpose restricted fund typically invests its cash and receives interest or dividends from its investments. A variety of investment transactions can affect the fund balance. Nevertheless, the specific fund is only a holding fund for temporarily restricted resources until they are released for use by the hospital.

The following entries record the transactions in Sol City Community Hospital's specific-purpose fund during the 20X2 fiscal year and are reflected in the balance sheet in Figure 19–6 and the statement of changes in net assets in Figure 19–8.

***Additions to Specific-Purpose Fund*** The specific-purpose fund receives $6,000 of interest income from its investment of funds from a restricted gift to support the hospital's research activity. Restricted gifts of $115,000 are received in response to a community fund-raising effort. The restricted gifts are allocated based on the donors' specifications. In addition, endowment fund earnings in the amount of $60,000 were deposited directly in the temporarily restricted fund:

| | | | |
|---|---|---:|---:|
| (27) | Cash | 6,000 | |
| |     Investment Income—Research | | 6,000 |
| |   Interest on investment of research gift resources. | | |
| | | | |
| (28) | Cash | 115,000 | |
| |     Contributions—Education | | 60,000 |
| |     Contributions—Research | | 55,000 |
| |   Receive restricted gifts. | | |
| | | | |
| (29) | Cash | 60,000 | |
| |     Investment Income—Endowment Earnings | | 60,000 |
| |   Earnings of endowment fund deposited in temporarily restricted funds until released for specified purposes. | | |

Entry (29) shows the earnings generated by the permanently restricted endowment fund's investments as reported by the temporarily restricted fund. **FASB 124** specifies that dividend, interest, and other investment income should be reported in the period earned as increases in unrestricted net assets unless there are donor-imposed restrictions on the use of the assets. However, in the case of Sol City Community Hospital, the earnings are reported as investment income of the temporarily restricted fund because of a donor-imposed restriction on those earnings. After clearance is given, the resources are then transferred to the general fund to be expended for the donor-specified purposes. If the donor-restricted investment income is permanently restricted, the income is reported in the permanently restricted net assets.

Gains or losses from valuation adjustments to fair value or from sales of securities must also be applied in accordance with any donor restrictions. For example, if the donor specifies that a specific investment be held for perpetuity, any valuation or sales transaction gain or loss on that investment is reported in the permanently restricted net asset class. The important point is to follow any restrictions imposed by the donor or applicable laws. If no restrictions are applicable, the investment income and gains or losses are reported in the unrestricted net asset class.

***Deductions from Specific-Purpose Fund*** The specific-purpose fund is notified that the general fund fulfilled the terms of agreements for specific restricted grants totaling $120,000. In addition to the $120,000, the specific-purpose fund also transferred $60,000 from endowment income to the general fund.

| (30) | Net Assets Released from Program Use Restriction—Education | 61,000 | |
| | Net Assets Released from Program Use Restriction—Research | 59,000 | |
| | Net Assets Released from Program Use Restriction—Endowment Income | 60,000 | |
| | Cash | | 180,000 |
| | Funds released from temporary restriction. | | |

This interfund transaction was also recorded in the general fund (see entries [14] and [15] earlier in the chapter).

### Time-Restricted Fund

Under **FASB 116,** procedures for recording contributions were changed. Earlier recognition of contribution revenue generally is now required for most not-for-profit organizations, including hospitals. Because of the critical nature of contributions to the operations of voluntary health and welfare organizations, a thorough treatment of this topic is included later in the chapter as part of the discussion of voluntary health and welfare organizations. For purposes of illustration in the hospital setting, it is assumed that in 20X1 the hospital received pledges for $12,000 to be collected in 20X2. During 20X2, the $12,000 in pledges was collected and immediately transferred to the general fund for unrestricted use (see entry [18] earlier in the chapter).

| (31) | Cash | 12,000 | |
| | Pledges Receivable | | 12,000 |
| | Collection of prior period pledge. | | |
| (32) | Net Assets Released from Time Restrictions | 12,000 | |
| | Cash | | 12,000 |
| | Funds released from time restrictions. | | |

### Plant Replacement and Expansion Fund

The plant replacement and expansion fund, sometimes called the "plant fund," is used to account for restricted resources given to the hospital to be used only for additions or major modifications to the physical plant. This fund is used as a holding fund until the expenditures for plant assets are approved in the general fund by the governing board. The resources are then transferred to the general fund.

A primary source of resources for the plant replacement and expansion fund is from fund-raising efforts in the communities served by the hospital. Hospitals often ask potential donors to sign pledges specifying a giving level for a period of time, for example, $100 per month for the next 12 months. The pledges become receivables of the fund and typically require a substantial allowance for uncollectibles. The fund records contribution revenue at the time the pledge is received.

The entries recorded in Sol City Community Hospital's plant replacement and expansion fund during 20X2 are presented next and are reflected in the balance sheet in Figure 19–6.

***Additions to Plant Fund***   Increases in the plant replacement and expansion fund during the period are a donation of equipment with a fair value of $25,000 that is recorded in the restricted plant fund until the equipment is placed into service; a donation of $60,000 for use to acquire additional equipment; and the receipt of $7,000 of interest on the plant fund's investments restricted to the purchase of plant. Entries to record these events follow:

| | | | |
|---|---|---:|---:|
| (33) | Property, Plant, and Equipment | 25,000 | |
| |     Contributions—Plant | | 25,000 |
| |     Receive donated equipment with fair value of $25,000. | | |
| (34) | Cash | 60,000 | |
| |     Contributions—Plant | | 60,000 |
| |     Receive restricted gifts for use to acquire equipment. | | |
| (35) | Cash | 7,000 | |
| |     Investment Income—Plant | | 7,000 |
| |     Receive interest on fund's investments. | | |

***Deductions from Plant Fund***   Deductions from the plant fund during the year are two interfund transfers to the general fund. The first is the transfer of $25,000 of donated equipment that is placed into service, and the second is the transfer of $200,000 to the general fund for expenditures for fixed assets. These two interfund transfers are also recorded in the general fund (see entries [16] and [17] earlier in the chapter):

| | | | |
|---|---|---:|---:|
| (36) | Net Assets Released—Plant Acquisition | 25,000 | |
| |     Property, Plant, and Equipment | | 25,000 |
| |     Transfer donated equipment to general fund at time of placement into service. | | |
| (37) | Net Assets Released—Plant Acquisition | 200,000 | |
| |     Cash | | 200,000 |
| |     Transfer cash to general fund for use in acquiring plant assets. | | |

***Other Transactions in Plant Funds***   Other transactions affecting only the asset or liability accounts of the plant funds represent a collection of pledges made by individual donors during the last capital fund-raising drive as well as the acquisition of additional investments in the fund. Entries for these transactions are presented here:

| | | | |
|---|---|---:|---:|
| (38) | Cash | 105,000 | |
| |     Pledges Receivable | | 105,000 |
| |     Collect pledges receivable. | | |
| (39) | Investments | 122,000 | |
| |     Cash | | 122,000 |
| |     Increase investments. | | |

## Endowment Fund

An endowment fund is a collection of cash, securities, or other assets. The use of its assets may be permanently restricted, temporarily restricted, or unrestricted based on the donor's wishes. Generally, endowment funds are established by donors to permanently restrict the capital of the donation and specify the use(s) of any income from those investments. The classification of an endowment fund is based, however, on the terms of the donor's contribution. If the endowment fund is temporarily restricted for a stated period of time after which the principal becomes available for the specified uses, it is normally described as a *term endowment*. If an endowment fund is permanently restricted into perpetuity, it is normally described as a *regular* or *permanent endowment*.

Sol City Community Hospital has a permanently restricted endowment fund to account for resources for which the donors have specified that the principal must be maintained in perpetuity. The income from the investments in the endowment fund is recorded in the appropriate fund based on the donor's specifications. If the investment income is restricted, it is recorded in the appropriate restricted fund. If no donor-imposed restriction is present, the investment income should be recorded and reported in the unrestricted net asset fund.

The balance sheet in Figure 19–6 and the statement of changes in net assets in Figure 19–8 include the entries in Sol City Community Hospital's endowment fund for 20X2.

***Additions to Endowment Fund***   The endowment fund earns $60,000 interest and dividends from its permanent investments that are deposited directly in the temporarily restricted fund (see entry [29]). In addition, a total of $415,000 in new permanent endowments is received and $400,000 is used to acquire additional investments:

| | | | |
|---|---|---|---|
| (40) | Cash | 415,000 | |
| | Contributions—Permanent Endowment | | 415,000 |
| | Receive additional endowments. | | |
| | | | |
| (41) | Investments | 400,000 | |
| | Cash | | 400,000 |
| | Acquire additional investments. | | |

## Summary of Hospital Accounting and Financial Reporting

The major operating activities of a hospital take place in the general fund. The restricted funds are holding funds that transfer resources to the general fund for expenditures upon satisfaction of their respective restrictions. The accrual basis of accounting is used in the general fund to fully measure the revenue and costs of providing health care. Patient services revenue is reported at gross amounts measured at standard billing rates. A deduction for contractual adjustments is then made to arrive at net patient services revenue. Other revenue is recognized for ongoing nonpatient services, such as cafeteria sales and television rentals, and donated supplies and medicines. Charity care services are presented only in the footnotes; no revenue is recognized for them. Operating expenses in the general fund include depreciation, bad debts, and the value of recognized donated services that are in support of the basic services of the hospital. Not all donated services are recognized. Donated property and equipment are typically recorded in a restricted fund, such as the plant fund, until placed into service, at which time they are transferred to the general fund. Donated assets are recorded at their fair market values at the date of gift.

The financial statements of a hospital are (1) the balance sheet, (2) the statement of operations, (3) the statement of changes in net assets, and (4) the statement of cash flows.

# VOLUNTARY HEALTH AND WELFARE ORGANIZATIONS

Voluntary health and welfare organizations (VHWOs) provide a variety of social services. Examples of such organizations are United Way, the American Heart Association, the March of Dimes, the American Cancer Society, the Red Cross, and the Salvation Army. These organizations solicit funds from the community at large and typically provide their services for no fee, or they may charge a nominal fee to those with the ability to pay.

As in the case of hospitals, accounting and financial reporting principles for VHWOs have undergone major change with the publication of **FASB 116** and **FASB 117.** Additional information on VHWOs may be obtained from a variety of sources. The AICPA Audit and Accounting Guide for Not-for-Profit Organizations requires the use of generally accepted accounting principles for VHWOs. VHWOs are typically audited, and the audited financial statements are made available to contributors and to others interested in knowing about the financial condition of the organization and how the resources are being used. The federal government normally provides tax-exempt status to these organizations. Another source for accounting and reporting guidelines for VHWOs is the *Standards of Accounting and Financial Reporting for Voluntary Health and Welfare Organizations,* published by the combined group of the National Health Council, the National Assembly of National Voluntary Health and Social Welfare Organizations, and the United Way of America. The standards book, known as "The Black Book," for the color of its cover, represents an effort to incorporate accounting and financial reporting standards as well as the actual experiences of the largest VHWOs in the United States in one manual.

## Accounting for a VHWO

The accrual basis of accounting is required for VHWOs in order to measure fully the resources available to the organization. Depreciation is reported as an operating expense each period because the omission of depreciation would result in an understatement of the costs of providing the organization's services. Therefore, accounting for VHWOs is similar to other not-for-profit organizations except for special financial statements that report on the important aspects of VHWOs. An overview of the accounting and financial reporting principles for a VHWO is presented in this section.

Even though not required to do so, VHWOs have been free to use fund accounting in their accounting and reporting processes. In the past, the typical VHWO has been portrayed as using a fund structure with (1) a current unrestricted fund, (2) a current restricted fund, (3) a land, building, and equipment fund, and (4) an endowment fund. Many VHWOs are considerably smaller in size and scope of activity than hospitals and may find it convenient to convert from the traditional fund structure to a single accounting entity or a fund structure that distinguishes between unrestricted, temporarily restricted, and permanently restricted assets. The journal entries for Voluntary Health and Welfare Service presented in this section assume the use of a single fund or accounting entity. When appropriate, designations have been added to the journal entry captions to show which of the three classes of assets (unrestricted, temporarily restricted, or permanently restricted) is affected. Thus, the entries could be used equally well if separate funds were established for each of the three asset classifications. Journal entries are presented in the following discussion for only a portion of the transactions of Voluntary Health and Welfare Service in 20X2.

## Financial Statements for a VHWO

**FASB 117** requires that VHWOs provide the following financial statements: (1) statement of financial position, (2) statement of activities, (3) statement of cash flows, and (4) statement of functional expenses.

The financial statements are designed primarily for those who are interested in the organization as "outsiders," not members of management. These include contributors, beneficiaries of services, creditors and potential creditors, and related organizations. A clear distinction should be maintained between restricted resources and those resources available for expenditure for the organization's major missions. As outlined in **FASB Concepts Statement No. 6,** "Elements of Financial Statements" (FAC 6), net assets of not-for-profit organizations are divided into three mutually exclusive classes: permanently restricted net assets, temporarily restricted net assets, and unrestricted net assets. Restricted resources are subject to externally imposed constraints, not internal or

**FIGURE 19–10**
Statement of
Financial Position
for a Voluntary
Health and Welfare
Organization

**VOLUNTARY HEALTH AND WELFARE SERVICE**
**Statement of Financial Position**
**December 31, 20X2 and 20X1**

| | 20X2 | 20X1 |
|---|---|---|
| **Assets** | | |
| Current: | | |
| Cash | $ 68,000 | $ 47,600 |
| Short-Term Investments | 39,000 | 48,000 |
| Accounts Receivable | 1,200 | 1,000 |
| Inventories | 6,400 | 8,300 |
| Net Pledges Receivable | 78,400 | 61,600 |
| Prepaid Expenses | 8,000 | 7,200 |
| Total Current Assets | $201,000 | $173,700 |
| Cash Restricted for Long-Term Use | 1,000 | -0- |
| Long-Term Investments | 383,000 | 351,900 |
| Property, Plant, and Equipment | 125,500 | 121,600 |
| Total Assets | $710,500 | $647,200 |
| **Liabilities and Net Assets** | | |
| Current: | | |
| Accounts Payable | $ 16,100 | $ 12,400 |
| Accrued Expenses | 4,800 | 4,300 |
| Total Current Liabilities | $ 20,900 | $ 16,700 |
| Noncurrent: | | |
| Mortgage Payable | $ 21,000 | $ 23,000 |
| Capital Leases | 8,000 | 7,000 |
| Total Liabilities | $ 49,900 | $ 46,700 |
| Net Assets: | | |
| Unrestricted | $498,200 | $437,800 |
| Temporarily Restricted by Donors | 22,900 | 24,100 |
| Permanently Restricted by Donors | 139,500 | 138,600 |
| Total Net Assets | $660,600 | $600,500 |
| Total Liabilities and Net Assets | $710,500 | $647,200 |

board-designated decisions that may be changed by the governing board of the VHWO. In addition, readers of the general-purpose financial statements should be able to clearly evaluate management's performance in accomplishing the objectives of the VHWO.

### Statement of Financial Position for a VHWO

Figure 19–10 presents a statement of financial position for a VHWO. The format used is similar to that used in the hospital illustration. Although it is not required by existing standards, the assets and liabilities are segregated into current and noncurrent classifications. The net assets section of the statement of financial position for VHWOs must be segregated into unrestricted, temporarily restricted, and permanently restricted, as illustrated. Major balance sheet accounts are as follows.

***Pledges from Donors***   Pledges may be unconditional or conditional promises to give. Conditional promises to give, which depend on the occurrence of a specified future and uncertain event, are recognized only after the conditions on which they depend are substantially met (i.e., when the conditional promise becomes unconditional). The pledges may be unrestricted, temporarily restricted, or permanently restricted based on the circumstances of the pledge and the donor's specifications.

For the VHWO example, the current unrestricted fund includes net ***pledges receivable*** of $78,400 in 20X2. The accrual basis of accounting recognizes the receivable and associated revenue when the unconditional pledge is received. If the contribution is available to support current-period activities, there is no restriction. An adequate allowance for uncollectibles for the pledges receivable is recognized by a debit to Contributions, as a direct reduction from the contribution revenue account, and a credit to Allowance for Uncollectible Pledges, which is a contra account to the pledges receivable asset account. Note that VHWOs do not have a bad debts expense account; the revenue account is charged directly for estimated uncollectible amounts. Pledges or other contributions applicable to future periods should be reported in temporarily restricted net assets as "Contributions—Temporarily Restricted" to show that these resources are not currently available for the entity's operations. Further accuracy could be attained by identifying the temporary restriction as "Contributions—Temporarily Restricted—Time Restrictions." Conditional pledges are not recognized until the conditions on which they depend have been substantially met.

The following illustrates the entries used in accounting for a portion of the pledges received by Voluntary Health and Welfare Service in 20X2. Note that this discussion is for only a part of the pledges, not all of the pledges received in the year, nor does the following discussion attempt to reconcile to the $78,400 balance in net pledges receivable at the end of the year. It shows the accounting for the pledges from only one of the organization's several pledge campaigns during the year.

A special pledge campaign resulted in $100,000 of new pledges received. Of this total, $5,000 is to be received in the current period but is to be held for use for unrestricted purposes in the following period. Experience shows that 20 percent of pledges are uncollectible for this organization. An allowance for uncollectibles is recognized in the amount of $20,000. Note that both the current and deferred pledges are reported as contribution revenue in the period the unconditional pledges are received and that provisions for estimated uncollectibles are then recorded as reductions of contribution revenue.

| | | | |
|---|---|---|---|
| (42) | Pledges Receivable—Unrestricted | 95,000 | |
| | Pledges Receivable—Temporarily Restricted | 5,000 | |
| |     Contributions—Unrestricted | | 95,000 |
| |     Contributions—Temporarily Restricted | | 5,000 |
| |   Receive pledges and recognize receivables. | | |
| | | | |
| (43) | Contributions—Unrestricted | 19,000 | |
| | Contributions—Temporarily Restricted | 1,000 | |
| |     Allowance for Uncollectible Pledges—Unrestricted | | 19,000 |
| |     Allowance for Uncollectible Pledges—Restricted | | 1,000 |
| |   Provide for estimated uncollectible pledges | | |
| |   as a reduction of contributions. | | |

Note that there is no separate bad debt expense recognition. Instead, the contributions accounts are reduced for the estimated amount of uncollectible pledges. **FASB 116** states that unconditional promises to give that are expected to be collected in less than one year may be measured at net realizable value (net settlement value). Pledged contributions expected to be collected in the future beyond one year can be valued at their present value of the estimated future cash flows. Subsequent increases in the present value of the future cash flows due to the reduction of the present value discount are accounted for as contribution income in the appropriate fund for which the pledge was received.

All $5,000 of the funds pledged for use the following year and $85,000 of unrestricted pledges are collected in the current period, requiring an adjustment to both unrestricted and temporarily restricted contribution revenue. Temporarily restricted contribution revenue is increased by $1,000 to the full $5,000 received, and $9,000 is added to unrestricted contribution revenue due to collections of $85,000 in pledges versus the initial estimate of $76,000 ($95,000 × .80). Of the remaining balance, $3,000 is written off as uncollectible, and the remainder is carried over to the following period:

| (44) | Cash—Unrestricted | 85,000 | |
| | Cash—Temporarily Restricted | 5,000 | |
| | Allowance for Uncollectible Pledges—Unrestricted | 9,000 | |
| | Allowance for Uncollectible Pledges—Restricted | 1,000 | |
| | Pledges Receivable—Unrestricted | | 85,000 |
| | Pledges Receivable—Temporarily Restricted | | 5,000 |
| | Contribution Revenue—Unrestricted | | 9,000 |
| | Contribution Revenue—Temporarily Restricted | | 1,000 |
| | Collect pledges including $10,000 above initial estimate of collectibility. | | |
| (45) | Allowance for Uncollectible Pledges—Unrestricted | 3,000 | |
| | Pledges Receivable—Unrestricted | | 3,000 |
| | Write off uncollectible pledges in unrestricted net asset class. | | |

In the following period when the $5,000 is available for unrestricted use, the balance is reclassified as unrestricted. Some organizations would use the terms "net assets released" instead of "reclassification," but the terms are synonymous, and both terms are used in this chapter to show their equality.

| (46) | Cash—Unrestricted | 5,000 | |
| | Reclassification of Contributions to Unrestricted | | 5,000 |
| | Reclassify time restricted funds to unrestricted. | | |
| (47) | Reclassification of Contributions from Temporarily Restricted | 5,000 | |
| | Cash—Temporarily Restricted | | 5,000 |
| | Reclassify time restricted funds from temporarily restricted. | | |

**FASB 116** also prescribes appropriate treatment for unconditional pledges to be received over a longer period of time. In general, contribution revenue is recognized at the present value of future cash receipts. As is the normal practice in utilizing present value procedures in the corporate sector, the present value is used to record contributions to be received in the following accounting periods. For example, if a donor agrees to contribute $10,000 per year at the end of each of the next five years, the stream of the payments is discounted at an appropriate rate (e.g., 8 percent), and the present value is recognized at the time the pledge is received:

| (48) | Pledges Receivable—Temporarily Restricted | 39,927 | |
| | Contributions—Temporarily Restricted | | 39,927 |
| | Receipt of pledge. | | |

At the end of the first year when the first payment of $10,000 is received, that amount is reclassified from temporarily restricted to unrestricted, and the increase in present value of the contributions receivable is recognized as an increase in temporarily restricted contributions and contributions receivable:

| (49) | Cash—Unrestricted | 10,000 | |
| | Reclassification of Contributions to Unrestricted | | 10,000 |
| | Reclassify time-restricted funds to unrestricted. | | |
| (50) | Reclassification of Contributions from Temporarily Restricted | 10,000 | |
| | Pledges Receivable—Temporarily Restricted | | 10,000 |
| | Reclassify time-restricted funds from temporarily restricted. | | |
| (51) | Pledges Receivable—Temporarily Restricted | 3,194 | |
| | Contributions—Temporarily Restricted | | 3,194 |
| | Increase in the present value of contributions receivable. | | |

***Investments***    Investments may be purchased or donated to the organization. Purchased investments should be recorded at acquisition cost. Securities donated to the organization should be recorded at their fair values at the dates of the gifts. Subsequently, equity investments (other than **APB 18** equity investments) and all investments in bonds are reported at fair value. Appreciation gains (or reductions in value) are separately identified as unrealized gains (losses) in the organization's statement of activity in accordance with **FASB 124.** Transfers of investments from one portfolio to another should be made at fair value, with any gains or losses in valuation recorded.

Investment earnings or losses should be reported as unrestricted, temporarily restricted, or permanently restricted, depending on how they are to be used. For example, the donor of a donor-restricted endowment fund may not specify any limitations on the uses of the income or losses from the fund. In that case, the income or losses on the investments are reported on the statement of activities as changes in unrestricted net assets. However, if the donor stipulates the treatment of the income or losses from the donor-restricted endowment fund, that treatment must be followed. In some cases, the donor may impose some time or dollar requirement on the earnings, such as requiring that the income for the first five years be added to the permanent endowment or that only income above some dollar amount can be transferred to an unrestricted fund while the income below that amount must be added to the principal of the permanent endowment. The key point is that the not-for-profit association must follow the donor's specifications as presented in the contribution agreement between the donor and the not-for-profit association and any applicable law regarding a not-for-profit association's management of restricted resources.

***Land, Buildings, and Equipment***    Land, buildings, and equipment, depreciation expense, and the accumulated depreciation on the fixed assets generally are reported as unrestricted unless restricted by the donor. The VHWO may have an accounting policy of retaining long-lived, restricted buildings and equipment in the restricted net asset class even though the assets are used in the operations of the entity. As the buildings and equipment are used in the operations, an allowance for depreciation is reclassified from the restricted net asset class to the unrestricted net asset class. This provides for depreciation and maintains the net book value of the restricted buildings and equipment in the restricted net asset class. The basis of fixed assets is cost, and donated assets are recorded at their fair values at the dates of the gifts. Donations of fixed assets that will be sold by the organization in the near future are equivalent to other contributions and should be separately reported as unrestricted assets until sold. For example, assume that the VHWO receives land as a donation. The VHWO plans to sell the land and use the proceeds from the sale in supporting the entity's program services. The land should be recorded at fair value as an unrestricted asset and reported as land held for resale, until sold.

A VHWO may use any one of the methods of depreciation available to commercial entities. Not-for-profit entities are not required to depreciate assets such as works of art or other historically valuable assets in instances in which the not-for-profit entity has made a commitment to preserve the value of the art or historically valuable assets, and has shown the capacity to do so.

***Liabilities***    Liabilities are recorded in the normal manner under the accrual model. In most situations, liabilities will be reported as part of the unrestricted net assets. For example, the mortgage payment made by Voluntary Health and Welfare Service in 20X2 was recorded as a $2,000 debit to Mortgage Payable and a $2,000 credit to Cash. In this illustration, property, plant, and equipment is classified as an unrestricted asset. In some cases, mortgage payments on assets classified as restricted are made from unrestricted funds. The following entries are needed in the latter case:

| | | | |
|---|---|---|---|
| (52) | Reclassification to Restricted Assets | 2,000 | |
| | Cash (Unrestricted) | | 2,000 |
| | Mortgage payment made from unrestricted assets. | | |
| | | | |
| (53) | Mortgage Payable—Restricted Assets | 2,000 | |
| | Reclassification from Unrestricted Assets | | 2,000 |
| | Reduction of carrying value of mortgage. | | |

**FIGURE 19–11** Statement of Activities for a Voluntary Health and Welfare Organization

### VOLUNTARY HEALTH AND WELFARE SERVICE
### Statement of Activities
### For the Year Ended December 31, 20X2

| | Unrestricted | Temporarily Restricted | Permanently Restricted | Total |
|---|---|---|---|---|
| Revenues, Gains, and Other Support: | | | | |
| Contributions | $627,000 | $42,300 | $ 9,900 | $679,200 |
| Legacies and Bequests | 15,000 | | | 15,000 |
| Collections through Affiliates | 2,800 | | | 2,800 |
| Allocated from Federated Fund-Raising Effort | 45,300 | | | 45,300 |
| Memberships | 6,100 | | | 6,100 |
| Program Fees | 700 | | | 700 |
| Sale of Materials | 200 | | | 200 |
| Investment Income | 36,400 | 500 | | 36,900 |
| Gain on Investments | 12,000 | | 1,000 | 13,000 |
| Donated Services | 3,000 | | | 3,000 |
| Net Assets Released from Restriction: | | | | |
| Program Use Restrictions | 25,000 | (25,000) | | |
| Passage of Time | 8,100 | (8,100) | | |
| Equipment Acquisition | 10,900 | (10,900) | | |
| Endowment Transfers | 10,000 | | (10,000) | |
| Total Revenues, Gains, and Other Support | $802,500 | $ (1,200) | $ 900 | $802,200 |
| Program Services and Operating Costs: | | | | |
| Research | $274,300 | | | $274,300 |
| Public Health Education | 92,000 | | | 92,000 |
| Professional Training | 106,000 | | | 106,000 |
| Community Services | 98,600 | | | 98,600 |
| Management and General | 91,700 | | | 91,700 |
| Fund-Raising | 64,500 | | | 64,500 |
| Payments to National Offices | 15,000 | | | 15,000 |
| Total Expenses | $742,100 | $ -0- | $ -0- | $742,100 |
| Change in Net Assets | $ 60,400 | $ (1,200) | $ 900 | $ 60,100 |
| Net Assets at Beginning of Year | 437,800 | 24,100 | 138,600 | 600,500 |
| Net Assets at End of Year | $498,200 | $22,900 | $139,500 | $660,600 |

***Net Assets*** Separate disclosure should be provided for the amounts of net assets designated as unrestricted, temporarily restricted, and permanently restricted. The VHWO's governing board also may show its intent to use unrestricted resources for specific needs in the future by creating one or more board-designated captions. For example, the $498,200 of unrestricted net assets at December 31, 20X2, shown in Figure 19–10 could be separated into board designated and undesignated. Board-designated purposes might be for purchases of new equipment, research, construction of new facilities, or other asset acquisitions. While the statement of financial position could reflect the designation of resources, the governing board may change these at any time.

### Statement of Activities

Figure 19–11 presents the major operating statement for Voluntary Health and Welfare Service, the statement of activities. The overall structure of the statement of activities for voluntary health and welfare organizations and other not-for-profit entities should be very similar as a result of **FASB 117.** As for other types of nonprofit entities, a number of organizations have issued standards relating to VHWOs. Both the National Health Council's "black book" of standards for VHWOs and the AICPA Audit and Accounting Guide for Not-for-Profit Organizations contain recommendations for accounting for VHWOs. Several of the unique aspects of VHWOs are discussed next.

***Public Support*** Historically, a distinction has been made in the sources of funding received by VHWOs. Nonprofit organizations generally provide services to those who cannot afford to pay for the benefits received or support programs for which little compensation is received. For VHWOs, the primary source of funds is likely to be contributions from individuals or organizations that do not derive any direct benefit from the VHWO for their gifts. The magnitude of funds received and the diversity of contributors are important in evaluating the effectiveness of VHWOs. Four sources of resources included in the 20X2 statement of activities for Voluntary Health and Welfare Service in Figure 19–11 are considered to fall in the category of support. They include contributions, legacies and bequests, collections through affiliates (other organizations in the same community or with similar goals), and contributions received from the federated (national or regional) organization's fund-raising efforts.

A recent change has occurred in accounting for support received from special events. In the past, the costs of providing the event were deducted from the total proceeds generated and the net amount was reported as support. Under the guidelines of **FASB 117,** total proceeds from a sponsored event such as a dance gala or marathon are reported as support from special events, and the costs of sponsoring the event are reported as fund-raising costs. Even though many of the necessary items are contributed for such activities, the costs of sponsoring an event can be rather substantial. The frequency of such events undoubtedly was a factor in the change in the tax laws that now require nonprofit organizations sponsoring a special event to provide participants with a statement detailing the portion of the cost of a ticket or other contribution that may be treated as a charitable contribution for tax purposes.

***Revenues*** Funds received in exchange for services provided or other activities are classified as revenues. Although the majority of a VHWO's resources are obtained from public support, funds also are received from memberships, fees charged to program participants, sales of supplies and services, and investment income.

***Gains*** Investments and other assets may be sold from time to time, and the difference between the sale price and the carrying value is included in the statement of activities as a gain or loss. Much of the time, gains received from sales of investments are reinvested in anticipation of future earnings; nevertheless, all gains and losses should be included in the statement of activities for the period.

***Donated Materials and Services*** A VHWO often relies heavily on ***donated materials and services.*** Donated materials should be recorded at fair value when received. If the donated materials are used in one of the VHWO's program services, their recorded value should be reported as an expense in the period used. If the donated materials simply pass through the VHWO to its charitable beneficiaries, the VHWO is acting as an agent, and the materials are not recorded as a contribution or an expense.

Donated services are an essential part of a VHWO. Because of the difficulty of valuing these services, they often are not recorded as contributions. However, if donated services are significant, the VHWO should recognize them if the services (1) create or enhance nonfinancial assets, or (2) require specialized skills, are provided by individuals possessing those skills, and typically need to be purchased if not provided by donation. If these conditions are satisfied, the value of donated services should be reported as part of the public support and as an expense in the period in which the services are provided. As an example of donated services, assume that a CPA donates audit services with an estimated value of $3,000. The VHWO makes the following entry in the current unrestricted fund to recognize the donated services:

| | | | |
|---|---|---|---|
| (54) | Expenses—Supporting Services | 3,000 | |
| | Support—Donated Services | | 3,000 |
| | CPA donates audit. | | |

Donated services that are directly related to restricted assets should be reported in the restricted net assets class. For example, an architect may provide donated services for the planning of the construction of a new building that is restricted for a specific purpose. In this case, the value of the donated services is capitalized to the construction in progress in the restricted net asset class and becomes part of the basis of the new building.

***Expenses***   The statement of activities should contain information about the major costs of providing services to the public, fund-raising, and general and administrative costs in order to provide contributors and others information that is useful in assessing the VHWO's effectiveness. Those costs of providing goods and services to beneficiaries, customers, or members in fulfilling the primary VHWO mission are referred to as *program service costs.* A VHWO's statement of activities normally should include the total costs of providing each of the major classes of program services. As shown in Figure 19–11, the primary activities for Voluntary Health and Welfare Service are research, public health education, professional training, and community services. **FASB 117** requires that all not-for-profit entities report total entity expenses in the unrestricted fund, even those financed by restricted fund resources. No expenses will be reported by restricted funds: the restricted fund will report a transfer out for the amount expended and the unrestricted fund will report a transfer in.

Information also is presented in the statement of activities on the costs of other activities needed for the organization to operate effectively but that may not be directly assignable to a particular program. These costs generally are reported either as management and general administrative costs or as fund-raising costs. Management and general activities include the costs of maintaining the general headquarters, recordkeeping, business management, and other management and administrative activities not directly assignable to program services or fund-raising activities. Fund-raising activities include the costs of special mailings, compiling potential donor lists, conducting campaigns through contacts with foundations and governmental agencies, and other similar costs. In those organizations whose membership contributions are an important source of funds, separate disclosure of the costs of soliciting members and providing special benefits to those who are members should be made.

Depreciation costs for 20X2 totaled $9,500. An allocation is made to each of the program services and supporting services based on square footage used or some other reasonable basis. For example, an allocation of the $9,500 of depreciation, based on square footage occupied, to each of the program and supporting services is recorded with the following entry:

| | | | |
|---|---|--:|--:|
| (55) | Research—Depreciation | 4,300 | |
| | Public Health—Depreciation | 1,000 | |
| | Professional Training—Depreciation | 2,000 | |
| | Community Services—Depreciation | 1,200 | |
| | Management and General—Depreciation | 500 | |
| | Fund-Raising—Depreciation | 500 | |
| | Accumulated Depreciation | | 9,500 |
| | Record depreciation for 20X2. | | |

***Costs of Informational Materials That Include a Fund-Raising Appeal***   Not-for-profit entities often prepare informational materials that include a direct or indirect message soliciting funds. The issue is how to record the cost of these materials. Should these costs be a program expense or a fund-raising expense? Many VHWOs prefer to classify such costs as program rather than fund-raising to highlight the fulfillment of their basic service mission and to present a better ratio of program expenses to total expenses. Users of the general-purpose financial statements are concerned with the amounts that VHWO organizations spend to solicit contributions, as opposed to the amounts spent for program services. If a not-for-profit entity cannot show that a program or management function has been conducted in conjunction with the appeal for funds, the entire cost of the informational materials or activities should be reported as a fund-raising expense. However, if it can demonstrate that a bona fide program or management function has been conducted in conjunction with the appeal for funds, then the ***costs of informational materials*** are allocated between programs and fund-raising. Evidence of a bona fide program intent in a brochure would be an appeal designed to motivate its audience to action other than providing financial support to the organization. The informational content of a brochure might include a description of the symptoms of a disease and the actions an individual should take if one or more of the symptoms occur. Thus, the content of the message and the intended audience are significant factors.

### Statement of Cash Flows

The third required financial statement for VHWOs is the statement of cash flows, as presented in Figure 19–12. The format of this statement is similar to that for hospitals as discussed earlier in the chapter. Note that under the indirect approach, the statement begins with the change in net assets and reconciles to the net cash provided by operating activities.

### Statement of Functional Expenses

The fourth statement specified by **FASB 117** for VHWOs is the *statement of functional expenses.* This statement details the items reported in the expenses section of the statement of activities in Figure 19–11. Figure 19–13 is a standard format for the statement of functional expenses. The expense categories are presented across the columns. The rows provide the specific nature of the items composing these expense categories from the various funds.

**FIGURE 19–12**
**Statement of Cash Flows for a Voluntary Health and Welfare Organization**

| VOLUNTARY HEALTH AND WELFARE SERVICE<br>Statement of Cash Flows<br>For the Year Ended December 31, 20X2 | | |
|---|---:|---:|
| Change in Net Assets | | $60,100 |
| Adjustments to Reconcile Changes in Net Assets to Net Cash | | |
| Provided by Operating Activities: | | |
| Depreciation | $ 9,500 | |
| Gain on Sale of Investments | (13,000) | |
| Decrease in Short-Term Investments | 9,000 | |
| Increase in Accounts Receivable | (200) | |
| Increase in Contributions Receivable (net) | (16,800) | |
| Decrease in Inventories | 1,900 | |
| Increase in Prepaid Expenses | (800) | |
| Increase in Accounts Payable | 3,700 | |
| Increase in Accrued Expenses | 500 | |
| Contributions Restricted for Equipment Acquisition | (10,900) | |
| Endowment Contributions Restricted for Acquisition | | |
| of Investments | (9,900) | (27,000) |
| Net Cash Provided by Operating Activities | | $33,100 |
| Cash Flows from Investing Activities: | | |
| Purchase of Property, Plant, and Equipment | $(13,400) | |
| Proceeds from Sale of Investments | 40,000 | |
| Purchase of Investments | (59,100) | |
| Investment Gain Restricted to Purchase of Investments | (1,000) | |
| Net Cash Used by Investing Activities | | (33,500) |
| Cash Flows from Financing Activities: | | |
| Mortgage Payments | $ (2,000) | |
| Capital Lease Agreements | 1,000 | |
| Contributions Restricted to Acquiring Fixed Assets | 10,900 | |
| Endowment Gain Restricted to Acquiring Investments | 1,000 | |
| Contributions Restricted for Permanent Endowment | 9,900 | |
| Net Cash Used in Financing Activities | | 20,800 |
| Net Increase in Cash | | $20,400 |
| Cash at the Beginning of Year | | 47,600 |
| Cash at the End of Year | | $68,000 |

**FIGURE 19–13**   Statement of Functional Expenses for a Voluntary Health and Welfare Organization

## VOLUNTARY HEALTH AND WELFARE SERVICE
### Statement of Functional Expenses
### Year Ended December 31, 20X2
(with comparative totals for 20X1)

| | Program Services | | | | | Supporting Services | | | Total Program and Supporting Services Expenses | |
| --- | --- | --- | --- | --- | --- | --- | --- | --- | --- | --- |
| | Research | Public Health Education | Professional Training | Community Services | Total | Management and General | Fund-Raising | Total | 20X2 | 20X1 |
| Salaries | $ 49,000 | $58,200 | $ 51,100 | $53,800 | $212,100 | $66,100 | $34,100 | $100,200 | $312,300 | $347,000 |
| Employee Benefits | 2,800 | 2,900 | 2,900 | 2,900 | 11,500 | 4,100 | 1,000 | 5,100 | 16,600 | 16,800 |
| Payroll Taxes, etc. | 2,400 | 3,100 | 2,600 | 2,900 | 11,000 | 3,600 | 1,800 | 5,400 | 16,400 | 15,500 |
| Total Salaries and Related Expenses | $ 54,200 | $64,200 | $ 56,600 | $59,600 | $234,600 | $73,800 | $36,900 | $110,700 | $345,300 | $379,300 |
| Professional Fees | 200 | 1,000 | 5,200 | 1,600 | 8,000 | 3,000 | 1,500 | 4,500 | 12,500 | 12,000 |
| Supplies | 400 | 600 | 1,000 | 1,000 | 3,000 | 2,100 | 3,000 | 5,100 | 8,100 | 7,900 |
| Telephone | 400 | 1,400 | 1,200 | 4,300 | 7,300 | 2,500 | 7,200 | 9,700 | 17,000 | 16,800 |
| Bad Debts and Other | 400 | 3,200 | 900 | 2,800 | 7,300 | 2,600 | 6,000 | 8,600 | 15,900 | 14,300 |
| Occupancy | 1,000 | 3,400 | 6,000 | 9,000 | 19,400 | 3,000 | 1,000 | 4,000 | 23,400 | 20,500 |
| Rental of Equipment | 200 | 800 | 3,400 | 400 | 4,800 | 600 | 100 | 700 | 5,500 | 4,800 |
| Printing and Publications | 600 | 11,200 | 6,500 | 1,400 | 19,700 | 900 | 7,400 | 8,300 | 28,000 | 23,000 |
| Travel | 1,600 | 2,000 | 10,800 | 4,200 | 18,600 | 1,100 | 200 | 1,300 | 19,900 | 21,500 |
| Conferences and Meetings | 800 | 1,800 | 10,500 | 1,600 | 14,700 | 1,400 | 600 | 2,000 | 16,700 | 16,300 |
| Awards and Grants | 209,300 | 1,200 | 600 | 10,300 | 221,400 | | | | 221,400 | 157,500 |
| Postage and Shipping | 900 | 200 | 1,300 | 1,200 | 3,600 | 200 | 100 | 300 | 3,900 | 4,200 |
| Total Expenses Before Depreciation | $270,000 | $91,000 | $104,000 | $97,400 | $562,400 | $91,200 | $64,000 | $155,200 | $717,600 | $678,100 |
| Depreciation of Buildings and Equipment | 4,300 | 1,000 | 2,000 | 1,200 | 8,500 | 500 | 500 | 1,000 | 9,500 | 6,500 |
| Total Functional Expenses | $274,300 | $92,000 | $106,000 | $98,600 | $570,900 | $91,700 | $64,500 | $156,200 | $727,100 | $684,600 |
| Payments to National Office | | | | | | | | | 15,000 | 12,000 |
| Total Expenses | | | | | | | | | $742,100 | $696,600 |

Bad Debts Expense is from estimated uncollectibles directly related to program services and operations, including membership fees. Note that any estimated uncollectible pledges are deducted directly from contribution revenue.

The statement of functional expenses includes depreciation of $9,500 for the year, allocated among the various programs and supporting services. Total expenses of $742,100 in Figure 19–11 are analyzed and reconciled on the statement of functional expenses in Figure 19–13.

### Summary of Accounting and Financial Reporting for VHWOs

The accounting and financial reporting requirements for VHWOs are specified in **FASB 116, FASB 117,** and the AICPA Audit and Accounting Guide for Not-for-Profit Organizations. The accrual basis of accounting is used. Primary activities of the VHWO are reported in the unrestricted asset class. Resources restricted by the donor for specific operating purposes or future periods are reported as temporarily restricted assets. Assets contributed by the donor with permanent restrictions are reported as permanently restricted assets.

A VHWO provides four financial statements: (1) a statement of financial position, (2) a statement of activities, (3) a cash flow statement, and (4) a statement of functional expenses. The statement of functional expenses is required of all VHWOs to provide an analysis of all of the organization's expenses, including depreciation. Expenses are broken down into types, such as salaries, supplies, and travel, and are summarized by individual program services and individual supporting services.

# OTHER NOT-FOR-PROFIT ENTITIES

There are many types of not-for-profit entities in addition to colleges and universities, hospitals, and voluntary health and welfare organizations. Our society depends heavily on such organizations for religious, educational, social, and recreational needs. Examples of other not-for-profit organizations (ONPOs) include the following:

| | |
|---|---|
| Cemetery organizations | Private and community foundations |
| Civic organizations | Private elementary and secondary schools |
| Fraternal organizations | Professional associations |
| Labor unions | Public broadcasting stations |
| Libraries | Religious organizations |
| Museums | Research and scientific organizations |
| Other cultural institutions | Social and country clubs |
| Performing arts organizations | Trade associations |
| Political parties | Zoological and botanical societies |

### Accounting for ONPOs

The issuance of **FASB 116** and **FASB 117** has done much to bring the financial reporting standards of hospitals, voluntary health and welfare organizations, and other not-for-profit organizations into agreement. In addition to the two FASB statements, the AICPA Audit Guide for Not-for-Profit Organizations provides guidance for accounting and financial reporting standards for ONPOs.

ONPOs vary significantly in size and scope of operations. While accrual accounting is required for all ONPOs, some small organizations operate on a cash basis during the year and convert to an accrual basis at year-end. Other ONPOs have thousands or even millions of members and hold assets worth substantial sums of money. From the viewpoint of asset management and control procedures, such organizations may be virtually identical to a large business entity. The fact that they are not in business to earn profits from selling goods and services continues to distinguish some aspects of financial reporting for ONPOs from that of business entities, however.

In the past, it has been assumed that fund accounting would be used by ONPOs in a manner similar to accounting for VHWOs. With the adoption of **FASB 116** and **FASB 117,** it is likely that the procedures used by ONPOs and VHWOs will move away from the traditional funds used and account for all transactions in a single entity or by establishing separate accounts for unrestricted, temporarily restricted, and permanently restricted net assets.

## Financial Statements of ONPOs

The principal purpose of the financial statements of an ONPO is to explain how the available resources have been used to carry out the organization's activities. Therefore, the statements should disclose the nature and source of the resources acquired, any restrictions on the resources, and the principal programs and their costs; they should also provide information on the organization's ability to continue to carry out its objectives. **FASB 117** requires that an ONPO provide the following financial statements: (1) a statement of financial position, (2) a statement of activities, and (3) a statement of cash flows. Although the statement of functional expenses is not required of ONPOs, it may be appropriate to prepare a statement providing information on expenses by function for each major program when an ONPO is involved in a broad range of activities or conducts activities that are very distinct from one another.

### Statement of Financial Position for an ONPO

Figure 19–14 presents a statement of financial position for Ellwood Historical Society, a nonprofit organization that renovates and preserves historical buildings in Sol City. The society has its own governing board and is not associated with a government. The illustrated statement of financial position is a very simple one in light of the well-defined mission of the organization.

***Land, Buildings, and Equipment***   Land, buildings, and equipment owned by the ONPO and used in its activities generally are recorded at historical cost and depreciated in the normal manner. Operating assets that are donated should be recorded at fair market value at the date of contribution. Unless the donor restricts the use of the asset, land, buildings, and equipment should be included in unrestricted net assets reported on the statement of financial position.

**FIGURE 19–14**
**Statement of Financial Position for an Other Not-for-Profit Organization**

| ELLWOOD HISTORICAL SOCIETY<br>Statement of Financial Position<br>June 30, 20X2 and 20X1 | | |
| --- | --- | --- |
| | **20X2** | **20X1** |
| Cash | $ 32,000 | $ 16,800 |
| Accounts Receivable | 17,500 | 1,500 |
| Contributions Receivable | 48,000 | 30,000 |
| Inventories | 3,000 | 1,000 |
| Prepaid Expenses | 6,500 | 6,500 |
| Cash Restricted for Long-Term Investments | 2,000 | -0- |
| Long-Term Investments (at fair value) | 184,000 | 87,000 |
| Property, Plant, and Equipment (net) | 242,000 | 246,000 |
| Total Assets | $535,000 | $388,800 |
| Accounts Payable | $ 28,000 | $ 28,000 |
| Mortgage Payable | 178,000 | 187,000 |
| Net Assets: | | |
|   Unrestricted | 179,000 | 130,800 |
|   Temporarily Restricted by Donors | 48,000 | 43,000 |
|   Permanently Restricted by Donors | 102,000 | -0- |
| Total Liabilities and Net Assets | $535,000 | $388,800 |

**FIGURE 19–15**
Statement of
Activities for an
Other Not-for-
Profit Organization
(ONPO)

**ELLWOOD HISTORICAL SOCIETY**
**Statement of Activities**
**For the Year Ended June 30, 20X2**

| | Unrestricted | Temporarily Restricted | Permanently Restricted | Total |
|---|---|---|---|---|
| Revenues, Gains, and Other Support: | | | | |
| Contributions | $130,000 | $78,000 | $100,000 | $308,000 |
| Donated Services | 3,000 | | | 3,000 |
| Membership Dues | 16,000 | | | 16,000 |
| Admissions | 12,000 | | | 12,000 |
| Investment Income | 12,200 | 2,600 | 12,000 | 26,800 |
| Gain on Investments | 5,000 | | | 5,000 |
| Net Assets Released from Restriction: | | | | |
| Program Use Restrictions | 62,600 | (62,600) | | |
| Equipment Acquisition | 13,000 | (13,000) | | |
| Endowment Transfers | 10,000 | | (10,000) | |
| Total Revenues, Gains, and Other Support | $263,800 | $ 5,000 | $102,000 | $370,800 |
| Program Services and Support: | | | | |
| Community Education | $139,400 | | | $139,400 |
| Research | 24,200 | | | 24,200 |
| Auxiliary Activities | 19,000 | | | 19,000 |
| General and Administrative | 20,000 | | | 20,000 |
| Fund-Raising | 13,000 | | | 13,000 |
| Total Expenses | $215,600 | $ -0- | $ -0- | $215,600 |
| Change in Net Assets | $ 48,200 | $ 5,000 | $102,000 | $155,200 |
| Net Assets at Beginning of Year | 130,800 | 43,000 | -0- | 173,800 |
| Net Assets at End of Year | $179,000 | $48,000 | $102,000 | $329,000 |

*Inexhaustible Collections*    Libraries, museums, art galleries, and similar entities often have collections of works of art or other historical treasures that are held for public viewing or for research. Some organizations recognize such works of art or other historical treasures as assets, but most do not. Moreover, when individual works of art or historical treasures are recorded, the Financial Accounting Standards Board in **FASB Statement No. 93,** "Recognition of Depreciation by Not-for-Profit Organizations" (FASB 93), concluded not-for-profit organizations are not required to record depreciation on those collections. Specific rules for disclosure of the costs of items purchased and funds generated from the sale of such items are presented in **FASB 116.**

### Statement of Activities

A statement of activities for Ellwood Historical Society, presented in Figure 19–15, reports the support, revenue, expenses, transfers, and changes in fund balance during the fiscal period.

The format for the statement of activities is comparable to the statement of activities for a VHWO. For the Ellwood Historical Society, contributions are the primary source of support. However, both membership dues and admissions provide a greater source of revenue than they do in the voluntary health and welfare setting. Memberships often provide free admission or admission at reduced rates in the case of a museum, art gallery, or library. Thus, memberships and admissions may be interrelated in these organizations. Other types of organizations may have very different sources of funds and major expense categories. The financial statement captions and presentation should be adjusted to focus on these attributes in such cases.

As with VHWOs, depreciation charges for the period have been apportioned to the ONPO's primary programmatic activities and reported as expenses in the unrestricted assets section of the statement of activities. Disclosure should be made of the depreciation charges for the period and the balance of accumulated depreciation in the financial statements or footnotes to the ONPO's financial statements to assist financial statement readers in assessing the ONPO's operating effectiveness and financial position.

**FIGURE 19–16**
Statement of Cash Flows for an Other Not-for-Profit Organization

| ELLWOOD HISTORICAL SOCIETY Statement of Cash Flows For the Year Ended June 30, 20X2 | | |
|---|---|---|
| Change in Net Assets | | $155,200 |
| Adjustments to Reconcile Changes in Net Assets to Net Cash Provided by Operating Activities: | | |
| Depreciation | $ 17,000 | |
| Gain on Sale of Equipment | (5,000) | |
| Increase in Accounts Receivable | (16,000) | |
| Increase in Contributions Receivable | (18,000) | |
| Increase in Inventories | (2,000) | |
| Contribution for Permanent Endowment | (100,000) | |
| Contribution Restricted for Plant | (13,000) | |
| Permanently Restricted Endowment Income | (2,000) | (139,000) |
| Net Cash Provided by Operating Activities | | $ 16,200 |
| Cash Flows from Investing Activities: | | |
| Purchase of Property, Plant, and Equipment | $ (16,000) | |
| Proceeds from Sale of Investments | 3,000 | |
| Purchase of Additional Investments | (100,000) | |
| Investment Income Restricted for Investments | (2,000) | |
| Proceeds from Sale of Equipment | 8,000 | |
| Net Cash Used by Investing Activities | | (107,000) |
| Cash Flows from Financing Activities: | | |
| Contributions Restricted for Permanent Endowment | $100,000 | |
| Investment Income Restricted for Permanent Endowment | 2,000 | |
| Contributions Restricted for Acquiring Fixed Assets | 13,000 | |
| Mortgage Payments | (9,000) | |
| Net Cash Provided by Financing Activities | | 106,000 |
| Net Increase in Cash | | $ 15,200 |
| Cash at Beginning of Year | | 16,800 |
| Cash at End of Year | | $ 32,000 |

Assets released from restriction during the period are shown as reclassifications in the statement of activities. Thus, a contribution of $21,000 for research on Civil War activities would be included in the $78,000 reported as temporarily restricted contributions in Figure 19–15. If $19,500 of the contribution is spent during 20X2, that amount is part of the $62,600 reclassified from temporarily restricted to unrestricted assets (net assets released from program use restrictions) in 20X2. The $19,500 expense incurred in conducting the research is included in the $24,200 total reported as research expense in 20X2.

### Statement of Cash Flows

Figure 19–16 presents the statement of cash flows for Ellwood Historical Society. It begins with the net change in assets for the combined entity taken from the statement of activities. Adjustments are made for noncash revenues and expenses and changes in account balances to arrive at cash provided by operating activities. Net cash flows from investing activities and financing activities are added (deducted) in arriving at the net increase (decrease) in cash for the period. The net cash flow for the period is added to the beginning cash balance in unrestricted assets to arrive at the balance at the end of the period.

## Summary of Accounting and Financial Reporting for ONPOs

Accounting for ONPOs is similar to that for VHWOs. The accrual basis of accounting is used for financial reporting purposes. A statement of financial position, a statement of activities, and a statement of cash flows are required for financial reporting purposes. When a large number of programs or a number of very different types of programs are part of the operations of an ONPO, it may be desirable to prepare a statement of expenses by functional area or major program as well. As a result of **FASB 116** and **FASB 117,** the reporting requirements of ONPOs are substantially the same as VHWOs.

## Summary of Key Concepts

Colleges and universities may be public or private. The accounting and financial reporting standards for public (governmental) colleges and universities are specified by the GASB, as provided in GASB 34 and GASB 35. Accounting and reporting for private colleges and universities are specified by the FASB. Five FASB standards are important for not-for-profit entities. FASB 93 specified that depreciation must be charged to operations and that the balance of net assets be reported. FASB 116 and FASB 136 presented the standards for accounting for contributions. FASB 117 presented the display standards for not-for-profit entities. FASB 124 specified the accounting for investments held by not-for-profit entities. Private not-for-profit colleges and universities must provide three financial statements: (1) a statement of financial position, (2) a statement of activities, and (3) a statement of cash flows. The net assets must be separated into three categories: (1) unrestricted, (2) temporarily restricted, and (3) permanently restricted, based on restrictions imposed by donors, law, or contract.

Health care providers, voluntary health and welfare organizations (VHWOs), and other not-for-profit organizations (ONPOs) use the accrual basis of accounting and account for a majority of transactions in the unrestricted assets class. The restricted funds of a health care provider and other not-for-profit entities are reported as temporarily or permanently restricted, depending on the terms established by the donor. Such funds are classified as restricted until the conditions of the restrictions are met and the resources are reclassified to the unrestricted net asset category. Hospitals deduct contractual adjustments from gross billings in arriving at net patient services revenue in the statement of operations. Donated medical supplies and medicines are included as revenue in the period of receipt. Nonprofit hospitals provide a statement of financial position, a statement of operations, a statement of changes in net assets, and a statement of cash flows. The statement of operations for a hospital must present a performance indicator, called something such as "Excess of revenues over expenses," that includes both operating income and other income such as investment income from trading securities in the general fund's investment portfolio. Below this operating indicator, hospitals present unrealized gains or losses on the general fund's other-than-trading securities, amounts for net assets released from restrictions used for purchase of property and equipment, and other nonoperating items.

VHWOs and ONPOs recognize contribution revenue, investment income, and gains and losses on investments for unrestricted, temporarily restricted, and permanently restricted asset classes. Contributions are reported in the unrestricted asset class unless they are specified by the donor for future periods or for specific-purpose use, in which case they are included as contributions in the temporarily or permanently restricted asset classes. When donor-imposed restrictions on temporarily restricted contributions are satisfied, a reclassification to unrestricted assets is shown in the statement of activities, and any expenses associated with the release from restricted funds are included in expenses for unrestricted assets for the period. Earnings of permanently restricted funds that are available for temporarily restricted or unrestricted purposes are shown as income in those net asset classes in the statement of activities for the period as well.

VHWOs and ONPOs prepare a statement of financial position, a statement of activities, and a statement of cash flows. VHWOs also must prepare a statement of functional expenses. Because of differences in the types and scope of activities of the various organizations, the statements may have differences in account titles and items included; however, many of the prior differences in financial presentation between not-for-profit organizations were eliminated by the requirements of FASB 116 and FASB 117.

## Key Terms

assets whose use is
   limited, *943*
board-designated
   resources, *941*
costs of informational
   materials, *965*
donated materials and
   services, *964*

general fund, *941*
performance indicator, *943*
permanently restricted net
   assets, *943*
pledges receivable, *959*
restricted funds, *941*
specific operating
   purposes, *941*

statement of functional
   expenses, *966*
temporarily restricted net
   assets, *943*
unrestricted net assets, *943*

## Questions

**Q19-1**   How are tuition scholarships reported by a private college or university?

**Q19-2**   What are the classifications of net assets reported in the statement of financial position by private colleges? Identify the types of assets assigned to each classification.

**Q19-3**   What are the major differences in financial reporting for a public university and a private university?

**Q19-4**   What is the basis of accounting in a hospital's general fund? In its restricted funds?

**Q19-5**   How are donated services accounted for by a hospital? How does it account for donated equipment and donated medical supplies?

**Q19-6**   A donor contributes $15,000 to a hospital to be used for operating costs in the intensive care unit. How does it account for this contribution? How does it account for the expenditure of the $15,000?

**Q19-7**   What are the components of a hospital's net patient service revenue?

**Q19-8**   Where is a gain on the sale of hospital properties recorded by a hospital? How is the gain reported in the hospital's financial statements?

**Q19-9**   Is depreciation accounted for by a hospital? Why or why not?

**Q19-10**   What is the basis of accounting for the unrestricted assets of a VHWO? What is the basis for the restricted assets?

**Q19-11**   Where are fixed assets recorded for a VHWO? Is depreciation recorded for a VHWO?

**Q19-12**   An individual contributes $10,000 to a VHWO for restricted use in a public health education service. How does the VHWO account for this contribution? How does it account for the expenditure of the $10,000?

**Q19-13**   Explain the accounting for pledges from donors to a VHWO.

**Q19-14**   Why do VHWOs not report all pledges received in the period in the unrestricted assets section of the statement of activities? Identify what is not included.

**Q19-15**   How do VHWOs account for donated services?

**Q19-16**   Describe the statement of functional expenses. What organizations must prepare this statement?

**Q19-17**   An alumna of a sorority donates $12,000 to it for restricted use in its community service activity. How is the contribution accounted for by this ONPO? How is the expenditure of the $12,000 accounted for?

**Q19-18**   Are donated services received by an ONPO accounted for in the same manner as those received by hospitals? Why or why not?

**Q19-19**   What is the market value unit method of accounting for investments?

**Q19-20**   Should a rotary club, an ONPO, report depreciation expense? Why or why not?

**Q19-21**   Describe the statement of activities for an ONPO. Compare it with the statement of activities for a VHWO.

**Q19-22**   Give two examples of contributions to an ONPO that should be reported as temporarily restricted and two that should be reported as permanently restricted.

---

# Cases

**C19-1**   **Accounting for Donations**

*Judgment*   Hospitals, voluntary health and welfare organizations, and other not-for-profit organizations often rely heavily on donations of volunteers' time as well as equipment, supplies, or other assets.

### Required

*a.* Specify the criteria to be used to determine the accounting for donated services to (1) hospitals, (2) voluntary health and welfare organizations, and (3) other not-for-profit organizations. Discuss the reasons for any differences in the accounting criteria used.

*b.* How are donations of capital assets, such as equipment, accounted for by hospitals? Is depreciation recorded on these donations? Why or why not?

*c.* How are cash contributions accounted for by (1) hospitals, (2) voluntary health and welfare organizations, and (3) other not-for-profit organizations?

**C19-2**   **Public Support to an Other Not-for-Profit Organization**

Leslie Dawnes has just been elected treasurer of the local professional association of registered nurses. The association provides public health messages for the community as well as services for

*Understanding*

members. Leslie is now preparing financial statements for the year and comes to you for advice on accounting for the proceeds from a major fund drive that occurred during the year. The nursing association received $25,000 in unrestricted donations and $15,000 in restricted donations that are restricted to public health advertisements. A total of $6,000 has been incurred for public health advertising since the restricted donations were received.

The former treasurer accounted for the $40,000 of donations as revenue in the unrestricted fund. Leslie believes that this may not be correct because it does not disclose the restricted nature of the donations for the public health messages.

### Required

a. Discuss the accounting and financial statement disclosure to be used to account for the $25,000 of unrestricted donations to the professional association.

b. How should the $15,000 of restricted contributions have been accounted for at the time of the donation? How should they have been reported on this year's financial statements?

**C19-3**

*Analysis*

### A Brief Analysis of the Financial Disclosures of United Way of America

Access the Web site for United Way of America (www.unitedway.org) and then look through the site until you locate the most recent Consolidated Financial Statements and Supplemental Schedule and the Form 990. Review the statements and Form 990 and then prepare a two- to three-page memo presenting your summary of the following items (the items refer to consolidated amounts for the most recent year available):

a. Briefly describe the reporting units that comprise the consolidated entity of United Way of America. How are they operationally interrelated?

b. Using the consolidated statement of financial position, first identify and briefly explain the consolidation eliminations. Then, describe the components and amounts of each of the major items comprising the consolidated net assets and equity. And finally, using the statement of financial position information along with the footnote information, describe the components of the custodial funds asset and custodial funds liability in the consolidated columns.

c. Using the consolidated statement of activities, what are the four largest revenue sources? What are the four largest expenses? What is the consolidated total of fund-raising expenses?

d. Using the supplemental schedule, the statement of functional expenses, along with the footnotes, describes the four largest program services categories. What are the three largest expense categories?

e. Accessing the Form 990, briefly describe the major types of information required on this Internal Revenue Service form.

**C19-4**

*Research FARS*

### Conditional Gift to a Not-for-Profit Organization

Betty Gardner is the treasurer for the Central Illinois chapter of a national not-for-profit organization, the Alzheimer's Association. Some of the money raised by the chapter is sent to the national organization to support research into Alzheimer's disease. The chapter also provides information about the disease and sponsors support programs for families of patients within the community. The chapter has just received a significant pledge from Victor Wyatt, who has offered to contribute $20,000 a year for the next five years on the condition that the Central Illinois chapter sponsor a series of annual educational programs about Alzheimer's disease. If it does not do so, he will direct future contributions elsewhere.

The donor has already contributed the first $20,000, and the chapter has made the arrangements for the first educational workshop, which will take place in six weeks, shortly after the chapter's fiscal year-end.

Betty Gardner is aware that the chapter intends to continue the educational workshops and has asked you, as a public accountant who volunteers to audit the chapter's financial statements each year, to research the appropriate accounting for Mr. Wyatt's $20,000 contribution and $80,000 pledge in the chapter's financial statements for the current fiscal year.

### Required

Obtain the most current accounting standards for accounting for conditional gifts to not-for-profit organizations. You can obtain access to accounting standards through the Financial Accounting Research System (FARS), your library, or some other source. Write a memo to Betty reporting on your research findings. Support your recommendations with citations and quotations from the authoritative financial reporting standards.

**C19-5** **Accounting for Contributions to and Activities of a Not-for-Profit Organization**

*Research*
*FARS*

Gerry Finley, a manager in a public accounting firm, has volunteered to audit the financial statements of the Community Chest, a not-for-profit organization that raises funds to assist people in central Illinois who are homeless or have low incomes. In reviewing the statement of activities, he notices the revenue item Auction Extravaganza. The Community Chest treasurer indicates that this amount is the net proceeds for this event, which is the organization's largest fund-raising event for the year.

The Auction Extravaganza combines a black-tie dinner, entertainment, and an auction of numerous donated items. Supporters buy tickets to the event and bid on the auction items. The treasurer informs Gerry that the dollar amount reported in the statement of activities is the total raised from ticket sales and from the auction, net of the expenses incurred for the event. These expenses include advertising and part of the cost of the dinner. The expenses, however, are comparatively low because a local hotel donates the ballroom and part of the cost of the dinner. A local auctioneer volunteers her time for the auction, the state university's music department provides the entertainment, and local businesses donate all auction items.

*Required*

Obtain the most current accounting standards for accounting for conditional gifts to not-for-profit organizations. You can obtain access to accounting standards through the Financial Accounting Research System (FARS), your library, or some other source. Gerry has asked you, as a staff accountant in his firm, to research the appropriate accounting for the Auction Extravaganza. Write him a memo reporting on your research findings. Support your recommendations with citations and quotations from the authoritative financial reporting standards.

**C19-6** **An Analysis of the Financial Statements for the American Red Cross, a Voluntary Health and Welfare Organization**

*Analysis*

The questions below can be answered by reading the most recent consolidated financial statements of the American Red Cross (ARC) at its Web site, www.redcross.org. (The financial statements may be under the Publications button of the header bar of the Web site.)

*a.* Why does the U.S. Army Audit Agency audit the financial statements of the American Red Cross?

*b.* For the most recent year, what was the ratio of program services expenses to total expenses? According to the Better Business Bureau, a ratio of program expenses to total expenses of 60 percent is considered acceptable. How does the ratio for the ARC compare with this benchmark?

*c.* What is the ARC's policy with respect to recognizing contribution revenue? Of the total contributions receivable at June 30 of the most recent year, what amount is temporarily restricted?

*d.* Of the total amount of unrestricted net assets at June 30 of the most recent year, what is the amount that is undesignated by the board of governors?

*e.* What interest rate is used to determine the present value for contributions that are receivable in years after June 30 of the current year?

*f.* For the most recent year ended June 30, what was the amount of net assets reclassified due to satisfaction of purpose and/or time restrictions?

*g.* Of all the program services provided, which one had the highest total cost for salaries and wages and employee benefits?

*h.* How does the ARC define temporarily restricted net assets?

*i.* How much contributed service revenue was reported for the most recent year?

*j.* At June 30 of the most recent year, what was the amount of conditional contributions? Did the ARC report these contributions in revenue for the current year?

*k.* Of the total amount of unrestricted investment income reported for the current year, what amount came from dividends and interest?

*l.* The ARC makes estimated income tax payments during each year for unrelated business income. State two sources of unrelated business income for the current year (you do not have to give dollar amounts for the income).

*m.* What does the ARC report when donor-imposed purpose restrictions are accomplished or donor-imposed time restrictions expire?

*n.* Assume the ARC received a cash contribution during the current year that was restricted by the donor for disaster relief. Also assume that the amount donated was spent in the current year for disaster relief. Specify whether the ARC would report this donation on its statement of activities for the current year: (1) as an increase in unrestricted net assets when the donation was received, or (2) as an increase in temporarily restricted net assets when the donation was received and as a reclassification of net assets from temporarily restricted to unrestricted when the donation was used.

o. Assume the ARC received a donation of equipment from a donor in the current year and the donor did not place any restrictions on the donated assets. Specify how the ARC would report this donation in its statement of activities for the current year: (1) as an increase in unrestricted net assets when the equipment was received, or (2) as an increase in temporarily restricted net assets when the equipment was received and as a reclassification of net assets from temporarily restricted to unrestricted when the equipment is depreciated.

**C19-7 An Analysis of the Financial Statements of the University of Notre Dame, a Private University**

*Analysis*

The questions below can be answered by reading the most recent annual report of the University of Notre Dame. This report can be accessed by going to www.nd.edu.

a. For the most recent year, how much cash was contributed by donors to the university for the acquisition of buildings and equipment?

b. On the statement of changes in unrestricted net assets, how does the university decide what information is disclosed in the nonoperating section?

c. On the statement of changes in unrestricted net assets for the most recent year, how much of the net assets released were for operations?

d. What is the university's accounting policy for its art collection?

e. What interest rate is used to determine the present value of multiyear pledges?

f. On the statement of financial position at June 30 for the most recent year, how much of the amount reported for contributions receivable is unrestricted?

g. At June 30 of the most recent year, what amount of unrestricted net assets is designated by the board?

h. True or false: Operating expenses on the statement of changes in unrestricted net assets for the most recent year are reported by functional categories.

i. During the most recent year, how many individual donors made contributions to support the university?

j. True or false: Land, buildings, and equipment, net of accumulated depreciation, are reported in unrestricted net assets on the university's statement of financial position.

k. For the most recent year, what was the total investment return on investments reported in all three net asset categories? How much of this amount represented an increase in unrestricted net assets?

l. True or false: The President's Circle consists of donors who make annual unrestricted contributions of at least $50,000.

m. For the 10-year period ending with the most recent year, what was the endowment pool's annualized return?

n. On the statement of financial position at June 30 of the most recent year, what amount of investments in endowments is reported in the permanently restricted net asset class?

o. Where is the university's endowment ranked in American higher education?

**C19-8 Profiles of Large Charitable Organizations**

*Analysis*

The Web site www.give.org is widely known for presenting profiles of nationally soliciting charitable organizations. The BBB Wise Giving Alliance provides the Web site to provide information to donors and to assist charities to operate responsibly.

**Required**

Go to the Give.org Web site and provide answers for each of the following questions.

a. Briefly describe the Standards for Charity Accountability used by the BBB Wise Giving Alliance. Explain why a charity might seek to be recognized as a BBB Accredited Charity.

b. Use the index of Charity Reports to obtain information for the American Red Cross. Provide an overview of the types of information provided for the American Red Cross, including its governance and its fund-raising.

*c.* Select another charity from the index of Charity Reports. You can select one with its name beginning with the same letter as your last name or, alternatively, a charity of your interest. Provide an overview of the types of information provided for your selected charity, including its governance and its fund-raising. How does your selected charity compare with the American Red Cross?

## Exercises

### E19-1  Multiple-Choice Questions on Colleges and Universities [AICPA Adapted]

Select the correct answer for each of the following questions.

1. For the summer session of 20X2, Pacific University assessed its students $1,700,000 (net of refunds) covering tuition and fees for educational and general purposes. However, only $1,500,000 was expected to be realized because scholarships totaling $150,000 were granted to students, and tuition remissions of $50,000 were allowed to faculty members' children attending Pacific. What amount should Pacific include as revenues from student tuition and fees?

 *a.* $1,500,000.
 *b.* $1,550,000.
 *c.* $1,650,000.
 *d.* $1,700,000.

2. Tuition remissions for graduate student teaching assistantships should be classified by a university as:

| | Revenue | Expenditures |
|---|---|---|
| *a.* | No | No |
| *b.* | No | Yes |
| *c.* | Yes | Yes |
| *d.* | Yes | No |

3. For the fall semester of 20X1, Dover University assessed its students $2,300,000 for tuition and fees. The net amount realized was only $2,100,000 because of the following revenue reductions:

| | |
|---|---|
| Refunds occasioned by class cancellations and student withdrawals | $ 50,000 |
| Tuition remissions granted to faculty members' families | 10,000 |
| Scholarships and fellowships | 140,000 |

How much should Dover report for the period for revenue from tuition and fees?

 *a.* $2,100,000.
 *b.* $2,150,000.
 *c.* $2,250,000.
 *d.* $2,300,000.

*Note:* Items 4 through 6 are based on the following information pertaining to Global University, a private institution, as of June 30, 20X1, and for the year then ended:
Unrestricted net assets comprised $7,500,000 of assets and $4,500,000 of liabilities (including deferred revenues of $150,000). Among the receipts recorded during the year were unrestricted gifts of $550,000 and restricted grants totaling $330,000, of which $220,000 was expended during the year for current operations and $110,000 remained unexpended at the close of the year.

Volunteers from the surrounding communities regularly contribute their services to Global and are paid nominal amounts to cover their travel costs. During the year, the amount for travel paid to these volunteers aggregated $18,000. The gross value of services performed by them, determined by reference to equivalent wages available in that area for similar services, amounted to $200,000. Global University normally purchases these types of contributed services, and the university believes the contributed services enhance its assets.

4. At June 30, 20X1, Global's unrestricted net asset balance was:

   a. $7,500,000.

   b. $3,150,000.

   c. $3,000,000.

   d. $2,850,000.

5. For the year ended June 30, 20X1, what amount should be included in Global's revenue for the unrestricted gifts and restricted grants?

   a. $550,000.

   b. $660,000.

   c. $770,000.

   d. $880,000.

6. For the year ended June 30, 20X1, what amount should Global record as contribution revenue for the volunteers' services?

   a. $218,000.

   b. $200,000.

   c. $18,000.

   d. $0.

E19-2   **Multiple-Choice Questions on Hospital Accounting [AICPA Adapted]**

Select the correct answer for each of the following questions.

*Note:* The following data are for questions 1 through 3:

Under Dodge Hospital's established rate structure, the hospital would have earned patient service revenue of $5,000,000 for the year ended December 31, 20X3. However, Dodge did not expect to collect this amount because of contractual adjustments of $500,000 to third party payors. In May 20X3, Dodge purchased bandages from Hunt Supply Company at a cost of $1,000. However, Hunt notified Dodge that the invoice was being canceled and that the bandages were being donated. On December 31, 20X3, Dodge had board-designated assets consisting of $40,000 in cash and investments of $700,000.

1. For the year ended December 31, 20X3, how much should Dodge report as net patient service revenue?

   a. $4,500,000.

   b. $5,000,000.

   c. $5,500,000.

   d. $5,740,000.

2. For the year ended December 31, 20X3, Dodge should record the donation of bandages as:

   a. A $1,000 reduction in operating expenses.

   b. A decrease in net assets released from restrictions.

   c. An increase in unrestricted revenue, gains, and other support.

   d. A memorandum entry only.

3. How much of Dodge's board-designated assets should be included in unrestricted net assets?

   a. $0.

   b. $40,000.

   c. $700,000.

   d. $740,000.

4. Donated medicines that normally would be purchased by a hospital should be recorded at fair value and should be credited directly to:

   a. Unrestricted revenue.

   b. Expense of medicines.

   c. Fund balance.

   d. Deferred revenue.

5. Which of the following would normally be included as revenue of a not-for-profit hospital?

   a. Unrestricted interest income from an endowment fund.

   b. An unrestricted gift.

   *c.* Tuition received from an educational program.

   *d.* All of the above.

6. An unrestricted gift pledge from an annual contributor to a not-for-profit hospital made in December 20X1 and paid in March 20X2 would generally be credited to:

   *a.* Contribution revenue in 20X1.

   *b.* Contribution revenue in 20X2.

   *c.* Other income in 20X1.

   *d.* Other income in 20X2.

7. An organization of high school seniors assists patients at Lake Hospital. These students are volunteers who perform services that the hospital would not otherwise provide, such as wheeling patients in the park and reading to patients. Lake has no employer–employee relationship with these volunteers, who donated 5,000 hours of service to Lake in 20X2. At the minimum wage, these services would amount to $18,750, while it is estimated that the fair value of these services was $25,000. In Lake's 20X2 statement of operations, what amount should be reported as donated services?

   *a.* $25,000.

   *b.* $18,750.

   *c.* $6,250.

   *d.* $0.

8. Which of the following would be included in the unrestricted funds of a not-for-profit hospital?

   *a.* Permanent endowments.

   *b.* Term endowments.

   *c.* Board-designated funds originating from previously accumulated income.

   *d.* Funds designated by the donor for plant expansion and replacement funds.

9. During the year ended December 31, 20X1, Greenacre Hospital received the following donations stated at their respective fair values:

| | |
|---|---:|
| Essential specialized employee-type services from members of a religious group | $100,000 |
| Medical supplies from an association of physicians that were restricted for indigent care and were used for such purpose in 20X1 | 30,000 |

  How much total revenue from donations should Greenacre report its 20X1?

   *a.* $0.

   *b.* $30,000.

   *c.* $100,000.

   *d.* $130,000.

10. Johnson Hospital's property, plant, and equipment (net of depreciation) consists of the following:

| | |
|---|---:|
| Land | $     500,000 |
| Buildings | 10,000,000 |
| Movable equipment | 2,000,000 |

  What amount should be reported as restricted assets?

   *a.* $0.

   *b.* $2,000,000.

   *c.* $10,500,000.

   *d.* $12,500,000.

11. Depreciation should be recognized in the financial statements of:

   *a.* Proprietary (for-profit) hospitals only.

   *b.* Both proprietary and not-for-profit hospitals.

   *c.* Both proprietary and not-for-profit hospitals only when they are affiliated with a college or university.

   *d.* All hospitals, as a memorandum entry not affecting the statement of revenue and expenses.

12. On March 1, 20X1, J. Rowe established a $100,000 endowment fund, the income from which is to be paid to Central Hospital for general operating purposes. Central does not control the fund's principal. The donor appointed Sycamore National Bank as trustee of this fund. What journal entry is required by Central to record the establishment of the endowment?

|  | Debit | Credit |
|---|---|---|
| *a.* Cash | 100,000 | |
|     Nonexpendable Endowment Fund | | 100,000 |
| *b.* Cash | 100,000 | |
|     Endowment Fund Balance | | 100,000 |
| *c.* Nonexpendable Endowment Fund | 100,000 | |
|     Endowment Fund Balance | | 100,000 |
| *d.* Memorandum entry only | — | — |

**E19-3 Entries for a Hospital's Unrestricted (General) Fund**

The following are transactions and events of the general fund of Sycamore Hospital, a not-for-profit entity, for the 20X6 fiscal year ending December 31, 20X6.

1. A total of $6,200,000 in patient services was provided.
2. Operating expenses total $5,940,000, as follows:

| | |
|---|---|
| Nursing services | $2,070,000 |
| Other professional expenses | 1,250,000 |
| Fiscal services | 225,000 |
| General services | 1,510,000 |
| Bad debts | 125,000 |
| Administration | 260,000 |
| Depreciation | 500,000 |

Accounts credited for operating expenses other than depreciation:

| | |
|---|---|
| Cash | $4,785,000 |
| Allowance for Uncollectibles | 125,000 |
| Accounts Payable | 210,000 |
| Inventories | 240,000 |
| Donated Services | 80,000 |

3. Contractual adjustments of $220,000 are allowed as deductions from gross patient revenue.
4. A transfer of $180,000 is received from specific-purpose funds. This transfer is for payment of approved operating costs in accordance with the terms of the restricted gift.
5. A transfer of $200,000 is received from the temporarily restricted plant fund to fund the purchase of new equipment for the hospital.
6. Sycamore Hospital receives $155,000 of unrestricted gifts.
7. Accounts receivable are collected except for $75,000 written off.
8. A valuation of the investment securities portfolio of the general fund reports a $70,000 increase in the market value from the beginning of the period. The board designated this entire income for other than current operations.

### Required

*a.* Prepare journal entries in the general fund for each of the transactions and events.

*b.* Prepare the statement of operations for the general, unrestricted fund of Sycamore Hospital.

### E19-4    Entries for Other Hospital Funds

The following are selected transactions of the specific-purpose fund, the plant fund, and the endowment fund of Toddville Hospital, a not-for-profit entity:

1. The endowment fund received new permanent endowments totaling $150,000 and new term endowments totaling $120,000.

2. The plant replacement and expansion fund received pledges of $1,500,000 for the new wing. Uncollectibles were estimated at 10 percent.

3. The specific-purpose fund received gifts of $50,000 for research and $30,000 for education.

4. Interest and dividends received on investments follow:

| | |
|---|---:|
| Endowment fund (permanent) | $100,000 |
| Plant fund | 45,000 |
| Specific-purpose fund (research) | 31,000 |

This year's interest and dividends in the endowment fund are permanently restricted by a donor-imposed requirement.

5. The specific-purpose fund was notified that the general fund fulfilled the agreements related to restricted gifts as follows:

| | |
|---|---:|
| Research | $55,000 |
| Education | 32,000 |

Cash of $70,000 was transferred to the general fund, with the balance to be sent later.

6. The following investments were made:

| | |
|---|---:|
| Endowment fund | $270,000 |
| Plant fund | 160,000 |
| Specific-purpose fund | 75,000 |

**Required**

Prepare journal entries for the transactions in the specific-purpose fund, plant fund, and endowment fund, as appropriate.

### E19-5    Multiple-Choice Questions on Voluntary Health and Welfare Organization Accounting [AICPA Adapted]

Select the correct answer for each of the following questions.

1. Which basis of accounting should a voluntary health and welfare organization use?

    *a.* Cash basis for all funds.

    *b.* Modified accrual basis for all funds.

    *c.* Accrual basis for all funds.

    *d.* Accrual basis for some funds and modified accrual basis for other funds.

*Note:* The following data are for questions 2 and 3:

Town Service Center is a voluntary health and welfare organization funded by contributions from the general public. During 20X6, unrestricted pledges of $800,000 were received, half of which were payable in 20X6, with the other half payable in 20X7 for use in 20X7. It was estimated that 10 percent of these pledges would be uncollectible. In addition, Helen Ladd, a social worker on Town's permanent staff, earning $30,000 annually for a normal workload of 1,500 hours, contributed an additional 600 hours of her time to Town at no charge.

2. How much should Town report as unrestricted contribution revenue for 20X6 with respect to the pledges?

    *a.* $0.

    *b.* $360,000.

    *c.* $720,000.

    *d.* $800,000.

3. How much should Town record in 20X6 for contributed service expenses?

    *a.* $0.

    *b.* $1,200.

    *c.* $10,000.

    *d.* $12,000.

4. A voluntary health and welfare organization received a pledge in 20X1 from a donor specifying that the amount pledged be used in 20X3. The donor paid the pledge in cash in 20X2. The pledge should be accounted for as:

    *a.* Contribution revenue in 20X3.

    *b.* Contribution revenue in 20X2.

    *c.* Contribution revenue in 20X1.

    *d.* Contribution revenue in the period in which the funds are spent.

5. Turner Fund, a voluntary health and welfare organization funded by contributions from the general public, received unrestricted pledges of $300,000 during 20X4. It was estimated that 10 percent of these pledges would be uncollectible. By the end of 20X4, $240,000 of the pledges had been collected. It was expected that $35,000 more would be collected in 20X5 and that the balance of $25,000 would be written off as uncollectible. What amount should Turner include as contribution revenue in 20X4?

    *a.* $300,000.

    *b.* $275,000.

    *c.* $270,000.

    *d.* $240,000.

*Note:* The following data are for questions 6 through 9:

On January 1, 20X2, State Center Health Agency, a voluntary health and welfare organization, received a bequest of a $200,000 certificate of deposit maturing on December 31, 20X6. The contributor's only stipulations were that the certificate be held to maturity and the interest revenue received annually be used to purchase books for the children to read in the preschool program run by the agency. Interest revenue each of the years was $9,000, and the full $9,000 was spent for books each year. When the certificate was redeemed, the board of trustees adopted a formal resolution designating $150,000 of the proceeds for future purchase of playground equipment for the preschool program.

6. What should be reported by the temporarily restricted fund in the 20X2 statement of activities?

    *a.* Legacies and bequests of $200,000.

    *b.* Investment income of $9,000.

    *c.* Transfers to unrestricted fund of $9,000.

    *d.* All of the above.

7. What amounts should be reported in the 20X2 statement of activities for the unrestricted fund?

    *a.* Legacies and bequests of $200,000.

    *b.* Investment income of $9,000.

    *c.* Transfers from the restricted fund of $9,000.

    *d.* Contributions of $209,000.

8. What should be reported in the 20X6 statement of activities for the unrestricted fund?

    *a.* Transfers from restricted fund of $209,000.

    *b.* Board-designated funds of $150,000.

    *c.* Playground equipment of $150,000.

    *d.* Transfers to plant and equipment fund of $150,000.

9. What should be reported in the December 31, 20X6, statement of financial position for the unrestricted fund?

   *a.* Liability for purchase of playground equipment, $150,000.

   *b.* Due to plant and equipment fund, $150,000.

   *c.* Board-designated funds, $150,000.

   *d.* Temporarily restricted funds, $200,000.

**E19-6**   **Entries for Voluntary Health and Welfare Organizations**

The following are the 20X2 transactions of the Midwest Heart Association, which has the following funds and fund balances on January 1, 20X2:

| | |
|---|---:|
| Unrestricted net assets | $281,000 |
| Temporarily restricted net assets | 87,000 |
| Permanently restricted (endowment) net assets | 219,000 |

1. Unrestricted pledges total $700,000, of which $150,000 is for 20X3. Uncollectible pledges are estimated at 8 percent.

2. Restricted use grants total $150,000.

3. A total of $520,000 of current pledges are collected, and $30,000 of remaining uncollected current pledges are written off.

4. Office equipment is purchased for $15,000.

5. Unrestricted funds are used to pay the $3,000 mortgage payment due on the buildings.

6. Interest and dividends received are $27,200 on unrestricted investments and $5,400 on temporarily restricted investments. An endowment investment with a recorded value of $5,000 is sold for $6,000, resulting in a realized transaction gain of $1,000. A donor-imposed restriction specified that gains on sales of endowment investments must be maintained in the permanently restricted endowment fund.

7. Depreciation is recorded and allocated as follows:

| | |
|---|---:|
| Community services | $12,000 |
| Public health education | 7,000 |
| Research | 10,000 |
| Fund-raising | 15,000 |
| General and administrative | 9,000 |

8. Other operating costs of the unrestricted current fund are:

| | |
|---|---:|
| Community services | $250,600 |
| Public health education | 100,000 |
| Research | 81,000 |
| Fund-raising | 39,000 |
| General and administrative | 61,000 |

9. Clerical services donated during the fund drive total $2,400. These are not part of the expenses reported in item 8. It has been determined that these donated services should be recorded.

**Required**

   *a.* Prepare journal entries for the transactions in 20X2.

   *b.* Prepare a statement of activities for 20X2.

**E19-7**   **Determination of Contribution Revenue**

Atwater Health Services, a voluntary health and welfare organization, has provided support for families with low income in the town of Atwater for approximately 20 years. In 20X6, Atwater Health Services conducted a major funding campaign to help replace facilities that are no longer adequate and to generate operating and endowment funds.

The community of Atwater ran a number of special events, and the chamber of commerce made the fund-raising campaign a major activity for 20X6. In 20X6, the following gifts and pledges were received:

1. The family of I. B. Plentiful donated a lot adjacent to the current building for future use as a playground and parking lot. The family had purchased the lot for $22,000 several years ago. It had a current value of $42,000 at the date contributed.

2. A number of new pledges were received and many were partially or fully paid in 20X6. The following information was compiled:

| | |
|---|---:|
| Unrestricted pledges for use in 20X6 | $120,000 |
| Unrestricted pledges for use in 20X7 | 70,000 |
| Pledges to support screening tests for children's hearing abilities | 90,000 |
| Pledge to assist in construction of addition to building; donor agrees to make eight annual payments of $50,000 each | 400,000 |
| | $680,000 |

3. Also during 20X6, $45,000 was spent in providing vision tests for grade school children. A total of $38,000 of funds collected in 20X4 and 20X5 for this purpose were used to help pay for the costs of providing the tests free of charge to all children in the community.

### Required

a. Prepare the journal entries for 20X6 for these activities, including receipt of the first installment on the pledge for building construction, which was received at the end of 20X6. Atwater currently earns an 8 percent return on its investments. The present value of the seven future payments of $50,000 is $260,318.

b. Prepare the journal entry or entries recorded at the end of 20X7 upon receipt of the second payment on the pledge for building construction.

**E19-8**  **Multiple-Choice Questions on Other Nonprofit Organizations [AICPA Adapted]**
Select the correct answer for each of the following questions.

1. On January 2, 20X2, a nonprofit botanical society received a gift of an exhaustible fixed asset with an estimated useful life of 10 years and no salvage value. The donor's cost of this asset was $20,000, and its fair market value at the date of the gift was $30,000. What amount of depreciation of this asset should the society recognize in its 20X2 financial statements?

   a. $3,000.
   b. $2,500.
   c. $2,000.
   d. $0.

2. In 20X1, a nonprofit trade association enrolled five new member companies, each of which was obligated to pay nonrefundable initiation fees of $1,000. These fees were receivable by the association in 20X1. Three of the new members paid the initiation fees in 20X1, and the other two new members paid their initiation fees in 20X2. Annual dues (excluding initiation fees) received by the association from all members have always covered the organization's costs of services provided to its members. It can be reasonably expected that future dues will cover all costs of the organization's future services to members. Average membership duration is 10 years because of mergers, attrition, and economic factors. What amount of initiation fees from these five new members should the association recognize as revenue in 20X1?

   a. $5,000.
   b. $3,000.
   c. $500.
   d. $0.

3. Roberts Foundation received a nonexpendable endowment of $500,000 in 20X3 from Multi Enterprises. The endowment assets were invested in publicly traded securities. Multi did not specify how gains and losses from dispositions of endowment assets were to be treated. No restrictions were placed on the use of dividends received and interest earned on fund resources. In 20X4, Roberts realized gains of $50,000 on sales of fund investments and received total interest and dividends of $40,000 on fund securities. The amount of these capital gains, interest, and dividends available for expenditure by Roberts's unrestricted current fund is:

   a. $0.
   b. $40,000.
   c. $50,000.
   d. $90,000.

4. In July 20X2, Ross donated $200,000 cash to a church with the stipulation that the revenue generated from this gift be paid to him during his lifetime. The conditions of this donation are that after Ross dies, the principal may be used by the church for any purpose voted on by the church elders. The church received interest of $16,000 on the $200,000 for the year ended June 30, 20X3, and the interest was remitted to Ross. In the church's June 30, 20X3, annual financial statements:

   a. $200,000 should be reported as temporarily restricted net assets in the balance sheet.
   b. $184,000 should be reported as revenue in the activity statement.
   c. $216,000 should be reported as revenue in the activity statement.
   d. Both *a* and *c*.

5. The following expenditures were among those incurred by a nonprofit botanical society during 20X4:

   | | |
   |---|---|
   | Printing of annual report | $15,000 |
   | Unsolicited merchandise sent to encourage contributions | 35,000 |

   What amount should be classified as fund-raising costs in the society's activity statement?

   a. $0.
   b. $5,000.
   c. $35,000.
   d. $40,000.

6. Trees Forever, a community foundation, incurred $5,000 in expenses during 20X3 putting on its annual fund-raising talent show. In the statement of activities of Trees Forever, the $5,000 should be reported as:

   a. A contra asset account.
   b. A contra revenue account.
   c. A reduction of fund-raising costs.
   d. Part of fund-raising costs.

7. In 20X3, the board of trustees of Burr Foundation designated $100,000 from its current funds for college scholarships. Also in 20X3, the foundation received a bequest of $200,000 from an estate of a benefactor who specified that the bequest was to be used for hiring teachers to tutor handicapped students. What amount should be accounted for as temporarily restricted funds?

   a. $0.
   b. $100,000.
   c. $200,000.
   d. $300,000.

*Note:* The following information is for questions 8 through 10:

United Together, a labor union, had the following receipts and expenses for the year ended December 31, 20X2:

| Receipts: | |
|---|---:|
| Per capita dues | $680,000 |
| Initiation fees | 90,000 |
| Sales of organizational supplies | 60,000 |
| Nonexpendable gift restricted by donor for loan purposes for 10 years | 30,000 |
| Nonexpendable gift restricted by donor for loan purposes in perpetuity | 25,000 |
| Expenses: | |
| Labor negotiations | 500,000 |
| Fund-raising | 100,000 |
| Membership development | 50,000 |
| Administrative and general | 200,000 |

The union's constitution provides that 10 percent of the per capita dues be designated for the strike insurance fund to be distributed for strike relief at the discretion of the union's executive board.

8. In United Together's statement of activities for the year ended December 31, 20X2, what amount should be reported under the classification of revenue from unrestricted funds?

   a. $740,000.

   b. $762,000.

   c. $770,000.

   d. $830,000.

9. In United Together's statement of activities for the year ended December 31, 20X2, what amount should be reported under the classification of program services?

   a. $500,000.

   b. $550,000.

   c. $600,000.

   d. $850,000.

10. In United Together's statement of activities for the year ended December 31, 20X2, what amounts should be reported under the classifications of temporarily and permanently restricted net assets?

    a. $0 and $55,000, respectively.

    b. $55,000 and $0, respectively.

    c. $30,000 and $25,000, respectively.

    d. $25,000 and $30,000, respectively.

**E19-9  Statement of Activities for an Other Nonprofit Organization**

The following is a list of selected account balances in the unrestricted operating fund for the Pleasant School:

| | Debit | Credit |
|---|---:|---:|
| Unrestricted Net Assets, July 1, 20X1 | | $  420,000 |
| Tuition and Fees | | 1,200,000 |
| Contributions | | 165,000 |
| Auxiliary Activities Revenue | | 40,000 |
| Investment Income (for current operations) | | 32,000 |
| Other Revenue | | 38,000 |
| Instruction | $1,050,000 | |
| Auxiliary Activities Expenses | 37,000 | |
| Administration | 250,000 | |
| Fund-Raising | 28,000 | |
| Transfer from Temporarily Restricted Assets | | 130,000 |
| Transfer from Permanently Restricted Assets | | 12,000 |

### Required

Prepare a statement of activities for the unrestricted operating fund of the Pleasant School for the year ended June 30, 20X2.

---

**Problems**  **P19-10**  **Financial Statements for a Private, Not-for-Profit College**

Friendly College is a small, privately supported liberal arts college. The college uses a fund structure; however, it prepares its financial statements in conformance with FASB 117.

Partial balance sheet information as of June 30, 20X2, is given as follows:

| | | |
|---|---|---|
| Unrestricted Items: | | |
| Cash | $210,000 | |
| Accounts Receivable (student tuition and fees, | | |
| less allowance for doubtful accounts of $9,000) | 341,000 | |
| State Appropriation Receivable | 75,000 | |
| Accounts Payable | | $ 45,000 |
| Deferred Revenue | | 66,000 |
| Unrestricted Net Assets | | 515,000 |
| Restricted Items: | | |
| Cash | $  7,000 | |
| Investments | 60,000 | |
| Temporarily Restricted Net Assets | | $ 67,000 |

The following transactions occurred during the fiscal year ended June 30, 20X3:

1. On July 7, 20X2, a gift of $100,000 was received from an alumnus. The alumnus requested that half the gift be restricted to the purchase of books for the university library and the remainder be used for the establishment of an endowed scholarship fund. The alumnus further requested that the income generated by the scholarship fund be used annually to award a scholarship to a qualified disadvantaged student. On July 20, 20X2, the board of trustees resolved that the funds of the newly established scholarship endowment fund would be invested in savings certificates. On July 21, 20X2, the savings certificates were purchased.

2. Revenue from student tuition and fees applicable to the year ended June 30, 20X3, amounted to $1,900,000. Of this amount, $66,000 was collected in the prior year, and $1,686,000 was collected during the year ended June 30, 20X3. In addition, on June 30, 20X3, the university had received cash of $158,000 representing deferred revenue fees for the session beginning July 1, 20X3.

3. During the year ended June 30, 20X3, the university had collected $349,000 of the outstanding accounts receivable at the beginning of the year. The balance was determined to be uncollectible and was written off against the allowance account. On June 30, 20X3, the allowance account was increased by $3,000 to $11,000.

4. During the year, interest charges of $6,000 were earned and collected on late student fee payments.

5. During the year the state appropriation was received. An additional unrestricted appropriation of $50,000 was made by the state but had not been paid to the university as of June 30, 20X3.

6. An unrestricted gift of $25,000 cash was received from alumni of the university.

7. During the year, restricted investments of $21,000 were sold for $26,000. Temporarily restricted investment interest income amounting to $1,900 was received.

8. During the year, unrestricted operating expenses of $1,777,000 were recorded, not including year-end accruals or transfers from other categories of net assets. On June 30, 20X3, $59,000 of these expenses remained unpaid.

9. Restricted current funds of $13,000 were released and spent for authorized operating purposes during the year.

10. The accounts payable on June 30, 20X2, were paid during the year.

11. During the year, $7,000 interest was earned and received on the savings certificates purchased in accordance with the board of trustees' resolutions, as discussed in transaction 1.

### Required

*a.* Prepare a comparative balance sheet for Friendly College as of June 30, 20X2, and June 30, 20X3.

*b.* Prepare a statement of activities for Friendly College for the year ended June 30, 20X3.

**P19-11**   **Balance Sheet for a Hospital**

Brookdale Hospital hired an inexperienced controller early in 20X4. Near the end of 20X4, the board of directors decided to conduct a major fund-raising campaign. They wished to have the December 31, 20X4, statement of financial position for Brookdale fully conform with current generally accepted principles for hospitals. The trial balance prepared by the controller at December 31, 20X4, is as follows:

|  | Debit | Credit |
|---|---|---|
| Cash | $  100,000 | |
| Investment in Short-Term Marketable Securities | 200,000 | |
| Investment in Long-Term Marketable Securities | 300,000 | |
| Interest Receivable | 15,000 | |
| Accounts Receivable | 55,000 | |
| Inventory | 35,000 | |
| Land | 120,000 | |
| Buildings and Equipment | 935,000 | |
| Allowance for Depreciation | | $  260,000 |
| Accounts Payable | | 40,000 |
| Mortgage Payable | | 320,000 |
| Fund Balance | | 1,140,000 |
| Total | $1,760,000 | $1,760,000 |

### Additional Information

1. Your analysis of the contributions receivable as of December 31, 20X4, determined that there were unrecognized contributions for the following:

| | |
|---|---|
| For unrestricted use | $  40,000 |
| For use in cancer research | 10,000 |
| For purchase of equipment | 20,000 |
| For permanently restricted endowment principal | 30,000 |
| Total | $100,000 |

2. Short-term investments at year-end consist of $150,000 of unrestricted funds and $50,000 of funds restricted for future cancer research. All of the long-term investments are held in the permanently restricted endowment fund.

3. Land is carried at its current market value of $120,000. The original owner purchased the land for $70,000, and at the time of donation to the hospital, the land had an appraised value of $95,000.

4. Buildings were purchased 11 years ago for $600,000 and had an estimated useful life of 30 years. Equipment costing $150,000 was purchased 7 years ago and had an expected life of 10 years. The controller had improperly increased the reported values of the buildings and equipment to their current fair value of $935,000 and had incorrectly computed the accumulated depreciation.

5. The board of directors voted on December 29, 20X4, to designate $100,000 of unrestricted funds invested in short-term investments for use in developing a drug rehabilitation center.

### Required

Prepare in good form a balance sheet for Brookdale Hospital at December 31, 20X4.

**P19-12** **Entries and Statement of Activities for an Other Nonprofit Organization [AICPA Adapted]**

A group of civic-minded merchants in Eldora organized the "Committee of 100" for the purpose of establishing the Community Sports Club, a nonprofit sports organization for local youth. Each of the committee's 100 members contributed $1,000 toward the club's capital and, in turn, received a participation certificate. In addition, each participant agreed to pay dues of $200 a year for the club's operations. All dues have been collected in full by the end of each fiscal year ending March 31. Members who have discontinued their participation have been replaced by an equal number of new members through transfer of the participation certificates from the former members to the new ones. Following is the club's trial balance for April 1, 20X2:

| | Debit | Credit |
|---|---|---|
| Cash | $ 9,000 | |
| Investments (at market, equal to cost) | 58,000 | |
| Inventories | 5,000 | |
| Land | 10,000 | |
| Building | 164,000 | |
| Accumulated Depreciation—Building | | $130,000 |
| Furniture and Equipment | 54,000 | |
| Accumulated Depreciation—Furniture and Equipment | | 46,000 |
| Accounts Payable | | 12,000 |
| Participation Certificates (100 at $1,000 each) | | 100,000 |
| Cumulative Excess of Revenue over Expenses | | 12,000 |
| Total | $300,000 | $300,000 |

Transactions for the year ended March 31, 20X3, were as follows:

| | |
|---|---|
| Collections from participants for dues | $20,000 |
| Snack bar and soda fountain sales | 28,000 |
| Interest and dividends received | 6,000 |
| Additions to voucher register: | |
| House expenses | 17,000 |
| Snack bar and soda fountain | 26,000 |
| General and administrative | 11,000 |
| Vouchers paid | 55,000 |
| Assessments for capital improvements not yet incurred (assessed on March 20, 20X3; none collected by March 31, 20X3; deemed 100% collectible during year ending March 31, 20X4) | 10,000 |
| Unrestricted bequest received | 5,000 |

### Adjustment Data

1. Investments are valued at market, which amounted to $65,000 on March 31, 20X3. There were no investment transactions during the year.

2. Depreciation for year:

| | |
|---|---|
| Building | $4,000 |
| Furniture and equipment | 8,000 |

3. Allocation of depreciation:

| | |
|---|---|
| House expenses | $9,000 |
| Snack bar and soda fountain | 2,000 |
| General and administrative | 1,000 |

4. Actual physical inventory on March 31, 20X3, was $1,000 and pertains to the snack bar and soda fountain.

### Required

a. Record the transactions and adjustments in journal entry form for the year ended March 31, 20X3. Omit explanations.

b. Prepare the appropriate all-inclusive statement of activities for the year ended March 31, 20X3.

**P19-13** **Entries and Statements for General Fund of a Hospital**

The postclosing trial balance of the general fund of Serene Hospital, a not-for-profit entity, on December 31, 20X1, was as follows:

| | Debit | Credit |
|---|---|---|
| Cash | $ 125,000 | |
| Accounts Receivable | 400,000 | |
| Allowance for Uncollectibles | | $ 50,000 |
| Due from Specific-Purpose Fund | 40,000 | |
| Inventories | 95,000 | |
| Prepaid Expenses | 20,000 | |
| Investments | 900,000 | |
| Property, Plant, and Equipment | 6,100,000 | |
| Accumulated Depreciation | | 1,500,000 |
| Accounts Payable | | 150,000 |
| Accrued Expenses | | 55,000 |
| Deferred Revenue—Reimbursement | | 75,000 |
| Bonds Payable | | 3,000,000 |
| Fund Balance—Unrestricted | | 2,850,000 |
| Total | $7,680,000 | $7,680,000 |

During 20X2 the following transactions occurred:

1. The value of patient services provided was $6,160,000.
2. Contractual adjustments of $330,000 from patients' bills were approved.
3. Operating expenses totaled $5,600,000, as follows:

| | |
|---|---|
| Nursing services | $1,800,000 |
| Other professional services | 1,200,000 |
| Fiscal services | 250,000 |
| General services | 1,550,000 |
| Bad debts | 120,000 |
| Administration | 280,000 |
| Depreciation | 400,000 |

Accounts credited for operating expenses other than depreciation:

| | |
|---|---|
| Cash | $4,580,000 |
| Allowance for Uncollectibles | 120,000 |
| Accounts Payable | 170,000 |
| Accrued Expenses | 35,000 |
| Inventories | 195,000 |
| Prepaid Expenses | 30,000 |
| Donated Services | 70,000 |

4. Received $75,000 cash from specific-purpose fund for partial reimbursement of $100,000 for operating expenditures made in accordance with a restricted gift. The receivable increased by the remaining $25,000 to an ending balance of $65,000.

5. Payments for inventories and prepaid expenses were $176,000 and $24,000, respectively.

6. Received $85,000 income from endowment fund investments.

7. Sold an X-ray machine that had cost $30,000 and had accumulated depreciation of $20,000 for $17,000.

8. Collected $5,800,000 in receivables and wrote off $132,000.

9. Acquired investments amounting to $60,000.

10. Income from board-designated investments was $72,000.

11. Paid the beginning balance in Accounts Payable and Accrued Expenses.

12. Deferred Revenue—Reimbursement increased $20,000.

13. Received $140,000 from the plant replacement and expansion fund for use in acquiring fixed assets.

14. Net receipts from the cafeteria and gift shop were $63,000.

### Required

a. Prepare journal entries to record the transactions for the general fund. Omit explanations.

b. Prepare comparative balance sheets for only the general fund for 20X2 and 20X1.

c. Prepare a statement of operations for the unrestricted, general fund for 20X2.

d. Prepare a statement of cash flows for 20X2.

**P19-14**   **Statements for Current Funds of a Voluntary Health and Welfare Organization [AICPA Adapted]**

Following are the adjusted current funds trial balances of Community Association for Handicapped Children, a voluntary health and welfare organization, on June 30, 20X4:

### COMMUNITY ASSOCIATION FOR HANDICAPPED CHILDREN
#### Adjusted Current Funds Trial Balances
#### June 30, 20X4

|  | Unrestricted | | Restricted | |
| --- | --- | --- | --- | --- |
|  | **Debit** | **Credit** | **Debit** | **Credit** |
| Cash | $ 40,000 | | $ 9,000 | |
| Bequest Receivable | | | 5,000 | |
| Pledges Receivable | 12,000 | | | |
| Accrued Interest Receivable | 1,000 | | | |
| Investments (at market) | 100,000 | | | |
| Accounts Payable and Accrued Expenses | | $ 50,000 | | $ 1,000 |
| Deferred Revenue | | 2,000 | | |
| Allowance for Uncollectible Pledges | | 3,000 | | |
| Fund Balances, July 1, 20X3: | | | | |
| Designated | | 12,000 | | |
| Undesignated | | 26,000 | | |
| Restricted | | | | 23,000 |
| Transfers of Expired Endowment Fund Principal | | 20,000 | 20,000 | |
| Contributions | | 300,000 | | 15,000 |
| Membership Dues | | 25,000 | | |
| Program Service Fees | | 30,000 | | |
| Investment Income | | 10,000 | | |
| Deaf Children's Program Expenses | 120,000 | | | |
| Blind Children's Program Expenses | 150,000 | | | |
| Management and General Services | 45,000 | | 4,000 | |
| Fund-Raising Services | 8,000 | | 1,000 | |
| Provision for Uncollectible Pledges | 2,000 | | | |
| Total | $478,000 | $478,000 | $39,000 | $39,000 |

### Required

a. Prepare a statement of activities for the year ended June 30, 20X4.

b. Prepare a statement of financial position as of June 30, 20X4.

**P19-15 Comparative Journal Entries for a Government Entity and a Voluntary Health and Welfare Organization [AICPA Adapted]**

Following are four independent transactions or events that relate to a local government and a voluntary health and welfare organization:

1. A disbursement of $25,000 was made from the general fund unrestricted assets for the cash purchase of new equipment.

2. An unrestricted cash gift of $100,000 was received from a donor.

3. Investments in common stocks with a total carrying value of $50,000 were sold by a permanently restricted endowment fund for $55,000 before any dividends were earned on these stocks. The gain is donor-restricted to remain in the permanently restricted fund.

4. General obligation bonds payable with a face amount of $1,000,000 were sold at par, with the proceeds required to be used solely for construction of a new building. This building was completed at a total cost of $1,000,000, and the total amount of bond issue proceeds was disbursed toward this cost. Disregard interest capitalization.

### Required

*a.* For each of these transactions or events, prepare journal entries without explanations, specifying the affected funds and showing how these transactions or events should be recorded by a local government whose debt is serviced by general tax revenue.

*b.* For each of these transactions or events, prepare journal entries without explanations, specifying the affected funds and showing how these transactions or events should be recorded by a voluntary health and welfare organization.

**P19-16 Matching Effects of Transactions on a Hospital's Financial Statements [AICPA Adapted]**

DeKalb Hospital, a large not-for-profit organization, has adopted an accounting policy that does not imply a time restriction on gifts of long-lived assets.

For each of the six items presented, select the best answer from the Answer List.

| Transactions | Answer List |
|---|---|
| 1. DeKalb's board designates $1,000,000 to purchase investments whose income will be used for capital improvements. | A. Increase in unrestricted revenues, gains, and other support |
| 2. Income from investments in item 1, which was not previously accrued, is received. | B. Decrease in an expense |
| 3. A benefactor provided funds for building expansion. | C. Increase in temporarily restricted net assets |
| 4. The funds in item 3 are used to purchase a building in the fiscal period following the period in which the funds were received. | D. Increase in permanently restricted net assets |
| 5. An accounting firm prepared DeKalb's annual financial statements without charge. | E. No required reportable event |
| 6. DeKalb received investments subject to the donor's requirement that investment income be used to pay for outpatient services. | |

**P19-17 Balance Sheet for a Hospital**

The following information is contained in the funds that are used to account for the transactions of the Hospital of Havencrest, which is operated by a religious organization. The balances in the accounts are as of June 30, 20X8, the end of the hospital's fiscal year.

| | General Fund | Specific-Purpose Fund | Plant Replacement and Expansion Fund | Endowment Fund |
|---|---|---|---|---|
| Cash | $ 30,000 | $32,000 | $140,000 | $ 20,000 |
| Accounts Receivable | 25,000 | | | |
| Allowance for Uncollectibles | (5,000) | | | |
| Inventories | 50,000 | | | |
| Prepaid Expenses | 10,000 | | | |
| Long-Term Investments | 100,000 | | 60,000 | 500,000 |
| Property, Plant, and Equipment | 300,000 | | | |
| Accumulated Depreciation | (140,000) | | | |
| Accounts Payable | 45,000 | | | |
| Accrued Expenses | 17,000 | | | |
| Deferred Revenue | 11,000 | | | |
| Current Portion—Long-Term Debt | 24,000 | | | |
| Mortgage Payable | 125,000 | | | |

### Additional Information

The $32,000 in the specific-purpose fund is restricted for research activities to be conducted by the hospital.

### Required

Prepare a balance sheet for Havencrest at June 30, 20X8.

**P19-18**   **Matching of Transactions to Effects on Statement of Changes in Net Assets for a Hospital**

Match the transactions on the left with the effects of the transactions on the statement of changes in net assets for a private, not-for-profit hospital.

| Transactions | Effects of Transactions on Statement of Changes in Net Assets |
|---|---|
| 1. Patients billed for services rendered. | A. Increases unrestricted net assets |
| 2. Realized a gain from the sale of securities that are permanently invested. | B. Decreases unrestricted net assets |
| 3. Recorded depreciation expense for the year. | C. Increases temporarily restricted net assets |
| 4. Designated assets for plant expansion. | |
| 5. Contributions restricted for research activities received. | D. Decreases temporarily restricted net assets |
| 6. Contributions restricted for equipment acquisition. | E. Increases permanently restricted net assets |
| 7. Acquired equipment with all of the contributions received in item 6. | F. Decreases permanently restricted net assets |
| 8. Earned endowment income. The donor placed no restrictions on the investment earnings. | G. Does not affect the statement of changes in net assets |
| 9. Expended 50 percent of the contributions restricted for research in item 5. | |
| 10. Received cash contribution from donor who stipulated the contribution be permanently invested. | |
| 11. Acquired investments with cash received in item 10. | |
| 12. Received tuition revenue from hospital nursing program and cash from sales of goods in the hospital gift shop. | |

**P19-19 Matching of Transactions to Effects on Statement of Activities for a Voluntary Health and Welfare Organization**

Match the transactions on the left with the effects of the transactions on the statement of activities for a voluntary health and welfare organization. A transaction may have more than one effect.

| Transactions | Effects of Transactions on Statement of Activities |
|---|---|
| 1. Received cash contributions restricted by donors for research. | A. Increases unrestricted net assets |
| 2. Incurred fund-raising costs. | B. Decreases unrestricted net assets |
| 3. Recorded depreciation expense for the year. | C. Increases temporarily restricted net assets |
| 4. Designated assets for plant expansion. | D. Decreases temporarily restricted net assets |
| 5. Realized a gain from the sale of securities that were permanently restricted. The donor specified that any gains from sales of these securities must be preserved and invested in other permanently restricted investments. | E. Increases permanently restricted net assets |
| 6. Earned endowment income. The donor specified that the income be used for community service. | F. Decreases permanently restricted net assets |
| 7. Received a multiyear pledge, with cash being received this year and for the next four years. Donors did not place any use restrictions on how the pledges were to be spent. | G. Is not reported on the statement of activities |
| 8. Earned income from investments of assets that the board designated in item 4. | |
| 9. Received pledges from donors who placed no time or use restrictions on how the pledges were to be spent. | |
| 10. Received cash contributions restricted by donors for equipment. | |
| 11. Acquired equipment with all of the contributions received in item 10. | |
| 12. Expended 75 percent of the contributions received in item 1 for research. | |

**P19-20 Net Asset Identification for Transactions Involving a Private Not-for-Profit University**

Buckwall University (BU), a private not-for-profit university, had the following transactions during the year ended June 30, 20X8:

1. Assessed students $2,000,000 for tuition for the winter semester, starting in January 20X8.

2. Received $1,000,000 from the federal government to be distributed to qualified students as loans and grants.

3. Recognized depreciation expense of $200,000 on university buildings and equipment for the fiscal year.

4. Received $1,500,000 in alumni contributions restricted to the construction of a new library building. Construction of the library is expected to begin in September 20X8.

5. Invested the contributions received in item 4 in equity securities that had a market value of $1,650,000 on June 30, 20X8.

6. Received $75,000 of investment revenue from investments in a term endowment. The donor stipulated that the investment revenue be used to fund scholarships for qualified entering freshmen.

7. Used $60,000 of the investment revenue in item 6 to fund scholarships during the year ended June 30, 20X8.

8. Designated $250,000 of cash to be used for refurbishing the steam tunnels used for heating the university during the winter.

9. Received from an alumnus a contribution of artwork with a fair value of $3,750,000. The donor has stipulated that the artwork be preserved, that it not be sold, and that it be on public view in the university museum. The university has a policy of recording donations of works of art and historical treasures.

10. Acquired debt securities at a cost of $400,000 during the year. Required by the governing board to keep these investments intact for the next five years and use interest revenue from the securities for funding summer research grants to faculty of BU.

11. Received during the year ended June 30, 20X8, interest revenue from the debt securities in item 10, which amounted to $18,000, of which $12,000 was used for research grants.

### Required

For each of the numbered transactions, indicate the net asset class affected by the transaction for the year ended June 30, 20X8. The three net asset classes are (1) unrestricted, (2) temporarily restricted, and (3) permanently restricted. Your answer should also specify the dollar amount and whether the asset class increased or decreased.

**P19-21** **Questions on Voluntary Health and Welfare Organization [AICPA Adapted]**

Items 1 through 6 represent various transactions pertaining to Crest Haven, a voluntary health and welfare organization, for the year ended December 31, 20X2. The information presented also includes a list of how transactions could affect the statement of activities (List A Effects) and the statement of cash flows (List B Effects). Crest Haven follows both FASB 116 and 117.

### Transactions

1. Pledges of $500,000 were made by various donors for the acquisition of new equipment. The equipment will be acquired in 20X3.

2. Dividends and interest of $40,000 were received from endowment investments. The donors have stipulated that the earnings from endowment investments be used for research in 20X3.

3. Cash donations of $350,000 were received from donors who did not stipulate how the donations were to be used.

4. Investments of $250,000 were acquired from cash donated in 20X0 by a donor who stipulated that the cash donation be invested permanently.

5. Depreciation expense of $75,000 was recorded for 20X2.

6. Of the amount pledged in transaction 1, $300,000 was received.

### Required

Indicate how Crest Haven should report each transaction on (1) the statement of activities and (2) the statement of cash flows prepared for the year ended December 31, 20X2. Crest Haven reports separate columns for changes in unrestricted, temporarily restricted, and permanently restricted net assets on its statement of activities. In addition, Crest Haven uses the direct method of reporting its cash flows from operation activities. The items in List A Effects and List B Effects may be used once, more than once, or not at all.

### Example

Cash paid to employees and suppliers:    List A = D    List B = I

| **Statement of Activities**<br>**List A Effects** | **Statement of Cash Flows**<br>**List B Effects** |
|---|---|
| A. Increases unrestricted net assets | H. Increases cash flows from operating activities |
| B. Increases temporarily restricted net assets | I. Decreases cash flows from operating activities |
| C. Increases permanently restricted net assets | J. Increases cash flows from investing activities |
| D. Decreases unrestricted net assets | K. Decreases cash flows from investing activities |
| E. Decreases temporarily restricted net assets | L. Increases cash flows from financing activities |
| F. Decreases permanently restricted net assets | M. Decreases cash flows from financing activities |
| G. Is not reported on the statement of activities | N. Transaction not reported on the statement of cash flows |

**P19-22** **Contributions to a Hospital [AICPA Adapted]**

Alpha Hospital, a large not-for-profit organization, has adopted an accounting policy that does not imply a time restriction on gifts of long-lived assets.

***Required***

For items 1 through 6, indicate the effect of the transaction on Alpha's financial statements by selecting the appropriate letter.

| Transactions | Effect |
| --- | --- |
| 1. Alpha's board designates $1,000,000 to purchase investments whose income will be used for capital improvements. | A. Increase in unrestricted revenues, gains, and other support |
| 2. Income from investments in item 1, which was not previously accrued, is received. | B. Decrease in expense |
| | C. Increase in temporarily restricted net assets |
| 3. A benefactor provides funds for a building expansion. | D. Increase in permanently restricted net assets |
| 4. The funds in item 3 are used to purchase a building in the fiscal period following the period the funds were received. | E. No required reportable event |
| 5. An accounting firm prepares Alpha's annual financial statements without charge to Alpha. | |
| 6. Alpha receives investments subject to the donor's requirement that investment income be used to pay for outpatient services. | |

**P19-23** **Evaluating Items for a Hospital's Statement of Operations**

Smallville Community Hospital, a not-for-profit hospital, has a number of items to be evaluated to determine their proper placement on the hospital's statement of operations (either above the performance measure of Excess of Revenues over Expenses or below the performance measure). It is possible that an item need not be reported on the hospital's statement of operations.

***Required***

Select the proper letter from the Where Reported column to match each item in the left-hand column. If an item is presented in two or more places on the statement of operations, provide the correct answer for each placement.

| Items | Where Reported |
| --- | --- |
| 1. Bad debts expense. | A. Above the performance measure line |
| 2. Donated supplies used in patient care. | |
| 3. Unrestricted investment interest income. | B. Below the performance measure line |
| 4. Gain on sale of hospital assets. | |
| 5. Net assets released from restriction for acquisition of equipment. | C. Not reported on the statement of operations |
| 6. Net assets released from restriction for use in hospital operations. | |
| 7. Gain on sale of permanently restricted endowment investments that the donor requires to be permanently restricted. | |
| 8. Investment interest income that donor restricted for use in medical care education programs, which the hospital plans to begin next year. | |
| 9. Pledges for a new hospital building wing to be constructed next year. | |
| 10. Revenue from cafeteria sales. | |

*(continued)*

11. Donations of specialized, professional-quality services.
12. Depreciation expense on hospital equipment.
13. Resources designated by the hospital board of directors to be set aside for the new hospital wing.
14. Gift of new heart-monitoring equipment received.
15. Charity care provided by the hospital in accordance with its state charter.
16. Contractual adjustment to the normal service charge for persons covered by an insurance company's health insurance.
17. Proceeds of a bond issue for the new wing.
18. Purchase of new operating tables for the operating rooms.
19. Recognition of unrealized holding gain for change in market value of investment securities. Income is in excess of amounts designated for current operations.

---

**P19-24   True-False Questions about Not-for-Profit Accounting and Reporting**

Determine whether each of the following is true or false. Assume that each organization is a private, nonprofit entity.

1. A statement of functional expenses is required for a musical arts association that is a not-for-profit organization.

2. Pledges received by a research organization should result in recording revenue net of estimated uncollectible pledges.

3. A college should account for a donor-restricted contribution to support student scholarships for the next three years as contribution revenue in its unrestricted net assets.

4. A hospital should record an insurance provider's contractual adjustment on a patient bill as an operating expense for the period in which the services were provided to the patient.

5. A university should account for its governing board's designation of resources for the development of a fine arts academic program as a transfer to a temporarily restricted net asset class.

6. An environmental watch organization received a donor-restricted donation for the purchase of equipment. The organization properly accounted for the donation when it was received. When the equipment is acquired, the organization should record "net assets released" from temporarily restricted net assets and an addition to unrestricted net assets.

7. A hospital used donated supplies for its patient services during the year. The hospital should not record the donation because it incurred no cost to obtain the supplies.

8. An organization earned investment income on its endowment fund that is permanently donor restricted for use in a specific organizational program. The investment income should be recorded directly into the temporarily restricted net asset class.

9. A hospital has a portfolio of securities that decreased in fair market value during the year. Because the securities were not sold during the year, the change in market value should not be recognized on the hospital's statement of operations.

10. A not-for-profit art museum receives for public display a donation of historical artifacts that the museum will care for and preserve. If any item in the collection is ever sold, the museum has agreed to use the proceeds for additional items for the collection. The museum is not required to record the contribution revenue and increase in collection assets.

11. All of a hospital's building and equipment should be recorded in its restricted building fund.

12. A local accountant donated significant professional services to a local fraternal organization, which should recognize the value of the donated services as both a contribution revenue and an operating expense.

13. A hospital has estimated uncollectibles on patient accounts that should be reported as a reduction of net patient service revenue.

14. A college received a conditional pledge based on the occurrence of a future event. The school should record the contribution at its fair value if it is determined that the future event is possible.

15. A hospital that received a donation restricted for a cancer awareness education program properly recorded the donation as contribution revenue in the temporarily restricted net asset

class. The cost of the program that the hospital offered should be recorded as an expense in the temporarily restricted net asset class to offset the contribution revenue for the program.

16. A voluntary health and welfare organization received a contribution that the donor specified could not be spent until the next year. Because the organization had received it in this year, the donation should be recorded as a debit to Cash and a credit to Deferred Revenue in the unrestricted net asset class.

17. Hospitals are required to use fund accounting, which specifies which funds are unrestricted, which are temporarily restricted, and which are permanently restricted.

18. Hospitals are required to report a performance measure in their statement of operations to separate the operating income from the nonoperating income.

19. A hospital's building fund transfers resources to the general fund for the purchase of new equipment. The building fund should record this as an expense of the period of the transfer, and the general fund should record this as an income of the period of the transfer.

20. A voluntary health and welfare organization conducted a major fund-raising effort that involved significant expenses. Because the expenses were incurred to obtain contribution revenue, the fund-raising costs should be accounted for as a direct reduction of contribution revenue to obtain the net contribution revenue reported on the organization's statement of activities.

**P19-25   Statement of Activities for a Voluntary Health and Welfare Organization**

The following information pertains to United Ways, a private voluntary health and welfare organization, for the year ended December 31, 20X3.

| Balances in net assets at January 1, 20X3: | |
| --- | --- |
| Unrestricted | $3,000,000 |
| Temporarily restricted | 5,000,000 |
| Permanently restricted | 6,000,000 |

The following transactions occurred during the year ended December 31, 20X3:

1. Received cash donations of $500,000 from donors who did not place any time or purpose restrictions on their donations.

2. Received $1,000,000 of pledges from donors to be received in 20X4; it was estimated that 5 percent of the pledges would not be collected. Donors did not place any restrictions on the use of their pledges.

3. Earned investment income of $200,000 on endowment investments that donors permanently restricted for research activities.

4. Designated $225,000 of the $500,000 of cash donations received in 20X3 for computer acquisitions.

5. Spent $150,000 of the $200,000 of investment income earned on endowment investments on research during the year ended December 31, 20X3. (This amount is included in the $250,000 shown below for research expenses.)

6. Acquired $100,000 of equipment from donations made in 20X2 that donors had restricted for that purchase. The governing board of United Ways reports acquisitions of capital assets as unrestricted.

7. Received donated audit services that would have cost $15,000 from the organization's accounting firm.

8. The organization learned that the fair value of endowment investments was $600,000 higher at the end of 20X3 than it had been at the beginning of 20X3. United Ways did not acquire or sell any endowment investments during 20X3. Gains and losses on endowment investments are treated as permanently restricted.

9. Incurred program and supporting services expenses during 20X3 as follows (depreciation expense for 20X3 has been properly allocated to the functional expenses):

| | |
|---|---:|
| Research | $250,000 |
| Public health education | 100,000 |
| Community services | 150,000 |
| Management and general (does not include the audit that was donated) | 125,000 |
| Fund-raising | 115,000 |

### Required

Prepare a statement of activities in good form for United Way for the year ended December 31, 20X3.

**P19-26**  **Reporting Transactions on the Statement of Cash Flows for Private, Not-for-Profit Entities**

Following is a list of transactions and events that may occur in private, not-for-profit entities. Indicate where each transaction or event should be reported on the entity's statement of cash flows. Assume that the indirect method of reporting operating activities is used. If a transaction or event is reported as an adjustment to the change in net assets in the operating activities section, your answer should indicate whether the adjustment is added to or subtracted from the change in net assets. If a transaction or event is reported in more than one section on the statement of cash flows, you should include all sections in your answer.

### Sample Question

A hospital recorded depreciation expense for the year of $50,000.

### Answer

Report the depreciation expense of $50,000 as an addition to the change in net assets in the operating activities section.

### Transactions and Events

1. A hospital's accounts receivable from patients increased $100,000 during the year.
2. A college received from a donor a $200,000 contribution restricted to acquiring fixed assets.
3. A voluntary health and welfare organization received $25,000 from a donor who stipulated that the amount be invested permanently.
4. A hospital's accounts payable for the purchase of medical supplies increased $20,000 during the year.
5. A botanical society borrowed $70,000 from the First National Bank on a long-term note payable.
6. A professional trade association invested $50,000 to acquire investments in bonds that it intends to keep until their maturity.
7. A college received investment income of $45,000 from endowment investments. The donor stipulated that the income be used for the acquisition of fixed assets.
8. A hospital spent $850,000 to acquire equipment.
9. A college made loans of $100,000 to students and faculty.
10. A zoological society made a payment of $30,000 to a local bank to repay the principal of a shortterm note payable.
11. A college's accrued interest receivable related to student and faculty loans increased $5,000 during the year.
12. A performing arts organization had an increase of $12,000 in deferred revenue for the year.
13. A college received $100,000 for the repayment of principal on loans made to students and faculty.
14. A hospital's prepaid assets increased $2,500 during the year.
15. A hospital's endowment investments increased in value by $35,000 during the year.

| Kaplan CPA Review | **Kaplan CPA Review Simulation on University and College Accounting and Reporting** |
|---|---|

Access to the online CPA Simulation can be attained by visiting the text's Web site at www.mhhe .com/baker8e.

### Situation

Jones University starts the current year with net assets of $1.5 million: $800,000 in unrestricted net assets, $500,000 in temporarily restricted net assets, and $200,000 in permanently restricted net assets. Unless otherwise stated, assume that Jones University is a private, not-for-profit organization.

### Topics Included in the Simulation

*a.* The required financial statements for a private, not-for-profit university versus the required financial statements for a public, not-for-profit university.

*b.* Accounting and reporting for transactions resulting in changes in unrestricted net assets, such as construction, and donations of money, property, and services.

*c.* Accounting for pledges, investments, and restricted donations.

*d.* Accounting for financial aid to students.

*e.* Accounting for future vacation costs of administration and staff.

*f.* Research on a conditional pledge.

*Supplemental Problems* for this chapter are available as part of the *Online Learning Center* on the textbook's Web site (URL:www.mhhe.com/baker8e)

# Corporations in Financial Difficulty

A life cycle exists for businesses as for individuals. The business press often carries stories of companies in financial difficulty, including large companies such as Kmart, United Airlines, Bethlehem Steel, Enron, and WorldCom. On average, there are 35,000 business filings in the U.S. bankruptcy courts each year. About 60 percent of these are filed under Chapter 7 as liquidations, and the remaining 40 percent are filed under Chapter 11 as reorganizations. Untold thousands of other companies use alternate courses of action, such as debt restructuring and agreements with creditors in order to work themselves out of financial difficulty.

Companies get into financial difficulty for a large variety of reasons. A company may suffer from continued losses from operations, overextended credit to customers, poor management of working capital, failure to react to changes in economic conditions, inadequate financing, and a host of other reasons for not sustaining a viable economic position. A company's liquidity problems often become cumulative. Failing to make a sufficient level of sales, a company cannot obtain adequate financing, then begins to miss debt payments, and the vicious cycle of financial difficulty is under way. At this point, outside creditors may decide to exercise their claims and demand payment of their receivables. The debtor company has a number of alternative courses open to it. It may try to reach an agreement with its creditors to postpone required payments, it may turn its assets over to its creditors for liquidation, or it may take the legal remedy of bankruptcy.

A company may petition the courts for bankruptcy for other reasons, such as to protect itself from an onslaught of legal suits. Several companies have also attempted to void union contracts by petitioning for bankruptcy. The courts are still defining the exact limits of bankruptcy, and each case must be decided individually.

*Insolvency* is defined as a condition in which a company is unable to meet debts as the debts mature. The insolvent company is unable to meet its liabilities. Before 1978, creditors had to show that the debtor was insolvent before they could petition for relief in a bankruptcy court. Because of changes in the bankruptcy law in 1978, insolvency is no longer a necessary precondition for bankruptcy.

A company in financial difficulty has a large number of alternatives, of which bankruptcy is only a final course. This chapter presents the range of major actions typically used by a company experiencing financial problems.

## COURSES OF ACTION

Bankruptcy is the final step for a financially distressed business. Prior to that, however, management usually tries to work closely with the company's creditors to provide for their claims while attempting to ensure the firm's continuing existence. A variety of nonjudicial arrangements with creditors are available. If these fail, the company usually ends up in a judicial action under the direction of a bankruptcy court.

## Nonjudicial Actions

Formal agreements between the company and its creditors are legally binding but are not administered by a court.

### Debt Restructuring Arrangements

Arrangements between a debtor company and one or more of its creditors are common for companies in temporary financial difficulty. The debtor may solicit an extension of due dates of its debt, ask for a decrease of the interest rate on the debt, or ask for a modification of other terms of the debt contract. Creditors are usually willing to extend concessions to a debtor rather than risk the legal expense and ill will from legal action against a previously valuable debtor. Many banks, for example, prefer to continue to work with a customer who is in temporary financial difficulty rather than force that customer into bankruptcy. Experience has shown that banks eventually realize a larger portion of their receivables and continue to have a future customer if they assist the debtor with financial problems by restructuring the debt. The debtors' accounting for these ***troubled debt restructurings*** is presented in **FASB Statement No. 15,** "Accounting by Debtors and Creditors for Troubled Debt Restructurings" (FASB 15). The creditor's accounting for impairments in the values of notes and loans is presented in **FASB Statement No. 114,** "Accounting by Creditors for Impairment of a Loan" (FASB 114), issued in May 1993 and superseding **FASB 15** for the creditor's accounting of troubled debt restructurings. In addition, **FASB Statement No. 118,** "Accounting by Creditors for Impairment of a Loan—Income Recognition and Disclosures" (FASB 118), was issued in October 1994 and makes minor changes to **FASB 114** for creditor accounting for the income from impaired loans. Examples of an impairment and a troubled debt restructuring are presented as supplementary information on this text's Web site.

Another form of debt restructuring arrangement is the *composition agreement.* In this case, creditors agree to accept less than the face amount of their claims. The advantage to the creditors is that they receive an immediate cash payment and usually negotiate the timing of the remaining cash payments. Although creditors receive less than the full amount, they are assured of receiving most of their receivables. Composition agreements typically involve all creditors, although some may not be willing to agree to the composition. In some cases, the consenting group of creditors agrees to allow the dissenting creditors to be paid in full if it is highly probable the debtor can eventually return to profitable operations.

### Creditors' Committee Management

Under ***creditors' committee management,*** the creditors may agree to assist the debtor in managing the most efficient payment of creditors' claims. Most creditors' committees are advisory and counsel closely with the debtor because the creditors do not want to assume additional liabilities and problems of actual operation of the debtor. Forming a creditors' committee is a nonjudicial action usually initiated with a *plan of settlement* proposed by the debtor. The plan of settlement is a detailed document that includes a schedule of payments listing the specific debts and the anticipated payments. The creditors then work closely with the debtor to enact the plan.

In some extreme cases, creditors may decide to assume operating control of the debtor company. The creditors appoint a trustee who assumes management responsibility for the debtor company. The trustee reports to the creditors with recommendations for the eventual settlement of claims. The trustee may attempt to work out a payment schedule or may recommend bankruptcy as the best alternative. The advantage of the creditors' committee management in these extreme cases is that creditors have operating control of the debtor and receive a full report of the debtor's financial condition. The disadvantage of assuming operating control to the creditors is that they incur an increased risk if the debtor enters bankruptcy because, as managers before the bankruptcy, they may be held responsible. The advantage to the debtor is that the creditors are attempting to assist the debtor out of its financial difficulty and may return operating control once the financial problems are solved without resorting to legal action.

## *Transfer of Assets*

Some debtors in financial difficulty may transfer assets, such as receivables or other financial instruments, in an effort to obtain quick cash. For example, debtors in need of cash may factor their trade receivables at a discount, and the contract may specify that the receivables are sold "with recourse" or "without recourse." The "with recourse" provision means that the debtor must accept the return of any uncollectible receivables that were initially transferred. The accounting issue is to determine whether these transfers should be accounted for as sales of the receivables or as a financing arrangement between the debtor company and the factor company. **FASB Statement No. 140,** "Accounting for Transfers and Servicing of Financial Assets and Extinguishment of Liabilities" (FASB 140), provides the accounting and reporting guidelines for these transfers. **FASB 140** specifies that a transfer of financial assets is considered a sale only if the transferor (the debtor company) has surrendered control over the transferred assets. Surrendering control means that the transferred assets have been isolated from the transferor, that the transferee (i.e., recipient) obtains the right to pledge or exchange the transferred assets, and that the transferor does not maintain effective control over the transferred assets such as through an agreement allowing the transferor to repurchase or redeem the transferred assets. **FASB Statement No. 156,** "Accounting for Servicing of Financial Assets: an amendment of FASB Statement No. 140" (FASB 156), requires that separately recognized servicing assets or liabilities in transactions such as these asset transfers be initially measured at fair value.

## Judicial Actions

Bankruptcy is a judicial action administered by bankruptcy courts and bankruptcy judges using the guidance provided in Title 11 of the United States Bankruptcy Code (Bankruptcy Code). This Bankruptcy Code provides the essential structure for bankruptcy proceedings, but periodically, amendments to this Bankruptcy Code have been made by the U.S. Congress. For example, the Bankruptcy Reform Act of 1994 (Reform Act of 1994) attempts to improve the efficiency and administration of bankruptcy cases while increasing creditors' legal protections. The Reform Act of 1994 also created a National Bankruptcy Review Commission to periodically investigate, analyze, and review bankruptcy issues and to improve the Bankruptcy Code. The Bankruptcy Abuse Prevention and Consumer Protection Act of 2005 (Bankruptcy Reform Act of 2005) made several changes for business filings, but most of the act pertains to personal filings. For example, the Bankruptcy Reform Act of 2005 makes it more difficult for persons to file for bankruptcy under Chapter 7 liquidations, and it changed Chapter 11 for personal filings to require the payment of debts such as credit card balances and other common forms of consumer debt. Personal bankruptcy filings are beyond the scope of this chapter; however, individuals considering filing for bankruptcy should first seek appropriate legal guidance.

The Bankruptcy Code is composed of eight chapters, numbered as follows:

| | |
|---|---|
| Chapter 1 | General Provisions |
| Chapter 3 | Case Administration |
| Chapter 5 | Creditors, the Debtor, and the Estate |
| Chapter 7 | Liquidation |
| Chapter 9 | Adjustment of Debts of a Municipality |
| Chapter 11 | Reorganization |
| Chapter 12 | Adjustment of Debts of a Family Farmer with Regular Annual Income |
| Chapter 13 | Adjustment of Debts of an Individual with Regular Income |

Chapters 1, 3, and 5 present the definitions and operating provisions of the Bankruptcy Code. Chapters 7 and 11 deal with corporations. Chapter 9 deals with municipal governments and Chapters 12 and 13 with individual bankruptcies.

Either the debtor or its creditors may decide that a judicial action is best in the individual circumstances. The debtor may file a *voluntary petition* seeking judicial protection in the form of an ***order of relief*** against the initiation or continuation of legal claims by the creditors against the debtor. Alternatively, creditors may file an *involuntary petition* against the debtor. Certain conditions must exist before creditors may file a petition. First, the debtor is generally not paying debts as they become due or within the last 120 days has had a custodian appointed by other creditors, by the debtor, or by some other agency to take possession of the debtor's assets. Second, if more than 12 creditors exist, 3 or more must combine to file the petition, and these must have aggregate unsecured claims of at least $5,000. The debtor is permitted to file an answer to an involuntary petition.

Once a petition has been filed, the bankruptcy court evaluates the company and determines whether present management should continue to manage the company or the court should appoint a trustee. Appointments of trustees are common when creditors make allegations of management fraud or gross management incompetence.

The Bankruptcy Code provides for two major alternatives under the protection of the bankruptcy court. These two alternatives are often known by the chapters of the Bankruptcy Code. The first is **reorganization under Chapter 11,** in which the debtor is provided judicial protection for a rehabilitation period during which it can eliminate unprofitable operations, obtain new credit, develop a new company structure with sustainable operations, and work out agreements with its creditors. The second alternative is a **liquidation under Chapter 7** of the Bankruptcy Code. A Chapter 7 liquidation is often administered by a trustee appointed by the court. The debtor's assets are sold and its liabilities extinguished as the business is liquidated. The major difference between a reorganization and a liquidation is that the debtor continues as a business after a reorganization, whereas the business does not survive a liquidation. Both of these alternatives are illustrated next.

# CHAPTER 11 REORGANIZATIONS

Chapter 11 of the Bankruptcy Code allows for legal protection from creditors' actions during a time needed to reorganize the debtor company and return its operations to a profitable level. The bankruptcy court administers reorganizations and often appoints trustees to direct the reorganization. Reorganizations are typically described by the four Ps of reorganization. A company in financial distress *petitions* the bankruptcy court for *protection* from its creditors. If granted protection, the company receives an order of relief to suspend making any payments on its prepetition debt. The company continues to operate while it prepares a **plan of reorganization,** which serves as an operating guide during the reorganization. The *proceeding* includes the actions that take place from the time the petition is filed until the company completes the reorganization.

The petition must discuss the alternative of liquidating the debtor and distributing the expected receipts to the creditors. The plan of reorganization is the essence of any reorganization. The plan must include a complete description of the expected debtor actions during the reorganization period and the way these actions will be in the best interest of the debtor and its creditors. A *disclosure statement* is transmitted to all creditors and other parties eligible to vote on the plan of reorganization. The disclosure statement includes information that would enable a reasonable investor or creditor to make an informed judgment about the worthiness of the plan and how it will affect that person's financial interest in the debtor company. The bankruptcy court then evaluates the responses to the plan from creditors and other parties and either confirms the plan of reorganization or rejects it. Confirmation of the plan implies that the debtor, or an appointed trustee, will fully follow the plan. The reorganization period may be as short as a few months or as long as several years. Most reorganizations require more than one year; however, the time span of the proceeding depends on the complexity of the reorganization.

**Statement of Position No. 90-7,** "Financial Reporting by Entities in Reorganization under the Bankruptcy Code" (SOP 90-7),[1] provides guidance for financial reporting

---

[1] *Statement of Position No. 90-7,* "Financial Reporting by Entities in Reorganization under the Bankruptcy Code" (New York: American Institute of Certified Public Accountants, 1990).

for companies in reorganization. The financial statements issued by a company during Chapter 11 proceedings should distinguish transactions and events directly associated with the reorganization from those associated with ongoing operations. Companies in reorganization are required to present balance sheets, income statements, and statements of cash flows, but **SOP 90-7** requires these three statements to clearly reflect the unique circumstances related to the reorganization.

The balance sheet of a company in reorganization has the following special attributes:

1. Prepetition liabilities subject to compromise as part of the reorganization proceeding should be reported separately from liabilities not subject to compromise. Liabilities subject to compromise include unsecured debt and other payables that were incurred before the company entered reorganization. Liabilities that are not subject to change by the reorganization plan include fully secured liabilities incurred before reorganization and all liabilities incurred after the company enters its petition for reorganization relief.

2. The liabilities should be reported at the expected amount to be allowed by the bankruptcy court. If no reasonable estimation is possible, the claims should be disclosed in the footnotes.

The income statement of a company in reorganization has the following special requirements:

1. Income statement amounts directly related to the reorganization, such as legal fees and losses on disposals of assets, should be reported separately as reorganization items in the period incurred. However, any gains or losses on discontinued operations, or extraordinary items, should be reported separately according to **APB Opinion 30**, "Reporting the Results of Operations" (APB 30).

2. Some of the interest income earned during reorganization is a result of not requiring the debtor to pay debt and thus investing the available resources in interest-bearing sources. Such interest income should be reported separately as a reorganization item. The extent to which reported interest expense differs from the contractual interest on the company's debt should be disclosed, either parenthetically on the face of the income statement or within the footnotes.

3. Earnings per share is disclosed as are any anticipated changes to the number of common shares or common stock equivalents outstanding as a result of the reorganization plan.

The statement of cash flows of a company in reorganization has the following special features:

1. **SOP 90-7** prefers the direct method of presenting cash flows from operations, but if the indirect method is used, the company must also disclose separately the operating cash flows associated with the reorganization.

2. Cash flows related to the reorganization should be reported separately from those from regular operations. For example, excess net interest received as a result of the company's not paying its debts during reorganization should be reported separately.

## Fresh Start Accounting

The basic view of a reorganization is that it is a fresh start for the company. However, it is difficult to determine whether a Chapter 11 reorganization results in a new entity for which fresh start accounting should be used or if it results in a continuation of the prior entity. **SOP 90-7** states that fresh start reporting should be used as of the confirmation date of the plan of reorganization if both the following conditions occur:[2]

1. The reorganization value of the assets of the emerging entity immediately before the date of confirmation is less than the total of all postpetition liabilities and allowed claims.

[2] *Statement of Position No. 90-7*, para. 36.

2. Holders of existing voting shares immediately before confirmation receive less than 50 percent of the voting shares of the emerging entity. This implies that the prior shareholders have lost control of the emerging company.

*Fresh start accounting* results in a new reporting entity. First, the company is required to compute the reorganization value of the emerging entity's assets. *Reorganization value* represents the fair value of the entity before considering liabilities and approximates the amount a willing buyer would pay for the entity's assets. The reorganization value is then allocated to the assets using the allocation of value method in **FASB Statement No. 141,** "Business Combinations" (FASB 141). A reorganization value in excess of amounts assignable to identifiable assets is reported as an intangible asset called Reorganization Value in Excess of Amounts Allocable to Identifiable Assets. This excess is then accounted for in conformity with **FASB Statement No. 142,** "Goodwill and Other Intangible Assets" (FASB 142). Intangibles with a finite life are amortized over that life span while intangibles with an indefinite useful life are reviewed annually for impairment to determine whether the carrying value exceeds its fair value. The emerging company's liabilities are recorded at the present values of the amounts to be paid. Any retained earnings or deficits are eliminated. A set of final operating statements is prepared just prior to emerging from reorganization. In essence, the company is a new reporting entity after reorganization.

### Companies Not Qualifying for Fresh Start Accounting

Those companies not meeting the two conditions for fresh start accounting should determine whether their assets are impaired in value. In addition, they should report liabilities at the present values of the amounts to be paid, with any gain or loss on the revaluation of the liabilities recorded in accordance with **APB 30** as to extraordinary or ordinary events.

Many companies decide to restructure their operations as part of the reorganization plan. Those companies not qualifying for fresh start accounting account for restructuring costs, such as the costs of closing a plant and reducing the work force, combining some of the remaining operations, and so on in accordance with **FASB Statement No. 146,** "Accounting for Costs Associated with Exit or Disposal Activities" (FASB 146). This statement establishes the recognition of a liability for a cost associated with an exit or disposal activity when the liability is incurred, not at the earlier time the company makes a commitment to an exit plan.

The accounting for long-lived assets should be performed in accordance with **FASB Statement No. 144,** "Accounting for Impairment or Disposal of Long-Lived Assets" (FASB 144). The long-lived assets are divided between (1) those to be held and used and (2) those to be disposed of by sale. An impairment loss on long-lived assets to be held and used is recognized only if the asset's carrying value is less than the estimated discounted cash flows from operations of the asset over its estimated useful life. The amount of the impairment loss is the difference between the asset's carrying amount and its fair value. Goodwill is not considered part of the long-lived assets to be tested for impairment under **FASB 144.** Note that **FASB 142** guides the accounting for any impairment of goodwill.

Individual long-lived assets that will be disposed of by sale are revalued to their lower of carrying amount or fair value less the selling costs. In addition, once the use of a long-lived asset is discontinued and set aside for disposal by sale, depreciation is stopped. A management decision to dispose of a component of the entity is accounted for as a discontinued segment under **APB 30.**

**FASB 15** does not apply to troubled debt restructurings in which debtors restate their liabilities generally under the purview of the bankruptcy court. **FASB 15** applies only to specific debt restructuring transactions. This exception is not an issue in the immediate settlement of debt in which the debtor's gain or loss is the difference between the fair value of the consideration given and the carrying value of the debt. The gain or loss is the same under **FASB 15** as under a general restatement of liabilities in a reorganization.

However, in cases of modification of terms in a reorganization involving a general restatement of liabilities, the debtor's restructuring gain is computed as the difference between the carrying value of the debt and the new principal after restructuring of the debt. The future cash flows from interest payments are not included in the computation of the new principal. Thus, in most cases of debt restructuring of companies in reorganization proceedings, the debtor's gain from the debt restructuring is greater than it would have been under **FASB 15.**

## Plan of Reorganization

The plan of reorganization is typically a detailed document with a full discussion of all major actions to be taken during the reorganization period. In addition to these major actions, management also continues to manufacture and sell products, collect receivables, and pursue other day-to-day operations. Most plans include detailed discussions of the following:

1. Disposing of unprofitable operations, through either sale or liquidation.
2. Restructuring of debt with specific creditors.
3. Revaluation of assets and liabilities.
4. Reductions or eliminations of claims of original stockholders and issuances of new shares to creditors or others.

The plan of reorganization must be approved by at least half of all creditors, who must hold at least two-thirds of the dollar amount of the debtor's total outstanding debt, although the court may still confirm a plan that the necessary number of creditors do not approve, provided the court finds that the plan is in the best interests of all parties and is equitable and fair to those groups not voting approval.

## Illustration of a Reorganization

A balance sheet for Peerless Products Corporation on December 31, 20X6, is presented in Figure 20–1. On January 2, 20X7, Peerless's management petitions the bankruptcy court for a Chapter 11 reorganization to obtain relief from debt payments and time to rehabilitate the company and return to profitable operations.

The following time line presents the dates relevant for this example:

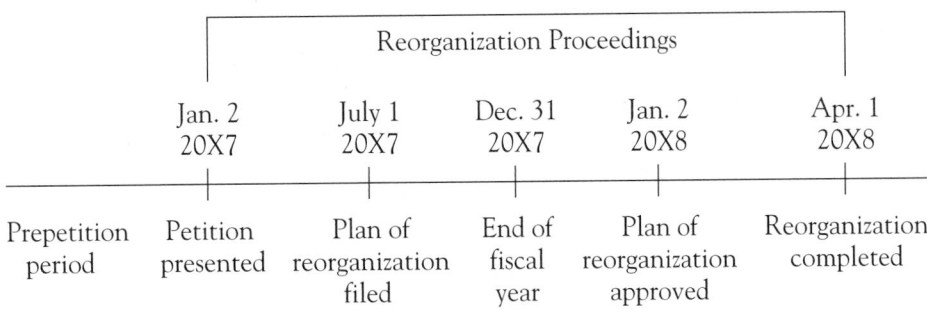

The bankruptcy court accepts the petition, and Peerless Products prepares its plan of reorganization. The plan is filed on July 1, 20X7, and the disclosure statement is sent to all creditors and other affected parties. On December 31, 20X7, the company presents its financial statements for the 20X7 fiscal period in which it was in Chapter 11 proceedings. The bankruptcy court approves the reorganization plan on January 2, 20X8, and the reorganization is completed by April 1, 20X8.

Peerless Products files the plan of reorganization presented in Figure 20–2, with audited financial statements and other disclosures requested by the bankruptcy court.

**FIGURE 20–1**
Balance Sheet on the
Date of Corporate
Insolvency

### PEERLESS PRODUCTS CORPORATION
### Balance Sheet
### December 31, 20X6

**Assets**

| | | | |
|---|---|---|---|
| Cash | | | $ 2,000 |
| Marketable Securities | | | 8,000 |
| Accounts Receivable | | $ 20,000 | |
| Less: Allowance for Uncollectible Accounts | | (2,000) | 18,000 |
| Inventory | | | 45,000 |
| Prepaid Assets | | | 1,000 |
| Total Current Assets | | | $ 74,000 |

Property, Plant, and Equipment:

| | Cost | Accumulated Depreciation | Undepreciated Cost | |
|---|---|---|---|---|
| Land | $ 10,000 | $ -0- | $ 10,000 | |
| Plant | 75,000 | 20,000 | 55,000 | |
| Equipment | 40,000 | 4,000 | 36,000 | |
| Total | $125,000 | $24,000 | $101,000 | 101,000 |
| Total Assets | | | | $175,000 |

**Liabilities**

| | | | |
|---|---|---|---|
| Accounts Payable | | | $ 26,000 |
| Notes Payable: | | | |
| Partially Secured | | $ 10,000 | |
| Unsecured, 10% interest | | 80,000 | 90,000 |
| Accrued Interest | | | 3,000 |
| Accrued Wages | | | 14,000 |
| Total Current Liabilities | | | $133,000 |
| Mortgages Payable | | | 50,000 |
| Total Liabilities | | | $183,000 |

**Shareholders' Equity**

| | | | |
|---|---|---|---|
| Preferred Stock | | $ 40,000 | |
| Common Stock ($1 par) | | 10,000 | |
| Retained Earnings (Deficit) | | (58,000) | |
| Total Shareholders' Equity | | | (8,000) |
| Total Liabilities and Shareholders' Equity | | | $175,000 |

**FIGURE 20–2**
Plan of
Reorganization

### PEERLESS PRODUCTS CORPORATION
### Plan of Reorganization
### Under Chapter 11 of the Bankruptcy Code
### (Filed July 1, 20X7)

a. The accounts payable of $26,000 will be provided for as follows: (1) $6,000 will be eliminated, (2) $4,000 will be paid in cash, (3) $12,000 of the payables will be exchanged for subordinated debt, and (4) $4,000 of the payables are to be exchanged for 4,000 shares of newly issued common stock.

b. The partially secured notes payable of $10,000 will be provided for as follows: (1) $2,000 will be paid in cash and (2) the remaining $8,000 will be exchanged for senior debt secured by a lien on equipment.

c. The unsecured notes payable of $80,000 will be provided for as follows: (1) $12,000 is to be eliminated, (2) $14,000 is to be paid in cash, (3) $49,000 is to be exchanged to senior debt secured by a lien against fixed assets, and (4) $5,000 is to be exchanged into 5,000 shares of newly issued common stock.

d. The accrued interest of $3,000 will be provided for as follows: (1) $2,000 will be eliminated and (2) the remaining $1,000 will be paid in cash.

e. The accrued wages of $14,000 will be provided for as follows: (1) $12,000 will be paid in cash and (2) the remaining $2,000 will be exchanged into 2,000 shares of newly issued common stock.

f. The preferred shareholders will receive 8,000 shares of newly issued common stock in exchange for their preferred stock.

g. The present common stockholders will receive 1,000 shares of newly issued common stock in exchange for their present common stock

Prior to the approval of the plan of reorganization, Peerless Products continues to operate under the protection of the granted petition of relief. The company makes only court-approved payments on the prepetition liabilities. The only court-approved payment on prepetition liabilities is a $2,000 payment on the mortgage payable. On December 31, 20X7, the company issues financial statements for the fiscal year. **SOP 90-7** prescribes the reporting guidelines for companies in reorganization proceedings. A most important reporting concern is that the reorganization amounts be reported separately from other operating amounts. Peerless Products prepares the following financial statements as of December 31, 20X7: balance sheet (Figure 20–3), income statement (Figure 20–4), and statement of cash flows (Figure 20–5). Note that "Debtor-in-Possession" indicates that Peerless Products continues to manage its own assets rather than having them managed by a court-appointed trustee.

On January 2, 20X8, the bankruptcy court approves the plan of reorganization, as filed. Peerless Products Corporation carries out the plan as shown in the recovery analysis presented in Figure 20–6.

**FIGURE 20–3**
**Balance Sheet for a Company in Reorganization Proceedings**

**PEERLESS PRODUCTS CORPORATION**
**(Debtor-in-Possession)**
**Balance Sheet**
**December 31, 20X7**

**Assets**

| | | |
|---|---:|---:|
| Cash | | $ 40,000 |
| Income Tax Refund Receivable | | 12,000 |
| Marketable Securities | | 8,000 |
| Accounts Receivable | $ 6,000 | |
| Less: Allowance for Uncollectibles | (1,000) | 5,000 |
| Inventory | | 37,000 |
| Total Current Assets | | $102,000 |
| Property, Plant, and Equipment | $104,000 | |
| Less: Accumulated Depreciation | (26,000) | 78,000 |
| Total Assets | | $180,000 |

**Liabilities**

Liabilities Not Subject to Compromise:

| | | |
|---|---:|---:|
| Current Liabilities (postpetition): | | |
| Short-Term Borrowings | $ 15,000 | |
| Accounts Payable—Trade | 10,000 | |
| Noncurrent Liability: | | |
| Mortgage Payable, Fully Secured | 48,000 | |
| Total Liabilities Not Subject to Compromise | | $ 73,000 |
| Liabilities Subject to Compromise (prepetition): | | |
| Accounts Payable | $ 26,000 | |
| Notes Payable, Partially Secured | 10,000 | |
| Notes Payable, Unsecured | 80,000 | |
| Accrued Interest | 3,000 | |
| Accrued Wages | 14,000 | |
| Total Liabilities Subject to Compromise | | 133,000 |
| Total Liabilities | | $206,000 |

**Shareholders' Equity**

| | | |
|---|---:|---:|
| Preferred Stock | $ 40,000 | |
| Common Stock ($1 par) | 10,000 | |
| Retained Earnings (deficit) | (76,000) | |
| Total Shareholders' Equity | | (26,000) |
| Total Liabilities and Shareholders' Equity | | $180,000 |

**FIGURE 20–4**
**Income Statement for a Company in Reorganization Proceedings**

| PEERLESS PRODUCTS CORPORATION | | |
|---|---:|---:|
| **(Debtor-in-Possession)** | | |
| **Income Statement** | | |
| **For the Year Ended December 31, 20X7** | | |
| Revenue: | | |
| Sales | | $120,000 |
| Cost and Expenses: | | |
| Cost of Goods Sold | $110,000 | |
| Selling, Operating, and Administrative | 21,000 | |
| Interest (contractual interest $6,000) | 3,000 | 134,000 |
| Loss before Reorganization Items and Income Tax Benefit | | $(14,000) |
| Reorganization Items: | | |
| Loss on Disposal of Assets | $(10,000) | |
| Professional Fees | (8,000) | |
| Interest Earned on Accumulated Cash Resulting from Chapter 11 Proceeding | 2,000 | |
| Total Reorganization Items | | (16,000) |
| Loss before Income Tax Benefit | | $(30,000) |
| Income Tax Benefit | | 12,000 |
| Net Loss | | $(18,000) |

An important concept for determining the appropriate accounting for entities in reorganization is the determination of reorganization value. Reorganization value is the fair value of the entity's assets. Typical methods of determining reorganization value are discounting future cash flows or appraisals. After extensive analysis, a reorganization value of $195,000 is determined for Peerless Products' assets. Recall that fresh start accounting

**FIGURE 20–5**
**Statement of Cash Flows for a Company in Reorganization Proceedings**

| PEERLESS PRODUCTS CORPORATION | |
|---|---:|
| **(Debtor-in-Possession)** | |
| **Statement of Cash Flows** | |
| **For the Year Ended December 31, 20X7** | |
| Cash Flows Provided by Operating Activities: | |
| Cash Received from Customers | $ 133,000 |
| Cash Paid to Suppliers and Employees | (109,000) |
| Interest Paid | (3,000) |
| Net Cash Provided by Operating Activities before Reorganization Items | $ 21,000 |
| Operating Cash Flows Used by Reorganization Activities: | |
| Professional Fees | $ (8,000) |
| Interest Received on Cash Accumulated Due to Chapter 11 Proceeding | 2,000 |
| Net Cash Used by Reorganization Items | $ (6,000) |
| Net Cash Provided by Operating Activities and Reorganization Items | $ 15,000 |
| Cash Flows Provided by Investing Activities: | |
| Proceeds from Sale of Assets Due to Chapter 11 Proceeding | $ 10,000 |
| Net Cash Provided by Investing Activities | $ 10,000 |
| Cash Flows Provided by Financing Activities: | |
| Net Borrowings under Short-Term Financing Plan | $ 15,000 |
| Principal Payments on Prepetition Debt Authorized by Court (Mortgage Payable) | (2,000) |
| Net Cash Provided by Financing Activities | $ 13,000 |
| Net Increase in Cash | $ 38,000 |
| Cash at January 1, 20X7 | 2,000 |
| Cash at December 31, 20X7 | $ 40,000 |

**FIGURE 20–6** Recovery Analysis for Plan of Reorganization

**PEERLESS CORPORATION**
**Plan of Reorganization**
**Recovery Analysis**

| | Elimination of Debt and Equity | Surviving Debt | Recovery Cash | Senior Debt | Subordinated Debt | Common Stock % | Common Stock Value | Total Recovery $ | Total Recovery % |
|---|---|---|---|---|---|---|---|---|---|
| Postpetition Liabilities | (73,000) | (73,000) | | | | | | (73,000) | 100% |
| Claims/Interest: | | | | | | | | | |
| Accounts Payable | (26,000) | 6,000 | (4,000) | | (12,000) | 20% | (4,000) | (20,000) | 77 |
| Notes Payable, partially secured | (10,000) | | (2,000) | (8,000) | | | | (10,000) | 100 |
| Notes Payable unsecured | (80,000) | 12,000 | (14,000) | (49,000) | | 25 | (5,000) | (68,000) | 85 |
| Accrued interest | (3,000) | 2,000 | (1,000) | | | | | (1,000) | 33 |
| Accrued wages | (14,000) | | (12,000) | | | 10 | (2,000) | (14,000) | 100 |
| Total | (133,000) | 20,000 | | | | | | | |
| Preferred Shareholders | (40,000) | 32,000 | | | | 40 | (8,000) | (8,000) | |
| Common Shareholders | (10,000) | 9,000 | | | | 5 | (1,000) | (1,000) | |
| Retained Earnings Deficit | 76,000 | (76,000) | | | | | | | |
| Total | (180,000) | (15,000) | (33,000) | (57,000) | (12,000) | 100% | (20,000) | (195,000) | |

*Note:* Parentheses indicate credit amount.

is appropriate only when both of the following conditions occur: (1) Reorganization value is less than total postpetition liabilities and allowed claims and (2) holders of existing shares of voting stock immediately before the plan of reorganization is approved retain less than 50 percent of the voting shares of the emerging entity. To determine the first condition for Peerless Products, a comparison is made on the date the plan of reorganization is approved:

| | |
|---|---:|
| Postpetition liabilities | $ 73,000 |
| Liabilities deferred pursuant to Chapter 11 proceedings | 133,000 |
| Total postpetition liabilities and allowed claims | $206,000 |
| Reorganization value | (195,000) |
| Excess of liabilities over reorganization value | $ 11,000 |

Note that the first condition for fresh start accounting is present. The second condition for fresh start accounting also occurs, as shown in Figure 20–6. The common shareholders immediately before the plan of reorganization is approved hold only 5 percent of the common stock of the emerging entity. Therefore, fresh start accounting is used for Peerless Products. If both conditions for fresh start accounting are not met, the emerging company is not a new reporting entity.

After intensive study of risk-equivalent companies, the profit potential of the emerging company, and the present value of future cash flows, the capital structure of the emerging company is established as follows:

| | |
|---|---:|
| Postpetition current liabilities | $ 25,000 |
| Postpetition mortgage payable | 48,000 |
| Senior debt | 57,000 |
| Subordinated debt | 12,000 |
| Common stock (new) | 20,000 |
| Total postreorganization capital structure | $162,000 |

Note that for purposes of the illustration, the newly issued common stock is no-par stock; therefore, no additional paid-in capital is carried forward to the emerging entity. If the assigned value of the newly issued stock is greater than its par value, an additional paid-in capital account is credited for the excess. The $162,000 of postreorganization capital is the reorganization value of $195,000 less the $33,000 paid out for the prepetition liabilities as part of the plan of reorganization.

Peerless Products prepares entries to record the execution of the plan of reorganization as it transpires between January 1, 20X8, and April 1, 20X8. Figure 20–7 presents a worksheet illustrating the effects of executing the plan of reorganization on Peerless Products' balance sheet accounts. The first journal entry (1) records the debt restructuring and the gain on the discharge of debt:

| | | | |
|---|---|---:|---:|
| January 1, 20X8–April 1, 20X8 | | | |
| (1) | Liabilities Subject to Compromise | 133,000 | |
| | Cash | | 33,000 |
| | Senior Debt | | 57,000 |
| | Subordinated Debt | | 12,000 |
| | Common Stock (new) | | 11,000 |
| | Gain on Debt Discharge | | 20,000 |
| | Record debt discharge. | | |

**FIGURE 20–7**  **Effect of Plan of Reorganization on Company's Balance Sheet**

| | Pre-confirmation | Adjustments to Record Confirmation of Plan | | | Company's Reorganized Balance Sheet |
| | | Debt Discharge | Exchange of Stock | Fresh Start | |
|---|---|---|---|---|---|
| **Assets** | | | | | |
| Cash | $ 40,000 | $ (33,000) | | | $ 7,000 |
| Income Tax Refund Receivable | 12,000 | | | | 12,000 |
| Marketable Securities | 8,000 | | | $ 2,000 | 10,000 |
| Accounts Receivable (net) | 5,000 | | | | 5,000 |
| Inventory | 37,000 | | | (4,000) | 33,000 |
| Total | $ 102,000 | | | | $ 67,000 |
| Property, Plant, and Equipment (net) | 78,000 | | | 7,000 | 85,000 |
| Reorganization Value in Excess of Amounts Allocable to Identifiable Assets | | | | 10,000 | 10,000 |
| Total Assets | $ 180,000 | $ (33,000) | | $ 15,000 | $ 162,000 |
| **Liabilities** | | | | | |
| Liabilities Not Subject to Compromise: | | | | | |
| Current Liabilities: | | | | | |
| Short-Term Borrowings | $ (15,000) | | | | $ (15,000) |
| Accounts Payable | (10,000) | | | | (10,000) |
| Noncurrent Liability: | | | | | |
| Mortgage Payable | (48,000) | | | | (48,000) |
| Total | $ (73,000) | | | | $ (73,000) |
| Liabilities Subject to Compromise: | (133,000) | $133,000 | | | |
| Senior Debt | | (57,000) | | | (57,000) |
| Subordinated Debt | | (12,000) | | | (12,000) |
| Total Liabilities | $(206,000) | $ 64,000 | | | $(142,000) |
| **Shareholders' Equity** | | | | | |
| Preferred Stock | $ (40,000) | | $40,000 | | |
| Common Stock (old) | (10,000) | | 10,000 | | |
| Common Stock (new) | | $ (11,000) | (9,000) | | $ (20,000) |
| Additional Paid-In Capital | | | (41,000) | $ 41,000 | |
| Retained Earnings (deficit) | 76,000 | (20,000) | | 20,000 | |
| | | | | (76,000) | -0- |
| Total Shareholders' Equity | $ 26,000 | $ (31,000) | -0- | $(15,000) | $ (20,000) |
| Total Liabilities and Shareholders' Equity | $(180,000) | $ 33,000 | -0- | $(15,000) | $(162,000) |

*Note:* Parentheses indicate credit amount.

The second journal entry (2) records the exchange of stock for stock. The prior preferred shareholders receive 8,000 shares of newly issued common stock. The prior common shareholders receive 1,000 shares of the newly issued common stock:

| January 1, 20X8–April 1, 20X8 | | | |
|---|---|---|---|
| (2) | Preferred Stock | 40,000 | |
| | Common Stock (old) | 10,000 | |
| | Common Stock (new) | | 9,000 |
| | Additional Paid-In Capital | | 41,000 |
| | Record exchange of stock for stock. | | |

The third and last journal entry (3) records the fresh start adjustments of the assigned values of the assets of the emerging entity and the elimination of any retained earnings, or deficit. A comparison between the book values and fair values of the company follows. The fair values are determined according to the procedures in **FASB Statement No. 144,** "Accounting for the Impairment or Disposal of Long-Lived Assets" (FASB 144), issued in 2001. An ***impairment loss*** is measured by the amount that the carrying value of a long-lived asset (or asset group) exceeds its fair value. Note that Reorganization Value in Excess of Amounts Allocable to Identifiable Assets is debited for an amount not assignable to other assets. The reorganization value excess is reported as an intangible asset and accounted for according to **FASB Statement No. 142,** "Goodwill and Other Intangible Assets" (FASB 142). **FASB 142** specifies that intangibles with finite useful lives should be amortized over their lives. However, for intangible assets determined to have an indefinite life, no amortization should be taken. Instead these indefinite life intangibles shall be tested for impairment at least annually to determine whether the asset is impaired and a loss should be recognized for a reduction in the asset's carrying amount.

Note that if prior to entering reorganization Peerless had goodwill that was judged to be impaired, it would recognize any impairment loss on the debtor-in-possession income statement. Typically, a company in reorganization proceedings is not expected to have goodwill because it is related to excess earnings potential. A case-by-case examination must be made, however, to determine whether the company's recognized goodwill was impaired.

| | Book Value | Fair Value | Difference |
|---|---|---|---|
| Cash | $ 7,000 | $ 7,000 | $ -0- |
| Income tax refund receivable | 12,000 | 12,000 | -0- |
| Marketable securities | 8,000 | 10,000 | 2,000 |
| Accounts receivable (net) | 5,000 | 5,000 | -0- |
| Inventory | 37,000 | 33,000 | (4,000) |
| Property, plant, and equipment | 78,000 | 85,000 | 7,000 |
| Reorganization value in excess of amounts allocable to identifiable assets | -0- | 10,000 | 10,000 |
| Totals | $147,000 | $162,000 | $15,000 |

The entry to record the fresh start revaluation of assets and elimination of the deficit follows:

April 1, 20X8

| | | | |
|---|---|---|---|
| (3) | Marketable Securities | 2,000 | |
| | Property, Plant, and Equipment | 7,000 | |
| | Reorganization Value in Excess of Amounts Allocable to Identifiable Assets | 10,000 | |
| | Gain on Debt Discharge | 20,000 | |
| | Additional Paid-In Capital | 41,000 | |
| | Inventory | | 4,000 |
| | Retained Earnings—Deficit | | 76,000 |
| | Record fresh start accounting and eliminate deficit. | | |

The last column in Figure 20–7 presents the postreorganization, new reporting entity's balance sheet.

Some reorganizations are unsuccessful, and the debtor must be liquidated. The major reason for unsuccessful reorganizations is continuing losses from operations and no reasonable likelihood of rehabilitation. Another common reason is the inability to consummate a reorganization plan because of the failure to dispose of an unprofitable subsidiary, a material default of the plan by either the debtor or a creditor, or the inability to effect part of the plan as a result of changes in the economic environment. The debtor company then moves from reorganization into liquidation; the latter is the topic of the next section of the chapter.

# CHAPTER 7 LIQUIDATIONS

Liquidations are administered by the bankruptcy courts in the interests of the corporation's creditors and shareholders. The intent in liquidation is to maximize the net dollar amount recovered from disposal of the debtor's assets. Bankruptcy courts appoint accountants, attorneys, or experienced business managers as trustees to administer the liquidation. The liquidation process is often completed within 6 to 12 months, during which the trustees must make periodic reports to the bankruptcy court. The entire liquidation process is governed by the Bankruptcy Code, which describes the specific procedures to be followed and reports to be made. A very important aspect of liquidation is determining the legal rights of each creditor and establishing priorities for those rights.

# CLASSES OF CREDITORS

The Bankruptcy Code specifies three classes of creditors whose claims have the following priorities: (1) secured creditors, (2) creditors with priority, and (3) unsecured creditors. The priority of claims determines the order and source of payment to each creditor.

## Secured Creditors

*Secured creditors* have liens, or security interests, on specific assets, often called "collateral." A creditor with such a legal interest in a specific asset has the highest priority claim on that asset. For example, in Figure 20–8, Peerless Products' $50,000 mortgage payable is secured by the company's land and plant. On December 31, 20X6, the land and plant have a combined net book value of $65,000 and a fair value of $55,000. The mortgage holders have first claim to the proceeds from the sale of the land and plant. Therefore, when the land and plant are sold for $55,000, $50,000 of the proceeds is used to discharge the Mortgage Payable account and the remaining $5,000 is available to the next-lower class of creditor.

## Creditors with Priority

As defined by the Bankruptcy Code, **creditors with priority** are unsecured creditors, that is, those having no collateral claim against specific assets, who have priority over other unsecured creditors. Creditors with priority are the first to be paid from any proceeds available to unsecured creditors. For businesses, the Bankruptcy Code presents the following as liabilities with priority:

1. Costs of administering the bankruptcy, including accounting and legal costs for experts appointed by the bankruptcy court.
2. Liabilities arising in the ordinary course of business during the bankruptcy proceedings.
3. Wages, salaries, or commissions, including severance and sick pay earned within 180 days of the date the petition was filed, but limited to $10,000 for each individual.
4. Contributions to employee benefit plans for the last 180 days remaining after elimination of compensation in item 3 but constrained by the remainder of the limit of $10,000 per individual.
5. Deposits of customers who made partial payments for the purchase or lease of goods or services that were not delivered. Priority is given to the first $1,800 per individual; any excess deposit is added to the unsecured claims.
6. Unsecured tax claims of governmental units, including income taxes, property taxes, excise taxes, and other taxes.

**FIGURE 20–8**  **Accounting Statement of Affairs**

### PEERLESS PRODUCTS CORPORATION
### Statement of Affairs
### December 31, 20X6

| Book Values | | | Estimated Current Values | Estimated Amount Available to Unsecured Claims | Estimated Gain or (Loss) on Realization |
|---|---|---|---|---|---|
| **Assets** | | | | | |
| | (1) | Assets pledged with fully secured creditors: | | | |
| $ 10,000 | | Land | $15,000 | | $ 5,000 |
| 55,000 | | Plant (net) | 40,000 | | (15,000) |
| | | | $55,000 | | |
| | | Less: Mortgage Payable | (50,000) | $ 5,000 | |
| | (2) | Assets pledged with partially secured creditors: | | | |
| 8,000 | | Marketable Securities | $ 9,000 | | 1,000 |
| | | Less: Notes Payable | (10,000) | | |
| | (3) | Free assets: | | | |
| 2,000 | | Cash | $ 2,000 | 2,000 | |
| 18,000 | | Accounts Receivable (net) | 18,000 | 18,000 | |
| 45,000 | | Inventory | 26,000 | 26,000 | (19,000) |
| 1,000 | | Prepaid Assets | -0- | -0- | (1,000) |
| 36,000 | | Equipment (net) | 12,000 | 12,000 | (24,000) |
| | | Estimated amount available | | $ 63,000 | |
| | | Less: Creditors with priority | | (18,000) | |
| | | Net estimated amount available to unsecured creditors (41 cents on the dollar: $45,000/$110,000) | | $ 45,000 | |
| | | Estimated deficiency to unsecured creditors | | 65,000 | |
| $175,000 | | | | | $(53,000) |
| | | Total unsecured debt (from liabilities) | | $110,000 | |

| | | | | Estimated Amount Unsecured |
|---|---|---|---|---|
| **Liabilities and Stockholders' Equity** | | | | |
| | (1) | Fully secured creditors: | | |
| $ 50,000 | | Mortgage Payable | $50,000 | |
| | (2) | Partially secured creditors: | | |
| 10,000 | | Notes Payable—Partially Secured | $10,000 | |
| | | Less: Marketable Securities | (9,000) | $ 1,000 |
| | (3) | Creditors with priority: | | |
| -0- | | Estimated liquidation expenses | $ 4,000 | |
| 14,000 | | Accrued wages | 14,000 | |
| | | | $18,000 | |
| | (4) | Remaining unsecured creditors: | | |
| 26,000 | | Accounts Payable | | 26,000 |
| 80,000 | | Notes Payable—Unsecured | | 80,000 |
| 3,000 | | Accrued Interest | | 3,000 |
| | (5) | Stockholders' equity: | | |
| 40,000 | | Preferred Stock | | |
| 10,000 | | Common Stock | | |
| (58,000) | | Retained Earnings (Deficit) | | |
| $175,000 | | (Carry up to asset section) | | $110,000 |

These six groups of creditors are paid from assets available to unsecured creditors. Any remaining monies are then distributed to the general unsecured creditors.

## General Unsecured Creditors

The lowest priority is given to claims by *general unsecured creditors.* These creditors are paid only after secured creditors and unsecured creditors with priority are satisfied to the extent of any legal limits. Often the general unsecured creditors receive less than the full amount of their claim. The amounts to be paid to these creditors are usually stated as a percentage of the total claim, such as 55 cents on the dollar, or whatever the specific percentage is. The payment to general unsecured creditors is often termed a "dividend." It is not uncommon for these dividends to be as low as 20 to 25 percent of the total remaining unsecured claims.

"Preference payments" made by the debtor to one creditor to the detriment of all other creditors within 90 days before the bankruptcy petition was filed may usually be recovered from the specific creditor and returned to the cash available for all creditors. Sometimes a member of the debtor's management may assure a creditor that the debtor will pay any claim to that specific creditor. This often occurs during the latter phases of financial difficulty, just before filing a petition for bankruptcy. These management assurances are not binding and do not increase the level of the legal claim against the debtor's assets. The priority of the claims is determined solely in accordance with the Bankruptcy Code.

## Statement of Affairs

The *accounting statement of affairs* is the basic accounting report made at the beginning of the liquidation process to present the expected realizable amounts from disposal of the assets, the order of creditors' claims, and the expected amount that unsecured creditors will receive as a result of the liquidation. A different report, also entitled the "statement of affairs," is a list of questions the debtor must answer as part of the bankruptcy petition. The following discussion is about the accounting report, not the legal questionnaire.

The statement of affairs is not a going-concern report; it is an important planning report for the anticipated liquidation of a company. The statement of affairs presents the book values of the debtor company's balance sheet accounts, the estimated fair market values of the assets, the order of the claims, and the estimated deficiency to the general unsecured creditors. Common stockholders rarely receive any monies from a liquidating company. The statement of affairs is a planning instrument: The actual liquidation process is recorded on the debtor's books as the transactions occur.

Assume that rather than reorganizing, Peerless decided on December 31, 20X6, to enter Chapter 7 bankruptcy on that date. The following illustration begins with the December 31, 20X6, statement of affairs for Peerless Products shown in Figure 20–8:

1. The report presents the balance sheet accounts in order of priority for liquidation. Current versus noncurrent accounts no longer have importance for Peerless Products.
2. The report presents estimated current fair values and expected gains or losses on the disposal of the assets. These are only estimates at the point the bankruptcy petition is filed. Actual gains or losses will be recorded as realized.
3. In this example, fully secured creditors are expected to have their entire claims of $50,000 satisfied with the proceeds from the disposal of the secured asset. The mortgage payable is expected to be fully satisfied with the proceeds of $55,000 from the sale of the land and plant. The remaining $5,000 will then be available to satisfy unsecured claims.
4. The claims of partially secured creditors will not be completely satisfied from the sale of the collateral asset. Marketable securities having an estimated fair value of $9,000 are used to secure notes payable of $10,000. The first $9,000 of the notes payable is satisfied; the remaining $1,000 is added to the general unsecured liabilities.
5. Free assets are available to unsecured creditors. The first unsecured creditors are those with priority as defined by the Bankruptcy Code. Peerless Products has accrued wages

of $14,000 payable to its employees, none of whom has more than $2,000 due. In addition, the company expects to incur $4,000 of expenses to administer the liquidation.

6. All remaining claims are added to the general unsecured liabilities. The total of unsecured claims is $110,000. Only $45,000 is expected to be available to meet these claims. Therefore, the estimated dividend to general unsecured creditors is 41 cents on the dollar ($45,000/$110,000). The estimated deficiency to unsecured creditors is $65,000.

7. The stockholders will not receive anything upon liquidation of Peerless Products. Stock is a residual claim to be settled only after all creditors' claims are fully settled. Stockholders typically do not receive anything from a bankruptcy liquidation.

The statement of affairs is a planning instrument prepared only at the beginning of the bankruptcy process. It provides important information to creditors and the bankruptcy court as to the expected monies available to each class of creditors. Once the bankruptcy is under way, the debtor records the transactions on its accounting records as they occur.

# ADDITIONAL CONSIDERATIONS

Presented now are the accounting and reporting practices for trustees who act as fiduciaries for the creditors' committee or for the bankruptcy court. Trustees' reports are different from the traditional financial statements because the trustees' legal rights and responsibilities differ from those of the debtor company's management.

Also included is a brief presentation on the bankruptcy provisions applicable to individuals. The area of individual bankruptcies is undergoing constant change, and thus the presentation is only a general guide.

## Trustee Accounting and Reporting

Bankruptcy courts appoint trustees to manage a company under Chapter 11 reorganization in cases of management fraud, dishonesty, incompetence, or gross mismanagement. The trustee then attempts to rehabilitate the business. In Chapter 7 liquidations, the trustee normally has the responsibility to expeditiously liquidate the bankrupt company and pay creditors in conformity with the legal status of their secured or unsecured interests. In some cases under Chapter 7, the court appoints a trustee to operate the company for a short time in an effort to obtain a better price for the company in entirety rather than selling it piecemeal.

Trustees examine the proofs of all creditors' claims against the debtor's bankruptcy estate, that is, the debtor's net assets. Sometimes the trustee receives title to all assets as a **_receivership,_** becomes responsible for the actual management of the debtor, and must direct a plan of reorganization or liquidation. A trustee who takes title to the debtor's assets in a liquidation must make a periodic financial report to the bankruptcy court, reporting on the progress of the liquidation and on the fiduciary relationship held. When the trustee accepts the assets, the trustee usually establishes a set of accounting records to account for the receivership. The trustee's accounting records include a liability of the trustee which is created to recognize the debtor's interest in the assets accepted by the trustee. This new account is credited for the book value of the assets accepted and is usually named for the debtor company in receivership. The trustee does not transfer the debtor's liabilities, because these remain the legal responsibility of the debtor company. The general form of the trustee's opening entry, accepting the assets of the debtor company, is as follows:

| | | |
|---|---|---|
| Assets | XXX | |
|     Debtor Company—In Receivership | | XXX |

The actual entry details the individual asset accounts and includes the debtor's company name.

### Statement of Realization and Liquidation

A monthly report, called a ***statement of realization and liquidation,*** is prepared for the bankruptcy court. It shows the results of the trustee's fiduciary actions beginning at the point the trustee accepts the debtor's assets. The statement has three major sections: assets, supplementary items, and liabilities. The debtor's liabilities are not transferred to the trustee, but the trustee may incur new liabilities that must be reported in the statement of realization and liquidation.

The assets section of the statement is divided into the following four groups:

| Assets | |
|---|---|
| Assets to be realized | Assets realized |
| Assets acquired | Assets not realized |

The assets to be realized are those received from the debtor company. The assets acquired are those subsequently acquired by the trustee. The assets realized are those sold by the trustee; the assets not realized are those remaining under the trustee's responsibility as of the end of the period. Cash is usually not reported in the statement of realization and liquidation because a separate cash flow report is typically made.

The supplementary items section of the report consists of the following two items:

| Supplementary Items | |
|---|---|
| Supplementary charges | Supplementary credits |

Supplementary charges include the trustee's administration fees and any cash expenses paid by the trustee. Supplementary credits may include any unusual revenue items.

Although the trustee does not record the debtor's liabilities, the trustee settles some of the debtor's payables and may incur new payables during the receivership. The liabilities section of the statement is divided as follows:

| Liabilities | |
|---|---|
| Liabilities liquidated | Liabilities to be liquidated |
| Liabilities not liquidated | Liabilities incurred |

The liabilities liquidated are creditors' claims settled during the period. The liabilities not liquidated are those outstanding at the end of the reporting period. The liabilities to be liquidated are those debts remaining on the books of the debtor company for whose liquidation the trustee is responsible as of the date of appointment. Finally, the liabilities incurred are new obligations incurred by the trustee.

### Illustration of Trustee Accounting and Reporting

On December 31, 20X6, D. Able was appointed trustee in charge of liquidating Peerless Products Corporation. Able will be allowed to operate the company for a short period of time to determine whether the company can be sold in entirety as opposed to piecemeal. During this time, the trustee must reduce the current short-term debts of Peerless Products. If a sale in entirety is infeasible, Able is directed to liquidate the company. Able accepts the assets on December 31, 20X6, and makes several transactions during January 20X7. The transactions and the entries made on Peerless's books and on the trustee's books are presented in Figure 20–9 and discussed in the following pages.

1. Entry (4) records the transfer of assets from Peerless Products to D. Able. Able recognizes the assets at their book values as reported by Peerless. Accounts receivable are dated as "old" to note that these were part of the transferred assets. The credit for $175,000 to Peerless Products Corporation—In Receivership is a liability of the

**FIGURE 20–9**  Trustee and Debtor Company Entries during Liquidation

| Trustee D. Able's Books | Debit | Credit | Peerless Products Corporation's Books | Debit | Credit |
|---|---|---|---|---|---|
| **(4)** Cash | 2,000 | | D. Able—Receiver | 175,000 | |
| Marketable Securities | 8,000 | | Allowance for Uncollectibles | 2,000 | |
| Accounts Receivable (old) | 20,000 | | Accumulated Depreciation | 24,000 | |
| Inventory | 45,000 | | Cash | | 2,000 |
| Prepaid Assets | 1,000 | | Marketable Securities | | 8,000 |
| Property, Plant, and Equipment | 125,000 | | Accounts Receivable | | 20,000 |
| Allowance for Uncollectibles (old) | | 2,000 | Inventory | | 45,000 |
| Accumulated Depreciation | | 24,000 | Prepaid Assets | | 1,000 |
| Peerless Products Corporation—In Receivership | | 175,000 | Property, Plant, and Equipment | | 125,000 |
| Transfer of Peerless's net assets to trustee. | | | | | |
| | | | | | |
| **(5)** Inventory | 20,000 | | (No entry) | | |
| Accounts Payable (new) | | 20,000 | | | |
| Purchases of inventory on account by trustee, $20,000. | | | | | |
| | | | | | |
| **(6)** Accounts Receivable (new) | 85,000 | | (No entry) | | |
| Sales | | 85,000 | | | |
| Sales on account by trustee, $85,000. | | | | | |
| | | | | | |
| **(7)** Cost of Sales | 50,000 | | (No entry) | | |
| Inventory | | 50,000 | | | |
| Cost of sales is $50,000, including all inventory transferred from Peerless Products Corporation. | | | | | |
| | | | | | |
| **(8)** Cash | 56,000 | | (No entry) | | |
| Accounts Receivable (old) | | 12,000 | | | |
| Accounts Receivable (new) | | 44,000 | | | |
| Receivables collected by trustee: | | | | | |
| Old receivables | $12,000 | | | | |
| New receivables | 44,000 | | | | |
| | | | | | |
| **(9)** Peerless Products Corporation—In Receivership | 30,000 | | Accounts Payable | 20,000 | |
| Accounts Payable (new) | 4,000 | | Notes Payable | 10,000 | |
| Operating Expenses | 13,000 | | D. Able—Receiver | | 30,000 |
| Trustee's Expenses | 5,000 | | | | |
| Cash | | 52,000 | | | |
| Disbursements by trustee: | | | | | |
| Old accounts payables | $30,000 | | | | |
| New accounts payables | 4,000 | | | | |
| Operating expenses | 13,000 | | | | |
| Trustee's expenses | 5,000 | | | | |

*(continued)*

(10) Cash 9,000
    Marketable Securities 8,000
    Gain on Sale of Securities 1,000
    Sales of marketable securities for $9,000.   (No entry)

Adjusting entries at end of the period:

(11) Uncollectibles Expense 3,000
    Depreciation Expense 10,000   (No entry)
      Allowance for Uncollectibles (old) 1,000
      Allowance for Uncollectibles (new) 2,000
      Accumulated Depreciation 10,000
    Provision for bad debts:
      Old receivables $1,000
      New receivables 2,000
    Recognize depreciation expense of $10,000
    for period.

(12) Allowance for Uncollectibles (old) 2,000
    Accounts Receivable (old) 2,000   (No entry)
    Old receivables of $2,000 are written off.

(13) Prepaid Costs Expense 1,000
    Prepaid Assets 1,000   (No entry)
    Recognize prepaid costs of $1,000
    expired during period.

Closing entry at end of the period:

(14) Sales 85,000
    Gain on Sale of Securities 1,000   D. Able—Receiver 4,000
      Cost of Sales 50,000     Retained Earnings 4,000
      Operating Expenses 13,000
      Trustee's Expenses 5,000
      Prepaid Costs Expense 1,000
      Uncollectibles Expense 3,000
      Depreciation Expense 10,000
      Peerless Products Corporation—In Receivership 4,000

trustee. On Peerless's books, the reciprocal account, D. Able—Receiver, is a receivable. Note that no liabilities are transferred. These remain on Peerless's books because they are legal responsibilities of the corporation.

2. The trustee's transactions are recorded in the normal manner in entries (5) through (8). The only difference is the differentiation between "old" accounts, which were part of the assets transferred, and "new" accounts, which result from the trustee's transactions.

3. The trustee pays $20,000 of Peerless's accounts payable and pays $10,000 for the partially secured note payable. In entry (9), the debit of $30,000 is made to the liability account Peerless Products Corporation—In Receivership. Peerless makes a corresponding entry to reduce its accounts payable and notes payable and to reduce the receivable, D. Able—Receiver.

4. The remaining entries (10) through (14) complete the transactions, adjust the books, and close the books at the end of the first period of receivership. Operations resulted in a net income of $4,000 for the period. The closing entry transfers the net income to the receivership account on the trustee's books. A corresponding entry on Peerless's books increases the receiver's account and the retained earnings account.

The entries are the basis of the statement of realization and liquidation for the month of January 20X7. This statement is reported to the bankruptcy court to show the current state of the liquidation process and to report on the fiduciary responsibility of D. Able, the trustee. The statement of realization and liquidation for Peerless Products Corporation, as reported by Able, is shown in Figure 20–10.

**FIGURE 20–10**
Receiver's
Statement of
Realization and
Liquidation

**PEERLESS PRODUCTS CORPORATION**
D. Able, Receiver
**Statement of Realization and Liquidation**
December 31, 20X6, to January 31, 20X7

### Assets

| Assets to Be Realized | | Assets Realized | |
|---|---|---|---|
| Old receivables (net) | $ 18,000 | Old receivables | $ 12,000 |
| Marketable securities | 8,000 | New receivables | 44,000 |
| Old inventory | 45,000 | Marketable securities | 9,000 |
| Prepaid assets | 1,000 | Sales of inventory | 85,000 |
| Depreciable assets (net) | 101,000 | | |
| **Assets Acquired** | | **Assets Not Realized** | |
| New receivables | 85,000 | Old receivables (net) | 5,000 |
| New inventory purchased | 20,000 | New receivables (net) | 39,000 |
| | | New inventory | 15,000 |
| | | Depreciable assets (net) | 91,000 |

### Supplementary Items

| Supplementary Charges | | Supplementary Credits | |
|---|---|---|---|
| Operating expenses paid | $ 13,000 | | |
| Receiver's expenses | 5,000 | | |
| Net gain from operations | 4,000 | | |

### Liabilities

| Debts Liquidated | | Debts to Be Liquidated | |
|---|---|---|---|
| Old current payables | $ 30,000 | Old current payables | $133,000 |
| New current payables | 4,000 | Mortgage payable | 50,000 |
| **Debts Not Liquidated** | | **Debts Incurred** | |
| Old current payables | 103,000 | New current payables | 20,000 |
| New current payables | 16,000 | | |
| Mortgage payable | 50,000 | | |
| | $503,000 | | $503,000 |

Following are observations concerning this statement:

1. The statement begins with an accounting of the assets received from Peerless Products Corporation and those acquired by the trustee. The assets realized section reports the proceeds of the sale of assets. For example, the marketable securities were sold for $9,000, which is $1,000 more than their book value. Sales of inventory are also reported for the amount of the total proceeds. This is the traditional approach used most often in practice, although an alternative sometimes found recognizes the disposal of the assets at their book values, with the profit or gain element recognized as a supplementary credit. Either method, using gross proceeds or book value, is allowed in practice. The assets not realized section shows the ending book values of remaining assets as of January 31, 20X7. Cash is not included on the statement because it is already a realized asset. Cash is reported in a separate statement by the trustee.

2. Supplementary items include $13,000 of operating expenses paid, receiver's expenses of $5,000, and the net gain of $4,000 as a balancing item. It is important to note that cost allocations are not included in the supplementary items. For example, the trustee recognized depreciation expense of $10,000, bad debt expense of $3,000, and expiration of prepaid assets of $1,000. These do not appear directly in the statement, but they are shown indirectly. For example, under assets to be realized, depreciable assets, net, are reported as $101,000 while under the assets not realized, the depreciable assets, net, are shown as $91,000. The $10,000 difference is the depreciation expense for the period. Bad debts expense and prepaid expense are treated in a similar way.

3. The last part of the statement is a report on the liabilities. The trustee is responsible for liquidating the preexisting debts of $183,000 and has incurred additional debt of $20,000 during the month. A total of $34,000 of debts has been liquidated, leaving $169,000 still to be liquidated.

4. The statement balances at a total of $503,000, indicating that all items are reported.

The trustee provides a statement of realization and liquidation to the bankruptcy court on a monthly basis. In addition, a short cash flow statement that summarizes the cash receipts and cash disbursements during the period is provided.

The fact that various bankruptcy courts are accepting alternative forms of the statement of realization may create some consternation for accountants providing professional services in several judicial districts. For example, should assets realized be shown at their gross proceeds, or should a net amount be shown with the gain or loss in supplementary items? The report format presented in this chapter is the traditional approach accepted by a large majority of courts. Some courts, however, are currently experimenting with other forms of trustee reporting. The experiments now taking place in trustee reporting may eventually lead to a new report that will be a modification of the present statement. Until then, accountants serving as trustees or advising trustees should ascertain from the specific bankruptcy court administering the estate which reporting form to use.

## Summary of Key Concepts

Various nonjudicial actions are available to companies in financial difficulty. A debtor may restructure its existing debt by agreeing to settle its obligation at less than current value or to modify some of the terms of the debt agreement. The debtor's payable may be settled with the transfer of equity or assets, or the terms of the debt may be modified. In some cases, creditors may form a committee to manage the debtor's business. In this nonjudicial action, the debtor agrees to comply with the creditors. The creditors' committee may attempt to rehabilitate the business or may find that liquidation is the best course of action.

Two judicial remedies are available under the Bankruptcy Code. The first is Chapter 11 reorganization, in which the debtor is given some relief from creditors' claims and can attempt to rehabilitate the business and return it to profitable operations. A trustee is sometimes appointed by the bankruptcy court to advise the debtor. SOP 90-7 requires that financial statements produced during reorganization proceedings clearly separate the reorganization items from operating items. In addition, SOP 90-7 prescribes the two conditions that must occur before fresh start accounting may be used by firms emerging from reorganization proceedings: (1) The postpetition liabilities, plus prepetition liabilities allowed as claims by the court, must be greater than the reorganization value assigned to the company's assets and (2) the holders of voting shares immediately prior to confirmation of the plan of reorganization must hold less than 50 percent of the voting shares of the emerging company. Fresh start accounting includes the revaluation of assets and the elimination of any retained earnings, or deficit.

The second judicial remedy is a Chapter 7 liquidation. At the beginning of a judicial action, a statement of affairs is prepared as a planning document to show the expected amounts that will be realized on the liquidation of the business and the order of the creditors' claims against the debtor's assets. During liquidation, the debtor's assets are sold, and the creditors' claims are settled in the order of priority defined by the Bankruptcy Code. Secured claims are satisfied with proceeds of the sale of the corresponding collateral; unsecured claims with priority are then settled. Any remaining cash is distributed to the general unsecured creditors.

Trustees are sometimes appointed by bankruptcy courts to administer the reorganization or liquidation process. A trustee provides a statement of realization and liquidation to the bankruptcy court to report on the progress of the judicial action and on the fiduciary actions of the trustee. The statement presents the assets transferred to the trustee, the additional assets acquired by the trustee, and the ending balance of unrealized assets still to be converted into cash. The statement also reports on the debtor's liabilities discharged by the trustee as well as the additional liabilities incurred by the trustee. Some minor variations of the statement format are found in bankruptcy courts.

## Key Terms

accounting statement
of affairs, *1017*
creditors' committee
management, *1002*
creditors with priority, *1015*
fresh start accounting, *1006*
general unsecured
creditors, *1017*

impairment loss, *1014*
liquidation under
Chapter 7, *1004*
order of relief, *1003*
plan of reorganization, *1004*
receivership, *1018*
reorganization under
Chapter 11, *1004*

reorganization value, *1006*
secured creditors, *1015*
statement of realization
and liquidation, *1019*
troubled debt
restructurings, *1002*

## Questions

**Q20-1** What are the nonjudicial actions available to a financially distressed company? What judicial actions are available?

**Q20-2** What is the difference between a Chapter 7 action and a Chapter 11 bankruptcy action?

**Q20-3** Under what circumstances may an involuntary petition for relief be filed? Who files this petition?

**Q20-4** What is usually included in the plan of reorganization filed as part of a Chapter 11 reorganization?

**Q20-5** Explain the use of the account Reorganization Value in Excess of Amount Assigned to Identifiable Assets during a Chapter 11 reorganization.

**Q20-6** What conditions must occur for a company in reorganization to use fresh start accounting?

**Q20-7** What financial statements must be filed by a company during a Chapter 11 reorganization?

**Q20-8** What are the rights of creditors with priority in a Chapter 7 liquidation?

**Q20-9** Describe the statement of affairs used in planning an anticipated liquidation.

**Q20-10\*** What are the financial reporting responsibilities of a trustee who accepts the debtor company's assets in a Chapter 7 liquidation?

**Q20-11\*** How are the sales of assets reported on the statement of realization and liquidation?

## Cases

*Communication*

**C20-1** **Creditors' Alternatives**

The creditors of the Lost Hope Company have had several meetings with the company's management to discuss the company's financial difficulties. Lost Hope currently has a significant deficit in Retained Earnings and has defaulted on several of its debt issues. The options currently open to the creditors are to (1) form a creditors' committee, (2) work with the company in a Chapter 11

*Indicates that the item relates to "Additional Considerations."

reorganization, or (3) go through a Chapter 7 liquidation. The creditors have come to you to seek your advice on the advantages and disadvantages of each of the three options from their viewpoint.

### Required

Discuss the advantages and disadvantages to the creditors of each of the three options available. Include a discussion of the probable recovery of each of the creditors' claims and the time period of that recovery.

**C20-2** **Research Related to Bankruptcy**

*Research*

You are working on a report regarding bankruptcies. You need to locate more information and have heard that the U.S. bankruptcy courts have a Web site that would be useful. Locate the Web site using a search engine. (*Hint:* A helpful search term may be "U.S. Bankruptcy Courts.") Locate the following information, and incorporate it into a one- to two-page report.

- *a.* How are bankruptcy judges assigned to specific cases? (You might look under the frequently asked questions, FAQs, for guidance on this question.)
- *b.* (1) How can a business obtain the appropriate filing forms for a voluntary petition for bankruptcy?
     (2) Briefly summarize the types of information required on the voluntary petition.
- *c.* Locate and summarize the following bankruptcy statistics:
     (1) First determine total business filings and then determine the number of filings by type (e.g., Chapter 7, Chapter 11, and so on) for the most recent calendar year ending on December 31.
     (2) Determine the number of filings by type for businesses in your specific federal judicial district. (*Hint:* Some circuits have several district courts, so select the one you feel is most appropriate based on the location of your educational institution.) Briefly discuss how the number of filings in your federal judicial district compares with those filed in other districts.

**C20-3\*** **Selection of Bankruptcy Trustee and Trustee's Responsibilities**

*Research*

The United States trustee in each of the federal judicial districts is a federal official appointed by the U.S. attorney general to oversee the administration of bankruptcy cases and private trustees in specific cases. You seek information on the selection of a trustee and the trustee's responsibilities in a Chapter 7 bankruptcy filing.

- *a.* Access Title 11 of the United States Bankruptcy Code and locate the material for a Chapter 7 filing. Summarize the procedure by which an interim trustee is appointed to a bankruptcy case. Then briefly summarize how a trustee may be elected by the creditors.
- *b.* Summarize the duties of the trustee under Chapter 7 of the Bankruptcy Code.

**C20-4** **The Bankruptcy of WorldCom**

*Analysis*

WorldCom Inc. was one of the largest companies to file for bankruptcy. This case requires the analysis of WorldCom's December 31, 2002, 10-K filed with the Securities and Exchange Commission. The 10-K can be obtained through EDGAR (www.sec.gov), Edgarscan (edgarscan. pwcglobal.com), or some other publicly available source. (*Note:* After its emergence from bankruptcy, WorldCom was merged into MCI, Inc.; however, that did not affect WorldCom's financial reporting for periods prior to the merger.)

### Required

Provide answers to the following questions, referencing the section(s) of the 10-K where you found the information.

- *a.* At what date and under which chapter of the Bankruptcy Code did WorldCom file for bankruptcy?
- *b.* Briefly discuss several reasons why WorldCom filed for bankruptcy at that time.
- *c.* Describe the major accounting irregularities of WorldCom prior to its bankruptcy.
- *d.* After the bankruptcy filing, WorldCom performed an extensive review and restatement of its consolidated financial statements for the two years prior to the bankruptcy. List the major categories and amounts of these restatements for each of the two years.
- *e.* Describe the company's financial accounting and reporting during the reorganization period. Include in your answer a brief discussion of the meaning of the title "Debtors-In-Possession" at the top of each of the company's financial statements during the reorganization period.
- *f.* Briefly discuss the form of accounting the company used as it emerged from bankruptcy.

## Exercises

### E20-1 Multiple-Choice Questions on Chapter 11 Reorganizations [AICPA Adapted]

Select the correct answer for each of the following questions.

1. A client has joined other creditors of Jet Company in a composition agreement seeking to avoid the necessity of a bankruptcy proceeding against Jet. Which statement describes the composition agreement?

   a. It provides for the appointment of a receiver to take over and operate the debtor's business.

   b. It must be approved by all creditors.

   c. It provides that the creditors will receive less than the full amount of their claims.

   d. It provides a temporary delay, not to exceed six months, in the debtor's obligation to repay the debts included in the composition.

2. Hardluck Inc. is insolvent. Its liabilities exceed its assets by $13 million. Hardluck is owned by its president, Blank, and members of her family. Blank, whose assets are estimated at less than $1 million, guaranteed the loans of the corporation. A consortium of banks is the principal creditor of Hardluck, having lent it $8 million, the bulk of which is unsecured. The banks have decided to seek reorganization of Hardluck, and Blank has agreed to cooperate. Regarding the proposed reorganization:

   a. Blank's cooperation is necessary since she must sign the petition for a reorganization.

   b. If a petition for bankruptcy is filed against Hardluck, Blank will also have her personal bankruptcy status resolved and relief granted.

   c. Only a duly constituted creditors' committee may file a plan of reorganization of Hardluck.

   d. Hardluck will remain in possession unless a request is made to the court for the appointment of a trustee.

3. Among other provisions, a Chapter 11 plan of reorganization must:

   a. Rank claims according to their liquidation priorities.

   b. Not impair claims of secured creditors.

   c. Provide adequate means for the plan's execution.

   d. Treat all claims alike.

4. A condition that must exist for the filing of an involuntary bankruptcy petition is:

   a. The debtor must have debts of at least $10,000.

   b. If the debtor has 12 or more creditors, a majority of the creditors must sign the petition.

   c. If the debtor has 12 or more creditors, only one creditor need sign the petition, but that creditor must be owed at least $5,000.

   d. If the debtor has 12 or more creditors, the required number of creditors signing the petition must be owed at least $5,000 in total.

5. The plan of reorganization must be approved by:

   a. At least one-third of all creditors who hold at least half of the total debt.

   b. At least half of all creditors who hold at least half of the total debt.

   c. At least half of all creditors who hold at least two-thirds of the total debt.

   d. At least two-thirds of all creditors who hold at least two-thirds of the total debt.

### E20-2 Recovery Analysis for a Chapter 11 Reorganization

The plan of reorganizing for Taylor Companies, Inc., was approved by the court, stockholders, and creditors on December 31, 20X1. The plan calls for a general restructuring of all debt of Taylor. The liability and capital accounts of the company on December 31, 20X1, are as follows:

| | |
|---|---:|
| Accounts Payable (postpetition) | $ 30,000 |
| Liabilities Subject to Compromise: | |
| Accounts Payable | 80,000 |
| Notes Payable, 10%, unsecured | 150,000 |
| Interest Payable | 40,000 |
| Bonds Payable, 12% | 200,000 |
| Common Stock, $1 par | 100,000 |
| Additional Paid-In Capital | 200,000 |
| Retained Earnings (deficit) | (178,000) |
| Total | $622,000 |

A total of $30,000 of accounts payable has been incurred since the company filed its petition for relief under Chapter 11. No other liabilities have been incurred since the petition was filed. No payments have been made on the liabilities subject to compromise that existed on the petition date.

Under the terms of the reorganization plan:

1. The accounts payable creditors existing at the date the petition was filed agree to accept $72,000 of net accounts receivable in full settlement of their claims.

2. The holders of the 10 percent notes payable of $150,000 plus $16,000 of interest payable agree to accept land having a fair value of $125,000 and a book value of $85,000.

3. The holders of the 12 percent bonds payable of $200,000 plus $24,000 of interest payable agree to cancel accrued interest of $18,000, accept cash payment of the remaining $6,000 of interest, and accept a secured interest in the equipment of the company in exchange for extending the term of the bonds for an additional year at no interest.

4. The common shareholders agree to reduce the deficit by changing the par value of the stock to $2 per share and eliminating any remaining deficit after recognition of all gains or losses from the debt restructuring transactions specified in the plan of reorganization. The deficit will be eliminated by reducing additional paid-in capital.

### Required

*a.* Prepare a recovery analysis for the plan of reorganization, concluding with the total recovery of each liability and capital component of Taylor Companies.

*b.* Prepare the journal entries to account for the discharge of the debt and the restructuring of the common equity in fulfillment of the plan of reorganization.

### E20-3  Multiple-Choice Questions on Chapter 7 Liquidations

Select the correct answer for each of the following questions.

1. Lear Company ceased doing business and is in bankruptcy. Among the claimants are employees seeking unpaid wages. The following statements describe the possible status of such claims in a bankruptcy proceeding. Which is the *incorrect* statement?

   *a.* They are entitled to priority.

   *b.* If a priority is afforded such claims, it cannot exceed $5,000 per wage earner.

   *c.* Such claims include wages earned within 180 days before the filing of the bankruptcy petition, but not to exceed $10,000 in amount per wage earner.

   *d.* The amounts of excess wages not entitled to a priority are mere unsecured claims.

2. The highest priority for payment of unsecured claims in a bankruptcy proceeding is:

   *a.* Administrative expenses of the bankruptcy.

   *b.* Unpaid federal income taxes.

   *c.* Wages of each employee up to $10,000 earned within 180 days before the petition.

   *d.* Wages owed to an insolvent employee.

3. The order of payments for unsecured priority claims in a Chapter 7 bankruptcy case is such that:

   *a.* Tax claims of governmental units are paid before claims for administrative expenses incurred by the trustee.

   *b.* Tax claims of governmental units are paid before claims of employees for wages.

   *c.* Claims of employees for wages are paid before administrative expenses incurred by the trustee.

   *d.* Claims incurred between the filing of an involuntary petition and appointment of a trustee are paid before the claims for contributions to employee benefit plans.

4. Narco is in serious financial difficulty and is unable to meet current unsecured obligations of $30,000 to some 14 creditors who are demanding immediate payment. Narco owes Johnson $5,000, and Johnson has decided to file an involuntary petition against Narco. Which of the following is necessary in order for Johnson to file validly?

   *a.* Johnson must be joined by at least two other creditors.

   *b.* Narco must have committed a fraudulent act within one year of the filing.

   *c.* Johnson must allege and subsequently establish that Narco's liabilities exceed Narco's assets upon fair valuation.

   *d.* Johnson must be a secured creditor.

5. Your client is insolvent under the federal bankruptcy law. Under the circumstances:

    *a.* So long as the client can meet current debts or claims by its most aggressive creditors, a bankruptcy proceeding is *not* possible.

    *b.* Such information—that is, insolvency—need *not* be disclosed in the financial statements reported on by your CPA firm so long as you are convinced that the problem is short-lived.

    *c.* A transfer of assets to a creditor less than 90 days before filing a petition may be a voidable transfer.

    *d.* Your client *cannot* file a voluntary petition for bankruptcy.

## E20-4 Chapter 7 Liquidation

The carrying values and estimated fair values of the assets of Penn Inc. are as follows:

|  | Carrying Value | Fair Value |
|---|---|---|
| Cash | $ 16,000 | $ 16,000 |
| Accounts Receivable | 60,000 | 50,000 |
| Inventory | 90,000 | 65,000 |
| Land | 100,000 | 80,000 |
| Building (net) | 220,000 | 160,000 |
| Equipment (net) | 250,000 | 100,000 |
| Total | $736,000 | $471,000 |

Debts of Penn Inc. are as follows:

| | |
|---|---|
| Accounts Payable | $ 95,000 |
| Wages Payable (all have priority) | 9,500 |
| Taxes Payable | 14,000 |
| Notes Payable (secured by receivables and inventory) | 190,000 |
| Interest on Notes Payable | 5,000 |
| Bonds Payable (secured by land and building) | 220,000 |
| Interest on Bonds Payable | 11,000 |
| Total | $544,500 |

### Required

*a.* Prepare a schedule to calculate the net estimated amount available for general unsecured creditors.

*b.* Compute the percentage dividend to general unsecured creditors.

*c.* Prepare a schedule showing the amount to be paid each of the creditor groups upon distribution of the $471,000 estimated to be realizable.

## E20-5* Statement of Realization and Liquidation

A trustee has been appointed for Pace Inc., which is being liquidated under Chapter 7 of the Bankruptcy Code. The following transactions occurred after the assets were transferred to the trustee:

1. Sales on account by the trustee were $75,000. Cost of goods sold were $60,000, consisting of all the inventory transferred from Pace.

2. The trustee sold all $12,000 worth of marketable securities for $10,500.

3. Receivables collected by the trustee:

| | |
|---|---|
| Old: | $21,000 of the $38,000 transferred |
| New: | $47,000 |

4. Recorded $16,000 depreciation on the plant assets of $96,000 transferred from Pace.

5. Disbursements by the trustee:

| | |
|---|---|
| Old current payables: | $22,000 of the $48,000 transferred |
| Trustee's expenses: | $4,300 |

**Required**

Prepare a statement of realization and liquidation according to the traditional approach illustrated in the chapter.

---

## Problems

### P20-6 Chapter 11 Reorganization

During the recent recession, Polydorous Inc. accumulated a deficit in retained earnings. Although still operating at a loss, the company posted better results during 20X1. Polydorous is having trouble paying suppliers on time and paying interest when it is due. The company files for protection under Chapter 11 of the Bankruptcy Code and has the following liabilities and stockholders' equity accounts at the time the petition is filed:

| | |
|---|---|
| Accounts Payable | $160,000 |
| Interest Payable | 20,000 |
| Notes Payable, 10%, unsecured | 340,000 |
| Preferred Stock | 100,000 |
| Common Stock, $5 par | 150,000 |
| Retained Earnings (deficit) | (80,000) |
| Total | $690,000 |

A plan of reorganization is filed with the court, which approves it after review and after obtaining creditor and investor votes. The plan of reorganization includes the following actions:

1. The prepetition accounts payable will be restructured according to the following: (*a*) $40,000 will be paid in cash; (*b*) $20,000 will be eliminated; and (*c*) the remaining $100,000 will be exchanged for a five-year, secured note payable paying 12 percent interest.

2. The interest payable will be restructured as follows: $10,000 of the interest will be eliminated, and the remaining $10,000 will be paid in cash.

3. The 10 percent, unsecured notes payable will be restructured as follows: (*a*) $60,000 of the notes will be eliminated; (*b*) $10,000 of the notes will be paid in cash; (*c*) $240,000 of the notes will be exchanged for a five-year, 12 percent secured note; and (*d*) the remaining $30,000 will be exchanged for 3,000 shares of newly issued common stock having a par value of $10.

4. The preferred shareholders will exchange their stock for 5,000 shares of newly issued $10 par common stock.

5. The common shareholders will exchange their stock for 2,000 shares of newly issued $10 par common stock.

After extensive analysis, the company's reorganization value is determined to be $510,000 prior to any payments of cash required by the reorganization plan. An additional $10,000 in current liabilities have been incurred since the petition was filed. After the reorganization is completed, the capital structure of the company will be as follows:

| | |
|---|---|
| Current liabilities (postpetition) | $ 10,000 |
| Notes payable, 12%, secured | 340,000 |
| Common stock ($10 par) | 100,000 |
| Postreorganization capital structure | $450,000 |

An evaluation of the fair values of the assets was made after the company completed its reorganization, immediately prior to the point the company emerged from the proceedings. The following information is available:

| | Book Value | Fair Value |
|---|---|---|
| Cash | $ 30,000 | $ 30,000 |
| Accounts receivable (net) | 140,000 | 110,000 |
| Inventory | 25,000 | 18,000 |
| Property, plant, and equipment (net) | 445,000 | 262,000 |
| Total | $640,000 | $420,000 |

### Required

*a.* Prepare a plan of reorganization recovery analysis for the liability and stockholders' equity accounts of Polydorous Inc. on the day the plan of reorganization is approved. (*Hint:* The liabilities on the plan's approval day are $530,000, which is $520,000 from prepetition payables plus $10,000 in additional accounts payable incurred postpetition.)

*b.* Prepare an analysis showing whether the company qualifies for fresh start accounting as it emerges from the reorganization.

*c.* Prepare journal entries for execution of the plan of reorganization with its general restructuring of debt and capital.

*d.* Prepare the balance sheet for the company on completion of the plan of reorganization.

**P20-7    Chapter 7 Liquidation, Statement of Affairs**

Name Brand Company is to be liquidated under Chapter 7 of the Bankruptcy Code. The balance sheet on July 31, 20X1, is as follows:

| Assets | |
|---|---|
| Cash | $ 5,000 |
| Marketable Securities | 30,000 |
| Accounts Receivable (net) | 105,000 |
| Inventory | 160,000 |
| Prepaid Insurance | 7,000 |
| Land | 80,000 |
| Plant and Equipment (net) | 412,000 |
| Franchises | 72,000 |
| Total | $871,000 |

| Equities | |
|---|---|
| Accounts Payable | $265,000 |
| Wages Payable | 20,000 |
| Taxes Payable | 12,000 |
| Interest Payable | 37,000 |
| Notes Payable | 280,000 |
| Mortgages Payable | 220,000 |
| Common Stock ($20 par) | 240,000 |
| Retained Earnings (deficit) | (203,000) |
| Total | $871,000 |

### Additional Information

1. Marketable securities consist of 1,000 shares of Wooly Inc. common stock. The market value per share of the stock is $22. The stock was pledged against a $28,000, 10 percent note payable that has accrued interest of $1,400.

2. Accounts receivable of $50,000 are collateral for a $40,000, 12 percent note payable that has accrued interest of $4,000.

3. Inventory with a book value of $79,000 and a current value of $75,000 is pledged against accounts payable of $105,000. The appraised value of the remainder of the inventory is $76,000.

4. Only $1,500 will be recovered from prepaid insurance.

5. Land is appraised at $110,000 and plant and equipment at $340,000.

6. It is estimated that the franchises can be sold for $30,000.

7. All the wages payable qualify for priority.

8. The mortgages are on the land and on a building with a book value of $162,000 and an appraised value of $150,000. The accrued interest on the mortgages is $14,600.

9. Estimated legal and accounting fees for the liquidation are $13,000.

### Required

a. Prepare a statement of affairs as of July 31, 20X1.

b. Compute the estimated percentage settlement to unsecured creditors.

**P20-8**   **Chapter 7 Liquidation, Statement of Affairs [AICPA Adapted]**

Tower Inc. advises you that it is facing bankruptcy proceedings. As the company's CPA, you are aware of its condition. Tower's balance sheet on December 31, 20X1, and supplementary data are presented here.

| Assets | |
|---|---:|
| Cash | $    2,000 |
| Accounts Receivable (net) | 70,000 |
| Inventory, Raw Materials | 40,000 |
| Inventory, Finished Goods | 60,000 |
| Marketable Securities | 20,000 |
| Land | 13,000 |
| Buildings (net) | 90,000 |
| Machinery (net) | 140,000 |
| Prepaid Expenses | 5,000 |
| Total Assets | $440,000 |

| Liabilities and Capital | |
|---|---:|
| Accounts Payable | $  80,000 |
| Notes Payable | 135,000 |
| Wages | 15,000 |
| Mortgages Payable | 130,000 |
| Common Stock | 100,000 |
| Retained Earnings (deficit) | (20,000) |
| Total Liabilities and Capital | $440,000 |

### Additional Information

1. Cash includes a $500 travel advance that has been expended.

2. Accounts receivable of $40,000 have been pledged in support of bank loans of $30,000. Credit balances of $5,000 are netted in the accounts receivable total.

3. Marketable securities consist of government bonds costing $10,000 and 500 shares of Dawson Company stock. The market value of the bonds is $10,000, and the stock is $18 per share. The bonds have $200 of accrued interest due. The securities are collateral for a $20,000 bank loan.

4. Appraised value of raw materials and finished goods is $30,000 and $50,000, respectively. For an additional cost of $10,000, the raw materials could realize $70,000 as finished goods.

5. The appraised value of fixed assets is $25,000 for land, $110,000 for buildings, and $75,000 for machinery.

6. Prepaid expenses will be exhausted during the liquidation period.

7. Accounts payable include $15,000 of withheld payroll taxes and $6,000 owed to creditors who have been reassured by the president of Tower that they will be paid. There are unrecorded employer's payroll taxes in the amount of $500.

8. Wages payable are not subject to any limitations under bankruptcy laws.

9. Mortgages payable consist of $100,000 on land and buildings and $30,000 for a chattel mortgage on machinery. Total unrecorded accrued interest for these mortgages amounts to $2,400.

10. Estimated legal fees and expenses in connection with the liquidation are $10,000.

11. The probable judgment on a pending damage suit is $50,000.

12. You have not rendered an invoice for $5,000 for last year's audit, and you estimate a $1,000 fee for liquidation work.

### Required

a. Prepare a statement of affairs. (The Book Value column should reflect adjustments that properly should have been made as of December 31, 20X1, in the normal course of business.)

b. Compute the estimated settlement per dollar of unsecured liabilities.

**P20-9    Financial Statements for a Firm in Chapter 11 Proceedings**

On January 2, 20X2, Hobbes Company files a petition for relief under Chapter 11 of the Bankruptcy Code. Hobbes had disastrous operating performance during the recent recession and needs time to reestablish profitable operations. The trial balance on January 2, 20X2, is as follows:

| | Debit | Credit |
|---|---|---|
| Cash | $ 15,000 | |
| Accounts Receivable (net) | 65,000 | |
| Inventory | 102,000 | |
| Property, Plant, and Equipment | 620,000 | |
| Accumulated Depreciation | | $140,000 |
| Accounts Payable | | 138,000 |
| Notes Payable, 10% | | 170,000 |
| Bonds Payable, 12% | | 250,000 |
| Interest Payable | | 47,000 |
| Preferred Stock | | 50,000 |
| Common Stock, $1 par | | 50,000 |
| Additional Paid-In Capital | | 75,000 |
| Retained Earnings (deficit) | 118,000 | |
| Total | $920,000 | $920,000 |

The following information applies to the 20X2 fiscal year, ending December 31, 20X2. Hobbes is in reorganization proceedings for the entire year, and the plan of reorganization has not been approved as of December 31, 20X2. The debtor remained in possession of the company during the year.

### Income Data for 20X2

1. Sales revenue of $246,000 is generated during the year.

2. Cost of goods sold is $170,000 as a result of cost reduction programs installed during the year.

3. Selling, operating, and administrative expenses are $50,000 for the year.

4. Interest expense is $4,000. Contractual interest would have been $51,000 for the year.

5. Reorganization items include $15,000 in fees paid to professionals and $3,000 of interest earned on cash accumulated as a result of the Chapter 11 proceedings.

6. The income tax of $5,000 on operating income was paid during the year.

7. Discontinued operations included a loss on operations, net of tax, of $16,000, and a gain on the sale of assets, net of tax, of $9,000. The sale of the assets was administered by the court under the Chapter 11 proceedings.

### Cash Flow Data for 20X2

1. A total of $264,000 is received from customers. This includes $18,000 received on the accounts receivable that were outstanding prior to filing the petition.

2. A total of $206,000 is paid to suppliers, employees, and others for operations.

3. The current interest expense of $4,000 on postpetition debt is paid during the year.

4. Professional fees of $15,000 are paid, and interest on cash accumulations of $3,000 is received.

5. Net cash used by discontinued operations, excluding the sale of assets, is $3,000.

6. The proceeds from the sale of the discontinued assets is $18,000. This sale was administered by the bankruptcy court.

7. Hobbes borrowed $10,000 in short-term debt as part of a financing plan administered by the court.

8. The court authorized a payment of $10,000 on the bonds payable. The ending cash balance of $72,000 represents an increase of $57,000 during the year.

### Other Data for 20X2

1. Through careful working capital management, the ending inventory is reduced to $88,000. Continued reduction is expected in 20X3.

2. The property, plant, and equipment, net of accumulated depreciation, at the end of 20X2 totaled $460,000.

3. In addition to the $10,000 short-term borrowings that are part of the court-approved financing plan, Hobbes has postpetition accounts payable of $7,000.

### Required

*a.* Prepare the income statement for Hobbes for the year ending December 31, 20X2.

*b.* Prepare the statement of cash flows for the company for the year ending December 31, 20X2.

*c.* Prepare the balance sheet for the company as of December 31, 20X2.

*Supplemental Problems* for this chapter are available as part of the *Online Learning Center* on the textbook's Web site (URL: www.mhhe.com/baker8e)

# Index

Page numbers followed by n indicate material in notes.

## H